Two week loan

Please return on or before the last
date stamped below.
Charges are made for late return.

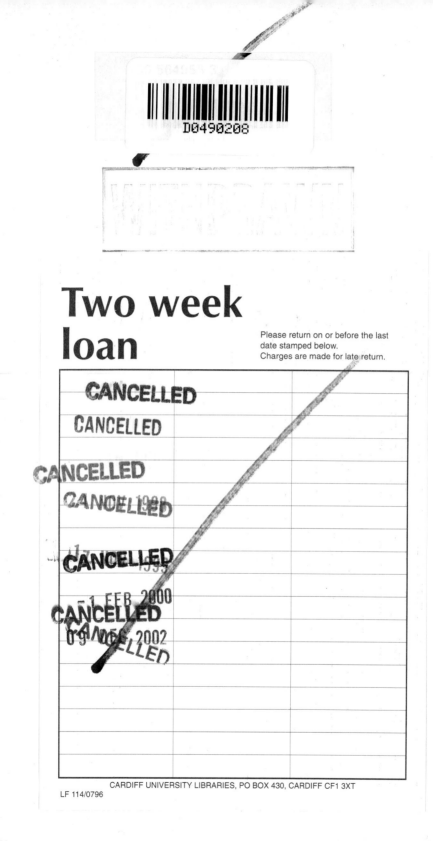

Contracts of Employment

Contracts of Employment

Seventh edition

Douglas Crump

David Pugsley

Butterworths
London, Edinburgh, Dublin
1997

United Kingdom	Butterworths, a Division of Reed Elsevier (UK) Ltd, Halsbury House, 35 Chancery Lane, LONDON WC2A 1EL and 4 Hill Street, EDINBURGH EH2 3JZ
Australia	Butterworths, SYDNEY, MELBOURNE, BRISBANE, ADELAIDE, PERTH, CANBERRA and HOBART
Canada	Butterworths Canada Ltd, TORONTO and VANCOUVER
Ireland	Butterworths (Ireland) Ltd, DUBLIN
Malaysia	Malayan Law Journal Sdn Bhd, KUALA LUMPUR
New Zealand	Butterworths of New Zealand Ltd, WELLINGTON and AUCKLAND
Singapore	Reed Elsevier (Singapore) Pte Ltd, SINGAPORE
South Africa	Butterworths Publishers (Pty) Ltd, DURBAN
USA	Michie, CHARLOTTESVILLE, Virginia

A CIP Catalogue record for this book is available from the British Library.

ISBN   0 406 01146 X

CARDIFF

4 JUN 1997

Typeset by Columns Design Ltd, Reading
Printed by Clays Ltd, Bungay, Suffolk

Preface

Pressures of practice have meant a long delay since the last edition of *Dix and Crump*. The distinctive characteristic of the early editions of *Dix* was that it recognised that much of employment law was statute based and it directed the attention of practitioners to the primary source of law. The indefatigable energy of Peter Wallington has produced in *Butterworths Employment Law Handbook* an indispensable source book. Yet the statutes on their own are a somewhat indigestible diet.

We hope there is still a place for a text which has the modest aim of providing an outline to the individual contract of employment. We trust that the text is sufficiently comprehensive to provide the answer to routine problems. We are well aware that in particular areas – such as discrimination – the text identifies, rather than resolves, complex problems. For those who have a difficult issue to consider we shall be satisfied if we have helped to identify it as such and if we provide a sign post to useful areas of exploration.

In Chapter 1 we give an overview to the practitioner who is innocent of the complexities of employment law. In each chapter we give a brief introduction to the topic. In the appendices we have set out the various practical tools which may be useful. The precedents are as a matter of deliberate policy drafted in the homespun way in which they are couched in practice.

Whilst we take responsibility for the text, we record with gratitude our thanks to those who have helped us. Two practising members of the Bar have assisted us. Mr James Tayler has contributed Chapter 14 on Trade Union and Related Rights and has read the proofs of the text. Ms Carolyn Hilder has assisted by reading the proofs and preparing some of the precedents. Mr Murray Creed, Chairman of Industrial Tribunals, has contributed material on maternity rights and has helped us read the proofs.

One of the insights of middle age is that much truth is lost in platitudes. We give thanks to the forbearance of our long suffering spouses and the patience of the staff at Butterworths. One of the editors is particularly grateful to his daughter, Alison, for her astringent comments as to the readability of certain of the earlier drafts of the text and to a friend, Mr Peter Petersen, who has taken on the task of seeking to make him computer literate.

The law is as stated on the materials available to us on 1 January 1997.

Douglas Crump
David Pugsley

Contents

Contents

Contents

Contents

Table of statutes

References in this table to *Statutes* are to Halsbury's Statutes of England (Fourth Edition) showing the volume and page at which the annotated text of the Act may be found. Page references printed in **bold** type indicate where the Act is set out in part or in full.

Table of statutory instruments

Page references printed in **bold** type indicate where the Regulation is set out in part or in full.

Table of statutory instruments

Table of cases

A

D

E

F

G

I

J

K

L

M

N

O

P

Q

R

S

T

U

V

W

Y

Z

Decisions of the European Court of Justice are listed below numerically. These decisions
  are also included in the preceding alphabetical list.

PARA

Table of cases

Chapter 1

Introduction

1.01 This book has been written for the practitioner, in particular for those practitioners who have to assimilate relevant issues of employment law before giving advice and preparing for a hearing. It will, however, also be of use to practitioners who have to advise at a much earlier stage and who are called upon to give more general advice.

1.02 In a book of this size we do not claim to give the same exhaustive treatment to every topic as that provided by *Harvey on Industrial Relations and Employment Law*. Our aim is a modest one – that the book is sufficiently comprehensive to deal with most routine matters and that we can identify those areas in which the practitioner will need to go to more specialised monographs.

1.03 Employment law reflects the compromises of expediency and accommodation to political pressure. There is an unresolved ambiguity in the legislation about the value of conferring employment rights. The common lawyer finds it an alien experience to be in a field of law in which in certain circumstances a right can only be acquired after a certain period of time and in which the amount of compensation which can be awarded is capped by statute at a particular level.

1.04 Employment law is largely statute based; the same legislation which gives to the industrial tribunal a wide discretion based on such philosophical concepts of fairness and equity also requires tribunals to construe a mass of detailed and, at times, opaque legislation about how to define such matters as a week's pay.

1.05 A textbook in this area of law which deals with only a general overview depicts a picture of misleading clarity. On the other hand, a textbook which seeks to qualify at every turn the broad proposition leaves the practitioner trapped in the tangled undergrowth of conflicting decisions and overlapping legislation.

1.06 We have dealt with the difficulty in this way. In this chapter a brief overview is given of the main principles of employment law and the rights and remedies. Subsequent chapters contain an introductory section giving an outline of the topic under consideration which precedes a more detailed exposition. The hard-pressed practitioner should first read the general introductory text before going on to the expanded commentary.

1.07 In researching a particular topic, an initial study of the general introduction in this chapter is also advisable, for a practitioner who fails to acquire a working knowledge of all the employment remedies may do his or her client a grave disservice. The issue which the client identifies as a redundancy case may in fact be an action for unfair dismissal and/or race, sex or disability discrimination. There have been cases where employers have ended up paying the much higher compensation of an unfair dismissal case as a result of putting forward a cast iron defence to a redundancy claim which has provoked the applicant into amending and presenting what is an unassailable case for unfair dismissal.

1.08 The precedents set out in Appendix 2 may appear of a somewhat homespun character. This is quite deliberate and aims to address what is a perennial problem in any form of litigation. A sophisticated pre-trial procedure may clarify and define issues, but it penalises the unrepresented litigant and makes litigation more expensive for the represented party. Although there are occasions when interlocutory procedures are used in general, in tribunal proceedings there is not the protracted correspondence and pre-trial procedures which characterise court litigation. It is therefore necessary for the pleadings to set out the issues. The majority of applicants are unrepresented. In drafting a notice of appearance it is prudent for a respondent to raise the issues on which it is intended to rely even if the issues do not arise directly from the originating application.

The historical perspective

1.09 The first edition of *Dix* was published in 1963. It originated as a commentary on the Contracts of Employment Act 1963. Few could have foreseen that this Act was to be the forerunner of a spate of legislation and case law. Employment law has been transformed and is no longer a discrete area of law of interest to specialist practitioners dealing with particular issues which can be safely ignored by practitioners in other specialities. The conveyancer, the insolvency practitioner, the pension fund trustee and the company lawyer can now no longer treat the impact of domestic and European legislation and case law on employment law as of marginal relevance to their own specialities.

1.10 In some ways the title of this book has become a misnomer. At common law the relationship between employer and employee was one of contract; yet statutory changes place numerous restrictions on the freedom of parties to negotiate terms of employment and grant to the employee and the job applicant rights of a non-contractual nature. Employment was perceived to be essentially a personal relationship. Whatever the economic reality, the legal theory was that both parties had equal freedom to create and terminate the relation of employer and employee. The suggestion that an employee could be compelled to work for an employer was regarded as equating service with servitude.

1.11 The right to chose for whom one worked was seen as one of the fundamental liberties and marked the distinction in feudal England between the serf and freeman. However, the imperatives of the two World Wars required that labour be directed to meet particular needs. In both wars the coalition governments gave greater weight to the leaders of the labour movement in the coalition than their political strength would have warranted because of their awareness of the sensitivity of compelling individuals to work for particular employers.

1.12 The personal nature of employment was reflected in the older text-books and cases which referred to employment law as the law of master and servant. Several developments have undermined that position. In particular, the growth of employment in large commercial and industrial undertakings and in the public sector increasingly made this terminology inappropriate to describe the relationship.

1.13 The employee's right to decide for whom he or she might work was matched by the employer's right to terminate that employment. At common law the only right that an employee had was that his employment should be lawfully terminated; namely that he been given the appropriate notice. In practice this rarely provided any great protection for the employee. Save for employees who had clearly defined lengthy periods of notice, an action for wrongful dismissal was a somewhat barren exercise. In any action an employee had to give credit for any other wages received if he obtained a job or any statutory benefits received if he had not. The employee was only enti-tled to notice and the employer was entitled to require the employee to work that notice.

1.14 No protection was given to the employee as to the reason for the dismissal. Few 20th century employers would follow the precedent of the Victorian employer who in the 1850s dismissed an employee because he had written to a local newspaper denying the existence of hell. However, until the introduction of unfair dismissal legislation and the race and sex legislation, an employee had no protection against being dismissed for his religious or politi-cal views, his ethnic origin or for any purely capricious reason. Moreover he had no right to know the reason for his dismissal and if he was told the reason he had no right to challenge the adequacy or fairness of that reason.

1.15 The introduction of the right to receive a redundancy payment, the right not to be unfairly dismissed and the right not to be discriminated against on grounds of race, gender or disability changed the whole context of employ-ment. An employer was no longer the sole judge of the standards of fairness with which he operated his undertaking. Certain of the legislative changes have in effect curtailed an employer's freedom to operate the business competi-tively. Changes in the rights of female workers have had a particular impact.

1.16 Traditionally females have been employed in the poorest paid jobs; the introduction of the right to be paid the same as male operatives doing the same work was therefore of limited utility. All an employer had to do was to ensure that only the female operatives did the low paid work. The introduction of the right for women to have their work reassessed as being of equal value to a male comparator was a radical limitation of the power of an employer to determine his own wage rates.

1.17 Employment law, therefore, no longer has as its conceptual image the engagement of a butler or servant who could be engaged or dismissed with relative ease. Instead it is concerned with a nexus of rights and obligations which often arise irrespective of the agreement of the parties and, with less sophisticated employers and employees, of their knowledge.

The general principles

The use of authority

1.18   The law of employment protection and equality is statute based. A plethora of case law has been reported. Nevertheless the Court of Appeal and the Employment Appeal Tribunal have repeatedly warned of the severe limitations that case law has in the main remedy, namely unfair dismissal.

1.19   As there are only appeals on questions of law, ingenious advocates often dress up as issues of law what are essentially issues of fact. This is not unique to employment law. When the Employment Appeal Tribunal dismisses an appeal by an employer who was found to have unfairly dismissed an apprentice for saying 'you couldn't have done any fucking better', it is not deciding as a matter of law that in all circumstances apprentices have the right to respond in that way. In dismissing the appeal all the Employment Appeal Tribunal is saying is that on the evidence that was a decision to which the tribunal could come *on the facts of that particular case.*

1.20   There is a more fundamental reason for being wary of the value of decided cases as to the central issue of the fairness of the decision. Section 98 of the Employment Rights Act 1996 now defines the statutory criteria of fairness. Section 98(4) in terms requires the tribunal to consider the size and administrative resources of the employer in reaching that decision. Even if there was a very high coincidence between the factual basis of two cases, there could well be a different result because a tribunal would have to consider the size and the administrative resources of the employer. If the company was a large multinational company, the range of options would be considerably greater than would be the case with a small company with a handful of employees.

Defeating the protection and the use of authority

1.21   Considerable ingenuity is often deployed by employers or their advisers to try to defeat the operation of employment legislation. The arrangements they make aim to ensure that the workforce will not be regarded as employees, or that the sale of an undertaking will be considered merely as a sale of the assets and not as the sale of a going concern. There is an increasing tendency for the appellate courts to accept that determining such issues is a matter for the tribunal or court at first instance, balancing the relevant factors, and that any attempt to lay down exhaustive definitions is inappropriate. Decided cases therefore tend to lay down general guidelines rather than definitive rulings on specific factual situations.

1.22   However, in considering the statutory definition of redundancy or the application of the Transfer of Undertakings (Protection of Employment) Regulations 1981 (hereafter 'the Transfer of Undertakings Regulations') then decided cases carry very much more weight. The definition of redundancy or the application of the Transfer of Undertakings Regulations is the same whether a tribunal is considering a sole employer of a private individual or a mass redundancy programme, or the transfer of a large or small organisation.

The contract of employment

1.23 The rights and responsibilities of employer and employee arise by virtue of the contract they make with each other. In many instances the contract is of a most informal nature. Employers are required to set out written particulars of employment although this is a requirement as much honoured in the breach as the observance by many small employers. The particulars of employment is not a contractual document but merely evidence of the contract. The contractual terms are those that are expressly agreed at the time the agreement is made or which are implied into the contract.

1.24 In the context of employment law the most important implied term is that the employee will act with fidelity towards his employer and that the employer will act with mutual trust and confidence towards the employee. In certain instances the provisions of a collective agreement are incorporated into the contract. Statutory provisions have modified the freedom to contract, either by conferring rights of a non-contractual nature or by the statutory imposition of contractual terms. This is evidenced by the provision of:

(1) minimum periods of notice;
(2) the right to a redundancy payment;
(3) the right not to be unfairly dismissed;
(4) the right not to be discriminated against on grounds of gender, race or disability;
(5) certain specific rights related to guarantee payments and the right to itemised pay statements;
(6) rights in relation to trade union membership;
(7) specific rights to women in respect of pregnancy and maternity leave.

1.25 Some of the above rights relate to issues which have arisen after termination of the contract of employment. The common law action for wrongful dismissal still survives although, save in the case of highly paid employees, the remedies it provides are of academic significance.

Rights conferred by statute

1.26 The cornerstone of the legislation is essentially that it protects employees who have had continuous employment for two years and that, apart from limited exceptions, it is impossible to contract out of the protection which such employees are afforded. The amount of the monetary award in both unfair dismissal cases and redundancy cases is related to the length of service and issues as to continuity of service may arise at that stage as well as in determining whether the applicant satisfies the qualifying period.

1.27 Whether an applicant is an employee, whether an applicant has continuous employment and whether there has been a dismissal are common threads of many different rights. In these circumstances it is helpful to give a brief analysis of these terms at this stage.

Employees

1.28 Statute has superimposed on the contractual relationship substantial obligations on employers. Moreover the employer has financial obligations to pay an employee's National Insurance contributions and to assume the administrative responsibility of collecting income tax from an employee's salary. It is inevitable that there has been a widespread movement on the part of many employers to free themselves from this burden by managing their businesses to ensure that work is carried out by contractors. In many cases this is a policy decision which can be easily recognised and defined.

1.29 Such operations as cleaning, catering or the provision of security services are frequently provided by outside firms. Although the individuals who carry out these functions may attend regularly at the office or factory and regard it as their workplace, they are employed by a different employer than the occupier of their workplace.

1.30 The more difficult area is where the parties come to a much less clearly defined arrangement, often with a single individual. An employer is free to organise the workload so as to use contractors rather than to engage employees, but an employer cannot avoid the obligations of employment merely by describing what is essentially a contract of employment in other terms. The categorisation by the Inland Revenue or National Insurance authorities as self-employed although relevant is not conclusive.

1.31 In general terms the test is that an employee is working under the direction of the employer and that the employer, rather than the employee, provides the equipment, the working capital and is taking the commercial risk and reward of the operation. Industrial tribunals are frequently confronted with a relationship in which some signs point to self-employment and some to employment. It is not unusual for national retailers to pay a manager a percentage of the turnover and to require him or her to employ the staff and to pay the outgoings. These matters point to self-employment. However, the conditions may also stipulate the hours the shop must open, the type of merchandise that must be sold and preclude the manager of the shop from selling any other items than those which he or she is supplied. The company may well retain the right to dictate how much holiday the manager takes and take it upon itself to provide a relief manager to cover holidays and sickness. These latter stipulations are as inconsistent with self-employment as the former requirements are with employment. In the final analysis the tribunal has to look at the whole picture and reach a decision as to how the manager's status should be construed. In homely language the question is this: *is he his own boss?*

1.32 The *employee* is to be distinguished from a mere *office holder*. A director of a company is an office holder. Whether he or she is also an employee will depend on the extent to which he or she works under the direction of the company and the extent to which such duties which are performed arise out of a contractual obligation to the company as opposed to the exercise of discretion of the office as a director.

Continuity of employment

1.33   In many cases whether or not an employee has been continuously employed is a matter free from any complexity. However, there can be difficulties when there has been a gap in the employment record. There are detailed statutory provisions which deal with absences of work and whether they break the continuity of employment.

1.34   Employees are given a certain limited protection by the provision that if they are dismissed immediately before the qualifying period, then they are entitled to have credited to the period of their employment the length of the notice to which they are entitled.

Continuity of employment and the change of employer

1.35   An issue which frequently arises is when the employee has remained in the same employment but the identity of the employer has changed. In law a company is a distinct legal entity; thus the 'take-over' of a company does not terminate the contract. Well before the Transfer of Undertakings Regulations became operative the essentially personal nature of employment had been lost for many employees.

1.36   The continuity of employment of an employee is protected when he or she is transferred to an associated employer, namely an employer which is controlled by the same body or company as the original employer.

1.37   However, the impact of the Transfer of Undertakings Regulations is substantial on employees of many small employers. The essence of these regulations is that where a business is bought as a 'going concern', then the contract of employment of existing employees is continued. The purchaser of a small shop found (often to his or her surprise) that he or she had assumed the obligations of being the employer of existing employees. If after the transfer the purchaser ran into difficulties and ceased trading, the obligation to pay a redundancy payment is calculated by reference to when the employment had first commenced and not to the date of the purchase of the business. Many purchasers of small businesses (and, in certain cases, their legal advisers) did not understand the implication of these regulations and the obligations which had been acquired. Equally many employees were ignorant of the implications. They assumed that the sale of the business had the effect of terminating the contract. They were reluctant to work for a new employer and when they left claimed they were entitled to a redundancy payment because their old employer 'did not want them any more'.

Dismissal

1.38   There are technical provisions which define certain matters as a dismissal, for example the expiry of a fixed term contract without renewal. However, for practical purposes there are essentially two types of dismissal.

The first is the direct dismissal when an employer terminates the employment by telling the employee to leave. The second type of dismissal is a *constructive dismissal* where an employee leaves because he or she considers that the employer has broken the contract in such a fundamental way that he or she is entitled to leave.

1.39 Tribunals look at the reality rather than the form. Thus if an employee is told to resign or be dismissed then this is clearly a dismissal since it is the employer who is bringing the contract to an end.

1.40 Many of the phrases used by employers and employees when they part company in acrimony are not readily susceptible to the type of forensic analysis which would be appropriate in construing a lease or a will. Whether telling an employer in graphic and specific terms what he can do with his job should be construed as a mere expression of irritation couched in colourful terms or a resignation is often a matter which will depend very much on the precise circumstances in which the words were said.

Redundancy

1.41 The basic statutory right is that an employee shall become entitled to a lump sum payment in those cases in which he has been dismissed by reason of redundancy. The first necessity is that an employee should have been dismissed; it is sometimes overlooked that this includes constructive dismissal. In certain situations such as the death of the employer or by frustration, the contract of employment is terminated by operation of law but the Employment Rights Act 1996 provides that it is to be treated as though terminated by the employer.

1.42 A redundancy payment is only payable if the dismissal is due wholly or mainly to redundancy. The statutory test defines three different types of situation: (1) the cessation of business; (2) the moving of the place of business and (3) when a business is over-manned in that it has more employees than the business requires.

1.43 There is one situation in which an employee may obtain what in effect is a declaratory judgment that he or she is entitled to a redundancy payment. Thus, if an employee is laid off or put on short time, he or she may, after activating a somewhat complicated procedure, obtain a declaration that there is an entitlement to redundancy.

1.44 There are certain circumstances in which an employee may effectively lose their entitlement to a redundancy payment. If an employee unreasonably refuses suitable alternative employment, or is guilty of gross misconduct after receiving notice of redundancy, then the employer will not be required to make a redundancy payment in whole or in part.

1.45 A redundancy payment is calculated according to a statutory formula, namely one week's pay (subject to a statutory maximum) for each year's continuous service and one and a half week's pay for each year over the age of 41.

1.46   The situation with regard to payment for redundancy vis-à-vis a claim for unfair dismissal has changed. Redundancy payments were the first statutory remedy for the employee and employers used to argue strenuously that dismissals were not due to redundancy. Since redundancy is now a potentially fair reason for dismissal, it is often the case that it is the employer rather than the employee who is arguing for the dismissal being due to redundancy – the employee's sword has become the employer's shield.

Unfair dismissal

1.47   In hearing claims for unfair dismissal, industrial tribunals do not sit as quasi-magistrates' courts trying employees for industrial misconduct. Their role is different. In the first instance their attention is directed to the decision of the employer rather than the action of the employee. The employer has to satisfy the tribunal as to the reason for the dismissal.

Automatically unfair dismissal

1.48   In certain circumstances, once it is proved that a dismissal was for a particular reason, for example dismissing an employee because she is pregnant, the dismissal is deemed to be automatically unfair. Further examples are dealt with in the chapters below.

Section 98 dismissals

1.49   In cases where dismissal is not automatically unfair, the provisions of s 98 of the Employment Rights Act 1996 apply. To be fair the reason for dismissal has to be one relating to:
(1)   capability;
(2)   conduct;
(3)   redundancy;
(4)   that the continued employment would be in breach of some enactment; or
(5)   be for some substantial other reason which justifies the dismissal.

1.50   If the employer discharges the burden of showing that the dismissal was for a reason that is potentially fair, the determination of the question whether the dismissal was fair or unfair, having regard to the reason shown by the employer, depends on whether in the circumstances (including the size and administrative resources of the employer's undertaking) the employer acted reasonably or unreasonably in treating it as a sufficient reason for dismissing the employee. The determination as to the reasonableness of the employer's actions shall be made in accordance with the equity and substantial merits of the case (1996 Act, s 98(4)).

1.51   An employer may establish that his reason for dismissing an employee was misconduct, but a tribunal may decide that it was unfair to dismiss him where the misconduct was the first blemish which was relatively minor. Subsumed within the issues raised by s 98(4) is the question of whether a dismissal can be fair if the employer goes about making the decision in a totally unfair way, as for example not making any attempt to interview the employee to ascertain his account. An employer who does not act fairly in arriving at the decision to dismiss is likely to have a finding of unfair dismissal made against him. However, an applicant may well find that the compensation he recovers in such circumstances is reduced or non-existent if he would have been dismissed in any event.

Summary of provisions

1.52 To come within the ambit of the s 98 provisions, the applicant must be an employee and have been continuously employed for a period of two years in order to have the right not to be unfairly dismissed. The applicant must make the application within three months of the dismissal. If the applicant fails to do so, the tribunal has no jurisdiction unless the 'escape clause' applies. See **15.156**.

1.53 The status of the applicant, the fact of continuous employment and the requirement to comply with the time limits are not matters that can be waived by the employer in any proceedings. An industrial tribunal has no inherent powers and only has such powers as are conferred by statute. If these conditions are not satisfied, the tribunal has no power to adjudicate upon an unfair dismissal claim.

Excluded employees

1.54 Contracting out of the provisions of the 1996 Act is not allowed except in certain limited circumstances. There are a number of categories of employees who are specifically excluded from the operation of the unfair dismissal provisions. The most important in numerical terms are police officers and members of the armed services.

1.55 An exclusion also exists based on age so that applicants who are over the age of 65 or who have reached the normal retiring age may not bring a claim for unfair dismissal. The normal retiring age may be ascertained from the contract of employment or from practice within the particular business.

1.56 Recent statutory change has, however, removed an exclusion for part-time workers which was based on sufficient hours of service per week. This limit no longer applies.

Essentials of the right to claim unfair dismissal

1.57 The employee must establish that there was a dismissal. If the issue is whether there was a constructive dismissal, it is important to note that it is still necessary for the tribunal to decide that the dismissal was unfair. For example, an employer may be forced to cut wages and this may be a fundamental breach of contract which allows an employee to claim successfully that he has been constructively dismissed. Yet an employer may equally argue that he had no alternative and that the changes were fair having regard to the provisions of s 98(4) of the 1996 Act and that therefore although there was a constructive dismissal, the dismissal was fair.

1.58 The employer must establish the reason for the dismissal and the dismissal must be for one of the potentially fair reasons. What matters is the state of affairs which forms the basis of the employer's belief rather than the legal label which he has attached to that state of affairs. A dismissal will be fair if the employer had reasonable grounds for that belief, reached after making such enquiries as were appropriate in all the circumstances, and if the decision to dismiss is within the range of responses of a reasonable employer.

1.59 The fairness of the decision is judged by the employer's knowledge at the time of the dismissal. An employer cannot rely on matters discovered after the decision to dismiss although such matters may be relevant to the issue of remedy. If an employer gives an employee no opportunity to give his side of the matter, then unless such an interview would on its particular facts be an empty charade, the dismissal is likely to be unfair. The industrial tribunal will have to decide whether the dismissal was fair in accordance with s 98(4). It is not for the tribunal to substitute its own view of the fairness but merely to ask whether the decision to dismiss was one to which a reasonable employer could come, bearing in mind that reasonable people can come to different decisions on the same set of facts.

Remedies

1.60 Under the Employment Rights Act 1996 the primary remedy for unfair dismissal is that of reinstatement or re-engagement. Reinstatement means the employee is put in the position as though he or she had never been dismissed. In re-engagement the applicant resumes work with the employer but not necessarily on the same terms. In practice the applicant for understandable reasons rarely wishes to be reinstated or re-engaged.

Compensation

1.61 An employee who has been unfairly dismissed receives a basic award based on similar criteria as in redundancy payments. In a case in which the employee has already received a redundancy award this extinguishes the basic award. The employee may receive a compensatory award to cover the loss of wages up to the hearing together with any continuing loss and any loss of pension rights. A sum is also included to reflect that in any new employment the employee will not have the right to bring a claim for redundancy payments and will not be protected from unfair dismissal for two years.

Reduction of the award

1.62 An award of compensation for unfair dismissal may be reduced on the basis that:
(1)   the employee contributed to his or her dismissal;
(2)   had the employer properly investigated the matter and given the employee an opportunity to be heard, there was a possibility that the employee may have been fairly dismissed;
(3)   events discovered after the making of the decision to dismiss would make it inequitable for the employee to receive compensation.

1.63 To reduce the award an industrial tribunal is not compelled to do so by means of an arithmetical deduction but may limit the period in respect of which compensation might be payable. For example, in a case involving selecting an employee for redundancy, if a dismissal is found to be unfair in that an employee was dismissed without any adequate consultation, a tribunal may conclude that even after full consultation an employee would still have been dismissed and such dismissal would have been fair. It is open to the tribunal to award the applicant the loss of wages for the time which adequate compensation would have postponed dismissal.

1.64 An ex gratia payment will generally be offset against the compensatory award. This may be contentious in cases where it is found as a fact that in any event the employee would have been dismissed and that he would then have received the ex gratia payment. If the applicant has received unemployment benefit, then there are provisions for recouping that figure from the sum awarded. This only applies if the tribunal makes an award and not if the parties reach agreement as to compensation.

Discrimination

1.65 The Race Relations Act 1976 and the Sex Discrimination Acts 1975 and 1986 make discrimination on grounds of gender and ethnic origin unlawful. Discrimination may be either direct or indirect. There is now similar legislation prohibiting discrimination against the disabled.

1.66 Direct discrimination occurs when an employee is treated less favourably on grounds of race or gender. The most blatant forms of discrimination come within this category (the 'we don't employ blacks or women here' type of case). Indirect discrimination occurs when an unjustifiable condition is imposed which is more difficult for a person of a particular gender or ethnic origin to comply with than the population as a whole. Because women are often out of the labour market in their twenties and early thirties a job which imposes age limits without good cause is likely to be held to be discriminatory.

1.67 The Race and Sex Discrimination Acts, but not the Disability Discrimination Act 1995, share a common conceptual framework. However, in the area of sex discrimination, unlike race discrimination, there is a two-tier system in that the courts and tribunals are concerned with European as well as domestic law.

1.68 The anti-discrimination legislation significantly extends the obligations of an employer in that it protects not just employees but those applying for jobs. Moreover, it also covers pension schemes and so protects the individual after the employment has ceased. Although the impetus behind the introduction of the Race and Sex Discrimination Acts was to improve the position of those who were perceived to be disadvantaged, namely ethnic minorities and women, the legislation provides protection for whites as well as blacks – for men as well as women. However, the sex discrimination legislation confers clearly defined protection for events which are biologically specific to women, ie childbirth and its consequences.

1.69 It has already been noted that the equal pay and equal value legislation affects decisions which lie at the very heart of the commercial viability of a business such as the wage structure of the workforce. The effect of this legislation has been far more wide-ranging than had been predicted at the time it came into force.

1.70 Within the United Kingdom the impact of European legislation and decisions of the European Court of Justice on issues of sexual discrimination has also been striking. It has led to fundamental changes in the pattern of employment and has challenged assumptions and attitudes which have been implicitly accepted for generations. Of particular note was the occasion of the House of Lords declaring that an Act of Parliament was in conflict with the requirements of European legislation.

1.71 At the very heart of English law has been the concept of reasonableness, which pervades both criminal and civil law. Although the equality legislation may allow justification of a requirement which is potentially discriminatory where indirect discrimination is being alleged, reasonableness is not a defence in an action based on direct discrimination. If the act constitutes discrimination, it is no defence to show that the intention was reasonable or even well-intentioned. In *Grieg v Community Industry*[1] a female trainee was not allowed to go on a building course due to the fact that another female had withdrawn; she would have then been the only female on the course and it was therefore felt that she might be subjected to unsolicited and unwanted attentions from the males on the course. Even though the reason for the decision was well-intentioned (even if somewhat patronising) it was held to be unlawful discrimination.

1 [1979] ICR 356, EAT.

The machinery of enforcement

1.72 In the area of employment law industrial tribunals have an exclusive jurisdiction to hear redundancy, unfair dismissal and sex and race and disability discrimination cases. There is now a concurrent jurisdiction for actions for breach of contract subject to certain financial limits. In certain cases a litigant may have a remedy for unfair dismissal in an industrial tribunal and an action for wrongful dismissal in the courts. In such cases the findings of fact of the industrial tribunal will be binding on the trial judge in the case before the courts.

1.73 In the industrial tribunal two lay members (representing both sides of industry) sit with a legally qualified chairman though in certain actions a chairman may sit alone. There are appeals on matters of law to the Employment Appeal Tribunal which consists of a High Court judge (or a designated circuit judge) and thereafter appeals to the Court of Appeal and the House of Lords.

The United Kingdom dimension

1.74 The United Kingdom has three quite separate legal systems although each has the House of Lords as its final appellate court. As employment law is now largely statute based there is considerable symmetry in all three jurisdictions. In no other area of the law is there such close judicial co-operation and contact. The presidents and chairmen of industrial tribunals of all three jurisdictions meet on formal and informal occasions. The President of the Employment Appeal Tribunal and the judicial member of the Scottish Employment Appeal Tribunal exchange places each year. In Northern Ireland there is no Employment Appeal Tribunal and appeals go direct to the Court of Appeal.

1.75 Although we do not trespass on the area of Scottish law as far as common law remedies[1] are concerned, with regard to employment legislation specific provisions are included in the text as to Scottish rules of procedure.

1 For such, see Craig and Miller *Employment Law in Scotland* (T & T Clark, 1991). A perusal of this or a similar book will reveal the very large level of congruence between the English and the Scottish systems.

Chapter 2

European law

Introduction

European law has had considerable impact on some aspects of United Kingdom employment law (in particular as to sex discrimination, equal pay and transfers of undertakings). European law has priority over domestic United Kingdom law to the extent that it may influence the construction of United Kingdom law and even result in the courts and tribunals disapplying domestic law; see **2.10–2.15**.

Certain rights conferred by European law can be directly enforceable by legal persons who are within member states, see **2.15–2.19**.

An article of the Treaty of Rome, if directly enforceable, may form the basis of a claim against private legal persons within member states, see **2.16**.

A Directive of the Council of Ministers of the European Union, if directly enforceable, may form the basis of an employment law claim against the state and state bodies. There may also be a right for individuals who have suffered because a member state has not implemented a European obligation to take direct proceedings against the member state in respect of his loss, see **2.21**.

European law in relation to employment rights is usually enforced by industrial tribunals if this is possible by construction of United Kingdom law, or by disapplying United Kingdom law, so as to comply with European law. Otherwise it is enforced through the courts, see **2.27**.

Background

2.01 Membership of the European Union (formerly the European Economic Community) has resulted in what are arguably some of the most significant developments in the law since 1970. Employment law is an area in which these developments have had particular effect and many problems in employment law today have a European dimension.[1]

1 Since it is the laws of the European Union which have had such far-reaching effects on the laws of the United Kingdom relating to employment relationships it is these which are referred to as European law. The European Convention on Human Rights and Fundamental Freedoms falls outside the main thrust of this work and is not considered. The European Court of Justice referred to is the European Court of Justice established under the Treaties creating the European Union.

The Treaties

2.02 The Treaty establishing the European Economic Community was the Treaty of Rome which was entered into by the original six members of the EEC in 1956.[1] The United Kingdom did not join the Community until 1 January 1973. The usual rule of United Kingdom laws is that treaties do not automatically become part of domestic law. The Treaty of Rome (and the other Treaties) were given some effect under domestic law by the European Communities Act 1972. Section 2(1) of the Act provides that all rights, powers, liabilities, obligations and restrictions from time to time created or arising by or under the Treaties, and all such remedies and procedures provided for by and under them, are without further enactment to be given legal effect and used in the United Kingdom. They are recognised and available in law and enforced, allowed, and followed, accordingly.[2] The intention of Parliament was that future, as well as existing, rights and obligations under the Treaties were to become part of domestic law and to take precedence over domestic legislation. Notwithstanding the significant constitutional and conceptual difficulties with regard to this, the European Court of Justice and the courts within the United Kingdom have proceeded on the basis that the Act was successful in implementing this intention.

1 Although of lesser importance to this work than the Treaty of Rome, it should not be overlooked that at the same time as the United Kingdom acceded to that Treaty it also acceded to the Treaties establishing the European Coal and Steel Community and the European Atomic Energy Community, and amending Treaties. References in the text are made to provisions of the Treaty of Rome, but the provisions of the other Treaties may be relevant too. The Treaties have themselves been subject to amendment, not the least by the Single European Act 1986 and the Maastricht Treaty. As with all other sources, European materials should always be referred to in their most up-to-date form.
2 European Communities Act 1972, s 2(1).

The European Court

2.03   The ultimate authority within the European Union which makes judicial decisions as to the interpretation of European law in cases referred to it, is the European Court of Justice. Decisions of the European Court of Justice have primacy, so far as decisions affecting the meaning or effect of the Treaties or the validity, meaning, or effect, of any Community instrument are concerned. Such matters are treated as questions of law.[1] Judicial notice is taken within the United Kingdom of European legislation and decisions.[2] Where a question arises in proceedings before a court or tribunal of a member state, as to the interpretation of the Treaty of Rome, the validity and interpretation of acts of institutions of the European Union, or the interpretation of the statutes of bodies established by the Council of Ministers, the domestic court or tribunal may, if it considers that a decision on the question is necessary for it to give judgment, request the European Court of Justice to give a ruling thereon.[3] Where such a question is raised in a case pending before a court or tribunal of a member state, against whose decisions there is no judicial remedy under national law, that court or tribunal should bring the matter before the European Court of Justice.[4] The reference is undertaken by posing questions to the European Court of Justice.[5]

1 European Communities Act 1972, s 3.
2 European Communities Act 1972, s 3(2).
3 Treaty of Rome, art 177. Under this provision infraction proceedings may be taken against member states. Member states may challenge Directives under art 173. See for example the ill-fated challenge to the Working Time Directive in Case C-84/94 *United Kingdom v EU Council* (1996) Times, 21 November.
4 Treaty of Rome, art 177, in the case of the United Kingdom the court referred to is usually the House of Lords.
5 The power is exercisable by all courts and tribunals. There have been references from industrial tribunals and the Employment Appeal Tribunal but this power should be exercised sparingly: *Jenkins v Kingsgate (Clothing Productions) Ltd* [1980] IRLR 6 at para 18, EAT. See

Industrial Tribunals (Constitution and Rules of Procedure) Regulations 1993, SI 1993/2687, Sch 1, para 19A and see **18.93** as to references by industrial tribunals. For the procedure on references from the High Court and Court of Appeal see Rules of the Supreme Court 1965, Ord 114. See also RSC Ord 14A which gives the High Court power to determine questions of law and construction without determining relevant facts. This was exercised in connection with the construction of the Transfer of Undertakings (Protection of Employment) Regulations 1981, SI 1981/1794, in *Kenny v South Manchester College* [1993] ICR 934, QBD.

Effect on United Kingdom law

2.04   In 1974 Lord Denning said '... when we come to matters with a European element, the treaty is like an incoming tide. It flows into the estuaries and up the rivers. It cannot be held back. Parliament has decreed that the treaty is henceforth part of our law. It is equal in force to any statute'.[1] Since then the flow has continued unabated and has had, and is having, ever greater effect on the domestic laws of the United Kingdom. As will be seen shortly, such is the extent of the penetration of some aspects of European law, that in certain circumstances, individual private legal persons are able to rely on (or be subject to) rules of European law, or domestic rules interpreted or modified to accommodate European obligations, where the domestic rules are not compatible with the European obligations. This may be so not only in connection with actions against the state or state bodies but also when taking action against other individual private legal persons in domestic courts and tribunals (including industrial tribunals).

1 *HP Bulmer Ltd v J Bollinger SA* [1974] 2 All ER 1226 at p 1231, CA.

European law-making actions

2.05   The provisions of the Treaties themselves may give rise to legally enforceable rights for individuals either directly or by way of modifying the application of domestic law.[1] There are several types of European legislative action.

1 For example Treaty of Rome, art 119.

2.06   The prime sources of European law are the provisions of the *Treaties* themselves. As well as the Treaties, other sources of European law have to be considered:
(1)   *Regulations* made by the Council of Ministers and the Commission are of general application, apply directly to individuals within member states, and are binding in their entirety.
(2)   *Council Directives* contemplate domestic legislation, or other means, for their implementation and bind member states as to the result to be achieved.
(3)   *Decisions* of the European Court of Justice and the Commission affect individual persons and bind the persons to whom they are addressed.
(4)   *Recommendations* of the Commission are not themselves enforceable but when appropriate will be taken into account by national courts and tribunals.[1]

1 Case 322/88 *Grimaldi v Fonds des Maladies Professionnelles* [1990] IRLR 400, ECJ.

The Social Chapter

2.07   In 1989 the then members of the EEC, with the exception of the United Kingdom, committed themselves to implement a regime of social rights for their citizens. Many of these rights will affect employees and members of the workforces within member states. The United Kingdom was not a signatory to this 'Social Chapter' and the Maastricht Treaty gave formal recognition to the exclusion of the United Kingdom from the obligations within the Social Chapter. The United Kingdom is bound by the other social provisions in and arising from the Treaty of Rome.

Effect of European law on employment law

2.08   Many of the provisions of European law are relevant to employment law practitioners. Those most likely to be encountered by employment lawyers include arts 119 and 48 of the Treaty of Rome,[1] the Equal Pay Directive,[2] the Directive on Collective Redundancies,[3] the Equal Treatment Directive,[4] the Acquired Rights Directive,[5] the Directive as to employees' rights in relation to Insolvent Employers[6] and the Directive as to Equal Treatment in relation to occupational pensions.[7] This list is not exhaustive and many other elements of European legislative activity are of relevance to employment lawyers.[8]

1 See Chapter 5. Article 119 relates to equal pay and art 48 to the freedom of movement of workers within the Community.
2 Directive 75/117/EEC.
3 Directive 75/129/EEC.
4 Directive 76/207/EEC.
5 Directive 77/187/EEC.
6 Directive 80/987/EEC.
7 Directive 86/378/EEC.
8 For instance Directive 79/7/EEC (social security), Directive 91/533/EEC (information as to conditions of employment relationship) and Directive 93/104/EEC (hours of work). Other matters of relevance to employment lawyers are under active consideration.

2.09   Several issues arise which are of particular importance to the subject matter covered by this work. First, the effect of European law on the rights and duties of individual legal persons has to be considered. Secondly, insofar as European law does affect domestic law, the effect which it has on the rights and duties of legal persons operating within the domestic legal system has to be determined. Thirdly, consideration must be given to the method of enforcement of 'European' rights.

Interpreting national law

2.10   It was long a tenet of statutory construction in English law that, so far as was possible, statutes (and secondary legislation made pursuant to them) would be construed without reference to external materials. Reference to international obligations and to materials such as the *Hansard* record was not normally resorted to when construing Acts of Parliament.[1] This occasioned particular difficulty when dealing with European sources where the expressed intention of domestic legislation was often to implement obligations contained in the Treaty, or Directives made pursuant to it. An approach which involved having regard to these extra-statutory materials required a change to the long-established rule of construction. This has been effected by the House of Lords. It established the rule that external matters are not considered when dealing with statutory materials, does not apply so far as European obligations are concerned. In *Pickstone v Freemans plc*,[2] after consideration of this issue, the House of Lords when construing the Equal Pay Act (Amendment) Regulations 1983 took into account statements made in the House of Commons by the Under-Secretary of State for Employment as to the intended purpose of the regulations.[3] The rule is that the regulations should be construed so as to take into effect the obligations contained in art 119 of the Treaty of Rome (see **5.02**) and Directive 75/117/EEC (see **5.03**). In *Litster v Forth Dry Dock & Engineering Co Ltd*,[4] a Scots case, Lord Oliver said:

'The approach to the construction of primary and subordinate legislation enacted to give effect to the United Kingdom's obligations under the E.E.C. Treaty have been the subject matter of recent authority in this House (see *Pickstone v Freemans plc* ...) and is not in doubt. If the legislation can reasonably be construed so as to conform with those obligations – obligations which are to be ascertained not only from the wording of the relevant Directive but from the interpretation placed upon it by the European Court of Justice at Luxembourg – such a purposive construction will be applied even though, perhaps, it may involve some departure from the strict and literal application of the words which the legislature has elected to use.'

1 *Fothergill v Monarch Airlines Ltd* [1980] 2 All ER 696 at pp 705–706, HL. Also contrast Bennion *Statutory Interpretation* (1984, Butterworths, London), p 531 onwards, with its second edition (1992, Butterworths, London), p 457 onwards.
2 [1988] ICR 697 at p 725, HL.
3 SI 1983/1794 which inserted s 1(2)(c) into the Equal Pay Act 1970, see **5.20**.
4 [1989] ICR 341 at p 354, HL.

2.11 It is now an established element of the laws of the United Kingdom that when construing domestic law which was bought into being to implement European obligations, courts and tribunals should do so as far as is possible to conform with the European obligations of the state. This 'purposive' approach to construction of domestic law has been adopted in relation to the provisions of the Equal Pay Act 1970 (as amended)[1] and the Transfer of Undertakings (Protection of Employment) Regulations 1981.[2] This approach must always be borne in when considering the increasing amount of domestic law which purports to implement European obligations. These developments have had an effect on domestic law. In part as a result of the decisions in *Pickstone* and *Litster*, the approach in construing domestic legislation which has no European dimension has changed and external materials such as records of parliamentary debates are now sometimes referred to by the courts in purely 'internal' cases.[3]

1 *Pickstone v Freemans plc* [1988] ICR 697, HL.
2 *Litster v Forth Dry Dock & Engineering Co Ltd* [1989] ICR 341, HL.
3 *Pepper v Hart* [1993] AC 593, [1993] 1 All ER 42, HL.

Direct enforceability

2.12 In some cases it may not be possible to achieve a result which is consistent with the United Kingdom's obligations to her partners simply by using the means of construction described by Lord Oliver. The requirement of

European law may have been imperfectly implemented into national law, or may not have been dealt with in national law at all. In these circumstances it has to be considered whether or not the individual legal person has a right or obligation which is directly enforceable against another in the national courts.

2.13 With the exception of Regulations and Decisions, which may of their nature be addressed to individual persons, the majority of European law-making actions are addressed to member states or to European organisations. For instance, art 119 of the Treaty of Rome begins 'Each Member State shall ... ensure and subsequently maintain [the principle of equal pay]'.[1] Thus, the primary obligation imposed by such European law-making actions is placed on the member state. What is contemplated is that the member state will take steps to ensure that the requirement of the European legislative act is given effect within the jurisdiction of the member state. At first sight it may appear unlikely that such a provision would grant rights to individuals within member states or impose obligations on others. Notwithstanding this, the European Court has held that some such provisions can be directly applicable within member states.[2] In consequence, in *Defrenne*[3] the European Court of Justice held that an airline stewardess could rely on art 119 in the Belgian courts in her action against the Belgian state airline.

1 For a consideration of Treaty of Rome, art 119 in greater detail, see 5.02–5.05.
2 Case 26/62 *Van Gend en Loos v Nederlandse Belastingadministratie* [1963] ECR 1, ECJ; Case 43/75 *Defrenne v Sabena* [1976] ICR 547, ECJ.
3 Case 43/75 *Defrenne v Sabena* [1976] ICR 547, ECJ.

Failure to implement European law

2.14 If the national law does not fully implement, or imperfectly implements, a European obligation which is a *directly enforceable* obligation, then it is now part of United Kingdom law that in certain circumstances the right may be enforced[1] in a national forum.[2] However, if there is a sufficient remedy under national law then the domestic remedy is the remedy which should be pursued. If there is a domestic remedy it is unnecessary, indeed impermissible, to explore the same complaint under the equivalent provisions in a Directive. It is only if there is a disparity between the two that it becomes necessary to explore whether there is a directly enforceable European right.[3] In addition, and as a separate claim, there may be the possibility of taking action against the state for failing to comply with its European obligations.[4]

1 See Case 43/75 *Defrenne v Sabena* [1976] ICR 547, ECJ.
2 For a discussion of the forum, see **2.27**.
3 *Blaik v Post Office* [1994] IRLR 280, EAT.
4 See **2.21**.

Direct effect

2.15 The European Court of Justice has held that arts 48 and 119 of the Treaty have direct effect. The circumstances in which Directives are directly enforceable are still to be made totally clear. Whether or not a Directive is directly enforceable, even to the limited extent mentioned below, depends on whether it imposes a clear, precise and unconditional obligation on the state which is subject to no limitation and 'the nature, general scheme, and wording of the provision'.[1] A well-known example of the application of these principles occurred in the *Miss Marshall's* second case[2] before the European Court of Justice when the Court held that by imposing a limit on the amount of compensation which the Miss Marshall could be awarded the United Kingdom had breached the Equal Treatment Directive which was directly enforceable. It is important to note that Miss Marshall's employer was an state body.

1 Case 41/74 *Van Duyn v Home Office (No 2)* [1975] 3 All ER 190, ECJ, see the opinion of the Advocate-General at pp 200 and 201.
2 Case C-271/91 *Marshall v Southampton and South West Hampshire Area Health Authority (Teaching) (No 2)* [1993] ICR 893, ECJ. The Sex Discrimination and Equal Pay (Remedies) Regulations 1993, SI 1993/2798, were made as result of this decision.

'Vertical' and 'horizontal' enforcement

Horizontal effect

2.16   Probably the principal provision of European law which is directly enforceable and which has had most significant effect on United Kingdom employment law is art 119 of the Treaty of Rome (see **5.02–5.05**).[1] A directly enforceable article in the Treaty may form the basis of an action by one private legal person against another in a national court. This is often referred to as the 'horizontal' effect of European law. An article which has horizontal effect may form the basis of an action by an employee against a private employer.

1 Other articles of the Treaty have direct effect, for instance art 48.

Vertical effect

2.17   Directives may themselves have direct effect, but only against member states, or against state bodies.[1] This is often called the 'vertical' effect of European law. The provisions of Directives cannot be relied on as having direct effect in actions against private individuals.[2] Thus a directly enforceable Directive cannot form the basis of a claim by an individual employee against a private employer.[3]

1 Case 222/84 *Johnston v Chief Constable of the Royal Ulster Constabulary* [1987] ICR 83, ECJ; Case 152/84 *Marshall v Southampton and South West Hampshire Area Health Authority (Teaching)* [1986] ICR 335, ECJ. Although it may appear that the Equal Pay Directive has been directly enforced in litigation between private individuals this has only been by way of explanation of the meaning of the article; see Case 96/80 *Jenkins v Kingsgate (Clothing Productions) Ltd* [1981] ICR 592 at p 614, para 22, ECJ, and *O'Brien v Sim-Chem Ltd* [1980] ICR 429, CA. The decision of the Court of Appeal was reversed in the House of Lords on other grounds.
2 For instance Treaty of Rome, art 48; Case 41/74 *Van Duyn v Home Office (No 2)* [1975] Ch 358, ECJ.
3 If the Directive merely explains the effect of a directly enforceable article in the Treaty it can be relied on, but only as a means of explaining the article.

Employers against which vertical claims may be brought

2.18   The decision whether or not a body is one which is subject to the direct effect of a Directive is a matter for national courts and tribunals[1] although the rules to be applied are rules of European law. In *Foster*[2] it was said that such a claim could be made against 'a body, whatever its legal form, which has been made responsible, pursuant to a measure adopted by the state, for providing a public service under the control of the state and has for that purpose special powers beyond those which result from the normal rules applicable in relations between individuals'. In a later case,[3] when giving judgment in the Court of Appeal, Mustill LJ expressed the view that this test is not intended to provide an answer to every category of case.

1 Case C-188/89 *Foster v British Gas plc* [1991] ICR 84, ECJ. The governing body of a voluntary aided school was held to be an organ of the state in *National Union of Teachers v Governing Body of St Mary's School* (1996) Times, 16 December, CA.
2 At p 108.
3 *Rolls Royce plc v Doughty* [1992] ICR 538 at p 552, CA. See also *St Mary's School*, n 1 above.

Imperfect implementation

2.19 Further complications arise when the national law, rather than failing to implement the European obligation, contains provisions which are in conflict with it. In Case 106/77 *Amministrazione delle Finanze dello Stato v Simmenthal SpA*[1] the European Court of Justice ruled:

'[A] national Court which is called upon, within the limits of its jurisdiction, to apply provisions of Community law is under a duty to give full effect to those provisions, if necessary refusing of its own motion to apply any conflicting provision of national legislation, even if adopted subsequently, and it is not necessary for the Court to request or await the prior setting aside of such provision by legislative or other constitutional means.'

1 [1978] ECR 629 at p 645, ECJ.

2.20 In *R v Secretary of State for Employment, ex p Equal Opportunities Commission*[1] (an action brought by the Equal Opportunities Commission) the House of Lords held that the threshold of 16 hours a week to be worked to become entitled to rights to redundancy payments and to be protected by the unfair dismissal provisions of the Employment Protection (Consolidation) Act 1978, was incompatible with art 119 of the Treaty of Rome and the Equal Treatment Directive. The House of Lords reached its decision without referring the matter to the European Court of Justice. The Court of Appeal has subsequently decided that the requirement of two years' service for two applicants who wished to complain of unfair dismissal discriminated against female employees and was incompatible with European law.[2] Although the national court will usually endeavour to use domestic rules of construction to enable a national provision to be applied in line with an obligation on the United Kingdom in European law, there is the ultimate power of adopting the approach in *Simmenthal*[3] and disapplying the provisions which are incompatible with European law. This is the approach which should be adopted by industrial tribunals if confronted with claims were it is necessary to disapply provisions of domestic law as being incompatible with European law.[4] Using this approach it may be possible for former employees to persuade an industrial tribunal to disapply the two years' continuous employment qualification for unfair dismissal.[5]

1 [1994] IRLR 176, HL.
2 *R v Secretary of State for Employment, ex p Seymour-Smith* [1995] IRLR 464, CA. An appeal against this decision is currently being heard by the House of Lords.

3 Case 106/77 *Amministrazione delle Finanze dello Stato v Simmenthal SpA* [1978] ECR 629 at
p 645, ECJ.
4 *Biggs v Somerset County Council* [1996] IRLR 203, CA; [1996] IRLR 203, CA.
5 See footnote 2 above.

Actions against the state for failure to transpose European obligations into national law

2.21   Where a legal person has suffered as a result of a failure by the state
to implement, or implement properly, its European obligations (for example
under art 119 of the Treaty of Rome) the person may have an action
against the state to remedy the loss which he has suffered as a result.[1] These
claims are often called 'Francovich' claims. Their extent is far from clear
and is likely to represent an active area of development in due course. It
appears that for claims to succeed (a) the rule of European law not transposed into domestic law must be intended to confer rights on individuals;
(b) the breach must be serious and (c) there has to be a direct causal link
between the breach by the state and the loss suffered by the individual.[2]

1 Case C-6/90 *Francovich v Italy* [1992] IRLR 84, ECJ; Case C-208/90 *Emmott v Minister for
Social Welfare* [1991] IRLR 387, ECJ.
2 *Brasserie du Pecheur SA v Germany* [1996] IRLR 267, ECJ; Case C-392/93 *R v HM Treasury,
ex p British Telecommunications plc* [1996] IRLR 300, ECJ.

Judicial review

2.22   If the decision which has lead to the failure to implement, or implement fully, European law has been taken by a minister or other public official
then the decision may be challenged by way of judicial review.[1] It is often difficult to establish locus standi to bring such actions, so that in *ex p EOC*,
although the Equal Opportunities Commission succeeded with its claim, an
individual applicant who had not brought a claim before an industrial tribunal because of the qualifying thresholds as to number of hours required
under provisions as to continuity of employment (formerly contained in Sch
13 to the Employment Protection (Consolidation) Act 1978) did not do so.[2]
The Court of Appeal have held that persons in private employment have sufficient standing to bring judicial review proceedings in reliance on the Equal
Treatment Directive.[3]

1 See for example *R v Secretary of State for Employment, ex p Equal Opportunities
Commission* [1994] ICR 176, HL.
2 For a case where applicants were found to have sufficient locus standi to bring their claims see
R v Secretary of State for Employment, ex p Seymour-Smith [1995] IRLR 464, CA.
3 *R v Secretary of State for Employment, ex p Seymour-Smith* [1995] IRLR 464, CA. This decision is presently under appeal in the House of Lords.

Time when European obligations take effect

2.23   When considering European obligations regard must be had to the
time at which the provision takes effect and at which it may be relied upon.
Not only has regard to be given to the time which the legislative act became
effective (as with domestic legislation) but also it falls to be considered

whether the European Court of Justice has, or will, set a limitation on the time before which conduct may not be the subject of complaint. Articles, Regulations and Directives usually state clearly when they are to be implemented or to become effective. Decisions of the European Court of Justice often deal expressly with this issue. So that in *Defrenne*[1] it was said that the direct effect of art 119 could not be relied on in order to support claims for pay periods prior to 8 April 1976, except by workers who at the time of the judgment had already bought proceedings or made equivalent claims.[2] A saving for those who have already bought proceedings or claims is regularly encountered in decisions of the European Court of Justice and should be borne in mind by those advising applicant's with possible claims in this still developing field.

1 Case 43/75 *Defrenne v Sabena* [1976] ICR 547, ECJ.
2 Case 43/75 *Defrenne v Sabena* [1976] ICR 547 at p 571, ECJ. In Case C-262/88 *Barber v Guardian Royal Exchange Assurance Group* [1990] ICR 616, ECJ, a similar approach was adopted when the European Court of Justice said its decision that an occupational pension was pay could not be relied upon to claim entitlement with effect prior to the date of the judgment (17 May 1990) except by workers who at the time of the judgment had already bought proceedings or made equivalent claims. See now Case C-435/93 *Dietz v Stichting Thuiszorg Rotterdam* [1996] IRLR 692, ECJ.

Time limits for claims based on European law

2.24   The question of time limits in which claims relying on European law may be brought to the tribunals and courts is also a vexed one. It appeared from *Emmott*[1] (a case involving a claim for invalidity benefits which was not properly transposed into domestic law) that in a claim against a member state pursuant to a Directive, the state cannot rely on the claimant's delay in bringing proceedings alleging a failure by the state to implement, or to implement fully, its obligations under the Directive. The time only begins to run when the obligation arising from the Directive is fully implemented. In *Emmott* it was not made clear whether the pronouncements of the European Court of Justice were limited to Directives, or whether they applied to directly effective Directives.

1 Case C-208/90 *Emmott v Minister for Social Welfare and A-G* [1991] IRLR 387, ECJ.

2.25   The lack of certainty in this respect is of considerable significance. As a result of the decision of the House of Lords in *ex p EOC*[1] many claims have been made to industrial tribunals by applicants claiming redundancy payments and/or remedies for unfair dismissal by part-time employees dismissed by both public and private employers years before the date their applications were presented to the industrial tribunal. In *Biggs v Somerset County Council*[2] the Court of Appeal considered the case of an applicant, a part-time employee, who was dismissed in 1976. At the time of the dismissal the applicant did not satisfy the requirement as to a minimum period of continuity of employment which was contained in the relevant statute. She did not present a claim of unfair dismissal to an industrial tribunal until 1 June 1994. The court upheld the decision that the application was out of time. It would have been practicable to present a claim to an industrial tribunal in 1976. At the time of the applicant's dismissal the tribunal had jurisdiction to hear such claims and, if appropriate, to disapply provisions of domestic law which were incompatible with European law. So, reasoned the court, her claim was out of time in accordance with the usual rules.[3]

1 *R v Secretary of State for Employment, ex p Equal Opportunities Commission* [1994] ICR 176, HL.
2 *Biggs v Somerset County Council* [1996] IRLR 203, CA. Contrast the earlier case of *Rankin v British Coal Corporation* [1995] ICR 774, EAT (in Scotland). For consideration of time limits regarding claims by part-time workers as to pension rights see *Preston v Wolverhampton Healthcare NHS Trust* [1996] IRLR 484, EAT; and *Levez v T H Jennings (Harlow Pools) Ltd* [1996] IRLR 499, EAT; and *Rastall v Midlands Electricity plc* [1996] ICR 644, EAT.
3 See also *Rastall v Midlands Electricity plc* [1996] ICR 644, EAT, where reference has been made to the European Court of Justice with regard to when time began to run in a pension claim. As to estoppel where a claim had been dismissed see *Barber v Staffordshire County Council* [1996] IRLR 209, CA.

2.26   If a claim is presented in time the amount recovered even against a public employer may itself be subject to temporal limitations. In *Johnston v Chief Adjudication Officer (No 2)*[1] it was held that it was compatible with European law to apply a national rule which limits the period in respect of which areas of benefit are payable to a claimant where the claim was based on the direct effect of the Social Security Directive 79/7/EEC, even where the Directive has not been properly transposed into domestic law in the member state within the prescribed period.

1 Case C-410/92 [1995] IRLR 157, ECJ, and see Case C-338/91 *Steenhorst-Neerings v Bestuur van de Bedrijfsverenging voor Detailhandel* [1994] IRLR 244, ECJ. Questions on similar issues have been referred to the European Court of Justice in *Levez v T H Jennings (Harlow Pools) Ltd* [1996] IRLR 499, EAT.

Jurisdiction of industrial tribunals

2.27   The High Court has a jurisdiction limited only by specific exclusion. This is known as the High Court's 'inherent jurisdiction'. Thus, unless there are statutory or other limitations to the contrary, the High Court can hear claims based on directly enforceable European rights. Industrial tribunals are creatures of statute and have only the restricted jurisdiction conferred on them. Industrial tribunals do not have inherent jurisdiction. Notwithstanding this, it has been held that industrial tribunals do have jurisdiction to hear claims based on European rights which are similar to specific statutory rights over which they have been given jurisdiction.[1] Industrial tribunals have power to apply European law to cases falling within their jurisdiction. The better view is that industrial tribunals have jurisdiction to hear claims bought within their jurisdiction under domestic law and, in doing so, to disapply any provisions which are incompatible with European law.[2] They do not have jurisdiction to hear claims for 'free standing' rights.[3] Industrial tribunals do not have jurisdiction to hear claims against the state as lawmaker for failing to fulfil its Treaty obligations ('Francovich' claims, see **2.21**).[4] Industrial tribunals do however have exclusive jurisdiction over many matters with which they deal. This must be taken into account by those advising as to the forum in which proceedings are to be brought.

1 *Pickstone v Freemans plc* [1987] ICR 867, CA. This was not an issue in the House of Lords: [1988] ICR 687, HL. See also *Biggs v Somerset County Council* [1996] IRLR 203, CA.
2 *Biggs v Somerset County Council* [1996] IRLR 203, CA; and *Barber v Staffordshire County Council* [1996] IRLR 209, CA.
3 See footnote 2 above.
4 *Mann v Secretary of State for Employment* [1996] IRLR 4, EAT.

Procedural rules

2.28 The procedural rules applicable by courts and tribunals to cases involving European law are designated by the national legal system.[1] They should be no less favourable than those relating to similar domestic actions and not be framed so as to render virtually impossible the exercise of the rights conferred by European law. In dealing with claims where European law is applicable the tribunals and courts follow, so far as is possible, the rules usually applicable to the forum.

1 Case 33/76 *Rewe-Zentralfinanz GmbH v Landwirtschaftskammer für Saarland* [1976] ECR 1989, ECJ and see Case C-410/92 *Johnson v Chief Adjudication Officer (No 2)* [1995] IRLR 157 at para 21, ECJ.

Chapter 3

Definition and formation of contracts of employment

Introduction

Although the relationship of employer and employee is founded on contract, rights of a contractual nature have been introduced by statute. Courts and tribunals recognise that employment rests on a relationship which changes and that the type of construction of a contract which would be appropriate in considering a mercantile contract is not relevant in this area of the law (see **3.07**).

Individual contracts of employment are often governed to some extent by collective agreements (see **3.12**).

It is necessary to distinguish between employees and independent contractors, office holders, directors and agents (see **3.15** et seq).

There are particular rules concerning certain parties such as minors, apprentices, aliens and Crown servants (see **3.24** et seq).

Contract and statute

3.01   At common law the relationship between employer and employee is one of contract. Statute places numerous restrictions on the freedom of the parties to negotiate terms of employment and grants to employees rights of a non-contractual nature. Recent legislative enactments superimpose provisions on the existing law. These developments are so far-reaching and are of such importance that, although knowledge of the common law is still an essential requirement for understanding their effects, the statutory provisions themselves are tending to distort the contractual basis of the relationship between employer and employee.

Formation of the contract

3.02   The formation of the contract of employment depends on the general law of contract. It is necessary for there to be to be both an offer and acceptance. Thus if a job applicant is offered a position subject to the receipt of satisfactory references this is a conditional offer of employment. The only obligation on the employer is to consider the references in good faith – whether the references are satisfactory is a matter for the employer.[1]

1 *Wishart v National Association of Citizens Advice Bureaux Ltd* [1990] IRLR 393, CA.

3.03   Offers of employment are often made subject to trial or probationary periods. Such a condition cannot avoid statutory rights. An employer would still be liable for an act of racial or sexual discrimination during the currency of such a period. Trial or probationary periods are normally of much shorter duration than the two years' continuous service necessary to acquire a right not to be unfairly dismissed. There is some authority that it might be fair to dismiss a probationary employee in circumstances in which it might be unfair to dismiss an established employee.[1] In reality this is probably no more than an application of the general proposition that an employer who has retained an employee for a number of years without complaint should have a cogent reason for deciding to dismiss such an employee for incompetence if there is no history of warnings. A lecturer appointed for a probationary lectureship of three years was held to be able to bring an action for unfair dismissal.[2]

1 *Hamblin v London Borough of Ealing* [1975] IRLR 354.
2 *Weston v University College of Swansea* [1975] IRLR 102.

3.04 There are certain advantages in including a term as to a trial period. It does bring home to an employee that his or her work is being assessed with particular scrutiny during the initial period. It makes it easier for an employer who dismisses an incompetent employee during such a period to show that incompetence was the reason for the dismissal. This might be of considerable evidential value in any action in which it is alleged that the dismissal was due to discrimination on grounds of race and/or sex or in cases of unfair dismissal in which there is no requirement for two years of continuous service.

3.05 For a contract to come into existence each party's promises must be supported by consideration, ie there must be obligations which bind each of them. The normal case will be the payment of remuneration by the employer and the provision of his labour or other services by the employee. Whether the consideration is adequate or not is immaterial provided that the quid pro quo exists.

Illegality

3.06 The courts and tribunals will not enforce rights and obligations arising under, or dependent on, an illegal contract of employment. The most frequent example is one which contains provisions intended to evade taxation.[1] However, if the employee does not receive direct benefit from the fraud, the contract may be enforceable.[2] Occasional payments made to the employee without deduction of tax which are not part of contractual remuneration have been held not to vitiate the contract on the ground of illegality.[3] Whilst it is open for a tribunal to take the point of illegality (even though the parties have not taken it) the tribunal should warn the parties of their concern and give them the opportunity of dealing with it.[4] Although the overwhelming proportion of cases concerns a fraud on the Inland Revenue, the rule applies to other situations if the fraudulent provisions are entered into for purposes which are forbidden by the law or which tend to promote sexual immorality.[5] In *Leighton v Michael* it was held that a sex discrimination case was still enforceable despite illegality.[6]

1 *Tomlinson v Dick Evans 'U' Drive Ltd* [1978] ICR 639, EAT (part of remuneration paid from petty cash to avoid tax); *Napier v National Business Agency Ltd* [1951] 2 All ER 264, CA; *Cole v Fred Stacey Ltd* (1974) 9 ITR 1193; *Holman v Johnson* (1775) 1 Cowp 341; *Davidson v Pillay* [1979] IRLR 275, EAT; *McConnell v Bolik* [1979] IRLR 422, EAT; *Corby v Morrison t/a Card Shop* [1980] ICR 564. See also *Salvesen v Simons* [1994] ICR 409, EAT (Scotland) where the authorities are reviewed.

2 *Hewcastle Catering Ltd v Ahmed* [1992] ICR 626.
3 *Annandale Engineering v Samson* [1994] IRLR 59, EAT. See also *Lightfoot v DJ Sporting Ltd* [1996] IRLR 64, EAT.
4 *Laurie v Holloway* [1994] ICR 32.
5 *Coral Leisure Group Ltd v Barnett* [1981] ICR 503, EAT.
6 [1995] ICR 1091, EAT.

Terms of the contract

3.07 It is not necessary, although it is usually wise, to set out the main terms of the contract. There is a statutory obligation to serve written particulars of employment not later than two months after the commencement of the employment.[1] However, it should be noted that the contract is what is agreed at the time when the contract was made. A common error is to assume that the particulars of employment invariably contain the terms of the contract. They do not; they are merely evidence of what the terms are and cannot override express terms agreed at the time when the contract was made. Frequently, as with other agreements, the relationship comes into being informally, when few terms are expressed, perhaps only those relating to salary and hours of work. In such cases the courts may imply such terms as are reasonably necessary to give effect to the contract. The common law rule applicable in such circumstances was expressed at the end of the 19th century by Lord Esher MR as follows:[2]

'A large number of cases have been cited, in some of which the Court implied a stipulation, and in others refused to do so. In my opinion, it is useless to cite such cases, so far as they merely show that in the particular case an implication was or was not made. The only use of citing such cases is where they lay down the rules as to such implications, upon which the Court will act in dealing with the particular case before it. I have for a long time understood that rule to be that the Court has no right to imply in a written contract any such stipulation, unless, on considering the terms of the contract in a reasonable and business manner, an implication necessarily arises that the parties must have intended that the suggested stipulation should exist. It is not enough to say that it would be a reasonable thing to make such an implication. It must be a necessary implication in the sense that I have mentioned.'

Although this remains an accurate summation of the law the courts and industrial tribunals have responded to social changes and have given the words *necessary implication*, an interpretation which reflects contemporary needs and realities.

1 But see the requirements of the Employment Rights Act 1996, s 1. In *Robertson v British Gas Corpn* [1983] IRLR 351, CA it was made clear that the written particulars are merely the evidence of the contract and not the contract itself. A written contract is conclusive: it is usually the sole evidence permissible of the express terms of the contract and evidence cannot be adduced to show that different terms were intended: *Gascol Conversions v Mercer* [1974] IRLR 155, CA. But see *Hawker Siddeley Power Engineering Ltd v Rump* [1979] IRLR 425, EAT in which it was held that an oral promise that a term to which the employee objected would not be enforced became a term of the contract and the employer could not treat a breach of the offending term as justifying dismissal. In construing a contract the normal rules of construction apply. The parties' subsequent behaviour is not admissible in construing a written contract: *Hooper v British Railways Board* [1988] IRLR 517. For a recent case see *Aparau v Iceland Frozen Foods* [1996] IRLR 119.
2 In *Hamlyn & Co v Wood & Co* [1891] 2 QB 488 at p 491, CA.

The changing nature of the job

3.08   Industrial tribunals and courts are alive to the fact that contracts of employment have a dynamic of their own which does not apply in other areas of contractual liability. An employee may have started life as a ledger clerk. If the employer decides to computerise the accounts, the ledger clerk may well be required to retrain and his or her job function may be very different, requiring skills which he or she may or may not be able to acquire. An employee's claim for a declaration that he should not be required to operate computerised systems failed in *Cresswell v Board of Inland Revenue*[1] on the basis that the employer was not in breach of contract in moving from manual to computerised systems and requiring the employee to acquire these new skills. The job content of many jobs will change over the years. Whether or not such changes constitute a breach of contract will depend on exactly how precisely the original post was defined and the extent of the change required. In *Redbridge Borough Council v Fishman*[2] a teacher who had been appointed as the teacher in charge of a resource centre was dismissed when she refused to take on an increased teaching load. Her dismissal was held to be unfair in that the employers were in breach of contract in requiring that teaching should be the main function of her job rather than an ancillary one. The citation of authority is of limited value in deciding such cases. Much depends on the facts of the particular case and in many cases such changes take place over a period of time with the result that in practice the employee will be held to have agreed with the changes, even though during that time the job content of the post may have become radically different. It should be noted that one of the particulars required to be given to an employee is the *title of the job* which the employee is employed to do or a *brief description of the work* for which he is employed and that if there is a change the employer is required to serve a written statement giving particulars of the change.[3] It is necessary to consider the realities. Although the employer may be in breach of contract the employee's remedy of wrongful dismissal is often a meagre financial recompense. If the employee refuses to co-operate with the changes, the employee may well be dismissed but the dismissal will not necesarily be unfair if the employer has good cause for imposing such changes and makes the changes with sensitivity. Whilst it may be possible for the employee to claim a redundancy payment, if the statutory requirements are satisfied this will be of scant financial consolation to an employee who is faced with a prolonged period of unemployment.

1 [1984] 2 All ER 713.
2 [1978] ICR 569.
3 Employment Rights Act 1996, ss 1(4)(f), 4(1) and (3).

General implied terms

3.09   Although each case does go on its own facts there are certain implied terms on the part of employer and employee which are of general application. These are dealt with in further detail at the appropriate place in the text. There are, however, certain implied terms of general application which may be noted here.

Terms commonly implied on behalf of the employer

3.10

(1)   Not to destroy the relationship of mutual trust and confidence between employer and employee. This does not extend to imposing an obligation on an employer to provide an employee – or former employee – with a reference.[1] If a reference is provided, then the employer may be liable to the recipient[2] and to the employee for negligent misstatements.[3] The most comprehensive formulation of the implied term of mutual trust and confidence is contained in the judgment of Browne Wilkinson J (as he then was) in *Woods v WM Car Services (Peterborough) Ltd*.[4] Where constructive dismissal is alleged, the underlying complaint is often that this is the term which has been broken. Indeed, the term is so wide in its effects that it has conferred a considerable discretion on tribunals to reach what they consider to be a just result.

(2)   To provide the employee with a safe system of work and safe equipment with which to work. In practice most claims arising out of personal injuries are covered by the rules as to tortious liability and in many cases by specific statutory duties.

1 *Gallear v Watson & Son Ltd* [1979] IRLR 306, EAT.
2 *Spring v Guardian Assurance plc* [1994] ICR 596, HL.
3 *Hedley Byrne & Co Ltd v Heller & Partners Ltd* [1964] AC 465.
4 [1981] ICR 666, EAT. The older textbooks, although emphasising the employee's duty of submissive obedience, nevertheless recognised that the employer had a duty of 'gentleness and moderation in his dealing with his servant'. See Lord Fraser *Master and Servant* (3rd edn) p 120.

Terms commonly implied on behalf of the employee

3.11

(1)   To act in good faith.
(2)   Obedience
(3)   Not to disclose confidential information.
(4)   To work with due care and diligence.

   It is not suggested that the above obligations are exhaustive and in particular companies or particular industries certain implied terms may well be implied by long-established custom.

Collective agreements

3.12   The terms of employment of a substantial section of the workforce are covered by collective agreements which are negotiated between a single employer, or a group of employers and the trade union or unions which represent those employees. Although this industrial practice is widespread it can give rise to a number of difficulties. It is beyond the scope of this book to consider in detail the extent to which collective agreements are legally enforceable by the trade unions and the employers. In effect such agreements will only be enforceable when they are in writing and there is an express provision that the agreement will be a legally enforceable contact.[1]

1 Trade Union and Labour Relations (Consolidation) Act 1992, s 179(1), (2). There are further rules as to incorporating a *no strike* clause into an individual contract (s 180). Even if the stringent test is met, a court will not order specific performance or an injunction which would compel an individual to attend work (s 236).

Incorporation into the individual contract

3.13 Although as between trade union and employer collective agreements will not be legally enforceable unless they satisfy the statutory test, collective agreements are frequently incorporated into the individual contract either because there is an implied term that they will be incorporated into the individual contract or because they are expressly incorporated into the individual contract.

3.14 When collective agreements which are incorporated into the individual contract deal with matters such as rates of pay, holiday entitlements and the like, no problem of construction usually arises since these are clearly issues of contractual entitlement. Difficulties can arise when collective agreements deal with rather more nebulous matters. It is not always clear whether what is being agreed is a general guideline of good industrial practice, a concession which may be withdrawn or an enforceable legal right. In *Cadoux v Central Regional Council*[1] C's letter of appointment stated that his post was subject to the conditions of service supplemented by the local authorities' rules as amended from time to time. One of these rules stated that the employing council had introduced a non-contributory life insurance policy. On the employee's complaint that the council was required to provide him with a life insurance scheme, it was held that the rules were made unilaterally by the employer and the facility could be withdrawn as the employer was entitled to vary, amend or cancel any of the provisions in the rules. If the collective agreement as varied from time to time is incorporated into the individual contract it matters not that the employee concerned does not approve of the term or that he has ceased to be a member of the union concerned.[2] An employee has been held to be able to enforce the terms of a collective agreement concerning redundancy procedures which was incorporated into his individual contract even though the collective agreement was expressed to be binding in honour only.[3] The particulars of employment are required to set out any collective agreements which directly affect the terms and conditions of employment including – where the employer is not a party – the persons by whom they were made.[4]

1 *Cadoux v Central Regional Council* [1986] IRLR 131, Ct of Sess and see *National Coal Board v National Union of Miners* [1986] ICR 736, ChD. Cf *Robertson v British Gas Corpn* [1983] ICR 351, CA.
2 *Tocher v General Motors (Scotland) Ltd* [1981] IRLR 55. For an example in which one group of employees sought to invoke a collective agreement to downgrade the status of other employees, see *Adams v British Airways plc* [1996] IRLR 574, CA.
3 *Marley v Forward Trust Ltd Group Ltd* [1989] ICR 891, CA.
4 Employment Rights Act 1996, s 1(4)(j).

Employed or self-employed

3.15 The relationship of employer and employee only arises where the contract is a 'contract of service', and not when it is a 'contract for services'.[1] The distinction is a fine one and may be difficult to apply in borderline cases. The distinction has assumed an increased importance for the purposes of social and fiscal legislation as well as for employment law.

1 Employment Rights Act 1996, s 230(1).

Distinguishing the employed from the self-employed

3.16 There are many incentives for an employer to ensure that as few as possible of the workforce are employees. This relieves an employer from having to pay National Insurance contributions, from the obligation of having to deduct income tax[1] and from the need to pay holiday or sickness pay or make a redundancy payment and from the risk of being sued for unfair dismissal. It also means that an employer is not vicariously liable for the acts of that particular individual. Yet employers often wish to retain their power to control and supervise those whom they are anxious to designate as self-employed. The position is best illustrated by the example of a company which has many small retail outlets. Experience may show that the turnover and profitability of such retail stores is better if a manager is not regarded as an employee, but as a self-employed manager working under a contract for services. The manager is likely to be allowed a percentage of turnover and from this he may be expected to employ such staff as he needs and to defray certain of the expenditure of the shop. The company may well wish to ensure that (1) the manager only sells its merchandise and does not use the floor space to sell goods on his own account; (2) the shop is open for a number of hours each week; (3) the manager keeps accounts in an approved form and deposits takings into a particular bank account and (4) the manager is subject to supervision and to a disciplinary code. The result is that many aspects of the manager's working life will point to his being an employee while many other aspects will suggest that he is self-employed. Faced with this complexity the recent trend in case law has been to accept that the nature of the relationship is not one that can be precisely defined and that the decision will be reached by an assessment of an accumulation of relevant factors which is best left to the court or tribunal of first instance to determine.

1 There are special rules in the building industry.

An issue of law or fact?

3.17 Whether or not the correct test to distinguish an employed from a self-employed person has been applied is a matter of law, but when the right test has been applied the conclusion to be drawn is usually regarded as a question of fact.[1] Thus, in the example given of the manager of a shop, whilst there will be a uniformity of approach there may well not be a uniformity of result since different courts or tribunals may give different weight to aspects of the relationship on the particular facts of the case. Exceptionally, if the relationship is dependent solely on the construction of a written document, it is regarded as a question of law.[2]

1 *Global Plant Ltd v Secretary of State for Health and Social Security* [1972] 1 QB 139; [1971] 3 All ER 385. See also the judgment of Browne LJ in *Ferguson v John Dawson & Partners (Contractors) Ltd* [1976] 3 All ER 817 at p 832, CA and *Nethermere (St Neots) Ltd v Taverna and Gardiner* [1984] IRLR 240, [1984] ICR 612, CA; *Lee Ting Sang v Chung Chi-Keung* [1990] ICR 409, PC; *Clifford v Union of Democratic Miners* [1991] IRLR 518, CA.
2 *Davies v Presbyterian Church of Wales* [1986] IRLR 194 and see *McMeechan v Secretary of State for Employment* [1995] ICR 444.

The control test

3.18 Traditionally, the existence of a contract of service was dependent in part on the amount of control exercised by the employer[1] but the test of control is not an absolute one.[2]

'The nature of the control which is required in order to bring the employment within the scope of a contract of service flows almost infinitely with the general nature of the duties involved. If, therefore, for example, one finds that the contract, whether a written contract or an oral contract, has laid down in considerable detail what the duties are which are to be performed, and that the employer has the right to dispense with the services of the employee if not satisfied with the manner in which he carries out the duty, the actual absence of any expressed provision as to the right of the employer to control the manner of carrying out the work may be of much less importance than it would be in other cases.'[3]

1 *Simmons v Heath Laundry* Co [1910] 1 KB 543, CA; *Amalgamated Engineering Union v Minister of Pensions and National Insurance* [1963] 1 All ER 864; [1963] 1 WLR 441; *Morren v Swinton and Pendlebury Borough Council* [1965] 2 All ER 349; [1965] 1 WLR 576: *Ready Mixed Concrete (South East) Ltd v Minister of Pensions and National Insurance* [1968] 2 QB 497; [1968] 1 All ER 433.
2 *Global Plant Ltd v Secretary of State for Health and Social Security* [1972] 1 QB 139; [1971] 3 All ER 385.
3 *Amalgamated Engineering Union v Minister of Pensions and National Insurance* [1963] 1 All ER 864 at p 871; [1963] 1 WLR 441 at p 453, per Megaw J.

The futility of a comprehensive definition

3.19 The reality is that it is almost impossible to provide a single comprehensive definition which embraces all situations. Over 40 years ago in *Stevenson Jordan and Harrison Ltd v MacDonald and Evans*,[1] Denning LJ (as he then was), said:

'it is almost impossible to give a precise definition of the distinction. It is often easy to recognise a contract of service when you see it, but difficult to say wherein the difference lies. A ship's master, a chauffeur, and a reporter on the staff of a newspaper are all employed under a contract of service; but a ship's pilot, a taximan, and a newspaper contributor are employed under a contract for services. One feature which seems to run through the instances is that, under a contract of service, a man is employed as part of the business, and his work is done as an integral part of the business. Whereas, under a contract for services, his work, although done for the business, is not integrated into it but is only accessory to it.'

In the plethora of cases which have been decided in the intervening period rather different tests have been formulated and the most dominant question to emerge is whether the person is *in business on his own account*. It is suggested that the best guidance as to the approach which any court or tribunal should adopt is contained in the decision of Mummery J (as he then was) in an Inland Revenue case *Hall v Lorimer*:[2]

'In order to decide whether a person carries on business on his own account it is necessary to consider many different aspects of that person's work. This is not a mechanical exercise of running through items on a checklist to see whether they are present in, or absent from, a given situation. The object of the exercise is to paint a picture from the accumulation of detail. The overall effect can only be appreciated by standing back from the detailed picture which has been painted, by viewing it from a distance and by making an informed, qualitative appreciation of the whole. It is a matter of evaluation of the overall effect of the detail, which is not necessarily the same as the sum total of the individual details. Not all details are of equal weight or importance in any given situation. The details may also vary in importance from one situation to another. The process involves painting a picture in each individual case.'

1 [1952] 1 TLR 101 at p 111.
2 [1994] ICR 218, CA, quoted with approval at p 226.

3.20 In a borderline case it is difficult for any practitioner to advise with confidence whether an applicant will be defined as an employee or as self-employed and, as long as the tribunal applies the correct test, it is difficult to mount a successful appeal against that finding in an appellate court. Frequently advocates in industrial tribunals overstate the importance of a decision in the Court of Appeal or the Employment Appeal Tribunal when they seek to bring the facts of their own case within the ambit of a decided case. Often on a close analysis of the judgment all the appellate court is saying is that the decision which an industrial tribunal reached is open to the tribunal on the facts of the particular case and it is not presuming to lay down a rule of law as to how persons carrying out that sort of work should be classified.

Formulating a test

3.21 In *Ready Mixed Concrete (South East) Ltd v Minister of Pensions and National Insurance*[1] MacKenna J used a 'multiple' test when he said:
'A contract of service exists if the following three conditions are fulfilled: (i) The servant agrees that in consideration of a wage or other remuneration he will provide his own work and skill in the performance of some service for his master. (ii) He agrees, expressly or impliedly, that in the performance of that service he will be subject to the other's control in a sufficient degree to make that other master. (iii) The other provisions of the contract are consistent with its being a contract of service.'
In applying the judge's third condition matters other than control are taken into account. Recent cases have emphasised the extent to which the person is carrying out the work as a person *in business on his own account*.[2] The terms of the contract and surrounding circumstances are looked at to see whether factors which categorise it as either one of service, or for services, are present. There is no exhaustive list of these characteristics, but items such as the provision of large capital assets, the right to delegate the work, the extent of the obligation to work, methods of payment, intention, the form of contractual documents, the power of selection and appointment, the power to dismiss or suspend, the fixing of times and places of work, and many others have been considered.[3] Perhaps the most pithy test is to ask what would the applicant's honest answer be to the question 'Are you your own boss?'[4]

1 [1968] 2 QB 497; [1968] 1 All ER 433, QBD.
2 Cooke J in *Market Investigations Ltd v Minister of Social Security* [1969] 2 QB 173 at p 187, affirmed by the Privy Council in *Lee v Chung* [1990] ICR 409. In that case the 'part and parcel' test was held to be misleading.
3 *Global Plant Ltd v Secretary of State for Health and Social Security* [1972] 1 QB 139; [1971] 3 All ER 385, QBD; *Maurice Graham Ltd v Brunswick* (1974) 16 ITR 158, DC; *Ferguson v John Dawson & Partners (Contractors) Ltd* [1976] 3 All ER 817; [1976] IRLR 346, CA; *Davis v New England College of Arundel* [1977] ICR 6, EAT; *Massey v Crown Life Insurance Co* [1978] 2 All ER 576; [1978] ICR 590, CA; *Tyne and Clyde Warehouses Ltd v Hamerton* [1978] ICR 661, EAT; *Market Investigations Ltd v Ministry of Social Security* [1969] 2 QB 173; [1968] 3 All ER 732, DC; *Thames Television Ltd v Wallis* [1979] IRLR 136, EAT. See also *Winfield v London Philharmonic Orchestra Ltd* [1979] ICR 726, EAT and *Hitchcock v Post Office* [1980] ICR 100,

EAT. *O'Kelly v Trusthouse Forte plc* [1983] ICR 457; *Airfix Footwear Ltd v Cope* [1978] ICR 1210; *Hall v Lorrimer* [1994] ICR 218, CA.
4 *Withers v Flackwell Heath Football Supporters Club* [1981] IRLR 307, EAT, per Bristow J.

Parties' definition of the relationship

3.22   Difficulty may still be experienced even where the parties have 'agreed' on the type of relationship.[1] A degree of judicial irritation has been expressed in certain of the decisions that a person has been anxious to agree to the status of being self-employed – with the more generous tax treatment which that allows – and equally anxious to assert that for the purpose of employment protection legislation he or she is an employee. The intention of the parties is an important, but not the determining, factor to be taken into account. Parties cannot change a status merely by putting a label on it and so describing a contract of service as self-employment will have no effect. Even if a worker has deliberately chosen to be classified as self-employed, he may still assert he is an employee when he is obviously an employee, since to deny him this right would deny him the protection of a statute passed for his benefit.[2] It is likely that when the parties deliberately agree that an individual is self-employed and he is so treated for all purposes he will be found to be engaged under a contract for services as long as the relationship is capable of this interpretation. The fact that the Inland Revenue or the Department of Social Security have accepted the relationship is, or is not, that of an employee is relevant but not conclusive.[3] An employee may be under a contract of service with his original employer while the use and benefit of his services are transferred to a temporary employer.[4]

1 *Ferguson v John Dawson & Partners (Contractors) Ltd* [1976] 3 All ER 817; [1976] IRLR 346, CA; *Massey v Crown Life Insurance Co* [1978] IRLR 31; [1978] ICR 590, CA; *Davis v New England College of Arundel* [1977] ICR 6, EAT; and *Tyne and Clyde Warehouses Ltd v Hamerton* [1978] ICR 661, EAT.
2 *Young & Woods Ltd v West* [1980] IRLR 201 at p 207, per Stephenson LJ; *Massey v Crown Life Insurance Co* [1978] ICR 590 at p 596, per Lord Denning, but see *Tyne and Clyde Warehouses Ltd v Hamerton* [1978] ICR 661, EAT.
3 *Narich Pty Ltd v Pay Roll Tax Comr* [1984] ICR 286.
4 *Denham v Midland Employers' Mutual Assurance Ltd* [1955] 2 QB 437; [1955] 2 All ER 561, CA.

Forms of contracts of employment

3.23   Apart from the provisions of s 1 of the Employment Rights Act 1996 (which provides that a written statement is to be given to the employee specifying certain particulars of the contract of employment), there are no formal requirements for a contract of service and it may even be inferred from conduct. Certain contracts of employment, by virtue of specific Acts of Parliament, must be in writing. These examples are the exception rather than the rule.

Parties to the contract

3.24   In general at common law any individual who was sui juris could enter into an employment contract and the limitations as to the bargains struck by the parties were small. Recent developments have meant that in addition to imposing significant limitations on the freedom of the employer and the employee as to the terms of the contract, an employer has to consider legislation relating to sex, race and disability as well as the abilities and other attributes of the candidate for employment.

Minors

3.25 Minors[1] (ie people under 18 years) are protected by the law of contract against disadvantageous bargains.[2] This aspect of the law in its detailed exposition belongs more properly to the law of contract as a whole, and reference should be made to works on that subject. In certain circumstances the question may have to be considered in relation to a minor employer or a minor employee. Broadly speaking, the position is that a contract to serve, or a contract to be bound as an apprentice, is voidable at the option of the minor if the contract as a whole is not for the minor's benefit. Because of the raising of school age modern cases are rare. In *Clements v London and North Western Rly Co*, Kay LJ said:[3]

'It has been clearly held that contracts of apprenticeship and with regard to labour are not contracts to an action on which the plea of infancy is a complete defence, and the question has always been, both at law and in equity, whether the contract, when carefully examined in all its terms, is for the benefit of the infant. If it is so, the Court before which the question comes will not allow the infant to repudiate it. I will take only one or two of the cases that illustrate this. In *R v Hindringham (Inhabitants)*[4] Lord Kenyon said: "I desire it may not be taken for granted that an infant who binds himself apprentice, a contract so notoriously for his own benefit, may put an end to that contract at any time during his minority." He did not decide the question, but he clearly expressed his opinion that an infant was not able to put an end to a contract that was for his benefit. I will only take one more of the cases that that of *Leslie v Fitzpatrick*.[5] There an apprenticeship agreement was pronounced to be not necessarily unfair because of certain unilateral provisions which were made against the infant. That was the case of an apprenticeship deed, giving the master power to terminate the agreement in certain events; and Lush J, in giving the judgment of the Court, said: "If such a provision were at the time common to labour contracts, or were in the then condition of trade such as the master was reasonably justified in imposing as a just measure of protection to himself, and if the wages were a fair compensation for the services of the youth, the contract is binding, inasmuch as it was beneficial to him by securing to him permanent employment, and the means of maintaining himself."'

1 Also called infants and so referred to in the older authorities. There are relatively few modern authorities relating to the employment of minors.
2 Infants Relief Act 1874.
3 [1894] 2 QB 482 at p 491, CA.
4 (1796) 6 Term Rep 557.
5 (1877) 3 QBD 229.

3.26 If a minor enters into a contract which he can subsequently avoid on the plea of his minority, the transaction will be valid and binding until he chooses to repudiate it, and any payment made by the minor of which he has obtained the benefit cannot be recovered by him after he has avoided the contract.[1]

1 *Valentini v Canali* (1889) 24 QBD 166.

Apprentices

3.27 At common law an apprentice is someone who by contract is to be taught a trade or calling, in contradistinction to a person who engages to serve another person generally.[1] In some trades and vocations apprenticeship is still a vital part of training, but in others its role is on the decline. Much of the case law on apprenticeship dates from the 19th century and so must be used with caution. Teaching and learning must be the principal object of the contracting parties and service is incidental.[2] In the past almost all apprentices were minors, but with the reduction of the age of majority and the increase in the school leaving age, this is less likely to be the case in future.

1 *R v Laindon Inhabitants* (1799) 8 Term Rep 379.
2 *R v Crediton Inhabitants* (1831) 2 B & Ad 493.

3.28 Many modern statutory definitions, for instance that in s 230(2) of the Employment Rights Act 1996, include within the definition of employee those working under contracts of apprenticeship. However, the fact that an employee is also an apprentice may not be irrelevant. An apprentice has been awarded damages not just for his immediate loss but also a sum representing the loss of future prospects as a qualified tradesman.[1] There is no reason why in principle this should not also apply to an action for unfair dismissal. Further, as apprentices were historically very much in loco parentis, an industrial tribunal might well be prepared to find that an employer should be more indulgent to lapses which would not be tolerated in other circumstances. Thus the apprentice who was criticised by his managing director and replied 'You couldn't have done any fucking better' was held to have been unfairly dismissed on the basis that an isolated act of insubordination did not justify the termination of an apprenticeship which had only ten months to run.[2]

1 *Dunk v George Waller & Son Ltd* [1970] 2 All ER 630, CA.
2 *Shortland (WF) Ltd v Chantrill* [1975] IRLR 208. See *Wallace v CA Roofing Services Ltd* [1996] IRLR 435 for a recent case on apprentices.

Holders of offices

3.29 At first sight some holders of offices may appear to fall within the category of employees. However, they may not be the subject of employment relationships. In considering an application by a secretary of a social club claiming that he had been unfairly dismissed, Phillips J said that important pointers in determining whether the applicant was an employee were:
'(1) The payment made to the secretary; was it an honorarium (*Shorter Oxford English Dictionary* (first meaning) 'an honorary reward') or was it a salary? So the question is whether the payment was made contractually for the services, and whether the services were rendered in return for the payment, or whether it was a mere grant or solatium.

(2) The tribunal may wish to consider whether the payment was fixed in advance, possibly on a periodical basis, or whether it was voted at the end of the year in token of the members' work. The former arrangement would

favour the view that the payment was a salary, the latter that it was not: though neither would be conclusive.

(3) It is material to see whether the arrangements confer upon the secretary a right to payment or whether what is paid is a mere bounty.

(4) The size of the payment.

(5) Whether he is exercising the functions of an independent office (somewhat in the way that a curate or a police officer does) or is subject to the control and orders of the club.

(6) The extent and weight of the duties performed; the smaller they are the less likely he is to be an employee.

(7) The description given to the payment in the minute or resolution authorising it, and its treatment in the accounts, and for tax and national insurance purposes.'[1]

The fact that the claimant was a member of the club, that there was no written agreement, that he also held an office, that he had another job, that he was elected and could be removed by a two-thirds majority were considered of little relevance. An office holder may be employed under a contract of service as well as being the holder of the office. The question is whether the duties which are performed arise out of the discretion of the office holder or as a result of a contractual obligation.

1 *Social Club (102) and Institute Ltd v Bickerton* [1977] ICR 911 at 919, EAT. For a decision in which the position of a barrister's clerk was considered, see *McMenamin (Inspector of Taxes) v Diggles* [1991] ICR 641.

Ministers of religion

3.30 The most widely accepted view is that ministers of religion cannot be regarded as employees.[1] This view has been recently reaffirmed in the Employment Appeal Tribunal when an appeal was allowed from an industrial tribunal decision that a curate was an employee.[2]

1 *Barthorpe v Exeter Diocesan Board of Finance Ltd* [1979] ICR 900, EAT (licensed reader in the Church of England engaged as full-time stipendary reader). See also *Re National Insurance Act 1911, Re Church of England Curates* [1912] 2 Ch 563 (curate); *Davies v Presbyterian Church of Wales* [1986] ICR 280, HL and *Methodist Conference v Parfitt* [1984] ICR 176, CA.
2 *Southwark Diocese v Coker* [1996] ICR 896, EAT.

Crown servants

3.31 There used to be some doubt whether or not a Crown servant is bound by an employment contract, but a modern view is that a contractual relationship does exist.[1] What is clear is that the Crown has an absolute right of dismissal which is unfettered unless it is expressly restricted by statute.[2] Anything falling short of a statute which purports to take away this right is void as contrary to public policy and, unless there is a statutory provision to the contrary, employment of a Crown servant is at the pleasure of the Crown and may be terminated without notice.[3] The relevant statutory provision is now s 191 of the Employment Rights Act 1996 which includes all the principal employment rights save for redundancy payments in respect of which the Civil Service has its own scheme.

1 *Kodeeswaran v A-G for Ceylon* [1970] AC 1111. In *R v Lord Chancellor's Department, ex p Nangle* [1991] IRLR 343 the Divisional Court decided that a contractual relationship existed on

the basis that there was an intention to create legal relations and therefore rights were enforceable by private law remedies.
2 *Riordan v War Office* [1959] 3 All ER 552 at p 447, per Diplock J quoting Stuart Robertson *Civil Proceedings by and Against the Crown* (1908 edn) p 357; affirmed [1960] 3 All ER 774n, CA.
3 As far as relevant to the statutory provisions considered in this book, the position of Crown servants is explained in each chapter below.

Directors

3.32 The position of a company director is somewhat anomalous. The director holds an office with the company but may in addition be an employee of it.[1] If he performs services for the company in circumstances where, but for his directorship he would be an employee, then he may have a dual relationship with the company being both an office holder and an employee. When there is no express contract of service the facts have to be closely examined to ascertain whether an implied contract of service exists. In a case where a director of a family company worked as managing director of subsidiary companies, where his remuneration was treated as part of 'fees and emoluments', and where a self-employed National Insurance stamp had been paid by him and no memorandum was kept pursuant to s 26(1) of the Companies Act 1967, a decision by an industrial tribunal that he was not an employee was restored by the Court of Appeal.[2] If an employee is also a director of his employing company, rules of company law have to be considered in addition to those governing his employment. He may be removed from his directorship in accordance with the articles of association of the employing company or under the Companies Act 1985. However, the relationship of employer and employee is governed by the usual employment law rules, and his removal from his directorship may well be in breach of contract and additionally give rise to the possibility of a claim under the statutory provisions.[3] A director who is not a shareholder, or holds only a small percentage of the company's capital, and who serves under a contract of employment is likely to be regarded as an employee.

1 See *Re TN Farrer Ltd* [1937] Ch 352; [1937] 2 All ER 505.
2 *Parsons v Albert J Parsons & Sons Ltd* [1979] ICR 271, CA.
3 See *Parsons'* case above.

3.33 Difficulties sometimes arise when the working director holds a substantial amount of the equity, or is able to exercise a large degree of control over the company's activities. Each case has to be judged on its merits and what is applicable for the purpose of one scheme of legislation is not necessarily so for another.[1] The issue is essentially one of fact for the tribunal and the crucial test is whether the functions which are carried out are consistent with a contractual obligation to perform those functions as opposed to being matters which are performed at the discretion of an office holder. In determining this, the relevant matters are the existence of a contract and whether payment is regular and pre-determined, for example in the case of a salary, as opposed to being essentially geared to the profitability of the company.[2]

1 *Robinson v George Sorby Ltd* (1966) 2 ITR 148.
2 *Eaton v Robert Eaton Ltd & Secretary of State for Employment* [1988] IRLR 83.

3.34 A distinction has to be drawn between terminating the employment of a director and terminating the directorship. Thus the board can terminate the employment relationship of a director but not the directorship. Unless there is specific provision to this effect in the company's articles of association, a director may be removed from his office only by retirement, removal under the terms of the articles of association, resignation, a requirement of the Companies Act or a resolution at a general meeting of the company.[1]

1 When drawing service agreements for directors of quoted companies and subsidiaries the requirements of the Stock Exchange have to be taken into account.

3.35   Under s 318 of the Companies Act 1985 a company must keep a copy of every written service agreement and a written memorandum of every oral contract. Section 319 further provides that without the approval of a resolution in general meeting a director may not be supplied with a contract of employment for more than five years.

Partners

3.36   An equity partner cannot be employed by the partnership, even though he is paid so-called wages for working in the partnership business. It is legally impossible to be under a contract of service with oneself and others as joint masters. In a case under the Workmen's Compensation Act 1897 (long since repealed) Mathew LJ said:

'The deceased man in this case was a partner; and the arrangement made between him and his co-partners as to payment of wages to him was really an agreement with regard to the mode in which accounts were to be taken between the partners, and to the share of profits to be received by him in excess of that received by the other partners in consideration of the work done by him. The Workmen's Compensation Act 1897 cannot in my opinion apply to such a case.'[1]

Although this dictum is of considerable antiquity it remains a correct statement of the present law.[2] If the reality is that the enterprise is a co-operative venture, then the participants do not turn themselves into employees merely by arranging their affairs in a corporate form with a board of directors.[3]

1 *Ellis v Joseph Ellis & Co* [1905] 1 KB 324 at p 329, CA. Contrast *Easdown v Cobb* [1940] 1 All ER 49, HL (workmen's compensation; partners executed a deed of assignment; former partner as manager).
2 *Cowell v Quilter Goodison & Co Ltd and QG Management Services Ltd* [1989] IRLR 392. Equity partner not governed by employment relationship and therefore the Transfer of Undertaking (Protection of Employment) Regulations 1981 had no application.
3 *Winfield v London Philharmonic Orchestra Ltd* [1979] ICR 726 but see *Drym Fabricators Ltd v Johnson* [1981] ICR 274.

Agents

3.37   So-called 'representatives' of commercial houses and traders are employed under so many varieties of contracts that it is often difficult to describe their exact legal position, and in each case the facts must be carefully studied. A number of decided cases will be found arising, for instance, out of actions for wrongful dismissal, claims by commercial travellers for commission, and cases on the law of principal and agent in addition to claims for redundancy payments, unfair dismissal and under other employment legislation. Agents per se are not the subject of contracts of service or contracts for services. Insofar as any person has authority to act on behalf of another, he is that other person's agent. All employees are in some matters agents of their employers. Many agents, however, are under no contract of employment.[1]

1 *Sellers v London Counties Newspapers* [1951] 1 KB 784; [1951] 1 All ER 544, CA (commercial traveller, remuneration by salary and commission); *Levy v Goldhill & Co* [1917] 2 Ch 297 (not 'employment', not contract of service, merely an agreement to remunerate in respect of orders accepted); *Tyne and Clyde Warehouses Ltd v Hamerton* [1978] ICR 661, EAT; *Massey v Crown Life Insurance Co* [1978] 2 All ER 576; [1978] ICR 590, CA; *Wickens v Champion Employment* [1984] ICR 365, EAT.

Chapter 4

Remuneration

Introduction

Remuneration is generally a matter of agreement; it is wider than the mere cash payment. An employer may not unilaterally reduce remuneration, but an employee has no implied contractual right to a pay increase. An employee cannot elect to carry out part of his duties. In many instances pay is the subject of national agreements which are incorporated into the individual's contract (see **4.01–4.11**).

The employer is under a statutory obligation to provide itemised pay statements (see **4.12–4.16**).

There is no general power to suspend an employee and such rights must arise out of express or implied terms (see **4.17–4.23**). There is a statutory power to suspend on medical grounds (see **4.24–4.28**).

Lay-off and short-time working depend on contractual rights (see **4.29–4.34**) and there is a statutory scheme of guarantee payments (see **4.35–4.45**).

Employers are under a duty to set out the position in regard to sick pay in their particulars of employment (see **9.16**). There is no universal rule that employees are entitled to sick pay and the right to payment depends on the express or implied terms of the contract (see **4.46–4.51**).

Contrary to popular belief there is no obligation, apart from statute, for an employer to allow paid or unpaid holidays (see **4.52–4.54**).

Employees are allowed time off for certain public duties although there is no requirement for employers to pay the employee concerned (see **4.55–4.61**).

Employees are protected against being dismissed or selected for redundancy on the basis of their refusal to work on Sundays (see **4.12**).

Remuneration and time off

Remuneration

4.01 Before the intervention of legislation the parties were free to decide the terms of the contract which existed between them. They could agree as to the amount of remuneration and when it would be paid. Statute has now taken away much of that freedom and at times an employee is entitled to payment whether or not he performs work for his employer. Governments have on occasion imposed statutory limits on the amount of pay increases and in certain industries wages councils have laid down minimum wages. Since 1979 the trend of recent legislation has been against intervention as a way of controlling inflation or, through wages councils, of ensuring a minimum wage. In default of agreement as to the amount of remuneration the courts have been prepared to imply a term that there is a contractual right to

43

reasonable remuneration.[1] In practice in the present climate there will be few occasions when there is no agreement as to the amount of remuneration. The statutory obligation to give written particulars of employment and itemised pay statements reduces the area of uncertainty.

1 *Way v Latilla* [1937] 3 All ER 759, HL. However, in *Re Richmond Gate Property Co Ltd* [1965] 1 WLR 335, ChD the court refused to imply a right of remuneration to a managing director in a provision that 'the managing director shall receive such payment ... as the directors may determine'.

Remuneration more than the cash payment

4.02   At common law the word 'remuneration' if unqualified in any way includes more than just the cash payment in the form of wages or salary. In *R v Postmaster General*,[1] Blackburn J said:

'I think the word "remuneration" means a *quid pro quo*. If a man gives his services, whatever consideration he gets for giving his services seems to me a remuneration for them.'

And a later passage in his judgment reads:[2]

'I liken it to a case of a domestic servant who receives wages at a certain rate, and also has board and lodging. There seems to me no doubt that his receipt of the board and lodging is part of the remuneration, and if he was dismissed improperly or unlawfully, the measure of the damages would be not only the money paid to him, but the money and money's worth in remuneration for his services, which he would have received if the contract had been carried out.'

When a tip which was included in a credit card or cheque for a restaurant meal was distributed among the waiters it was held to be remuneration for the purposes of minimum wage legislation.[3]

1 (1876) 1 QBD 658 at p 663 (on appeal (1878) 3 QBD 428, CA).
2 *R v Postmaster General* (1876) 1 QBD 658 at p 664. This proposition now seems settled law; see *Skailes v Blue Anchor Line Ltd* [1911] 1 KB 360, CA; *Costello v Pigeon (Owners)* [1913] AC 407 and *S and U Stores Ltd v Wilkes* [1974] ICR 645, NIRC; and *Gould v Balliol College, Oxford* (1966) 1 ITR 534.
3 *Nevra v RL & G Ltd* [1995] IRLR 200; affirmed [1996] IRLR 461, CA.

A contractual right or a concession

4.03   Thus many of the 'fringe benefits' received by employees may be included in the term 'remuneration', as for example, use of a company car, pension and life assurance schemes, and the provision of rent-free accommodation. Subject to certain limited exceptions the Inland Revenue tax expenses when there is a profit element. In many cases in which basic pay is supplemented by additional benefits and bonus or performance related pay it is clear that such payments are included within the remuneration package. In certain cases it depends on the express or implied terms of the agreement. In *Powell v Braun*[1] the Court of Appeal construed an employer's promise to his secretary that instead of a salary increase a bonus would be paid on the net profits of the previous year as an undertaking to pay a reasonable bonus. The more usual cases to come before industrial tribunals and courts concern implied terms. There is a distinction between those cases in which an established practice, such as paying a Christmas bonus, is likely to be construed as an implied term[2] and a concession or act of kindness, such as allowing an employee the occasional use of a company car or to use the office telephone which do not give rise to a contractual entitlement. Although the fact that the facility applies to all the workforce and the length of time which it has existed are relevant matters, they are not in themselves conclusive. Thus payment of sick pay does not give rise to a contractual right to sick pay if an employer makes it clear that this is done on an ex gratia basis.[3]

Employers who introduce early retirement schemes are well advised to make it clear that these provisions are by way of a concession rather than giving any contractual right. Decided cases are of limited value as precedents since much depends on the facts of the individual case. Although not all the benefits which an employee enjoys are matters of a contractual entitlement this does not mean that an employee is necessarily without remedy. If an employee acts capriciously as between different employees, this could give rise to an action for unfair dismissal based on the breach of the implied term of mutual trust and confidence. Further, if such disparate treatment can be referable to gender, race or disability, an employer could face an action for sex, race or disability discrimination.

1 [1954] 1 WLR 401, CA.
2 *Frischers Ltd v Taylor* [EAT] 386/79 in which case there was held to be a contractual right to a Christmas bonus which had been paid for several years.
3 *Petrie v MacFisheries Ltd* [1940] 1 KB 258, CA.

Reduction in pay

4.04 The employer has no right to reduce wages or salaries unilaterally.[1] The payment of wages is a term of such fundamental importance in the contract that it is difficult to imagine circumstances in which a unilateral reduction of wages could be construed as other than a repudiatory breach of contract which would allow the employee to treat the employer as guilty of constructive dismissal. This does not mean that the employee will as of right succeed in an action for unfair dismissal.[2] A company may be in grave financial difficulties and its bankers may refuse to continue its finance of the operation unless a business plan is produced which shows substantial cuts in costs. The management consults with the workforce and decides to reduce wage rates by 10%. The majority of the workforce accept this as being preferable to the inevitable collapse of the business which would otherwise occur. The minority who do not accept this cut in wages leave and sue for unfair dismissal. There would be no issue that there was a dismissal but an industrial tribunal may not determine that this dismissal is unfair by virtue of s 98(4) of the Employment Rights Act 1996 if they accept that there was a genuine need for such reductions and that the management had made real attempts to consult with the employees about the imposition of the changes. A tribunal which has listened to endless criticisms of the failure of management to explore alternatives to redundancies in cases alleging unfair selection for redundancy might well be of the opinion that such a measure was an appropriate response.

1 *Miller v Hamworthy Engineering Ltd* [1986] ICR 846, CA and see *Davies v Hotpoint* [1994] IRLR 538, EAT.
2 For the test which applies when a company unilaterally varies terms and conditions because of adverse trading conditions, see *Catamaran Cruisers Ltd v Williams* [1994] IRLR 386, EAT.

The employee's remedy

4.05 In *Rigby v Ferodo Ltd*[1] the employer was unable to secure agreement with the union for a reduction in wages. The employers then unilaterally reduced the plaintiff's wages by £30 per week. The plaintiff continued to work on at the lower rate and his contract was terminated by 12 weeks' notice. The plaintiff had not accepted the repudiation of the contract. The House of Lords decided the plaintiff was entitled to recover for the whole period of the breach and not just for the period of 12 weeeks' notice when the employers could lawfully have terminated the employment.

1 [1988] ICR 29.

Summary

4.06 The position may be summarised by the following propositions:
(1) A unilateral reduction in wages is a breach of contract.
(2) An employee may elect to treat this as such a fundamental breach that he may leave and claim unfair dismissal. If there were good reasons for the reduction in wages, although an employee will probably establish that he was constructively dismissed, it does not necessarily follow that a tribunal will consider it was an unfair dismissal.
(3) An employee may refuse to treat a reduction in wages as a repudiatory breach and sue for his wages in which case he is entitled to sue for the whole period of the breach.
(4) The real protection afforded to the employee is limited. If the employee refuses to accept the reduction, then the employer will not be liable for wrongful dismissal as long as he gives the requisite notice. For the reasons set out above the employee will not necessarily succeed in an action for unfair dismissal.

Pay increases

4.07 In all employment there is a general expectation that pay will increase normally on an annual basis. But the courts have declined to imply a term that there will be an annual pay rise.[1] If there is a general overall pay increase but a particular employee is not given the increase, then the employee may, depending on the circumstances, have a claim for unfair dismissal based on constructive dismissal. If the employer can show that there was good cause for that particular employee not to receive a pay increase – the most obvious example being poor performance – the employer would not be in breach of the term as to mutual confidence. When an employee had negotiated for himself an hourly rate in December and in the following month all operatives were given a general increase, he was successfully able to claim he had been constructively dismissed since it was held that it was reasonable to imply a term that he would also receive general increases.[2] In times of high unemployment an employee's right to sue for unfair dismissal based on constructive dismissal may well be somewhat academic. There is a further obstacle. In cases in which there is a real dispute about the construction of the contract or a genuine misunderstanding as to matters of fact or law tribunals will not necessarily find that the employer's conduct is a repudiation of the contract. If that conduct is based on a bona fide belief as to the employer's contractual responsibility, it may not be regarded as repudiatory conduct.[3]

1 *Murco Petroleum Ltd v Forge* [1987] IRLR 50, EAT. In *Leyland Vehicles Ltd v Reston* [1981] ICR 403, EAT it was held that a practice which had continued for ten years of negotiating a pay rise in April and backdating it to the previous January did not establish that there was an implied term that any future increases would be backdated.
2 *Pepper & Hope v Daish* [1980] IRLR 13, EAT.
3 *Brigden v Lancashire County Council* [1987] IRLR 58, CA.

Payment and industrial action short of going on strike

4.08   In cases in which an employee takes industrial action short of going on strike issues can arise as to the employer's right to refuse in whole or in part payment for work done. In *Miles v Wakefield Metropolitan District Council*[1] the House of Lords held that a registrar of births, deaths and marriages could not attend work on Saturday morning but decline to conduct weddings. His employers were entitled not to pay him for Saturday morning. In *Wiluszynarski v Tower Hamlets London Borough Council*[2] the Court of Appeal went further. In that case an employee refused as part of a pay dispute to answer queries from council officers which normally took some three hours of his time per week. He continued with his other duties. The employer made it clear at the outset that they would pay no wages to employees who took this action. The Court of Appeal upheld the employer's right to refuse any payment for part performance. The judgment made it clear that the basis of its decision was that the employers had spelt out the position in clear terms before industrial action was taken. They had in terms told the employee that if he attended and did not do the whole range of duties required of him he would not be paid; if he did attend work under these circumstances he would be doing so voluntarily.

1 [1987] ICR 368.
2 [1989] ICR 493. See also *British Telecommunications plc v Ticehurst* [1992] ICR 383, CA.

Collective agreements

4.09   Apart from statutory regulation the parties to a contract of employment are at liberty to make such arrangements with regard to remuneration, and the other terms of their relationship, as they wish. In practice, however, the theoretical equality of the contracting parties, if it ever existed, disappeared long ago, and the provisions of individual agreements are often dictated by external influences. Of these the two most often encountered are statutory regulation and collective agreements made between employers and their representatives and trade unions.

4.10   One of the major factors dealt with in agreements between employers or employers' associations and trade unions is the question of wages and wage rates. If an agreement containing details of remuneration is incorporated into the employee's individual contract of employment, then he is entitled to rely on it in actions for remuneration. Indeed since the imposition of requirements to furnish employees with written statements of the major terms of their contracts of employment, it has been common practice for the employer to refer to collective agreements which give details of remuneration and wage rates. The collective agreement need not be incorporated verbatim.[1]

1 *Burroughs Machines Ltd v Timmoney* [1977] IRLR 404, Ct of Sess.

Incorporation of rules

4.11 In *Camden Exhibition and Display Ltd v Lynott*[1] Lord Denning MR said with regard to the negotiated working rules of the National Joint Council for the exhibition industry:

'In an ordinary contract of employment a man is bound to work his proper hours during his working week. But he is not bound to do overtime. Overtime is a matter for agreement between him and his employers. Do these working rules alter the position? It seems to me that, since the Contracts of Employment Act 1963, these working rules are incorporated into the terms of employment of all men in the industry. A notice was issued under that Act saying to every man: Your rate of wages, hours of work, holidays and holiday pay are in accordance with the provisions of the constitution and working rules agreement issued by and under the authority of the National Joint Council. In view of that notice these working rules are not only a collective agreement between the union and the employers. They are incorporated into the contract of employment of each man, insofar as they are applicable to his situation.'

1 [1966] 1 QB 555 at p 562; [1965] 3 All ER 28, CA, per Lord Denning at p 31 and per Davies LJ at p 33.

Itemised pay statements

4.12 Sections 8–10 of the Employment Rights Act 1996 make provision for employees to be provided by their employers at, or before, the time of payment of wages or salary, with an itemised written pay statement containing the particulars set out in s 8. They are:

'(a) the gross amount of the wages or salary;
(b) the amounts of any variable[1] and, subject to section 9, any fixed deductions from that gross amount and the purposes for which they are made;
(c) the net amount of wages or salary payable; and
(d) where different parts of the net amount are paid in different ways, the amount and method of payment of each part payment'.[2]

1 'Miscellaneous deduction/payment' is not sufficient; *Milsom v Leicestershire County Council* [1978] IRLR 433. The right is not conditional upon the employee requesting it: *Coales v John Wood & Co (Solicitors)* [1986] ICR 71.
2 'Employee' is as defined in the Employment Rights Act 1996, s 230(1). Any agreement to exclude or limit the operation of the provision or to preclude any person from presenting a complaint to, or bringing proceedings before an industrial tribunal is void (s 203). The right extends to those in Crown employment (s 191); for the position of the armed service, see s 192. Those employed, or engaged under a contract of employment in police service are excluded (s 200).

The particulars

4.13 The statement given in accordance with the requirements of ss 8–10 need not contain separate particulars of fixed deductions, if it instead contains an aggregate amount of fixed deductions, and the employer has given to the employee at the time, or before, a pay statement is given, a written standing statement of fixed deductions which is effective as defined below and contains particulars of the amount of the deduction, the intervals at which the deduction is made and the purpose for which it is made, in respect of each deduction comprised in the aggregate amount.[1] The standing statement may be amended from time to time by notice in writing given by the employer to the employee containing particulars of the amendment and within 12 months of the date on which the first standing statement was given, and at intervals of not more than 12 months thereafter, the statement should be reissued in consolidated form incorporating any amendments.[2] A standing statement becomes effective on the date on which it is given to the employee and ceases to be effective for the purposes of s 9 on the expiration of the period of 12 months beginning with that date or where it has been reissued the expiration of the period of 12 months beginning on the date when it was last reissued. The Secretary of State for Employment has power by order to add or remove items from the specified particulars and to shorten or extend the period of 12 months.[3]

1 Employment Rights Act 1996, s 9(1).
2 Employment Rights Act 1996, s 9(3).
3 Employment Rights Act 1996, ss 9(5) and 10.

The remedy

4.14 If the employer does not provide the pay statement as required, the employee may require a reference to be made to an industrial tribunal to determine what particulars ought to be included in the statement.[1] When a statement, or a standing statement of fixed deductions which purports to comply with ss 8 and 9(1) has been given to an employee and a question arises as to the particulars which ought to have been included, either the employer, or the employee, may require the question to be referred to and determined by the industrial tribunal.[2] In this connection a question as to the particulars which ought to have been included does not include a question solely as to the accuracy of an amount stated in any such particulars.[3] The application may be made while the employment continues, or within three months of the date on which the employment ceased.[4]

1 Employment Rights Act 1996, s 11(1). Note the difficult wording of the subsection. The assistance of a conciliation officer may also be sought: Industrial Tribunals Act 1996, s 18(d).
2 Employment Rights Act 1996, s 11(2).
3 Employment Rights Act 1996, s 11(3), nor any question as to whether the employment is, has been or will be, contracted out employment for the purposes of Pt III of the Pension Schemes Act 1993.
4 Employment Rights Act 1996, s 11(4). If not, within the three months the reasonably practicable test applies: s 11(4)(b).

The award

4.15 Should the tribunal find that the employer has failed to give a pay statement in accordance with ss 1, 4, or 8, or that the pay statement, or standing statement of fixed deductions, does not, in relation to a deduction, constitute the particulars required by that section or s 9(1), the tribunal will make a declaration to that effect. Where it finds further that any unnotified deduction had been made from the pay of the employee during the period of 13 weeks immediately preceding the date of the application for the reference (whether or not the deduction was made in breach of contract) it may order the employer to pay the employee a sum not exceeding the deductions made without the employer giving the employee particulars of those deductions in any pay statement or standing statement of fixed deductions, as required.[1]

1 Employment Rights Act 1996, s 12. This can have a penal effect, but see *Scott v Creager* [1979] ICR 403, EAT where a tribunal awarded the applicant only the difference between what she should have received and what was paid.

Exceptions

4.16 The provisions as to itemised pay statements do not apply to the police,[1] to merchant seamen,[2] to share fishermen[3] or to employees who ordinarily work outside Great Britain.[4]

1 Employment Rights Act 1996, s 200.
2 Employment Rights Act 1996, s 199(4).
3 Employment Rights Act 1996, s 199(2).
4 Employment Rights Act 1996, s 196(3).

Suspension

4.17 In some cases the contract of employment contains power for the employer to suspend the employee temporarily for misconduct. Such a power can exist only by statute,[1] or by an express or implied term in the contract.[2] Such a power was held not to be contrary to s 1 of the Truck Act 1896.[3] An established practice at a particular factory may be incorporated in a workman's contract of service whether he knows of it or not; he may be presumed to have accepted employment on the same terms as those applied to other members of the factory.[4] The same may apply to an established practice in a particular trade or district. The legal effect of the power to suspend is dependent upon the precise nature of the particular power under consideration.[5]

1 *Wallwork v Fielding* [1922] 2 KB 66.
2 *Warburton v Taff Vale Rail Co* (1902) 18 TLR 420; *Pirie and Hunter v Crawford* IDS Brief 155.
3 *Marshall v English Electric Co Ltd* [1945] 1 All ER 653 at p 655, CA; *Sagar v Ridehalgh & Son Ltd* [1931] 1 Ch 310, CA.
4 See *Marshall's* case, above.
5 It raises analogous issues as to whether there is a duty on the employer to provide work.

Basis and scope of the power to suspend

4.18 In *Bird v British Celanese Ltd*[1] the employer was entitled 'temporarily to suspend the workman from his employment ... if he was guilty of misconduct or breach of duty or breach of an order'. Explaining this clause Scott LJ said in the course of his judgment:[2]

'The suspense clause may act in two ways. It may be a merciful substitute for the procedure of dismissal, and a possible re-engagement. Under the suspense clause the right to wages ceases and the wages are not earned, and no deduction can be made from wages which are not payable. In the present case, as the workman was adjudged guilty of serious misconduct, the operation of the clause was merely merciful. It enabled the workman, when the suspension ended, to claim as of right to continue in his old job. The clause operates in accordance with its terms; the whole contract is suspended, in the sense that the operation of the mutual obligations of both parties is suspended; the workman ceases to be under any present duty to work and the employer ceases to be under any consequential duty to pay. That is the natural meaning of the word 'suspend' when applied to a contract of employment, and I think it is also its legal meaning.'

1 [1945] KB 336; [1945] 1 All ER 488, CA.
2 [1945] KB 336 at p 341.

4.19 The case of *Hanley v Pease & Partners Ltd*[1] is illustrative of the contractual position where an employer purports to suspend an employee when he has no power to do so. A workman absented himself from work for one day without leave from his employers. The employers did not dismiss him, but suspended him from working on the following day, as a result of which he was prevented from earning a day's wages. It was held that the employee's claim in such circumstances is technically one for damages for refusing to allow him to perform his contract of service. Further, it was held that although the employers might have a right to damages against the employee, they had no right to suspend him in that by so doing they were taking upon themselves to assess their own damages at one day's wages. After declining to dismiss the employee they had elected to treat the contract as continuing.

1 [1915] 1 KB 698. See also *Gorse v Durham County Council* [1971] 2 All ER 666; [1971] 1 WLR 775, QBD, where teachers were suspended, but the proper procedure for suspension was not complied with.

4.20 A right to suspend without payment of wages analogous to that in *Bird v British Celanese Ltd*[1] is not a termination of the contract. However, in some cases suspension may amount to dismissal.

1 [1945] KB 336; [1945] 1 All ER 488, CA.

4.21 In *Marshall v English Electric Co Ltd*[1] which related to a contract of service liable to be determined by an hour's notice given by either side, there was also a well-established practice at the particular works of suspending without pay for breaches of discipline, and this was held to be a condition of employment. Lord Goddard said:[2]
'In my opinion what is called suspension is in truth dismissal with an intimation that at the end of so many days, or it may be hours, the man will be reemployed if he chooses to apply for reinstatement.'

1 [1945] 1 All ER 653, CA.
2 [1945] 1 All ER 653 at p 655.

4.22 An employer who purports to exercise a right of suspension when he is not entitled to do so, may be guilty of repudiating the contract of employment and, if the employee elects to accept it as such, the employer's action may amount to dismissal.[1]

1 *Powell Duffryn Wagon Co Ltd v House* [1974] ICR 123, NIRC; *McKenzie Ltd v Smith* [1976] IRLR 345, Ct of Sess; *McArdle v Scotbeef Ltd* 1974 SLT (Notes) 78.

4.23 In view of the new requirement to include a note of details of disciplinary procedure in the statement issued to employees pursuant to s 1 of the Employment Rights Act 1996, employers who wish to exercise a power of suspension as a mode of discipline should ensure that it is expressly contained in that note or the document referred to in it.[1] An employer will find it increasingly difficult to claim to have a right to suspend employees if it is not clearly stated in disciplinary rules which are contained or referred to in the note.

1 But note that the duty to give rules of disciplinary procedures is qualified in the case of small employers, ie those who employ less than 20 employees (Employment Rights Act 1996, s 3).

Suspension on medical grounds

4.24 By virtue of s 64 of the Employment Rights Act 1996 an employee who is suspended from work on medical grounds in consequence of:

(a) any statutory requirement, or the requirement of any subordinate legislation, or

(b) any recommendation in any provision of a code of practice issued or approved under s 16 of the Health and Safety at Work etc Act 1974,

which is a provision for the time being set out in s 64(3) of the 1996 Act, is entitled to be paid by his employer remuneration while he is so suspended for a period not exceeding 26 weeks.[1] The provisions leading to suspension on medical grounds are:

(1) Control of Lead at Work Regulations 1980, SI 1980/1284, reg 16;

(2) Ionising Radiations Regulations 1985, SI 1985/1333, reg 16;

(3) Control of Substances Hazardous to Health Regulations 1988, SI 1988/1657, reg 11.

Under s 64(4) of the 1996 Act the minister has power to add or remove provisions from the Act. It should be noted that if an employee is dismissed by reason of any requirement or recommendation as is referred to in s 64(2), the qualifying period for the unfair dismissal provisions is reduced to one month (s 108(2)). The usual restrictions on contracting out apply.

1 Employment Rights Act 1996, s 64.

4.25 The employee is regarded as suspended from work if he continues to be employed by the employer (ie the contract of employment still exists) but he is not provided with work, or does not perform the work which he normally performed before the suspension.[1] The provisions for payment on suspension for medical grounds do not apply unless the employee has been continuously employed for one month ending with the last complete week before the day on which the suspension begins.[2] The employee is not entitled to remuneration by virtue of these provisions if he is incapable of work by reason of disease, or bodily or mental disablement,[3] is a share fisherman,[4] or under his contract of employment the employee ordinarily works outside Great Britain.[5] The provisions do not apply to employment under a contract for a fixed term of three months or less, or to employment under a contract made in contemplation of a performance of a specific task which is not expected to last for more than three months, unless in either case, the employee has been continuously employed for a period of more than three months.[6] Crown employees are included,[7] but not those employed or engaged under a contract of employment in police service.[8]

1 Employment Rights Act 1996, s 64(4).
2 Employment Rights Act 1996, s 65(1).
3 Employment Rights Act 1996, s 65(3).
4 Employment Rights Act 1996, s 199(2).
5 Employment Rights Act 1996, s 196(3).
6 Employment Rights Act 1996, s 65(2).

7 Employment Rights Act 1996, s 191(2).
8 Employment Rights Act 1996, s 200.

4.26 The employee is not entitled to remuneration on suspension for medical grounds if the employer has offered to provide him with suitable alternative work, whether or not it is work which the employee is employed to perform under his contract, or was employed to perform under the contract in force before the suspension, and the employee has unreasonably refused to perform that work, or he does not comply with reasonable requirements imposed by his employer with a view to ensuring his services are available.[1] The remuneration payable is a week's pay for each week of suspension and in proportion for any part of a week.[2] Chapter 2 of Pt XIV of the Employment Rights Act 1996 applies for the purposes of calculating a week's pay[3] and the calculation date is the day before that on which the suspension begins.[4] The statutory right to remuneration does not affect any contractual right to pay,[5] and payment under a contractual obligation goes towards discharging the statutory liability and vice versa,[6] so that the employee is entitled to receive either contractual payment or statutory payment whichever is the greater.

1 Employment Rights Act 1996, s 65(4).
2 Employment Rights Act 1996, s 69(1).
3 Employment Rights Act 1996, s 220 et seq.
4 Employment Rights Act 1996, s 225(5)(a).
5 Employment Rights Act 1996, s 69(2).
6 Employment Rights Act 1996, s 69(3).

4.27 An employee can present a complaint to an industrial tribunal that his employer has failed to pay the whole or any part of the remuneration to which he is entitled.[1] The complaint must be presented before the end of the period of three months beginning with the day in respect of which the complaint is made, or within such further period as the tribunal considers reasonable when it is satisfied that it was not reasonably practicable for the complaint to be presented within that period.[2] If it finds the complaint well founded, the tribunal must order the employer to pay to the employee the amount of remuneration due to him.[3]

1 Employment Rights Act 1996, s 70(1).
2 Employment Rights Act 1996, s 70(2).
3 Employment Rights Act 1996, s 70(3).

4.28 An employer may engage an employee to replace a suspended employee. If the employer informs the new employee in writing, on engaging him, that his employment will be terminated at the end of such suspension, and he so dismisses him in order to make it possible to allow the suspended employee to resume his original work, then for the purposes of the unfair dismissal provisions the reason for the dismissal is 'a substantial reason of a kind such as to justify dismissal of an employee holding the position which that employee held'.[1] On a complaint to an industrial tribunal by the dismissed employee claiming compensation for unfair dismissal, the tribunal will still have to be satisfied that the employer in the circumstances acted reasonably in treating the reason as a sufficient reason for dismissing the employee.[2]

1 Employment Rights Act 1996, s 106(3).
2 Employment Rights Act 1996, s 106(4).

Lay-off and short-time

4.29 The old common law cases indicate that employers are not under an obligation to provide work for their employees save in special circumstances[1] such as for those employees on piecework[2] and actors.[3] In *Turner v Sawdon & Co*[4] the Court of Appeal had expressed surprise at the suggestion that an employer was under obligation to provide employment for an employee and had dismissed his claim to carry out his work. However, when considering this case in *Breach v Epsylon Industries Ltd*,[5] Phillips J said in the Employment Appeal Tribunal:

> 'It seems to us at least possible that the tribunal was saying to themselves that *Turner v Sawdon & Co* lays down a principle of law to the effect that employers are under no obligation to provide their employees with work to do. If that is so, then, with respect, there was a misdirection because it was necessary to look at the background to the contract to see how it should be construed, and whether a term ought not to be implied that in the circumstances of this case there was an obligation on the employers to provide work suitable for a chief engineer.'

1 *R v Welch* (1853) 2 E & B 357; *Aspdin v Austin* (1844) 5 QB 671; *Dunn v Sayles* (1844) 5 QB 685.
2 *Whittle v Frankland* (1862) 2 B & S 49.
3 *Fechter v Montgomery* (1863) 33 Beav 22.
4 [1901] 2 KB 653, 85 LT 222.
5 [1976] ICR 316 at p 321. See also *Bosworth v Angus Jowett & Co Ltd* [1977] IRLR 374 and *Langston v Amalgamated Union of Engineering Workers* [1974] ICR 180, CA.

Lay-off

4.30 The term 'lay-off', except when used in connection with redundancy where it has a technical meaning,[1] is not a clearly defined legal concept. It is often used by employers and employees but not always in the same sense and appears to be used to cover at least two distinct situations. The first is where the contract of employment is terminated. The termination can be by dismissal, agreement between the parties, or frustration, so that the employment comes to an end and there is no existing employment relationship between the employer and the employee. If the employee is subsequently re-employed by the employer, the interim period may be spoken of as one of lay-off.[2] The second alternative arises when, either by agreement at the time, or as a result of provision in the contract, the employment relationship subsists between the employer and the employee, but the obligation on the employer to provide work for the employee is temporarily suspended. The stipulation as to lay-off in these cases can be either express or implied, and an implied term has been found to arise by way of custom of the trade or of the individual business.[3] During this type of lay-off there may be a contractual obligation on the employer to make payment of wages, or of a guaranteed minimum wage, and but for the suspension of the employer's obligation to provide work (if such there be), the relationship of employer and employee continues.

1 See Chapter 16.
2 *McCarthy v Burroughs Machines Ltd* (1975) 10 ITR 46, but see *Sneddon v Ivorycrete (Builders) Ltd* (1966) 1 ITR 538, where it was said that dismissal could not be a 'lay-off'.
3 But it is not easy to establish a right to lay off by custom: *Waine v Oliver (Plant Hire) Ltd* [1977] IRLR 434, EAT and *Johnson v Cross* [1977] ICR 872, EAT. If an employer claims a right

to lay off his employees he should make certain that it is clearly expressed, see for example *Burroughs Machines Ltd v Timmoney* [1977] IRLR 404, Ct of Sess.

4.31 An example of this type of lay-off occurred in *Puttick v John Wright & Sons (Blackwall) Ltd*[1] when Lord Thompson delivering the judgment of the court said:

'We think it quite possible to envisage circumstances in which A may consider it in his best interests to undertake to do such work of a particular kind as B provides for him, A holding himself available to do such work as required and being paid only for the work he actually does, while B undertakes to make available to A such work of that particular kind as from time to time comes to hand. In such an arrangement between A and B, A in effect agrees to be "temporarily suspended" or "laid off" for such periods as no work is in fact available. It may well be that in the present case the parties never put their minds to the full legal implications of such an arrangement, but it does not seem to be disputed that such an arrangement was in fact what they contemplated and intended and believed they had entered into. This is in our view borne out by the history of the relationship between the parties, particularly the basic continuity of the appellant's employment with the respondents over some 23 years, the fact that at no time when he was laid off was he given notice of dismissal and the fact that he always held himself available for work from the respondents and they always gave him work to do with only very short periods of interruption between jobs. We are unable to find anything in any of the quoted cases to suggest that such an arrangement does not amount to a contract of employment binding in its terms.'

1 (1972) 7 ITR 438 at p 442, NIRC.

4.32 In this sense of the word lay-off the obligations which continue during the suspension of work vary from case to case. In some situations the relationship between the parties is still close, payment being made to the employee who reports to the place of work regularly; in others no payment is due to the employee, he collects unemployment pay and returns to work only when required.

4.33 The present position regarding lay-off is far from clear.[1] If the lay-off is of a type which amounts to dismissal, then it is treated as such for the purposes of the employee's claims both under the terms of his contract and arising from the employee's statutory rights. It is unlikely that the courts or tribunals will accept that lay-off does not operate as a dismissal unless a clear term of the contract, such as an express agreement to that effect, can be shown and if employers wish to rely on such a right to lay-off they will be well advised to include it expressly in the rules which are referred to in the statement given to the employee pursuant to s 1 of the Employment Rights Act 1996.[2] When lay-off of this type takes place the employer will be liable to pay the employee any guaranteed wage prescribed by contract or statute. The provisions governing redundancy payments may also have to be considered.

1 See for instance *Waine v Oliver (Plant Hire) Ltd* [1977] IRLR 434, EAT.
2 For difficulties which can be encountered when the terms of the contract are not precise, see *Burroughs Machines Ltd v Timmoney* [1977] IRLR 404, Ct of Sess.

Short-time

4.34 When the employer provides the employee with work and payment for less than the normal number of hours per week it is said that the employee is on 'short-time'. The position is very similar to that of lay-off. Unless the employer has the power pursuant to the contract of employment to reduce the number of hours or payment, a unilateral attempt at introducing short-time could amount to repudiation of the contract by the employer and hence dismissal. An employer who claims to have the right to put his employees on to short-time is best advised to express it in documentary form available to the employees. When an attempt to put employees on short-time amounts to dismissal then all the effects of dismissal have to be considered in the usual way. If there is a contractual right for the employees to be placed on short-time working, the employer should consider his contractual and statutory obligations to provide a guaranteed minimum wage.[1] The special provisions in redundancy cases may also be relevant.[2]

1 For the position of guarantee payments, see **4.35**.
2 See **16.54** et seq.

Guarantee payments

4.35 This is a statutory scheme to give the employee some financial recompense for the employer's failure to provide work. Not all failure to provide work comes within the ambit of the provisions. The failure to provide work must be due to a shortage of work or an *occurrence*[1] which affects the normal running of the business. The amount of financial recompense is limited both as to amount and duration. The amount does not exceed £14.50 and the sum is only payable for a maximum of five days in any period of three months. To qualify an employee must have been continously employed for one month and not be employed for a fixed period of under three months. Seasonal workers are not covered since there is no right to a guarantee payment if the contract of employment is not anticipated to last more than three months. If the workless day is due to industrial action, this disentitles an employee from a guarantee payment as does the unreasonable refusal of suitable alternative employment.

1 A threatened power cut has been held to be such an occurrence (*Miller v Harry Thornton (Lollies) Ltd* [1978] IRLR 430) but when a Jewish owner closed down the factory for the observance of a religious festival this was held not to be within the ambit of an occurrence: *North v Pavleigh Ltd* [1977] IRLR 461.

The statutory basis

4.36 The statutory provisions are contained in s 28 of the 1996 Act which provides:
'(1) Where throughout a day[1] during any part of which an employee would normally be required[2] to work in accordance with his contract of employment is not provided with work by his employer by reason of—
(a) a diminution in the requirements of the employer's business for work of the kind which the employee is employed to do, or

(b)   any other occurrence affecting the normal working of the employer's business in relation to work of the kind which the employee is employed to do,

the employee is entitled to be paid in respect of that day.

(2) In this Act a payment to which an employee is entitled under subsection (1) is referred to as a guarantee payment.'

1 'Day' means the period of 24 hours from midnight to midnight. Where a period of employment straddles midnight or would normally do so, if the longer period is, or would normally be, worked before midnight then the period of employment is treated as falling wholly on the first day. In other cases it is treated as falling wholly on the second day (s 28(4) and (5)).
2 If the employee has the right to turn down an offer of work as he or she is not *normally required to work*, the employee is therefore not entitled to a guarantee payment: *Mailway (Southern) Ltd v Willsher* [1978] ICR 511.

Excluded occupations

4.37   The provisions with regard to guarantee payments apply to employees and those in Crown employment are also included,[1] but not those in the armed forces[2] or the police force.[3] Share fishermen[4] and those working outside Great Britain[5] are not within the provisions.

1 Employment Rights Act 1996, s 191.
2 Employment Rights Act 1996, s 192(2).
3 Employment Rights Act 1996, s 200.
4 Employment Rights Act 1996, s 199(2).
5 Employment Rights Act 1996, s 196(3).

Eligibility

4.38   An employee has to have been continously employed for a period of one month ending with the day before the *workless day* in respect of which a claim is made.[1] The provisions do not apply to employment under a contract for a fixed term of three months or less, or to employment under a contract made in contemplation of the performance of a specific task which is not expected to last for more than three months, unless in either case, the employee has been continuously employed for a period of more than three months.[2] It is to be noted that where there is not any obligation on the employer to provide work (ie there are no normal working hours) the provisions do not apply.[3]

1 Employment Rights Act 1996, s 29(1).
2 Employment Rights Act 1996, s 29(2).
3 Employment Rights Act 1996, s 30(1).

Exclusions

4.39   An employee is not entitled to a guarantee payment if the failure to provide the employee with work occurs in consequence of a trade dispute involving any employee of the employer, or of an associated employer.[1] The employee will not be entitled to a guarantee payment in respect of a workless day if his employer has offered to provide alternative work for that day which is suitable in all the circumstances, whether or not it is work the employee is contractually bound to perform and the employee has unreasonably refused the offer, or he does not comply with reasonable requirements imposed by his employer with a view to ensuring that his services are available.[2]

1 Employment Rights Act 1996, s 29(3). See *Thomson v Priest (Lindley) Ltd* [1978] IRLR 99 and also *Garvey v J & J Maybank (Oldham) Ltd* [1979] IRLR 408.
2 Employment Rights Act 1996, s 29(4). For the 'casual worker' situation, see *Mailway (Southern) Ltd v Willsher* [1978] ICR 511, EAT and *Miller v Harry Thornton (Lollies) Ltd* [1978] IRLR 430. The employee does not automatically disentitle himself by registering as unemployed: *Robinson v Claxton and Garland (Teesside) Ltd* [1977] IRLR 159. As to the 'reasonableness' of the employer's action, see *Meadows v Faithfull Overalls Ltd* [1977] IRLR 330 and *Purdy v Willowbrook International Ltd* [1977] IRLR 388.

The calculation of the amount

4.40 Subject to the limits set out below the amount of a guarantee payment payable to an employee in respect of any day is the sum produced by multiplying the number of normal working hours on that day by the guaranteed hourly rate.[1] No guarantee payment is payable in respect of a day if there are no normal working hours on that day. The guaranteed hourly rate is the amount of a week's pay[2] divided by the employee's normal working hours in a week under the contract of employment in force on the day in respect of which the guarantee payment is payable or, if the number of normal working hours in a week differs from week to week, or over a longer period, it is the amount of one week's pay divided by the average number of such hours over the 12-week period ending with the last complete week before the day in respect of which the guarantee payment is payable.[3] If the employee has not been employed for a sufficient period, it is the amount of one week's pay divided by a number which fairly represents the number of normal working hours in a week having regard to the average number of normal working hours in a week which the employee could expect in accordance with the terms of his contract and the average number of such hours of other employees engaged in relevant comparable employment with the same employer, as appropriate in the circumstances.[4] If an employee's contract has been varied or a new contract has been entered into in connection with a period of short-time working, these provisions have effect as if for references to the day in respect of which guarantee payment is payable there are substituted references to the last day on which the original contract was in force.[5]

1 Employment Rights Act 1996, s 30(1).
2 Employment Rights Act 1996, s 30(2).
3 Employment Rights Act 1996, s 30(3)(a).
4 Employment Rights Act 1996, s 30(3)(b).
5 Employment Rights Act 1996, s 30(5).

The limitations

4.41 The amount of guarantee payment payable to an employee in respect of any day shall not exceed £14.50[1] and the employee is not entitled to guarantee payments in respect of more than the specified number of days, not exceeding five, in any three-month period.[2] There is a statutory formula for the calculation of the specified number of days when the number of days worked under the contract of employment varies.[3] If an employee's contract has been varied, or a new contract entered into, in connection with a period of short-time working, then in calculating the specified number of days references to the day in respect of which the guarantee payment is claimed are construed as if they are to the last day on which the original contract was in force.[4]

1 Employment Rights Act 1996, s 31(1). This may be varied by order of the Secretary of State for Employment and he is under a duty to review the limit annually (ss 31(7) and 208).
2 Employment Rights Act 1996, s 31(2). The period may be varied by order of the Secretary of State from time to time (s 31(7)).
3 Employment Rights Act 1996, s 31(4). If an employee works only four days a week the specified number of days is four: *Trevethan v Sterling Metals* [1977] IRLR 416.
4 Employment Rights Act 1996, s 31(6).

The contractual rights preserved

4.42 The provisions as to guarantee payments do not affect the validity of contractual rights to payment during absence from work and payment under the contract in respect of a workless day goes towards discharging the statutory liability to pay a guarantee payment in respect of that day, and payment of a guarantee payment goes towards discharging the contractual liability.[1] The effect is that the employee should receive whichever is the greater of the payments due under the statutory scheme and under his contract.[2] The payment under the contract is treated as paid in respect of a workless day if it is expressed to be calculated or payable by reference to that day to the extent that it is so expressed, and in any other case to the extent that it represents guaranteed remuneration rather than remuneration for work actually done, and is referable to that day when apportioned rateably between that day and any other workless period falling within the period in respect of which the remuneration is paid.[3]

1 Employment Rights Act 1996, s 32(1).
2 Employment Rights Act 1996, s 32(2).
3 Employment Rights Act 1996, s 32(3).

Secretary of State's power to modify the provisions

4.43 The Secretary of State for Employment may by order modify various provisions of the guarantee payment scheme.[1]

1 Employment Rights Act 1996, s 33.

Enforcement

4.44 An employee may present a complaint to the industrial tribunal that his employer has failed to pay the whole or any part of a guarantee payment to which the employee is entitled.[1] The complaint should be presented before the end of the period of three months beginning with the day in respect of which the complaint as to the guarantee payment is made, or if it is satisfied that it was not reasonably practicable for the complaint to be presented in that time, within such further period as the tribunal considers reasonable.[2] When a tribunal finds a complaint well founded it will order the employer to pay to the complainant the amount of the guarantee payment it finds due to him.[3]

1 Employment Rights Act 1996, s 34(1).
2 Employment Rights Act 1996, s 34(2).
3 Employment Rights Act 1996, s 34(3).

Exemption orders

4.45 The Secretary of State for Employment may by order exclude employees from the operation of the statutory guarantee payment scheme.[1] There must be in force a collective agreement or wages order whereby the employees to whom the agreement or order relates have a right to guaranteed remuneration. The Secretary of State will not make the order unless the agreement provides procedures to be followed (whether upon arbitration or otherwise) in cases where an employee claims his employer has failed to pay the whole or any part of any guaranteed remuneration to which the employee is entitled under the agreement and that the procedure includes the right to arbitration or adjudication by an independent referee or body, in cases where (by reason of an equality of votes or otherwise) a decision cannot otherwise be reached, or the agreement indicates that the employee can present a complaint to an industrial tribunal that his employer has failed to pay the whole or any part of any guaranteed payment to which the employee is entitled under the agreement.[2] The application to the Secretary of State has to be by all parties to the agreement or, as the case may be of the wages council or board making the order and the appropriate minister has to be satisfied that the provisions as to statutory guarantee payments should not apply to those employees.[3]

1 Employment Rights Act 1996, s 35(1).
2 Employment Rights Act 1996, s 35(4). When such an order is in force industrial tribunals have jurisdiction to decide such matters.
3 Employment Rights Act 1996, s 35(1) and (2).

Sickness

The problem

4.46   With the reduction in manning which has taken place over the last few years absenteeism has become a major problem in the efficient running of many undertakings. Employers are justifiably sceptical as to some claims of ill-health especially when the illness manifests itself at the end of a holiday or on a Friday and a Monday. Self-certification has increased this suspicion and even a doctor's sick note does not always allay doubts about the reasons for absence. Medical practitioners are often placed in a difficult position in that they see themselves in a relationship based on trust and to confront or challenge their patients would undermine that trust. Any practitioner in the area of personal injuries will know that even when there has been an objective event like an industrial or motor accident the extent of the injury often turns on whether the plaintiff is being honest about his condition or malingering. In some cases a plaintiff may genuinely believe that he has symptoms which disable him or her from work but there may be no organic basis for those symptoms. In many cases of illness as opposed to injuries there is no way in which a doctor can verify the symptoms of which the patient complains. The problem for employers is not so much the specific absence for a pre-planned medical operation – for which cover can be planned – as the frequent short-term absence without warning for a wide variety of relatively trivial illnesses.

Issues raised by sickness

4.47   Although this chapter is only concerned with remuneration it is relevant to note that ill-health has wide ramifications:
(1)   In certain circumstances the prolonged ill-health of an employee may frustrate the contract (see **13.13** et seq).

(2) The ill-health of an employee may be a potentially fair reason for his or her dismissal (see **15.101**).

(3) Certain industrial processes expose employees to potential health hazards and it may be necessay to suspend employees on medical grounds (see **4.24**).

(4) Pregnancy can cause certain health problems and there are detailed safe-guards to protect the position of pregnant women (see Chapter 7).

(5) Employers are under an obligation to set out the terms concerning sick pay in the particulars of employment (see **9.16**).

(6) The right to sickness payment may arise from the express or implied terms of the contract (see **4.48**).

(7) The burden of administering the statutory sick pay scheme for the first 28 weeks has been delegated to employers (see **4.51**).

Remuneration during sickness

4.48   There is no universal rule of law that an employee is entitled to wages or other remuneration during sickness.[1] There are special provisions which apply during the minimum statutory notice period.[2] The question to be asked is: what were the terms of the contract between employer and employee, and what did those terms provide in regard to payment of wages during absence by reason of illness? The ordinary principles of the law of contract must be applied. In many cases there are express conditions as to the payment of sick pay: in the absence of such conditions it is for the courts to consider whether it is right to imply such a term.

1 *Mears v Safecar Security Ltd* [1982] ICR 626, CA which stated there was no general presumption of entitlement to sick pay as suggested in *Orman v Saville Sportswear Ltd* [1960] 1 WLR 1055.
2 Employment Rights Act 1996, s 88 (1)(b). See **13.36**.

4.49   It is submitted that the authorities[1] establish that the following propo-sitions will be relevant in determining whether there is an implied term that sickness payments will be made.

(1) Whether there is a precedent for paying wages during sickness to opera-tives in a comparable position.

(2) Even if there is a precedent for paying sickness payments, this may be negated by an express stipulation that sickness payment would be paid as a matter of grace only.

(3) If under the contract the consideration for the payment of wages is the actual performance of the work this will point to there being no implied term, but if mere readiness and willingness, if able to do so, is the consideration this will suggest that there is an implied term to make payments during sickness. When payment is for piecework the con-sideration for the wages will be the actual performance of the work. In the case of employment by the hour the actual performance of the work is likely to be the consideration for the wages. Similarly when payment is by the day, the actual performance of each day's work is likely to be the consideration for that day's wages.[2] When payment is by the week much depends on the nature of the work. In the case of employees engaged for a longer period, usually the consideration will be found to be the mere readiness and willingness to do the work, if able to do so, and not the actual performance of the work.

(4) It is in the interests of both parties that the precise right, if any, to remuneration during absence while incapacitated be defined at the time of engagement and clarified in the contract of employment and there is an obligation on the employer to give details of any provisions for sick pay in the written particulars of the contract of employment issued pursuant to s 1 of the Employment Rights Act 1996. If the employer has failed in this obligation it is at least arguable that industrial tribunals may well be more liberal in their views as to implying a term and treat with a degree of reservation older decisions which were decided before there was any such obligation upon the employer.

1 *Petrie v MacFisheries Ltd* [1940] 1 KB 258; [1939] 4 All ER 281, CA explaining *Marrison v Bell* [1939] 2 KB 187; [1939] 1 All ER 745, CA; *O'Grady v M Saper Ltd* [1940] 2 KB 469 at p 473; [1940] 3 All ER 527, CA. Every effort should be used to make the contractual provisions clear: *Roberts v BICC Ltd* [1976] IRLR 404.
2 *Hancock v BSA Tools Ltd* [1939] 4 All ER 538 (notice displayed in works – hourly basis – custom of trade – driller); *Hanley v Pease & Partners* [1915] 1 KB 698.

The amount of sick pay

4.50 If under the terms of his contract, express or implied, the employee is entitled to wages during temporary sickness, he is entitled during such absence to receive his full remuneration in accordance with the terms of his employment. This may, in certain circumstances, include a bonus.[1] In *Mears v Safeway Security Ltd*[2] the Court of Appeal affirmed the view of the Employment Appeal Tribunal that if there is an implied term of payment during sickness payments this is subject to the right of the employer to deduct the amounts due from the statutory sickness schemes. Many schemes expressly limit the duration of the time for which sickness payment is payable. Typically in the public sector the employee is paid fully for the first six months and then receives half pay for the next six months. In the absence of agreement as to the duration of the payment of sick pay the courts will imply a term which is reasonable having regard to what is the usual practice in the industry concerned.[3]

1 *Orman v Saville Sportswear Ltd* [1960] 3 All ER 105; [1960] 1 WLR 1055 (production manager).
2 [1982] IRLR 183; [1982] ICR 626, CA.
3 *Howman & Son v Blyth* [1983] ICR 183.

Statutory sick pay

4.51 The government has sought to shift the burden of paying statutory sick pay for the first 28 weeks to the employer.[1] Employers are entitled to recoupment of the costs through deduction from their liabilities for National Insurance contributions.[2] In a nutshell there is no payment for the first three days of illness although two periods of incapacity separated by not more than two weeks will be regarded as one period of incapacity. The amounts of payment are related to the normal salary of the employee. Employers can easily obtain details of the scheme from the Department of Social Security.

1 Social Security Contributions and Benefits Act 1992.
2 Statutory Sick Pay Percentage Threshold Order 1995, SI 1995/513.

Holidays

4.52 Holidays with pay are now a common practice, but there is no duty on an employer, apart from statute[1] to allow his employees holidays, with or without pay, unless the contract contains a term, express or implied, to that effect. Contrary to popular belief there is no absolute right to statutory bank holidays. Article 120 of the EC Treaty provides that member states should endeavour to maintain existing equivalence between paid holiday schemes. A term of the contract as to pay during holidays may be implied by custom as in *R v Stoke-upon-Trent (Inhabitants)*.[2]

1 There may be direct statutory intervention, for example the Factories Act 1961, s 94 provided that women and children should not be required to work on public holidays. The Sex Discrimination Act 1986 and the Employment Act 1989 removed these entitlements. The right of the employee to be paid for holidays taken during the minimum statutory period of notice is discussed at **13.36**.
2 (1843) 5 QB 303.

A matter of construing the contract

4.53 As with other terms of contracts of employment, those relating to holidays should be expressed without ambiguity to prevent misunderstandings. In particular the position when an employee leaves before taking a holiday should be covered, and also the question whether a holiday accrues from day to day or requires a completed minimum period of work before the employee is entitled to a holiday with pay. In *Hurt v Sheffield Corpn*,[1] a resolution provided that:

> 'all the workmen in the employ of the Corporation with not less than twelve months' service shall have one week's holiday in each year between the beginning of April and the end of October with pay ...'

A workman who was dismissed and whose employment ended on 5 August was held not to be entitled to a week's wages in lieu of a holiday which he had not had. On the wording of the resolution it was decided that he must in fact be in the service of the Corporation during the whole period from the beginning of April to the end of October in order to be entitled to the holiday or payment in lieu. The contract being lawfully terminated at an earlier date the employer had committed no breach of contract. When the contract governs the position with regard to holidays and holiday pay it can, of course, only be changed if both parties agree.[2]

1 (1916) 85 LJKB 1684. This does not accord with modern practice but the Court of Appeal did not overrule *Hurt* in the case of *Morley v Heritage plc* [1993] IRLR 400.
2 See for example *Tucker v British Leyland Motor Corpn Ltd* [1978] IRLR 493, Cty Ct.

4.54 In the overwhelmimgly majority of cases no problem arises as to when holidays may be taken since there is often an annual shut down in major manufacturing industries and there is then the right to take the balance of the holidays. However a prudent employer should be careful to set out the position. For example, garages selling cars are particularly busy with new registrations in August which is a time when because of school holidays many employees wish to take their holidays. In such circumstances an employer would be well advised to reserve the right to ensure that the workplace was not denuded of employees.

Time off work in certain circumstances

Time off for public duties

4.55   An employer shall permit his employee to take time off during the employee's working hours in accordance with s 50(1) of the Employment Rights Act 1996 for carrying out public duties as a justice of the peace. In addition a number of other public offices are covered such as membership of a local authority, a statutory tribunal, and a relevant health or educational body.[1] Interestingly the Act does not provide a specific right for time off for jury service or for attendance at court as a witness. As preventing a person from discharging either of these functions would amount to a contempt of court the reality is that it is difficult to see that any employer could prevent an employee from discharging these obligations.

1 See s 50(2) for the full range of public duties and positions covered.

Who qualifies?

4.56   It should be noted that the right only applies to employees. Since the rules restricting the rights of part-timers have been abrogated, part-time employees now also qualify for this right. There is no requirement for continuity of service. There are specific exclusions:
(1)   Those who ordinarily work outside Great Britain.[1]
(2)   Crown employees whose work involves national security and in respect of which such work there is a certificate of exemption.[2]
(3)   Those employed in the 'police service'(which no longer includes prison officers by virtue of s 126(1) of the Criminal Justice and Public Order Act 1994).[3]
(4)   Share fishermen or merchant seamen.[4]

1 Employment Rights Act 1996, s 196.
2 Employment Rights Act 1996, s 193(2)(c).
3 Employment Rights Act 1996, s 200.
4 Employment Rights Act 1996, s 199(2) and (4).

Duties to which s 50 applies

4.57   The duties to which the section applies, other than those of justices of the peace, are attendances at meetings of the body, or of any of its committees or sub-committees, and the doing of any other thing approved by the body or of any of a class so approved, for the purpose of the discharge of the functions of the body, or of any of its committees or sub-committees.[1] The amount of time off which the employee is permitted, and the occasions on which, and any conditions subject to which, the time off may be so taken are those which are reasonable in all the circumstances. In determining this regard has to be given to how much time off is required for the performance of the duties of the office or as a member of the body in question and how much time off is required for the performance of the particular duties; how much time off the employee has already been permitted for trade union duties and activities and public duties; and the circumstances of the employer's business, and the effect of the employee's absence on the running of the business.[2] The industrial tribunal does not have power to impose conditions upon the parties as to the way in which the time off shall be granted.[3] There is no requirement for time off in accordance with these provisions to be with pay.[4]

1 Employment Rights Act 1996, s 50(3).
2 Employment Rights Act 1996, s 50(4). There is no express provision for the issue of a code of practice to assist by giving guidance in these cases. See *Borders Regional Council v Maule* [1993] IRLR 199 for an examination of the issues which a tribunal ought to consider.
3 *Corner v Buckinghamshire County Council* [1978] ICR 836, EAT.
4 For an example of the application of these provisions see *Corner's* case, above, *Emmerson v IRC* [1977] IRLR 458, and *Ratcliffe v Dorset County Council* [1978] IRLR 191. Some employers do pay their employees. Under the Local Government and Housing Act 1989, s 10, local authorities are precluded from allowing employees more than 208 hours' paid time off in any financial year for the purpose of performing duties as councillors (though the provision does not apply to council chairman).

4.58 An employee may present a complaint to an industrial tribunal that his employer failed to permit him to take time off as required by s 50.[1] So far as Crown servants are concerned if the terms of an employee's employment restrict the right to take part in certain political activities or activities which may conflict with his official functions, nothing in s 50 shall require him to be allowed time off for public duties in connection with any such activities).[2]

1 Employment Rights Act 1996, s 51.
2 Employment Rights Act 1996, s 191(5).

Complaints to industrial tribunals

4.59 Complaints by an employee relating to time off for public duties should be presented within three months of the date when the failure occurred, or within such further period as the tribunal considers reasonable in a case where it is satisfied that it was not reasonably practicable for the complaint to be presented within the period of three months.[1] When it finds that a complaint of an employer's failure to permit the employee to take time off is well founded, the tribunal will make a declaration to that effect[2] and may award compensation to be paid by the employer to the employee of such amount as the tribunal considers just and equitable in all the circumstances, having regard to the employer's default and to the loss sustained by the employee which is attributable to the matters complained of.[3]

1 Employment Rights Act 1996, s 51(2). The assistance of a conciliation officer may also be sought.
2 Employment Rights Act 1996, s 51(3).
3 Employment Rights Act 1996, s 51(4).

Redundancy, trade union activities and pregnancy

4.60 Employees dismissed by reason of redundancy have the right to be allowed time off to look for new employment and to make arrangements for training for future employment. This is discussed more fully below (see Chapter 16). The provisions for time off for trade union activities are covered in Chapter 14. For the rights of pregnant women to have time off for antenatal care, see Chapter 7.

Occupational pension trustees

4.61 Occupational pension trustees have the right to have time off for the performance of their duties and for receiving training relevant to such duties.[1] A right exists for payment for such time off.[2] A formula is provided for the calculation of the remuneration depending on whether the work is paid at a flat rate or a performance related basis.[3]

4.61 *Remuneration*

1 Employment Rights Act 1996, s 58.
2 Employment Rights Act 1996, s 59.
3 Employment Rights Act 1996, s 59(2) and (3).

Sunday trading

4.62 The laws as to Sunday trading were clarified by the Sunday Trading Act 1994 and are now consolidated in the Employment Rights Act 1996. In general terms[1] the Act protects an employee from being compelled to work on a Sunday if he or she was not required to do so before the legislation came into force or alternatively she or he has given a written 'opting out notice'.

1 See **15.76** and for the provisions in detail, see *Harvey on Industrial Relations and Employment Law.*

Chapter 5

Equal pay

Introduction

The rules governing equal pay are intended to ensure that men and women receive equal benefits (not just pay) for the same or equal work. This is provided for in European law by art 119 of the Treaty of Rome and Directives made by the Council of the European Union, and in United Kingdom law by the Equal Pay Act 1970. The Equal Pay Act operates through the contract of employment of individual employees. It provides that every contract to which it relates contains an equality clause to ensure equality of benefits to those received by a man employed on equal work are received by the woman working under the contract.

Sources of the law

5.01 When considering the rules governing equal pay for workers both the laws of the United Kingdom and of the European Union may have to be considered. The Equal Pay Act 1970 is the principal source of the law of equality of payment, but in the light of the primacy of European law[1] it is important to have a knowledge of the relevant European provisions since these provide an aid to construction of the Equal Pay Act and may themselves be directly effective where they have not been, or only imperfectly have been, implemented in to English and Scots law.[2]

1 See 2.02.
2 For a more full discussion of these matters, see 2.19–2.21.

The law of the European Union

5.02 Article 119 of the Treaty of Rome provides:
'Each Member State shall during the first stage ensure and subsequently maintain the application of the principle that men and women should receive equal pay for equal work.

For the purposes of this Article, "pay" means the ordinary basic or minimum wage or salary and any other consideration, whether in cash or in kind, which the worker receives, directly or indirectly, in respect of his employment from his employer.

Equal pay without discrimination based on sex means:

(a) that pay for the same work at piece rates shall be calculated on the basis of the same unit of measurement;
(b) that pay for work at time rates shall be the same for the same job.'

5.03   A Council Directive of 10 February 1975[1] states:

'The principle of equal pay for men and women outlined in Article 119 of the Treaty, hereinafter called "principle of equal pay", means, for the same work or for work to which equal value is attributed, the elimination of all discrimination on grounds of sex with regard to all aspects and conditions of remuneration. In particular, when a job classification system is used for determining pay, it must be based on the same criteria for both men and women, and so drawn up as to exclude any discrimination on the ground of sex.'

1 Directive 75/117/EEC. For a helpful discussion of 'pay' for the purposes of art 119 see Case C-457/93: *Kuratorum Fur Dialyse und Nierentransplantation eV v Lewark* [1996] IRLR 637, ECJ.

5.04   A further Directive of 9 February 1976[1] seeks to bring into effect the principle of equal treatment for men and women as regards access to employment, including promotion, as to practical training and as regards working conditions.

1 Directive 76/207/EEC.

5.05   The Equal Pay Act 1970 when it came into force was intended to carry the obligations of the United Kingdom under art 119 of the Treaty of Rome into effect. The failure of the United Kingdom to implement, or implement fully, its obligations in this respect has lead to a considerable jurisprudence in the European Court of Justice and national courts and tribunals.[1] Article 119 is directly applicable in the courts and tribunals of member states[2] and has been regularly so applied in the United Kingdom.[3]

1 The European Commission have taken infraction proceedings against the United Kingdom in respect of some of the failings, for instance Case 61/81 *EC Commission v United Kingdom* [1982] ICR 578, ECJ (which lead to the Equal Pay (Amendment) Regulations 1983, SI 1983/1794).
2 Case 43/75 *Defrenne v Sabena* [1976] ICR 547, ECJ. In this case it was decided that art 119 was directly applicable internally by the courts of member states. The direct effect of art 119 cannot be relied on in order to support claims concerning pay periods prior to 8 April 1976, except as regards those workers who had already brought legal proceedings or made an equivalent claim. Decisions under art 119 should always be considered in connection with claims under the Equal Pay Act 1970.
3 See Chapter 2 above as to the relationship between European law and the domestic laws of the United Kingdom.

Equal Pay Act 1970

5.06   The Equal Pay Act 1970 came fully into force on 29 December 1975. In general terms its purpose is to eliminate discrimination between the sexes as regards terms and conditions of employment. The Act forms part of the overall legislation with regard to the effect of sex on employment and it should be construed together with the Sex Discrimination Act 1975 as one harmonious code. A case in the employment field which could be brought under the Equal Pay Act 1970 must be brought under that Act, and not under Pt II of the Sex Discrimination Act 1975.[1] The method adopted by the statute of achieving its purpose is by the use of an 'equality clause'. If the terms of a contract under which a woman is employed at an establishment in Great Britain do not include (directly or by reference to a collective agreement or otherwise) an equality clause they are deemed to include one.[2] Although the Act is expressed in terms of providing protection to women it provides similar protection for men.[3]

1 *Steel v Union of Post Office Workers* [1977] IRLR 288 at 290, EAT.
2 Equal Pay Act 1970, s 1(1).
3 Equal Pay Act 1970, s 1(13).

5.07 The concept of an equality clause was new to the laws of the United Kingdom and was devised by the draftsmen of the Equal Pay Act 1970.[1] The equality clause operates in three sets of circumstances; where the woman is employed on like work with a man; where she is employed on work rated as equivalent with that of a man; and where she is employed on work not falling within those categories which is of equal value in terms of demand to that of a man.

1 European law does not require an employee on maternity leave to be paid full pay during her absence. She should receive the benefit of a pay award prior to or during her absence: Case C-342/93 *Gillespie v Northern Health and Social Services Board* [1996] IRLR 214, ECJ.

The equality clause has effect in the following three circumstances.

Like work

5.08 A woman is to be regarded as employed on like work with men if, but only if, her work and theirs is of the same or a broadly similar nature, and the differences (if any) between the things she does and the things they do are not of practical importance in relation to terms and conditions of employment; and accordingly in comparing her work with theirs regard should be had to the frequency or otherwise with which any such differences occur in practice as well as to the nature and extent of the differences.[1]

1 Equal Pay Act 1970, s 1(4).

5.09 The work has to be of the same or of broadly similar nature to a man's work[1] and it is for the applicant to choose the man with whom comparison is to be made.[2] The comparator has to be 'a man'. There is no requirement that he should be a 'representative man'.[3] The man must be employed in the same employment as explained in s 1(6) of the Equal Pay Act 1970, if not the equality clause cannot benefit the applicant.[4] Comparison can be made by the woman with a man who was previously in the employment or a successor.[5]

1 There must be comparison with a man: *Meeks v National Union of Agricultural and Allied Workers* [1976] IRLR 198; *Rice v Scottish Legal Life Assurance Society* [1976] IRLR 330. What is compared must be 'work': *Manor Bakeries Ltd v Nazir* [1996] IRLR 604, EAT, but see 5.03, n 1.
2 *Ainsworth v Glass Tubes and Components Ltd* [1977] ICR 347, EAT.
3 *Thomas v National Coal Board* [1987] IRLR 451, EAT.
4 *Rice v Scottish Legal Life Assurance Society* [1976] IRLR 330.
5 *Macarthys Ltd v Smith* [1980] ICR 672, CA; *Hallam Diocese Trustee v Connaughton* [1996] IRLR 505, EAT.

5.10 In deciding whether the work of the man and the woman is like work considerable assistance will be found in the decision of the Employment Appeal Tribunal in *Capper Pass Ltd v Lawton*.[1] A woman cook worked a 40-hour week to prepare lunches for 1,020 people. Two male assistant chefs worked in a different kitchen and produced approximately 350 meals daily. The men worked 40 hours and overtime each week. The tribunal explained that when deciding whether there is work of a broadly similar nature the industrial tribunal should be the sole judge. Phillips J said:[2]

'It seems to us that in most cases the inquiry will fall into two stages.
First, is the work of the same, or, if not, "of a broadly similar" nature?
This question can be answered by a general consideration of the type of
work involved, and of the skill and knowledge required to do it. It seems to
us to be implicit in the words of subsection (4) that it can be answered
without a minute examination of the detail of the differences between the
work done by the man and the work done by the woman. But, secondly, if
on such an examination the answer is that the work is of a broadly similar
nature, it is then necessary to go on to consider the detail and to inquire
whether the differences between the work being compared are of "practical
importance in relation to terms and conditions of employment". In answering
that question the industrial tribunal will be guided by the concluding
words of the subsection. But again, it seems to us, trivial differences, or
differences not likely in the real world to be reflected in the terms and
conditions of employment, ought to be disregarded. In other words, once it
is determined that work is of a broadly similar nature it should be regarded
as being like work unless the differences are plainly of a kind which the
industrial tribunal in its experience would expect to find reflected in the
terms and conditions of employment. This last point requires to be emphasised. There seems to be a tendency, apparent in some of the decisions
of industrial tribunals cited to us, and in some of the arguments upon the
hearing of this appeal, to weigh up the differences by reference to such
questions as whether one type of work or another is or is not suitable for
women, or is the kind of work which women can do, or whether the
differences are important, and so on. These are not the tests prescribed by
the Act. The only differences which will prevent work which is of a
broadly similar nature from being "like work" are differences which in
practice will be reflected in the terms and conditions of employment.'
This clearly sets out the two-stage process in deciding whether or not the
woman was employed on like work with that of the man. Adopting this
approach the decision of the industrial tribunal that the work of the woman
cook was broadly similar to the men's work, was upheld by the Employment
Appeal Tribunal.

1 [1977] QB 852; [1977] 2 All ER 11, EAT.
2 [1977] ICR 83 at p 85. See also *Waddington v Leicester Council for Voluntary Services* [1977]
2 All ER 633; [1977] ICR 266, EAT and *Redland Roof Tiles Ltd v Harper* [1977] ICR 349, EAT.

5.11   What happens in practice is what is considered. It is not a relevant
difference for these purposes that the man is obliged to be available to do additional further duties unless the man performs them to a significant extent.[1] It is
not permissible in ordinary circumstances to ignore part of the work actually
done in practice, except where it is a separate and distinct job.[2] What is important is what occurs in practice. The tribunal should look at the circumstances in
which apparently similar work is done rather than the theoretical possibilities
arising out of the terms of the contract.[3] Merely doing the work at a different
time, for example on a night shift, does not mean that the work is not like
work.[4] Factors which have been found to be of practical importance include
the responsibility undertaken, and the consequences of error, by the man.[5]

1 *Electrolux Ltd v Hutchinson* [1977] ICR 252, EAT; *British Leyland (UK) Ltd v Powell* [1978]
IRLR 57, EAT.
2 *Maidment v Cooper & Co (Birmingham) Ltd* [1978] ICR 1094, EAT.
3 *Thomas v National Coal Board* [1987] ICR 757, EAT.

4 *Dugdale v Kraft Foods Ltd* [1977] ICR 48, EAT. Contrast *Kerr v Lister & Co Ltd* [1977] IRLR 259, EAT.
5 *Eaton Ltd v Nuttall* [1977] 3 All ER 1131; [1977] ICR 272, EAT (female production scheduler dealt with 2, 400 items each with a value of up to £2.50, male dealt with 1, 200 items with a value of from £5 to £1, 000).

5.12 Difficulties are frequently encountered when it is said that the man's work requires greater physical strength than does the work undertaken by the woman. Such differences may mean that the work undertaken by the woman is not like work, but the difference must be of practical importance to satisfy the statutory requirement if the work is not to be found to be like work. Further, an employer should not assume that an individual is not capable of undertaking particular work solely on the basis of the sex of the employee. Whether a woman can do a particular job is a matter of judgment for the employer. He should base his judgment on the personal qualities of the individual employee not on an assumption based on the employee's sex. Employers should not assume that all women are incapable of doing a particular job or work.[1]

1 *Noble v David Gold & Son (Holdings) Ltd* [1980] ICR 543, CA.

Work rated as equivalent

5.13 A woman is regarded as employed on work rated as equivalent with that of any man if, but only if, her job and his job have been given an equal value, in terms of the demand made on a worker under various headings (for instance effort, skill, decision), on a study undertaken with a view to evaluating in those terms the jobs to be done by all or any of the employees in an undertaking or group of undertakings, or would have been given an equal value but for the evaluation being made on a system setting different values for men and women on the same demand under any heading.[1]

1 Equal Pay Act 1970, s 1(5).

5.14 It has been said obiter in the Employment Appeal Tribunal:[1]
'It seems to us that subsection (5) can only apply to what may be called a valid evaluation study. By that, we mean a study satisfying the test of being thorough in analysis and capable of impartial application. It should be possible by applying the study to arrive at the position of a particular employee at a particular point in a particular salary grade without taking other matters into account except those unconnected with the nature of the work. It will be in order to take into account such matters as merit or seniority, etc, but any matters concerning the work (eg responsibility) one would expect to find taken care of in the evaluation study. One which does not satisfy that test, and requires the management to make a subjective judgment concerning the nature of the work before the employee can be fitted into the appropriate place in the appropriate salary grade, would seem to us not to be a valid study for the purpose of subsection (5).'

1 *Eaton Ltd v Nuttall* [1977] ICR 272 at p 277, EAT. In the Appendix to this judgment the Employment Appeal Tribunal sets out a note of the principal methods of job evaluation based on the ACAS Guide *Job Evaluation Guide No 1*. This quotation was referred to in the Court of Appeal in *Bromley v H & J Quick Ltd* [1988] ICR 623, CA. See also *England v Bromley London Borough Council* [1978] ICR 1, EAT.

5.15 No job evaluation study can be truly objective. 'Objective' has a special meaning in these circumstances since there is no universally accepted method of undertaking a job evaluation. All methods of job evaluation involve an element of subjective assessment. It is in the application of these judgments that discrimination can taint an apparently innocent job evaluation.[1] What is required is a study undertaken with a view to evaluating jobs under various headings, for instance effort, skill and decision. The jobs of each worker covered by the study must have been valued in terms of the demand on the worker under the appropriate headings.[2] Thus job ranking by paired comparisons on a 'whole job basis' which was the method used by the employers in *Bromley's* case was not a job evaluation study for the purposes of s 1(5).

1 Case 237/85 *Rummler v Dato-Druck GmbH* [1987] ICR 774, ECJ.
2 *Bromley v H & J Quick Ltd* [1988] ICR 623, CA. Dillon LJ thought that this meant that the study should consist of a detailed analysis of each job (see p 633). Woolf LJ thought that employers can identify a group of jobs which when evaluated under headings have no material difference (at p 639).

5.16 A merit assessment scheme is not necessarily part of a job evaluation study. The job evaluation study should grade jobs not persons. A job evaluation study does not directly have anything to do with remuneration. Remuneration may be fixed by separate salary rules determined as agreed to be appropriate to the different grades assessed in accordance with the job evaluation rules.[1] It does not matter that the scheme has not been applied in practice if it is complete since at that time the comparison is feasible. Notwithstanding this, the job evaluation study will not be complete unless and until the parties who have agreed to carry out the study have accepted its validity.[2]

1 *O'Brien v Sim-Chem Ltd* [1980] ICR 573, HL.
2 *Arnold v Beecham Group Ltd* [1982] IRLR 307, EAT.

5.17 The terms of the woman's contract must be of such kind that the rating of the job is relevant to its application. When there has been a properly constituted job evaluation study an industrial tribunal is bound to act on the conclusions and the content of the job evaluation study. The job evaluation study can only be challenged if it is shown that there is a fundamental error in it, or there is a plain error on the face of the record. An industrial tribunal cannot disregard a job evaluation study just because the employers and employees regard it as being unsatisfactory to some extent.[1] The position is not affected because the employer undertook the job evaluation study voluntarily.[2]

1 *Green v Broxtowe District Council* [1977] 1 All ER 694; [1977] ICR 241, EAT.
2 *O'Brien v Sim-Chem Ltd* [1980] ICR 573, HL.

5.18 The provision as to work rated as equivalent has now assumed a differing importance from that when it was first enacted. This is the result of the implementation of the equal value provisions. Those provisions do not apply where the employee is employed on like work with, or work rated pursuant to a valid job evaluation study as being equivalent to that of, a man. In some cases in an attempt to avoid claims pursuant to the equal value provisions employers claim that there has been a valid job evaluation study. In such cases the onus of proof to show the existence of a valid job evaluation study rests on the employer.[1]

1 *Bromley v H & J Quick Ltd* [1988] ICR 623, CA.

Work of equal value

5.19   The provisions relating to the application of the equality clause when a woman is employed on work of equal value with her male comparator were introduced by the Equal Pay (Amendment) Regulations 1983, SI 1983/1794. The regulations were made following the decision of the European Court of Justice[1] that the Equal Pay Act as then in force did not effect all the United Kingdom's obligations arising from art 119 of the Treaty of Rome.[2]

1 Case 61/81 *EC Commission v United Kingdom* [1982] ICR 578, ECJ.
2 See 5.05, n 1.

5.20   The Equal Pay (Amendment) Regulations 1983 introduced a new paragraph (c) in s 1(2) of the Equal Pay Act 1970. Its effect is that where a woman is employed on work which, not being work in relation to which paragraph (a) (like work) or (b) (job evaluation study) applies, is, in terms of the demands made on her (for instance under such headings as effort, skill and decision), of equal value to that of a man in the same employment, then an equality clause applies.

5.21   Industrial tribunals have a special procedure which is applicable to these 'equal value' cases.[1] This may involve the preparation by an expert of a report to the tribunal on whether in his or her opinion the work of the applicant is of equal value using the statutory test to that of the comparator. This report if requested is considered by the tribunal before it decides whether or not the applicant's work is of equal value to that of the comparator.

1 See Chapter 18. The procedure is almost universally thought to be too complex and slow. The effect of the amendment to the rules allowing an industrial tribunal to decide the issue without appointing an expert (see **18.104**) remains to be seen. An example of judicial criticism of the earlier procedure is to be found in the decision of the Employment Appeal Tribunal in *British Coal Corp v Smith* [1993] IRLR 308, EAT.

5.22   The words in the new paragraph 'not being work in relation to which paragraph (a) or (b) applies' have caused difficulties. Employers have claimed either that the applicant was employed on like work with a man or that the applicant's work had been the subject of a job evaluation study to avoid a claim based on equal value. In *Pickstone v Freemans plc*[1] it was held that the presence of a man doing the same work as the applicant's did not prevent them from relying on s 1(2)(c) of the 1970 Act. The House of Lords held that the applicant was only excluded from claiming that she was employed on work of equal value with a man if *that* man was employed on like work with her (or on work rated as equivalent to that man). As has been noted the strange result is that with the coming into force of the equal value provisions, employers, who previously may have wished to resist claims that employees are employed on like work or work rated as equivalent to that of a man, may now seek to show that such a situation applies to resist a claim for equal value. In such cases the onus of proof lies on the employers.[2]

1 [1988] IRLR 357, HL. Mrs Pickstone's case is also important in helping to lay the foundations for significant developments in the rules of statutory interpretation, see **2.10**.
2 *Bromley v H & J Quick Ltd* [1988] ICR 623, CA.

5.23   The preparation of the report by the expert is expensive and takes time and even if an expert is not appointed the issues are complex. In these circumstances it is obviously in the interests of all parties that the issue of whether or not the applicant is employed on like work or work rated as equivalent to that of the comparator is determined before consideration is given to whether her work is of equal value to that of the male comparator. It is expressly provided that there are no reasonable grounds for determining that the work of a woman is of equal value to that of a man if her work and the work of the man have been given different values on a job evaluation study and there are no reasonable grounds for determining that the evaluation contained in the study was made on a system which discriminates on grounds of sex.[1]

1 Equal Pay Act 1970, s 2A(2). Section 2A(3) provides that a study discriminates on grounds of sex where there is a difference, or coincidence, between values set by that system on different demands under the same or different headings which is not justifiable irrespective of the sex of the person on whom those demands are made.

The material factor defence

5.24 An equality clause does not operate in relation to a variation between the woman's contract and the man's contract if the employer proves that the variation is genuinely due to a material factor which is not the difference of sex. In a case where the woman is employed on like work with, or work rated as equivalent to that of, the man, the factor must be a material difference between the woman's case and the man's. Where the woman's work is of equal value to that of a man the material factor may be such a material difference.[1] The difference between cases of women employed on like work with (or work rated as equivalent to that of) a man and cases where the woman's work is of equal value is not clear. It is apparently intended to provide a wider range of defences for the employer but the extent of this remains to be ascertained.

1 Equal Pay Act 1970, s 1(3). There is no distinction between 'direct' and 'indirect' discrimination for the purposes of the Equal Pay Act 1970. If a woman shows she is employed on like work with, work rated as equivalent to that of, or of equal value to that of, a man she is entitled to her remedy unless the Equal Pay Act 1970, s 1(3) is satisfied: *Ratcliffe v North Yorkshire County Council* [1995] IRLR 439, HL.

5.25 When considering whether or not the employer has a material factor defence the important issues to be decided are:
(1) whether there was a material factor other than sex which was a material difference between the woman's case and the man's case, or other material difference; and
(2) has the employer proved that it was more probable than not that the variation was genuinely due to that material factor?
In an equal value case the relevant factors to be considered are the same whether raised at the hearing prior to the determination of whether the work is of equal value, or at the hearing which takes place after the tribunal has decided that the work is of equal value to that of the comparator.[1] The burden to prove the defence lies fully on the employer.[2] There is no obligation on the employer to show that the explanation for the difference in pay is objectively justified. All he has to show is that the variation was genuinely due to a material factor which was not the difference of sex.[3]

1 *McGregor v GMBATU* [1987] ICR 505, EAT. Refer to **18.104–18.115** for details of the procedure.

2 *Financial Times v Byrne (No 2)* [1992] IRLR 163, EAT; *National Vulcan Engineering Insurance Group Ltd v Wade* [1979] QB 132; [1978] 3 All ER 121, CA.
3 *Tyldesley v TML Plastics Ltd* [1996] IRLR 395, EAT. For example a genuine mistake. See also *Calder v Rowntree Mackintosh Confectionery Ltd* [1993] IRLR 212, CA and contrast with the approach in Case 109/88 *Handels-og v Danflos* [1991] ICR 74, ECJ. See also *Rainey v Greater Glasgow Health Board* [1987] ICR 129, HL.

5.26 The tribunal should hear evidence as to the alleged defence. The issue should be determined on its merits and even if the respondent claims that the regulations providing for the difference are an act of the executive, the respondent is still required to satisfy the requirements of the defence.[1] Material means 'significant and relevant'. All relevant circumstances of a person's case are to be considered. They may go beyond the personal qualifications or merits of the individual by way of skill, experience and training. In particular, provided that there is no direct or indirect discrimination based on sex, they may apply where the difference in pay was reasonably necessary to obtain a result for economic or administrative efficiency.[2] This is in line with decisions of the European Court of Justice to the effect that a difference in pay can be justified on objective economic grounds unrelated to sex.[3]

1 *R v Secretary of State for Social Services, ex p Clarke* [1988] IRLR 22, QBD. See also *Oxford v Department of Health and Social Security* [1977] ICR 884, EAT.
2 *Rainey v Greater Glasgow Health Board* [1987] ICR 129, HL.
3 Case 170/84 *Bilka-Kaufhaus GmbH v Weber von Hartz* [1987] ICR 110, ECJ; Case 171/88 *Rinner-Kuhn v FWW Spezial-Gebaudereinigung GmbH & Co KG* [1989] IRLR 493, ECJ.

5.27 Whether or not there was an intention to discriminate is not relevant.[1] The proper approach is to ascertain whether the difference in pay was genuinely due to a material factor other than sex. It is not sufficient for the employer to show that the cause of the variation was entirely free from any kind of sex discrimination. There can be 'causes' which are not 'material factors'. The two questions arising from s 1(3) of the 1970 Act – was there a difference in pay?; and was there a material factor other than sex which justified it? – must constantly be borne in mind by the tribunal.[2]

1 *McPherson v Rathgael Centre for Children and Young People* [1991] IRLR 206, NICA.
2 *Barber v NRC Manufacturing Ltd* [1993] IRLR 95, EAT.

5.28 A wide variety of circumstances have been found to satisfy the requirements of the genuine material factor defence. However, it must be stressed that to provide the employer with a defence all the requirements referred to must be satisfied. Examples of circumstances found to amount to material factors include seniority and length of service,[1] a personal skill or qualification,[2] larger output or productivity, a difference in the place of work such as a 'London weighting'[3] and differences in the degree of responsibility if that is the genuine reason for the difference. 'Red circling' or the creation of a personal protected salary on transfer to another job is also permitted, provided that it does not perpetuate unlawful discrimination. It is clear that an employer cannot: 'establish in the terms of [the material factor defence] that the variation between the woman's contract and the man's contract is genuinely due to a material difference (other than the difference of sex) between her case and his when it can be seen that past sex discrimination has contributed to the variation'.[4] Motherhood is not a material difference other than sex.[5]

1 *ARW Transformers Ltd v Cupples* [1977] IRLR 228, EAT; *Boyle v Tennent Caledonian Breweries Ltd* [1978] IRLR 321, EAT. Or a high grading for personal skill or qualifications:

National Vulcan Engineering Insurance Group Ltd v Wade [1979] QB 132; [1978] 3 All ER 121, CA. A trainee cannot claim equal pay with a fully experienced person: *de Brito v Standard Chartered Bank Ltd* [1978] ICR 650, EAT.
2 See footnote 1 above.
3 *Navy, Army and Air Force Institutions v Varley* [1977] ICR 11, EAT.
4 *Snoxell v Vauxhall Motors Ltd* [1977] ICR 700 at p 717, EAT where the argument failed because the original wages were discriminatory. Red circling may amount to a genuine material difference even if it is permanent, if it can be justified on the grounds of good industrial relations practice; see *Outlook Supplies Ltd v Parry* [1978] 2 All ER 707; [1978] ICR 388, EAT. However, past discrimination should not be perpetuated *Sun Alliance and London Insurance Ltd v Dudman* [1978] ICR 551, EAT; *Clay Cross (Quarry Services) Ltd v Fletcher* [1979] 1 All ER 474; [1979] ICR 1, CA; *United Biscuits Ltd v Young* [1978] IRLR 15, EAT; and *Methven v Cow Industrial Polymers Ltd* [1979] ICR 613, EAT.
5 *Coyne v Export Credits Guarantee Department* [1981] IRLR 51.

5.29   The difference between the case of the woman and that of the man must be genuine (and not a sham)[1] and material, justifying the variation.[2] If the employer cannot show this to be so he will not discharge the burden of proof which rests upon him and will fail.

1 *National Vulcan Engineering Insurance Group Ltd v Wade* [1979] QB 132; [1978] 3 All ER 121, CA. See for example *Electrolux Ltd v Hutchinson* [1977] ICR 252, EAT.
2 *Enderby v Frenchay Health Authority* [1992] IRLR 15, CA. See **5.30**, n 2.

5.30   Difficulties have been encountered over differences arising from collective bargaining. In *Enderby v Frenchay Health Authority*[1] a female speech therapist (a profession carried on mainly by women) claimed that her work was of equal value to that of male pharmacists and clinical psychologists. One defence advanced by the respondents was that the differing pay scales were determined by separate negotiating structures. The case was referred to the European Court of Justice which held that the fact that the collective bargaining processes which, although distinct, were carried out by the same parties and were undertaken without any discriminatory effect within each group was not sufficient justification for the difference in pay. The Court did say that the state of the employment market which may lead an employer to increase the pay of a particular job to attract candidates may constitute an objective justification for a difference in pay. If the national court is able to determine precisely what proportion of the increase in pay is attributable to the market forces, it must necessarily accept that the pay differential is objectively justified to the extent of that proportion. If that is not the case, the national court should ascertain whether the role market forces had in determining the rate of pay was sufficiently significant to provide objective justification for all or part of the differential. This decision raises important questions as to proportionality in connection with this defence which remain to be answered.[2]

1 Case C-127/92: [1993] IRLR 591, ECJ.
2 Compare the judgment in *Enderby* with those in the Court of Appeal in *Calder v Rowntree Mackintosh Confectionery Ltd* [1993] IRLR 212, CA.

5.31   Problems often arise in connection with part-time employment. Historically part-time employees were often paid less than full-time employees. Women were predominant amongst part-time employees. In Case 96/80 *Jenkins v Kingsgate (Clothing Productions) Ltd*[1] the European Court of Justice held that if it was established that a considerably smaller number of women worked sufficient hours to be entitled to the full-time rate there was a prima facie breach of art 119 of the Treaty of Rome. It was said that it is for the national court to decide in each particular case whether or not a difference in rates of pay for full or part-time workers was in reality discrimination based on the sex of the worker. In a later case the Court found that the exclusion of part-time workers, where the majority of them were women, from a pension scheme infringed art 119 unless the employer shows that the exclusion is based on objectively justified factors unrelated to any discrimination on grounds of sex.[2] Thus unless an employer is able to justify differences in benefits between full-time and part-time workers where part-time workers are predominantly of one sex the differences will be unlawful.[3] It is noted elsewhere that there are other important developments as to the rights of part-time workers (see **11.17**).[4] For equally important developments in the pension rights of men and women employees, see Chapter 8.[5]

1 [1981] IRLR 228, ECJ.
2 Case 170/84 *Bilka-Kaufhaus GmbH v Weber von Hartz* [1987] ICR 110, ECJ.
3 Case C-33/89 *Kowalska v Freie und Hansestadt Hamburg* [1992] ICR 29, ECJ.
4 The effect of the Finance Act 1996, s 119 is that employee share ownership plans do not discriminate against part-time workers.
5 For developments in connection with claims by part-time workers for pension benefits following the decisions of the European Court of Justice in *Vroege* [1994] IRLR 651, ECJ, and *Fischer* [1994] IRLR 662, ECJ, see *Preston v Wolverhampton Healthcare NHS Trust* [1996] IRLR 484, EAT; *Levez v T H Jennings (Harlow Pools) Ltd* [1996] IRLR 499; and Case C-435/93 *Dietz v StichtingThuiszorg Rotterdam* [1996] IRLR 692, ECJ.

Effect of the equality clause

5.32 The equality clause is deemed to be included in the woman's contract of employment. Notwithstanding the short name of the Equal Pay Act 1970 it relates to all contractual benefits to which the employee is entitled. It is very wide in its effect and includes any other consideration whether in cash or kind, whether immediate or future, provided that the worker receives it, albeit indirectly, in respect of his employment from his employer.[1] Following the decision of the European Court of Justice which established this principle, 'pay' has been held to include a statutory redundancy[2] payment, payment for time off[2] and pensions.[3] Remedies for unfair dismissal constitute pay.[4] Terms are looked at individually. This is the case notwithstanding that, when looked at as a whole, the woman's contract may have been no less favourable than the contract of the comparator.[5]

1 Case 12/81 *Garland v British Rail Engineering Ltd* [1982] ICR 420, ECJ and HL. In that case travel facilities for employees after retirement were held to be pay.
2 Case C-360/90 *Arbeiterwohlfahrt der Stadt Berlin v Botel* [1992] IRLR 423, ECJ.
3 Case C-262/88 *Barber v Guardian Royal Exchange Assurance Group* [1990] ICR 616, ECJ.
4 *Mediguard Services Ltd v Themes* [1994] ICR 751, EAT, where it was said this was an *acte clair*. This was questioned by the Court of Appeal in *R v Secretary of State for Employment, ex p Seymour-Smith and Perez* [1995] IRLR 464, CA, currently being appealed to the House of Lords.
5 *Hayward v Cammell Laird Shipbuilders Ltd* [1988] ICR 464, HL.

5.33 The equality clause operates in each of the following three situations where a woman claims equal pay.

Like work

5.34 An equality clause is a provision which relates to the terms of a contract under which a woman is employed. It relates to all terms whether concerned with pay or not. It has the effect that:

'(a)   where the woman is employed on like work with a man in the same employment—

(i)   if (apart from the equality clause) any term of the woman's contract is or becomes less favourable to the woman than a term of a similar kind in the contract under which that man is employed, that term of the woman's contract shall be treated as so modified as not to be less favourable, and

(ii)   if (apart from the equality clause) at any time the woman's contract does not include a term corresponding to a term benefiting that man included in the contract under which he is employed, the woman's contract shall be treated as including such a term'.[1]

1 Equal Pay Act 1970, s 1(2)(a). *Pointon v University of Sussex* [1979] IRLR 119, CA. Argument that the employee should have been paid better than the man cannot be sustained under the 1970 Act on the basis of a 'like work' claim.

Work rated as equivalent

5.35 An equality clause is a provision which relates to the terms of a contract under which a woman is employed. It relates to all terms whether concerned with pay or not. It has the effect that:

'(b)   where the woman is employed on work rated as equivalent with that of a man in the same employment—

(i)   if (apart from the equality clause) any term of the woman's contract determined by the rating of the work is or becomes less favourable to the woman than a term of a similar kind in the contract under which that man is employed, that term of the woman's contract shall be treated as so modified as not to be less favourable, and

(ii)   if (apart from the equality clause) at any time the woman's contract does not include a term corresponding to a term benefiting that man included in the contract under which he is employed and determined by the rating of the work, the woman's contract shall be treated as including such a term.'[1]

1 Equal Pay Act 1970, s 1(2)(b).

Work of equal value

5.36 An equality clause is a provision which relates to the terms of a contract under which a woman is employed. It relates to all terms whether concerned with pay or not. It has the effect that:

'(c)   where a woman is employed on work which, not being work in relation to which paragraph (a) or (b) above applies, is, in terms of the demands made on her (for instance under such headings as effort, skill and decision), of equal value to that of a man in the same employment—

(i)   if (apart from the equality clause) any term of the woman's contract is or becomes less favourable to the woman than a term of a similar kind in the contract under which that man is employed, that term of the woman's contract shall be treated as so modified as not to be less favourable, and

(ii)   if (apart from the equality clause) at any time the woman's contract does not include a term corresponding to a term benefiting that man included in the contract under which he is employed,

the woman's contract shall be treated as including such a term'.[1]

1 Equal Pay Act 1970, s 1(2)(c), inserted by the Equal Pay (Amendment) Regulations 1983, SI 1983/1794, with effect from 1 January 1984.

Application of the Equal Pay Act 1970

5.37   For the purposes of the Equal Pay Act 1970 'employed' means employed under a contract of service or of apprenticeship or a contract personally to execute any work or labour. Accordingly it applies to others besides employees. Related expressions are construed accordingly.[1] Men are treated as in the same employment with a woman if they are men employed by her employer or any associated employer at the same establishment or at establishments in Great Britain which include that one and at which common terms and conditions of employment are observed, either generally or for employees of the relevant classes.[2] Two employers are treated as associated if one is a company of which the other (directly or indirectly) has control or if both are companies of which a third person (directly or indirectly) has control (see **11.45**).[3]

1 Equal Pay Act 1970, s 1(6)(a).
2 Equal Pay Act 1970, s 1(6). Common terms and conditions means terms and conditions which are substantially comparable on a broad basis, rather than the same terms and conditions, subject only to minor differences: *British Coal Corpn v Smith* [1996] IRLR 404, HL. See also *Leverton v Clwyd County Council* [1989] ICR 33, HL, for consideration of 'the same employment'.
3 Equal Pay Act 1970, s 1(6)(c). It is to be noted that art 119 of the Treaty of Rome is wider than s 1(6). The test is whether the employees are employed in the 'same establishment or service'. Thus in an appropriate case the limit in s 1(6) will be displaced: *Scullard v Southern Regional Council for Education and Training* [1996] IRLR 344, EAT.

Crown servants

5.38   The provisions of the 1970 Act apply to service for purposes of a minister of the Crown or government department, other than service of a person holding a statutory office, and to service on behalf of the Crown for purposes of a person holding a statutory office or for purposes of a statutory body, as they apply to employment by a private person. They also so apply as if references to a contract of employment included references to the terms of service.[1] This is not the case in relation to service in the naval, military or air forces of the Crown.[2] Members of the House of Commons and House of Lords staff are covered as in relation to service for the purposes of a minister of the Crown or government department.[3]

1 Equal Pay Act 1970, s 1(8). 'Statutory body' means a body set up by or in pursuance of an enactment, and 'statutory office' means an office so set up. Service 'for purposes of' a minister of the Crown or government department does not include service in any office set out in Sch 2 to the House of Commons Disqualification Act 1975 (ministerial disqualification) as for the time being in force: Equal Pay Act 1970, s 1(10).
2 Equal Pay Act 1970, s 1(9).
3 Equal Pay Act 1970, s 1(10A) and (10B). The section applies as if references to a contract of employment included references to the terms of service of such a member of House of Commons staff.

Members of the armed services

5.39   There are special provisions relating to service pay.[1] Their effect is that the terms and conditions of service of members of the naval, military or air forces of the Crown should not have the effect of making a distinction, as regards pay, allowances or leave, between men and women who are members of those forces not being a distinction fairly attributable to differences between the obligations undertaken by men and those undertaken by women as such members.[2]

1   Equal Pay Act 1970, s 7(1).
2   The Secretary of State or Defence Council may refer to the Central Arbitration Committee for their advice on any question whether a provision made or proposed to be made ought to be regarded for the purposes of this section as making a distinction not permitted by s 7(1): Equal Pay Act 1970, s 7(2).

Special circumstances

5.40   Under the Equal Pay Act 1970 an equality clause does not operate in relation to terms affected by compliance with the laws regulating the employment of women, or affording special treatment to women in connection with pregnancy or childbirth.[1] An equality clause does operate in relation to terms relating to membership of an occupational pension scheme being terms in relation to which, by reason only of any provision made by or under ss 62 or 64 of the Pensions Act 1995 (equal treatment), an equal treatment rule would not operate if the terms were included in the scheme.[2]

1   Equal Pay Act 1970, s 6(1).
2   Equal Pay Act 1970, s 6(1B). 'Occupational pension scheme' has the same meaning as in the Pension Schemes Act 1993 and 'equal treatment rule' has the same meaning given by the Pensions Act 1995: Equal Pay Act 1970, s 6(1C): see Chapter 8.

Complaints to industrial tribunals

5.41   Three types of claim can be brought before industrial tribunals under the Equal Pay Act 1970. Any claim in respect of a contravention of a term which is modified, or included, by virtue of the equality clause including a claim for areas of remuneration or damages in respect of the contravention may be presented to an industrial tribunal.[1] An employer can apply to an industrial tribunal for an order declaring the rights of the employer and employee where a dispute arises in relation to the effect of an equality clause.[2] The Secretary of State can refer a question to an industrial tribunal when it appears to him that there may be a question whether an employer of any woman is, or has been, contravening a term modified, or included, by virtue of their equality clauses, but it is not reasonable to expect them to take steps to have the question determined. Such a reference may be in respect of all the cases, or an individual case, and is dealt with as if the reference was by the women or woman against the employer.[3] The civil courts have a concurrent jurisdiction.[4]

1   Equal Pay Act 1970, s 2(1). In addition the woman can seek the assistance of a conciliation officer. See Chapter 18.
2   Equal Pay Act 1970, s 2(1A).

3 Equal Pay Act 1970, s 2(2).
4 For the relationship with proceedings in industrial tribunals see Equal Pay Act 1970, s 2(3).

Time limit

5.42 Claims may be made during and after termination of the employment, but must be referred to the industrial tribunal within six months of the woman ceasing to be in the employment in respect of which the reference is made. The woman is entitled to claim what she has lost as a result of the equality clause not operating.[1] If the claim succeeds, the employee is entitled to be awarded any payment by way of arrears of remuneration, or damages, for her loss but these cannot be recovered in respect of a time earlier than two years before the date on which the proceedings were instituted.[2] If, in proceedings before the courts, it appears to the court seized of the case that a claim or counterclaim in respect of the operation of an equality clause could be more conveniently disposed of separately by an industrial tribunal, there is a procedure for referring, or directing reference of the question to an industrial tribunal and the proceedings may be struck out or the claim or counterclaim stayed in the meantime.[3] The time limit for reference to the industrial tribunal does not apply in these cases.[4] The usual civil time limits apply to cases before the ordinary courts.

1 For the position as to claims as to entry to, or benefits under pension schemes, see the Occupational Pension Schemes (Equal Treatment) Regulations 1995, SI 1995/3183, and Chapter 8. The terms of the contract are altered by the operation of the equality clause and alterations require the agreement of both parties: *Sorbie v Trust Houses Forte Hotels Ltd* [1976] IRLR 371, EAT.
2 Equal Pay Act 1970, s 2(5). But not in respect of the period before 29 December 1975. Issue estoppel applies to applications under the Act: *McLoughlin v Gordons (Stockport) Ltd* [1978] IRLR 127, EAT. A question as to whether the two year limitation is contrary to European law has been referred to the European Court of Justice; *Levez v T H Jennings (Harlow Pools) Ltd* [1996] IRLR 499, EAT. For interest on awards see Industrial Tribunals (Interest on Awards in Discrimination Regulations) 1996, SI 1996/2803.
3 Equal Pay Act 1970, s 2(3).
4 The Equal Opportunities Commission may advise or assist an employee in connection with proceedings, see Chapter 7. It also can conduct formal investigations, issue non-discrimination notices and obtain injunctions in relation to the Equal Pay Act 1970 as well as under the Sex Discrimination Act 1975 itself. The Equal Opportunities Commission has powers in connection with persistent infringements of the Equal Pay Act 1970, see Chapter 7.

Other provisions

5.43 The Act also contains detailed provisions for references to be made to the Central Arbitration Committee relating to agricultural wages orders which are beyond the scope of this work.[1]

1 Equal Pay Act 1970, s 5.

Chapter 6

Unlawful deductions from wages

Introduction

The Truck Acts 1831 to 1940 were concerned with two types of abuse; the payment to workers in kind or in tokens (redeemable only at an employer's shop) and the arbitrary deduction of wages by an employer to cover deficiencies. The statutes which imposed limitations on employers' actions in these circumstances have been repealed and replaced by restrictions on deductions from wages (see **6.01**). With the exception of specified situations, it is not possible to contract out of these provisions (see **6.24**).

The restrictions apply to workers and include those in Crown employment other than those serving as members of the armed forces (see **6.02** and **6.03**). In general terms the provisions do not apply to employment wholly or mainly outside Great Britain (see **6.04**).

The basic rule is that an employer is not entitled to make any deduction from the wages, or to receive a payment from the worker, unless authorised to do so by statute or a contractual term, or the worker has previously signified in writing his agreement or consent to the deduction (see **6.05–6.09**).

The rule applies not only to basic wages but includes such items as fees, bonus, commission and holiday pay. It does not cover such items as expenses, pension payments, or compensation for loss of employment or office. For detailed provisions, see **6.10** and **6.11**.

If during a claim made pursuant to the unlawful deduction provisions there is a dispute as to whether a sum is properly payable to the worker, this is determined by the industrial tribunal hearing the claim. See **6.12** and **6.17**. This issue is resolved according to general contractual principles.

It is common for the contracts of those working in retail employment to contain provisions requiring the worker to reimburse the employer for cash shortages, or in respect of stock deficiencies. For those working where there is a high volume of sales – such as petrol pump attendants – this could leave workers receiving little or no wages at all. There are detailed rules which limit the employer's right to make deductions in these circumstances. See **6.12–6.18**. An unauthorised deduction the subject of a declaration by an industrial tribunal precludes an employer from recovering the amount of the deduction thereafter. See **6.22–6.24**.

Claims that there have been unlawful deductions from wages can be made to industrial tribunals. See **6.19**. Claims must be made within three months, but the 'not reasonably practicable' escape clause applies; see **6.20**.

Before jurisdiction to hear contractual claims was conferred on industrial tribunals much legal learning and expense was wastefully expended on pursuing claims for deductions or non-payment of wages in industrial tribunals and claims for money in lieu of notice in the courts. Now both types of claim can be dealt with together.

General

6.01   The present provisions as to unlawful deductions from wages which are contained in Pt II of the Employment Rights Act 1996 were originally contained in the Wages Act 1986 which effectively replaced the Truck Acts which it repealed.[1] The Truck Acts had the effect of providing workers with some protection against employers who wished to pay employees other than with coin of the realm, or who wished to make certain deductions from their wages. The 1986 Act imposed a new regime of control and its interpretation has not been without problems.[2] Save in specified circumstances agreements to exclude or limit the operation of the provisions are void.[3]

1 Wages Act 1986, s 11. As originally enacted the Wages Act 1986 contained provisions relating to wages councils. Those provisions were repealed with effect from 30 August 1993 by the Trade Union Reform and Employment Rights Act 1993, ss 35 and 51 and Sch 10.
2 Further difficulties arise because the provisions still do not lie easily with the jurisdiction conferred on tribunals to deal with claims for breach of contract.
3 See **6.25**.

6.02   The provisions apply to wages to be paid to a 'worker' by his employer. 'Worker' is wider than employee. A worker is an individual who has entered into, or works under (or, where the employment has ceased, worked under) a contract of employment and any other contract whereby the individual undertakes to do or perform personally any work or services for another party to the contract whose status is not by virtue of the contract that of a client or customer of any profession or business undertaking carried on by the individual. The contract may be express or implied, or oral or in writing.[1] 'Employer', in relation to a worker, means the person by whom the worker is (or, where the employment has ceased, was) employed; 'employment', in relation to a worker, means employment under his contract; and 'employed', in relation to a worker, accordingly means employed under his contract.[2]

1 Employment Rights Act 1996, s 230(3).
2 Employment Rights Act 1996, s 230(4) and (5).

6.03   The restrictions do not apply to service as a member of the naval, military or air forces of the Crown, but do apply to employment by any association established for the purposes of Pt VI of the Reserve Forces Act 1980.[1] Otherwise the Act applies to Crown employment.[2] There are provisions for appropriate consequential construction of statutory references.[3]

1 Employment Rights Act 1996, ss 191 and 192(1) and (2).
2 Employment Rights Act 1996, s 191(1) and (2). 'Crown employment' means employment under or for the purposes of a government department or any officer or body exercising on behalf of the Crown functions conferred by any statutory provision: Employment Rights Act 1996, s 191(3).
3 Employment Rights Act 1996, s 191(4).

6.04   In general the provisions do not apply to employment where under his contract the person employed ordinarily works outside Great Britain.[1] The requirements do not apply to a person employed under a crew agreement of a kind approved by the Secretary of State.[2]

1 Employment Rights Act 1996, s 196(2) and (3). For these purposes a person employed to work on board a ship registered in the United Kingdom (not being a ship registered at a port outside Great Britain) unless the employment is wholly outside Great Britain or he is not ordinarily resident in Great Britain is regarded as a person who ordinarily works in Great Britain: Employment

Rights Act 1996, s 196(5). There is power to extend the provisions to employment outside the United Kingdom contained in the Employment Rights Act 1996, s 201.
2 Employment Rights Act 1996, s 199(1).

Authorised deductions

6.05 The basic requirement of the provisions forbidding unlawful deductions from wages is that an employer should not make any deduction from any wages of any worker employed by him, unless the deduction is required, or authorised to be made, by virtue of any statutory provision, or a relevant provision of the worker's contract, or the worker has previously signified in writing his agreement or consent to the making of it.[1] A similar rule applies to payments made by a worker to his employer. A 'relevant provision' means any provision of the worker's contract comprised in one or more written terms of the contract of which the employer has given the worker a copy on any occasion prior to the employer making the deduction in question (or prior to his receiving the payment in question). Alternatively it may be contained in one or more terms of the contract (whether express or implied and, if express, whether oral or in writing) whose existence and effect, or combined effect, in relation to the worker the employer has notified to the worker in writing on any such occasion. Any relevant provision of a worker's contract having effect by virtue of any variation of the contract, or any agreement or consent signified by a worker, will not operate to authorise the making of any deduction, or the receipt of any payment, on account of any conduct of the worker, or any other event occurring, before the variation took effect or (as the case may be) the agreement or consent was signified.[2]

1 Employment Rights Act 1996, s 13(1).
2 Employment Rights Act 1996, s 13(5) and (6). Notified to the worker in writing means notified to him individually in writing; display on a notice board is not enough: *Kerr v Sweater Shop (Scotland) Ltd* [1996] IRLR 424, EAT. Deductions which are not authorised by a contract as continued by the Transfer of Undertakings (Protection of Employment) Regulations 1981 are unlawful deductions: *Wilson v St Helens Borough Council* [1996] IRLR 320, EAT.

Deductions

6.06 A total failure by the employer to pay wages is a deduction for these purposes,[1] as is an unauthorised 'reduction' in wages by the employer.[2] Where the total amount of any wages paid on any occasion by an employer to any worker employed by him is less than the total amount of the wages properly payable by him to the worker on that occasion (after deductions) then, except insofar as the deficiency is attributable to an error of computation, the amount of the deficiency is treated for these purposes as a deduction made by the employer from the worker's wages.[3] This does not apply insofar as the deficiency is attributable to an error of any description on the part of the employer affecting the computation by him of the gross amount of the wages properly payable by him to the worker. For these purposes an error of computation is an error of any description on the part of the employer affecting the computation by him of the gross amount of the wages that are properly payable by him to the worker on that occasion.[4]

1 *Delaney v Staples* [1992] ICR 483, HL.
2 *Delaney v Staples* [1992] ICR 483, HL.

3 Employment Rights Act 1996, s 13(3). A non-payment of a sum on the day when it should be paid is a deduction. The Employment Rights Act 1996, s 13(3) brings all failures to pay wages within the ambit of the Employment Rights Act 1996. See *Delaney v Staples* [1992] ICR 483, HL. Intentional non-payment or deduction which arises otherwise than from an error, whether or not it is made after a dispute, is a deduction for these purposes: *Kournavous v JR Masterton & Sons (Demolition) Ltd* [1990] ICR 387, EAT. See also *Foster Wheeler (London) Ltd v Jackson* [1990] ICR 757, EAT and *Yemm v British Steel plc* [1994] IRLR 117, EAT.
4 Employment Rights Act 1996, s 13(4). An employer who makes a conscious decision not to make a payment because he believes that the contract of employment entitles him to take that course of action is not making an 'error of computation': *Yemm v British Steel plc* [1994] IRLR 117, EAT.

6.07 The effect of the provisions is that an employer may only make a deduction from a worker's wages or receive a payment from him if the deduction or payment satisfies one of five conditions. These are:
(1) it is required or authorised by a statutory provision; or
(2) it is required or authorised by a relevant provision of the worker's written contract;[1] or
(3) the contractual term permitting the deduction or payment, although not in writing, is notified to the worker in written form;[2] or
(4) the worker has previously signified in writing his agreement or consent;[3] or
(5) the requirements do not apply by virtue of the provisions referred to in **6.09**.

1 Employment Rights Act 1996, s 13(2).
2 Employment Rights Act 1996, s 13(2).
3 A worker's written agreement or consent to the making of a deduction must have been given *before* the conduct or event giving rise to the deduction: *Discount Tobacco & Confectionery Ltd v Williamson* [1993] IRLR 327, EAT.

6.08 An employer should not receive any payment from any worker employed by him unless the payment satisfies similar conditions to those applicable to deductions.[1] For these purposes a reference to an employer receiving a payment from a worker employed by him is a reference to his receiving such a payment in his capacity as the worker's employer.[2]

1 Employment Rights Act 1996, s 15.
2 Employment Rights Act 1996, s 15(5).

Exclusions

6.09 The requirements do not apply:
(a) to any deduction from a worker's wages made by his employer, or any payment received from a worker by his employer, where the purpose of the deduction or payment is the reimbursement of the employer in respect of—
(i)   any overpayment of wages, or
(ii) any overpayment in respect of expenses incurred by the worker in carrying out his employment,
made (for any reason) by the employer to the worker;[1]
(b) to any deduction from a worker's wages made by his employer, or any payment received from a worker by his employer, in consequence of any disciplinary proceedings if those proceedings were held by virtue of any statutory provision;[2]

(c)   to any deduction from a worker's wages made by his employer in pursuance of any requirement imposed on the employer by any statutory provision to deduct and pay over to a public authority amounts determined by that authority as being due to it from the worker, if the deduction is made in accordance with the relevant determination of that authority;[3]

(d)   to any deduction from a worker's wages made by his employer in pursuance of any arrangements which have been established—

  (i)   in accordance with any relevant provision of his contract to which the worker has signified his agreement or consent in writing, or

  (ii)   otherwise with the prior agreement or consent of the worker signified in writing,

  and under which the employer is to deduct and pay over to a third person amounts notified to the employer by that person as being due to him from the worker, if the deduction is made in accordance with the relevant notification by that person;[4]

(e)   to any deduction from a worker's wages made by his employer, or any payment received from a worker by his employer, where the worker has taken part in a strike or other industrial action and the deduction is made, or the payment has been required, by the employer on account of the worker having taken part in that strike or other action;[5] or

(f)   to any deduction from a worker's wages made by his employer with his prior agreement or consent signified in writing, or any payment received from a worker by his employer, where the purpose of the deduction or payment is the satisfaction (whether wholly or in part) of an order of a court or tribunal requiring the payment of any amount by the worker to the employer.[6]

1 Employment Rights Act 1996, ss 14(1) and 16(1). In *Home Office v Ayres* [1992] ICR 175, EAT, it was said that it is necessary for the tribunal to consider the lawfulness of the deduction and the general law relating to such matters as estoppel falls to be considered. However, in *Sunderland Polytechnic v Evans* [1993] IRLR 196, EAT, it was said that this was inconsistent with statements made by ministers during the passage of the Wages Act 1986 through Parliament. The approach adopted in *Evans* is to be preferred: *SIP Industrial Products Ltd v Swinn* [1994] ICR 473, EAT. In *Swinn* it was held that the effect of what are now ss 14 and 16 is that s 13 does not apply in the six categories of wages set out irrespective of whether the deduction was lawful or unlawful. It was held that the tribunal had no jurisdiction to hear the claim when the employers sought the reimbursement of an overpayment of expenses.
2 Employment Rights Act 1996, ss 14(2) and 16(2).
3 Employment Rights Act 1996, s 14(3).
4 Employment Rights Act 1996, s 14(4).
5 Employment Rights Act 1996, ss 14(5) and 16(3).
6 Employment Rights Act 1996, s 14(6).

Wages

6.10   Wages, in relation to a worker, means any sums payable to the worker by his employer in connection with his employment, including any fee, bonus, commission, holiday pay, or other emolument referable to his employment, whether payable under his contract or otherwise.[1] Wages also include sums payable in pursuance of an order for reinstatement or re-engagement under s 115 of the Employment Rights Act 1996, any sum payable by way of pay in pursuance of an order under s 164 of the Trade Union and Labour Relations (Consolidation) Act 1992 for the continuation of a contract of employment and guarantee payments and other statutory payments in lieu of wages. Statutory sick pay is also included, as is in the case of a female worker, statutory maternity pay under Pt XII of the Social Security Contributions and Benefits Act 1992.[2] For these purposes 'wages' do not include payment in kind, eg free meat, petrol or accommodation. Any voucher, stamp or similar document which is of a fixed value expressed in monetary terms, and is capable of being exchanged (whether on its own or together with other vouchers, stamps or documents, and whether immediately or only after a time) for money, goods or services (or for any combination of two or more of those things) is included within the definition of wages.[3]

1 Employment Rights Act 1996, s 27(1)(a). In *Kent Management Services Ltd v Butterfield* [1992] ICR 272, EAT, it was held that commission which was described as discretionary and ex gratia was payable for these purposes. The full definition is in the Employment Rights Act 1996, s 27. See *Nerva v RL & G Ltd* [1996] IRLR 461, CA, for the position as to tips paid to waiters.
2 Employment Rights Act 1996, s 27(1).
3 Employment Rights Act 1996, s 27(5). The Apportionment Act 1870 may be referred to as to apportionment of wages. In which case the expression 'day to day' refers to calendar days not working days: *Thames Water Utilities v Reynolds* [1996] IRLR 186, EAT.

6.11 Certain payments are excluded from the definition of wages and are not wages for the purposes of the Employment Rights Act 1996. These are:
(1) any payment by way of an advance under an agreement for a loan or by way of an advance of wages (but without prejudice to the application of s 13 of the Employment Rights Act 1996 to any deduction made from the worker's wages in respect of any such advance);
(2) any payment in respect of expenses incurred by the worker in carrying out his employment;[1]
(3) any payment by way of a pension, allowance or gratuity in connection with the worker's retirement or as compensation for loss of office;
(4) any payment referable to the worker's redundancy; and
(5) any payment to the worker otherwise than in his capacity as a worker.[2]
Where any payment in the nature of a non-contractual bonus is for any reason made to a worker by his employer, then the amount of the payment is treated as wages of the worker, and is treated as payable to him as such on the day on which the payment is made.[3]

1 This means 'referring to' or 'relating to' or 'concerning in a general way' expenses. It does not have to be an exact reimbursement of the expenses: *Southwark London Borough v O'Brien* [1996] IRLR 420, EAT.
2 Employment Rights Act 1996, s 27(2).
3 Employment Rights Act 1996, s 27(3).

6.12 If there are disputes as to the amount which is payable to the worker these fall to be determined as preliminary issues by the industrial tribunal.[1] Whether or not a sum is payable is determined using the rules of the common law of contract.[2] The sums in respect of which partial payment and non-payment of which can be a deduction include accrued holiday pay on the termination of employment,[3] and supplements paid as a result of an agreement entered into when salaries were to be paid by credit transfer.[4] The obligation to pay the worker on which the claim for wages is founded can arise from express or implied contractual terms of the contract.[5] Although payment due to an employee pursuant to a 'garden leave' arrangement is payment for a period during which the employment relationship subsists and does fall within the definition of wages for these purposes, payment of wages in lieu of notice does not.[6]

1 *Delaney v Staples* [1992] ICR 483, HL. The tribunal should decide whether the deduction was justifiable: *Fairfield Ltd v Skinner* [1992] ICR 836, EAT.
2 *Greg May (Carpet Fitters and Contractors) Ltd v Dring* [1990] ICR 188, EAT, affirmed in *Delaney's* case above.
3 *Delaney v Staples* [1992] ICR 483, HL.
4 *McCree v Tower Hamlets London Borough* [1992] ICR 99, EAT.
5 *Morley v Heritage plc* [1993] IRLR 400, CA.
6 *Delaney v Staples* [1992] ICR 483, HL. Such payments are related to the termination of the employment and not to the provision of services thereunder. Wages include unpaid commission when a quantifiable contractual entitlement: *Blackstone Franks Investment Management Ltd v Robertson* (1996) Times, 12 November.

Retail employment

6.13   There are specific provisions relating to deductions from wages of workers in retail employment (retail workers) on account of cash shortages, stock deficiencies and the like. Employers of retail workers who wish to make deductions or receive payments should comply with the basic rules set out above and in addition observe further limitations:
(1)   the amount deducted must not exceed one-tenth of the gross amount payable on the appropriate day. This does not apply to the final instalment; and
(2)   the deduction to cover a shortage must be made before the end of the 12-month period starting with the date when the employer discovered the shortage or deficiency, or when the employer ought reasonably to have established the shortage or deficiency.

6.14   Where the employer of a retail[1] worker makes, on account of one or more shortages or stock deficiencies, a deduction or deductions from any wages payable to the worker on a pay day, the amount, or aggregate amount, of the deduction or deductions must not exceed one-tenth of the gross amount of the wages payable to the worker on that day.[2] 'Cash shortage' is defined as a deficit arising in relation to amounts received in connection with retail transactions and 'pay day' as a day on which wages are payable to the worker.[3] Where the employer of a retail worker makes a deduction from the worker's wages on account of a cash shortage or stock deficiency, the employer is not treated as making a lawful deduction unless (in addition to satisfying the requirements of s 13) the deduction is made, or in the case of a deduction which is one of a series of deductions relating to the shortage or deficiency, the first deduction in the series was made, not later than the end of the period of 12 months beginning with the date when the employer established the existence of the shortage or deficiency or (if earlier) the date when he ought reasonably to have done so.[4] There are specific provisions applicable where it is agreed by the retail worker and his employer that the amount of the worker's wages or any part of them is, or may be, determined by reference to the incidence of cash shortages or stock deficiencies. These provisions apply if the gross amount of the wages payable to the worker on any pay day is, on account of any such shortages or deficiencies, less than the gross amount of the wages that would have been payable to him on that day if there had been no such shortages or deficiencies. When these requirements are satisfied the amount representing the difference between the two amounts referred to ('the relevant amount') is treated as a deduction from the wages payable to the worker on that day made by the employer on account of the cash shortages or stock deficiencies in question. The gross amount of the wages that would have been payable to him on that day if there had been no such shortages or deficiencies is treated as the gross amount of the wages payable to him on that day.[5]

1 Retail employment, in relation to a worker, means employment involving (whether on a regular basis or not) the carrying out by the worker of retail transactions directly with members of the public or with fellow workers or other individuals in their personal capacities, or the collection by the worker of amounts payable in connection with retail transactions carried out by other persons directly with members of the public or with fellow workers or other individuals in their personal capacities. Retail transaction means the sale or supply of goods, or the supply of services (including financial services). Stock deficiency is a stock deficiency arising in the course of retail transactions: Employment Rights Act 1996, s 17(1), (2) and (3).
2 Employment Rights Act 1996, s 18(1). Section 18(1) does not operate to restrict the amount of any deductions that may (in accordance with s 13(1)) be made by the employer of a retail worker from the worker's final instalment of wages: Employment Rights Act 1996, s 22.
3 Employment Rights Act 1996, s 17(6).
4 Employment Rights Act 1996, s 18(2) and (3).
5 Employment Rights Act 1996, s 19. The general provisions as to deductions have effect in relation to the relevant amount accordingly: Employment Rights Act 1996, s 19(4).

6.15   Payments made by retail workers to their employers have to satisfy requirements which are similar to those applicable to deductions.[1]

1 Employment Rights Act 1996, s 20.

6.16   Where the employer of a worker in retail employment receives from the worker any payment on account of a cash shortage or stock deficiency the employer is not treated as receiving the payment in accordance with the provisions as to unlawful payment in respect of payments received by employers unless (in addition to the requirements of s 15 being satisfied with respect to the payment) two requirements are satisfied. First, he should have previously notified the worker in writing of the worker's total liability to him in respect of that shortage or deficiency. Secondly, he should have previously required the worker to make the payment by means of a demand for payment made in accordance with the appropriate stipulations.[1] These include requirements that any relevant demand for payment should be in writing and be made on one of the worker's pay days.[2] A demand for payment in respect of a particular cash shortage or stock deficiency, or (in the case of a series of such demands) the first such demand, should not be made earlier than the first pay day of the worker following the date when he is notified of his total liability in respect of the shortage or deficiency in pursuance of the provisions or, where he is so notified on a pay day, earlier than that day.[3] Further, the demand for payment should not be made later than the end of the period of 12 months beginning with the date when the employer established the existence of the shortage or deficiency or (if earlier) the date when he ought reasonably to have done so.[4] Where the employer of a retail worker makes on any pay day one or more demands for payment in accordance with these provisions, the amount or aggregate amount required to be paid by the worker in pursuance of the demand or demands must not exceed one-tenth of the gross amount of the wages payable to the worker on that day. Where one or more deductions[5] are made by the employer from those wages, the amount required to be paid by the worker must not exceed such amount as represents the balance of that one-tenth after subtracting the amount or aggregate amount of the deduction or deductions.[6] Once any amount has been required to be paid by means of a demand for payment that amount is not taken into account as it applies to any subsequent pay day, notwithstanding that the employer is obliged to make further requests for it to be paid.[7] A demand for payment will be treated as made by the employer on one of the worker's pay days if it is given to the worker, or posted to, or left at, his last known address on that pay day, or in the case of a pay day which is not a working day of the employer's business, on the first such working day following that pay day.[8]

1 Employment Rights Act 1996, s 20(1). Nothing in s 20 applies to any payment falling within s 20(1) that is made on or after the day on which any such worker's final instalment of wages is paid, but (notwithstanding that the requirements of s 15 would otherwise be satisfied with respect to it) his employer is not treated as receiving any such payment in accordance with s 15 if the payment was first required to be made after the end of the period referred to in s 20(3)(b).
2 Employment Rights Act 1996, s 20(2).
3 Employment Rights Act 1996, s 20(3)(a).
4 Employment Rights Act 1996, s 20(3)(b).
5 Falling within the Employment Rights Act 1996, s 18(1).
6 Employment Rights Act 1996, s 21(1).
7 Employment Rights Act 1996, s 21(2).
8 Employment Rights Act 1996, s 20(4).

6.17 Legal proceedings by the employer of a retail worker for the recovery from the worker of any amount in respect of a cash shortage or stock deficiency should not be instituted by the employer after the end of the period referred to in s 20(3)(b) unless the employer has within that period made a demand for payment in respect of that amount in accordance with s 20.[1] Where in any legal proceedings the court finds that the employer of a retail worker is (in accordance with s 15, as it applies apart from s 20(1)) entitled to recover an amount from the worker in respect of a cash shortage or stock deficiency, the court will, in ordering the payment by the worker to the employer of that amount, make such provision as appears to the court to be necessary to ensure that it is paid by the worker at a rate not exceeding that at which it could be recovered from him by the employer in accordance with s 21.[2] This provision does not apply to any amount which is to be paid by a worker on or after the day on which his final instalment of wages is paid.[3]

1 Employment Rights Act 1996, s 20(5).
2 Employment Rights Act 1996, s 21(3).
3 Employment Rights Act 1996, s 22(4).

6.18 For the purposes of the provisions relating to deductions from wages of, and payments by, retail workers in respect of cash shortages and the like, 'final instalment of wages' means the amount of wages payable to the worker which consists of or includes an amount payable by way of contractual remuneration in respect of the last of the periods for which he is employed under his contract prior to its termination for any reason (but excluding any wages referable to any earlier such period) or where an amount in lieu of notice is paid to the worker later than that amount the amount so paid, in each case whether the amount in question is paid before or after the termination of the worker's contract.[1] References to a deduction made from any wages of a retail worker, or to a payment received from such a worker by his employer, on account of a cash shortage or stock deficiency, include references to a deduction or payment so made or received on account of any dishonesty or other conduct on the part of the worker which resulted in any such shortage or deficiency, or any other event in respect of which he (whether together with any other workers or not) has any contractual liability and which so resulted, in each case whether the amount of the deduction or payment is designed to reflect the exact amount of the shortage or deficiency or not.[2] Accordingly, references to recovery from a worker of an amount in respect of a cash shortage or stock deficiency include references to the recovery from him of an amount in respect of any such conduct.[3]

1 Employment Rights Act 1996, s 22(1).
2 Employment Rights Act 1996, s 17(4).
3 Employment Rights Act 1996, s 17(5).

Enforcement

6.19   A complaint may be presented by a worker to an industrial tribunal that his employer has made a deduction from his wages in contravention of these provisions rendering deductions unlawful,[1] or that his employer has received from him a payment in contravention of the provisions making payments unlawful.[2] Complaints may also be presented to a tribunal by a worker that his employer has recovered from his wages by means of one or more deductions falling within the provision relating to deductions from the wages of retail workers an amount or aggregate amount exceeding the limit applying to the deduction or deductions under that provision, or that his employer has received from him in pursuance of one or more demands for payment made (in accordance with the provision relating to payments by retail workers) on a particular pay day, a payment or payments of an amount or aggregate amount exceeding the prescribed limit applying to the demand or demands.[3]

1 Including a deduction made in contravention of the provision as it applies by virtue of the Employment Rights Act 1996, s 18(2): Employment Rights Act 1996, s 23(1)(a).
2 Including a payment received in contravention of that provision as it applies by virtue of the Employment Rights Act 1996, s 20(1): Employment Rights Act 1996, s 23(1)(b).
3 Employment Rights Act 1996, s 23(1)(c) and (d).

6.20   An industrial tribunal will not entertain the complaint unless it is presented within the period of three months beginning with, in the case of a complaint relating to a deduction by the employer, the date of payment of the wages from which the deduction was made, or in the case of a complaint relating to a payment received by the employer, the date when the payment was received.[1] In a case where the tribunal is satisfied that it was not reasonably practicable for the complaint to be presented within the relevant period of three months the tribunal will entertain the complaint if presented within such further period as the tribunal considers reasonable.[2] Where a complaint is brought in respect of a series of deductions or payments, or a number of payments made in pursuance of demands for payment subject to the same limit but received by the employer on different dates, the time limits are read as referring to the last deduction or payment in the series, or to the last of the payments so received (as the case may require).[3]

1 Employment Rights Act 1996, s 23(2).
2 Employment Rights Act 1996, s 23(4). These time limits are similar to those applicable to claims of unfair dismissal and reference should be made to the decisions applicable in such cases, see **15.155–15.166.** Time runs from the time a payment which is unpaid should have been paid: *Delaney v Staples* [1991] ICR 331, CA. Assistance in deciding when bonus payments are due may be obtained from *Marshall v Industrial Systems and Control Ltd* [1992] IRLR 294, EAT.
3 Employment Rights Act 1996, s 23(3).

6.21 When deciding if an application is in time the tribunal should ask the following questions:

(1) Does the complaint relate to one deduction or a series of deductions by the employer?

(2) If a single deduction, what was the date of payment of the wages from which the deduction was made?

(3) If a series of deductions, what was the date of the last deduction?

(4) Was the relevant date under (2), or alternatively (3), within the period of three months prior to the presentation of the claim?

(5) If the answer to question (4) is negative, was it reasonably practicable for the complaint to be presented within the relevant three-month period?

(6) If the answer to question (5) is in the negative, does the tribunal consider that the complaint was nevertheless presented within a reasonable time?[1]

1 *Taylorplan Services Ltd v Jackson* [1996] IRLR 184, EAT.

6.22 Where a tribunal finds a complaint to be well founded, it will make a declaration to that effect.[1] In addition, subject to that mentioned below, in the case of a complaint relating to an unlawful deduction or payment, the tribunal will order the employer to pay to the worker the amount of any deduction, or to repay to him the amount of any payment, made or received in contravention of the provisions. In the case of a complaint of a deduction or payment rendered unlawful by the provisions relating to deductions from the wages of, or payments by, retail workers the tribunal will order the employer to pay, or (as the case may be) repay, to the worker any amount recovered or received from him in excess of the relevant limit.[1] Where, in the case of any complaint of an unlawful deduction a tribunal finds that, although neither of the conditions set out in s 13(1)(a) and (b) of the Employment Rights Act 1996 was satisfied with respect to the whole amount of a deduction or payment, one of those conditions was satisfied with respect to any lesser amount, the amount of the deduction or payment is for these purposes treated as reduced by the amount with respect to which that condition was satisfied.[2] An employer will not be ordered by a tribunal to pay or repay to a worker any amount in respect of a deduction or payment, or (as the case may be) in respect of any combination of deductions or payments, in so far as it appears to the tribunal that he has already paid or repaid any such amount to the worker.[3] Where a tribunal has ordered an employer to pay or repay to a worker an amount in respect of a particular unlawful deduction or payment ('the specified amount') under these provisions, the amount which the employer is entitled to recover (by whatever means) in respect of the matter in respect of which the deduction or payment was originally made or received is treated as reduced by the specified amount.[4] The effect of this provision is that if an employer has a valid claim against the employee and purports to make a deduction from the employee's wages which is not authorised under the provisions of the provisions in respect of the claim, then the amount of the claim is reduced (or extinguished) by the amount of the unlawful deduction. Where a tribunal has ordered an employer to pay or repay to a worker any amount in respect of any combination of deductions or payments in respect of retail employment ('the relevant amount') the aggregate amount which the employer is entitled to recover (by whatever means) in respect of the cash shortages or stock deficiencies in respect of which the deductions or payments were originally made or required to be made is treated as reduced by the relevant amount.[5]

1 Employment Rights Act 1996, s 24.
2 Employment Rights Act 1996, s 25(1).
3 Employment Rights Act 1996, s 25(3).
4 Employment Rights Act 1996, s 25(4). These provisions were intended as a sanction and so when the employer is ordered by the tribunal to pay the amount of the unlawful deduction he loses the right to recover the amount of the deduction in other ways: *Potter v Hunt Contracts Ltd* [1992] ICR 337, EAT, a decision under the Wages Act 1986, s 5(7). This is a potential minefield for the unwary.
5 Employment Rights Act 1996, s 25(5).

6.23   Section 205 of the Employment Rights Act 1996 states that a worker's remedy in respect of any contravention of ss 13, 15, 18(1) or 21(1) of the Employment Rights Act 1996 is by way of a complaint to an industrial tribunal and not otherwise.[1] The right to claim to an industrial tribunal under the Employment Rights Act 1996 does not affect the jurisdiction of an industrial tribunal to entertain a reference under s 11 of the Employment Rights Act 1996 (see **4.14**) in relation to any deduction from the wages of a worker, but the aggregate of any amounts ordered by an industrial tribunal to be paid under ss 12(4) and 24 of the Employment Rights Act 1996 (whether on the same or different occasions) in respect of a particular deduction should not exceed the amount of the deduction.[2] Industrial tribunals also have the jurisdiction to hear complaints of breach of contract (see **13.60**).

1 Employment Rights Act 1996, s 205(2).
2 Employment Rights Act 1996, s 26.

6.24   The words 'and not otherwise' in what is now s 205(2) of the Employment Rights Act 1996 cause difficulties. Such authority as there is, namely *Rickard v PB Glass Supplies Ltd*[1] and *Delaney's* case,[2] makes it clear that a worker still has the right to pursue his claim for unpaid wages in the courts. It is suggested that this is correct, but anomalies result. A common situation is that an employer admits making a deduction but justifies it on the basis that a worker has by his carelessness or otherwise, such as damaging the employer's van, caused the employer financial loss. The deduction may well be unlawful if challenged in proceedings under the Employment Rights Act 1996 before a tribunal. In such proceedings the employer would lose his right to set off this sum.[3] If the worker does not proceed in the tribunal under the provisions relating to the unlawful deduction of wages, s 25(4) may not apply. If this interpretation is correct the employer has a defence in proceedings relating to unpaid wages in the courts which is not available to him in the tribunal. The same analysis appears to apply by analogy to claims made before tribunals for breach of contract.

1 [1990] ICR 150, CA.
2 [1992] ICR 483, HL; [1991] ICR 331, CA at p 341 (Nicholls LJ).
3 Employment Rights Act 1996, s 25(4).

6.25   Any term in an agreement insofar as it purports to exclude or limit the operation of any provision relating to unlawful deductions or payments, or to preclude any person from presenting a complaint to a tribunal in respect of them is void. This is not so in the case of an agreement to refrain from presenting or continuing with a complaint where a conciliation officer has taken action,[1] or of an agreement to refrain from presenting or continuing with a complaint if the conditions regulating compromise agreements are satisfied in relation to the agreement.[2]

1 In accordance with the Industrial Tribunals Act 1996, s 18.
2 Employment Rights Act 1996, s 203.

Chapter 7

Discrimination (including pregnancy)

Introduction

Sex, race and disability discrimination

The law against sex, race and disability discrimination is based on specific statutory enactments. In the case of sex discrimination there is a European dimension (see **7.01**). There is no right to contract out of the obligation of the Sex Discrimination Act 1975, the Race Relations Act 1976 or the Disability Discrimination Act 1995. Settlements of cases are only binding if they satisfy statutory criteria.

In the context of employment the rights and remedies are enforced in industrial tribunals, but the equality legislation differs from an application for unfair dismissal in certain important respects:

(1) There is no requirement for a qualifying period of employment.
(2) There is a wider definition of those to whom it applies than the definition of employee for the purposes of the unfair dismissal (see **7.19**).
(3) Job applicants have rights and remedies (see **7.21**).
(4) There is the more liberal test of 'just and equitable' in cases in which applications are not in time.
(5) Compensation is not subject to a statutory ceiling (see **7.46**).
(6) In each case there are provisions which provide protection against victimisation (see **7.17**).

The problem of proof   The courts and tribunals have recognised that where race and/or sex discrimination is alleged, applicants face particular problems in establishing that they were the victims of discrimination (see **7.02**). In cases of race and sex discrimination the courts have laid down an approach (see **7.04**) which may prove to be a guideline in disability cases. In discrimination cases an applicant, or a potential applicant, has the right to serve a questionnaire (see **7.51**) on a respondent and adverse inferences can be drawn from a failure to respond or evasive answers (see **7.52**).

The public interest in enforcement   It has been accepted that there is a public interest in outlawing discrimination by the creation of the Equal Opportunities Commission (see **7.48**); the Commission for Racial Equality (see **7.82**) and the National Disability Council (see **7.163**). The National Disability Council has considerably less power than the former two bodies. In all three types of discrimination a code of practice has been drawn up (see Appendix 3).

Sex and race discrimination   In the case of sex and race discrimination there is a distinction between direct and indirect discrimination (see **7.10** et seq). In cases of direct discrimination the motive of the discriminator is irrelevant and there is no concept of reasonable discrimination as opposed to unlawful discrimination (see **7.10**). Indirect discrimination arises when a condition is imposed which has a discriminatory effect on those of a particular gender or racial group (see **7.13**). It is open to a respondent to show that such a condition is justified (see **7.16**). There is a distinction between the imposition of a mandatory requirement and the expression of a preference (see **7.14**).

Disability discrimination   The distinction between direct and indirect discrimination is not replicated in the disability discrimination legislation (see **7.122**). Less favourable treatment is always subject to the defence of justification (see **7.139**). There is a positive duty to make arrangements to reduce the obstacles to the disabled obtaining or retaining employment (see **7.142**). A small employer's exclusion exists for those with less than 20 employees (see **7.154**).

Exceptions in the law with regard to sex, race and discrimination   In all the cases of discrimination there are exceptions to the overall provisions of the legislation. At its most obvious it is now not unlawful for a director to arrange for Desdemona to be played by a woman and Othello to be played by a male actor of Afro-Caribbean descent. The exceptions are set out in the text.

Similarities and differences   The legislation on sex and race discrimination shares a common conceptual analysis and matters relevant to both forms of discrimination are set out in the text relating to sex discrimination. There are differences of detail between the race and sex discrimination provision. The disability discrimination has a very different conceptual analysis.

Discrimination and the European dimension

7.01   Much discussion about discrimination is dominated by the assertion of the moral value that it is unjust to discriminate against a person on the ground of colour, gender, creed or disability. In the context of employment it is germane to point out there are economic as much as ethical arguments for the equality legislation. An organisation which is blinded by misleading racial or sexual stereotypes or by the perception that disability in a physical impairment reflects itself in an intellectual impairment limits the reservoir of talent from which it can draw. It is of interest that in all parts of the United Kingdom – with the exception of Northern Ireland – discrimination on the ground of creed, in that it is given any consideration at all, would be perceived as subsumed within the context of discrimination on ethnic grounds. Yet until well into the 20th century in England any discussion of discrimination would have been in the context of the religious inequality. The battles of non-conformists against the injustices and disabilities they suffered at the hands of the Established Church are now of purely historical interest and their struggle for religious equality has not provided any template for courts and tribunals grappling with the impact of the equality legislation in the area of employment. Both the race and sex equality legislation draw a distinction between direct and indirect discrimination. Indirect discrimination consists of imposing a condition which is not justifiable with which a considerably smaller proportion of one gender of one ethnic group cannot comply. Direct discrimination is when a person is treated less favourably on grounds of race or gender. As will be seen this is not an analysis which has been replicated in the disability legislation. In sex discrimination there is the added dimension that our membership of the European Union has imposed obligations to which domestic legislation is subordinate (see Chapter 2).[1] Where art 119 of the Treaty of Rome (see Chapter 2) is infringed it can be directly enforced by an individual. In the case of an infringement of the Equal Treatment Directive, then an individual can only rely on its provisions if they are employed by the *state* which includes any body which is an emanation of the state.[1] This doctrine has an established history in English law in that there are many strands of authority for the simple proposition that no party can rely on their own default to establish a defence. If the government has failed to implement the legislation required by the Directive then it cannot set up its own failure to afford it a defence in its capacity as an employer.[2]

1 See *Foster v British Gas* [1991] 2 AC 306 and *Doughty v Rolls Royce* [1992] IRLR 126, CA.
2 See *Marshall v Southampton Area Health Authority* [1986] QB 401; [1986] 2 All ER 584, ECJ.

Identifying discrimination

7.02   It is now well accepted that cases of direct discrimination pose particular problems. Employers are far too sophisticated to say 'we do not employ women or blacks' – still less use the offensive phrases in which such views were once couched. If any explanation is given it will be along the euphemistic lines that the applicant for a job or for promotion *would not fit in*.[1] Qualities praised in a man as exhibiting qualities of leadership can in a woman be stigmatised as bossiness or stridency. An appointments panel imbued – whether consciously or not – with the belief in the innate superiority of the white over the black will regard the absence of deference as arrogance. The woman or the black who is not appointed faces a heavy burden since the probability is that there were many white and/or male candidates who were similarly disappointed. This problem received its first authoritative recognition in the judgment of Browne-Wilkinson J in *Chattopadhyay v Headmaster of Holloway School*[2] when he said:

'As has been pointed out many times, a person complaining that he has been unlawfully discriminated against faces great difficulties. There is normally not available to him any evidence of overtly racial discriminatory words or action used by the respondents. All that the applicant can do is to point towards certain facts which, if unexplained, are consistent with his having been treated less favourably than others on racial grounds. In the majority of cases it is only the respondents and their witnesses who are able to say whether in fact the allegedly discriminatory act was motivated by racial discrimination or by any other, perfectly innocent, motivations.

Although concerned with issues of racial discrimination the judgment is equally applicable to other forms of discrimination.

1 *Noone v North West Thames Regional Health Authority* [1988] IRLR 195, CA.
2 [1982] ICR at 137, and see 7.05.

Statistical evidence

7.03 Courts and tribunals do not receive independent evidence of social and economic patterns. A tribunal may be considerably impressed by a respondent's assertion that it does not have any policy or wish to discriminate on grounds of race and gender and produces credible evidence for its failure to appoint or promote the applicant in the particular case. Yet if the tribunal knew that case was merely part of a pattern – although it might still reject the applicant's claim – it would only do so after considerably more scrutiny of the respondent's reasons.

7.04 In *West Midlands Transport Executive v Singh*[1] the Court of Appeal approved the admission of statistical evidence even though it accepted that as a matter of strict logic it may not be probative:

'The fact that the statistical evidence might show that the employers had between October 1984 and 1985 rejected all coloured applicants for the post of traffic supervisor would not of itself prove racial discrimination; in every case there may have been good, non-racial reasons for the rejection of the particular applicant. And, even if there had been racial discrimination by the employers on the other occasions, it would not in itself prove racial discrimination against the applicant on this particular occasion. As a matter of strict logic both these propositions are true.'

The court went on to point out that in deciding what is relevant evidence courts regard matters as relevant that which makes the matter requiring proof more or less probable and that in judging whether one fact is probative of another experience plays as much part as logic. The matter was put in this way by Balcombe LJ:

'Direct discrimination involves that an individual is not treated on his merits but receives unfavourable treatment because he is a member of a group. Statistical evidence may establish a discernible pattern in the treatment of a particular group: if the pattern demonstrates a regular failure of members of a group to obtain promotion to particular jobs and the under-representation in such jobs, it may give rise to an inference of discrimination against the group ... Statistics obtained through monitoring are not conclusive in themselves, but if they show racial or ethnic imbalance or disparities, then they may indicate areas of racial discrimination.'[2]

The judgment observed that statistical evidence concerning a group may well be more persuasive than previous treatment of the applicant which may be indicative of matters peculiar to the applicant and not be racially motivated. Furthermore there are subjective judgments in the assessment of any job applicant and a high percentage failure rate of a particular group to be promoted may indicate that the real reason for their failure is conscious or unconscious racial attitudes which may involve stereotyped assumptions about members of that group.

1 [1988] IRLR 186 at p 189.
2 [1988] IRLR 186.

Burden of proof

7.05 There have been a plethora of cases dealing with the issues of the burden of proof and much argument as to *legal* or *evidential* or *shifting* burdens of proof. In *King v Great Britain China Centre*[1] the Court of Appeal laid down what it is hoped will be the definitive guidelines on the subject in the judgment of Neill LJ:[2]

(1) It is for the applicant who complains of racial discrimination to make out his or her case. Thus, if the applicant does not prove the case on the balance of probabilities, he or she will fail.

(2) It is important to bear in mind that it is unusual to find direct evidence of racial discrimination. Few employers will be prepared to admit such discrimination even to themselves. In some cases the discrimination will not be ill-intentioned but merely based on the assumption 'that he or she would not have fitted in'.

(3) The outcome of the case will therefore usually depend on what inferences it is proper to draw from the primary facts found by the tribunal. These inferences can include, in appropriate cases, any inferences that it is just and equitable to draw in accordance with s 65(2) of the Race Relations Act 1976 from an evasive or equivocal reply to a questionnaire.

(4) Though there will be some cases where, for example, the non-selection of the applicant for a post or for promotion is clearly not on racial grounds, a finding of discrimination and a finding of a difference of race will often point to the possibility of racial discrimination. In such circumstances the tribunal will look to the employer for an explanation. If no explanation is then put forward or if the tribunal considers the explanation to be inadequate or unsatisfactory, it will be legitimate for the tribunal to infer that the discrimination was on racial grounds. This is not a matter of law but, as May LJ put it in *Noone*,[3] 'almost common sense'.

(5) It is unnecessary and unhelpful to introduce the concept of a shifting evidential burden of proof. At the conclusion of all the evidence the tribunal should make findings of fact as to the primary facts and draw such inferences as it considers proper from those facts. The tribunal should then reach a conclusion on the balance of probabilities which face a person who complains of unlawful discrimination and the fact that it is for the complainant to prove his or her case.'

Although the cases cited were drawn from cases involving racial discrimination, exactly the same considerations apply in cases of sexual discrimination and will no doubt be considered apt when tribunals consider cases of disability.

1 [1992] ICR 516.
2 [1992] ICR 528.
3 [1988] ICR 813 at p 822.

Establishing direct discrimination

7.06 On the basis of these authorities it is submitted that in considering a case of direct discrimination on grounds of race or sex, the following questions emerge:

(1) Has the applicant been less favourably treated than others?

(2) If yes, are the circumstances consistent with the treatment being on grounds of race or sex?

(3) If yes, what is the respondent's explanation for the less favourable treatment? Is that explanation credible? Is it consistent with a reasonable and innocent[1] explanation for the less favourable treatment?

(4) If not, on the evidence is it appropriate to draw the inference that the less favourable treatment was due to race or sex?[2]

(5) If it is, the applicant has proved that he or she was discriminated against. The motive or intention of the respondent is not a relevant consideration. The question is ultimately: would the applicant have received the same treatment from the respondent but for his or her race or sex?

(6) If discrimination is proved it is still necessary to consider whether it was unlawful under s 6 of the Sex Discrimination Act 1975 or s 4 of the Race Relations Act 1976.

(7) If the answer is yes, it is still necessary to decide whether the unlawful act of discrimination was done by the discriminator in the course of his or her employment.

(8) If the answer is yes, then the employer (assuming he is the respondent) will be liable unless he proves that he took all such steps as were reasonably practicable to prevent the employee from carrying out such act or acts of discrimination.

1 'Innocent' in this context means other than due to a reason based on gender or race. It sometimes happens that an employer treats an employee with the most blatant unfairness but the employee does not have the requisite continuity for an action for unfair dismissal. On hearing the evidence a tribunal may well conclude that the reason the employer treated this employee badly was due to a reason relating to race or gender. But it is not unknown for a tribunal to draw a rather different (though equally unflattering) inference, namely that this employer treats all his employees badly.

2 As a matter of common sense where a tribunal rejects an employer's explanation as not credible the likelihood is that it will go on to make a finding of racial or sexual discrimination. But there may be cases in which a tribunal rejects the employer's explanation but nevertheless a claim based on race or sex discrimination fails. On the evidence it has heard a tribunal, for example, may find that the employer's *real* reason for the less favourable treatment was his dislike of the applicant's political views or the fact that he feared the applicant might wish to recruit employees into a trade union. In *Leicester University Students Union v Mahomed* [1995] IRLR 292 it was pointed out that *King* allows inferences to be drawn from inadequate or unsatisfactory explanations but that it is not authority for the proposition that such inferences must always be drawn.

Discrimination on grounds of sex and marital status

Discrimination

7.07 The provisions of the Sex Discrimination Act 1975 dealing with discrimination on the grounds of sex came into force by 29 December 1975. The Act applies equally to men[1] as women, and insofar as employment is concerned makes unlawful discrimination on the ground of married status[2] as well as on the grounds of sex. The provisions of the Act are referred to only insofar as they are relevant for the purpose of this book. The object is to give an outline of the Act as it applies to employers and employees although the Act does deal with discrimination in other fields.

1 Sex Discrimination Act 1975, s 2.

2 Sex Discrimination Act 1975, s 3. Discrimination on grounds of marital status is defined in a similar way to discrimination on the grounds of sex with appropriate modifications. There are

difficult issues for those about to be married. Contrast *Bick v Royal West of England Residential School for the Deaf* [1976] IRLR 326 and *McLean v Paris Travel Services Ltd* [1976] IRLR 202. For a case in which an employee was dismissed because she became engaged to an employee of a competitor, see *Skyrail Oceanic Ltd v Coleman* [1981] IRLR 398. It is suggested that if an employee was dismissed because her job entailed access to highly confidential information and she became engaged to, or married, an employee of the principal competitor, it would not necessarily be either sex discrimination or unfair dismissal if the employer could show that this course would have been taken in any case in which there was an intimate relationship irrespective of gender or married status and that it was not taken on the assumption that the man was the *breadwinner.*

7.08 Sex discrimination is defined by s 1 of the Sex Discrimination Act 1975 as follows:

'(1) A person discriminates against a woman[1] in any circumstances relevant for the purposes of any provision of this Act if—

(a) on the ground of her sex he treats her less favourably than he treats or would treat a man, or

(b) he applies to her a requirement or condition which he applies or would apply equally to a man but—

(i) which is such that the proportion of women who comply with it is considerably smaller than the proportion of men who can comply with it, and

(ii) which he cannot show to be justifiable irrespective of the sex of the person to whom it is applied, and

(iii) which is to her detriment because she cannot comply with it.

(2) If a person treats or would treat a man differently according to the man's marital status, his treatment of a woman is for the purposes of subsection (1)(a) to be compared to his treatment of a man having a like marital status.'

1 'Woman' includes a female of any age: Sex Discrimination Act 1975, s 82(1).

7.09 Central to the race and sex discrimination legislation is a distinction between direct and indirect discrimination. In the former the issue is whether a person has been treated less favourably on grounds of gender and race. In deciding that issue it is necessary for the woman to show that she is treated less favourably on grounds of her sex. It is not necessary for the woman to claim that her employers are acting in a manner that is inherently adverse or hostile to the interests of women. So when male examiners were included on a rota to do a particularly dirty job and women of the same grade were not, the men were discriminated against unlawfully.[1] The fact that the males received an additional payment when doing the dirty work did not mean that they were not discriminated against. It has been held by the Court of Appeal that arrangements made in the interests of safety or in the interests of good administration are not infringements of the law even though they may be more favourable to women than to men: or conversely more favourable to men than to women.[2] In *Ministry of Defence v Jeremiah* Lord Denning MR said[3] that this ground for the earlier decision was per incuriam and should not be relied upon. Section 1 defines what is discrimination but does not set out when it is unlawful. This is dealt with later in the Act. In the case of indirect discrimination what is prohibited is the imposition of an unjustifiable condition with which a considerably smaller number of persons of a particular gender or race can comply. In determining whether a condition is justifiable, then elements of reasonableness do arise.

1 *Ministry of Defence v Jeremiah* [1979] IRLR 436, CA. See in particular the judgment of Brandon LJ at p 439.
2 *Peake v Automotive Products Ltd* [1977] ICR 968, CA. A rule which had applied for 30 years provided that although men and women stopped work at the same time, women were allowed to leave immediately whereas men had to wait for five minutes before doing so. The decision that the rule did not amount to unlawful discrimination is probably still good on the ground of the maxim *de minimis non curat lex.*
3 [1979] IRLR 436 at p 438, CA. Brandon and Brightman LJJ did not express any opinion on the point.

Direct discrimination

7.10   Cases which fall within s 1(1)(a) of the Sex Discrimination Act 1975 are generally referred to as 'direct discrimination'. The test of direct discrimination within s 1(1)(a) is whether a person of one gender would have received the same treatment *but for his or her sex*. Where there is a different pension age based on gender it was direct discrimination to make free entry to a swimming pool dependent upon being of pensionable age.[1] It is not necessary to show the treatment was objectively worse: it is sufficient to show that on grounds of gender a person of one gender was denied an opportunity which was valued by them on reasonable grounds.[2] Thus in *Birmingham City Council v Equal Opportunities Commission*[3] it was held that it was not necessary to show that selective education was better: it was sufficient to show that persons of one gender were denied a choice which they – or more realistically their parents – on reasonable grounds believed was a benefit. Moreover it is not necessary to show that the reason for the differential treatment was ill-intentioned. Thus, where a woman was not allowed to start work because another woman had failed to attend and it was felt that as the only woman amongst an exclusively male workforce she would be the subject of unwanted attentions, it was nevertheless held to be sex discrimination even though the motive was well-intentioned.[4] Domestic case law suggests discrimination on the basis of sexual orientation is not within the ambit of sex discrimination legislation.[5] The European Court has held it is discriminatory to dismiss a transsexual employee who has had a sex change operation.[6]

1 *James v Eastleigh Borough Council* [1990] ICR 554.
2 *Humphreys v Board of Managers of St Georges Church of England (Aided) Primary School* [1978] ICR 546, EAT. Only in exceptional or frivolous cases should the tribunal find against the applicant at the end of her case without hearing the respondents. See also *Saunders v Richmond-upon-Thames London Borough Council* [1978] ICR 75, EAT.
3 [1989] AC 1155.
4 *Grieg v Community Industry* [1979] IRLR 158.
5 See *Smith v Gardner Merchant Ltd* [1996] IRLR 342, EAT; *R v Ministry of Defence, ex p Smith and Grady* and *R v Admiralty Board of the Defence Council, ex p Lustig-Pream and Beckett* [1996] IRLR 100.
6 *P v S and Cornwall County Council* [1996] IRLR 347.

Making the comparison

7.11   For a woman to establish that she has been discriminated against, a comparison must be possible. A female employee required to wear a skirt in the public part of a shop was not discriminated against, since no comparable condition could be applied to men.[1] It is to be noted however that in contrast to the Equal Pay Act 1970 it is not necessary for the woman to show an actual employee who has been more favourably treated. By virtue of s 5(3) of the Sex Discrimination Act 1975 a comparison of the cases of persons of different sex or marital status under s 1(1) or 3(1) must be such that the relevant circumstances in the one case are the same, or not materially different, in the other.[2] Section 1(1)(a) deals with those who are treated less favourably than a man and also those who *would* be so treated.

1 *Schmidt v Austicks Bookshops Ltd* [1977] IRLR 360, EAT, and see *Stewart v Cleveland Guest (Engineering) Ltd* [1994] IRLR 440 for a case in which it was held that the display of photographs of partially clad women was not discriminating since men might find it equally distasteful. It has been held not to be discrimination to insist on different length of hair for men and women: *Smith v Safeway plc* [1996] IRLR 456.
2 See *Bullock v Alice Ottley School* [1993] ICR 138 and see Chapter 8. The differential retirement ages in this case were justified on grounds that they were not gender based since the position of the gardeners was different in that they were more difficult to recruit and retain.

Sexual harassment

7.12 Many of the types of conduct which come within the description of sexual harassment constitute behaviour which would establish a criminal offence of indecent assault or intentional harassment under the Criminal Justice and Public Order Act 1994. Further, such conduct would normally constitute a tortious wrong which would enable an individual to obtain an injunction to deter the harasser from repetition of such conduct. There is nothing in terms in the Sex Discrimination Act 1975 which specifically deals with this problem. In *Porcelli v Strathclyde Regional Council*[1] the applicant was a laboratory technician and complained that she was subject to suggestive remarks and innuendos and unwanted physical contact. This was held to be unlawful sexual discrimination since she had been subjected to treatment to which a man would not have been vulnerable. Other cases have followed this decision.[2] Such harassment must take place within the course of the employment.[3] Although an employer is vicariously liable for the acts of an employee it is a defence to show that he took such steps as were reasonably practicable to prevent the employee from perpetrating the act.[4] A woman who makes such a complaint may be cross-examined on her own sexual attitudes to show that the injury to her feelings would have been minimal in view of the attitudes she has exhibited.[5]

1 [1986] ICR 564.
2 *Bracebridge Engineering Ltd v Darby* [1990] IRLR 3 and *Insitu Cleaning v Heads* [1995] IRLR 4. A single incident if sufficiently serious can constitute harassment.
3 *Waters v Metropolitan Police Comr* [1995] ICR 510, but see **7.41**.
4 *Balgobin v Tower Hamlets London Borough Council* [1987] ICR 829.
5 *Snowball v Gardner Merchant Ltd* [1987] ICR 719.

Indirect discrimination

7.13 Discrimination which falls within s 1(1)(b) of the Sex Discrimination Act 1975 is 'indirect discrimination'.[1] The onus of proof to show discrimination is on the applicant but in the case of indirect discrimination once the applicant shows that s 1(1)(b)(i) and (iii) apply, the employer who seeks to rely on s 1(1)(b)(ii), has to establish that the requirement or condition is justifiable irrespective of the sex of the person to whom it is applied. In examining the provisions of s 1(1)(b)(i), Phillips J has said:[2]

'The test is whether the condition is such that the proportion of women who can comply with it is considerably smaller than the proportion of men who can comply with it. Examples usually given are of physical attributes such as height or strength or weight. But the subparagraph goes much further than that, and would extend to educational or professional qualifications, if they are of a kind which few women but many men possess. Thus an advertisement which required as a condition for appointment to a post a degree in engineering, or the status of a barrister at law,[3] would seem to be prima facie discriminatory in that the proportion of women who can comply with the condition is considerably smaller than the proportion of men who can comply with it. No doubt in those and other similar cases the advertiser would have no difficulty in showing the condition to be justifiable. Accordingly such cases are not brought in practice because it is known that though they might pass the test of subparagraph (i) they will fail at that of sub-paragraph (ii).'

1 See for instance *Steel v Union of Post Office Workers* [1978] 2 All ER 504; [1978] ICR 181, EAT (allocation of walks depended on seniority and rules operated against women).
2 *Price v Civil Service Commission* [1978] 1 All ER 1228; [1978] ICR 27, EAT at p 29. A majority decision of the Employment Appeal Tribunal.
3 No judge would now chose this example now that law faculties have a far more equal balance in terms of gender.

7.14 Tribunals have had to grapple with far more sophisticated conditions. It is by no means unusual for a job to have three requirements:
(1)   that the job is full-time;
(2)   that the employee should be prepared to travel extensively;
(3)   that the employee should be prepared to move to different parts of the country.
The difficulty is that in making the decision that these conditions are potentially discriminatory, a tribunal, in the absence of detailed statistical evidence, is making a sexual stereotyped assumption that women are unable to fulfil these conditions because they have assumed the responsibility for looking after young children or elderly relatives. Often subsumed within this assumption is the further assumption that women are more suited to these roles or that they always have had the less prestigious and less lucrative jobs. This conflict is illustrated in *Clarke v Eley (IMI Kynock) Ltd*[1] where the Employment Appeal Tribunal upheld the industrial tribunal's decision that selecting part-time workers for redundancy before full-time employees was discriminatory, yet in *Kidd v DRG (UK) Ltd*[2] the Employment Appeal Tribunal also upheld another industrial tribunal's decision that the practice was not discriminatory against married women since in the absence of detailed statistical evidence the tribunal was not prepared to assume that a considerably greater proportion of married women than unmarried women or men assumed a childcaring role. The position was complicated in that case by the fact that all the employees from whom the selection for redundancy was made were women. In *Home Office v Holmes*[3] the requirement that a job had to be full-time was held to be discriminatory, but the Employment Appeal Tribunal was anxious to emphasise that each case was decided on its own facts. It is suggested that in the light of *Bilka-Kaufhaus GmbH v Weber van Hartz*[4] tribunals would be far more likely to make the assumption that the requirement that work was full-time was potentially discriminatory in that it was more difficult for women to comply with it. Even if that is the case it by no means follows that it is not *justifiable* to impose such a condition. There is an important qualification which narrows the scope of a claim for indirect discrimination. The Act refers to a *requirement* or a *condition*. If all

an employer does is to set out a series of preferences that is looked for in a candidate and not an absolute condition with which the candidate *must* comply, then the employer does not fall foul of the legislation.[5]

1 [1982] IRLR 482.
2 [1985] ICR 405. In *Kidd's* case there were arguments about the marginal advantages of retaining full-timers.
3 [1984] ICR 678. And see *Clymo v Wandsworth London Borough Council* [1989] ICR 250.
4 [1987] ICR 110; see also the decision of the House of Lords in *R v Secretary of State for Employment, ex p Equal Opportunities Commission* [1994] ICR 317.
5 *Meer v Tower Hamlets London Borough Council* [1988] IRLR 399 and see also *Perera v Civil Service Commission (No 2)* [1982] ICR 350.

Can comply

7.15   In determining whether a woman 'can comply' with a requirement or condition, the test is not what is a 'theoretical possibility' but it is necessary to see whether the employee 'can comply in practice'.[1] It then falls to be determined whether the proportion of women who can comply with it is *considerably smaller* than the proportion of men who can comply. The 'pool' of persons being compared may well be less than the total male and female population. An employee cannot merely select as a pool one that is convenient to her case. In *Jones v Manchester University*[2] the Court of Appeal held that the pool should have consisted of all those who could satisfy the relevant criteria apart from the alleged potentially discriminatory requirement rather than limiting the pool to all mature graduates (which was a group into which the applicant herself fell). An employee cannot complain if she *can* comply but chooses not to do so because of a decision which she has taken as to her future matrimonial status. Thus a divorced woman who was required to join a pension scheme which included benefits for a surviving spouse cannot claim the scheme is discriminatory since she has no intention of remarrying.[3]

1 *Price v Civil Service Commission* [1978] ICR 27 at p 32, EAT. An upper age limit of 28 for applicants was found to be discrimination within s 1(1)(b) in *Price v Civil Service Commission* [1978] 1 All ER 1228; [1978] ICR 27, EAT and *Price v Civil Service Commission (No 2)* [1978] IRLR 3.
2 [1993] ICR 474.
3 *Turner v Labour Party* [1987] IRLR 101, CA.

Test of justifiability

7.16   It is obvious that in the example cited by Phillips J at **7.12** that the fact that only a small percentage of engineering graduates are female would not make it unlawful discrimination to require an engineering degree for certain jobs. Normally one is dealing with considerably more difficult tests than that. A balance has to be struck between the discriminatory effects of the condition and the objectively considered reasonable needs of the employer.[1] The House of Lords has equated the test of justifiability in relation to unlawful discrimination with the test of material difference in the Equal Pay Act 1970.[2] There is a great danger that decided cases wrenched from their factual context can cease to be helpful guidelines and instead become tram lines which divert both employers (and later tribunals) from their proper task. Striking a balance between the discriminatory impact of a condition and the reasonable and proper needs of the employer is not a metaphysical exercise which can be answered in the abstract. The imposition of a condition that the employee will travel extensively, often at short notice, within a wide area which will require frequent nights away from home may well be a potentially discriminatory condition in that it will be more difficult for a woman to comply with such a condition. It may be justifiable in the case of a small company which wants to recruit one salesperson to cover a wide area, but not in the case of a large employer which has found no problem at all in finding members of its workforce happy to volunteer to travel extensively. Such an example reveals that there is an incipient conflict between an employer's natural desire to make a working pattern a matter of contractual obligation and the requirements of the equality legislation not to impose without good cause contractual obligations which are discriminatory in their effect.

1 *Briggs v North Eastern Education and Library Board* [1990] IRLR 181 (requirement on a teacher to take out of hours school games was justifiable irrespective of gender or matrimonial status).
2 See *Rainey v Greater Glasgow Health Board* [1987] ICR 129.

Victimisation

7.17 Discrimination is by way of victimisation in circumstances relevant to any provision of the Sex Discrimination Act 1975 where a person treats ('the person victimised') less favourably than in those circumstances he treats, or would treat, other persons. The reason for this less favourable treatment must be that the person victimised:[1]

(a) has brought proceedings or threatens to do so against the discriminator or any other person under the Sex Discrimination Act 1975 or the Equal Pay Act 1970, or

(b) has given evidence or information in connection with proceedings brought by any person under those Acts, or

(c) has done anything otherwise under or by reference to those Acts in relation to the discriminator or any other person, or

(d) has alleged that the discriminator, or any other person, has committed an act which would amount to a contravention of either of those statutes, or

(e) by reason that the discriminator knows the person victimised intends to do any of those things, or suspects that the person victimised has done or intends to do any of them.

The person victimised cannot rely on an allegation which was false and not made in good faith.[2] If the employer would not have been liable under the Act for the original conduct, then the less favourable treatment does not amount to victimisation. In *Waters v Metropolitan Police Comr*[3] a policewoman complained that she had been sexually harassed by a colleague. The incident had occurred when both she and the alleged harasser were off duty and therefore her employer would not have been vicariously liable for these acts. An employee cannot rely on the victimisation provisions if the abrasive and disruptive manner in which the complaint has been made, rather than the complaint itself, has been the reason for the less favourable treatment.[4]

1 Sex Discrimination Act 1975, s 4(1).
2 Sex Discrimination Act 1975, s 4(2).
3 [1995] ICR 510.
4 *Re York Truck Equipment* IDS Brief 439 p 10.

7.18 A complainant has to show that someone who had not done any of the acts would have been treated differently.[1] This is illustrated by a case under the Race Relations Act 1976. In *Aziz v Trinity Street Taxis Ltd*[2] the applicant was expelled from a trade association for making a tape recording for use in discrimination proceedings. His claim for victimisation failed since there was a finding of fact that others would have been treated in the same way even if such treatment would not have been done in the context of there being no discrimination claim. The issue was one of causation. The protection is limited to an act that takes place whilst the applicant is an employee. In a case under the Race Relations Act 1976 there was no redress when a former employer gave an unfavourable reference to a former employee.[3]

1 *Cornelius v University College of Swansea* [1987] IRLR 141, CA.
2 [1988] ICR 534, CA.
3 *Nagarajan v Agnew* [1994] IRLR 61.

Employment

7.19 Part II of the Sex Discrimination Act 1975 sets out situations of discrimination in the employment field which it makes unlawful. Employment is defined widely as employment under a contract of service or of apprenticeship or *a contract personally to execute any work or labour.*[1] This is a wider definition than that contained in the Employment Rights Act 1996. The Sex Discrimination Act 1975 binds the Crown and Crown service is included within Pt II, as is service on behalf of the Crown for purposes of statutory officers or bodies. The armed services are now included save that nothing is rendered unlawful which is done to ensure *combat effectiveness.*[2] A justice of the peace does not come within the definition.[3] Rent officers are also not included.[4] In making appointments and offering offices or posts where s 6 (see **7.21**) does not apply to the appointment, ministers and government departments should not do acts which would be unlawful under s 6 if the Crown were the employer.[5] For further exceptions see **7.22** et seq. The offers of a pupillage and a tenancy[6] in chambers as well as partnerships[7] are within the ambit of the Act.

1 Sex Discrimination Act 1975, s 82. See *Tanna v Post Office* [1981] ICR 374; *Ganning v Mirror Newspapers* [1986] ICR 145; *Post Office v Adekeye* [1995] ICR 540.
2 For detailed provisions see the Sex Discrimination Act 1975, s 85 generally and for the armed services, see s 85(4).
3 *Knight v A-G* [1979] ICR 194, EAT.
4 *Department of the Environment v Fox* [1979] ICR 736, EAT.
5 Sex Discrimination Act 1975, s 86.
6 Sex Discrimination Act 1975, s 35(a).
7 Sex Discrimination Act 1975, s 11.

Advertisements

7.20 Section 38 makes it unlawful to publish or cause to be published an advertisement which indicates or might be reasonably understood as indicating an intention to discriminate unlawfully and the use of job descriptions with sexual connotations (such as 'waiter', 'salesgirl', 'postman' or 'stewardess') is taken as showing an indication to discriminate in that way unless the advertisement includes an indication to the contrary'.[1] There are provisions similar to these mentioned in connection with employment agencies. It is a defence for the publisher of an advert to show that he reasonably relied on the assurance of the person placing the advert that it was not unlawful. A person who knowingly or recklessly makes such a statement[2] which is in a material respect false, or misleading, commits an offence.[3]

1 The sanctions are the issue of a non-discrimination notice pursuant to the Sex Discrimination Act 1975, s 67 or an application to a county court for an injunction.
2 Sex Discrimination Act 1975, s 38(4).
3 Sex Discrimination Act 1975, s 38(5).

The unlawful acts

7.21 Whilst the particular statutory provisions should be studied, in general terms discrimination on grounds of sex or marital status is unlawful at every stage of employment, ie in recruitment, training, promotion or dismissal. The statutory provisions are contained in s 6 of the Sex Discrimination Act 1975:

'(1)   It is unlawful for a person, in relation to employment by him at an establishment in Great Britain to discriminate against a woman—
(a)   in the arrangements[1] he makes for the purpose of determining who shall be offered that employment, or
(b)   in the terms on which he offers her that employment, or
(c)   by refusing or deliberately omitting to offer her that employment.[2]
   (2) It is unlawful for a person in the case of a woman employed by him at an establishment in Great Britain, to discriminate against her—
(a)   in the way he affords her access to opportunities for training, or to any other benefits, facilities or services, or by refusing or deliberating omitting to afford her access to them, or
(b)   by dismissing[3] her or subjecting her to any other detriment.'[4]

1 In *Saunders v Richmond Borough Council* [1978] ICR 75 it was assumed that the questions (asked by a woman chairman) to a prospective golf professional such as 'are you blazing a trail?' were part of the arrangements. See also *Brennan v Dewhurst Ltd* [1984] ICR 52.
2 *Roadburg v Lothian Regional Council* [1976] IRLR 283 suggests that it is still unlawful discrimination even if no one is ultimately offered the job, but for a decision to the opposite effect, see *Thorn v Meggitt Engineering* [1976] IRLR 241.
3 Dismissal is given an extended definition in that in the case of partners, it includes expelling a woman from a partnership: s 11(1)(d)(ii).
4 Sexual harassment comes within the ambit of detriment.

Contracting out of the Sex Discrimination Act 1975 and exceptions

7.22 It is not possible to contract out of the provisions of the Sex Discrimination Act 1975 and the Act applies unless covered by a specific statutory exception.[1]

1 Section 77 prohibits contracting out of the Act. A settlement of a case is only enforceable in circumstances which pertain to unfair dismissal (s 77(4)). Certain other exceptions are dealt with along with miscellaneous provisions of the Act at 7.23 et seq.

Genuine occupational qualifications[1]

7.23 It is not unlawful discrimination to choose a man for a particular job if the essential nature of the job calls for a man for reasons of physiology (excluding physical strength or stamina), or in dramatic performances, or other entertainment, for reasons of authenticity, so that the essential nature of the job would be materially different if carried out by a woman.[2] Thus, there is nothing to prevent a drama director requiring an actor to play Hamlet or an actress to play Ophelia or for an advertising agency to recruit according to gender for a model to fashion male or female clothes. What is unlawful is to discriminate against a woman on the grounds of physical strength and stamina providing a woman is capable of carrying out the task concerned. It is unlawful to assume that a woman would be unable to be a labourer, but it is not unlawful to decide on objective grounds that a particular job applicant whether male or female does not have the strength and stamina to do a particular job. An employer who failed to interview a female applicant and make such enquiries as were appropriate in all the circumstances would have some difficulty in convincing a tribunal that he was not merely making assumptions on the basis of a sexist stereotype.

1 Sex Discrimination Act 1975, s 7(1). Note that s 7 does not exclude s 6(1)(b).
2 Sex Discrimination Act 1975, s 7(2)(a).

Decency and privacy
7.24   It is also a genuine occupational qualification if the job needs to be held by a man to preserve decency, or privacy, because it is likely to involve physical contact with men in circumstances where they might reasonably object to it being carried out by a woman[1] or the holder of the job is likely to do his work in circumstances where men might reasonably object to the presence of women because they are in a state of undress, or using sanitary facilities.[2] The exception applies when the holder of the job is likely to do his work, or live in a private home, and the job needs to be done by a man because objection might reasonably be taken to allowing a woman the degree of physical or social contact with a person living in the house, or the knowledge of the intimate details of a person's life arising from holding the job.[3] Another type of genuine occupational qualification is where the nature or location of the employer's establishment makes it impracticable for the holder of the job to live elsewhere than in the premises provided by the employer, and the only such premises available are lived in, or normally lived in, by men and are not equipped with separate sleeping accommodation for women and sanitary facilities which could be used by women in privacy from men, and it is not reasonable to expect the employer to equip those premises with such accommodation and facilities or to provide other premises for women.[4]

1 Sex Discrimination Act 1975, s 7(2)(b)(i). See *Wylie v Dee & Co (Menswear) Ltd* [1978] IRLR 103.
2 Sex Discrimination Act 1975, s 7(2)(b)(ii).
3 Sex Discrimination Act 1975, s 7(2)(b)(i).
4 Sex Discrimination Act 1975, s 7(2)(c).

Occupational environment
7.25   Yet another type of genuine occupational qualification occurs when the nature of the employer's establishment, or the part in which the work is done, requires the job to be done by a man because it is, or is part of a hospital, prison, or other establishment, for persons requiring special care, supervision or attention and those persons are all men, save any woman whose presence is exceptional, and it is reasonable having regard to the essential character of the establishment that the job should not be held by a woman.[1] When the holder of a job provides individuals with personal services promoting their welfare or education or similar personal services and those services can be most effectively performed by a man that again can be a genuine occupational qualification.[2]

1 Sex Discrimination Act 1975, s 7(2)(d).
2 Sex Discrimination Act 1975, s 7(2)(e).

Religious or cultural prohibition on women abroad or the need to preserve the marriage bond

7.26 If a job needs to be held by a man because it is likely to involve the performance of duties outside the United Kingdom in a country, whose laws and/or customs are such that the duties could not, or could not effectively, be performed by a woman, that is also a genuine occupational qualification.[1] The final exclusion of this type is where the job is one of two which are to be held by a married couple.[2]

1 Sex Discrimination Act 1975, s 7(2)(g).
2 Sex Discrimination Act 1975, s 7(2)(h).

When only part of the job is a genuine occupational qualification

7.27 The job is still one for which sex is a genuine occupational qualification where some only of the duties fall within the heads in **7.23–7.26**,[1] but with the exception of the exclusion relating to two related jobs held by a married couple, the genuine occupational qualification exclusion does not apply to the filling of a vacancy when the employer already has male employees capable of carrying out the duties, whom it would be reasonable to employ on those duties, and whose numbers are sufficient to meet the employer's likely requirement in respect of them without undue inconvenience.[2] There is a similar exclusion where the employee would be caused to share communal accommodation being residential accommodation which includes dormitories or other shared sleeping accommodation which for reasons of privacy should be used by one sex only.[3]

1 Sex Discrimination Act 1975, s 7(3).
2 Sex Discrimination Act 1975, s 7(4). See *Wylie v Dee & Co (Menswear) Ltd* [1978] IRLR 103.
3 Sex Discrimination Act 1975, s 46 which sets out the extent of this exclusion. It can only be relied on if such arrangements as are reasonably practicable are made to compensate for the detriment caused by the discrimination: s 46(6).

Particular occupations

Police

7.28 The office of police constable is treated as employment for the purposes of the Sex Discrimination Act 1975 and subject to certain minor amendments the Act applies to it.[1] Regulations under ss 50, 51 or 52 of the Police Act 1996 should not treat men and women differently except as to requirements relating to height, uniform or equipment or allowances in lieu thereof, so far as special treatment is accorded to woman in connection with pregnancy or childbirth, or in relation to pensions to, or in respect of, special constables or police cadets.[2]

1 Sex Discrimination Act 1975, s 17.
2 Sex Discrimination Act 1975, s 17(2).

Prison officers

7.29 The Act also applies to prison officers but it does not render unlawful any discrimination between male and female prison officers as to requirements relating to their height.[1]

1 Sex Discrimination Act 1975, s 18.

Ministers of religion

7.30 The Act does not apply to employment for purposes of an organised religion where the employment is limited to one sex so as to comply with the doctrines of the religion, or to avoid offending the religious susceptibilities of a significant number of its followers.[1]

1 Sex Discrimination Act 1975, s 19(1).

Compliance with statutory enactment or needs of national security

7.31 It is not unlawful to do any act necessary to comply with a statutory requirement[1] or for the purpose of safeguarding national security.[2]

1 Sex Discrimination Act 1975, s 51. This includes enactments passed before the Sex Discrimination Act 1975 and instruments made under such Acts: *Hugh-Jones v St John's College, Cambridge* [1979] ICR 848, EAT; *Greater London Council v Farrar* [1979] LS Gaz R 1253, EAT.
2 Sex Discrimination Act 1975, s 52. The usual rules as to ministerial certificates apply: s 52(2) and (3).

Small employers exception

7.32 The previous exclusion for employers who together with any associated employers do not employ more than five employees has been repealed by the Sex Discrimination Act 1986.

Death and retirement

7.33 As originally drafted it was not unlawful to differentiate as to provisions in relation to death or retirement of the employee or prospective employee. However, in the celebrated case of *Marshall*,[1] the European Court of Justice held that this offended the Equal Treatment Directive and new provisions as to retirement have been substituted.[2] The Pensions Act 1995 has now sought to deal with the question of access to pensions provision.[3]

1 *Marshall v Southampton Area Health Authority* [1986] QB 401; [1986] 2 All ER 584, ECJ. The original terms of the Sex Discrimination Act 1975, s 6(4) have now been amended. From 6 April 1978 there should be equal access to most occupational pension schemes: Equal Pay Act 1970, s 6(1A).
2 See Chapter 8 for the current position.
3 See Chapter 8 for the effect of sex discrimination on pensions.

Pregnancy and childbirth

7.34 It is not unlawful to discriminate by affording special treatment to women in connection with pregnancy or childbirth.[1]

1 Sex Discrimination Act 1975, s 2(2). For pregnancy dismissals see maternity rights, 7.88 et seq.

Territorial limitations

7.35 The employment provisions of the Sex Discrimination Act 1975 are limited to employment by the employer at an establishment in Great Britain.[1] This is defined as including such of the territorial waters of the United Kingdom as are adjacent to Great Britain.[2] By virtue of s 10(1) employment is regarded as being at an establishment in Great Britain unless the employee does his work wholly or mainly outside Great Britain.

7.35 *Discrimination (including pregnancy)*

Employment on a ship registered in Great Britain, or on a United Kingdom registered aircraft or hovercraft operated by a person whose principal place of business is, or who is ordinarily resident, in Great Britain, is treated as an establishment in Great Britain unless the employment is wholly outside Great Britain.[3]

1 Sex Discrimination Act 1975, s 6.
2 Sex Discrimination Act 1975, s 82(1).
3 Sex Discrimination Act 1975, s 10(3)

Contract worker and employment agencies

7.36 There are special provisions relating to discrimination against contract workers.[1] These cover the case of work for a person ('the principal') which is done by individuals (the 'contract workers') who are not employed by the principal himself, but by another person who supplies them under a contract made with the principal.[2] It is unlawful for the principal to discriminate against a woman who is a contract worker in the terms on which he allows her to do that work, or by not allowing her to do it, or continue to do it, or in the way in which he affords her access to benefits, facilities or services or by refusing or deliberately omitting to afford her access to them,[3] or by subjecting her to any other detriment.[4] However, when being a man would be a genuine occupational qualification for the job if directly employed, it is not unlawful discrimination for the principal not to allow a woman to do the job or continue to do it.[5] It is unlawful for an employment agency[6] to discriminate against a woman either in the terms on which the agency offers to provide any of its services,[7] or by refusing or deliberately omitting to provide any services, or in the way it provides any of its services. The reference to services includes guidance on careers and other services related to employment, but it is not unlawful for the agency to carry out such acts if the discrimination only concerns employment which the employer could lawfully refuse to offer the woman.[8] There is a saving for an employment agency if it proves that it acted in reliance on a statement made to it by the employer that the employer could lawfully refuse to employ a woman, that its action would not be unlawful and that it was reasonable for it to rely on the statement.[9] There is a criminal liability on a person who knowingly or recklessly makes a statement which is in a material respect false or misleading.[10]

1 Sex Discrimination Act 1975, s 9.
2 Sex Discrimination Act 1975, s 9(1). The wide definition of 'employee' is of particular importance in these cases, see *BP Chemicals v Gillick* [1995] IRLR 128, EAT.
3 Sex Discrimination Act 1975, s 9(2). This provision does not apply to benefits, facilities or services of any description if the principal is concerned with the provision of benefits, facilities or services of that description to the public, or to a section of the public to which the woman belongs unless that provision differs in a material respect from the provision of benefits, facilities or services by the principal to his contract workers: Sex Discrimination Act 1975, s 9(4).
4 Sex Discrimination Act 1975, s 9(2)(d).
5 Sex Discrimination Act 1975, s 9(3).
6 'Employment agency' means a person who, for profit or not, provides services for the purpose of finding employment for workers or supplying employers with workers: Sex Discrimination Act 1975, s 82(1).
7 Sex Discrimination Act 1975, s 15(1). See *Rice's* case above.
8 Sex Discrimination Act 1975, s 15(4).
9 Sex Discrimination Act 1975, s 15(5).
10 Sex Discrimination Act 1975, s 15(6).

Trade unions, employer's organisations, qualifying bodies

7.37 The Sex Discrimination Act 1975 seeks to prevent organisations of workers, organisations of employers and other organisations whose members carry on a particular profession or trade for the purposes of which the organisation exists, from discriminating unlawfully.[1] It is unlawful for an authority or body which can confer authorisation or qualifications to discriminate contrary to the Act[2] and for vocational training bodies[3] and the Secretary of State in the provision of facilities under section 2 of the Employment and Training Act to discriminate against women.[4]

1 Sex Discrimination Act 1975, s 12.
2 Sex Discrimination Act 1975, s 13.
3 Sex Discrimination Act 1975, s 14.
4 Sex Discrimination Act 1975, s 16.

Partners

7.38 As a result of amendments introduced by the Sex Discrimination Act 1986 the legislation applies to partners irrespective of the number of partners.[1] The right to contract out of the provisions if there is a genuine occupational qualification is preserved.[2]

1 Sex Discrimination Act 1975, s 11(1).
2 Sex Discrimination Act 1975, s 11(3).

Miscellaneous cases

7.39 There are savings to cover the cases of sports, games and other activities[1] of a competitive nature where the physical strength, stamina or other physique of the average woman puts her at a disadvantage to the average man and also with regard to life assurance and accident insurance policies.[2] There is a general exception which applies to a provision conferring benefits on persons of one sex only (disregarding only benefits to persons of the opposite sex which are exceptional or are relatively insignificant) which is contained in a charitable instrument.[3]

1 Sex Discrimination Act 1975, s 44.
2 Sex Discrimination Act 1975, s 45.
3 Sex Discrimination Act 1975, s 43 as amended by the Sex Discrimination Act 1975 (Amendment of Section 43) Order 1977, SI 1977/528. See *Hugh-Jones v St John's College, Cambridge* [1979] ICR 848, EAT.

Discriminatory practices

7.40 A person is guilty of a discriminatory practice on the application by him of a requirement or condition resulting in an act of discrimination which is unlawful by virtue of any provision of Pt II or Pt III of the Sex Discrimination Act 1975 taken with s 1(1)(b) or s 3(1)(b), or which would be likely to result in such an act of discrimination if the persons to whom it is applied were not all one sex. If and so long as the person applies the discriminatory practice, or he operates practices or other arrangements which in any circumstances would call for the application by him of a discriminatory practice he contravenes s 37. Proceedings in respect of contravention of this provision may only be brought by the Equal Opportunities Commission.[1] Similarly, it is unlawful for a person who has authority over another person, or in accordance with whose wishes that other person is accustomed to act, to instruct him to do any act which is unlawful by virtue of Pt II of the Sex Discrimination Act 1975, or procure or attempt to procure the doing by him of any such act.[2] It is unlawful to induce, or attempt to induce, a person to do any act in contravention of Pt II of the Act, by providing or offering to provide him with any benefit, or subjecting, or threatening to subject, him to any detriment.[3] This applies whether the offer is direct or indirect.[4] Enforcement in these cases also lies with the Equal Opportunities Commission.

1 Sex Discrimination Act 1975, s 37(3).
2 Sex Discrimination Act 1975, s 39.
3 Sex Discrimination Act 1975, s 40(1).
4 Sex Discrimination Act 1975, s 40(2).

Aiding another to do an unlawful act and vicarious liability

7.41 A person who knowingly aids another person to do an unlawful act is himself guilty of an unlawful act[1] and anything done by a person in the course of his employment is treated as done by his employer as well as by him, whether or not it was done with the employer's knowledge or approval.[2] However, in proceedings taken under the Sex Discrimination Act 1975 against any person in respect of an act alleged to have been done by an employee of his, it is a defence for the person to prove that he took such steps as were reasonably practicable to prevent the employee from doing that act, or from doing in the course of his employment acts of that description.[3] Anything done by a person as agent for another person with the authority (express, implied, precedent or subsequent) of the other is treated as done by the principal as well as by the agent.[4]

1 Sex Discrimination Act 1975, s 42. A person does not knowingly aid another to do an unlawful act if he acts in reliance on a statement made by the other person that by reason of the Act the act which he aids would not be unlawful and it is reasonable for him to rely on the statement: s 42(3). See *Johnson v HM Prison Service* (1996) Times, 31 December where an award was upheld against fellow employees.
2 Sex Discrimination Act 1975, s 41.
3 Sex Discrimination Act 1975, s 41(3).
4 Sex Discrimination Act 1975, s 41(2). See *Jones v Tower Boot Co Ltd* [1997] NLJR 60 in which the Court of Appeal held that the words 'in the course of employment' are wider than in tortious liability; and see also *Burton v De Vere Hotels* [1996] IRLR 596.

Positive discrimination

7.42 In certain cases the Sex Discrimination Act 1975 does allow discrimination to take place. For instance when a training body affords one sex only access to facilities for training, which would help to fit them for that work, or encourages women only, or men only, to take advantage of opportunities of doing that work when it appears to the training body that any time within the 12 months immediately preceding the doing of the discriminatory act, there were no persons of the sex in question doing the work in Great Britain, or the number of persons of that sex doing the work in Great Britain was comparatively small.[1] Further provisions relating to training when similar shortages apply locally and when training is provided for those in special need by reason of the period for which they have been discharging domestic or family responsibilities to the exclusion of regular full-time employment are contained in s 47. There are also exceptions allowing certain discrimination in training by employers, employers' associations, trade unions and professional and trade associations.[2] These organisations may reserve seats on constituent bodies for persons of a particular sex, or make extra seats on the body available (by election, co-option or otherwise) for persons of that sex when the number of persons of that sex is below the minimum, where in the organisation's opinion the provision is needed in the circumstances to secure a reasonable lower limit to the number of members of that sex serving on the body.[3]

1 Sex Discrimination Act 1975, s 47.
2 Sex Discrimination Act 1975, s 48.
3 Sex Discrimination Act 1975, s 49(1). This does not make lawful discrimination in arrangements for determining entitlement to vote in an election of members of the body, or otherwise to choose the persons to serve on the body, or discrimination in any arrangements concerning membership of the organisation itself: s 49(2).

Relationship with the Equal Pay Act 1970

7.43   In the broadest of terms if an employer contravenes the equality clause, then the employee's ground for complaint lies under the Equal Pay Act 1970; in other cases of discrimination, then the Sex Discrimination Act 1975 applies. The position is dealt with by s 8(2)–(5) of the Sex Discrimination Act 1975[1] which are as follows:

'(2)   Section 1 (1) of the Equal Pay Act 1970 (as set out in subsection (1) above) does not apply in determining for the purposes of section 6(1)(b) of this Act the terms on which employment is offered.

(3)   Where a person offers a woman employment on certain terms, and if she accepted the offer then, by virtue of an equality clause, any of those terms would fall to be modified, or any additional term would fall to be included, the offer shall be taken to contravene section 6(1)(b).

(4)   Where a person offers a woman employment on certain terms, and subsection (3) would apply but for the fact that, on her acceptance of the offer, section 1(3) of the Equal Pay Act 1970 (as set out in subsection (1) above) would prevent the equality clause from operating, the offer shall be taken not to contravene section 6(1)(b).

(5)   An act does not contravene section 6(2) if:
   (a)   it contravenes a term modified or included by virtue of an equality clause, or
   (b)   it would contravene such a term but for the fact that the equality clause is prevented from operating by section 1(3) of the Equal Pay Act 1970.'

1 See also *Meeks v National Union of Agricultural and Allied Workers* [1976] IRLR 198.

Enforcement – time limits

7.44   If an employee, or prospective employee considers that she has been discriminated against contrary to Pt II of the Sex Discrimination Act 1975, she may present a complaint to an industrial tribunal.[1] This should be done before the end of the period of three months beginning when the act complained of was done,[2] unless the tribunal considers that in all the circumstances of the case it is just and equitable to consider the complaint out of time.[3]

1 Sex Discrimination Act 1975, s 63. This is not the case where the complaint is against a qualifying body under s 13(1) of the Act and there is a statutory right of appeal: s 63(2). Facilities for conciliation are available, see Chapter 18.

2 Sex Discrimination Act 1975, s 76(1). Section 76(6) is as follows:

'(6) For the purposes of this section:

(a) where the inclusion of any term in a contract renders the making of the contract an unlawful act that act shall be treated as extending throughout the duration of the contract, and

(b) any act extending over a period shall be treated as done at the end of that period, and

(c) a deliberate omission shall be treated as done when the person in question decided upon it,

and in the absence of evidence establishing the contrary a person shall be taken for the purposes of this section to decide upon an omission when he does an act inconsistent with doing the omitted act or, if he has done no such inconsistent act, when the period expires within which he might reasonably have been expected to do the omitted act if it was to be done.'

3 Sex Discrimination Act 1975, s 76(5). This differs from the test in unfair dismissal cases, see Chapter 15. In *Hutchinson v Westward Television Ltd* [1977] ICR 279, EAT, it was held that the industrial tribunal is entitled to take into account anything which it adjudges relevant and is unlikely to be assisted by decisions under the unfair dismissal legislation.

Remedies

7.45 If the tribunal finds that the complaint is well founded it will make such of the following orders as it considers just and equitable:

(1) An order declaring the rights of the complainant and the respondent in relation to the act to which the complaint relates.[1]

(2) An order requiring the respondent to pay to the complainant compensation of an amount corresponding to any damages which could have been ordered by a county court if the complaint had been under s 66 of the Act.[2]

(3) A recommendation that the employer take within a specified period action appearing to the tribunal to be practicable for the purposes of obviating, or reducing, the adverse effect on the complainant of any act of discrimination to which the complaint relates.[3] If the respondent without reasonable justification fails to comply with a recommendation made by an industrial tribunal, then if it thinks it is just and equitable to do so, it may increase the amount of compensation required to be paid to the complainant in respect of the complaint and, if an order to pay compensation had not previously been made, it may make such an order.[4]

1 Sex Discrimination Act 1975, s 65(1)(a).
2 Sex Discrimination Act 1975, s 65(1)(b).
3 Sex Discrimination Act 1975, s 65(1)(c).
4 Sex Discrimination Act 1975, s 65(3)(3).

Compensation

7.46 The Sex Discrimination and Equal Pay (Remedies) Regulations 1993[1] made two fundamental changes. The first is that they remove the ceiling which hitherto existed and now compensation is at large. Secondly, the regulations conferred a right to interest. The position used to be that where the complaint was one of indirect discrimination on grounds of sex or married status no damages were awarded at all if the respondent proved that the requirement or condition was not applied with the intention of treating the claimant unfavourably on the ground of his sex or marital status. This provision has now been amended by the Sex Discrimination and Equal Pay (Remedies) Regulations 1996[2] and a tribunal may make such an order if it is just and equitable to do so.[3] The damages may include compensation for injury to feelings, whether or not they include compensation under any other head.[4] It would be beyond the scope of this book to set out in any detail the decisions as to the assessment of compensation. In the leading case of *Ministry of Defence v Cannock*[5] Morison J set out helpful guidelines as to the basis upon which compensation should be assessed under the new unlimited jurisdiction.

1 SI 1993/2798. See now the Industrial Tribunal (Interest on Awards in Discrimination Cases) Regulations 1996, SI 1996/2803.
2 SI 1996/438.
3 Sex Discrimination Act 1975, s 65(1A) and (1B) as amended.
4 Sex Discrimination Act 1975, s 66(4).
5 [1994] IRLR 509. See also *Johnson v HM Prison Service* (1996) Times, 31 December for an award of £28,500 for injury to feelings and aggravated damages.

Restriction on publicity

7.47 For many years there have been restrictions on the reporting of the identity of the victims of sexual offences. Whilst industrial tribunals are not, of course, criminal courts and cases in which salacious details are given in evidence form only a small part of their workload, nevertheless it was an anomaly that such details could be given and reported. Under what is now s 11 of the Industrial Tribunals Act 1996 regulations have been made which restrict what may be reported in cases involving sexual misconduct and there are similar regulations governing proceedings in the Employment Appeal Tribunal.

Equal Opportunities Commission

7.48 The Equal Opportunities Commission may play several distinct types of role in connection with discrimination in the employment field. It can take a positive action by instituting formal investigations, issuing non-discrimination notices[1] and in instituting legal proceedings itself in respect of discrimination, and also it has powers to assist individual complainants on the ground that the case raises a question of principle, or it is unreasonable having regard to the complexity of the case, or the applicant's position in relation to the respondent or another person involved, or any other matter, to expect the applicant to deal with the case unaided or by reason of any other special consideration.[2] The Commission has power to conduct formal investigations either of its own volition or when required to do so by the Secretary of State.[3] A non-discrimination notice may be issued during the course of a formal investigation if the Commission decides that a breach of the Sex Discrimination Act 1975 or the Equal Pay Act 1970 has occurred.[4] The requirements as to non-discrimination notices are beyond the scope of this book, but there is a right of appeal against the notice[5] and the Commission is obliged to establish and maintain a register of such notices which have become final.[6]

1 Sex Discrimination Act 1975, s 67.
2 Sex Discrimination Act 1975, s 75(1).
3 Sex Discrimination Act 1975, s 57.
4 Sex Discrimination Act 1975, s 67.

5 Sex Discrimination Act 1975, s 68.
6 Sex Discrimination Act 1975, s 70.

Persistent discrimination

7.49 If during a period of five years beginning on the date on which either a non-discrimination notice served on an employer became final, or a court or tribunal has determined that an employer had committed an unlawful act of discrimination, or an act in breach of a term modified or included by virtue of an equality clause under s 2 of the Equal Pay Act 1970, it appears to the Commission that unless the employer is restrained he is likely to commit one or more further such acts the Commission may apply to a county court for an injunction restraining him from doing so. If the court is satisfied that the application is well founded it may grant the injunction in the terms applied for, or in more limited terms.[1] The Commission should not allege that a person to whom proceedings relate has done an act which is within the jurisdiction of the industrial tribunal unless a finding by the industrial tribunal that he did the act, has become final.[2]

1 Sex Discrimination Act 1975, s 71(1).
2 Sex Discrimination Act 1975, s 71(2). A finding by a tribunal becomes final when an appeal against the finding is dismissed, withdrawn or abandoned, or when the time for appealing expires without an appeal having been brought: s 82(4). With a view to making an application under s 71(1) (and also s 72(4) which relates to discrimination in advertising and pressure and instructions to discriminate) the Commission may present a complaint to an industrial tribunal that the respondent has done an act within the tribunal's jurisdiction. The tribunal can make similar orders to those mentioned at **7.45**, other than an order for compensation: s 73(1). A finding by an industrial tribunal under the Equal Pay Act 1970 or the Sex Discrimination Act 1975, if final, is treated as conclusive by the county court on an application under s 71(1) or s 72(4) or in proceedings on an equality clause and by an industrial tribunal on a complaint made by a person affected by the act in relation to an equality clause: s 73(3).

Codes of practice

7.50 The Race Relations Act 1976 introduced s 56A into the Sex Discrimination Act 1975. This provides that the Equal Opportunities Commission may issue codes of practice containing such practical guidance as the Commission thinks fit for either or both the elimination of discrimination in the field of employment and the promotion of equality of opportunity in that field between men and women.[1] The codes of practice may include such practical guidance as the Commission thinks fit as to what steps it is reasonably practicable for employers to take for the purpose of preventing their employees from doing in the course of their employment acts made unlawful by the Act.[2] There are the usual provisions for publication and consultation regarding draft codes laid before both Houses of Parliament. A failure on the part of any person to observe any provision of a code of practice does not of itself render him liable to any proceedings but in any proceedings under the Sex Discrimination Act 1975 before an industrial tribunal any code of practice issued under the Act is admissible in evidence and if any provision of such a code appears to the tribunal to be relevant to any question arising in the proceedings it shall be taken into account in determining that question.[3]

1 Sex Discrimination Act 1975, s 56A(1). The only code which has been issued is the Code of Practice for the Elimination of Discrimination on the Grounds of Sex and Marriage and the Promotion of Equality of Opportunity in Employment (1985). See Appendix 3 for the Code. The Commission has published guidance for employers.

2 Sex Discrimination Act 1975, s 56A(11).
3 Sex Discrimination Act 1975, s 56A(10).

Obtaining information

7.51   Under the provisions of s 74 of the Sex Discrimination Act 1975 the Secretary of State is empowered to prescribe forms to assist aggrieved persons to question the respondent on his reasons for doing any relevant act, or on any matter which may be relevant. The Sex Discrimination (Questions and Replies) Order 1975[1] has been made in pursuance of these powers and sets out a form of questionnaire to be completed by the aggrieved person as well as a reply by the respondent. The forms are available both from the Equal Opportunities Commission and from local offices of the Employment Service Agency. Where the aggrieved person questions the respondent, whether using the prescribed form or not, the questions and the replies of the respondent are admissible as evidence in proceedings.

1 SI 1975/2048.

7.52   If it appears to the court or tribunal that the respondent deliberately and without reasonable excuse omitted to reply within a reasonable period, or that his reply is evasive or equivocal, the court or tribunal may draw any inference from that fact that it considers just and equitable to draw, including an inference that the respondent committed an unlawful act.[1] In proceedings before an industrial tribunal[2] a question and reply is only admissible as evidence when the question was served before a complaint had been presented to a tribunal, if it was so served within the period of three months beginning when the act complained of was done, and where it was served when a complaint had been presented to a tribunal either, if it was so served within the period of 21 days beginning with the day on which the complaint was presented, or if it was so served later with leave given, and within a period specified by a direction of the tribunal. The question and reply procedure may be of great assistance in preparing cases for hearing before industrial tribunals in employment cases. For this reason it may be important from the employee's point of view that they are raised of the employer at the appropriate time and, from the employer's point of view, that they are properly replied to

1 Sex Discrimination Act 1975, s 74(2).
2 See the Sex Discrimination (Questions and Replies) Order 1975, SI 1975/2048 (as amended by SI 1977/844), art 5.

Discrimination on grounds of race, colour, nationality or ethnic origins

7.53   The Race Relations Act 1976 came fully into effect on 13 June 1977. The Act follows the form of the Sex Discrimination Act 1975 and is framed in similar terms to it. In considering various aspects of the Sex Discrimination Act 1975 above, cases under the Race Relations Act 1976 have been cited. It is not intended to set out those matters again, but to cross-refer to relevant matters which have already been decided. The 1976 Act also distinguishes between direct and indirect discrimination.

7.53 *Discrimination (including pregnancy)*

Discrimination falling within s 1(1)(a) is 'direct' discrimination and discrimination falling within s 1(1)(b) is 'indirect' discrimination. See **7.10** et seq for a fuller analysis.

7.54 Racial discrimination is defined by s 1 of the Race Relations Act 1976 as follows:

'(1)   A person discriminates against another in any circumstances relevant for the purposes of any provision of this Act if—

(a)   on racial grounds he treats that other less favourably than he treats or would treat other persons; or

(b)   he applies to that other a requirement or condition which he applies or would apply equally to persons not of the same racial group as that other but

    (i)   which is such that the proportion of persons of the same racial group as that other who can comply with it is considerably smaller than the proportion of persons not of that racial group who can comply with it; and

    (ii)   which he cannot show to be justifiable irrespective of the colour, race, nationality or ethnic or national origins of the person to whom it is applied; and

    (iii)   which is to the detriment of that other because he cannot comply with it.

(2)   It is hereby declared that, for the purposes of this Act, segregating a person from other persons on racial grounds is treating him less favourably than they are treated.'

Direct discrimination

7.55   In *Zarczynska v Levy*[1] the Employment Appeal Tribunal held that a barmaid sacked for refusing to obey instructions not to serve coloured customers had been sacked on racial grounds. Motive is irrelevant. Thus when a local authority withdrew an offer of employment because it was feared that other employees would take industrial action this was held to be discrimination.[2] It is not unlawful to discriminate to comply with the law. Thus to require evidence of permission to work from those who were not EC citizens was permitted.[3] See **7.10** for a fuller analysis.

1 [1978] IRLR 532; see also *Johnson v Timber Tailors (Midlands) Ltd* [1978] IRLR 146.
2 *R v Commission for Racial Equality, ex p Westminster City Council* [1985] ICR 827, CA.
3 *Dhatt v McDonalds Hamburgers* [1991] ICR 238, CA.

Indirect discrimination

7.56   It is not unknown for employers to stipulate that employees must live within close proximity to their workplace. If such a condition is not justifiable, then it would be indirect discrimination. In reality in some cases such adverts are a thinly disguised attempt to exclude those of ethnic origin. A rule forbidding beards on grounds of hygiene has been held to be justified.[1] Justification requires a balancing act between the reasonable, objective needs of the employer and the potentially discriminatory effect of the imposition of a condition.[2]

1 *Panesar v Nestle Co Ltd* [1980] ICR 144n, [1980] IRLR 64, CA.
2 See **7.13** et seq for further discussion of justification.

Racial grounds and racial group

7.57 The statutory definition is contained in s 3 of the Race Relations Act 1976 which provides:

'(1) In this Act, unless the context otherwise requires—

"racial grounds" means any of the following grounds, namely colour, race, nationality or ethnic or national origins;

"racial group" means a group of persons defined by reference to colour, race, nationality or ethnic or national origins, and references to a person's racial group refer to any racial group into which he falls.

(2) The fact that a racial group comprises two or more distinct racial groups does not prevent it from constituting a particular racial group for the purposes of this Act.

(3) In this Act—
  (a) references to discrimination refer to any discrimination falling within section 1 or 2; and
  (b) references to racial discrimination refer to any discrimination falling within section 1, and related expressions shall be construed accordingly.

(4) A comparison of the case of a person of a particular racial group with that of a person not of that group under section 1 must be such that the relevant circumstances in the one case are the same, or not materially different, in the other.'

Racial grounds

7.58 In *Ealing London Borough Council v Race Relations Board*[1] a distinction was drawn between racial origin and citizenship. The issue in each case is one of causation: was the less favourable treatment due to racial considerations? As noted above in *Zarczynska's* case a white employee dismissed for refusing to obey an instruction not to serve a black customer is the victim of racial discrimination.

1 [1972] 1 All ER 105, HL.

Racial group

7.59 The definitive ruling is that of the House of Lords in *Mandla v Dowell Lee*[1] in which it was held that the word ethnic embraced a wider group than the biological concept of descending from a common racial stock. It was a group which had a long shared history with a sense of a cultural identity which distinguished it from the wider society. A common language, geographical origin, literary tradition and religious belief are all matters which would be relevant. Thus Sikhs were held to be a racial group within the Act but Rastafarians were not.[2] Language is not conclusive. In *Gwynedd County Council v Jones*[3] the Employment Appeal Tribunal reached the not unsurprising conclusion that there are not two racial groups depending upon whether they are Welsh or non-Welsh speaking. There is no requirement that the comparison should be with only one ethnic group. A number of ethnic groups defined by colour may be regarded as a racial group.[4] Although there is no prohibition against discrimination against religions as such, it has been held that the word 'Jews' refers to a racial group.[5]

1 [1983] ICR 385.
2 *Crown Suppliers (Property Services Agency) v Dawkins* [1993] ICR 517.
3 [1986] ICR 833.
4 *Lambeth London Borough v Commission for Racial Equality* [1990] ICR 768.
5 *Seide v Gillette Industries Ltd* [1980] IRLR 427.

Victimisation

7.60 Discrimination is by way of victimisation in circumstances relevant for any provision of the Race Relations Act 1976 if a person treats another ('the person victimised') less favourably than in those circumstances he treats or would treat other persons and does so by reason that the person victimised has brought proceedings against the discriminator or any other person under the Race Relations Act 1976, or has given evidence or information in connection with proceedings brought by any person against the discriminator or any other person under the Act or otherwise done anything under or by reference to the Act in relation to the discriminator or any other person, or has alleged that the discriminator or any other person has committed an act which (whether or not the allegation so states) would amount to a contravention of the Race Relations Act 1976, or by reason that the discriminator knows that the person victimised intends to do any of those things, or suspects that the person might have done, or intends to do any of them[1] unless the allegations are false and not made in good faith.[2] Some of the limitations placed on the remedy against victimisation have already been explored (see **7.17**).

1 Race Relations Act 1976, s 2(1).
2 Race Relations Act 1976, s 2(2).

Employment

7.61 Part II of the Race Relations Act 1976 sets out situations of discrimination in the employment field. Employment is defined widely as employment under a contract of service or of apprenticeship or a contract personally to execute any work or labour and related expressions are construed accordingly.[1]

1 Race Relations Act 1976, s 78(1). Crown employees are included, including members of the armed services: s 75. See s 75 for the detailed provisions. The holding of office as a police constable is treated as employment for the purposes of Pt II of the Act: s 16. See **7.19** for a fuller analysis. For partners see s 10 and for barristers s 26A of the Act.

Discrimination

7.62 It is unlawful for a person in relation to employment by him at an establishment in Great Britain to discriminate against another in the arrangements which he makes for the purpose of determining who shall be offered employment, in the terms of which he offers that employment, or by refusing or deliberately omitting to offer him that employment.[1] So far as an existing employee is concerned it is unlawful for the employer to discriminate against the employee in the terms of the employment which he affords him, or in the way he affords him access to opportunities for promotion, transfer or training, or any other benefits, facilities or services, or by refusing or deliberately omitting to afford him access to them, or by dismissing him or subjecting him to any other detriment.[2] The Court of Appeal has considered[3] whether it was a detriment for a black typist to hear one manager say to another manager 'get the typing done by the wog'. There were a number of procedural issues in that case. It is suggested that there is now clear authority that racial abuse is a detriment.[4]

1 Race Relations Act 1976, s 4(1).
2 Race Relations Act 1976, s 4(2). The subsection applies to employment at an establishment in Great Britain as defined in s 8. The area of operation may be extended in manner similar to that of the Sex Discrimination Act 1975.
3 *De Sousa v Automobile Association* [1986] ICR 514.
4 *Burton v De Vere Hotels* [1996] IRLR 596 and *Johnson v HM Prison Service* (1996) Times, 31 December.

Public facilities

7.63   Under s 4(4) the employment discrimination provisions do not apply when the employer operates an undertaking which is open to the public and the discrimination from which the employee suffers is as a member of the public rather than as an employee. Subject to the exceptions set out in s 4 the remedy for the employee is an action in the county court.

Exceptions

7.64   There is no power to contract out of the Act (s 72(3)) and its provisions apply unless there is a specific statutory exception.

Genuine occupational qualifications

7.65   The scope of this exception is narrower than in the case of sexual discrimination. Effectively it involves dramatic performances and employment as a model in which a person of a racial group is required for authenticity. The other exceptions are those concerned with restaurants in which a racial group is required for authenticity and working for an employer which promotes the welfare of a particular racial group and that can be done most effectively by a member of that racial group. Section 5(2) provides that it is a genuine occupational requirement where:

(a)   the job involves participation in a dramatic performance or other entertainment in a capacity for which a person of that racial group is required for reasons of authenticity; or

(b)   the job involves participation as an artist or photographic model in the production of a work of art, visual image or sequence of visual images for which a person of that racial group is required for reasons of authenticity; or

(c)   the job involves working in a place where food or drink is provided to and consumed by members of the public or a section of the public in a particular setting for which, in that job, a person of that racial group is required for reasons of authenticity; or

(d)   the holder of the job provides persons of that racial group with personal services promoting their welfare and those services can most effectively be provided by a person of that racial group.

The job is still one for which being of a particular racial group is a genuine occupational qualification where some only of the duties fall within the above heads, but the genuine occupational qualification exclusion does not apply to the filling of a vacancy at a time when the employer already has employees of the racial group in question who are capable of carrying out the duties, whom it would be reasonable to employ on those duties and whose numbers are sufficient to meet the employer's likely requirements in respect of those duties without undue inconvenience.[1]

1 Race Relations Act 1976, s 5(3) as qualified by s 5(4). For the similar provisions in sex discrimination, see 7.23.

Training for a job abroad

7.66 Acts done by an employer for the benefit of a person not ordinarily resident in Great Britain, in or in connection with employing him at an establishment in Great Britain, where the purpose of that employment is to provide him with training in skills which in the understanding of the employer he intends to exercise wholly outside Great Britain are not included.[1]

1 Race Relations Act 1976, s 6.

Recruiting seamen abroad

7.67 Acts done by an employer in, or in connection with, employment by him on a ship in the case of a person who applied or was engaged for that employment outside Great Britain are not unlawful.[1]

1 Race Relations Act 1976, s 9. A person brought to Great Britain with a view to entering into an agreement in Great Britain to be employed on any ship is treated as having applied for employment outside Great Britain: s 9(4). See also s 9(2) and (3).

Employment in a private household

7.68 Employment for the purposes of a private household is excluded, but not if the discrimination is by victimisation.[1]

1 Race Relations Act 1976, s 4(3).

Complying with a statutory enactment

7.69 It is not unlawful to do any act necessary to comply with a statutory enactment,[1] nor is it unlawful to discriminate against another on the basis of that other's nationality or place of ordinary residence, or the length of time which he has been present, or resident, in or outside the United Kingdom, or an area within the United Kingdom, if done in pursuance of arrangements made or approved by a minister of the Crown or in order to comply with any condition imposed by a minister of the Crown.[2]

1 Race Relations Act 1976, s 41(1).
2 Race Relations Act 1976, s 41(2).

National security

7.70 It is not unlawful to do any act for the purpose of safeguarding national security.[1]

1 Race Relations Act 1976, s 42. The usual rules for ministerial certificates apply: s 69(2) and (3).

Contract workers

7.71 There are special provisions relating to discrimination against contract workers which apply to any work for a person ('the principal') which is available for doing by individuals who are employed not by the principal himself but by another person, who supplies them under a contract made with the principal.[1] The provisions are very similar to those of the Sex Discrimination Act 1975, and there is a similar exception with regard to genuine occupational qualifications for the job. It is unlawful for an employment agency to discriminate either in the terms on which the agency offers to provide any of its services, or by refusing or deliberately omitting to provide any of its services, or in the way it provides any of its services.[2] 'Services' are widely defined and there is a saving for an employment agency if it proves that it acted in reliance on a statement made to it by the employer that its action would not be unlawful and it was reasonable for it to rely on that statement.[3] There is criminal liability on the part of a person who knowingly or recklessly makes a statement which is in a material respect false or misleading.[4]

1 Race Relations Act 1976, s 7. See in particular s 7(4) and s 9(2).
2 Race Relations Act 1976, s 14.
3 Race Relations Act 1976, s 14(5).
4 Race Relations Act 1976, s 14(6).

Advertisements

7.72   Section 29 makes it unlawful to publish or cause to be published an advertisement which indicates, or might reasonably be understood as indicating, an intention to discriminate unlawfully. It does not apply to an advertisement which indicates that persons of any class defined otherwise than by reference to colour, race, ethnic or national origin are required for employment outside Great Britain. There are provisions similar to those outlined in relation to employment agencies (see **7.36**) allowing the publisher of an advertisement who published it in reliance on a statement made to him by the person who caused it to be published to the effect that the publication would not be unlawful and that it was reasonable for him to rely on the statement to escape liability.[1] A person who knowingly or recklessly makes such a statement which is in a material respect false or misleading commits an offence.[2]

1 Race Relations Act 1976, s 29(4).
2 Race Relations Act 1976, s 29(5).

Trade unions, bodies conferring qualifications or providing vocational training

7.73   There are provisions in the Race Relations Act 1976 which seek to prevent organisations of workers, employers' organisations and other organisations whose members carry on a particular profession or trade for the purposes of which the organisation exists, from discriminating unlawfully.[1] It is unlawful for an authority or body which can confer authorisation or qualifications to discriminate contrary to the Act[2] and for vocational training bodies[3] to discriminate unlawfully. It is unlawful for a firm consisting of six or more partners to discriminate in relation to a position as a partner in a firm[4] and in making an appointment by a minister of the Crown, or government department, to an office or post, no act should be done which would be unlawful discrimination if the Crown were an employer for the purposes of the Race Relations Act 1976.[5]

1 Race Relations Act 1976, s 11.
2 Race Relations Act 1976, s 12.
3 Race Relations Act 1976, s 13.
4 Race Relations Act 1976, s 10.
5 Race Relations Act 1976, s 76, but see s 75(5) and the Race Relations (Prescribed Public Bodies) Regulations 1977, SI 1977/1774.

Discriminatory practice

7.74 A person is guilty of a discriminatory practice on the application by him of a requirement or condition which results in an act of discrimination which is unlawful by virtue of any provision of Pt II or Pt III of the Act taken with s 1(1)(b), or which would be likely to result in such an act of discrimination if the persons to whom it is applied included persons of any particular racial group as regards which there has been no occasion for applying it. If and so long as the person applies the discriminatory practice, or operates practices or other arrangements which in any circumstances would call for the application by him of a discriminatory practice, he contravenes s 28.[1] Proceedings in respect of contravention of this section may only be brought by the Commission for Racial Equality.[2] Similarly it is unlawful for a person who has authority over another person, or in accordance with whose wishes that other person is accustomed to act to instruct him to do any act which is unlawful by virtue of Pt II or Pt III or procure or attempt to procure the doing by him of any such act.[3] It is unlawful to induce or attempt to induce a person to do any act[4] in contravention of Pt II or Pt III of the Act.[4] This applies whether the attempt is direct or indirect.[5]

1 Race Relations Act 1976, s 28(2).
2 Race Relations Act 1976, s 28(3).
3 Race Relations Act 1976, s 30.
4 Race Relations Act 1976, s 31(1).
5 Race Relations Act 1976, s 31(2).

Vicarious liability

7.75 A person who knowingly aids another person's unlawful act is himself treated as doing the unlawful act[1] and anything done by a person in the course of his employment is treated (except as regards criminal offences) as done by his employer as well as by him, whether or not it is done with the employer's knowledge or approval.[2] However, in proceedings taken under the Race Relations Act 1976 against any person in respect of an act alleged to have been done by an employee of his, it is a defence for that person to prove that he took such steps as were reasonably practicable to prevent the employee from doing that act, or from doing in the course of his employment acts of that description.[3] Anything done by a person as agent for another person with the authority (whether express or implied, precedent or subsequent) of that other person is treated for the purposes of the Act (except as regards criminal offences) as done by that person as well as by him.[4] See **7.41** for a fuller analysis.

1 Race Relations Act 1976, s 33.
2 Race Relations Act 1976, s 32.
3 Race Relations Act 1976, s 32(3).
4 Race Relations Act 1976, s 32(2).

Positive discrimination

7.76   In certain cases the Race Relations Act 1976 does allow discrimination to take place. It is not unlawful to do acts in affording persons of a particular racial group access to facilities or services to meet the special needs of the persons of that group in relation to their education, training or welfare or any ancillary benefits.[1]

1 Race Relations Act 1976, s 35.

Training

7.77   Acts are not unlawful in accordance with the Act when done by a training body in relation to particular work in, or in connection with, affording only persons of a particular racial group access to facilities for training which would help to fit them for that work, or encouraging only persons of a particular racial group to take advantage of opportunities for doing that work where it appears to the training body that at any time within the 12 months immediately preceding the doing of the act, there were no persons of that group among those doing that work in Great Britain, or the proportion of persons of that group among those doing that work in Great Britain was small in comparison with the proportion of persons of that group among the population of Great Britain.[1] There is also an exception which applies where access to training facilities, or encouragement to take advantage of opportunities for doing particular work at an establishment is given by an employer when at any time during the preceding 12 months no person of the racial group, or only a small proportion of them compared with the proportion of those employed by the employer there, or among the population of the area from which the employer normally recruits persons for work in his employment at the establishment do that work.[2] There is a similar exception which applies to training to fit persons for holding posts of any kind in organisations where at any time during the preceding 12 months persons of the racial group are not represented, or only a small proportion of them is represented, in comparison with the proportion of persons of that group among the members of the organisation.[3] A similar rule applies to membership of organisations.[4]

1 Race Relations Act 1976, s 37(1) and (2).
2 Race Relations Act 1976, s 38(1).
3 Race Relations Act 1976, s 38(3).
4 Race Relations Act 1976, s 38(5).

Games and charities

7.78   There are savings with regard to sports and competitions.[1] A provision which is contained in a charitable instrument and which provides for conferring benefits on persons of a class defined by reference to colour shall have effect for all purposes as if it provided for conferring the like benefit on persons of the class which results if the restriction by reference to colour is disregarded, or where the original class is defined by reference to colour only, on persons generally.[2]

1 Race Relations Act 1976, s 39.
2 Race Relations Act 1976, s 34(1) and see remaining provisions of the section.

Enforcement

Industrial tribunals

7.79   If an employee, or prospective employee, considers that he has been discriminated against contrary to Pt II of the Act he may present a complaint to an industrial tribunal.[1] This should be done before the end of the period of three months beginning when the act complained of was done,[2] unless the tribunal considers that in all the circumstances of the case it is just and equitable to consider the complaint out of time.[3] An industrial tribunal will only entertain a complaint by the Commission for Racial Equality under s 64(1) if it is presented before the end of the six months beginning when the act complained of was done.[4] There is a similar saving when in all the circumstances of the case the industrial tribunal considers it just and equitable to consider the complaint.[5]

1 Race Relations Act 1976, s 54(1). The services of a conciliation officer are available, see Chapter 18. With the exception of seeking prerogative orders the only possible proceedings in respect of acts which are unlawful by virtue of a provision of the Race Relations Act 1976 are those provided for by the Act: s 53. By virtue of s 75(9) servicemen apply not to an industrial tribunal but to the appropriate service tribunal.
2 Race Relations Act 1976, s 68(1).
3 Race Relations Act 1976, s 68(6).
4 Race Relations Act 1976, s 68(5).
5 Race Relations Act 1976, s 68(5).

Remedies

7.80   If the tribunal finds that the complaint is well founded it will make such of the following orders that it considers just and equitable:
(1)   an order declaring the rights of the complainant and the respondent in relation to the act to which the complaint relates;
(2)   an order requiring the respondent to pay to the complainant compensation of an amount corresponding to any damages he may have been awarded by a county court if the complaint had been made under s 57 of the Act;[1]
(3)   a recommendation that the respondent take action within a specific period appearing to the tribunal to be practicable for the purpose of obviating or reducing the adverse effect on the complainant of any act of discrimination to which the complaint relates.[2] If the respondent without reasonable justification fails to comply with a recommendation made by an industrial tribunal, then if it thinks it is just and equitable to do so, it may increase the amount of compensation required to be paid to the complainant in respect of the complaint and if an order to pay compensation had not previously been made it may make such an order.[3]

1 Race Relations Act 1976, s 56(1).
2 Race Relations Act 1976, s 56(1)(c).
3 Race Relations Act 1976, s 56(4), if it could have been made under s 56(1)(b).

Compensation

7.81   The damages may include compensation for injury to feelings whether or not they include compensation under any other head.[1] There is now no limit on compensation since the Race Relations (Remedies) Act 1994 came into force in July 1994. Since August 1994 interest is payable.[2] In the case of indirect discrimination no award of damages is payable if the respondent proves that the requirement or condition was not applied with the intention of treating the claimant unfavourably on racial grounds.[3]

1 Race Relations Act 1976, s 57(4). See **7.46** and *Johnson v HM Prison Service* (1996) Times, 31 December.
2 Race Relations (Interest on Awards) Regulations 1994, SI 1994/1748 and now the Industrial Tribunal (Interest on Awards in Discrimination Cases) Regulations 1996, SI 1996/2803.
3 Race Relations Act 1976, s 57(3). A similar provision in respect of sex discrimination has been amended, see **7.46**.

Commission for Racial Equality

7.82   The Commission for Racial Equality may play several distinct types of role in connection with discrimination in the employment field. It can take positive action by instituting a formal investigation, issuing non-discrimination notices and itself taking legal proceedings in respect of discrimination. Also it has power to assist individual complainants on the ground that the case raises a question of principle, or on the ground that it was unreasonable, having regard to the complexity of the case, or to the applicant's position in relation to the respondent or another person involved, or to any other matter, to expect the applicant to deal with the case unaided or by reason of any other special consideration.[1] The Commission has power to conduct formal investigations either of its own volition or if required to do so by the Secretary of State.[2] A non-discrimination notice may be issued during the course of the formal investigation if the Commission decides that a breach of the Race Relations Act 1976 has occurred.[3] The requirement of non-discrimination notices are beyond the scope of this book, but there is a right of appeal against the notice[4] and the Commission is obliged to establish and maintain a register of such notices which have become final.[5]

1 Race Relations Act 1976, s 66(1).
2 Race Relations Act 1976, s 48.
3 Race Relations Act 1976, s 58.
4 Race Relations Act 1976, s 59.
5 Race Relations Act 1976, s 61.

Power to seek injunctions

7.83   If during a period of five years beginning on the date on which either a non-discrimination notice served on the employer became final, or a court or tribunal has determined that an employer has committed an unlawful act of discrimination, it appears to the Commission for Racial Equality that unless the employer is restrained he is likely to commit one or more further such acts, the Commission may apply to a county court for an injunction restraining him from doing so.[1] If the court is satisfied that the application is well founded it may grant the injunction in the terms applied for, or in more limited terms. The Commission should not allege that a person to whom the proceedings relate has done an act which is within the jurisdiction of the industrial tribunal unless a finding by the industrial tribunal that he did the act has become final.

1 Race Relations Act 1976, s 62. The Commission has a power in s 64 to present a complaint to an industrial tribunal similar to that of the Equal Opportunities Commission, see **7.49**. A finding of an industrial tribunal when it has become final is conclusive in proceedings under the Act: s 69(1).

Functions of the Commission

7.84 The circumstances in which the Commission for Racial Equality may assist an individual are set out in s 66 of the Act. In cases where the section applies the Commission may give advice, procure or attempt to procure a settlement of any matter in dispute, arrange for the giving of advice or assistance by a solicitor or counsel, arrange for representation by any person including all such assistance as is usually given by a solicitor or counsel in the steps preliminary or incidental to proceedings, or in arriving at or in giving effect to a compromise to avoid or bring to an end any proceedings, or any other form of assistance which the Commission may consider appropriate.[1]

1 Race Relations Act 1976, s 66. Expenses incurred by the Commission constitute a first charge on any costs or expenses ordered or agreed to be paid to the applicant: s 66(5).

Codes of practice

7.85 There is provision for the Commission for Racial Equality to issue codes of practice containing such practical guidance as the Commission thinks fit for either or both the elimination of discrimination in the field of employment and the promotion of equality of opportunity in that field between persons of different racial groups.[1] There are the usual provisions for preparation and publication of draft codes and a requirement that the Commission shall consult with trade unions and employers' organisations and such other organisations or bodies as appear to the Commission to be appropriate. If the Commission determines to proceed with the draft the same is transmitted to the Secretary of State who shall, if he approves it, lay it before both Houses of Parliament, or if not, publish details of his reasons for withholding approval.[2] When the code or codes have become effective failure on the part of any person to observe any provision of a code of practice shall not in itself render him liable to any proceedings, but in any proceedings under the Act before an industrial tribunal any code of practice shall be admissible in evidence and if any provision of such a code appears to the tribunal to be relevant to any question arising in the proceedings it shall be taken into account in determining that question.[3]

1 Race Relations Act 1976, s 47(1). The only code which has been issued is the Code of Practice for the Elimination of Racial Discrimination and the Promotion of Equality of Opportunity in Employment 1983. The codes of practice may include such practical guidance as the Commission thinks fit as to what steps it is reasonably practicable for employers to take for the purpose of preventing their employees from doing in the course of their employment acts made unlawful by the Race Relations Act 1976: s 47(11). See Appendix 3 for the Code.
2 Race Relations Act 1976, s 47(4).
3 Race Relations Act 1976, s 46(10).

Obtaining information

7.86 Under the provisions of the Race Relations Act 1976 the Secretary of State is empowered to prescribe forms to assist aggrieved persons to question the respondent on the reasons for doing any relevant act or any matter which may be relevant.[1] The Race Relations (Questions and Replies) Order 1977[2] has been made in pursuance of these powers and sets out a form of questionnaire which may be completed by the aggrieved person, together with a form which a respondent may, if he so wishes, use to reply to such questions. The forms are available both from the Commission for Racial Equality and from local offices of the job centres. Where the aggrieved person questions the respondent, whether using a prescribed form or not, the questions and the replies of the respondent are admissible as evidence in proceedings. If it appears to the court or tribunal that the respondent, deliberately and without reasonable excuse, omitted to reply within a reasonable period, or that his reply is evasive or equivocal the court or tribunal may draw any inference from the fact that it considers just and equitable to draw, including an inference that a respondent committed an unlawful act.[3] In proceedings before an industrial tribunal a question and reply is only admissible as evidence when the question was served before a complaint had been presented to a tribunal, if it was so served within the period of three months beginning when the act complained of was done and where it was served when a complaint had been presented to a tribunal, either if it was so served within the period of 21 days beginning with the day on which the complaint was presented, or if it was served later with leave given, and within a period specified, by direction of a tribunal.[4]

1 Race Relations Act 1976, s 65.
2 SI 1977/842.
3 Race Relations Act 1976, s 65(2).
4 Race Relations (Questions and Replies) Order 1977, art 5.

Questionnaires

7.87   The question and reply procedure is of great assistance in preparation for hearings before industrial tribunals. For this reason it may be important from the employee's point of view that questions are raised of the employer at the appropriate time and from the employer's point of view that they are properly replied to.

Maternity issues

Introduction

In many professions and occupations the ten years from the ages of the late twenties to the late thirties are critical in terms of career development. They are also the years in which a significant number of women are engaged in child bearing. Any policy which seeks to promote equality of opportunity for women needs to have specific measures to protect women from the inevitable consequences of pregnancy.

In most cases the appropriate course for a woman who has been dismissed due to her pregnancy is to bring claims for both sex discrimination (see **7.88**) and for unfair dismissal (see **7.91**). It should be noted that there are differences between the two claims. The sex discrimination legislation has a wider ambit than the statutory right not to be unfairly dismissed in that it has a wider definition of employment (see **7.19**) and protects the job applicant (see **7.21**). Compensation can be recovered for injury to feelings in a sex discrimination claim (see **7.46**) and if the claim is out of time there is a more liberal test than in unfair dismissal (see **7.44**).

7.87 Discrimination (including pregnancy)

The Employment Rights Act 1996 confers specific rights on the pregnant woman. She has the right to take time off for ante-natal care (see 7.91) and the right to be paid if suspended from work due to medical reasons associated with her pregnancy (see 7.92). The most fundamental right is that it is automatically unfair to dismiss an employee by reason of her pregnancy or a reason connected with it (see 7.93). The employee has a right to have maternity leave (see 7.94); to retain certain benefits whilst away from work (see 7.95) and either an implicit (see 7.95) or express (see 7.96 et seq) right to return to work depending on her length of service. Whilst away from work a woman may, subject to certain conditions, receive maternity pay (see 7.101) or maternity allowance (see 7.119).

Dismissal for pregnancy and sex discrimination

7.88 The earlier authorities decided that dismissal on the ground of pregnancy could not be sex discrimination on the basis that pregnancy could only affect one gender and therefore comparisons could not be made. The law then developed by equating pregnancy with an illness and suggested that the test was whether a comparable male – suffering from a medical condition which would require a period of absence from work – would have been dismissed.[1] The current trend, heavily influenced by European decisions,[2] is to regard dismissal for pregnancy as direct dismissal.

1. *Hayes v Malleable Working Men's Club and Institute* [1985] ICR 703.
2 *Dekker v Stichting VJV-Centrum Plus* [1992] ICR 325.

Direct discrimination

7.89 The matter was considered at length in *Webb v Emo Air Cargo Ltd*. The facts are important. Mrs Webb was employed as a temporary replacement for a member of staff who was pregnant and taking maternity leave. Several weeks after starting work Mrs Webb informed her employer she was pregnant and was dismissed. The industrial tribunal dismissed her claim on the basis that a man in a comparable position would have been dismissed. This approach was accepted at all the appellate stages but the House of Lords referred the case to the European Court.[1] The European Court decided[2] that *comparator approach* was inappropriate and that dismissal of a pregnant woman was direct discrimination. When the House of Lords reconsidered the matter[3] they allowed Mrs Webb's appeal. The judgment posits the possibility that there may be an exception to the general rule that to dismiss a woman because of her pregnancy is direct discrimination when a woman is recruited for a limited period and during the whole, or a substantial, part of the time she would be away due to pregnancy. An obvious example would be a seasonal worker employed for a limited period such as a hotel worker taken on for the Christmas break. Since *Webb* it has been decided that it was unlawful sexual discrimination to dismiss an employee who was absent on maternity leave because her replacement was more efficient[4] and not to renew a fixed-term contract because the employee would not be available at its commencement due to pregnancy.[5]

1 [1993] ICR 175.
2 [1994] ICR 770.
3 [1995] ICR 1021.
4 *Rees v Apollo Watch Repairs plc* [1996] ICR 466.
5 *Caruana v Manchester Airport plc* [1996] IRLR 378.

The reason for dismissal

7.90 An employee who is dismissed will not succeed in an action for sex discrimination if the employer does not know of her pregnancy.[1] Difficulties have arisen when the dismissal has not been so much for the fact of pregnancy but for the consequences of employing an unmarried mother. In *Berrisford v Woodward School (Midland Division) Ltd*[2] the applicant was a matron of a Church of England school. She was not dismissed because she was pregnant – indeed the headmaster made suggestions about the provision of married accommodation – but because she refused to marry the father and the school did not think it would convey the right example to have an unmarried pregnant woman on the staff. The industrial tribunal had made a finding that a comparable man would have been dealt with in this way. The Employment Appeal Tribunal dismissed her appeal. A very different conclusion was reached in the later case of *O'Neill v Governors of St Thomas Moore RCVA Upper School and Bedford County Council*[3] which was decided after *Webb*. In that case an unmarried religious education teacher became pregnant by a Roman Catholic priest and she was dismissed. The Employment Appeal Tribunal reversed the industrial tribunal and found that she was the victim of sexual discrimination. Motive was not a relevant factor and the pregnancy precipitated and permeated the decision to dismiss.

1 *Del Monte Foods Ltd v Mundon* [1980] ICR 694.
2 [1991] ICR 564.
3 [1996] IRLR 372.

The rights under the Employment Rights Act

Time off for ante-natal care

7.91 Section 55 confers upon a pregnant woman the right to have paid time off for ante-natal care in certain circumstances. If advised by a registered medical practitioner, midwife or health visitor to make an appointment she is entitled to take time off in her working hours to enable her to keep such an appointment. Save for the first appointment,[1] the employee must, if requested, produce a certificate that she is pregnant and produce the appointment card or other evidence of the appointment.[2] She is entitled to be paid for the time that is thus taken and the Act sets out the formula as to how such remuneration shall be calculated.[3] If the employer refuses to allow her to take such time off or fails to pay her the remuneration she may make application to an industrial tribunal.[4] The Act provides that the normal time limit of three months should apply.[5] Civil servants are within the provisions[6] but not those in the armed forces,[7] the police,[8] or those working wholly or mainly outside Great Britain.[9]

1 Section 55(3).
2 Section 55(2).
3 Section 56(2) and (3).
4 Section 57(1).
5 Section 57(2).
6 Section 191.
7 Section 192.
8 Section 200.
9 Section 196.

Suspension from work on maternity grounds

7.92   The Management of Health and Safety at Work Regulations 1992,[1] as amended, require, in certain circumstances, an assessment to be made of risks to a new or an expectant mother or her baby. If the new or expectant mother is suspended from work pursuant to the powers contained in the health and safety legislation, she must first be offered suitable alternative employment[2] and if that is not available she is entitled to be paid during the period of suspension.[3] If she unreasonably refuses to take such alternative employment she forfeits the right to remuneration.[4] The Act provides for the method of calculation of the remuneration[5] and the right to remuneration is enforceable in an industrial tribunal in the same way as infringement of the right to time off for ante-natal care.[6] There is no requirement for any continuity of employment to enforce this right.[7]

1 Regulation 13(a) and (b).
2 Section 67.
3 Section 68(1).
4 Section 68(2).
5 Section 69.
6 Section 70.
7 This contrasts with cases of medical suspension where there is a requirement of one month's continuity of employment: s 65(1).

The right not to be dismissed by reason of pregnancy or childbirth
7.93   Section 99 of the Act is the lynchpin of the statutory protection. There is no requirement for any length of service. A dismissal is automatically unfair where the reason, or the principal reason:
(1)   is her pregnancy or for a reason connected with the pregnancy;[1]
(2)   her maternity leave is ended by a dismissal and the reason is that she gave birth or any reason connected with childbirth;[2]
(3)   where after the end of her maternity leave she is dismissed and the reason is that she took maternity leave or availed herself of the benefits of maternity leave;[3]
(4)   where she is dismissed because of a recommendation or requirement to suspend her on health and safety grounds;[4]
(5)   where her maternity leave is ended by her dismissal due to redundancy and she had not been offered suitable alternative employment[5] as required by section 77 of the Act;[6]
(6)   where she has informed her employer she cannot return to work because of illness, produced a sick note from a medical practitioner and within four weeks of the end of the maternity leave she is dismissed and the reason is because of childbirth or a reason connected with it.[7]

Under section 104 of the Act it is automatically unfair to dismiss a woman for asserting a maternity right[8] and by virtue of section 105[9] it is automatically unfair to select a woman for dismissal on the basis that she is pregnant or for any of the reasons set out in section 99(1)(a), (b), (c) or (d).

1 Section 99(1)(a). This would obviously include pregnancy-related sickness and conditions. Even if the initial absence was due to non-pregnancy-related ill health, if the absence which actually led to her dismissal was pregnancy-related, such as a miscarriage, it would be automatically unfair: *George v Beecham Group* [1977] IRLR 43. See also *Clayton v Vigers* [1990] IRLR 177 where the EAT held that 'connected' means 'associated with'.
2 Section 99(1)(b).
3 Section 99(1)(c).
4 Section 99(1)(d). See **7.92**.
5 Section 99(1)(e).

6 Section 77 requires an employer (or his successor or an associated company) *where there is a suitable available vacancy* to offer it to the employee. The new contract must be such that it is suitable and appropriate (s 77(3)(a)) and its provisions as to its terms and conditions of her employment must not be substantially less favourable to her than if she had continued under the old contract (s 77(3)(b)).
7 Section 99(3)(a), (b) or (c).
8 See **15.80**.
9 Section 105(2) and see *Brown v Stockton-on-Tees Borough Council* [1988] ICR 410, HL and see **15.81**.

The right of a pregnant woman to take maternity leave
7.94 Irrespective of her length of service, a woman has the right to take maternity leave[1] subject to complying with certain conditions.[2] The length of such leave is 14 weeks from its commencement or until the birth of the child, if later.[3] It cannot start before the 11th week before the expected date of childbirth.[4] It may be extended beyond the 14-week period if return would breach a statutory enactment.[5] The right to maternity leave is forfeited if the woman does not comply with the obligations imposed by section 74 (requirement to notify commencement of leave) and section 75 (requirement to notify pregnancy). In summary these provisions require a woman to give written notice at least 21 days before the commencement of maternity leave that she is pregnant, the expected week of childbirth (or if childbirth has occurred the date on which it occurred)[6] and if it is not reasonably practicable within these requirements she must do so as soon as is reasonably practicable.[7] If required to do so by her employer she must produce a certificate from a registered medical practitioner or registered midwife stating the expected week of childbirth.[8] In addition the woman must inform her employer at least 21 days before the commencement of her maternity leave of the date of its commencement.[9] If this is not reasonably practicable she must do so as soon as is reasonably practicable.[10] If a woman wants to return to work earlier than the end of the 14th week she must give her employer seven days' notice.[11] If the woman attempts to return to work earlier without having given the seven days' notice, the employer has the right to postpone her return by seven days,[12] subject to the qualification that he cannot postpone her return beyond the end of the 14-week period.[13]

1 Section 71.
2 Set out in ss 74 and 75.
3 Section 73(1).
4 Section 74(2).
5 Section 73(2).
6 Section 75(1).
7 Section 75(1).
8 Section 75(8).
9 Section 74(1).
10 Section 74(3).
11 Section 76(1).
12 Section 76(2).
13 Section 76(3).

The implicit right to return to work
7.95 The combined effect of sections 99 (the right not to be dismissed) and 71 (the right to take maternity leave) is such that irrespective of the length of service a pregnant woman has an implied right to return to work. Indeed the use of the words 'right to work' is a misnomer. The effect of section 71 is that the contract continues and she is entitled to all the benefits, save remuneration,[1] that she would have been entitled to had she not been absent. Thus a

woman on maternity leave has the right to holiday entitlements, share options schemes, BUPA membership and all other contractual rights. If an employee has a contractual right to maternity leave she may take advantage of whichever right is, in any particular respect, the more favourable.[2]

1 Section 71(2).
2 Section 78(1).

The position of a woman who has been employed for a period of at least two years at the beginning of the 11th week prior to the expected week of confinement

7.96 Such an employee has the additional right that she has the right to return to work at any time up to 29 weeks after the beginning of the week in which she gave birth.[1] To qualify the woman must be employed at the beginning of the 11th week prior to her confinement[2] so that if she resigns before that date she has lost the right. A mere statement of general intent that she does not intend to return to work when no leaving date is fixed does not preclude a woman from claiming the right as long as the contract is still subsisting at the 11th week prior to the expected week of confinement.[3] An employee is only entitled to the right to return if she has the right conferred by section 71 (see **7.97**) and she complies with the requirements of section 75(1) (see **7.94**). In addition, when complying with the requirements of section 75(1), she has to notify her employer in writing that she intends to exercise her right to return to work.[4] This requirement is subject to the same considerations as is reasonably practicable.[5] The employee exercises her right to return to work by giving at least 21 days' notice of the date of her return.[6] The employer may postpone her return to work for four weeks[7] and the employee may postpone her return to work for four weeks due to medical incapacity.[8] The period can be extended if there is an interruption of work due to industrial action or any other cause.[9] An employee can lose her right to return to work if she is requested by her employer to confirm her intention to return and she fails to do so.[10]

1 Section 79(1).
2 Section 79(2).
3 *Hughes v Gwynedd Area Health Authority* [1977] IRLR 436.
4 Section 80(1) and see *FW Woolworths plc v Smith* [1990] ICR 45, EAT.
5 *Nu-Swift International Ltd v Mallinson* [1978] ICR 157 held that despite worries about whether the child would be born deformed and whether appropriate child-care arrangements could be made, it was reasonably practicable for the woman to have given the notice.
6 Section 82(1).
7 Section 82(2).
8 Section 82(3) and (4) but she can only exercise the right to postpone on one occasion: s 82(5).
9 Section 82(7).
10 Section 80(2). The employer must warn the employee of the consequences of failing to give the confirmation: s 80(3)(b).

The status of a woman absent from work due to pregnancy

7.97 The terms in which section 71 is drafted presupposes that the contract subsists for the 14-week period of maternity leave. If the employee is absent beyond that period but has a right to return to work pursuant to section 79, the position is less clear and it seems that the contract is in a state of suspended animation ready to be reactivated by the exercise of the right to return to work. Where the statutory requirements have not been complied with there is considerable uncertainty about whether the contract is to be regarded as terminated or still subsisting.[1] An employee who has a contractual right to return to work may take advantage of whichever right is in the circumstances the more favourable.[2]

1 See *Lucas v Norton of London Ltd* [1984] IRLR 86; *Institute of the Motor Industry v Harvey* [1992] ICR 470. In *Hilton International Hotels (UK) Ltd v Kassi* [1994] ICR 578 the EAT considered that where the employee had failed to give notice of her intention to return did not mean that the contract was thereby terminated, but a rather different view was taken in *Crouch v Kidsons Impey* [1996] IRLR 79 when it was held that if a woman merely leaves and the employer stops paying her, the appropriate inference was that there was a mutual termination. The factual matrix was rather different than in *Kassi's* case. See also *Lavery v Plessey Telecommunications Ltd* [1983] ICR 534, CA.
2 Section 85(1) and note the parallel provision in relation to maternity leave at s 78.

The return to work

7.98 If the woman has the right to work under section 79 (see **7.96**) and complied with the requirements of section 82 (see **7.96**) the failure to permit her to return to work constitutes a dismissal for the purposes of a claim for unfair dismissal[1] and redundancy.[2] If the denial of her right to return to work arises because it is not reasonably practicable by reason of redundancy, then the dismissal will be automatically unfair[3] unless she is offered such suitable alternative employment as is available by her employer, his successor or an associated employer.[4] There are two defences open to an employer. If the employer, together with the number employed by any associated employer, employs five or fewer employees, can show[5] that it was not reasonably practicable for him to offer her her old job or some other suitable alternative then she is not deemed to be dismissed by virtue of section 96(1).[6] It is a defence for any employer to show that it is not reasonably practicable to offer her her old job for reasons other than redundancy[7] and that he has offered her suitable alternative employment[8] which she has either accepted or unreasonably refused.[9]

1 Section 96(1).
2 Section 137(1).
3 Section 99(4).
4 Section 81. See the parallel provisions of s 77 and see *Phillip Hodges & Co Ltd v Kell* [1994] ICR 656.
5 Section 96(5). The burden is on the employer.
6 Section 96(2)(a) and (b).
7 If the reason is redundancy then s 81 applies.
8 Section 96(3)(a).
9 Section 96(3)(b).

The nature of the work

7.99 The right to return does not mean that an employee has the inalienable right to return to exactly the same job. Minor alterations may occur but there is the overriding requirement that the terms and conditions must not be less favourable.[1] There is no right to return to work on different conditions. For example, two employees who want to work on a job-share basis can only succeed if they can show indirect sex discrimination.[2]

1 Section 79(2)(a)(b)(c). See *Edgell v Lloyd's Register of Shipping* [1977] IRLR 463 where a minor alteration in the work was held not to be less favourable.
2 *British Telecommunications plc v Roberts* [1996] ICR 625.

The replacement employee

7.100 In reality those who are taken on as a replacement employee for the pregnant employee will rarely acquire the requisite continuity of service to bring an action for unfair dismissal. There are specific statutory provisions[1] which allow an employer to give written warning that the employment will be terminated on the resumption of work of the original employee and in such circumstances the reason for dismissal will constitute a substantial other reason for the purposes of section 98(1)(b). The tribunal would still have to consider the issue of fairness by the criteria set out in section 98(4) of the Act.

1 Section 106.

Rights of the pregnant woman during her absence from work

Maternity pay

The statutory framework

7.101 The provisions governing the right to receive statutory maternity pay ('SMP') are set out in Pt XII of, and Sch 13 to, the Social Security Contributions and Benefits Act 1992 ('the SCBA') and the rules governing the rights are to be found in the Statutory Maternity Pay (General) Regulations 1986[1] ('the SMP Regulations').[2]

1 SI 1986/1960 as amended by SI 1988/532 and SI 1990/662.
2 The rights provided for by the Pregnant Workers Directive (Directive 92/85/EEC) are implemented by the Maternity Allowance and Statutory Maternity Pay Regulations 1994, SI 1994/1230.

7.102 The regulations came into effect in all circumstances where the expected date of confinement began on or after 16 October 1994 with the exception of reg 5 (concerning the recovery of SMP by employers). The Social Security Maternity Benefits and Statutory Sick Pay (Amendment) Regulations 1994[1] set the lower rate of SMP at the same level as statutory sick pay. It is currently set at £54.55.

1 SI 1994/1230, supplemented by SI 1994/1367.

The operation of the scheme

7.103 The employer administers SMP. It follows the statutory sick pay scheme. An employee is entitled to payment at a prescribed rate for up to 18 weeks unless she is excluded from the entitlement. The right is not affected by termination of the employee's contract of employment at the commencement of the maternity leave. The employer can claim reimbursement from the state of a proportion (or all, in the case of a small employer) of the sum paid by way of SMP.

Qualification necessities for SMP

7.104 The qualification requirements for SMP are that a woman must:
(1) still be pregnant at the 11th week before her expected week of confinement ('the EWC'), or have had a baby at that time;[1] and
(2) have been continuously employed for at least 26 weeks ending with the week immediately preceding the 14th week before the expected week when the baby is due. This week is known as the 'qualifying week' ('the QW'); and

(3) have normal weekly earnings for the period of eight weeks ending with the QW, of not less than the lower earnings limit in force at the time for the payment of National Insurance contributions;[2] and

(4) have stopped working for the employer, that is,[3] the employee must be absent from work.

'Absent from work' includes a woman who leaves work to have the baby and who does not want to return to work and does not do so. She can claim SMP as her absence from work is during her statutory notice period.

1 SCBA, ss 164 and 171.
2 SCBA, s 164.
3 SCBA, s 165.

7.105 The employee's contract of employment must subsist until immediately before the 14th week before the baby is due and it is immaterial whether she physically works in the 14th week. SMP is payable for 18 weeks no matter how close to the birth a woman works.

7.106 A former employer will be liable to make payments of SMP to any woman who was employed by him continuously for at least eight weeks where her contract has been terminated solely or mainly for the purpose of avoiding liability for SMP.[1]

1 See SMP Regulations, reg 3.

Maternity pay period

7.107 The maternity pay period is the period of claim for SMP which is of a maximum duration of 18 weeks when the employee is absent from work due to pregnancy or confinement. The maternity pay period cannot start earlier than the 11th week before the EWC, the expected week of confinement.[1]

1 SCBA, s 165.

SMP rates

7.108 SMP is set at two rates. The higher rate is a weekly rate equivalent to nine-tenths of a woman's normal weekly earnings.[1] The lower rate is a regulated sum which is adjusted from time to time.[2]

1 SMP Regulations, reg 21. See Statutory Maternity Pay (General) Amendment Regulations 1996, SI 1996/1335 which require backdated increases to be included in the calculation of pay.
2 SMP Regulations, reg 6.

7.109 Higher rate SMP is payable to all women who can show 26 weeks' service with their employers by the QW. After six weeks' payment at the higher rate, all women will receive payment at the lower rate. SMP is not payable to an employee whose average weekly earnings are below the lower earnings limit for the purposes of National Insurance contributions. An employee may be paid her contractual entitlement or the amount of her SMP whichever is the greater which would have the effect of discharging the other.

7.110 SMP is regarded as earnings for social security purposes and as regards income tax, National Insurance and other deductions from pay. It can be paid in the same way as other remuneration.

Formal notification of intention to be absent

7.111 An employee must give the employer formal notification of her intention to be absent from work due to pregnancy or confinement but she does not have to state that she will return. It must normally be 21 days' notice but it does not have to be in writing unless requested by the employer.[1] Notice is not required where the employee leaves for a reason wholly unconnected with her pregnancy after the beginning of the 15th week before the EWC, or where she is fairly dismissed because it is physically or legally impossible for her to continue in employment.

1 SCBA, s 164(5).

Failure to give notice or late notice

7.112 If the employee does not give notice, then she will not be entitled to SMP unless it was not reasonably practicable to give notice and she gives notice as soon as is reasonably practicable thereafter.[1] Evidence should be provided not later than the end of the third week of the maternity pay period, but may be presented up to the end of the 13th week of the maternity pay period. Whether the employer accepts the employee's reason for not submitting the details on the appropriate date, the onus is on the employer to decide whether the employee's reason is justified.

1 SCBA, s 164(4)(b).

Decision as to whether SMP is paid

7.113 The employer must determine whether to pay SMP in situations where the employee does not give notice at an acceptable time of the date she will stop work, or does not provide medical evidence of her EWC. If the employer decides against SMP, the employer is required to explain the decision to the employee if a 'reasonable enquiry' is made by her, and the employer must provide a written statement in respect of the period before the request is made, covering one or more of the following matters:
(1) the weeks in the period the employer regards as weeks when there is a liability to pay SMP;
(2) the reasons why the employer does not include other weeks in the period;
(3) an opinion as to the SMP level to which the employee is entitled in respect of each of the weeks which the employer regards himself as liable to make a payment;
(4) the response must be within a reasonable time.

Complaints against a failure to pay SMP

7.114 Where the employee does not accept the employer's decision regarding payment of SMP, a complaint can be referred to an adjudication officer of the DSS by the employee or an officer of the DSS. An appeal lies from the adjudication officer to the Social Security Appeals Tribunal and thereafter to the Social Security Commissioner. The decision of any of the appeal officers obliges the employer to pay[1] and failure so to do is an offence. Appeal from the commissioner lies to the Court of Appeal.

1 SMP Regulations, reg 29.

Attempts to sign away the right to SMP

7.115 An employee cannot validly sign away her right to SMP nor can an employer validly require her to contribute towards the cost incurred by the employer and any purported agreement to this end is void.[1]

1 SCBA, s 164(6).

Enforcing rights against the Secretary of State for Social Services

7.116 An employee may be able to claim against the Secretary of State for Social Services if she is unable to obtain her SMP from her employer on two grounds:
(1) Where an adjudicating body has concluded that an employer is liable to make payments of SMP and the time for appeal has expired and an appeal has not been lodged or leave has been refused for an appeal out of time and the employer has failed to pay.[1]
(2) Where the employer is insolvent. The employer is taken to be insolvent in England and Wales if:
    (a) the employer has been adjudged bankrupt or has made an arrangement with his creditors;
    (b) a winding-up or administration order has been made in the case of a company, or a voluntary winding-up resolution passed, or a receiver or manager appointed, or possession is taken of a floating charge or a voluntary arrangement proposed for the purposes of Pt I of the Insolvency Act 1986 has been approved.
In order to investigate a claim the Secretary of State may call for information from the employee of others and failure to comply may lead upon conviction to a fine.

1 SMP Regulations, reg 30.

Recovery of SMP

7.117 SMP is paid by the employer but recovered through National Insurance contributions. Small employers with National Insurance contributions in the previous tax year of £20,000 or less will recover 104% of the cost of SMP[1] and all other employers will recover 92% of the cost.

1 SMP Regulations, reg 5.

Those excluded from the benefit

7.118 The exclusions from entitlement to SMP are those on overseas employment, share fisherwomen and the police service. There are restrictions on the application of SMP to mariners. A woman does not qualify for SMP for any week that she is outside the European Union, or she is in legal custody or is serving a period of imprisonment when she would be otherwise entitled to claim.

Maternity allowance

7.119 Those who are not eligible for statutory maternity pay may be eligible for maternity allowance paid by the Benefits Agency. It is paid for the same 18-week period as statutory maternity pay and it has two rates of payment which are set at a lower level than statutory maternity pay. To be eligible the woman must have worked and paid National Insurance contributions for 26 weeks in a 66-week period ending immediately before the baby is due.

Disability

Background to the Disability Discrimination Act 1995

7.120 Although the last 30 years have witnessed a stream of statutory changes concerning nearly every aspect of employment the position of the disabled employee has been almost totally untouched by legislation. Employment lawyers would know that the Disabled Persons (Employment) Act 1944 had certain provisions concerning the registration of disabled persons and that it imposed an obligation on certain employers to have a quota of disabled persons in their employment. However, it would be rare to find any lawyer who had ever dealt with a case involving non-compliance with those statutory provisions. Company lawyers would be aware that companies which employ, on average, more than 250 employees in the financial year are obliged to include in their annual report a policy statement on the employment of disabled persons.[1] Lawyers specialising in personal injury cases would have noticed that the move towards contracting out many jobs means that the prospects of light work for the severely injured employee with the existing employer were, compared with a generation ago, remote. The sad truth is that the practitioner has been able to ignore the position of the disabled. The dearth of legislative change has not been because the disabled have been without their champions. Between 1982 and 1994 there were 17 attempts by back-bench MPs to introduce legislation.[2] The Disability Discrimination Act 1995 has itself all the hallmarks of legislation passed in haste and it has already been the subject of serious criticism. Translating a laudable objective into workable legislation which gives enforceable rights and defined responsibilities is a difficult task. Nevertheless, to the practitioner who has experience of the problems of conflicting medical evidence as to physical or psychiatric conditions, the prospect of some of the issues which may arise under the somewhat nebulous definitions of the Act is daunting. Despite such criticisms and concerns the Act will radically alter the law in relation to disabled employees. The Act repeals the provisions of the Disabled Persons (Employment) Act 1944, introduces a new definition of 'disabled person' and takes the radical step of making it unlawful to discriminate against disabled persons in employment as well as in other areas. The equality legislation of the 1970s has had an impact on working practices far greater than was ever envisaged and there is every reason to think that introduction of employment rights for the disabled will be as far-reaching.

1 Companies Act 1985, s 234. This obligation will continue under the new legislation, see s 234 as amended by the Disability Discrimination Act 1995, Sch 6, para 4.
2 See Caroline Gooding *Guide to the Disability Discrimination Act 1995* (Blackstone, 1996) for a history of the gestation of the Act.

No contracting out

7.121 As with the other equality and employment protection legislation contracting out is precluded. Section 9(1) provides:

'(1) Any term in a contract of employment or other agreement is void so far as it purports to—

(a) require a person to contravene any such provision;

(b) exclude or limit the operation of any such provision; or

(c) prevent any person from presenting a complaint to an industrial tribunal under this Part.'

Relationship of the Disability Discrimination Act 1995 with other equality employment protection legislation

7.122 Sex and race equality legislation draws a distinction between direct and indirect discrimination. This analysis is not replicated in the Disability Discrimination Act 1995 and the justification defence is more broadly based. There is an exclusion for small businesses which is far wider than was ever the case in the sex and race discrimination legislation. There is a different emphasis in the disability equality legislation since a positive duty is put on employers to make adjustments to assist disabled employees. Just as the race and sex equality legislation is intertwined with the employment protection legislation and in certain cases an applicant may properly allege that the dismissal was unfair and an act of discrimination, it is likely that a similar pattern will emerge with the disability legislation. The incapacity of an employee is a potentially fair reason for a dismissal. It is likely that some applicants will now allege discrimination on the ground of disability as well as unfair dismissal in cases in which there has been a dismissal due to medical incapacity. It may safely be predicted that there is likely to be a plethora of cases in which the old case law (and the assumptions on which such cases were based) on medical incapacity dismissals will now need to be reconsidered in the light of the responsibilities under the new Act.

Proving the case

7.123 The difficulties which beset an applicant in proving discrimination in cases of race and gender have already been adverted to at 7.02 et seq. Although there are differences in the conceptual framework of the Act and that of other equality legislation, nevertheless it is likely that the case law that has developed will be held to be equally applicable in cases founded on discrimination due to disability. As in the other equality legislation applicants will be able to use questionnaires to elicit from the respondents the basis of their actions. The tribunal may draw inferences from the way in which such questionnaires are answered.[1]

1 Disability Discrimination Act 1995, s 56(3)(a), (b).

Definition of 'disability' and 'disabled person'

7.124 Whether or not an employee has a disability as defined by the Act is the crucial lynchpin to the operation of the statutory provisions. Before considering the statutory definition it is important to note the difference between the disability and race and sex discrimination legislation. Although the purpose of the race and sex discrimination legislation was to prevent discrimination against ethnic minorities and women, the way in which this was achieved was to prevent discrimination on grounds of *race* and *gender* and therefore the indigenous white population and men may rely on the remedies it affords. In contrast the only persons who can rely on the provisions of the Disability Discrimination Act 1995 are those who come within the statutory definition and an employee who suffers from mental or physical health problems, but who does not satisfy the provisions of the Act has no remedy under the Act. Thus, an employee who is selected for redundancy on the basis of the frequency of his or her absences from work – all of which may be due to ill-health – cannot rely on the Act if he or she fails to meet the statutory definition.

Supplementing the statutory definition

7.125   Legislation in this area creates the most difficult problems of definition. Although the Act contains its own definition, s 3 provides that the Secretary of State may issue guidance about matters to be taken into account in determining whether an impairment has a substantial adverse effect on a person's ability to carry out normal day-to-day activities or whether such impairment has a long-term effect. Further, there is the most extensive power to make regulations as to what condition is to be treated, or not treated, as an impairment; for prescribing circumstances in which the effect of an impairment is, or is not, to be treated as of long-term effect; for prescribing circumstances in which the likelihood of a substantial adverse effect recurring is to be disregarded; for prescribing circumstances in which an impairment is to be taken to affect, or not affect, the ability to carry out day-to-day activities and for prescribing the kinds of effect on day-to-day activities which are to be treated as a substantial adverse effect. Further the Act provides for the issue of a code of practice. The code of practice and the guidance are essential documents for the understanding of the practical implications of the Act and references are made to them at frequent intervals. It is possible that commentators will find it necessary to refer extensively to ministerial statements made during the passage of the legislation as an aid to statutory construction.[1]

1 See *Pepper v Hart* [1993] 1 All ER 42, HL. See Appendix 3 for the code of practice and guidance relating to the definition of disability.

Changes in the statutory definition

7.126   The definition of 'disabled person' in the Disabled Persons (Employment) Act 1944 is replaced by a new statutory definition and any reference to a disabled person in subordinate legislation making reference to the 1944 Act will be construed as a reference to the new statutory definition.[1] A person has a disability for the purposes of the 1995 Act if he has a physical or mental impairment which has a substantial and long-term adverse effect on his ability to carry out normal day-to-day activities.[2]

1 Disability Discrimination Act 1995, s 61(8).
2 Disability Discrimination Act 1995, s 1(1).

7.127   In effect there are five categories of persons who are protected by the Act:
(1)   Those who are *deemed* to have a disability (see **7.128**).
(2)   Those who are currently suffering from a disability (see **7.129**).
(3)   Those who in the past have suffered from a disability (see **7.132**).
(4)   Those who suffer from a progressive condition which is likely to lead to them suffering from a disability (see **7.133**).

(5)   Those who have been victimised for asserting a right under the Act (see **7.136**).

Those protected by the Act

Persons deemed to be disabled

7.128   Any person who under the old legislation was on the register of disabled persons both on 12 January 1995 and upon the coming into force of the Disability Discrimination Act 1995 on 2 December 1996 shall be deemed, for a period of three years, to have a disability for the purposes of the 1995 Act.[1] Thus, although the old registration provisions ceased on 2 December 1996, the position of those registered under the old legislation is safeguarded for a period of three years from that date.[2] Paragraph 7(5) of Sch 1 to the 1995 Act allows the minister to make regulations which deem those afflicted by certain conditions as being disabled persons within the statutory definition. Subject to such deeming provisions the 1995 Act provides its own exclusive definition with which those seeking its protection have to comply.[3]

1 Disability Discrimination Act 1995, Sch 1, para 7(1) and (2).
2 Disability Discrimination Act 1995, s 61(7)(b).
3 See Appendix 3 for the code and guidance.

Physical impairment

7.129   Where such deeming provisions do not apply the responsibilities of a tribunal will be daunting. Whilst in practice the fact that a person's condition has been recognised as entitling him or her to a statutory benefit such as a disability living allowance will no doubt carry weight with a tribunal, in the final analysis it will not be conclusive. Of course in many cases there will be no issue that the applicant is suffering from a disability by reason of a physical impairment. But when this in dispute this means that a tribunal will be burdened with all the problems that disputed medical evidence causes and the parties will have all the attendant expense that expert medical evidence dictates. Those innocent of the problems of the diagnosis of conditions such as repetitive strain injury will have a rude awakening as to the divergence of view of the medical profession. The guidance relating to the definition of disability set out in Appendix 3 should be consulted.

Mental impairment

7.130   A mental impairment includes impairment resulting from or consisting of a clinically well-recognised mental illness.[1] What is a 'clinically well-recognised illness' is likely to be a fertile field of debate. The government resisted attempts to incorporate the wider definition contained in the Mental Health Acts and s 68 in terms provides that the words mental impairment do not have the same meaning as in the Mental Health Act 1983 or the Mental Health Act 1984 (Scotland). Indeed it might be argued that those with learning difficulties do not come within the statutory definition on the basis that a mental handicap is not a mental illness. However, ministerial pronouncements suggest that it was intended that those suffering from learning difficulties should be regarded as coming within the Act.[2] The government indicated that it intended to use its powers under regulations to exclude from the ambit of the Act certain anti-social conditions even though they come within the ambit of being a recognised illness and thus under the Disability Discrimination (Meaning of Disability) Regulations 1996,[3] reg 4 provides:

'(1) For the purposes of the Act the following conditions are to be treated as not amounting to an impairment—
(a)   a tendency to set fires,
(b)   a tendency to steal,
(c)   a tendency to physical or sexual abuse of other persons,
(d)   exhibitionism, and
(e)   voyeurism.'

1 Disability Discrimination Act 1995, Sch 1, para 1(1).
2 See Brian Doyle *Discrimination: The New Law* (Jordans, 1996) p 19. Professor Doyle provides an excellent guide to those areas in which ministerial views have been expressed and will be an invaluable guide to those who are considering further research with regard to ministerial statements which may assist in statutory construction.
3 SI 1996/1455.

Long-term impairment

7.131   The effect of an impairment is a long-term effect if it has lasted at least 12 months, or if it is likely to last at least that long, or if it is likely to last for the rest of the affected person's life, or if it is likely to recur if in remission.[1] An impairment is to be taken to affect the ability to carry out normal day-to-day activities only if it affects one of the following:[2]
(1)   mobility;
(2)   manual dexterity;
(3)   physical coordination;
(4)   continence;
(5)   the ability to lift, carry or otherwise move everyday objects;
(6)   speech, hearing or eyesight;
(7)   memory or ability to concentrate, learn or understand; or
(8)   perception of the risk of physical danger.

1 Disability Discrimination Act 1995, Sch 1, para 2(1) and (2).
2 Disability Discrimination Act 1995, Sch 1, para 4(1) and see Appendix 3, para 4 et seq of Annex 1 of the code and the guidance.

Past disabilities

7.132   During the passage of the legislation the government changed its original stance with the result that the Act now protects those who in the *past* have had a disability from which they no longer suffer and all references to disabled persons are to be read accordingly.[1] In any proceedings under the employment related provisions of the Act, the question whether a person had a disability at a certain time ('the relevant time') shall be determined as if the provisions of, or made under, the Act in force when the act complained of was done had been in force at the relevant time.[2] The relevant time may be a time before the passing of the Act.[3] This change is likely to have a profound effect on recruitment procedures and provides a remedy for those who are discriminated against because of their medical history. To come within the section an applicant will still have to show that at the relevant time in the past he or she came within the statutory definition. The Act does not expressly deal in terms with the practice of pre-employment health screening. But if a job applicant was rejected because of information obtained during such a screening process and the rejection was based on a generalised blanket policy rather than on an individualised assessment of the particular candidate applying for a specific job in the light of the requirements of the Act and in particular the duty to make reasonable adjustments, then an employer might well have considerable difficulties in justifying the decision. It may assist by focusing on a particular factual context. See Appendix 3, para 9 of Annex 1 of the code.

1 Disability Discrimination Act 1995, s 2(1).
2 Disability Discrimination Act 1995, s 2(4).
3 Disability Discrimination Act 1995, s 2(5).

Progressive conditions

7.133 It has already been noted that the definition of impairment includes the position in which there is a remission but the underlying condition is likely to recur. The Act goes further in dealing in terms with progressive conditions. The Act cites the following as examples of a progressive condition: cancer, multiple sclerosis, muscular dystrophy, or AIDS. If as a result of that condition, the sufferer has an impairment which has (or had) an effect on his ability to carry out normal day-to-day activities, but that effect is not (or was not) a substantial adverse effect he shall be taken to have an impairment which has such a substantial adverse effect if the condition is likely to result in his having such an impairment.[1] This provision will give a much needed protection, but its practical application is fraught with difficulties in that the Act rests on a premise which many medical practitioners would dispute, namely that the course of a condition can be predicted with the precision which the wording of the provision presupposes. It is probable that tribunals and courts would construe the word *likely* as meaning more probable than not. On this basis a person with a 51% chance of the condition degenerating into an impairment which will have a substantial adverse effect comes within the provision, but a person with only a 49% chance does not. The provision does not cover those who by virtue of genetic inheritance or other medical testing would be regarded as at risk from developing such conditions as multiple sclerosis, Huntingdon's chorea or various forms of cancer. The distinction may be a fine one. See Appendix 3, paras 14 and 16 of Annex 1 of the code.

1 Disability Discrimination Act 1995, Sch 1, para 8(1).

Other disabilities

Severe disfigurement

7.134 Subject to regulations made under the Act, an impairment which consists of a severe disfigurement is to be treated as a disability.[1] Under the Disability Discrimination (Meaning of Disability) Regulations 1996[2] a tattoo (which has not been removed) or a piercing of the body for decorative or non-medical reasons is excluded from the statutory protection.[2] See Appendix 3, paras 13 and 17 of Annex 1 of the code.

1 Disability Discrimination Act 1995, Sch 1, para 3.
2 SI 1996/1455, reg 5.

Controlled or corrected impairments

7.135 An impairment which would have a substantial adverse effect on the ability to carry out normal day-to-day activities were it not controlled by medical treatment or corrected by prosthesis or other aid still ranks as a disability.[1] This provision does not apply to impaired eyesight which is correctable by spectacles or contact lenses.[2] The ambit of wording could be very wide. An employee who suffered from diverticular disease which has the effect that without medication he or she is prone to acute diarrhoea would probably not wish to publicise the condition. But the employer may well have knowledge of the condition through a sick note. In the absence of a further statutory definition it is at least arguable that this condition could be one that comes within the definition of disability since it affects his or her continence. In such circumstances an employee might well argue that he or she has the right to refuse to move to an area in which there was not ready access to lavatory facilities. The strength of such an argument would, despite the statutory provisions, probably depend on the extent to which the condition was controlled by medication. See Appendix 3, paras 11 and 12 of Annex 1 of the code.

1 Disability Discrimination Act 1995, Sch 1, para 6(1) and (2).
2 Disability Discrimination Act 1995, Sch 1, para 6(3)(a).

Discrimination by victimisation

7.136 A person (A) discriminates against another person (B) if he treats him less favourably than he treats or would treat other persons, whose circumstances are the same as B's, and the reason for such less favourable treatment is that B has:
(1) brought proceedings under the Act; or
(2) given evidence or information in connection with such proceedings brought by any person; or
(3) otherwise done anything under the Act in relation to A or any other person; or
(4) alleged that A or any other person has contravened the Act,
or by reason that A believes or suspects that B has done or intends to do any of these things.[1] Where B is a disabled person, or a person who has had a disability, the disability should be disregarded in comparing his circumstances with the comparator in s 55(1)(a).[2] Where it is established that the allegation was false and was not made in good faith the victimisation provisions do not apply.[3] It is likely that these provisions will be construed in the light of the decisions on the comparable provisions of the race and sex discrimination legislation (see **7.17**).

1 Disability Discrimination Act 1995, s 55(1), (2). See Appendix 3, para 4.53 of the code.
2 Disability Discrimination Act 1995, s 55(3).
3 Disability Discrimination Act 1995, s 55(4).

Scope of the duty not to discriminate

7.137 In place of the obligation on employers with 20 or more employees to employ a quota of registered disabled persons, and related obligations under the old Act[1] there is now a much more far-reaching duty imposed on employers not to discriminate against a disabled person at every stage of employment. An employer discriminates against a disabled person if, for a reason that relates to the disabled person's disability, he treats him less favourably than he treats or would treat others to whom that reason does not or would not apply, and the employer cannot show that such treatment is justified.[2] An employer is under a duty to take such steps as are reasonable to prevent any arrangements made by him on his behalf, or any physical features of the employer's premises from placing a disabled applicant or employee at a substantial disadvantage compared to those applicants or employees who are not disabled.[3] Failure to comply with this duty in relation to a disabled person amounts to discrimination against that person if that failure cannot be justified.[4] There is nothing in the disability discrimination legislation analogous to the concept of indirect discrimination which is found in the sex and race legislation. Yet whereas in cases of direct discrimination under the sex and race discrimination legislation there is no defence of reasonableness or justification, under the Disability Discrimination Act 1995 the employer may have a defence of justification. In deciding whether a person has been discriminated against, there is no express obligation to compare the disabled employee with the employee who is not disabled, rather the Act concentrates on the reason for the disparate treatment. Whereas in a case of sex discrimination it would be extremely rare, and in the case of race discrimination very unusual, for an employer not to know the gender or ethnic origin of the employee concerned this would not necessarily be so in the case of disability. The Act does not impose any duty on an employer in relation to a disabled person if the employer does not know and could not be reasonably expected to know that a person has a disability which places him at a substantial disadvantage.[5]

1 Disability Discrimination Act 1995, s 61(7)(c).
2 Disability Discrimination Act 1995, s 5(1).
3 Disability Discrimination Act 1995, s 6(1).
4 Disability Discrimination Act 1995, s 5(2).
5 Disability Discrimination Act 1995, s 6(6)(b). See Appendix 3, para 4.56 of the code.

Treating disabled person less favourably

7.138   If a disabled person applies for a job and is not appointed because there are other better qualified candidates he or she has no cause for complaint under the Act. What the Act prohibits is failing to appoint the best candidate because that candidate is in a wheelchair when that disability reason cannot be justified. Obviously the Act does not preclude dismissing a disabled employee, but it does require that if it is a reason related to the employee's disability, then the action should be justified. An employee suffering from severe arthritis may for that reason be both absent from, and late for, work. If he was dismissed from work it would not be relevant (as it would be if race or sex discrimination was alleged) to show that the company had dismissed able-bodied employees who had lost similar time from work. The defence open to the employer would be one of justification. In order to establish the defence of justification the employer must show that the reason for the treatment in question of the disabled person is both material in the circumstances and substantial.[1] Regulations may prescribe circumstances in which the treatment is to be taken as justified for these purposes.[2] If the employer has not discharged his duty to make adjustments (see **7.139**), the defence of justification is only available if the treatment in question would have been justified even if the duty had been complied with.[3] An area in which the defence of justification is likely to be extensively adopted is where the employment of a disabled employee would place him or his fellow employees at risk of physical injury. It is difficult to imagine that any employer could be criticised for refusing to employ someone suffering from the spasticity which arises from multiple sclerosis in a foundry or in any job which required proximity to moving equipment. See Appendix 3, para 4.02 of the code.

1 Disability Discrimination Act 1995, s 5(3).
2 Disability Discrimination Act 1995, s 5(6).
3 Disability Discrimination Act 1995, s 5(5).

Duty of employer to make reasonable adjustments

7.139 Unlike other areas of discrimination law a positive duty is imposed on employers. It requires employers to make reasonable adjustments to work arrangements and the workplace. Such failure can only be justified if the reason for the failure is both material in the circumstances and substantial.[1] 'Arrangements' mean arrangements for determining to whom employment should be offered and any term, condition or other arrangements on which employment or any other benefit connected with employment is offered or afforded.[2] The Disability Discrimination (Employment) Regulations 1996[3] made pursuant to the powers contained in the Act set out circumstances in which physical features are or are not to be taken to place a disabled person at a substantial disadvantage and as to things which are or are not to be treated as physical features. For example, under reg 8 it is deemed that it is never reasonable for an employer to have to take steps to alter a physical characteristic which was adopted to meet the requirements of building regulations designed to afford access and facilities for disabled persons. Regulation 9 sets out what constitutes physical features.

1 Disability Discrimination Act 1995, s 5(4).
2 Disability Discrimination Act 1995, s 6(2).
3 SI 1996/1456. See Appendix 3, para 4.12 et seq of the code.

Recruitment procedures

7.140 Section 6(5) of the Act requires that in making arrangements for determining to whom employment should be offered, the employer's duty extends not just to an applicant for the job but to to any disabled person who has notified the employer that he may be an applicant for that employment. This is an extension of the duty owed to job applicants since an employer may be required to ensure that application procedures are not discriminatory when the employer is put on notice as to the possibility of such an application. See Appendix 3, para 5.1 et seq of the code.

Employers occupying premises under leases

7.141 Employers who occupy premises as tenants may not be entitled to make the alterations to the premises necessary for compliance with the s 6 duty. Section 16 of the Act modifies the terms of the lease to allow the tenant to make alterations subject to the consent of the landlord who cannot withhold his consent unreasonably. The Disability Discrimination (Employment) Regulations 1996 provide in reg 10(1) that it is always reasonable for an employer to have to take steps to obtain that consent and that it is never reasonable for an employer to have to make that alteration before the consent is obtained. Regulations 11–15 of the 1996 Regulations apply to the construction of s 16 and Pt 1 of Sch 4 to the Act. The effect of this latter provision is that when considering the duty to make adjustments under s 6, any constraint arising from the fact that the employer occupies the premises under a lease is to be ignored unless the employer has applied in writing for consent to the making of the alteration. See Appendix 3, para 4.35 et seq of the code.

Complying with the duty

7.142   The prime duty imposed on employers is the general one set out in s 6(1). Section 6(3) gives examples of steps an employer *may* have to take in order to comply with his duty not to place a disabled applicant or employee at a substantial disadvantage. They are to:

(1)   make adjustments to premises;
(2)   allocate some of the disabled person's duties to another person;
(3)   transfer him to fill an existing vacancy;
(4)   alter his working hours;
(5)   assign him to a different place of work;
(6)   allow him to be absent during working hours for rehabilitation, assessment or treatment;
(7)   give him (or arrange for him to be given) training;
(8)   acquire or modify equipment;
(9)   modify instructions or reference materials;
(10) modify procedures for testing or assessment;
(11) provide a reader or interpreter; or
(12) provide supervision.

7.143   Section 6(4) of the Act itself provides certain criteria which should apply in determining whether it is reasonable for an employer to have to take the steps set out in s 6(1).[1] Regard must be had to the extent to which the step would prevent the discriminatory effect, whether it would be practical for the employer to take such steps, the costs incurred, the disruptive effect, the employer's resources and the availability to the employer of financial or other assistance. Section 6(8) confers power to make regulations which will define more specifically the scope of the duty. The Act does not impose any free-standing duty to make adjustments, the breach of which is actionable. The duties are solely imposed for the limited purposes of determining whether an employer has discriminated against a disabled person.[2]

1 It should be noted that the steps referred to are those under the mandatory general duty imposed in s 6(1) not the examples contained in s 6(3). The examples cannot, and do not, purport to provide an exhaustive code and nor is there a mandatory requirement to take the specific steps set out in s 6(3) as the subsection uses the permissive word 'may'.
2 Disability Discrimination Act 1995, s 6(12).

Pensions etc excluded under s 6

7.144   Section 6(11) excludes from the the duty to make adjustments matters relating to any benefit under an occupational pension scheme or any other benefit in money or money's worth under a scheme in respect of termination of service, retirement, old age, death, accident, injury, sickness, invalidity or any other prescribed matter. These are covered by other provisions in the Act (see **7.150**).

Discrimination in employment

7.145   The Act provides that an employer is prohibited from discriminating against a disabled person prior to and during employment. Employment is defined in the same terms as other discriminatory legislation,[1] namely as employment under a contract of service or of apprenticeship or a contract personally to do any work, and thus carries a broader meaning than in other employment protection legislation. This definition may be limited by regulations which gives the minister a power to restrict the ambit of protection which is not contained in the sex and race discrimination legislation. As with other discrimination claims, there is no requirement for a qualifying period of service.

1 Disability Discrimination Act 1995, s 68(1). See **7.19** for a fuller analysis.

Advertisements

7.146   A discriminatory advertisement is not, per se, unlawful. But the placing of such an advertisement by an employer might well create a presumption that he had discriminated against the disabled candidate. The statutory provisions are contained in s 11 which provides that:

(1) 'Where:

(a)   a disabled person has applied for employment with an employer;

(b)   the employer has refused to offer, or has deliberately not offered him the employment;

(c)   the disabled person has presented a complaint under section 8 against the employer;

(d)   the employer has advertised the employment (whether before or after the disabled person applied for it); and

(e)   the advertisement indicated, or might reasonably be understood to have indicated, that any application for the authorised employment would, or might, be determined to any extent by reference to—

  (i)   the successful applicant not having any disability or any category of disability which includes the disabled person's disability; or

  (ii)   the employer's reluctance to take any action of a kind mentioned in section 6.

(2) The tribunal hearing the complaint shall assume, unless the contrary is shown, that the employer's reason for refusing to offer, or deliberately not offering, the employment to the complainant was related to the complainant's disability.'

Job applicants

7.147   Section 4(1) provides that:

'It is unlawful for an employer to discriminate against a disabled person—

(a)   in the arrangements he makes for the purpose of determining who should be offered that employment; or

(b)   in the terms on which the employment is offered; or

(c)   by refusing or deliberately omitting to offer employment.'

Promotion, training and other benefits

7.148   Section 4(2) provides that an employer shall not discriminate against a disabled employee in the terms of employment offered to him, or in the opportunities for promotion, training or the receipt of any other benefit afforded to him, or by refusing to afford him or deliberately not affording him, any such opportunity.

Dismissal or subjection to any other detriment

7.149 Section 4(2)(d) provides that it is unlawful for an employer to discriminate against a disabled employee by dismissing him, or subjecting him to any other detriment. By analogy with the decisions on sexual harassment, a disabled employee subject to abuse related to his disability might well be able to complain that this amounts to a detriment within the meaning of the Act.

Membership of occupational pension schemes

7.150 Section 17 provides that every occupational pension scheme shall be taken to include a 'non-discrimination' rule relating to the terms on which persons become members of the scheme and the terms on which members are treated. The trustees or managers of the scheme are required to refrain from any act of omission which, if done in relation to a person by an employer, would amount to unlawful discrimination against the person. However, if due to a medical condition the costs are substantially greater, such differential treatment would be justifiable.[1]

1 See Disability Discrimination (Employment) Regulations 1996, reg 4. See Appendix 3, para 6.9 of the code.

Insurance services

7.151 Section 18 provides that where an insurer enters into an arrangement with an employer under which employees receive benefits in respect of the termination of service, retirement, old age, death, accident, injury, sickness, invalidity or any other prescribed matter, it will be unlawful for the insurer to discriminate against a disabled employee in refusing to provide or deliberately not providing the disabled employee with such benefits or in the terms on which such benefits are provided to the disabled employee.[1]

1 For a practical example, see para 6.17 of the code. An employee is entitled to receive the same protection against discrimination as a member of the public, s 18(2)(a)–(b).

Exceptions

Excluded employment

7.152 Discrimination in employment is unlawful under the Act only in respect of employment at an establishment in Great Britain.[1] Where an employee does his work wholly or mainly outside Great Britain, his employment will not be treated as being work at an establishment in Great Britain.[2] Section 68(5) defines the position in the case of the itinerant employee and the employee who works from home. Section 68(3) and (4) deals with the position with regard to aircraft, hovercraft and ships. In a nutshell the provisions do not apply to such employment unless prescribed exceptions are made. Under s 68(4) the minister has power to exclude certain kinds of employment or employment in certain circumstances as not being employment in Great Britain. Where facilities are provided by the employer to the public, then an employee cannot rely on the statutory protection save in the limited circumstances set out in s 4(3)(a)–(c). Section 64(5) excludes certain offices such as policemen, firemen and the armed forces.

7.152 *Discrimination (including pregnancy)*

1 Disability Discrimination Act 1995, s 4(6).
2 Disability Discrimination Act 1995, s 68(2).

Acts done under statutory authority

7.153 By virtue of s 59(1)–(3) the Act does not make unlawful any act done pursuant to any enactment or statutory instrument or in order to comply with a ministerial condition or requirement imposed pursuant to statute or for the purpose of safeguarding national security.

Exemption for small businesses

7.154 Under s 7(1) the provisions of the Act in relation to employment do not apply to any employer who has fewer than 20 employees. This provision is one of beguiling simplicity. It may well require a tribunal to spend considerable time examining the status of a number of the workforce to determine whether they are *really* employees despite the label that is given to their position. See Appendix 3, para 7.7 of the code.

Charities

7.155 Section 10(1) provides that any act done by a charity pursuant to any charitable purpose connected with categories of persons determined by reference to any physical or mental capacity will not be unlawful under the employment provisions of the Act. This protects charities specifically concerned with those suffering from particular disabilities.

Discrimination against contract workers

7.156 It is unlawful[1] for a principal who hires contract labour to discriminate against a contract worker:
(1)   in the terms on which he allows him to do that work; or
(2)   by not allowing him to work or continue working;
(3)   in the way he affords him access to any benefits or refusing or deliberately omitting to afford him access to them; or
(4)   by subjecting him to any other detriment.

1 Disability Discrimination Act 1995, s 12(1).

Public facilities

7.157 The principal[1] who hires contract labour is exempt from the provisions of the Act where he is concerned with the provision (whether or not for payment) of benefits (including facilities and services) of any description to the public or to a section of the public which includes the contract worker in question, unless that provision differs in a material respect from the provision of the benefits by the principal to contract workers.

1 Disability Discrimination Act 1995, s 12(2).

Discrimination by trade organisations

7.158 Trade organisations, which are defined as organisations of workers or employers, or any other organisation whose members carry on a particular profession or trade for the purpose of which the organisation exists, may not discriminate against a disabled person:[1]

(a) in the terms on which they are prepared to admit him to membership; or

(b) by refusing to accept or deliberately not accepting, his application for membership.

Trade organisations may not discriminate[2] against a disabled member:

(a) in the way they afford him access to any benefits or by refusing or deliberately omitting to afford him access to them; or

(b) by depriving him of membership or varying the terms on which he is a member; or

(c) subjecting him to any other detriment.

1 Disability Discrimination Act 1995, s 13(1).
2 Disability Discrimination Act 1995, s 13(2).

Discrimination

7.159 Sections 5 and 14 are drafted in almost identical terms and thus the test for 'discrimination' is the same whether by an employer or trade organisation. Trade organisations are under a similar duty to make adjustments[1] in occupying premises. They are in the same position as employers in terms of alterations to their premises.[2]

1 Disability Discrimination Act 1995, s 15(1).
2 Disability Discrimination Act 1995, s 16(1)(a).

Other unlawful acts

7.160 Any unlawful act (other than an offence under s 57(4))[1] committed by an employee in the course of his employment shall be treated as also done by his employer, whether or not it was done with the employee's knowledge or approval.[2] The employer has a defence if he can prove that he took such steps as were reasonably practicable to prevent the employee from doing that said act, or from doing, in the course of his employment, acts of that description.[3]

1 Disability Discrimination Act 1995, s 57(4) imposes criminal liability for making false statements.
2 Disability Discrimination Act 1995, s 58(1).
3 Disability Discrimination Act 1995, s 58(5). See **7.41** for a fuller analysis.

Liability for unlawful act of an agent

7.161 Any unlawful act (except for an offence under s 57(4)) done by an agent with the express or implied authority of his principal (whether such authority was given before or after the act in question was done), is treated as also done by his principal.[1]

1 Disability Discrimination Act 1995, s 58(2).

Aiding unlawful acts

7.162 By virtue of s 57 a person who knowingly aids another person to do an act made unlawful by the Act is to be treated as if he himself did the same kind of unlawful act. A person does not knowingly aid another to do an unlawful act if:

7.162 *Discrimination (including pregnancy)*

(1) he acts in reliance upon a statement made to him by that person that the act would not be unlawful; and
(2) it is reasonable for him to rely on that statement.

National Disability Council

7.163 The National Disability Council does not have the wider investigative powers of the Commission for Racial Equality and the Equal Opportunities Commission. Its function is an advisory one and though it may assume further duties there is no power under the Act to give it the role of the other two bodies. In preparing proposals for inclusion in a code of practice it is at all times subject to ministerial authority.

Enforcement

7.164 No civil or criminal proceedings may be brought against any person in respect of unlawful acts of discrimination except as provided by the Act.[1] This does not preclude an application for judicial review in respect of an act of a public body.[2] The National Disability Council has no enforcement powers under the Act to investigate discriminatory practices or issue non-discrimination notices.

1 Disability Discrimination Act 1995, Sch 3, para 2(1).
2 Disability Discrimination Act 1995, Sch 3, para 2(2).

Enforcement by an individual: application to an industrial tribunal

7.165 Under s 8(1) the industrial tribunal has jurisdiction in relation to employment matters. The time limit for the presentation of such complaints is three months; there is power to extend that time limit if it is just and equitable to do so and definitions apply as to identifying the time of the act about which complaint is made.[1]

1 Disability Discrimination Act 1995, Sch 3, para 3(1)–(4).

Powers of the industrial tribunal

7.166 Under s 8(2)–(6) a tribunal shall, if it finds a complaint well founded, take such of the following steps as it considers just and equitable:
(1) Make a declaration as to the rights of the complainant and the respondent in relation to the matters to which the complaint relates (s 8(2)(a)).
(2) Order the respondent to pay compensation to the complainant (s 8(2)(b)). The amount of compensation shall be calculated on principles applicable to the calculation of damages in claims of tort (s 8(3)). Compensation may include compensation for injury to feelings (s 8(4)). There is no upper limit on the amount of such compensation. The award may include interest (s 8(6)(a)). See **7.46** for provisions as to interest.
(3) Recommend that the respondent takes, within a specified period, action appearing to the tribunal to be reasonable in the circumstances for the purpose of obviating or reducing the adverse effect on the complainant of any matter to which the complainant relates (s 8(2)(a)). Failure, without any reasonable justification, to comply with such a recommendation may lead to an increase in the amount of compensation to be

paid, if such an increase is considered by the tribunal to be just and equitable (s 8(5)(a)).

Preserving medical confidentiality: restricted reporting orders in the industrial tribunal

7.167 In many hearings evidence will be given of intimate personal medical matters. Under s 12, Industrial Tribunals Act 1996, the Secretary of State is enabled to make regulations in respect of the power of industrial tribunals to restrict reporting of such matters and comparable powers are given to the Lord Chancellor in respect of appeals in the Employment Appeal Tribunal.

Settlement of claim

7.168 Just as in other employment claims, unless an applicant has received independent legal advice in relation to a written compromise agreement, any agreement to settle a complaint must be made with the assistance of a conciliation officer.[1]

1 Disability Discrimination Act 1995, s 9(2) and (3).

Chapter 8

Pensions

Introduction

Although there has been little growth in absolute terms in individual longevity in the course of this century there has been a fundamental demographic change in that a much higher proportion of the population is now living to old age. This has been paralleled by a widespread reduction in the length of the working life. Inevitably the issue of pensions is a matter which generates a lively interest. Many will live on a pension for as long as they received a salary.

From philanthropy to contractual obligation

8.01 Employers have often recognised a moral obligation to provide for their former employees and their families in old age, yet the essential feature of such provision was that it was the voluntary philanthropic gesture for past services. The concept that an employee has a right to pension provision not only on his or her retirement but on transferring to other employment is a comparatively recent development. Shades of the old paternalistic philanthropy still linger in the wide residual area of discretion in deciding such issues as early retirement. Nevertheless such discretion has to be exercised according to the general requirements that an employer must not act in a manner which is inconsistent with the the implied term of mutual trust and confidence. In *Imperial Group Pension Trust Ltd v Imperial Tobacco Ltd*[1] the matter was put thus by Browne-Wilkinson V-C:

> 'As the Court of Appeal has pointed out in *Mihlenstedt v Barclays Bank International*[2] a pension scheme is quite different. Pension schemes are part of the consideration which the employee receives in return for tendering his services. In many cases, including the present, membership of the pension scheme is a requirement of employment. In contributory schemes, such as this, the employee is himself bound to pay his or her contributions.... The company employer is not conferring a bounty....
>
> In every contract of employment there is an implied term "that the employers will not, without reasonable and proper cause, conduct themselves in a manner calculated or likely to destroy or seriously damage the relationship of confidence and trust between employer and employee ..."[3]
> ... I will call this *the obligation of good faith*. In my judgment, that obligation of an employer applies as much to the exercise of his rights and powers under a pension scheme as they do to the other rights and powers of an employer. Say, in a purported exercise of its right to give or withhold consent, the company were to say, capriciously, that it would consent to an

increase in the pension benefits of members of a union A but not of the members of union B, the members of union B would have a good claim in contract for breach of an implied obligation of good faith (see *Mihlenstedt's* case).'

In *Scally v Southern Health and Social Services Board*[4] the House of Lords unanimously found that an employer was under a duty to bring to an employee's attention the facility for buying in extra years of a pension. The plaintiff was a doctor whose pension entitlement was subject to a statutory scheme which allowed the employee to purchase extra years, but there was a time limit within which this had to be done. The plaintiff was not informed of this facility and only became aware of it after the time had expired for exercising this option.

1 [1991] ICR 524.
2 [1989] IRLR 522, CA.
3 *Woods v WM Car Services (Peterborough) Ltd* [1981] ICR 666 at p 670, approved by the Court of Appeal in *Lewis v Motorworld Garages Ltd* [1986] ICR 157.
4 [1991] ICR 771.

Tax incentives

8.02   Because of the very considerable tax advantages which accrue to pension schemes there are detailed rules which the Inland Revenue apply. To look at pension provision purely in terms of Inland Revenue approved schemes which are fiscally attractive is to ignore the informal arrangements which employer and employee often made; at its most informal sums of cash from the till which were collected weekly by the former employee. As late as the 1970s universities provided pensions to lecturers by means of life insurance policies. Although there are still recipients of informal pension arrangements, existing employees are covered by more formal arrangements.

State pension provision

8.03   There is no statutory duty on employers to set up an occupational pension scheme and their obligation is limited to contributing to state provision. Although occupational pension schemes have increased, many of the less well paid are solely reliant on state provision. There are three elements of state pension. The basic pension is paid to all those who have made certain contributions and is part of the general social security system which seeks to provide a minimum safety net for all its citizens. Contributions can be made by those who are not employed. All who have made the requisite contributions receive the basic state pension.

8.04   There are two further elements which supplement the basic state pension. There is a graduated pension scheme which provided an additional pension according to the amount of graduated National Insurance contributions paid between April 1961 and April 1975. That was superseded by the State Earnings Related Pension Scheme (SERPS) which is an earnings related pension based on the individual's earnings in respect of which full National Insurance contributions have been paid.

Contracting out

8.05 Since its introduction it has been possible for employees to contract out of SERPS in respect of those employees whose final salary occupational pension satisfies certain criteria. The result is that smaller National Insurance contributions are paid. Such a final salary sheme must at least provide a guaranteed minimum pension (GMP) which would be equivalent to the additional pension provided by SERPS. At the very least an employee of a contracted out scheme must have an additional pension with an inflation protection element. In reality most occupational pension schemes which are contracted out aim to provide much greater financial provision than would be available under SERPS.

8.06 Since April 1988 it has been posssible for employers to contract out of SERPS by money purchase schemes, as well as by final salary schemes. Since 1 July 1988 employees have been able to make their own pension arrangements and opt out of both their employer's pension schemes and out of SERPS. In this case both the employer and the employee pay the full National Insurance contributions and part of these (grossed up for tax) is paid by the the Department of Social Security into the employee's pensional scheme.

Occupational pension schemes

8.07 Those with occupational pension schemes still qualify to receive the basic state pension. There is a fundamental difference between the two main categories of occupational pension; one is salary related (final salary schemes) and the other contribution based (money purchase schemes).

Final salary schemes

8.08 In a final salary scheme an employee's pension is based on a fraction of a year's pensionable pay for every year of service. In the best private sector pension scheme the fraction is 1/60th. Thus an employee who retires on a pensionable salary of £21,000 with 40 years' service will receive a pension of £14,000. In reality the pensioner will probably commute part of his pension for a capital sum and receive a lump sum of his annual salary, namely £31,500 and a pension of £10,500. In the normal public sector scheme the fraction is 1/80th but the lump sum based on the final year's salary is in addition. Thus in the example given the public service employee would receive broadly the same pension as the private sector employee.

8.09 The final salary scheme has as its stereotype the young man joining a large company, a local authority or the civil service and retiring 40 years later. Yet this pattern of employment and family life is increasingly ceasing to be the norm. Traditionally it was married women with family responsibilities who chose to work part-time when their children were small or when approaching the end of their working life where there may be responsibilities for elderly parents. However, it is not now the invariable rule that the husband earns more than his wife or that his job is more secure. With something like a third of marriages ending in divorce and a marked increase in cohabitation as opposed to marriage women need their own pension provision. The whole concept of a job for life is one which has proved to be an illusion, even in those jobs which were perceived to have security as one of their principal attractions.

8.10 The fundamental feature of final salary schemes is that it is the employer rather than the employee who bears the burden of ensuring that the pension fund is adequately funded to provide the benefits due. When inflation was high in the 1970s pension fund managers were concerned as to the enormous cost that final salary schemes were imposing on the employer. Low inflation, a buoyant stock market and the reduced liabilities which ensued from widespread redundancies meant that by the mid-1980s many employers were not required to make any contribution to their pension funds.

8.11 The usual though not invariable pattern is that the pension is funded by contributions from employee and employer. Commonly this at the rate of 5% or 6% for the employee and 10% or 12% for the employer. The Civil Service has a non-contributory scheme but its salary structure reflects this.

8.12 Many final salary schemes have other features than the provision of a pension for the employee on retirement. Life insurance benefits for death in service are often included as are benefits for spouses and dependent children. From the age of 50 Inland Revenue rules permit employers to offer early retirement. In the public sector early retirement is normally reserved to those who positions are made redundant or who retire in the efficiency of the service which is a polite euphemism for the fact that it is cheaper to employ new entrants on the bottom of an incremental scale rather than long-service employees on higher salaries. There are certain occupations which are regarded as exceptional in which the Revenue allows earlier retiring ages, consequently boxers, footballers and National Hunt jockeys may retire aged 35.

The problem of the early leaver

8.13 It has already been noted that final salary schemes benefit the long-term employee who works the whole of his life with the same employee. The employee who left before retirement was heavily penalised and was entitled to a pension payable at what would have been his retirement date as an annuity for the rest of his or her life. This was known as a deferred pension. Until recent legislative changes this deferred pension was frozen and there are still many employees and pensioners who are suffering as a result of this rule. The effects could be dramatic as the following example shows:

X and Y work for the same employee for 20 years and each has a salary of £18,000. X decides to leave. His basic deferred pension is 20/60th of £18,000 namely £6,000. Y stayed on with the company. His salary increased at 7% per annum and his final salary on retirement was £72,000. His pension would then have been 40/60ths of his final salary of £72,000, namely £48,000, although he elects to commute part of that to provide a lump sum.

X on leaving his first employer had immediately worked for another company at an identical salary. He received identical pay increases and retired at exactly the same time as Y. On joining his new employer he joined their pension scheme which like his previous scheme provided a final salary based on 1/60th of the final salary for each year of service. His pension in respect of his first employer would still be £6,000; his pension in respect of the second employer would be 20/60th of £72,000 namely £24,000.

By moving job even though X had remained on the same salary with the new employer and was a member of exactly the same type of pension scheme, because his pension in respect of his first 20 years of employment was frozen at £6,000, his total pension was £30,000 as opposed to £48,000. Though like Y he can commute part of his pension to provide a lump sum the reality is that he is dramatically worse off than had he remained with the same company. Depending on annuity rates at the time and the age of retirement he would probably need a capital sum of in the order of £180,000 to £220,000 to purchase an annuity to make up the difference.

8.14 By the Social Security Act 1990 this unfairness to the early leaver is somewhat mitigated by the requirement that a deferred pension increases by 5% per annum up to retirement or by the rate of inflation whichever is the lower. In the case of public sector employees, the pension is fully linked to the rate of price inflation. In the private sector the early leaver is penalised by the fact that the increases can at best match inflation and can if inflation rises above 5% be seriously disadvantaged. The public sector early leaver knows that at least his or her pension will match inflation. There is the disadvantage that the pension will only keep pace with the rise in prices and not with salaries and of course the early leaver will not have the benefit of the enhanced pension which any promotion later in his or her career would have brought.

Transfer of pension

8.15 Since 1985 an employee has the right to require his former employer to transfer the value of his or her accrued pension rights either to the pension scheme of his new employer or to a pension scheme run by an insurance company. A common misconception is to assume that the employee does not lose financially if his or her pension is transferred from his or her old employer's pension fund to his or her new employer's pension fund or to a private scheme run by an insurance company.

8.16 A transfer value has only to be calculated on the basis of the limited indexing required under the Social Security Act 1990 and actuarial rules thereto and thus it may not reflect the greater advantages which the employee had accrued and would have accrued had he remained in the pension scheme run by his former employer.

Money purchase pensions

8.17 The essential difference between a final salary scheme and a money purchase scheme is that, whereas in a final salary scheme the employee has no right to any particular 'pot' of money to be used to provide a pension for him or her, in a money purchase scheme an employee has a defined fund which will be used to fund the employee's pension. An employee with a final salary pension may view with complete indifference the buoyancy of the stock market; the level of interest rates and, if he or she is the recipient of a public sector pension which is completely index linked, the rate of inflation. To those who have a money purchase scheme the pension position is totally dependent on the investment performance of the fund to which payments have been made.

8.18 There is a distinction between the company money purchase scheme and personalised plans which were introduced by the Social Security Act 1985. These later policies are similar to the personal pensions which have been available to the self-employed since 1956. The main difference between these plans and company money purchase schemes is that the employee and not the employer chooses in which fund the money is to be invested.

8.19 From the employer's point of view there are distinct advantages in money purchase schemes. The employer agrees to pay a specific sum of the salary and does not have the open-ended commitment which a final salary scheme entails. The converse of this is that in a money purchase scheme the employee and not the employer gets the advantage of any favourable investment returns and the employer cannot have the contribution holidays which certain major companies enjoyed in the late 1980s.

8.20 To the employee a money purchase scheme is undoubtedly less secure than a final salary scheme. Yet it does give the employee certain advantages such as the fact that his or her pension is genuinely portable. This can be a real asset in those areas of employment in which it is quite usual to move employment at frequent intervals. Some money pension schemes will provide superior growth than the statutory formula of 5% or the rate of inflation, whichever is the less. There may well be greater flexibility in being able to take the pension at an earlier stage than a final salary scheme allows or indeed deferring the taking of the pension if there is no immediate need for income.

The hybrid position

8.21 The rigid distinction between a final salary pension scheme and a money pension scheme is blurred to a certain extent by the requirement under the Social Security Act 1986 that employers should allow employees to take out additional voluntary contributions (AVCs). These operate in a similar way to money purchase schemes whereby the employee alone makes the contribution (which together with other contibutions made to pension policies must not exceed 15% of the gross salary).

8.22 The object of AVCs is to allow employees to make good deficiencies in pension provision. AVCs cannot be used to obtain a pension in excess of the Inland Revenue permitted limits. One of the drawbacks of AVCs is that there is no provision for taking a lump sum and the total fund has to be paid as a pension unlike certain pension schemes in the public sector which allow employees to buy in added years to make good the deficiency of their service. In these circumstances the added years do lead to an enhancement of the lump sum.

Transferring out of the occupational pension scheme

8.23 Despite adverse publicity with regard to employees having been given inappropriate advice about transferring from occupational pension schemes to personal pension schemes, there may be occasions when that course could be considered. In cases, for example, in which an employee is capable of working, but suffers from a life threatening condition, there may be circumstances in which there are guarantees available in a private pension which are not available in an occupational pension.

Compensation for loss of pension rights on dismissal

8.24 It has been noted that increased general longevity and the reduction in the working life have provoked a greater interest in pension provision. It is inevitable that the flow of litigation has reflected this. The dismissed employee who remains unemployed loses not only his present income but also the increase in the occupational pension payment that further years of service would have given. However, in a final salary scheme even if the employee immediately gains comparable employment with a final salary scheme pension, it still remains the case that there may well be a pension loss for the reasons which have been set out, namely that growth in the pension is limited at best to the rate of inflation and not to the growth of salaries. In the case of a money purchase scheme the accrued fund goes on growing, subject to any cancellation charges, at exactly the same rate as if the employee was still employed unfettered by the ceiling which those leaving occupational pensions suffer. The only loss is that if the employee does not obtain further employment no further contributions will be made to the fund. Compensation for loss of accrued pension rights is primarily a matter which arises in final salary schemes.

Wrongful dismissal

8.25 In the overwhelming number of cases of wrongful dismissal the period of notice is such that the impact on the pension scheme is of little consequence. Where there is a service contract in the case of a highly paid executive, the contract itself may well set out the terms of pension provision.

8.26 However, there are cases in which the existence of a pension may be of importance. In *Hopkins v Norcros plc*[1] the Court of Appeal dismissed an appeal from Mr David Latham QC (as he then was) sitting as a Deputy High Court Judge in which he had decided that where an employee had been dismissed, his damages were not to be reduced by virtue of the company pension he received.

1 [1994] ICR 11, CA.

Unfair dismissal

8.27 The assessment of pension loss more frequently occurs in the cases of unfair dismissal. Parties are of course free to produce such actuarial evidence as they wish before tribunals. In view of the relatively limited amount of compensation which can be recovered the expenditure of fees on the obtaining of actuarial evidence would prove an onerous burden to the parties. In order to avoid this guidelines have been prepared for the assessment of compensation for loss of pension rights and these have been published by the HMSO.

The guidelines make very broad brush assumptions and are not appropriate to all situations. Within their modest aims they have been widely used in tribunals. Its main conclusions are summarised in Appendix 3.

Pensions and sex equality

8.28 It was commonplace to have a different retirement age for women as opposed to men and this reflected the fact that women were eligible for a state pension at 60 whereas men only received such a pension at 65. As a result of the decision of *Marshall v Southampton and South West Hampshire AHA (Teaching)*,[1] when the European Court of Justice decided that such differing age limits for retirement were unlawful under the Equal Treatment Directive, the Sex Discrimination Act 1986 rendered different retirement ages unlawful. It is nevertheless an over-simplification to say that the law requires a common retirement and pension age. There may be circumstances in which a group of workers may have different retirement ages and this is lawful. An example of this is the case of *Bullock v Alice Otley School*[2] where the majority of its teaching and domestic staff were female whereas the gardening staff were male. The first group retired at 60; the latter at 65. It was held that this different retirement age was not unlawful discrimination because it was based on considerations other than gender. Whilst the Court of Appeal accepted that there had been discrimination it accepted that it was objectively justified because of the particular difficulty in recruiting and retaining garden staff.[2]

1 [1986] ICR 335.
2 [1993] ICR 138, CA.

Sex discrimination and occupational pension schemes.

8.29 Since s 6(4) of the Sex Discrimination Act 1986, as amended, excluded from its ambit provision for benefits relating to death or retirement, there was no domestic legislation which requires equality of access to or equality of pension age. In *Barber v Guardian Royal Exchange Assurance Group Ltd*[1] it was decided that an occupational pension scheme was pay and therefore fell within art 119 of the Treaty of Rome. It was therefore unlawful to have a pension scheme which discriminated on the grounds of gender as to when the pension might become payable. It was later held in *Coloroll Pension Trustees v Russell*[2] that this applies to all pension schemes whether contracted in or contracted out; whether contributory or non-contributory. It would be beyond the ambit of this book to deal with the complications which can arise in the provision of occupational pension schemes and issues of sex discrimination and readers are referred to specialist works.[3]

1 Case C-262/88: [1990] ICR 616, ECJ.
2 Case C-200/91: [1995] ICR 179, ECJ.
3 Eg Jaques and Lewis *Sex Discrimination and Occupational Pension Schemes* (1992, Butterworths).

Access to pension provision

8.30 There is no duty on an employer to set up an occupational pension scheme. If an employer does do so, then the employer must not discriminate on grounds of gender in providing access to the pension scheme. Some 90%

of part-time employees are female in the United Kingdom. In *Vroege v NCIV Instituut voor Volkshuisvesting BV* and *Fisscher v Voorhuis Hengelo BV*[1] the European Court of Justice made it clear that it is unlawful under art 119 to operate a pension scheme from which married women employees are excluded. The Court also held that where part-time employees are excluded art 119 was contravened if the exclusion affected a much greater number of women then men, unless the employer can show that the exclusion is objectively justified on grounds unrelated to gender. The Pensions Act 1995 has introduced an equality clause in relation to access to pensions and so domestic legislation has now sought to enshrine the European obligations in statutory form.[2]

1 [1995] ICR 635.
2 Pensions Act 1995, s 62 and see Occupational Pension Schemes (Equal Treatment) Regulations 1995, SI 1995/3183.

Time limits

8.31 In *Barclays Bank plc v Kapur*[1] it was held that where a pension scheme was discriminatory, the operation of a pension scheme was a continuing act and that the time limit only runs from the end of the time when the discrimination took place. In *Fletcher v Midland Bank plc*[2] it was held that claims by part-timers excluded from pension schemes were governed by the domestic time limits in the Equal Pay Act, namely six months and arrears limited to two years prior to the commencement of proceedings.

1 [1991] ICR 208, HL.
2 [1996] IRLR 484, EAT.

Summary of options

For employee

Considerations which favour electing for a final salary scheme

8.32

1   The job is secure and it is intended to stay within the organisation on a permanent basis.

2   There is a likelihood of promotion within the organisation.

3   Whether the contribution which the employer makes to the occupational scheme exceeds the rebate of the National Insurance contribution which the employee receives if the employee elects to have a personal pension scheme.

4   Employees who have a medical condition affecting their mortality may be able to obtain life insurance benefits in an employer's scheme which would not be available on a personal pension scheme.

5   The employer may have schemes for enhancing the pension on early retirement; on redundancy or on grounds of ill-health.

6   In the case of public sector employees the fact that the pension is index linked, both for the early leaver and when the pension becomes payable.

Considerations in favour of contracting out of an occupational final salary pension scheme

1   It is not intended to stay with the company for any great length of time.

2   The income may fluctuate and in particular earnings may fall at the end of the career.

3   There are few prospects of promotion without moving.

4   The job is such that there may well be times when the occupation could be conducted on a self-employed basis.

5   The undertaking is not soundly based and the employment could be terminated on grounds of redundancy.

6   The employee may wish to take time out for a personal reason, eg to have a family or nurse elderly parents.

7   The employee wishes to have the right of retiring early (namely from the age of 50 onwards). This may well be relevant when a partner is considerably older.

8   The employee is not solely reliant on pension provision. As there is no obligation to take the proceeds of a personal pension on retiring, it can be left as a tax-free exempt fund which need only be taken on reaching the age of 75.

For employer

Considerations in favour of a final salary scheme

8.33

1   There is difficulty in recruiting and retaining the workforce and a final salary scheme will deter employees from leaving.

2   With skilled investment and with a proportion of early leavers the final salary scheme may mean that the company can reduce its liabilities to the pension fund.

3   A final salary scheme will attract able employees and be an inducement for them to remain with the company.

Considerations in favour of money purchase schemes

1   The employer knows that the pension provision will be a fixed percentage of the wages bill and there is not the open-ended commitment which a final salary scheme entails.

2   There are real deterrents for employees in leaving employment at the later part of their working lives with final salary schemes. A final salary scheme makes older employees reluctant to look for other employment and to be reluctant to take on less onerous, but less remunerative work.

3   The age profile of the workforce is elderly and this makes a final salary scheme proportionately more expensive to operate.

4   If the pension fund is well or over-funded, there is a danger that this may make the company attractive for unwelcome take-over bids which would not be the case with a money purchase scheme.

Chapter 9

Written particulars of terms of employment

Introduction

The requirement for employees to be provided with a written statement of employment particulars was included in the Contracts of Employment Act 1963, which in some respects was the first piece of modern employment legislation affecting most employees as individuals. The requirements have been added to and improved upon and are now contained in the Employment Rights Act 1996.

The requirements benefit employees only, see **9.02**. Some employees are excluded, see **9.03–9.10**.

For the vast majority of employees, not more than two months after the beginning of their employment, their employer should give them a statement setting out the major terms of the particulars of their employment. See **9.14–9.21**. Some of the requirements may be complied with by referring to other documents, see **9.18**.

If there are changes to the particulars these should be notified to the employee at the earliest opportunity and in any event not later than a month after the change. See **9.22–9.24**.

Contracting out of these requirements is forbidden. See **9.25**.

The statements provided under these provisions are important evidence of the terms of the relationship between the parties. See **9.26–9.29**.

Enforcement of the requirement is through industrial tribunals. The tribunal will determine the terms of the statement of employment particulars or of the change to it. See **9.30–9.35**.

Application of the requirement

9.01   Employers are required to give employees a statement of employment particulars not later than two months after the beginning of the employee's employment.[1] The statement should be given to the employee notwithstanding that his employment ends before the end of the period within which the statement is required to be given.[2]

1 Employment Rights Act 1996, s 1(2).
2 Employment Rights Act 1996, s 2(6).

Employee

9.02   'Employee' means an individual who has entered into or works under (or, where the employment has ceased, worked under) a contract of employment. A contract of employment is a contract of service or apprenticeship, whether express or implied, and (if it is express) whether it is oral or in writing.[1] 'Employer' in relation to an employee means the person by whom the employee is (or in a case where the employment has ceased, was) employed.[2] Thus the provisions relating to the provision of employment particulars do not benefit those working pursuant to contracts for services.[3]

1 Employment Rights Act 1996, s 230(1) and (2). For contract of service, see Chapter 3.
2 Employment Rights Act 1996, s 230(4).
3 For the distinction between contracts of service and contracts for services, see **3.15–3.22**.

Special cases

Special cases should be considered as follows:

Very short-term employees

9.03   The requirement does not apply to an employee if his employment continues for less than one month.[1]

1 Employment Rights Act 1996, s 198.

Merchant seamen and fishermen

9.04   The provisions do not apply to a person employed as a seaman in a ship registered in the United Kingdom under a crew agreement the provisions and form of which are of a kind approved by the Secretary of State.[1] The requirement to provide a statement of employment particulars applies to an employee who at any time comes, or ceases to come, within this exception as if his employment with his employer terminated or began at that time.[2] In such cases there is an obligation to specify the date on which the employee's employment actually began.[3]

1 Employment Rights Act 1996, s 199.
2 Employment Rights Act 1996, s 5(1).
3 Employment Rights Act 1996, s 5(2).

Police officers

9.05   Members of police forces are not employees in the strict legal sense (see **3.29**) and so the provisions do not apply to them, unless working under a contract of employment.

National security

9.06   Where in the opinion of a minister of the Crown the disclosure of any information would be contrary to the interests of national security, the provisions do not require any person to disclose the information and the information should not be disclosed in any proceedings in any court or tribunal relating to those provisions.[1]

1 Employment Rights Act 1996, s 202(1) and (2).

Employment outside Great Britain

9.07   The provisions as to written statements do not apply in relation to employment during any period when the employee is engaged in work wholly or mainly outside Great Britain, unless the employee ordinarily works in Great Britain and the work outside Great Britain is for the same employer, or the law which governs his contract of employment is the law of England and Wales or of Scotland.[1] The requirement to provide a statement of employment particulars applies to an employee who at any time comes, or ceases to come, within this exception as if his employment with his employer terminated or began at that time.[2] This provision does not affect the obligation to specify the date on which his employment actually began.[3] Subject to this exclusion, the provisions apply whatever the law governing the contract between the employer and the employee.[4]

1 Employment Rights Act 1996, s 196(1).
2 Employment Rights Act 1996, s 5(1).
3 Employment Rights Act 1996, s 5(2).
4 Employment Rights Act 1996, s 204.

9.08 There is power in the Employment Rights Act 1996, s 201 for the provisions as to statements of terms and particulars of employment (and others) to be extended by Order in Council to employment for the purpose of any activities in the territorial waters of the United Kingdom, connected with the exploration of the seabed or subsoil, or the exploitation of their natural resources, in the United Kingdom sector of the continental shelf, or connected with the exploration or exploitation, in a foreign sector of the continental shelf, of a cross-boundary petroleum field.[1]

1 By virtue of the Employment Protection (Offshore Employment) Order 1976, SI 1976/766 (as amended by SI 1977/588, SI 1981/208 and SI 1984/1149), which came into operation on 21 June 1976, the provisions apply to employment for the purposes of the following activities:
(a) any activities (other than activities connected with a ship which is in the course of navigation or is a survey ship or is engaged in dredging or fishing) in the territorial waters;
(b) any activities connected with the exploration of the sea bed or subsoil or the exploitation of their natural resources in any designated area (other than an area or part of an area in which the law of Northern Ireland applies) being activities carried out on or from an offshore installation in any such designated area;
(c) any activities in the foreign sector of the continental shelf connected with the exploration or exploitation of the Frigg Gas Field.
The order does not apply to any employment wholly or mainly for the purpose of any activities connected with the Ekofisk Field. In applying the provisions appropriate consequential amendments are made by the Order.

Employees about to work outside the United Kingdom

9.09 Where before the end of the period of two months after the beginning of his employment an employee is to begin to work outside the United Kingdom for a period of more than one month, the statement of employment particulars should be given to him not later than the time when he leaves the United Kingdom in order to begin that work.[1]

1 Employment Rights Act 1996, s 2(5).

Further exclusions

9.10 Additional excluded classes may be prescribed by the Secretary of State for Employment by statutory instrument laid before Parliament and approved by each House of Parliament.[1] The requirement to provide a statement of employment particulars applies to an employee who at any time comes or ceases to come within this exception as if his employment with his employer terminated or began at that time.[2] This provision does not affect the obligation to specify the date on which his employment actually began.[3]

1 Employment Rights Act 1996, s 209(1).
2 Employment Rights Act 1996, s 5(1).
3 Employment Rights Act 1996, s 5(2).

Employees no longer excluded

Part-time employees

9.11   Until 6 February 1995 there was a provision in the Employment Protection (Consolidation) Act 1978,[1] which purported to exclude from the provisions as to written statements an employee if employed under a contract which normally involved employment for less than eight hours weekly. This provision has now been repealed.[2]

1 Employment Protection (Consolidation) Act 1978, s 5(1)(b).
2 By the Employment Protection (Part-time Employees) Regulations 1995, SI 1995/31, reg 2.

Crown servants and members of the services

9.12   At one time Crown servants were excluded from the benefit of these provisions, but they are now included within them.[1] Members of the armed forces are covered by the provisions.[2]

1 As a result of amendments to the Employment Protection (Consolidation) Act 1978 made by the Trade Union Reform and Employment Rights Act 1993, s 49(1) and Sch 7.
2 Employment Rights Act 1996, s 192, which should be referred to for detail.

Parliamentary staff

9.13   Although at one time there was no requirement to provide a statement of employment particulars to relevant members of the House of Commons staff they are now entitled to the benefit of the provisions.[1] The provisions apply in relation to employment as a relevant member of the House of Lords staff as they apply to other employment.[2]

1 See Employment Rights Act 1996, s 195.
2 Employment Rights Act 1996, s 194.

Written particulars of employment

Employer's duty to give statement of employment particulars

9.14   The employer is required to give to the employee a written statement of particulars of employment.[1] The statement may be given in instalments before the end of the period of two months from the commencement of the employment.[2] The statement should contain the information required by ss 1, 2 and 3 of the Employment Rights Act 1996.[3]

1 Employment Rights Act 1996, s 1(1).
2 Employment Rights Act 1996, s 1(2) subject to s 2(3).
3 The Secretary of State may by order provide that the Employment Rights Act 1996, s 1 has effect as if particulars of such further matters as may be specified in the order were included in the particulars required by that section; and, for that purpose, the order may include such provisions amending that section as appear to the Secretary of State to be expedient: Employment Rights Act 1996, s 7.

Contents of the statement

Parties and period of employment

9.15   The statement should contain particulars of:
(1)   the names of the employer and employee;[1]
(2)   the date when the employment began; and
(3)   the date on which the employee's period of continuous employment began (taking into account any employment with a previous employer which counts towards that period).[2]

1 Employment Rights Act 1996, s 1(3)(a). See *Smith v Blandford Gee Cementation Co Ltd* [1970] 3 All ER 154, DC and *Clifford v Union of Democratic Mineworkers* [1991] IRLR 518, CA.
2 Employment Rights Act 1996, s 1(3)(c).

9.16   The statement should also contain particulars, as at a specified date not more than seven days before the statement or instalment of the statement containing them is given, of:

(1)   the scale or rate of remuneration or the method of calculating remuneration;[1]

(2)   the intervals at which remuneration is paid (that is, weekly, monthly or other specified intervals);

(3)   any terms and conditions relating to hours of work (including any terms and conditions relating to normal working hours);

(4)   any terms and conditions relating to any of the following:

(a)   entitlement to holidays, including public holidays, and holiday pay (the particulars given being sufficient to enable the employee's entitlement, including any entitlement to accrued holiday pay on the termination of employment, to be precisely calculated);

(b)   incapacity for work due to sickness or injury, including any provision for sick pay; and

(c)   pensions and pension schemes;[2]

(5)   the length of notice which the employee is obliged to give and entitled to receive to terminate his contract of employment;

(6)   the title of the job which the employee is employed to do or a brief description of the work for which the employee is employed;

(7)   where the employment is not intended to be permanent, the period for which it is expected to continue or, if it is for a fixed term, the date when it is to end;

(8)   either the place of work or, where the employee is required or permitted to work at various places, an indication of that and of the address of the employer;

(9)   any collective agreements which directly affect the terms and conditions of the employment including, where the employer is not a party, the persons by whom they were made; and

(10)   where the employee is required to work outside the United Kingdom for a period of more than one month:

(a)   the period for which he is to work outside the United Kingdom;

(b)   the currency in which remuneration is to be paid while he is working outside the United Kingdom;

(c)   any additional remuneration payable to him, and any benefits to be provided to or in respect of him, by reason of his being required to work outside the United Kingdom; and

(d)   any terms and conditions relating to his return to the United Kingdom.

1 This should be in clear and unambiguous terms. See for example *Owens v Multilux Ltd* [1974] IRLR 113, NIRC and *Cole v Midland Display Ltd* [1973] IRLR 62, NIRC.
2 This does not apply to the employees of any body or authority if the employee's pension rights depend on the terms of a pension scheme established under any provision contained in or having effect under any Act of Parliament, and the body or authority is required by any such provision to give to new employees information concerning their pension rights or the determination of questions affecting their pension rights: Employment Rights Act 1996, s 1(5).

9.17 If there are no particulars to be entered under any of the heads, that fact should be stated.[1] The statement should also include a note about disciplinary procedures and other matters referred to below (see **9.20**).

1 Employment Rights Act 1996, s 2(1).

Reference to other documents

9.18 For particulars of any matters relating to incapacity for work and sick pay and pensions and pension schemes a statement of employment particulars may refer the employee to the provisions of some other document which either the employee has reasonable opportunities of reading in the course of his employment, or is made reasonably accessible to him in some other way.[1] A statement of employment particulars given to an employee may refer the employee to the law,[2] or to the provisions of any collective agreement[3] which directly affects the terms and conditions of the employment, for particulars of the length of notice which the employee is obliged to give, and entitled to receive, to terminate his contract of employment.[4]

1 Employment Rights Act 1996, s 2(2).
2 In practice this normally means referring to such provisions as Employment Rights Act 1996, s 86 (or its predecessor Employment Protection (Consolidation) Act 1978, s 49) which sets out minimum periods of notice.
3 If and only if, it is an agreement which the employee has reasonable opportunities of reading in the course of his employment, or is made reasonably accessible to him in some other way: Employment Rights Act 1996, s 6.
4 Employment Rights Act 1996, s 2(3).

The principal statement

9.19 Certain particulars must be included in one single document. This document is referred to as the 'principal statement'.[1] The particulars which must be included in the principal statement are those relating to the names of employer and employee, the date when the employment began and when the employees's period of continuous employment began, together with the particulars as to:
(1) the scale or rate of remuneration or the method of calculating remuneration;
(2) the intervals at which remuneration is paid (that is, weekly, monthly or other specified intervals);
(3) any terms and conditions relating to hours of work (including any terms and conditions relating to normal working hours);
(4) entitlement to holidays, including public holidays, and holiday pay (the particulars given being sufficient to enable the employee's entitlement, including any entitlement to accrued holiday pay on the termination of employment, to be precisely calculated);
(5) the title of the job which the employee is employed to do or a brief description of the work for which the employee is employed; and
(6) either the place of work or, where the employee is required or permitted to work at various places, an indication of that and of the address of the employer.

1 Employment Rights Act 1996, s 2(4).

*Note about disciplinary and grievance procedures and contracting
out certificate*

9.20   The statement of employment particulars should include a note:

(1)   specifying any disciplinary rules applicable to the employee. In this
connection the statement can refer the employee to the provisions of a
document which the employee has reasonable opportunities of reading
in the course of his employment, or which is made reasonably accessible
to him in some other way, and which specifies such rules;

(2)   specifying, by description or otherwise:

(a)   a person to whom the employee can apply if he is dissatisfied with
any disciplinary decision relating to him; and

(b)   a person to whom the employee can apply for the purpose of
seeking redress of any grievance relating to his employment;

and in each case the manner in which any such application should be
made;

(3)   where there are further steps consequent on any such application,
explaining those steps. Again for these purposes the statement may refer
to the provisions of a document which the employee has reasonable
opportunities of reading in the course of his employment, or is made
reasonably accessible to him in some other way, and which explains
them;[1] and

(4)   stating whether a contracting out certificate is in force for the employment.[2]

In practice this note can be of considerable importance. Disciplinary procedures are very frequently referred to in proceedings relating to employment.

1 Employment Rights Act 1996, s 3(1). This does not apply to rules, disciplinary decisions,
grievances or procedures relating to health or safety at work: Employment Rights Act 1996,
s 3(2).
2 Employment Rights Act 1996, s 3(5).

Small employers

9.21   There are special provisions if on the date when the employee's
employment began the relevant number of employees[1] was less than 20.[2] In
these circumstances the note need not specify any disciplinary rules applicable
to the employee, the person to whom the employee can apply if dissatisfied
with a disciplinary decision relating to him and further steps consequent on
such an application.

1 'The relevant number of employees', in relation to an employee, means the number of
employees employed by his employer added to the number of employees employed by any
associated employer: Employment Rights Act 1996, s 3(4). Any two employers are treated as
associated if one is a company of which the other (directly or indirectly) has control, or if both
are companies of which a third person (directly or indirectly) has control. The expression
'associated employer' is construed accordingly: Employment Rights Act 1996, s 231. See 11.45.
2 Employment Rights Act 1996, s 3(3). It is still good practice to have a suitable disciplinary
procedure and to include a note so that there is no doubt as to the position.

Changes in terms

Employer's obligation

9.22   If, after the date to which a statement given under s 1 relates, or,
where no such statement is given, after the end of the period within which a
statement of employment particulars is required to be given, there is a change

in any of the matters particulars of which are required to be included, or referred to, in the statement, the employer should give to the employee a written statement containing particulars of the change. This should take place at the earliest opportunity and, in any event, not later than one month after the change. Where the change results from the employee being required to work outside the United Kingdom for a period of more than one month, the latest time for giving the statement is when the employee leaves the United Kingdom in order to begin so to work, if that is earlier.[1]

1 Employment Rights Act 1996, ss 4(1) and 4(3). For the detailed provisions as to the material date where the statement is provided in instalments see the Employment Rights Act 1996, s 4(2).

Reference to other documents

9.23 For a change in any of the terms relating to incapacity and sick pay and pensions and pensions schemes and disciplinary rules (other than specifying the person to whom the employee can apply if dissatisfied with any disciplinary decision or if he has a grievance), the statement of the change may refer the employee to the provisions of some other document.[1] This must be a document which the employee has reasonable opportunities of reading in the course of his employment, or is made reasonably accessible to him in some other way.[2] The statement of change may refer the employee to the law, or to the provisions of any collective agreement which directly affects the terms and conditions of the employment, for a change in the length of notice which the employee is obliged to give and entitled to receive to terminate his contract of employment.[3]

1 Employment Rights Act 1996, s 4(4).
2 If, and only if, it is an agreement which the employee has reasonable opportunities of reading in the course of his employment, or is made reasonably accessible to him in some other way: Employment Rights Act 1996, s 6.
3 Employment Rights Act 1996, s 4(5).

Changes in name or identity of the employer

9.24 There are specific provisions applicable where, after an employer has given to an employee a statement of employment particulars, the only change is in the name or identity of the employer. These apply when the name of the employer (whether an individual or a body corporate or partnership) is changed without any change in the identity of the employer, or the identity of the employer is changed in circumstances in which the continuity of the employee's period of employment is not broken, and in each case the change does not involve any change in any of the matters (other than the names of the parties) particulars of which are required[1] to be included in the statement of employment particulars.[2] In these circumstances the person who immediately after the change is the employer is not required to give to the employee a new statement of employment particulars, but the change is treated as a change in the statement of employment particulars.[3] A statement of change which informs an employee of a change in the identity of the employer in circumstances in which the continuity of the employee's period of employment is not broken should specify the date on which the employee's period of continuous employment began.[4]

1 By the Employment Rights Act 1996, ss 1–3.
2 Employment Rights Act 1996, s 4(6).
3 Ie falling within the Employment Rights Act 1996, s 4(1).
4 Employment Rights Act 1996, s 4(8).

Contracting out of provision of written particulars

9.25   Any provision in an agreement (whether in a contract of employment or not) is void insofar as it purports to exclude or limit the operation of any provision of the Employment Rights Act 1996, including those as to statements of employment particulars and changes thereto.[1] Similarly any provision in any agreement is void insofar as it purports to preclude any person from presenting, or bringing proceedings as to statements of employment particulars and changes thereto.[2]

1 Employment Rights Act 1996, s 203(1)(a).
2 Employment Rights Act 1996, s 203(1)(b). This is subject to exceptions where a conciliation officer has taken action or where there is a compromise agreement, see **18.19**.

Effect of the written particulars

9.26   The relationship between employee and employer is governed by the terms of the contract which were agreed by them. The statements of employment particulars given to employees under the provisions of the Employment Rights Act 1996 as to written particulars of employment are usually good evidence of the terms of that relationship so far as the particulars included in the statements are concerned. Thirty years ago it was said by an industrial tribunal in *Moore v RH McCulloch Ltd*[1] 'It should perhaps be added that particulars of a contract of employment delivered [under s 1 of the Employment Rights Act 1996] by the employer to the employee, are not conclusive evidence of what the terms of the contract of employment were'.[2] However, it may be extremely difficult for an employer in proceedings before a court or tribunal to claim that the statement by him wrongly sets out terms and conditions of employment, when it is to the employee's advantage to contend that the statement is correct.[3] As Lord Denning MR said in the Court of Appeal, when discussing a statement of terms and conditions of employment, 'It is well settled that where there is a written contract of employment, as there was here, and the parties have reduced it to writing, it is the writing which governs their relations. It is not permissible to say they intended something different.' In many cases the statement given pursuant to the statutory obligation is not itself the contract of employment. It is the contract which binds the parties and contains the agreement between them whether or not it is in written form.[4] Considerable care should be exercised in preparing the statements to ensure that they correctly represent the contractual position.

1 (1966) 1 ITR 484.
2 At p 486.
3 *Gascol Conversions Ltd v Mercer* (1974) 9 ITR 282 at p 286, CA. See also *Turriff Construction Ltd v Bryant* [1967] 2 KIR 659, DC, and *Parkes Classic Confectionery Ltd v D Ashcroft* (1973) 8 ITR 43, DC.
4 *Robertson v British Gas Corpn* [1983] ICR 351, CA, approved in *Marley v Forward Trust Group Ltd* [1986] ICR 891, CA.

9.27   The document given to the employee has to provide only the particulars required by statute and it is not necessary for other terms of the contract of employment to be included. Notwithstanding this, there are circumstances where it is preferable for stipulations of the contract which are not required to be recorded in the written particulars to be set out. Each case must be looked at individually, but it is often helpful to the parties to include other matters which have been agreed. An example being where the employer has a contractual right to require the employee to change jobs or to undertake additional or differing work in certain circumstances. It is good practice for the terms of this arrangement to be set out precisely. If the appointment of the employee is probationary or temporary this may helpfully be stated, as can any special requirements for the employee to fulfil. Any restrictive agreement should be carefully drawn and included (see **10.13–10.26**). In many such situations it is convenient to include the appropriate clauses in the written particulars of terms of employment given pursuant to the statutory obligation or at least refer to their existence in it.

9.28   It is undoubtedly good practice from the employer's point of view to retain a copy of the statement and to obtain the signature of the employee to it, although there is no statutory requirement as to this. A signature acknowledging receipt of the statement does not of itself amount to an acknowledgement that it contains the terms of the contract unless it says so, although it is strong prima facie evidence of its terms.[1]

1 *System Floors (UK) Ltd v Daniel* [1982] ICR 54, EAT.

9.29   It is important to realise that the obligation to provide the written statement does not alter the common law rules relating to contracts. The requirement of mutuality applies and so an employer cannot unilaterally alter the terms of the contract of employment by issuing a statement of change of those terms.[1] An interesting case on the point is *Turner v Yates Wine Lodges Ltd*[2] when the employee was given a statement under a forerunner of the present obligation. The employee sought advice from his trade union as to whether to sign a copy for the employers. The employers claimed that since the employee had not signed his copy of the statement, the employee had resigned. Mr Turner's application involved other matters, but the tribunal had no difficulty in deciding that he was dismissed. It was not unreasonable for the employee to take advice on the statement which had been given to him.

1 *Jones v Associated Tunnelling Co Ltd* [1981] IRLR 477, EAT; *System Floors (UK) Ltd v Daniel* [1982] ICR 54, EAT; and see *Lee v GEC Plessey Telecommunications* [1993] IRLR 383, HC; and *Aparau v Iceland Frozen Foods plc* [1996] IRLR 119, EAT.
2 [1972] IRLR 84.

Enforcement

Application to industrial tribunal

9.30   Where an employer does not give an employee a statement of employment particulars, or of a change in those particulars, as required (that is to say, either because he gives him no statement or because the statement he gives does not comply with the statutory requirements), the employee may require a reference to be made to an industrial tribunal. The employee asks the tribunal to determine what particulars ought to have been included or referred to in a statement so as to comply with the requirements of the relevant section.[1] Where a statement purporting to be a statement of employment particulars, or of change, has been given to an employee, and a question arises as to the particulars which ought to have been included, or referred to, in the statement so as to comply with the requirements, either the employer or the employee may require that question to be referred to and determined by an industrial tribunal.[2] A question as to the particulars which ought to have been included in the note as to contracting out certificate to be included in the statement of employment particulars does not include any question whether the employment is, has been, or will be, contracted out employment for the purposes of Pt III of the Pensions Schemes Act 1993.[3] An applicant cannot seek damages in the courts for breach of statutory duty by his employer in failing to provide the required written particulars.[4]

1 Under the Employment Rights Act 1996, s 1 or s 4(1).
2 Employment Rights Act 1996, s 11(2).
3 Employment Rights Act 1996, s 11(3).
4 *Scally v Southern Health and Social Services Board* [1991] IRLR 522, HL.

Time limit

9.31 An industrial tribunal will not entertain a reference under these provisions in a case where the employment to which the reference relates has ceased, unless an application requiring the reference to be made was made to the industrial tribunal before the end of the period of three months beginning with the date on which the employment ceased or within such further period as the tribunal considers reasonable, in a case where it is satisfied that it was not reasonably practicable for the application to be made before the end of that period of three months.[1]

1 Employment Rights Act 1996, s 11(4). See the cases referred to at **15.155–15.166**.

Remedy

9.32 On a reference to an industrial tribunal it will determine what particulars ought to have been included, or referred to, in a statement so as to comply with the statutory requirements. Where, on a reference under these provisions, an industrial tribunal determines particulars as being those which ought to have been included, or referred to, in a statement of employment particulars or a change in those particulars, the employer is deemed to have given to the employee a statement in which those particulars were included, or referred to, as specified in the decision of the tribunal.[1]

1 Employment Rights Act 1996, s 12(1). For a recent use of the provisions in relation to a transfer of an undertaking, see *Meade v British Fuels Ltd* [1996] IRLR 541, EAT.

9.33 On determining a reference where a statement purporting to be a statement of employment particulars or of change has been given to an employee, an industrial tribunal may either confirm the particulars as included or referred to in the statement given by the employer, or may amend those particulars. The tribunal may also substitute other particulars for them as the tribunal may determine to be appropriate. The statement is deemed to have been given by the employer to the employee in accordance with the decision of the tribunal.[1]

1 Employment Rights Act 1996, s 12(2).

Determination of particulars by tribunal

9.34 The industrial tribunal will seek to determine the particulars which should have been included in the statement given to the employee. It will determine, confirm or amend the particulars or substitute new particulars accordingly. In performing this function it will use the usual rules of contractual construction. It will decide first whether a term was expressly agreed between the parties. If so, the particulars will be determined, confirmed, amended or substituted, in accordance with that term.[1] When there is no express term the tribunal will determine whether an appropriate clause should be implied into the contract of employment. When there is an implied term the tribunal will determine, confirm, amend or substitute, the particulars to accord with that term. If, using these rules, the tribunal decides that there were no terms in the employee's contract of employment in respect of which particulars should be included in the written statement it will so decide and determine the appropriate particular.

1 *Eagland v British Telecommunications plc* [1993] ICR 644, CA; see pp 652 and 654. Compare with *Mears v Safecar Security Ltd* [1982] IRLR 183, CA. See also *Howman & Son v Blyth* [1983] IRLR 139, EAT.

9.35 The tribunal does not have power under these provisions, to determine terms of a contract of employment particulars of which are not required to be given to the employee.[1] The tribunal may have to determine other provisions in a case brought under the breach of contract provisions (see **13.60**) but does not have to determine particulars which should be given, or should have been given, to the employee in those circumstances.

1 *Eagland v British Telecommunications plc* [1993] ICR 644, CA.

Chapter 10

The employee's duty of good faith

Introduction

An employee is under a duty to act in good faith towards his employer. He should not accept a secret commission or a bribe and he is under a duty to account to his employer for any sums so received (see **10.01**) even if such sums have been obtained under an illegal transaction (see **10.02**). An employee should not utilise information acquired in the course of his own employment for his own use and should not work in his own time for a competitor while the contract of employment subsists (see **10.03** and **10.05**).

The employee should not utilise confidential information either during or after his employment. This does not preclude an employee using the general expertise and experience he has acquired; what is precluded is the use of special or particular information peculiar to his employment (see **10.04** et seq). Apart from the duty of confidentiality the rules of equity will preclude disclosure of confidential information (see **10.10**), but confidentiality will not be protected if it is in the public interest that information be disclosed (see **10.11**).

Employers may seek to limit the employee's right to set up business on his own account or work for a competitor after his employment has ceased. Such conditions are regarded as being void as being in restraint of trade unless they are reasonable as to the limitations which are imposed (see **10.13**).

A provision may be held to be in restraint of trade even though it is not expressed as such (see **10.18**). Courts may sever oppressive terms from unobjectionable terms, but they will not rewrite the contract (see **10.19**).

An employer may seek an injunction or a declaration as well as damages against a former employee. An employer who has repudiated the contract is precluded from enforcing a covenant against an employee or former employee (see **10.23**). A breach of an employee's duties may be a ground for dismissal, but this dismissal has to satisfy the requirements as to fairness. Employers may use garden leave provisions as well as, or instead of, restrictive covenants (see **10.25**). A covenant in restraint of trade which applies during the subsistence of employment is more likely to be enforced (see **10.26**).

Issues of title to inventions and improvements can arise (see **10.27**). Statutory provision for inventions exists and there is provision for compensation. Rights as to copyright and design material are covered by statute (see **10.27**).

Duty of fidelity and duty to account

10.01 An employee is in a position of trust and his or her responsibilities may well encompass handling large sums of money or possessing confidential information either with regards to customers and suppliers or industrial and technical matters. An employee is often in a vulnerable position in relation to his employer in terms of bargaining power. If he wishes to work for another employer or to set up in business on his own, it is likely that he will wish to do so in an area in which he has some experience. There is therefore a balancing act between the protection of the employer's legitimate interests and the protection of the employee's right to work for other employers or to set up in business on his own account, even if this involves working in competition with his former employer. At common law a basic element of the relationship of employer and employee is the obligation of the employee to render loyal service to the employer. The employee must be faithful to his employer, both in dealing with the employer's property and in exercising the trust which the employer places in him. He should not accept any payment or inducement from other persons to influence him in the activities which he carries on for his employer.[1] When performing his services he should do so entirely for the employer's benefit and should not further his own interests (save in earning remuneration), or those of any third party contrary to his employer's interests. It is a breach of this obligation if he makes secret profits for himself in carrying out his duties and he must account for any such profits to his employer. For instance, in *Boston Deep Sea Fishing and Ice Co v Ansell*[2] the employee, who was the employing company's managing director, placed contracts with shipbuilders and received a secret commission. He also made arrangements on the company's behalf, overtly in his own name, which resulted in him receiving moneys from a third party. Although this state of affairs did not come to light until after the employee was dismissed (before the time of his fixed term contract had expired), it was held that the acceptance of secret commission was a sufficient ground to enable the employers to dismiss the employee. The other benefits which the employee had received were bonuses which were paid to him in his personal capacity as a shareholder in the third party and could not have been received by the employer. Even so the employee was held liable to account to the employer for these bonuses. Although the company could not have received them itself, by acting in a way to further his own interests, he had abused the trust placed in him by his employer.

1 *Bartram & Sons v Lloyd* (1903) 88 LT 286; *Harrington v Victoria Graving Dock Co* (1878) 3 QBD 549.
2 (1888) 39 Ch D 339, CA; *Sinclair v Neighbour* [1967] 2 QB 279; [1966] 3 All ER 988. But see *Horcal Ltd v Gatland* [1984] IRLR 288, CA. As for conduct discovered after dismissal in cases of unfair dismissal as opposed to wrongful dismissal, see *W Devis & Sons Ltd v Atkins* [1977] 3 All ER 40; [1977] ICR 662, HL. For a case involving a director in which, on very different facts, there was held to be no duty to declare the terms of new employment which included shares in consideration of business the director was bringing to the new employer, see *Framlington Group v Anderson* [1995] Dec CL 199 and [1995] 1 BCLC 475. The common law does not regard the relationship as one of *uberrimae fidei*, see *Bell v Lever Bros* [1932] AC 161, HL.

Duty to account extends to profits arising from criminal acts

10.02 The obligation to account to the employer extends to circumstances where the moneys arise as a result of criminal actions. *Reading v A-G* was a case where a British Army sergeant in Egypt used his position to enable a criminal practice to be carried on. As a result of the sergeant in uniform accompanying lorries, making it unlikely that the lorries would be stopped by the civilian police, it was easier for criminals to participate in illicit trade in alcoholic spirits. The employee made an enormous profit in doing this, which was claimed by the Crown. In delivering his judgment in the House of Lords, Lord Oaksey said:[1]

> 'I do not think there is any difficulty in imputing to a servant an implied promise that he will account to his master for any moneys he may receive in the course of his master's business, or by the use of his master's property, or by the use of his position as his master's servant. There is nothing illegal in such a promise. On the contrary, in substance it is the basis for the equitable principle that an agent is accountable for profits made in the course of his agency without the knowledge and consent of his principal and no less accountable if the profits arise out of corrupt transactions.'

This principle was reasserted and *Reading's* case was followed by the Privy Council in the case of *A-G for Hong Kong v Reid*.[2] In that case the defendant had been Acting Director of Prosecutions in Hong Kong. He had been convicted of receiving bribes and the case proceeded on the basis that certain property in New Zealand had been purchased with the proceeds of these bribes. The Privy Council held that where a bribe was accepted by a fiduciary in breach of his duty, he held that bribe in trust to the person to whom he owed the duty. If property representing the bribe decreased in value, he had to pay the difference between that value and the initial amount, and if the property increased in value, the employee was not entitled to any surplus in excess of the initial value of bribe because he was not allowed by any means to make a profit out of that breach of duty.

1 [1951] AC 507; [1951] 1 All ER 617 at 621, HL.
2 See [1994] 1 AC 324; [1994] 1 All ER 1, PC.

Duty not to profit from information and not to compete with employer whilst the contract of employment subsists

10.03   When information which would benefit his employer comes into an employee's possession he should disclose it to the employer and should not terminate his employment to utilise the information for his own benefit, or pass it on to some third party.[1] An express or implied term of the contract of employment may impose on the employee a duty to disclose to his employer the fraud of fellow employees.[2] Employees should not take part-time employment which competes with, and harms, the business of their employers. This application of the duty of loyalty was made in *Hivac Ltd v Park Royal Scientific Instruments Ltd*.[3] The employees, who were skilled workers, were employed by a company making hearing aids and in their spare time worked for a direct competitor, and also persuaded other employees of the employer to work for the competitor on a part-time basis. Although no confidential information was passed on by the part-time employees, the plaintiffs were granted an interlocutory injunction to prevent the defendants (the part-time employers) employing the employees of the plaintiffs on this basis. It was said that in assessing the duty of the employees in such cases, all circumstances had to be looked at, but the employees had deliberately set themselves on a course which would harm their employers and so were in breach of this duty of loyalty to them. Morton LJ said:[4]

'In all the circumstances of the case, have these five employees observed the obligations of good faith and fidelity? I do not propose to recapitulate the facts, but I must start from this point, that the work done for the defendants was done in what is usually described as the employees' spare time. No cases were cited to us in which work so done was held to be a breach of the obligation of fidelity to the employer. I do not propose to express any view of such a general nature as that all work done for a firm in the same line of business as the employers in the spare time of the employees is a breach of contract, but I do say that in my view the obligation of fidelity subsists so long as the contract of service subsists, and even in his spare time an employee does owe that obligation of fidelity.'

This decision needs to be set in context in that not every job for a rival company would necessarily justify dismissal. For a case in which an odd job man was held to be unfairly dismissed for working for a competitor see *Nova Plastics Ltd v Froggat*.[5]

1 *Cranleigh Precision Engineering Ltd v Bryant* [1964] 3 All ER 289, [1965] 1 WLR 1293; *Thomas Marshall Exports Ltd v Guinle* [1979] Ch 227; [1978] 3 All ER 193.
2 *Swain v West (Butchers) Ltd* [1936] 3 All ER 261, CA. In *Sybron Corpn v Rochem Ltd* [1984] Ch 112, CA an employee was held to be in such a senior position that he was under an obligation to report misconduct of those above and below him in the hierarchy even though this might well incriminate himself. But see *Horcal Ltd v Gatland* [1984] IRLR 288 and *Bell v Lever Bros* [1932] AC 161. It is suggested that whilst an employee is not under a duty to reveal his own misdeeds because it is not a contract *uberrimae fidei* an employee who fraudulently covers up his misconduct would be in breach of his duty of fidelity. The reality is that industrial tribunals in considering whether a dismissal is unfair frequently attach considerable importance to the frankness of an employee during the investigation. If an employee is guilty of quite minor misconduct, but attempts to deceive his employer about the matter, it is open to a tribunal to conclude that the employee has broken the bond of trust and that the dismissal is fair even though dismissal for the misconduct alone might well not have been fair.
3 [1946] 1 All ER 350, CA. See also *Provident Financial Group plc v Hayward* [1989] ICR 160, CA.
4 [1946] 1 All ER 350 at p 357.
5 [1982] IRLR 146, EAT.

Duty to protect employer's interest

10.04   In *Sanders v Parry*[1] an employed solicitor agreed with one of his principal's clients that he would commence practice on his own account and the client would instruct the defendant to carry out his legal work for a period of seven years. The employee left his principal's employ for this purpose and at the same time his secretary also terminated her employment with the principal and shortly afterwards joined him in the new practice. It was held that during employment there is a duty on the employee to protect his employer's interests and to maintain his contacts. By accepting the offer from the client the employee was looking after his own interests and was in breach of the duty of good faith and fidelity. If the employee had known his secretary was dissatisfied it was his duty to give the opportunity to his principal of dealing with any complaint which she may have had.

1 [1967] 2 All ER 803 and see *Marshall v Industrial Systems and Control Ltd* [1992] IRLR 294 but see *Laughton and Hawley v Bapp Industrial Supplies Ltd* [1986] ICR 634, EAT and **10.24**. See also *GFI Group Ltd v Eaglestone* [1994] IRLR 119.

Duty of confidentiality

10.05 The duty of the employee to look after and preserve the employer's property extends to the employer's physical property[1] and also his intangible property such as his trade secrets, lists of customers and secret processes. The obligation exists while the employee is employed and continues after the employment has terminated. The former employee is free to compete with his ex-employer, either directly by operating his own business, or as an employee of another employer, so long as he does not disclose, or make use of, confidential information belonging to the employer. Indeed the preparation by an employee to set up on his own or join a competitor will not in itself constitute a breach of the duty of loyalty.[2] The extent of the duty of confidentiality will depend on the facts of the particular case. In *Robb v Green*[3] the defendant was the manager of the plaintiff's business. Before he left his employment he copied out lists of his employer's customers to enable him to approach those customers on behalf of the business which he intended to operate when the employment terminated. The court had no difficulty in deciding that the employee was obligated to the employer to keep good faith between them, and the employee had clearly contravened this duty by copying out the lists for his own use.

1 *Leck v Maestaer* (1807) 1 Camp 138, NP; *Superlux v Plaisted* (1958) Times, 12 December; *Cranleigh Precision Engineering Ltd v Bryant* [1964] 3 All ER 289; [1965] 1 WLR 1293.
2 See for example *Hart v Colley* (1890) 6 TLR 216 and on the unfair dismissal aspect, see *Laughton and Hawley v Bapp Industrial Supplies Ltd* [1986] IRLR 245; [1986] ICR 634, EAT approving a judgment of Sir Hugh Griffiths of the NIRC in *Harris and Russell Ltd v Slingsby* [1973] IRLR 221; [1973] ICR 454. But see *Marshall v Industrial Systems and Control Ltd* [1992] IRLR 294 for a case in which a managing director was summarily dismissed; and *Adamson v B & L Cleaning Services Ltd* [1995] IRLR 193.
3 [1895] 2 QB 315, CA; *Floydd v Cheney* [1970] 1 All ER 446 at p 449.

10.06 A recent comprehensive statement of the employee's obligations is contained in the judgment of Neill LJ in *Faccenda Chicken Ltd v Fowler*. He summarised the principles as follows:

'Where the parties are, or have been linked by a contract of employment, the obligations of the employee are to be determined by the contract between him and his employer.

In the absence of any express term, the obligations of the employee in respect of the use and disclosure of information are the subject of implied terms.

While the employee remains in the employment of the employer, the obligations are included in the implied term which imposes a duty of good faith or fidelity on the employee ...

(a)   that the extent of the duty of good faith will vary according to the nature of the contract;
(b)   that the duty of good faith will be broken if an employee makes or copies a list of the customers of the employer for use after his employment ends or deliberately memorises such a list, even though, except in special circumstances, there is no general restriction on an employee canvassing or doing business with customers of his former employer.

The implied term which imposes an obligation on the employee as to his conduct after the determination of the employment is more restricted in its scope than that which imposes a general duty of good faith. It is clear that the obligation not to disclose information may cover secret processes of the manufacture such as chemical formulae ... or designs or special methods and other information. The obligation does not extend, however, to cover all information which is given or acquired by the employee while in the employment, and in particular does not cover information which is only "confidential" in the sense that an unauthorised disclosure of such information to a third party while the employment subsisted would be a clear breach of the duty of good faith.'[1]

In order to determine whether any particular item of information falls within the implied term so as to prevent its use or disclosure by an employee after his employment has ceased, it is necessary to consider all the circumstances of the case.'[2]

1 *Faccenda Chicken Ltd v Fowler* [1986] ICR 297; [1986] IRLR 69, CA.
2 For an example see *Roger Bullivant Ltd v Ellis* [1987] ICR 464, CA.

The extent of confidentiality

10.07 What is protected is information or 'know how' which is special to the employer and it is extremely difficult to define its limits. The best that can be said is that each case is looked at on its facts to ascertain if the employer has an interest which he properly seeks to protect. For instance in *Wessex Dairies Ltd v Smith*[1] a milkman solicited business from his employer's customers when he intended to leave the employment to commence business on his own account. This was found to be an obvious infringement of the employee's obligations. When former employees of a furniture polish manufacturers set up a business in competition with their former employers to sell a similar product, under a name which would manifestly be confused with that of the employers, an injunction was granted to prevent the trade continuing.[2]

1 [1935] 2 KB 80, CA. See also *Bullivant* (**10.06**) and *Johnson & Bloy (Holdings) Ltd and Johnson & Bloy Ltd v Wolstenholme Rink plc and Fallon* [1987] IRLR 499, CA.
2 *Liquid Veneer Co Ltd v Scott* (1912) 29 RPC 639.

Balance between employee utilising experience and expertise and the protection of confidential information

10.08 The employee must be allowed to use his own skill and expertise acquired while working for the employer, but is not entitled to make use of any information which is special or peculiar to his employer. Cross J in *Printers and Finishers Ltd v Holloway*[1] tried to differentiate between the two interests. He said:

'The mere fact that the confidential information is not embodied in a document but is carried away by the employee in his head is not, of course, of itself a reason against the granting of an injunction to prevent its use or disclosure by him. If the information in question can fairly be regarded as a separate part of the employee's stock of knowledge which a man of ordinary honesty and intelligence would recognise to be the property of his old employer and not his own to do as he likes with, then the court, if it thinks that there is a danger of the information being used or disclosed by the ex-employee to the detriment of the old employer, will do what it can to prevent that result by granting an injunction. Thus an ex-employee will be restrained from using or disclosing a chemical formula or a list of customers which he has committed to memory.'

The judge envisaged a case where the ex-employee tells his new employers how the former employers have overcome minor difficulties encountered in the manufacturing process. He continued:

'Recalling matters of this sort is, to my mind, quite unlike memorising a formula or list of customers or what was said (obviously in confidence) at a particular meeting. The employee might well not realise that the feature or expedient in question was in fact peculiar to his late employer's process and factory; but even if he did such knowledge is not readily separable from his general knowledge of the ... process and his acquired skill in manipulating a ... plant, and I do not think that any man of average intelligence and honesty would think that there was anything improper in his putting his memory of particular features of his late employer's plant at the disposal of his new employer. The law will defeat its own object if it seeks to enforce in this field standards which would be rejected by the ordinary man. Afer all, this involves no hardship on the employer. Although the law will not enforce a covenant directed against competition by an ex-employee it will enforce a covenant reasonably necessary to protect trade secrets (see the recent case of *Commercial Plastics Ltd v Vincent*),[2] in which the plaintiff only failed because the covenant was too widely drawn as regards area.'

1 [1964] 3 All ER 731 at pp 735 and 736. It had been said in the past that the distinction was that the employee was entitled to utilise the information he memorised, but no more. Cf *Worsley & Co Ltd v Cooper* [1939] 1 All ER 290.
2 [1965] 1 QB 623; [1964] 3 All ER 546, CA.

Confidential information and trade secrets which will be protected

10.09 In *Thomas Marshall (Exports) Ltd v Guinle*[1] Sir Robert Megarry V-C identified four elements which might be of assistance in identifying confidential information or trade secrets which the court will protect:

'First, I think that the information must be information the release of which the owner believes would be injurious to him or of advantage to his rivals or others. Second, I think the owner must believe that the information is confidential or secret, ie that it is not already in the public domain. It may be that some or all of his rivals already have the information: but as long as the owner believes it to be confidential I think he is entitled to try and protect it. Third, I think that the owner's belief under the two previous heads must be reasonable. Fourth, I think that the information must be judged in the light of the usage and practices of the particular industry or trade concerned. It may be that information which does not satisfy all these requirements may be entitled to protection as confidential information or trade secrets: but I think that any information which does satisfy them must be of a type which is entitled to protection.'

1 [1978] 3 All ER 193 at p 209, ChD; *Amway Corpn v Eurway International Ltd* [1974] RPC 82, ChD, Digest Cont Vol D 997.

Application of equitable principles

10.10 In addition to the duty of confidentiality which arises from the employment relationship, the rules of equity which apply generally to information communicated in confidence are particularly relevant in employment situations. For instance, in *Seager v Copydex Ltd*,[1] an inventor had in confidence provided a potential customer with details of an invention which he had not then patented. Later after negotiations to purchase the invention had broken down the customer, who had not made a bargain with the inventor, sought to patent a similar invention itself. When considering the inventor's claims, Lord Denning MR, said in the Court of Appeal:

'The law on this subject does not depend on any implied contract. It depends on the broad principle of equity that he who has received information in confidence shall not take unfair advantage of it. He must not make use of it to the prejudice of him who gave it without obtaining ... his consent. The principle is clear enough when the whole of the information is private. The difficulty arises when the information is in part public and in part private. As for instance in this case ... When the information is mixed, being partly public and partly private, then the recipient must take special care to use only the material which is in the public domain. He should go to the public source and get it: or, at any rate, not be in a better position than if he had gone to the public source. He should not get a start over others by using the information which he received in confidence. At any rate, he should not get a start without paying for it. It may not be a case for injunction but only for damages, depending on the worth of the confidential information to him in saving him time and trouble.'

1 [1967] 2 All ER 415 at p 417. See also *Saltman Engineering Co Ltd v Campbell Engineering Co Ltd* [1963] 3 All ER 413n and *Terrapin Ltd v Builders Supply Co (Hayes) Ltd* [1960] RPC 128, CA.

Exception to the duty of confidentiality

10.11 An exception to the obligation of confidentiality arises when it is in the public interest to disclose the matters which the employer has revealed to the employee. This was expressed by Lord Denning MR in *Initial Services Ltd v Putterill*[1] in the following way:

'In support of the appeal, counsel for Initial Services Ltd said that in the employment of every servant there is implied an obligation that he will not, before or after his service, disclose information or documents which he has received in confidence. Now I quite agree that there is such an obligation. It is imposed by law. But it is subject to exceptions. Take a simple instance. Suppose a master tells his servant: "I am going to falsify these sale notes and deceive the customers. You are not to say anything about it to anyone." If the master thereafter falsifies the sale notes, the servant is entitled to say: "I am not going to stay any longer in the service of a man who does such a thing. I will leave him and report it to the customers." It was so held in the case of *Gartside v Outram*.[2] Counsel suggested that this exception was confined to a case where the master has been "guilty of a crime or fraud"; but I do not think that it is so limited. It extends to any misconduct of such a nature that it ought in the public interest to be disclosed to others. Wood V-C put it in a vivid phrase:[2] "There is no confidence as to the disclosure of iniquity".'

There is a similar exception to the obligation where the employer seeks publicity to his advantage and he cannot complain if an ex-employee afterwards discloses the truth.[3] It has been held an employee is not in breach of his duty of confidentiality in reporting suspected breaches of regulatory provisions to the body charged with supervising the regulations of financial irregularities to the Inland Revenue.[4] An employee summonsed to answer questions of a liquidator pursuant to s 236 of the Insolvency Act 1986 is not required to give a transcript of his evidence to his employers. Although the information which he gives arises in the course of his employment the employee gives the information because of a statutory requirement and it would be contrary to public policy to require him to disclose a transcript of his evidence.[5] It might be a relevant consideration if an ex-employee sought to make a profit from his breach of confidence.[6]

1 [1967] 3 All ER 145 at p 148, CA; *Fraser v Evans* [1969] 1 QB 349; [1969] 1 All ER 8, CA; *D v National Society for the Prevention of Cruelty to Children* [1976] 2 All ER 993, CA.
2 (1856) 26 LJCh 113 at pp 114 and 116.
3 *Woodward v Hutchins* [1977] 2 All ER 751; [1977] 1 WLR 760, CA.
4 *Re a Company's Application* [1989] ICR 449.
5 *Macmillan Inc v Bishopsgate Investment Trust plc* [1993] IRLR 393.
6 In *A-G v Guardian Newspapers Ltd (No 2)* [1990] 1 AC 109 there was said to be a duty not to profit from a breach of confidence.

Confidentiality and trade union membership

10.12   It was held in *Bent's Brewery Co Ltd v Hogan*[1] that an employee should not disclose confidential information to his trade union. It is not certain whether this would be the common law rule today, but the situation must be affected by the duty as to the disclosure of information to representatives of recognised independent trade unions and the code of practice relating to this issued by the Advisory, Conciliation and Arbitration Service.

1 [1945] 2 All ER 570 (where the information related to payments to employees). See *Archer v Cheshire and Northwich Building Society* [1976] IRLR 424, EAT.

Restrictive agreements

10.13   Employers obviously wish to protect themselves against competition either from an employee setting up in business himself or by working for a competitor. As a result of uncertainties surrounding the common law obligation of confidentiality on employees, employers often try to obtain express covenants or agreements from their employees to restrict their activities, insofar as they involve the disclosure of information which is peculiar to the employer. It is usual for the restraint to purport to operate both whilst the contract subsists and after its termination. Such covenants raise issues of public policy. A balance has to be struck to ensure that the protection of an employer's legitimate interests does not become a device to protect that employer against competition and to render his ex-employee unemployable. All covenants in restraint of trade are prima facie unenforceable at common law.

10.14   Whether or not a restraint on trade is enforceable depends on its reasonableness, both from the point of view of the public and of the parties to it. It is for the person propounding the agreement to prove that it is valid and the restriction, will be regarded as being void unless the contrary is proved.[1] To be enforceable a restraint must be:

'reasonable ... in reference to the interests of the parties concerned and reasonable in reference to the interests of the public, so framed and so guarded as to afford adequate protection to the party in whose favour it is imposed, while at the same time it is in no way injurious to the public'.[2]

10.14 *The employee's duty of good faith*

Although the leading case of *Esso Petroleum Co Ltd v Harper's Garage (Stourport) Ltd*[3] was not concerned with the employment law aspect of the doctrine of restraint of trade, the dictum of Lord Wilberforce that 'the common law has often (if sometime unconsciously) thrived on ambiguity and it would be mistaken, even if it were possible, to try and crystallise the rules of this or any aspect of public policy into neat propositions. The doctrine of restraint of trade is one to be applied to factual situations with a broad and flexible rule of reason' is equally applicable to cases concerning employers and employees.

1 *Herbert Morris Ltd v Saxelby* [1916] 1 AC 688, HL. For other cases showing the approach of the Court of Appeal to apparently wide restraints, see *Littlewoods Organisation Ltd v Harris* [1978] 1 All ER 1026; [1977] 1 WLR 1472, CA and *Greer v Sketchley Ltd* [1979] IRLR 445, CA.
2 Per Lord Macnaughten in *Nordenfelt v Maxim Nordenfelt Guns and Ammunition Co* [1894] AC 535 at p 565, HL.
3 [1968] AC 269 at p 331, HL.

The test of reasonableness

10.15 The courts look with great care at restrictive covenants and agreements in view of the economic inequality between the parties. The employer cannot protect himself from competition by a former employee but he is entitled to protect his confidential information and trade secrets.[1] The tests which are to be applied were explained by Sellers LJ in the Court of Appeal in *Gledhow Autoparts Ltd v Delaney*[2] as follows:

'first, that it is for the covenantee to show that the restriction sought to be imposed on the covenantor goes no further than is reasonable for the protection of his business; secondly, that the restraint must be reasonable not only in the interests of the covenantee but in the interests of both the contracting parties; and thirdly, that an employer is not entitled by a covenant taken from his employee to protect himself after the employment has ceased against his former servant's competition, although a purchaser of goodwill is entitled to protect himself against such competition on the part of the vendor.'

1 *Herbert Morris Ltd v Saxelby* [1916] 1 AC 688, HL.
2 [1965] 3 All ER 288 at p 291, CA.

Restrictions not enforced

10.16 In *Delaney's* case the restrictions sought to prohibit transactions with potential, as well as existing, customers and the covenant was held to be invalid. In applying the test of reasonableness all the circumstances are looked at to see if the agreement is reasonable. *Instone v A Schroeder Music Publishing Co Ltd*[1] is a case, not actually involving a contract of service, when the question of reasonableness was examined by the Court of Appeal. An unknown songwriter, aged 21, entered into an agreement with a music publisher giving the publisher the exclusive right to his songwriting services for five years, renewable in certain circumstances for a further period of five years. The publisher could at any time determine the agreement on a month's notice and there was no obligation on it to exploit the writer's songs. It was held that the contract was unreasonable, as it operated in restraint of trade in view of its 'onesided' nature. Russell LJ said:[2] 'this contract is restrictive of the ability of the plaintiff to turn to account his compositions to an extent and in a manner that is against the public interest.'

1 [1974] 1 All ER 171, CA. See also *Clifford Davis Management Ltd v WEA Records Ltd* [1975] 1 All ER 237; [1975] 1 WLR 61, CA.
2 [1974] 1 All ER 171 at p 178. See *Austin Knight (UK) Ltd v Hinds* [1994] FSR 52, Vinelott J for a further example in which a restrictive covenant was unreasonably wide.

10.17 A covenant the effect of which would be to prevent an employee working in a similar business for a period of seven years after leaving the employer's employment was held by the House of Lords to be void.[1] The contract was contrary to public policy because it would have prevented both the employee and the world at large from having the benefit of the employee's skills.

Attempts to ensure that restrictions are reasonable usually involve several types of limitation on their application, for instance by restricting the employee from dealing with existing customers or suppliers of the employer and no more, or by providing that the restraint is in respect of a closely defined geographic area only or a combination of such restrictions. In addition such agreements are frequently expressed to apply within a time limit after the expiration of the termination of employment. Each case falls to be decided on its merits. In one situation which was brought before the courts, albeit some time ago, a worldwide restriction was considered to be reasonable,[2] as was a covenant not to participate in a solicitor's practice within seven miles of a country town.[3] A covenant not to engage in trade as a tailor within a three mile radius has been upheld[4] and so has a restriction which forbade an estate agent from acting in any capacity as such agent within three miles of a town for three years after the ending of the employment.[5] In *Commercial Plastics Ltd v Vincent*[6] an agreement 'not to seek employment with any of our competitors ... for at least one year after leaving our employ' was held to be void because there was no geographic restriction and the description of the area of operations to which the restriction applied was too wide. This case must now be read in the light of *Littlewoods Organisation Ltd v Harris.*[7] A clause in the contract of service of a very senior executive stated that the employee should not   at   any   time   within 12 months of the determination of his employment, enter into a service agreement with a named competitor company, or be engaged, concerned or interested in the business of the competitor or any of its subsidiaries. The competitor had many subsidiaries which did not compete with the business of the former employer and it carried on its activities throughout the world, whereas the former employer's relevant activities were limited to the United Kingdom. The Court of Appeal held that where a covenant in restraint of trade was drafted in general terms which without alteration of wording could be construed in a sense which was not unreasonably wide in relation to the confidential information or trade secrets to which the former employer was entitled to seek protection, the court should construe the covenant in a way which rendered it valid and enforceable. Courts tend to take a robust attitude towards merely speculative possibilities. Thus in one case[8] a milkman had agreed that he would not serve or sell 'milk or dairy produce' to any customer of his ex-employer. It was argued that the covenant was too wide since it would prevent the employee working for a grocery shop which might sell milk and butter if there was a possibility that customers of the milkman's former employer were also customers of the grocery shop. Although this argument

10.17 *The employee's duty of good faith*

found favour with the trial judge it was rejected by the Court of Appeal. The court found that it was obvious that the restraint was intended to restrict the employee's activities only when engaged in the same type of business as that of the employer. As Cross LJ observed '... the validity of a covenant is not to be tried by the improbabilities that might fall within its wording'.[9] A restrictive covenant is more likely to be upheld if it forms part of a business carried on by the person restrained even if he or she is an employee.[10]

1 *Herbert Morris Ltd v Saxelby* [1916] 1 AC 688, HL.
2 *Nordenfelt v Maxim Nordenfelt Guns and Ammunition Co* [1894] AC 535, HL.
3 *Fitch v Dewes* [1921] 2 AC 158, HL. See *Office Angels Ltd v Rainer Thomas* [1991] IRLR 214, CA.
4 *Putsman v Taylor* [1927] 1 KB 741, CA.
5 *Calvert Hunt and Barden v Elton* (1974) 233 Estates Gazette 391.
6 [1965] 1 QB 623; [1964] 3 All ER 546, CA. See also *Spencer v Marchington* [1988] IRLR 392.
7 [1978] 1 All ER 1026; [1977] 1 WLR 1472, CA. Contrast *Greer v Sketchley Ltd* [1979] IRLR 445, CA in which a director of their dry cleaning operation was restrained from working within the United Kingdom for 12 months. It was held that this was too wide since he had only had responsibility for part of that area.
8 *Home Counties Dairies Ltd v Skilton* [1970] 1 WLR 526, CA.
9 [1970] 1 WLR 526 a p 537, per Cross LJ.
10 See *Systems Reliability Holdings plc v Smith* [1990] IRLR 377; for the position as far as partners is concerned see *Bridge v Deacons* [1984] AC 705, PC.

Courts look at substance not form

10.18 A provision in an agreement may be a restraint on trade even though not expressed as such.[1] In *Eastham v Newcastle United Football Club Ltd*[2] the football clubs who were members of the Football Association had agreed to a rule that if a footballer's employment contract was terminated other football clubs would not employ him without the consent of the previous club. This agreement was held to be void as being in restraint of trade because it restricted the freedom of footballers to earn their living.

1 *Stenhouse Australia Ltd v Phillips* [1974] AC 391; [1974] 1 All ER 117, PC when one of the obligations was to pay half of an insurance broker's gross commission to the former employer was dealt with as an agreement in restraint of trade: *Wyatt v Kreglinger and Fernau* [1933] 1 KB 793, CA; *Bull v Pitney-Bowes Ltd* [1966] 3 All ER 384; [1967] 1 WLR 273.
2 [1964] Ch 413; [1963] 3 All ER 139; *Cooke v Football Association* (1972) Times, 24 March. See also *Greig v Insole* [1978] 3 All ER 449; [1978] 1 WLR 302, QBD. See also *R v Jockey Club, ex p RAM Racecourses Ltd* [1993] 2 All ER 225, DC.

Severance

10.19 If the contract in its entirety is against public policy, then it is un-enforceable. However, an issue arises when certain terms of the contract are in breach of public policy but other terms are unobjectionable. The question then arises as to whether certain parts of the contract may be enforced although other parts are unenforceable. The courts have been prepared to enforce the contract if they can sever the unenforceable parts of the contract. It is often difficult for employers to predict whether their employee's agreement will be enforced. If the restriction which the employer has sought to impose is found to be void by the court, it will not rewrite a new contract for the parties and substitute a reasonable covenant in its place.[1] In such circumstances all the employer can do is to rely on the obligation of confidentiality at common law. The problem for employers is that they are unable to know whether agreements entered into by their employees are enforceable, until the restriction has been considered by the court, by which time it is too late for the matter to be put right. In drafting restrictions for inclusion in service agreements great care should be exercised to ensure that only such limitations as are necessary to protect the employer's proprietorial interests are included. One method adopted as an attempt to overcome this difficulty was to have several covenants contained in one agreement document, but in *Atwood v Lamont*[2] the Court of Appeal refused to apply the previous 'blue pencil' approach. It considered the covenant imposed by the employer to be oppressive and would not do anything to render it enforceable. However, if the covenants are drawn in such a way as to be totally independent of each other severance may still be used to benefit the employer. In *T Lucas & Co Ltd v Mitchell*[3] one of the two restrictions which had been imposed was reasonable and the other was not. The reasonable restriction depended on the other covenant for the definition of the goods in respect of which it applied. Pennycuick V-C said:

'I conclude then that cl 16 cannot be severed. The first restriction is unreasonable and unenforceable and the second, standing alone, would be reasonable and enforceable but as the two restrictions cannot be severed one must treat the entirety of the restrictions as being unreasonable and unenforceable. I must say I come to this conclusion with considerable regret. What is actually happening is that the defendant is canvassing the plaintiff company's customers with whom he dealt during his employment. Had cl 16 been framed as two separate restrictions there is no doubt in my mind that the plaintiff company could have prevented him from doing what he is now doing.'

The learned judge was clearly of the opinion that if the two restrictions were entirely separate, the second restriction would have been reasonable and would have been enforceable.

1 *Commercial Plastics Ltd v Vincent* [1965] 1 QB 623; [1964] 3 All ER 546, CA; *Littlewoods Organisation Ltd v Harris* [1978] 1 All ER 1026; [1977] 1 WLR 1472, CA.
2 [1920] 3 KB 571.
3 [1972] 2 All ER 1035 at p 1046. For other cases on severance see *Rex Stewart Jeffries Parker Ginsberg Ltd v Parker* [1988] IRLR 483, CA; *Spencer v Marchington* [1988] IRLR 392; and *Sadler v Imperial Life Assurance Co of Canada Ltd* [1988] IRLR 388.

Construction

10.20   The covenants must be limited to the circumstances which the court considers the parties had in their contemplation when the relationship was entered into.

'Another matter which requires attention is whether a restriction on trade must be treated as wholly void because it is so worded as to cover cases which may possibly arise, and to which it cannot be reasonably applied ... Agreements in restraint of trade, like other agreements, must be construed with reference to the object sought to be attained by them. In cases such as the one before us, the object is the protection of one of the parties against rivalry in trade. Such agreements cannot be properly held to apply to cases which, although covered by the words of the agreement, cannot be reasonably supposed ever to have been contemplated by the parties, and which on a rational view of the agreement are excluded from its operation by falling, in truth, outside, and not within its real scope.'[1]

This general proposition is of particular relevance when the Transfer of Undertaking (Protection of Employment) Regulations 1981 apply. In *Morris*

Angel & Son Ltd v Hollande[2] the defendant was employed as a managing director of A Ltd and its subsidiaries. His service agreement contained a covenant restricting him, for one year following the termination of his employment, from dealing with any person who had done business with A Ltd or its group in the previous year. A Ltd was purchased by the plaintiff company who dismissed the defendant. The plaintiff sought to enforce the restrictive covenant. An issue arose as to whether the plaintiff was entitled by virtue of reg 5(1) of the 1981 Regulations to enforce the covenants in relation to those who had done business with A Ltd or with the plaintiff. At first instance it was held that the restrictive covenant should apply as though it was made between the defendant and the plaintiff. The Court of Appeal allowed the appeal; the obligations of the covenant would apply to those people who had dealt with A Ltd during the relevant time since that was in the contemplation of the parties when the covenant was made. The effect of the regulations was merely to give the plaintiff the same right to enforce the agreement as A Ltd would have enjoyed. As Dillon LJ said of the decision at first instance:

'Such an obligation was not remotely in the contemplation when the service agreement was entered and I see no reason why the regulation should have been thought to change the burden on the employee.'[3]

1 Per Lindley MR in *Haynes v Doman* [1899] 2 Ch 13 at pp 24 and 25, CA.
2 [1993] IRLR 169; [1993] 3 All ER 569, CA.
3 Per Dillon LJ at p 575.

10.21   The construction of restrictions gives rise to considerable difficulties. The agreement must be approached without reference to the question of its legality or illegality.[1] In *Moenich v Fenestre*[2] Lopes LJ said:

'There are two canons of construction to be considered where questions of this kind arise. One is, that you must examine whether the restraint, having regard to the circumstances of the case, the business of the employer, and the nature of the employment, is greater than is reasonably required for the protection of the employer in his trade or business. The other is, you must construe the agreement according to the reasonable meaning of the words used, without regard to what may be the effect of such construction.'

1 *Mills v Dunham* [1891] 1 Ch 576, CA.
2 (1892) 67 LT 602, CA.

10.22   In *Home Counties Dairies Ltd v Skilton*[1] it was held that a restriction not to sell dairy produce to those persons who had been customers within six months of the termination of the contract of employment was reasonable. It could be reasonably expected that such persons might return their custom to the employer even if they had left during the six-month period. The more liberal approach of the Court of Appeal in *Littlewoods Organisation Ltd v Harris*[2] may be adopted but the only adequate solution for employers is to err on the side of caution when drawing up restrictive covenants for employees to enter into.

1 [1970] 1 All ER 1227; [1970] 1 WLR 526, CA.
2 *Littlewoods Organisation Ltd v Harris* [1978] 1 All ER 1026; [1977] 1WLR 1472, CA. See also *Office Overload Ltd v Gunn* (1976) 120 Sol Jo 147, CA and *Greer v Sketchley Ltd* [1979] IRLR 445, CA. For recent examples in financial services see *Cantor Fitzgerald International v George* [1996] 5 CL 196, CA and *GFI Group Inc v Eaglestone* [1994] IRLR 119, QBD.

Remedies against ex-employees and the new employer

10.23 If a former employee breaks a valid restriction, or does not comply with his obligations as to confidentiality, the employer may be able to claim both damages and an injunction to prevent the breach continuing, against the former employee. In many cases the remedy which will be most effective will be the injunction. In addition to an injunction against the former employee, the employer may be able to obtain a similar remedy against a new employer. This can be extremely effective if obtained quickly and an interlocutory injunction[1] will often be a final solution to the former employer's problem. The right to sue the former employee for damages tends to be of more academic than practical interest. In certain circumstances it may also be possible to obtain an award of damages against the new employer.[2] If the employers have repudiated the contract they cannot then enforce a covenant against the former employee.[3] A party to a restriction may also be able to seek a declaration as to the validity of the restriction.[4] The plaintiff employer is unlikely to obtain an order that the costs of an action against the former employee be paid by the new employer if the new employer was not joined in the action. In *Symphony Group plc v Hodgson*[5] the plaintiff had employed the defendant under a contract of employment which provided a restrictive covenant that the defendant should not work for a competitor for a year. The defendant left the plaintiff's employment and worked for H Ltd, a competitor. The defendant signed a letter drafted by H Ltd's solicitors claiming that the plaintiff had repudiated the contract. The defendant was at all times represented by H Ltd's solicitors under the terms of a legal aid cerificate. The defendant lost the action and an order was made against him for costs which were likely to exceed £100,000. However, as the defendant was legally aided the order was that the order of costs was not to be enforced without leave of the court. The reality was that there was no realistic prospect of the order for costs being met and therefore the plaintiffs applied for an order for costs against H Ltd under s 51(1) of the Supreme Court Act 1981. In allowing H Ltd's appeal it was held that it would only be in very exceptional circumstances that a non-party to an action could be ordered to pay the costs if the successful plaintiff could have joined the non-party as a party to the original proceedings.

1 See for instance *Standex International Ltd v Blades* [1976] FSR 114, CA, but contrast *Consolidated Agricultural Suppliers Ltd v Rushmere* (1976) 120 Sol Jo 523, CA. See as well *Barry Artist Ltd v Baumal* [1975] LS Gaz R 123, ChD. As to when an interlocutory injunction may be obtained see *American Cyanamid Co v Ethicon Ltd* [1975] AC 396; [1975] 1 All ER 504, HL and *Dairy Crest Ltd v Pigott* [1989] ICR 92, CA. For recent examples in which injunctive relief was granted, see *Poly Lina v Finch* [1995] FSR 751 and *Hanover Insurance Brokers Ltd v Shapiro* [1994] IRLR 82, CA, but cf *Alliance Paper Group plc v Prestwich* [1996] IRLR 25 at first instance.
2 See *Printers and Finishers Ltd v Holloway* [1964] 3 All ER 731; [1965] 1 WLR 1.
3 *General Billposting Ltd v Atkinson* [1909] AC 118, HL. See *D v M* [1996] IRLR 192 and *PR Consultants Scotland Ltd v Mann* [1996] IRLR 188. *D v M* was overruled by *Rock Refrigeration Ltd v Jones* [1997] 1 All ER 1, CA.
4 *Greer v Sketchley Ltd* [1979] IRLR 445, CA.
5 [1993] 4 All ER 143, CA.

Remedies against existing employees

10.24 If an employee is still in the injured employer's employment at the time of the breach of the obligation as to confidentiality, or breach of a valid restrictive agreement, it has to be considered whether the employee has repudiated the contract of employment such as to justify dismissal. The position both at common law and under the unfair dismissal provisions has to be considered. A breach of the duty of confidentiality would doubtless amount to a reason as to the employee's conduct for the purpose of the unfair dismissal provisions, but it still has to be shown that having regard to the reason the employer has in all the circumstances acted reasonably in treating it as sufficient reason for dismissing the employee.[1] As Sir Hugh Griffiths put it in *Harris and Russell Ltd v Slingsby*:[2]

'This court ... would regard it as a wholly insufficent reason to dismiss a man, that he was merely seeking employment with a competitor, unless it could be shown there were reasonably solid grounds for supposing that he was doing so in order to abuse his confidential postion and information with his present employer. By the very nature of things, when a man changes his employment, it is more likely he will be seeking fresh employment with someone in the same line of business and therefore a competitor of his present employers.'

1 The decision to dismiss has to satisfy the reasonableness test of s 98(4) of the Employment Rights Act 1996.
2 See *Laughton and Hawley v Bapp Industrial Supplies Ltd* [1986] IRLR 245; [1986] ICR 634; approving dicta of Sir Hugh Griffiths in *Harris and Russell Ltd v Slingsby* [1973] IRLR 221; [1973] ICR 454. But see *Adamson* (10.05).

10.25 In addition to, or in place of, a restrictive covenant employers have resorted to the expedient of what has become known as a 'garden leave' provision. Such a clause reserves to the employer the right to require the employee to spend the period of notice at home in the hope that the value of his contacts and confidential information will diminish.[1] However, courts will not allow analogies of garden leave cases to be applied when the contract has actually been terminated.[2] A garden leave provision coupled with a restriction operating from the termination of employment can give the employer a very considerable period of protection. In *Crédit Suisse Asset Management Ltd v Armstrong*[3] A was employed in the private client department of his employer. He handed in his notice and was placed on garden leave. He was also subject to a restrictive covenant of six months after the end of his employment. He wished to take up other employment with a competitor. He argued that the garden leave period and the restrictive covenant extended the period of protection to 12 months. In dismissing his appeal the Court of Appeal made it clear that in all but an exceptional case there was no power to set off the period of garden leave against the period of the restrictive covenant. As long as the restrictive covenant was valid it would be enforced by the court.

1 *Provident Financial Group plc v Haywood* [1989] IRLR 84; [1989] ICR 160, CA. In that case the court refused to grant an injunction since there was no real evidence that there was a serious prospect of damage if the employee took up a new job and in any event there was only 10 weeks of the notice unexpired. See also *GFI Group Inc v Eaglestone* [1994] IRLR 119 and *EuroBrokers Ltd v Rabey* [1995] IRLR 206.
2 *JA Mont (UK) v Mills* [1993] IRLR 172, CA.
3 [1996] ICR 882, CA.

10.26 The courts look on restrictions on trade during an employment or engagement, in a different light from those afterwards. It is generally regarded as less likely that a restriction during the continuance of the employment would be inimical to the public interest'.[1]

1 See *William Robinson & Co Ltd v Heuer* [1898] 2 ChD 451, CA and *Rely-A-Bell Burglar and Fire Alarm Co Ltd v Eisler* [1926] Ch 609. *Esso Petroleum Co Ltd v Harper's Garage (Stourport) Ltd* [1968] AC 269; [1967] 1 All ER 699 at p 727, HL. See **10.05** and the authorities quoted therein.

Inventions, copyright and registered designs

10.27   The question of title to inventions or improvements in processes made by employees occasionally gives rise to problems and it falls to be decided in whose ownership the invention, patent or improvement should be vested. It would be beyond the ambit of this work to deal with these issues which are mainly governed by the provisions of the Copyright, Designs and Patents Act 1988 and are the subject of specialist monographs.[1]

1 See Butterworth's *Intellectual Property Law Handbook* (2nd edn, 1994).

Chapter 11

Continuity of employment and a week's pay

Introduction

Continuity of employment is an artificial concept which bristles with difficulties of definition. It is relevant for determining whether a former employee qualifies for certain employment rights and also the quantum of some awards which may be made in a former employee's favour, see **11.01**.

Continuity of employment cannot be waived or the employer estopped so as to confer jurisdiction on an industrial tribunal, see **11.09**.

It is not possible for the employer and employee to agree what the period of continuous employment is, see **11.09**. If an employer gives an employee assurance that his continuity of employment will be preserved but on the statutory construction it has not been then no question of estoppel arises and if the statutory requirement is not satisfied then the tribunal does not have jurisdiction.

There are rules which enable the beginning and end of periods of continuity of employment to be determined, see **11.03** and **11.04**.

There is a presumption of continuity of employment, see **11.07**. Continuity of employment only counts if it is under a lawful contract of employment, see **11.07**.

The fundamental rule is that a week which does not count under the rules breaks continuity of employment, see **11.05**. Weeks count if during the week the employee works for the employer, or there is a contract of employment between him and the employer, see **11.10**.

There are certain exceptions to this. These cover absences because of sickness and injury (see **11.20** and **11.21**); arrangement or custom (see **11.30–11.33**); pregnancy or childbirth (see **11.34–11.35**); a strike (see **11.36–11.37**) and temporary cessation of work (see **11.22–11.29**).

There are many cases of intermittent work today, for instance in fishing, catering and teaching. These employments pose problems when considering continuity of employment. They raise questions as to whether the employee is employed under one contract or a series of contracts of short duration, and whether in the later case continuity is preserved by construing the absences as a temporary cessation of work? Assistance in dealing with these questions will be found at **11.18–11.34**.

At common law employment was personal and it would have been regarded as contrary to the common law for an employee to be transferred from one employer to another. There are specific provisions to preserve continuity on the death of an employer (see **11.46**), a change in partners, personal representatives, and trustees who employ an employee (see **11.47**). Continuity is preserved when employees transfer between associated employers and those with common control, see **11.45**.

Continuity is also preserved when there is a change in ownership of a business, see **11.41–11.43**. In this connection the Transfer of Undertakings (Protection of Employment) Regulations 1981 have to be considered as well as the provisions of the Employment Rights Act 1996, see **11.41**.

A week's pay is an important concept for calculating redundancy payments, basic awards and certain other payments which are payable to employees. There are technical rules for calculating a week's pay, see **11.48–11.59**.

Continuity of employment

The concept

11.01   Continuity of employment is a concept which is used to ascertain qualification for, and the amount of entitlement to, certain statutory employment rights. The general rule is that if an employee is employed by his employer during a week that week counts as a week of employment. A period of employment consists of the continuous period during which the employment with that employer continues without a break.

Calculation

11.02   References to a period of continuous employment in any provision of the Employment Rights Act 1996[1] are, except where provision is expressly made to the contrary, to a period computed in accordance with the provisions of Pt XIV, Ch I of the Act.[2] In computing an employee's period of continuous employment any question arising as to whether a period of employment counts towards a period of continuous employment, or whether periods (consecutive or otherwise) are to be treated as forming a single period of continuous employment, is determined in accordance with Pt XIV.[3] Periods of employment are calculated week by week, but the length of an employee's period of employment is computed in months and years of 12 months in accordance with the statutory rules.[4] A month means a calendar month and a year means a year of 12 calendar months.

1 Employment Rights Act 1996, Pt XIV, Ch I provides an exhaustive definition of continuous employment: *Secretary of State for Employment v Globe Elastic Thread Co Ltd* [1979] IRLR 327, HL. The provisions as to continuity apply to periods before they came into force as well as to later periods. Weeks which counted under the former rules relating to continuity of employment for the purposes of the Contracts of Employment Act 1972, the Redundancy Payments Act 1965, the Trade Union and Labour Relations Act 1974 and the Employment Protection Act 1975 count under the present provisions. Any week which did not break the continuity of a person's employment for the purpose of those Acts does not do so for the purpose of the Employment Rights Act: Employment Rights Act 1996, Sch 2, para 6.
2 Employment Rights Act 1996, s 210(1).
3 Employment Rights Act 1996, s 210(3).
4 Employment Rights Act 1996, s 210(3).

Commencement date

11.03   Subject to the special provision as to redundancy payments, an employee's period of continuous employment for the purposes of any provision of the Act begins with the day on which he starts work and ends with the day by reference to which the length of his period of continuous employment falls to be ascertained for the purposes of the provision in question.[1] 'Starts work' is not given a literal interpretation as being the time when the employee commences his duties. It refers to the commencement of the relevant employment, so that the period of continuous employment of an employee whose contract begins on a bank holiday on which work is not carried out commences on the bank holiday. For the purposes of an employee's entitlement to redundancy payment, an employee's period of continuous employment is treated as beginning on his 18th birthday, if that date is later than the starting date.[3]

1 Employment Rights Act 1996, s 211(1).
2 *General of the Salvation Army v Dewsbury* [1984] IRLR 222, EAT.
3 Employment Rights Act 1996, s 211(2).

Termination date

11.04 The date at which the relevant period of continuous employment ends is determined in accordance with the rules applicable to the right in respect of which the period of employment is being considered.[1] It is to be noted that for some purposes in connection with claims for redundancy payments and remedies for unfair dismissal, when the employment is terminated by the employer without proper (ie minimum statutory) notice the period of continuous employment is extended (see **15.67–15.68**).

1 Reference should be made to the relevant paragraphs in the text and to the relevant checklists.

Breaks in continuity

11.05 A most important feature of the concept of continuity of employment is that a week which does not count breaks the continuity of the period of employment, unless it is otherwise provided.[1]

1 Employment Rights Act 1996, s 210(4).

Particular weeks which do not break the period

11.06 The provisions as to continuity apply to a period of employment even though during that period the employee was excluded by or under the Employment Rights Act 1996 from any right conferred by the Act.[1] If an employee's period of continuous employment includes one or more periods which, by virtue of the provisions, do not count in computing the length of the period but do not break continuity, in calculating the length of a period of continuous employment the beginning of the period is treated as postponed by the number of days which do not count.[2] There are special rules in such cases.[3] For instance, if an employee takes part in a strike for three weeks during the period of his employment then, when calculating the length of his period of continuous employment with the employer, the commencing date is treated as being postponed by three weeks.[4]

1 Employment Rights Act 1996, s 215(1)(b).
2 Employment Rights Act 1996, s 211(3).
3 For the specific rules see the Employment Rights Act 1996, ss 214, 215, 216 and 217.
4 Employment Rights Act 1996, s 216(2).

Presumption of continuity

11.07 A person's employment during any period is, unless the contrary is shown, presumed to have been continuous.[1] Thus the onus of proof is on the employer, or former employer, who alleges that employment has not been continuous to prove that there was no continuity. This involves proving a negative and so is usually effected by producing evidence of a break in the employment. Continuous employment means continuous employment under a legal contract of employment. Thus when an untaxed lodging allowance was received as an expense for a month when not incurred the period of continuous employment was broken.[2]

1 Employment Rights Act 1996, s 210(5). For an interesting consideration of this provision where there had been a change of employer, see *Secretary of State for Employment v Cohen and Beaupress Ltd* [1987] ICR 570, EAT.
2 *Hyland v JH Barker Ltd* [1985] ICR 861, EAT.

11.08 Subject to the express exemptions, continuity of employment must be with one employer and the statutory presumption of continuity only applies to employment by that employer.[1]

1 *Secretary of State for Employment v Globe Elastic Thread Co Ltd* [1979] IRLR 327, HL. See the judgment of Lord Wilberforce in particular at p 329.

Contractual continuity?

11.09 Since continuity of employment is a statutory concept it occurs only when the statutory requirements are satisfied. If this is not the case the parties cannot enter into an agreement to produce a 'contractual' continuity of employment. At one time it was suggested[1] that in circumstances where there was no continuity of employment in accordance with the statutory provisions, an employer could be 'estopped' by reason of his conduct[2] from denying that continuity of employment existed. It is now clear that estoppel will not operate in these circumstances. Accordingly, an employer who gives assurances to a new employee that his employment will be treated as continuous with that with a previous employer when there is no continuity pursuant to the statutory provisions will not be estopped from denying that there was no continuity of employment. The employer may be liable to that employee pursuant to the contract, but the agreement will not give an industrial tribunal jurisdiction to take the period of employment with the former employer into account when determining the employee's statutory rights.[3]

1 *Evenden v Guildford City Association Football Club Ltd* [1975] QB 917; [1975] 3 All ER 269; [1975] ICR 367, CA.
2 For instance by assuring an employee that his rights as an employee will be preserved on a change from one employer to another when continuity is not provided for by the Act.
3 *Secretary of State for Employment v Globe Elastic Thread Co Ltd* [1979] IRLR 327, HL.

Weeks which count

The basic principle

11.10 In general the concept of continuity of employment depends upon the relationship of employer and employee existing at the relevant time. Any week during the whole, or part, of which the employee's relations with the employer are governed by a contract of employment counts in computing a period of employment, as does any week during which the employee is employed by the employer.[1] All weeks which meet either of these criteria count in computing the period of continuous employment. Periods of absence for illness and holidays are normally included by reason of these rules since the contract of employment continues to subsist during such absences. However, a contract of employment must subsist for there to be continuity of employment unless continuity is otherwise preserved by the statutory provisions.[2]

1 Employment Rights Act 1996, s 212(1). Prior to the decision of the House of Lords in *R v Secretary of State for Employment, ex p Equal Opportunities Commission* [1995] 1 AC 1, HL and consequent regulations there were thresholds of 16 hours a week (or eight hours a week after five years' service) before weeks counted.
2 *Hellyer Bros Ltd v McLeod* [1987] ICR 526, CA.

A series of contracts

11.11 It frequently happens in a period of service with one employer that the employer and employee enter into a succession of contracts; for example there may be a new contract of employment each time an employee is promoted. To be continuous, employment does not have to be pursuant to a single contract of service.[1] A series of contracts can provide the basis of a period of continuous employment provided that the employment is continuous. On the other hand a series of contracts with breaks between them may not together amount to a period of continuous employment. An example of this can occur where those who work on a ship spend periods ashore during which there is no contract of employment with the employer. Unless the periods when there is no contract are preserved by the other provisions of the Act they do not count and break the period of continuity. When the Court of Appeal was considering such a case, Slade LJ said: 'Though the series of short-term crew agreements had continued in sequence for a long time, and it was no doubt desirable in everyone's interest that stable crews should if possible be maintained, the existence of this series does not show that there was any umbrella contract which imposed mutual obligations between each man and [the employer], during such terms as the short-term contracts were not subsisting'.[2]

1 *Hellyer Bros Ltd v McLeod* [1987] ICR 526 at p 531, CA.
2 *Wood v York City Council* [1978] ICR 840, CA; *Re Mack Trucks (Britain) Ltd* [1967] 1 All ER 977; [1967] 1 WLR 780, ChD.

Preservation of continuity

11.12 There are regulations[1] which preserve continuity when an employee is reinstated or re-engaged by his employer, or engaged by a successor or associated employer in certain circumstances.[1] These apply when the reinstatement or engagement takes place following the presentation of a claim to an industrial tribunal of a relevant complaint of dismissal,[2] or after the intervention of a conciliation officer, or after a claim is made in accordance with a dismissals procedure agreement,[3] or after the making of a relevant compromise agreement.[4] In these circumstances the period beginning with the date of dismissal took effect and ending with the date of reinstatement or re-engagement, as the case may be, counts in the computation of the employee's period of continuous employment and its continuity is preserved.

If the terms of the re-engagement or engagement include provision for the employee to repay the amount of the redundancy payment paid in respect of the dismissal, s 214 of the Employment Rights Act 1996 (which requires the period of continuity to be broken for redundancy payment purposes when a redundancy payment is paid) does not apply so long as the provision in the terms is complied with.[5]

1 Employment Protection (Continuity of Employment) Regulations 1996, SI 1996/3147.
2 Employment Protection (Continuity of Employment) Regulations 1996, r 2(b).
3 Designated under the Employment Rights Act 1996, s 110.
4 Employment Protection (Continuity of Employment) Regulations 1996, r 2(d).
5 Employment Protection (Continuity of Employment) Regulations 1996, r 4.

Extension of period of continuous employment

11.13 Where s 97(2) or s 97(4) of the Employment Rights Act 1996 apply and as a result a date is treated as the effective date of termination of employment which is later than the effective date of termination of employment as determined by s 97(4), then for the purposes of ss 108(1) and 119(1) of the Employment Rights Act 1996 the period to the later date is included in the period of continuous employment.[1] Specific provisions apply when an employee is treated as not being dismissed by reason of renewal or re-engagement under s 138(1) of the Employment Rights Act 1996[2] and where the relevant date is extended by s 145(5) of that Act.[3]

1 Employment Rights Act 1996, s 213 which should be referred to in detail.
2 Employment Rights Act 1996, s 213(2).
3 Employment Rights Act 1996, s 213(3).

Continuity of employment and redundancy payments

11.14 For the purposes of determining whether an employee is entitled to a redundancy payment, and the period of continuous employment on calculation of a redundancy payment, special provisions apply. If a redundancy payment is paid to an employee who is dismissed, or laid off, or put on short-time, within the meaning of the Act but the contract of employment is renewed, or he is re-engaged, the continuity of the period of employment is treated for the purposes of redundancy payments as being broken at the date which was the relevant date in respect of the payment of the redundancy payment.[1] Accordingly no account is taken for the purposes of redundancy payments in any subsequent calculation of the period of employment of any time before that date.[2] Payment includes actual payment by the employer and also payment made by the Secretary of State. Similar provisions apply when, instead of a redundancy payment, a payment has been made under s 1 of the Superannuation Act 1972 or similar payments to other public employees[3] so that the continuity is broken by such payment.[4] This provision applies only to calculations carried out for the calculation of entitlement to, and the amount of, a redundancy payment.

1 Employment Rights Act 1996, s 214.
2 However, there must be a true redundancy for this to apply. So that when a payment was made which was described as a redundancy payment but the employee was not redundant this provision did not apply: *Rowan v Machinery Installations (South Wales) Ltd* [1981] ICR 386, EAT. See also *Boorman v Allmaker* [1995] ICR 842, CA.
3 Those referred to in the Employment Rights Act 1978, s 177(3).

4 Employment Rights Act 1996, s 214(3). There is an appropriate exclusion applicable on rein-statement and re-engagement: Employment Protection (Continuity of Employment) Regulations 1993, reg 5.

Employment abroad

11.15 Subject to the special provisions relating to redundancy payments, for the purpose of computing an employee's period of employment (but not for other purposes) the provisions as to continuity apply to a period of employment notwithstanding that during the period the employee was engaged in work wholly or mainly outside Great Britain or was excluded by or under the Employment Rights Act 1996 from any right conferred by it.[1]

1 Employment Rights Act 1996, s 215.

Crown employment and the armed services

11.16 The statutory provisions as to continuity have effect for the purpose of computing an employee's period of employment in relation to Crown employment. The provisions apply to persons in Crown employment as they have effect in relation to other employment and to other employees with appropriate amendments so far as construction is concerned.[1] This is also the case of service as a member of the naval, military or air forces of the Crown, and the provisions apply to employment by any association for the purposes of Part XI of the Reserve Forces Act 1996.[2]

1 Employment Rights Act 1996, s 191. The provisions also apply to members of House of Commons and House of Lords staff: Employment Rights Act 1996, ss 194 and 195.
2 Employment Rights Act 1996, s 192.

Part-time employees

11.17 As originally enacted and continued into the Employment Protection (Consolidation) Act 1978 employees had to satisfy requirements as to the number of hours worked or contracted to be worked to qualify for a period of continuous employment. In the provisions most recent form the employee had to work for 16 hours a week or more (or for eight hours a week or more if he or she had five years' service) for a week to count. In *R v Secretary of State for Employment, ex p Equal Opportunities Commission*[1] the House of Lords decided that the requirement was not consistent with the obligations of the equal pay requirements of European law. As a result Sch 13 to the Employment Protection (Consolidation) Act 1978 was amended to exclude this requirement.[2] Thus there is no requirement of a minimum number of hours worked or contracted to be worked for a week to count towards a period of continuity in the Employment Rights Act 1996. This relates to weeks both before and after the amendment.

1 [1995] 1 AC 1, HL.
2 Employment Protection (Part-time Employees) Regulations 1995, SI 1995/31.

Temporary absences

11.18 Problems are often encountered when considering employees who are temporarily absent from work. These problems may arise in connection with one or two specific periods of absence, or in relation to seasonal or 'intermittent' workers. If the contract of employment subsists during the period of temporary absence from employment, continuity is preserved in accordance with the usual rules.[1] If this is not the case the special provisions should be taken into account. In approaching a case where there have been apparent breaks in the period of working it should be considered first whether the contract of employment has continued to exist during the break. If so, continuity is preserved. If not, it should be investigated whether continuity is preserved by the special provisions relating to temporary absences. It is possible that more than one of these provisions may operate during a period of employment and each should be considered. In the case of a seasonal or intermittent worker it may be that he was regarded as continuing in employment for some purpose during one period of absence, and on another occasion his absence was on account of a temporary cessation of work.

1 This is in part as a result of the removal of the requirement to work for above a specified number of hours to qualify. The contract must have ceased to exist for s 212(3) to be relied on: *Ford v Warwickshire County Council* [1983] ICR 273, HL; *Lewis v Surrey County Council* [1987] ICR 982, HL, must be read in the light of this amendment.

Special provisions as to temporary absence

11.19 There are special provisions as to temporary absences. They preserve continuity in some cases of temporary absence during which the contractual relationship has not continued. They provide that if in any week for the whole or part of the week the employee is:

'(a) incapable of work in consequence of sickness or injury,
 (b) absent from work on account of a temporary cessation of work,
 (c) absent from work in circumstances such that, by arrangement or custom, he is regarded as continuing in the employment of his employer for all or any purposes, or
 (d) absent from work wholly or partly because of pregnancy or childbirth'
that week counts as a period of employment.[1]

1 Employment Rights Act 1996, s 212(3). A dismissal need not be expressed as being for one of the specified reasons for s 212(3) to apply: *Scarlett v Godfrey Abbott Group Ltd* [1978] ICR 1106, EAT.

Sickness or injury

11.20 The employee must be 'incapable of work in consequence of the sickness or injury'. Not more than 26 weeks between periods can count under this provision.[1] The incapacity need only relate to the incapability to carry out the type of work actually undertaken by the employee.[2]

1 Employment Rights Act 1996, s 212(4).
2 *Donnelly v Kelvin International Services* [1992] IRLR 496, EAT.

11.21 There must be a causal link between the absence and the incapacity.[1] Balcombe LJ, when hearing a case relating to an employee who took early retirement on medical grounds from a senior post and ten days later was re-employed in a more junior post, said:

'what the Industrial Tribunal has to do is to look backwards and decide what was the reason for the employee's absence considered week by week during the period when he seeks to rely on [s 212(3)(a)]. Where during a particular week the work on offer by the employer differs from that for which the employee was previously employed – and it is possible to envisage a scenario where the work on offer changes over the whole period, for example where an employee disabled by injury becomes fit for light work, although not necessarily for the heavier work for which he had been previously employed – then the Industrial Tribunal will have to consider whether the work offered by the employer was of a kind which the employee was willing to accept or, even though unwilling, was suitable for his particular circumstances. It would then have to decide whether his absence from that work was due to incapacity in consequence of sickness or injury.'[2]

It is possible for the effect of the provisions to result in a period after a dismissal being part of a period of continuous employment.[3]

1 *Pearson v Kent County Council* [1993] IRLR 165, CA. See also *Scarlett v Godfrey Abbott Group Ltd* [1978] IRLR 456, EAT.
2 *Pearson v Kent County Council* [1993] IRLR 165 at p 164, CA.
3 For an example see *Kolatsis v Rockware Glass Ltd* [1974] ICR 580, NIRC.

Temporary cessation of work

General approach

11.22 Section 212(3)(b) is often considered by asking three questions:
(1) Was there a cessation of the employee's work or job?
(2) Was the employee's absence on account of that cessation? and
(3) Was the cessation a temporary one?
The statutory provision itself must always be considered but these questions above are a useful aid to doing so. If the questions are used to assist in deciding whether continuity is preserved the result must be tested by asking the determining question: Was the claimant absent from work on account of a temporary cessation of work?[1]

1 *Bentley Engineering Co Ltd v Crown* [1976] ICR 225, DC. See Parker J at p 228.

Temporary cessation of work

11.23 It is important to note that what is referred to is absence on account of a temporary cessation in work. A temporary absence from work of itself is not enough. Section 212(3)(b) requires the absence to be causally linked to the temporary cessation of work. The provision relates to a lack of availability of work for the employee.[1] 'Work' is construed as limited to paid work, so the fact that work exists does not prevent the provision being used to benefit an employee if the employer is not able to pay the employee for carrying out the work.[2]

1 *Byrne v Birmingham City District Council* [1987] ICR 519, CA which deals with a 'pool' of workers. See *Letheby & Christopher Ltd v Bond* [1988] ICR 480, EAT, for a case concerning casual catering staff.
2 *Fitzgerald v Hall Russell & Co Ltd* (1969) 5 ITR 1 at p 16, HL.

11.24 In deciding whether a period of cessation of work was temporary or not, a subjective approach is adopted.[1] The meaning of a forerunner to the present provision was considered by the House of Lords in *Fitzgerald v Hall Russell & Co Ltd*[2] when during the course of his judgment Lord Upjohn said:

'In my opinion, the words "absent from work on account of temporary cessation or work" mean that he was laid off or dismissed because his employer had no longer work available for him personally any longer ... So the question – was the cessation temporary? – in most cases cannot be answered at the time of dismissal ... you must look at the original dismissal with hindsight, that is to say, with knowledge of all that has happened since the original dismissal until the second dismissal, and then decide whether in all the circumstances of the case the original dismissal can properly be described as due to a *temporary* cessation of work ...'

1 *Hunter v Smith's Dock Co Ltd* [1968] 2 All ER 81; [1968] 1 WLR 1865, QBD. This dictum was approved by the House of Lords in *Fitzgerald's* case. See *Thompson v Bristol Channel Ship Repairers and Engineers Ltd* (1970) 5 ITR 85, CA. Contrast *Newsham v Dunlop Textiles Ltd (No 2)* (1969) 4 ITR 268, DC.
2 (1969) 5 ITR 1 at p 16, HL.

11.25 'Temporary cessation' should be assessed by reference to successor and predecessor contracts in the same series.[1] All the relevant circumstances should be taken into account. In particular the length of period of absence should be considered in the context of the period of employment as a whole.[2] Looking at the circumstances 'as the historian of a completed chapter of events' it was held in the case of *Bentley Engineering Co Ltd v Crown*[3] that the decisions of an industrial tribunal that absences of 21 months and two years (during the shorter one of which the employee took other employment) were absences which fell within what is now s 212(3)(b) notwithstanding that after the absences the employees worked in different jobs for an associated company of their former employer.

1 *Lewis v Surrey County Council* [1987] ICR 982, HL.
2 *Flack v Kodak Ltd* [1986] ICR 775 at p 782, CA.
3 [1976] ICR 225, DC. The facts of this case are thought to extend the application of this provision to its limits.

Seasonal workers

11.26 The position of seasonal workers can give rise to difficulties. 'Temporary' connotes a period which is of relatively short duration when contrasted with the periods of work. In one case employees regularly worked for their employer six or seven months each year and were out of work for the remaining part of the year. It was held that the absences were not for a 'relatively short time' and the employment was not continuous.[1] The fact that the employee obtained employment with another employer during the period of the cessation of work does not of itself mean that the continuity is broken.[2] However it may be more difficult for an employee to show that his absence was on account of a temporary cessation of work if he resigns.[3] It is clear that regularity or predictability of the cessation does not prevent it from being a temporary cessation of work.[4]

1 *Sillars v Charringtons Fuels Ltd* [1989] ICR 475, CA. See also *Berwick Salmon Fisheries Co Ltd v Rutherford* [1991] IRLR 203, EAT. These decisions are very helpful when considering the position of seasonal workers. See also *Ford v Warwickshire County Council* [1983] ICR 273, HL.
2 *Bentley Engineering Co Ltd v Crown* [1976] ICR 225, DC, and *Thompson v Bristol Channel Ship Repairers and Engineers Ltd* (1970) 5 ITR 85, CA.
3 *Roach v CSB (Moulds) Ltd* [1991] ICR 349, EAT; *Wessex National Ltd v Long* (1978) 13 ITR 413, EAT.
4 *Ford v Warwickshire County Council* [1983] ICR 273, HL. For a recent example see *Pfaffinger v City of Liverpool Community College* [1996] IRLR 508, EAT, where it was made clear that the expiry of fixed term contracts amounted to dismissal.

Fixed term contracts

11.27   The provisions apply to fixed term contracts of employment which are not renewed in the same way as they apply to employment contracts of an indefinite duration. In these cases it is necessary to ascertain the reasons for the employer's failure to renew the contract on the expiry of the fixed term and decide if it was on account of a temporary cessation of work.[1] It is likely that for the contracts to be linked they should form part of a series of contracts.[2]

1 *Ford v Warwickshire County Council* [1983] ICR 273, HL.
2 *Lewis v Surrey County Council* [1987] ICR 982, HL.

Strikes

11.28   It will be seen (see **11.36**) that a week does not count if in that week, or any part of that week, the employee takes part in a strike.[1] Employees who do not themselves strike but are involved in a temporary cessation of work resulting from it do not have such period of enforced idleness subtracted from their period of continuous employment.

1 Employment Rights Act 1996, s 216(1). See *Hanson v Fashion Industries (Hartlepool) Ltd* [1981] ICR 35, EAT.

11.29   An interesting point arose in *Clarke Chapman-John Thompson Ltd v Walters*.[1] The applicant and others went on strike. When he returned to work he was informed that he was discharged but would be allowed to apply for employment again. He did so. Some of the employees receiving similar offers started to work for the employer immediately. The applicant was not required to return to work for 16 days. It fell to be decided whether the 16 days' absence broke the continuity of his employment. It was held that the absence did not do so. Mr Walters had not resumed work after the strike because there was a temporary cessation of work. A somewhat similar problem was considered in *Kolatsis v Rockware Glass Ltd*.[2] The employee was dismissed whilst in Cyprus after a holiday having been unable to return home because of ill-health. In due course he returned and was told that he could either start on another shift immediately, or on his old shift in ten days' time. He preferred his old shift, and made the appropriate arrangements. It was held that continuity of employment was not broken, the interval of absence between the incapacity because of sickness and return was absence on account of temporary cessation of work.

1 [1972] 1 All ER 614; [1972] ICR 83, NIRC.
2 [1974] 3 All ER 555; [1974] ICR 580, NIRC.

Arrangement or custom

11.30   The provisions preserve continuity when the employee was absent from work in circumstances such that, by arrangement or custom, he is regarded as continuing in the employment of his employer for all or any purposes. The words 'absent from work' are given their ordinary and literal meaning.[1]

1 *Lloyds Bank Ltd v Secretary of State for Employment* [1979] ICR 258, EAT. For a discussion of whether the expression means simply not working or not at the employee's place of work, or absent from work when under the employee's contract of employment he would normally be present see *Corton House Ltd v Skipper* [1981] ICR 307, EAT.

11.31 The essential element is that there must be a positive arrangement or custom whereby the employee is regarded as continuing in the employment of the employer. A series of separate and distinct contracts of employment may not be linked together under this provision unless such an arrangement or custom exists.[1] The question to be decided is whether, when the absence took place, the parties regarded the employment as continuing. So that where a casual worker running a bar at race meetings took a holiday when there were few race meetings the Employment Appeal Tribunal said that there was no continuity of employment over the holiday because there was no agreement by the parties that the employment was continuing.[2] An agreement to work alternative weeks only has been held to fall within the paragraph and continuity was preserved.[3] The employee's absence from work was by arrangement with her employers and so the requirements of what is now s 212(3)(b) were satisfied.

1 Voyage leave of a registered seafarer is not included under this head: *Duff v Evan Thomas Radcliffe & Co Ltd* [1979] ICR 720, EAT.
2 *Letheby & Christopher Ltd v Bond* [1988] ICR 480, EAT.
3 *Lloyds Bank Ltd v Secretary of State for Employment* [1979] ICR 258, EAT.

11.32 The arrangement or custom cannot be made retrospectively. The arrangement or custom must exist at the commencement of the absence.[1] However, this was found not to be the case where an employee was reinstated after a dismissal by the employer which the employee considered to be unfair and a conciliation officer had not taken action or the employee applied to a tribunal.[2]

1 *Murphy v A Birrell & Sons Ltd* [1978] IRLR 458, EAT.
2 *Ingram v Foxon* [1984] ICR 685, EAT.

11.33 'For all or any purposes' covers, for example, an employee's absence during periods which are ignored for purposes of pension provisions and holiday entitlement. A good example was *Wishart v National Coal Board*[1] where the employee had worked for the Coal Board but, requiring lighter work, was employed by a contractor, itself carrying out work for the Coal Board. After 18 months he returned to work for the Coal Board. During the period of absence he remained in the Mineworkers Pension Scheme. It was held that the period did not break the continuity because the employers regarded Mr Wishart as not having left the industry permanently and by custom treated him as continuing in their employ.

1 [1974] ICR 460, NIRC. See also *O'Reilly v Hotpoint Ltd* (1969) 5 ITR 68, QBD.

Pregnancy or childbirth

11.34 The absence must arise wholly or partly from pregnancy or childbirth.[1] If the absence is because of one of these reasons, it does not matter if a termination of employment has taken place as a result of a resignation by the employee. Provided the conditions are satisfied continuity is preserved.[2] Subject to the provisions mentioned below, not more than 26 weeks count under this paragraph between any periods.

1 Employment Rights Act 1996, s 212(3)(d).
2 *Mitchell v Royal British Legion Club* [1981] ICR 18, EAT.

Special provisions

Maternity

11.35 If an employee returns to work in accordance with s 79 of the Employment Rights Act 1996, or in pursuance of an offer made of re-engagement[1] after a period of absence from work wholly or partly occasioned by pregnancy or childbirth, every week during that period counts in computing the period of employment. This so notwithstanding that the period does otherwise count.[2]

1 As described in the Employment Rights Act 1996, s 96(3).
2 Employment Rights Act 1996, s 212(2).

Strikes and lockouts

11.36 A week does not count in computing a period of continuous employment if in that week, or in any part of it, the employee takes part in a strike.[1] In contrast to the usual rule continuity of employment is not broken if during a week or any part of it the employee takes part in a strike.[2]

1 Employment Rights Act 1996, s 216(1). Section 216 should be referred to for the detailed provisions.
2 Employment Rights Act 1996, s 216(2). This is so even if the employee is dismissed during the strike: *Hanson v Fashion Industries (Hartlepool) Ltd* [1981] ICR 35, EAT.

Strike

11.37 A strike[1] includes an unofficial as well as an official strike and for this purpose can continue after the employee has been dismissed.[2] 'The fact that the employer terminates [the strikers'] contracts of employment does not take them outside this category, unless and until he engages other persons on a permanent basis to do the work which the strikers had been doing or he permanently discontinues the activity in which they were employed. Similarly the fact that the striker takes other temporary employment pending the settlement of the dispute, does not prevent him claiming that he is taking part in a strike.'[3] If a short period of time elapses to allow an orderly return to work after a strike it is likely to be found to be a temporary cessation of work.[4]

1 '"Strike" means (a) the cessation of work by a body of persons employed acting in combination, or (b) a concerted refusal or a refusal under a common understanding of any number of persons employed to continue to work for an employer in consequence of a dispute, done as a means of compelling their employer or any person or body of persons employed, or to aid other employees in compelling their employer or any person or body of persons employed, to accept or not to accept terms or conditions of or affecting employment' unless the context otherwise requires: Employment Rights Act 1996, s 235(5).
2 *Bloomfield v Springfield Hosiery Finishing Co* [1972] 1 All ER 609; [1972] ICR 91, NIRC. See also *Winnett v Seamarks Bros Ltd* [1978] ICR 1240, EAT and *Williams v Western Mail & Echo Ltd* [1980] ICR 366, EAT.
3 Per Sir John Donaldson in *Bloomfield's* case above at p 613.
4 *Clarke Chapman-John Thompson Ltd v Walters* [1972] 1 All ER 614; [1972] ICR 83, NIRC; *McGorry v Earls Court Stand Fitting Co Ltd* [1973] ICR 100, NIRC, employee dismissed as being redundant whilst on strike.

Lockout

11.38 Whether or not a week during which an employee is absent from work during the course of a lockout[1] by the employer counts as a period of continuous employment depends upon the general provisions. Thus, if he is absent from work on account of a temporary cessation of work, the week counts. Even if the week does not count under the usual rules the continuity is not broken by the lockout.[2]

1 ' "Lockout" means (a) the closing of a place of employment, (b) the suspension of work, or (c) the refusal by an employer to continue to employ any number of persons employed by him in consequence of a dispute, done with a view to compelling those persons, or to aid another employer in compelling persons employed by him, to accept terms or conditions of or affecting employment': Employment Rights Act 1996, s 235(4).
2 Employment Rights Act 1996, s 216(3).

Reserve forces

11.39 When an employee is entitled to claim reinstatement under the Reserve Forces (Safeguard of Employment) Act 1985, and is re-employed by his former employer within six months of the end of his service, the period of service in the reserve forces did not break the continuity of employment.

1 Employment Rights Act 1996, s 217(1).

Change of employer

11.40 The usual rule is that employment is only continuous if it is employment by one employer.[1] There are however certain important exceptions.

1 Employment Rights Act 1996, s 218(1). See *Harold Fielding Ltd v Mansi* [1974] ICR 347, NIRC.

Transfer of trade or business

11.41 Continuity of employment is preserved if a trade or business or undertaking (whether or not it is an undertaking established by or under an Act of Parliament) is transferred from one person to another. A period of employment in the trade or business or undertaking at the time of transfer counts as a period of employment with the transferee and the transfer does not break continuity of the period of employment.[1] Although the wording of s 218(2) of the Employment Rights Act 1996, differs from that in the Transfer of Undertakings (Protection of Employment) Regulations 1981[2] the provisions in the Act as to continuity of employment should be read in such a way as to be consistent with the regulations. It has been said in the Employment Appeal Tribunal that a forerunner of the provision should not be given the restricted meaning of a moment in time.[3] The transfer itself can take place over a period of time.[4] Further, gaps in employment of short duration at the time the business is transferred may not prevent continuity being preserved.[5] The better view is that continuity of employment is preserved as a right by the Transfer of Undertakings (Protection of Employment) Regulations 1981 (see **12.11**).[6]

1 Employment Rights Act 1996, s 218(2). A transfer of the entire equity in the goodwill of a business to one of two former partners is included: *Allen & Son v Coventry* [1979] IRLR 399, EAT and see *Jeetle v Elster* [1985] ICR 389, EAT.
2 SI 1981/1794. See Chapter 12. The provisions of the 1981 Regulations should always be borne in mind when considering the Employment Rights Act 1996, s 218(2).
3 *Macer v Abafast Ltd* [1990] ICR 234, EAT.
4 *A & G Tuck Ltd v Bartlett* [1994] ICR 379, EAT.

5 *Justfern Ltd v Skaife D'Ingerthorpe* [1994] ICR 286, EAT.
6 SI 1981/1794. See *Kaur v Ghosh* [1996] COIT 00156/95.

11.42 Reference should be made to the Transfer of Undertakings (Protection of Employment) Regulations 1981 and decisions made under them. If there is a transfer of a trade or business or an undertaking, continuity is preserved even if the technical requirements of s 141[1] (as to renewal of contract or re-engagement in circumstances of redundancy) have not been complied with. The position may be that the employee could have claimed a redundancy payment against the former employer, but since he did not do so, he is able to include the period of employment with the former employer along with that with the transferee.[2]

1 Substituted for s 13(1) of the Redundancy Payments Act 1965. See **16.64**.
2 *Lord Advocate v de Rosa* [1974] 2 All ER 849; [1974] ICR 480, HL.

11.43 All manner of businesses can be transferred whether or not there is a transfer of the goodwill.[1] An activity may be an identifiable business if it was carried on as such after the transfer even if there is a question as to whether it was such beforehand.[2] Difficulty may be experienced in deciding whether there has been a transfer of a business as distinct from a transfer of assets used in the business. In *Melon v Hector Powe Ltd*[3] Lord Fraser of Tullybelton said 'It seems to me that the essential distinction between the transfer of a business, or part of a business, and a transfer of physical assets, is that in the former case the business is transferred as a going concern "so that the business remains the same business but in different hands"'. Whether or not this has occurred is a matter of fact to be decided by the tribunal.[4]

1 See for instance *Lloyd v Brassey* [1969] 2 QB 98; [1969] 1 All ER 382, CA (farm); *Young v Daniel Thwaites & Co Ltd* [1977] ICR 877, EAT (business as a publican).
2 *Rastill v Automatic Refreshment Services Ltd* [1978] ICR 289, EAT.
3 [1981] ICR 43 at p 49, HL.
4 *Melon v Hector Powe Ltd* [1981] ICR 43 at p 49, HL.

Act of Parliament

11.44 There is express provision to preserve the continuity of employment when under an Act of Parliament a contract of employment is modified and another body corporate is substituted as the employer. This provision may be of considerable importance when considering those employees affected by 'privatisation' of their employers. Continuity is preserved and the period of employment with the former employer counts with the new employer.[1]

1 Employment Rights Act 1996, s 218(3). The effect is not to modify the employment contract: *Gale v Northern General Hospital NHS Trust* [1994] IRLR 292, EAT.

Associated employers

11.45 If an employee is taken into the employment of another employer, which at the time he is taken into employment is an associated employer of the first employer, then continuity is preserved and the period of employment with the first employer counts as a period of employment with the second employer.[1] Any two employers are treated as associated if one is a company of which the other (directly or indirectly) has control, or if both are companies of which a third person (directly or indirectly) has control.[2] The better view is that 'control' is by the person holding voting control,[3] but views have been expressed to the contrary.[4]

1 Employment Rights Act 1996, s 218(6).
2 Employment Rights Act 1996, s 231. This definition of associated employers is exhaustive: *Merton London Borough Council v Gardiner* [1981] ICR 186, CA.
3 *South West Launderettes Ltd v Laidler* [1986] ICR 455, CA; *Secretary of State for Employment v Newbold* [1981] IRLR 305, EAT; *Washington Arts Association Ltd v Forster* [1983] ICR 346, EAT. Where control is exercised by several persons acting together refer to *Poparm Ltd v Weekes* [1984] IRLR 388, EAT and *Strudwick v Iszatt Bros Ltd* [1988] ICR 796, EAT.
4 See *Zarb v British and Brazilian Produce Co (Sales) Ltd* [1978] IRLR 78, EAT.

Death of individual employer

11.46 If on the death of an employer the employee is taken into the employment of the personal representatives or trustees of the deceased, the employee's period of employment at the time of death counts as a period of employment with the employer's personal representatives or trustees, and the death does not break the continuity.[1]

1 Employment Rights Act 1996, s 218(4). See *Rowley Holmes & Co v Barber* [1977] ICR 387, EAT.

Changes of partners, personal representatives and trustees

11.47 If there is a change in the partners, personal representatives, or trustees, who employ an employee, the employee's period of employment at the time of the change counts as a period of employment with the partners, personal representatives, or trustees after the change and does not break the continuity of employment.[1] The position of general medical practitioners practising under National Health Service contracts is covered by these provisions.[2]

1 Employment Rights Act 1996, s 218(5). In *Harold Fielding Ltd v Mansi* [1974] 1 All ER 1035; [1974] ICR 347, NIRC, the employee had been employed by a partnership when presenting a theatrical show and immediately afterwards he was employed on a different show by one of the partners individually. The National Industrial Relations Court held that there was no continuity of employment to enable the applicant to claim that he had been employed for the requisite period. First, what is now s 218(5) did not appear to cover a case where there was only a sole proprietor after the change and secondly the two theatrical productions were separate ventures and so not covered by the provision. But see *Allen & Son v Coventry* [1979] IRLR 399, EAT; *Lee v Barry High Ltd* [1970] 3 All ER 1040; [1970] 1 WLR 1549, CA; and *Jeetle v Elster* [1985] ICR 389, EAT.
2 *Jeetle v Elster* [1985] ICR 389, EAT, and see *Kaur v Ghosh* [1996] COIT 00156/95.

A week's pay

11.48 A 'week's pay' is important for the calculation of an employee's entitlement under a number of provisions of the Employment Rights Act 1996. It is defined in the Act.

Normal working hours

11.49 The first stage in determining the amount of a week's pay in respect of any employment is to ascertain whether it is an employment for which there are normal working hours. Where an employee is entitled to overtime pay when employed for more than a fixed number of hours in a week, or other period, then he is said to be employed for 'normal working hours'. The normal working hours are usually the fixed number of hours.[1] Where the contract of employment fixes the number, or the minimum number, of hours of employment in a week or other period (whether or not it also provides for the reduction of that number or minimum in certain circumstances), and that number or minimum number of hours exceeds the number of hours without overtime, it is that number or minimum number of hours (and not the number of hours without overtime) which is the normal working hours.[2]

1 Employment Rights Act 1996, s 234(2).
2 Employment Rights Act 1996, s 234(3).

11.50 Thus if there is a contractually fixed number, or minimum fixed number, of overtime hours they are included as normal working hours. Otherwise they are excluded from the calculation. When considering the Contracts of Employment Act 1963, Sch 2, para 1 which was in similar terms Lord Denning MR said in the Court of Appeal in *Tarmac Roadstone Holdings Ltd v Peacock*:[1]

'Those provisions are very complicated, but on analysis, they can be applied to these situations—

First, where there is a fixed number of compulsory working hours, and thereafter overtime is voluntary on both sides – so that the employer is not bound to employ the man for any overtime and the employee is not bound to serve it – then, although the overtime is worked regularly each week, nevertheless being voluntary, it does not count as part of the normal working hours. Such a situation is covered by [s 234(1) and (2)].

Second, when there is a fixed number of compulsory working hours and in addition a fixed period of overtime which is obligatory on both sides – so that the employer is bound to provide that overtime and the employee bound to serve it – then that fixed period of overtime is added to the fixed period of compulsory working hours so that the total number counts as the normal working hours. Such a situation is covered by [section 234(3)]. In short, "guaranteed overtime" counts as part of normal working hours.

Third, where there is a fixed number of compulsory working hours, and overtime is obligatory on the man if asked but not on the employer – so that the employer is entitled to call on the man to work overtime but is not bound to call upon him to do so: then the overtime does not come within the normal working hours. Such a case seems to me to come within [s 234(1) and (2)]. It comes within the words "the employee is entitled to overtime pay when employed for more than a fixed number of hours in a week ...". It does not come within the words of [s 234(3)], because the contract of employment does not "fix" the number of hours of employment. The overtime is not fixed but is at the option of the employer.'

1 (1973) 8 ITR 300 at p 303, CA. Substituted in square brackets are references to the corresponding provisions in the 1996 Act. See also *Gascol Conversions Ltd v Mercer* [1974] ICR 420, CA; *Fox v C Wright (Farmers) Ltd* [1978] ICR 98, EAT; and *Barrett v National Coal Board* [1978] ICR 1101, EAT.

11.51 To fall within s 234(3) of the Employment Rights Act 1996, the obligation to work overtime must arise from a contractual duty of the employer to provide the work and of the employee to carry it out. In *Peacock's* case above the employee's hours of work were fixed by reference to a national agreement which gave the normal working hours of 40 per week.

There was obligation to work overtime 'if required to do so' and regularly the employees worked 57 hours a week. It was held that since the employers were only obliged to employ the employees for 40 hours a week, the number of 'normal working hours' a week was 40.

Amount of a week's pay

11.52 Chapter II of Pt XIV of the Employment Rights Act 1996 lays down the rules for calculating the amount of a week's pay for the purposes of the Act. If there is a statutory provision providing a minimum amount for the hours worked, but the employee was paid less than the minimum, the minimum is the amount of the week's pay.[1]

1 *Cooner v PS Doal & Sons* [1988] ICR 495, EAT.

11.53 Where there are normal working hours for an employee when employed under the contract of employment in force on the calculation date,[1] if the employee's remuneration[2] for employment in the normal working hours whether calculated by the hour, week, or other period, does not vary with the amount done, the amount of a week's pay is the amount[3] which is payable by the employer if the employee works throughout his normal working hours in a week under the contract of employment in force on the calculation date.[4] Section 222 provides for cases where there are normal working hours for an employee when employed under the contract of employment in force on the calculation date, but he is required under the contract to work during those hours on days of the week, or at times of the day, which differ from week to week, or over a longer period, so that the remuneration payable for, or apportionable to, any week varies according to the incidence of the days or times. In those cases the amount of a week's pay is the amount of remuneration for the average weekly number of normal working hours at the average hourly rate.[5] The average is taken over a 12-week period.[6] The week's pay does not include a backdated increase if the agreement for it is made after the employment has come to an end.[7]

1 The calculation date to be used in particular circumstances is ascertained in accordance with Employment Rights Act 1996, ss 225 and 226, discussed elsewhere in this book.
2 For remuneration, see Chapter 4. In general terms it means all financial benefits to which the employee is contractually entitled. Benefits in kind are disregarded, as will be payments from third parties, but the profit element in 'expenses' will be included: *S and U Stores Ltd v Wilkes* [1974] 3 All ER 401, NIRC; see also *Weevsmay Ltd v Kings* [1977] ICR 244, EAT (remuneration includes commission); *J & S Bickley Ltd v Washer* [1977] ICR 425, EAT (commission to be rateably apportioned over the financial year). An 'attendance allowance' may be included, *London Brick Co Ltd v Bishop* [1979] LS Gaz R 102, EAT.
3 Ie the contractual gross pay; see *Murphy Telecommunications (Systems) Ltd v Henderson and Craig* [1974] IRLR 51, NIRC; *NG Bailey & Co Ltd v Preddy* [1971] 3 All ER 225; [1971] 1 WLR 796, QBD. It was held that for the purposes of what is now the Employment Rights Act 1996, s 184(1) a week's pay was net of tax: *Secretary of State for Employment v Jobling* [1980] ICR 380, EAT. This appears to be wrong in principle; see *Secretary of State for Employment v John Woodrow & Sons (Builders) Ltd* [1983] ICR 582, EAT.
4 Employment Rights Act 1996, s 221(2). This can include a bonus paid by main contractors (*Donelan v Kerrby Construction Ltd* [1983] ICR 237, EAT) and a service charge levied by employers and distributed to employees (*Keywest Club Ltd v Choudhury* [1988] IRLR 51, EAT); and see *Nerva v RL & G Ltd* [1996] IRLR 461, CA. References to remuneration varying with the amount of work done include references to remuneration which may include commission or similar payment which varies in amount: Employment Rights Act 1996, s 221(4).
5 Employment Rights Act 1996, s 222(2). It is the actual hourly rate even if it includes a notional amount in respect of holidays: *Cole v Birmingham District Council* [1978] ICR 1004; [1978] IRLR 394, EAT. The position may have been different if a full explanation had been given

at the time of engagement. The average hourly rate is the rate paid less any overtime premium: *British Coal Corpn v Cheesbrough* [1990] ICR 317, HL.
6 Employment Rights Act 1996, s 222(3) and (4). Where the calculation date is the last day of a week the 12-week period ends with that week, in other cases it is the 12-week period ending with the last complete week before the calculation date. 'Week' means for an employee whose remuneration is calculated weekly by a week ending with a day other than Saturday, a week ending with that other day, and in relation to any other employee, means a week ending with Saturday: Employment Rights Act 1996, s 235(1).
7 *Leyland Vehicles Ltd v Reston* [1981] IRLR 19, EAT.

11.54　In other cases of employments for which there are normal working hours, the amount of a week's pay is the amount of remuneration for the number of normal working hours in a week calculated at the average hourly rate of remuneration payable by the employer to the employee in respect of the period of 12 weeks (a) where the calculation date is the last day of the week, ending with that week; or (b) in any other case ending with the last complete week before the calculation date.[1]

1 Employment Rights Act 1996, s 221(3). Incentive bonuses and the like are included: *Ogden v Ardphalt Asphalt Ltd* [1977] 1 All ER 267; [1977] 1 WLR 1112, EAT.

11.55　In arriving at the average hourly rate of remuneration only the hours when the employee was working, and only the remuneration payable for, or apportionable to, those hours of work will be brought into the calculation. If, for any of the 12 weeks mentioned, no remuneration was payable by the employer to the employee, account will be taken of remuneration in earlier weeks so as to bring the number of weeks of which account is taken up to 12.[1] Where in arriving at the hourly rate of remuneration account has to be taken of remuneration payable for, or apportionable to, work done in hours other than normal working hours, and the amount of that remuneration is greater than it would have been if the work had been done in normal working hours, account is taken of that remuneration as if the work had been done in normal working hours and the amount of that remuneration had been reduced accordingly.[2] In such a case where the minimum number of hours of employment exceeds the number of hours without overtime[3] the remuneration for the hours other than normal working hours is taken as if the work had been done in 'non-overtime hours' and the amount of the remuneration had been reduced accordingly.[4]

1 Employment Rights Act 1996, s 223(1) and (2).
2 Employment Rights Act 1996, s 223(3). The average hourly rate is the rate paid less any overtime premium: *British Coal Corpn v Cheesbrough* [1990] ICR 317, HL.
3 Ie falling within Employment Rights Act 1996, s 234(3).
4 Employment Rights Act 1996, s 223(3).

11.56　Differing rules apply to employment when under the contract of employment in force on the calculation date there are no normal working hours for the employee.[1] The amount of a week's pay in this situation, is the amount of the employee's average weekly remuneration in the period of 12 weeks ending on the calculation date, if it is the last day of the week, or in any other case ending with the last complete week before the calculation date.[2] No account is taken of a week in which no remuneration was payable by the employer to the employee and remuneration in earlier weeks is brought in so as to bring the number of weeks of which account is taken up to 12.[3]

1 Employment Rights Act 1996, s 224.
2 Employment Rights Act 1996, s 224(2).
3 Employment Rights Act 1996, s 224(3).

11.57 Whether or not there are normal working hours applicable to the employment, if the employee has not been employed for a sufficient period to enable a calculation to be made as above, the amount of a week's pay is the amount which fairly represents the week's pay. The tribunal in determining that amount applies as nearly as may be such of the above provisions as it considers appropriate, and may have regard to such of the following considerations as it thinks fit:

(1) any remuneration received by the employee in respect of the employment in question,

(2) the amount offered to the employee as remuneration in respect of the employment in question,

(3) the remuneration receivable by other persons engaged in the relevant comparable employment with the same employer, and

(4) the remuneration received by other persons engaged in relevant comparable employment with other employers.[1]

Account is taken of work with former employers where continuity has been preserved for the purposes of the Employment Rights Act 1996.[2]

1 Employment Rights Act 1996, s 228.
2 Employment Rights Act 1996, s 229(1).

11.58 If bonuses or other payments are receivable but do not coincide with the periods for which the remuneration or other payments are calculated then they are apportioned in such manner as the tribunal considers to be just.[1] The Secretary of State may by regulations provide that in prescribed cases the amount of a week's pay shall be calculated in such manner as the regulations may prescribe.[2]

1 Employment Rights Act 1996, s 229(2).
2 Employment Rights Act 1996, s 228(4).

Statutory maximum

11.59 The amount of a week's pay for the purposes of calculating an additional award of compensation, a basic award of compensation in unfair dismissal cases, a redundancy payment and certain other rights will not in each case exceed a prescribed limit. This is at present £210.[1] The Secretary of State is under an obligation imposed by s 208 of the Employment Rights Act 1996 to review these limits in each calendar year and in making such review he will consider the general level of earnings obtaining in Great Britain at the time of the review, the national economic situation as a whole and such other matters as he thinks relevant.[2]

1 Employment Rights Act 1996, s 227.
2 Employment Rights Act 1996, s 208(2). He may also carry out further reviews: Employment Rights Act 1996, s 208(6).

Chapter 12

Transfers of undertakings

Introduction

The Transfer of Undertakings (Protection of Employment) Regulations 1981 have a substantial effect on the position of employers and employees in circumstances where undertakings are transferred. In general the Regulations apply where a person transfers an undertaking, or part of it, to another person, see **12.02–12.10**.

The effect of a transfer of an undertaking is that it does not terminate the contracts of employment of employees employed in the undertaking, but the employment contracts continue as if made between the transferee and the employees. This reverses the position at common law which regards the relationship between employer and employee as a personal one, see **12.11–12.16**.

After a transfer of an undertaking collective agreements made with the transferor continue as if made with the transferee, see **12.17**.

Employees dismissed by reason of the transfer are automatically unfairly dismissed, subject only to the saving that those dismissed because of economic, technical or organisational reasons are regarded for the purposes of the unfair dismissal provisions as dismissed for a substantial reason of a kind such as to justify the dismissal of an employee holding the position which the employee held. In that case the usual test of fairness has to be applied to see whether or not the employee was unfairly dismissed, see **12.19–12.22**.

The Transfer of Undertakings Regulations

12.01 The Transfer of Undertakings (Protection of Employment) Regulations 1981[1] were introduced to implement Council Directive 77/187 of the then European Economic Community (the Acquired Rights Directive). The Regulations came into force in 1982 and have since been the subject of amendment, in part because they were held by the European Court of Justice not to implement fully the Directive.[2] The Council Directive is itself being reviewed by the European Commission. It is now clearly established as a rule of United Kingdom law that the 1981 Regulations should be construed so far as is possible to give effect to the Directive and relevant decisions of the European Court of Justice.[3]

---

1 SI 1981/1794.
2 In (Cases C-382/92 and C-383/92) *EC Commission v United Kingdom* [1994] ICR 664, ECJ.
3 *Litster v Forth Dry Dock and Engineering Co Ltd* [1989] ICR 341, HL; *Dines v Initial Healthcare Services Ltd* [1995] ICR 11, CA; *Webb v Emo Air Cargo (UK) Ltd* [1993] ICR 175 at p 186, HL.

12.02   *Transfers of undertakings*

Application

12.02   The Regulations apply to a *relevant transfer of an undertaking*.

Undertaking

12.03   Regulation 2(1) describes undertaking as including 'any trade or business'.[1] Part of an undertaking refers to a transfer of a part which is being transferred as a business. The transfer of a ship without more is not a transfer of an undertaking.[2] There must be an identifiable economic entity for an undertaking, or part of one to exist. The economic entity is often a going concern of some nature.[3] It may simply comprise activities and employees and therefore tangible assets are not an essential requirement for an activity to be an undertaking and they may not be appropriate for an undertaking in certain circumstances, for instance in the case of some service industries.[4] It has been held that the contracting out of canteen services resulted in a transfer of an undertaking for the purpose of the Directive.[5] An undertaking has been held to be comprised of one individual cleaner at a bank.[6] Not only is the definition of undertaking broad, but it is established that the economic entity does not have to be the same after as before the transfer.[7] It is clear that there is no universal test for whether an activity is an undertaking. Decisions of the European Court of Justice with regard to the Directive are of considerable assistance in ascertaining whether an activity is an undertaking. Whether or not there is an economic undertaking is a matter of fact to be decided by the tribunals or courts in each case. Decisions setting out the principles as to whether or not a business has been transferred for the purposes of deciding whether employment has been continuous under the provisions of the Employment Rights Act 1996, and the earlier statutes replaced by it, should be referred to with considerable caution when considering the Regulations.[8]

1 As originally enacted the 1981 Regulations contained an exclusion of any undertaking, or part of an undertaking, which was not in the nature of a commercial venture. This exclusion was repealed following the decision of the European Court of Justice in (C-382/92) *EC Commission v United Kingdom* [1994] IRLR 392, ECJ.
2 Transfer of Undertakings (Protection of Employment) Regulations 1981, reg 2(2).
3 (Case 24/85) *Spijkers v Gebroeders Benedik Abbatoir CV* [1986] 2 CMLR 296, ECJ, a decision on the Directive. In Case C-48/95 *Ledernes Hovedorganisation v Dansk Arbejdsgiverforening* [1996] IRLR 51, ECJ it was held that an undertaking must be a stable economic entity whose activity is not limited to performing one specific works contract. It is thought that the effect of this decision may be limited; see for instance *BSG Property Services v Tuck* [1996] IRLR 134, EAT.
4 *Scilly Isles Council v Brintel Ltd* [1995] ICR 249, EAT. See also *Merckx v Ford Motor Co Belgium SA* [1996] IRLR 467, ECJ.
5 (Case C-209/91) *Rask v ISS Kantineservice* [1992] ECR I-5755, ECJ.
6 *Schmidt v Spar-und Leihkasse der fruheren Ämter Bordesholm, Kiel und Cromshagen* [1995] ICR 237, ECJ.
7 See footnote 4 above. The reorganisation of public administrative functions does not constitute a transfer of an undertaking within the meaning in the Directive; *Henke v Gemeinde Schierke* [1996] IRLR 701, ECJ.
8 *Scilly Isles Council v Brintel Helicopters Ltd* [1995] ICR 249, EAT. It is likely that the 1981 Regulations and provisions as to continuity of employment in the Employment Rights Act 1996 will be construed so far is as possible to like effect. All cases on the construction of the regulations prior to *Litster v Forth Dry Dock and Engineering Co Ltd* [1989] ICR 341, HL, should be viewed with considerable caution. In *Marleasing SA v La Comercial Internacional de Alimentacion SA* [1992] 1 CMLR 305, ECJ, it was held that national laws passed before, as well as those passed after European obligations came into existence, should be construed to conform with the European obligation.

Transfer

12.04 The Transfer of Undertakings Regulations apply to a transfer from one person to another of an undertaking situated immediately before the transfer in the United Kingdom, or part of one which is so situated.[1] This does not require a transfer of ownership of the undertaking. The regulations apply whether the transfer is effected by sale or by some other disposition or by operation of law.[2] Further, the regulations apply notwithstanding that the transfer is governed or effected by the law of a country or territory outside the United Kingdom. They also apply even though persons employed in the undertaking, or part, transferred ordinarily work outside the United Kingdom, and when the employment of any of the persons employed is governed by any other system of law.[3]

1 Transfer of Undertakings (Protection of Employment) Regulations 1981, reg 3(1).
2 Transfer of Undertakings (Protection of Employment) Regulations 1981, reg 3(2). See for example *Betts v Brintel Helicopters Ltd* [1996] IRLR 45, QBD.
3 Transfer of Undertakings (Protection of Employment) Regulations 1981, reg 3(3).

12.05 A transfer of an undertaking, or part of one, may be effected by a series of two or more transactions, and may take place whether or not any property is transferred to the transferee by the transferor.[1] However, care must be taken to ensure that a succession of events causally linked to one another, which did not as a series effect the transfer, are not treated as a series of transactions effecting the transfer. This was made clear by the Employment Appeal Tribunal in *Longden v Ferrari Ltd*.[2] A prospective purchaser, who was negotiating with a receiver to purchase a business, paid a sum of money to enable the business to trade while negotiations were taking place. Employees were dismissed shortly afterwards, but a fortnight elapsed before the prospective purchaser and the receiver agreed terms for the sale. The Employment Appeal Tribunal upheld the decision of the industrial tribunal that there was not a series of transactions within the meaning of reg 5(3). There are special provisions relating to ships within the meaning of the Merchant Shipping Act 1894.[3]

1 Transfer of Undertakings (Protection of Employment) Regulations 1981, reg 3(4).
2 [1994] ICR 443, EAT.
3 Transfer of Undertakings (Protection of Employment) Regulations 1981, reg 3(5) to the effect that where, in consequence (whether directly or indirectly) of the transfer of an undertaking or part of one which was situated immediately before the transfer in the United Kingdom, a ship within the meaning of s 313, Merchant Shipping Act 1995 registered in the United Kingdom ceases to be so registered, the regulations do not affect the right conferred by s 29 (right of seamen to be discharged when ship ceases to be registered in the United Kingdom) on a seaman employed in the ship.

12.06 A relevant transfer may occur in a variety of ways. A transfer occurs when there has been a change in the identity of the legal person who is responsible for employing the employees of the economic entity.[1] This so even if the change occurs without arrangements as to the business activities as such. An example of this can occur when a business is run at leased premises. If the first tenant ceases to trade and the premises revert to the landlord and the landlord, or another tenant, carries on a similar business in the premises there may be a relevant transfer to the landlord or new tenant.[2] The transfer can occur in more than one stage, as for instance, the surrender of the lease and the granting of a new lease to an unrelated person who carries on the economic entity in the same premises. The decisive criterion is whether the economic entity has retained its identity and whether there is a causal connection between the events.[3]

1 *Scilly Isles Council v Brintel Helicopters Ltd* [1995] ICR 249, EAT.

2 *Landsorganisationen i Danmark v Ny Molle Kro* [1989] IRLR 37, ECJ; *P Bork International A/S (in liquidation) v Foreningen af Arbejdsledere i Danmark* [1989] IRLR 41, ECJ; *Berg and Busschers v Besselsen* [1989] IRLR 447, ECJ.
3 *Longden v Ferrari Ltd* [1994] ICR 443, EAT.

12.07 The application of these principles to 'contracting out' by public authorities of some of their activities has occasioned considerable difficulties. It is now reasonably clear that the contracting out of an economic entity is a relevant transfer, as it the situation when the contract changes hands, or where the contract reverts to the body which contracted out the activities.[1] In these circumstances canteen services, cleaning services, fire-fighting, baggage handling and the like have been held to be economic entities (and hence undertakings) which have transferred.[2]

1 *Scilly Isles Council v Brintel Helicopters Ltd* [1995] ICR 249, EAT; *Dines v Initial Healthcare Services Ltd* [1995] ICR 11, CA.
2 (Case C-209/91) *Rask v ISS Kantineservice* [1992] ECR I-5755, ECJ; *Scilly Isles Council v Brintel Helicopters Ltd* [1995] ICR 249, EAT; *Dines v Initial Healthcare Services Ltd* [1995] ICR 11, CA.

12.08 It should be noted that the Regulations apply only where there is a change in the legal personality of the employer. If there is no such change, for instance where the employer remains the same on a sale and purchase of shares in a corporate employer, the Regulations do not apply.

Transfers by receivers and liquidators

12.09 The Acquired Rights Directive does not apply to circumstances where there is a liquidation proceeding with a view to the realisation and distribution of the assets of the insolvent employer on behalf of its creditors rather than to enable the trade to continue.[1] If the transfer by the liquidator has the purpose of enabling the undertaking to continue to trade, the Directive does apply.[2] Thus, if the liquidator continues the business and then transfers it to a third party, the Directive (and the 1981 Regulations) do apply.[3]

1 *Abels v Administrative Board of the Bedrijfsvereniging etc* [1985] ECR 469, ECJ.
2 (Case C-362/89) *d'Urso v Ercole Marelli Elettromeccanica Generale SpA* [1992] IRLR 136, ECJ.
3 (Case C-472/93) *Spano v Fiat Geotech Spa* [1995] ECR I-4321, ECJ.

12.10 There are special provisions in the Regulations which apply to transfers by receivers, administrators and liquidators to wholly owned subsidiaries.[1] In these circumstances the transfer is deemed not to have been effected until immediately before the transferee company ceases (otherwise than by reason of its being wound up) to be a wholly owned subsidiary of the transferor company, or the relevant undertaking is transferred by the transferee company to another person, whichever occurs first. The transfer of the relevant undertakings is taken to have been effected immediately before that date by one transaction only.[2]

1 Transfer of Undertakings (Protection of Employment) Regulations 1981, reg 4. These apply where the receiver of the property, or part of the property, of a company, or the administrator of a company appointed under Pt II of the Insolvency Act 1986 or, in the case of a creditors' voluntary winding up the liquidator of a company, transfers the company's undertaking, or part of the company's undertaking (the 'relevant undertaking') to a wholly owned subsidiary of the company.
2 Transfer of Undertakings (Protection of Employment) Regulations 1981, reg 4(1).

Effect of relevant transfer on contracts of employment

12.11 A relevant transfer does not operate so as to terminate the contract of employment[1] of any person employed by the transferor in the undertaking, or part, transferred. Contracts of employment, which would otherwise have been terminated by the transfer, have effect after the transfer as if originally made between the person so employed and the transferee.[2] On completion of a relevant transfer all the transferor's rights, powers, duties and liabilities under, or in connection with, any such contract, are transferred by the operation of the Regulations to the transferee. Anything done before the transfer is completed by or in relation to the transferor in respect of that contract or a person employed in that undertaking or part, is deemed to have been done by or in relation to the transferee.[3] This provision does not transfer or otherwise affect the liability of any person to be prosecuted for, convicted of and sentenced for any offence.[4] It is unlikely that the provision affords protection to an employee who voluntarily leaves his employment.[5]

1 'Employee' means any individual who works for another person whether under a contract of service or apprenticeship or otherwise, but does not include anyone who provides services under a contract for services. References to a person's employer are construed accordingly. 'Contract of employment' means any agreement between an employee and his employer determining the terms and conditions of his employment. See **3.15–3.22**.
2 Transfer of Undertakings (Protection of Employment) Regulations 1981, reg 5(1). In *Photostatic Copiers (Southern) Ltd v Okuda* [1995] IRLR 11, EAT, it was held that the transfer of the undertaking did not transfer an employee's contract of employment when the employee did not know of the transfer. This is an area of the law which remains to be developed and the editors have doubts as to the merits of the decision.
3 Transfer of Undertakings (Protection of Employment) Regulations 1981, reg 5(2). Thus liability for an act of sex discrimination passes to the transferee: *DJM International Ltd v Nicholas* [1996] IRLR 76, EAT.
4 Transfer of Undertakings (Protection of Employment) Regulations 1981, reg 5(4).
5 (Case 105/84) *Mikkelsen v Danmols Inventar A/S* [1986] 1 CMLR 316, ECJ.

Employment to which the Regulations relate

12.12 References to a person employed in an undertaking, or part of one, transferred by a relevant transfer, are to a person so employed immediately before the transfer, including, where the transfer is effected by a series of two or more transactions, a person so employed immediately before any of those transactions.[1] When the 1981 Regulations were first introduced it was thought that it may be possible to defeat their operation by arranging for employees to be dismissed shortly before a transfer took place. However, this was held by the European Court of Justice to be contrary to the provisions of the Directive.[2] The matter was put beyond doubt as a matter of United Kingdom law by the House of Lords in *Litster v Forth Dry Dock and Engineering Co Ltd*.[3] The House decided that the words 'immediately before the transfer' in reg 5 should be construed as if they were followed by the words 'or would have been so employed if he had not been unfairly dismissed in the circumstances described in regulation 8(1)' (ie the provision as to dismissal because of, or for a reason connected with, the transfer).

1 Transfer of Undertakings (Protection of Employment) Regulations 1981, reg 5(3).
2 Article 4(1) of the Directive makes a dismissal because of the transfer unlawful (except where it is for 'economic, technical or organisational reasons entailing changes in the workforce'). In *Bork International A/S (in liquidation) v Foreningen af Arbejdsledere i Danmark* [1989] IRLR 41, ECJ, it was held that national courts should have regard to this provision when deciding whether an employee was employed in the undertaking at the date of the transfer. So that an

employee dismissed because of the transfer is considered as employed on the date of the transfer even though dismissed before that date.
3 [1989] ICR 341, HL.

12.13 Where only part of an undertaking is transferred the tribunal has to decide whether the employee was assigned, or allocated, to the part of the undertaking which was transferred.[1] The test applied is to ascertain whether the employee was employed in that part of the undertaking on the day on which the transfer took place, so that if the employee satisfied this test his contract is transferred even though he continues to work for the transferee for some time after the transfer.[2]

1 (Case 186/83) *Botzen v Rotterdamsche Droogdok Maatschappij BV* [1986] 2 CMLR 50, ECJ; *Michael Peters Ltd v Farnfield and Michael Peters Group plc* [1995] IRLR 190, EAT; *Buchanan-Smith v Schleicher & Co International Ltd* [1996] ICR 613, EAT; and *Securicor Guarding Ltd v Fraser Security Services Ltd* [1996] IRLR 552, EAT.
2 *Sunley Turriff Holdings Ltd v Thomson* [1995] IRLR 184, EAT.

12.14 When the Regulations preserve the contract of employment of an employee it is treated as if made with the transferee. This does not mean that the employee's rights are immutable. The transferee, as employer, is bound by the 'original' contract, but nonetheless has such rights as exist under the national law to seek to change the terms of the contract.[1] Notwithstanding this, if the operative reason for the purported variation in the employee's terms and conditions is the transfer of the undertaking, the variation is ineffective and the terms of the original contract remain in force.[2]

1 *Foreningen af Arbejdsledere i Danmark v Daddy's Dance Hall A/S* [1988] IRLR 315, ECJ.
2 *Wilson v St Helens Borough Council* [1996] IRLR 320, EAT. Nonetheless an employee may still be validly, although unfairly, dismissed before a transfer: *Meades v British Fuels Ltd* [1996] IRLR 541, EAT.

Objections by employees

12.15 The provisions do not operate to transfer an employee's contract of employment, and the rights, powers, duties and liabilities under, or in connection with, it if the employee informs the transferor or the transferee that he objects to becoming employed by the transferee.[1] Where the employee so objects the transfer operates so as to terminate the employee's contract of employment with the transferor, but he is not treated for any purpose as dismissed by the transferor.[2]

1 Transfer of Undertakings (Protection of Employment) Regulations 1981, reg 5(4A). The word 'object' means actual refusal to consent to the transfer. The refusal can be communicated in a variety of ways: *Hay v George Hanson (Building Contractors) Ltd* [1996] IRLR 427, EAT.
2 Transfer of Undertakings (Protection of Employment) Regulations 1981, reg 5(4B).

Existing right for employee to terminate his employment

12.16 The provisions operate without prejudice to any right of an employee, arising apart from the Regulations, to terminate his contract of employment without notice if a substantial change is made in his working conditions to his detriment. No such right arises by reason only that as a result of the operation of the Regulations the identity of his employer changes, unless the employee shows that, in all the circumstances, the change is a significant change and is to his detriment.[1]

1 Transfer of Undertakings (Protection of Employment) Regulations 1981, reg 5(5).

Effect of relevant transfer on collective agreements

12.17 Where at the time of a relevant transfer there is in existence a collective agreement made by, or on behalf of, the transferor with a trade union recognised[1] by the transferor in respect of any employee whose contract of employment is preserved by the Regulations, the collective agreement remains in force after the transfer. The agreement, in its application in relation to the employee, after the transfer, has effect as if made by or on behalf of the transferee with the trade union.[2] Accordingly, anything done under, or in connection with it in its application, by or in relation to the transferor before the transfer, is after the transfer, deemed to have been done by or in relation to the transferee.[3] Any order made in respect of the agreement, in its application in relation to the employee, has effect after the transfer as if the transferee were a party to the agreement.[4]

1 Transfer of Undertakings (Protection of Employment) Regulations 1981, reg 6. 'Recognised', in relation to a trade union, means recognised to any extent by an employer, or two or more associated employers.
2 This is without prejudice to the general law as to collective agreements presumed to be unenforceable in specified circumstances now contained in the Trade Union and Labour Relations (Consolidation) Act 1992, ss 179 and 180.
3 Transfer of Undertakings (Protection of Employment) Regulations 1981, reg 6(a).
4 Transfer of Undertakings (Protection of Employment) Regulations 1981, reg 6(b).

Exclusion of occupational pension schemes

12.18 The Regulations as to the effect of relevant transfers on contracts of employment and collective agreements do not apply to so much of a contract of employment, or collective agreement, as relates to an occupational pension scheme.[1] Nor do they apply to any rights, powers, duties or liabilities under or in connection with any such contract, or subsisting by virtue of any such agreement, and relating to such a scheme or otherwise, arising in connection with that person's employment and relating to such a scheme.[2] For these purposes, any provisions of an occupational pension scheme which do not relate to benefits for old age, invalidity or survivors are treated as not being part of the scheme, and so are transferred by the Regulations.[3] Notwithstanding that this leaves a serious gap in the protection of employees affected by transfers, reg 7 has been held to comply with the obligation in Directive.[4]

1 Within the meaning of the Social Security Pensions Act 1975 or the Social Security Pensions (Northern Ireland) Order 1975 in Northern Ireland. See the Transfer of Undertakings (Protection of Employment) Regulations 1981, reg 7(1)(a).
2 Transfer of Undertakings (Protection of Employment) Regulations 1981, reg 7(1)(b).
3 Transfer of Undertakings (Protection of Employment) Regulations 1981, reg 7(2).
4 *Adams v Lancashire County Council* [1996] IRLR 154, ChD.

Dismissal of employee because of relevant transfer

12.19 Where either before, or after, a relevant transfer, any employee of the transferor or transferee is dismissed, that employee is treated for the purposes of the unfair dismissal provisions of the Employment Rights Act 1996 as unfairly dismissed if the transfer, or a reason connected with it, is the reason or principal reason for his dismissal.[1] The only exception to this occurs where an economic, technical or organisational reason entailing changes in the workforce of either the transferor or the transferee, before or after a relevant transfer, is the reason or principal reason for dismissing an employee. In those circumstances it is possible for the dismissal to be fair. For the purposes of the unfair dismissal provisions, the dismissal is regarded as having been for a substantial reason of a kind such as to justify the dismissal of an employee holding the position which that employee held.[2] Thus, such a dismissal may be fair subject to the test in s 98(4) of the Employment Rights Act 1996. It is to be noted that these provisions apply whether or not the employee in question is employed in the undertaking, or part of the undertaking, transferred or to be transferred.[3] The complaint of unfair dismissal is made to an industrial tribunal in the usual way. Injunctions are unlikely to be granted by the courts to restrain a transferee from dismissing employees in breach of the Regulations.[4]

1 Transfer of Undertakings (Protection of Employment) Regulations 1981, reg 8(1). This does not apply in relation to the dismissal of any employee which was required by reason of the application of s 5 of the Aliens Restriction (Amendment) Act 1919 to his employment: Transfer of Undertakings (Protection of Employment) Regulations 1981, reg 8(4). If dismissal is with notice it is the reason for the dismissal when the notice is given which has to be considered by the tribunal: *BSG Property Services v Tuck* [1996] IRLR 134, EAT
2 Transfer of Undertakings (Protection of Employment) Regulations 1981, reg 8(2).
3 Transfer of Undertakings (Protection of Employment) Regulations 1981, reg 8(3).
4 *Betts v Brintel Helicopters Ltd* [1996] IRLR 45, QBD.

12.20 There is no definition or description of an 'economic, technical or organisational reason' in the 1981 Regulations. As with the Regulations as a whole reg 8 should be construed so far as is possible consistently with the relevant provisions of the Directive.[1] The Directive is described as being 'on the approximation of the laws ... relating to the safeguarding of employees' rights in the event of transfers of undertakings, businesses or parts of businesses'. This has been recognised both by the European Court of Justice and domestic courts as the purpose of the Directive and also of the Regulations. The Directive refers to reasons which entail changes in the workforces of either the transferee or transferor. For the partial exemption to apply the reason for the dismissal must relate to the workforces of either party to the transfer.[2] This requirement causes difficulties when a transferee wishes to bring the terms and conditions of its new employees into line with those of its existing employees. If this is done, and a dismissal results, the exemption can only be relied upon if there are changes in job functions and not merely the employment terms.[3] There is some doubt, but the better view is that the 'economic, technical or organisational reason' should relate to the individual employee, in a similar manner to the potentially fair reasons of capability or conduct in a straightforward unfair dismissal case.[4]

1 Article 4(1). It has been suggested that the Directive does not provide for any defence where the dismissal related to the transfer (in (Case C-362/89) *d'Urso v Ercole Marelli Elettromeccanica Generale SpA* [1992] IRLR 136, ECJ) but this approach was rejected in *Trafford v Sharp & Fisher (Building Supplies) Ltd* [1994] IRLR 325, EAT.
2 *Berriman v Delabole Slate Ltd* [1985] ICR 546, CA.
3 *Crawford v Swinton Insurance Brokers Ltd* [1990] ICR 85, EAT.
4 *Gateway Hotels v Stewart* [1988] IRLR 287, EAT See also *Anderson and McAlonie v Dalkeith Engineering Ltd* [1985] ICR 66, EAT and *Wheeler v Patel & J Golding Group* [1987] ICR 631, EAT.

12.21 As has been noted, an 'economic, technical or organisational reason' is not an automatically fair reason for dismissing the employee. The industrial tribunal determines whether or not the employer acted fairly within the meaning of s 98(4) of the Employment Rights Act 1996. In deciding such cases the tribunal first decides what was the reason for the dismissal and whether or not it was an 'economic, technical or organisational reason'. If it was, the tribunal treats the reason for the dismissal as being for a substantial reason of a kind such as to justify the dismissal of an employee holding the position which that employee held, in the same way as it would treat any other such reason. The tribunal then applies the usual test of reasonableness to the dismissal to ascertain whether it was fair or unfair.[1] An employee unfairly dismissed in circumstances of a transfer is entitled to remedies according to the usual unfair dismissal rules (see Chapter 15). The entitlement of the former employee to a redundancy payment is not affected by its operation.[2]

1 *Meikle v McPhail (Charleston Arms)* [1983] IRLR 351, EAT.
2 *Gorictree Ltd v Jenkinson* [1985] ICR 51, EAT, and *Anderson and McAlonie v Dalkeith Engineering Ltd* [1985] ICR 66, EAT. Contrast *Canning v Niaz and McLoughlin* [1983] IRLR 431, EAT, which is probably wrongly decided.

12.22 A division of the Employment Appeal Tribunal held that the effect of reg 8 as originally enacted was such that the usual qualification period was not necessary to claim a remedy for unfair dismissal under the regulation.[1] This has been the subject of amending regulations. An employee must have been employed for the usual qualifying period to be entitled to a claim for unfair dismissal under the Regulations.[2]

1 *Milligan v Securicor Cleaning Ltd* [1995] IRLR 288, EAT subsequently reversed in the Court of Appeal. *MRS Environmental Services Ltd v Marsh* (1996) 140 Sol Jo LB 186, CA.
2 Transfer of Undertakings (Protection of Employment) Regulations 1981, reg 8(5). This may have to be re-considered in the light of the House of Lords in *R v Secretary of State for Employment, ex p Seymour-Smith and Perez* [1995] ICR 889, CA. See **15.1**.

Effect of relevant transfer of trade union recognition

12.23 There are provisions which relate to trade union recognition where after a relevant transfer the undertaking, or part of the undertaking, transferred maintains an identity distinct from the remainder of the transferee's undertaking.[1] The provisions apply in circumstances where before such a transfer an independent trade union is recognised to any extent by the transferor in respect of employees of any description who in consequence of the transfer became employees of the transferee. In such cases the union is deemed to be recognised by the transferee after the transfer to the same extent in respect of those employees so employed and any agreement for recognition is varied or rescinded accordingly.[2]

1 Transfer of Undertakings (Protection of Employment) Regulations 1981, reg 9(1).
2 Transfer of Undertakings (Protection of Employment) Regulations 1981, reg 9(2).

Duty to inform and consult employee representatives

12.24 An employer of any employee likely to be affected by a transfer should consult all persons who are appropriate representatives of any of those affected employees with regard to the transfer.[1] The employer of affected employees should provide the representatives with the information specified in reg 10 long enough before a relevant transfer to enable consultation to take place. The specified information consists of:

(1) the fact that the relevant transfer is to take place, when, approximately, it will be and the reasons for it;[2] and

(2) the legal, economic and social implications of the transfer for the affected employees; and

(3) the measures which the employer envisages he will take in relation to those employees in connection with the transfer. If he envisages that no measures will be so taken, he should inform the representatives of that fact; and

(4) if the employer is the transferor, the measures which the transferee envisages he will, in connection with the transfer, take in relation to such of those employees as become employees of the transferee after the transfer. If he envisages that no measures will be so taken, he should inform the representatives of that fact.[3]

Tribunals will look at the information which is to be disclosed broadly. It is unlikely that they will not conduct a line by line examination of the information available to, and disclosed by, the employer.[4]

1 In relation to a relevant transfer, references to affected employees, are to any employees of the transferor or the transferee (whether or not employed in the undertaking or the part of the undertaking to be transferred) who may be affected by the transfer, or who may be affected by measures taken in connection with it: Transfer of Undertakings (Protection of Employment) Regulations 1981, reg 10(1). References to the employer are construed accordingly.

2 The obligation is only to divulge the employer's appraisal or judgment, not the calculations and assumptions on which the appraisal or judgment is based: *Institution of Professional Civil Servants v Secretary of State for Defence* [1987] IRLR 373, ChD.

3 Transfer of Undertakings (Protection of Employment) Regulations 1981, reg 10(2).

4 *Institution of Professional Civil Servants v Secretary of State for Defence* [1987] IRLR 373, ChD (obiter).

12.25 The information which is to be provided should be given to each of the appropriate representatives by being delivered to them, or sent by post to an address notified by them to the employer. In the case of representatives of a trade union it should be sent by post to the union at the address of its head or main office.[1]

1 Transfer of Undertakings (Protection of Employment) Regulations 1981, reg 10(4).

Appropriate representatives

12.26 The obligation is to consult with appropriate representatives. Appropriate representatives of any employees are the employee representatives elected by them.[1] If the employees are of a description in respect of which an independent trade union is recognised by the employer, representatives of the trade union are appropriate representatives. In the case of employees who both elect employee representatives, and are of a description in respect of which a union is recognised, the employer may choose to notify either the employee representatives elected by the employees, or representatives of the trade union.[2] For these purposes persons are employee representatives if they have been elected by employees for the specific purpose of being given information and consulted by their employer under reg 10. If they have been elected by employees otherwise than for that specific purpose and it is appropriate (having regard to the purposes for which they were elected) for their employer to inform and consult them under that regulation, they are employee representatives for the purpose. In either case they must employed by the employer at the time when they are elected.[3]

1 The absence of specific rules for the election of representatives in the 1981 Regulations does not constitute a breach of the Directive: *R v Secretary of State for Trade and Industry, ex p Unison* [1996] IRLR 438, HC.
2 Transfer of Undertakings (Protection of Employment) Regulations 1981, reg 10(2A).
3 Transfer of Undertakings (Protection of Employment) Regulations 1981, reg 11A.

12.27 The transferee is under an obligation to give the transferor such information at such a time as will enable the transferor to perform the duty to consult.[1]

1 Transfer of Undertakings (Protection of Employment) Regulations 1981, reg 10(3).

12.28 Where an employer of any affected employees envisages that he will, in connection with the transfer, be taking measures in relation to any such employees, he should consult all persons who are appropriate representatives of any of the affected employees in relation to whom he envisages taking measures. This should be with a view to seeking their agreement to the measures to be taken.[1] In the course of those consultations the employer should consider any representations made by the appropriate representatives. He should reply to the representations and, if he rejects any of those representations, state his reasons.[2] The employer should allow the appropriate representatives access to the affected employees, and afford to those representatives such accommodation and other facilities, as may be appropriate.[3]

1 Transfer of Undertakings (Protection of Employment) Regulations 1981, reg 10(5).
2 Transfer of Undertakings (Protection of Employment) Regulations 1981, reg 10(6).
3 Transfer of Undertakings (Protection of Employment) Regulations 1981, reg 10(6A).

12.29 If, in any case, there are special circumstances which render it not reasonably practicable for an employer to perform a duty imposed on him by the consultation obligations, he should take all such steps towards performing the duty as are reasonably practicable in the circumstances.[1]

1 Transfer of Undertakings (Protection of Employment) Regulations 1981, reg 10(7).

12.30 There is specific provision for circumstances where the employer has invited any of the affected employees to elect employee representatives. If the invitation was issued long enough before the time when the employer is required to give the required information to allow them to elect representatives by that time, the employer is treated as complying with requirements in relation to those employees if he complies with those requirements as soon as is reasonably practicable after the election of the representatives.[1]

1 Transfer of Undertakings (Protection of Employment) Regulations 1981, reg 10(8).

Failure to inform or consult

12.31 Where an employer has failed to comply with the requirements to inform and consult, a complaint may be presented to an industrial tribunal. The complaint may be presented by any of the employee representatives where the employer failed to consult the employee representative. In the case of a failure relating to representatives of a trade union, it may be presented by the trade union. In any other case, the complaint may be presented by any employees who are affected employees.[1]

1 Transfer of Undertakings (Protection of Employment) Regulations 1981, reg 11(1).

12.32 The Regulations deal with the onus of proof on some complaints. Provision is made for cases where a question arises as to whether or not it was reasonably practicable for an employer to perform a particular duty, or what steps he took towards performing it. In those circumstances it is for the employer to show that there were special circumstances which rendered it not reasonably practicable for him to perform the duty and that he took all such steps towards its performance as were reasonably practicable in those circumstances.[1] On a complaint against a transferor that he has failed to perform the duty imposed upon him to provide information as to the measures which the transferee will take in respect of employees, or there is a question as to whether it was reasonably practicable for the employer to do so, he may not show that it was not reasonably practicable for him to perform the duty in question for the reason that the transferee had failed to give him the requisite information at the requisite time, unless he gives the transferee notice of his intention to show that fact. The giving of the notice automatically makes the transferee a party to the proceedings.[2]

1 Transfer of Undertakings (Protection of Employment) Regulations 1981, reg 11(2).
2 Transfer of Undertakings (Protection of Employment) Regulations 1981, reg 11(3).

12.33 Where the tribunal finds the complaint against the employer to be well founded, it will make a declaration to that effect. In addition, it may order the employer to pay appropriate compensation to such descriptions of affected employees as may be specified in the award. If the complaint is that the transferor did not perform the duty to provide information as to the measures which the transferee will take in respect of employees and the transferor (after giving due notice) shows the facts so mentioned, the tribunal may order the transferee to pay appropriate compensation to such descriptions of affected employees as may be specified in the award.[1] 'Appropriate compensation' means such sum not exceeding four weeks' pay for the employee in question as the tribunal considers just and equitable having regard to the seriousness of the failure of the employer to comply with his duty.[2]

1 Transfer of Undertakings (Protection of Employment) Regulations 1981, reg 11(4).
2 Transfer of Undertakings (Protection of Employment) Regulations 1981, reg 11(11).

Complaints by employees

12.34 An employee may present a complaint to an industrial tribunal on the ground that he is an employee of a description to which an order under these provisions relates and that the transferor or the transferee has failed, wholly or in part, to pay him compensation in pursuance of the order.[1] Where the tribunal finds the complaint is well founded, it will order the employer to pay the complainant the amount of compensation which it finds is due him.[2]

1 Transfer of Undertakings (Protection of Employment) Regulations 1981, reg 11(5).
2 Transfer of Undertakings (Protection of Employment) Regulations 1981, reg 11(6).

Time limit

12.35 An industrial tribunal will not consider a complaint under these provisions unless it is presented to the tribunal before the end of the period of three months beginning with the date on which the relevant transfer is completed, in the case of a complaint made by a representative, or the date of the tribunal's order, in the case of a complaint made by an individual employee. In a case where the tribunal is satisfied that it was not reasonably practicable for the complaint to be presented before the end of the period of three months, the complaint may have been presented within such further period as the tribunal considers reasonable.[1] Complaints can also be made before the transfer.[2]

1 Transfer of Undertakings (Protection of Employment) Regulations 1981, reg 11(8). There are appropriate provisions to the effect that the complaint is the sole remedy for breach of relevant rights and to provide for the functions of a conciliation officer: Transfer of Undertakings (Protection of Employment) Regulations 1981, reg 11(9). The High Court has no jurisdiction to grant injunctions restraining dismissals following a transfer of an undertaking: *Betts v Brintel Helicopters Ltd* [1996] IRLR 45, QBD.
2 *Banking Insurance and Finance Union v Barclays Bank plc* [1987] ICR 495, EAT and *South Durham Health Authority v UNISON* [1995] ICR 495, EAT.

Appeals

12.36   Appeals from the decisions of industrial tribunals lie, and lie only, to the Employment Appeal Tribunal on a question of law arising from any decision of, or arising in any proceedings before, an industrial tribunal under or by virtue of the Regulations.[1]

1 Transfer of Undertakings (Protection of Employment) Regulations 1981, reg 11(10).

Restriction on contracting out

12.37   Any provision of any agreement (whether a contract of employment or not) is void insofar as it purports to exclude or limit the operation of the Regulations as to their effect on employment contracts, dismissals because of the transfer and the duty to inform and consult with representatives, or to preclude any person from presenting a complaint to an industrial tribunal under the Regulations.[1]

1 Transfer of Undertakings (Protection of Employment) Regulations 1981, reg 12. See *Wilson v St Helens Borough Council* [1996] IRLR 320, EAT.

Work outside the United Kingdom

12.38   The Regulations relating to dismissals because of relevant transfers and as to consulting and informing representatives, do not apply to employment where under the employee's contract of employment he ordinarily works outside the United Kingdom.[1] A person employed to work on board a ship registered in the United Kingdom is regarded as a person who under his contract ordinarily works in the United Kingdom, unless the employment is wholly outside the United Kingdom, or he is not ordinarily resident in the United Kingdom.[2]

1 Transfer of Undertakings (Protection of Employment) Regulations 1981, reg 13(1).
2 Transfer of Undertakings (Protection of Employment) Regulations 1981, reg 13(2).

Chapter 13

Termination of employment

Introduction

The law relating to the termination of employment reflects a recurrent tension in employment law. In that employment law is based on contract, the general contractual principles apply but these are often modified, either by specific statutory provisions or by case law, in order to ensure that employees do not lose the right to a redundancy payment or the right not to be unfairly dismissed. Sometimes, as in the case of frustration, a gloss is put on general contractual principles to ensure that a party does not gain from his own default.

At common law performance of a contract is discharged either by completion of the task or by the expiry of the term of the contract. However statutory enactments provide that the expiry of a fixed term contract constitutes a dismissal (see **13.01** et seq).

Whilst a contract of employment may be terminated by agreement the courts and tribunals have analysed the circumstances which have led to the agreement with particular scrutiny to ensure that an employee's statutory rights are not defeated by a side-wind (see **13.03** et seq).

The doctrine of frustration and supervening impossibility applies to a contract of employment, but the courts have been careful to ensure that in the cases of illness amounting to a frustrating event statutory rights are not easily lost. Moreover, by specific statutory enactment (Employment Rights Act 1996, s 136(5)) a frustrating event affecting an employer cannot defeat the employee's claim to a redundancy payment. In the case of imprisonment being the frustrating event, the courts have developed a doctrine that an employee cannot contend that the fact that his misconduct has led to the imprisonment precludes the contract from being frustrated (see **13.09** et seq).

Contracts may contain express provisions as to notice or periods of notice may be implied (see **13.28** et seq). However, there is a minimum statutory period of notice (see **13.33**).

Statute has conferred certain rights to an employee during notice (see **13.35**).

The relationship of employer and employee may be terminated by either party repudiating the contract (see **13.44**).

There are special rules concerning repudiation in the case of apprentices (see **13.51**).

Employees have, on request, a right to have written reasons for the reason for their dismissal (see **13.54**). There are special rules in relation to those dismissed for reasons connected with maternity (see **13.46**).

The primary remedy for breach of contract is the wages from the date of dismissal until the earliest point at which the employer could lawfully have terminated the contract (see **13.58**). Damages may include other benefits apart from mere wages or salary (see **13.63**).

From this gross sum certain deductions have to be made in respect of other benefits which have been received (see **13.64**). The employee is in general under a duty to mitigate his loss by obtaining other employment (see **13.67**) although there is no duty to mitigate when the contract provides in terms that the employer has a right to pay money in lieu of notice (see **13.62**).

In a limited category of cases damages are payable for lost opportunities (see **13.71**), but it is not possible to recover damages for lost prestige, injured feelings or the stigma of having being employed by a company which collapsed in well-publicised circumstances (see **13.71**).

In particular circumstances employees may use equitable remedies such as an injunction (see **13.73**) or a declaration (see **13.75**). When issues arise for which there is not a private law remedy then a judicial review is possible (see **13.76**).

Performance

13.01   A contract of employment may be for a fixed period or for carrying out a particular task and that task only. The general law of contract provides that in such cases when the time expires or the task is performed, and the other stipulations have been complied with, the contract is discharged. The common law regards the relationship of employer and employee as entirely one of contract and after compliance with all the provisions of the agreement the parties are released from their obligations between themselves.

13.02   The expiry of a fixed term contract is deemed to be a dismissal for the purposes of the redundancy[1] and the unfair dismissal provisions.[2] However, when the contract is not for a fixed term but its duration is governed by the continuance of funding by a third party, then it has been held that on the cessation of such funding there has been no dismissal. In *Brown v Knowsley Borough Council*[3] there was no dismissal in law when a contract of employment specified that the appointment was to last only as long as funding was provided by outside sponsors. When the funding ceased it was held that the contract came to an event automatically and there was no dismissal. When a contract is for the carrying out of a particular task or amount of work there is no dismissal; the contract expires on the completion of the particular task.[4] In *Ryan v Shipboard Maintenance Ltd*[5] over a five-year period the applicant worked on numerous tasks varying from one to 11 weeks. In the periods when there was no work he claimed unemployment pay. After a period of eight weeks with no work he made a claim for redundancy payment. His claim failed. It was held by the EAT that he was engaged on a job to job basis and was discharged by performance. In practice such contracts rarely come before tribunals since a 'purpose contract' is normally completed well before the employee has the requisite two years' qualifying service. Moreover, where the contract is for the carrying out of a particular task, steps are often taken to ensure that the person carrying out the task does so as an independent contractor rather than as an employee.

1 Employment Rights Act 1996, ss 83 and 136.
2 Employment Rights Act 1996, s 95.
3 [1986] IRLR 102, EAT.
4 See *Wiltshire County Council v National Association of Teachers in Further and Higher Education* [1980] ICR 455, CA and *Ironmonger v Movefield Ltd* [1988] IRLR 461, EAT.
5 [1980] ICR 88, EAT (approved by the Court of Appeal in *Wiltshire* above).

Agreement

13.03 As employment is based on contract it may be terminated by mutual consent like any other contract and in such cases there is no dismissal.[1] This agreement may finally discharge the relationship of employer and employee or terminate the existing contract substituting a new one in its place.[2] Whether a not a contract has been terminated by agreement or by dismissal has assumed great importance with the advent of statutory employment rights. The employee has to prove that he or she has been dismissed in a claim for unfair dismissal or redundancy. It is not open to the employer and employee to contract out of the Act save for the limited exception that the Act itself allows. Very fine distinctions can arise in considering whether there has been a consensual termination of employment or a dismissal and whether or not any agreement which has been made offends the statutory prohibition of attempting to exclude the operation of the Act.

1 *R v Bottesford (Inhabitants)* (1825) 4 B & C 84.
2 *R v Buckingham (Inhabitants)* (1834) 5 B & Ad 953.

13.04 Whilst a contract can come to an end by mutual agreement to terminate the contract, courts and tribunals will look very carefully at circumstances which, at first blush, may look like a resignation by the employee or a mutual agreement by the employer and the employee to terminate the contract but are, in reality, cases in which the employer has brought the contract to an end. This is particularly the case when the events which are claimed as constituting the mutual termination of contract occur after notice has been given. From its inception courts and tribunals have been concerned that the protection given by employment legislation should not be eroded. In *Lees v Arthur Greaves (Lees) Ltd*[1] the employee was given six months' notice to expire on 31 March 1972. He left the employment on 28 January, so the employers contended, by agreement (the date was of particular importance because the unfair dismissal provisions of the Industrial Relations Act 1971 came into force on 28 February 1972). The majority in the Court of Appeal expressly approved the statement by Sir John Donaldson in the National Industrial Relations Court in *McAlwane v Boughton Estates Ltd*:[2]

'We would further suggest that it would be a very rare case, indeed, in which it could properly be found that the employer and the employee had got together and, notwithstanding that there was a current notice of termination of the employment, agreed mutually to terminate the contract, particularly when one realises the financial consequences to the employee involved in such an agreement.'

Courts and tribunals look at the reality of the facts rather than the form of the transaction in deciding whether the contract has been terminated by the employer. The test, as formulated by Sir John Donaldson MR in *Martin v Glynwed Distribution Ltd*[3] is:

'Whatever the respective actions of the employer and employee at the time when the contract of employment is terminated, at the end of the day the question always remains the same. "Who *really* terminated the contract of employment?"'

1 [1974] 2 All ER 393, CA; but see *Hempel v Parrish* (1968) 3 ITR 240.
2 [1973] ICR 470 at p 473. See also *Tunnel Holdings Ltd v Woolf* [1976] ICR 387, EAT; *Hudson v Fuller-Shapcott* (1970) 5 ITR 266; *Glacier Metal Co Ltd v Dyer* [1974] 3 All ER 21; [1974] IRLR 189, NIRC, and *Oldham & Son Ltd v Heyd-Smith* (1973) 16 KIR 177, NIRC.
3 [1983] ICR 511 at p 519, CA.

Dismissal or resignation

13.05 Thus, if an employee resigns under the threat of being dismissed, or under a threat of calling the police or is inveigled into resigning, this will be a dismissal.[1] A resignation on acceptable terms even if there remains the lurking possibility of dismissal in default of agreement is not a dismissal.[2] Essentially the issue of causation is one of fact and degree for the tribunal to determine in the light of the findings of fact it makes as to the employee's freedom of choice.

1 *East Sussex County Council v Walker* (1972) 7 ITR 280, but contrast *Haseltine Lake & Co v Dowler* [1981] IRLR 25, EAT; *Allders International Ltd v Parkins* [1981] IRLR 68; or *Caledonian Mining Co v Bassett* [1987] ICR 425.
2 *Sheffield v Oxford Controls Ltd* [1979] ICR 396 and see also *Logan Salton v Durham County Council* [1989] IRLR 99, EAT. Rather than go through a disciplinary hearing an employee agreed to terminate his employment on agreed terms; such an agreement was held not to fall foul of s 140 and *Scott v Coalite Fuels & Chemicals Ltd* [1988] ICR 355, EAT when even after notice had been given for redundancy mutual termination was held to apply. See also *Hellyer Bros Ltd v Atkinson* [1992] IRLR 540, EAT. See **15.29** et seq and particularly **15.38** for a fuller exposition of the issues.

Voluntary redundancy and consensual termination

13.06 An employee who volunteers for redundancy or an employee director who votes for a board decision to cease trading and therefore by inference ensures that his own employment is terminated is still regarded as being dismissed.[1] That position has to be contrasted with the position in *Birch v University of Liverpool*.[2] In that case the applicant volunteered for early retirement. Although the employers had the long-term aim of reducing their workforce, there was no suggestion that failure to take early retirement would lead to an employee being made redundant. A distinction was drawn between a unilateral termination of the contract as in a redundancy exercise even though the employee might welcome the dismissal and where there has been a consensual termination as in *Birch's* case (for a fuller analysis, see **16.29**).

1 *Burton, Allton & Johnson Ltd v Peck* [1975] ICR 193, EAT; *Morley v CT Morley Ltd* [1985] ICR 499 in which it was held that the fact that an employee director agreed in a board meeting to cease trading with the result that his contract was terminated did not mean that the termination was by mutual consent.
2 [1985] ICR 470, CA.

Circumventing the protection

13.07 Tribunals will not allow a party to agree terms which in effect allow for contracting out of the provisions of the Act. In *British Leyland (UK) Ltd v Ashraf*[1] decided by the Employment Appeal Tribunal, an employee was given leave of absence and agreed to return to work on a specific date. It was agreed that if the employee did not attend on that date the contract of employment would terminate. In that instance it was held that the contract of employment came to an end by agreement when he failed to return on the date. However *Ashraf's* case was overruled in the case of *Igbo v Johnson Matthey's Chemicals Ltd*[2] on the ground that such an agreement infringed the provisions of what is now s 203 of the Employment Rights Act 1996 which renders an agreement void in that it purports to exclude the Act. As Parker LJ commented:

'The whole object of the Act can easily be defeated by the inclusion of a term in the contract of employment that if the employee is late for work on the first Monday in the month, or indeed any date, no matter whatever the reason, the contract will automatically terminate.'

Igbo's case makes it clear that employers cannot circumvent the provisions of the Act by making an agreement with the employee that the failure to carry out a particular term of the contract will lead to the automatic termination of the contract. A related issue is whether an employee who commits a repudiatory breach that goes to the root of the contract can be said to have dismissed himself. The matter is not free from doubt but the balance of authority is that there is no concept known to English law as self-dismissal and that the employer dismisses the defaulting employee when he elects to treat the employee's breach as repudiatory.[3]

1 [1978] ICR 979.
2 [1986] ICR 82, EAT.
3 *London Transport Executive v Clarke* [1981] ICR 355, CA disapproving earlier cases such as *Gannon v Firth* [1976] IRLR 415, EAT.

13.08 When termination takes place by agreement it will probably be in the employer's interests to record the terms in writing so that it is clear that a dismissal did not take place.

Frustration and supervening impossibility of performance

13.09 The classic formulation of the doctrine of frustration is contained in the speech of Lord Radcliffe in *Davies Contractors Ltd v Fareham UDC*:

'Frustration occurs whenever the law recognises that without default of either party a contractual obligation has become incapable of being performed because the circumstances in which performance is called for would make it radically different from that which was undertaken by the contract.'[1]

The House of Lords have expressly upheld this formulation.[2]

1 [1956] AC 696 at p 729, HL.
2 *National Carriers Ltd v Panalpina (Northern) Ltd* [1981] AC 675, HL and *Paal Wilson & Co A/S v Partenreederei Hannah Blumenthal* [1983] 1 AC 854 at p 900.

13.10 Subject to the exception that by statutory enactment (Employment Rights Act 1996, s 136(5)(b)) a frustrating event affecting an employer cannot defeat an employee's claim for redundancy (for which see **16.34**) the doctrine of discharge by frustration and supervening impossibility of performance apply to contracts of employment. Indeed the personal nature of the relationship means that they are particularly susceptible to determination in this way. For practical purposes the two areas in which the doctrine of frustration are most frequently met are in the cases of illness and imprisonment. It should be noted that in both these cases in appropriate circumstances these can be fair reasons for a dismissal. However, frustration can take place in circumstances in which dismissal would be inappropriate. If performance of the contract becomes impossible, or it cannot be performed in the manner contemplated when it was entered into, it may be discharged. An early example occurred in *Poussard v Spiers and Pond*[1] where an opera singer was unable to perform at the opening of a new opera because of illness and her contract was held to be frustrated. In another case[2] a doctor employed as School Medical Officer by Preston Corporation was interned for nine months during the Second World War and the resulting absence from his post brought the contract to an end.

1 (1876) 1 QBD 410. See also *Condor v Barron Knights Ltd* [1966] 1 WLR 87.
2 *Unger v Preston Corpn* [1942] 1 All ER 200. See also *Tarnesby v Kensington and Chelsea Area Health Authority* [1981] ICR 615, HL for a distinction between frustration and a contract terminated by operation of law.

Situations where the doctrines of frustration and supervening impossibility of performance has to be considered include the following.

Death of the employer or employee

13.11 Unless there is a provision in the contract to the contrary the death of either party to the contract will discharge it.[1] Where the employer is a partnership the death of a partner will terminate the contract of employment if it is dependent upon the deceased's membership of the partnership.[2] There are special provisions affecting statutory rights which may apply on the death of either party which are set out in the chapters on unfair dismissal and redundancy.

1 *Farrow v Wilson* (1869) LR 4 CP 744.
2 *Robson v Drummond* (1831) 2 B & Ad 303.

Physical impossibility

13.12 The contract may also be discharged if it becomes physically impossible to perform. For instance, illness of the employee going to the root of the relationship, can bring the contract to an end, as in *Poussard*'s case, above. In another reported decision a contract of apprenticeship was terminated when the apprentice contracted a permanent illness. Other cases of physical impossibility are encountered where the employee is, through no fault of his own, put in a position, where he cannot render the service he has agreed to carry out for his employer.[2] The doctrine of frustration may seem to be alien to employers and employees in cases of illness and certainly there are difficulties in applying it in such circumstances.[3]

1 *Boast v Firth* (1868) LR 4 CP 1.
2 *Unger v Preston Corpn* [1942] 1 All ER 200; *Morgan v Manser* [1947] 2 All ER 666.
3 *Hart v AR Marshall & Sons (Bulwell) Ltd* [1978] 2 All ER 413; [1977] ICR 539, EAT; *Hebden v Forsey & Son* [1973] ICR 607, NIRC; *Egg Stores (Stamford Hill) Ltd v Leibovici* [1976] IRLR 376, EAT.

Frustration and illness

13.13 In *Marshall v Harland and Wolff Ltd*, a case under the Redundancy Payments Act 1965, Sir John Donaldson, in a seminal judgment, explained the tests to be applied in determining whether a contract of employment has been frustrated by the employee's illness.[1]

'The tribunal must ask itself: "Was the employee's incapacity, looked at before the purported dismissal, of such a nature, or did it appear likely to continue for such a period, that further performance of his obligations in the future would either be impossible or would be a thing radically different from that undertaken by him and agreed to be accepted by the employer under the agreed terms of his employment?"'

1　*Marshall v Harland and Wolff Ltd* (1972) 7 ITR 150 at p 154, NIRC.

In considering the answer to this question, the tribunal should take account of the following:

(1)　*Terms of the contract, including provisions as to sickness pay*
13.14
'The whole basis of weekly employment may be destroyed more quickly than that of monthly employment and that in turn more quickly than annual employment. When the contract provides for sick pay, it is plain that the contract cannot be frustrated so long as the employee returns to work, or appears likely to return to work, within the period during which such sick pay is payable. But the converse is not necessarily true, for the right to sick pay may expire before the incapacity has gone on, or appears likely to go on, for so long as to make a return to work impossible or radically different from the obligations undertaken under the contract of employment.'

(2)　*How long the employment was likely to last in the absence of sickness*
13.15
'The relationship is less likely to survive if the employment was inherently temporary in its nature or for the duration of a particular job, than if it was expected to be long-term or even lifelong.'

(3)　*Nature of the employment*
13.16
'Where the employee is one of many in the same category, the relationship is more likely to survive the period of incapacity than if he occupies a key post which must be filled and filled on a permanent basis if his absence is prolonged.'

(4)　*Nature of the illness or injury and how long it has already continued and the prospects of recovery*
13.17
'The greater the degree of incapacity and the longer the period over which it has persisted and is likely to persist, the more likely it is that the relationship has been destroyed.'

(5)　*Period of past employment*
13.18
'A relationship which is of long standing is not so easily destroyed as one which has but a short history. This is good sense and, we think, no less good law, even if it involves some implied and scarcely detectable change in the contract of employment year by year as the duration of the relationship lengthens. The legal basis is that over a long period of service the parties must be assumed to have contemplated a longer period or periods of sickness than over a shorter period.'

13.19
'These factors are interrelated and cumulative, but are not necessarily exhaustive of those which have to be taken into account. The question is and remains—

"Was the employee's incapacity, looked at before the purported dismissal, of such a nature, or did it appear likely to continue for such a period, that further performance of his obligations in the future would either be impossible or would be a thing radically different from that undertaken by him and accepted by the employer under the agreed terms of his employment?"'

13.20 Although the *Marshall* formulation still remains a classic formulation it does not lay down completely comprehensive guidelines. In *Egg Stores (Stamford Hill) Ltd v Leibovici*[1] the Employment Appeal Tribunal mentioned other factors to be taken into account as follows:
(1)   The need of the employer for the work to be done and the need for a replacement employee to do it.
(2)   The risk to the employer of acquiring obligations in respect of redundancy payments and compensation for unfair dismissal to the replacement employee.
(3)   Whether wages have continued to be paid.
(4)   The acts and statements of the employer in relation to the employment, including dismissal of or failure to dismiss the employee.
(5)   Whether in all the circumstances a reasonable employer could be expected to wait any longer.
To establish frustration it is not necessary for the employers to have taken some action in respect of it but particular importance may be attached to the fact that the employee has not been dismissed. Phillips J has said:[2]
'It seems to us that considerable importance attaches to the failure of an employer in such circumstances to dismiss the employee. We have wondered whether in truth the doctrine of frustration has anything much to do with short-term periodic contracts of employment, for there is no doubt that the concept is alien both to employers and employees, and is often not matched by the reality of the situation as they see it. The automatic ending of a contract by operation of law in a case where the subject matter is destroyed is easily understood and matches experience. So is the case where a sudden calamity overtakes an employee which there and then renders any future service by him impossible. But in the case of an illness of uncertain duration the situation is quite different and neither employer nor employee thinks in terms approaching those underlying the concept of frustration.'

1 [1976] IRLR 376 at p 378, EAT.
2 *Hart v AR Marshall & Son (Bulwell) Ltd* [1977] ICR 539 at p 542. See also *Williams v Watson's Luxury Coaches* [1990] ICR 536, EAT in which Wood J warned against too easy an application of the doctrine in cases of ill-health.

13.21 There are no easy answers as to when a contract is frustrated by illness. The decided cases provide guidelines but not clear practical answers. The difficulty which an employer faces is that there is often a clash between humanitarian instincts and commercial pressures. If a long-serving employee suffers a debilitating or life threatening illness, understandably an employer may be reluctant to make the somewhat insensitive enquiries which would be necessary to dismiss on grounds of ill-health. A failure to do so may mean that it will be more difficult to argue the contract has been frustrated and the employer may still retain certain obligations such as the making of a redundancy payment. The Disability Discrimination Act 1995 now needs to be considered: see Chapter 7.

Sickness – a practical guide
13.22
(1) If an employee is engaged for a short-term project – such as series of concerts or dramatic productions extending over a period of two weeks – and is incapable of honouring the engagement because of illness, then the contract is likely to be regarded as being frustrated.
(2) If an employee is frequently away for periods of short duration with a range of minor ailments, then the doctrine of frustration is unlikely to apply. Frustration only applies when the contract is incapable of performance not when temporary illness merely affects the performance. In such circumstances an employer would need to consider whether dismissal is the appropriate option.
(3) In the case of long-term illness frustration may apply. Frustration arises by operation of law not by the decision of the parties. However, the actions or inaction of the employer will be among the considerations which will determine whether frustration has taken place. Compassion may well deter a benevolent employer from taking action to formalise the position by initiating dismissal procedures. In initiating dismissal procedures an employer may run the risk of an unfair dismissal action: in failing to act an employer exposes himself to the danger that he retains residual obligations to the employee concerned. Although the illness may not be of such duration to frustrate a contract, it may well be the justification for the employee's failure to work while the illness continues.[1]
(4) As a matter of practice it might well be wiser for an employer in the case of long-term illness to dismiss rather than rely on the prospect of establishing frustration at a later date.

1 *Notcutt v Universal Equipment Co (London) Ltd* [1986] ICR 414, CA.

Imprisonment

13.23 A prisoner sentenced to a period of less than four years' imprisonment receives remission of half the sentence. The time spent in custody on remand counts toward his sentence. Thus if D is arrested on 1 January, is remanded in custody and on 15 June receives a sentence of 12 months' imprisonment he will be released on 30 June. There is no easy answer to the employer's dilemma as to how to deal with such a problem.

13.24 Each case where frustration is considered must be looked at on its own facts. For instance in *Hare v Murphy Bros Ltd*[1] the employee was sentenced to a year in prison and the Court of Appeal held that this frustrated the contract. The general formulation referred to in the classic expositions of frustration emphasise that the essence of frustration is that it occurs without fault on either side. However in the context of employment law this could lead to inequitable results. In *FC Shepherd & Co Ltd v Jerrom*[2] the applicant was a plumber with some 24 months of his apprenticeship left to run when he was sentenced to borstal training which was for a minimum of six months and a maximum of two years. The company refused to employ him when he returned. The Court of Appeal held the contract had been frustrated. Relying on the general proposition that *no man can profit from his own wrong* the court held that it was not open to the applicant to rely on his own misconduct to deny that frustration had occurred. The length of imprisonment which will frustrate a contract is very much a matter of fact for the industrial tribunal. Appellate courts will only intervene if the fact-finding tribunal is clearly wrong.[3] The practical conclusion is that a substantial period of imprisonment will frustrate the contract.

1 [1974] 3 All ER 940; [1974] ICR 603, CA. In *Harrington v Kent County Council* [1980] IRLR 353, EAT 12 months was held to frustrate the contract even though the employers knew the employer was going to appeal and was successful.
2 [1986] IRLR 358; [1986] ICR 802, CA.
3 In *Pioneer Shipping Ltd v BTP Tioxide Ltd* [1982] AC 724 the House of Lords emphasised that what constituted a frustrating event was essentially a matter for the fact-finding tribunal, in that case the arbitrator.

Imprisonment – a practical guide
13.25   In *Chakki v United Yeast Ltd*[1] Neill J laid down three tests for determining whether a prison sentence imposed on an employee amounted to frustration:
(1)   From a practical commercial point of view, was it necessary for the employer to decide as to the employee's future and whether an employee would have to be engaged?
(2)   At the time when the decision had to be taken, what would a reasonable employer have considered to be the likely length of the employee's absence over the next few months?
(3)   If, therefore, it appeared necessary to engage a replacement, was it reasonable to engage a permanent, not a temporary, one?
This does not mean that the employer is powerless. If the offence which led to this imprisonment either arose from his employment or reflected on his capacity to carry out his job, it may well be that the employer will be able to dismiss the employee fairly. The fact that the employee has been absent from work due to his incarceration may in itself be a ground for a fair dismissal. In *Kingston v British Railways Board*[2] a three-month sentence involving a two-month absence from work constituted a reason for a fair dismissal.

1 [1982] ICR 140, EAT.
2 [1982] IRLR 274; [1982] ICR 392, EAT.

Legal impossibility

13.26   The parties may be released from their obligations if it becomes legally impossible to comply with them. This usually arises as a result of new statute law, Act of State, or change in the law of a foreign jurisdiction in some way governing the contract or the work to be carried out in accordance with it. In *Reilly v R*,[1] Reilly was appointed a member of the Federal Appeal Board but when the position was abolished by statute his contract was frustrated. The new situation need not go as far as making the employee's position obsolete, it is sufficient if another essential requirement of the contract is vitiated, for instance the method of calculation of remuneration.[2]

1 [1934] AC 176, PC and see *Tarnesby v Kensington and Chelsea and Westminster Area Health Authority (Teaching)* [1981] IRLR 369; [1981] ICR 615.
2 *Studholme v South Western Gas Board* [1954] 1 All ER 462, QBD.

Consequences of termination of the contract by frustration or supervening impossibility

13.27 The termination of the contract of employment in accordance with the doctrines of frustration and supervening impossibility of performance, does not amount to a breach entitling the employee to damages or payment in lieu of notice. The claim of an employee whose engagement has been so terminated is limited to the wages and other benefits accrued. The rules as to frustration and impossibility of performance applied to contracts of employment are those generally prevailing and when relevant the Law Reform (Frustrated Contracts) Act 1943 may have to be considered.

Termination by notice

13.28 Employment contracts may contain express provisions enabling either party to terminate the contract upon notice being given to the other. There is no requirement that notice to be given by the employer is the same as that given by the employee or, save where expressly so provided, for the notice to terminate to be in writing.

One of the particulars to be included in the written particulars of terms of employment is that specifying the length of notice to which the employee is entitled[1] although this may be done by reference to the rights conferred by the Employment Rights Act 1996 itself. In addition the Act lays down minimum periods of notice which apply to the majority of employment contracts.[2] When the Act applies and the employee is entitled to notice of determination of the contract, the period should be either that expressed or implied in the contract, or the statutory minimum period, whichever is the longer.

1 Employment Rights Act 1996, ss 1 and 2(3).
2 Employment Rights Act 1996, s 86.

Notice when the contract is silent

13.29 Difficulties are encountered where the length of notice is not dealt with expressly. Only very rarely are the courts prepared to accept that the parties intended employment to be for life.[1] In all other cases where the contract is not for a fixed period or task, a term will be implied as to the notice necessary for termination. Two approaches are adopted to this problem. The first is to ascertain from the contract and surrounding circumstances whether there is a period of notice which the employer and employee must have intended to be applicable thereto. Many factors may be taken into account in showing that the parties had in mind specific provisions as to notice. In the older cases reference was made to usages and customs of particular trades, and a distinction grew up between customs which had been judicially noticed and those which had not.[2] These usages and customs were established when society was evolving slowly, being common knowledge amongst those to whom they applied, but their relevance today is questionable.

1 *Salt v Power Plant Co Ltd* [1936] 3 All ER 322, CA; *Wallis v Day* (1837) 2 M & W 273. But see *Ivory v Palmer* [1975] ICR 340, CA, where the Court of Appeal by majority upheld the

decision of a county court that an employment contract was for life in surprising circumstances and also *McClelland v Northern Ireland General Hospital Services Board* [1957] 2 All ER 129; [1957] 1 WLR 594, HL.
2 *Paxton v Courtnay* (1860) 2 F & F 131, quoted by Horridge J in *Produce Brokers Co Ltd v Olympia Oil and Cake Co Ltd* [1916] 2 KB 296 at p 298.

13.30 The second approach operates where the contract is silent as to notice and it cannot be said that the parties clearly intended a specific period to apply. In such cases the courts will imply that the relationship can be terminated on reasonable notice by either party.[1]

1 *Payzu Ltd v Hannaford* [1918] 2 KB 348; *SW Strange Ltd v Mann* [1965] 1 All ER 1069; [1965] 1 WLR 629, ChD (three months held to be reasonable notice – manager of credit betting business); *James v Thomas H Kent & Co Ltd* [1951] 1 KB 551; [1950] 2 All ER 1099, CA.

13.31 Problems frequently arise (for example in calculating damages for wrongful dismissal) as to what is reasonable notice. Reasonableness is a question of fact which depends upon the circumstances of the particular case and although no definite rules can be laid down some help may be found in the reports. A ship's Chief Officer has been held to be entitled to 12 months' notice,[1] a photographer and journalist six months,[2] and three months' notice was reasonable for the manager of a bookmaker's credit department.[3]

1 *Savage v British India Steam Navigation Co Ltd* (1930) 46 TLR 294.
2 *Bauman v Hulton Press Ltd* [1952] 2 All ER 1121, QBD.
3 *SW Strange Ltd v Mann* [1965] 1 All ER 1069; [1965] 1 WLR 629, ChD.

13.32 Previous decisions must be referred to with caution, and should be used as no more than a guide. This uncertainty makes it difficult to advise with accuracy, and decided cases show considerable variation, even in the same type of employment. The introduction of statutory minimum periods of notice has undoubtedly had a restrictive effect with regard to the length of notice, and in many instances it may be difficult, if not impossible, to argue that the employee is entitled to notice longer than that required by the Act. This is so even where the balance of reasonableness is heavily on that side, for the statutory minimum period will normally have been expressed in the statement given pursuant to the Act, which will in many cases have been accepted as being correct by the employee.

Statutory provisions as to notice

13.33 The imposition of minimum periods of notice was one of the first examples of statutory changes being superimposed on the contract of employment. In general terms the position is that after one month's continuous employment an employee is entitled to receive one week's notice until such time as he has two years' continuous employment at which time he is entitled to one week's notice for every year of continuous employment. After one month's continuous employment an employee is required to give one week's notice. This requirement does not alter with the employee's length of service. The statutory periods are the minimum required and both employer and employee can agree longer, but not shorter, periods than that the statutory requirement. Section 86 of the Employment Rights Act 1996 reads as follows:

'**86.** – (1) The notice required to be given by an employer to terminate the contract of employment of a person who has been continuously employed[1] for one month or more—

(a) is not less than one week's notice if his period of continuous employment is less than two years;

(b) is not less than one week's notice for each year of continuous employment if his period of continuous employment is two years or more but less than twelve years; and

(c) is not less than twelve weeks' notice if his period of continuous employment is twelve years or more.

(2) The notice required to be given by an employee who has been continuously employed for one month or more to terminate his contract of employment is not less than one week.[2]

(3) Any provision for shorter notice in any contract of employment with a person who has been continuously employed for one month or more shall have effect subject subsections (1) and (2); but this section shall not be taken to prevent either party from waiving his right to notice on any occasion, or from accepting a payment in lieu of notice.[3]

(4) Any contract of employment of a person who has been continuously employed for three months or more which is a contract for a term certain of one month or less shall have effect as if it were for an indefinite period and, accordingly, subsections (1) and (2) shall apply to the contract.[4]

(5) Subsections (1) and (2) do not apply to a contract made in contemplation of the performance of a specific task which it is not expected to last for more than three months unless the employee has been continuously employed for a period of more than three months.[5]

(6) This section does not affect any right of either party to treat the contract as terminable without notice by reason of such conduct of the other party.'[6]

1 In the majority of cases calculation of a period of continuous employment should prove of little difficulty since the employer will have provided most employees to whom the section applies with a statement in accordance with the statutory requirements setting out the date from which the period is to be calculated. Continuous employment need not be pursuant to one contract but can be under a succession of them: *Re Mack Trucks (Britain) Ltd* [1967] 1 All ER 977; [1967] 1 WLR 780, ChD.

2 It is of course possible to increase this by agreement, but it is to be noted that the statutory provision with regard to notice *by the employee* does not vary with the length of service.

3 If the contract provides for shorter notice it is of no effect, but the parties at the time may waive notice, or the employee accept payment in lieu of notice. There appears to be no power to waive payment in such cases. Section 87 makes provision for payment during notice. Any agreement whether in a contract of employment or not to exclude or limit the employer's obligations is void unless it satisfies the requirement of s 203.

4 In a fixed term contract no notice is necessary, and a series of short fixed term contracts might, in the absence of this subsection, defeat the object of the Act. This subsection enables a person who has in fact been employed for three months or more under a contract for a term certain of one month or less to receive the statutory notice and requires him to give not less than one week's notice.

5 This subsection in effect takes the seasonal worker out of the ambit if the section.

6 This subsection was included out of an abundance of caution. It makes clear beyond doubt that the existing common law position, enabling an employer or employee to terminate the contract summarily, is preserved.

Exceptions

13.34 Section 86 of the Employment Rights Act 1996 applies to all employees, as defined by s 230(1) of the Act[1] subject to certain exceptions. It does not apply to merchant seamen subject to a crew agreement approved by the Secretary of State for Employment[2] but does apply to share fishermen[3] and to merchant seaman.[4] It applies to the police force,[5] but not to to civil servants[6] and the armed services.[7] Employees who are engaged in work wholly or mainly outside Great Britain are not covered unless the employee ordinarily works in Great Britain and the work outside Great Britain is for the same employer or the law which governs the contract of employment is the law of England and Wales or the law of Scotland.[8]

1 In general terms employees are those serving under contracts of service.
2 Employment Rights Act 1996, s 199(1).
3 Employment Rights Act 1996, s 199(2).
4 Employment Rights Act 1996, s 199(4).
5 Employment Rights Act 1996, s 200.
6 Employment Rights Act 1996, s 191(2)(d).
7 Employment Rights Act 1996, s 192(d).
8 Employment Rights Act 1996, s 196(1)(a) and (b).

Rights during the period of notice

13.35 If an employee has been continuously employed for one month or more and the employment is terminated by either the employer or the employee giving notice, then the employee is given certain statutory rights during the period of notice.[1] This general proposition is subject to the important exception that it does not apply when the notice to be given by the employer under the contract exceeds the statutory minimum notice by at least one week. Thus if under the contract an employee is entitled to three months' notice which he is duly given and he has eight years' service the section does not apply.[2]

1 Employment Rights Act 1996, s 87.
2 Section 87(4). When the statutory provisions as to the rights of the employee during the period of notice do not apply the position depends entirely on the terms of the contract existing between the parties.

The rights conferred

13.36 The main right conferred on an employee is to be paid in those cases in which an employee is ready and willing to work but no work is provided for him or her,[1] or where the the employee is incapable for work because of injury or sickness,[2] or when absent wholly or partly because of pregnancy or childbirth[3] or where the employee is, and is contractually entitled to be, away on holiday.[4] An employee who works throughout the currency of the notice only benefits when he or she is absent from work, for example as a result of sickness, and his or her contract does not contain provisions as beneficial as the provisions of the Act.

1 Employment Rights Act 1996, s 88(1)(a).
2 Employment Rights Act 1996, s 88(2)(b).
3 Employment Rights Act 1996, s 88(2)(c).
4 Employment Rights Act 1996, s 88(2)(d).

Employment with normal working hours

13.37 The employer is liable to pay the employee for that part of the normal working hours in respect of which he was so absent, a sum not less than the remuneration for that part of his normal working hours calculated at the average hourly rate of remuneration produced by dividing a week's pay by the number of normal working hours. Any payments made by the employer during the notice period by way of sick pay, statutory sick pay, maternity pay, holiday pay or otherwise, go towards meeting the employer's liability.[1]

1 Employment Rights Act 1996, s 88(2).

Employment without normal working hours
13.38 In situations where there are no normal working hours the employer should pay the employee for each week of the period of notice, not less than a week's pay.[1] The week's pay is computed in accordance with the Employment Rights Act 1996,[2] which in broad terms, defines it as the average weekly rate of remuneration during the previous 12 weeks.

1 Employment Rights Act 1996, s 89(1).
2 See ss 220 et seq and, in particular, s 221. See **11.48** et seq.

13.39 It should be noted that the obligation on the employer is conditional on the employee being ready and willing to do work of a reasonable nature and amount to earn a week's pay,[1] save when the employee is incapable of work because of sickness or injury, wholly or partly due to pregnancy or childbirth or is absent in accordance with the terms of the contract of employment as to holidays.[2] Any payment made whether by way of sick pay, statutory sick pay, maternity pay, statutory maternity pay, holiday pay or otherwise shall be regarded as if it were remuneration paid by the employer during the notice period.[3]

1 See Employment Rights Act 1996, s 89(2).
2 See s 89(3).
3 See s 89(4).

Provisions applicable to employment with and without normal working hours
13.40 The employer is not liable to make payments in respect of a period of absence with leave granted by the employer at the request of the employee[1] (including any time off in accordance with the provisions as to time off for trade union duties and activities, public duties or to look for work or make arrangements for training).[2] No payment is due in consequence of a notice to terminate given by the employer, if after the notice is given and on or before termination of the contract, the employee takes part in a strike of the employer's employees.[3] No payments will be due in respect of any period of notice after the employer has rightfully treated a breach of the contract of employment by the employee as terminating the contract.[4] Where notice was given by the employee the employer's liability does not arise unless and until the employee leaves the employment.[5] Short-term incapacity and industrial injury benefits are taken into account as if paid by the employer and are taking account as meeting any liability.[6]

1 Employment Rights Act 1996, s 91(1).
2 Employment Rights Act 1996, s 91(a) and (b).
3 Employment Rights Act 1996, s 91(3).
4 Employment Rights Act 1996, s 91(4).
5 Employment Rights Act 1996, s 88(3) and 89(5).
6 Employment Rights Act 1996, s 90.

13.41 The provisions as to occupations which are excluded are the same as for the requirements as to notice (see **13.34**).

Remedies

13.42 The employee's claim for infringement of rights under s 87 is a claim in contract. Originally such a claim could only be pursued in the courts, but it can now be pursued in an industrial tribunal. Should the employer fail to give the notice required by statute, the rights conferred by s 86 are taken into account in arriving at the employer's liability for the breach.[1] If the employer breaks the contract during the period of notice, any payments made after the breach go towards mitigating the damages payable to the employee for loss of earnings due during the period of notice.[2] It is probable that the amount of damages should be reduced by earnings from other employment during the notice period.[3]

1 Employment Rights Act 1996, s 91(7).
2 Employment Rights Act 1996, s 91(3).
3 *Secretary of State for Employment v Wilson* [1977] IRLR 483, EAT.

13.43 Even if the employer gives the correct notice and pays all the sums due to the employee pursuant to his contractual obligations this may not absolve the employer from liability to the employee for unfair dismissal or a redundancy payment.

Repudiation and wrongful dismissal

13.44 If an employer or employee repudiates the contract of employment, the relationship may be terminated. A party to a contract is guilty of repudiatory conduct if he acts in such a manner as to indicate that he no longer considers himself bound by, or does not intend to comply with, his obligations under it.[1] Not every breach entitles the innocent party to rescind the contract, but the misconduct must be such as goes to the foundation or 'root' of the relationship itself.[2]

1 *Freeth v Burr* (1874) LR 9 CP 208. In the case of an employer repudiating a contract a mass of case law has built up as to the circumstances in which an employee may be held to have been constructively dismissed. This is considered at **15.47** et seq.
2 *Mersey Steel and Iron Co v Naylor Benzon & Co* (1884) 9 App Cas 434; *Cornwall v Henson* [1900] 2 Ch 298, CA.

13.45 It used to be a matter of debate as to whether it is necessary for repudiation by an employer of the employment contract to be 'accepted' by the employee to bring it to an end. In *Sanders v Ernest A Neale Ltd*[1] Sir John Donaldson said: '... the obvious, and indeed the only, explanation is that repudiation of a contract of employment is an exception to the general rule. It terminates the contract without the necessity for acceptance by the injured party.' The opposing view that the usual rule of contract law applies, namely that the injured party has the right to elect to bring the contract to an end by clearly showing that he considers himself released from the obligations, now seems to be have triumphed in the light of the Court of Appeal decision in *Boyo v Lambeth Borough Council*.[2] In that case the plaintiff was employed as an accountant by the defendant local authority with a provision that the contract could be terminated by either party on a month's notice or, subject to the appropriate disciplinary procedures, by the council on the grounds of gross misconduct. Following his arrest for an offence of conspiracy to defraud he was suspended on full pay. On 28 October 1991 he was charged with conspiracy to pervert the course of justice. The council wrote to him on 29 October saying that as it was a term of his bail that he was prohibited from any contact with council employees, he was absent from work without permission, so that his contract had been frustrated and his salary would cease. He was barred from work on 3 November when he tried to return. In March 1992 the charges against him were abandoned. In May 1992 he issued proceedings against the council. It was held that an unlawful repudiation of a contract by an employer which was not accepted by an employee did not result in the automatic termination of the contract. In the absence of special circumstances an employer's liability for damages did not extend beyond the time at which the employer could lawfully have brought the contract to an end. The plaintiff was held to be entitled to the loss of one month's notice notionally served after the disciplinary hearing, if there had been one, could reasonably be expected to have been concluded. In the view of Gibson LJ it was unreal to allow for any period for the carrying out of a disciplinary procedure in the assessment of damages, but that was a concession made by the defendant from which they did not feel it proper to resile on appeal.[3]

1 [1974] ICR 565 at p 571, NIRC; *Kolatsis v Rockware Glass Ltd* [1974] ICR 580 at p 583, NIRC. See also the judgment of Lord Denning MR in *Hill v CA Parsons & Co Ltd* [1972] Ch 305; [1971] 3 All ER 1345, CA; but contrast Sachs LJ in *Vine v National Dock Labour Board* [1957] AC 488; [1956] 3 All ER 939, HL; *Cranleigh Precision Engineering Ltd v Bryant* [1964] 3 All ER 289; [1965] 1 WLR 1293, QBD.
2 In *Boyo v Lambeth Borough Council* [1994] ICR 727 the Court of Appeal followed an earlier case of *Gunton v Richmond upon Thames London Borough Council* [1981] Ch 448; [1980] ICR 755 though with a certain reluctance. For other cases see the judgments of Salmon and Sachs LJ in *Decro-Wall International SA v Practitioners in Marketing Ltd* [1971] 2 All ER 216; [1971] 1 WLR 361, CA; and also *Denmark Productions Ltd v Boscobel Productions Ltd* [1969] 1 QB 699; [1968] 3 All ER 513, CA. The famous dictum 'an unaccepted repudiation is a thing writ in water' appears in *Howard v Pickford Tool Co Ltd* [1951] 1 KB 417 at p 421, CA (per Asquith LJ). See also *Dietman v London Borough of Brent* [1987] ICR 737 and affirmed [1988] ICR 842.
3 [1994] ICR 727 at p 745 et seq.

13.46 The most frequently encountered example of repudiation by an employer is where he wrongfully dismisses the employee, then the employee's right to bring action for damages following such dismissal is in theory an action for wrongful repudiation of the contract.[1] Repudiation by the employer is not confined to wrongful dismissal and includes other conduct falling within the definition outlined above. For example, the test was satisfied when the employer failed to comply with an important stipulation of the contract,[2] when the master of a ship treated a seaman with unreasonable harshness,[3] when the employer exposed the employee to unacceptable dangers,[4] when the employer gave notice he was to move his plant depot[5] and when an employer refused to pay an agreed guaranteed minimum wage.[6] More modern examples will be found in Chapters 15 and 16 (unfair dismissal and redundancy).[7] The employer may also repudiate the contract if he suspends or lays off the employee in a situation where he does not have the contractual right to do so (see **4.17** et seq and **4.28** et seq) and in some cases by failing to provide suitable work for the employee.[8] In such cases, the employee can accept the repudiation by summarily terminating the employment. The law as to constructive dismissal is dealt with in Chapter 15 at **15.47**.

1 *Re Rubel Bronze & Metal Co and Vos* [1918] 1 KB 315.
2 *The Castilia* (1822) 1 Hag Adm 59.
3 *Edward v Trevellick* (1854) 4 E & B 59.
4 *Limland v Stephens* (1801) 3 Esp 269; *British Aircraft Corpn Ltd v Austin* [1978] IRLR 332, EAT.
5 *Maher v Fram Gerrard Ltd* [1974] 1 All ER 449, NIRC.
6 *Powell Duffryn Wagon Co Ltd v House* [1974] ITR 46, NIRC.
7 See in particular *Western Excavating (ECC) Ltd v Sharp* [1978] QB 761; [1978] 1 All ER 713.
8 *Breach v Epsylon Industries Ltd* [1976] IRLR 180, EAT.

13.47 Where repudiation is by the employee, the employer frequently decides to treat the contract at an end by summarily dismissing him. To justify summary dismissal the employee must be guilty of conduct which is inconsistent with the express or implied conditions of service.[1] On entering into a contract of employment an employee is not under a duty to disclose his prior misconduct or criminal convictions,[2] unless requested to do so by the employer, and if they subsequently come to light, the employer is not entitled to rely on them as grounds for summary dismissal except where the employee has been guilty of misrepresentation or fraud.[3] Not all misconduct by an employee is of sufficient gravity to warrant summary dismissal,[4] and when considering whether or not the employer has the right to dismiss summarily a distinction must be drawn between employee's subject to contracts of service, and apprentices subject to contracts of apprenticeship.

1 *Clouston & Co Ltd v Corry* [1906] AC 122 at p 129, PC.
2 *Healey v Francaise Rubastic SA* [1917] 1 KB 946; *Hands v Simpson Fawcett & Co Ltd* (1928) 44 TLR 295; *Bell v Lever Bros Ltd* [1932] AC 161, HL.
3 See 15.122 for the effect of the Rehabilitation of Offenders Act 1974.
4 *Laws v London Chronicle (Indicator Newspapers) Ltd* [1959] 2 All ER 285 at p 287; [1959] 1 WLR 698 at p 700, CA.

Employees subject to a contract of service

13.48 Before deciding whether or not summary dismissal is lawful it is necessary to look at the obligations of the employee under the contract of service. There must be a grave breach of such an obligation in order to justify summary dismissal by the employer. A catalogue of breaches which have been held in the past to justify such dismissal will be found in all the standard works on the law of contract, but whether conduct of sufficient gravity exists in the given circumstances is a question of fact in each case. The conduct, according to Parke J[1] must come within the ambit of 'moral misconduct, either pecuniary or otherwise, wilful disobedience, or habitual neglect'.

1 *Callo v Brouncker* [1831] 4 C & P 518.

13.49 In *Laws v London Chronicle (Indicator Newspapers) Ltd*[1] Lord Evershed explained the law as follows:

'since a contract of service is but an example of contracts in general, so that the general law of contract will be applicable, it follows that, if summary dismissal is claimed to be justifiable, the question must be whether the conduct complained of is such as to show the servant to have disregarded the essential conditions of the contract of service. It is, no doubt, therefore, generally true that wilful disobedience of an order will justify summary dismissal, since wilful disobedience of a lawful and reasonable order shows a disregard – a complete disregard – of a condition essential to the contract of service, namely, the condition that the servant must obey the proper orders of the master and that, unless he does so, the relationship is, so to speak, struck at fundamentally.'

For the overwhelming majority of the population the remedy of unfair dismissal rather than wrongful dismissal has been more appropriate because the claim is of greater value and more easily asserted. The enlargement of the tribunal's jurisdiction to include wrongful dismissal may mean that a body of case law may now develop which has a less dated character[2] than the authorities which see employment in personal terms as one of master and servant.

1 [1959] 2 All ER 285 at p 287; [1959] 1 WLR 698 at p 700, CA.
2 See *Edwards v Levy* (1860) 2 F & F 94 in which Hill J said: '... a single instance of insolence on the part of a gentleman employed in such a capacity [newspaper critic] would hardly justify dismissal.' In *Wilson v Racher* [1974] ICR 428, CA the Court of Appeal had to consider the case of a gardener who, when provoked, had used foul and offensive language on one occasion in front of his employer and his employer's wife and children. The employee, who was dismissed as a result, claimed damages for wrongful dismissal. The decision of the county court judge, which was upheld, was that the employee was wrongfully dismissed. The judgment of Edmund Davies LJ, although at one point couched in the vernacular, gives an interesting insight into the durable nature of the idea of personal service:
> 'In these circumstances would it be just to say that the plaintiff's use of this extremely bad language on a solitary occasion made impossible the continuance of the master and servant relationship, and showed that the plaintiff had indeed resolved to follow a line of conduct which made the continuance of the relationship impossible?'

He continued:
> 'In my judgment, in the light of the findings of fact the judge arrived at a just decision. That is not to say that language such as that employed by the plaintiff is to be tolerated. On the contrary, it requires very special circumstances to entitle a servant who expresses his feelings in such a grossly improper way to succeed in an action for wrongful dismissal. But there were special circumstances here, and they were of the defendant's own creation. The plaintiff, probably lacking the educational advantages of the defendant, and finding himself in a frustrating situation despite his efforts to escape from it, fell into the error of explosively using this language. To say that he ought to be kicked out because on this solitary occasion he fell into such grave error would, in my judgment, be wrong.'

Conduct justifying summary dismissal

13.50 Examples of conduct held to be sufficient to amount to repudiation are: taking money from the till even though subsequently repaid,[1] persistent insolence to the employer's wife,[2] incompetence,[3] and speculation on the Stock Exchange by a confidential clerk.[4] In seeking to justify summary dismissal an employer may rely on misconduct which came to his knowledge after the dismissal had taken place.[5] As a matter of reality courts and tribunals have little difficulty in identifying cases of gross misconduct and many employers give in their disciplinary codes examples of what constitutes gross misconduct. It should be noted that there are two fundamental distinctions between justifying summary dismissal and meeting an action for unfair dismissal based on misconduct. In a case of wrongful dismissal the issue is whether the employee *has* breached the contract and, as has been noted, events discovered after the dismissal has taken place may be relied on to justify the dismissal. In the case of unfair dismissal the tribunal is concerned with the employer's perception of the employee's actions – namely whether the employer believed on reasonable grounds that the employee had been guilty of misconduct. In such circumstances events discovered after the dismissal cannot effect the fairness of the decision to dismiss but only the extent to which it is equitable to award compensation.[6]

1 *Sinclair v Neighbour* [1967] 2 QB 279; [1966] 3 All ER 988, CA.
2 *Pepper v Webb* [1969] 2 All ER 216; [1969] 1 WLR 514, CA.
3 *Harmer v Cornelius* (1858) 5 CBNS 236. However, many of the cases which suggest that summary dismissal is appropriate for incompetence are of considerable antiquity and predate the development of the principle that summary dismissal only applies when the breach is a fundamental or repudiatory breach. It is submitted that an isolated act of carelessness is unlikely to justify summary dismissal save where the employee is engaged in an occupation – such as an airline pilot – in which such an act of carelessness could have draconian consequences.
4 *Pearce v Foster* (1886) 17 QBD 536, CA.
5 *Boston Deep Sea Fishing and Ice Co v Ansell* (1888) 39 ChD 339, CA; *Cyril Leonard & Co Ltd v Simo Securities Trust Ltd* [1971] 3 All ER 1313; [1972] 1 WLR 80, CA.
6 *Devis (W) & Sons Ltd v Atkins* [1977] AC 931; [1977] ICR 662.

Apprentices

13.51   The right of summary dismissal, ie dismissal without notice, is more limited in the case of apprentices than when the relationship is merely that of employer and employee. This is probably due to the historical development and peculiar nature of the relationship. In earlier days masters of apprentices had considerable powers without the need of recourse to the courts; further, the contract being one for the benefit of an infant, special circumstances under the law of contract had to be applied. Although the case law is old and to some extent apprenticeship has itself been overtaken by other methods of training, apprenticeship is still used in some industries. A graphic review of the history of apprenticeship is to be found in the judgment of Shearman J in *Waterman v Fryer*.[1]

1 [1922] 1 KB 499 at p 506 (on appeal from county court).

13.52   Exceptionally bad conduct is necessary to justify summary dismissal of an apprentice. Nonetheless in many contracts of apprenticeship, conduct which falls short of that giving the right to summary dismissal may, under the terms of the contract itself, give the master a remedy. For instance, the contract may permit termination by notice before the end of the full period of apprenticeship if the apprentice 'be wilfully disobedient or be slothful or negligent or otherwise grossly misbehave himself'.[1] However, the effects of such stipulations remain to be tested in modern circumstances and apprenticeship deeds in current use make frequent reference to arbitration to resolve differences. Whether or not an employee's employment has been rightfully or wrongfully terminated it remains to be considered whether the dismissal was by reason of redundancy or unfair.[2]

1 See, for instance *Newell v Gillingham Corpn* [1941] 1 All ER 552. (The learned judge's views on conscientious objection provide a fascinating social commentary on wartime attitudes.) The dismissal of an apprentice for his retort to the managing director 'You couldn't have done any fucking better' was held to unfair in *Shortland v Chantrill* [1975] IRLR 208 and a court or tribunal would probably reach the same conclusion as to summary dismissal.
2 For a modern case re-emphasising the special nature of apprenticeship see *Wallace v CA Roofing Services* [1996] IRLR 435, QBD.

Insolvency of the employer

13.53   Where the employer is an individual his bankruptcy may not operate as a determination of the employment contract[1] but it is usual for the trustee in bankruptcy to dismiss employees on his appointment. The making of a compulsory winding-up order,[2] or the appointment of a receiver by the court,[3] of a corporate employer automatically determines employment contracts, as does the appointment of a receiver by debenture holders, if there is no provision making him the company's agent.[4] Most modern debentures provide that the receiver shall be the agent of the company, in which case the appointment out of court does not terminate the contracts of employment.[5] If there is a determination of the employment relationship in accordance with the above rules, it operates as a wrongful dismissal unless proper notice has been given. For the effect of insolvency on the employees' claims, see Chapter 17.

1 *Thomas v Williams* (1834) 1 Ad & El 685.
2 *Re Oriental Bank Corpn (McDowall's Case)* (1886) 32 ChD 366; *Fox Bros (Clothes) Ltd v Bryant* [1979] ICR 64.
3 See *Re Foster Clark Ltd's Indenture Trust, Loveland v Horscroft* [1966] 1 All ER 43; [1966] 1 WLR 125, ChD; *Reid v Explosives Co* (1887) 19 QBD 264, CA.
4 *Deaway Trading Ltd v Calverley* [1973] ICR 546.
5 *Re Mack Trucks (Britain) Ltd* [1967] 1 All ER 977; [1967] 1 WLR 780, ChD.

Written statement of reasons for dismissal

13.54 At common law an employer is under no obligation to provide an employee with reasons for dismissal. However an employee who on the effective date of termination has been, or will have been, continuously employed for a period of two years ending with that date, is entitled to be provided by his employer on request within 14 days of that request, with a written statement giving particulars of the reasons for his dismissal.[1] This requirement applies when an employee is given notice of termination of his contract of employment by his employer, his contract of employment is terminated by his employer without notice, or, where he is employed under a contract for a fixed term, that term expires without being renewed under the same contract.[2] A complaint may be presented to an industrial tribunal by the employee against his employer on the ground that the employer unreasonably refused to provide the written statement,[3] or that the particulars of reasons given in purported compliance with this requirement are inadequate or untrue.[4] The complaint has to be made within the time limit applicable for a complaint under the unfair dismissal provisions[5] and if the tribunal finds that the complaint is well founded it may make a declaration as to what it finds the employer's reasons were for dismissing the employee, and it must make an award that the employer pay the employee a sum equal to the amount of two weeks' pay.[6] The written statement provided under the Employment Rights Act 1996, s 92 is admissible in evidence in any proceedings.[7] Accordingly it is of great importance to the employer and employee. Considerable weight is given to the contents of the written statement by industrial tribunals and it should be carefully prepared by the employer and preserved by the employee.

1 Employment Rights Act 1996, s 92. But note there is no requirement for any length of continuity of service when an employee is dismissed for maternity reasons. See **13.57**.
2 Employment Rights Act 1996, s 92(1)(a), (b), (c).
3 Employment Rights Act 1996, s 93(1)(a).
4 Employment Rights Act 1996, s 93(1)(b).
5 Employment Rights Act 1996, s 93(3).
6 Employment Rights Act 1996, s 93(2).
7 Employment Rights Act 1996, s 92(5).

13.55 To be adequate the written statement should disclose the reasons for the dismissal. 'The document must be of such a kind that the employee, or anyone to whom he may wish to show it, can know from reading the document itself why the employee was dismissed.'[1] The document can refer to other documents but must itself contain a simple statement of the essential reason for the dismissal. It is not certain whether constructive dismissal is included.[2] It may not be reasonable to refuse to provide a written statement of reasons for dismissal if there is a general request from the police investigating a crime not to communicate with the ex-employee.[3] Mere failure to comply with a request for written reasons does not necessarily amount to an unreasonable refusal.[4] Save in maternity cases there has to be a request by the employee.[5] In deciding whether the statement is true the tribunal has to decide whether the employer has truthfully stated the reason for the dismissal; it does not have to decide whether the employer was justified in reaching that view.[6]

1 *Horsley Smith & Sherry Ltd v Dutton* [1977] IRLR 172 at p 173, EAT. However in *Marchant v Earley Town Council* [1979] IRLR 311, EAT, it was held that by referring to an earlier document setting out the reason the respondent may not have acted 'unreasonably'. In *Gilham v Kent County Council* [1985] ICR 227 distinguishing *Horsley's* case it was held to be sufficient to refer to documentation already given providing that copies of that documentation were enclosed.
2 See *Marriott v Oxford and District Cooperative Society (No 2)* [1970] 1 QB 186; [1969] 3 All ER 1126, CA; and *Sutcliffe v Hawker Siddeley Aviation Ltd* [1973] ICR 560, NIRC.
3 *Daynecourt Insurance Brokers Ltd v Iles* [1978] IRLR 335, EAT. But see a decision of the Employment Appeal Tribunal in Scotland, *Charles Lang & Sons Ltd v Aubrey* [1977] IRLR 354, EAT, where inaction for a short time was not found to be an unreasonable refusal.
4 *Lawson v Percy Main and District Social Club* [1979] IRLR 83, but failure to respond may eventually amount to a refusal (*Keen v Dymo Ltd* [1977] IRLR 118).
5 *Catherine Haigh Harlequin Hair Design v Seed* [1990] IRLR 175, EAT.
6 *Harvard Securities plc v Younghusband* [1990] IRLR 17, EAT.

13.56 The employee is entitled to be provided with the statement whatever the reason for the dismissal and even if the employee has been rightfully and fairly dismissed the employer should comply with his request for written particulars of the reason for the dismissal. If he refuses to do so, the tribunal will make the award in favour of the employee. An employee may well know why he has been dismissed but a failure to provide written reasons may still be unreasonable since the object of the section is to enable an employee to show the written reasons to an employer.[1] The requirements as to the provision of written reasons for dismissal do not apply when the employee is a share fisherman,[2] is employed under a contract of employment in the police service[3] or when the employee under his contract ordinarily works outside Great Britain,[4] but do apply to civil servants[5] and the armed services.[6]

1 *McBreaty v Thompson* IDS Brief 450, p 15.
2 Employment Rights Act 1996, s 199(2).
3 Employment Rights Act 1996, s 200.
4 Employment Rights Act 1996, s 196(2).
5 Employment Rights Act 1996, s 191(2)(d).
6 Employment Rights Act 1996, s 192(2)(d).

Maternity provisions

13.57 If an employee is dismissed whilst she is pregnant or after childbirth in which her maternity leave ends by reason of the dismissal, she is entitled to written reasons for dismissal irrespective of the length of time of her service and irrespective of any request.[1]

1 Employment Rights Act 1996, s 92(4).

Employee's remedies on breach of contract

13.58   It has been noted at **13.47** et seq that where the employee has repudiated the contract his employer is entitled to dismiss him summarily. In such circumstances the employee has no claim for wrongful dismissal (and any claim he might have for unfair dismissal is likely to be of limited value).[1] The employee is wrongfully dismissed when his employer terminates his contract without sufficient cause, in the case of a contract for a fixed period, prior to the expiration of the term, or where the contract is terminable on notice, without giving proper notice. If the employer has repudiated the contract the employee can summarily determine the relationship and sue for breach.

1 An employee may have a claim for unfair dismissal but not for wrongful dismissal and vice versa. If an employer was entitled to dismiss an employee summarily then as a matter of practical reality it is difficult to envisage a case in which a tribunal would not reduce any reward very considerably either because the employee had contributed to the dismissal and/or because it was just and equitable to reduce any compensation.

13.59   For practical purposes in the overwhelming number of cases the only remedy for the employee is to sue for damages. The circumstances in which an employee may obtain the equitable remedies of an injunction are limited (see **13.73** et seq).

13.60   Where an employer has purported to dismiss the employee, even though not in accordance with the procedure laid down in the contract, it has been held that the employee cannot treat the contract as still subsisting but must proceed as if wrongfully dismissed.[1] Remedies for breaches of employment contracts may be pursued either before the ordinary courts or in appropriate cases before an industrial tribunal.[2] There are limits to the jurisdiction of industrial tribunals in breach of contract claims. The sum awarded must not exceed £25,000. It may only be made if the claim arises out of, or is outstanding at the time of the termination of, the contract of employment. The time limit is the same as for unfair dismissal cases. Contract cases are the only area in which the employer may make a counterclaim in an industrial tribunal. There is the proviso that the counterclaim must be presented when the applicant's claim is before the tribunal. There are certain categories of contractual claim which are excluded.[3]

1 See *Barber v Manchester Regional Hospital Board* [1958] 1 All ER 322; *Gunton v Richmond upon Thames London Borough Council* [1981] Ch 448, CA and *Marsh v National Autistic Society* [1993] ICR 453, but see *Boyo* at **13.35**.
2 Industrial Tribunals Act 1996, s 8. See Industrial Tribunals Extension of Jurisdiction Orders 1994 (SI 1994/1623, England and Wales), (SI 1994/1624, Scotland).
3 See article 5. There is only a six week time limit for a counter claim (article 8).

Assessment of loss

13.61   The fundamental contractual principle applies namely that the party who has suffered the breach is entitled to recover the extent of his or her loss.

However, the loss which is recoverable is limited to compensation for lost wages from the date of dismissal until the earliest point at which the employer could have lawfully terminated the employment. For the employee engaged in employment terminable by notice, the starting point in the calculation is the total of the benefits he would have been entitled to receive if proper notice had been given at the time of the wrongful dismissal. If the contract is for a fixed period, that figure is the sum of the benefits which would have accrued due from the time of actual termination, to the earliest time at which the contract could rightfully have been terminated.

13.62 If there is a term of the contract providing for liquidated damages, for instance the payment of wages for a period in lieu of notice, that is the sum which is payable. In *Abrahams v Performing Right Society*[1] it was held that where there was a term in the contract providing for the payment of a sum in lieu of notice, the employer committed no breach if the payment was made. The money in lieu was a contractual entitlement and therefore there was no duty to mitigate.[2]

1 [1995] IRLR 486, CA.
2 Whilst *Abrahams* may seem a generous decision to the employee the existence of a clause empowering the employer to make a payment in lieu can have adverse effects for the employee. In *Marshall (Cambridge) Ltd v Hamblin* [1994] ICR 362, EAT it was held that in these circumstances the employee had no right to work out his notice even if his income was largely derived from commission if the employer chose to make the payment. See *Beckham v Drake* (1849) 2 HL Cas 579 for the position as far as the payment of liquidated damages. However, this is subject to the normal contractual rule prohibiting the enforcement of a penalty. See Halsbury 12 *Halsbury's Laws* (4th edn) para 1116 (Damages).

13.63 In addition to salary there may be included amounts in respect of commission,[1] pension benefits,[2] gratuities and pension and life assurance contributions,[3] (which the employer has a contractual obligation to provide. Employees are taxed on the fringe benefits (such as a car or mobile phone) which they receive and standard formulae are often applied. In assessing the value of such benefits the courts have adopted the robust view of determining what the employee has actually lost rather than applying the Inland Revenue formula. Thus in *Shove v Downs Surgical plc* [4] Sheen J assessed the employee's loss of the use of a company car by reference to figures provided by the AA rather than the Inland Revenue tables of the tax due on the benefit of the provision of a company car. If such benefits were a matter of discretion and there was no contractual obligation to provide them, then such benefits are not recoverable as damages.[5]

1 See *Bold v Brough, Nicholson and Hall Ltd* [1963] 3 All ER 849.
2 See *Manubens v Leon* [1919] 1 KB 208.
3 See *Acklam v Sentinel Insurance* [1959] 2 Lloyd's Rep 683.
4 [1984] 1 All ER 7.
5 See *Lavarack v Woods of Colchester Ltd* [1967] 1 QB 278, CA.

Deductions from the gross sum

13.64 Because the basic rule is that an employee is only to be compensated for that which he has lost by being dismissed without proper notice or before the expiry of a fixed term contract, certain sums are deducted from the gross sum. From the figures so calculated should be deducted all items which should be taken into account in minimising or mitigating damages. Deductions frequently occurring, are the actual earnings of the employee during the period, and/or job seeker's allowance,[1] income support[2] and any payment in lieu of notice or ex gratia payment.[3] Although it has been held that a redundancy payment is deductible[4] it is respectfully suggested that those decisions in which redundancy payments[5] have not been deducted are of greater authority. The purpose of a redundancy payment is not to compensate an employee for loss of wages. As a matter of practice employers do not deduct from the money in lieu of notice the amount of the redundancy payment. It has been held that compensation for unfair dismissal is not deductible.[6] However, in that case the industrial tribunal had not particularised the basis for the loss. For a further analysis see Chapter 17.

1 *Parsons v BNM Laboratories Ltd* [1963] 2 All ER 658, CA.
2 *Lincoln v Hayman* [1982] 2 All ER 819, CA.
3 *Addison v Babcock FATA Ltd* [1987] ICR 805, CA.
4 *Stocks v Magna Merchants Ltd* [1973] 2 All ER 329; *Colledge v Bass Mitchells & Butlers Ltd* [1988] 1 All ER 536, CA.
5 *Basnett v J and A Jackson Ltd* [1976] ICR 63. It has been suggested (16 *Halsbury's Laws* (4th edn) para 308) that *Colledge* above has overruled all cases in which a redundancy payment has not been deducted. However *Basnett's* case was not cited in *Colledge's* case. In *Colledge* the Court of Appeal was considering a personal injury case and there was a crucial finding of fact that the plaintiff would have been unlikely to have been made redundant but for sustaining injury.
6 *O'Laoire v Jackel International Ltd (No 2)* [1991] ICR 718, CA. In *Shove v Downs Surgical plc* [1984] ICR 532 the basic award was not deducted.

13.65 It is suggested that as a matter of general principle if an employee has received compensation which is clearly defined as covering the period of notice to which he was entitled, then it would be deductible. The courts have recently had to consider[1] whether the occupational pension to which the employee had become entitled should be deducted from the damages for wrongful dismissal. In the event it was decided that an employer could not deduct from the sums recoverable the amount of the pension which the plaintiff was receiving. It is submitted that in the light of this decision and of analogous decisions on personal injuries, no deduction should be made from the damages for any private insurance cover the employee has made such as, for example, to pay his mortgage.[2]

1 *Hopkins v Norcros plc* [1994] ICR 11, CA.
2 See *Parry v Cleaver* [1970] AC 1, HL.

Deductions of unemployment benefit

13.66 The effect of the requirement to deduct unemployment benefit may not be as great as first appears since unemployment benefit is not payable in respect of any day in respect of which money has been paid in lieu of notice.[1] It has been held[2] that a payment made in consideration of resignation falls within this paragraph.[3] In *Westwood v Secretary of State for Employment*[4] it was held that the deduction of unemployment benefit only applied in that it was a benefit to the claimant and consideration had to be given for the fact that a claimant may exhaust his or her entitlement to job seeker's allowance.

1 SI 1975/564.
2 National Insurance Tribunal Decision R (U) 9/73.
3 But see *Parry v Cleaver* [1970] AC 1; [1969] All ER 555, HL, when in a personal accident case the House of Lords held by a majority of one that a disability pension was not deductible in calculating loss of earning capacity. In *Basnett v J and A Jackson Ltd* [1976] ICR 63, QBD Crichton J held that supplementary benefits were not deductible. See also *Foxley v Olton* [1965] 2 QB 306; [1964] 3 All ER 248n.
4 [1985] ICR 209, HL.

The duty to mitigate: finding alternative employment

13.67 The employee is under a duty to find alternative employment in respect of which earnings will be taken into account but he cannot be expected to take any job; it must be suitable to his circumstances and status. This does not mean that an employee is necessarily able to argue that he is justified in refusing a job merely because it is less well paid than the job from which he has been wrongfully dismissed.

Taxation

13.68 Taxation is taken into account as shown at **17.21** and the total sum payable may be reduced because damages are paid earlier than the salary and benefits would have been received if the contract had continued. In addition to these damages, the employee can recover the wages and benefits accrued up to the time of the termination of the contract.[1] For a helpful schedule which illustrates the assessment of damages see *Harvey on Industrial Relations and Employment Law* (Butterworths) vol 1, A Para 685.

1 See *The Halcyon Skies* [1977] QB 14, [1976] 1 All ER 856, QBD (pension contributions were deducted from the employee's wages).

Quantum meruit

13.69 There is another pecuniary remedy available to the employee, that of an action for quantum meruit. Proceedings for an award of damages on this basis are rarely encountered in relation to employment contracts other than those where the employee has agreed to carry out a task certain.[1] The claim is for reasonable payment for the work carried out prior to the termination, and precludes claims for future loss and wages accrued due.[2]

1 For example writing a book, *Planche v Colburn* (1831) 5 C & P 58.
2 *Lilley v Elwin* (1848) 11 QB 742.

13.70 Where the contract is repudiated by the employer before the time for actual performance by the employee has arrived,[1] the employee can immediately proceed for damages if he wishes, or he may wait until the time for performance before presenting proceedings. In such cases the question of quantum meruit does not arise.

1 *Hochster v De La Tour* (1853) 2 E & B 678.

Loss of opportunity and injured feelings

13.71 Apprentices who are wrongfully dismissed can recover damages for the loss of future prospects and the opportunity of completing their apprenticeship,[1] and artists such as actors and authors may be able to recover additional damages for a missed chance of furthering their reputation and careers.[2] It is not possible to recover damages for reduction in prestige or injured feelings. This view was based on the decision of the House of Lords in *Addis v Gramophone Co Ltd*[3] and has been followed in subsequent cases. There is no claim for damages arising out of the stigma of having been employed by a particular company which had collapsed in widely publicised circumstances.[4] It is to be noted that in unlawful discrimination cases there is compensation for injury to feelings (see Chapter 7).

1 *Dunk v George Waller & Son Ltd* [1970] 2 QB 163; [1970] 2 All ER 630, CA.
2 *Herbert Clayton and Jack Waller Ltd v Oliver* [1930] AC 209, HL; *Withers v General Theatre Corpn Ltd* [1933] 2 KB 536, CA.
3 [1909] AC 488. See also *Re Golomb and William Porter & Co Ltd's Arbitration* (1931) 144 LT 583, CA and *Bliss v South East Thames Regional Health Authority* [1987] ICR 700, CA.
4 *Malik v BCCI* [1995] IRLR 593, CA.

13.72 When considering claims for damages for wrongful dismissal it is also necessary to consider the possibility of claims for redundancy payment and reinstatement or re-engagement and compensation for unfair dismissal (see Chapters 15 and 16) and for unlawful discrimination (see Chapter 7).

Equitable remedies

13.73 In *Hill v CA Parsons & Co Ltd*[1] an injunction was granted to an employee in very unusual circumstances. As a result of pressure brought upon the employers by a trade union which was attempting to establish a closed shop, Mr Hill was given one month's notice by his employers to terminate his employment. He held a senior position with the company which, said the majority of the Court of Appeal, entitled him to reasonable notice of at least six months. The length of notice was of crucial significance for if the employee had been given six months' notice by the time it expired the provisions of the now repealed Industrial Relations Act 1971 would have been in force. The court, by a majority, granted Mr Hill an injunction restraining his employers from acting on the dismissal. Such cases are however very rare.

1 [1972] Ch 305; [1971] 3 All ER 1345, CA. An injunction has also been granted to an employee restraining dismissal or purported dismissal in *Jones v Lee* [1980] ICR 310.

13.74 In *Chappell v Times Newspapers Ltd*[1] Stephenson LJ said:
'In this developing situation there may arise cases in which it is proper for the court to exercise its discretion in favour of a workman and grant an injunction which will hold an employer against his will to the continued performance of his contract of employment. Such a case was *Hill v CA Parsons & Co Ltd* but it was "highly exceptional", as Sachs LJ said at p 317; and was in my judgment rightly described by Sir John Donaldson when presiding in the National Industrial Relations Court in *Sanders v Ernest A Neale Ltd*[2] as "unusual, if not unique". Like Stamp LJ dissenting in *Hill v CA Parsons & Co Ltd*:[3] "I would be far from holding that in a changed and changing world there can be no new exception to the general rule" that a court will not grant an injunction in aid of specific performance of a contract of personal service, so that if the servant has been wrongfully dismissed, it will consider his contract unilaterally terminated by the master and leave the servant to his remedy in damages. I would not, however, look for new categories in which to pigeonhole new exceptions to this rule as it works either for the employer or the employee, but I would make exceptions in accordance with the general principle on which discretionary remedies are granted, namely, where, and only where, an injunction is required by justice and equity in a particular case, and, at the interim stage, by the balance of convenience. Applying those general principles, I do not find this a suitable case for making an exception to this sensible but flexible rule.'

In a number of recent cases the courts have shown their willingness to grant injunctions. The precise ambit of the circumstances in which injunctions will be granted is not easy to define. Until recently the one matter which appeared to be central to the granting of an injunction was that the employer should not have lost confidence in the employee although some later decisions have reduced the importance of this.[4] In *Marsh v National Autistic Society*[5] the plaintiff was the principal of a school. The contract stipulated that depending on when it was to take effect the contract could be terminated by either side with either three or four months' notice. A series of incidents took place involving a member of the staff and the plaintiff's handling of the situation was subject to criticism. A disciplinary panel was convened. It decided that although the allegations were in some respects well founded they did not merit dismissal as a disciplinary measure but that it would be in the best interests of the school if he did not resume his duties. The plaintiff was dismissed with immediate effect. The plaintiff contended that, in the absence of notice properly terminating his contract, in summarily dismissing him the defendants had repudiated the contract. He argued that as he had not accepted the repudiation the contract continued until lawfully brought to an end either by notice given by him or by notice given by the defendant in compliance with the contractual entitlement. Ferris J refused to grant an interlocutory judgment as the plaintiff's claim for wrongful dismissal was a claim for damages and that as damages were an adequate remedy an interlocutory injunction would not be granted. It is suggested that the refusal to grant an injunction could have been justified on the basis that although the dismissal was expressly stated not to be a disciplinary measure it was equally clear the employers did not consider that it was in the best interests of the school for the plaintiff to remain as the headmaster.

1 [1975] 2 All ER 233 at p 241, CA. See also *IPC Business Press Ltd v Gray* [1977] ICR 858, EAT.
2 [1974] 3 All ER 327 at p 333.
3 [1972] Ch 305 at p 323.
4 See *Irani v Southampton & South West Hampshire Health Authority* [1985] ICR 590; *Powell v Brent London Borough Council* [1988] ICR 176; *Hughes v Southwark London Borough Council* [1988] IRLR 55 and *Ali v Southwark London Borough Council* [1988] ICR 567. In *Wadcock v London Borough of Brent* [1990] IRLR 223 the High Court granted an injunction although it was not a case in which it could be said trust and confidence remained, but the employee was required to give an undertaking to work according to instructions. See also *Jones v Gwent County Council* [1992] IRLR 521.
5 [1993] ICR 453. See also *Alexander v Standard Telephones and Cables Ltd* [1990] IRLR 55, ChD.

Declarations

13.75 The courts have recently shown a far greater inclination than in the past to grant judicial declarations and it may be that in the future the declaration will play an important role in employment law.[1]

1 Cf *Vine v National Dock Labour Board* [1957] AC 488; [1956] 3 All ER 939, HL. An example of the use of an application for a declaration in an employment case is *Greer v Sketchley Ltd* [1979] IRLR 445, CA and see *R v BBC, ex p Lavelle Pty* [1983] 1 All ER 241 and *Shook v London Borough of Ealing* [1986] ICR 314, EAT.

Judicial review

13.76 If the complaint is not primarily a contractual one, but has wider implications of a public law nature as when the employment is in the nature of an office, then a claim for judicial review may be made. A nursing officer failed because he was seeking what was in effect a private contractual right;[1] a prison officer succeeded because as the holder of the office of constable he had no contract of employment and no private contractual rights which he could enforce.[2] Judicial review is most likely to apply in cases in which an employee of a public body is entitled or required to seek redress to a body established under statute or under the prerogative.

1 *R v East Berkshire Health Authority, ex p Walsh* [1984] ICR 743, CA.
2 *R v Secretary of State for the Home Department, ex p Benwell* [1984] ICR 723. For an analysis of the somewhat quixotic examples as to the way in which public law remedies have been allowed, see 16 *Halsbury's Laws* (4th edn) para 303. In *McClaren v Home Office* [1990] ICR 824, CA Wolfe LJ set out the relevant criteria which apply in determining whether a judicial review is the appropriate remedy.

Action short of dismissal

Constructive dismissal

13.77   It has been noted at **13.74** that an employee who has been dismissed cannot elect to treat the contract as subsisting even if the dismissal has been in breach of a procedure laid down in the contract. However, if the employer has not expressly dismissed the employee, but the employee is entitled to regard himself as constructively dismissed, there are circumstances in which an employee can elect to treat the contract as still subsisting and sue for damages. If an employer has breached a substantial term of the contract so as to repudiate the contract, the employee may accept the repudiation and sue for damages and/or claim unfair dismissal. However, it is open to the employee to refuse to accept the repudiation, treat the contract as subsisting and sue for his wages. This is of particular relevance when an employee has cut the wages, the hours, withdrawn a contractual facility or put the employee on short-term working.[1] Whereas in an unfair dismissal case based on constructive dismissal it is always open for an employer to argue that although there was a constructive dismissal it was not unfair since the reasons for making the changes were within the ambit of the Employment Rights Act 1996, s 98(4), this defence would not be open to an employer in a breach of contract action.[2]

1 See *Rigby v Ferodo Ltd* [1988] ICR 29, HL and *Burdett-Coutts v Hertfordshire County Council* [1984] IRLR 91, QBD, but see *Boyo* at **13.46**.
2 See *Fosca Services (UK) Ltd v Birkett* [1996] IRLR 325 for a case in which the EAT emphasised the difference between wrongful and unfair dismissal. See also the decision of *Wilson v Housing Corpn* (1996) Times, 18 December in which it was held that there was no such tort as inducing unfair dismissal.

Chapter 14

Trade union and related rights

Introduction

Trade union membership and activities   Part III of the Trade Union and Labour Relations (Consolidation) Act 1992 (TULR(C)A) sets out employees' rights concerning their membership or non-membership of trade unions. The provisions have complex legislative histories related to the changing political fortunes of the trade union movement.

Employers are under no general duty to recognise trade unions. However, employers may not discriminate against members or non-members of trade unions by refusing to offer them employment, taking action short of dismissal against them or dismissing them. The protection is similar to that offered by the anti-discrimination provisions of the Race Relations Act 1976 and the Sex Discrimination Act 1986.

Officials of recognised independent trade unions have a right to paid time off to carry out their trade union duties and to undergo certain training. Members of independent trade unions recognised by their employers are entitled to unpaid time off to take part in the activities of the union.

Dismissals during strike and other industrial action   An employee dismissed while taking part in unofficial industrial action has no right to claim unfair dismissal. In the case of other industrial action, the industrial tribunal has no jurisdiction to hear a complaint of unfair dismissal if:
(1)   all employees taking part in the action are dismissed, and
(2)   none is re-engaged within three months.

Health and safety   A recognised trade union may appoint safety representatives from amongst the workforce. Safety representatives take part in consultations with their employer and have a series of specific functions related to the investigation of and prevention of risks to employees' health. They are entitled to paid time off to carry out their duties. Where no such safety representatives are appointed, the employer must consult either directly with employees or with 'representatives of employee safety' who have similar rights and duties to union appointed safety representatives. Individual employees are protected from being subjected to a detriment or being dismissed because they take part in certain defined health and safety activities.

Employee representatives   Employee representatives are appointed to consult with employers where there are to be collective redundancies or on transfers of undertakings. They are protected against being subjected to a detriment or being dismissed as a result of their activities and are entitled to paid time off to carry out their duties.

Trade union membership and activities

Access to employment

Employers

14.01   TULR(C)A, s 137 protects applicants for employment[1] from dis-crimination on the grounds of their trade union membership. In particular, s 137(1)(a) makes it unlawful to refuse[2] a person employment because he is or is not a member of a trade union.[3]

1 Defined by TULR(C)A, s 143(1).
2 By TULR(C)A, s 137(5) a person is treated as having been refused employment where the employer:
  (a)   refuses or deliberately omits to entertain and process his application or enquiry;
  (b)   causes him to withdraw or cease to pursue his application or enquiry;
  (c)   refuses or deliberately omits to offer him employment;
  (d)   makes him an offer of employment on terms that no reasonable employer who wished to fill the post would offer and where the offer is refused;
  (e)   makes an offer but withdraws it or causes the applicant not to accept it.
By TULR(C)A, s 137(6) where a person is offered employment on terms that include a requirement that he is or is not a member of a trade union or includes a requirement outlawed by s 137(1)(b) and he does not accept the job because he is not willing to accept the requirement or condition he shall be treated as having refused employment for that reason.
3 See also s 137(1)(b) which makes it unlawful to refuse a person employment who will not accept a requirement to take steps to become, cease to be, remain or not become a member of a trade union or who will not accept that he will have to make payments or suffer deductions in the event of him not being a member of a trade union. See s 143(3) for interpretation of references to membership of a trade union.

14.02   It is also unlawful to publish an advertisement which indicates or might reasonably be understood as indicating that employment will be lim-ited to those who are or are not members of a trade union.[1] Where an appli-cant does not comply with the terms of such an advertisement and is not offered the job it will be conclusively presumed that he has been turned down as a result of his trade union membership.[2]

1 Or who will accept a requirement outlawed by s 137(1)(b).
2 TULR(C)A, s 137(3).

14.03   These provisions concluded the legislative attack on the closed shop by rendering the pre-entry closed shop illegal. It is not permissible to agree with a trade union that employment will be limited to its members. The provisions cannot be avoided by limiting employment to those put forward or approved by a union which only puts forward or approves its own members.[1] There is, however, a saving provision that allows trade unions to limit those who can be considered for office to its own members.[2]

1 TULR(C)A, s 137(4). A person who is not a member of the union and is refused employment pursuant to such an arrangement or practice will be taken to have been refused employment because he is not a member of the union.
2 TULR(C)A, s 137(7). Office is defined as a position by which the holder is an official of the union or to which TULR(C)A, Pt I, Ch IV (duty to hold election) applies.

14.04   In addition to outlawing the pre-entry closed shop, s 137 makes it unlawful to refuse a person employment because he *is* a member of a trade union. It is uncertain to what extent a distinction is to be drawn between trade union membership and activities. Section 146 (action short of dismissal) and s 152 (dismissal for trade union reasons) specifically refer to both trade union *membership* and trade union *activities* whereas s 137 refers only to trade union membership. If a clear distinction is to be drawn it may be open to an employer to claim that an applicant has been refused employment, not because he is a member of a trade union, but because of his past trade union activities. This may be of great significance where a job applicant has a long history as a trade unionist and, for example, has been involved in organising industrial action at a previous workplace.

14.05 In *Harrison v Kent County Council*[1] the applicant was refused employment because he had a history as a trade union activist. The Employment Appeal Tribunal held that the industrial tribunal was entitled to conclude that he was refused employment as a result of his trade union membership. The Employment Appeal Tribunal stated that a rigid distinction should not be drawn between union membership and activities. However, in reaching this conclusion, the Employment Appeal Tribunal relied upon *Discount Tobacco & Confectionery Ltd v Armitage*[2] in which it was concluded that use of union services was the 'outward and visible manifestation of trade union membership'. However, *Armitage* has since been doubted by the House of Lords in *Associated Newspapers Ltd v Wilson; Associated British Ports v Palmer.*[3] Thus the weight to be attached to *Harrison* is uncertain and it is unclear whether an employer can refuse a person employment because he has a reputation as a trade union activist.

1 [1995] ICR 434.
2 [1995] ICR 431n.
3 [1995] ICR 406. See discussion at **14.17**.

Employment agencies

14.06 Section 137(8) prevents an employment agency[1] which acts (or purports to act) on behalf of an employer discriminating against members or non-members of a trade union in breach of s 137. Section 138 prevents employment agencies refusing any of their services because a person is or is not a member of a trade union.

1 Employment agencies are defined in TULR(C)A, s 143(1). Other services are to be ignored (s 143(2)(a)). A trade union is not to be considered as an employment agency in respect of its members (s 143(2)(b)).

Complaint and remedies

14.07 A person refused employment in breach of s 137 or refused the services of an employment agency in breach of s 138 may complain to the industrial tribunal.[1] The complaint must be presented before the end of the period of three months beginning with the date of the conduct[2] complained of. If it was not reasonably practicable to do so the tribunal has a discretion to extend the period for such time as it considers reasonable.[3]

1 TULR(C)A, ss 137(2) and 138(2). No other liability is created by the sections (s 143(4)). Where a complaint lies against both a prospective employer and an employment agency the applicant may bring his claim against either or both (s 141). If one is joined initially, the other may be added at a later stage (s 141(2)). Where a complaint succeeds against both, the tribunal may order that any compensation is split between the two respondents in any manner it considers just and equitable.
2 The date of the conduct complained of is defined in relation to a complaint under s 137 by s 139(2) and in relation to a complaint under s 138 by s 139(3).
3 TULR(C)A, s 139(1).

14.08   If the applicant succeeds, the industrial tribunal will make a declaration and may award compensation. Compensation is assessed on a breach of statutory duty basis and may include a claim for injury to feeling.[1] The unfair dismissal compensation limit applies.[2] The tribunal may also recommend that the respondent takes action to obviate or reduce the effect of its conduct.[3] For example, an applicant may obtain compensation for the wages that he would have earned if he had been given the job. Alternatively, the tribunal might recommend that the applicant should be given the job. If an employer refuses to comply with a recommendation, compensation may be increased. However, the industrial tribunal has no power to force a respondent to employ the applicant.

1 TULR(C)A, s 140(2).
2 TULR(C)A, s 140(4). For limit on compensation for unfair dismissal, see Employment Rights Act 1996, s 124.
3 TULR(C)A, s 140(1).

Industrial pressure

14.09   A trade union may attempt to apply industrial pressure to ensure that employment is offered only to its members. Section 142 aims to prevent this. If it is claimed that a trade union caused the respondent to refuse the applicant employment (or otherwise act in breach of s 137 or s 138) by calling, organising, procuring or financing a strike or other industrial action, the union may be joined in the proceedings[1] and may be ordered to pay part or all of any compensation awarded.[2]

1 If the request is made prior to the hearing, it shall be granted. If made during the hearing, it may be allowed prior to the tribunal reaching is decision (TULR(C)A, s 142(2)).
2 TULR(C)A, s 142(3).

Protection of trade union members and activists

14.10   Employees are protected from action short of dismissal (s 146), from being dismissed (s 152) or being selected for redundancy (s 153) as a result of their trade union membership, activities or to compel them to join a trade union.[1] Much of the case law is generally applicable and will be considered together below.

1 TULR(C)A, s 146(3) and (4) also prevents such action to enforce a requirement that, in the event of the employee not being a member of a trade union, he must make one or more payment.

Action short of dismissal

14.11   Section 146 is a complex provision which should be considered with care. It states as follows:
    '(1)   An *employee*[1] has the right not to have *action short of dismissal* taken against him *as an individual* by his employer for the purpose of:
    (a)   preventing or deterring him from being or seeking to become a member of an independent trade union,[2] or penalising him for doing so,
    (b)   preventing or deterring him from taking part in the *activities* of an independent trade union *at an appropriate time*, or penalising him for doing so, or
    (c)   *compelling him to become a member* of any trade union or of a particular trade union or of one of a number of particular trade unions.'
(Italics supplied.)

1 The terms employee and employer are defined in TULR(C)A, s 295.
2 For the meaning of trade union, see TULR(C)A, s 1; for the meaning of independent trade union, see TULR(C)A, s 5.

14.12   Action short of dismissal is not defined but the term would appear to be relatively wide. Taking disciplinary action against an employee can amount to action short of dismissal[1] as can refusing an employee promotion.[2] However, the section will not be allowed to operate as a cloak or excuse for conduct which ordinarily would justify dismissal. Wholly unreasonable, extraneous or malicious acts done in support of trade union activities may provide grounds for a fair dismissal.[3]

1 *British Airways Board v Clark* [1982] IRLR 238, EAT.
2 *Department of Transport v Gallacher* [1994] ICR 967, CA.
3 *Lyon and Scherk v St James Press Ltd* [1976] ICR 413, EAT.

Action or omission

14.13   In *Associated Newspapers Ltd v Wilson; Associated British Ports v Palmer*[1] a pay rise was withheld from employees who would not give up rights to collective bargaining and enter into personal contracts of employment. The House of Lords concluded that a failure to make the payments could not amount to *action* short of dismissal. It was an omission and so was not caught by the section.[2] This decision could give rise to considerable difficulties in practice. It is unfortunate that the lawfulness of conduct should depend on whether it is defined as an action or omission. It is also surprising that an employer who demotes an employee because he is a trade unionist will be caught by the section whereas an employer who refuses to promote will not.

1 [1995] ICR 406, HL.
2 Section 298 defines action as including omission. However, the House of Lords decided the legislative history of the section was such that s 298 did not apply to s 146.

Purpose of action

14.14   The House of Lords also concluded that the purpose of the payments had not been to deter union membership. The aim was to move away from collective bargaining in the *Wilson* case and to increase flexibility in the *Palmer* case. In reaching this decision the House of Lords overruled the Court of Appeal.[1] The decision of the Court of Appeal had resulted in a late amendment to TULR(C)A to introduce s 148(3). Where an employer's intention was to further a change in relationship with his employees, such as a move from collective bargaining to individual contracts, and he also had a purpose that falls within s 146, such as deterring trade union membership, s 148(3) provides a statutory presumption that the tribunal shall have regard only to the former purpose unless no reasonable employer could have taken the action complained of.

1 *Associated Newspapers Ltd v Wilson; Associated British Ports v Palmer* [1994] ICR 97, CA.

Taken against him as an individual

14.15   Section 146 protects an employee against action taken against him as an individual. In *National Coal Board v Ridgway*[1] the National Coal Board decided not to grant NUM members a pay rise agreed with the UDM. The Court of Appeal held that although the NUM was the primary target of the action, all members of the NUM were effected as individuals and so the action breached s 146.

1 [1987] ICR 641. Note that *Ridgeway* was overruled by the House of Lords on the point that failure to make such a payment was an omission not action.

Membership of an independent trade union

14.16 Section 146 refers to deterring membership of an independent trade union. In *Ridgeway* it was suggested that the conduct of the NCB would only deter employees from being members of the NUM rather than of any trade union at all. The Court of Appeal rejected this argument and held that the phrase *an independent trade union* referred to a particular union as well as to any union.

Union membership and use of the services of the union

14.17 In *Discount Tobacco & Confectionery Ltd v Armitage*[1] Mrs Armitage was dismissed after invoking the help of her trade union in a dispute about the terms of her contract of employment. It was concluded that use of union services was the 'outward and visible manifestation of trade union membership'. However, *Armitage* was later considered by the House of Lords in *Associated Newspapers Ltd v Wilson; Associated British Ports v Palmer*.[2] Lord Lloyd stated that, although *Armitage* might have been correctly decided on its facts, it was not authority for the general proposition that membership of a union should be equated with making use of the union's services. The question has since been revisited by the Employment Appeal Tribunal in *Speciality Care plc v Pachela*.[3] The Employment Appeal Tribunal noted that the House of Lords decided *Wilson* and *Palmer* on the basis that action did not include omission. Thus the comments about *Armitage* were obiter. The Employment Appeal Tribunal considered that *Armitage* was still applicable and that 'it will be for the tribunal to find as a fact whether or not the reason or principal reason for dismissal related to the applicant's trade union membership not only by reference to whether he or she had simply joined a union, but also by reference to whether the introduction of union representation into the employment relationship had led the employer to dismiss the employee.'

1 [1995] ICR 431n.
2 [1995] ICR 406.
3 [1996] IRLR 248.

Trade union activities

14.18 Tribunals are encouraged to apply common sense in deciding what are trade union activities. For example, seeking to recruit fellow employees as members of the union will generally amount to a trade union activity.[1] Another example is provided by *British Airways Engine Overhaul Ltd v Francis*.[2] An employee made a statement to the press criticising her union for failing to secure equal pay for its members. The statement was made after a meeting that she had organised in her capacity as a shop steward. The Employment Appeal Tribunal accepted that making such a statement could amount to a trade union activity although it was critical of the union.

1 *Brennan and Ging v Ellward (Lancs) Ltd* [1976] IRLR 378, EAT.
2 [1981] ICR 278.

14.19 Employees may be protected against action taken because of activities with a previous employer. In *Fitzpatrick v British Railways Board*[1] the applicant was dismissed when it was discovered that he had been a trade union activist in his previous job. The Court of Appeal held that the only rational reason for his dismissal was the fear that he would engage in such actions again. Therefore he was protected.

1 [1992] ICR 221, CA.

14.20 A greater range of activities are protected where the individual is a union official.[1] However, the protection does not extend to taking part in industrial action[2] although it may extend to activities preparatory to a strike.[3]

1 *Post Office v Union of Post Office Workers* [1974] ICR 378, HL.
2 *Drew v St Edmundsbury Borough Council* [1980] ICR 513, EAT.
3 *Britool Ltd v Roberts* [1993] IRLR 481, EAT.

14.21 To gain the protection the activity must be carried out by the individual acting as a member of a trade union rather than on his own behalf.[1] An employee who campaigned about a health and safety issue for personal reasons was not protected.[2]

1 *Chant v Aquaboats Ltd* [1978] ICR 643, EAT.
2 *Drew v St Edmundsbury Borough Council* [1980] ICR 513, EAT but see below for discussion of dismissals for health and safety reasons.

14.22 On the other hand, an employee is not protected against action taken because of something done by his union rather than himself. In *Carrington v Therm-A-Stor Ltd*[1] a number of employees were dismissed after the district secretary of their union wrote to their employer seeking recognition. The Court of Appeal decided that, because the section refers to the activities of *an* employee, the activities must be of *that individual*. Thus the employees were not protected from action taken as a result of the letter written by their convenor. The case highlights a disturbing gap in the protection offered to employees.

1 [1983] ICR 208.

At an appropriate time

14.23 For activities to be protected they must take place at an appropriate time. A time outside the employee's working hours will be appropriate. Alternatively the employer may agree to the activity taking place in working hours.[1] An appropriate time may be established by custom and practice: see *Marley Tile Co Ltd v Shaw*[2] and *Zucker v Astrid Jewels Ltd*[3]. However, if the employer refuses permission for the activities to take place then they cannot be at an appropriate time: *Robb v Leon Motor Services Ltd*.[4]

1 TULR(C)A, s 146(2).
2 [1980] ICR 72, CA.
3 [1978] ICR 1088, EAT.
4 [1978] ICR 506, EAT.

Complaint and remedies

14.24 Complaint is made to the industrial tribunal.[1] The complaint must be presented before the end of the period of three months beginning with the date of the action complained of (or the last action if the complaint refers to a series of acts). However, if it was not reasonably practical to submit the claim within the three-month period the tribunal may extend time for such further period as it considers reasonable.[2]

1 TULR(C)A, s 146(5).
2 TULR(C)A, s 147.

14.25 It is for the employer to establish the purpose for which the action was taken.[1] Where there is evidence that the employer intended to further a change in relationship with all or a class of employees and had a purpose that falls within s 146, the tribunal shall have regard only to the former purpose, unless no reasonable employer could have taken the action complained of.[2]

1 TULR(C)A, s 148(1).
2 TULR(C)A, s 148(3); but see discussion of *Associated Newspapers Ltd v Wilson; Associated British Ports v Palmer* [1995] ICR 406, HL at **14.14**.

14.26 No account is taken of pressure put on the employer as a result of strike or other industrial action.[1] However, in such a case the trade union may be joined as a party to the action and ordered to pay some or all of any compensation awarded.[2]

1 TULR(C)A, s 148(2).
2 TULR(C)A, s 150.

14.27 If an application succeeds, the tribunal makes a declaration and may award such compensation as it considers just and equitable having regard to any loss sustained or expenses incurred by the applicant.[1] Thus, if the employer demotes the employee, compensation could be awarded for any loss of salary involved. An award in respect of injury to feeling may also be made.[2] If the applicant caused or contributed to his loss the award may be reduced.[3]

1 TULR(C)A, s 149.
2 *Brassington v Cauldon Wholesale Ltd* [1978] ICR 405, EAT.
3 TULR(C)A, s 149(6).

Dismissal for trade union reasons

14.28 TULR(C)A, s 152 protects employees from being dismissed as a result of their trade union membership, activities or in order to compel them to become members of a trade union. A dismissal for refusing to agree to make payments or suffer deductions if the employee ceases to be a trade union member is also rendered unfair.[1]

1 TULR(C)A, s 152(3).

14.29 As with s 146 (action short of dismissal) the section requires careful consideration. It states:

'For the purposes of Part X of the Employment Rights Act 1996 (unfair dismissal) the dismissal of an employee shall be regarded as unfair if the reason for it (or, if more than one, the principal reason) was that the employee—

(a) was, or proposed to become, a *member* of an *independent trade union*, or

(b) had taken part, or proposed to take part, in the *activities* of an independent trade union at an *appropriate time,*

(c) was *not a member* of any trade union, or of a particular trade union, or of one of a number of particular trade unions, or had refused, or proposed to refuse, to become or remain a member.'

(Italics supplied.)

14.30 The protection extends to members of an independent trade union, non-members of trade unions and those who take part in trade union activities at an appropriate time. The relevant case law and definitions are considered at **14.16–14.23**.

Selection for redundancy

14.31 Employees are protected from selection for redundancy for one of the reasons set out in TULR(C)A, s 152(1) if the circumstances constituting the redundancy applied equally to one or more other employee who was not dismissed despite holding a similar position to the applicant at the undertaking where he was employed.[1] Thus an employer will not be able to use a redundancy situation as an opportunity to rid himself of trade union activists. The discussion at **14.16–14.23** is also applicable to this section.

1 TULR(C)A, s 153.

Complaint and remedies (interim relief)

14.32 Employees dismissed in contravention of s 152 may complain of unfair dismissal to the industrial tribunal. There is no qualifying period.[1] Where a complaint is made that the dismissal is unfair by reason of s 152 an application can be made for interim relief.[2] The application must be made before the end of the period of seven days immediately following the effective date of termination.[3] Special provisions ensure that such applications are considered promptly.[4] If the industrial tribunal concludes that it is likely that the applicant will succeed in his claim it may order that the applicant be reinstated (if the employer agrees), re-engaged (if the employer and employee agree), or that the employee's contract of employment continues for the purpose of pay, other benefits and continuity pending the hearing of the full complaint.[5] If an application for interim relief is not made the usual unfair dismissal time limit will apply.

1 TULR(C)A, s 154.
2 TULR(C)A, s 161.
3 TULR(C)A, s 161(2).
4 TULR(C)A, s 162.
5 TULR(C)A, ss 163 and 164.

14.33 Where the complaint succeeds at the full hearing special compensation provisions apply. There is a minimum compensatory award (presently £2,770 prior to any permitted deduction).[1] Where the applicant applies for reinstatement or re-engagement the compensatory award will include a special award (presently the *greater* of one week's pay multiplied by 104 or £13,775 subject to a maximum of £27,500).[2] If an employer refuses to comply with an order to reinstate or re-engage the applicant, the amount of the special award shall be the *greater* of one week's pay multiplied by 156 or £20,600 unless it was not reasonably practicable to comply.[3] Special provisions apply to the deduction that may be made from any award in respect of contributory conduct.[4] In particular, the industrial tribunal may not reduce any award of compensation for a reason relating to the employee's trade union membership or non-membership.[5]

1 TULR(C)A, s 156.
2 See TULR(C)A, ss 157 and 158(1).
3 TULR(C)A, s 158(2).
4 See TULR(C)A, s 158.
5 TULR(C)A, s 155.

Time off for trade union activities

14.34 An official of an independent trade union[1] that is recognised by his employer is entitled to paid time off to carry out his trade union duties.[2] Trade union duties are limited to negotiations[3] concerned with collective bargaining and other duties that the employer has agreed may be performed. Paid time off is also permitted to undergo certain training which is relevant to the duties carried out by the official and approved by the TUC or the official's trade union.[4]

1 See TULR(C)A, s 5 for a definition.
2 TULR(C)A, ss 168 and 169.
3 The section applies not only to negotiations, but can include work preparatory to negotiations where there is a sufficient factual matrix between the duty carried out and the relevant collective bargaining: *London Ambulance Service v Charlton* [1992] ICR 773, EAT.
4 TULR(C)A, s 168(2).

14.35 An individual member of an independent trade union that is recognised by his employer is entitled to take unpaid time off during working hours to take part in the activities of the union and activities in which he acts as a representative of the union.[1] The protection does not extend to activities which constitute industrial action.

1 TULR(C)A, s 170.

14.36 In the case of both trade union officials and members the amount of time off allowed, the occasions on which it can be taken and any conditions applied are judged by the test of reasonableness in the light of the ACAS code of conduct.[1] Where a complaint is made that time off was not allowed the industrial tribunal should consider whether the decision was within the range of reasonable responses.[2]

1 ACAS code of conduct (SI 1991/968).
2 See *Ministry of Defence v Crook and Irving* [1982] IRLR 488, EAT.

14.37 A complaint that time off has not been allowed is brought before the industrial tribunal.[1] The complaint must be presented within three months of the date of the failure unless the tribunal is satisfied that it was not reasonably practical to do so in which case the period may be extended for such period as the tribunal considers reasonable.[2] Where the application is successful the industrial tribunal makes a declaration and may award such compensation as it considers just and equitable having regard to the employer's default in not allowing the time off and any loss suffered by the employee as a result of the refusal.[3]

1 TULR(C)A, ss 168(4) and 170(4).
2 TULR(C)A, s 171.
3 TULR(C)A, s 172.

Dismissals during industrial action

Unofficial strike or industrial action

14.38   An employee who is dismissed while taking part in unofficial industrial action has no right to claim unfair dismissal.[1] The employer's reason for dismissing the employee is irrelevant (unless it is outlawed by the Employment Rights Act 1996, s 100 (health and safety), s 103 (employee representatives) or s 99 (pregnancy)). It does not matter whether the employee was dismissed for taking part in the action, for leading it or for an unconnected reason.

1 TULR(C)A, s 237.

14.39   A strike or other industrial action[1] is unofficial in relation to an employee unless
(1)   he is a member of a trade union which has authorised or endorsed the action, or
(2)   if he is not a member of a trade union, there are employees taking part who are members of the trade union that has authorised or endorsed the action.[2]

1 See discussion of meaning of strike and industrial action discussed at **14.47**.
2 TULR(C)A, s 237(2).

14.40   As a strike or other industrial action is treated as unofficial in relation to *an* employee, it may be unofficial for some taking part but not others. However, action is not considered unofficial if none of those taking part is a member of a union.[1]

1 TULR(C)A, s 237(2): in the case of such a strike or other industrial action the provisions of TULR(C)A, s 238 apply.

14.41   The industrial tribunal will decide whether the action was authorised or endorsed by application of TULR(C)A, s 20(2).[1] The tribunal must decide whether the action was so authorised or endorsed at the time of the dismissal. This is defined as the date when notice is *given*, the date of summary dismissal or the date that a fixed term contract expires.

1 Action can be authorised or endorsed by (1) any person empowered by the union's rules, (2) the principal executive committee, (3) the president, (4) the general secretary, (5) any committee of the union, (6) any official of the union, paid or not, (7) any group or member of a group, which a union official is a member, the purpose of which included organising or co-ordinating industrial action. Where the authorisation is by a person within categories (5)–(7) the action will cease to be authorised if it is repudiated by the principal executive committee, the president or the general secretary pursuant to the provisions of TULR(C)A, s 21.

14.42   Action may cease to be official if it is repudiated[1] by the union. However, it shall not cease to be treated as official until the end of the next working day after the repudiation took place.[2] This gives employees an opportunity to cease taking part before they lose all rights to claim unfair dismissal. Where a person is a member of a relevant trade union when he began to take part in the action he will continue to be treated as a member even if he resigns before the end of the action.[3]

1 See TULR(C)A, s 21.
2 See TULR(C)A, s 237(4).
3 See TULR(C)A, s 237(6).

Other strike and industrial action

14.43   TULR(C)A, s 238 applies when employees are dismissed during a strike or other industrial action (that is not unofficial within the meaning of s 237) or while an employer is conducting a lockout. The industrial tribunal will not have jurisdiction to determine a complaint of unfair dismissal unless:
(1)   one or more of the employees taking part in the action or locked out is not dismissed, or
(2)   one or more of the employees who took part in the action or was locked out is offered re-engagement within three months of his dismissal, but the applicant is not.

14.44   To protect himself from complaints of unfair dismissal, the employer must dismiss all those who take part in such action and may not selectively re-engage strikers within three months of their dismissals.

14.45   The industrial tribunal also has jurisdiction if the reason or principle reason for the dismissal is one that is outlawed by the Employment Rights Act 1996, s 100 (health and safety), s 103(employee representatives) or s 99 (pregnancy).

Lockout

14.46   The term lockout is not defined in the Act. In *Express and Star Ltd v Bunday*[1] the Court of Appeal considered that industrial tribunals might obtain assistance from the dictionary definition as 'a refusal on the part of an employer ... to furnish work to their operatives except on conditions to be accepted by the latter collectively'. The definition in the Employment Rights Act 1996, s 235(4) (formerly Sch 13 to the Employment Protection (Consolidation) Act 1978) also gives an indication of the sort of ingredients that should be looked for. However, these definitions are not to be treated as though part of the statute. The Court of Appeal emphasised that the question of what amounts to a lockout is a question of fact for the industrial tribunal.

1 [1988] ICR 379.

Strike or other industrial action

14.47   A strike is defined as a concerted stoppage of work.[1] Other industrial action is not defined. What amounts to other industrial action is a question of fact for the industrial tribunal.[2] A work to rule or go slow will generally amount to other industrial action. It is not necessary that the action amount to a breach of the employee's contract. In *Power Packing Casemakers v Faust*[3] the Court of Appeal accepted that an embargo on voluntary overtime could amount to industrial action although it involved no breach of contract. Much will turn on the motives behind the action.

1 TULR(C)A, s 246.
2 *Express and Star Ltd v Bunday* [1988] ICR 379, CA; see **14.46**.
3 [1983] ICR 292, CA.

14.48 Action cannot be both industrial action, for the purposes of s 138, and trade union activities, for the purposes of s 152.[1] However, the dividing line is thin. For example, holding a union meeting at work with the implied consent of the employer may amount to taking part in trade union activities at an appropriate time. An employee dismissed for attending such a meeting would be able to claim that the dismissal was automatically unfair. However, if the industrial tribunal concludes that there was no implied consent, attendance could amount to taking part in industrial action. In those circumstances the industrial tribunal would have no jurisdiction to hear the complaint (unless the case came within one of the exceptions in s 238).[2]

1 *Drew v St Edmundsbury Borough Council* [1980] ICR 513, EAT.
2 See for example *Rasool v Hepworth Pipe Co Ltd* [1980] ICR 494, EAT.

14.49 An individual may take part in industrial action alone. In *Lewis and Britton v E Mason and Sons*[1] the applicant was not prepared to take out a lorry with a broken overnight heater unless he was paid the cost of bed and breakfast accommodation. The Employment Appeal Tribunal accepted that this could amount to industrial action.

1 [1994] IRLR 4.

Taking part

14.50 If an employee is absent from work during a strike the courts will generally treat him as taking part. His motives for staying away will be irrelevant. In *Coates and Venables v Modern Methods and Materials Ltd*[1] an employee was absent during a strike, not because she supported the strike, but because she feared abuse from her workmates if she attended for work. The industrial tribunal held that she was taking part in the strike. The Court of Appeal accepted that this was a question of fact for the industrial tribunal and were not prepared to overturn the decision. Lord Justice Stephenson stated at p 777A 'If he [the employee] stops work when his workmates come out on strike and does not say or do anything to make plain his disagreement, or which could amount to a refusal to join them, he takes part in their strike. The line between unwilling participation and not taking part may be difficult to draw, but those who stay away from work with the strikers without protest for whatever reason are to be regarded as having crossed that line to take part in the strike. In the field of industrial action those who are not openly against it are presumably for it.' Lord Justice Kerr took an even stricter line stating at p 783B 'their reasons or motives for staying out cannot be regarded as relevant. Nor would it be relevant to consider whether their utterances or actions, or silence or inaction, showed support, opposition or indifference in relation to the strike.' Eveleigh LJ dissented. In practice it will be difficult for an employee who was absent at the time of the strike to show that he was not taking part. Participation is determined objectively and the employer's knowledge is irrelevant.[2]

1 [1982] ICR 763, CA.
2 *Bolton Roadways Ltd v Edwards* [1987] IRLR 392, EAT.

14.51 An employee who is away sick or on holiday at the time of the strike can still be taking part if he associates himself with the strike by, for example, attending on the picket line.[1] An employee who goes out on strike, but subsequently becomes sick or starts his holiday, will be treated as remaining on strike unless he communicates a clear intention to cease taking part and return to work at the end of his absence.[2]

1 *Bolton Roadways Ltd v Edwards* [1987] IRLR 392. See also *Hindle Gears Ltd v McGinty* [1984] IRLR 477, EAT; cf *Rogers v Chloride Systems* [1992] ICR 198, EAT.
2 *Williams v Western Mail and Echo Ltd* [1980] ICR 366, EAT.

14.52 The threat or advance warning of industrial action will not itself amount to industrial action.[1] However, once some employees have started the action, an employee who is not yet due in for work will be treated as taking part if he makes it plain that he intends to withdraw his labour when his shift begins.[2]

1 *Midland Plastics v Till* [1983] ICR 118, EAT; cf *Lewis and Britton v E Mason and Sons* [1994] IRLR 4, EAT.
2 *Winnett v Seamarks Bros Ltd* [1978] ICR 1240, EAT.

14.53 Section 238 applies to an employee who was taking part in a strike or other industrial action 'at the date' of his dismissal. Usually 'date' is interpreted as a full day. If that interpretation was applied to s 238, an employer would have the remainder of the day on which industrial action was called off to dismiss those taking part. However, 'date' is interpreted as 'time' of dismissal[1] and s 238 ceases to apply from the time that the industrial action ends.

1 *Heath v Longman Ltd* [1973] ICR 407, NIRC.

Relevant employee

14.54 The industrial tribunal has jurisdiction if a 'relevant employee' was not dismissed or was re-engaged within three months of his dismissal. The definition of relevant employee depends on whether there is a lockout or industrial action.

14.55 In the case of a lockout, a relevant employee is one who had a direct interest in the dispute in contemplation or furtherance of which the lockout occurred.[1] Thus an employer may not instigate a lockout as a ruse to dismiss his workforce. There must be a genuine trade dispute before the section can bite.

1 TULR(C)A, s 238(3)(a).

14.56 The employer cannot selectively lockout and dismiss certain employees who, for example, are leading the industrial action. All those with a direct interest must be dismissed. The courts will consider who had a direct interest at the date that the lockout commenced: *H Campey and Sons Ltd v Bellwood*.[1]

1 [1987] ICR 311, EAT.

14.57 Thus an employer may not issue an ultimatum to employees to return to work, dismiss only those who do not obey and then rely on s 238 to oust the jurisdiction of the industrial tribunal.

14.58 In the case of strike or other industrial action relevant employees are those employed at the *establishment* where the applicant worked *at the date of his dismissal*.[1]

1 TULR(C)A, s 238(3)(b).

14.59   The industrial tribunal will determine whether all relevant employees were dismissed on or before the date of the jurisdiction hearing. In *P & O European Ferries (Dover) Ltd v Byrne*[1] the Court of Appeal held that an employee could be required to divulge, at an interlocutory stage, who he claimed was a relevant employee for the purposes of s 238 even though this would allow the employer to dismiss that employee and prevent the applicant pursuing his claim.

1 [1989] ICR 779.

Offer of re-engagement

14.60   There is no statutory definition of an offer of re-engagement. Generally it will not be difficult to assess whether such an offer has been made. The courts have shown a willingness to adopt a relatively broad approach. A tacit acceptance of continuance of employment can be sufficient.[1]

1 *Bolton Roadways Ltd v Edwards* [1987] IRLR 392, EAT.

14.61   However, problems may arise where an applicant claims that he was unaware of the offer. In *Williams v National Theatre Board Ltd*[1] an employee had not received a letter offering re-engagement as it had been wrongly addressed. However, he knew that the offer had been made and that it applied to him. The Employment Appeal Tribunal accepted that this was sufficient to comply with the section.

1 [1982] ICR 715, CA.

14.62   The mere fact that an employer advertises for staff does not mean that he will be taken to have offered re-engagement[1] unless the applicant is made aware that he will definitely be taken on if he applies.[2] The offer of re-engagement need not be on the same terms and conditions as the original job in all respects.[3]

1 *Crossville Wales Ltd v Tracey* [1993] IRLR 60, EAT.
2 *Williams v National Theatre Board Ltd* [1982] ICR 715.
3 *Williams v National Theatre Board Ltd* [1982] ICR 715.

Complaint and remedy

14.63   Where an employee is able to establish that the industrial tribunal has jurisdiction to hear a complaint of unfair dismissal because, for example, not all those taking part in a strike were dismissed, it must go on to consider whether the dismissal was fair. A failure to re-engage is treated as a dismissal.[1] The mere involvement of an employee in the industrial action will not amount to contributory conduct so as to reduce any award of compensation. However, if the employee has been involved in any particular activity such as leading the strike, this is a matter that the industrial tribunal may consider.[2] The complaint must be made before the end of the period of six months beginning with the date of the complainant's dismissal. If it was not reasonably practicable to do so the tribunal may extend the time for such further period as it considers reasonable.[3]

1 TULR(C)A, s 239(3).
2 *Tracey v Crosville Wales Ltd* [1996] ICR 237, CA.
3 TULR(C)A, s 239(2).

Health and safety

14.64 Detailed consideration of the law of health and safety at work is beyond the scope of this book. Consideration will be limited to the principal areas of overlap between employment and heath and safety law.

Safety representatives

14.65 The Safety Representatives and Safety Committees Regulations 1977 (as amended in 1992)[1] provide that a recognised trade union may appoint safety representatives from amongst the employees at a workplace.[2] Safety representatives take part in consultations with their employer and have a series of specific functions related to the investigation of and prevention of risks to employees' health.[3] Employers are required to allow safety representatives paid time off to carry out their functions and to undergo reasonable training.[4]

1 SI 1977/500, enacted pursuant to Health and Safety at Work &c Act 1974, s 2(4).
2 Regulation 3(1). The right does not extend to coal mines within the meaning of the Mines and Quarries Act 1954, s 180.
3 Regulation 4(1) sets out the relevant list of duties.
4 Regulation 4(2).

14.66 A safety representative who is not allowed time off or is not paid for time taken may complain to the industrial tribunal.[1] The complaint must be made within three months of the date when the failure occurred. If it was not reasonably practical to do so, the industrial tribunal may extend time for such further period as it considers reasonable.[2] Where a complaint that time off has not been allowed succeeds, the industrial tribunal will make a declaration and may order that the respondent pay compensation of such an amount as is equitable having regard to the employer's default and the loss suffered by the employee.[3] Where a complaint that an employee has not been paid for time off succeeds, the industrial tribunal shall order the employer to pay the sum that should have been due.[4]

1 Regulation 11(1).
2 Regulation 11(2).
3 Regulation 11(3).
4 Regulation 11(4).

14.67 The regulations also set out detailed provision relating to consultation and the provision of information, facilities and assistance to safety representatives which are beyond the scope of this work.

Where there are no union appointed safety representatives, the Health and Safety (Consultation with Employees) Regulations 1996, SI 1996/1513, provide that the employer must consult either with employees directly or with 'representatives of employee safety'. Representatives of employee safety have similar rights and duties to safety representatives.

Right not to suffer detriment or dismissal for health and safety reasons

14.68 The Trade Union and Employment Rights Act 1993 added similar anti-discrimination provisions to protect employees in relation to health and safety activities as protect employees from discrimination in respect of trade union membership and activities.

14.69 Employees have a right not to suffer any detriment by any act or deliberate failure to act by his employer[1] or to be dismissed[2] on the grounds that:

'(a) having been designated by the employer to carry out activities in connection with preventing or reducing risks to health and safety at work, he carried out, or proposed to carry out, any such activities,

(b) being a representative of workers on matters of health and safety at work, or a member of a safety committee—

   (i) in accordance with arrangements established under or by virtue of any enactment, or

   (ii) by reason of being acknowledged as such by the employer

   he performed, or proposed to perform, any functions as such a representative or member of such a committee,

(c) being an employee at a place where—

   (i) there was no such representative or safety committee, or

   (ii) there was such a representative or safety committee but it was not reasonably practicable for the employee to raise matters by those means,

   he, brought to his employer's attention, by reasonable means, circumstances connected with his work which he reasonably believed were harmful or potentially harmful to health or safety,

(d) in circumstances of danger which he reasonably considered to be serious, and imminent and which he could not reasonably have been expected to avert, he left, or proposed to leave, or (while the danger persisted) refused to return to, his place of work or any dangerous part of his place of work, or

(e) in circumstances of danger which he reasonably believed to be serious and imminent, he took, or proposed to take, appropriate steps to protect himself or other persons from the danger.[3]

1 Employment Rights Act 1996, s 44.
2 Employment Rights Act 1996, s 100.
3 Employment Rights Act 1996, ss 44(3) and 100(3) provide exceptions where the employer can show that the steps which the employee took or proposed to take were so negligent that a reasonable employer could treat the employee in the manner complained of.

Detriment

14.70 Section 44 of the Employment Rights Act 1996 prevents employers subjecting employees to a detriment on health and safety grounds. The protection is similar to that members of trade unions have against action short of dismissal taken to deter union membership or activities. In many cases there may be some overlap between the two provisions where health and safety activities are carried out by an employee in his role as a member or official of a trade union. However, the provisions are drafted differently and it is important to consider the health and safety provisions with care. For instance, it is interesting to note that detriment is defined to include both action and omission, so avoiding the unfortunate result arrived at in the *Wilson* and *Palmer* cases whereby union members are protected only against action taken against them but not against omissions (see **14.13**).

Complaint and remedy

14.71 An employee who has suffered a detriment on health and safety grounds may complain to an industrial tribunal.[1] It is for the employer to show the reason for the action or omission.[2] The complaint must be presented before the end of the period of three months beginning with the date of the act or failure to act[3] complained of unless it was not reasonably practicable to do so in which case the industrial tribunal may extend time for such further period as it considers reasonable.

1 Employment Rights Act 1996, s 48(1).
2 Employment Rights Act 1996, s 48(2).
3 Employment Rights Act 1996, s 48(3), see s 48(4) for a definition of date of act where an act extends over a period and for a definition of date of failure to act.

14.72 Where a complaint succeeds the industrial tribunal will make a declaration and may award such compensation as it considers just and equitable. This shall include any expense reasonably incurred by the complainant and any benefit he might reasonably have expected.[1] Common law rules on mitigation of loss apply.[2] The tribunal may reduce compensation where the complainant caused or contributed to the loss.[3]

1 Employment Rights Act 1996, s 49.
2 Employment Rights Act 1996, s 49(4).
3 Employment Rights Act 1996, s 49(5).

Dismissal

14.73 Where an employee is dismissed or selected for redundancy for a health and safety reason, he will have an action for unfair dismissal. The dismissal will be automatically unfair.[1] There is no qualifying period of employment or upper age limit.[2] Where the employee is a health and safety official[3] he may seek interim relief,[4] there is a minimum basic award[5] and he may obtain a special award of compensation.[6] The provisions are similar to those relating to dismissals for trade union membership and activities discussed at **14.28–14.30**.

1 Employment Rights Act 1996, s 100.
2 Employment Rights Act 1996, ss 108(3) and 109(2).
3 A health and safety official is a person as set out in s 100(1)(a) or (b).
4 Employment Rights Act 1996, s 128(1)(b).
5 Employment Rights Act 1996, s 120(1)(b).
6 See Employment Rights Act 1996, s 118, see s 124 for calculation.

Employee representatives

14.74 Consultation when there are to be collective redundancies or on transfers of undertakings were formerly limited to consultation with recognised trade unions. The United Kingdom was found to be in breach of European law in imposing this limit on consultation.[1] As a result regulations[2] were passed that provide for employee representatives to be consulted in such cases. The detail of the role of such representatives is beyond the scope of this book. However, it is to be noted that employee representatives have similar protections to those where employees are subjected to a detriment or are dismissed on health and safety grounds.

1 (C-383/92) *EC Commission v United Kingdom* [1994] ICR 664.
2 Collective Redundancies and Transfer of Undertakings (Protection of Employment) (Amendment) Regulations 1995, SI 1995/2587.

14.75 Employee representatives are protected from suffering a detriment by reason of their activities.[1] They are entitled to paid time off to carry out their activities.[2] If an employee representative or candidate for election is dismissed for carrying out or proposing to carry out his duties, the dismissal will be automatically unfair.[3] It is not permissible to select an employee for redundancy for such a reason.[4] There is no qualifying period to claim unfair dismissal and no upper age limit.[5] An applicant dismissed in such circumstances may claim interim relief.[6] Where an applicant succeeds at a full hearing there is a minimum basic award[7] and he may obtained a special award of compensation.[8]

1 Employment Rights Act 1996, s 47. See **14.70**.
2 Employment Rights Act 1996, s 61.
3 Employment Rights Act 1996, s 103.
4 Employment Rights Act 1996, s 105.
5 Employment Rights Act 1996, ss 108(3) and 109(2).
6 Employment Rights Act 1996, s 128(b).
7 Employment Rights Act 1996, s 120(1)(b).
8 See Employment Rights Act 1996, s 118, see s 124 for calculation.

Chapter 15

Unfair dismissal

Introduction

In unfair dismissal cases the right not to be unfairly dismissed only arises if the applicant is an employee; if he has the requisite period of continuous employment and if he makes the application in time (see **15.12–15.16** and **15.06**). All these issues go to the jurisdiction of the industrial tribunal to hear an application for a remedy for unfair dismissal. If the applicant does not surmount these hurdles the tribunal has no jurisdiction to adjudicate on the matter however meritorious the claim. Moreover there are certain classes of employment which are exempted from unfair dismissal protection (see **15.01–15.28**). There are only limited provisions for contracting out of the Employment Rights Act 1996 (see **15.17–15.21**).

There are two species of unfair dismissal cases. If employees are dismissed for certain reasons, then the dismissals are automatically unfair (see **15.70–15.85**).

In other cases – and by far the most significant numerically – an employer who wishes to defend a claim has to establish the reason for the dismissal and that it was one of the reasons set out in s 98(1) and (2) of the Act (see **15.88**). What is considered is the reason for the dismissal at the time of the dismissal (see **15.91–15.94**). The tribunal then has to determine whether it was fair to treat that reason as a sufficient reason for the dismissal having regard to the provisions of s 98(4) of the Act. In considering whether the employer acted fairly an industrial tribunal considers whether the employer had reasonable grounds for his belief in the reason for the dismissal, after making such enquiries as were appropriate in all the circumstances of the case (see **15.96–15.100**). The tribunal then looks to see if an employer acting reasonably could have dismissed in the circumstances.

In some unusual situations an employee who claims to be unfairly dismissed can obtain interim relief – an order that his contractual conditions continue (see **15.168**).

Claims as to unfair dismissal are heard by industrial tribunals. If the employee is found to be unfairly dismissed he may ask the tribunal to make an order for his reinstatement or re-engagement (see **15.169–15.188**). These may be accompanied by financial orders.

If an order for reinstatement or re-engagement is not made, or it is not complied with, compensation can be ordered. This will normally consist of a basic award (see **15.190–15.193**) and compensatory award (see **15.194–15.218**). In some cases there may be an additional (see **15.187–15.188**) or special award as well (see **15.219**).

Awards of compensation may subject to recoupment in favour of the Secretary of State (see **15.220–15.221**).

Those who are and are not protected by the unfair dismissal provisions

15.01 As a general principle, the right not to be unfairly dismissed applies to employees (see **3.15–3.22**) only. An employee is an individual who has entered into, or works under (or where the employment has ceased, worked under), a contract of service or apprenticeship (whether express, implied, oral or in writing). Thus those working under contracts for services do not have the benefit of the unfair dismissal provisions. Reference should be made to the decisions on the distinction between contracts of service and contracts for services given when discussing the position at common law and with regard to redundancy payments.

Part-time employees

15.02 Some part-time employees were at one time excluded by the requirements for minimum numbers of hours for weeks to count for the purposes of computing periods of continuous employment. The effect was to exclude many part-time employees from the benefit of the unfair dismissal provisions. This was found to be discriminatory and unlawful and the requirement has been repealed.[1] Thus if part-time employees satisfy the service qualification, which now does not discriminate against them, they have the benefit of unfair dismissal protection.

1 Following the decision in *R v Secretary of State for Employment, ex p Equal Opportunities Commission* [1995] 1 AC 1, [1994] 1 All ER 910. See **11.17**.

Crown servants

15.03 Notwithstanding that there is considerable doubt whether they work under contracts of service, unfair dismissal protection is expressly extended to most Crown servants.[1] In these cases, references in the unfair dismissal provisions to 'employee' are construed as references to 'persons in Crown employment',[2] and references to dismissal as if to 'termination of Crown employment'. Most members of parliamentary staff are included.[3]

1 Employment Rights Act 1996, s 191.
2 Employment Rights Act 1996, s 191(4).
3 Employment Rights Act 1996, ss 194 and 195; apart from the Employment Rights Act 1996, ss 101 and 102. For ss 101 and 102, see **15.76–15.78**.

Teachers in aided schools

15.04 There are special provisions relating to teachers in aided schools.[1] When such a teacher is dismissed by the governors or managers of the school in pursuance of a requirement of the local education authority under paragraph (a) of the proviso to s 134(3) of the Education Act 1996, the unfair provisions have effect as if the local education authority had at all material times been the teacher's employer, the local education authority had dismissed him and the reason, or principal reason, for which they did so had been the reason, or principal reason, for which they required the dismissal.[2]

1 Employment Rights Act 1996, s 134.
2 Employment Rights Act 1996, s 134(1). There are appropriate modifications so far as remedies are concerned: Employment Rights Act 1996, s 134(2).

Illegal contracts

15.05 As a rule of policy the courts and tribunals will not grant remedies the effect of which will be to enforce, or give effect to, illegal contracts. Thus, if the purpose of an employment contract is for illegal, or immoral, purposes, the employee will not be able to rely on it to make a claim for unfair dismissal.[1] Where the contract is known by the employer and the employee to be illegal, for instance wages are to be paid in cash and hidden from the Inland Revenue, the employee will not be able to claim unfair dismissal.[2] If the employee is not party to the illegality, he does not lose the statutory protection.[3] However, a pragmatic approach may be adopted so long as employees are not encouraged to act illegally in doing so.[4] A period of illegality breaks continuity of employment.[5]

1 Because of the rule as to illegal contracts he will not have the necessary continuity of service to qualify for the right in any event. If the intention of the applicant when entering into the contract was not illegal, he may be able to rely on it: *Coral Leisure Group Ltd v Barnett* [1981] IRLR 204, EAT. See **3.06**.
2 *Tomlinson v Dick Evans U Drive Ltd* [1978] IRLR 77, EAT.
3 *Newland v Simons & Willer (Hairdressers) Ltd* [1981] IRLR 359, EAT.
4 *Hewcastle Catering Ltd v Ahmed* [1991] IRLR 473, CA, where the Court of Appeal appears to be much influenced by the public interest in uncovering VAT fraud and the fact that the employees did not themselves benefit from the fraud.
5 *Hyland v JH Barker (North West) Ltd* [1985] ICR 861, EAT.

Claims made out of time

15.06 The complaint to an industrial tribunal must be made within the statutory time limit,[1] ie three months from the effective date of termination, or within such period as the tribunal considers reasonable in a case where it is satisfied that it was not reasonably practicable to present the complaint within that period. If it is not, the employee cannot proceed with his claim.

1 Employment Rights Act 1996, s 111(2). See **15.155–15.165**.

Retiring age

15.07 An employee will generally be excluded from unfair dismissal protection if, on or before the effective date of termination, he attained the age of 65 or the age which, in the undertaking in which he was employed, was the normal retiring age for an employee holding the position which he held (so long as that normal retiring age was the same for men and women).[1] However, even if the employee has attained the specified age, he is entitled to claim he has been unfairly dismissed if the following provisions apply:
(1)   as to employees dismissed at or after the end of maternity leave period or failure to permit return after childbirth;[2]
(2)   as to dismissal for pregnancy or childbirth;[3]
(3)   as to dismissals for health and safety reasons;[4]
(4)   as to shop workers and betting shop workers who refuse Sunday work;[5]
(5)   as to dismissals of trustees of occupational pension schemes;[6]
(6)   as to the dismissal of employee representatives for consultation as to redundancies and transfers of undertakings;[7]
(7)   as to dismissals for asserting a statutory right;[8]
(8)   as to redundancy dismissals which are automatically unfair;[9]

(9)   relating to trade union membership and activities, see **14.32**.
In these cases there is no age limit for complainants.[10]

1 Employment Rights Act 1996, s 109(1). The forerunner of this section referred to pensionable
ages for men and women, which should be borne in mind when considering earlier decided cases.
2 Employment Rights Act 1996, s 109(2)(a); s 84 or s 96(1). See Chapter 7.
3 Employment Rights Act 1996, s 109(2)(b); s 99(1) read with s 99(2) or (3). See Chapter 7.
4 Employment Rights Act 1996, s 109(2)(c); s 100 read with s 100(2) and (3). See **15.74–15.75**.
5 Employment Rights Act 1996, s 109(2)(d); s 101 read with s 101(2) and (3). See **15.76–15.77**.
6 Employment Rights Act 1996, s 109(2)(e); s 102. See **15.78**.
7 Employment Rights Act 1996, s 109(2)(f); s 103. See Chapter 16 and Chapter 12.
8 Employment Rights Act 1996, s 109(2)(g); s 104(1) read with s 104(2) and (3). See **15.80**.
9 Employment Rights Act 1996, s 109(2)(h); s 105. See **15.81–15.88**.
10 The burden of proof is on the employee to show that the exclusions do not apply, *Smith v
Hayle Town Council* [1978] ICR 996, CA (a majority decision of the Court of Appeal, Lord
Denning MR delivered a judgment in dissent); *Goodwin Ltd v Fitzmaurice* [1977] IRLR 393,
EAT.

15.08   At first the retiring age exclusion was interpreted as a double barrier,
so that an employee retained unfair dismissal protection rights only if he had
reached neither the normal retiring age in his undertaking, nor the statutorily
specified age. However, it is now established[1] that an employee is excluded
where there is a normal retiring age, if he has reached that age; and where
there is no normal retiring age, where he has reached the age of 65.

1 *Nothman v Barnet London Borough* [1979] IRLR 35, HL.

15.09   How is the 'normal retiring age' ascertained? Section 109(1) of the
Employment Rights Act 1996 refers to the normal retiring age of 'an
employee holding the position' which the complainant held. 'Position' is
defined in s 235(1) as 'the following matters taken as a whole ... (a) his status
as an employee, (b) the nature of his work, and (c) his terms and conditions
of employment'. The relevant conditions are those at the time of consideration; it is not further restricted by consideration of employment history.[1]
Where employees joining the company at different times are subject to
different contractual retirement ages, that difference is one of the 'terms and
conditions' to be taken into account when deciding whether they fall into the
same 'position' as the complainant employee.[2]

1 *Hughes v Department of Health and Social Security* [1985] IRLR 263; [1985] ICR 419, HL.
2 *Barber v Thames Television plc* [1992] IRLR 410; [1992] ICR 661, CA. *Bratko v Beloit
Walmsley Ltd* [1995] IRLR 629, EAT, appears to limit the wide managerial discretion apparently
recognised in *Barber*.

15.10   Having ascertained the group of employees in the same 'position',
the approach to be adopted in establishing their normal retirement age is
not merely statistical. Although there is a presumption that the contractual
retiring age is the normal one, the presumption can be displaced by evidence
that in practice there is some other age at which they regularly retire. The
reasonable expectation or understanding of the relevant employees must be
ascertained.[1] The evidence required to displace the presumption will need to
be quite significant but does not have to amount to a full-scale departure
from the contractual provision.[2] Once the presumption is displaced, the effect
may be either to establish an independent normal retiring age, or to reveal
that there is in fact no 'normal' practice,[3] in which case the age stipulated by
statute will apply.

1 *Waite v Government Communications Headquarters* [1983] IRLR 161; [1983] ICR 359, CA. In *Bratko v Beloit Walmsley Ltd* [1995] IRLR 629, EAT, it was said that the House of Lords in *Waite* had in mind the raising of the retiring age only.
2 *Secretary of State for Scotland v Meikle* [1986] IRLR 208. Conversely, where a normal retiring age is established by a new policy, the allowance of limited exceptions will not undermine it: *Barclays Bank plc v O'Brien* [1993] ICR 347, EAT.
3 *Swaine v Health & Safety Executive* [1986] IRLR 205; [1986] ICR 498, EAT, in which employees were retired at ages within a given band, so that it could not be said that any particular age was the 'normal retiring' one.

15.11   Where there are no other employees in the same position as the complainant, it cannot be argued that he constitutes a 'group' and so the contractual provision is the normal retiring age. The proper analysis is that there can be no comparisons and therefore no broad normality. Consequently the age specified by statute will apply.[1]

1 *Age Concern Scotland v Hines* [1983] IRLR 477, EAT.

Qualifying period of service

15.12   As a general rule an employee does not have the benefit of the unfair dismissal provisions, unless he has been continuously employed for a period of not less than two years, ending with the effective date of termination.[1] This requirement is subject to challenge as being unlawful discrimination against women which is presently being considered by the House of Lords.[2]

1 Employment Rights Act 1996, s 108(1). A power to vary or exclude s 108(1) is conferred on the Secretary of State by s 209(5). As to effective date of termination, see **15.59–15.69**.
2 In *R v Secretary of State for Employment, ex p Seymour-Smith and Perez* [1995] IRLR 464, CA; *Thomas v National Training Partnership* [1996] EAT 1126/95; *Arbuthnott v Mount Carmel School* [1996] EAT 1379/95 and *Street v Peacock* [1996] EAT 217/96.

Circumstances where there is a reduced, or no, qualifying period

15.13   In some circumstances the two-year qualification period does not apply.

15.14   The period of two years is reduced to one month if the employee is dismissed by a requirement as is referred to in the statutory provisions as to payment during suspension on medical grounds.[1]

1 Employment Rights Act 1996, s 108(2). See **4.24–4.28**.

15.15   There is no qualifying period at all if the following provisions apply:
(1)   as to employees dismissed at or after the end of maternity leave period or as to a failure to permit return after childbirth;[1]
(2)   as to dismissal for pregnancy or childbirth;[2]
(3)   as to dismissals for health and safety reasons;[3]
(4)   as to shop workers and betting shop workers who refuse Sunday work;[4]
(5)   as to dismissals of trustees of occupational pension schemes;[5]
(6)   as to the dismissal of employee representatives for consultation as to redundancies and transfers of undertakings;[6]
(7)   as to dismissals for asserting a statutory rights;[7]
(8)   as to redundancy dismissals which are automatically unfair;[8]
(9)   relating to trade union membership and activities, see **14.32**.

15.15   *Unfair dismissal*

In these cases there is no qualifying period of continuous service for complainants.

1 Employment Rights Act 1996, s 108(2)(a); s 84 or s 96(1). See Chapter 7.
2 Employment Rights Act 1996, s 108(2)(b); s 99(1) read with s 99(2) or (3). See Chapter 7.
3 Employment Rights Act 1996, s 108(2)(c); s 100 read with s 100(2) and (3). See **15.74–15.75**.
4 Employment Rights Act 1996, s 108(2)(d); s 101 read with s 101(2) and (3). See **15.76–15.77**.
5 Employment Rights Act 1996, s 108(2)(e); s 102. See **15.78**.
6 Employment Rights Act 1996, s 108(2)(f); s 103. See Chapter 16 and Chapter 12.
7 Employment Rights Act 1996, s 108(2)(g); s 104(1) read with s 104(2) and (3). See **15.80**.
8 Employment Rights Act 1996, s 108(2)(h); s 105. See **15.81–15.82**.

Calculating the qualifying period

15.16   When calculating the qualifying period account must be taken of the provisions of s 97(2) and (4) of the Employment Rights Act 1996 which provides that the effective date of termination is to be the date when a notice of the minimum period provided for in s 86 to be given by the employer would have expired, if given when notice of termination was given; or if there was no notice, when the contract was terminated, if later than the effective date of termination as otherwise defined.[1] Continuous employment is calculated in accordance with the provisions of the Act (see Chapter 11).[2]

1 Employment Rights Act 1996, s 97(2); see **15.67–15.69**. In these circumstances the period during the interval between the actual date of termination and the effective date of termination counts towards a period of continuous employment: Employment Rights Act 1996, s 213.
2 In the Employment Rights Act 1996, Ch I, Pt XIV.

Agreements to exclude the unfair dismissal provisions

15.17   The power to agree to exclude the unfair dismissal provisions is very limited. The intention is that employees cannot contract away their statutory rights. As a general principle, agreement by an employee to forego the right of protection against unfair dismissal is no effect. Thus any agreement to exclude or limit any of the provisions or to preclude a person from bringing any proceedings before an industrial tribunal in respect of them is void.[1] This rule does not apply in certain circumstances where there are agreements to exclude the operation of the unfair dismissal provisions affecting some fixed term contracts and in settlement and compromise agreements and dismissals procedures agreements.

1 Employment Rights Act 1996, s 203(1).

Fixed term contracts

15.18   The non-renewal of a fixed term contract constitutes a dismissal for the purposes of the unfair dismissal provisions (see **15.43–15.46**). However, the right to unfair dismissal protection does not extend to dismissal from employment under a contract for a fixed term of one year or more, where the dismissal consists only of the expiry of the term without its being renewed, if, before the term expires, the employee has agreed in writing to exclude any claim in respect of rights under Pt X of the Employment Rights Act 1996 in relation to that contract.[1] The written agreement can be made at any time before the expiry of the contractual term, and may be contained either in the contract itself or in a separate document. If the agreement is made when the period of employment has already started, there must be some fresh consideration from the employer.[2] The exclusion does not apply to dismissals taking effect during the currency of the contract.

1 Employment Rights Act 1996, s 197(1). For an interesting case where there was a short extension to the contract, see *Mulrine v University of Ulster* [1993] IRLR 545, NICA.
2 Dismissal at the end of a fixed term contract when there is no agreement in writing to exclude the unfair dismissal provisions will not automatically be unfair. The fairness or otherwise will depend on the usual tests. Where the fixed term is for a genuine purpose, and the temporary nature of the employment was made clear to the employee from the outset, the non-renewal of the contract may be a fair dismissal 'for some other substantial reason': *Terry v East Sussex County Council* [1976] ICR 536.

Conciliated settlements and compromise agreements

15.19   There are limited exceptions to the rule in s 203(1) in order to facilitate settlements where the employee has had access to advice, and in very limited circumstances, where a collective agreement has the effect of excluding the provisions.

Thus agreements made after a conciliation officer has taken action,[1] and where the employee enters a compromise agreement[2] can exclude the operation of the section.

1 Employment Rights Act 1996, s 203(2)(e). See **18.18**.
2 Employment Rights Act 1996, s 203(2)(f). See **18.19**.

Dismissal procedures agreements

15.20   The other method of avoiding the operation of section 203(1) by agreement is by way of a dismissal procedures agreement. This is provided for in s 110 of the Employment Rights Act 1996. The requirements of the section should be studied in detail. The order is made following an application made jointly to the Secretary of State by all the parties to the dismissal procedures agreement. The effect of such an agreement is to substitute for the statutory provisions those laid out in the agreement,[1] except in relation to the right not to be unfairly dismissed for certain inadmissible reasons.[2] At present there is one order in force, relating to some employees in the electrical contracting industry.

1 Employment Rights Act 1996, s 110(1).
2 Employment Rights Act 1996, s 110(2). This should referred to for the detail, but in general the provisions not affected by the order are those:
 (a) as to employees dismissed at or after the end of maternity leave period or failure to permit return after childbirth,
 (b) as to dismissal for pregnancy or childbirth,
 (c) as to shop workers and betting shop workers who refuse Sunday work,
 (d) as to dismissals for asserting a statutory rights, and
 (e) as to redundancy dismissals of shop and betting shop workers which are automatically unfair.

15.21   The Secretary of State may make an order designating a dismissals procedure agreement if he is satisfied that:
(1)   every trade union which is a party to the dismissal procedures agreement is an independent trade union;
(2)   the agreement provides for procedures to be followed in cases where an employee claims he has been, or is in the course of being, unfairly dismissed;

(3) those procedures are available without discrimination to all employees falling within any description to which the agreement applies;

(4) the remedies provided by the agreement in respect of unfair dismissal are, on the whole, as beneficial as (but not necessarily identical with) those provided in respect of unfair dismissal by the statutory unfair dismissal provisions;

(5) the procedures provided by the agreement include a right to arbitration or adjudication by an independent referee, or by a tribunal or other independent body, in cases where (by reason of an equality of votes or for any other reason) a decision cannot otherwise be reached; and

(6) the provisions of the agreement are such that it can be determined with reasonable certainty whether a particular employee is one to whom the agreement applies.[1]

1 Employment Rights Act 1996, s 110(3).

Members of the armed services

15.22 Notwithstanding the general application of the unfair dismissal provisions to the Crown, members of the Naval, Military or Air Forces of the Crown are excluded at present.[1]

1 The provisions can be applied to those persons by order; Employment Rights Act 1996, s 192(1). Refer to s 192 for full details.

National security

15.23 Wherever there is in force a certificate signed by or on behalf of a minister of the Crown certifying that the employment described, or of a particular person, is required to be excepted from the unfair dismissal provisions for the purpose of safeguarding national security, the provisions do not apply.[1] If on a complaint before an industrial tribunal under the unfair dismissal provisions it is shown that the action to which the complaint relates was taken for the purpose of safeguarding national security, the industrial tribunal should dismiss the complaint.[2] A certificate purporting to be signed by or on behalf of a minister of the Crown certifying that the action specified in the certificate was taken for the purpose of safeguarding national security is conclusive evidence of that fact.[3]

1 Employment Rights Act 1996, s 193.
2 Industrial Tribunals Act 1996, s 10(4).
3 Industrial Tribunals Act 1996, s 10(5). Except where the dismissal is unfair by virtue of the Employment Rights Act 1996, ss 99(1)–(3), 100, 103 or 105(1) as applied by s 105(2), (3) or (6). See Chapter 7, **15.74–15.75**, Chapter 16, Chapter 12 and **15.81–15.82**.

Police

15.24 Employment as a member of the constabulary is expressly excluded from the unfair dismissal provisions.[1] This exclusion no longer applies to prison officers (who are in law constables) who are now protected by the unfair dismissal provisions.[2] A police cadet is not an employee or an apprentice. Accordingly the termination of his cadetship does not fall within the unfair dismissal provisions.[3]

1 Employment Rights Act 1996, s 200, which should be referred to in detail.

2 Employment Rights Act 1996, s 200(2)(b) effectively reversing *Home Office v Robinson* [1981] IRLR 524; [1982] ICR 31.
3 *Wiltshire Police Authority v Wynn* [1980] ICR 649, CA.

Share fishermen

15.25   Employment as a master, or as a member of the crew of a fishing vessel, where the employee is remunerated only by a share in the profits, or gross earnings, of the vessel (a 'share fisherman') is excluded[1].

1 Employment Rights Act 1996, s 199(2). This exclusion may be varied or excluded by order of the Secretary of State: Employment Rights Act 1996, s 209.

Those who ordinarily work outside Great Britain

15.26   The unfair dismissal provisions do not apply to any employment where under his contract of employment, the employee ordinarily works outside Great Britain.[1] Persons employed to work on board a ship registered in the United Kingdom are regarded as persons who under their contracts ordinarily work in Great Britain, unless the ship is registered at a port outside Great Britain, the employment is wholly outside Great Britain, or the employee is not ordinarily resident in Great Britain.[2]

1 Employment Protection (Consolidation) Act 1978, s 196(2). Whether or not the employee ordinarily works outside Great Britain depends on the terms of his contract of employment. The forerunner of this provision has been construed by the Court of Appeal in *Wilson v Maynard Shipbuilding Consultants AB* [1978] 2 All ER 78, CA, cf Megaw LJ at p 83. See also *Todd v British Midland Airways Ltd* [1978] ICR 959, CA. Earlier cases should be approached with considerable caution in the light of these decisions of the Court of Appeal. For maternity and return to work dismissals, see Chapter 7.
2 Employment Rights Act 1996, s 196(5).

State immunity

15.27   Until the State Immunity Act 1978 an employer entitled to diplomatic privilege was not bound by the unfair dismissal provisions unless he waived his privilege. In *Omerri v Uganda High Commission*,[1] Sir John Donaldson said:

'The basis of diplomatic immunity is that of international law, international comity and respect of one sovereign state for another. It is mutual. In foreign countries, British missions enjoy the same immunity as this country and its courts extend to foreign and Commonwealth missions in London. It has always been a matter of general law. It is not to be thought from the fact that Parliament did not mention diplomatic missions, that Parliament intended, in breach of international law and the accepted standards of international behaviour, to make foreign and Commonwealth missions subject to the Act.'[1]

1 (1973) 8 ITR 14 at p 15, NIRC. See also International Organisations Act 1968.

15.28   Section 4 of the State Immunity Act 1978[1] provides that a state is not immune with respect to proceedings relating to a contract of employment between the state and an individual where the contract was made in the United Kingdom, or the work is to be wholly or partly performed there.[2] This provision does not apply if, at the time when the proceedings are brought, the individual is a national of the state concerned, or at the time when the contract was made the individual was neither a national of the United Kingdom nor habitually resident there, nor where the parties to the contract have agreed otherwise in writing.[3] However where the work is for an office, agency or establishment maintained by the state in the United Kingdom for commercial purposes, the employer is not immune on the grounds that at the time when the proceedings are brought the individual is a national of the state concerned, or at the time when the contract was made the individual was neither a national of the United Kingdom nor habitually resident there, unless at the time when the contract was made the individual was habitually resident in the state.[4]

1 State Immunity Act 1978, s 3, lifts the immunity of states from proceedings in respect of many commercial transactions, subject to some limitations. Proceedings in respect of statutory rights and duties are included: State Immunity Act 1978, s 4(6).
2 State Immunity Act 1978, s 4(1).
3 State Immunity Act 1978, s 4(2). For definition of 'national of the United Kingdom' see State Immunity Act 1978, s 4(5). State Immunity Act 1978, s 4(2)(c) does not exclude the application of where the law of the United Kingdom requires the proceedings to be brought before a court of the United Kingdom: State Immunity Act 1978, s 4(4).
4 State Immunity Act 1978, s 4(3).

Dismissal

15.29 The first essential requirement for a successful claim for unfair dismissal made by a qualified claimant is for the ex-employee to have been dismissed. Dismissal is defined in s 95 of the Employment Rights Act 1996 which provides as follows:

'95.–(1) For the purposes of [the unfair dismissal provisions] an employee is dismissed by his employer if (and, subject to subsection (2) and section 96[1], only if)—
  (a) the contract under which he is employed is terminated by the employer (whether with or without notice),
  (b) he is employed under a contract for a fixed term and that term expires without being renewed under the same contract, or
  (c) the employee terminates the contract under which he is employed (with or without notice) in circumstances in which he is entitled to terminate it without notice by reason of the employer's conduct.
  (2) An employee shall be taken to be dismissed by his employer for the purposes of [the unfair dismissal provisions] if—
  (a) the employer gives notice to the employee to terminate his contract of employment, and
  (b) at a time within the period of that notice the employee gives notice to the employer to terminate the contract of employment on a date earlier than the date on which the employer's notice is due to expire;
  and the reason for the dismissal is to be taken to be the reason for which the employer's notice is given.'

1 Relating to failure to permit to return after childbirth, see Chapter 7.

15.30 An employee who is entitled to return to work after childbirth and is not permitted to do so by her employer is taken to be dismissed.[1]

1 Employment Rights Act 1996, s 96. See Chapter 7.

15.31 The burden of proof to show that there has been a dismissal is on the applicant.[1]

1 *GEC Telecommunications Ltd v McAllister* [1975] IRLR 346.

15.32 Not every termination of employment is a dismissal. Termination by agreement, performance and frustration do not fall within the definition (see **13.01–13.04** and **13.09–13.27**).[1] Other circumstances of termination by operation of law, unless they fall within s 95, do not amount to dismissal. An agreement that there will be automatic termination of employment in certain circumstances will almost certainly be caught by s 203 of the Employment Rights Act 1996 and so will be void.[2] Thus the employee will be protected by the provisions. The definition of dismissal contained in s 95(1) is similar to that in section 136 of the Act relating to redundancy payments and assistance can be obtained from decisions under that section and previous provisions relating to redundancy payments.

1 Early retirement if by agreement is not dismissal: *Birch v Liverpool University* [1985] ICR 470, CA. There can even be termination by agreement after notice of redundancy has been given: *Scott v Coalite Fuels and Chemicals Ltd* [1988] ICR 355, EAT, although the tribunals and courts will subject such cases to considerable scrutiny.
2 *Igbo v Johnson Matthey Chemicals Ltd* [1986] ICR 505, CA, compare *Salton v Durham County Council* [1989] IRLR 99, EAT. See **13.28**.

Termination of employment by the employer

15.33 In the majority of cases the fact of dismissal is clear. The employment has come to an end and it is not in dispute who terminated it. However there are circumstances where the language which was used or facts surrounding the termination render the matter less certain. Unfortunately, the authorities are not totally consistent as to the principles to adopt in resolving any ambiguity.

15.34 The intention of the speaker is not the relevant test, as was made clear in *Tanner v DT Kean Ltd*.[1] It is suggested that this is correct, since an employer should not be able to rely on undisclosed intentions when they are at apparent variance with his actions.

1 [1978] IRLR 110. See *BG Gale Ltd v Gilbert* [1978] IRLR 453 and *Sothern v Franks Charlesly & Co* [1981] IRLR 278 for judicial comment on this point.

15.35 The weight of decisions supports an objective test. Considered in the light of all the surrounding circumstances: how would the words or events have been understood by a reasonable listener? If the listener honestly and reasonably understood the words to constitute a dismissal, he is entitled to rely on that understanding, irrespective of the speaker's intention.[1] On the other hand, what if the listener genuinely understands words to constitute a dismissal in circumstances where a reasonable listener considering the statement in all the circumstances would not? The objective test still applies, albeit with the caveat that courts and tribunals will be careful not to find that unambiguous words do not mean what they say, particularly where the listener so understood them.[2]

15.35 *Unfair dismissal*

1 *BG Gale Ltd v Gilbert* [1978] IRLR 453; *Martin v Yeoman Aggregates Ltd* [1983] IRLR 49; *J & J Stern v Simpson* [1983] IRLR 52.
2 *Sothern v Franks Charlesly & Co* [1981] IRLR 278; *Sovereign House Security Services Ltd v Savage* [1989] IRLR 115, per May LJ; *Barclay v City of Glasgow District Council* [1983] IRLR 313.

15.36 What if the words are unambiguous and the speaker says that they were intended to have a meaning different from that which was apparent? Whilst there is no general duty to ensure that apparently unambiguous words are actually so intended, there may be special circumstances in which it would be unreasonable for words to be construed at face value.[1] Such circumstances, though rare, can exist where words are given in the heat of the moment, or in temper, or when under extreme pressure.

1 *Kwik-Fit (GB) Ltd v Lineham* [1992] ICR 183; [1992] IRLR 156.

Questions of law

15.37 Even if the factual question is clear, there may be an issue of law as to whether there was a dismissal as defined in s 95. There may be a dismissal for the purposes of the unfair dismissal provisions even where the employee remains in the employment of his employer, if the employer terminates the contract of employment and the employee works for the employer pursuant to a new contract. In such circumstances a claim for unfair dismissal remains a possibility.[1] There can be no dismissal if a contract of employment is brought to an end by an agreement[2] even after notice has been given to bring the contract of employment to an end. However, the courts and tribunals are very slow to find that the employment has been terminated by agreement prior to the expiry of notice[3] (such situations may arise, for example, where the employee wishes to leave earlier than the stipulated date in order to take up his new employment). In such circumstances s 95(2) should be considered (see **15.29**). In some cases it may be possible to sever some duties from a contract without amounting to a termination.[4]

1 *Hogg v Dover College* [1990] ICR 39, EAT. This decision rests on the finding that the former contract was terminated by the employer and the employee accepted the new contract by way of mitigation of his loss. See also *Alcan Extrusions Ltd v Yates* [1996] IRLR 327, EAT
2 *British Leyland (UK) Ltd v Ashraf* [1978] ICR 979; *Harvey v Yankee Travellers Restaurant* [1976] IRLR 35; *Sheffield v Oxford Controls Co Ltd* [1979] ICR 396.
3 *McAlwane v Boughton Estates Ltd* [1973] 2 All ER 299; *Lees v Arthur Greaves (Lees) Ltd* [1974] 2 All ER 393; [1974] ICR 501; *CPS Recruitment Ltd v Bowen & Secretary of State for Employment* [1982] IRLR 54.
4 *Land v West Yorkshire Metropolitan County Council* [1981] ICR 334, CA.

Resign or be dismissed

15.38 If an employee is given the alternative of resigning or being dismissed, and resigns, this constitutes dismissal since the contract was terminated by the employer.[1] If an employee is told to follow a course of action and that in the event of his failure to do so his employment will be deemed to be terminated, then again the contract of employment has been terminated by the employer if the employee does not do as told.[2] The employee has been dismissed within the statutory definition.

1 *Robertson v Securicor Transport Ltd* [1972] IRLR 70. Contrast *Sheffield v Oxford Controls Co Ltd* [1979] IRLR 133.

2 *Jones v Liverpool Corpn and Liverpool Polytechnic* [1974] IRLR 55. A dismissal has been held to take place when the employee requested the employer to dismiss him: *Thomas v General Industrial Cleaners Ltd* (1972) (COIT No 3964/72); *Fisher v York Trailer Co Ltd* [1979] ICR 834; [1979] IRLR 385.

15.39 Dismissal under s 95(1)(a) is termination by the employer. An employee cannot claim to be dismissed if he resigns when the employer has not repudiated the contract of employment.[1] There is a requirement for certainty for both notice of dismissal and of resignation; to be effective each must specify the date when it is to take effect or, if it does not specify that date, at least make it possible for the other party to ascertain that date with certainty.[2] Intimation, or advance warning, of future termination does not amount to notice of dismissal or repudiatory breaches of contract,[3] unless the employer indicates that the future action will be in breach of contract so as to amount to an anticipatory breach of contract in circumstances which, if accepted, amount to constructive dismissal.[4]

1 For example, *Elliott v Waldair (Construction) Ltd* [1975] IRLR 104.
2 *Haseltine Lake & Co v Dowler* [1981] ICR 222.
3 *Burton Group Ltd v Smith* [1977] IRLR 351; *Haseltine Lake & Co v Dowler* [1981] IRLR 25.
4 *Maher v Fram Gerrard Ltd* [1974] 1 All ER 449; see **15.47–15.58**.

15.40 Once notice has been given to terminate (whether by the employer or the employee) it cannot be unilaterally withdrawn,[1] save that withdrawal of a dismissal or resignation has been allowed in special circumstances where it was given in the heat of the moment and the withdrawal followed immediately upon the cooling of tempers.[2]

1 *Chesham Shipping Ltd v Rowe* [1977] IRLR 391.
2 *Martin v Yeoman Aggregates Ltd* [1983] IRLR 49.

15.41 As has been seen at **13.09–13.27** the doctrine of frustration applies to contracts of employment. In such cases the employment is terminated by operation of law and not by the parties. As a consequence the employee whose employment is ended is not dismissed and is unable to make a claim for unfair dismissal. The doctrine of frustration depends upon some unforeseen extraneous event making it impossible for the contract to be performed at all, and operates independently of fault on either side. However, an event may arise due to the fault of one party (eg a sentence of imprisonment for an employee) and still constitute frustration, albeit that the party at fault cannot make the allegation.[1]

1 *FC Shephard & Co Ltd v Jerrom* [1986] IRLR 358, CA.

15.42 Very exceptionally there may be an issue whether the act allegedly constituting the dismissal can be attributed to the employer at all. The situation may arise when there is question as to the actual and ostensible authority of officers of the employer.[1]

1 An employer may not rely on lack of power under its constitution or lack of actual or ostensible authority unless both sides appreciated that what was done was of no practical effect. For a recent example, see *Warnes v Trustees of Cheriton Oddfellows Social Club* [1993] IRLR 58.

Expiry of a fixed term contract

15.43   At the end of the specified period a fixed term contract expires by effluxion of time rather than by an act of either party. This does not amount to termination by the employer at common law or in the vernacular, and so without statutory provision, failure to renew the contract would not amount to a dismissal. Thus the creation of a series of fixed term contracts may have provided a device to avoid the protective provisions relating to unfair dismissal. Consequently, the situation is specifically provided for in s 95(1)(b). Notwithstanding this, an employee can agree to forego his right to claim for unfair dismissal by virtue of the expiry of the contract without its being renewed, if the fixed term contract is for one year or more.[1]

1 Employment Rights Act 1996, s 197(1). See **15.18**.

What is a contract for a fixed term?

15.44   A contract for a fixed term is one which comes to an end on a fixed date. A contract may be for a fixed term notwithstanding that it may be terminable by notice within the term.[1] A contract is not for a fixed term where it is to run for a specified time and thereafter until terminated by notice.[2] Where a contract is specified to run for a particular period of indefinite duration it is not for a fixed term.[3] Unfortunately, there may be circumstances where it is not easy to determine whether a contract is for a particular purpose or one of fixed duration, as the *Wiltshire* case, where there was doubt whether the employee was employed for an academic year or to teach a course while it ran, demonstrates.

1 *BBC v Ioannou* [1975] ICR 267, CA.
2 *Weston v University College Swansea* [1975] IRLR 102.
3 *Wiltshire County Council v National Association of Teachers in Further and Higher Education* [1980] IRLR 198, CA.

15.45   Difficulties may arise where an employee accepts a continuation of the employment relationship, but under a different contract. In such a situation there is still a dismissal. It should be noted that, in order to avoid a dismissal, the provision does not require the renewal to be on the same terms and conditions, merely to be under the same contract. What alterations of terms and conditions are permissible before it must be said that the contract is a new one? In general, it seems that changes are permissible unless they go to the root of the contract.

15.46   Acceptance by the employee that the contract expires at the end of a fixed term, even where the employee agrees to take an ex gratia payment, does not automatically mean there was no dismissal.[1]

1 *Thames Television Ltd v Wallis* [1979] IRLR 136.

Termination of the contract by the employee

15.47   As has been seen, termination of his employment by an employee may amount to dismissal under the terms of the Employment Rights Act 1996. This situation is often referred to as 'constructive dismissal'. Whether or not what takes place amounts to dismissal depends upon common law contractual concepts. At one time there were two competing tests suggested for assessing whether the employer's conduct was such that the employee was entitled to terminate the contract of employment without notice by reason of it. One of these involved deciding whether or not the employee was entitled, according to the law of contract, to bring the employment to an end ('the contract test'); the other stated that dismissal occurred if the employee terminated the contract in circumstances where the employer had conducted himself or his affairs so unreasonably that the employee could not be fairly expected to put up with it any longer ('the reasonableness test').

15.48 The uncertainty was resolved by the Court of Appeal in the case of *Western Excavating (ECC) Ltd v Sharp*[1] where it was clearly laid down that the contract test determines whether or not there has been a dismissal pursuant to what is now s 97(1)(c). The industrial tribunal will decide whether or not the employer has conducted himself in such a way that under the law of contract the employee was entitled to terminate the relationship without notice. If the employer commits 'a significant breach going to the root of the contract of employment, or which shows that the employer no longer intends to be bound by one or more of the essential terms of the contract, the employee is entitled to treat himself as discharged from any further performance' of the contract. If he does so, then he terminates the contract by reason of the employer's conduct and can claim to be dismissed pursuant to s 95(1)(c). It is likely that in such circumstances the dismissal will be found to be unfair, but this should not be assumed. The usual tests of fairness apply.[2]

1 [1978] IRLR 27, [1978] ICR 221 at p 226. Confirmed in *Spafax Ltd v Harrison* [1980] IRLR 442. See also *Wadham Stringer Commercials (London) Ltd & Wadham Stringer Vehicles Ltd v Brown* [1983] IRLR 46.
2 *Gaelic Oil Co Ltd v Hamilton* [1977] IRLR 27, but see *Industrial Rubber Products v Gillon* [1977] IRLR 389; *Stephenson & Co (Oxford) Ltd v Austin* [1990] ICR 609, CA.

15.49 Whether or not there has been a constructive dismissal can be approached in seven stages:
(1)   Was there a contractual term?
(2)   If so, what were its provisions?
(3)   Was the term broken?
(4)   If so, was the breach repudiatory?
(5)   Was the employment terminated by the employee?
(6)   Was the termination of the employment contract by the employee an 'acceptance' of the employer's breach by the employee?
(7)   Was the 'acceptance' before the employee had affirmed the contract?
In answering these questions the usual common law rules apply (see **13.44–13.52**).

Contractual term

15.50 Contractual terms are ascertained in the usual way. First, it has to be ascertained if there is a relevant express term of the contract. There can be no constructive dismissal if the employers had contractual authority to carry out the conduct which is complained of.[1] The employer is entitled to make rules for the conduct of employees in their place of work, and he is entitled to give lawful orders.[2] Exceptionally, the courts and tribunals may imply a very limited power to vary specific terms.[3]

15.50 *Unfair dismissal*

1 See for example *Atherton v John Crankshaw Co Ltd* (1970) 5 ITR 201; *Simms Motor Units Ltd v Hinds* (1971) 6 ITR 113; *Dal v Orr* [1980] IRLR 413; *Spafax v Harrison* [1980] IRLR 442, CA.
2 See for example *Dryden v Greater Glasgow Health Board* [1992] IRLR 469, where it was held not to be a repudiatory breach of contract when the employer banned smoking.
3 *Millbrook Furnishings Industries Ltd v McIntosh* [1981] IRLR 309. See also *Tocher v General Motors Scotland Ltd* [1981] IRLR 55.

15.51 Often employees claim that the employer has broken an implied term of the contract. Whether or not a term can be implied and the content of the implied term is determined in accordance with the common law rules (see **3.07–3.11**). The distinction between the contractual and reasonableness test can become blurred. Implied contractual duties of the employer can come close to accepting that the employer is under a duty to behave reasonably towards his employees. Brown-Wilkinson J has said that:

'In our view it is clearly established that there is implied in a contract of employment a term that the employers will not, without reasonable and proper cause, conduct themselves in a manner calculated or likely to destroy the relationship of trust and confidence between employer and employee.'[1]

The implied obligation of an employer most frequently relied on in practice is that the employer must not behave in such a way as to undermine trust and confidence in the employment relationship. This is an essential requirement of all employment contracts and is specifically recognised.[2]

1 *Woods v WM Car Services (Peterborough) Ltd* [1981] IRLR 347, EAT at p 350. See also *British Aircraft Corpn Ltd v Austin* [1978] IRLR 332. See also the comments of Slynn J in *Palmanor Ltd v Cedron* [1978] IRLR 303.
2 *Courtaulds Northern Textiles Ltd v Andrew* [1979] IRLR 84;. *Bliss v South East Thames Regional Health Authority* [1985] IRLR 308; [1987] ICR 700; *Lewis v Motorworld Garages Ltd* [1985] IRLR 465; [1986] ICR 157, CA.

Breach of contract

15.52 In deciding whether the breach is a repudiatory breach, the contractual term and the employer's conduct are considered by the tribunal. The breach of the contractual term may occur as a result of one act of the employer. It can also consist of a series of actions, perhaps leading to the final 'last straw'.[1] In such cases a series of actions can constitute the breach, each of which may be individually justified as falling within the contract, but taken as a whole may not be.[2]

1 *Lewis v Motorworld Garages Ltd* [1985] IRLR 465, CA.
2 *United Bank Ltd v Akhtar* [1989] IRLR 507, which relied on dicta of Browne-Wilkinson J in *Woods v WM Car Services (Peterborough) Ltd* [1981] IRLR 347.

15.53 Once the employee can establish that there was a breach of contract (either actual or anticipatory) by the employer, he should also show that the breach was sufficiently important (either in itself or as the last of a series of incidents) to justify resignation. To do this the employee should satisfy the tribunal that the breach was a repudiatory breach of the employment contract. This is a breach which goes to the heart of the employment contract.[1]

1 A belief by the employer that the breach was not repudiatory is irrelevant: *Milbrook Furnishing Industries Ltd v McIntosh* [1981] IRLR 309, EAT.

'Acceptance' of the employer's conduct

15.54   An essential ingredient of constructive dismissal is that the employee terminates the employment. There must be a causal connection between the employee's leaving and the employer's breach of contract. The employee must show not only that he left the employment, but also that he did so as a response to the breach and not for some other reason.[1]

1 *Logabax Ltd v Titherley* [1977] IRLR 97; [1977] ICR 369; *Walker v Josiah Wedgwood & Sons Ltd* [1978] IRLR 105; [1978] ICR 744.

Non-affirmation of contract

15.55   The employee cannot claim to be constructively dismissed if he has affirmed the contract after he is aware of the repudiatory breach. Delay between the breach and the departure may be taken to be waiver of the breach and/or agreement to vary the contract. If he cannot satisfy all these conditions, his departure will be a resignation, not a dismissal (see **13.44–13.46**). Conduct by the employee which is unequivocal and is consistent with the contract being kept alive results in the employee losing the right to leave and claim he was dismissed.[1] An employee may continue to work under protest and preserve his right to terminate the contract.[2] Mere delay does not amount to affirmation of the contract, but after a time is likely to be good evidence that the employee has affirmed the contract.[3]

1 *Spencer v Marchington* [1988] IRLR 392.
2 Even if the employee did not expressly do so: *Bliss v South East Thames Regional Health Authority* [1987] ICR 700, CA.
3 *WE Cox Toner (International) Ltd v Crook* [1981] IRLR 443, EAT. Contrast *Post Office v Roberts* [1980] IRLR 347, EAT, where the position was being ascertained by the applicant's trade union.

15.56   What conduct of the employer will justify an employee leaving and claiming dismissal? Resort may be had to a survey of the authorities. The following random examples are illustrative:
(1)   unilateral reduction of pay;[1]
(2)   unilateral change of duties;[2]
(3)   demanding work during hours not provided for in the contract;[3]
(4)   unilateral alteration from nights only to days;[4]
(5)   transfer of employee beyond reasonable travelling distance of his house in the absence of a mobility clause;[5]
(6)   failure to deal with complaint about protective eye wear.[6]

1 *Industrial Rubber Products v Gillon* [1977] IRLR 389.
2 *Pederson v Camden London Borough Council* [1981] IRLR 173, CA.
3 *Derby City Council v Marshall* [1979] IRLR 261.
4 *Simmonds v Dowty Seals Ltd* [1978] IRLR 211.
5 *Courtaulds Northern Spinning Ltd v Sibson and Transport & General Workers' Union* [1988] IRLR 305; [1988] ICR 451; but see also *Little v Charterhouse Magna Assurance Co Ltd* [1980] IRLR 19.
6 *British Aircraft Corpn Ltd v Austin* [1978] IRLR 332.

15.57   A claim for constructive dismissal may be founded on an anticipatory breach of contract by the employer,[1] but caution must be exercised in considering whether the proposed action constitutes a breach of contract. The mere fact that an employer misunderstands his powers under the contract will not of itself constitute an anticipatory breach; only when entrenched positions have been taken up and the time for performance of the contractual term in dispute has arisen will the action amount to anticipatory breach.[2] If an employer withdraws a threat of a breach, then an employee who resigns after the withdrawal is not dismissed.[3]

1 *Norwest Holst Group Administration Ltd v Harrison* [1985] IRLR 240; [1985] IRLR 668 CA.
2 *Financial Techniques (Planning Services) Ltd v Hughes* [1981] IRLR 32, CA; *Blyth v Scottish Liberal Club* [1983] IRLR 245.
3 *Northwest Holst Group Administration Ltd v Harrison* [1985] ICR 668, CA.

15.58 Particular problems may arise in deciding whether a contract has been terminated or consensually varied by the parties. This arose in a case considered by the Court of Appeal before there was a statutory right for employees who terminated the employment contract to claim to be dismissed. In *Marriott v Oxford and District Co-operative Society Ltd (No 2)*[1] the employers wrote to Mr Marriott stating that as a result of re-organisation they did not require him as an electrical foreman. They wished to retain his services and were prepared to do so reducing his wages by £3 a week. Mr Marriott objected and after discussions another letter was written by the employers stating that the arrangements to reduce his wages by £3 had been rescinded, but they would be reduced by £1 a week subject to a review after three months. Mr Marriott left after three or four weeks, having been paid less the £1 reduction for two or three weeks. The Court of Appeal held that the second letter was a dismissal within the meaning of a provision similar to s 95(1)(a) of the Employment Rights Act 1996 in that the employer clearly stated that it would not fulfil its contract with Mr Marriott. He had not been party to a consensual variation by receiving reduced wages for two or three weeks since he had never accepted the position. Although the statutory position has now changed, it may still be that in some circumstances what at first sight may appear to be a constructive dismissal is in reality termination by the employer.

1 [1969] 3 All ER 1126; see also *Alcan Extrusions v Yates* [1996] IRLR 327, EAT.

Effective date of termination

15.59 The concept of 'effective date of termination' is an important one. Only by establishing this date can it be decided whether the employee has been employed by the employer for a sufficient period of continuous employment to qualify for protection, whether he has reached a relevant age and whether his claim has been presented to the tribunal in time. In addition the effective date of termination is a key factor in establishing the amount of the basic award if his claim is successful. The effective date of termination is the date from which the period for presenting a claim relating to a request for written reasons for his dismissal runs. Very occasionally it may even be necessary to identify the precise moment of dismissal, to determine the fairness of the dismissal.[1]

1 *Octavius Atkinson & Sons Ltd v Morris* [1989] IRLR 158; [1989] ICR 431.

15.60 'Effective date of termination' is defined in s 97 of the Employment Rights Act 1996. Section 97(1) is as follows:
  '(1) Subject to the following provisions of this section '... the effective date of termination'—

(a) in relation to an employee whose contract of employment is terminated by notice, whether given by his employer or by the employee, means the date on which that notice expires,

(b) in relation to an employee whose contract of employment is terminated without notice, means the date on which the termination takes effect, and

(c) in relation to an employee who is employed under a contract for a fixed term which expires without being renewed under the same contract, means the date on which that term expires.'

15.61 The Employment Appeal Tribunal has held, somewhat surprisingly, that parties can agree a date which will be treated as the effective date of termination.[1] The parties can also agree to extend or shorten a notice period so as to postpone or advance the effective date of termination.[2]

1 *Crank v Her Majesty's Stationery Office* [1985] ICR 1.
2 *Mowlem Northern Ltd v Watson* [1990] IRLR 500. However when the alteration is made at the request of the employer, it may be construed simply as an agreement to waive the employee's duty to work: *Lees v Arthur Greaves (Lees) Ltd* [1974] 2 All ER 393; [1974] IRLR 93, CA.

15.62 Once notice has been given by the employer the effective date of termination is the date when it expires, even if the employee is allowed, or ordered, to attend work no longer.[1] Where the employer, after giving notice, seeks to terminate the contract on a date earlier than that originally specified, the tribunals are reluctant to treat this as affecting the effective date of termination, at least where to do so would be disadvantageous to the employee, unless the employer's intention to do this is absolutely unambiguous.[2] However, if the employer terminates the employment with immediate effect then – subject to s 97(2) (see **15.67**) the effective date of termination is when the termination takes place.[3] This is of particular importance when considering the time limit in which an application has to be made to an industrial tribunal since the 'extension' provided by the subsection does not apply in such circumstances.

1 This is often referred to as 'garden leave'. See also **10.25**. *Brindle v HW Smith (Cabinets) Ltd* [1973] 1 All ER 230, [1972] IRLR 125; *IPC Business Press Ltd v Gray* [1977] ICR 858.
2 For an example where the effective date of termination was foreshortened, see *Stapp v Shaftesbury Society* [1982] IRLR 326, CA.
3 *Dedman v British Building and Engineering Appliances Ltd* [1974] 1 All ER 520; [1974] 1 WLR 171; *Robert Cort & Son Ltd v Charman* [1981] IRLR 437; [1981] ICR 816.

15.63 It may not be easy to tell whether an employee has been dismissed with notice or not. For example, where the employer terminates the contract, pays a sum of money to the employee and dispenses with his services, it may be that the employee is dismissed with notice but given a payment instead of working out that notice, or he may be dismissed immediately with the payment made in lieu of notice. The effective date of termination will clearly be different – when the notice terminates in the former case, and when the employment terminates in the latter case. It is a matter of construction which category the situation falls into.[1]

1 See *Adams v GKN Sankey Ltd* [1980] IRLR 416; *Chapman v Letheby and Christopher Ltd* [1981] IRLR 440 and *Leech v Preston Borough Council* [1985] IRLR 337.

15.64 When an employer has given notice to terminate the employment contract, the employee may at any time during the notice period give a counter-notice to terminate the employment at an earlier date.[1] The dismissal is still deemed to have been by the employer, but the effective date of termination is the date when the counter-notice expires rather than when the employer's notice expires.[2]

1 Employment Rights Act 1996, s 95(2).
2 *Thompson v GEC Avionics Ltd* [1991] IRLR 488.

15.65 After a dismissal there may be a conciliation process or appeal procedure. If the conciliation breaks down or the appeal fails, the determination of the effective date of termination depends upon the interpretation to be given to the particular disciplinary procedure. The effective date of termination is determined in accordance with s 97. The effective date of termination is not 'extended' by the appeal process if the employment has been terminated at the outset. However, if the employment continues during the conciliation and appeal process, the position is different. The provision under which the conciliation and appeal took place and the terminating event and their effect has to be construed. In *J Sainsbury Ltd v Savage*[1] the Court of Appeal upheld a finding of the Employment Appeal Tribunal which decided that a suspension during the appeal process did not necessarily involve the continuation of the relationship of employer and employee until the period of suspension ended. A distinction was drawn between a suspension pending a decision whether to dismiss or not, and a suspension after dismissal, pending appeal.[2] In the latter type of case, if the appeal is successful and the employee is effectively reinstated, he will be treated as not having broken his continuity of employment, irrespective of whether there is a term in his contract to that effect or not.[3]

1 [1980] IRLR 109, CA.
2 This reasoning was approved by the House of Lords in *West Midland Co-operative Society Ltd v Tipton* [1986] IRLR 112; [1986] ICR 192. See also *Crown Agents for Overseas Governments and Administration v Lawal* [1978] IRLR 542; [1979] ICR 103, where no distinction was drawn between cases turning on medical issues and cases turning on issues of misconduct or capability.
3 *Howgate v Fane Acoustics Ltd* [1981] IRLR 161.

15.66 If an employee is taken as dismissed for the purposes of the unfair dismissal provisions where there is a failure to permit her to return to work after childbirth,[1] the effective date of termination is the notified date of return.[2]

1 Ie under Employment Rights Act 1996, s 96; see Chapter 7.
2 Employment Rights Act 1996, s 97(6).

'Extension' of effective date of termination for certain purposes

15.67 Section 97(2) provides:
'(2) Where—
   (a) the contract of employment is terminated by the employer, and
   (b) the notice required by section 86 to be given by an employer would, if duly given on the material date,[1] expire on a date later than the effective date of termination (as defined by subsection (1)),
for the purposes of sections 108(1), 119(1) and 227(3) that later date is the effective date of termination.'

1 The 'material date' is the date when notice was given by the employer, or where no notice was given, the date the contract of employment was terminated by the employer: Employment Rights Act 1996, s 97(3).

15.68   Section 97(4) provides:

'(4)   Where—

(a)   the contract of employment is terminated by the employee,

(b)   the material date does not fall during a period of notice given by the employer to terminate that contract, and

(c)   had the contract been terminated not by the employee but by notice given on the material date[1] by the employer, that notice would have been required by section 86 to expire on a date later than the effective date of termination (as defined by subsection (1)),

for the purposes of sections 108(1), 119(1) and 227(3) that later date is the effective date of termination.'

1 The 'material date' is the date when notice was given by the employee, or where no notice was given, the date the contract of employment was terminated by the employee: Employment Rights Act 1996, s 97(5).

15.69   The effect of s 97(2) and (4) is that for specified purposes the effective date of termination will be later than the actual date of termination of the employment if no notice, or less than the minimum statutory notice (to be given by the employer) has been given to terminate the contract. The purposes for which this extension applies all relate to calculation of qualification periods – for entitlement to request a written statement of reasons for dismissal; for entitlement to claim for unfair dismissal; and for the calculation of the basic award. It is to be noted that the extension is only for the statutory minimum notice period, not for the contractual notice period,[1] but it applies even where the employee has waived his right to notice or accepted wages in lieu of notice.[2] The extension operates only for the specified purposes and for no others. It does *not* operate to extend the time in which to present a complaint to an industrial tribunal.

1 *Fox Maintenance Ltd v Jackson* [1977] IRLR 306; [1978] ICR 110.
2 *Staffordshire County Council v Secretary of State for Employment* [1989] IRLR 117; [1989] ICR 664, CA.

Reasons for dismissal

15.70   There are certain circumstances where if the tribunal is satisfied as to the reason for the dismissal it is unfair without the application of any further requirement or test. These are often referred to as dismissals which are automatically unfair. There are other circumstances where there is no jurisdiction to decide whether or not the dismissal is fair or unfair.

Automatically unfair dismissals

15.71   As has just been mentioned, in some cases, if the industrial tribunal is satisfied that the reason for dismissal was for a particular reason (or if more than one the principal reason was for that reason) the dismissal is automatically unfair. By this is meant that once the tribunal is satisfied as to the reason for the dismissal (or in the case of redundancy, the selection for dismissal) the dismissal is unfair without need to resort to a further test of fairness.

15.72 The cases of automatically unfair dismissal are as follows.

Pregnancy and childbirth

15.73 Employees who are dismissed for reasons related to pregnancy and childbirth will be unfairly dismissed if the provisions of s 99 of Employment Rights Act 1996 are satisfied (see Chapter 7).

Health and safety cases

15.74 An employee who is dismissed is regarded as unfairly dismissed if the reason (or, if more than one, the principal reason) for the dismissal is one of several relating to health and safety.[1] These occur where the reason (or principal reason) for the dismissal is that the employee:

(1) having been designated by the employer to carry out activities in connection with preventing or reducing risks to health and safety at work, carried out (or proposed to carry out) any such activities,[2]

(2) being a representative of workers on matters of health and safety at work or member of a safety committee,[3] he performed (or proposed to perform) any functions as such a representative or a member of such a committee,[4]

(3) being an employee[5] at a place where there was no such representative or safety committee[5] brought to his employer's attention, by reasonable means, circumstances connected with his work which he reasonably believed were harmful or potentially harmful to health or safety,[6]

(4) in circumstances of danger which he reasonably believed to be serious and imminent and which he could not reasonably have been expected to avert, he left (or proposed to leave) or (while the danger persisted) refused to return to his place of work or any dangerous part of his place of work,[7] or

(5) subject to what is mentioned in the next paragraph, in circumstances of danger which the employee reasonably believed to be serious and imminent, he took (or proposed to take) appropriate[8] steps to protect himself or other persons from the danger.[9]

Interim relief and a special award may be available in these cases (see **15.168** and **15.219**).

1 This provision was introduced to comply with Directive 89/391/EEC.
2 Employment Rights Act 1996, s 100(1)(a).
3 In accordance with arrangements established under or by virtue of any enactment, or by reason of being acknowledged as such by the employer: Employment Rights Act 1996, s 100(1)(b).
4 Employment Rights Act 1996, s 100(1)(b). This is also the case where the employee took part (or proposed to take part) in consultations or elections of representatives (whether as a candidate or not) pursuant to the Health and Safety (Consultation with Employees) Regulations 1996; Employment Rights Act 1996, s 100(1)(ba).
5 Or there was such a representative or safety committee but it was not reasonably practicable for the employee to raise the matter by those means: Employment Rights Act 1996, s 100(1)(c)(ii).
6 Employment Rights Act 1996, s 100(1)(c).
7 Employment Rights Act 1996, s 100(1)(d).
8 Whether steps which an employee took (or proposed to take) were appropriate is to be judged by reference to all the circumstances including, in particular, his knowledge and the facilities and advice available to him at the time: Employment Rights Act 1996, s 100(2).
9 Employment Rights Act 1996, s 100(1)(e).

15.75 Where the reason (or, if more than one, the principal reason) for the dismissal of the employee, was that in circumstances of danger which the employee reasonably believed to be serious and imminent, he took (or proposed to take) appropriate steps to protect himself or other persons from the danger, he is not regarded as unfairly dismissed if the employer shows that it was (or would have been) so negligent for the employee to take the steps which he took (or proposed to take) that a reasonable employer might have dismissed him for taking (or proposing to take) them.[1]

1 Employment Rights Act 1996, s 100(3).

Sunday working

15.76   Shop workers who were in their current employment on 26 August 1994 (who have not opted in to work on Sundays) are protected against dismissal (or selection for dismissal) because they refuse to undertake Sunday working. Those who are not so covered can 'opt out' of Sunday working on giving notice under s 40 of the Employment Rights Act 1996. Betting shop workers have similar rights. Where an employee who is a member of one of the categories mentioned in s 101(1) of the Employment Rights Act 1996 is dismissed, the dismissal is regarded as unfair if the reason (or, if more than one, the principal reason) for the dismissal was that he refused (or proposed to refuse) to do shop work, or betting work, on Sunday or on a particular Sunday. The workers enjoying this protection are protected shop workers or an opted-out shop worker, protected betting workers and opted-out betting workers.[1] A shop worker or betting worker who is dismissed is also regarded as unfairly dismissed if the reason (or, if more than one, the principal reason) for the dismissal is that the shop worker or betting worker gave (or proposed to give) an opting-out notice to the employer.[2]

1 Employment Rights Act 1996, s 101(1). Shop worker is widely defined in the Employment Rights Act 1996, s 232. Betting worker is defined in the Employment Rights Act 1996, s 233. 'Opted-out' is as defined in the Employment Rights Act 1996, s 41.
2 Employment Rights Act 1996, s 101(3). For the purposes of the Employment Rights Act 1996, s 36(2)(b) or s 41(1)(b), the appropriate date in relation to s 101 is the effective date of termination: Employment Rights Act 1996, s 101(4).

15.77   This does not apply in relation to an opted-out shop worker or an opted-out betting worker where the reason (or principal reason) for the dismissal is that he refused (or proposed to refuse) to do shop work, or betting work, on any Sunday or Sundays falling before the end of the opting-out notice[1] period.[2]

1 The notice is the notice given under the Employment Rights Act 1996, s 40.
2 Employment Rights Act 1996, s 101(2).

Trustees of occupational pension schemes

15.78   An employee who is dismissed is regarded as unfairly dismissed if the reason (or, if more than one, the principal reason) for the dismissal is that, being a trustee of a relevant occupational pension scheme which relates to his employment, the employee performed (or proposed to perform) any functions as such a trustee.[1] Interim relief and a special award may be available in these cases (see **15.168** and **15.219**).

1 Employment Rights Act 1996, s 102(1). 'Relevant occupational pension scheme' means an occupational pension scheme (as defined in s 1 of the Pension Schemes Act 1993) established under a trust: Employment Rights Act 1996, s 102(2).

Employee representatives

15.79　An employee who is dismissed is regarded as unfairly dismissed if the reason (or, if more than one, the principal reason) for the dismissal is that the employee, being:

(1)　an employee representative for the purposes of consultation as to redundancies[1] or the transfer of an undertaking, [2] or

(2)　a candidate in an election in which any person elected will, on being elected, be such an employee representative,

performed (or proposed to perform) any functions or activities as such an employee representative or candidate.[3] Interim relief and a special award may be available in these cases (see **15.168** and **15.219**).

1　For the purposes of the Trade Union and Labour Relations (Consolidation) Act 1992, Pt IV, Ch II; see **16.112–16.124**.
2　For the purposes of the Transfer of Undertakings (Protection of Employment) Regulations 1981, regs 10 and 11; see **12.24–12.25**.
3　Employment Rights Act 1996, s 103.

Assertion of a statutory right

15.80　An employee who is dismissed is regarded as unfairly dismissed if the reason (or, if more than one, the principal reason) for the dismissal is that the employee brought proceedings against the employer to enforce a right of his which is a relevant statutory right, or alleged that the employer had infringed a right of his which is a relevant statutory right.[1] Relevant statutory rights are any right conferred by the Employment Rights Act 1996 for which the remedy for its infringement is by way of a complaint or reference to an industrial tribunal, the statutory right to minimum notice, and the rights conferred by the Trade Union and Labour Relations (Consolidation) Act 1992[2] as to deductions from pay, union activities and time off.[3] For these purposes it is immaterial whether or not the employee had the right, or whether or not the right had been infringed, but the claim to the right and that it has been infringed must be made in good faith.[4] It is sufficient for this provision to apply that the employee, without specifying the right, made it reasonably clear to the employer what the right claimed to have been infringed was.[5]

1　Employment Rights Act 1996, s 104(1). It includes dismissal for refusing to enter a contract which would have allowed the employer to make deductions from wages; *Mennell v Newell & Wright (Transport Contractors) Ltd* [1996] ICR 607, EAT.
2　Trade Union and Labour Relations (Consolidation) Act 1992, ss 68, 86, 146, 168, 169 and 170.
3　Employment Rights Act 1996, s 104(4).
4　Employment Rights Act 1996, s 104(2).
5　Employment Rights Act 1996, s 104(3).

Redundancy

15.81　The selection of employees for dismissal by reason of redundancy for reasons of trade union membership or activities is automatically unfair (see **14.31–14.33**). The Employment Rights Act 1996 makes certain other dismissals by reason of redundancy, or selection for such dismissals, unfair. An employee who is dismissed is regarded as unfairly dismissed if the reason (or, if more than one, the principal reason) for the dismissal is that the employee was redundant and it is shown that the circumstances constituting the redundancy applied equally to one or more other employees in the same undertaking who held positions similar to that held by the employee, and who have not been dismissed by the employer, and the reason for selection of the employee for dismissal was one of the reasons set out in s 105(2)–(7).[1]

1 See **15.82**.

15.82 The provision applies where the employee was selected for dismissal by reason of redundancy for a reason:
(1)   as to pregnancy or childbirth as specified in s 99(1)(a)–(d) of the Employment Rights Act 1996,[1]
(2)   as to dismissals for health and safety reasons,[2]
(3)   as to shop workers and betting shop workers who refuse Sunday work,[3]
(4)   as to dismissals of trustees of occupational pension schemes,[4]
(5)   as to the dismissal of employee representatives for consultation as to redundancies and transfers of undertakings,[5] and
(6)   as to dismissals for asserting a statutory rights.[6]

1 Employment Rights Act 1996, s 105(2); s 99(1)(a) to (d) read with s 99(2) or (3).
2 Employment Rights Act 1996, s 105(3); s 100 read with s 100(2) and (3).
3 Employment Rights Act 1996, s 105(4); s 101 read with s 101(2) and (3). For the purposes of s 36(2)(b) or s 41(1)(b), the appropriate date in relation to s 105 is the effective date of termination: Employment Rights Act 1996, s 105(8).
4 Employment Rights Act 1996, s 105(5); s 102(1).
5 Employment Rights Act 1996, s 105(6); s 103.
6 Employment Rights Act 1996, s 105(7); s 104(1) read with s 104(2) and (3).

Trade union membership and activities

15.83 Selection for dismissal by reason of redundancy and certain other dismissals in connection with trade union membership and activities are automatically unfair (see **14.28–14.33**).

Transfer of undertakings

15.84 Subject to the exception where the reason for the dismissal is an economic, technical or organisational reason entailing changes of the workforce of either transferor or transferee,[1] an employee who is dismissed is unfairly dismissed if the transfer of an undertaking, or a reason connected with it, is the reason for the dismissal.[2]

1 Transfer of Undertakings (Protection of Employment) Regulations 1981, reg 8(2); see **14.20–14.22**.
2 Transfer of Undertakings (Protection of Employment) Regulations 1981, reg 8(1); see **14.19**.

Other cases

15.85 Dismissal which is an act of unlawful discrimination on grounds of sex, race or disability is unfair.[1] Dismissal for having a conviction which is spent as provided in the Rehabilitation of Offenders Act 1974 (in respect of employment which is not excluded by order) is almost certainly unfair.[2]

1 Employees who consider they have been unfairly dismissed by reason of unlawful discrimination should claim under all heads of claim. See Chapter 7.
2 *Property Guards Ltd v Taylor and Kershaw* [1982] IRLR 175, EAT. See also *Wood v Coverage Care Ltd* [1996] IRLR 264, EAT.

Dismissals in connection with industrial action

15.86 Special provisions apply where an employee is dismissed for taking part in industrial action (see **12.38–12.63**).

General provisions as to fairness

The meaning of 'fair' and 'unfair'

15.87 The general provisions as to fairness of dismissals are set out in s 98 of the Employment Rights Act 1996. There is a large volume of decided cases as to its application, but whenever the fairness of a dismissal is to be considered the statute itself should be referred to. Where it is applicable, the test of fairness is that set out in the Act. The statutory test is the only definitive test for fairness of the dismissal. There are numerous reported and unreported cases as to the application of the section and its forerunners. These can be of assistance in deciding whether or not a dismissal is fair or unfair, but care should be taken not to assume that they prescribe whether or not a dismissal is fair. The only definitive test is whether or not the dismissal is fair as determined in accordance with the statutory provision.

15.88 Section 98(1)–(5) of the Employment Rights Act 1996 is as follows:
'(1) In determining for the purposes of [the unfair dismissal provisions] whether the dismissal of an employee is fair or unfair, it is for the employer to show—
    (a)   the reason (or, if there was more than one, the principal reason) for the dismissal, and
    (b)   that it is either a reason falling within subsection (2) or some other substantial reason of a kind such as to justify the dismissal of an employee holding the position which the employee held.

(2) A reason falls within this subsection if it—
    (a)   relates to the capability or qualifications of the employee for performing work of the kind which he was employed by the employer to do,
    (b)   relates to the conduct of the employee,
    (c)   is that the employee was redundant, or
    (d)   is that the employee could not continue to work in the position which he held without contravention (either on his part or on that of his employer) of a duty or restriction imposed by or under an enactment.

(3) In subsection (2)(a)—
    (a)   "capability", in relation to an employee, means his capability assessed by reference to skill, aptitude, health or any other physical or mental quality, and
    (b)   "qualifications", in relation to an employee, means any degree, diploma or other academic, technical or professional qualification relevant to the position which he held.

(4) Where the employer has fulfilled the requirements of subsection (1), the determination of the question whether the dismissal is fair or unfair (having regard to the reason shown by the employer)—

(a) depends on whether in the circumstances (including the size and administrative resources of the employer's undertaking) the employer acted reasonably or unreasonably in treating it as a sufficient reason for dismissing the employee, and

(b) shall be determined in accordance with equity and the substantial merits of the case.

(5) Where the employee is taken to be dismissed for the purposes of [the unfair dismissal provisions] by virtue of section 96 [failure to permit return after childbirth], subsection (4)(a) applies as if for the words "acted reasonably" onwards there were substituted the words "would have been acting reasonably or unreasonably in treating it as a sufficient reason for dismissing the employee if she had not been absent from work, and" '.[1]

1 Subsections (4) and (5) are subject to the Employment Rights Act 1996, ss 99–107 and the Trade Union and Labour Relations (Consolidation) Act 1992, ss 152, 153 and 238, ie the situations where the dismissal is 'automatically' unfair and other matters; see **14.28–14.31**.

15.89 The effect of the section is that – subject to special cases dealt with above – for a tribunal to decide that the dismissal of the employee was not unfair the employer has to show first, what was the reason (or principal reason) for the dismissal; and secondly, that it fell within the four heads set out in s 98(2), or was some other substantial reason of a kind such as to justify the dismissal of an employee holding the position which that employee held. The tribunal then determines whether in all the circumstances (having regard to equity and the substantial merits of the case) the employer acted reasonably in treating the reason as a sufficient one for dismissing the employee. These three stages should be considered in all cases where s 98 applies.

15.90 The onus of proof lies on the employer to show the reason for the dismissal and that it was one of the five specified reasons.[1] Thus, if the employer does not appear before, or make representations to, the tribunal he is likely to fail in his contention that the dismissal was fair.[2] Even in constructive dismissal cases, where the employer is not actually intending to dismiss at all, if he wishes to claim in the alternative that the dismissal is fair, the onus is still on him to establish the reason for dismissal if the employee is dismissed. The employer should show the tribunal the reason for his conduct in terminating the employment contract.[3] If he seeks to show several reasons for the dismissal he should satisfy the tribunal as to them all, or those on which he seeks to rely when the tribunal considers whether or not the dismissal is fair.[4]

1 *W Devis & Sons Ltd v Atkins* [1977] 3 All ER 40; [1977] ICR 662. The burden remains with the employer even where the employee alleges that the dismissal was for a reason that is automatically unfair; *Maund v Penwith District Council* [1984] IRLR 21; [1984] ICR 143, CA.
2 *Rigby v British Steel Corpn* [1973] ICR 160.
3 *Berriman v Delabole Slate Ltd* [1985] ICR 546. See also *Savoia v Chiltern Herb Farms Ltd* [1981] IRLR 65.
4 *Smith v City of Glasgow District Council* [1987] ICR 796, HL.

Reason for the dismissal

15.91 A reason for the dismissal of an employee is a set of facts known to the employer, or of beliefs held by him, which cause him to dismiss the employee. If at the time of the dismissal the employer gives a reason for it, that is evidence, at any rate as against him, as to the real reason, but it does not necessarily constitute the real reason. He may knowingly give a reason different from the real reason out of kindness.[1]

1 *Abernethy v Mott Hay and Anderson* [1974] ICR 323, CA. Per Cairns LJ and approved by the Viscount Dilhorne in *W Devis & Sons Ltd v Atkins* [1977] AC 931. See also *Trust House Forte Leisure Ltd v Aquilar* [1976] IRLR 251, EAT.

15.92 It is the task of an industrial tribunal to establish what was the reason for the employer's conduct in dismissing the employee. The tribunal does not have to dissect the reason with excessive and analytical detail; a broad approach may be adopted.[1] All the circumstances surrounding the dismissal are looked at to find the reason for the dismissal, not just the final incident which leads to it.[2] There may be a finding that there were several constituent reasons.[3]

1 *Bates Farms and Dairy Ltd v Scott* [1976] IRLR 214.
2 See *Turner v Wadham Stringer Commercials (Portsmouth) Ltd* [1974] ICR 277, NIRC.
3 *Patterson v Messrs Bracketts* [1977] IRLR 137.

15.93 Information coming to light after the dismissal cannot constitute the reason for it – whether that be to the employee's advantage or not – but an employer may seek to persuade the tribunal that the actual reason for the dismissal differed from that which he expressed at the time.[1] If, after the dismissal, information comes to light which indicates that the employer should not have dismissed the employee, the dismissal may become unfair where the employer should have withdrawn the notice.[2] Exceptionally, evidence of subsequent events may also be permissible to help establish the truth of evidence given in relation to events occurring before the dismissal. Such evidence may also be relevant in the context of remedies; and, where the evidence emerges in the course of an internal appeal, in determining the fairness of the employer[3] (but not to justify a fresh reason for the dismissal).[4]

1 In *Abernethy v Mott Hay and Anderson* [1974] ICR 323 the employee was held to have been dismissed because of lack of capability even though at the time of the dismissal took place it was expressed as redundancy.
2 *Williamson v Alcan (UK) Ltd* [1977] IRLR 303, EAT; *Stacey v Babcock Power Ltd* [1986] IRLR 3.
3 *West Midlands Co-operative Society Ltd v Tipton* [1986] IRLR 112, HL.
4 *Monie v Coral Racing Ltd* [1979] IRLR 54; [1979] ICR 254.

15.94 When an employer has provided an employee with written reasons for his dismissal pursuant to the statutory obligation[1] it is possible, but difficult, for an employer to go beyond the reasons which it specifies in the written statement of reasons for dismissal.[2] Because of this great care should be taken when preparing this statement, but it is sufficient to refer unambiguously to an earlier letter sent to the employee wherein the reasons have previously been set out.[3]

1 Employment Rights Act 1996, s 92, see **13.54–13.57**.
2 For an example where the employer relied on a different reason at the hearing, see *Clarke v Trimco Motor Group Ltd* [1993] IRLR 148. But see also *Nelson v British Broadcasting Corpn* [1977] IRLR 148; [1977] ICR 649, CA; *Murphy v Epsom College* [1983] IRLR 395 and *Hannan v TNT-IPEC (UK) Ltd* [1986] IRLR 165.
3 *Kent County Council v Gilham* [1985] IRLR 16; [1985] ICR 227, CA.

Reasonableness

15.95 The tribunal decides what was the reason for the dismissal of the employee and whether it was one of the reasons specified in s 98. Unless the reason is found to be one which is automatically unfair, the industrial tribunal will decide whether the employer acted reasonably in treating this reason as one which justified dismissal. The onus of proof in this third stage is cast in neutral terms and the matter is determined 'in accordance with equity and the substantial merits of the case'.[1]

1 Employment Rights Act 1996, s 98(4).

15.96   The test to be applied by the industrial tribunal was reformulated by the Employment Appeal Tribunal (presided over by Browne-Wilkinson J) as follows:
  '(1)   the starting point should always be the words of [s 98(4)] themselves;
  (2)   in applying the section an Industrial Tribunal must consider the reasonableness of the employer's conduct, not simply whether they (the members of the Tribunal) consider the dismissal to be fair;
  (3)   in judging the reasonableness of the employer's conduct an Industrial Tribunal must not substitute its decision as to what the right course to adopt for that of the employer;
  (4)   in many (though not all) cases there is a band of reasonable responses to the employee's conduct within which one reasonable employer might reasonably take one view, another quite reasonably take another;
  (5)   the function of the Industrial Tribunal, as an industrial jury, is to determine whether in the particular circumstances of each case the decision to dismiss the employee fell within the band of reasonable responses which a reasonable employer might have adopted. If the dismissal falls within the band the dismissal is fair; if the dismissal falls outside the band it is unfair.' [1]

1 *Iceland Frozen Foods v Jones* [1982] IRLR 439.

15.97   When considering all the circumstances in deciding upon the reasonableness of the employer's conduct, the tribunal should take note of the size and administrative resources of the employer[1] and any relevant code of practice (see Appendix 3). The House of Lords has put an emphasis on procedural propriety.[2] In *Polkey v AE Dayton Services Ltd*,[3] the importance of procedural safeguards was re-emphasised, indicating that a tribunal will not err in law if it starts from the premise that breach of procedure (at least where it embodies significant safeguards for the employee) will render a dismissal unfair.

1 Employment Rights Act 1996, s 98(4). See *MacKellar v Bolton* [1979] IRLR 59; *Bevan Harris Ltd v Gair* [1981] IRLR 520 and *De Grasse v Stockwell Tools Ltd* [1992] IRLR 269.
2 *West Midlands Co-operative Society v Tipton* [1986] IRLR 112; [1986] ICR 192, and more strongly, *Polkey v AE Dayton Services Ltd* [1987] IRLR 503; [1988] ICR 142, HL.
3 [1987] IRLR 503, [1988] ICR 142, HL.

15.98   Failure to allow an employee to exercise his right of appeal may render an otherwise fair dismissal unfair;[1] and procedural defects in the handling of the appeal may have the same effect. The kind of defects which will have this effect is a matter of interpretation. It seems that minor defects may be ignored,[2] but a defect in the sense that the appeal 'could and should have found and demonstrated a flaw in the decision at first instance in the internal procedures of the employer'[3] cannot.

1 *West Midlands Co-operative Society Ltd v Tipton* [1986] IRLR 112; [1986] ICR 192, HL.

2 *Whitbread & Co plc v Mills* [1988] IRLR 501.
3 *Post Office v Marney* [1990] IRLR 170.

15.99 What if the employee has not been adversely affected by the procedural defect? The House of Lords' decision in *Polkey*[1] effectively ended what had become a substantial erosion of the protection of the employee by what used to be referred to as 'the *British Labour Pump* principle'.[2] According to this principle, a dismissal based upon conduct of an employer which was unfair if judged in the circumstances known at the time of the dismissal, could still be fair if, on facts proved before the tribunal, the tribunal came to the conclusion that – had the employer followed a fair procedure – he could reasonably have decided to dismiss. After *Polkey*, a failure to apply full procedural safeguards will not automatically render the dismissal unfair, but if the employer was acting unreasonably at the time, a dismissal will not retrospectively be rendered fair simply because the employee has not – or probably has not – been adversely affected by the breach of procedure. *Polkey* focuses on the reasonableness of the employer in the light of matters known to him at the time of his actions.

1 *Polkey v AE Dayton Services Ltd* [1987] IRLR 503; [1987] ICR 301, HL. All cases relating to procedural matters which were decided prior to *Polkey* must be looked at with caution.
2 Based on *British Labour Pump Co Ltd v Byrne* [1979] ICR 347, EAT.

15.100 Other factors often taken into account in judging the employer's reasonableness include length of service, whether dismissal is a fair sanction,[1] where evidence is in conflict,[2] where capability is in issue,[3] and consistency (of treatment of employees or of conduct)[4].

1 *Johnson Matthey Metals v Harding* [1978] IRLR 248.
2 *O'Brien v Boots Pure Drug Co* [1973] IRLR 261.
3 *Tiptools Ltd v Curtis* [1973] IRLR 276.
4 *Post Office v Fennell* [1981] IRLR 221; *Proctor v British Gypsum Ltd* [1992] IRLR 7. A difference in personnel deaing with the matter may be no answer; *Cain v Leeds Western Health Authority* [1990] IRLR 168.

Particular reasons

Reason related to employee's capability or qualifications

Capability
15.101 Capability is defined in s 98(3)(a) of the Employment Rights Act 1996 as capability 'assessed by reference to skill, aptitude, health or any other physical or mental quality'. For the effect of the Disability Discrimination Act 1995 on dismissals in these circumstances, see Chapter 7.

15.102 Physical incapability often involves illness on the part of employees. The possibility of the illness frustrating the contract must be considered (see **13.09–13.26**). Although there can be overlap between the criteria used to determine whether a contract of employment has been frustrated, and whether the employee has been dismissed fairly because of the lack of capability, the tests are not identical.[1] When deciding whether the employer has acted fairly in dismissing the employee in these cases, factors such as the nature of the illness, the likely length of continuing absence, the employer's requirements to have the work carried out for which the employee was engaged and the circumstances of the case are all likely to be taken into account.[2]

1 *Tan v Berry Bros and Rudd Ltd* [1974] ICR 586, NIRC.
2 *Spencer v Paragon Wallpapers Ltd* [1976] IRLR 373.

15.103 An employer acting reasonably should ascertain the facts with regard to the employee's illness. Unless there are wholly exceptional circumstances, the employer should consult the employee and discuss the matter with him. The employer should take steps to ascertain the true medical position before dismissing an employee because of his ill-health.[1] The results of the employer's own medical advice as to the state of the employee's health should be discussed with the employee, for he may be able to cast new light on the matter and/or seek to obtain alternative medical advice.[2] When the employer does obtain a medical report unless it is clearly wrong as to the facts in some way, or indicates that no proper examination has taken place, the employer is unlikely to be required to evaluate it in terms of medical expertise.[3]

1 *East Lindsey District Council v Daubney* [1977] ICR 566, EAT.
2 *Williamson v Alcan (UK) Ltd* [1978] ICR 104, EAT; *Cadbury Ltd v Doddington* [1977] ICR 982, EAT; *Owen v Funditor Ltd* [1976] ICR 350, EAT.
3 *Liverpool Area Health Authority (Teaching) Central and Southern District v Edwards* [1977] IRLR 471, EAT.

15.104 The employer has no inherent power to compel an employee to undergo a medical examination. If he seeks to do so without the employee's consent, in the absence of an express contractual power, it is likely to constitute a repudiatory breach of contract by the employer.[1] However, if an employee refuses to be examined, an employer is entitled to act on the information available to him. This may mean that a dismissal will be fair, even if – had a medical opinion been available – it would have been unfair.

1 *Bliss v South East Thames Regional Health Authority* [1985] IRLR 308; [1987] ICR 700, CA.

15.105 In deciding an issue of competence (often 'mental' capacity within the statutory definition), there are two questions to be considered by the tribunal: did the employer honestly and reasonably hold the belief that the employee was not competent and did he have reasonable grounds for that belief?[1] It is not the tribunal's function to substitute its members' own views of the employee's competence for that of the employer.

1 Per Sir Geoffrey Lane LJ in *Alidair Ltd v Taylor* [1978] IRLR 82. Lord Denning MR thought that the employer could have dismissed the employee on the strength of his belief alone, but that may have been limited to the special circumstances of *Taylor's* case.

15.106 In order to ensure fairness, it may be that an employer must carry out a careful appraisal of the employee's performance and discuss it with him; warn the employee of the consequences of there being no improvement; and give him a reasonable opportunity to improve.[1] Exceptionally, it may be reasonable to dismiss for incompetence without warning; for example where even a simple error leads to serious consequences, or where the employee's conduct has significantly damaged the employer's interests.[2]

1 See *James v Waltham Holy Cross UDC* [1973] IRLR 202, per Sir John Donaldson.
2 *Alidair Ltd v Taylor* [1978] IRLR 82 (airline pilot); *Turner v Pleasurama Casinos Ltd* [1976] IRLR 151 (gaming inspector); *Retarded Children's Aid Society Ltd v Day* [1978] IRLR 128, CA.

15.107 An employee may be fairly dismissed for lack of capability indicated by a number of small incidents; and there is no rule of law that the employee is entitled to have the employer's judgment tested by results.[1] However, there may be an issue as to whether the employer has fulfilled his responsibilities to create conditions which enable the employee to carry out his duties satisfactorily, particularly on a question of training.[2]

1 *Miller v Executors of John Graham* [1978] IRLR 309, EAT.
2 See for example *White v London Transport Executive* [1981] IRLR 261 and *Davison v Kent Meters Ltd* [1975] IRLR 145.

15.108 It may be appropriate for an employer to investigate the possibility of alternative employment where an employee has been dismissed for incompetence, but this is not always the case.[1] The argument for not seeking alternative employment may be stronger where the employee has been promoted beyond his capacity. Where an employee is incapable of performing his job through no fault of his own it cannot be said that the incapability was a 'contribution' to the dismissal when assessing compensation.[2]

1 *Bevan Harris Ltd (t/a Clyde Leather Co) v Gair* [1981] IRLR 520.
2 *Kraft Foods Ltd v Fox* [1978] ICR 311, EAT.

Qualifications
15.109 Qualifications are defined in s 98(3)(a) of the Act as 'any degree, diploma or other academic, technical or professional qualification relevant to the position which [the employee] held'. This definition has been narrowly interpreted, so that mere licence, permit or authorisation will not fall within the definition;[1] an aptitude test, however, will.[2] Trustworthiness is not a qualification within the meaning of the subsection.[3]

1 For example, registration as a seafarer: *Blue Star Ship Management Ltd v Williams* [1979] IRLR 16; [1978] ICR 770.
2 *Blackman v Post Office* [1974] ICR 151, NIRC.
3 *Singh v London County Bus Service Ltd* [1976] IRLR 176, EAT.

Conduct

15.110 The reasons for dismissal given by employers are most frequently related to the employee's conduct. In the majority of these cases the employer is readily able to show a reason for the dismissal, but whether or not the conduct of the employee was in fact the reason for the dismissal is a matter for the industrial tribunal to determine.

15.111 Difficulties can arise when dealing with the requirement that the employer must have acted reasonably. The 'circumstances' which the industrial tribunal should consider in deciding whether the employer's action was reasonable are those circumstances that were known to exist at the time of the dismissal. Matters of which the employer was not aware at the time of the dismissal cannot be relied upon as evidence that the dismissal was fair.[1]

1 *W Devis & Sons Ltd v Atkins* [1977] 3 All ER 40; [1977] ICR 662, HL.

15.112 In order to show that a dismissal for misconduct is fair, it used to be said it was for the employer to establish that he believed that the employee was guilty of the misconduct; that he had reasonable grounds for the belief when he formed it and that he had carried out as much investigation as was reasonable in the circumstances[1]. These are still valuable guidelines, but the onus of proof on the last two elements is no longer on the employer, and the test does not apply where the employer believes the misconduct is the act of one of two or more employees, or possibly both, or all.[2]

1 *British Home Stores Ltd v Burchell* [1978] IRLR 379; [1980] ICR 303n, as approved by the Court of Appeal in *W Weddel & Co Ltd v Tepper* [1980] IRLR 96; [1980] ICR 286; and see *Boys and Girls Welfare Society v McDonald* [1996] IRLR 129, EAT, and *Scottish Daily Record and Sunday Mail v Laird* [1996] IRLR 665, Ct of Sess.
2 In such a case it may be sufficient if the employer reasonably believes that one of them committed the misconduct, eg *Monie v Coral Racing Ltd* [1980] IRLR 464; [1981] ICR 109; *McPhie & Dermott v Wimpey Waste Management Ltd* [1981] IRLR 316. For a case of more than two suspects, see *Parr v Whitbread & Co plc* [1990] IRLR 39. Nonetheless, each employee should be considered individually: *Gibson v British Transport Docks Board* [1982] IRLR 228.

15.113 It is a logical consequence of these guidelines that a dismissal may be fair even though a criminal court subsequently decides that the employee is not guilty of suspected criminal misconduct,[1] and a dismissal may be unfair notwithstanding subsequent discovery of serious misconduct.[2]

1 *Harris (Ipswich) Ltd v Harrison* [1978] IRLR 382.
2 *W Devis & Sons Ltd v Atkins* [1977] 3 All ER 40; [1977] ICR 662, HL.

15.114 The extent of the investigation required will depend on the facts of the case but, even though appellate courts have avoided laying down rigid criteria, the basic expectations of the procedure are now well established.[1] The tendency in recent cases has been to require fuller safeguards of fairness. Delay in carrying out the investigation may make an otherwise fair dismissal unfair.[2] The task of hearing the employee will normally be undertaken by the person ultimately deciding on the dismissal.[3]

1 See *Clark v Civil Aviation Authority* [1991] IRLR 412.
2 *RSPCA v Cruden* [1986] IRLR 83.
3 *Budgen & Co v Thomas* [1976] IRLR 174; [1976] ICR 344. In view of *Polkey*, earlier criticisms of this case are difficult to maintain.

Inefficiency and failure to comply with employer's orders

15.115 Generally an employee must obey the lawful (which usually means 'in accordance with the contract') and reasonable orders of the employer, and failure to do so will be an act of misconduct.[1] An employee cannot automatically refuse to comply with his employer's directions where the latter is in breach of a statutory duty.[2] However, all circumstances of the case must be considered and personal factors of the employee should be taken into account;[3] even if a non-compliance is misconduct, it may not justify dismissal.

1 Examples of cases under this head include *Courtney v Babcock and Wilcox (Operations) Ltd* [1977] IRLR 30, EAT; *St Anne's Board Mill Co Ltd v Brien* [1973] IRLR 309; [1973] ICR 444; *Turner v Pleasurama Casinos Ltd* [1976] IRLR 151, QBD; *Ferodo Ltd v Barnes* [1976] IRLR 302, [1976] ICR 439, EAT; *Alidair Ltd v Taylor* [1978] ICR 445, CA.
2 *Lindsay v Dunlop Ltd* [1980] IRLR 93. For contrast, where the Health & Safety Executive considered a process to be safe, but the employee refused to perform the task, see *Piggott Bros & Co Ltd v Jackson* [1991] IRLR 309, CA.
3 See *Lewis v John Adamson & Co Ltd* [1982] IRLR 233.

15.116 Conversely, if the employer is insisting on the employee doing something outside the terms of his contract, and the employee refuses and is dismissed, the dismissal may be unfair.[1] Even if ostensibly within the scope of his contract, an employee may refuse to comply with an order in limited circumstances, eg the term of the contract is illegal,[2] or if compliance would oblige him to put himself in direct and immediate danger.[3]

1 *Graham v Anthony Todd (Haulage) Ltd* [1975] IRLR 45; *Kemp v Robin Knitwear Ltd* [1974] IRLR 69.
2 *Riley v Joseph Frisby Ltd* [1982] IRLR 479.
3 *Ferrie v Western No 3 DC* [1973] IRLR 162; *Associated Tunnelling Co Ltd v Wasilewski* [1973] IRLR 346.

Absenteeism

15.117   Although each case has to be looked at on its merits, it is often said that before dismissal can take place for poor attendance there should be enquiries as to the reason for the poor attendance and appropriate warning.[1] The tribunal will apply the reasonableness test if satisfied as to the reason for the dismissal.

1 See *Mooney v Rowntree Mackintosh Ltd* [1974] IRLR 277; *Moore v Central Electricity Generating Board (Midlands Region)* [1974] IRLR 296; *Wallace v EJ Guy Ltd* [1973] ICR 117, NIRC.

Insubordination, uncooperative attitude and breach of rules

15.118   Again the factors have to be looked at most carefully in the light of all the circumstances to ascertain whether the employer was justified in accordance with s 98 to dismiss the employee. Any disciplinary rules should be documented and made available to employees.[1] If the offence is explicitly covered in a rule, the employer will find it easier to justify his dismissal; conversely, failure to adopt a specific rule may make it harder,[2] although some areas of misconduct are so well known that it is hardly necessary to spell them out.[3]

1 Examples are *Farnborough v Governors of Edinburgh College of Art* [1974] IRLR 245, NIRC; *Coendo v Midland Bank Ltd* [1975] IRLR 172; *Shortland v Chantrill* [1975] IRLR 208, NIRC; *Glitz v Watford Electric Co Ltd* [1979] IRLR 89, EAT.
2 In accordance with the note on the statement of employment particulars and the ACAS Code of Practice on Disciplinary Practice and Procedures in Employment; see Appendix 3.
3 *Singh v Lyons Maid Ltd* [1975] IRLR 328; *Distillers Co (Bottling Services) Ltd v Gardner* [1982] IRLR 47; *CA Parsons & Co Ltd v McLoughlin* [1978] IRLR 65; *Denco Ltd v Joinson* [1991] IRLR 63; [1991] ICR 172.

Criminal offences by the employee away from work

15.119   The basic principle is illustrated in para 15(c) of the ACAS Code of Practice on Disciplinary Practice and Procedures in Employment:
'*Criminal offences outside employment.* These should not be treated as automatic reasons for dismissal regardless of whether the offence has any relevance to the duties of the individual as an employee. The main considerations should be whether the offence is one that makes the individual unsuitable for his or her type of work or unacceptable to other employees. Employees should not be dismissed solely because a charge against them is pending or because they are absent through having been remanded in custody.'

15.120   An industrial tribunal is likely to consider this principle and look at all the circumstances of the case to determine whether the employer has acted fairly in accordance with the requirements of s 98(4).[1] However, it is not necessary for the employer to prove that the employee committed the alleged offence; it is likely to be sufficient if he honestly believes on reasonable grounds that the employee did so.[2] It is not likely that a tribunal will consider it fair for an employee to be discharged because a criminal charge is being made without more.[3]

1 See *McLaren v National Coal Board* [1988] IRLR 215, [1988] ICR 370, CA and *Saeed v Inner London Education Authority* [1986] IRLR 23; [1985] ICR 637.
2 *Alidair v Taylor* [1978] IRLR 82, CA; *P v Nottinghamshire County Council* [1992] IRLR 362.
3 *Securicor Guarding Ltd v R* [1994] IRLR 633, EAT.

15.121 Industrial tribunals have considered that enquiries and proper investigations as to the allegations should be undertaken prior to the dismissal. Other factors which would influence a reasonable employer, such as the status of the employee, the length of his period of employment and personal factors have all been taken into account.[1] It may also be relevant to take account of the effect the offence may have on what an employer can properly allow or expect an employee to do.[2]

1 See *Jones v RM Douglas Construction Ltd* [1975] IRLR 175, IT; *Moore v C & A Modes* [1981] IRLR 71.
2 For example a groundsman convicted of indecent assault, likely to come in contact with young girls; *P v Nottinghamshire County Council* [1992] IRLR 362, CA.

Past criminal convictions

15.122 Sometimes an employee may have concealed past criminal convictions, and thereby obtained employment which he would not otherwise have obtained. Unless the employee is entitled to withhold such information under the Rehabilitation of Offenders Act 1974, a dismissal for false concealment may well be fair, at least where it may reasonably be inferred that the information was deliberately withheld.[1]

1 *Torr v British Railways Board* [1977] IRLR 184; [1977] ICR 785.

Clocking offences

15.123 Particular problems arise in connection with timekeeping and operation of 'clocking-in' arrangements. Industrial tribunals have been called upon to determine whether or not employees dismissed as a result of improper use of procedures have had their employment terminated unfairly. Tribunals generally recognise the view that false clocking-in in the industrial scene is serious dishonesty and, depending on the clarity of the rules, can justify dismissal.[1]

1 See *Dalton v Burton's Gold Medal Biscuits Ltd* [1974] IRLR 45, NIRC; *Meridian Ltd v Gomersall* [1977] ICR 597, EAT; *Stewart v Western SMT Co Ltd* [1978] IRLR 553, EAT; *Elliott Bros (London) Ltd v Colverd* [1979] IRLR 92, EAT.

Redundancy

15.124 When considering the position of employees dismissed by reason of redundancy, in addition to s 98 of the Employment Rights Act 1996, s 105 of that Act has to be considered (see **15.81–15.82**). This provides that in certain circumstances dismissal by reason of redundancy is automatically unfair. In approaching a redundancy dismissal, once the tribunal is satisfied that the dismissal was by reason of redundancy it will next determine whether or not the dismissal was automatically unfair. Only when it has decided that the redundancy was not automatically unfair will it go on the consider whether the dismissal was fair or unfair in accordance with the test in s 98(4).

15.125 It is a matter for an employer to decide on the size of his labour force. The employee may challenge whether his dismissal was by reason of redundancy and the method of his selection for dismissal by reason of redundancy. Provided the employer acted in good faith in deciding on the need for the redundancy it is unlikely the employee will challenge successfully the decision to effect redundancies.[1]

1 *Moon v Homeworthy Furniture (Northern) Ltd* [1976] IRLR 298; [1977] ICR 117; *Ladbroke Courage Holidays Ltd v Asten* [1981] IRLR 59; *Orr v Vaughan* [1981] IRLR 63; *James W Cook & Co (Wivenhoe) Ltd v Tipper* [1990] IRLR 386; [1990] ICR 716.

15.126 For the purposes of proceedings where an employee claims to have been unfairly dismissed the onus of proof is on the employer to show the reason for dismissal, and this applies in cases of redundancy just as it does in situations where the employer claims the dismissal took place for other reasons. It will be seen that for the purposes of a claim for a redundancy payment where an employer seeks to deny the claim the onus of proof is on the employer to disprove redundancy (see **16.38**). It is possible in the case of an application claiming both a remedy for unfair dismissal and a redundancy payment, for the employer to fail to discharge the onus of proof so far as the unfair dismissal application is concerned, and yet for the tribunal to resolve that for the purposes of the claim for a redundancy payment the employee was dismissed by reason of redundancy.[1] Moreover, an employee may allege that the dismissal is unfair on the ground that the dismissal was not by reason of redundancy having received what was accepted as a redundancy payment.[2]

1 See *Midland Foot Comfort Centre Ltd v Richmond* [1973] ICR 219.
2 *Clarkson International Tools Ltd v Short* [1973] IRLR 90, [1973] ICR 191, NIRC.

15.127 Prior to the implementation of the Employment Protection Act 1975 there were difficulties and anomalies in computing compensation when the employee was both redundant and unfairly dismissed since compensation for unfair dismissal did not include a basic award (which roughly equates to the amount of a redundancy payment). The Employment Rights Act 1996 contains provisions which cover the situation so that an employee who is unfairly dismissed for whatever reason may be entitled to the basic award, but will not receive a redundancy payment as well if dismissed by reason of redundancy (see **15.193**). Employers who wish to claim a dismissal was a fair redundancy dismissal will usually have paid a redundancy payment and so the employee has little to gain by claiming a redundancy payment as well. A claim for unfair dismissal which is in time, prevents a later claim for a redundancy payment being out of time. Accordingly claims by an applicant that he was dismissed by reason of redundancy as well as unfairly dismissed are now more rarely encountered than they were.

15.128 Formerly s 59(1)(b) of the Employment Protection (Consolidation) Act 1978 made it automatically unfair to select a candidate for redundancy contrary to a customary arrangement or agreed procedure, but for dismissals taking effect after 3 January 1995 this provision was repealed by the Deregulation and Contracting Out Act 1994.

Reasonableness in connection with redundancy

15.129 If the dismissal is not rendered unfair by the provisions rendering the dismissal automatically unfair the industrial tribunal has to consider whether or not the employer acted reasonably in accordance with s 98(4) before it can be decided that the dismissal was fair. When considering whether an employer has acted reasonably in dismissing an employee by reason of redundancy as in connection with other unfair dismissal claims the tribunal will have regard to good industrial relations practice.

15.130   The Employment Appeal Tribunal provided assistance in determining the fairness of redundancy dismissals in *Williams v Compair Maxam Ltd.*[1] The guidance given in this case does not lay down tenets of law, but suggested standards of behaviour which may alter with time. The prevailing expectation at present is that they should not be departed from without good reason. Browne-Wilkinson J expressed the five principles thus:

'(1)   The employer will seek to give as much warning as possible of impending redundancies so as to enable the union and employees who may be affected to take early steps to inform themselves of the relevant facts, consider possible alternative solutions and, if necessary, find alternative employment in the undertaking or elsewhere.

(2)   The employer will consult the union as to the best means by which the desired management result can be achieved fairly and with as little hardship to the employees as possible. In particular, the employer will seek to agree with the union the criteria to be applied in selecting the employees to be made redundant. When a selection has been made, the employer will consider with the union whether the selection has been made in accordance with those criteria.

(3)   Whether or not an agreement as to the criteria to be adopted has been agreed with the union, the employer will seek to establish criteria for selection which so far as possible do not depend solely upon the opinion of the person making the selection but can be objectively checked against such things as attendance record, efficiency at the job, experience or length of service.

(4)   The employer will seek to ensure that the selection is made fairly in accordance with these criteria and will consider any representations the union may make as to such selection.

(5)   The employer will seek to see whether instead of dismissing an employee he could offer him alternative employment.'

1 [1982] IRLR 83, EAT.

15.131   In *Polkey*[1] it was said that an employer will not normally have acted reasonably on a redundancy dismissal unless he warns and consults affected employees or their representatives, he adopts a fair basis on which to carry out the selection of those to be dismissed and takes reasonable steps to avoid or reduce the effects of the redundancy by redeployment of the affected employees. Since that decision the importance of consultation has been re-emphasised in numerous cases.[2] The distinction between the obligation to consult and the obligation to warn has also been drawn.[3] Whilst there are no fixed rules as to what consultation should cover, it has been said[4] that fair consultation means:

(1)   consultation when the proposals are still at a formative stage;
(2)   the provision of adequate information on which to respond;
(3)   allowing adequate time in which to respond; and
(4)   conscientious consideration by an authority of the response to consultation.

15.131 *Unfair dismissal*

1 *Polkey v AE Dayton Services Ltd* [1987] IRLR 503; [1987] ICR 142, HL.
2 See for example *Robertson v Magnet Ltd (Retail Division)* [1993] IRLR 512; *Dyke v Hereford & Worcester County Council* [1989] ICR 800; *Heron v Citylink-Nottingham* [1993] IRLR 372; *King v Eaton Ltd* [1996] IRLR 199, Ct of Sess.
3 *Rowell v Hubbard Group Services Ltd* [1995] IRLR 195.
4 Glidewell LJ in *R v British Coal Corpn & Secretary of State for Trade and Industry, ex p Price* [1994] IRLR 72, quoting Hodgson J in *R v Gwent County Council, ex p Bryant* [1988] COD 19.

15.132 An employer may be expected to look for alternative employment for the affected employee. Failure to make appropriate efforts to find alternative employment may make the dismissal unfair.[1] The steps to be taken depend on the circumstances. It may be that less has been expected of employers as to efforts to be taken to seek alternative employment for the employee.[2] It may be that a failure to consider the employee for alternative employment which arises after the dismissal itself, will not make a dismissal unfair. The tribunal should examine the fairness of the dismissal itself. The selection of the individual for the new post may have taken place afterwards.[3] The employee should be consulted as to work which is available. Employers should not assume that an employee will reject alternative employment if it involves demotion,[4] and should endeavour to ensure that any offer of alternative employment is made on a reasonable basis.[5]

1 *Vokes Ltd v Bear* [1973] IRLR 363; [1974] ICR 1, NIRC.
2 *Quinton Hazell Ltd v Earl* [1976] IRLR 296, [1976] ICR 296; *British United Shoe Machinery Co Ltd v Clarke* [1977] IRLR 297; [1978] ICR 70; *Barratt Construction Ltd v Dalrymple* [1984] IRLR 385.
3 *Labour Party v Oakley* [1987] IRLR 79; [1987] ICR 178. The decision in this case was overturned by the Court of Appeal [1988] IRLR 34, [1988] ICR 403, but the principle that unfair conduct after dismissal cannot render an otherwise fair dismissal unfair was confirmed in *Octavius Atkinson & Sons Ltd v Morris* [1989] IRLR 158, CA.
4 *Avonmouth Construction Co Ltd v Shipway* [1979] IRLR 14; *Huddersfield Parcels Ltd v Sykes* [1981] IRLR 115.
5 *Elliot v Richard Stump Ltd* [1987] IRLR 215; [1987] ICR 579.

15.133 A lack of consultation or a failure to make reasonable efforts to find other employment for the dismissed employee may make the dismissal unfair. It must be remembered that the fairness of dismissal by reason of redundancy which is not automatically unfair is assessed in accordance with the provisions of s 98(4) of the Employment Rights Act 1996 in the same way as other reasons for dismissal.[1] The section must always be referred to. If the employer does not appear at the hearing, the tribunal is likely to find the employee was unfairly dismissed as well as redundant.[2]

1 *Clarkson International Tools Ltd v Short* [1973] ICR 191, NIRC.
2 *Rigby v British Steel Corpn* [1973] ICR 160, NIRC.

15.134 Once it is established that the claimant was dismissed by reason of redundancy and he was not unfairly selected for dismissal, and the employer otherwise acted fairly, the industrial tribunal should decide that the dismissal was fair. The tribunal should guard against temptation of making a finding of unfair dismissal in such cases as a means of 'topping up' what is sometimes considered an inadequate redundancy payment.[1]

1 *British United Shoe Machinery Co Ltd v Clarke* [1977] IRLR 297; [1978] ICR 70; *Hinckley and Bosworth Borough Council v Ainscough* [1979] IRLR 224, EAT.

Contravention of a duty or restriction imposed by or under an enactment

15.135 Section 98(2)(d) of the Employment Rights Act 1996 allows an employer to dismiss an employee fairly if he can show that 'the employee could not continue to work in the position which he held without contravention (either on his part or that of his employer) of a duty or restriction imposed by or under any enactment'. This ground is encountered rarely. The majority of cases which do arise involve employees disqualified from driving, although they may be said to fall within the category of reason relating to capability and qualifications as well. The usual requirement that the tribunal decides whether the dismissal was fair or unfair pursuant to s 98(4) applies. Factors such as the extent to which driving is required for the performance of the employee's duties, whether or not alternative employment could be found for the employee, and difficulties in obtaining a temporary replacement, have all been taken into account.[1] An employer may find it difficult to rely on s 98(2)(d) where it is within his control to prevent, or avoid the effects of the statutory restriction.[2]

1 For examples see *Appleyard v FM Smith (Hull) Ltd* [1972] IRLR 19; *Fearn v Tayford Motor Co Ltd* [1975] IRLR 336.
2 *Sutcliffe and Eaton Ltd v Pinney* [1977] IRLR 349, EAT; *Sandhu v Department of Education and Science and London Borough of Hillingdon* [1978] IRLR 208, EAT. With regard to 'non-qualified' teachers see *Birmingham District Council v Elson* [1979] EAT 609/79.

Some other substantial reason

15.136 Even if the reason for a dismissal cannot be established under any of the categories outlined above, it may be justified under the residual category of 'some other substantial reason of a kind such as to justify the dismissal of an employee holding the position which the employee held'. The words 'other substantial reason' do not have to be construed in a similar manner (ie ejusdem generis) with the other reasons in s 98(1) and (2).[1] Provided the reason is substantial, it is capable of falling within this category. Although potentially open-ended, most of the dismissals which employers seek to justify under this head occur because the trust and confidence between the employer and employee has broken down or the employer is acting to safeguard his business or other interests. It could be that the employee has refused to accept a reorganisation or other changes in work practices, or changes in his terms and conditions of employment (eg placing a restriction on the employee's use of knowledge of a new technical process). If an employee refuses to accept the change, the employer may dismiss him and seek to justify the dismissal as being for the substantial reason of the necessity to protect business interests.[2] Like any other ground for dismissal, the decision to dismiss is subject to considerations of reasonableness as provided in s 98(4).[3]

1 *RS Components Ltd v Irwin* [1974] 1 All ER 41; [1973] ICR 535, NIRC.
2 *RS Components Ltd v Irwin* [1974] 1 All ER 41; [1973] ICR 535; *Bowater Containers Ltd v McCormack* [1980] IRLR 50; *Genower v Ealing, Hammersmith and Hounslow Area Health Authority* [1980] IRLR 297.
3 See *Evans v Elemeta Holdings Ltd* [1982] IRLR 143; *Chubb Fire Security Ltd v Harper* [1983] IRLR 311; *St John of God (Care Services) Ltd v Brooks* [1992] IRLR 546.

15.137 Each case has to be considered in the light of its particular facts. The non-renewal of temporary engagements may fall in this category as could a contention that the employer has not renewed a contract which was always known to be temporary.[1] The sexual orientation of the employee, where it impinges on the employment, may also fall in this category.[2] An employer's belief that the reason was substantial where he dismissed the employee because of facts which he honestly and genuinely but erroneously believed to be true (and which if true would have justified dismissal) was found to satisfy the requirement,[3] as have personality differences,[4] requests by important customers,[5] imprisonment[6] and the imposition of new terms and conditions of employment.[7]

1 *Terry v East Sussex County Council* [1977] 1 All ER 567; [1976] ICR 536; *Fay v North Yorkshire County Council* [1985] IRLR 247.
2 *Saunders v Scottish National Camps Association Ltd* [1980] IRLR 174.
3 *Taylor v Cooperative Retail Services Ltd* [1981] IRLR 1; [1981] ICR 172; *Bouchaala v Trusthouse Forte Hotels Ltd* [1980] IRLR 382; [1980] ICR 721.
4 *Treganowan v Robert Knee & Co Ltd* [1975] IRLR 247; [1975] ICR 405.
5 *Scott Packing & Warehousing Co Ltd v Paterson* [1978] IRLR 166. However, the employer must still show consideration for potential injustice: *Dobie v Burns International Security Services (UK) Ltd* [1984] IRLR 329; [1984] ICR 812, CA.
6 *Kingston v British Railways Board* [1984] IRLR 146, CA.
7 *Catarmaran Cruisers Ltd v Williams* [1994] IRLR 386, EAT.

15.138   There are circumstances where it is expressly provided that a dismissal is to be regarded as dismissal for a substantial reason of a kind such as to justify the dismissal of an employee which the employee held.[1] This occurs when an employer engages an employee having informed him in writing that his employment will be terminated either:
(a)   on the resumption of work of another employee who is, or will be, absent wholly or partly because of pregnancy or childbirth,[2] or
(b)   at the end of a period of suspension of another employee on medical or maternity grounds,[3]
and the employer dismisses him in order to make it possible to give work to the other employee. Such dismissals are not automatically fair; the test of fairness in s 98(4) still has to be applied to ascertain whether the employee was fairly or unfairly dismissed.

1 Employment Rights Act 1996, s 106.
2 Employment Rights Act 1996, s 106.
3 Within the meaning of the Employment Rights Act 1996, Pt VII; s 106(3).

Transfer of undertakings

15.139   When on a transfer of an undertaking an employee is dismissed where the reason, or principal reason, is an economic, technical or organisational reason entailing changes in the workforce, the dismissal is regarded as having been for a substantial reason of a kind such as to justify the dismissal of an employee holding the position which that employee held.[1] Such dismissals are not automatically fair; the test of fairness in s 98(4) has to be applied to ascertain whether the employee was fairly dismissed.

1 Transfer of Undertakings (Protection of Employment) Regulations 1981, reg 8(2). See **12.19–12.22**.

Did the employer act reasonably in the circumstances?

15.140   The determination of the question whether the dismissal was fair, or unfair when the employer has shown that the reason for the dismissal fell within s 98(1) or (2) depends on the application of s 98(4).[1]

1 It should be noted that the original forerunner of the Employment Rights Act 1996, s 98(4) placed the onus of proof on the employer to show that he had acted fairly. This is not the position now, see the comment in *Boys and Girls Welfare Society v McDonald* [1996] IRLR 129, EAT, where the Employment Appeal Tribunal stressed the importance of the change as to the onus of proof. See also *Scottish Daily Record and Sunday Mail v Laird* [1996] IRLR 665, Ct of Sess.

15.141 The tribunal must not substitute its own decision for that of the employers.[1] It should start its consideration of whether the respondents acted fairly by considering the words of s 98.[2] The tribunal should consider whether the dismissal falls within the band of responses in all the circumstances of an employer acting reasonably.[3] This does not mean that very little short of a perverse decision has to be shown for the applicant to succeed.[4] The tribunal should examine the employer's conduct, not whether or not the applicant has suffered injustice.[5]

1 *Iceland Frozen Foods Ltd v Jones* [1982] IRLR 439, EAT; *Union of Construction Allied Trades and Technicians v Brain* [1981] IRLR 224, CA.
2 *Conlin v United Distillers* [1994] IRLR 169, Ct of Sess.
3 *British Leyland (UK) Ltd v Swift* [1981] IRLR 91, CA.
4 *Rentokil Ltd v Mackin* [1989] IRLR 286, EAT.
5 *W Devis & Sons Ltd v Atk ins* [1977] IRLR 314, HL; *Polkey v AE Dayton Services Ltd* [1987] IRLR 503, HL.

15.142 This factor is examined by the industrial tribunal after the reason for the dismissal has been shown to it and in very many cases is the matter of greatest contention before the tribunal. As with so many other factors relating to unfair dismissal, it depends to a large extent on the facts as determined by the tribunal. Each case is looked at in the light of these and although previous decisions may be of assistance they must be treated with caution. All that can be done is to highlight some of those factors which have in previous cases been of relevance in determining the question of reasonableness. The cases which are mentioned were decided under earlier provisions in the Industrial Relations Act 1971, the Trade Union and Labour Relations Act 1974 and the Employment Protection (Consolidation) Act 1978 which were not in the same terms as s 98(4) of the Employment Rights Act 1996.[1] Many of the decisions cited were made on a version of the forerunner of s 98(4) when there was an onus of proof on the employer to show he acted reasonably and this must not be overlooked when considering them.[2]

1 See *Boys and Girls Welfare Society v McDonald* [1996] IRLR 129, EAT.
2 *Boys and Girls Welfare Society v McDonald* [1996] IRLR 129, EAT; *Post Office Counters Ltd v Heavey* [1989] IRLR 513, EAT and see *Scottish Daily Record and Sunday Mail v Laird* [1996] IRLR 665, Ct of Sess.

15.143 The procedure adopted in connection with the dismissal is of considerable importance. An employer should take the procedural steps necessary to justify dismissal.[1] The employer is expected to comply with its own procedure unless there are cogent reasons for departing from it.[2] If there is a procedural defect, this will result in the dismissal being unfair if it is of such seriousness that it results in the dismissal looked at as a whole being unfair.[3]

1 *Polkey v AE Dayton Services Ltd* [1987] IRLR 503, HL.
2 *Stocker v Lancashire County Council* [1992] IRLR 75, CA.
3 *Fuller v Lloyds Bank plc* [1991] IRLR 336, EAT. See also *Westminster City Council v Cabaj* [1996] IRLR 399, CA.

15.144   The tribunal will pay attention to such matters as whether or not codes of practice have been complied with, whether the employee has received warnings of the consequences of continuance or repetition of the conduct upon which the employers seek to rely, whether a warning or warnings were promptly given, the length of time the employee has been employed by the employer, his status and whether the employer acted fairly in the employment situation. Disciplinary procedures may be looked at to see whether they are fair and whether in the circumstances they were properly applied. The interests of both the employer and the employee should be considered.

15.145   The reasons or facts giving rise to the reason for the dismissal should generally be made known to the employee at the time of the dismissal[1] and he should be given an opportunity to explain the reason for his behaviour. However, it is for the tribunal to decide whether the management reasonably came to the decision which it did, and not for the tribunal to impose its own decision on the management.[2] The employer should be seen to have acted fairly and given the employee a reasonable time to set any matters complained of to rights. It will usually be necessary for the employee to have an opportunity of being heard[3] and to explain his behaviour and how it might be remedied. Factors such as the length of time which an employee has worked for the employer,[4] personal factors affecting the employee and all the circumstances are taken into account. Each case is looked at on its merits and the industrial tribunal will apply the test set out in s 98(4) in those circumstances.[5]

1 *Abernethy v Mott Hay and Anderson* [1974] ICR 323, CA; *St Anne's Board Mill Co Ltd v Brien* [1973] ICR 444, NIRC.
2 *Grundy (Teddington) Ltd v Willis* [1976] ICR 323, DC; *Vickers Ltd v Smith* [1977] IRLR 11, EAT; *Mitchell v Old Horse Exchange and Palantine Club Ltd* [1978] IRLR 160, EAT.
3 *Jamieson v Aberdeen County Council* [1975] IRLR 348, Ct of Sess.
4 *Tiptools Ltd v Curtis* [1973] IRLR 276, NIRC.
5 *Hollister v National Farmers Union* [1979] ICR 542, CA.

15.146   Although each case must be looked at in the light of its own particular circumstances the matters mentioned below have been regarded as of particular importance.

Codes of practice

15.147   Great importance is attached to the codes of practice issued pursuant to employment legislation (for relevant provisions of the codes, see Appendix 3). Whilst not legally binding on the parties, a failure on the part of any person to observe any provision of a code of practice which is for the time being in force whilst not rendering the party liable in the proceedings, is admissible in evidence before industrial tribunals. Any provision of a code which appears to the tribunal to be relevant to any question which arises should be taken into account by the tribunal in determining that question.[1] The obligation is for the industrial tribunal to take into account the provisions of the codes of practice; this does not mean that because a code has not been complied with to the letter the dismissal is unfair.

1 Trade Union and Labour Relations (Consolidation) Act 1992, s 207; *Lowndes v Specialist Heavy Engineering Ltd* [1977] ICR 1, EAT; *Courtney v Babcock and Wilcox (Operations) Ltd* [1977] IRLR 30, EAT. See also *Dacres v Walls Meat Co Ltd* [1976] ICR 44, QBD; *Mansfield Hosiery Mills Ltd v Bromley* [1977] IRLR 301, EAT.

Disciplinary and grievance procedures

15.148 In many cases the industrial tribunal will look at the grievance or disciplinary procedures adopted by the employers to see if appropriate procedures have been made available to the dismissed employee and whether or not they have been properly applied. The absence of a disciplinary procedure as recommended by the code of practice does not of itself make the dismissal unfair.[1] As in other areas of unfair dismissal the facts of the individual case are gone into. If there is a procedure, it should be followed properly but there is no automatic right to an oral hearing. What is required is that the employer should know the complaints against him, have an opportunity to state his case and those deciding on the dismissal and the appeals committee should take their decisions in good faith.[2]

1 *Ayanlowo v IRC* [1975] IRLR 253, CA; *Ladbroke Racing Ltd v Arnott* [1979] IRLR 192, EAT. Industrial tribunals must not overlook the words of the statute when considering dismissals procedures; *Hollister v National Farmers Union* [1979] ICR 542, CA.
2 Guidelines for the conduct of a disciplinary hearing appear in *Clark v Civil Aviation Authority* [1991] IRLR 412, EAT.

15.149 Disciplinary procedures usually contain a right of appeal for the dismissed employee. Again, the absence of an appeal procedure does not automatically render a dismissal unfair. It is just one of the many factors which the tribunal should take into account when deciding if the employer acted fairly.[1] If the employee is contractually entitled to the right to appeal and is not allowed to do so by the employer, the employer may well be acting unfairly.[2] A procedural defect at the initial disciplinary hearing can be corrected by an appeal in the nature of a rehearing,[3] but not if the person conducting the appeal is a judge in his own cause.[4] An applicant who did not appeal did not thereby acquiesce in his dismissal.[5]

1 *Shannon v Michelin (Belfast) Ltd* [1981] IRLR 505, NICA; *Rowe v Radio Rentals Ltd* [1982] IRLR 177, EAT.
2 *West Midlands Co-operative Society Ltd v Tipton* [1986] IRLR 112, HL.
3 *Sartor v P&O European Ferries (Felixstowe) Ltd* [1992] IRLR 271, CA; but not if by way of review only.
4 *Byrne v BOC Ltd* [1992] IRLR 505, EAT.
5 *Chrystie v Rolls-Royce (1971) Ltd* [1976] IRLR 336, EAT.

Consistency

15.150 The conduct of the employer may be examined to ascertain whether he has acted consistently in dealing with other employees who have behaved similarly to the applicant. This arises from the use of the word 'equity' in s 98(4).[1] However, the individual case should be looked at carefully. A dismissal is not unfair solely because of a breach of a contractual disciplinary procedure.[2] A consistent approach to misconduct or other failure by employees (or the lack of it) is a factor to be taken into account, but employers and tribunals should be careful not to adopt a 'tariff' approach to misconduct.[3] An employer who has an established practice of dealing with types of misconduct in certain ways should not change this without warning. The employer can take into account not merely the misconduct but the surrounding and personal circumstances of the employee,[4] and in doing so it should consider the position of the employees being compared.[5]

1 *Post Office v Fennell* [1981] IRLR 221, CA.
2 *Westminster City Council v Cabaj* [1996] IRLR 399, CA; *Blundell v Christie Hospital National Health Service Trust* [1996] ICR 347, EAT.

3 *Hadjioannous v Coral Casinos Ltd* [1981] IRLR 352, EAT. The tribunal has to decide whether an employer could reasonably have treated the employees differently: *Securicor Ltd v Smith* [1989] IRLR 356, CA.
4 *Paul v East Sussex District Health Authority* [1995] IRLR 305, CA; *Harrow London Borough v Cunningham* [1996] IRLR 256, EAT.
5 *Wood v Coverage Care Ltd* [1996] IRLR 264, EAT.

Warnings

15.151   The code of practice lays great stress on warnings and they are clearly of great importance if an employer is to contend that a dismissal is fair. Warnings may not be necessary where the employer could have reasonably concluded a warning would be utterly useless[1]; if it is likely that they would have had an effect on the employee's conduct then industrial tribunals regard them of the utmost importance. In such cases whether an employee has been given a warning is a matter of substance and not one of procedure alone.[2] The fact that warnings have been given and their number and nature are factors which a tribunal is entitled to take into account in reaching its decision.[3] Where a warning taken into account at the time of the dismissal decision is itself the subject of appeal, it is likely this will be taken into account when the tribunal decides whether or not the employer has acted reasonably.[4] Although each case must depend upon its own particular facts, warnings are unlikely to be restricted solely to cases where there has been misconduct.[5] There may be some matters which are so obviously most serious that a warning is unnecessary.[6]

1 *Polkey v AE Dayton Services Ltd* [1987] IRLR 503, HL.
2 *AJ Dunning & Sons (Shop Fitters) Ltd v Jacomb* [1973] ICR 448, NIRC. For codes of practice, see Appendix 3.
3 *Auguste Noel Ltd v Curtis* [1990] IRLR 326, EAT.
4 *Tower Hamlets Health Authority v Anthony* [1989] IRLR 394, CA.
5 *Winterhalter Gastronom Ltd v Webb* [1973] ICR 245, NIRC; *Judge International Ltd v Moss* [1973] IRLR 208, NIRC; *Retarded Children's Aid Society v Day* [1978] 1 WLR 763; [1978] ICR 437, CA; *McPhail v Gibson* [1977] ICR 42, EAT;
6 *Ulsterbus Ltd v Henderson* [1989] IRLR 251, NICA.

Pressure on an employer to dismiss unfairly

15.152   Section 107 of the Employment Rights Act 1996 provides:
   '107. – (1) This section applies where there falls to be determined for the purposes of [the unfair dismissal provisions] a question—
      (a)   as to the reason, or principal reason, for which an employee was dismissed,
      (b)   whether the reason or principal reason for which an employee was dismissed was a reason fulfilling the requirement of section 98(1)(b), or
      (c)   whether an employer acted reasonably in treating the reason or principal reason for which an employee was dismissed as a sufficient reason for dismissing him.

   (2)   In determining the question no account shall be taken of any pressure which by calling, organising, procuring or financing a strike or other industrial action, or threatening to do so, was exercised on the employer to dismiss the employee; and the question shall be determined as if no such pressure had been exercised.'

15.153   Upon making a decision on the application of an employee claiming that he has been unfairly dismissed the industrial tribunal ignores any pressure of the type to which s 107 relates.[1] It is not necessary for the employee to show that those exerting pressure on the employer explicitly seek the employee's dismissal. Conduct short of that may amount to pressure to dismiss. The appropriate test in deciding whether such pressure has been exerted is whether the pressure on the employers is such that it can be foreseen that it is likely to result in the employee's dismissal.[2]

1 If the pressure is the only reason for the dismissal then it must be unfair: *Hazell Offsets Ltd v Luckett* [1977] IRLR 430, EAT.
2 *Ford Motor Co Ltd v Hudson* [1978] ICR 482, EAT.

Complaints to industrial tribunals

15.154 A person alleging that he was unfairly dismissed may present a complaint against an employer to an industrial tribunal.[1] When the dismissal is with notice, the complaint may be presented after the notice is given notwithstanding that it is presented before the effective date of termination.[2] In these circumstances the provisions of the Act are construed as if references to dismissal, reinstatement, effective date of termination and the employee ceasing to be employed are altered appropriately.[3]

1 Employment Rights Act 1996, s 111(1). For a discussion of the role of conciliation officers, see **18.17–18.18.** For the relationship between complaints under the unfair dismissal provisions and under the Sex Discrimination Act 1975, the Race Relations Act 1976, the Disability Discrimination Act 1995 and for breach of contract, see **17.10–17.20.**
2 Employment Rights Act 1996, s 111(3). This applies on a termination by notice not on the occasion of a prior indication that a fixed term will not be renewed; *Throsby v Imperial College of Science and Technology* [1979] IRLR 114, CA. It is not limited to notice by the employer but may apply to a situation where the employee terminates the contract when he has been 'constructively dismissed': *Presley v Llanelli Borough Council* [1979] ICR 419, EAT.
3 Employment Rights Act 1996, s 111(4).

Time limit

15.155 The time limit for presenting complaints of unfair dismissal is crucial. It goes to the jurisdiction of the industrial tribunal to hear the application and is very short.

15.156 Section 111(2) and (3) of the Employment Rights Act 1996 state:
'(2) Subject to subsection (3), an industrial tribunal shall not consider a complaint... unless it is presented to the tribunal—
  (a) before the end of the period of three months beginning with the effective date of termination, or
  (b) within such further period as the tribunal considers reasonable in a case where it is satisfied that it was not reasonably practicable for the complaint to be presented before the end of that period of three months.

(3) Where a dismissal is with notice, an industrial tribunal shall consider a complaint under this section if it is presented after the notice is given but before the effective date of termination.'

15.157 In view of the time limit it is essential that complaints claiming remedies for unfair dismissal are presented to industrial tribunals as soon as possible. The requirement is jurisdictional and so cannot be waived by the parties.[1] A complaint is presented to the industrial tribunal when the originating application is received by the tribunal office.[2] If the application is sent by post, and is delayed in reaching the office, the tribunal will consider whether, taking into account the class of postage, the application could reasonably have been expected to arrive in time.[3]

1 *Rogers v Bodfari (Transport) Ltd* [1973] ICR 325, NIRC; *Hammond v Haigh Castle & Co Ltd* [1973] 2 All ER 289; [1973] ICR 148, NIRC.
2 *Hammond v Haigh Castle & Co Ltd* [1973] 2 All ER 289; [1973] ICR 148, NIRC.
3 *St Basil's Centre v McCrossan* [1991] IRLR 455, EAT. It is reasonable for tribunals to follow the Queen's Bench Practice Direction which indicated that for first class delivery subject to proof to the contrary first class post will be taken as arriving the second working day after posting and second class post will be taken as arriving the fourth working day after posting. See also *Capital Foods Retail Ltd v Corrigan* [1993] IRLR 430, EAT, and *Camden and Islington NHS Trust v Kennedy* [1996] IRLR 381, EAT.

15.158 The three-month period begins with and includes the whole of the effective date of termination, so that it expires on the date three months after the date prior to the effective date of termination, ie if the dismissal takes place on 20 June the period terminates on 19 September.[1] What is required is that the application arrives during the three-month period. The time runs from the date of dismissal even though at the time it was thought there was no right to claim.[2] The three-month time limit does not apply to adding a new respondent outside the period to a claim which was made in time.[3]

1 *Hammond v Haigh Castle & Co Ltd* [1973] 2 All ER 289; [1973] ICR 148, NIRC; *Pruden v Cunard Ellerman Ltd* [1993] IRLR 317, EAT. The claim should not be delayed were there is a domestic appeals or conciliation procedure: *Palmer v Southend on Sea Borough Council* [1984] ICR 372, CA. If the contract of employment continues during the appeals procedure there is no termination until the procedure is exhausted; *High v British Railways Board* [1979] IRLR 52, EAT.
2 *Biggs v Somerset County Council* [1996] IRLR 203, CA.
3 *Gillick v BP Chemicals Ltd* [1993] IRLR 437, EAT.

15.159 The words 'it was not reasonably practicable' have given rise to considerable difficulties. If an employee seeks to present a complaint out of time, the onus of proof is on him to satisfy the industrial tribunal that he did not know of his rights during the whole of the period and that there was no reason why he should have been put on enquiry.[1] May LJ has said the question that should be asked is whether it was reasonably feasible to present the complaint to the industrial tribunal within the relevant three months.[2] The Court of Appeal had to consider the provisions of the Industrial Relations Act 1971 which differed slightly in that the word 'reasonably' did not appear in *Dedman v British Building and Engineering Appliances Ltd*.[3] The employee, after his dismissal, knew he had rights under the unfair dismissal provisions, but did not know of the time limit in which to present the complaint (then four weeks). Approximately 14 days after the effective date of termination the employee consulted his legal advisers who did not advise him to make the complaint within the necessary period. The complaint was not made until seven weeks after the effective date of termination. Lord Denning MR explained the tests to be applied (at p 526), as follows:

'Summing up, I would suggest that in every case the tribunal should enquire into the circumstances and ask themselves whether the man or his advisers were at fault in allowing the four weeks to pass by without presenting the complaint. If he was not at fault, nor his advisers – so that he had just cause or excuse for not presenting his complaint within the four weeks – then it was "not practicable" for him to present it within that time. The court has then a discretion to allow it to be presented out of time, if it thinks it right to do so. But, if he was at fault, or is his advisers were at fault, in allowing the four weeks to slip by, he must take the consequences. By exercising reasonable diligence, the complaint could and should have been presented in time.'

Scarman LJ concurred in that approach, but Stamp LJ dissented on this point. Mr Dedman had consulted his lawyers during the period and so it was practicable for the complaint to be presented and the tribunal did not have jurisdiction.

1 *Porter v Bandridge Ltd* [1978] 1 WLR 1145; [1978] ICR 943, CA.
2 In *Palmer v Southend on Sea Borough Council* [1984] ICR 372, CA.
3 [1974] 1 All ER 520, CA, but see the dissenting judgments of Ormerod LJ and that of Shaw LJ in *Walls Meat Co Ltd v Khan* [1978] IRLR 499, CA. Although each case turns on its own facts there have been cases where it has been held that trade union officials and Citizens Advice Bureaux have been treated as skilled advisers; *Riley v Tesco Stores Ltd* [1979] ICR 223, EAT; *Harvey's Household Linens Ltd v Benson* [1974] ICR 306, NIRC; *W Press & Son Ltd v Hall* [1974] ICR 21, NIRC. 'Astonishing ignorance' was held not to be sufficient excuse in *Avon County Council v Haywood-Hicks* [1978] ICR 646, EAT. If the applicant claims that there is a reasonable excuse for the delay, or that his advisers should have the opportunity to explain why it was not reasonably practicable to present the complaint in time, the applicant should call the advisers to give evidence: *Riley v Tesco Stores Ltd* (above).

15.160   It is important to note that the test is applied in two stages. First, the tribunal has to decide whether it was reasonably practicable for the complaint to be presented in time, and secondly, if it was not, the tribunal determines if it was presented within a reasonable period thereafter. Although the wording of s 111(2) of the Employment Rights Act 1996 differs slightly from that in corresponding provisions in the Employment Protection (Consolidation) Act 1978 and the Industrial Relations Act 1971 a similar approach is likely to be adopted.[1]

1 See *Walls Meat Co Ltd v Khan* [1978] IRLR 499, CA.

15.161   In the case of *Wall's Meat Co Ltd v Khan*[1] Lord Denning MR said he: 'would venture to take the simple test given by the majority in *Dedman's* case. It is simply to ask this question: Had the man just cause or excuse for not presenting his complaint within the prescribed time? Ignorance of his rights – or ignorance of the time limit – is not just cause or excuse, unless it appears that he or his advisers could not reasonably be expected to have been aware of them. If he or his advisers could reasonably have been so expected, it was his or their fault, and he must take the consequences. That was the view adopted by the Employment Appeal Tribunal in Scotland in *House of Clydesdale Ltd v Foy*[2] and in England in *Times Newspapers v O'Regan*[3] – decisions with which I agree.'

Mr Khan was dismissed and proceedings were commenced for his case to be heard by the local tribunal under the National Insurance Acts. Mr Khan knew of the unfair dismissals legislation before the end of the three-month period but wrongly thought that it was being dealt with. It was not until the local tribunal determined his case that he found that his claim for unfair dismissal could not be prosecuted before that forum. Mr Khan acted fairly promptly after that and applied to an industrial tribunal. The industrial tribunal held that he was not barred by the time limit and their decision was affirmed by the Court of Appeal.

1 [1978] IRLR 499 at p 500.

2 [1976] IRLR 391.
3 [1977] IRLR 101.

15.162 Ignorance of a fact which is essential to the claim may be a reason for it not being reasonably practicable to present the claim in time.[1]

1 *Machine Tool Industry Research Association Ltd v Simpson* [1988] ICR 558, CA; *Churchill v Yeates & Sons Ltd* [1983] ICR 380, EAT; *Marley (UK) Ltd v Anderson* [1996] IRLR 163, CA.

15.163 Particular difficulties arise where the ex-employee was dismissed for theft or some other criminal offence and criminal proceedings are instituted. Often the applicant does not make a claim for a remedy for unfair dismissal until outside the time period, perhaps not until he has been acquitted. Such a case was considered in *Porter v Bandridge Ltd*[1] Waller LJ said:

'When a man is dismissed for stealing there are three possible situations. The first is that he is completely innocent – it was a terrible mistake. The second is that he is guilty. And the third is that he has done something which, while not quite in accordance with the rules of his employers, is not stealing and is not dishonest. As it seems to me, in the first case the man would do everything in his power to obtain redress and it would be astonishing if he had not started proceedings for unfair dismissal within a comparatively short time and well within the period of three months. In the second case, on the assumption that he was not going to plead guilty when tried, the probability is that no proceedings for unfair dismissal would be started and that it would only be after an acquittal that proceedings would be thought to be worth trying. In those circumstances they would be much too late. In the third case the man is innocent but has broken some rule of the establishment. As a result of their complaint he is being prosecuted for stealing. I find it difficult to believe that he would not behave very much as the first man. As it seems to me he would wish to establish as soon as possible that what was really only a technical mistake was not dishonest. He would wish to take steps against his employer to show that was so. I would expect this man to take proceedings quickly. It is in this last category that the appellant in this case falls, because his defence is that he was doing something that he had done on a previous occasion that there was no dishonesty involved, that he was taking the clock for somebody he knew and that he would be paying for it in due course. He would, of course, have to explain the absence of any documentation, but the sooner he took steps to do this the more likely he would be to succeed both in showing that there was no dishonesty and in showing that he had been unfairly dismissed. I would have thought that there was only one answer to a delay of the dimension of this eleven months, namely that the appellant was put on enquiry or, alternatively, certainly ought to have known and, were it not that I know that a different view is taken in this case, I would have thought the view taken by the Industrial Tribunal and the Employment Appeal Tribunal was the only possible view on the facts.'

1 [1978] IRLR 271 at p 273, CA.

15.164 When deciding whether a late application can be entertained the tribunal should clearly differentiate between the two parts of the enquiry set out above. In coming to a decision whether it was reasonably practicable to present the application within the period, events which take place afterwards are irrelevant. The tribunal should consider all the relevant facts and apply a 'strict but common sense approach' to the questions.[1] The finding whether or not it was practicable to present the claim in time is a finding of fact. Accordingly appeals against the decision of the industrial tribunal will rarely succeed. When the tribunal finds that it was not reasonably practicable to present the complaint in time, the second part of the enquiry involves the tribunal exercising its discretion whether, or not, to entertain the complaint out of time. There are no time limits on what can be the reasonable period after the initial three-month period.[2]

1 Per Kilner Brown J in *Crown Agents for Overseas Governments and Administration v Lawal* [1978] IRLR 542 at p 544, EAT.
2 *Marley (UK) Ltd v Anderson* [1994] IRLR 152, EAT.

15.165 Lord Denning MR said in *Khan's* case[1] that there is a danger in referring to too many decided cases when considering the subsection. Each case turns very much on its own facts and the industrial tribunal should come to a conclusion having ascertained the facts of the case before it and applying the rules set out above. It should be noted that the important date is when the claim is presented to the industrial tribunal and presentation takes place when the originating application is received by an Office of Industrial Tribunals.[2]

1 *Walls Meat Co Ltd v Khan* [1978] IRLR 499, CA.
2 *Anglo Continental School of English (Bournemouth) Ltd v Gardiner* [1973] ICR 261, NIRC.

15.166 As a matter of practice, in view of the provisions of s 116 of the Employment Rights Act 1996 it should be stated in the originating application whether or not the applicant wishes to be reinstated or re-engaged if the tribunal finds the grounds of the complaint well founded. The forms at present available from Job Centres and the Regional Offices of Industrial Tribunals make provision for this (see **18.20–18.23**).

Interim relief

15.167 The provisions for interim relief must be considered in appropriate cases and the very short time limits and strict procedural requirements taken into account (see **15.168**). Tribunals have an accelerated procedure for dealing with such cases (see **18.13**).

Remedies for unfair dismissal

Interim relief

15.168 Interim relief may be granted by the tribunal where the employee complains that he has been unfairly dismissed and the reason (or if more than one, the principal reason) is a specified health and safety reason,[1] relates to trusteeship of an occupational pension scheme[2] or relates to activities of an employee representative or candidate employee representative.[3] The provisions as to the procedure for applying for interim relief and also the order for continuation of the contract of employment are similar to those where the applicant claims the reason for the dismissal is trade union membership or activities.[4] In particular the claim must be presented to the tribunal within seven days of the effective date of termination.[5]

15.168   *Unfair dismissal*

1 Specified in the Employment Rights Act 1996, s 100(1) (a) and (b).
2 Specified in the Employment Rights Act 1996, s 102(1).
3 Specified in the Employment Rights Act 1996, s 103.
4 For these purposes they are contained in the Employment Rights Act 1996, ss 128, 129 and 130. See also ss 131 and 132.
5 Employment Rights Act 1996, s 128(2).

Reinstatement and re-engagement

15.169   Having found that a complaint of unfair dismissal was well founded, the tribunal will go on to consider the appropriate remedy to be awarded in favour of the applicant.[1]

1 For interim relief and special awards in the case of dismissals related to trade union membership and activities, see **14.33**.

15.170   The tribunal will explain to the former employee the meaning of orders for reinstatement and re-engagement and ask him whether he wishes such an order to be made.[1] Only if he does can the tribunal make such an order; otherwise the tribunal will go on to consider compensation. A failure to indicate a desire for an order on his originating application form does not prevent the employee requesting it at the hearing.

1 Employment Rights Act 1996, s 112(2). This must be done even if the claimant is professionally represented; *Pirelli General Cable Works Ltd v Murray* [1979] IRLR 190, EAT. A failure to follow the procedure does not make an award of compensation a nullity. The order for compensation can be set aside if the failure to comply with the procedure has led to a possibility of injustice or unfairness; *Cowley v Manson Timber Ltd* [1995] IRLR 153, CA.

Reinstatement

15.171   An order for reinstatement is 'an order that the employer shall treat the complainant in all respects as if he had not been dismissed'.[1] All previous contractual rights must be restored to the applicant and he must be given the additional benefit of any improvement in his job conditions (eg pay rises) which occurred whilst he was dismissed, with effect from the date on which he would have received them if his working had been un-interrupted. In making such an order, the tribunal will specify any such contractual rights to be restored; the amount payable by the employer in respect of any such benefit; and the date by which the order must be complied with.

1 Employment Rights Act 1996, s 114(1).

Re-engagement

15.172   An order for re-engagement is much wider. It 'is an order, on such terms as the tribunal may decide, that the complainant be engaged by the employer, or by a successor of the employer or by an associated employer, in employment comparable to that from which he was dismissed or other suit-able employment'.[1] The employee's re-engagement may be with an employer who succeeded, or is associated with, the dismissing employer. The job itself may be different from the former one provided that it satisfies the statutory test. In making a re-engagement order, the tribunal will specify the identity of the employer, the nature of the employment, the remuneration, the amount payable in respect of benefits missed during the period of dismissal, the restoration of any rights and privileges and the date by which the order must be complied with.[2] So far as reasonably practicable, these terms must be 'as favourable as an order for reinstatement'.[3]

1 Employment Rights Act 1996, s 115(1).
2 Employment Rights Act 1996, s 115(2). See also *Electronic Data Processing Ltd v Wright* [1986] IRLR 8, [1986] ICR 76.
3 Employment Rights Act 1996, s 116(4), except where the tribunal takes into account contributory fault.

15.173 The tribunal has a discretion in deciding whether either order is appropriate.

15.174 In exercising its discretion the industrial tribunal should first consider whether to order reinstatement. In so doing, the tribunal should take into account whether the employee wishes to be reinstated; whether it is practicable for the employer to comply with an order for reinstatement; and where the complainant caused or contributed to some extent to his dismissal, whether it would be just and equitable to order reinstatement.[1] These reasons for refusing to make an order are exhaustively set out in the Employment Rights Act. An industrial tribunal should not add 'expediency' to the list.[2]

1 Employment Rights Act 1996, s 116(1).
2 *Qualcast (Wolverhampton) Ltd v Ross* [1979] ICR 386.

Terms of the orders

15.175 If it makes a reinstatement order the tribunal will specify:
'(a) any amount payable by the employer in respect of any benefit which the complainant might reasonably be expected to have had but for the dismissal (including arrears of pay) for the period between the date of termination of employment and the date of reinstatement,
(b) any rights and privileges (including seniority and pension rights) which must be restored to the employee, and
(c) the date by which the order must be complied with.'[1]
If the complainant would have benefited from an improvement in his terms and conditions of employment had he not been dismissed, an order for reinstatement will require him to be treated as if he had benefited from that improvement from the date on which he would have done so but for being dismissed.[2]

1 Employment Rights Act 1996, s 114(2).
2 Employment Rights Act 1996, s 114(3).

15.176 If the tribunal decides not to make an order for reinstatement, it will consider whether to make an order for re-engagement and if so on what terms.[1] In so doing the tribunal will take into account any wish expressed by the complainant as to the nature of the order to be made; whether it is practicable for the employer (or a successor or an associated employer) to comply with an order for re-engagement; and where the employee caused, or contributed to some extent to, his dismissal whether it would be just to order re-engagement and (if so) on what terms.[2]

1 Employment Rights Act 1996, s 116(2).
2 Employment Rights Act 1996, s 116(3).

15.177 The re-engagement order will specify the terms on which re-engagement is to take place, including:

'(a) the identity of the employer,
(b) the nature of the employment,
(c) the remuneration for the employment,
(d) any amount payable by the employer in respect of any benefit which the complainant might reasonably be expected to have had but for the dismissal (including arrears of pay) for the period between the date of termination of employment and the date of re-engagement,
(e) any rights and privileges (including seniority and pension rights) which must be restored to the employee, and
(f) the date by which the order must be complied with'.[1]

1 Employment Rights Act 1996, s 115(2).

Practicability

15.178 Considerations of practicability may arise at two stages when considering reinstatement or re-engagement orders. The first is when exercising the discretion whether or not to make an order for reinstatement or re-engagement. As will be seen, the second occurs when an order has been made which is not complied with. This two-stage consideration of practicability has been construed as allowing an industrial tribunal to make an order for reinstatement or re-engagement providing it was thought that it stood some chance of success.[1] If the employer succeeds in showing at either stage that the order was not practicable, the tribunal will move on to consider compensation in the usual way.

1 *Timex Corpn v Thomson* [1981] IRLR 522; *Port of London Authority v Payne* [1994] IRLR 9, CA.

15.179 Practicability should be looked at in a subjective and pragmatic way. Factors considered by tribunals as rendering it impracticable to make an order have included a poisoned atmosphere in the workplace,[1] a distrustful employee likely to make a poor worker,[2] and lack of trust in the employee in a job which involves contact with the public.[3] When dealing with a small employer, special consideration may be given to the closeness of the personal relationship between the employer and employee.[4]

1 *Meridian Ltd v Gomersall* [1977] ICR 597, EAT.
2 *Nothman v London Borough of Barnet (No 2)* [1980] IRLR 65, CA.
3 *ILEA v Gravett* [1988] IRLR 497.
4 *Enessy Co SA (t/a the Tulchen Estate) v Minoprio & Minoprio* [1978] IRLR 489, EAT.

15.180 In determining the practicability of compliance with an order for reinstatement or re-engagement, the tribunal may not take into account the fact that the employer has engaged a permanent replacement for the dismissed employee, unless the employer shows that it was not practicable for him to arrange for the dismissed employee's work to be done without engaging a permanent replacement. The only other exception is where the employer has engaged the replacement after the lapse of a reasonable period, without having heard from the dismissed employee that he wished to be reinstated or re-engaged, and when the employer engaged the replacement, it was no longer reasonable for him to arrange for the dismissed employee's work to done except by a permanent replacement.[1]

1 Employment Rights Act 1996, s 116(5) and (6).

Payment to the employee

15.181 Once an order for reinstatement or re-engagement has been made, the terms of the order require that an employee receives all payment he could reasonably have expected from the employment, including arrears of pay, from the date of dismissal to the date of reinstatement or re-engagement, unless the industrial tribunal finds that the employee contributed to his dismissal. If the employee has been found to have contributed to his dismissal, there is no obligation on the tribunal to ensure that the terms of re-engagement are as favourable as in an order for reinstatement.

15.182 For the purposes of calculating the amounts ordered to be paid by the employer when reinstatement and re-engagement orders are made the tribunal will take into account, so as to reduce the employer's liability, any sums received by the complainant in respect of the period between the date of termination of employment and the date of reinstatement or re-engagement by way of:
(1) wages in lieu of notice or ex gratia payments paid by the employer, or
(2) remuneration paid in respect of employment with another employer,
and such other benefits as the tribunal thinks appropriate in the circumstances.[1]

1 Employment Rights Act 1996, ss 114(4) and 115(3).

15.183 The quantification of the amount payable by the employer is not stated as a lump sum, but the order refers to rates of pay or other some formulae, so that the due amount can be calculated when the precise date of reinstatement or re-engagement is known.[1] Credit must be given for sums received by the employee in the period of the dismissal by way of wages in lieu of notice or ex gratia payments,[2] remuneration from employment with another employer and such other benefits as the tribunal considers appropriate. However, the payment should not be reduced by notional amounts which an employer might have received had she mitigated her loss.[3]

1 *O'Laoire v Jackel International Ltd* [1990] IRLR 70; [1990] ICR 197, CA.
2 *Darr v LRC Products Ltd* [1993] IRLR 257.
3 *City and Hackney Health Authority v Crisp* [1990] IRLR 47; [1990] ICR 95.

Failure to comply with the order

15.184 Where an order has been made and the complainant is reinstated or re-engaged and the terms are not fully complied with, the tribunal awards compensation of the amount as it thinks fit having regard to the loss sustained by the complainant in consequence of the failure to comply fully with the terms of the order.[1] In some cases of purported reinstatement or re-engagement, the conditions actually afforded the employee may be so inferior to those ordered as to amount to a failure to reinstate or re-engage at all, and should be so treated.[2]

1 Employment Rights Act 1996, s 117(2), subject to the statutory maximum for the compensatory award contained in the Employment Rights Act 1996, s 124.
2 *Artisan Press Ltd v Srawley & Parker* [1986] IRLR 126, EAT.

15.185 If the employee has not been reinstated or re-engaged in accordance with the order, the tribunal will assess compensation in the normal way. In addition it will consider whether to make an 'additional award' in favour of the complainant. It will make the additional award unless the employer satisfies the tribunal that it was not practicable to comply with the order. It will not do so if the reason (or principal reason) for dismissing the employee or selecting an employee for dismissal by reason of redundancy was a health and safety reason,[1] related to the employee's functions as a trustee of an occupational pensions scheme,[2] or was because the employee performed the functions of a representative.[3] In these circumstances it may make a special award, see **15.219**.

1 Ie specified in the Employment Rights Act 1996, s 100(1)(a) and (b).
2 Ie specified in the Employment Rights Act 1996, s 102(1).
3 Ie specified in the Employment Rights Act 1996, s 103.

15.186   Where an industrial tribunal finds that the complainant has unreasonably prevented the order for reinstatement or re-engagement from being complied with, in making the award of compensation for unfair dismissal in accordance with the usual rules, the tribunal will take that conduct into account as a failure on the part of the complainant to mitigate his loss.[1] In such circumstances it is likely that an additional award will not be made because it was not practicable for the employer to comply with the order.

1 Employment Rights Act 1996, 117(8).

The additional award

15.187   The amount of the additional award of compensation depends on the reason for dismissal. Where the dismissal is an act of discrimination under either the Sex Discrimination 1975 or the Race Relations Act 1976 the amount of the additional compensation will be an amount of not less than 26, nor more than 52, weeks' pay. In any other case, the range is between 13 and 26 weeks' pay.[1] The amount of the 'week's pay' is calculated in accordance with the usual rules in the Employment Rights Act 1996 (see **15.52–15.58**) subject to a maximum (currently £210). Where dismissal is for trade union or certain health and safety, occupational pension scheme and 'representative' related reasons, the tribunal may also award a 'special award' (see **15.219**).

1 Employment Rights Act 1996, s 117(5) and (6).

15.188   In assessing the additional award within the appropriate band, the tribunal has a wide discretion. The exercise of the discretion should reflect the purpose of the award, ie to provide a general solatium rather than a precisely calculated substitute for financial loss.[1] It is not intended to cover matters adequately covered in the compensatory award, nor merely to cover any additional loss suffered by the failure to reinstate or re-engage. The employer's conduct should be reflected in the award, so that deliberate refusal to comply with the order is likely to be met with a higher award than a genuine belief of good reason for non-compliance.

1 *Mabirizi v National Hospital for Nervous Diseases* [1990] IRLR 133; [1990] ICR 281.

Compensation

15.189   If the industrial tribunal finds that the complainant was unfairly dismissed and no order is made for reinstatement or re-egagement, or such an order has been made but the complainant is not in fact reinstated or re-engaged in accordance with the order, the tribunal will make an award of compensation for unfair dismissal.[1] The award of compensation consists of the basic award and a compensatory award.[2] An additional award or special award may also be made (see **15.187–15.188**). If the dismissal was automatically unfair for trade union reasons, there may be a special award (see **15.219**). When the complainant has unreasonably prevented an order for reinstatement or re-engagement from being complied with the industrial tribunal will take this conduct into account as a failure on the part of the complainant to mitigate his loss.[3]

1 Employment Rights Act 1996, ss 112(4) and 117(3).
2 See **15.194–15.218**.
3 Employment Rights Act 1996, s 117(8).

Basic award

15.190   The rules as to calculation of the basic award are set out in s 119 of the Employment Rights Act 1996 which reads:

'**119.** – (1) Subject to the provisions of this section, sections 120 to 122 and section 126, the amount of the basic award shall be calculated by—

(a)   determining the period, ending with the effective date of termination, during which the employee has been continuously employed,

(b)   reckoning backwards from the end of that period the number of years of employment falling within that period, and

(c)   allowing the appropriate amount for each of those years of employment.

(2)   In subsection (1)(c) 'the appropriate amount' means—

(a)   one and a half weeks' pay for a year of employment in which the employee was not below the age of forty-one,

(b)   one week's pay for a year of employment (not within paragraph (a)) in which he was not below the age of twenty-two, and

(c)   half a week's pay for a year of employment not within paragraph (a) or (b).

(3)   Where twenty years of employment have been reckoned under subsection (1), no account shall be taken under that subsection of any year of employment earlier than those twenty years.

(4)   Where the effective date of termination is after the sixty-fourth anniversary of the day of the employee's birth, the amount arrived at under subsections (1) to (3) shall be reduced by the appropriate fraction.

(5)   In subsection (4) 'the appropriate fraction' means the fraction of which—

(a)   the numerator is the number of whole months reckoned from the sixty-fourth anniversary of the day of the employee's birth in the period beginning with that anniversary and ending with the effective date of termination, and

(b)   the denominator is twelve.

(6)   Subsections (4) and (5) do not apply to a case within section 96(1).'[1]

1 A week's pay is as defined in Employment Rights Act 1996, Pt XIV, see **11.48–11.58**. It is subject to the statutory maximum, currently £210, see **11.59**. For a table assisting with the calculation of the basic award, see Appendix 4. It is to be noted that the method of calculation is similar to that for redundancy payments, but there is no lower age limit for the basic award.

Special cases affecting the basic award

15.191   The amount of the basic award (before any reduction under s 122) will not be less than £2,770[1] where the reason (or, if more than one, the principal reason) in a redundancy case, for selecting the employee for dismissal, or otherwise, for the dismissal, is a specified health and safety reason,[2] relates to trusteeship of an occupational pension scheme[3] or relates to activities of an employee representative or candidate employee representative.[4] There is a similar position where the reason for the dismissal is trade union membership or activities (see **14.33**).

1 The Secretary of State may by order increase the sum of £2,770: Employment Rights Act 1996, s 120.
2 Specified in the Employment Rights Act 1996, s 100(1)(a) and (b).
3 Specified in the Employment Rights Act 1996, s 102(1).
4 Specified in the Employment Rights Act 1996, s 103.

15.192   The amount of the basic award is two weeks' pay in certain cases where the tribunal finds that the reason (or, where there is more than one, the principal reason) for the dismissal of the employee is that he was redundant and the employee is not entitled to a redundancy payment by virtue of the provisions as to renewal or re-engagement.[1]

1 Employment Rights Act 1996, s 121. Where by virtue of the Employment Rights Act 1996, s 138 he is not regarded as dismissed for the purposes of Pt XI, or by virtue of the Employment Rights Act 1996, s 141, he is not, or (if he were otherwise entitled) would not be, entitled to a redundancy payment.

Reductions in the basic award

15.193   The basic award is subject to possible reduction on the following grounds:
(1)   Where the tribunal considers that any conduct of the complainant before the dismissal (or, where the dismissal was with notice, before the notice was given) was such that it would be just and equitable to reduce or further reduce the amount of the basic award to any extent, the tribunal will reduce or further reduce that amount accordingly.[1]
(2)   The amount of the basic award will be reduced, or further reduced, by the amount of any statutory redundancy payment awarded by the tribunal in respect of the same dismissal, or any payment made by the employer to the employee on the ground that the dismissal was by reason of redundancy (whether a statutory redundancy payment or otherwise).[2]
(3)   Where the tribunal finds that the complainant has unreasonably refused an offer by the employer which (if accepted) would have the effect of reinstating the complainant in his employment in all respects as if he had not been dismissed, the tribunal will reduce or further reduce the amount of the basic award to such extent as it considers just and equitable having regard to that finding.[3]

Although clearly established that an ex gratia payment will reduce the compensatory award, it is not clear whether any excess of the ex gratia payment which does not fall within category (2) above can be set off against the basic award.[4]

1 Employment Rights Act 1996, s 122(2). In the case of a dismissal referred to in **15.191** and **15.192** the basic award will not be reduced below the minimum figure, presently £2,770: Employment Rights Act 1996, s 122(3).
2 Employment Rights Act 1996, s 122(4).
3 Employment Rights Act 1996, s 122(1).
4 See *Chelsea Football Club and Athletic Co Ltd v Heath* [1981] IRLR 73.

The compensatory award

15.194   The function of the compensatory award is to compensate for loss actually suffered, not to penalise the employer or confer gratuitous benefit on the employee. In accordance with the statutory provisions, the tribunal will award what is just and equitable in the circumstances; nothing more, nothing less.[1]

1 See *W Devis & Sons Ltd v Atkins* [1977] IRLR 314; [1977] ICR 662; *Tele-Trading Ltd v Jenkins* [1990] IRLR 430; *Vaughan v Weighpack Ltd* [1974] ICR 261, NIRC.

15.195   Calculation of the compensatory award is in accordance with s 123 of the Employment Rights Act 1996. The section should always be referred to when calculating the compensatory award. It is as follows:

'**123.** – (1) Subject to the provisions of this section and sections 124 and 126, the amount of the compensatory award shall be such amount as the tribunal considers just and equitable in all the circumstances having regard to the loss sustained by the complainant in consequence of the dismissal in so far as that loss is attributable to action taken by the employer.

(2) The loss referred to in subsection (1) shall be taken to include—
- (a)   any expenses reasonably incurred by the complainant in consequence of the dismissal, and
- (b)   subject to subsection (3), loss of any benefit which he might reasonably be expected to have had but for the dismissal.

(3) The loss referred to in subsection (1) shall be taken to include in respect of any loss of—
- (a)   any entitlement or potential entitlement to a payment on account of dismissal by reason of redundancy (whether in pursuance of Part XI or otherwise), or
- (b)   any expectation of such a payment,

only the loss referable to the amount (if any) by which the amount of that payment would have exceeded the amount of a basic award (apart from any reduction under section 122) in respect of the same dismissal.

(4) In ascertaining the loss referred to in subsection (1) the tribunal shall apply the same rule concerning the duty of a person to mitigate his loss as applies to damages recoverable under the common law of England and Wales or (as the case may be) Scotland.

(5) In determining, for the purposes of subsection (1), how far any loss sustained by the complainant was attributable to action taken by the employer, no account shall be taken of any pressure which by—
- (a)   calling, organising, procuring or financing a strike or other industrial action, or
- (b)   threatening to do so,

was exercised on the employer to dismiss the employee; and that question shall be determined as if no such pressure had been exercised.

(6) Where the tribunal finds that the dismissal was to any extent caused or contributed to by any action of the complainant, it shall reduce the amount of the compensatory award by such proportion as it considers just and equitable having regard to that finding.

(7) If the amount of any payment made by the employer to the employee on the ground that the dismissal was by reason of redundancy (whether in pursuance of [the redundancy payment provisions of the Act] or otherwise) exceeds the amount of the basic award which would be payable but for section 122(4), that excess goes to reduce the amount of the compensatory award.'

15.196 Save for certain instances where the employer has refused reinstatement or re-engagement, or failed to comply with such orders, the amount of compensatory award to a person calculated in accordance with s 123 will not exceed the limit for the time being imposed by s 124(1), currently £11,300.[1]

1 For further details refer to the Employment Rights Act 1996, s 124.

15.197 Section 126 of the Employment Rights Act 1996 provides that where compensation falls to be awarded in respect of any act, under the provisions relating to unfair dismissal and under either or both of the Sex Discrimination Act 1975 and the Race Relations Act 1976, an industrial tribunal should not award compensation under any head of claim in respect of any loss or other matter which is, or has been, taken into account under the other statute by the tribunal, or another industrial tribunal, in awarding compensation on the same or another complaint in respect of that act.[1]

1 The losses in respect of which compensation is payable under the various enactments are not always the same. For instance, injury to feelings may be compensated under the Sex Discrimination Act 1975 and the Race Relations Act 1976 but probably not under the unfair dismissal provisions. It is important that originating applications to tribunals do include complaints in respect of violations of every statute which may be involved. See **18.20–18.26**.

15.198 The objective of a compensatory award is to compensate the complainant for the loss sustained as a result of the dismissal. The amount of the award must be just and equitable. Thus the fact that the employee may well have been dismissed in any event, quite apart from the unfairness, can properly be reflected in a percentage reduction under s 123(1).[1] The tribunal can in principle make a deduction under s 123(1) and also under s 123(6). The tribunal should first assess the ex-employee's loss (including an assessment of the likelihood of the employment continuing if he had not been unfairly dismissed) and then, in the light of that finding, decide the extent to which the complainant caused or contributed to his dismissal and the extent to which it is just and equitable to reduce the award on that basis.[2] The only statutory indication of what should be included in the assessment of loss is contained in s 123(2) and (3), which provide for the inclusion of expenses reasonably incurred by the employee in consequence of the dismissal.[3] The employee is also entitled to be compensated for the loss of benefits which he might reasonably be expected to have had but for the dismissal.[4] The loss may be solely the time taken for consultation if it were properly carried out.[5]

1 *Campbell v Dunoon & Cowal Housing Association* [1993] IRLR 496, Ct of Sess, applying *Polkey v AE Dayton Services Ltd* [1987] IRLR 503, HL. See also *Slaughter v C Brewer & Sons Ltd* [1990] IRLR 426, EAT.
2 *Rao v Civil Aviation Authority* [1994] IRLR 240, CA.
3 This head of compensation encompasses a claim for the costs of looking for new employment: *Leech v Berger, Jensen & Nicholson Ltd* [1972] IRLR 58, even to the point of including home removal costs; *Nohar v Granitstone (Galloway) Ltd* [1974] ICR 273, NIRC.
4 See *York Trailer Co Ltd v Sparkes* [1973] ICR 518, NIRC.
5 *Abbotts and Standley v Wesson-Glynwed Steels Ltd* [1982] IRLR 51, EAT.

15.199 The decision of *Norton Tool Co Ltd v Tewson*,[1] although made under the original unfair dismissal provisions contained in the Industrial Relations Act 1971, is still referred to regularly as to the calculation of the compensatory award. The National Industrial Relations Court assessed compensation under four heads:
(1) immediate wage loss,
(2) future wage loss,

(3)   loss of fringe benefits, and

(4)   loss of protection in respect of unfair dismissal and redundancy.

In calculating wage loss for compensatory awards, unlike for basic awards, tribunals take account of *net* value.

1 [1973] 1 All ER 183; [1972] IRLR 86, NIRC.

15.200   In assessing loss, tribunals should set out in the decision document details of the heads of compensation.[1]

1 Industrial Tribunals (Constitution and Rules of Procedure) Regulations 1993, SI 1993/2687, Sch 1, para 10(3). For an exposition of the reasons why see *Blackwell v GEC Elliott Process Automation Ltd* [1976] IRLR 144, per Phillips J.

Immediate loss

15.201   The tribunal will calculate the loss of earnings of the complainant to the date of the hearing, or award, whichever is later. The compensation will include all the complainant's losses during that period. This will include his loss in receiving less than he would receive in accordance with good industrial relations practice[1] but should not result in him receiving more than his actual loss.[2] Any calculation of compensation for income lost during the notice period may be subject to special consideration protecting it from deduction because of sums actually earned elsewhere. The employee is not absolutely entitled to compensation equal to full wages during the notice period, but the employer should pay such sums as good industrial practice requires, and sums earned by way of mitigation may not be taken into account to reduce that sum on this basis.[3]

1 *Addison v Babcock FATA Ltd* [1987] IRLR 173, CA.

2 *Isleworth Studios v Rickard Ltd* [1988] IRLR 137, EAT.

3 *Norton Tool Co Ltd v Tewson* [1972] IRLR 86 as applied in *Addison v Babcock FATA Ltd* [1987] IRLR 173, CA.

Future loss

15.202   The tribunal will assess the loss which the complainant will sustain in the future from the unfair dismissal. This may involve the tribunal in assessing whether the applicant is likely to obtain employment in the future, and if so when, and at what rate of pay and with what benefits. The tribunal may also have to decide if the applicant's employment would have come to an end fairly in any event, and if so when. Even if the applicant has obtained, or is likely to obtain other employment the compensation may include a continuing loss of wages and other benefits. It can include a loss which goes beyond normal retirement age.[1] A tribunal need not take into account receipt of a grant to follow an educational course on the basis that it was not just and equitable for the respondent to take advantage of the former employee's efforts to improve himself.[2]

1 *Barrel Plating and Phosphating Co Ltd v Danks* [1976] IRLR 262, EAT.

2 *Justfern Ltd v D'Ingerthorpe* [1994] IRLR 164, EAT.

Loss of fringe benefits

15.203   The employee is entitled to be compensated for all losses which the tribunal considers flow from the wrong done to him, whether he is contractually entitled to them or not. This can include a wide variety of benefits such as overtime earnings,[1] the provision of a car which can be used for private purposes, loss of the availability of discount schemes and the like. All benefits which have been lost may be included. However there must be a loss of a real benefit. The loss of the right to be reimbursed expenses where there is no profit element will not be compensated.[2]

1 *Brownson v Hire Service Shops Ltd* [1978] IRLR 73, EAT.
2 *Tradewinds Airways Ltd v Fletcher* [1981] IRLR 272, EAT.

Loss of protection in respect of unfair dismissal and redundancy

15.204 The dismissed employee will have lost the benefit of the protection given by the provisions as to unfair dismissal, redundancy payments and other rights for which a qualification period is necessary. If it is just and equitable to do so, this loss too will be compensated since the employee will have to re-qualify for unfair dismissal, redundancy and certain other statutory protection. At present awards for this loss are often in the region of £200.

Other heads of claim indicated by decisions are:

Losses in respect of pension rights

15.205 The pensions element of the complainant's loss is often one of the most difficult to calculate, and frequently the largest loss. There may be a loss in the value of accrued pension rights as well as the loss of future contributions paid by the employer. Reference should be made to the HMSO publication, prepared by a committee of industrial tribunal chairmen after consultation with the Government Actuary's Department and used widely in tribunals and elsewhere, entitled *Industrial Tribunals – Compensation for Loss of Pension Rights*. This booklet is frequently referred to when such awards are made or negotiated by way of settlement (see Appendix 4).[1]

1 Although the booklet is in practice regularly referred to, there is no obligation on the tribunal invariably to do so: *Bingham v Hobourn Engineering Ltd* [1992] IRLR 298, EAT.

Loss of service related notice period

15.206 If and when he starts new employment, the employee will probably be on shorter notice than he was with his former employers.[1] If so, this can provide a further head of compensation. Whereas this always used to attract a fairly nominal sum of compensation, in times of economic recession the increased value of such rights has been recognised by higher awards, exceptionally amounting to half the statutory notice entitlement.[2]

1 *Hilti (Great Britain) Ltd v Windridge* [1974] ICR 352, NIRC.
2 *Daley v AE Dorset (Almar Dolls) Ltd* [1981] IRLR 385, not overruled but definitely restricted by *SH Muffett Ltd v Head* [1986] IRLR 488; [1987] ICR 1, EAT.

Expenses in setting up business

15.207 The expenses incurred by the complainant in setting up a business to mitigate his loss may be recoverable.[1]

1 *Gardiner-Hill v Roland Beiger Technics Ltd* [1982] IRLR 498, EAT.

Reductions in compensation

15.208 There may be reasons for a tribunal to award compensation at a level lower than the remuneration the employee may have expected to earn had he remained employed by the respondent. The tribunal may award such reduced sums where it would not be just and equitable to award the full sum; where the employee would or might have been dismissed anyway; where the employer has already paid him compensation; or where the employee has either caused or contributed to his own dismissal, or failed to mitigate his loss thereafter.

Just and equitable

15.209 The industrial tribunal awards as a compensatory award such amount as is considered just and equitable in all circumstances having regard to the loss sustained by the complainant in consequence of the dismissal, insofar as that loss is attributable to action taken by the employer. There may be circumstances where in the light of justice and equity no compensatory award will be made.[1] A common instance of this occurs where it can be shown that the employee suffered no loss because he could have been fairly dismissed in the circumstances and that the dismissal was only 'technically unfair'.[2] The industrial tribunal should in its decision spell out the facts which are the basis for determining that the complainant was at fault and the reason for deciding the amount of the contribution assessed by it.[3]

1 *Polkey v AE Dayton Services Ltd* [1987] IRLR 503, HL; *Devis & Sons Ltd v Atkins* [1977] 3 All ER 40; [1977] ICR 662, HL; *Dunlop Ltd v Farrell* [1993] ICR 885. A percentage reduction may be applied, see *Polkey* and *Red Bank Manufacturing Co Ltd v Meadows* [1992] IRLR 209.
2 *Clyde Pipeworks Ltd v Foster* [1978] IRLR 313, EAT; *Earl v Slater and Wheeler (Airlyne) Ltd* [1973] 1 All ER 145; [1972] ICR 508, NIRC; *Sutton and Gates (Luton) Ltd v Boxall* [1978] IRLR 486, EAT; *UBAF Bank Ltd v Davis* [1978] IRLR 442, EAT. For the position as to invalidity benefit see the conflicting decisions of *Puglia v C James & Sons* [1996] IRLR 70, EAT and *Rubenstein v McGloughlin* [1996] IRLR 557, EAT.
3 *Pirelli General Cable Works Ltd v Murray* [1979] IRLR 190, EAT.

Payment from employer

15.210 Where an employee is summarily dismissed he may claim for both unfair and wrongful dismissal. However it is now clear that the employer must be given credit for payments made. Therefore where an employee is awarded damages for wrongful dismissal, those sums must be credited to the employer in considering compensation for unfair dismissal.[1] Unless the employer states that any such payment is intended to be in respect only of the notice period, it seems that even compensation for future loss can be reduced by the requirement to give credit for the sums already paid. For example, where an employer pays more in lieu of notice than an employee is contractually entitled to, the correct approach is to assess the period of future loss; calculate the net salary for that period, and deduct from that figure the sum paid by the employer.[2]

1 *Addison v Babcock FATA Ltd* [1987] IRLR 173; *Digital Equipment Co Ltd v Clements* (1996) Times, 11 December, EAT.
2 *MBS Ltd v Calo* [1983] IRLR 189; [1983] ICR 459.

15.211 Where the unfair dismissal is by way of redundancy, and a redundancy payment was made, such payment will first be deducted from the basic award (which is usually the same), but any payment over and above the statutory minimum may then be set off against the compensatory award too.

Contributory fault

15.212 As has been seen, s 123(6) of the Employment Rights Act 1996 provides that where the dismissal was to any extent caused, or contributed to, by any action of the complainant, the tribunal will reduce the award by such proportion as it considers to be just and equitable having regard to that finding. Section 122(2) is a somewhat similar provision although for that section to operate there need be no causal connection between the conduct in respect of which the reduction is made and the dismissal. The onus of proof is on the employer to show that there has been a contribution to the dismissal by the former employee.[1] In deciding whether to make a reduction in the compensatory award the tribunal should consider three factors: (1) whether the employee had been guilty of conduct in connection with his dismissal which was culpable or blameworthy; (2) whether that conduct contributed to the dismissal; and (3) whether it is just and equitable to reduce the assessment to a specified extent.[2] It is only the conduct of the employee himself which is taken into consideration, but the fault of his agent will be attributed to the employee. Even where blameworthy conduct was embarked upon following advice from a solicitor, a reduction in compensation may be justified.[3]

1   *AC Bracey Ltd v Iles* [1973] IRLR 210, NIRC.
2   *Nelson v British Broadcasting Corpn (No 2)* [1979] IRLR 346, CA.
3   *Allen v Hammett* [1982] IRLR 89, EAT.

15.213   The correct approach is to assess the gross compensation, itemising it fully. Only after this sum had been worked out can the deduction be assessed. The amount of any reduction in compensation depends on the facts of each particular case but there should be no reduction if the employee is not in any way to 'blame' for the dismissal.[1] It is open to an industrial tribunal to find that an employee contributed to his dismissal even where pressure is exerted on the employer by a third party.[2] The amount of contribution is a matter for the tribunal to decide, but it may take into account any agreement between the parties.[3]

1   *Kraft Foods Ltd v Fox* [1977] IRLR 431, EAT. In that case it was said that in a true incapability case it may well be that there is no degree of contribution at all, eg where the employee tries desperately hard but cannot cope at all. If he is at fault in an incapability case an order of contribution may be appropriate: *Sutton and Gates (Luton) Ltd v Boxall* [1978] IRLR 486, EAT; *Moncur v International Paint Co Ltd* [1978] IRLR 223, EAT; *Slaughter v C Brewer & Sons* [1990] ICR 730.
2   *Ford Motor Co Ltd v Hudson* [1978] ICR 482; *Sulmanji v Toughened Glass Ltd* [1979] ICR 799, but contrast *British United Trawlers (Grimsby) Ltd v Carr* [1977] ICR 622, EAT.
3   *Weatherill v Shipton Automation Ltd* (1977) 12 ITR 123, EAT. In exceptional cases the contribution can be 100%: *Sulemanji v Toughened Glass Ltd* [1979] ICR 799, EAT.

Failure to mitigate

15.214   The employee is under a duty to mitigate his loss and the usual rules of contract law apply,[1] but the duty does not arise until the employee is actually dismissed, so that a refusal to agree to a transfer, which leads to dismissal, cannot be a failure to mitigate.[2] The test is to consider whether the applicant who is said to have failed to mitigate his loss acted reasonably in all the circumstances, and the burden of proof is on the employer.[3]

1   Employment Rights Act 1996, s 123(4).
2   *McAndrew v Prestwick Circuits Ltd* [1988] IRLR 514; *Savoia v Chiltern Herb Farms Ltd* [1981] IRLR 65. However, if the offer to transfer remains open after the dismissal, a refusal to accept it at that stage probably will be a failure to mitigate, and the existence of the offer is likely to be a factor indicating that the employer has acted reasonably.
3   *Bessenden Properties Ltd v Corness* [1974] IRLR 338, CA; *Sturdy Finance Ltd v Bardsley* [1979] IRLR 65; [1979] ICR 249; *Fyfe v Scientific Furnishings Ltd* [1989] IRLR 331; [1989] ICR 648.

15.215   If an ex-employee unreasonably refuses an offer of reinstatement, he may be solely responsible for his loss.[1] It is unlikely that an employee will be found to have failed to mitigate his loss after a constructive dismissal by reason only of a failure to use a grievance procedure.[2] The industrial tribunal will expect the complainant to have made reasonable efforts to obtain other employment[3] and to give evidence as to those efforts. When assessing the amount of a deduction for failure to mitigate loss the tribunal should not reduce the compensatory award by a percentage, but should decide on a date by which the employee should have found work and assess his loss until that date.[4] A decision to elect to receive payment of pension contributions rather than for a future pension has been held not to be a failure to mitigate.[5]

1 *Sweetlove v Redbridge and Waltham Forest Area Health Authority* [1979] ICR 477, EAT.
2 *Seligman and Latz Ltd v McHugh* [1979] IRLR 130, EAT. See also *William Muir (Bond 9) Ltd v Lamb* [1985] IRLR 95; *Lock v Connell Estate Agents* [1994] IRLR 444.
3 See for example *Bristol Garage (Brighton) Ltd v Lowen* [1979] IRLR 86, EAT. If the employment obtained is subsequently lost through no fault of the former employee he will not be found to have failed to mitigate: *Barrel Plating and Phosphating Co Ltd v Danks* [1976] 3 All ER 652; [1976] ICR 503, EAT.
4 *Peara v Enderlin Ltd* [1979] ICR 804, EAT; *Gardiner-Hill v Roland Beiger Technics Ltd* [1982] IRLR 498.
5 *Sturdy Finance Ltd v Bardsley* [1979] IRLR 65, EAT.

Method of calculation

15.216 Where the statutory maximum applies the gross amount of the compensation is calculated, then the deductions are made, and finally the statutory maximum is applied (rather than applying the maximum before the deduction, which would work to the employer's advantage).[1] There is considerable uncertainty as to the order in which deductions are made for the *Polkey* factor, contribution and payments made by the employer and the application of the statutory maximum to the compensation. Which approach is correct where there is a deduction due to the employee's conduct is not clear. Tribunals have held both that the award of compensation should be reduced for contributory fault, and then the employer's payment deducted;[2] and that the payment should be credited before the deduction for contributory fault.[3] The better view is the latter approach is more consistent with the intention of s 123 of the 1978 Act (namely to have regard to the loss actually suffered by the employee) and the wording (s 123(6) refers to a reduction for fault of the 'compensatory award') of s 123. It is also thought that the *Polkey* deduction should be made prior to the reduction for contributory fault.[4]

1 See Employment Rights Act 1996, s 124(5).
2 *Clement-Clarke International Ltd v Manley* [1979] ICR 74; *Derwent Coachworks v Kirby* [1994] IRLR 639.
3 *UBAF Bank Ltd v Davis* [1978] IRLR 442; *Parker and Farr Ltd v Shelvey* [1979] IRLR 434; [1979] ICR 896.
4 *Rao v Civil Aviation Authority* [1994] IRLR 240, CA. For an extensive and thorough analysis of the relevant authorities see *Digital Equipment Co Ltd v Clements* (1996) Times, 11 December, EAT.

15.217 Where a dismissed employee obtains permanent employment at a higher rate of remuneration than the job from which he is dismissed, two differing methods of assessing loss have been used, which can give significantly varying results. Loss may be calculated up to the date of obtaining the new job, with no credit given for increased income thereafter;[1] or up to the date of the tribunal hearing, giving credit for all income, including the element of increased income.[2] On current authorities, the latter approach is to be preferred. Yet a third approach has been suggested, of calculating the applicant's income by reference to the period by which it may be expected that the higher paid job will be maintained, thereby giving credit for the future element of increased pay. In the Employment Appeal Tribunal it has been said that this method is flawed in that it effectively means that the employer pays for only a fraction of the loss suffered in the period of unemployment. The observation is correct, but if the purpose of the award is to compensate actual loss, rather than to compensate for the status of being unemployed, the incidental benefit to the employer is a logical consequence.

1 *Lytlarch Ltd v Reid* [1991] ICR 216, EAT; *Fentiman v Fluid Engineering Products Ltd* [1991] IRLR 150.
2 *Ging v Ellward (Lancs) Ltd* [1991] ICR 222n; 13 ITR 265; *Courtaulds Northern Spinning Ltd v Moosa* [1984] IRLR 43; [1984] ICR 218.

Information available after award

15.218   If after a compensation award it comes to light as a result of events following the tribunal's decision, that it was in some way misconceived a party should consider whether or not to seek a review. The test to be applied by the tribunal in such cases is explained by Sir John Donaldson in *Yorkshire Engineering and Welding Co Ltd v Burnham*[1]as follows:

'In such circumstances the test to be applied in deciding whether or not to review a decision is as follows: the tribunal must ask itself whether the forecasts which were the basis of its decision have been falsified to a sufficiently substantial extent to invalidate the assessment and whether this occurred so soon after the decision, that a review was necessary in the interests of justice. There must be some finality in these matters. But at the same time, if very shortly after a tribunal has reached a decision it comes to its notice, upon an application for review, that the facts are so different from those which it had assumed, that the whole substratum of its award has gone, then, subject to such considerations as whether the party applying could have obtained that evidence before the hearing, there is manifestly a case for review.'

1 [1973] 3 All ER 1176; [1974] ICR 77, NIRC. See **18.95–18.103**.

Special award

15.219   In addition to those cases of certain trade union dismissals (see **14.33**) the tribunal may make a special award if the employee requests the tribunal to make an order under s 113 in certain limited circumstances if s 121 is inapplicable (see **15.192**). These are where the reason (or principal reason) for dismissing the employee, or for selecting the employee for dismissal by reason of redundancy, was for certain reasons relating to health and safety,[1] the employee's functions as a trustee of an occupational pension scheme,[2] or because the employee performed the particular functions as a representative.[3] Special awards are rarely encountered in practice but if an order for reinstatement or re-engagement is made, unless the employer satisfies the tribunal that it was not practicable to comply with the order,[4] the special award is the greater of 156 weeks' pay or £20,600, but not exceeding £27,500. In other cases the special award is the greater of 104 weeks' pay or £13,775.[5] There are provisions for the reduction of the award if the effective date of termination is after the employee's 64th birthday, where by reason of the employee's conduct it is just and equitable to reduce the amount of the award, and where the employee prevented the order from being complied with, or refused, an offer of re-instatement.[6]

1 As referred to in the Employment Rights Act 1996, s 100(1)(a) and (b).
2 As referred to in the Employment Rights Act 1996, s 102(1).

3 As referred to in the Employment Rights Act 1996, s 103.
4 Employment Rights Act 1996, s 125(2) and see s 125(6).
5 Employment Rights Act 1996, s 125(1).
6 Employment Rights Act 1996, s 125(3), (4) and (5) which should be referred to in detail. The Secretary of State can by order increase the specified sums; s 125(7). The usual maximum does not apply to the week's pay.

Recoupment

15.220   When an industrial tribunal makes a financial award in favour of a former employee recoupment has to be considered. Section 16 of the Industrial Tribunals Act 1996 gives the Secretary of State power to make provision for recoupment of state benefits from industrial tribunal awards of compensation. The Employment Protection (Recoupment of Jobseeker's Allowance and Income Support) Regulations 1996[1] are in force under these provisions. Where an employee has applied for jobseeker's allowance or income support (previously unemployment benefit and supplementary benefit) and a monetary award is made by the tribunal in favour of the complainant, the industrial tribunal must set out:

(a)   the 'monetary award'; ie the whole award made by the industrial tribunal;

(b)   the amount of the 'prescribed element', ie the payment made in respect of loss of wages for a period before the conclusion of the proceedings;

(c)   the dates of the period to which the prescribed element is attributable;[2] and

(d)   the amount, if any, by which the monetary award exceeds the prescribed element.

1 SI 1996/2349 replacing the Employment Protection (Recoupment of Unemployment Benefit and Supplementary Benefit) Regulations 1977, SI 1977/674. In addition to unfair dismissal, recoupment may take place when an award is made of guarantee payments, payments in respect of a collective agreement excluded from the guarantee payment provisions, payments made under orders for reinstatement and re-engagement, under an order for continuation of a contract, in respect of a period of medical suspension and on default by an employer to make payments under a protective award. When a protective award is made the Employment Protection (Recoupment of Jobseeker's Allowance and Income Support) Regulations 1996, regs 5 and 6 have also to be considered.
2 It is only in respect of the period for which compensation is awarded: *Homan v A1 Bacon Co Ltd* [1996] ICR 721, EAT.

15.221   At the end of the hearing the tribunal should inform the employer that he should pay the applicant the difference between the two elements; but that he should not pay the employee any part of the prescribed element until the employer has received a copy of the 'recoupment notice' (or is informed that no notice will be issued) from the Secretary of State. This notice sets out the amount of jobseeker's allowance or income support payments made to the employee, which is recouped from the prescribed element, directly from the employer. Once the employer has paid the amount set out in the notice to the Secretary of State, any remaining balance of the prescribed element should be paid to the employee. These regulations do not apply to private settlements, where there is generally no power of recoupment. The effect is that the possibility of recoupment can be an incentive to both parties to settle and thus avoid a financial award.

Interest on awards

15.222 Interest is payable on awards made by industrial tribunals[1] if they are unpaid after 42 days from the day when the decision is recorded as having been sent to the parties.[2] It is calculated as simple interest at the rate for the time being specified in s 17 of the Judgments Act 1838.[3] The interest accrues on a daily basis. It does not accrue on money which is the subject of a recoupment order or on tax or National Insurance payable to the appropriate authorities.[4] If the decision is the subject of appeal or review the interest is calculated on the sum confirmed or varied.[5]

1 Under the Industrial Tribunals (Interest) Order 1990, SI 1990/479.
2 For calculation date, see the Industrial Tribunals (Interest) Order 1990, art 2(1).
3 Industrial Tribunals (Interest) Order 1990, SI 1990, art 4.
4 Industrial Tribunals (Interest) Order 1990, SI 1990, art 3.
5 Industrial Tribunals (Interest) Order 1990, SI 1990, arts 5–10.

Death of employer or of employee

15.223 Section 133 of the Employment Rights Act 1996 provides the rules applicable when the death of either party takes place after a dismissal which is claimed to be unfair has taken place.[1] If the employer has given notice to the employee to terminate his contract of employment and before the termination the employer, or employee, dies, the unfair dismissal provisions apply as if the contract had been duly terminated by the employer by notice expiring on the date of death.[2] When the contract of employment has been terminated and s 97(2) and (4) (the provisions which apply when notice is of less than the obligatory statutory period has been given) provides for an effective date of termination later than would otherwise have been the case and before that later date the employee or the employer dies, then s 97 has effect as if the notice to which it refers would have expired on the date of death.[3]

1 For institution and continuance of tribunal proceedings and rights and liabilities accruing after death, see **18.85–18.87**.
2 Employment Rights Act 1996, s 133(1).
3 Employment Rights Act 1996, s 133(2).

15.224 Where an employee has died, then unless an order of reinstatement, or re-engagement has been made, the unfair dismissal provisions relating to reinstatement and re-engagement do not apply. If the industrial tribunal finds the case is well founded, then for the purposes of compensation the case is treated as one in which no order for reinstatement or re-engagement has been made.[1] When an order for reinstatement or re-engagement has been made, and the employee dies before it is complied with, if the employer has before the death refused to reinstate, or re-engage, the employee in accordance with the order, the usual provisions as to non-compliance apply and compensation may be awarded for that reason unless the employer satisfies the tribunal that it was not practicable at the time of the refusal to comply with the order.[2] If there has been no such refusal, the tribunal may still make an award in respect of ancillary terms of the order which are capable of fulfilment after the employee's death if the employer fails to comply with the order in just the same way as if there was a failure to comply with the order where the employee had been reinstated, or re-engaged.[3]

1 Employment Rights Act 1996, s 133(3).
2 Employment Rights Act 1996, s 133(5)(a).
3 Employment Rights Act 1996, s 133(5)(b).

Chapter 16

Redundancy

Introduction

The statutory provision of redundancy payment was introduced in 1965. Subject to certain exceptions, in general terms employees with continuous service of two years or more are entitled to a redundancy payment when they are dismissed by reason of redundancy or, in certain clearly defined circumstances, laid off or put on short-time. There are specific rules which deal with the death of an employee and an employer. An employee may lose the right to a redundancy payment to which he or she would otherwise be entitled. A redundancy payment is calculated according to a formula based on a week's pay and length of continuous service, but there are certain rules which limit the amount of income and the number of years which count and increase payments in respect of older employees. If the employer is insolvent, then the employee may recoup the redundancy payment under the insolvency provisions.

Employees with two years, or more continuous service To qualify for a redundancy payment the applicant must be an employee (see **16.01**). Certain types of employment not falling within the statutory definition of employment are nevertheless covered by the redundancy payment provisions (see **16.22**). An employee cannot recover a redundancy payment if the contract is illegal (see **16.01**).

Two years, or more continuous service For the general provisions as to continuity of service (see **16.02**) and for the particular requirements in redundancy (see **16.02**). The Employment Rights Act 1996 contains detailed rules dealing with the change of ownership of a business and these have to be viewed together with the Transfer of Undertakings (Protection of Employment) Regulations 1981 (see Chapter 12).

An employee cannot count on the same period of employment for two different entitlements to a redundancy payment. Thus, if an employee has received a redundancy payment, then continuity of employment is deemed to have been broken (see **16.02** et seq).

There are specific rules dealing with continuity of employment when an employer refuses to permit a woman to return to work after confinement (see **11.34** and **11.35**).

As in unfair dismissal cases there are detailed rules which extend the period of continuity of employment to include the statutory period of notice (see **16.03**).

The exceptions Employees who have reached retirement age (see **16.09** and for fuller analysis of comparable provisions in relation to unfair dismissal, **15.07**).

There is a power in certain limited cases to exclude the obligation to make a redundancy payment (see **16.10**) or obtain an exemption order (see **16.11**).

Employment wholly or partially abroad (see **16.12**) or with a government of an overseas territory (see **16.14**).

Certain occupations such as a civil servant (see **16.15**) or as a share fisherman (see **16.19**) are excluded.

Dismissal Subject to the detailed and complex rules concerning lay-off and short-time (see **16.54**) it is an essential prerequisite of redundancy that an employee should be dismissed. There is a statutory definition of dismissal for the purposes of redundancy (see **16.26**). Whilst in the majority of cases the dismissal for redundancy is the termination by the employer, the right of the employee to leave and claim that he or she has been constructively dismissed is expressly allowed by the Employment Rights Act 1996. This has important consequences when employees wish to change working practices (see **16.32**).

An employee is still dismissed even if he or she volunteers for redundancy (see **16.28**) but there is no dismissal if there is a mutual termination of the contract (see **16.29**). An employee's entitlement to a redundancy payment is preserved when there is a frustrating event which affects the employer (see **16.34**).

By reason of redundancy There is a specific statutory definition of redundancy (see **16.36**). A redundancy payment is payable if the dismissal is attributable wholly or mainly to situations within the statutory definition (see **16.39**). Unless the contrary is proved an employee who is dismissed is presumed to be dismissed due to redundancy (see **16.38**). Nevertheless a tribunal is still required to consider cases in which there may be more than one reason for a dismissal and to decide whether the statutory test is met (see **16.39**).

The first limb of the definition covers the position when an employer ceases or intends to cease carrying out the business altogether or at the place where the employee was employed (see **16.40**). The place where the employee was employed will often involve more detailed consideration of any express or implied mobility term in the contract (see **16.41**).

The second limb deals with the position in which the employer intends to continue to carry on the business but the requirements for employees to carry out work of a particular kind have ceased or diminished or are expected to cease or diminish (see **16.43**). The main difficulties which are encountered deal with the construction of the words 'work of a particular kind' (see **16.45** et seq).

Redundancy when the employee is laid off or put on short-time The *time off* provisions deal with the situation in which the employee is not dismissed, but is not provided with any work or with only reduced work (see **16.54**). There are statutory definitions of lay-off and short-time working (see **16.55**).

The provisions require a detailed procedure to be followed (see **16.56**). An employer may successfully resist a claim if he can show that work is likely to become available (see **16.57**).

These provisions have to be viewed in the context of general contractual principles as to constructive dismissal (see **16.56**).

Death of an employer or employee The death of an individual employer operates as a dismissal (see **16.33**). The employee is entitled to a redundancy payment if he is not re-engaged due to redundancy (see **16.80**). The employee may lose his or her entitlement of a redundancy payment in certain circumstances (see **16.81**).

Death of an employee   A case may be brought by the deceased employee's personal representatives (see **16.86**) or by a person authorised by the tribunal (see **16.88**) for the benefit of the estate.

In general terms the effect of the legislation is that the entitlement to a redundancy payment is equated with the position which would have pertained had the employee been dismissed on the date of his death (see **16.80** et seq). If the employer had offered alternative employment, the tribunal has to consider the speculative issue of whether it would have been unreasonable for the deceased, had he survived, to have refused the offer (see **16.82**). There are special provisions as to time limits (see **16.104**).

Losing the entitlement
Offers of renewal and re-engagement   The general purpose of the Employment Rights Act 1996 would be defeated if an employee was entitled to receive a redundancy payment even though the employer offered to renew the contract on the same terms or offered suitable alternative employment. There are therefore specific statutory provisions (see **16.60** et seq) which provide that if the employee is offered a new contract on the same terms, or if the employee unreasonably refuses the offer of suitable alternative employment, he forfeits his right to redundancy payment (see **16.63**). The interpretation of what constitutes the unreasonable refusal of suitable alternative employment has spawned considerable case law (see **16.67**). It suffices if the offer comes from an associated employer (see **16.61**).

If the offer is made on the basis of new terms and conditions the employee has the right to a four-week trial period (see **16.64**). This statutory right is in addition to the common law right. Thus, if the employer's action amounts to constructive dismissal (as for example a significant change of location where there is no mobility clause), the employee has a reasonable time to make up his mind whether to accept the repudiation or to carry on with the new contract. It is only when a reasonable time has elapsed that the statutory trial period commences (see **16.66**).

Misconduct   An employee who is guilty of misconduct may forfeit his redundancy entitlement in whole or in part (see **16.76**).

Strikes   An employee may in certain circumstances forfeit in whole or in part his redundancy entitlement if he goes on strike after he has been given notice due to redundancy (see **16.73**).

Leaving early   An employee who has been given notice due to redundancy may wish to leave earlier than the date of the expiry of the notice. In certain circumstances an employee may lose his entitlement to a redundancy payment if he leaves prior to the expiry of the notice (see **16.72**).

Pension   In certain circumstances (in practice confined to the public sector) the receipt of a pension may reduce or extinguish a redundancy payment (see **16.78**).

Calculation of the redundancy payment   There are particular rules as to the way in which the redundancy payment is calculated (see **16.89**) and there are specific requirements as to the documentation which must be provided by the employer when making a redundancy payment. Industrial tribunals have an exclusive jurisdiction and certain time limits apply (see **16.100**).

Handling redundancies   Employers are required to consult appropriate representatives as to redundancies (see **16.113**). If they do not carry out their obligations industrial tribunals may make protective awards (see **16.119**). Employers may also be under an obligation to notify the Secretary of State as to proposed redundancies. There are criminal penalties for not doing so (see **16.126**).

Employees with two years' or more continuous service

Employees

16.01   An employee does not have any right to a redundancy payment unless he has been continuously employed for a period of not less than two years ending with the relevant date.[1] Until the decision in *R v Secretary of State for Employment, ex p Seymour-Smith*[2] is resolved by the House of Lords there must be some doubt as to the legality of the two-year period. The issue of the definition of employment has already been considered (see **3.15** et seq). It is for the applicant to prove that he is an employee.[3] If the contract is entered into for an illegal purpose, for instance to defraud the Inland Revenue, it may be that the industrial tribunal will not allow the employee to enforce a claim based upon it.[4] In some cases it is possible for a person to be technically employed by one organisation and paid for by another. Numerically the most significant group are schoolteachers who are employed by the governors but paid by the local authority. In such cases it is the body which pays the employee which is regarded as the employer for the purposes of a redundancy payment.[5]

1 Employment Rights Act 1996, s 155.
2 [1995] IRLR 464. See **15.12**.
3 In some circumstances a company which is not the applicant's employer may be estopped from denying that it was the employer; see *Smith v Blandford Gee Construction Ltd* [1970] 3 All ER 154, DC where the respondent company was not allowed to deny that it employed the applicant having served him with a written statement of terms and conditions of employment stating that the applicant was employed by the respondent company, but see *Secretary of State for Employment v Globe Elastic Thread Co Ltd* [1979] ICR 706, HL and *Hammett v Livingstone Control Ltd* (1970) 5 ITR 136, DC.
4 *Tomlinson v Dick Evans 'U' Drive Ltd* [1978] IRLR 77, EAT. See also *Chang Chao v Dommett* (1976) 11 ITR 93, IT, and **3.06**.
5 See Employment Rights Act 1996, s 173(1).

Continuous employment

16.02   The issues of continuity of employment (see Chapter 11) and an employee's rights on the transfer of the business[1] have already been outlined. Redundancy payments do not become payable until the employee has been continuously employed for the 'requisite period' namely the period of two years ending with the relevant date.[2] The 'relevant date' is important for two reasons. It determines whether there is a liability to pay a redundancy payment[3] and also the multiplier for the calculation of redundancy payments.[4] Although the detailed provisions of the section should be considered, in the vast majority of cases the relevant date is the day when either the employer's or the employee's notice expires or when there is a dismissal without notice when the contract is terminated. As regards redundancy claims, continuity of service only commences from the employee's 18th birthday.[5] Further, if an employee has already received a redundancy period in respect of that employment, he cannot count the period covered by that redundancy payment as continuous employment for the purpose of any subsequent redundancy payment.[6] For example:

> An employee commences employment on 6 January 1989 and is dismissed with proper notice due to redundancy so that the relevant date is 4 April 1992. He will receive a redundancy payment based on three years' service. If the company then receives a large order on 5 April 1992 and the employee is then re-engaged on 8 April 1992 because he has not been away from the same employment for a week he will have continuous service from 6 January 1989 for the purpose of unfair dismissal proceedings but not for the purpose of a redundancy payment. If there is then a further redundancy exercise so that he is dismissed due to redundancy with the relevant date being 6 June 1996 he will be entitled to a redundancy payment based on four years' continuous service.[7]

1 By virtue of the Transfer of Undertakings (Protection of Employment) Regulations 1981, SI 1981/1794, the existing employees' contracts are not terminated but the rights, duties and obligations are transferred to the transferee (see Chapter 12). The provisions contained in ss 94 and 95 of the Employment Protection (Consolidation) Act 1978, have been repealed.
2 Employment Rights Act 1996, s 145 defines 'relevant date' in relation to dismissal:
 '(2) Subject to the following provisions of this section 'the relevant date'—
   (a) in relation to an employee whose contract of employment is terminated by notice, whether given by his employer or the employee, means the date on which that notice expires,
   (b) in relation to an employee whose contract of employment is terminated without notice, means the date on which his termination takes effect, and
   (c) in relation to an employee who is employed under a contract for a fixed term which expires without being renewed under the same contract, means the date on which the term expires.'
3 See the Employment Rights Act 1996, s 155.
4 See the Employment Rights Act 1996, s 162(1).
5 See the Employment Rights Act 1996, s 211 (2) which provides:
 'For the purposes of Section 155 and 162(1) an employee's period of service of continuous service shall be treated as beginning on the employee's eighteenth birthday if that is later than the day on which the employee starts work.'
6 See the Employment Rights Act 1996, s 214(2), **11.14**.
7 Continuity can be preserved if the redundancy payment is repaid, see **11.12**.

Adding the notice period

16.03   There is a provision which extends the period of employment for the purposes of continuity of service by the time of the statutory (though not the contractual) notice in cases in which notice has not been given.[1] The provision applies even if the employee has waived the period of notice [2] but does not apply if the employer was entitled to dismiss the employee without statutory notice.[3] If in the last week before he acquires the two-year qualifying period an employee is lawfully dismissed for dishonesty, then his claim for a redundancy payment would fail for two reasons. He does not have the requisite qualifying period nor would the dismissal have been for redundancy. If it is accepted that the employer had the right to dismiss the employee summarily, then no problem arises. As the following example illustrates if there is an issue as to the employer's right to dismiss the employee summarily, then the position is a complicated one:

> X is engaged on 5 March 1994. In mid-February 1996 it is clear that the company is going to have make substantial cuts in manpower. On 3 March 1996 X is accused of an offence of dishonesty and dismissed forthwith. X denies the allegation. He feels that the company has acted unfairly and believes that the company is seeking to save itself a redundancy payment.
>
> The first issue the tribunal has to decide is whether as a matter of contract X has acted dishonestly, thereby entitling the company to dismiss him summarily. If the tribunal decides that has been guilty of such a fundamental breach of contract so as to entitle the company to dismiss him summarily, that is the end of the matter.
>
> If the tribunal decides that X has not breached his contract in the way alleged so that the company was not entitled to dismiss him, then X is entitled to damages in lieu of notice and the extra period of statutory notice means that he his entitled to bring both a claim for redundancy and for unfair dismissal.
>
> As X believes that the real reason for his dismissal is that the company wanted to effect redundancies and as there is a presumption that dismissal is due to redundancy,[4] X in such circumstances would be well advised to claim a redundancy payment.
>
> In addition X should claim unfair dismissal since the company has not purported to dismiss him due to redundancy, but due to dishonesty and the company will have evidential difficulties in seeking to limit the applicant's claim to a redundancy payment. However, although the tribunal found that X had not been in breach of contract, it does not necessarily follow X will win his unfair dismissal case. Whereas in considering the issue of contract the tribunal has to determine whether X had *acted dishonestly,* in the unfair dismissal case the tribunal must consider the employer's perception, namely whether the employers *believed on reasonable grounds* that X had acted dishonestly.[5]

1 Employment Rights Act 1996, s 145(5). It is to be noted that the extended period for calculating the relevant date applies for three purposes (see ss 155, 162(1) and 227(3)) and does not apply to other provisions affecting the issue of continuity of employment: *Slater v John Swain & Son Ltd* [1981] ICR 554, EAT.
2 *Staffordshire County Council v Secretary of State for Employment* [1989] IRLR 117, CA.
3 Employment Rights Act 1996, s 86(6) preserves the right of an employer and employee to dismiss or resign without notice by reason of the conduct of the other party. If the employer was entitled to dismiss the employee without notice, then there is no notice *required* by s 145(5).
4 Employment Rights Act 1996, s 163(2)
5 *Bonner v H Gilbert Ltd* [1989] IRLR 475, EAT.

Part-time employees

16.04 As a result of the statutory changes[1] following the decision of *R v Secretary of State for Employment, ex p Equal Opportunities Commission*[2] part-time employment counts towards continuity of employment in the same way as full-time employment. As domestic servants are included within the ambit of the redundancy payments scheme,[3] this change is likely to have a profound impact on the position of the domestic help who comes in for a few hours per week. Tribunals will probably have to consider with far greater frequency the status of the intermittent worker – the employee who helps out in the shop or on the farm at various times (see Chapter 11 and **11.26**).

1 Employment Protection (Part-time Employees) Regulations 1995, SI 1995/31, but now see the Employment Rights Act 1996, Part XIV, ss 210 et seq for provisions as to continuity of employment. For fuller analysis see Chapter 11.
2 [1994] ICR 317, HL.
3 Employment Rights Act 1996, s 161(1) although certain categories of family relations are excluded (see **16.18**).

Local government employees

16.05   Local government employees stand in a special position as far as continuous service is concerned in that in general terms an employee may count his or her period in local government as a whole rather than with a particular local authority.

16.06   When considering employment with the local authorities specified in the Redundancy Payments (Local Government) (Modification) Order 1983[1] that order must always be referred to. For those local authorities included within the order, the words 'has been employed in relevant local government service for the requisite period' are substituted for 'has been continuously employed for the requisite period'. The order must be looked at in order to ascertain whether particular employment is 'local government service', but in general service with all local authorities is included, as is service with kindred bodies such as development agencies, grant maintained schools, certain Fire Service authorities and museums.[2]

1 SI 1983/1160, as amended by SI 1988/907, SI 1989/532, SI 1990/862, SI 1990/1432 and SI 1991/818.
2 For an example of consideration of the Redundancy Payments (Local Government) (Modification) Order 1983 by the courts, see *West Midlands Residuary Body v Deebank* [1990] ICR 349, CA.

16.07   Those employed in schools are included within the redundancy payments provisions.[1] If their employment has been with a local authority of a grant maintained school, they are likely to have the advantage of the Redundancy Payments (Local Government) (Modification) Order 1983 (see **16.06**).

1 Specific provision was made on the abolition of the Inner London Education Authority: Education Reform Act 1988, s 178(2)(b).

Exclusions, exemptions and special cases

16.08   Not every employee with two years' continuous service is eligible for a redundancy payment if dismissed due to redundancy. As will be noted later, there are situations in which an employee is prima facie entitled to a redundancy payment but forfeits that entitlement for some reason.[1] However, there are certain employees who have the requisite continuity of employment but for a variety of reasons relating to their age, the place of their employment, the identity of their employer or the nature of their occupation are excluded from the right to a redundancy payment. These special cases now fall to be considered.

1 Such as unreasonably refusing suitable alternative employment, see **16.60**, and for the position generally, see **16.72** et seq.

Age

16.09 Employees who have reached the age of 65 or the *normal retiring age* of the business concerned are not eligible for a redundancy payment.[1] Until the statutory amendment in 1989, women over 60 had to claim their right to a redundancy payment by direct enforcement of art 119 of the Treaty of Rome.[2] Now there is no gender-based differential in age.[3]

1 See the Employment Rights Act 1996, s 156. For a fuller analysis see comparable provisions on unfair dismissal, **15.07**.
2 *McKechnie v UBM Building Supplies (Southern) Ltd* [1991] ICR 710, EAT.
3 See the Employment Rights Act 1996, s 156(1)(b).

Agreement to exclude entitlement to redundancy payment

16.10 There is power in the case of a fixed term contract[1] of two years or more to exclude the obligation to make a redundancy payment in respect of the expiry of that term, without it being renewed. The agreement to exclude the redundancy payment must be made before the expiration of the term and it is usual to include it in the service agreement when it is entered into. However, the agreement to exclude the operation of the Act may be made at any time before the term expires.[2] The agreement must be in writing. It is permissible to include an exclusion of this type in a contract of apprenticeship.[3] If there is such an agreement and the fixed term is renewed the original exclusion agreement is not construed as applying to the term as renewed. Where it is sought to rely on this provision, a new agreement in writing to exclude the right to redundancy payment must be entered into.[4] The exclusion does not apply to contracts with mariners (including apprentices) on a British ship.[5]

1 For an explanation of the meaning of the expression 'fixed term contract', see **15.44**. See also *Fuller-Shapcott v Chilton Electric Ltd* (1970) 5 ITR 186 (contract for ten years and to continue until determined by at least six months' notice: held not to be a contract for a fixed term); *Warren v D Ferranti Ltd* (1968) 3 ITR 284 (contract could be terminated at any time after 30 June 1967 on three months' notice: held not a fixed term).
2 Employment Rights Act 1996, s 197(3).
3 For the position where the employee is engaged in employment in United Kingdom territorial waters or offshore installations, see ss 199 and 201.
4 Employment Rights Act 1996, s 197(5). In calculating the two-year period it is not permissible to amalgamate the cumulative total of several contracts and regard that as constituting a single fixed term: *Open University v Triesman* [1978] IRLR 114, EAT; *British Broadcasting Corpn v Ioannou* [1975] QB 781; [1975] 2 All ER 999, CA.
5 Employment Rights Act 1996, s 199(6).

Agreement for exemption

16.11 Employers or employers' associations and the relevant trade union or unions representing employees may agree on a redundancy scheme which in their view is more suitable than the statutory scheme. In such a case they can apply to the Secretary of State for Employment for an exemption order under s 157 of the Employment Rights Act 1996. If the Secretary of State is satisfied as to the provisions of the agreement, then he may make the order.[1] The Secretary of State will only make such an order if the agreement contains a provision that any entitlement to a redundancy payment or any issue as to the amount of redundancy payment is referred to an industrial tribunal.[2] Orders made under this section are extremely rare.[3]

1 Employment Rights Act 1996, s 157(1)
2 Employment Rights Act 1996, s 157(4))
3 The only orders at the moment are: SI 1969/207 (affecting employees of Centrax Ltd and associated companies), SI 1970/354 (relating to North of Scotland Hydro Electricity Board and South of Scotland Electricity Board) and SI 1980/1052 (affecting some employees of Lancashire schools).

Employment with a foreign element

Working abroad

16.12   When under the contract of employment the employee ordinarily works outside Great Britain and on the relevant date of termination he is outside Great Britain, then no redundancy payment is payable.[1] When an employee ordinarily works outside Great Britain he is only entitled to a redundancy payment if at the relevant date he is in Great Britain in accordance with instructions given to him by his employer.[2] If the contract of employment provides for the employee ordinarily to work in Great Britain, he is entitled to a redundancy payment even if he is outside Great Britain when the contract terminates.[3]

1 Employment Rights Act 1996, s 196(6)(a).
2 Employment Rights Act 1996, s 196(6)(b). Being in England on paid leave is not sufficient: *Costain Civil Engineering Ltd v Draycott* [1977] ICR 335, EAT.
3 Employment Rights Act 1996, s 196(6)(a).

Continuity of service and employees working outside Great Britain

16.13   Issues of continuity are governed by the provisions of s 215(2) of the Employment Rights Act 1996. A week will not count if the employee was outside Great Britain during the whole or part of the week and he was not during that week an employed earner for the purposes of the Social Security Contributions and Benefits Act 1992 in respect of whom a secondary Class 1 contribution was payable (whether or not the contribution was in fact paid). There are provisions in the Act for determining matters of doubt in these cases.[1] However, where as a result of the rules, a week does not count in computing the period of continuous employment, it does not break the continuity of employment.[2]

1 Employment Rights Act 1996, s 215(5).
2 Employment Rights Act 1996, s 215(3). For continuity generally, see Chapter 11.

Employment by a foreign government

16.14   Redundancy payments are not payable to any person in respect of employment in any capacity under the government of an overseas territory.[1]

1 Employment Rights Act 1996, s 160. 'Government of an overseas territory' is defined in s 160(3) as any territory or country outside the United Kingdom. See for example *Antoni and Louka v United Kingdom Area Exchange* (1968) 3 ITR 136 (no power to award a redundancy payment to a hairdresser employed by the US government in Great Britain), but contrast *Bagga v Heavy Electricals (India) Ltd* [1972] ICR 118, NIRC (although not raised in notice of appeal, 'somewhat unlikely' that a company whose capital was wholly owned by the Indian government could avail itself of the exemption). An employee of the Commonwealth Secretariat was held to be excluded by virtue of the Commonwealth Secretariat Act 1966: *Gadhok v Commonwealth Secretariat* (1977) 12 ITR 440, CA.

Particular occupations

Civil servants

16.15 Crown servants are not entitled to redundancy payments since the Act is not expressed to bind the Crown.[1] The redundancy provisions do not apply to public offices for the purposes of s 39 of the Superannuation Act 1965,[2] or to employment which is treated for the purposes of pensions and superannuation benefits as service in the Civil Service of the state.[3]

1 Employment Rights Act 1996, s 191(2).
2 Employment Rights Act 1996, s 159(a).
3 Employment Rights Act 1996, s 159(b).

16.16 These exclusions also apply to employees of certain public bodies such as the Forestry Commission and the Nature Conservatory who are not technically Crown servants, but whose conditions of employment are similar.

16.17 A government undertaking has been given with regard to those employees who are excluded under these provisions, see *Hansard*, Standing Committee D, Official Report for 3 June, p 437 and 15 June, p 471, 1965.

Domestic servants

16.18 Domestic employees prima facie benefit from the redundancy payments scheme. A household is treated as a business, and its maintenance, the carrying on of that business.[1] There are special provisions which apply should the employer die (see **16.83**) but otherwise such employment is dealt with in accordance with the usual rules. The employee is not entitled to a redundancy payment if in such a case the employer is the parent (or step-parent), grandparent, child (or step-child) grandchild or brother or sister (or half-brother or half-sister) of the employer.[2] Significantly a spouse is not excluded from receiving a redundancy payment though experience does not suggest that this is a fertile field for redundancy applications.

1 Employment Rights Act 1996, s 161 (2).
2 Employment Rights Act 1996, s 161(1).

Share fishermen

16.19 Employment as a member or master of a crew of a fishing vessel who is not remunerated otherwise than by a share in profits, or gross earnings, of the vessel (commonly called 'share fishermen') is excluded.[1]

1 Employment Rights Act 1996, s 199(2), save for the rather academic case of such a fisherman being refused the right to return after childbirth and being deemed to be dismissed by virtue of s 137. The provision is construed strictly so that a fisherman paid by reference to the profits of the fleet was held not to be excluded in *Goodeve v Gilsons* [1985] ICR 401, CA.

National Health Service employees

16.20 Those employed in the National Health Service were at one time excluded from the benefit of the redundancy payments scheme but are now included.[1]

1 National Health Service and Community Care Act 1990, s 66(2) which came into force on 1 April 1991. For those who transferred to National Health Service employment from the Civil Service, see the National Health Service Act 1977, s 18.

Office holders

16.21   Section 171 of the Employment Rights Act 1996 enables the Secretary of State to make regulations relating to employment in certain offices in respect of which the office holders are technically not employees under a contract of service. The effect of such regulations is that the office holders concerned are treated as employees for the purposes of the provisions of the Act relating to redundancy payments.[1] The Redundancy Payments Office Holders Regulations 1965[2] have been made pursuant to a similar power contained in the Redundancy Payments Act 1965 and bring such persons as justices' clerks and registrars of births and deaths within the scope of the provisions.

1 Employment Rights Act 1996, s 172(2).
2 SI 1965/2007. Also includes a rent officer or deputy rent officer appointed under the Rent Act 1965 and medical inspectors appointed under the Aliens Order 1953 and the Commonwealth Immigrants Act 1962.

The minister's powers

16.22   The Redundancy Payments Termination of Employment Regulations 1965[1] bring redundant chief constables and chief fire officers and assistant chief fire officers within the scope of the provisions relating to redundancy payments and they are treated as employees for the purposes of its provisions. By virtue of reg 3 if, in accordance with the statutes therein referred to, an officer is transferred to and becomes a member of another force or brigade and he does not accept a fresh appointment, the redundancy payments provisions have effect as if he were dismissed by reason of redundancy.

1 SI 1965/2022 made pursuant to the Redundancy Payments Act 1965, s 50. The authority to make such regulations is now contained in the Employment Rights Act 1996, s 172.

Secretary of State's powers

16.23   The Secretary of State may by order provide that the statutory redundancy payments scheme does not apply to persons or employments as prescribed by the order, or shall apply to persons or employments so prescribed.[1] The Secretary of State for Employment also has power to make regulations on the transfer of persons who by virtue of statutory provisions are transferred from a statutory body even though they are not employees within the meaning of the Act.[2]

1 Employment Rights Act 1996, s 209(1).
2 Employment Rights Act 1996, s 172(2).

Losing the right to a redundancy payment

16.24   In certain circumstances an employee who is prima facie dismissed by redundancy may not be entitled to a redundancy payment or may lose his entitlement or the amount of his claim may be reduced (see **16.72** et seq).

Redundancy and unfair dismissal

16.25   If there is any doubt it is always much wiser to claim both a redundancy payment and unfair dismissal. A body of case law has built up concerning unfair selection for redundancy (see **15.124** et seq).

Dismissal

16.26   Apart from the complicated provisions relating to lay-off and short-time there can be no redundancy payment unless the employee is first dismissed within the meaning of the Act. Section 136 defines dismissal[1] and it will be seen that, broadly speaking,[2] an employee is dismissed:

(1)   when the contract is terminated by the employer, or

(2)   on expiry of a fixed term contract, or

(3)   if the employee with justification 'walks out'.

1 Section 136(2) of the Employment Rights Act 1996 provides as follows:

'(2) ... an employee shall be treated as dismissed by his employer if (but only if)—

  (a) the contract under which he is employed by the employer is terminated by the employer (whether with or without notice),

  (b) where under that contract he is employed for a fixed term, that term expires without being renewed under the same contract, or

  (c) the employee terminates the contract under which he is employed (with or without notice) in circumstances in which he is entitled to terminate it without notice by reason of the employer's conduct.

2 There are other circumstances which are held to constitute a dismissal which are dealt with elsewhere in the text. Many employees suffer from the illusion that if the business is sold they can claim a redundancy payment from their former employer (see Chapter 12).

Termination by the employer

16.27   In the overwhelming majority of cases involving redundancy which come before tribunals the employer has terminated the contract. Warning by an employer that employment will be terminated at some future unspecified date is not a dismissal, and if as a result the employee finds fresh employment he is not entitled to a redundancy payment.[1]

1 *Morton Sundour Fabrics Ltd v Shaw* (1966) 2 ITR 84, DC; *British Leyland UK Ltd v McQuilken* [1978] IRLR 245, EAT; *Devon County Council v Cook* [1977] IRLR 188, EAT; *Burton Group Ltd v Smith* [1977] IRLR 351, EAT. See also *International Computers Ltd v Kennedy* [1981] IRLR 28, EAT and *Doble v Firestone Tyre and Rubber Co Ltd* [1981] IRLR 300, EAT.

Voluntary redundancies

16.28   The fundamental prerequisite of a dismissal, namely that it should not be a consensual parting, sits somewhat uneasily with the precept of good industrial practice that employers should, if possible, accept voluntary redundancies. The question of the distinction between a dismissal and a consensual parting has already been considered (see **13.04** and **15.33**).

Dismissal and mutual termination of employment: defining the boundary

16.29   Problems may be encountered with 'voluntary redundancies'. An employee who is expressly invited to resign when his job is at an end is dismissed for the purposes of what is now s 136[1] and the fact that an employee agreed to his selection for redundancy does not prevent the termination amounting to dismissal.[2] This situation has to be contrasted with a voluntary agreement which precludes dismissal as in the case of *Birch v University of Liverpool*.[3] The facts of that case were that the employer recognised that its funding was such that over the next few years it was going to have to slim down its workforce by about 300. The employer therefore invited applications for early retirement. There was no evidence that it was suggested to the employees that there was any question of any of them being compulsory retired before normal retiring age if they did not apply for the scheme. It was also not suggested to any of the employees that they would be eligible for a redundancy payment if they applied for the early retirement scheme. Indeed in terms the document stated it was not a redundancy scheme. On these facts it was held that there was a mutual termination of employment.

1 *East Sussex County Council v Walker* (1972) 7 ITR 280, NIRC.
2 *Burton Allton and Johnson Ltd v Peck* [1975] ICR 193, DC; *Glencross v Dymoke* [1979] ICR 536, EAT.
3 [1985] IRLR 165, CA.

Establishing dismissal: the crucial test

16.30 The onus of proof to show that he has been dismissed lies on the applicant. It it is suggested that the crucial test is contained in the words of Sir John Donaldson MR in *Martin v Glwnwed Distribution Ltd*:[1]

'Whatever the respective actions of the employer and the employee at the time when the contract of employment is terminated, at the end of the day the question always remains the same, "Who *really* terminated the contract of employment". If the answer is the employer, there was a dismissal within paragraph (a) of section 55(2) of the Act of 1978.[2] If the answer is the employee, a further question may then arise, namely, "Did he do so in circumstances such that he was entitled to do so without notice by reason of the employer's conduct?" '

This dictum was approved in *Birch's* case although it was pointed out that Sir John Donaldson MR was not purporting to deal with the issue of mutual termination which arose in that case.

1 [1983] ICR 511 at p 519, CA.
2 This was the test for unfair dismissal, but exactly the same principles apply to the construction of the Employment Rights Act 1996, s 136.

The non-renewal of a fixed term contract

16.31 It will be noted that s 136(2) is in terms which are essentially the same as s 95(2) of the Act which defines dismissal for the purposes of the unfair dismissal provisions and reference should be made to decisions with regard to that section. The position with regard to fixed term contracts at common law has been discussed (see **15.44**). For the special provisions relating to some fixed term contracts and redundancy, see **16.10**.

Constructive dismissal

16.32 The Employment Rights Act 1996 preserves the right of the employee to claim constructive dismissal and to claim a redundancy payment. In many situations in which an employer is faced with financial difficulties the action which he wishes to take may well constitute a fundamental breach of contract. The scope of the doctrine of constructive dismissal has already been discussed at **15.47**. In *Kykot v Smith Hartley Ltd*[1] the applicant was a weaver who worked on the night shift. Orders were falling off and he was asked to fill a vacancy on a day shift and the night shift was terminated. There was no contractual power to move him to the day shift. It was held that he was constructively dismissed and as the reason for the change was the reduced manning needs of the company he was entitled to a redundancy payment. However, the employee cannot rely on this provision as a dismissal for the purposes of entitlement to a redundancy payment if he terminates the contract without notice in circumstances in which he is entitled to do so by reason of a lockout by the employer.[2]

1 [1975] IRLR 372, EAT.
2 Employment Rights Act 1996, s 136(2).

Implied or constructive termination of contract

16.33   If any act of an employer, or an event affecting an employer (including in the case of an individual, his death) operates in accordance with any enactment or rule of law so as to terminate an employment contract, then for the purposes of the redundancy payments provisions that act or event is treated as a termination of the contract by the employer.[1] The most common examples of this occur on the death of an individual employer, or the compulsory winding up of a company.[2]

1 See the Employment Rights Act 1996, s 136(5) which provides:
   'Where in accordance with any enactment or rule of law—
   (a)   any act on the part of an employer, or
   (b)   any event affecting an employer (including, in the case of an individual, his death),
   operates to terminate a contract under which an employee is employed by him, that act or event shall for the purposes of [the redundancy payments provisions] be treated as a termination of the contract by the employer.'
2 The rules applicable on the death of the employer are described at **16.80**.

Frustration

16.34   If the contract of employment is frustrated by an event affecting the employee there can be no dismissal (see **13.09**). The burden of proof to show that the employment contract has been frustrated lies on the employer. Reference should be made to the cases discussed at **13.12** to ascertain whether frustration has taken place. It should be noted however that a frustrating event affecting an employer operates as a dismissal by virtue of s 136(5).

Failure to permit woman to return to work after confinement

16.35   Where an employee who has been absent from work wholly or partly because of pregnancy or confinement has a statutory right to return to work under s 79 and has exercised that right in accordance with s 82 of the Act, but is not permitted to return to work, she is treated for the purposes of the redundancy payments provisions as if she had been dismissed on the notified day of return.[1]

1 Employment Rights Act 1996, s 137(1).

Redundancy

16.36   Subject to the exceptions already noted an employer is required to make a redundancy payment to an employee who has been continuously employed for the requisite period of two years, if the employee is:

(1) dismissed by his employer by reason of redundancy, or
(2) laid off or kept on short-time as defined for redundancy payment purposes in the Act.[1]

1 Employment Rights Act 1996, s 135.

16.37 Section 139(1) of the Employment Rights Act 1996[1] contains the following definition of dismissal by reason of redundancy:

'(1) For the purposes of this Act an employee who is dismissed shall be taken to be dismissed by reason of redundancy if the dismissal is attributable wholly or mainly to[2]—
  (a) the fact that his employer has ceased, or intends to cease—
    (i) to carry on the business for the purposes of which the employee was employed by him, or
    (ii) to carry on that business in the place where the employee was so employed, or
  (b) the fact that the requirements of that business—
    (i) for employees to carry out work of a particular kind, or,
    (ii) for employees to carry out work of a particular kind in the place where he was so employed, have ceased or diminished or are expected to cease or diminish.'[3]

1 It is to be noted that the fact that a dismissal falls under the Transfer of Undertakings (Protection of Employment) Regulations 1981, SI 1981/1794, reg 8(2) does not prevent the dismissal constituting a dismissal by reason of redundancy: *Gorictree Ltd v Jenkinson* [1984] IRLR 391, EAT, notwithstanding the decision of the EAT in *Canning v Niaz and McLoughlin* [1983] IRLR 431, EAT. See also *Anderson and McAlonie v Dalkeith Engineering Ltd* [1984] IRLR 429, EAT; *Chapman and Elkin v CPS Computer Group plc* [1987] IRLR 462, CA.
2 An industrial tribunal should look carefully to ascertain whether the dismissal is attributable wholly or mainly to redundancy: *Tipper v Roofdec Ltd* [1989] IRLR 419, EAT.
3 For the purposes of s 139(1) the business of the employer together with the business or businesses of his associated employers are treated as one unless either of the conditions in s 139(1)(a) or (b) would be satisfied without so treating them (s 139(2)). For 'associated employer' see **11.45**. 'Cease' means cease either permanently or temporarily for whatever cause and 'diminish' has a corresponding meaning: s 139(6). When considering s 139 it is important to appreciate the distinction between an employer's 'requirements' and 'needs' . It is the 'fact of the redundancy' and not the 'reason' for it which is the material matter: *Association of University Teachers v University of Newcastle-upon-Tyne* [1988] IRLR 10, EAT. The decision of the EAT in *Delanair Ltd v Mead* [1976] IRLR 340 should be read as explained in *Association of University Teachers v University of Newcastle-upon-Tyne*.

The reason

16.38 Unless the contrary is proved an employee who has been dismissed by his employer is presumed to have been so dismissed by reason of redundancy. Thus the burden of proof rests on the employer and he has to prove to the industrial tribunal that on the balance of probabilities the employee is not redundant. Since this involves proof of a negative, the onus is usually discharged by proving a reason for dismissal other than redundancy.[1] Difficulty has been experienced in deciding whether a subjective or objective test is to be applied in determining whether a dismissal is 'attributable' to redundancy. Widgery LJ (as he then was) in *Hindle v Percival Boats Ltd*[2] said:

'I agree that the tribunal must look at the facts objectively to discover the true causes to which the dismissal is attributable but I do not find the distinction between objective and subjective tests to be either helpful or conclusive.'

The dismissal is attributable to the facts which caused it to occur. The tribunal must consider the evidence to see what those facts were and must bear in mind that the claimant succeeds on this issue unless the employer demonstrates that a diminution in the requirements of the business was *not* the main cause.[3] The employer's evidence may be highly material because he knows what prompted him to dismiss the claimant and if his evidence is believed it may go a long way to establishing the true causes of his action. The reality is that any tribunal would scrutinise with particular care a claim that a dismissal was not for redundancy when an employee was not replaced. Since the introduction of the right not to be unfairly dismissed in 1972, the tendency of employers has been to claim that dismissals are by reason of redundancy to assist in defending claims for unfair dismissal and the older authorities should be viewed with a degree of reservation since points were argued then which an employer would be unlikely to assert in the present climate.

1 Employment Rights Act 1996, s 163(2) sets out the presumption. When considering an application for a redundancy payment the industrial tribunal must not overlook the presumption. See *Wilcox v Hastings* [1987] IRLR 298, CA and in the light of this case *Parkes v B and M Bodyworks Ltd* (1972) 7 ITR 48, NIRC should be regarded with caution. See also Sachs LJ in *Hindle v Percival Boats Ltd* [1969] 1 All ER 836; [1969] 1 WLR 174, CA and *Wagstaff v Trade and Industrial Press Ltd* (1967) 3 KIR 339, DC.
2 [1969] 1 All ER 836; 4 ITR 86, CA.
3 The dismissal (as defined) of an employee whose apprenticeship term comes to an end and who is not taken on as a qualified employee because there is a diminution of requirements for skilled men, is not dismissal by reason of redundancy because his dismissal is attributable to the expiry of the apprenticeship term and not to the shortage of work for skilled men. It is the refusal of new employment which is attributable to the work shortage: *North East Coast Shiprepairers Ltd v Secretary of State for Employment* [1978] ICR 755, EAT; *Small v Lex Mead (Southampton) Ltd* [1977] IRLR 48.

Multiple reasons

16.39   There may be some cases where there are several reasons for dismissal; for instance it could be due to a combination of circumstances such as redundancy and unsuitability or lack of ability. It will then have to be considered whether the employee has been unfairly dismissed, but he will be entitled to redundancy payment only if the dismissal is attributable 'wholly or mainly' to redundancy. Dismissal may in certain cases be to neither redundancy nor misconduct.[1] In delivering the decision of the National Industrial Relations Court in *MacFisheries Ltd v Willgloss*[2] Lord Thompson said:

'It seems to us that, broadly speaking the employer can discharge this onus in two ways ... In the first place, if the employer negatives the proposition that "the requirements of the employer's business for employees to carry out work of a particular kind has diminished or was expected to diminish", then the employee's case must fail. If on the other hand a "redundancy situation" is established by the evidence to the satisfaction of the tribunal, then the employers must go on to establish to the tribunal's satisfaction that the dismissal was not attributable wholly or mainly to the redundancy situation.'

Lord Thompson went on to say that where two causes contributed to the dismissal it is for the industrial tribunal to decide whether the employers have discharged the onus of proving that redundancy was not the sole, or main, cause of dismissal. The tribunal had taken the view that the employers had not proved that the cause other than redundancy went more towards the dismissal than the redundancy, so the employers must fail in their appeal.

1 See for example *Arnold v Thomas Harrington Ltd* [1969] 1 QB 312; [1967] 2 All ER 866, DC where the reason was to obtain possession of a flat. Reference should be made to the judgment of Widgery LJ in *Hindle v Percival Boats Ltd* [1969] 1 All ER 836; [1969] 1 WLR 174, CA and also *North Riding Garages Ltd v Butterwick* [1967] 2 QB 56; [1967] 1 All ER 644, DC.
2 (1972) 7 ITR 57 at p 58, NIRC.

Carrying on a business

16.40 It might be thought that the use of the word business limited redundancies to a commercial undertaking. This is not the case. For the purposes of the definition of redundancy 'business' includes a trade or profession and includes any activity carried on by a body of persons, whether corporate or unincorporated[1] and 'activity' in this context means 'a combination of operations undertaken by the corporate body whether or not amounting to a business trade or profession in the ordinary sense'.[2] A private household is a business for the purposes of the redundancy provision.[3] Activities carried on by a local education authority with respect to the schools maintained by it and the activities carried on by the governors of those schools are treated as one business.[4] An employer can operate a business which he or she does not own. Thus a postmistress retired and dismissed her employee. The Post Office continued to operate but it was held by the Employment Appeal Tribunal that the employee was entitled to a redundancy payment as there was no requirement that the employer should own the business.[5] In view of the attempt by many national retail outlets to make the managers *self-employed* and require them to employ their own staff, it may well be that this decision will have a wider importance.

1 Employment Rights Act 1996, s 235. For a discussion of this definition see *Lloyd v Brassey* [1969] 2 QB 98; [1969] 1 All ER 382, CA and *Kenmir v Frizzell* [1968] 1 All ER 414, DC.
2 Per Diplock LJ in *Dallow Industrial Properties Ltd v Else* [1967] 2 QB 449, [1967] 2 All ER 30, CA.
3 Employment Rights Act 1996, s 161(2); although immediate family (although not the spouse) are excluded (s 161(1)).
4 Employment Rights Act 1996, s 139(3).
5 *Thomas v Jones* [1978] ICR 274 EAT.

Place where employee was employed

The static employee

16.41 In the overwhelming majority of cases of redundancy which arise when a workplace is closed it is obvious that the statutory requirement is met. There can be difficulties when an employee worked at one place but there was a contractual term that the employee might be required to work elsewhere. There is conflicting authority as to whether the place of work refers to the geographical location of where the employee does work or to any of the places at which he or she may be required to work under the contract. There is a stream of authority for saying that the place where the employee was so employed is the place where he was contractually obliged to be employed but in *Bass Leisure Ltd v Thomas*[1] the Employment Appeal Tribunal reasserted the older line of cases that the place of work is established by a factual enquiry. It was held that in answering that question the tribunal will take into account the contractual provisions in that they help to decide where the employee *in fact* worked but will not concern itself with the question of where under the contract the employee *might* have been required to work. In reality the practical difference between a geographic test and a contract test in cases where the proposed transfer is in fairly close proximity may not be great since an employee who unreasonably refuses an offer of suitable alternative employment loses his or her entitlement to a redundancy payment. Where the contractual, as opposed to the geographic test, is applied, if the employer is entitled to transfer the employee from place to place and he refuses to be transferred, the dismissal is not by reason of redundancy. In such a situation it would be essential to establish the exact terms of the contract. In some instances there are express terms permitting transfer by the employer[2] and in other circumstances a term allowing transferability may be implied.[3] Whether such a term can be implied is a question of law and not of fact and is therefore the subject of appeal.[4] Each case must be judged on its merits. If the employer wishes to rely on the mobility clause to defeat a claim for a redundancy payment, it should clearly invoke the mobility clause prior to the dismissal.[5] An employer who wishes to have the right to transfer the geographic location of the employment should include a provision to that effect in the contract of employment.[6] It is suggested that it gives a far more natural meaning of the Act to apply the geographic test and that the employer is protected against the unreasonable refusal of suitable alternative employment by the sanction of the employee losing or her entitlement to a redundancy payment.

1 [1994] IRLR 104, EAT. But see *Johnson v Peabody Trust* [1996] IRLR 387. Cases such as *Rank Xerox Ltd v Churchill* [1988] IRLR 280, EAT which proceeded on the basis of a contractual test should be viewed with caution.
2 See for instance *Briggs v Imperial Chemical Industries Ltd* (1968) 3 ITR 276, DC (transfer within a factory); *Parry v Holst & Co Ltd* (1968) 3 ITR 317, DC (transfer from South Wales to Somerset); *Sutcliffe v Hawker Siddeley Aviation Ltd* [1973] ICR 560, NIRC (contract to work anywhere in the United Kingdom; employee required to work long distance from home: held no redundancy); and *United Kingdom Atomic Energy Authority v Claydon* [1974] ICR 128, NIRC (requirement to work at any of employer's establishments in Great Britain or in post overseas). The clause must be unambiguous. In *Litster v Fram Gerrard Ltd* [1973] IRLR 302, NIRC a turner was employed at a plant depot in Swindon. A term of the National Working Rule Agreement stated that the employee could be required to transfer from site to site. The employers wished to transfer Mr Litster to their depot at Aldington. It was held that the agreement did not entitle the employers to transfer the employee; 'site' meant civil engineering site and did not include permanent depots. It is important to ensure that the contract has not been varied or a 'concession' granted to the employee: *Hawker Siddeley Power Engineering Co Ltd v Rump* [1979] IRLR 425, EAT; *Wilson-Undy v Instrument and Control Ltd* [1976] ICR 508, EAT.
3 See *O'Brien v Associated Fire Alarms Ltd* [1969] 1 All ER 93; [1968] 1 WLR 1916 CA; *Stevenson v Teesside Bridge and Engineering Ltd* [1971] 1 All ER 296, DC; *Rowbotham v Arthur Lee & Sons Ltd* [1975] ICR 109, DC; *Managers (Holborn) Ltd v Hohne* [1977] IRLR 230, EAT.
4 *O'Brien v Associated Fire Alarms Ltd* [1969] 1 All ER 93; [1968] 1 WLR 1916, CA. See also *Jones v Associated Tunnelling Co Ltd* [1981] IRLR 477, EAT.
5 If the employers seek to rely on a clause allowing transfer they must invoke it when they seek to do so: *RH McCulloch Ltd v Moore* [1968] 1 QB 360; [1967] 2 All ER 290, DC. An employer who does not invoke a mobility clause cannot be heard to say that its mere existence entitles him to claim after a workplace has closed that he might have required them to work elsewhere if he did not do so: *Curling v Securicor Ltd* [1992] IRLR 549, EAT.
6 If there is an express mobility clause which is clear and unambiguous it is wrong to attempt to superimpose a test of reasonableness: *Rank Xerox Ltd v Churchill* [1988] IRLR 280, EAT.

The itinerant employee

16.42   If an employee does not work from any one centre but works as a salesman or as a construction worker on a site, then obviously there is no one place of work. If such an itinerant worker objects to moving on, the dismissal will be for refusal to obey an instruction rather than for redundancy.[1]

1 *McCaffrey v EE Jeavons & Co Ltd* (1967) 2 ITR 636.

Work of a particular kind

Employees

16.43 Much of the case law has centred on what is meant by *work of a particular kind*. It is worth pointing out that a frequent complaint made by unrepresented employees is that it is unfair that they have been dismissed for redundancy when their jobs have not disappeared and are being done by outside contractors. If an employer decides to sub-contract the same work which hitherto was done by a dismissed employee, this is a dismissal which is by reason of redundancy because the employer no longer has a requirement for *employees* to carry out that work.

Part-time and full-time employees

16.44 There are conflicting authorities as to whether part-time work is a different *kind of work*.[1] It is suggested that if the whole of the statutory definition is considered then the position is that if an employer decides to rearrange the same hours which are currently done by five part-time employees to three full-time employees and there is no change in function then there is a redundancy because there is an overall reduction for *employees* to carry out *work of a particular kind* but that if there is a reallocation of three full-time jobs to five part-time jobs then there is no redundancy because there is no reduction of *employees*.[2]

1 *Rosie v Watt* and *Pollock v Victor Value (Holding) Ltd* suggest part-time work is a different *kind of work* but *Brown v Dunlop Textiles Ltd* suggests it is not. All three cases are to be found in one volume (1966) 2 ITR at pp 201, 338 and 531.
2 There are two unreported tribunal decisions to this effect.

Meaning of 'work of a particular kind'

16.45 Considerable difficulty may be experienced with the meaning of *work of a particular kind* in s 139(1)(b). Whether or not the requirements of a business for employees to carry out work of a particular kind have ceased or diminished will depend upon the employee's contractual obligations. Work of a particular kind does not mean *work of a particular kind on the existing terms and conditions of employment*. In *Chapman v Goonvean and Rostowrack China Clay Co Ltd*[1] the Court of Appeal considered employees whose employment was treated as terminated and who claimed redundancy payments when their employers withdrew a free bus service because of increased per capita costs. It was decided that the absence of the bus service could not be said to result in the employers' requirements for work of a particular kind having ceased or diminished. Buckley LJ explained the position as follows:

'The section does not pose the question, what might be expected to happen if the employees were not dismissed but continued under their prior contracts of employment. It poses the question whether the employers' requirement for employees to carry out work of the particular kind in question "is expected to cease or diminish". That is a question which needs to be answered objectively in the light of all the circumstances affecting the employers' business, but not, in my opinion, with any special relation to the particular contracts of employment under which the dismissed employees were previously employed.'

The work to which the section refers is the particular kind of work which the employee was under his contract of employment employed to do.[2]

1 [1973] 2 All ER 1063 at p 1070, CA. See also *Murphy v Epsom College* [1985] ICR 80, CA.
2 *Cowen v Haden Ltd* [1982] IRLR 314, CA; *Pink v White and White & Co (Earls Barton) Ltd* [1985] IRLR 489, EAT but see *Amos v Max Arc Ltd* [1973] IRLR 285, NIRC. If an employee is contractually bound to perform a wide range of duties but in practice is only required to carry out one function then if that function disappears there may well be an issue as to whether one should apply a *function* or *contractual* test. For a discussion, see *Harvey on Industrial Relations* vol 1, para E868.

Changing the image and time of work

16.46 It is by no means unusual for employers to wish to change the image of their workforce and in some case this means replacing older staff with younger staff especially when the employees are female. When considering the case of a barmaid dismissed because the respondents wished to give a public house a modern image and to replace her with a younger woman, the Divisional Court said[1] the test was whether the requirements of the business for employees to carry out work of a particular kind had ceased or diminished not whether there had been a diminution in the requirements for a barmaid of her type. In that case the type of work was the same and it was held that the application for a redundancy payment failed. Whilst replacing middle-aged barmaids with young 'bunny girls' might well not have constituted a redundancy that case was decided before the unfair dismissal and sex discrimination legislation was in force and it would be foolhardy for any employer to adopt such a course today. The word 'requirements' in the section means 'needs'.[2]

1 *Vaux and Associated Breweries Ltd v Ward (No 2)* (1970) 5 ITR 62, DC.
2 *Bromby and Hoare Ltd v Evans* [1972] ICR 113, NIRC (amount of work on hand had increased but more efficient organisation had reduced the 'need' for the employees; held to be redundancy); *McCrea v Cullen & Davison Ltd* [1988] IRLR 30, NICA.

16.47 In *Johnson v Nottinghamshire Combined Police Authority*[1] the Court of Appeal was concerned with whether there was a redundancy when the employers wished to reallocate shifts. Lord Denning MR said:

'It is settled by those cases that an employer is entitled to reorganise his business so as to improve its efficiency and, in so doing, to propose to his staff a change in the terms and conditions of their employment: and to dispense with their services if they do not agree. Such a change does not automatically give the staff a right to redundancy payments. It only does so if the change in the terms and conditions is due to a redundancy situation. The question in every case is: Was the change due to a redundancy situation, or not? If the change is due to a redundancy situation, he is entitled to a redundancy payment. If it is not due to it, he is not. Typical of redundancy situations are these: There may be a recession in trade so that not so many men are needed. There may be a change in the kind of work done, as from wood to fibreglass, so that woodworkers are no longer needed (see *Hindle v Percival Boats Ltd).*[2] The business may be no longer profitable so that the employer has to cut down somewhere. Or, he may be overstaffed. The employer may meet such a situation by dispensing with the services of some of the men; or alternatively he may lower the wages; or put them on part time. If he does it by making a change in the terms and conditions of employment, it is due to a redundancy situation. Those who lose or leave their work in consequence are entitled to redundancy payments.'

It is clear that the mere fact that the employee is required to work a different pattern of hours does not mean that if he or she refuses and is dismissed then a claim for a redundancy payment will be successful. If however the change is accompanied by an overall reduction in manning levels as in *Kykot's*,[3] then a claim for redundancy is likely to be successful. In that case the applicant was required to change from night shift to day shift. He left and claimed he was constructively dismissed. His claim for redundancy was successful on the basis that there was an overall reduction in employees.

1 (1974) 9 ITR 164 at p 167, CA; see *Kykot v Smith Hartley Ltd* [1975] IRLR 372, DC. In *Kykot's* case *Johnson* could be distinguished in two respects. Not only were shifts reorganised but there was a reduction in the total number of people employed and a falling off of trade. See also *Macfisheries Ltd v Findlay* [1985] ICR 160, EAT.
2 [1969] 1 All ER 836; [1969] 1 WLR 174, CA.
3 [1975] IRLR 372, DC.

Redundancy situation

16.48 Care must be used to ensure that the 'shorthand' expression 'redundancy situation' does not direct attention away from the statutory provisions.[1] Whether or not dismissals in consequence of a reorganisation are dismissals by reason of redundancy depends solely on whether the statutory definition is satisfied. For instance, if as a result of a reorganisation, the applicant's job disappears and his duties are assigned to a more senior employee there may be a fundamental change in the nature of the work to be done so that the requirement for employees to carry out work of a particular kind had ceased or diminished.[2] When deciding whether the requirements of section 139 have been satisfied the overall requirement of the business are looked at. In *North Riding Garages Ltd v Butterwick*[3] Widgery J (as he then was) said:

'It is, we think, important to observe that a claim under [s 81(2)(b)] is conditional upon a change in the requirements of the business. If the requirement for the business for employees to carry out work of a particular kind increases or remains constant no redundancy payment can be claimed by an employee, in work of that kind, whose dismissal is attributable to personal deficiencies which prevent him from satisfying his employer. The very fact of dismissal shows that the employee's services are no longer required by his employer and that he may, in a popular sense, be said to have become redundant, but if the dismissal was attributable to age, physical disability or inability to meet his employer's standards he was not dismissed on account of redundancy within the meaning of the Act. For the purpose of this Act an employee who remains in the same kind of work is expected to adapt himself to new methods and techniques and cannot complain if his employer insists on higher standards of efficiency than those previously required; but if new methods alter the nature of the work required to be done it may follow that no requirement remains for employees to do work of the particular kind which has been superseded and that they are truly redundant. Thus if a motor manufacturer decides to use plastics instead of wood in the bodywork of his cars and dismisses his woodworkers, they may well be entitled to redundancy payments on the

footing that their dismissal is attributable to a cessation of the requirement
of the business for employees to carry out work of a particular kind,
namely woodworking.'

This attention to the overall requirements of the business means that an
employee can be dismissed by reason of redundancy when the job of the
employee who is dismissed continues but he is replaced in that job by another
employee whose job has disappeared.[4] This situation is variously called
'shunted' , 'bumped' or 'transferred' redundancy.[5]

1 In *Lesney Products & Co Ltd v Nolan* [1977] ICR 235, CA, Lord Denning MR said (at
p 238) when considering *Johnson's* case (see **16.47**) 'Whilst I adhere to what I there said, I think
that the phrase "a redundancy situation" may be misleading. It is shorthand: and it is better
always to check it by the statutory words.' In *Nolan's* case machine setters who had worked a
day shift with overtime were changed to a double day shift. The number of operatives was not
reduced and the amount of work for *day* shift machine setters was no less. The Court of Appeal
found that the employees who left were not dismissed by reason of redundancy.
2 *Robinson v British Island Airways Ltd* [1978] ICR 304, EAT; *Delanair Ltd v Mead* [1976]
ICR 522, EAT.
3 (1967) 2 ITR 229 at p 232, DC. See also *European Chefs (Catering) Ltd v Currell* (1971)
6 ITR 37, DC which illustrates a nice distinction. The applicant was a chef specialising in eclairs
and meringues. He was replaced because the employers wanted a chef who would specialise in
continental pastries. The tribunal, applying the presumption, found he was entitled to a
redundancy payment and this was affirmed by the Divisional Court.
4 *W Gimber & Sons Ltd v Spurrett* (1967) 2 ITR 308, QBD. Notwithstanding the express
provision of the Employment Protection (Consolidation) Act 1978, s 81(2) (now s 139(2) of the
Employment Rights Act 1996) that the business of the employer together with the business of his
associated employer shall be treated as one in *Babar Indian Restaurant v Rawat* [1985] IRLR
57, EAT, the EAT upheld a decision of an industrial tribunal which did not do so for these
purposes.
5 It is important to draw the distinction between a 'bumped' redundancy and the loss of the
chance to apply for employment. The former case is redundancy, the latter is not: *Fay v North
Yorkshire County Council* [1985] IRLR 247, CA.

Analysing work of a particular kind

16.49 It is of course essential to decide the particular kind of work carried
out by the employee. This may be made easier by the inclusion of the title of
the job the employee is employed to do in the written particulars and terms of
employment which is to be given to him. However, considerable difficulties
have been occasioned in this regard in the past. In *Amos v Max-Arc Ltd*[1] Sir
John Donaldson said:

'The phrase "work of a particular kind" in [s 81(2)(b)] of the Act, means,
in our judgment, work which is distinguished from other work of the same
general kind by requiring special aptitudes, skills or knowledge.'

The test is whether there is a cessation or diminution in the particular kind of
work under his contract of employment the employee is employed to carry
out.[2] The question for the tribunal to decide is what are the terms of the
employee's contract of employment and do they restrict him to one kind of
work.[3] If the employment contract contains an express provision defining the
type of work for which the employee is employed the industrial tribunal
should not try and imply a restriction in it.[4]

1 (1973) 8 ITR 65 at 67, NIRC. See also *Lane Fox and Co Ltd v Binns* (1972) 7 ITR 125,
NIRC; *O'Donnell v George Wimpey & Co Ltd* (1972) 7 ITR 343, NIRC and *Weed v AE Smith
& Son (Kettering) Ltd* (1972) 7 ITR 352, NIRC.
2 *Cowen v Haden Ltd* [1982] IRLR 314, CA.
3 *O'Neill v Merseyside Plumbing Co Ltd* [1973] ICR 96, NIRC.
4 *Nelson v British Broadcasting Corpn* [1977] ICR 649, CA.

16.50 At one time it was suggested that if an employee had been responsible or partly responsible for the redundancy situation arising he may not be entitled to redundancy payment. In *Sanders v Ernest A Neale Ltd*[1] this idea was finally dispelled. Sir John Donaldson said:

'The court would like to take this opportunity of exorcising the ghost of self-induced redundancy. It can certainly occur, but as such it has no legal significance. Interruption of service due to industrial action can cause customers to look to competitors or to turn to substitute materials or services. This can lead to a diminution in the requirements of the business for employees to carry out work of a particular kind and to workers being dismissed. But the mere fact that the employees' action created the redundancy situation does not disentitle them to a redundancy payment. The entitlement depends upon the words of the statute and there is no room for any general consideration of whether it is equitable that the employee should receive a payment.'

1 [1974] ICR 565 at p 573, NIRC.

16.51 Each case depends on its own particular circumstances. When deciding whether or not an employee is redundant an industrial tribunal should determine and set out clearly the facts on which it relies to justify the conclusion in the terms of s 139.[1]

1 *Elliott v University Computing Co (Great Britain) Ltd* [1977] ICR 147, EAT. Although each case depends on its own facts some assistance may be obtained from previous cases of which there are some examples below.

Cases where the employee was held not to be redundant

16.52 It should be noted that many of these cases refer to events which took place before the coming into force of the unfair dismissal provisions in 1972 and so the employer was more inclined to argue that the employee was not redundant than may be the case today.

(1) *Hindle v Percival Boats Ltd* [1969] 1 All ER 836; [1969] 1 WLR 174, CA (Hindle skilled woodcraftsman employed by boat builders and repairers. Earlier employees dismissed because of movement to glass-fibre boats but Hindle was retained for repair work. He was an excellent skilled craftsman but was dismissed because he took such a long time in doing a thorough job).

(2) *J Styles & Son Ltd v Saunders* (1968) 3 ITR 6, DC (one-eyed carpenter, although contract permitted transfer he refused to go to site where exposed to danger to existing eye).

(3) *Malton v Crystal of Scarborough Ltd* (1971) 6 ITR 106, DC (redundancy situation but dismissed because of unsatisfactory work).

(4) *Stride v Moore (Metal Spinners) Ltd* (1968) 3 ITR 117, DC (redundancy situation but dismissed because of unsatisfactory work).

(5) *Jones v Star Associated Holdings Ltd* (1970) 5 ITR 178, DC (manager of casino and theatre, employer reduced applicant's status to theatre manager only and appointed new casino manager).

(6) *Vaux and Associated Breweries Ltd v Ward (No 2)* (1970) 5 ITR 62, DC (elderly barmaid replaced by younger woman).

(7) *Wagstaff v Trade and Industrial Press Ltd* (1967) 3 ITR 1, DC (employers dissatisfied with employee).

(8)   *North Riding Garages Ltd v Butterwick* [1967] 2 QB 56; [1967] 1 All ER 644, DC.

(9)   *Arnold v Thomas Harrington Ltd* [1969] 1 QB 312; [1967] 2 All ER 866, DC (reason for dismissal to obtain possession of flat).

(10)   *Auld v Trocoll Industries (Scotland) Ltd* (1971) 6 ITR 64, Ct of Sess (dispute with his employers resulted in dismissal).

(11)   *Bradley v Plastocraft Products (Darwen) Ltd* (1971) 6 ITR 217, DC (clash of personalities with chairman).

(12)   *Kleboe v Ayr City Council* (1972) 7 ITR 201, NIRC (art teacher dismissed when unable to comply with statutory requirement for registration – the business was that of teaching children not teaching by unregistered lecturer).

(13)   *Blakely v Chemetron Ltd* (1972) 7 ITR 224, NIRC (change to night shift not a change in requirement for work of a particular kind).

(14)   *Johnson v Nottinghamshire Combined Police Authority* [1974] 1 All ER 1082; [1974] ICR 170, CA (change for clerical workers to shift working; held no diminution of work but see *Kykot's* case at **16.32**).

(15)   *North East Coast Shiprepairers Ltd v Secretary of State for Employment* [1978] ICR 755, EAT (apprentice not offered employment on expiry of apprenticeship term).

(16)   *Dal v Orr* [1980] IRLR 413, EAT (reduction in workforce by attrition – no redundancy at time of dismissal).

Cases where the employee was held to be redundant and redundancy payments were awarded

16.53

(1)   *Hall v Farrington Data Processing Ltd* (1969) 4 ITR 230, DC (branch manager of Cardiff office offered employment as salesman with same salary on closing of office).

(2)   *Monckton v Atkins* (1969) 4 ITR 254, DC (gamekeeper whose work was reduced because of foot and mouth disease – his employer did not appear before tribunal).

(3)   *Etherington v Henry Greenham (1929) Ltd* (1969) 4 ITR 226, DC (employee told he was to be replaced by younger man, but not replaced; presumption of redundancy not rebutted).

(4)   *Walley v Morgan* (1969) 4 ITR 122, DC (farm worker persuaded employer to dismiss him shortly after foot and mouth disease outbreak).

(5)   *Watts, Watts & Co Ltd v Steeley* (1968) 3 ITR 363, DC (ship's master off sick for month during which chief officer takes over as captain; employers no longer required his services, but preferred the chief officer who was a foreign going captain).

(6)   *Royle v Pointer Group Holdings Ltd* (1971) 6 ITR 124, DC (oil tanker driver dismissed for refusing to do general haulage work).

(7)   *European Chefs (Catering) Ltd v Currell* (1971) 6 ITR 37 DC (pastry cook replaced by another with a different speciality).

(8)   *City Tote Ltd v Johnson* (1972) 7 ITR 44, NIRC (security man doing some photographic work transferred to photography department after reorganisation).

(9)   *Marshall v Harland and Wolff Ltd (No 2)* [1972] ICR 97, NIRC (an employee incapable of work at the time can be held to be entitled to a redundancy payment).

(10) *Robinson v British Island Airways Ltd* [1978] ICR 304, EAT (two managerial posts eliminated and work undertaken by holder of more important post; the two dismissed employees were redundant).

(11) *Nottinghamshire County Council v Lee* [1980] IRLR 284, CA (lecturer engaged on temporary basis because of diminishing work; dismissed at end of temporary appointment).

(12) *Huddersfield Parcels Ltd v Sykes* [1981] IRLR 115, EAT (reduction in number of employees to be looked at overall).

(13) *Carry All Motors Ltd v Pennington* [1980] ICR 806, EAT (employees reduced but work remained the same).

(14) See also *O'Hare v Rotaprint Ltd* [1980] ICR 94, EAT (a case on the Employment Protection (Consolidation) Act 1978, s 81(2). Kilner Brown J said 'when a workforce was expanded to meet a scale of production that never materialised, it might well be that there was no cessation or diminution of work because the requirement never materialised').

Lay-off and short-time

The problem

16.54 Many small employers, especially in such areas as the construction industry, are subject to peaks and troughs of demand for their work. They do not wish to disband their workforce but equally they do not want to pay them whilst there is insufficient work. They often resort to either laying the employee off (sending him home) or putting him on short-time (reducing the hours that the employee works). Whilst the employee might well be prepared to accept this as a temporary expedient it can obviously be unjust if it continues for any great length of time.

Statutory solution in outline

16.55 The statutory solution to this dilemma is to provide a mechanism whereby an employee may resolve the issue and require the employer to either provide work or pay a redundancy payment. It enables an employee to serve a notice on the employer indicating a claim for redundancy payment. The employer may then serve a notice contesting liability on the basis that it is reasonable to be expected that further work will be forthcoming. If no notice is served by an employer (or a notice is served but subsequently withdrawn), the employee has to terminate the employment in order to claim a redundancy payment. If the employer's notice is served, the employee may contest the matter before an industrial tribunal and must serve notice to terminate after notification of the tribunal's decision. If the employee has remained in the same employment and in the four weeks after service of the notice of intention to claim he has been laid off or kept on short-time for each of those weeks, the employer's defence of reasonable expectation of employment is defeated.

The statutory provisions

Lay-off and short-time

16.56 An employee is *laid off* for a week if his remuneration is dependent upon being provided with work of the kind which he is employed to do and he is not paid if he is not provided with such work.[1] An employee is deemed to be on *short-time* if by reason of a diminution of work the employee's remuneration is less than half a week's pay.[2] Thus there is no protection under these provisions for the employee who continues to receive a half or more of his week's pay.[3]

1 Employment Rights Act 1996, s 147(1)(a) and (b). It is important to distinguish between lay-off and short-time and dismissal; the decision of an industrial tribunal in *Sneddon v Ivorycrete (Builders) Ltd* (1966) 1 ITR 538 is illustrative. The employers wished to lay off an employee for about three weeks, but his trade union advised that there was no provision in the working agreement for suspension and the employee should be dismissed. He was dismissed and after about three weeks was recalled to work. He refused and claimed redundancy payment. The employers contended that he was laid off and not dismissed, but the tribunal decided (by majority) that he had been dismissed and pointed out that in law the contract of employment was still in being in a case of lay-off (though in a modified form), whereas it was terminated where an employee is dismissed. Reference may also be made to *Jones v Harry Sherman Ltd* (1969) 4 ITR 63, and *Powell Duffryn Wagon Co Ltd v House* [1974] ICR 123, NIRC. As is illustrated by *Sneddon's* case not all contracts contain the power for the employer to lay off their employees and great care must be exercised before purporting to lay off an employee. If the lay-off constitutes a dismissal whether or not the dismissal is by reason of redundancy is determined in accordance with the usual rules. The employee in such a case can also claim unfair dismissal: *Jewell v Neptune Concrete Ltd* [1975] IRLR 147. The terms of the contract must be examined most carefully. In *Burroughs Machines Ltd v Timmoney* [1977] IRLR 404, Ct of Sess, in confused circumstances a contract was construed as entitling the employer to suspend the guaranteed pay provisions of the individual's contract when there was an industrial dispute at the employers not involving Mr Timmoney. Contrast *Waine v R Oliver (Plant Hire) Ltd* [1977] IRLR 434, EAT. It was held in *A Dakri & Co Ltd v Tiffin* [1981] IRLR 59, EAT, that a contractual right to lay off was subject to an implied limitation that it was for a reasonable period only. However, there can be no implied term where there is an express term giving the right to lay off indefinitely. If an employee thinks that too long has elapsed his remedy is to follow the statutory procedure. See *Kenneth MacRae & Co Ltd v Dawson* [1984] IRLR 5, EAT. *Tiffin's* case should be read in the light of the decision in *Dawson*. See *McClory v Post Office* [1992] ICR 758.
2 Employment Rights Act 1996, s 147(2).
3 For week's pay, see **11.48** et seq.

Relation between short-time and lay-off

16.57 For the purposes of the provisions as to lay-off and short-time it is immaterial whether a series of weeks consists wholly of weeks during which the employee is laid off or kept on short-time, or partly one and partly of the other.[1] However, no account is taken of any week in which the employee is laid off or kept on short-time where the lay-off or short-time is wholly or mainly attributable to a strike or lockout, whether or not the strike or lock-out is in the trade or industry in which the employee is employed, and whether or not it is in Great Britain or elsewhere.[2]

1 Employment Rights Act 1996, s 154(a).
2 Employment Rights Act 1996, s 154(b).

The entitlement

16.58 Under s 148 of the Act an employee is only eligible for a redundancy payment if, after lay-off or short-time lasting four or more consecutive weeks, or a total of six or more weeks (of which not more than three were consecutive) in any 13 weeks, he gives notice to his employer of his intention to claim a redundancy payment. This 'notice of intention to claim' which must be in writing, has to be given four weeks or less after the end of the period of lay-off or short-time.[1] When an employee has given notice of his intention to claim, he is not entitled to a redundancy payment in pursuance of the notice unless he terminates his employment by a week's notice[2] which is given before the end of the period allowed for this purpose.[3] If he is obliged by his contract to give more than a week's notice to terminate the employment, then the reference to a week's notice is construed as being to the minimum period of notice he is required to give to bring his employment to an end.[4] The employee is not entitled to a redundancy payment by virtue of his notice of intention to claim, if the employer dismisses him (but this is without prejudice to the usual rules as to redundancy payments which may apply to the dismissal).[5] Within seven days after service of the notice of intention to claim the employer can serve on the employee notice in writing 'a counter-notice' that he will contest any liability to pay a redundancy payment in pursuance of the notice of intention to claim. For the employer to resist the claim for a redundancy payment successfully he must satisfy the industrial tribunal that on the date of the notice of intention to claim it was reasonably expected that the employee (if he continued to be employed by the same employer) would, not later than four weeks after that date, enter upon a period of employment[6] of not less than 13 weeks during which he would not be laid off or on short-time for any week.[7]

1 Employment Rights Act 1996, s 141(1)(a), (b) and (2). See *Fabar Construction Ltd v Race and Sutherland* [1979] IRLR 232, EAT. The provisions of the section must be strictly complied with: *Allinson v Drew Simmons Engineering Ltd* [1985] ICR 488, EAT.
2 Section 150(1). This notice must be a full seven days' notice: *Hamson v FMS (Farm Products) Ltd* (1967) 2 ITR 326 and see *Vennard v Deal* (1969) 4 ITR 315. No particular terms of art are required to indicate termination of employment: *Walmsley v C & R Ferguson Ltd* [1989] IRLR 112, Ct of Sess.
3 Employment Rights Act 1996, s 150(3) defines the relevant period as follows:
'(a) if the employer does not give a counternotice within seven days after the service of the notice of intention to claim, that period is three weeks after the end of those seven days;
(b) if the employer gives a counternotice within those seven days, but withdraws it by a subsequent notice in writing, that period is three weeks after the service of the notice of withdrawal; and
(c) if
(i) the employer gives a counter-notice within those seven days and does not so withdraw it, and,
(ii) a question as to the right of the employee to a redundancy payment in pursuance of the notice of intention to claim is referred to a tribunal, that period is three weeks after the tribunal has notified to the employee its decision on that reference.'

(4) For the purposes of subsection 3(c) no account shall be taken of—
(a) any appeal against the decision of an industrial tribunal, or
(b) of any proceedings or decision in consequence of any such appeal.'
4 Employment Rights Act 1996, s 150(2)(a) and (b).
5 Employment Rights Act 1996, s 151.
6 The period of employment refers to employment under the contract of employment in relation to which the employee was laid off or put on short-time: *Neepsend Steel and Tool Corpn Ltd v Vaughan* [1972] 3 All ER 725, NIRC, where the employment offered differed from that previously carried out and s 88(3), as it then was, was held not to have been complied with.
7 Employment Rights Act 1996, s 152(1). See *Hulse v Harry Perry (t/a Arthur Perry & Son)* [1975] IRLR 181.

Defeating the employer's defence

16.59 The employer cannot rely on the defence of the likelihood of future employment if the employee continues or has continued for four weeks after the notice of intention to claim was served to be employed by the same employer and he is, or has been, laid off or kept on short-time for each of those weeks.[1] If a counter-notice is served and not subsequently withdrawn by notice in writing, the employee is not entitled to a redundancy payment in pursuance of his notice of intention to claim except in accordance with a decision of an industrial tribunal.[2]

1 Employment Rights Act 1996, s 152(2).
2 Employment Rights Act 1996, s 149.

Loss and/or reduction of the redundancy payment

Offers of renewal and re-engagement

General position

16.60   For the purposes of the redundancy payment provisions an offer of alternative employment may defeat an employee's claim for a redundancy payment. In certain circumstances where an employee's contract is renewed, or he is re-engaged under a new contract of employment, then he is not regarded as being dismissed and hence there is no entitlement to a redundancy. The unreasonable refusal to take either a job on the same terms or suitable alternative employment disentitles an employee from a redundancy payment.

The offer

16.61   It is not necessary for the offer of renewal, or re-engagement, to be in writing. The offer must be made by the original employer or an associated employer. It must be made before the ending of the employment under his previous contract. The alternative employment must take effect immediately on the ending of the employment or not more than four weeks thereafter. The offer must be a serious and proper one with a realistic estimate of future earnings.[1] It has been held that an employer who procures an offer of employment with another employer is not making an offer of alternative employment within the meaning of the provision[2] and an employer is not able successfully to contend that the employee is excluded from the right to redundancy payment if no offer of renewal or re-engagement is made because the employee has indicated that he is not willing to accept any such offer.[3] Thus even where the employer knows that the employee will refuse it is necessary for the employer to make the offer. There are detailed statutory provisions as to the offer and how the four weeks are computed.[4]

1 *Clark v Wolsey* [1975] IRLR 42, EAT.
2 *Farquharson v Ross* (1966) 1 ITR 335 and *Scott v Salisbury* (1970) 5 ITR 22.
3 *Simpson v Dickenson* (1973) 8 ITR 40, NIRC.
4 Employment Rights Act 1996, s 138(3).

Effect of a valid offer

16.62   If an employee accepts the renewal of his contract on the same terms and conditions or accepts suitable alternative employment then he is not regarded as being dismissed and he is not entitled to a redundancy payment.[1] If the new contract differs as to capacity or place of employment, the employee is entitled to a four-week trial period to test the new job. If the employee does not like it he can resign and can claim a redundancy payment and he is deemed to have been dismissed for the purposes of redundancy.

1 See s 138(1).

16.63   If the new contract does not differ from the old contract as to capacity or place of employment there is no right to a trial period and it takes effect immediately, or after an interval of not more than four weeks after the ending of the contract of employment, and there is no dismissal.[1] But if the employee unreasonably refuses:

(1)   an offer on the same terms;[2]

(2)   an offer of suitable alternative unemployment;[3] or

(3)   unreasonably terminates the employment within the trial period;[4]

he will lose his entitlement to redundancy.[5] At the risk of stating the obvious if the employee accepts the offer and, where appropriate, works beyond the trial period there is no entitlement to a redundancy payment.[6]

1 See the Employment Rights Act 1996, s 138(1) and *SI (Systems & Instrumentation) Ltd v Grist and Riley* [1983] ICR 788, EAT and *Ebac Ltd v Wymer* [1995] ICR 466, EAT.
2 Employment Rights Act 1996, s 141(2) and (3)(a).
3 Employment Rights Act 1996, s 141(2) and (3)(b).
4 Employment Rights Act 1996, s 141(4)(d).
5 Employment Rights Act 1996, s 141.
6 Employment Rights Act 1996, s 138(1).

The trial period

16.64   This period of four weeks is construed strictly as calendar weeks even if that period includes bank holidays.[1] The effect of section 138 is that an offer falling within the statutory provisions incorporates a trial period of four weeks whether the parties to the contract agree that or not.[2] The section only applies for the purposes of the redundancy payments provisions; different considerations are taken into account for unfair dismissal.[3]

1 *Benton v Sanderson Kayser Ltd* [1989] IRLR 19, CA.
2 *Elliot v Richard Stump Ltd* [1987] IRLR 215, EAT
3 *Hempell v WH Smith & Sons Ltd* [1986] IRLR 95, EAT and see *Elliot v Richard Stump Ltd* [1987] IRLR 215, EAT

Extending the trial period

16.65   The trial period may be extended for the purposes of retraining[1] by agreement between the parties. Whereas there is no requirement that the original offer should be in writing an agreement to extend the trial period must:[2]

(1)   be made before the employee starts work under the new or renewed contract;

(2)   be in writing;[3]

(3)   specify the terms and conditions which will apply in the employee's case after the end of that period;[4]

(4)   specify the date on which the retraining will end.[5]

1 Employment Rights Act 1996, s 138(3)(b)(ii). Such an extension must be for the purpose of retraining: *Meek v J Allen Rubber Co Ltd and Secretary of State of Employment* [1980] IRLR 21, EAT.
2 Employment Rights Act 1996, s 138(6).
3 Employment Rights Act 1996, s 138(6)(b).This does not mean formal probative writing as is required under Scots law: *McKindley v William Hill (Scotland) Ltd* [1985] IRLR 492, EAT.
4 Employment Rights Act 1996, s 138(6)(d). This does not necessarily mean the same particulars as required by the written particulars of employment. It must however embody the most important matters such as remuneration and job description, see *McKindley's* case above.
5 Employment Rights Act 1996, s 138(6)(c).

The trial period – the common law position

16.66   In many situations in which an employer is seeking to transfer staff from one workplace to another place, or one job function to another job function, on its true analysis the employer is repudiating the contract. In decisions which predated the statutory right to a trial period the tribunals established that an employee had a reasonable time to make up his or her mind as to whether to agree to the fundamental change or whether to leave and treat themselves as having been constructively dismissed.[1] It has been held that this trial period is in addition to the statutory trial period.[2]

1 *Air Canada Ltd v Lee* [1978] ICR 1202, EAT; *Shields Furniture Ltd v Goff* [1973] 2 All ER 653; [1973] ICR 187, NIRC.
2 *Turvey v CW Cheyney & Son Ltd* [1979] ICR 341, EAT.

Suitability

16.67 Whether or not employment is suitable is a question of fact and degree for the tribunal to decide and is looked at in relation to the employee in question.[1] In *Taylor v Kent County Council*[2] Lord Parker CJ dealing with the section as first enacted said: '... it does seem to me that by the words "suitable employment", suitability means employment which is substantially equivalent to the employment which has ceased.' Whether or not the employment is suitable should be considered in the light of facts as known at the time when the offer was made.[3] Suitability must be considered separately from the reasonableness of the refusal. They are each matters for the tribunal to evaluate.[4]

1 *Collier v Smiths Dock Co Ltd* (1969) 4 ITR 338, DC; *Hitchcock v St Anne's Hosiery Co Ltd* (1971) 6 ITR 98, DC; and *Curling v Securicor Ltd* [1992] IRLR 549, EAT.
2 [1969] 2 QB 560; [1969] 2 All ER 1080, DC; *Goode and Cooper Ltd v Thompson* [1974] IRLR 111, NIRC.
3 *Smith v Spicers Ltd* (1966) 1 ITR 470. Guidance can also be obtained from *Johnston v St Cuthbert's Co-operative Association Ltd* (1969) 4 ITR 137, Ct of Sess and *Eltringham v Sunderland Co-operative Society Ltd* (1971) 6 ITR 121, DC. A multiplicity of insufficiently specific offers may not be an adequate substitute for an offer of a single suitable alternative employment: *Curling v Securicor Ltd* [1992] IRLR 549, EAT.
4 *Spencer and Griffin v Gloucestershire County Council* [1985] IRLR 393, CA.

Reasonableness of the refusal

16.68 This is a matter of fact to be determined by the tribunal in the light of the employee's attributes. Although special circumstances affecting the employee personally must be considered it is unlikely that a personal preference for a complete change of employment is a circumstance (however 'reasonable' from the employee's own standpoint) to be taken into account under these provisions.[1] The reason for the redundancy may be relevant to the question of reasonableness.[2] Each case has to be looked at on its merits but questions of status, pay, changes to shift working and the time at which the offer was made have all been considered as relevant factors by tribunals and the courts. In *Dutton v Hawker Siddeley Aviation Ltd*[3] Phillips J, said when delivering the decision of the Employment Appeal Tribunal:

'Great care has to be exercised before it can be said that an employee who is skilled and with a particular trade can be required to move to some other in a case where his contract does not provide for it.'

In that case however a temporary transfer was suggested only and the decision reached by the industrial tribunal that the employee had acted unreasonably was upheld.

1 *Pilkington v Pickstone* (1966) 1 ITR 363; *Paton Calvert & Co Ltd v Westerside* [1979] IRLR 108, EAT. The test is a subjective one: *JF Everest (Executors) v Cox* [1980] 1 ICR 415,

EAT. See *Fuller v Stephanie Bowman Ltd* [1977] IRLR 87 in which an applicant failed in her claim for a redundancy payment on the basis she was being required to move from Mayfair to work in Soho in premises above a sex shop. The tribunal actually inspected the premises.
2 *Freer v Kayser Bondor Ltd* (1966) 2 ITR 4.
3 [1978] IRLR 390 at p 391, EAT.

16.69 Although each case turns on its own facts some assistance may be obtained by referring to decided cases.

Unreasonable rejection of employer's offer

16.70

(1) *Johnston v St Cuthbert's Co-operative Association Ltd* (1969) 4 ITR 137, Ct of Sess (office worker offered post on same terms save that office at Fountainbridge, Edinburgh and not Portobello).
(2) *Hitchcock v St Ann's Hosiery Co Ltd* (1971) 6 ITR 98, DC (offered work at Newark instead of Nottingham, other terms comparable, employers would pay travelling expenses for nine months and alter shifts to suit travelling arrangements).
(3) *Collier v Smith's Dock Co Ltd* (1969) 4 ITR 338, DC (chargehand shipwright transferred to other dockyard as shipwright).
(4) *Eltringham v Sunderland Co-operative Society Ltd* (1971) 6 ITR 121, DC (branch manager of shop offered job as assistant manager with prospects – status 'is not the only consideration').
(5) *Morganite Crucible Ltd v Street* [1972] 2 All ER 411, NIRC (one reason given by clerk/typist for refusal to accept an offer of alternative employment was that she thought that the new employment would only last between 12 to 18 months. Sir John Donaldson (at p 413) said, 'In our judgment save in exceptional cases, if the offer is of regular employment, the time which it is anticipated that the employment will last is irrelevant either under the heading of "suitability" or "reasonableness". There may be exceptional cases which would qualify the general rule, but we are satisfied that that should be the general rule.' If the offer is of 'regular' (as opposed to 'temporary') employment the length of time which it is likely to last is not to be taken into account in assessing either suitability or reasonableness).
(6) *Dutton v Hawker Siddeley Aviation Ltd* [1978] ICR 1057; EAT (offer of 'sideways' move on temporary basis).

Employment not suitable and/or reasonably rejected by employee

16.71

(1) *Taylor v Kent County Council* [1969] 2 QB 560; [1969] 2 All ER 1080, DC (on amalgamation of schools a headmaster with ten years' experience offered post in pool of mobile staff: held unsuitable).
(2) *Lee v British Wagon Co Ltd* (1970) 5 ITR 192, DC (branch manager of finance company offered post as new business representative).
(3) *Allied Ironfounders Ltd v Macken* (1971) 6 ITR 109, DC (refused double shift work because he had to attend invalid wife).
(4) *Universal Fisher Engineering Ltd v Stratton* (1971) 7 ITR 66, NIRC (shift worker working four nights per week offered job on different work five nights per week: held suitable employment but reasonably refused).

(5) *E and J Davis Transport Ltd v Chattaway* [1972] ICR 267, NIRC (offer made to all employees in context of an industrial dispute: held not suitable offer for all employees).

(6) *Harris v Turner & Sons (Joinery) Ltd* [1973] ICR 31, NIRC (joiner who had been promoted to 'apprentice instructor' paid at higher rate than other joiners and 'on the staff', offered job as joiner: held not suitable; regard should be had to the employee's status and history) but contrast *Kane v Raine & Co Ltd* [1974] ICR 300, NIRC, where a slight change of status did not render the new employment unsuitable.

(7) *Thomas Wragg & Sons Ltd v Wood* [1976] ICR 313, EAT (after notice was given by his employers an employee obtained other employment to begin immediately the notice expired; offer of alternative employment not made until the day before the notice was due to expire).

(8) *Hindes v Supersine Ltd* [1979] IRLR 343, EAT (£10 per week reduction in pay; acceptance conditional on liking the new job; employee left after a few days because he did not like the job).

(9) *Spencer and Griffin v Gloucestershire County Council* [1985] IRLR 393, CA (cleaners refused alternative employment on the ground that they considered that they would not be able to do their jobs adequately and to a proper standard with reduced number of cleaners).

Loss of the redundancy payment in whole or in part – other cases

Employee anticipating expiry of employer's notice

16.72   Although an employee has not been dismissed if he is merely warned that at some future unspecified date there are going to be redundancies, once an employee has been given notice the position is rather different. Obviously an employee in such circumstances does not want to lose an opportunity to take up fresh employment by having to work out his notice. If during the notice the employee gives a written counter-notice stating that he intends to leave before the expiry of his notice he is still regarded as being dismissed.[1] The employer may then give the employee written notice that he requires him to work out the original notice and warning him that if he does not do so, the employer will contest his right to a redundancy payment.[2] If the employee refuses and leaves, the tribunal has power to make a redundancy payment or to reduce it in whole or in part. In reaching the decision as to what is just and equitable the tribunal has to have regard for the reasons for which the employee wished to leave and the reasons for which the employer wished the employee to work out his notice.[3] This procedure is virtually never used. It is rare for employers to require employees to work out their notice in large scale redundancies and it is inevitable that the cases on the topic are of some antiquity.[4] Indeed a frequent complaint on the part of employees is the unceremonious way in which they are escorted from the premises immediately they are told they are to be made redundant. Employers point out that they are apprehensive a distraught employee might be tempted to tamper with computer systems and wreak havoc with company records.

1 See the Employment Rights Act 1996, s 136(3)(b). This must be in the obligatory period of notice which is defined in s 136(4).
2 See the Employment Rights Act 1996, s 142.
3 Employment Rights Act 1996, s 142(3).

4 See *Armit v McLauchlan* (1965) 1 ITR 280; *Meger v Green's Food Fare Ltd* (1966) 1 ITR 244
and *McAlwane v Boughton Estates Ltd* [1973] 2 All ER 299, NIRC.

Strikes during period of employer's notice[1]

16.73   Section 143 of the Employment Rights Act 1996 provides a safeguard for an employer if the employee takes part in a strike during the period
of his notice given on dismissal by reason of redundancy. If during the period
of notice the employee strikes, the employer may serve on him a written
notice ('a notice of extension')[2] requesting him to agree to extend the employment contract beyond the time of expiry of the dismissal notice by an additional period comprising as many available days as the number of working
days lost by striking.[3] The notice of extension should be served prior to the
expiry of the dismissal notice. The additional period is called 'the proposed
period of extension'. The notice of extension should indicate the employer's
reasons for the request and should state that unless, either the employee
complies with the request, or the employer is satisfied that in consequence of
sickness, injury or otherwise the employee is unable to comply with it, or that
notwithstanding that he is able to comply with it in the circumstances it is
reasonable for him not to do so, then the employer will contest any liability
to a redundancy payment in respect of the dismissal.[4] To comply the
employee must attend at his proper or usual place of work on each available
day during the proposed period of extension and be ready and willing to
work.[5] Signifying his agreement to the request in any other way is not good
enough within the technical provisions of the section, although it would be
taken into account by a tribunal in the proceedings mentioned below.

1 For the situation when the employee is guilty of misconduct, see **16.76**.
2 Employment Rights Act 1996, s 143(2).
3 Employment Rights Act 1996, s 143(2)(a).
4 Employment Rights Act 1996, s 143(2)(c).
5 Employment Rights Act 1996, s 144 (1).

Applications to an industrial tribunal

16.74   If the employee does not comply with the request, he is not entitled
as of right to a redundancy payment in respect of that dismissal in circumstances where his employer does not agree to pay it.[1] He does have the right
to apply to the tribunal. When a notice of extension has been served and it
appears to the tribunal that the employee has not complied with the request,
and the employer has not agreed to pay a redundancy payment in respect of
the dismissal in question, the tribunal does have a discretion to award the
redundancy payment in whole or in part. If the employee was unable to
comply with the request, or it was reasonable for him not to comply with it
because in the circumstances he was unable to comply with it as a result of
sickness, injury or otherwise or notwithstanding that he was able to comply
with it, in the circumstances it was reasonable for him not to do so, the
tribunal may determine that the employer is liable to pay to the employee the
whole of the redundancy payment which would otherwise be due, or such
part of it as the tribunal thinks fit.[2]

1 Employment Rights Act 1996, s 143(3).
2 Employment Rights Act 1996, s 143(5). For a case which shows that taking part in a strike
can be misconduct notwithstanding, see *Simmons v Hoover Ltd* [1977] QB 284; [1977] 1 All ER
775, EAT.

Summary dismissal preserved

16.75 Neither the service of a notice of extension, nor any extension of the notice period, affects the right of the employer or employee to terminate the contract.[1]

1 Employment Rights Act 1996, s 144(4).

Misconduct (other than strikes) during notice period

16.76 If an employer is entitled to dismiss the employee for misconduct, then the employee loses his entitlement to a redundancy payment.[1] If the employer does give notice he must, if he wants to rely on this provision, accompany it with a written statement that the employer would be entitled to terminate the contract without notice.[2] The employee may apply to the tribunal which has a discretion to order the employer to make an appropriate payment if the tribunal considers it just and equitable.[3] An appropriate payment may include the whole or part of the redundancy payment.[4] When an employer raises a defence under the section the burden is on the employer to show that the employee was guilty of conduct which was a significant breach going to the root of the contract or which showed that the employee no longer intended to be bound by one or more of the essential terms of the contract.[5]

1 Employment Rights Act 1996, s 140.
2 Employment Rights Act 1996, s 140(1)(c).
3 Employment Rights Act 1996, s 140(3).
4 Employment Rights Act 1996, s 140(4)(a), (b). The misconduct may have taken place before or during the obligatory notice period. In *Lignacite Products Ltd v Krollman* [1979] IRLR 22, EAT, the industrial tribunal awarded an employee 60% of the normal redundancy payment when he was dismissed for theft. The Employment Appeal Tribunal did not set the decision aside although the award was greater than it would have made. See also *Cairns v Burnside Shoe Repairs Ltd* (1966) 2 ITR 75, two-thirds of the redundancy payment was paid; in *Jarmain v Pollard Son & Co Ltd* (1967) 2 ITR 406, £90 out of £180 was awarded – larceny after seven years' service with the company. In *Clark v EN Heath & Co Ltd* (1966) 2 ITR 42, the whole of the redundancy payment was paid.
5 In other words a 'contractual' test is used: *Bonner v H Gilbert Ltd* [1989] IRLR 475, EAT.

Redundancy and pension entitlement

16.77 The amount of redundancy payment may be reduced in accordance with regulations made under s 158 of the Employment Rights Act 1996 where the redundant employee has a right or claim (whether legally enforceable or not) to a periodical payment, or lump sum, by way of pension gratuity or superannuation allowance which is to be paid by reference to his employment by a particular employer[1] and is to be paid, or begin to be paid, at any time when he leaves that employment or within such period as is prescribed by the regulations. The present rules are contained in the Redundancy Payments Pensions Regulations 1965.[2] These must be looked at in detail when they are applicable. Broadly they apply when there is a statutory scheme, or a scheme or arrangement established by an irrevocable trust subject to the laws of any part of Great Britain, or secured by a contract of assurance, or an annuity contract with an insurance company, registered friendly society, or industrial and provident society, for provision of periodical payments, or a lump sum,[3] by way of pension, gratuity or superannuation allowance, having for its object or one of its objects, the provision of retirement benefits for persons serving in particular employments.[4] Payments made to an employee which consist solely of a return of his own contributions, with or without interest, payments to an employee which are attributable solely to additional voluntary contributions by that employee made in accordance with the scheme or arrangement, and periodical payments, or lump sums, which represent statutory compensation, are all ignored.[5]

1 See *Royal Ordnance plc v Pilkington* [1989] ICR 737, CA.
2 SI 1965/1932. Included in the Employment Rights Act 1996, s 158(1) is power to exclude the right to a redundancy payment or reduce the amount.
3 There is no requirement that the lump sum should be secured as mentioned when it has been paid. The notice required by reg 5 of the 1965 Regulations must be served within a reasonable time of the employee's claim: *British Telecomunications plc v Burwell* [1986] ICR 35, EAT.
4 Redundancy Payments Pensions Regulations 1965, reg 3(1). Certain other arrangements are also included, for instance some schemes equivalent to those of the Civil Service and certain Commonwealth pension arrangements.
5 Redundancy Payments Pensions Regulations 1965, reg 3(3).

Exclusion or reduction of the redundancy payment

16.78   The right to the payment may be excluded or the amount of the payment reduced where an employee who is entitled, or but for the regulations would be entitled, to a redundancy payment from an employer, has a right or claim to a benefit as mentioned above for himself which is to be paid by reference to the employee's last period of continuous employment with that employer, and if it is a lump sum is to be paid, or if it is a periodical payment is to begin to accrue, at the time when the employee leaves the employment with that employer, or within 90 weeks thereafter.[1] In addition if the pension consists of periodical payments the conditions specified in reg 4(2) of the 1965 Regulations must be satisfied. To exercise the right the employer must by notice in writing to the employee claim to exclude the right of the employee to a redundancy payment, or reduce its amount to be the extent permitted, and the employee in those circumstances is not entitled to a redundancy payment or, as the case may be, entitled only to the reduced amount.[2] The right of the employer to exclude, or reduce, the amount of the redundancy payment is discretionary.

1 Redundancy Payments Pensions Regulations 1965, reg 4. The words 'the employee's last period of continuous employment with that employer' in the regulation are construed as referring to the complete period of continuous employment: *Royal Ordnance plc v Pilkington* [1988] IRLR 466, EAT.
2 Redundancy Payments Pensions Regulations 1965, reg 5. The notice must be served within a reasonable time: *Stowe-Woodward BTR Ltd v Beynon* [1978] ICR 609, EAT. If by virtue of a statutory provision an employee 's remuneration is payable to him by a person other than his employer any reference to employer is construed as a reference to the person paying the remuneration (reg 6).

Old statutory compensation schemes

16.79   The Secretary of State is empowered[1] to make provision by regulation for securing that where a person is entitled to compensation under a statutory provision for loss of employment, or loss, or diminution, of emoluments or pension rights, in consequence of the operation of another statutory provision, the amount of any redundancy payment to which the employee is also entitled should be set off against the compensation which is otherwise payable. The Redundancy Payments Statutory Compensation Regulations

1965[2] have been made under this power and the amount of compensation payable pursuant to the listed statutory compensation provisions should be reduced by the amount of the redundancy payment paid to the employee under the redundancy payments provisions.[3]

1 Employment Rights Act 1996, s 178.
2 SI 1965/1988.
3 Redundancy Payments Statutory Compensation Regulations 1965, reg 4.

Death of employee or of employer

Death of employer

16.80 The death of an individual employer terminates the employment of the employee and as such operates as a dismissal.[1] If the contract is not renewed or the employee is not re-engaged under a new contract under the provisions of s 138 of the Employment Rights Act 1996 he is taken as being dismissed by reason of redundancy if the fact that he is not so re-engaged is wholly or mainly attributable to redundancy for the purpose of the Act.[2]

1 Employment Rights Act 1996, s 136(5).
2 Employment Rights Act 1996, s 139(4)(b). Section 138 applies as modified for the purpose. See *Narang v Trustees of J Hodge* (1969) 4 ITR 81, where an application for a redundancy payment made by an employee who refused to work for his dead employer's widow was dismissed.

Renewal of contract or re-engagement of the employee

16.81 By virtue of s 174(1) of the Employment Rights Act 1996 the personal representative has the right to renew or re-engage the employee and has the concession of a more generous timescale, namely of eight as opposed to four weeks. The effect of the section is that when an employee's contract is terminated by the death of his employer, he is not entitled to a redundancy payment if he is re-engaged by the personal representative to take effect not later than eight weeks after the death. This is subject to the qualification that if the provisions of the contract as renewed, or the new contract, as to the capacity and place in which the employee is employed or as to the other terms and conditions of his employment, differ (wholly or in part) from the corresponding provisions of the previous contract, the rules as to trial period on offer of renewal or re-engagement apply. The reference to the employer shall be construed as reference to the personal representatives of the deceased employer.[1]

1 Employment Rights Act 1996, s 174.

Employee's unreasonable refusal defeats his claim for redundancy

16.82 An employee is not entitled to a redundancy payment if he unreasonably refuses such an offer of re-engagement by the personal representatives, if the employment offered is either on the same terms as before, or if on different terms, suitable in relation to the employee.[1] In deciding whether the employment offered is suitable or whether the employee acted unreasonably in refusing it, the mere fact that the personal representative is now the employer is irrelevant.[2]

1 Employment Rights Act 1996, s 174(4).
2 Employment Rights Act 1996, s 174(4)(b).

Domestic servants

16.83 Where the employee is a domestic servant employed in a private household[1] references to the personal representative are construed as including references to any person (eg a relative) to whom management of the household has passed in consequence of the death, otherwise than on a sale or other disposal for valuable consideration.

1 Employment Rights Act 1996, s 174(6).

Time off provisions

16.84 If the employee has been laid off or put on short-time immediately before the employer's death and has not served notice of intention to claim, s 175 contains provisions for aggregating a period before death with that afterwards as if the week in which the former employer died and the first week of employment by the personal representative were consecutive weeks. The periods of four and 13 weeks are construed accordingly.[1] Section 175(3) deals with cases where the employee has served notice of intended claim within the four weeks preceding the death.

1 Employment Rights Act 1996, s 175(2). If he is not re-engaged or his contract is not renewed within four weeks after the service of notice of intention to claim, the usual provisions apply as if the employer had not died and the employee had terminated the employment by notice expiring at the end of the four weeks: s 175 (4). If the contract is renewed, or the employee re-engaged, and the employee was laid off or put on short-time for one or more weeks before the employer's death and he is laid off or kept on short-time by the personal representative for the week or more weeks following the renewal or re-engagement, the weeks are treated as consecutive and the periods for lay-off and short-time are extended by any week or weeks any part of which was after the death of the deceased employer and before the date on which the renewal or re-engagement took effect: s 175(5). The periods set out in s 150(3)(a) and (b) (see **16.58**) are extended by the interval between the death of the employer and the date of the renewal or re-engagement (s 175(6)).

Continuity

16.85 On a renewal or re-engagement by a personal representative within the provisions mentioned the employee is not regarded as having been dismissed and continuity is preserved.[1] The obligation of the personal representative so far as payment of a redundancy payment which is payable as a result of the termination occasioned by the death is a liability which is treated as accruing immediately before the former employer's death.[2]

1 Employment Rights Act 1996, ss 174(1) et seq.
2 Employment Rights Act 1996, s 207(3).

Death of the employee

16.86 Under s 207 of the Employment Rights Act 1996 a right which has accrued after the death of the employee devolves as if it had accrued before his death.

16.87 There are provisions in s 176 of the Act to cover cases where the employee dies after notice has been given, where he dies after notice has been given and an offer to renew the employment contract or re-engage him has been made and also if the employee dies during the trial period.[1] There are also provisions applicable if the employee dies having given notice anticipating the expiry of the employer's notice.[2]

1 If an employee has been given notice and dies before it expires the notice is treated as expiring on the date of the employee's death: Employee Rights Act 1996, s 176(2). Offers to renew, or re-engage, both before and during the trial period defeat a claim 'if it would have been unreasonable' for the employee to refuse them: s 176(2) and (3).
2 Employment Rights Act 1996, s 176(5).

16.88   If there is no personal representative of the deceased employee, tribunal proceedings may be instituted, or continued, on behalf of the estate of the deceased employee by such person as the tribunal may appoint, being either a person authorised by the employee to act in connection with the proceedings before his death, or the widower, widow, child, father, mother, brother or sister of the deceased employee. References to a personal representative are construed as including such person.[1] In such a case any award made by the tribunal shall be in such terms and shall be enforceable in such manner as may be provided by regulations made by the Secretary of State.[2] The effect of death on the time limits in which to claim redundancy payments is discussed at **16.104**.

1 Employment Rights Act 1996, ss 206(4) et seq.
2 Employment Rights Act 1996, s 206(6). See the Industrial Tribunals Awards (Enforcement in Case of Death) Regulations 1976, SI 1976/663.

Redundancy payments

Calculation of redundancy payments

16.89   Redundancy payments are calculated by reference to periods of continuous employment ending with the relevant date and reckoning backwards the number of years of continuous employment falling within that period and allowing:
(1)   one and a half weeks' pay for each such year of employment which consists wholly of weeks in which the employee was not below the age of 41 years;
(2)   one week's pay for each such year of employment (not falling within (1)) in which the employee was not below the age of 22 years;
(3)   half a week's pay for each such year (not falling within (1) or (2)).[1]

1 Employment Rights Act 1996, s 162(1). It is to be noted that a statutory redundancy payment is one which is calculated strictly in accordance with the statutory formula: *Secretary of State for Employment v Cheltenham Computer Bureau Ltd* [1985] IRLR 333, EAT.

No period counts in excess of 20 years

16.90   When reckoning the number of years no account of any year is taken of years earlier than 20 years before the relevant date.[1]

1 Employment Rights Act 1996, s 162(3).

Reduction after reaching the age of 64

16.91   When the relevant date is after the employee's 64th birthday the amount of a redundancy payment is reduced by one-twelfth for each complete month of employment after that birthday prior to the relevant date.[1]

1 Employment Rights Act 1996, s 162(4) and (5).

Continuity of employment

16.92 Continuity is calculated by reference to s 210 of the Employment Rights Act 1996. However, there are specific provisions which affect continuity of employment in relation to the calculation of redundancy payments:
(1) No period before the age of 18 counts.[1]
(2) There is no break in continuity if the employee is re-engaged or his contract renewed.[2]
(3) A period does not count in respect of which an employee has received a redundancy payment[3] or in particular circumstances received a pension.[4]
(4) Where an employee has not received his statutory notice, then he can add on the statutory notice.[5]

Thus if X started work on 5 of April 1989 and is dismissed without notice on 5 March 1996, as he is entitled to one week's notice for each completed year of service,[6] he is entitled to six weeks' notice and therefore (as this would take him beyond 5 April) he is entitled to a redundancy payment based on seven years' continuity of service.

1 Employment Rights Act 1996, s 211(2).
2 Employment Rights Act 1996, s 214(2)(b).
3 Employment Rights Act 1996, s 214(1).
4 Employment Rights Act 1996, s 214(3)(a).
5 Employment Rights Act 1996, s 145(5).
6 Employment Rights Act 1996, s 86.

Statutory limit to a week's pay

16.93 When calculating a redundancy payment there is a statutory limit to a week's pay which has to be taken into account and at present this is £210.[1] The Secretary of State has power to vary this limit by order when carrying out the statutory annual review of limits. The computation and definition of a week's pay is dealt with elsewhere (see Chapter 11).

1 Employment Rights Act 1996, s 227.

Written statement of amount of redundancy payment

16.94 On making a redundancy payment, otherwise than in pursuance of a decision of an industrial tribunal which specifies the amount of the payment to be made, the employer should give to the employee a written statement indicating how the payment has been calculated.[1] Forms for this purpose are available from local job centres although there is no statutory requirement to use them. An employer who fails to comply, without reasonable excuse, is guilty of an offence and is liable on summary conviction to a fine not exceeding level 1 on the standard scale.[2] In addition the employee can require the employer to provide such a statement by a notice in writing[3] within such period (not being less than one week beginning with the day on which the notice is given) as may be specified in the notice. If the employer without reasonable excuse fails to comply with that notice he is guilty of an offence and is liable on summary conviction to a fine not exceeding level 3 on the standard scale.[4]

1 Employment Rights Act 1996, s 165(1).
2 Employment Rights Act 1996, s 165(2).
3 Employment Rights Act 1996, s 165(3).
4 Employment Rights Act 1996, s 165(4).

Time off to look for work or make arrangements for training

16.95 An employee who is given notice of dismissal by reason of redundancy has in certain circumstances the right to be allowed reasonable time to look for work or make arrangements for training for future employment.[1] To qualify the employee must have been continuously employed for two years when the notice expires[2] or on the date on which it would expire if he was given the minimum statutory required notice.[3]

1 Employment Rights Act 1996, s 52(1). The claim can be made even if for some reason the employee is not entitled to a redundancy payment, for instance because of unreasonable refusal of an offer of suitable alternative employment: *Dutton v Hawker Siddeley Aviation Ltd* [1978] ICR 1057, EAT. In *Dutton's* case it was also held that it was not necessary for the employee to have a definite appointment or interview for a new position so long as the time off was used for training or to look for work.
2 Employment Rights Act 1996, s 52(2).
3 Employment Rights Act 1996, s 86(1).

16.96 The provisions as to time off in these circumstances apply to employees,[1] but not to employment where the employee is a share fisherman,[2] a merchant seaman[3] or engaged in employment where under his contract he ordinarily works outside Great Britain.[4] Crown servants are included other than members of the armed forces and women's services administered by the Defence Council.[5]

1 Employment under a contract of employment in the police service and persons engaged in such employment are excluded: Employment Rights Act 1996, s 200.
2 Employment Rights Act 1996, s 199(2).
3 Employment Rights Act 1996, s 199(4).
4 Employment Rights Act 1996, s 196(3).
5 Employment Rights Act 1996, ss 191 and 192(2). Members of the staff at the Houses of Parliament are included: ss 194 and 198.

Remuneration

16.97 An employee who is accordingly allowed time off during his working hours is entitled to be paid limited remuneration by his employer for the period of absence at the appropriate hourly rate. This is the amount of a week's pay divided by the number of normal working hours in a week for that employee when employed under the contract of employment in force on the day when the notice was given.[1] When the number of normal working hours differs from week to week, or over a longer period, the average number of such hours is calculated by dividing the total number of the employee's normal working hours during the period of 12 weeks ending with the last complete week before the date on which notice was given, by 12.[2] The amount of the employer's liability cannot exceed 40% of a week's pay for that employee for time off during the notice period.[3] If an employer unreasonably refuses to allow an employee time off under s 52 of the Employment Rights Act 1996 the employee is entitled to be paid an amount equal to the amount to which he would have been entitled under these provisions if he had been allowed time off, subject to the limitation.[4] An employee may present a complaint to an industrial tribunal that his employer has unreasonably refused to allow him time off under the provisions, or has failed to pay the whole or any part of any amount to which the employee is entitled in respect thereof.[5] If the tribunal finds the grounds of the complaint well founded it should make a declaration to that effect and order the employer to pay to the employee the amount due to him.[6] The statutory provisions do not affect the right of an employee to remuneration under his contract of employment,[7] but the amount of any contractual remuneration in respect of the period when he takes the time off goes towards discharging liability under s 52 and vice versa.[8]

1 Employment Rights Act 1996, s 53(1). The calculation date for these purposes is the day on which the employer's notice was given; s 53(2).
2 Employment Rights Act 1996, s 53(3).
3 Employment Rights Act 1996, s 53(5).
4 Employment Rights Act 1996, s 53(4).
5 Employment Rights Act 1996, s 54(1).
6 Employment Rights Act 1996, s 54(3).
7 Employment Rights Act 1996, s 53(6).
8 Employment Rights Act 1996, s 53(7).

16.98 It should be noted that although there is a limitation as to the amount of remuneration which an employer is required to pay, namely 40% of a week's pay, the employee is allowed *reasonable* time off which ultimately is a matter for a tribunal to determine. The maximum amount of entitlement to remuneration is 40% of a week's pay, but an employee who has 12 weeks' notice might well quite reasonably argue that he ought to be allowed a half-day a week albeit that this would mean some of that time he was not entitled to be paid. In reality it is by no means clear how an employee could assert this right in a tribunal given the time limits. In most large scale redundancies an employee is given payment in lieu of notice and applications under this section are rare.

Time limits

16.99 The industrial tribunal has jurisdiction to entertain complaints under s 52 only if the complaint is presented to the tribunal within the period of three months beginning with the day on which it is alleged that the time off should have been allowed, or within such further period as the tribunal considers reasonable, in a case where it is satisfied that it was not reasonably practicable for the complaint to be presented within the period of three months.[1]

1 Employment Rights Act 1996, s 54 (2).

Claims for redundancy payments

The exclusive jurisdiction of the industrial tribunal

16.100 Any question under Pt XI of the Employment Rights Act 1996 as to the right of an employee to a redundancy payment or as to the amount of the payment shall be referred to and determined by an industrial tribunal.[1] Any question as to the right of any person as to a payment equivalent to a redundancy payment as is mentioned in s 157(1) (namely an exemption order) of the Employment Rights Act 1996 or as to amount of the payment shall be referred to and determined by an industrial tribunal.[2] It is to be noted that the exclusive jurisdiction refers to a claim under Pt XI of the Act. There may be occasions in which courts might be required to determine issues as to the entitlement of a redundancy payment. Thus a person who insures himself so as to maintain the repayment instalments on a loan in the event of his redundancy may, if it is contended, for example, that the dismissal was due to misconduct, be required to bring his claim in the county court. If the industrial tribunal had adjudicated upon the matter, whatever the technical issues as to estoppel, it is unlikely that a court would not accept the adjudication of the industrial tribunal. There might be circumstances in which the tribunal did not have jurisdiction to hear the claim as when an employee did not have two years' continuous employment or if the claim was not brought within time. In such cases it would be for a court rather than a tribunal to determine the issue, but the presumption of redundancy would not apply.

1 Employment Rights Act 1996, s 163(1).
2 Employment Rights Act 1996, s 163(4). See *Greenwich Health Authority v Skinner; Greenwich Health Authority v Ward* [1989] IRLR 238, EAT.

Time for bringing the claim

16.101   In general terms an applicant has six months in which to make a redundancy claim. Moreover, the tribunal has a discretion to extend the time limit by a further six months if it is just and equitable to do this having regard to the reasons for the failure to take such action within the first six months. There are detailed statutory provisions which provide further exceptions to this general proposition.

16.102   Section 164 of the Employment Rights Act 1996 provides:
'(1)   An employee does not have the right to a redundancy payment unless, before the end of the period of six months[1] beginning with the relevant date[2]—
   (a)   the payment has been agreed and paid,[3] or
   (b)   the employee has made a claim for the payment by notice in writing given to the employer,[4] or
   (c)   a question as to the employee's right to, or the amount of, the payment has been referred to an industrial tribunal,[5] or
   (d)   a complaint relating to his dismissal has been presented by the employee under section 111.[6]

(2)   An employee is not deprived of his right to a redundancy payment by subsection (1) if, during the period of six months immediately following the period mentioned in that subsection, the employee—
   (a)   makes such a claim for the payment in writing given to the employer,
   (b)   refers to a tribunal a question as to his right to, or the amount of, the payment, or
   (c)   presents a complaint relating to his dismissal under section 111,
and it appears to the tribunal to be just and equitable that the employee should receive a redundancy payment.'

1 As originally enacted the time limit in which to claim redundancy payments was more strict in that there was no equivalent of s 164(2) and this led to a tendency to look liberally at the provision. Cases decided under the former provision should be looked at with caution. An application for a redundancy payment is 'referred' to an industrial tribunal when it is received by the office of the industrial tribunal: *Secretary of State for Employment v Banks* [1983] ICR 48, EAT. The applicant in *Hetherington v Dependable Products Ltd* (1970) 6 ITR 1, CA, did not apply to the industrial tribunal within the six-month period but a union official wrote to the employers 're the position of Mrs Hetherington, who was made redundant whilst off sick'. In the Court of Appeal Lord Denning MR said that the requirements as to notice should be construed liberally in favour of the employee, but that the letter from the union official could not be held to be such notice. Contrast *Gerrard v James Linton Co Ltd* (1969) 4 ITR 135, DC, where the letter referred to taking the case to the tribunal. This was found by the Divisional Court to be sufficient notice in writing.

2 For the definition of 'relevant date', see s 145. If the claim is made before the relevant date, s 164 is not complied with: *Watts v Rubery Owen Conveyancer Ltd* [1977] 2 All ER 1; [1977] ICR 429, EAT; *Pritchard-Rhodes Ltd v Boon and Milton* [1979] IRLR 19, EAT.

3 The time limit applies to the right to a redundancy payment but does not apply to claims as to its amount: *Bentley Engineering Co Ltd v Crown* [1976] ICR 225, EAT.

4 Notice in writing by or on behalf of employees was generally construed liberally in the employees' favour: *Hetherington v Dependable Products Ltd* (1970) 6 ITR 1, CA; *North Western Electricity Board v Secretary of State for Employment* (1973) 8 ITR 209. In *Price v Smithfield and Zwanenberg Group Ltd* [1978] ICR 93, EAT, a letter containing the statement 'so far I have not heard from you in respect of the employee's claim for wrongful dismissal including his claim for redundancy payment' was found to be a good claim. That the letter was written 'without prejudice' was a factor to be taken into consideration but did not prevent it from being a valid claim. Contrast the decision of an industrial tribunal in *Stoughton v Bancroft Folding Machines Ltd* (1967) 2 ITR 32. Once the claim is made a complaint may be presented to a tribunal at any time; see *Bentley Engineering Co Ltd v Crown* [1976] ICR 225, EAT 'the Doomsday argument' and *Price* (above).

5 The application cannot be effectively made to an industrial tribunal before the date of termination of the employment contract: *Pritchard-Rhodes Ltd v Boon and Milton* [1979] IRLR 19, EAT.

6 See an unfair dismissal claim. If the claim is made within the six-month period, it does not render it out of time even if the claim for unfair dismissal is itself out of time: *Duffin v Secretary of State for Employment* [1983] ICR 766, EAT.

The just and equitable test

16.103   In deciding whether it is just and equitable the tribunal has to have regard to the reason shown by the employee for his failure to take any such step as is referred to in s 164(2) within the sixth-month period and all the other relevant circumstances.[1]

1 Employment Rights Act 1996, s 164(3).

Time limits when the employee dies

16.104   If the employee dies before the end of the six-month period beginning with the relevant date, the initial period of six months is extended to a year.[1] If the former employee dies after the period of six months from the relevant date and before the end of the following period of six months, the 'discretionary' period of six months is extended to one year.[2]

1 Employment Rights Act 1996, s 176(7)(a).
2 Employment Rights Act 1996, s 176(7)(b).

Time limits for application under s 177 (equivalent payments)

16.105   There is no express statutory time limit for references to an industrial tribunal under s 177 of the Employment Rights Act 1996. The only time limit applicable is that of six years under the Limitation Act 1980.[1]

1 *Greenwich Health Authority v Skinner; Greenwich Health Authority v Ward* [1989] IRLR 238, EAT; a decision under s 111 of the Employment Protection (Consolidation Act) 1978, as amended.

Claims against the National Insurance Fund

16.106   The Redundancy Payments Act 1965 established a Redundancy Fund from which payments were made to employers and employees in certain circumstances. With effect from 1 February 1991 the assets and liabilities of the Redundancy Fund became assets and liabilities of the National Insurance Fund.[1] Over the years the right of employers to rebates in respect of redundancy payments was whittled away and rebates payable to employers were finally abolished as from 16 January 1990.[2]

1 Employment Act 1990, s 13.
2 Employment Act 1989, s 17.

Payments out of the National Insurance Fund to employees

16.107   When an employee has taken all reasonable steps (other than legal proceedings) to recover a redundancy payment from his employer and the employer has refused or failed to pay it, or has paid part of it, and refused, or failed, to pay the balance, or the employer is insolvent and the whole or part of the redundancy payment remains unpaid the employee may apply to the Secretary of State for payment from the National Insurance Fund.[1] When the Secretary of State is satisfied of the employee's entitlement, that the employee has taken all reasonable steps to obtain payment from the employer, or the employer is insolvent and the redundancy payment or part of it remains unpaid, he must make a redundancy payment computed in accordance with the Act. So long as the employee is not affected by an agreement exempted under s 157 the sum paid is the whole of the redundancy payment less any amount already paid. If the Secretary of State is satisfied that a sum is due under an exempted agreement under s 157, he must similarly make a payment.[2] A payment under the section is not pay for the purpose of art 119 of the Treaty of Rome.[3] In cases where the employer admits his liability to make a payment but fails to pay, application to a tribunal is not a necessary 'step to recover payment' within s 106(1).[4] An employee can claim against the employer before a tribunal even though the employer is insolvent.[5]

1 Employment Rights Act 1996, s 166. The phrase 'legal proceedings' does not include any proceedings before a tribunal but includes any proceedings to enforce a decision or award of a tribunal: s 166(4).
2 Employment Rights Act 1996, s 166(2). The payment includes statutory redundancy payment and the employer's payment under an agreement which leads to an exemption order under s 157. If a tribunal determines that an employer is to pay only part of a redundancy payment, references are construed as being to that part of the redundancy payment: s 166(3).
3 *Secretary of State for Employment v Levy* [1989] IRLR 469, EAT.
4 *Jeffrey v Grey* (1967) 2 ITR 335.
5 *Barcza v Potomac Restaurants Ltd* (1968) 3 ITR 234.

The rights of the Secretary of State when a payment is made

16.108   If the Secretary of State makes a payment, all rights and remedies of the employee with respect to the employer's payment (or if appropriate that part paid from the National Insurance Fund) are transferred to and vest in the Secretary of State. Any decision of a tribunal requiring the employer's payment to be paid to the employee has effect as if it required that payment, or as the case may be, that part of it paid from the Fund to be paid to the Secretary of State for payment into the National Insurance Fund.[1] Insolvency is defined in England and Wales for these purposes by s 166(5) of the Employment Rights Act 1996 as being, in the case of an individual, if he has been adjudged bankrupt, or made a composition or arrangement, with his creditors, or he has died and an order has been made under s 421 of the Insolvency Act 1986 for the administration of his estate, or where the employer is a company, a winding-up order or an administration order has been made with respect to it, or a resolution for voluntary winding up has been passed, or a receiver or manager of its undertaking has been duly appointed, or possession has been taken by, or on behalf of, the holders of any debentures secured by a floating charge, of any property of the company comprised in or subject to the charge or a voluntary arrangement proposed for the purposes of Pt I of the Insolvency Act 1986 is approved under that Part of the Act.[2] In Scotland an employer is taken as being insolvent (if he is an individual) if an order of sequestration has been made of his estate or he has executed a trust deed for his creditors or has entered into a composition contract or he has died and a judicial factor appointed under s 11A of the Judicial Factors (Scotland) Act 1889 is required by the provisions of that section to divide his insolvent estate among his creditors. Where the employer is a company it is insolvent if a winding-up order or an administration order has been made or a resolution for voluntary winding up is passed with respect to it or a receiver of its undertaking is duly appointed or a voluntary arrangement proposed for the purposes of Pt I of the Insolvency Act 1986 is approved under that Part.[3] In cases of insolvency where the Secretary of State makes payment to the employee he is able to prove in the insolvency for the redundancy payment. An employee who has made a claim to the Secretary of State for payment under s 166 may refer the matter to the tribunal to determine liability, or the amount of any payment to be made.[4] A tribunal does not have jurisdiction to decide whether or not employees have rightly received redundancy payments paid to them on a reference by the Secretary of State.[5] The employer does not have to be a party to the claim.[6]

1 Employment Rights Act 1996, s 167(3).
2 It is to be noted that a company may not be able to pay its debts and yet not be insolvent within the meaning of the Employment Rights Act 1996, s 166(5).
3 Employment Rights Act 1996, s 166(6) and (7).
4 Employment Rights Act 1996, s 170. For the purposes of such a reference an employee who has been dismissed by his employer shall, unless the contrary is proved, be presumed to have been so dismissed by reason of redundancy: s 170(2).
5 *Secretary of State for Employment v Wellworthy Ltd* [1973] 3 All ER 488; [1973] ICR 477, NIRC; *Secretary of State for Employment v Nortons (Cardiff) Ltd* (1972) 7 ITR 136 (as to this point). This is within the jurisdiction of the High Court: *Secretary of State for Employment v Wellworthy Ltd (No 2)* [1976] ICR 13, QBD.
6 *Jones v Secretary of State for Employment* [1982] ICR 389, EAT, although it may help procedurally to do so: *Bradley v Secretary of State for Employment* [1989] ICR 69, EAT.

Information relating to applications

16.109 Where an employee makes an application to the Secretary of State for Employment for payment out of the National Insurance Fund, the Secretary of State may by notice in writing given to the employer require the employer to provide him with such information and to produce for examination documents in his custody or under his control of such descriptions as the Secretary of State may reasonably require for the purpose of determining whether the application is well founded.[1] A person on whom notice is served who fails without reasonable excuse to comply with a requirement of the notice is guilty of an offence and is liable on summary conviction to a fine not exceeding level 3 on the standard scale.[2] Any person who in providing any information required by such notice makes a statement which he knows to be false in a material particular, or recklessly makes a statement which is false in a material particular, or produces for examination in accordance with any such notice a document which to his knowledge has been wilfully falsified is guilty of an offence.[3] He is liable on summary conviction to a fine not exceeding the statutory maximum or imprisonment for a term not exceeding three months or both, or on conviction on indictment to a fine or to imprisonment of a term not exceeding two years or both.[4]

1 Employment Rights Act 1996, s 169(1).
2 Employment Rights Act 1996, s 169(2).
3 Employment Rights Act 1996, s 169(3).
4 Employment Rights Act 1996, s 169(4).

Procedure for handling redundancies

16.110   Part IV of the Employment Protection Act 1975[1] was enacted to comply with Directive 75/129/EEC[2] and introduced a new statutory procedure for handling redundancies of employees.[3] These provisions are now contained in the Trade Union and Labour Relations (Consolidation) Act 1992. The provisions have been the subject of considerable amendment.[4] The procedure has two elements – consultation and notification. For the purposes of proceedings involving these procedures, dismissals and proposed dismissals are presumed to be by reason of redundancy unless the contrary is proved.[5]

1 Which came into force on 8 March 1976.
2 It is the duty of the courts, if possible, to construe the legislation so as to comply with the Directive, but that must be achieved by proper processes of construction: *Re Hartlebury Printers Ltd* [1992] IRLR 516, EAT. See also *R v British Coal Corpn, ex p Vardy* [1993] 1 CMLR 721, DC. Article 1(1)(a) of the Directive determines the Directive's scope but does not prescribe the internal organisations of undertakings; *Rockfon A/S v Specialarbejderforbundet i Danmark* [1996] IRLR 168, ECJ.
3 Reference to dismissal as redundant are references to dismissal for a reason not related to the individual concerned or for a number of reasons all of which are not so related; Trade Union and Labour Relations (Consolidation) Act 1992, s 195.
4 Principally by the Trade Union Reform and Employment Rights Act 1993 and Collective Redundancies and Transfer of Undertakings (Protection of Employment) (Amendment) Regulations 1995, SI 1995/2587.
5 Trade Union and Labour Relations (Consolidation) Act 1992, s 195(2) and for redundancy generally, see **16.38**.

16.111   The provisions apply to employees but not to those in Crown employment, House of Commons and House of Lords staff, those in the police service, and share fishermen.[1] Those who under their contracts of employment ordinarily work outside Great Britain and those employed under a fixed term contract for three months or less or made in contemplation of the performance of a specific task which is not expected to last for more than three months, unless in either case the employee has been continuously employed for a period of more than three months, are excluded.[2] There is power to make further provision as to excluded classes of employment so that the requirement relating to the handling of redundancies will or will not, apply to the classes of employees specified in the order, or varying or revoking the excluded classes of employees.[3]

1 Trade Union and Labour Relations (Consolidation) Act 1992, ss 273, 278, 280, 284.
2 Trade Union and Labour Relations (Consolidation) Act 1992, ss 285 and 282. See *National Association of Teachers in Further and Higher Education v Manchester City Council* [1978] ICR 1190, EAT.
3 Trade Union and Labour Relations (Consolidation) Act 1992, s 286.

Consultation

16.112 An employer proposing[1] to dismiss as redundant 20 or more employees at one establishment[2] within a period of 90 days or less, should consult about the dismissals all the persons who are appropriate representatives of any of the employees who may be so dismissed.[3] Consultation should begin in good time and if the employer is proposing to dismiss as redundant 100 or more employees at one establishment, this should be at least 90 days before the first of those dismissals takes effect;[4] otherwise consultation should begin at least 30 days before the first of those dismissals takes effect.[5] No account is taken in computing the figures of employees who are to be dismissed because they are redundant, of those employees in respect of whom redundancy consultation has already begun.[6]

1 Proposing means 'having in view or expecting'; *Re Hartlebury Printers Ltd* [1992] IRLR 516, DC. That is when a specific proposal has been formulated: *Hough v Leyland Daf Ltd* [1991] ICR 696, EAT.
2 Trade Union and Labour Relations (Consolidation) Act 1992, s 188(2)(b). Whether or not employees employed at several locations can be counted as employed at one establishment is a matter to be decided by the industrial tribunal in the light of the facts before it; *Barratt Developments (Bradford) Ltd v Union of Construction Allied Trades and Technicians* [1978] ICR 319, EAT. See also a case relating to selective employment tax: *Lord Advocate v Babcock and Wilcox (Operations) Ltd* [1972] 1 All ER 1130; [1972] 1 WLR 448, HL (Sc).
3 Trade Union and Labour Relations (Consolidation) Act 1992, s 188(1). There is limited power to vary the periods; Trade Union and Labour Relations (Consolidation) Act 1992, s 197. Dismissal is as defined for unfair dismissal; Trade Union and Labour Relations (Consolidation) Act 1992, s 298 referring to the Employment Rights Act 1996, Pt X. As to establishment see *Rockfon A/S v Specialarbejderforbundet i Danmark* [1996] IRLR 168, ECJ.
4 Trade Union and Labour Relations (Consolidation) Act 1992, s 188(1A)(a).
5 Trade Union and Labour Relations (Consolidation) Act 1992, s 188(1A)(b).
6 Trade Union and Labour Relations (Consolidation) Act 1992, s 188(3).

16.113 The consultation should be with appropriate representatives. Appropriate representatives of any employees are the employee representatives elected by them,[1] or if the employees are of a description in respect of which an independent trade union is recognised[2] by the employer, representatives of the trade union are appropriate representatives. In the case of employees who both elect employee representatives, and are of a description in respect of which a union is recognised, the employer may choose to notify either the employee representatives elected by the employees, or representatives of the trade union.[3]

1 Trade Union and Labour Relations (Consolidation) Act 1992, s 188(1B). For these purposes persons are employee representatives if they have been elected by employees for the specific purpose of being given information and consulted by their employer about dismissals proposed by him. If they have been elected by employees (whether before or after the dismissals were proposed) otherwise than for that specific purpose and it is appropriate (having regard to the

purposes for which they were elected) for their employer to consult them about the proposed dismissals, they are employee representatives for the purpose. In either case they must be employed by the employer at the time when they are elected; Trade Union and Labour Relations (Consolidation) Act 1992, s 196(1). The absence of specific rules for the election of representatives does not constitute a breach of Directive 75/129/EEC; *R v Secretary of State for Trade and Industry, ex p Unison* [1996] IRLR 438, HC.
2 Whether or not a union has been recognised depends upon what has been agreed between the parties. It must be recognition for the purposes of negotiating terms and conditions of employment; *Union of Shop, Distributive and Allied Workers v Sketchley Ltd* [1981] ICR 644, EAT. It must be true recognition. It cannot be enforced or automatic recognition thrust upon an employer by a third party over whom he has no control; *Cleveland County Council v Springett* [1985] IRLR 131, EAT. Representatives of the trade union are officials or other persons authorised by the union to carry on collective bargaining with the employer; Trade Union and Labour Relations (Consolidation) Act 1992, s 196(2).
3 Trade Union and Labour Relations (Consolidation) Act 1992, s 188(1B).

16.114   Consultation should include consultation about ways of avoiding dismissals, reducing the numbers of employees to be dismissed, and mitigating the consequences of the dismissals. It should be undertaken with a view to reaching agreement with the appropriate representatives.[1] The employer should disclose in writing to the appropriate representatives:
  '(a)   the reasons for his proposals;
  (b)   the numbers and descriptions of employees whom it is proposed to dismiss as redundant;
  (c)   the total number of employees of any such description employed by the employer at the establishment in question;
  (d)   the proposed method of selecting the employees who may be dismissed;
  (e)   the proposed method of carrying out the dismissals, with due regard to any agreed procedure, including the period over which the dismissals are to take effect; and
  (f)   the proposed method of calculating the amount of any redundancy payments to be made (otherwise than in compliance with an obligation imposed by or by virtue of any enactment) to employees who may be dismissed'.[2]

1 Trade Union and Labour Relations (Consolidation) Act 1992, s 188(2).
2 Trade Union and Labour Relations (Consolidation) Act 1992, s 188(4).

16.115   The employer should allow the appropriate representatives access to the affected employees, and afford to those representatives such accommodation and other facilities, as may be appropriate.[1]

1 Trade Union and Labour Relations (Consolidation) Act 1992, s 188(5A).

16.116   The information which is to be provided should be given to each of the appropriate representatives by being delivered to them, or sent by post to an address notified by them to the employer. In the case of representatives of a trade union it may be sent by post to the union at the address of its head or main office.[1]

1 Trade Union and Labour Relations (Consolidation) Act 1992, s 188(5).

16.117   If there are special circumstances[1] rendering it not reasonably practicable to carry out such consultation, the employer should take all such steps towards compliance as are reasonably practicable in those circumstances.[2] Where the decision leading to the proposed dismissals is that of a person controlling the employer (directly or indirectly), a failure on the part of that person to provide information to the employer does not constitute special circumstances rendering it not reasonably practicable for the employer to comply with the requirement.[3] There is specific provision for circumstances where the employer has invited any of the affected employees to elect employee representatives. If the invitation was issued long enough before the time when the employer is required to consult in accordance with requirements to begin to allow them to elect representatives by that time, the employer is treated as complying with requirements if he complies with those requirements as soon as is reasonably practicable after the election of the representatives.[4]

1 'Special' means that the event must be something out of the ordinary or something uncommon. Insolvency on its own is not a special circumstance; *Clarks of Hove Ltd v Bakers Union* [1978] IRLR 366, CA where the appointment of a receiver was not considered to be a special circumstance. However, the suddenness of the circumstances bringing about the insolvency may make it special; *Union of Shop, Distributive and Allied Workers v Leancut Bacon Ltd* [1981] IRLR 295, EAT. See *Hamish Armour v Association of Scientific, Technical and Managerial Staffs* [1979] IRLR 24, EAT (delaying consultation until outcome known of application by company for government aid when already received such assistance amounted to special circumstances). See also *Association of Pattern Makers and Allied Craftsmen v Kirvin Ltd* [1978] IRLR 318, EAT. When an employer discharges the burden of proof placed on him by s 188 of the 1992 Act he is provided with a defence, thereafter there can be no question of a protective award (see **16.121**) being made against him; *Clarks of Hove Ltd v Bakers Union* (above).
2 Trade Union and Labour Relations (Consolidation) Act 1992, s 188(7). See *Hamish Armour v Association of Scientific, Technical and Managerial Staffs* [1979] IRLR 24, EAT and *Union of Shop, Distributive and Allied Workers v Leancut Bacon Ltd* [1981] IRLR 295, EAT. The onus of proof is on the employer. It does not make it not reasonably practicable if a Government Department mistakenly says consultation is not necessary when dismissing one employee although the tribunal may in the exercise of its discretion decide not to make a protective award; *Union of Construction, Allied Trades and Technicians v H Rooke & Son (Cambridge) Ltd* [1978] ICR 818, EAT.
3 See footnote 2 above.
4 Trade Union and Labour Relations (Consolidation) Act 1992, s 188(7A).

16.118 It may be in order for the employer to give notice to the employees during the period of consultation but the consultation period must begin before the notices of dismissal are given.[1] It is to be noted that the obligation to consult contained in s 188 is not transferred pursuant to the Transfer of Undertakings (Protection of Employment) Regulations 1981.[2]

1 However, there must be an opportunity for 'meaningful' consultation before notices of dismissal are given, see *National Union of Teachers v Avon County Council* [1978] ICR 626, EAT where the 'consultation' took place after dismissal notices had been dispatched. There must be time for the union representatives to consider the proposals and sufficient 'meaningful' consultation before the dismissal notices are sent out; *GEC Ferranti Defence Systems Ltd v MSF* [1993] IRLR 101, EAT.
2 SI 1981/1794; *Angus Jowett & Co Ltd v National Union of Tailors and Garment Workers* [1985] IRLR 326, EAT.

Failure to consult

16.119 Complaints may be presented to an industrial tribunal alleging failures to comply with the obligations. The complaint can be presented by any of the employee representatives where the employer failed to consult the employee representative. In the case of a failure relating to representatives of a trade union, it can be presented by the trade union. In any other case, the complaint can be presented by any employees who are affected employees.[1]

1 Trade Union and Labour Relations (Consolidation) Act 1992, s 189(1). There are no other remedies, see the Trade Union and Labour Relations (Consolidation) Act 1992, s 188(8). The tribunal will refer the matter to the Advisory Conciliation and Arbitration Service so that conciliation may be attempted. For the relevance of these provisions in unfair dismissal cases, see Chapter 15.

16.120 Subject to the exception noted above, an individual employee is not able to present such a complaint. The onus of proof in this respect is on the complainant,[1] save that if the employer seeks to show that he did not comply with the obligation because of special circumstances rendering it not reasonably practicable to do so, it is for the employer to show that there were such circumstances and that he took all steps towards compliance with the requirements as were reasonably practicable in the circumstances.[2]

1 Subject to the presumption which will operate so far as the reasons for the dismissals are concerned, see **16.117**.
2 Trade Union and Labour Relations (Consolidation) Act 1992, s 189(6).

16.121 If the tribunal finds that the complaint is well founded it must make a declaration to that effect and may also make a protective award.[1] A protective award is an award that in respect of such descriptions of employee as may be specified, being employees who have been dismissed, or whom it is proposed to dismiss, as redundant, and in respect of whose dismissal or proposed dismissal the employer has failed to comply with the consultation requirements, the employer should pay remuneration for the 'protected period'.[2] The protected period is a period, beginning with the date on which the first of the dismissals to which the complaint relates takes effect,[3] or the date of the award, whichever is the earlier, of such length as the tribunal determines as being just and equitable in all circumstances having regard to the seriousness of the employer's default in complying with the consultation requirement. The period must not exceed 90 days when the 90-day consultation period was applicable or 30 days when the 30-day period applied.[4] The purpose of the protective award is to compensate for the failure to consult. The industrial tribunal should consider the loss of days of consultation which has occurred not the loss or potential loss of actual remuneration during the relevant period by specific employees. The tribunal should have regard to the seriousness of the employer's default, the length of the period of actual consultation, the nature of the default and justice and equity.[5]

1 Trade Union and Labour Relations (Consolidation) Act 1992, s 189(2) and (4).
2 Trade Union and Labour Relations (Consolidation) Act 1992, s 189(3).
3 The proposed date of the first dismissal: *E Green & Son (Castings) Ltd v Association of Scientific, Technical and Managerial Staffs* [1984] IRLR 135, EAT and *Transport & General Workers Union v Ledbury Preserves (1928) Ltd* [1986] IRLR 492, EAT. Contrast *GKN Sankey Ltd v National Society of Motor Mechanics* [1980] ICR 148, EAT.
4 Trade Union and Labour Relations (Consolidation) Act 1992, s 189(4). For the power to vary the periods, see the Trade Union and Labour Relations (Consolidation) Act 1992, s 197.
5 *Spillers-French (Holdings) Ltd v Union of Shop Distributive and Allied Workers* [1979] IRLR 339, EAT. Contrast with *Talke Fashions Ltd v Amalgamated Society of Textile Workers and Kindred Trades* [1977] ICR 833, EAT. Where an employer had been advised by the Department of Employment that no consultation was necessary no protective award was made; *Union of Construction, Allied Trades and Technicians v H Rooke & Son (Cambridge) Ltd* [1978] ICR 818, EAT. The fact that consultations will have no effect on the decision is not by itself sufficient reason to make no protective award; *Transport and General Workers Union v Gainsborough Distributors (UK) Ltd* [1978] IRLR 460, EAT. An interesting example of the calculation of the protection award is set out in *Barratt Developments (Bradford) Ltd v Union of Construction, Allied Trades and Technicians* [1977] IRLR 403, EAT. See also *General and Municipal Workers Union v British Uralite* [1979] IRLR 413. Employment

Protection (Recoupment of Jobseeker's Allowance and Income Support) Regulations 1996, SI 1996/2349.

16.122 The complaint to the industrial tribunal must be made before the date on which the last of the dismissals to which the complaint relates takes effect, or during the period of three months beginning with that date, or within such further period as the tribunal considers reasonable in a case where it is satisfied that it was not reasonably practicable for the complaint to be presented during the period of three months.[1]

1 Trade Union and Labour Relations (Consolidation) Act 1992, s 189(5).

16.123 If a protective award is made every employee of the description to which the award relates is entitled to be paid remuneration for the protected period.[1] This is calculated at the weekly rate of a week's pay as defined for the purposes of the Employment Rights Act 1996.[2] Remuneration for a period of less than a week is calculated by reducing proportionately the amount of a week's pay.[3] An employee is not entitled to remuneration during the protected period unless he would have been so entitled by virtue of his contract of employment or by virtue of the provisions of the Employment Rights Act 1996 as to rights of an employee during the notice period if the period fell within the minimum statutory period of notice.[4] Nor is he entitled to remuneration, where he is fairly dismissed (otherwise than as redundant) during the period for a reason other than redundancy, or when he unreasonably terminates the contract of employment, in respect of any period during which but for the dismissal or termination he would have been so employed.[5]

1 Trade Union and Labour Relations (Consolidation) Act 1992, s 190(1). The Employment Protection (Recoupment of Jobseeker's Allowance and Income Support) Regulations 1996, SI 1996/2349 apply; see Chapter 15.
2 Employment Rights Act 1996, s 220; Trade Union and Labour Relations (Consolidation) Act 1992, s 190(5). The calculation date is the usual date for redundancy purposes if the dismissal has taken effect and in other cases it is the date on which the protective award was made: Trade Union and Labour Relations (Consolidation) Act 1992, s 190(5).
3 Trade Union and Labour Relations (Consolidation) Act 1992, s 190(2).
4 Trade Union and Labour Relations (Consolidation) Act 1992, s 190(4). This applies in respect of a period during which the employee is employed by the employer.
5 Trade Union and Labour Relations (Consolidation) Act 1992, s 191(1).

16.124 There are special provisions to cover situations where the employer makes an offer (whether in writing or not and whether before or after the ending of his employment under the previous contract) to renew the contract of employment or re-engage the employee under a new contract, when the renewal or re-engagement would take effect before or during the protected period.[1] If the provisions of the renewed contract, or the new contract (as the case may be) would not differ from the corresponding terms of his previous contract as to the capacity or place in which he would be employed and as to the other terms and conditions of his employment, or they differ, but the offer constitutes an offer of suitable employment in relation to the employee, and in each case he unreasonably refused the offer, he is not entitled to any remuneration under the protective award in respect of any period during which, but for the refusal, he would have been employed.[2] There are similar provisions as to a trial period of four weeks, or longer if agreed, in accordance with the statutory procedure, as are applicable on offers of renewal or re-engagement in relation to redundancy payments.[3]

1 Trade Union and Labour Relations (Consolidation) Act 1992, s 191(2)–(7).
2 Trade Union and Labour Relations (Consolidation) Act 1992, s 191(3).
3 Trade Union and Labour Relations (Consolidation) Act 1992, s 191(4)–(7). See **16.64**.

Failure to pay remuneration during protected period

16.125 An employee[1] can present a complaint to an industrial tribunal on the ground that he is an employee of a description to which a protective award relates and his employer has failed wholly, or in part, to pay his remuneration under the award.[2] The complaint should be presented before the end of the period of three months beginning with the day, or if applicable, last of the days in respect of which the complaint is made of failure to pay remuneration, or within such further period as the tribunal considers reasonable in a case where it is satisfied it was not reasonably practicable for the complaint to be presented within the period of three months.[3] If the industrial tribunal finds the complaint is well founded it will order the employer to pay the amount of remuneration due to him.[4]

1 It should be noted that it is the individual employee and not the employee representatives or trade union who makes the complaint under this head. The industrial tribunal will refer the matter to the Advisory Conciliation and Arbitration Service so that conciliation may be attempted; see **18.17** and **18.18**.
2 Trade Union and Labour Relations (Consolidation) Act 1992, s 192(1).
3 Trade Union and Labour Relations (Consolidation) Act 1992, s 192(2).
4 Trade Union and Labour Relations (Consolidation) Act 1992, s 192(3). If the employee has died during the protected period, the award is treated as if the protected period ended on his death: Trade Union and Labour Relations (Consolidation) Act 1992, s 190(6). For supplementary provisions applicable on the death of the employee or the employer, see the Trade Union and Labour Relations (Consolidation) Act 1992, s 292.

Notice to the Secretary of State

16.126 An employer who proposes to dismiss as redundant 100 or more employees at one establishment within a period of 90 days or less, must notify the Secretary of State, in writing, of his proposal at least 90 days before the first of the dismissals takes effect.[1] If he proposes to dismiss 20 or more employees at one establishment within a period of 90 days or less, he should notify the Secretary of State in writing at least 30 days before the first of the dismissals takes place.[2] Where there are representatives to be consulted under the provisions as to consultation, the employer should give them a copy of the notice.[3] The form of the notice and the particulars to be given to the Secretary of State have been prescribed by him and copies of an appropriate form are obtainable from local offices of the Department. If it is a case where consultation is required the notice should identify the representatives concerned and state the date when the consultation began.[4] On receiving the notice the Secretary of State may in writing require the employer to give him such further information as he specifies. There is a similar proviso to that relating to consultation, in that if there are special circumstances rendering it not reasonably practicable for the employer to comply with the requirements as to notice, he is obliged to take all steps towards compliance with that requirement as are reasonably practicable in those circumstances.[5]

1 Trade Union and Labour Relations (Consolidation) Act 1992, s 193(1). For limited power to vary the period see the Trade Union and Labour Relations (Consolidation) Act 1992, s 197.
2 Trade Union and Labour Relations (Consolidation) Act 1992, s 193(2). In determining whether notice should be given or which period is applicable, no account is taken of employees

the employer proposes to dismiss as redundant in respect of whose proposed dismissal notice has already been given to the Secretary of State, s 193(3).
3 Trade Union and Labour Relations (Consolidation) Act 1992, s 193(6).
4 Trade Union and Labour Relations (Consolidation) Act 1992, s 193(4).
5 Trade Union and Labour Relations (Consolidation) Act 1992, s 193(7). Where the decision leading to the proposed dismissals is that of a person controlling the employer (directly or indirectly) a failure on the part of that person to provide information to the employer does not constitute special circumstances rendering it not reasonably practicable for the employer to comply with the requirement.

Failure to notify the Secretary of State

16.127   If an employer[1] fails to give notice to the Secretary of State in accordance with s 193 of the Trade Union and Labour Relations (Consolidation) Act 1992 he commits an offence and is liable on summary conviction to a fine not exceeding level 5 on the standard scale.[1] Proceedings can only be instituted by, or with the consent of, the Secretary of State or an officer authorised for the purpose by him.[2] Officers of the Department may be authorised to conduct proceedings themselves before magistrates' courts.[3] A director, manager, secretary or other similar officer of a body corporate, or any person purporting to act in any such capacity, is guilty of the offence jointly with the body corporate if it is proved to have been committed with his consent or connivance or to have been attributable to his neglect.[4]

1 In the case of a school with a delegated budget the governing body is the employer for these purposes: Education (Modification of Enactments Relating to Employment) Order 1989, SI 1989/901.
2 Trade Union and Labour Relations (Consolidation) Act 1992, s 194(1).
3 Trade Union and Labour Relations (Consolidation) Act 1992, s 194(2).
4 Trade Union and Labour Relations (Consolidation) Act 1992, s 194(3). When the affairs of a body corporate are managed by its members s 194(3) applies in relation to the acts and defaults of a member in connection with his functions of management as if he were a director of the body corporate: Trade Union and Labour Relations (Consolidation) Act 1992, s 194(4).

16.128   There is provision for the Secretary of State, by order, to vary the periods given above (with certain limitations) subject to approval by both Houses of Parliament.[1] In circumstances where there is a collective agreement on redundancies the Secretary of State may make an order adapting, modifying or excluding any of the consultation and notification provisions. For such an order to be made there must be a collective agreement in force relating to the employees concerned, which establishes arrangements for providing alternative employment for employees to whom it relates if dismissed as redundant, or arrangements for the handling of the dismissal of employees as redundant. All parties to the agreement must apply to the Secretary of State and he must be satisfied that having regard to the provisions of the agreement the arrangements on the whole are at least as favourable as those created by the Trade Union and Labour Relations (Consolidation) Act 1992.[2] The agreement must contain independent arbitration or adjudication arrangements, or indicate that an aggrieved employee can complain to an industrial tribunal on the ground that the employer or another person has not complied with the provisions of the agreement.[3] An order so made may confer on an industrial tribunal such powers and duties as the Secretary of State considers appropriate.[4]

1 Trade Union and Labour Relations (Consolidation) Act 1992, s 197.
2 Trade Union and Labour Relations (Consolidation) Act 1992, s 198(2). The order may be varied or revoked by subsequent order on application by all or any of the parties to the

agreement or without any such application: Trade Union and Labour Relations (Consolidation) Act 1992, s 198(5).
3 Trade Union and Labour Relations (Consolidation) Act 1992, s 198(3).
4 Trade Union and Labour Relations (Consolidation) Act 1992, s 198(4). There have been no such orders at the moment.

Miscellaneous provisions relating to redundancy

When remuneration is paid by someone other than the employer

16.129 When by virtue of a statutory provision an employee's remuneration is payable to him by a person other than his employer, s 173 of the Employment Rights Act 1996 provides that reference to the 'employer' should be construed as reference to the person responsible for paying remuneration.

Notices

16.130 Section 179 of the Employment Rights Act 1996 sets out the rules applicable for serving notices pursuant to Pt XI of the Act. A notice to be given by an employer to an employee may be delivered to the employee, or left at his usual or last known place of residence or sent to him by post there. Notices to the employer may be given either by the employee himself, or by a person authorised by him to act on his behalf, and can be delivered to the employer, sent by post addressed to him at the place where the employee is, or was, employed by him or, if arrangements in that behalf have been made by the employer, can be given by being delivered to a person designated by the employee in pursuance of the arrangements or left for such a person at a place so designated, or sent by post to that person at the designated address. Notices left for a person at the appropriate place mentioned are presumed, unless the contrary is proved, to have been received by him on the day on which it was left there.

Criminal offences

16.131 When a criminal offence under Pt XI of the Employment Rights Act 1996 committed by a body corporate is proved to have been committed with the consent or connivance of, or to be attributable to any neglect on the part of any director, manager, secretary, or other similar officer of the body corporate, or any person purporting to act in any such capacity, he is guilty of the offence as well as the body corporate and is liable to be proceeded against and be punished accordingly.[1]

1 Employment Rights Act 1996, s 180(1). 'Director' is defined in s 180(2).

Chapter 17

Insolvency, calculation of composite claims on termination of employment and taxation

Introduction

This chapter deals with three matters which impact on payments to employees and former employees: insolvency of the employer; calculation of composite awards; and taxation.

If an employer is insolvent certain payments due to employees are preferential claims in the insolvency, see **17.01**. Some debts due to the employee may be paid out of the National Insurance Fund, see **17.02–17.05**. If these are not paid by the Secretary of State, an aggrieved employee may complain to an industrial tribunal, see **17.06**.

On some occasions an employee may have claims against his former employer under several heads, for instance unfair dismissal, one or more types of unlawful discrimination and breach of contract. There are statutory and other rules to prevent the same loss being recovered twice, see **17.10–17.20**.

Taxation on payments to an employee on the termination of employment may be of considerable significance to employer and employee. This may affect the calculation of the sum to be paid to the employee, see **17.28**; the taxation position of the former employee, see **17.29**; and the employer, see **17.30–17.35**.

The effect of insolvency on an employee's claims

Preferential claims

17.01 As has been seen above (see **16.106**) there are provisions enabling the Secretary of State to pay redundancy payments from the National Insurance Fund in certain circumstances including where the employer is unable to make payment as a result of insolvency. There are provisions contained in the Insolvency Act 1986 which give certain claims by ex-employees preference when his employer is insolvent.[1] In general terms these provide that not more than four months' arrears of wages, or salary of employees together with holiday pay, not exceeding £800, ranks as a preferential debt in the insolvency. Entitlements under the Employment Rights Act 1996 for guarantee payments (see **4.35–4.45**), remuneration payable on suspension on medical grounds and payment for time off, in accordance with the statutory provisions as to time off for carrying out trade union duties (see **14.34–14.37**), for ante-natal care (see Chapter 7), to look for work or make arrangements for training (see **16.95–16.99**) and remuneration to be paid under a protective award made by an industrial tribunal pursuant to s 189 of the Trade Union and Labour Relations (Consolidation) Act 1992 (see **16.121**), rank as preferential debts.[2]

1 Insolvency Act 1986, s 386 and Sch 6.
2 The debts are those falling in Category 5 in the Insolvency Act 1986, Sch 6. Insolvency Act 1986, Sch 6, paras 13–15 contain detailed provisions as to their interpretation.

Claims against the National Insurance Fund

Insolvency of employer

17.02 In certain circumstances an employee may be entitled to payment from the National Insurance Fund of sums due to him from an insolvent employer. An employee who wishes to take advantage of this right must make a written application for payment to the Secretary of State for payment. If the Secretary of State is satisfied that the employer has become insolvent,[1] and that the employment of the employee has been terminated and on the appropriate date,[2] the employee was entitled to the debt, or any part of any debt, mentioned below, the Secretary of State should pay to the employee, out of the National Insurance Fund, the amount which in the opinion of the Secretary of State he is entitled in respect of the debt.[3]

1 Insolvency is defined in the Employment Rights Act 1996, s 183. An individual employer is insolvent for these purposes, in England and Wales, if he has been adjudged bankrupt or has made a composition or arrangement with his creditors or he has died and his estate falls to be administered under s 421 of the Insolvency Act 1986: Employment Rights Act 1996, s 183(2)(a). In Scotland an individual employer is insolvent for these purposes if sequestration of his estate has been awarded or he has executed a trust deed for his creditors or has entered into a composition contract or he has died and a judicial factor appointed under s 11A of the Judicial Factors (Scotland) Act 1889 is required by that section to divide his insolvent estate among his creditors: Employment Rights Act 1996, s 183(2)(b). If the employer is a company the provision is satisfied if a winding-up order or an administration order is made or a resolution for voluntary winding up is passed with respect to the company. It is also satisfied in relation to a company if a receiver or (in England and Wales only) a manager of its undertaking has been duly appointed, or (in England and Wales only) possession has been taken, by or on behalf of the holders of any debentures secured by a floating charge, of any property of the company comprised in or subject to the charge or a voluntary arrangement proposed for the purposes of Pt I of the Insolvency Act 1986 is approved under that Part: Employment Rights Act 1996, s 183(3). A company may be in so much debt that there are insufficient funds to pay for the liquidation and yet not be insolvent within this definition! (See *Pollard v Teako (Swiss) Ltd* (1967) 2 ITR 35.)
2 Appropriate date is defined in the Employment Rights Act 1996, s 185 which should be referred to for the detail. In round terms, for arrears of pay it is the date on which the employer became insolvent and for unfair dismissal and protective awards it is the latest of that date, the date of termination of the employment, or the award. In other cases it is the later of the date of the insolvency and the date of termination of the employment.
3 Employment Rights Act 1996, s 182. Similar rights for employees are harmonised by EU Council Directive 80/987/EEC. See *Francovich v Italy* [1996] IRLR 355, ECJ.

Debts to which the provisions apply

17.03 The debts to which the provisions apply are:
(1) Any arrears of pay in respect of one or more (but not more than eight) weeks.[1] Arrears of pay include, guarantee payments, remuneration on suspension on medical grounds, payment for time off in accordance with Pt VI of the Employment Rights Act 1996 or under s 169 of the Trade Union and Labour Relations (Consolidation) Act 1992, remuneration on suspension on maternity grounds under s 64 of the Employment Rights Act 1996 and remuneration under a protective award under s 189 of the Trade Union and Labour Relations (Consolidation) Act 1992.[2]

(2) Any amount which the employer is liable to pay the employee in respect of the statutory minimum period of notice or failure to give such notice.[3]

(3) Any holiday pay in respect of a period, or periods, of holiday, not exceeding six weeks in all, to which the employee became entitled during the 12 months immediately preceding the appropriate date.[4]

(4) Any basic award of compensation for unfair dismissal.[5]

(5) Any reasonable sum by way of reimbursement of the whole, or part, of any premium paid by an apprentice, or articled clerk.[6]

1 Employment Rights Act 1996, s 184(1)(a). See *Namyslo v Secretary of State for Employment* [1979] IRLR 450.
2 Employment Rights Act 1996, s 184(2).
3 Employment Rights Act 1996, s 184(1)(b). The minimum statutory period of notice is that required by Employment Rights Act 1996, s 86(1) or (2). The amount recovered from the Secretary of State must not exceed the amount which would have been payable by the employer and so earnings during the period of notice and debts due to the employer should be deducted: *Secretary of State for Employment v Wilson* [1996] IRLR 330, EAT; *Secretary of State for Employment v Stewart* [1996] IRLR 335, EAT, but the sum paid under a protective award cannot be set off against pay in lieu of notice: *Secretary of State for Employment v Mann* [1996] IRLR 4, EAT. There is no liability to pay a woman absent because of pregnancy although if damages for failing to give notice are paid the employee may have a right under art 119: *Clark v Secretary of State for Employment* [1996] IRLR 578, CA.
4 Employment Rights Act 1996, s 184(1)(c). 'Holiday pay' means pay in respect of a holiday actually taken, or any accrued holiday pay which, under the employee's contract of employment would in the ordinary course have become payable to him in respect of the period of a holiday if his employment with the employer had continued until he became entitled to a holiday: Employment Rights Act 1996, s 184(3).
5 Employment Rights Act 1996, s 184(1)(d).
6 Employment Rights Act 1996, s 184(1)(e).

17.04 The amount in respect of payments referable to time, is subject to a statutory limitation, at present £210 in respect of any one week, reduced in proportion for lesser periods.[1] The Secretary of State may increase the limit by statutory instrument after the annual review.[2] The reasonable sum by way of reimbursement of fee, or premium, on apprenticeship, or articles of clerkship, is the sum admitted to be reasonable by the trustee in bankruptcy, or permanent or interim trustee or the liquidator, for the purposes of the bankruptcy or winding up or sequestration.[3] The Secretary of State will not make payment normally until he has received from the relevant officer a statement of the amount of the debt which appears to have been owed to the employee on the appropriate date and to remain unpaid.[4] The relevant officer is a trustee in bankruptcy, a permanent or interim trustee, a liquidator, an administrator, a receiver or manager, or a trustee under a composition or arrangement or trust deed for the benefit of the employer's creditors, or a trustee under a trust deed for his creditors executed by the employer as the case may be.[5] There is a duty on the relevant officer, on the request of the Secretary of State, to provide the statement as soon as reasonably practicable.[6] If the Secretary of State is satisfied that he does not require such a statement in order to determine the amount of the debt that was owed to the employee on the appropriate date and remains unpaid, he may make payment even though the statement has not been received.[7]

1 Employment Rights Act 1996, s 186(1). The maximum is not contrary to Directive 80/987/EEC: *Secretary of State for Employment v Mann* [1996] IRLR 4, EAT.
2 Employment Rights Act 1996, s 186(2). The review is carried out under s 208.
3 Employment Rights Act 1996, s 184(4). The reasonable sum by way of reimbursement of fee, or premium, on apprenticeship, or articles of clerkship, is the sum accepted by the person specified in the subsection.
4 Employment Rights Act 1996, s 187(1).

5 Employment Rights Act 1996, s 187(4).
6 Employment Rights Act 1996, s 187(3).
7 Employment Rights Act 1996, s 187(2).

Payment of unpaid contributions to pension schemes

17.05 There are specific provisions relating to the payment of certain contributions to occupational pension schemes when these have not been paid by insolvent employers.

Complaints to industrial tribunals

17.06 A person who has made an application to the Secretary of State for payment of any such sums from the National Insurance Fund may present a complaint to an industrial tribunal, when he claims the Secretary of State has failed to make payment, or the payment is less than should have been paid.[1] The complaint to the industrial tribunal should be made within the period of three months beginning with the date on which the decision of the Secretary of State was communicated to the employee, or if that was not reasonably practicable within such further period as is reasonable.[2] When the industrial tribunal finds that the Secretary of State ought to have made such payment, it will make a declaration to that effect and also declare the amount of any such payment the Secretary of State ought to make.[3]

1 Employment Rights Act 1996, s 188(1).
2 Employment Rights Act 1996, s 188(2).
3 Employment Rights Act 1996, s 188(3).

Rights of the Secretary of State

17.07 If the Secretary of State makes payment to the employee in accordance with the provisions of s 182 of the Employment Rights Act 1996, any rights or remedies in respect of the payments, or the part payment made by the Secretary of State, become rights and remedies of the Secretary of State, and any decision of an industrial tribunal requiring the employer to pay the debt is treated as if it were an order for it to be paid to the Secretary of State.[1] The rights which are vested in the Secretary of State include any right to be paid in preference to other creditors in accordance with the Insolvency Act 1986, the Companies Act 1985 and the Bankruptcy (Scotland) Act 1985 (including and such provision as applied by s 11A of the Judicial Factors (Scotland) Act 1889)[2] as the case may be, and the Secretary of State is entitled to be so paid in priority to other unsatisfied claims of the employee.[3] If the Secretary of State receives payment under these provisions the moneys are paid into the National Insurance Fund.[4]

1 Employment Rights Act 1996, s 189(1) and (3).
2 Employment Rights Act 1996, s 189(2).
3 Employment Rights Act 1996, s 189(3) which should be considered in detail if relevant.
4 Employment Rights Act 1996, s 189(5).

17.08 The Secretary of State has power to require the employer to provide him with such information as he reasonably requires to decide if the claims under s 182 of the Employment Rights Act 1996 are well founded[1] and to require any person having the custody, or control, of any relevant records or documents to produce them for examination on behalf of the Secretary of

State, if of a description he requires to be so produced.[2] The requirements of the Secretary of State should be given in writing and can be varied or revoked.[3] A person who refuses or wilfully neglects to furnish any information, or to produce any document he has been required to furnish or produce by such a notice is guilty of an offence and is liable on summary conviction to a fine not exceeding level 3 on the standard scale.[4] A person purporting to comply with the requirement of such a notice who knowingly, or recklessly, makes a false statement is guilty of an offence and is liable on summary conviction to a fine not exceeding level 5 on the standard scale.[5]

1 Employment Rights Act 1996, s 190(1)(a).
2 Employment Rights Act 1996, s 190(1)(b).
3 Employment Rights Act 1996, s 190(2).
4 Employment Rights Act 1996, s 190(3).
5 Employment Rights Act 1996, s 190(4).

Employees who benefit

17.09   All employees serving under contracts of service are entitled to take advantage of these provisions with the exception share fishermen[1] and employees who ordinarily work outside the territory of the member states of the European Communities and of Norway and Iceland.[2] Merchant seamen do not enjoy the benefit of the right to seek payments by the Secretary of State from the National Insurance Fund.[3] It is to be noted that this protection applies to employees who are over usual retirement age.[4]

1 Employment Rights Act 1996, s 199(2).
2 Employment Rights Act 1996, s 196.
3 Employment Rights Act 1996, s 199(4).
4 The exclusions may be varied or revoked by order of the Secretary of State, who may in the same way provide that the provisions do, or do not, apply to persons or employments of such classes as may be prescribed, subject to such exceptions and modifications as may be so prescribed: Employment Rights Act 1996, s 209.

Composite claims

17.10   As a result of the same dismissal the employee may be entitled to financial awards of damages, and/or compensation, against the employer under several different heads, whilst proceedings for wrongful dismissal may be heard by the ordinary courts as well as in industrial tribunals, in more than one forum.[1] An employee who commences proceedings for damages for wrongful dismissal at common law, or presents a complaint to an industrial tribunal under a particular statute, is not precluded from seeking remedies under other statutes, or the common law. The total amount recovered by the employee as a result of a dismissal can consist of one, or more, of the following.[2]

1 As to the jurisdiction to hear claims for breach of contract, see **13.60**.
2 In addition to the other claims considered.

Payment in lieu of notice, or damages for wrongful dismissal

17.11   These claims only arise if the contract is not rightfully terminated at common law. In general, damages for wrongful dismissal do not put the dismissed employee in a position better than he would have been in if the contract had been terminated at the earliest time at which it could lawfully have been brought to an end (see **13.61–13.72**). Although not beyond doubt, the better view is that a redundancy payment is not deducted in computing damages for wrongful dismissal. In *Stocks v Magna Merchants Ltd*[1] Arnold J held, on assize, that a redundancy payment should be deducted in computing damages for wrongful dismissal. However, this was strongly disapproved by Sir John Donaldson in *Yorkshire Engineering and Welding Co Ltd v Burnham*,[2] when he said in the National Industrial Relations Court:

'The essence of the cause of action for wrongful dismissal is that the employee is dismissed prematurely. If it is a fixed term contract, he is dismissed before the end of the term. If it is a running contract, his contract is terminated without notice or with less notice that to which he is entitled under the contract. The damages to which he is entitled consist of the net loss flowing from the *premature* nature of the dismissal. *Prima facie* the measure of damage is what the employee would have earned between the time of dismissal and the earliest moment at which he could properly have had his contract terminated, less any benefits which he has received and which he would not have received if he had been properly dismissed, ie had been allowed to work until the end of the notice or the end of the fixed term contract. We are unable to agree with and follow *Stocks'* case because it appears to overlook the fact that Mr Stocks' would have received his redundancy payment even if his contract had been allowed to run to the end of its term, that being the earliest date upon which it could properly have been determined. If, contrary to our view, the decision in *Stocks'* case is correct and of general application it would produce some very startling results. To take simple figures, suppose that a man aged 40 or over is dismissed on account of redundancy. He is then entitled, under the [redundancy payments provisions], to a lump sum calculated at the rate of one and a half weeks' wages for every year of his service, provided only that he has a minimum of 104 weeks' continuous service. If one assumes a man with only four years' service, his redundancy payment will amount to a sum equal to six week's pay and his entitlement to notice will be only two weeks [Contracts of Employment Act 1972]. Accordingly, if the decision in *Stocks v Magna Merchants Ltd* is right, any employer can dismiss such an employee summarily without wages in lieu of notice, because the redundancy payment will be set off against and exceed the amount of money due in lieu of notice.'[3]

1 [1973] 2 All ER 329; [1973] ICR 530, QBD.
2 (1973) 8 ITR 621, at p 623, NIRC. The employee would be entitled to four weeks' notice under the Employment Rights Act 1996, s 86 which replaces the corresponding provision in the Contracts of Employment Act 1972.
3 *Burnham's* case was approved and *Stocks* expressly disapproved in *Millington v TH Goodwin & Sons Ltd* [1975] ICR 104, QBD and *Basnett v J & A Jackson Ltd* [1976] ICR 63, QBD.

17.12 When an award of compensation for unfair dismissal has already been made, insofar as it relates to matters which would be taken into account in calculating damages for wrongful dismissal, the amount of the compensation for items so taken into account, will be deducted by the tribunal, or court, in assessing damages for wrongful dismissal. For instance, if an industrial tribunal makes an award which includes an element for loss of wages during the period in respect of which the employee would have been employed, had his employment been rightfully terminated, the amount of compensation awarded for loss of wages during that period, will be deducted when the damages are computed.[1] The basic award, on the other hand, is not related to the loss arising from the unlawful nature of the termination, and although it is far from clear, it is considered that no part of the basic award will be taken into account when assessing damages for wrongful dismissal.[2] It is possible that damages may be recovered for the loss of the right to qualify for statutory rights if dismissed wrongfully before reaching a qualifying period.[3] Now that industrial tribunals have jurisdiction to hear claims for breach of contract if there are claims for both unfair and wrongful dismissal it is preferable for these claims to be heard together in an industrial tribunal.

1 On the principle that the same loss cannot be recovered twice.
2 *Shove v Downs Surgical plc* [1984] ICR 532, QBD. The reasoning being similar to that in *Burnham's* case; *Berry v Aynsley Trust Ltd* (1977) 127 NLJ 1052, CA; *Basnett v J & A Jackson Ltd* [1976] ICR 63, QBD.
3 *Stapp v Shaftesbury Society* [1982] IRLR 326, CA; *Robert Cort & Son Ltd v Charman* [1981] ICR 816, EAT; and *HW Smith (Cabinets) Ltd v Brindle* [1972] IRLR 125, CA.

17.13 It has been seen in Chapter 7 that a compensation award consequent upon discrimination contrary to Pt II of the Sex Discrimination Act 1975,[1] although awarded by an industrial tribunal, is of an amount corresponding to any damages which the employee could have been awarded by a county court under the provisions of s 66 of that Act.[2] Similarly, an award of compensation following a finding that the respondent has committed an act of discrimination against the complainant which is unlawful by virtue of Pt II of the Race Relations Act 1976, is of an amount which corresponds to damages which could have been ordered by a county court had the complaint fallen to be dealt with under s 57 of the Race Relations Act 1976.[3] Awards of compensation for unlawful discrimination on grounds of disability made against employers are calculated by applying the principles applicable to the calculation of claims for damages in claims in tort or (in Scotland) in reparation for breach of statutory duty.[4] This means that the calculations are made as if the claims were in tort. The compensation can include an element in respect of injury to feelings.[5] It is probable that insofar as an award of such compensation takes into account factors which form the basis of an award for damages for wrongful dismissal, the damages will be reduced by the amount of compensation awarded in respect thereof if the damages are assessed after the compensation has been awarded. A claim pursuant to the Equal Pay Act 1970 is technically a claim for breach of the equality clause (see **5.32–5.36**).

1 Complaints under the Sex Discrimination Act 1975, s 41 (liability of employers and principals) and s 42 (aiding unlawful acts) are also included within the jurisdiction of industrial tribunals when related to employment matters: Sex Discrimination Act 1975, ss 65(1) and 63(1).
2 Sex Discrimination Act 1975, s 65(1)(b).
3 Complaints under the Race Relations Act 1976, s 32 (liability of employers and principals) and s 33 (aiding unlawful acts) are also included within the jurisdiction of industrial tribunals when related to employment matters: Race Relations Act 1976, ss 56(1) and 54(1).
4 Disability Discrimination Act 1995, s 8(3).
5 Sex Discrimination Act 1975, s 66(4); Race Relations Act 1976, s 57(4); and Disability Discrimination Act 1995, s 8(4).

17.14 If an employee is reinstated, or re-engaged, following an order of an industrial tribunal, the loss resulting from a breach of contract could be reduced to nil and if so the damages would be similarly affected. A payment, whether described as ex gratia, or not, referring expressly to a payment consequent upon wrongful dismissal, may be held to reduce the damages for such dismissal.

17.15 The right of former employers to counterclaim when claims are made for breach of contract should not be overlooked. The operation of s 25(4) of the Employment Rights Act 1996 may make it preferable for the employee to claim expressly under the provisions of the Employment Rights Act 1996 relating to unlawful deductions from wages rather than claim for breach of contract.

Redundancy payments

17.16 A redundancy payment is calculated in accordance with the statutory formula (see **16.89–16.93**) and so is not affected by the amount of any damages for wrongful dismissal, payment in lieu of notice, or compensation for unfair dismissal, or discrimination. In certain circumstances, a payment not expressly referable to the redundancy payments provisions, may be held to be a redundancy payment (see **16.78**), otherwise an ex gratia payment may not go towards discharging the employer's liability for redundancy payments. A payment made in respect, or on account, of damages for wrongful dismissal will not reduce the amount of redundancy payment, nor will the compensatory award of compensation for unfair dismissal, or compensation awarded as a result of discrimination on the ground of sex, or marital status.[1] A payment expressed to include a redundancy payment is not deducted from the basic award if the employee is found to be dismissed for a reason other than redundancy.[2]

1 *Stocks v Magna Merchants Ltd* [1973] 2 All ER 329; [1973] ICR 530, QBD; *Basnett v J & A Jackson Ltd* [1976] ICR 63, QBD. For the effect of the basic award of compensation for unfair dismissal, see **17.12**.
2 *Boorman v Allmakes Ltd* [1995] IRLR 553, CA.

Compensation for unfair dismissal

17.17 The amount of the compensatory award for unfair dismissal may be affected by any damages awarded as a result of a claim for wrongful dismissal. If the employee has already received payment in respect of such a claim, the loss which he has suffered will be reduced to the extent that the loss has already been compensated.[1] A court when seized of a claim for wrongful dismissal after compensation for unfair dismissal has been awarded, may consider that insofar as an element of the compensation was in respect of the period during which the contract would have existed if it were rightfully terminated, then damages for wrongful dismissal should be reduced accordingly. Before the coming of the basic award, the loss of any entitlement, or potential entitlement, to a redundancy payment was taken into account in calculating compensation for unfair dismissal.[2] Section 123(3) of the Employment Rights Act 1996 now governs the position, and provides that such element of compensation should include only the loss referable to the amount, if any, by which the amount of that payment would have exceeded the amount of the basic award (apart from any reduction under s 122 of the Employment Rights Act 1996) in respect of the same dismissal. Although compensation for unfair dismissal is subject to the statutory maximum, compensation for unlawful discrimination is not (see Chapter 7). It is likely that there will be overlap between the heads of claim under the statutes, and when the same factors are taken into account for the purpose of calculating the sum to be paid to the employee, each factor will be taken into account only once, on the basis that the ex-employee should not recover his loss twice.[3] It should not be overlooked that the interest provisions applicable to awards of compensation for unfair dismissal and unlawful discrimination differ and so it may be of benefit to a successful applicant for his or her award to be made under the discrimination legislation (see Chapter 7). Gratuitous payments to the employee after the dismissal will be taken into account in computing the compensatory award for unfair dismissal.[4]

1 See *Wellman Alloys Ltd v Russell* [1973] ICR 616, NIRC.
2 See *Norton Tool Co Ltd v Tewson* [1973] 1 All ER 183; [1972] ICR 501, NIRC and **15.194–15.218**.
3 Employment Rights Act 1996, s 126.
4 *Digital Equipment Co Ltd v Clements* (1996) Times, 11 December.

Compensation for discrimination on the grounds of sex, or marital status

17.18 The principles of assessment of compensation under the Sex Discrimination Act 1975 provide that damages will be computed in claims made 'in like manner as any other action in tort'.[1] The tribunal will be careful not to duplicate an award of compensation arising from the same cause.[2] The position with regard to exemplary and aggravated damages has already been discussed in Chapter 7. Payment of a redundancy payment will probably not affect compensation awarded under the Sex Discrimination Act 1975 and the relationship with damages for wrongful dismissal has been dealt with above. It is likely that all claims relating to the same dismissal falling within the jurisdiction of industrial tribunals will be heard together, if possible, and compensation will be calculated at the same time.[3]

1 Sex Discrimination Act 1975, s 66(1). For claims for equal pay, see **15.32–15.39**.
2 Employment Rights Act 1996, s 126.
3 For instance, the form of originating application available from Job Centres and its note of explanation encourage applicants to include all grounds in the application.
4 Race Relations Act 1976, s 56(3).

Compensation for discrimination on racial grounds

17.19 The principles of assessment of compensation under the Race Relations Act 1976 being similar to those in the Sex Discrimination Act 1975, the 1976 Act provides that damages will be computed in claims made 'in like manner as any other claim in tort'.[1] The tribunal will be careful not to duplicate an award of compensation arising from the same loss arising from the same cause. Payment of a redundancy payment will probably not affect compensation under the Race Relations Act 1976 and the relationship with damages for wrongful dismissal has been dealt with above. It is preferable for all claims relating to the same dismissal falling within the jurisdiction of industrial tribunals to be heard together and compensation calculated at the same time.

1 Disability Discrimination Act 1995, s 8(3).

Compensation for discrimination on grounds of disability

17.20 The principles of assessment of compensation under the Disability Discrimination Act 1995 being similar to those in the other anti-discrimination legislation, provide that awards of compensation for unlawful discrimination on grounds of disability made against employers are calculated 'by applying the principles applicable to the calculation of claims for damages in claims in tort or (in Scotland) in reparation for breach of statutory duty'.[1] The tribunal will be careful not to duplicate an award of compensation for the same loss arising from the same cause (see **17.12**). Payment of a redundancy payment will probably not affect compensation under the Disability Discrimination Act 1995 and the relationship with damages for wrongful dismissal has been dealt with above. It is preferable for all claims relating to the same dismissal falling within the jurisdiction of industrial tribunals to be heard together and compensation calculated at the same time.

1 Disability Discrimination Act 1995, s 8(3).

Taxation

General

17.21 The payment of damages and/or compensation to the former employee may be subject to charge to tax. There are three distinct contexts in which the effects of taxation have to be considered when making payment to an employee, or former employee, on the termination of his employment. First, taxation may have to be taken into account in calculating the sum to be paid to the former employee; secondly, the taxation consequences for the recipient have to be examined; and thirdly, it has to be decided whether the payment is deductible in computing the taxable profits of the employer.

17.22 If the employer is under a contractual obligation arising from the contract of employment (as opposed to an obligation arising from breach of contract) to make a payment to an employee on termination of employment, subject to what is said below, the sum paid is taxable as an emolument of the employment.[1] Ex gratia pensions to the ex-employee, his spouse or dependant are treated as income chargeable under Schedule E.[2]

1 Under the Income and Corporation Taxes Act 1988, s 19. See *Williams v Simmonds* [1981] STC 715.
2 Inland Revenue Statement of Practice SP 13/91, para 5.

17.23 Originally damages for breach of employment contracts and payments made on termination of contracts of employment were not brought into charge for tax. However, provisions were introduced in the Finance Act 1960 which taxed 'golden handshakes', ie payments made on a person's retirement, or removal, from employment (including damages awarded as a result of wrongful dismissal) leaving only the first £5,000 excluded from the charge. The present regime is to treat the golden handshake as income and, subject to certain exemptions, tax it as such. The provisions are contained in s 148 of the Income and Corporation Taxes Act 1988.[1] Subject to the exemptions, tax is charged in respect of any payment (not otherwise chargeable to tax) which is made, whether in pursuance of a legal obligation or not, either directly or indirectly in consideration, or in consequence of, or otherwise in connection with, the termination of the holding of an office or employment.[2] Payments are included in the charge if made to the holder or past holder of the office or employment, or to his personal representatives, whether made by the person under whom he held the office or employment or any other person.[3] The payments which are caught within the charging net include any payment in commutation of annual or periodical payments (whether chargeable to tax or not) which would otherwise have been so made.[2] Payments made to or on behalf of, or to the order of, the employee's or former employee's spouse, other relative or dependant are also caught.[4] Statutory redundancy payments are exempt from the 'normal' charge to tax, but are included in this charge.[5]

1 The former 'top-slicing' provisions ceased to have effect on 6 April 1988.
2 Income and Corporation Taxes Act 1988, s 148(2). Also included are such payments relating any change in the functions or emoluments of the office or employment.
3 Income and Corporation Taxes Act 1988, s 148(1). The Inland Revenue may be prepared to treat the payment to the widow as her income.
4 Income and Corporation Taxes Act 1988, s 148(3). Any valuable consideration other than money is treated as payment of money equal to the value of the consideration on the day on which it is given.
5 Subject to the £30,000 exemption. In practice non-statutory redundancy payments (if genuine redundancy payments) are similarly treated: Inland Revenue Statement of Practice 1/94. Advance clearance may be sought.

17.24 Payments treated as chargeable to tax under these provisions are treated as received:
(1) in the case of a payment in commutation of annual or other periodical payments on the date on which the payment is effected; or
(2) in the case of any other payment, on the date of termination or change in respect of which the payment is made.[1]

The payment is treated as income of the employee or former employee and taxed as such. In the case of death of the employee, or the former employee, the tax is assessed and charged on his personal representatives.[2]

1 Income and Corporation Taxes Act 1988, s 148(4).
2 Income and Corporation Taxes Act 1988, s 148(5).

17.25 There special rules applicable to ex gratia payments from retirement benefits schemes. These are dealt with by an Inland Revenue Statement of Practice.[1] In general the most significant of these for the purposes of this book may summarised as follows:
(1) if from an approved retirement benefits scheme, the payment is exempt up to the prescribed maximum for the scheme;[2] and
(2) if from a non-approved retirement benefits scheme, then the payment is taxable.[3]

1 Inland Revenue Statement of Practice SP 13/91 which should be studied carefully for its detailed provisions. An ex gratia payment made to an employee on severance of employment due to redundancy or loss of office, or because of death or disability due to an accident is not affected by the Statement of Practice: Inland Revenue Statement of Practice SP 13/91, para 10.
2 Inland Revenue Statement of Practice SP 13/91, paras 6–8.
3 Inland Revenue Statement of Practice SP 13/91, para 9, which includes benefits not falling in para 7 or 8.

17.26 The provisions of s 148 of the Income and Corporation Taxes Act 1988 relate only to payments on loss of office and employment (often called compensation for loss of office) and so payments such as damages for industrial injury, or on death are not taxable under them. Payments from some occupational pension schemes are also excluded, but may themselves be taxable under provisions which are beyond the scope of this book. Terminal grants and gratuities paid under Royal Warrant, Queens Order or Order in Council relating to members of Her Majesty's forces are also not taxable under s 148. A payment made to an employee should he enter a restrictive covenant on the termination of his employment, or when he releases the employer from such a covenant, would be taxable under different provisions.[1] To the extent that the compensation for loss of employment exceeds the sum of £30,000 the sum received by the employee is taxable. The exemption of the sum of £30,000 is of particular importance to employment lawyers.

1 This is a broad summary of the Income and Corporation Taxes Act 1988, s 188. The Revenue construe arrangements for payment in a wide sense to include any system, plan, pattern or policy connected with the payment: Inland Revenue Statement of Practice SP/13/91, para 2.

17.27 In calculating the sum to be brought into charge the taxpayer is not entitled to deduct from the damages or compensation legal costs and the expenses of obtaining other employment.[1]

1 *Warnett v Jones* [1980] ICR 359, ChD.

Calculation of sum paid

17.28 Unless there is a provision in the contract providing for liquidated damages by reference to gross remuneration,[1] as there is in contracts very occasionally encountered providing for pay in lieu of notice, the employee can recover his net loss only, on a claim for breach of contract. Where the claim is for loss of earnings which, if the contract had been performed, would have been subject to tax, the damages may be reduced by the amount of the tax saving, if the sum recovered or payment is itself not taxable, or is taxable at a lower rate, in the former employee's hands. This is, of course, an application of the principle that damages paid on breach of contract will not, save in most unusual cases, put the employee in a position better than that in which he would have been had the contract continued (see **13.64**). Despite the fact that golden handshakes are brought into charge for taxation the rule in *British Transport Commission v Gourley*,[2] to the effect that the employee can only recover his net loss, is applied in calculating damages to the £30,000 ceiling. A deduction is made from the damages equivalent to the amount of tax which would fall to be paid if the sum was received by way of emoluments,[3] ie where the notional figure for damages is less than £30,000, the adjusted notional sum is apportioned over the unexpired term of employment, or period of notice, and reduced by the tax which would be payable by the employee thereon if the same was received by way of remuneration. Where the payment is over £30,000 the position is not totally clear. One approach is to treat the total award as being £30,000 for the application of the *Gourley* principle as if it were the total award for loss of income during the period in respect of which the damages are claimed (ie the length of notice, or the unexpired period of a fixed term contract), the taxation likely to be charged on such income is computed and that figure is then deducted from the notional gross amount of damages.[4] In other cases the total award is taken into account in the calculation, the tax payable on the amount over the sum of £30,000 being added back to the award.[5] In certain cases, for instance those involving foreign service, payments may not be caught by the Income and Corporation Taxes Act 1970, s 148.[6] In such circumstances liability to foreign taxation will be taken into account in computing the employee's, or former employee's, net loss.

1 In cases where payments to be made when the contract is determined are agreed when it is entered into, the Inland Revenue are likely to contend that they are emoluments taxable under Schedule E.

2 [1956] AC 185; [1955] 3 All ER 796, HL; see also *Beach v Reed Corrugated Cases Ltd* [1956]
2 All ER 652; [1956] 1 WLR 807, QBD.
3 *Parsons v BNM Laboratories Ltd* [1964] 1 QB 95; [1963] 1 All ER 658, CA.
4 See footnote 3 above.
5 *Stewart v Glentaggart* 1963 SLT 119; *Shove v Downs Surgical plc* [1984] 1 All ER 7, QBD.
See also *Lyndale Fashion Manufacturers v Rich* [1973] 1 WLR 73, CA.
6 Income and Corporation Taxes Act 1970, s 188(3).

Consequences of payment for the employee

17.29 When a payment is made while the employment relationship subsists (ie before the termination), then prima facie it is liable to taxation under Schedule E and the employee should receive it subject to the deduction of PAYE. Where the sum is paid after the employment relationship has been determined, then the £30,000 exemption, mentioned above, normally applies and a payment under £30,000 may be made gross, providing that it is properly payable as being 'wholly and exclusively' for the purposes of trade and it is not taxable under Schedule E. This is also the case when the payment is made on the termination, and it is reasonable compensation (the term includes damages for wrongful dismissal, compensation for unfair dismissal, or payment in lieu) for loss of office, or employment, there being no further obligation of service thereafter.[1] To put this matter beyond doubt, it is preferable from the employee's point of view for the payment to be made after termination. Even if the payment is made after termination, but it is in effect payment for services rendered under the contract of employment, it is taxable under Schedule E.[2] The Inland Revenue are also likely to challenge any payment made gross, if the ex-employee continues to carry out work for the employer after the termination.[3]

1 *Clayton v Lavender* [1965] TR 461, ChD.
2 *Hochstrasser v Mayes* [1960] AC 376; [1959] 3 All ER 817, HL; *Henry v Foster* (1932) 145 LT 225, CA. See also *Heywood v Comptroller General of Inland Revenue* [1975] AC 229; [1974] 3 All ER 872, PC.
3 Payments which are to be made gross should never be paid until the position has been cleared with the local tax office. If tax is not deducted when it is deductible, the employer may be liable to pay to the Inland Revenue the tax which should have been deducted and may be unable to recover it from the ex-employee. The Inspector of Taxes should be given details as soon as convenient and whenever possible he will authorise a reduced tax deduction in line with the employee's actual liability.

Consequences of payment for the employer

17.30 It is most important for employers to be aware that when a payment chargeable under s 148 of the Income and Corporation Taxes Act 1988 is made, it is the duty of the person making it to deliver particulars of it in writing to HM Inspector of Taxes not later than 30 days after the year of assessment in which it is paid.[1]

1 Income and Corporation Taxes Act 1988, s 148 (7). For a limited exemption, see Inland Revenue Statement of Practice SP 13/91, para 8.

17.31 For an employer liable to income tax, if an individual or partnership, or to corporation tax if a corporate body, payments made 'wholly and exclusively' for the purpose of the trade, profession or vocation are deductible in computing profits brought into account for such taxes.[1] Where the employer is continuing in trade, payments made to an ex-employee on dismissal, or retirement, of the employee, if made for the purposes of trade and at arm's length, are allowable.[2] This is on the ground that such payments to former employees may affect the employer's relations with present employees and so benefit his business.

1 Income and Corporation Taxes Act 1988, s 74.
2 *Smith v Incorporated Council of Law Reporting for England and Wales* [1914] 3 KB 674, KBD.

17.32   A payment made to compromise an action, or threat of proceedings for damages, or compensation, which is properly calculated would be so deductible. Ex gratia payments pose a more difficult problem. They are allowed as deductions when calculating the employer's profit only if the employer, be it an individual, or company, has considered the matter properly and thoroughly in its own interests and those of its trade.[1] At first sight the application of these principles appears to be simple, but difficulties arise if the payment is made at, or close to, the time when the employer's business is sold or closes down, or when in the case of a company there are changes in the ownership of shares in the employer. On the sale of the business redundancy payments made to employees, are an allowable deduction.[2] Other payments are allowable if made from revenue sources and if they fall within the requirements set out above but not if they are set aside as part of the sale price.[3] On the cessation of a business, redundancy payments are allowed but not other payments for the discontinuance of the trade. This is because they could not have been made for the benefit of the employer's trade since it was not continuing.[4] However, when the cessation is on a liquidation, which is part of a reconstruction involving a transfer of trade, so long as the payment is made before the liquidator is appointed, then it is likely to be allowed. Payment for services already rendered is also deductible even if paid after cessation.[5]

1 *Snook & Co Ltd v Blasdale* (1952) 33 TC 244, CA.
2 Income and Corporation Taxes Act 1988, s 579.
3 *George Peters & Co v Smith; Williams v JJ Young & Son* [1963] TR 329.
4 *Godden v A Wilsons Stores (Holdings) Ltd* [1962] TR 19, CA; *Strong & Co of Romsey Ltd v Woodifield* [1906] AC 448, HL.
5 *IRC v Patrick Thompson Ltd (in liquidation)* [1956] TR 471, Ct of Sess. Such payments would be subject to taxation under Schedule E, in the ex-employee's hands.

17.33   When the former employee was also a shareholder in the employing company and there is a transfer of his shares at, or about, the same time as the termination of his employment, the principle in *Snook's* case (above) is applied but the practice of the Inland Revenue is to look more carefully at the payment to ensure that decisions as to payment and quantum have been taken solely in the company's interests. In that case Donovan J (as he then was) said[1]:

'The mere circumstances that compensation to retiring directors is paid on a change of shareholding control does not of itself involve the consequence that such compensation can never be a deductible trading expense. So much is common ground. But it is essential in such cases that the company should prove to the Commissioners' satisfaction that it considered the question of payment wholly untrammelled by the terms of the bargain its shareholders had struck with those who were to buy their shares and came to a decision to pay solely in the interests of its trade. This may be very difficult at times, because the persons who have to take the decision are often the persons who are to get the compensation; but any difficulty in securing an independent decision by or on behalf of the Company does not do away with the necessity of securing it if a title to deduct the compensation as a trade expense is to be sought.'

1 (1952) 33 TC 244 at p 251. This statement was expressly approved in the Court of Appeal. See also *George J Smith & Co Ltd v Furlong* [1969] 2 All ER 760, ChD.

17.34 A further difficulty can be encountered when the former employee, or director, was, or is, a member of the paying company, since the payment could be treated as being a distribution by the former employer.[1] The Inland Revenue may give sympathetic consideration to such cases where the terminal payment was made by a continuing company at arm's length, and was reasonable having regard to the circumstances and admissible as a deduction for corporation tax purposes.[2]

1 Reference should be made to specialist works such as *Simon's Taxes* (Butterworths).
2 [1974] BTR 412.

Chapter 18

Conciliation and industrial tribunals

Introduction

For the statutory basis, constitution and ambit of industrial tribunals (see **18.01–18.16.**)

Conciliation and settlement of cases In general terms the settlement of cases between the parties does not oust the jurisdiction of the tribunals unless the agreement has been reached in certain specified ways; namely assisted by a conciliation officer from the Advisory, Conciliation and Arbitration Service or cases in which the employee has received independent legal advice (see **18.16–18.18**). With the assistance of a qualified lawyer a compromise agreement may be entered into (see **18.19**).

Commencement of proceedings There are pro forma forms provided for the use by applicants but the use of such forms is not mandatory. Tribunals have interpreted the procedural requirements in a non-legalistic way (see **18.20–18.23**).

Amendments There are liberal powers to allow amendments both as to the parties and the substance of the claim (see **18.24–18.26**).

Time limits In civil litigation in the courts the fact that an action is out of time affords the defendant a defence. If that defence is not raised, then the action proceeds. In the case of litigation before industrial tribunals if a claim is not in time it goes to the jurisdiction of the tribunal and the point has to be considered even if the respondents do not raise the issue; the respondents have no right to waive the issue. There are restricted escape clauses if claims are not made in time; these are dealt with elsewhere in the text as appropriate. There are detailed rules as to where claims should be presented (see **18.28**).

Practice and procedure The industrial tribunals have a wide discretion in the procedure which they operate. Where there are civil or criminal cases pending arising out of the same, or a related, issue which the tribunal has to determine the industrial tribunal has a difficult balancing act to perform in deciding whether to allow the tribunal case to proceed. To allow the tribunal case to be heard may prejudice the forthcoming trial but to adjourn the tribunal case until the other litigation has taken place may deny the parties the expeditious hearing and remedy which tribunals give (see **18.57**). Industrial tribunals are not bound by the usual rules of evidence so that evidence will be admissible in a tribunal which is not admissible in civil or criminal litigation (see **18.69**).

The tribunal's power to intervene   Unlike courts, tribunals to a large extent control the litigation which takes place before them. They have a wide discretion, of their own motion to order discovery, join parties and summon witnesses. Tribunals often manage cases to control the course of litigation (see **18.54**).

The hearing   Although it is preferable for parties to attend and give evidence on oath there is a procedure for them to rely on written submissions (see **18.67**). As a matter of practice hearings normally follow a uniform pattern, but there is no rigidity in the way in which cases are heard (see **18.71–18.72**).

The decision   Industrial tribunals provide written decisions and reasons. Reasons may be given either in summary or extended form (see **18.89–18.91**).

Review   One of the fundamental values of any legal system is finality. In keeping with the informality of their approach tribunals have extensive powers to review their decisions. These powers do not extend to reviewing a decision merely because one of the parties does not like the decision. There is a distinction between parties appealing a decision because it is claimed the decision is wrong in law and reviewing a decision because the tribunal did not have before it matter which was relevant to the decision which it reached or for the other reasons on which decisions may be reviewed (see **18.95–18.103**).

Procedure in equal value cases   There are special procedures applicable in equal value cases. The issues raised are complex and the procedure involved is cumbersome (see **18.104–18.115**).

Procedure in Scotland   Procedure in industrial tribunals in Scotland is very similar to that in England and Wales, but there are some differences (see **18.116**).

Industrial tribunals

18.01   The industrial tribunals were created by the Industrial Training Act 1964 to hear appeals against levies imposed by Industrial Training Boards. Their scope and jurisdiction has been extended on numerous occasions so they now have jurisdiction conferred by many enactments including, amongst others, under the Safety Representatives and Safety Committees Regulations 1977,[1] the Equal Pay Act 1970, the Sex Discrimination Act 1975, the Race Relations Act 1976, the Disability Discrimination Act 1995 and complaints under the Employment Rights Act 1996 relating to unfair dismissal and individual employment protection rights. They also have jurisdiction in respect of claims for damages for breach of contracts of employment.[2]

1 SI 1977/500.
2 Industrial Tribunals Extension of Jurisdiction (England and Wales) Order 1994, SI 1994/1623 and the Industrial Tribunals Extension of Jurisdiction (Scotland) Order 1994, SI 1994/1624.

Constitution

18.02   The President of Industrial Tribunals (England and Wales) (at present His Honour Judge Timothy Lawrence) is appointed by the Lord Chancellor, subject to provisions as to resignation, retirement and revocation.[1] There are similar provisions relating to the President of Industrial Tribunals (Scotland) (presently Mrs Doris Littlejohn).[2] The chairman of each tribunal is a barrister or solicitor of not less than seven years' standing appointed by the Lord Chancellor. Subject to what is mentioned below, the chairman sits with two other members.[3]

1 Industrial Tribunals (Constitution and Rules of Procedure) Regulations 1993, SI 1993/2687, reg 3. The Rules of Procedure are contained in Sch 1 to the 1993 Regulations and references below to 'rule' or 'the Rules' are to these Rules of Procedure. See **18.13**.
2 The Industrial Tribunals (Constitution and Rules of Procedure) (Scotland) Regulations 1993, SI 1993/2688, reg 3.
3 Hearings of applications are heard by tribunals composed in accordance with the Industrial Tribunals Act 1996, s 4: rule 8(1). For the provisions relating to Scotland, see the Industrial Tribunals (Constitution and Rules of Procedure) (Scotland) Regulations 1993, SI 1993/2688, reg 7.

18.03   The tribunals sit at suitable centres. The two members of the tribunal, other than the chairman, are selected by the President or a nominated chairman, as to one from the panel of persons appointed by the Secretary of State after consultation with organisations or associations of organisations representative of employers, and as to the other member from the panel of persons appointed by the Secretary of State after consultation with organisations or associations of organisations representative of employees.[1]

1 Industrial Tribunals (England and Wales) Regulations 1965, reg 5(3).

18.04   A person is appointed Secretary of Tribunals and there are Regional Secretaries who act as the secretary of a Regional Office of the Industrial Tribunals. Any function of the Secretary of Tribunals can be performed by a Regional Secretary, or by a person acting with the authority of the Secretary, or of a Regional Secretary.[1] The Secretary maintains the register of applications, appeals and decisions. This open to inspection of any person without charge, at all reasonable hours.[2]

1 Industrial Tribunals (Constitution and Rules of Procedure) Regulations 1993, SI 1993/2687, Sch 1, rule 13(10). See also the Industrial Tribunals (Constitution and Rules of Procedure) (Scotland) Regulations 1993, SI 1993/2688, Sch 1, rule 13(10) where the title 'Assistant Secretary' is retained.
2 Industrial Tribunals (Constitution and Rules of Procedure) Regulations 1993, SI 1993/2687, reg 9. See also the Industrial Tribunals (Constitution and Rules of Procedure) (Scotland) Regulations 1993, SI 1993/2688, reg 9. In part it is kept by electronic means: reg 9(2).

Transfer of proceedings

18.05   The President or a Regional Chairman may at any time, on the application of a party made by notice to the Secretary of Tribunals or of his own motion, with the consent of the President of the Industrial Tribunals (Scotland), direct any proceedings to be transferred to the Office of the Industrial Tribunals (Scotland). This direction is made if it appears to him that the proceedings could be, and would more conveniently be, determined in an industrial tribunal (Scotland). No such direction is made unless notice has been sent to all parties concerned giving them an opportunity to show cause why a direction should not be made.[1] Where proceedings have been transferred to the Office of the Industrial Tribunals (England and Wales) under Scottish rule 19(1) they are treated as if in all respects they had been commenced by an originating application pursuant to the Rules.[2]

1 Rule 19(1).
2 Rule 19(2). The Scottish Rules contain similar provisions.

Constitution for hearings

18.06　Unless there is provision to the contrary, tribunal hearings take place before a tribunal consisting of a chairman and two other members.[1] In the absence of any one member of the tribunal, other than the chairman, proceedings may, with consent of the parties, be heard in the absence of such member and in that event the tribunal is properly constituted.[2]

1 Industrial Tribunals Act 1996, s 4(1).
2 Industrial Tribunals (Constitution and Rules of Procedure) Regulations 1993, SI 1993/2687, reg 7(3). Efforts are made to ensure that in cases relating to the Equal Pay Act 1970 and the Sex Discrimination Acts that there is one member of the tribunal of each sex and that in cases under the Race Relations Act 1976 that there is at least one member with experience of race relations.

Chairmen sitting alone

18.07　The circumstances in which a chairman on his own may act for the tribunal have been extended. Chairmen sit on their own without members in the following circumstances.

General
18.08　Pre-hearing reviews are usually heard by a chairman sitting alone. The tribunal may consist of the President, the chairman of the tribunal, or a nominated chairman only, for the purpose of making an order dismissing the proceedings where the appellant or applicant has given notice of the abandonment of his appeal or application, deciding an appeal or application in accordance with the written agreement of the parties, dealing with any interlocutory matter or application, or making any order for costs in connection with such an order or decision.

18.09　Any act required or authorised by the Rules to be done by a tribunal may be done by a chairman except:
(1)　the hearing of an originating application;
(2)　an act in connection with the procedure of the hearing, or the giving of a decision which the Rules imply is to be done by the tribunal which is hearing or has heard the originating application; or
(3)　the review of a decision and the confirmation, variation or revocation of a decision or ordering a rehearing.[1]

1 Industrial Tribunals (Constitution and Rules of Procedure) Regulations 1993, SI 1993/2687, Sch 1, rule 13(8).

Entitlement to bring or contest proceedings
18.10　The new rule 6 contains provision that the tribunal may at any time before the hearing of an application on the application of a party, or of its own motion, hear and determine any issue relating to the entitlement of any party to bring or contest the proceedings to which the originating application

relates.[1] Hearings under this rule may be conducted by a chairman alone. The better view is that at such hearings the chairman alone can hear evidence[2] and so many preliminary issues may be dealt with under this rule.[3] A tribunal will not determine the issue unless the Secretary has sent notice to each of the parties giving them an opportunity to submit representations in writing and to advance oral argument before the tribunal.[4]

1 Rule 6(1). For this purpose the tribunal may consist of a chairman alone: see rule 13(8).
2 *Tsangacos v Amalgamated Chemicals Ltd* [1997] IRLR 4, EAT; strongly disapproving *Mobbs v Nuclear Electric plc* [1996] IRLR 536, EAT; but see *Fleming v Secretary of State* (17 October 1996, unreported) EAT.
3 See Practice Direction issued by the President on 22 November 1994.
4 Rule 6(2).

Jurisdiction conferred by the Industrial Tribunals Act 1996, s 4(2)[1]

18.11 Subject to what is said in the following paragraph, the following proceedings are heard by a chairman alone:

(1) proceedings on an application for and relating to interim relief,[2]

(2) proceedings on a complaint under s 126 of the Pension Schemes Act 1993 (see Chapter 8),

(3) proceedings on a complaint or application under ss 23, 128, 131, 132 or 188 of the Employment Rights Act 1996,[3]

(4) proceedings in respect of which an industrial tribunal has jurisdiction by virtue of an order under s 3 of the Industrial Tribunals Act 1996 (see **13.60**),

(5) proceedings in which the parties have given their written consent to the proceedings being heard by a chairman alone[4] (whether or not they have subsequently withdrawn it),

(6) proceedings in which the person bringing the proceedings has given written notice withdrawing the case, and

(7) proceedings in which the person (or, where more than one, each of the persons) against whom the proceedings are brought does not, or has ceased to, contest the case.[5]

1 See the Industrial Tribunals Act 1996, s 4 for the specific provisions.
2 Under the Trade Union and Labour Relations (Consolidation) Act 1992, ss 161, 165 or 166.
3 Only suitable cases should be heard by a chairman sitting alone: *Southwark London Borough v O'Brien* [1996] IRLR 420, EAT.
4 Under the Industrial Tribunals Act 1996, s 4(3)(e).
5 Industrial Tribunals Act 1996, s 4(3)(g). The Secretary of State may by order amend the provisions of s 4(3): Industrial Tribunals Act 1996, s 4(4). No such order will be made unless a draft of the order has been laid before Parliament and approved by a resolution of each House of Parliament: Industrial Tribunals Act 1996, s 41(2).

18.12 Proceedings to which these provisions apply are heard by a tribunal including lay members if a chairman of an industrial tribunal decides (at any stage of the proceedings) that the proceedings are to be heard by a tribunal so constituted.[1] In making this decision the chairman should have regard to:

(1) whether there is a likelihood of a dispute arising on the facts which makes it desirable for the proceedings to be heard by a tribunal with lay members;

(2) whether there is a likelihood of an issue of law arising which would make it desirable for the proceedings to be heard by a chairman alone;

(3) any views of any of the parties as to the matter; and

(4) whether there are other proceedings which might be heard concurrently but which are not proceedings to which a chairman can hear alone under s 4(3) of the Industrial Tribunals Act 1996.

1 Industrial Tribunals Act 1996, s 4(5). Where a minister of the Crown so directs in relation to proceedings on grounds of national security, the proceedings are heard and determined, and acts are done by, the appropriate President: Industrial Tribunals Act 1996, s 4(7).

The Rules

18.13 The procedure of industrial tribunals is laid down in regulations.[1] In cases where s 101(1)(a) and (b), s 102(1) or s 103 of the Employment Rights Act 1996 and ss 161, 165 and 166 of the Trade Union and Labour Relations (Consolidation) Act 1992[2] are applicable the Rules apply as modified by s 129 of the 1996 Act or s 163 of the 1992 Act, as appropriate. A complaint presented to an industrial tribunal in accordance with s 128 or s 161 should be determined by the industrial tribunal as soon as practicable after receiving the application and, where appropriate the relevant certificate, and the tribunal should, at least seven days before the date of the hearing, give the employer a copy of the application and certificate in support together with notice of the date, time and place of hearing.[2] An industrial tribunal will not exercise its powers of postponing the hearing in the case of an application under these provisions, except where the tribunal is satisfied that special circumstances exist which justify it in doing so.[3] Otherwise the usual rules apply to such applications. Where proceedings are referred to a tribunal by a court the Rules apply, except where they are inappropriate, as if the proceedings have been instituted by the presentation of an originating application.[4]

1 New rules relating to the constitution and procedure of industrial tribunals came into force on 16 December 1993. In England and Wales these are contained in the Industrial Tribunals (Constitution and Rules of Procedure) Regulations 1993, SI 1993/2687, 'the Regulations'. The Rules of Procedure have been amended by the Industrial Tribunals (Constitution and Rules of Procedure) (Amendment) Regulations 1994, SI 1994/536 and the Industrial Tribunals (Constitution and Rules of Procedure) (Amendment) Regulations 1996, SI 1996/1757. The Rules of Procedure contained in the Sch 1 to the Regulations (as amended) are 'the Rules' referred to in this chapter. The Rules applicable in Scotland are contained in the Industrial Tribunals (Constitution and Rules of Procedure) (Scotland) Regulations 1993, SI 1993/2688 as amended by the Industrial Tribunals (Constitution and Rules of Procedure) (Scotland) (Amendment) Regulations 1994, SI 1994/538 and the Industrial Tribunals (Constitution and Rules of Procedure) (Amendment) (Scotland) Regulations 1996, SI 1996/1758. The Scottish Rules are not specifically referred to in the text and reference should be made to **18.166**.
2 Employment Rights Act 1996, s 128 and the Trade Union and Labour Relations (Consolidation) Act 1992, s 162(1) and (2). If a request under s 160 (awards against third parties) is made three days or more before the date of the hearing, the tribunal also gives the person to whom the request relates, as soon as reasonably practicable, a copy of the application and any certificate, together with notice of the date, time and place of the hearing: Trade Union and Labour Relations (Consolidation) Act 1992, s 162(3).
3 Employment Rights Act 1996, s 128(5) and the Trade Union and Labour Relations (Consolidation) Act 1992, s 162(4).
4 Rule 1(5).

Codes of practice

18.14 In proceedings before an industrial tribunal the codes of practice issued pursuant to certain statutory provisions are admissible in evidence and relevant provisions should be taken into account by the tribunal in determining the question before it.[1] Generally, a failure on the part of any person to observe any provision of the codes of practice does not of itself render him liable to any proceedings.[2]

1 Trade Union and Labour Relations (Consolidation) Act 1992, s 207 and Sch 3, para 1. Codes of practice are provided for and have been issued under the Sex Discrimination Act 1975 and the Race Relations Act 1976. At present there are ACAS codes of practice, those relating to 'Disciplinary Practice and Procedures in Employment' (1977), 'Disclosure of Information to Trade Unions for Collective Bargaining Purposes' (1977), and 'Time off for Trade Union Duties and Activities' (1991). Codes of practice have been made by the Secretary of State for Employment on 'Trade Union Ballots on Industrial Action' (1991) and 'Picketing' (1992). Codes of practice have also been made under health and safety legislation and under the Disability Discrimination Act 1995.
2 See footnote 1 above.

Enforcement

18.15   Industrial tribunals do not have their own machinery for the enforcement of their decisions. Any sum payable in pursuance of a decision of an industrial tribunal in England and Wales which has been registered in accordance with the regulations will, if a county court so orders, be recoverable by execution issued from the county court or otherwise as if it were payable under an order of that court.[1] Contempt of an industrial tribunal is punishable by the Queens Bench Division of the High Court.[2]

1 Industrial Tribunals Act 1996, s 15(1). In Scotland any order for payment of any sum made by an industrial tribunal is enforced in like manner as an extract registered decree arbitral bearing a warrant for execution issued by a Sheriff Court of any Sheriffdom in Scotland: Industrial Tribunals Act 1996, s 15(2).
2 *Peach Grey & Co v Sommers* [1995] ICR 549, QBD.

Legal aid

18.16   Legal aid is not available for representation at hearings of industrial tribunals although legal advice may be given under the Green Form Scheme provided by the Legal Aid Act 1988 in respect of employment matters. The assistance can include the drafting of documents in relation to proceedings before an industrial tribunal and even the production of proofs and documents to assist presentation of the case before the tribunal.

Conciliation

18.17   The Employment Protection Act 1975[1] gave statutory recognition to the establishment of the Advisory, Conciliation and Arbitration Service (ACAS) which is now charged with the general duty of promoting the improvement of industrial relations in particular by exercising its functions in relation to the settlement of trade disputes. Besides its conciliation powers in connection with trade disputes ACAS designates officers to perform the functions of conciliation officers under enactments in respect of matters which are, or could be the subject of proceedings before an industrial tribunal.[2] References to a conciliation officer in such enactments are treated as being references to officers so designated by ACAS. When a complaint or claim is presented to an industrial tribunal under the provisions of any enactment providing for conciliation a copy is sent by the Secretary of Tribunals to the conciliation officer.[3] It is the duty of a conciliation officer, if he is requested to do so both by the complainant and the person against whom the complaint is presented, or if in the absence of any such request, the conciliation officer considers that he could act under the appropriate subsection with a reasonable prospect of success, to endeavour to promote a settlement of the complaint without it being determined by an industrial tribunal.[4] In proceeding in accordance with these powers the conciliation officer has regard, where appropriate, to the desirability of encouraging the use of other procedures available for the settlement of grievances. In all those cases a request may be made to a conciliation officer before a complaint or claim has been presented to an industrial tribunal by the complainant, or by the person against whom the complaint could be made, for the conciliation officer to make his services available to him, and the conciliation officer then acts as if a complaint had been presented to an industrial tribunal.[5]

1 Section 1. ACAS is continued in existence under the Trade Union and Labour Relations (Consolidation) Act 1992, s 247. The functions of ACAS are set out in the Trade Union and Labour Relations (Consolidation) Act 1992, ss 209–214.
2 Trade Union and Labour Relations (Consolidation) Act 1992, s 211.
3 Industrial Tribunals (Constitution and Rules of Procedure) Regulations 1993, SI 1993/2687, Sch 1, rule 20(7) and the Industrial Tribunals (Constitution and Rules of Procedure) (Scotland) Regulations 1993, SI 1993/2688, Sch 1, rule 20(7). All documents and notices are sent to the appropriate conciliation officer, unless the Secretary and ACAS agree otherwise (rule 20(7A)).
4 Industrial Tribunals Act 1996, s 18(1) which sets out in detail particulars of claims presented to industrial tribunals in respect of which conciliation officers endeavour to promote settlement.
5 Industrial Tribunals Act 1996, s 18(3).

18.18   The assistance of a conciliation officer is of particular significance when settling complaints to an industrial tribunal pursuant to the Equal Pay Act 1970, the unfair dismissal provisions, the Sex Discrimination Act 1975, the Race Relations Act 1976, the Disability Discrimination Act 1995 and the individual rights granted by the Employment Rights Act 1996. There are specific exclusions from the restrictions on contracting out of the statutes in circumstances where the contract to settle a complaint is made with the assistance of a conciliation officer in the case of the Equal Pay Act 1970, the Sex Discrimination Act 1975, and the Race Relations Act 1976 and the Disability Discrimination Act 1995 (see Chapter 7) or is to refrain from presenting, instituting or proceeding with a complaint for unfair dismissal or in respect of the individual rights granted by the Employment Rights Act 1996 if a conciliation officer has taken action.[1]

1 Employment Rights Act 1996, s 203(2)(e). An attendance by a conciliation officer and recording an agreement in a Form COT3 was held to be sufficient action for this purpose in *Moore v Duport Furniture Products Ltd* [1982] ICR 84, HL. The Secretary of State may add to the list of provisions in the Industrial Tribunals Act 1996, s 18(1): Industrial Tribunals Act 1996, s 18(8).

Compromise agreements

18.19   The restrictions rendering void an agreement excluding or limiting the operation of the Employment Rights Act 1996 and the anti-discrimination legislation or preventing a person from bringing proceedings under them before an industrial tribunal do not themselves apply if the agreement is a compromise agreement.[1] A compromise agreement is an agreement to refrain from instituting or continuing any proceedings where conciliation is available.[2] The following conditions have to be met:

(1) the agreement must be in writing;

(2) the agreement must relate to the particular complaint;

(3) the employee or worker must have received independent[3] legal advice from a qualified lawyer[4] as to the terms and effect of the proposed agreement and, in particular, its effect on his ability to pursue his rights before an industrial tribunal;

(4) there must be in force, when the adviser gives the advice, a policy of insurance covering the risk of a claim by the employee or worker in respect of loss arising in consequence of the advice;

(5) the agreement must identify the adviser; and

(6) the agreement must state that the conditions regulating compromise agreements under the 1996 Act are satisfied.[5]

1 Employment Rights Act 1996, s 203(2).
2 Employment Rights Act 1996, s 203(2)(f).
3 'Independent', in relation to legal advice received by an employee or worker, means that the advice is given by a lawyer who is not acting in the matter for the employer or an associated employer: Employment Rights Act 1996, s 203(4).
4 'Qualified lawyer' means
   (a) as respects England and Wales, a barrister (whether in practice as such or employed to give legal advice), or a solicitor who holds a practising certificate, and
   (b) as respects Scotland, an advocate (whether in practice as such or employed to give legal advice), or a solicitor who holds a practising certificate: Employment Rights Act 1996, s 203(4).
5 Employment Rights Act 1996, s 203(3).

The originating application

18.20 The originating application to the industrial tribunal is made by the person seeking the tribunal's decision. It should be in writing setting out the name and address of the applicant and if different, an address within the United Kingdom to which he requires notices and documents relating to the proceedings to be sent, the name and address of the person or persons against whom relief is sought and the grounds, with particulars thereof, upon which the relief is sought.[1] Forms for completion of originating applications are readily available from local Job Centres, but are not essential. In *Smith v Automobile Proprietary Ltd*[2] the National Industrial Relations Court had to decide whether a letter addressed to the Central Office of Industrial Tribunals by a prospective applicant's solicitors amounted to an originating application. Sir Hugh Griffiths delivering the judgment of the now defunct National Industrial Relations Court stated, 'be it observed that there is no requirement that any particular form shall be used. In fact for the convenience of litigants a form has been prepared and is available throughout the country ... but we repeat that it is not mandatory, and an application will not fail merely because the form is not used, provided such application contains the necessary information required by rule 1.' It is important to note that the requirement of rule 1(1)(c) is for the 'grounds ... on which the relief is sought' to be shown and not the relief which is sought. In *Coates v CJ Crispin Ltd*[3] the applicant had deleted the reference to the Industrial Relations Act 1971 (the statute which gave employees the right not to be unfairly dismissed at that time) when filling in the form of originating application then available from local offices of the Department of Employment. Thus the form read 'I HEREBY APPLY for a decision of a tribunal under REDUNDANCY

PAYMENTS ACT, 1965'. When completing the section of the form entitled 'the grounds of the application are as follows:' Mr Coates wrote 'Sir, I have been employed by Mr. Crispin for five years. About seven weeks ago approximately the first week in October, I had a disagreement about one particular job. On 25th October, he gave me one month's notice and told me I would not receive redundancy payments. Yours Mr. H. Coates.'

1 Rule 1(1).
2 [1973] 2 All ER 1105 at p 1107, NIRC. See also *Smith v Automobile Proprietary Ltd (No 2)* (1973) 8 ITR 376, NIRC.
3 [1973] ICR 413, NIRC. It is to be noted that the Rules now require the grounds, with particulars thereof, upon which relief is to be sought, to be included.

18.21   During Mr Coates' evidence to the tribunal it had been clear that he was not asking the tribunal to award a redundancy payment but was seeking redress for unfair dismissal. When asked by the chairman of the tribunal whether, in view of the error, the respondents were prepared to allow the case to proceed on the basis of a claim for unfair dismissal, they indicated that they would not make any concessions in the matter. The National Industrial Relations Court held that the grounds which he set out suggested that what Mr Coates was seeking was a remedy for unfair dismissal and pointed out[4] that the note to the form of application used at the time stated that the applicant was fully entitled 'to amplify (and, as we would add, clarify) the grounds of his complaint at the hearing' . If the ground of complaint is dismissal 'the tribunal should always be prepared on the facts to consider whether either a redundancy payment or compensation for unfair dismissal or both, is due unless, (a) on the facts the tribunal has been deprived of jurisdiction in relation to compensation for unfair dismissal by ... [the time bar], (b) the validity of one or other claim has been determined in previous proceedings between same parties, or (c) there has been an unequivocal abandonment of one or other claim in such circumstances that even if there was an adjournment of the hearing, consideration of the abandoned claim would be unjust to the respondent employer'.[2]

1 (1973) 8 ITR 446 at p 451.
2 (1973) 8 ITR 446 at p 452.

18.22   In the case of an originating application in respect of a complaint under s 6(4A) of the Sex Discrimination Act 1986 (see Chapter 7) relating to a collective agreement, the following, whether or not identified in the originating application, are regarded as the persons against whom relief is sought and are treated as respondents: the applicant's employer (or prospective employer) and such employers or workers organisations their associations and representatives as would, if the term was to be varied voluntarily, be likely in the opinion of the tribunals, to negotiate a variation. There is, however, the proviso that such an organisation or association will not be treated as a respondent if the tribunal, having made such enquiries of the applicant and otherwise as it thinks fit, is of the opinion that it is not reasonably practicable to identify the organisation or association.[1]

1 Rule 1(4).

Formalities

18.23   It is obviously good practice when making an originating application to set out fully the grounds on which the claim is made. The only imperative requirement of rule 1 is that the application should be in writing. The remaining requirements are directory only. Thus when a claim was for unfair dismissal and gave no particulars of the claim the Employment Appeal Tribunal upheld the decision of an industrial tribunal that it had jurisdiction to hear the complaint.[1] An order for further and better particulars should be sought by a respondent who is in doubt about the nature of the applicant's claim or of the grounds in support. As will be seen, the tribunal can also make an order for further particulars of its own motion (see **18.39**).

1 *Burns International Security Services (UK) Ltd v Butt* [1983] ICR 547, EAT. See also *Dodd v British Telecommunications plc* [1988] IRLR 16, EAT, where an applicant included a date under the head on the form relating to claims under the Sex Discrimination Act 1975 and the Race Relations Act 1976 but no other details of the claim, and was held to have made a valid application. A deficiency in particulars can be remedied subsequently. This should be done as soon as possible.

Amendments: parties and claims

18.24   A tribunal has allowed a claim by an employee that he was unfairly dismissed when the company named by the applicant as the employer was not the employing company but the named company, had a common managing director and majority shareholder with the employer. Since the respondents knew of the application and were not caused any prejudice, an amendment substituting the name of the employing company as respondents was allowed.[1] Nevertheless problems often arise where the employer is a member of a group of companies and the employee, though employed by one of their number, performs tasks for one or more others. Such a case was considered by the National Industrial Relations Court in *Cocking v Sandhurst (Stationers) Ltd*[2] when, although employed by the holding company, the applicant was a director of a subsidiary which was named as the respondent in the originating application. The applicant wished to amend the application to substitute the name of his employer as the respondent. Sir John Donaldson gave the judgment of the court and said:[3]

'In every case in which a tribunal is asked to amend a complaint by changing the basis of the claim or by adding or substituting respondents it should proceed as follows—

(1) It should ask itself whether the unamended originating application complied with rule 1 of the Rules of Procedure (see in relation to homemade forms of complaint *Smith v Automobile Proprietary Ltd)* (see **18.20** and **18.25**).

(2) If it did not, there is no power to amend and a new originating application must be presented.

(3) If it did, the tribunal should ask itself whether the unamended originating application was presented to the Secretary of Tribunals within the time limit appropriate to the type of claim being put forward in the amended application.

(4) If it was not, the tribunal has no power to allow the proposed amendment.

(5) If it was, the tribunal has a discretion whether to allow the amendment.

(6) In deciding whether or not to exercise its discretion to allow an amendment which will add or substitute a new party, the tribunal should only do so if it is satisfied that the mistake sought to be corrected was a genuine mistake and was not misleading or such as to

cause reasonable doubt as to the identify of the person intending to claim or, as the case may be, to be claimed against.

(7) In deciding whether or not to exercise its discretion to allow an amendment, the tribunal should in every case have regard to all the circumstances of the case. In particular it should consider any injustice or hardship which may be caused to any of the parties, including those proposed to be added, if the proposed amendment were allowed or, as the case may be, refused ... If, however, the tribunal considered that the defect in the originating application had caused any party to incur unnecessary expense it could properly conclude that leave to amend should only be given if the party seeking to amend agreed to make some payment in respect of that expense and could order accordingly.'

In reaching its decision whether to allow the amendment they should balance the interests of the parties.[4]

1 *Fellows v Rock Rippers Ltd* (1973) 8 ITR 348.
2 (1975) 10 ITR 6, NIRC. See also *Sheringham Development Co Ltd v Browne* [1977] ICR 20, EAT.
3 (1975) 10 ITR 6 at p 12. In *Selkent Bus Co Ltd v Moore* [1996] IRLR 661, EAT, Mummery J said that when considering an application to add a new head of claim, a tribunal should take into account all the circumstances and balance the interests of both parties. Amongst relevant circumstances are the nature of the amendment, applicability of time limits and the timing and manner of the application.
4 *British Newspaper Printing Corpn (North) Ltd v Kelly* [1989] IRLR 222, CA. See also *Ketteman v Hansel Properties Ltd* [1987] AC 189, HL; *Gillick v BP Chemicals Ltd* [1993] IRLR 437, EAT; and *Linbourne v Constable* [1993] ICR 698, EAT.

18.25   In *Smith v Automobile Proprietary Ltd*,[1] the letter addressed to the Central Office of Industrial Tribunals did not set out the address of the respondents but since the respondents were the proprietary company of the RAC, the National Industrial Relations Court was of the opinion that the application was not rendered bad by this omission. It is suggested that the same would be true of any company named as respondent in the application which is incorporated in the United Kingdom fully and correctly named. The Registrar of Companies does not allow more than one company on the register with a particular name. Since the major purpose of the address is to identify the respondent there should be no question of mistaken identity in such circumstances.[2]

1 [1973] ICR 306, NIRC.
2 An application naming the respondents and giving their phone number, so enabling them to be identified, was accepted in *Gosport Working Mens and Trade Union Club Ltd v Taylor* (1978) 13 ITR 321, EAT. In the same case it was held that it was in order for two applications to be made in the same document. In a claim against the Secretary of State for Trade and Industry for the payment of a redundancy payment from the Redundancy Fund it is not necessary for the employer to be a party to the proceedings: *Jones v Secretary of State for Employment* [1982] ICR 389, EAT. The applicant should be careful to include his own address: *Hopes v Miller* (1978) 13 ITR 64, EAT.

18.26   In *Chapman v Goonvean and Rostowrack China Clay Co Ltd*[1] Sir John Donaldson made another major statement of policy as to the treatment of applications and to the exercise by tribunals of their right to amend applications:

'Accordingly, if there is the slightest doubt whether an applicant's claim is or should be for a redundancy payment or compensation for unfair dismissal, or for both ... the applicant should be encouraged to put forward or maintain both such claims until all the facts are known. The adoption of this course will not usually increase the time or expense involved as all or most of the evidence will be common to both claims. Even when the full facts are known and a decision has been made as to the true basis of claim, if there is any chance of this Court taking a different view on appeal, the claim which is considered inappropriate should be dismissed rather than withdrawn, thus allowing this Court to restore it if necessary. In all circumstances industrial tribunals should make the widest use of their powers to allow amendment of claims and to extend time limits in order to ensure that justice is done not only to the applicant, but to the respondent, who must always be granted any adjournment necessary to enable him to answer a new basis of claim which emerges at a late stage.'

1 (1972) 8 ITR 77 at p 86, NIRC. Upheld on appeal [1973] 2 All ER 1063; [1973] ICR 310, CA; *Home Office v Bose* [1979] ICR 481, EAT.

Finality

18.27   Tribunals will not entertain applications amounting to a challenge to a previous decision. The parties cannot test a previous decision otherwise than by way of review or appeal.[1] Industrial tribunals will not hear applications where it has been determined that they fall outside their jurisdiction.

1 *Curtis v James Paterson (Darlington) Ltd* [1974] IRLR 88, NIRC. See *O'Laoire v Jackel International Ltd* [1990] ICR 197, CA and *Barber v Staffordshire County Council* [1996] IRLR 209, CA, as to issue estoppel and cause of action estoppel. A tribunal can review its decision; see **18.95–18.103**.

Presenting an application

18.28   Applications should be sent to the Secretary of Tribunals at the Office of Industrial Tribunals or a Regional Office of Industrial Tribunals in England and Wales or the Office of the Industrial Tribunals (Scotland), The Eagle Building, 215 Bothwell Street, Glasgow G2 7TS if the matter to which the complaint relates arose in Scotland.[1] Originally in England and Wales the originating application had to be presented at the Central Office of Tribunals. However it became established that if an application was accepted by a Regional Office of Industrial Tribunals, then it was treated as 'delivered' to the Central Office of Industrial Tribunals.[2] From 1 September 1996 the rule has been changed so that in England and Wales an originating application may be presented at the Office of Industrial Tribunals or at any Regional Office of the Industrial Tribunals.[3] The position is different in Scotland. In Scotland all applications should be presented at the Central Office of the Industrial Tribunals (Scotland).[4] A legible application received by fax at an appropriate office within the time limit is treated as being in time.

1 So far as proceedings discussed in this book are concerned there is jurisdiction under the Industrial Tribunals (Constitution and Rules of Procedure) Regulations 1993 SI 1993/2687, where:
  '(a) the respondent or one of the respondents resides or carries on business in England or Wales; or
  (b) had the remedy been by way of action in the county court, the cause of action would have arisen wholly or in part in England or Wales; or
  (c) the proceedings are to determine a question which has been referred to the tribunal by a court in England or Wales.' (reg 8).
Having a registered office in London is sufficient to establish residence in England and Wales.

There is jurisdiction under the Industrial Tribunals (Constitution and Rules of Procedure) (Scotland) Regulations 1993, SI 1993/2688, reg 8, where:

'(a) the respondent or one of the respondents resides or carries on business in Scotland; or

(b) the proceedings relate to a contract of employment the place of execution or the performance of which is in Scotland; or

(c) the proceedings are to determine a question which has been referred to the tribunal by a sheriff in Scotland.'

For a discussion as to the transfer of proceedings, see **18.28**.

2 *Bengey v North Devon District Council* [1977] ICR 15, EAT.
3 See Appendix 2 for addresses.
4 See *Craig v Associated Dairies* (1980) unreported.

Registering an application

18.29   If the Secretary of Tribunals is of the opinion that the originating application does not seek, or on the stated facts cannot entitle the applicant to, relief which an industrial tribunal has power to give, he can give notice of this to the applicant stating his reasons for his opinion and informing the applicant that the application will not be registered unless the applicant states in writing that he wishes to proceed with it.[1] If no such intimation is forthcoming then the application will not be proceeded with by the industrial tribunal. It will be proceeded with upon receipt of a written intimation that the applicant wishes to proceed with it.[2] The better view is that a tribunal will not entertain an academic or hypothetical application where there is no dispute between the parties.[3]

1 Rule 1(2).
2 Rule 1(3).
3 *Secretary of State for Employment v Nortons (Cardiff) Ltd* (1972) 7 ITR 136, IT and NIRC.

Presentation and time limits

18.30   Presentation of the originating application to the industrial tribunal is of the utmost importance. In an action in the courts a claim which is statute barred presents a defence for the defendant. In an industrial tribunal a question as to whether or not an application is made in time goes to the jurisdiction of the industrial tribunal to hear the case. It is therefore essential to the applicant that the application is presented in time.[1] An originating application is presented when it is received by an Office of Industrial Tribunals.[2] If the Office is closed when the time for presenting an originating application expires the time is not extended to the next day on which the Office is open if it is physically possible to present the application in time.[3] It is the time of receipt which is important not the time of dispatch[4] but where an application was delayed in the post so that it should have arrived in time in the ordinary course of post it was held 'not reasonably practicable' for the application to be made in time.[5]

1 The time limits applicable to claims dealt with in this work are to be found in the relevant chapters.
2 Placing an application through a letter box or other authorised means of communication was sufficient: *Hetton Victory Club Ltd v Swainston* [1983] ICR 341, CA. If there is no letter box or authorised means of communication available on a bank holiday, the bank holiday is a *dies non*: *Ford v Stakis Hotels and Inns Ltd* [1987] ICR 943, EAT. If there is a special arrangement with the Post Office for the post to be held over on Saturdays until the office reopens, an application held over in accordance with the arrangement will be in time. In *Bengey v North Devon District Council* [1977] ICR 15, EAT, it was held that an application was presented when it was received

and accepted by an Assistant Secretary of Tribunals in a Regional Office. Presentation cannot be made at an Area Office in Scotland.

3 *Hetton Victory Club Ltd v Swainston* [1983] ICR 341, CA. This case was decided before the introduction of regional registration and when applications had to be presented at the Central Office of the Industrial Tribunals. It is likely to be followed in circumstances when the Regional Office is closed.

4 *Reeves v Marley Tile Co Ltd* (1975) 10 ITR 192.

5 For example for the purposes of the Employment Rights Act 1996, s 111(2); *Burton v Field Sons & Co Ltd* [1977] ICR 106, EAT; *Sturges v AE Farr Ltd* [1975] ICR 356, QBD.

18.31   The Secretary of Tribunals will deal with the originating application in accordance with rule 2. Upon receiving the application he sends a copy (usually a photographic copy) to the respondent and informs the parties of the case number of the application (which constitutes the title of the proceedings) and the address to which notices and other communications to the Secretary of Tribunals should be sent. The notice to the respondent is accompanied by information as to the means and time for entry of an appearance, the consequences of failure to do so and the right to receive a copy of the decision.[1] At the same time, in redundancy and other appropriate cases a copy of the application is sent to the Secretary of State for Trade and Industry and/or to the Advisory, Conciliation and Arbitration Service. The Secretary notifies the parties in every case where an enactment provides for conciliation that the services of a conciliation officer are available to them.[2] Copies of all documents and notices arising later in the proceedings are also sent to the Secretary of State and/or the appropriate conciliation officer, as the case may be.

1 Rule 2. Subject to rule 13(6), see **18.94**, the Secretary enters particulars in the register either within 28 days of receiving it or, if that is not practicable, as soon as reasonably practicable thereafter: rule 2(2). Where the application appears to involve allegations of the commission of a sexual offence rule 13(6) is applicable; see **18.94**.

2 Rule 2(3).

Appearance by the respondent

18.32   Within 21 days of receiving the copy of the originating application the respondent should enter an appearance to the proceedings by presenting to the Secretary of Tribunals a written notice of appearance. This should set out his full name and address, and if different, an address within the United Kingdom to which he requires notices and documents relating to the proceeding to be sent. The notice of appearance should state whether or not the respondent intends to resist the application and, if so, set out sufficient particulars to show on what grounds.[1] A respondent who wishes to raise a counterclaim pursuant to the provisions enabling a tribunal to hear claims for breach of contract should do so when entering his notice of appearance.[2]

1 Rule 3(1).

2 See **13.60** and the Industrial Tribunals Extension of Jurisdiction (England and Wales) Order 1994, SI 1994/1623 and the Industrial Tribunals Extension of Jurisdiction (Scotland) Order 1994, SI 1994/1624.

18.33   On receipt of the appearance the Secretary of Tribunals sends a copy to each other party to the proceedings. Unless an extension of time in which to enter the appearance is granted, the respondent who does not enter an appearance in the time cannot take any part in the proceedings otherwise than to apply for such extension and seek further and better particulars of the grounds of the application and to be called as a witness by another person.[1] He can of course apply for review of a decision by the tribunal on the grounds that he did not receive notice of the proceedings leading to the decision.[2] The party who has not entered an appearance will be sent a copy of the tribunal decision and of the revoked, varied or amended decision.[3] His consent is not necessary for a tribunal to sit with a chairman and one member only.[4] A failure to comply fully with the rule relating to appearances by the respondent does not automatically mean that he has not entered an appearance.[5] It is good practice to set out the matters in issue clearly and precisely. This is particularly so in complex proceedings, such as those in many discrimination cases. A respondent who considers that there are preliminary matters which go to the jurisdiction of the tribunal to hear the claim is best advised to set these out clearly in the notice of appearance.

1 Rule 3(2). Copies of the documents are also sent to the Secretary of State or conciliation officer, if appropriate.
2 See footnote 1 above.
3 Rule 3(2)(e).
4 *Comber v Harmony Inns Ltd* [1993] ICR 15, EAT.
5 *Seldun Transport Services Ltd v Baker* [1978] ICR 1035, EAT. The requirement to provide particulars of grounds of resistance is directory and not mandatory.

18.34 The prescribed time for entering a notice of appearance was 14 days until 31 July 1996 when it was extended to 21 days. At the same time other amendments were made to rule 3 which it was hoped would help reduce delays in lodging notices of appearance. A notice of appearance which is presented to the Secretary after the time appointed for entering appearances, and sets out the reasons why the notice has been presented after that time, is deemed to include an application for an extension of the time to enter the appearance on the grounds disclosed by those reasons. The amended rule provides that where a chairman grants an application[1] for an extension of the time to enter the appearance (including a deemed application) he will determine whether, having regard to the grounds of the application, it would have been reasonably practicable for the respondent to present his notice of appearance within the 21 days' time limit. If the chairman determines that it would have been so practicable, the respondent will be treated as having acted unreasonably for the purposes of the costs rule and the chairman should make an order under that rule if he considers it appropriate.

1 Under rule 15(1). See *St Mungo Community Trust v Colleano* [1980] ICR 254, EAT, and *S Aspris & Sons Ltd v Demetriou* [1989] ICR 246, EAT. Failure to enter an appearance within the time limit for entering an appearance does not have the same serious effect on the respondent as failure to make an application in time has on the applicant. This is because the failure to enter the notice of appearance does not go to the tribunal's jurisdiction to hear the application. Extension of time in which to enter a notice of appearance is usually granted by a tribunal chairman ex parte. In this respect the guidance given by Mummery J in *Reddington v S Straker & Sons Ltd* [1994] ICR 172 at p 176, EAT, that ex parte orders are in essence provisional should be borne in mind.

18.35 The effect of the new rule remains to be seen. If it is applied too strictly, dealing with the matter of costs may delay the case coming to hearing. It may also be an obstruction to settlement between the parties. In each case defeating the object of the amendment. It could be that difficulties will be avoided by chairmen granting extensions of time of their own motion.

18.36 If an extension is granted a copy of the appearance is sent to the other parties to the proceedings.[1] An application for extension of time can be made both before and after the time limit in which to enter the appearance has gone by. Industrial tribunals are slow to exclude a respondent from taking part in the proceedings. In *St Mungo Community Trust v Colleano*[2] the Employment Appeal Tribunal said that a notice of appearance could be admitted even after a tribunal has made its decision. In a case where the notice of appearance did not raise the issue of the applicant's capability, although the respondents attempted to prove to the tribunal that the applicant's employment was terminated because of his lack of capability, the National Industrial Relations Court found that the applicant had not been prejudiced and so did not remit the case to the tribunal.[3] It may be that an adjournment will be necessary for the applicant to consider the new arguments being advanced by the respondents and make appropriate arrangements for further evidence. The chairman of the tribunal should, in an appropriate case, give the applicant the opportunity to call further witnesses or evidence.[4] However, industrial tribunals will not always allow amendments at a late stage other than those of a technical nature .[5] Although industrial tribunals frequently, in the interests of justice, are prepared to allow appearances to be entered out of time their patience is not unending. For example, a tribunal had to consider whether to extend the time to allow an appearance entered over 60 days after the receipt by the respondent of the originating application. In view of the explanations or excuses offered in the case the tribunal considered it not to be reasonable to extend the limit in the circumstances.[6]

1 Rule 3(1). See *S Aspris & Sons Ltd v Demetriou* [1989] ICR 246, EAT.
2 [1980] ICR 254, EAT.
3 *Dean v Polytechnic of North London* [1973] ICR 490, NIRC.
4 (1973) 8 ITR 526 at p 529.
5 *Blue Star Ship Management Ltd v Williams* [1978] ICR 770, EAT, and see *Nelson v British Broadcasting Corpn* [1977] ICR 649, CA.
6 *Cook v Pardor Engineering Co Ltd* (1975) 10 ITR 28. See also *Ryan Plant International Ltd v Price and Secretary of State for Employment* [1976] IRLR 25, DC, where in a situation when there were many applications to the tribunal, extension of time to enter an appearance was granted in some cases only.

Interlocutory matters

18.37 The industrial tribunals have powers to make interlocutory orders. Decisions on interlocutory matters are often made ex parte by a chairman alone.[1] The industrial tribunal may require the party applying for an order to give notice of the application to the other party or parties. The notice should give particulars of the application and indicate the address to which, and the time within which, any objection to the application should be made, being an address and time specified for the purposes of the application by the tribunal.[2] When an interlocutory requirement has been made on a party in his absence, or on a person other than a party, the party or person to whom the order has been directed may apply to the tribunal requesting that it be varied or set aside before the time at which or, as the case may be, the expiration of the time within which, the requirement is to be complied with. In such cases the Secretary gives notice of the application to each party, or where applicable, to each party other than the party making the application.[3] An interlocutory order, other than an order to strike out under rule 4(7) or 13(2) is not a decision within the meaning of the Rules.[4] An order which is not a decision for the purposes of the Rules is not capable of review.[5] The tribunal's discretion is wide. A chairman cannot fetter a discretion which is to be exercised by the full tribunal. The decision of the chairman in exercising his discretion is only likely to be overturned on appeal if perverse.[6] The chairman should keep a note of the reasons for his decision.[7] There is a growing tendency, particularly in complex cases and those involving multiple applications, to hold interlocutory or directions hearings to clarify and identify the issues between the parties.[8]

1 The practice of the tribunals is, where it appears appropriate to do so, to invite the party from whom the particulars have been requested to provide them voluntarily before making an order. A similar approach is also often used when an application is made for discovery and inspection of documents.
2 Rule 13(5).
3 Rule 4(5).
4 Industrial Tribunals (Constitution and Rules of Procedure) Regulations 1993, SI 1993/2687, reg 2(2). For the position beforehand, see *Jones v Enham Industries Ltd* [1983] ICR 580n, EAT.
5 *Nikitas v Metropolitan Borough of Solihull* [1986] ICR 291, EAT and see *Casella London Ltd v Banai* [1990] ICR 215, EAT.
6 *Medallion Holidays Ltd v Birch* [1985] ICR 578, EAT; *Adams v West Sussex County Council* [1990] ICR 546, EAT.
7 *ASTMS v Mucci* (1973) 8 ITR 118, NIRC.
8 See rule 16 and the views expressed in *Barking and Dagenham London Borough v Camara* [1988] ICR 865, EAT.

18.38 In *Copson v Eversure Accessories Ltd*[1] the National Industrial Relations Court said that industrial tribunals should be vigilant to ensure that the parties are aware of their interlocutory powers in appropriate cases and in such circumstances tribunals should take the initiative by telling parties that they are entitled to apply for orders. The action taken by tribunals in this regard is to include information as to their interlocutory powers in the booklet issued to parties.

1 [1974] ICR 636, NIRC.

Further particulars

18.39 Industrial tribunals have power, on the application of a party by notice to the Secretary or at the hearing, or of their own motion, to require a party to furnish further particulars of the grounds on which he relies and of any facts or contentions relevant thereto.[1] The tribunal may (and invariably does) appoint the time at or within which and the place at which any such act is to be done.[2] Often, prior to making an order, a tribunal will enquire of the other party if he is prepared to provide the information requested without the need for a formal order, but there is no requirement to do this. The tribunal should not be unduly legalistic in considering whether to order a party to provide further and better particulars of the grounds on which he relies, or of any relevant facts and contentions. Amongst the general principles applied by tribunals in considering such matters are those that parties should not be taken by surprise at the last minute, further particulars should only be ordered when necessary in order to do justice or prevent adjournment, the order should not be oppressive, the particulars should identify the issues and are not intended merely to produce evidence, and complicated pleading battles should be avoided.[3] More formal pleadings are almost inevitable in complicated cases such as many involving allegations of unlawful discrimination.[4] The object of the order is to ensure that the parties know the case which they have to meet.[5]

1 Rule 4(1). This extends the power under the former rule. In *White v University of Manchester* [1976] ICR 419, EAT, it was held that an employee who had applied should have been granted an order for further and better particulars to enable her to know the details of the case she had to meet with sufficient particularity to enable her to prepare an answer. See also *Wilcox v HGS* [1976] ICR 306, CA. Orders for further and better particulars are more frequently granted today than in the past.
2 See footnote 1 above.
3 *Byrne v Financial Times Ltd* [1991] IRLR 417, EAT.
4 *Halford v Sharples* [1992] ICR 146, EAT.
5 *Honeyrose Products Ltd v Joslin* [1981] IRLR 80, EAT; *Colonial Mutual Life Assurance Society Ltd v Clinch* [1981] ICR 752, EAT.

Discovery or inspection

18.40 Industrial tribunals have power of their own motion, or on the application of a party, or, by notice to the Secretary at the hearing, to require one party to grant to another such discovery or inspection (including the taking of copies) of documents as might be granted by a county court.[1] Tribunals may (and invariably do) appoint the time at, or within, which and the place at which any such act is to be done.[2] In the absence of a formal order for discovery there is no general duty on a party to proceedings before an industrial tribunal to disclose any documents in his possession, but no document should be withheld if the effect of non-disclosure would be to mislead another party as to the true meaning of any document which has been voluntarily disclosed[3] and no party should suffer any avoidable damage as a result of not being aware of a document in the other side's possession.[4] In deciding whether or not to order discovery and inspection the ultimate test to be applied by an industrial tribunal is whether the order is necessary for disposing fairly of the proceedings. The order should not be oppressive on the party to which it is directed.[5]

1 Rule 4(1)(b). For the position in Scotland see **18.116**.
2 Rule 4(1)(b).
3 *Birds Eye Walls Ltd v Harrison* [1985] ICR 278, EAT. This was expressed as 'a high duty' at p 288.
4 *Harrison's* case above.
5 *Perera v Civil Service Commission* [1980] ICR 699, IT.

18.41 The power of industrial tribunals to make orders for discovery and inspection of documents is that 'as might be granted by a county court'.[1] Order 14 of the County Court Rules 1981 contains the provisions relating to the relevant powers of county courts. The order and decisions made pursuant to it should be referred to in cases of difficulty. Particular reference should be made to CCR Ord 14, rr 2, 5, 6, 8 and 9. The basic principle is that discovery, disclosure and production should only be ordered if it is necessary for fairly disposing of the action or for saving costs.[2] The power is to order a party to grant discovery and inspection. In appropriate cases it may be appropriate to join a person as party to proceedings to enable the tribunal to make an order for discovery or inspection.[3] Although discovery should not be ordered which relates solely to credit,[4] evidence relating to the treatment of another employee in similar circumstances may be the subject of an order.[5] 'Documents' include a tape recording (whether on audio[6] or video[7] tape) and information stored on the hard disk of a computer.[8]

1 Rule 4(1)(b).
2 CCR Ord 14, r 8(1). See also *Science Research Council v Nasse* [1979] ICR 921, HL. If a party has produced a document to the tribunal voluntarily he can be ordered to disclose documents which alter or seriously affect the true meaning of the document: *Colonial Mutual Life Assurance Society Ltd v Clinch* [1981] ICR 752, EAT. 'Fairly' means fairly 'to the other party': *British Library v Palyza* [1984] ICR 504, EAT.
3 *Bradley v Secretary of State for Employment* [1989] ICR 69, EAT but see *Douihech v Findlay* [1990] 3 All ER 118.
4 *George Ballantine & Son Ltd v Dixon & Son Ltd* [1974] 2 All ER 503, DC. See also *Sphere Drake Insurance plc v Denby* (1991) Times, 20 December, DC.
5 *Eagle Star Insurance Co Ltd and Dunbar v Hayward* [1981] ICR 860, EAT.
6 *Grant v Southwestern and County Properties Ltd* [1974] 2 All ER 465, DC.
7 *Senior v Holdsworth, ex p Independent Television News Ltd* [1975] 2 All ER 1009, CA, but there must be a relevance as to the extent of what is ordered to be produced.
8 *Alliance and Leicester Building Society v Ghahremani* [1992] RVR 198, DC.

Discovery and confidentiality

18.42 Considerable difficulty is encountered by industrial tribunals when dealing with applications seeking discovery or inspection when claims of privilege and confidentiality are raised by the party against which the order is sought. There is no special rule applicable to confidential documents, but in exercising its discretion a tribunal should have regard to the fact that the documents are confidential and that disclosure would be a breach of confidence. In deciding whether to grant an order of discovery in such circumstances the tribunal should consider how to reconcile the competing interests of the parties and of the public.[1]

1 *Science Research Council v Nasse* [1979] ICR 921, HL; *British Railways Board v Natarajan* [1979] 2 All ER 794; [1979] ICR 326, EAT.

18.43 The difficulty in connection with confidential documents arises regularly in discrimination cases. It is clear that public interest immunity exists independent of the parties to the action. It is a public right and cannot be waived.[1] Wood P said in *Halford v Sharples*:[2]

'When faced with issues of public interest immunity we ask ourselves the following questions in the following order:

1. Is the class of documents – regarded as a class – of such standing, importance and sensitivity that in balancing the two public interests namely the proper administration of justice and the proper and secure functioning of some public or quasi-public body, the weight to be given is so strongly in favour of the latter that there can be no question of disclosure? This is only likely to be so on rare occasions.

2. If the position is not abundantly obvious and perhaps where the details and reasoning of the affidavit or other evidence supporting the claim are insufficiently cogent, then in considering the question further it may be legitimate for a judge to "peep" at a particular document for two purposes: (a) to decide whether that document is within the class – "properly in that file", and/or (b) to decide the importance of that document to the issue. The document is examined as a whole – the type of document – and not as to the details of its contents, which would only be relevant to a "contents" claim. This would only arise where it is common ground that the document is disclosable but the public interest immunity claim is made as to part of its contents.'

If public interest immunity is claimed, the applicant for the order for discovery should satisfy the tribunal that the contents are likely to give substantial support for his contentions and that if they were not available he might be deprived of a proper opportunity to present his case before the tribunal which will inspect them.[3] Whether a class of documents is a type to which public immunity attaches depends on the nature and status of the procedure in which they were generated.[4]

1 *Halford v Sharples* [1992] ICR 146, EAT.
2 [1992] ICR 146 at p 158.
3 *Air Canada v Secretary of State for Trade (No 2)* [1983] 1 All ER 910, HL.
4 *Metropolitan Police Comr v Locker* [1993] ICR 440, EAT.

18.44 So far as documents which have arisen in circumstances of confidence there is no public interest immunity which arises from confidentiality alone. When considering applications for discovery the tribunal should have regard to the fact that their disclosure would involve a breach of confidence. In these circumstances relevance alone does not provide an automatic test for making the order. The tribunal may have regard to the sensitivity of the information, the interests of third parties (such as those providing references and those to whom they relate), to the interests of employers and employees and wider interests in preserving systems of confidential personal assessments. The ultimate test is whether discovery is necessary for disposing fairly of the proceedings. If discovery is so necessary, it should be ordered. When the tribunal is impressed with the need to preserve confidentiality it should consider whether the necessary information has been, or can be, obtained by other means not involving a breach of confidence. In order to reach a decision in such circumstances as to whether discovery is necessary, the tribunal can inspect the documents and see whether confidentiality can be protected by 'covering up' , obliterating names, using other means of identification and the like. In extreme cases it may be that the hearing or part of it will be heard in private.[1] The tribunal should consider whether the documents have a prima facie relevance before inspecting them. Inspection can take place at an interlocutory or full hearing, as convenient.[2]

1 *Science Research Council v Nasse* [1979] ICR 921, HL. See in particular the speech of Lord Wilberforce stating at p 925 upon which the above passage is heavily based.
2 *British Railways Board v Natarajan* [1979] ICR 326, EAT, approved in this respect in *Nasse*.

Legal privilege

18.45 The usual rules as to privilege apply in an industrial tribunal, so those as to privileged communications between a party and his legal advisers have to be considered. This privilege applies only to professionally qualified legal advisers and not to the other representatives frequently appearing before tribunals.[1] There is no legal professional privilege in statements taken by the police under s 49 of the Police Act 1964 but they may be protected under public interest immunity.[2] 'Without prejudice' correspondence is not usually admitted in evidence, subject to the usual rules.[3]

1 *New Victoria Hospital v Ryan* [1993] ICR 201, EAT.
2 *Neilson v Laugharne* [1981] 1 All ER 829, CA. With regard to police disciplinary files, see *Halford v Sharples* [1992] ICR 583, CA. See also *Goodwin v Chief Constable of Lancashire* [1992] 44 LS Gaz R 35, CA. As to documents generated as part of police internal grievance procedures see *Metropolitan Police Comr v Locker* [1993] ICR 440, EAT.

3 *Independent Research Services Ltd v Catterall* [1993] ICR 1, EAT. The usual exceptions apply so that if there would be an abuse of process to exclude the 'without prejudice' document it would be admitted; *Catterall's* case above at p 6.

Discovery and discrimination

18.46   Although at one time there were doubts, it is now clearly established that statistical evidence showing the racial mix of a workforce may be subject to discovery.[1] Medical evidence also may give rise to problems from time to time. The rules encountered in the courts are usually applied.[2]

1 *West Midlands Passenger Transport Executive v Singh* [1988] ICR 614, CA overruling *Jalota v Imperial Metal Industry (Kynoch) Ltd* [1979] IRLR 313, EAT.
2 *Ford Motor Co Ltd v Nawaz* [1987] IRLR 163, EAT. See also *Department of Health and Social Security v Sloan* [1981] ICR 313, EAT.

Witness orders

18.47   On the application of a party, or of its own motion, the tribunal can require the attendance of any person (including a party to the proceedings) as a witness, wherever such witness may be within Great Britain, and if it does so may require him to produce any document relating to the matter to be determined.[1]

1 Rule 4(2).

18.48   In *Dada v Metal Box Co Ltd*[1] the National Industrial Relations Court considered the circumstances in which industrial tribunals should issue witness orders. Tribunals no longer have jurisdiction to hear claims such as that forming the substance of Mr Dada's application, but Sir John Donaldson delivering the judgment of the court gave the following statement of matters to be considered by industrial tribunals when considering an application for a witness order which still provides helpful guidance:
'We are quite clear that tribunals have a discretion in deciding whether or not to issue witness orders. There is no automatic right to witness orders. But that discretion must be exercised judicially and it must be exercised with due regard to the fact that a tribunal is dealing with litigants in person who may not have the benefit of any advice.

It seems to us that there are only two matters of which tribunals should be satisfied before they issue a witness order. The first is that the witness prima facie can give evidence which is relevant to issues in dispute. For that purpose they will no doubt wish to ask the applicant what evidence can be given by the person who is the proposed subject of the witness order. We do not suggest that the tribunal should ask the applicant to give a full proof of that evidence, but applicants should indicate the subject matter of the evidence and show the extent to which it is relevant. The second matter of which the tribunal should be satisfied is that it is necessary to issue a witness order. In the present case the tribunal seems to have taken the view that it would be wrong ... to issue a witness order, unless they could be satisfied that the person concerned was unwilling to attend voluntarily. We think that this policy is erroneous to the point of amounting to an error of law.

The necessity for issuing a witness order can arise in a number of ways. We agree that witnesses should always be invited to attend by the applicant before he applies for witness orders. If they agree to attend and the applicant is quite satisfied that they will attend, then it is unnecessary to issue witness orders. If in such circumstances he asks for an order, it should be refused. But there are a number of other cases which can arise. A witness may not reply to the request for an undertaking that he will attend. In those circumstances it may be necessary to issue such an order. He may refuse, in which case no problem arises for a witness order is clearly needed. Again, he may equivocate or give an answer which at any rate leaves the applicant in reasonable doubt whether the witness will attend in the absence of such an order. In such circumstances it will, of course, be a matter for the judgment of the tribunal, but we should not be in the least surprised if the tribunal thought it proper to issue a witness order. Finally, although not exclusively (because these problems arise in many shapes, forms and sizes), there is the case of the witness who says, 'Certainly I will come and give evidence, but it would be very much easier for me to come if I had a witness order requiring me to come.' That situation can arise if an employer is unwilling to release a witness. Again that would be a reason for granting a witness order. We do not seek in any way to fetter the discretion of tribunals. What we are saying is that tribunals should be satisfied that the witness can give relevant evidence and that it is necessary to issue a witness order. But if they are satisfied on both these matters they ought to issue such an order.'

The witness order can require a proper officer of a company or other corporation to bring documents in its possession to the hearing.[2]

1 [1974] ICR 559, NIRC. In *Gowans v UBM Motors Ltd* (1978) 13 ITR 163, a tribunal set aside a witness order previously made by it against a police officer. The principles on which witness orders may be set aside are explained in *Rogers v Secretary of State for the Home Department* [1973] AC 388; [1972] 2 All ER 1057, HL.
2 *Penn-Texas Corpn v Murat Anstalt (No 2)* [1964] 2 All ER 594, CA.

18.49   In *Wilcox v HGS Ltd*[1] a case was remitted so that a new chairman could decide whether to make a witness order directed to a third party enabling documentary evidence required by an applicant to be made available at a tribunal hearing, when the chairman who had made the decision not to make the order had seen a letter prejudicial to the applicant's case.

1 [1976] ICR 306, CA.

Interrogatories

18.50   A power included in the 1993 Rules enables a tribunal, on the application of a party, or of its own motion, to require a party in writing to furnish to the tribunal a written answer to any question if it considers that the answer of the party to that question may help to clarify any issue likely to arise for determination in the proceedings and that it would be likely to assist the progress of the proceedings for that answer to be available to the tribunal before the hearing. The requirement may (and invariably does) appoint the time within which the written answer is to be furnished. Upon the imposition of the requirement, the Secretary sends a copy to each other party and he sends a copy of the answer to each other party.[1]

1 Rule 4(3). There was no such power prior to 16 December 1993: *Carrington v Helix Lighting* [1990] ICR 125, EAT. The tribunal takes account of a written answer furnished pursuant to rule 4(3) in the same way as it takes into account written representations pursuant to rule 8(5): rule 4(4).

Failure to comply with interlocutory orders

18.51 The order for discovery, inspection of documents, ordering the attendance of a witness, or production of documents, should contain a reference to the fact that under s 7(4) of the Industrial Tribunals Act 1996 any person who without reasonable excuse fails to comply with any such requirement will be liable on summary conviction to a fine and the amount of the current maximum fine.[1]

1 Rule 4(6). The amount of the fine is presently fixed at £1, 000.

18.52 If after an order for further particulars, discovery or inspection, or requiring a party to furnish a written answer, has been made, it is not complied with, a tribunal may, either before or at the hearing, strike out the whole or part of the originating application, or as the case may be, the notice of appearance, and where appropriate direct that a respondent be debarred from defending altogether. A tribunal will not so strike out or direct unless it has sent notice to the party who has not complied with the requirement giving him an opportunity to show cause why the tribunal should not do so.[1]

1 Rule 4(7).

Pre-hearing reviews

18.53 Prior to 16 December 1993 a tribunal could hold a pre-hearing assessment in connection with an application. The 1993 Rules introduce the pre-hearing review in its place. A tribunal may at any time before the hearing of an originating application, either on the application of a party, or of its own motion, conduct a pre-hearing review consisting of a consideration of the contents of the originating application and notice of appearance, any representations in writing and any oral argument advanced by or on behalf of a party.[1] The decision whether or not to hold a pre-hearing review is usually taken by a chairman alone.[2] The tribunal which hears the pre-hearing review is usually constituted of a chairman alone. The pre-hearing review is held after notice has been sent to the parties giving them an opportunity to submit representations in writing and advance oral argument at the pre-hearing review if they so wish.[3] If on the pre-hearing review the tribunal considers that the contentions put forward by any party in relation to a matter required to be determined by the tribunal have no reasonable prospect of success the tribunal may make an order against that party requiring the party to pay a deposit. The deposit will be of an amount not exceeding £150 as a condition of being permitted to continue to take part in the proceedings relating to that matter.[4] No order for payment of a deposit will be made unless the tribunal has taken reasonable steps to ascertain the ability of the party against whom it is proposed to make the order to comply with such an order, and has taken account of any information so ascertained in determining the amount of the deposit.[5] Orders made under the rule and the tribunal's reasons for considering the contentions in question have no reasonable prospect of success are recorded in summary form. A copy of the document is sent to each of the parties and is accompanied by a note explaining that if the party against whom the order is made persists in participating in proceedings relating to the matter to which the order relates, he may have an award of costs made against him and could lose his deposit.[6] The party against whom the order has been made should pay the amount specified in the order to the Secretary of Tribunals within the period of 21 days beginning with the day on which the document recording the order is sent to him, or within such further period, not exceeding 14 days, as the tribunal allows in the light of representations made by that party within the said period of 21 days. If he does not do so the tribunal will strike out the originating application or notice of appearance of that party or, as the case may be, the part of it to which the order related.[7] The deposit is refunded in full to the party who made it, except where the tribunal has made an order of costs against him in which case it goes in settlement or part settlement of the costs order. The balance of the deposit is refunded to the party who paid it.[8] The tribunal which hears the originating application will not include any member of the tribunal which conducted the pre-hearing review.[9]

1 Rule 7(1).
2 This procedure was approved by the Employment Appeal Tribunal in connection with pre-hearing assessments in *Ferodo Ltd v Bradbury* [1990] ICR 209, EAT. See also the Practice Direction issued by the President on 11 November 1994. If a party applies for a pre-hearing review and the tribunal determines that there shall be no review the Secretary sends notice of the determination to the party: rule 7(2).
3 Rule 7(3).
4 Rule 7(4). There is no power to dismiss a claim at a pre-hearing review: *Wellcome Foundation v Darby* [1996] IRLR 538, EAT.
5 Rule 7(5).
6 Rule 7(6). It was not usual for a tribunal to give reasons for expressing its opinion under the previous pre-hearing assessment procedure. The decision to express an opinion under that procedure was probably not subject to appeal: *Mackie v John Holt Vintners Ltd* [1982] ICR 146, EAT. It is likely that orders under the new rule will similarly not be subject to appeal.
7 Rule 7(7).
8 Rule 7(8).
9 Rule 7(9). This provision does not apply where in accordance with a direction of a minister of the Crown the President has conducted a pre-hearing review alone: rule 7(10).

Other preliminary matters

Directions

18.54   A tribunal may at any time, on the application of a party, or of its own motion, give directions on any matter arising in connection with the proceedings.[1] An application for directions is made by presenting to the Secretary of Tribunals notice of the application which states the title of the proceedings and sets out the grounds of the application.[2] In complex cases, and other cases where it is considered appropriate, the Secretary of Tribunals may arrange for a directions hearing to take place. This will deal with such matters as the clarification of issues and others which it is hoped will result in the hearing being conducted to best effect in the interests of the parties and the tribunal.

1 Rule 16(1). There is an increasing tendency for tribunals to exercise this power.
2 Rule 16(2).

Arranging the hearing

18.55   The President of Industrial Tribunals, or the Regional Chairman, fixes the date, time and place of the hearing of the originating application. Not less than 14 days before the hearing date[1] the Secretary of Tribunals will send to each party entitled to receive the same, notice of the hearing which will include information and guidance as to attendance at the hearing, witnesses and the bringing of documents (if any), representation by another person and written representations.[2] The parties may consent to a hearing being held at short notice. A chairman may, if he thinks fit, postpone the day or the time fixed for, or adjourn, any hearing (particularly as respects cases under the provisions of any enactment providing for conciliation for the purpose of giving an opportunity for the complaint to be settled by way of conciliation and withdrawn).[3] Chairmen of industrial tribunals have a wide discretion to postpone hearings.[4]

1 Rule 5(2). In *Derrybaa v Castro-Blanco* [1986] ICR 546, EAT, it was held that 'send' referred to the date the letter was received or was deemed to have been received. No reference was made to the earlier decision of the Court of Appeal under another jurisdiction in *R v Secretary of State for the Home Department, ex p Yeboah* [1987] 3 All ER 999, CA, where 'sent' was construed as 'dispatched' although in that case the Interpretation Act 1978 was not cited!
2 Rule 5(l). Notice can be less than 14 days where the Secretary of Tribunals has agreed a shorter time with the parties and on an application for interim relief under the Employment Rights Act 1996, s 128 and the Trade Union and Labour Relations (Consolidation) Act 1992, s 161. A former President has expressed the need for speed in bringing matters to hearing before industrial tribunals: Practice Note, July 1976. Unfortunately pressure of work has resulted in cases being heard less expeditiously than was hoped for at that time.
3 Rule 13(7). But for the position where the application relates to interim relief, see **15.168**.
4 *Bastick v James Lane (Turf Accountants) Ltd* [1979] ICR 778, EAT and *Medallion Holidays Ltd v Birch* [1985] ICR 578, EAT. Reference can also be made to *Carter v Credit Change Ltd* [1980] 1 All ER 252, CA.

18.56 A chairman may vary any a postponement or adjournment of a hearing.[1] It may be that it will be advantageous to the parties and to the tribunal if a preliminary matter or matters are heard before the main hearing. This will often be a matter as to entitlement to bring or contest proceedings. In such cases it may be directed that there is a hearing of the preliminary issue in advance of the hearing as to the merits of the application. This approach should be used only when the anticipated savings can be achieved.[2]

1 Rule 13(7).
2 *Wellcome Foundation v Darby* [1996] IRLR 538, EAT. The matter should be one which is properly taken in advance of the full hearing which will dispose of the full case.

Adjournment and concurrent cases before the courts

18.57 From time to time cases occur when other proceedings have arisen, or are likely to arise, from the same or overlapping facts or in which the same or similar issues are likely to arise. The other proceedings may be in the civil or criminal courts. Findings of fact by tribunals can bind civil courts. There may be cases where the commission of a criminal offence is the reason for, or is closely related to, the dismissal. If the tribunal proceedings go ahead before the criminal trial takes place, the witnesses may be forewarned of the defence case and the defendant's advisers may be in professional difficulties when interviewing witnesses. The allegations which form the basis of the criminal trial may go to the merits of the application and also to the remedy to be awarded to a successful applicant.[1] In such circumstances the industrial tribunal may be asked to consider whether or not to stay the proceedings before it to enable the other trial to go ahead first. In these cases the tribunal proceedings may be stayed until the other proceeding have been tried.[2] The question which should be asked is 'In which court is this action most conveniently and appropriately to be tried bearing in mind all the surrounding circumstances including the complexity of the issue, the amount involved, the technicality of the evidence, and the appropriateness of the procedures?'.[3] The other factors which should be taken into account include who is making the application (it may be that a respondent will be less likely to be affected by the existence of industrial tribunal proceedings in parallel with High Court proceedings than the applicant), the amount likely to be at stake in the industrial tribunal compared with those in the High Court, the fact that a successful litigant in the High Court is more likely to recover costs than before an industrial tribunal and whether the issues are such that a decision by the High Court will probably determine the issue before the industrial tribunal.[4] The Rules do not allow the tribunal to apply conditions to the adjournment.[5] In rare instances tribunals adjourn cases to be heard by newly constituted tribunals.[6]

1 *Bastick v James Lane (Turf Accountants) Ltd* [1979] ICR 778, EAT; *W Devis & Sons Ltd v Atkins* [1977] 3 All ER 40, HL.
2 See for instance *Jacobs v Norsalta Ltd* [1977] ICR 189, EAT and *Carter v Credit Change Ltd* [1979] ICR 908, CA.
3 As expressed by Wood J in *Bowater plc v Charlwood* [1991] ICR 798 at p 804, EAT. The applicability of the principles of estoppel were considered by the Court of Appeal in *O'Laoire v Jackel International Ltd (No 2)* [1991] ICR 718, CA.
4 *Warnock v Scarborough Football Club* [1989] ICR 489, EAT.
5 *Cooper v Weatherwise (Roofing) Ltd* [1993] ICR 81, EAT and see *Rajguru v Top Orders Ltd* [1978] ICR 565, EAT.
6 *Charman v Palmers Scaffolding Ltd* [1979] ICR 335, EAT; *R v Industrial Tribunals, ex p Cotswold Collotype Co Ltd* [1979] ICR 190 but see *Automobile Proprietary Ltd v Healy* [1979] ICR 809, EAT.

Withdrawals and decisions enshrining agreements

18.58 There are most useful rules empowering industrial tribunals to dismiss proceedings if the applicant at any time gives notice of withdrawal of his originating application.[1] Tribunals are permitted to make formal decision in accordance with a written agreement between parties (and the Secretary of State for Employment, if appropriate) as to the terms of decision.[2]

1 Rule 13(2)(a).
2 Rule 13(2)(b).

Extending time and directions

18.59 A chairman of tribunals may, on the application of a party, or of his own motion, extend the time for doing any act appointed by or by under the Rules both before and after the time has passed.[1] If an extension of time is granted, notice is given to the parties. A tribunal may at any time on the application of a party or of its own motion, give directions on any matter arising in connection with proceedings.[2] The application may be made by presenting to the Secretary of Tribunals a notice stating the title of the proceedings and setting out the grounds of the application.[3] The Secretary of Tribunals gives notice to the parties of any extension of time granted under rule 15.[4] The chairman's power of granting extensions of time may be done by a tribunal or on the direction of a chairman.[5]

1 Rule 15(1).
2 Rule 16(1).
3 Rules 15(2) and 16(2).

4 Rule 15(3).
5 Rule 13(9).

Joinder and representative respondents

18.60   An industrial tribunal may at any time, either upon application of any person made by notice to the Secretary, or of its own motion, direct that any person against whom any relief is sought be joined as a party to the proceedings and give such consequential directions as it considers necessary.[1] There is a similar power, exercised in the same way, to dismiss from the proceeding a respondent who appears to the tribunal not to have been, or to have ceased to be, directly interested in the subject of the originating application.[2] Where there are a number of persons having the same interest in an originating application, one or more of them may be cited as the person or persons against whom relief is sought, or may be authorised by the tribunal, before or at the hearing, to defend on behalf of all the persons so interested.[3] The industrial tribunal may require the party applying for such an order to give notice of the application to the other party or parties. The notice should give particulars of the application and indicate the address to which and the time within which any objection to the application should be made, being an address and time specified for the purposes of the application by the tribunal.[4] A fully constituted tribunal can rescind the order for joinder.[5]

1 Rule 17(1).
2 Rule 17(2).
3 Rule 17(3).
4 Rule 13(5).
5 *Reddington v Straker & Sons Ltd* [1994] ICR 172, EAT.

Combined proceedings

18.61   An industrial tribunal may order that some (as specified in the order) or all of several originating applications should be considered together, and may give such consequential directions as may be necessary. The order can be made on the application of a party made by notice to the Secretary of Tribunals or by the tribunal of its own motion. The tribunal may make the order if in relation to two or more originating applications pending before the industrial tribunal, it appears to the tribunal that:
(1)   a common question of law or fact arises in some or all the originating applications, or
(2)   the relief claimed in some or all of those originating applications is in respect of or arises out of the same set of facts, or
(3)   for any other reason it is desirable to make such an order.[1]
   The tribunal will only make an order under this provision if each of the parties concerned has been given an opportunity at a hearing to show cause why such an order should not be made, or it has sent notice to all the parties concerned giving them an opportunity to show such cause.[2] The tribunal may, on the application of a party made by notice to the Secretary, or of its own motion, vary or set aside such an order but will not do so unless it has given each party an opportunity to make either oral or written representations before the order is varied or set aside.[3]

1 Rule 18(1).
2 Rule 18(2).
3 Rule 18(3).

Notices

18.62 Notices given under the Rules should be in writing. All notices and documents required by the Rules to be presented to the Secretary of Tribunals may be presented at the Office of Industrial Tribunals or such other office as may be notified by the Secretary of Tribunals to the parties.[1] Notices and documents required or authorised to be sent or given under the Rules may be sent by post or delivered to parties at the addresses for service specified in the originating application, or notice of appearance. If no address is so specified, or if a notice sent to such an address has been returned, the notices and documents may be sent to any other known address or place of business in the United Kingdom. If notices are to be sent to a corporate body, they may be sent to the body's registered or principal office in the United Kingdom. In any case they may be sent to such address or place outside the United Kingdom as the President or Regional Chairman shall allow. Notices and documents, if sent or given to the authorised representative of a party, are deemed to have been sent or given to the party.[2] A party may by notice in writing to the Secretary of Tribunals and to the other party or parties (and, where appropriate, to the appropriate conciliation officer) change his address for service.[3] The recorded delivery postal service is used if a second set of documents or notices is sent to a party who has not entered an appearance, and for serving witness orders.[4] The President of the Industrial Tribunals, or a Regional Chairman, may direct substituted service in such manner as he may deem fit in any case he considers appropriate.[5]

1 Rule 20(2).
2 Rule 20(3).
3 Rule 20(4).
4 Rule 20(5). It is no longer the practice to send reminders to respondents who have not entered notice of appearance.
5 Rule 20(6).

18.63 In proceedings brought under the provisions of any enactment providing for conciliation, or which may involve a payment out of the National Insurance Fund, the Secretary will send all documents and notices or, as the case may be, will where appropriate send copies of all such documents to the appropriate conciliation officer and to Secretary of State, respectively.[1] In proceedings under the Equal Pay Act 1970, the Sex Discrimination Acts or the Race Relations Act 1976 the Secretary will send to the Equal Opportunities Commission or, as the case may be, the Commission for Racial Equality, copies of every decision and reasons and every review, revocation and variation thereof.[2]

1 Rule 20(7) and (8), subject to rule 20(7A).
2 Rule 20(9).

Striking out

18.64 At any stage of the proceedings a tribunal can order to be struck out, or amended, any originating application or notice of appearance, or anything in such application or notice of appearance, on the ground that it is scandalous, frivolous or vexatious.[1] Also, at any stage of the proceedings, the tribunal may order to be struck out any originating application or notice of appearance on the grounds that the manner in which the proceedings have been conducted by or on behalf of the applicant or, as the case may be, the respondent have been scandalous, frivolous or vexatious.[2] The tribunal may also, on the application of the respondent, or of its own motion, order to be struck out any originating application for want of prosecution.[3] This power will be exercised in accordance with the principles set out by Lord Diplock in *Birkett v James*[4] applied mutatis mutandis. Lord Diplock said:[5]

'The power should be exercised only where the court is satisfied either (1) that the default has been intentional or contumelious, eg disobedience to a peremptory order of the court or conduct amounting to an abuse of the process of the court; or (2) (a) that there has been inordinate and inexcusable delay on the part of the plaintiff or his lawyers, and (b) that such delay will give rise to a substantial risk that it is not possible to have a fair trial of the issues in the action or is such as is likely to cause or to have caused serious prejudice to the defendants either as between themselves and the plaintiff or between each other or between them and a third party.'

These powers to strike out are only exercised after notice has been given to the party against whom it is proposed to make such an order giving him an opportunity to show cause why such an order should not be made.[6] A striking out order is now subject to review.[7]

1 Rule 13(2)(d). The categories of what is frivolous or vexatious are not closed but depend on all the relevant circumstances of the particular case. Public policy and the interests of justice being very material considerations: *Ashmore v British Coal Corpn* [1990] ICR 485, CA, where the Court of Appeal upheld the decision of an industrial tribunal chairman to strike out the application of a person not selected as a sample case after a full investigation by the tribunal into the sample cases had resulted in their being dismissed. However, it is not frivolous or vexatious for an applicant to continue with a claim for unfair dismissal just because the applicant refused an offer of a maximum award: *Telephone Information Services Ltd v Wilkinson* [1991] IRLR 148, EAT. The rule does not extend to conduct at the hearing: *O'Keefe v Southampton Council* [1988] IRLR 424, EAT.
2 Rule 13(2)(e).
3 Rule 13(2)(f). In considering this provision great assistance can be gained from the decision of the House of Lords in *Birkett v James* [1977] 2 All ER 801, HL.
4 [1977] 2 All ER 801, HL. See *Evans v Metropolitan Police Comr* [1992] IRLR 570, CA.
5 [1977] 2 All ER 801 at p 805, HL. Reference should also be made to *Department of Trade v Chris Smaller Transport Ltd* [1989] 1 All ER 897, HL.
6 Rule 13(3). This does not require the tribunal to send written notice to the party if the party has been given an opportunity to show cause orally why the order should not be made. This proviso is newly introduced into the Rules and effectively reverses *O'Keefe v Southampton Council* [1988] IRLR 424, EAT, which held that the notice must be written notice, verbal warnings not being enough. Where notice is sent in relation to an order to strike out for want of prosecution, service is treated as having been effected if it has been sent by post or delivered in accordance with rule 20(3). The tribunal may strike out the originating application notwithstanding that there has been direction for substituted service if the party does not avail himself of the opportunity given by the notice: rule 13(4).
7 See the definition of 'decision' in the Industrial Tribunals (Constitution and Rules of Procedure) Regulations 1993, SI 1993/2687, reg 2(2) which so far as striking out orders under rules 4(7) and 13(2) has the effect of reversing *Casella London Ltd v Banai* [1990] ICR 215, EAT.

The hearing

Duty to sit in public except in limited circumstances

18.65 The tribunal will be composed in accordance with the requirements of the Industrial Tribunals Act 1996. Hearings before industrial tribunals take place in public,[1] unless in the opinion of the tribunal a private hearing would be appropriate for the purpose of hearing evidence which relates to matters of such a nature that it would be against the interests of national security to allow the evidence to be given in public,[2] or for hearing evidence from any person which in the opinion of the tribunal is likely to consist of:

'(a) information which he could not disclose without contravening a prohibition imposed by or under any enactment; or

(b) any information which has been communicated to him in confidence, or which he has otherwise obtained in consequence of the confidence reposed in him by another person; or

(c) information the disclosure of which would cause substantial injury to any undertaking of his or any undertaking in which he works for reasons other than its effect on negotiations with respect to any of the matters mentioned in section 244(1) of the [Trade Union and Labour Relations (Consolidation) Act 1992]'.[3]

In such cases a member of the Council of Tribunals is entitled to attend in his official capacity.[4]

1 Rule 8(2).
2 Rule 8(2) except where a minister of the Crown has directed a tribunal to sit in private on grounds of national security in accordance with the Industrial Tribunals Act 1996, s 10(1).
3 Rule 8(3). The Trade Union and Labour Relations (Consolidation) Act 1992, s 244(1) is as follows:

'(1) In this Part a "trade dispute" means a dispute between workers and their employer which relates wholly or mainly to one or more of the following –
   (a) terms and conditions of employment, or the physical conditions in which any workers are required to work;
   (b) engagement or non-engagement, or termination or suspension of employment or the duties of employment, of one or more workers;
   (c) allocation of work or the duties of employment between workers or groups of workers;
   (d) matters of discipline;
   (e) a worker's membership or non-membership of a trade union;
   (f) facilities for officials of trade unions; and
   (g) machinery for negotiation or consultation, and other procedures, relating to any of the above matters, including the recognition by employers or employers' associations of the right of a trade union to represent workers in such negotiation or consultation or in the carrying out of such procedures.'

There is no obligation on the tribunal to consider whether a hearing should be in private in advance of the hearing. Indeed it could be that the decision should only be made by the full tribunal itself: *Milne & Lyall v Waldren* [1980] ICR 138, EAT. The application by a party for the hearing is likely to be held in private, but the decision whether or not the hearing will be heard in private should be announced publicly.
4 Rule 8(4).

Restricted reporting orders

18.66 In any case which involves allegations of sexual misconduct[1] the tribunal may at any time before the promulgation of its decision in respect of the originating application either on the application of a party made to the Secretary or of its own motion make a restricted reporting order.[2] There is a similar power in proceedings on a complaint under s 8 of the Disability Discrimination Act 1995 in which evidence of a personal nature is likely to be heard.[3] The tribunal will not make a restricted reporting order unless it has given each party an opportunity to advance oral argument at the hearing if they so wish.[4] A restricted reporting order will specify the persons who may not be identified and it will remain in force until the promulgation of the decision of the tribunal on the originating application to which it relates unless it is revoked earlier. The Regional Secretary will ensure that a notice of that fact is displayed on the notice board of the tribunal with any list of proceedings taking place before the industrial tribunal and on the door of the room in which the proceedings are taking place.[5] A tribunal may revoke a restricted reporting order at any time if it thinks fit.[6]

1 This is wider than the term 'sexual offence' used in rule 13(6), see **18.94**.
2 Rule 14(1). See *R v Southampton Industrial Tribunal, ex p INS* [1995] IRLR 247, QBD.
3 Rule 14(1A). If an order is made under this power and the complaint is being dealt with together with other proceedings the tribunal may direct that the order applies also in relation to those other proceedings or such part of them as it directs: rule 14(1B).
4 Rule 14(2).
5 Rule 14(3). Promulgation occurs for this purpose on the date recorded as the date on which the document recording the determination of the originating application was sent to the parties: rule 14(5).
6 Rule 14(4).

Oral hearings with right to make written representations

18.67   Hearings usually take the form of oral hearings, but a party who wishes to submit representations in writing for consideration at the hearing may do so, provided that he presents such representations to the Secretary of Tribunals not less than seven days before the hearing, at the same time sending a copy or copies to the other party or parties.[1] The Rules now make it clear that a tribunal may consider representations in writing which have been submitted by a party to the Secretary of Tribunals less than seven days before the hearing.[2] The better view beforehand was that an industrial tribunal had a discretion to admit such written statements.[3] The representations contemplated by this rule are those given in place of evidence[4] on oath. The rule does not apply to the situation where a witness who is sworn reads from his proof of evidence. Such evidence, which is increasingly used in industrial tribunals, is treated as evidence given on oath in the usual way.

1 Rule 8(5) and see the Civil Evidence Act 1968, s 2(1).
2 Rule 13(2)(c).
3 *Lawrence v Newham London Borough Council* [1978] ICR 10, EAT. See in particular the note at p 14.
4 *Hardisty v Lowton Construction Group Ltd* (1973) 8 ITR 603, NIRC.

Representation

18.68   At the hearing those entitled to be present may appear in person, be represented by counsel, solicitor, representative of trade union or employers association, or any other person who they desire to represent them.[1] The Secretary of State, if he so elects, is entitled to appear as if he is a party and be heard at any hearing on, or in connection with, an originating application in proceedings which may involve payments out of the National Insurance Fund.[2]

1 As a matter of practice, it may be undesirable for the employer's representative to have been a member of the domestic appeal panel: *Singh v London Country Bus Services Ltd* [1976] IRLR 176, EAT.
2 Rule 8(6). If he does so, the Secretary of State is treated as if a party.

Conduct of the hearing

18.69   The tribunal, so far as it appears to it appropriate, will avoid formality in its proceedings and it is not bound by any enactment or rule of law relating to the admissibility of evidence in proceedings before courts of law.[1] The tribunal will make such enquiries of the persons appearing before it and witnesses as it considers appropriate and will otherwise conduct the hearing in such manner as it considers most suitable to the clarification of the issues before it and generally to the just handling of the proceedings.[2] So far as appears to the tribunal to be appropriate, it will seek to avoid formality in its proceedings. Those entitled to appear may give evidence, call and question witnesses and address the tribunal.[3] The tribunal may require witnesses to give evidence on oath or affirmation and administer such oath or affirmation.[4] If a party wishes to raise a question relating to a transient concern or matter, such as tribunal member failing to pay attention or falling asleep, it should be raised at the time in the course of the proceedings.[5] If a party fails to appear or to be represented at the relevant time and place fixed for the hearing, the tribunal may, if that party is an applicant dismiss, or, in any case, dispose of the application in the absence of that party or may adjourn the hearing to a later date. Before dismissing or disposing of any application in the absence of a party, the tribunal will consider his originating application, or notice of appearance, and if the absent party has made written representations pursuant to rule 8(5) these will be considered by the tribunal, as will any answer to an interrogatory furnished to the tribunal.[6] The hearing is usually conducted in an accusatory manner but, as has been seen, the tribunal will make such enquiries of the persons appearing before it and of the witnesses as it considers appropriate. The tribunal has no duty to ensure that all the relevant evidence is before it. It is for the parties to present their cases to the tribunal.[7] The tribunal may assist the parties in presenting their cases, particularly where they are not represented, or are manifestly unversed in the legal procedure before a tribunal,[8] but the tribunal is not under a duty to raise points not raised by the parties or in the pleadings.[9] If the other party does not object the industrial tribunal may of its own volition amend the pleadings.[10]

1   Rule 9(1). The tribunal should not exclude normally admissible evidence; *Rosedale Mouldings Ltd v Sibley* [1980] ICR 816, EAT.
2   See footnote 1 above. The reference to an inquisitorial approach did not appear in the Rules before the amendments in 1993.
3   Rule 9(2). A party, who when invited to call evidence refuses to do so, may in some circumstances be precluded from changing his mind: *Stokes v Hampstead Wine Co Ltd* [1979] IRLR 298, EAT.
4   Rule 9(4).
5   *Red Bank Manufacturing Co Ltd v Meadows* [1992] ICR 204, EAT.
6   Rule 9(3).
7   *Bagga v Heavy Electricals (India) Ltd* [1972] ICR 118, NIRC.
8   *Craig v British Railways (Scottish Region)* (1973) 8 ITR 636, NIRC.
9   *Dimtsu v Westminster Council* [1991] IRLR 450, EAT.
10   *Sheringham Development Co Ltd v Browne* [1977] ICR 20, EAT; *Cocking v Sandhurst (Stationers) Ltd* [1974] ICR 650, NIRC.

Adjournments during the course of hearings; the right to be heard

18.70   Where at the hearing a party is taken by surprise, for instance because he has been mislead by a conciliation officer into believing that the case would not proceed,[1] or because the other party seeks to rely on grounds which were not referred to in the originating application or notice of appearance, the tribunal may decide that it is appropriate to grant an adjournment to reconsider the case in the light of the new circumstances and to allow the party taken by surprise to prepare his case accordingly. In *Dean v Polytechnic of North London*[2] Sir John Donaldson said:

'It is of the greatest importance that parties to proceedings before courts or tribunals should have the fullest opportunity of presenting their cases. If, due to the necessary informality of the proceedings, they are in any way taken by surprise they should be offered the opportunity of calling or themselves giving further evidence and if there is any need for an adjournment it should be granted without hesitation.'

It is important that the parties have an opportunity to be heard on all allegations against them.[3] If a party seeks to change the grounds of his contentions, it is essential that the other party is fully able to respond.[4] A tribunal may refuse to allow a late amendment which goes beyond attaching a different label to established facts.[5] A tribunal which is minded to reach a decision on a point which has not been raised by either side, and which will take them by surprise, should recall the parties, put the point to them and hear argument and submissions on the point.[6] This is particularly the case where the tribunal is likely to decide that the reason for a dismissal is different from that pleaded or argued.[7]

1 *Berkeley Garage (Southampton) Ltd v Edmunds* (1975) 10 ITR 70, DC.
2 [1973] ICR 490, NIRC. The parties or their representatives should prepare numbered bundles of correspondence and documents to be used in evidence. A list should be supplied to the other party and, if possible, a single bundle prepared and agreed. Three sets of documents should be available for the tribunal.
3 *Murphy v Epsom College* [1985] ICR 80, CA.
4 *Hotson v Wisbech Conservative Club* [1984] ICR 859, EAT
5 *Blue Star Ship Management Ltd v Williams* [1979] IRLR 16, EAT.
6 *Zim Israel Navigation Co Ltd v Edmonds* (1990) unreported, EAT, referred to in *Vauxhall Motors Ltd v Ghafoor* [1993] ICR 376, EAT.
7 *Burkett v Pendletons (Sweets) Ltd* [1992] ICR 407, EAT.

Presentation of case: who goes first?; reading proofs

18.71 The usual procedure is for the tribunal to call upon the person on whom the burden of proof lies to present his case first. In a case of an application alleging unfair dismissal where dismissal is accepted as having taken place by the respondent employers, even though the burden of proof is 'neutral' the respondents usually present their case first and put forward the grounds which they allege justify the dismissal.[1] Although, as has been noted, the tribunal has power to admit written representations, the best evidence is usually that given on oath and subject to the possibility of cross-examination. Tribunals try to adopt a flexible and informal approach and do not apply the usual rules of evidence in every case.[2] The parties should be aware of the procedure to be adopted by the tribunal and it is essential that the hearing is conducted fairly and appropriately.[3] It is becoming a widely used practice for witnesses to read their proofs of evidence by way of examination in chief.[4] Parties entitled to take part in the hearing have the right to cross-examine witnesses called by the other parties or party.[5]

1 *Gill v Harold Andrews Sheepbridge Ltd* [1974] ICR 294, NIRC. There is no binding rule that the person who has to discharge the onus of proof should present his case first: *Hawker Siddeley Power Engineering Ltd v Rump* [1979] IRLR 425, EAT, although he often does so; see for instance *H Goodwin Ltd v Fitzmaurice* [1977] IRLR 393 (dismissal related to trade union

membership or activities); *Chapman v Goonvean & Rostowrack China Clay Co Ltd* (1973) 9 ITR 379, CA (redundancy).
2 The industrial tribunal has a discretion to admit hearsay evidence 'but should exercise its good sense in weighing the matters which come before it, unless it feels that the evidence which it is proposed to tender is such that its admission could in some way adversely affect the reaching of a proper decision in the case: *Coral Squash Clubs Ltd v Matthews* [1979] ICR 607 at p 611, EAT. The wide discretion given to tribunals does not allow them to exclude evidence which is normally admissible and probative: *Matthews'* case (above) and *Rosedale Mouldings Ltd v Sibley* [1980] ICR 816, EAT.
3 *Aberdeen Steak Houses v Ibrahim* [1988] ICR 550, EAT.
4 See *Hardisty v Lowton Construction Group Ltd* (1973) 8 ITR 603, NIRC.
5 *McBride v British Railways Board* (1972) 7 ITR 84, NIRC; see also *Vickers v Hudson Bros (Middlesbrough) Ltd* (1970) 5 ITR 259, DC.

18.72 The general practice is that, notwithstanding where the balance of proof lies, the industrial tribunal should hear evidence and what is said on behalf of both the applicant and the respondent.[1] Submissions of no case to answer rarely succeed before industrial tribunals. If there is an arguable case, both sides should be heard.[2] Save in the most exceptional cases, both sides will be heard in cases concerning discrimination.[3] Although there may be exceptions to this rule where for instance the applicant's case is so hopeless that it would be a complete waste of time for the respondent to be called upon in reply.[4]

1 *Buskin v Vacutech Successors Ltd* (1977) 12 ITR 107, EAT.
2 *H Goodwin v Fitzmaurice* [1977] IRLR 393, EAT.
3 *Owen and Briggs v James* [1981] ICR 377, EAT and *Hammington v Berker Sportcraft Ltd* [1980] ICR 248, EAT.
4 *Ridley v GEC Machines Ltd* (1978) 13 ITR 195, EAT; *Coral Squash Clubs Ltd v Matthews* [1979] ICR 607, EAT.

Hearing cases together

18.73 If cases involve similar issues, proceedings are often combined under rule 18 (see **18.61**). Occasionally tribunals are aware that there is more than one application against the same respondents and several cases may be heard together to ensure consistency and on grounds of economy, without a formal order under the rule. This approach should only be used when appropriate. *Strowger v David Rosenfield Ltd*[1] was a case where the tribunal ordered that the evidence of a second applicant be given after the conclusion of the evidence of the first and before evidence given on behalf of the respondent. The National Industrial Relations Court held that the tribunal should not have made the order. Sir John Brightman, giving judgment, said that there would have been no objection to hearing the two cases consecutively and the tribunal giving its decision in both cases after both cases had been closed. Nor would it have been objectionable if, after the close of the first applicant's case, the second applicant's case was commenced and, following the conclusion of the second applicant's evidence, his representative had been invited to cross-examine the respondent's witnesses on the basis that both sides would agree that the evidence in chief given on the first application by the employer should be read into the second application so as to avoid repetition.[2]

1 (1972) 7 ITR 375, NIRC.
3 But see *Green v Southampton Corpn* [1973] ICR 153, NIRC (husband and wife superintendent and matron of boys' home: held to be right to hear both cases together, but should consider each separately). When several applications are dealt with together it is essential

that in coming to a decision in an individual's case that the position of each applicant is considered separately taking into account any peculiarities of his case: *John Fowler (Don Foundry) Ltd v Parkin* [1975] IRLR 89, DC.

Admissibility of communications promoting settlement

18.74   Anything communicated to a conciliation officer designated by the Advisory, Conciliation and Arbitration Service in connection with the performance of his function in endeavouring to promote a settlement of an issue which is being considered by an industrial tribunal is not admissible in any proceedings before the industrial tribunal, except with the consent of the person who communicated it to that officer.[1] A similar provision was included in the Industrial Relations Act 1971 which was considered by the National Industrial Relations Court in *M and W Grazebrook Ltd v Wallens*.[2] Sir John Donaldson, who delivered the judgment of the court, pointed out that the provision was not intended to render inadmissible evidence which could have been given if there had been no communication to the conciliation officer. Documents passing between parties and those representing them and conciliation officers relating to proceedings before industrial tribunals pose a special problem and their admissibility depends upon rules of privilege established in the interests of the administration of justice. The privilege is however limited. 'It exists only in relation to communications with an actual view to the litigation in hand and the mode of conduct of it. It does not exist in relation to the situation at the time when the matters complained of were arising'.[3] The privilege extends to any document which was prepared solely for the purpose of communication to a conciliation officer whether in connection with his function as such or more generally with a view to achieving a settlement of the subject matter of proceedings before the tribunal. 'The basis of this privilege (which extends to "without prejudice" communications between parties or in the field of family law, to communications through marriage guidance counsellors, probation officers and others) is the public interest in achieving an agreed settlement of disputes.'

1 Industrial Tribunals Act 1996, s 18(6) and (7). As to 'without prejudice' correspondence, see 18.45.
2 (1973) 8 ITR 258, NIRC.
3 (1973) 8 ITR 258 at p 260.

Order of witnesses

18.75   Within reasonable limits the parties before the tribunal and those representing them may present their cases as they wish. A strange situation arose in *Barnes v BPC (Business Forms) Ltd*.[1] For reasons of business efficacy, counsel for the respondents asked the chairman of the tribunal hearing a case if certain witnesses, who were employees of the respondents and were attending the hearing in response to witness orders, could be called prior to the cross-examination of the applicant. The applicant's solicitor objected to this course of action but the chairman directed that it should take place and it did. On appeal, Phillips J, in the Queen's Bench Division, although describing the action as unfortunate, thought that in the case before him it had worked no injustice and so found against the appellants. In the conduct of the hearing, the evidence and documents used should be kept within reasonable bounds.[2] Parties are able to call witnesses in the order they decide[3] and, although the tribunal can impose reasonable restrictions, cross-examination should not be the subject of arbitrary limitation.[4]

1 [1975] ICR 390, QBD.
2 *Inner London Education Authority v Lloyd* [1981] IRLR 394 at p 398, CA, per Watkins LJ.
3 *Barnes and Taylor v BPC (Business Forms) Ltd* [1975] ICR 390, QBD.
4 *Vickers v Hudson Bros (Middlesbrough) Ltd* (1970) 5 ITR 259, QBD.

Liability and remedy; 'split' hearings

18.76 In view of the complex nature of the remedies available before industrial tribunals and their factual bases, tribunals often determine the issue of liability separately from compensation. Then, if the applicant has succeeded, the tribunal will consider the remedies to be granted after the decision as to the merits of the application.[1] When dealing with involved cases the hearing may take several days and in such instances the tribunal will, if possible, arrange to list the case for consecutive days of hearing to avoid difficulties in recalling evidence occasioned by long adjournments.[2] In practice this may not be easy to arrange since the lay members of tribunals are always part-time. Parties who anticipate that the hearing of their case will occupy the tribunal for more than one day should notify the tribunal as soon as possible.

1 See *Copson v Eversure Accessories Ltd* [1974] ICR 636, NIRC and Employment Rights Act 1996, s 112. Matters relating to the jurisdiction of the tribunal, or not directly affecting the main substantive issues of the case but which may determine the outcome of the case are often taken separately at an earlier hearing.
2 *Barnes v BPC (Business Forms) Ltd* [1976] 1 All ER 237; [1975] ICR 390, DC.

Chairman's note

18.77 The chairman of the tribunal will take a note of the substance of the evidence which is adduced before it. He is not obliged to write down every word of evidence, but justice does require that in appropriate cases an appellant should be able to refer to the evidence which was given to the tribunal. The chairman may be ordered by the Employment Appeal Tribunal to provide copies of his notes or part of them.[1] The practice of supplying notes of evidence was described by Phillips J in *Moore v Aluminium Platers (Leeds) Ltd*[2] as being of 'the greatest possible assistance' to appellate bodies. Where there is a conflict between the chairman's notes of evidence and the findings of fact in the formal reasons given by the tribunal, the appellate court is guided by the findings of facts in the reasons, unless there are compelling circumstances which lead it to the conclusion that the reasons may inaccurately state the substance of the evidence.[3]

1 See **18.38–18.40**. *Archbold Freightage Ltd v Wilson* (1974) 9 ITR 133, NIRC; *Houston v Lightwater Farms Ltd* [1990] ICR 502, EAT. If words are inserted in the chairman's note after consideration of the recollection of the members they are treated as if heard by the chairman: *Keskar v Governors of All Saints C of E School* [1991] ICR 493, EAT.
2 [1976] IRLR 23, DC.
3 *Ogidi-Olu v Guys Hospital Board of Governors* [1973] ICR 645, NIRC.

18.78 It is mentioned elsewhere (see **15.23**) that on certain applications, if it is shown that the action to which the complaint relates was taken for the purposes of safeguarding national security, the tribunal will dismiss the complaint.[1] Subject to exceptions, a certificate purporting to be signed by or on behalf of a minister of the Crown certifying that the action specified was taken for the purpose of safeguarding national security, or that a particular request for information could not be complied with except by disclosing information the disclosure of which would have been against the interest of national security, is treated as conclusive evidence of the fact so certified.

1 Industrial Tribunals Act 1996, s 10(4) and (5).

Costs

18.79 Subject to the exceptions mentioned below, an industrial tribunal does not normally award costs, but may do so where in its opinion a party to the proceedings (and if he is the respondent, whether or not he has entered an appearance) has, in bringing or conducting the proceedings, acted frivolously, vexatiously, abusively, disruptively, or otherwise unreasonably.[1] In such cases the tribunal may make an order containing an award against that party in respect of the costs of another party. The award is either a specified sum, not exceeding £500, a sum agreed between the parties in respect of costs, or the whole or part of the costs incurred by the party in whose favour the award is made as taxed (if not otherwise agreed).[2] In practical terms in many cases if costs are taxed they are likely to be considerably in excess of £500. If costs are required by an order to be taxed, they are taxed in the county court according to such of the scales prescribed by the County Court Rules for proceedings in the county court as directed by the order.[3] The power to award costs is entirely in the discretion of the tribunal and those who wish to apply for costs should do so promptly.[4] The tribunal has to decide if the conduct complained of falls within the categories referred to in rule 12(1). Sir Hugh Griffiths said of an earlier provision (which did not include the words 'abusively, disruptively or otherwise unreasonably') 'It is a serious finding to make against an applicant, for it will generally involve bad faith on his part and one would expect the discretion to be sparingly exercised'.[5] Costs may also be awarded in certain circumstances under the special procedure applicable in 'equal value claims' (see **18.114**). In addition, in similar circumstances to those where costs may be ordered to be paid by a party, the tribunal can order that a party pays to the Secretary of State the whole, or any part, of any allowances (other than allowances paid to members of tribunals or assessors) paid by the Secretary of State under the relevant provisions for the purpose of, or in connection with, his attendance at the tribunal.[6]

1 Rule 12(1). This applies to a respondent who has not entered an appearance in relation to the conduct of any part in the proceedings which he has taken: rule 12(2). The words 'shall not normally make an award in respect of the costs or expenses' which appeared in the former Rules do not appear in the Rules. It is thought that this omission will have little effect on the practice of tribunals.
2 Rule 12(3).
3 Rule 12(6).
4 *Colin Johnson t/a Richard Andrew Ladies Hairstylists v Baxter* [1985] IRLR 96, EAT.
5 In *ET Marler Ltd v Robertson* [1974] ICR 72 at p 76, NIRC; *Bhardwaj v Post Office* (1977) 12 ITR 459, EAT.
6 Rule 12(1)(b).

18.80 Before deciding whether to award costs the tribunal should hear submissions on the point.[1] The costs of 'in house' lawyers are recoverable and although the ability (or lack of it) of the person against the award is sought should be considered it is not a compelling reason to prevent an order being made.[2]

1 *Meagher v Holland & Hannen and Cubbitts (Southern) Ltd* (1968) 3 ITR 104, DC.
2 *Wiggin Alloys Ltd v Jenkins* [1981] IRLR 275, EAT.

18.81 In *ET Marler Ltd v Robertson*[1] Sir Hugh Griffiths said, in the National Industrial Relations Court:

'If the employee knows that there is no substance in his claim and that it is bound to fail, or if the claim is on the face of it so manifestly misconceived that it can have no prospect of success, it may be deemed frivolous and an abuse of the procedure to pursue it. If an employee brings a hopeless claim not with any expectation of recovering compensation but out of spite to harass his employers or for some other improper motive, he acts vexatiously, and likewise abuses the procedure. In such cases the tribunal can and doubtless usually will award costs against the employee.'

The correct test as to whether behaviour is frivolous is what the party knew, or ought to have known, if he had gone about the matter sensibly.[2] The fact that legal advice has been taken is a relevant, but not decisive, factor to be taken into account.[3]

1 [1974] ICR 72 at p 76, NIRC; *Cartiers Superfoods Ltd v Laws* [1978] IRLR 315, EAT; *Lothian Health Board v Johnstone* [1981] IRLR 321, EAT.
2 *Cartiers Superfoods Ltd v Laws* [1978] IRLR 315, EAT.
3 See *Stannard & Co (1969) Ltd v Wilson* [1983] ICR 86, EAT, a decision on a similar rule in the Employment Appeal Tribunal Rules where costs were awarded against employers who had pursued an appeal after taking legal advice.

Exceptions to the general rule as to costs

18.82 The first exception to the general rule is where on the application of a party to the proceedings the tribunal has postponed the day or time fixed for the hearing or has adjourned the hearing, then the tribunal may order costs incurred or allowances paid as a result of a postponement or adjournment against, or in favour of, that party.[1] Such an award may be made irrespective of any question whether the party acted 'frivolously or vexatiously' etc. This is also the case when the second exception applies. This is where a postponement or adjournment of a hearing has been caused by the respondent when the applicant has expressed a wish to be reinstated or re-engaged which was communicated to the respondent at least seven days before the hearing of the complaint, or the proceedings arise out of the employer's failure to permit the employee to return to work after an absence due to pregnancy or confinement (see Chapter 7). In these circumstances the tribunal will, in the absence of a special reason for failure to adduce reasonable evidence as to the availability of the job from which the applicant was dismissed, or as the case may be, which she held before her absence, or of comparable or suitable employment, make orders against the employer as respects any costs incurred or any allowances paid as a result of the postponement or adjournment.[2] The final exception applies when a pre-hearing review has taken place.

1 Rule 12(4). See for example *Ladbroke Racing Ltd v Hickey* [1979] ICR 525, EAT and *Rajguru v Top Order Ltd* [1978] ICR 565, EAT. The award should be compensatory in nature and not contain a punitive element: *Cooper v Weatherwise (Roofing & Walling) Ltd* [1993] ICR 81, EAT. For special rules applicable where a notice of appearance is filed late and in connection with equal value claims, see **18.34** and **18.109**.
2 Rule 12(5).

Costs after a pre-hearing review

18.83   Where a party has been ordered to pay a deposit at a pre-hearing review as a condition of being permitted to continue to participate in proceedings relating to a matter, a further question may arise as to costs. If the tribunal finds against that party in respect of the matter and there has been no award of costs against the party arising out of the proceedings on that matter, the tribunal will consider whether to award costs against that party on the ground that he conducted the proceedings relating to the matter unreasonably in persisting in having the matter determined by a tribunal. The tribunal will not make an award of costs on that ground unless it has considered the document recording the order on the pre-hearing review and is of the opinion that the reasons which caused the tribunal to find against the party in its decision were substantially the same as the reasons recorded in that document for considering that the contentions of the party had no reasonable prospect of success.[1] Where an award of costs is made against a party against whom an order was made at a pre-hearing review (whether the award arises out of the proceedings relating to the matter in respect of which the order was made, or out of proceedings relating to any other matter considered with that matter), his deposit is used in part or full settlement of the award of costs. Where an award of costs is made in favour of one party the deposit is used to pay the costs of that party. Where awards of costs are made in favour of more than one party, the deposit is paid to all of them or any one or more of them as the tribunal thinks fit, and if to all or more than one, in such proportions as the tribunal considers appropriate. If the amount of the deposit exceeds the amount of the award of costs, the balance is refunded to the party who paid it.[2]

1 Rule 12(7).
2 Rule 12(8).

Allowances

18.84   Subsistence allowances may be paid to a party, witnesses and the person representing a party, unless the representative is a full-time officer of a workers or employers association, or a solicitor, barrister, accountant or consultant. In addition allowances for loss of earnings occasioned by attendance at the tribunal may be granted. The allowances vary from time to time and details can be obtained from a local tribunal office. The tribunal may refuse the payment of an allowance if it considers the attendance was not reasonably justified or the applicant acted frivolously or vexatiously.[1]

1 Unless it can be shown that the industrial tribunal has misdirected itself as to the law, the Employment Appeal Tribunal is unlikely to overrule a decision of an industrial tribunal as to costs and allowances. See for example: *ET Marler Ltd v Robertson* [1974] ICR 72, NIRC.

Death of a party

18.85   Where an employee has died tribunal proceedings may be instituted or continued by his personal representative under the provisions relating to discrimination, redundancy, unfair dismissal and appropriate provisions of the Employment Rights Act 1996 conferring rights on employees. If there is no personal representative, then the proceedings may be instituted or continued on behalf of the estate of the deceased employee by such person as the industrial tribunal appoints. The tribunal can appoint either a person authorised by the employee to act in connection with the proceedings before the employee's death or the widower, widow, child, father, mother, brother or sister of the deceased employee.[1] In such cases the award is made by the industrial tribunal in favour of the estate, or as the case may be, of the employee who has since died. The person appointed by the tribunal may enforce such award on behalf of the estate without his obtaining letters of administration or probate of any will. The receipt of the person so appointed is a sufficient discharge to the employer for any sum payable to the estate under the award.[2] Where there is no person so appointed the award made in favour of the estate, or in favour of an employee who has since died, is enforceable on behalf of the estate by the person to whom a grant of letters of administration or probate has been made in respect of that estate. The personal representative or appointed person is put in a similar position to the applicant in proceedings where death is not involved.[3]

1 Employment Rights Act 1996, s 206 which should be referred to for the detailed provisions.
2 Industrial Tribunals Awards (Enforcement in Case of Death) Regulations 1976, SI 1976/663, reg 5. The regulations should be referred to for the detailed provisions.
3 Employment Rights Act 1996, s 206(3).

18.86 The personal representative of a deceased employer may defend proceedings in a similar way but there is no corresponding provision for appointment by the tribunal of a person to act on behalf of the deceased's estate. Where under the relevant provisions a personal representative of a deceased employer is liable to pay an amount and that liability had not accrued before the death of the employer in question it will be treated for all purposes as if it was a liability of the deceased employer which accrued immediately before the death.[1]

1 Employment Rights Act 1996, s 207(3).

18.87 If a protective award is made pursuant to s 189 of the Trade Union and Labour Relations (Consolidation) Act 1992 and an employee of a description to which the award relates dies during the protected period the award is treated in his case as if it specified a protected period of such length as to end on the date of his death.[1] There are specific provisions relating to death in situations of redundancy and unfair dismissal and they are discussed above.[2]

1 Trade Union and Labour Relations (Consolidation) Act 1992, s 190(6).
2 For redundancy, see **16.86–16.88** and unfair dismissal, see **15.223–15.224**.

The decision

18.88 Where the tribunal is composed of three members its decision may be taken by majority. If the tribunal is composed of two members, the chairman has a second or casting vote.[1] The decision of the industrial tribunal is often given orally at the conclusion of the hearing. The decision may be reserved.[2] A document setting out the decision and the reasons for it is dispatched to the parties in due course. Although the decision is that of all members of the tribunal, or the majority of them, the document is under the hand of the chairman only.[3]

1 Rule 10(1).
2 Rule 10(2). If by reason of death or incapacity the chairman is unable to sign the decision, the document is signed by the other members or member of the tribunal who should certify that the chairman is unable to sign: rule 10(12).
3 See footnote 2 above.

Summary or extended reasons

18.89 The reasons may be in summary or extended form. The decision will set out whether the reasons are in summary or extended form.[1] Reasons are usually given in summary form except that they are given in extended form where:

(a) the proceedings involve the determination of an issue of equal pay, unlawful sex or race discrimination or disability discrimination;

(b) a request for extended reasons is made by a party orally at the hearing;

(c) a request is made in writing by a party after the hearing either before the summary reasons are sent to the parties or within 21 days of the date on which that document was sent to the parties; or

(d) the tribunal considers that reasons given in summary form would not sufficiently explain the grounds of its decision.[2]

1 Rule 10(3).
2 Rule 10(4).

18.90 Extended reasons should be detailed and it is essential that they set out the findings of the primary facts.[1] If the decision of the tribunal is made by a majority it is desirable that the views and findings of the majority and those of the minority should are set out clearly and distinctly in separate paragraphs so the parties may easily ascertain precisely the view of the majority and minority respectively.[2] The conclusions drawn from the facts should also be made clear. In cases where there is an allegation of dismissal for redundancy the tribunal should specify the facts justifying the conclusion that the case either fell within, or outside, the statutory definition of redundancy.[3] If a tribunal has drawn inferences from primary facts the inferences and the reasons for drawing them should be made clear. The rules of law being applied by the tribunal should be set out. For instance, in cases where unfair dismissal is alleged it is highly desirable that the industrial tribunal expressly refers to s 98(4) of the Employment Rights Act 1996 wherever it is applicable together with the matters which the parties have claimed have a bearing on the question and those which the tribunal themselves (if additional) have taken into account and the conclusions which they have reached upon them.[4] If the tribunal determines that the applicant by his behaviour has contributed to the loss, the tribunal should set out details of the behaviour, action or conduct which they are taking into account, and then specify the extent of such contribution to the dismissal.[5] The decision should be so constructed that an appellate body is be able to determine upon precisely what grounds the tribunal's decision was reached.[6]

1 *Parkers Bakeries Ltd v Palmer* [1977] IRLR 215, EAT and *Porter v Bandridge Ltd* [1978] IRLR 271 at p 273, CA. A decision of an industrial tribunal is a judicial decision of a judicial tribunal for the purposes of the doctrine of res judicata: *Green v Hampshire County Council* [1979] ICR 861, ChD.
2 See footnote 1 above.
3 *Elliott v University Computing Co (Great Britain) Ltd* [1977] ICR 147, EAT.
4 *Gentles v Harvey Fabrication Ltd* (1976) 11 ITR 228, EAT; *Elliotts'* case above.

5 *Parkers Bakeries Ltd v Palmer* [1977] IRLR 215, EAT.
6 See for example *Cooper v British Steel Corpn* [1975] ICR 454, DC; *Beardmore v Westinghouse Brake and Signal Co Ltd* [1976] ICR 49, DC.

18.91 The statement of reasons must provide both parties with the material which would enable them to know whether or not the tribunal has made an error of law in making its decision.[1] The absence of evidence to support a finding of fact is an error of law, as is a conclusion which no tribunal properly directing itself could reach on the basis of the evidence which had been given to and accepted by it. The tribunal should in its reasons set out the facts found, and the legal rules applied, by it. The tribunal has not exhausted its jurisdiction when the oral decision is given but does have power to recall the parties for further argument. If this power is exercised, the tribunal should inform the parties precisely and in detail what it is that it requires to be done at the further hearing.[2] Obvious errors or omissions which come to light soon after the hearing before the order is drawn up may be dealt with in this way rather than by way of review. This approach should only be used as a method of rectifying errors and should be used carefully, sparingly and not as a matter of course.[3]

1 *Speciality Care plc v Pachela* [1996] IRLR 248, EAT; *Meek v City of Birmingham District Council* [1987] IRLR 250, CA.
2 *Hanks v Ace High Productions Ltd* [1978] ICR 1155, EAT, where *Jowett v Earl of Bradford* [1977] ICR 342, EAT is distinguished. In *Jowett's* case it was held that a second tribunal did not have jurisdiction to determine an application for a remedy for unfair dismissal when the chairman of the first tribunal was taken seriously ill before the decision was promulgated.
3 *Hanks'* case at p 1158. In special circumstances the tribunal may discontinue a hearing and order a rehearing. This must be done most sparingly and only for very good reason: *Charman v Palmers Scaffolding Ltd* [1979] ICR 335, EAT and *Automobile Proprietary Ltd v Healy* [1979] ICR 809, EAT.

Calculation of compensation

18.92 Where the tribunal makes an award of compensation or comes to any other determination by virtue of which one party is required to pay a sum to another (excluding an award of costs or allowances) this should be set out. The decision and reasons should contain a statement of the amount of the compensation awarded, or of the sum required to be paid, followed either by a table showing how the amount or sum has been calculated, or by a description of the manner in which it has been calculated.[1]

1 Rule 10(3). When making monetary awards the industrial tribunal must comply with the Employment Protection (Recoupment of Jobseeker's Allowance and Income Support) Regulations 1996, SI 1996/2349. See **15.220**. Interest is payable on tribunal awards, see **15.222**.

References to the European Court of Justice

18.93 Where a tribunal makes an order referring a question to the European Court of Justice for a preliminary ruling under art 177 of the Treaty of Rome the Secretary of Tribunals will not send a copy of the order to the Registrar of the Court until the time for appealing against the order has expired or, if an appeal is made within that time, until the appeal has been determined or otherwise disposed of.[1]

1 Rule 19A. See *Practice Direction* [1997] All ER (EC) 1, ECJ.

Formal matters

18.94 The Secretary enters the decision and reasons in the register and sends a copy of the entry to each of the parties. Where the proceedings were referred to the tribunal by a court, a copy is sent to the court.[1] The document is omitted from the register in any case in which evidence has been heard in private, and the tribunal so directs, and where a minister of the Crown has directed[2] the tribunal to sit in private on grounds of national security.[3] In these cases the Secretary sends the document to each of the parties. Where there are proceedings before a superior court relating to the decision in question the Secretary sends a copy of the decision to that court, together with a copy of the entry in the register. In any case appearing to involve allegations of a sexual offence the decision and reasons are entered in the register with deletions of any identifying matter which is likely to lead members of the public to identify any person affected by or making such an allegation.[4] If a decision and reasons is corrected, or a decision is revoked or varied on review or altered in any way by a superior court, the Secretary alters the record to conform. A copy of the altered entry is sent to the parties and, if appropriate, to the court.[5] Clerical mistakes in decisions and reasons or errors arising in those documents from an accidental slip or omission may at any time be corrected by the chairman by a certificate under his hand.[6]

1 Rule 10(5). Copies are also sent to the Equal Opportunities Commission in all cases under the Equal Pay Act 1970 and the Sex Discrimination Acts and the Commission for Racial Equality in all cases under the Race Relations Act 1976: rule 20(9). A document purporting to be certified by the Secretary to be a true copy of an entry of a decision in the register is, unless the contrary be proved, sufficient evidence of the document and the fact stated therein: Industrial Tribunals (Constitution and Rules of Procedure) Regulations 1993, SI 1993/2687, reg 10.
2 In accordance with the Industrial Tribunals Act 1996, s 10(1).
3 Rule 10(6).
4 Rules 10(7) and 13(6).
5 Rule 10(10). There is similar provision appropriately amended applicable if the document is omitted from the register under rule 10(6): rule 10(11).
6 Rule 10(9).

Review

18.95 The Industrial Tribunals (Industrial Relations etc) Regulations 1972 were the first regulations which gave an express right to industrial tribunals to review their decisions. The Rules give tribunals the power to review, revoke or vary,[1] by certificate under the chairman's hand, any decision in a case in which a county court has power to order a new trial on grounds that:

'(a) the decision was wrongly made as a result of an error on the part of tribunal staff;
 (b) a party did not receive notice of the proceedings leading to the decision;[2]
 (c) the decision was made in the absence of a party;[3]
 (d) new evidence has become available since the conclusion of the hearing to which the decision relates, provided that its existence could not have been reasonably known of or foreseen at the time of the hearing;[4] or
 (e) the interests of justice require such a review.'[5]

1 Rule 11(1). Before the express power of review was given a similar approach was adopted by tribunals on rare occasions, see for instance *Taylor v France* (1967) 2 ITR 661 (notice not sent);

Summers v British Railways Board (1969) 4 ITR 395 (power to vary decision before entered in the register). If a respondent who has not entered an appearance seeks a review he should first obtain leave to enter an appearance: *St Mungo Community Trust v Colleano* [1980] ICR 254, EAT.

2 'Receipt' equates with 'send': *T & D Transport (Portsmouth) Ltd v Limburn* [1987] ICR 696, EAT.

3 See *Habib v Elkington and Co Ltd* [1981] IRLR 344, EAT.

4 There can be no review under this head when a conscious decision has been taken not to use evidence: *Bingham v Hobourn Engineering Ltd* [1992] IRLR 298, EAT.

5 This may have given the tribunal power to review of its own motion prior to the amendment of the Rules: *Lamont v Fry's Metals Ltd* [1983] ICR 778, EAT. However it does not give power to review interlocutory orders: *Nikitas v Solihull Metropolitan Borough* [1986] ICR 291, EAT.

18.96 An application for review may be refused by the President of Industrial Tribunals, or the chairman of the tribunal which decided the case, or a Regional Chairman, if in his opinion it has no reasonable prospect of success.[1] If not so refused the application is heard by the tribunal which decided the case, or where it is not practicable for it to be heard by that tribunal, or where the decision was made by a chairman acting alone in accordance with the rules, by a tribunal appointed by the President or a Regional Chairman.[2]

1 Rule 11(5).
2 Rule 11(6). Where the application for review relates to a matter of substance all parties should have the opportunity of being present: *Ali v Nilgun Fashions* (1978) 13 ITR 443, EAT.

18.97 Application for review by a party may be made at the hearing, but if it is not made then it can be made to the Secretary of Tribunals at any time from the date of hearing until 14 days after the date on which the decision was sent to the parties. The application must be in writing stating the grounds in full.[1] The industrial tribunal is empowered to extend this time limit[2] but, since to do so is a discretion of the tribunal, an appellate court does not have such power.[3] A tribunal may not review a decision of its own motion unless it is the tribunal which issued the decision.[4] A tribunal may review a decision of its own motion if, within the period beginning with the date of hearing and ending the 14th day after the date on which the decision was sent to the parties, it has sent to the parties an explanation in summary form of the ground upon which and the reasons why it is proposed to review the decision. The parties should be given the opportunity to show cause why there should be no review.[5]

1 Rule 11(4). The reasons for contending that the original decision is wrong should be included: *PJ Drakard & Sons Ltd v Wilton* [1977] ICR 642, EAT.
2 Rule 15.
3 *Archbold Freightage Ltd v Wilson* [1974] IRLR 10, NIRC, and see also *Ryan Plant International Ltd v Price* [1976] ICR 424, DC.
4 Rule 11(2).
5 Rule 11(3).

18.98 When making an application for review on the basis of new evidence, the ordinary practice is to submit to the tribunal the substance of the evidence which it is intended to put before the tribunal. The matter should have been investigated to the point of taking proofs and the proofs should be submitted in support of the application.[1] In *Yorkshire Engineering and Welding Development Co Ltd v Burnham*[2] a tribunal had to consider an application for review on grounds that at the hearing the applicant had given evidence that he would only be able to earn £86.50 gross per week, whereas at the time he had already made enquiries about a post which he had subsequently taken, the pay for which was greatly in excess of that sum. Sir John Donaldson delivering the decision of the National Industrial Relations Court said:[3]

'In such circumstances the test to be applied in deciding whether or not to review a decision is as follows. The tribunal must ask itself whether the forecasts which were the basis of its decision have been falsified to a sufficiently substantial extent to invalidate the assessment and whether this occurred so soon after the decision, that a review was necessary in the interests of justice. There must be some finality in these matters. But at the same time, if very shortly after a tribunal has reached a decision it comes to its notice, upon an application for review, that the facts are so different from those which it had assumed, that the whole substratum of its award has gone, then, subject to such considerations as whether the party applying could have obtained that evidence before the hearing, there is manifestly a case for review.

As the interval of time between the original decision and the application lengthens, it becomes more and more difficult to justify a review, for two reasons: first, because of the need for certainty and finality in litigation, and second, because any tribunal which is looking into the future should recognise that the further into the future it looks, the more impossible it is to be accurate. Longer term inaccuracies do not therefore strike at the foundations of the tribunal's award because they will have been contemplated.'

1 *Simmons v Medway Welding Ltd* (1973) 8 ITR 373, NIRC.
2 (1973) 8 ITR 621, NIRC.
3 (1973) 8 ITR 621 at p 625 .

18.99 *Bateman v British Leyland (UK) Ltd*[1] concerned an applicant who at the first hearing by the industrial tribunal was awarded compensation based on an assumption that he had obtained a reasonably secure job with new employers. Unfortunately the new employers went out of business almost immediately and he lost the employment. A review was applied for on the grounds that there was new evidence not available to the tribunal. Although the event in respect of which the evidence was to be given had occurred since the hearing, the National Industrial Relations Court said that the tribunal was entitled to carry out a review. The fact that an estimate had been made as to the security of the job did not preclude such a decision. Where the facts which it is intended to put before the tribunal on review were known to the party seeking to put them forward at the time of the original hearing no review will be granted save in exceptional circumstances.[2] In one case an employee, who was represented at the tribunal hearing by a union representative, did not give a medical reason for refusing to accept alternative employment which had been offered to him.[3] He did not tell his representative of his incapacity until after the hearing and a review was applied for. In giving his decision Phillips J discussed the relationship between what are now paragraphs (1)(d) and (e) of rule 11[4] and reached the conclusion that paragraph (d) cannot be regarded as exhaustive of cases where the ground of the application is the desire to call fresh evidence. He said paragraph (e) was intended to be a residual category of case designed to confer a wide discretion on industrial tribunals but must be applied in practice with some regard to the kind of case which is intended to come within paragraph (d). Paragraph (e) exists for the case which although it may be put forward under paragraph (d) has in it some special additional circumstance which leads to the conclusion that justice does require a review, for instance a case where although all the evidence could be foreseen or indeed reasonably foreseen or actually known, it was for some reason or another not available. Having weighed the arguments for both sides the judge concluded that the majority of the tribunal was right in not granting a review. In giving his decision Phillips J considered the earlier case of *Stevensons (Dyers) Ltd v Brennan*[5] which has been the subject of some adverse criticism. In that case the National Industrial Relations Court had, in a reserved decision, determined first, that the power of the review under the predecessor of rule 11 was a once and for all power and that when it had been used once it could not be used again for a similar reason. In the later case Phillips J having carefully considered the matter decided reluctantly[6] to follow *Brennan's* case, although it is open to the Court of Appeal to decide that the familiar rules of practice which have been laid down over the years in the courts should be taken into account when deciding whether a decision should be reviewed.

1 [1974] ICR 403, NIRC.
2 *Richler v North Thames Gas Board* (1973) 8 ITR 177, NIRC.
3 *Flint v Eastern Electricity Board* [1975] ICR 395, DC; *Morris v Griffiths* [1977] ICR 153, EAT. See also *House v Haughton Bros (Worcester) Ltd* [1967] 1 All ER 39; [1967] 1 WLR 148, CA and *Skrzypkowski v Silvan Investments Ltd* [1963] 1 All ER 886; [1963] 1 WLR 525, CA. The shortcomings of a representative are usually not grounds for review: *Ironsides Ray & Vials v Lindsay* [1994] IRLR 318, EAT.
4 The judgment actually relates to the Industrial Tribunals (Industrial Relations etc) Regulations 1972, SI 1972/38, Sch, rule 12(d) and (e) which were in similar terms.
5 [1974] ICR 194, NIRC.
6 See [1975] ICR 395 at p 401.

18.100 Although the power to grant a review on the grounds that 'the interests of justice require such a review' is very wide, it will be exercised with caution.[1] Applications for review are looked at very much in the circumstances of each individual case. It is not appropriate for a tribunal to review its decision simply because there is an error of law on its face.[2] A review was refused by a tribunal when sought on the grounds that it was in the interests of justice to do so when the reason for the application was that the solicitors acting for the respondents had by telephone requested an adjournment of the hearing without explanation only two and a half hours before it was due to take place and, notwithstanding the request, the hearing proceeded. When applying for review no explanation for the solicitors' conduct was given.[3]

1 *Ironsides Ray & Vials v Lindsay* [1994] IRLR 318, EAT.
2 *Trimble v Supertravel Ltd* [1982] IRLR 451, EAT.
3 *Pigott v Sidney Jacobs (Bettan) Co Ltd* (1973) 8 ITR 367.

18.101 An interesting situation arose on review in *Estorffe v Smith*[1] an employee applied to an industrial tribunal for compensation for unfair dismissal and redundancy payment and at the first hearing was awarded compensation for unfair dismissal. A factor not brought to the tribunal's attention was that the employer employed three employees only and so was not at the time subject to the unfair dismissal provisions.[2] The employer applied for a review. At the review hearing he produced his wages book to show that he had only three employees. The tribunal revoked that part of their decision awarding compensation for unfair dismissal, but having seen the rundown of staff from the wages book, also reversed its earlier decision not to award a redundancy payment and the appropriate sum was awarded to the employee. The National Industrial Relations Court said that having been asked to review the finding of unfair dismissal (but not redundancy) the tribunal did have power to review the previous decision as to redundancy as well. There was one decision, so it was said, although it dealt with two issues. The employer who appealed against the decision as reviewed did succeed and the case was remitted for rehearing by another tribunal because the tribunal's attitude on the question of redundancy was a matter the employer had not come prepared to meet. If the tribunal intended to base an inference on the wages book, the employer should have been given an opportunity of considering whether to call further evidence as to the reason why other employees had left.

1 [1973] ICR 542, NIRC.
2 At that time an employee of such an employer was excluded from the unfair dismissal provisions.

18.102　Once a tribunal has determined an application for review on one ground then it does not have power to entertain another application for review on that ground. The argument being that having granted or refused an application the tribunal is functus officio.[1] In exceptional circumstances however a second application for review may be favourably heard.[2]

1 *Stevensons (Dyers) Ltd v Brennan* [1974] ICR 194, NIRC.
2 *Raybright TV Services Ltd v Smith* [1973] ICR 640, NIRC.

18.103　On reviewing its decision a tribunal may confirm the decision, or vary or revoke the decision under the chairman's hand. If the tribunal revokes the decision, it orders a rehearing before the same or a differently constituted tribunal.[1] Application for review is not as such an alternative, or preliminary, to an appeal to an appellate body[2] but if the result of the review could be to remove or alter the ground of appeal, or alter the findings of fact, the application should be dealt with before the hearing of the appeal. A tribunal can review its decision even though notice of appeal has been filed.[3] An industrial tribunal will in such circumstances attempt to dispose of the application to review as speedily as possible. In some cases the Employment Appeal Tribunal will interfere with a tribunal's discretion whether or not to review a decision although such cases are likely to be rare.[4] The better view is that the decision of a tribunal may be reviewed even though it is not possible to convene the same tribunal because, for instance, a member has reached retiring age, died or becomes ill.[5]

1 Rule 11(7).
2 *Dean v Polytechnic of North London* [1973] ICR 490, NIRC.
3 *Dean's* case above, but see *Simmons v Medway Welding Ltd* (1973) 8 ITR 373, NIRC.
4 *Morris v Griffiths* [1977] ICR 153, EAT.
5 *Coates v CJ Crispin Ltd* (1973) 8 ITR 446 at p 452, NIRC.

Equal value claims

18.104　It has been seen at **5.19–5.23** that s 2A of the Equal Pay Act 1970 makes specific reference to the procedure before tribunals.[1] Where on a complaint to an industrial tribunal under s 2 of that Act a dispute arises as to whether any work is of equal value with that of the comparator the tribunal may either proceed to determine that question, or unless it is satisfied that there are no reasonable grounds for determining that the work is of equal value, require a member of the panel of independent experts to prepare a report with respect to that question and has received that report. Originally the tribunal was obliged to appoint an expert if the question whether the work was of equal value to that of the comparator had to be resolved. Tribunals are now able to determine the issue without involving an expert as part of attempt to speed up and simplify proceedings in equal value cases. The regulations contain complementary rules of procedure for use in proceedings involving claims to the benefit of an equality clause by virtue of the operation of s 1(2)(c) of the Equal Pay Act 1970.[2] The complementary rules applicable in these circumstances are contained in Sch 2 to the regulations.[3] The scheme of the Equal Value Rules is that the usual rules apply with a new Equal Value Rule 8A and rules 4, 9, 10, 12, 13 and 20 replaced by Equal Value Rules which are similarly numbered.[4] The intention of the Equal Value Rules is to ensure that the expert is adequately provided with information to enable him to carry out his task and to provide procedures to deal with the expert's report and make the appropriate incidental provisions.

1 It is important to remember that the burden of proof lies with the complainant. The burden does not become heavier if the independent expert's report is against the applicant, nor does it shift to the employer if the expert's report favours the applicant: *Tennants Textile Colours Ltd v Todd* [1989] IRLR 3, NICA.
2 For a discussion of these provisions see **5.19–5.23**.
3 In this chapter the rules contained in Industrial Tribunals (Constitution and Rules of Procedure) Regulations 1993, Sch 2 are called 'the Equal Value Rules'. It is to be noted that the Equal Value Rules are part of the general structure of the rules of procedure applicable to industrial tribunals and must be viewed in this light: see *Aldridge v British Telecommunications plc* [1989] ICR 790, EAT.
4 Industrial Tribunals (Constitution and Rules of Procedure) Regulations 1993, reg 8(2).

Interlocutory matters

18.105 The Equal Value Rules make similar provision to the Rules with regard to interlocutory matters.[1] In addition the tribunal may make certain orders at the request of any expert it requires to report to it. A tribunal may, on the application of an expert who has been required by the tribunal to prepare a report, require any person who the tribunal is satisfied may have information which may be relevant to the question or matter on which the expert is required to report to furnish in writing such information as the tribunal may require. The tribunal may also require any person to produce any documents which are in the possession, custody or power of that person and which the tribunal is satisfied may contain matter relevant to the question on which the expert is required to report.[2] Any information required to be furnished, or document required to be produced, should be furnished or produced, at or within the time the tribunal appoints, to the Secretary of Tribunals who will send the information or document to the expert.[3] A person, whether or not a party, upon whom such a requirement has been made may apply to the tribunal by notice to the Secretary of Tribunals before the appointed time at, or within which, the requirement is to be complied with to vary or set aside the requirement. Notice of such application should be given to the parties and to the expert upon whose application the requirement was made.[4]

1 Equal Value Rules, rule 4.

2 Equal Value Rules, rule 4(2A). A tribunal will not make a requirement under rule 4(2A) of a conciliation officer who has acted in connection with the complaint under the Sex Discrimination Act 1975, s 64, or if it is satisfied that the person so required would have good grounds for refusing to comply with the requirement if it were a requirement made in connection with a hearing before the tribunal: Equal Value Rules, rule 4(2B).
3 See footnote 2 above.
4 Equal Value Rules, rule 4(5A).

Procedure relating to expert's report

18.106   The amendments to the Equal Value Rules which came into effect on 31 July 1996 sought to speed up the procedure in equal value cases in three ways. First, they allow the tribunal to carry out the assessment without the involvement of an expert and, secondly, they stipulate for the provision of a timetable as to the expert's activities. They also provide for sanctions against those whose activities delay the expert's work. In any case involving an equal value claim where a dispute arises as to whether work is of equal value to other work in terms of the demands made on the person employed on the work, the tribunal will, except in cases where it is satisfied that there are no reasonable grounds for determining the question in the affirmative, determine whether to require an expert to prepare a report with respect to the question.[1] Before determining whether to require an expert to prepare a report the tribunal will give the parties an opportunity to make representations to the tribunal as to whether an expert should be so required.[2] Where the tribunal has determined not to require an expert to prepare a report it may nevertheless, at any time during its consideration of the question, require an expert to prepare a report, but will not do so unless it has given the parties a further opportunity to make representations to the tribunal as to whether an expert should be so required.[3]

1 Equal Value Rules, rule 8A. The delays inherent in the expert procedure have been the subject of much adverse comment. See for example *Aldridge v British Telecommunications plc* [1989] ICR 790, EAT. There is no power to require the complainant to be interviewed by the employer's expert: *Lloyds Bank plc v Fox* [1989] IRLR 103, EAT. The power to administer interrogatories is of course available and the sanctions which may be imposed on those delaying the preparation of the experts report may assist.
2 Equal Value Rules, rule 8A(2).
3 Equal Value Rules, rule 8A(3).

18.107   Where the tribunal requires the preparation of a report the requirement to prepare a report is made in writing. It sets out the name and address of each of the parties, the address of the establishment at which the applicant is (or, as the case may be, was) employed, the question to be determined, the identity of the person with reference to whose work the question arises, the date by which the expert is required to send his report to the tribunal and the length of the intervals, during the currency of the requirement to prepare the report, before the expiration of which the expert must send progress reports to the tribunal.[1] The Secretary of Tribunals sends a copy of the requirement to each of the parties together with a notice informing them that a party who unreasonably delays the preparation of the expert's report may have an award of costs made against him, which may include an award in respect of the expert's fees, or have his originating application or notice of appearance struck out.[2] The requirement stipulates that the expert should take account of all such information supplied and all such representations made to him as have a bearing on the question and before drawing up his report, the expert should produce and send to the parties a written summary of the said information and representations and invite the representations of the parties upon the material contained therein. It will require the expert to make his report to the tribunal in a document which reproduces the summary and contains a brief account of any representations received from the parties upon it, any conclusion he may have reached upon the question and the reasons for that conclusion or, as the case may be, for his failure to reach such a conclusion. It will state that the expert should take no account of the difference of sex and at all times act fairly.[3] Where a tribunal requires an expert to prepare a report, it adjourns the hearing so the report can be prepared.[4]

1 Equal Value Rules, rule 8A(4).
2 Equal Value Rules, rule 8A(4).
3 Equal Value Rules, rule 8A(5).
4 Equal Value Rules, rule 8A(6).

18.108 Before the expiration of each interval specified in the requirement given to the expert he should send a progress report to the tribunal. The progress report should state whether the expert considers that he will be able to send his report to the tribunal by the required date[1] and if he considers that he will be unable to do so, give the reasons for the delay and the date by which he now expects to send his report to the tribunal. Where a progress report states that the expert considers that he will be unable to send his report to the tribunal by the required date the Secretary of Tribunals sends a copy to each party.[2] If at any time when a progress report is not imminent, the expert comes to the view that he will be unable to send his report to the tribunal by the required date, he should give notice in writing to the tribunal stating that fact and giving the reasons for the delay and the date by which he now expects to send his report to the tribunal. The Secretary sends a copy of any such notice to each party.[3] In giving the reasons for any delay the expert should, in particular, state whether he considers that any action (including an omission) by a party has contributed to the delay. If he so considers he should identify the party, give particulars of the action, describe how it has contributed to the delay, and give an assessment of the extent to which the delay is attributable to it.[4]

1 'The required date' means the most recent date specified as the date by which the expert must send his report to the tribunal either in the requirement made upon him under rule 8A(4) or in a notice given to him under rule 8A(10A): Equal Value Rules, rule 8A(7).
2 Equal Value Rules, rule 8A(8).
3 Equal Value Rules, rule 8A(9).
4 Equal Value Rules, rule 8A(10).

18.109 On receiving a progress report, or a notice stating that the expert considers that he will be unable to send his report to the tribunal by the required date, the tribunal may take one of three steps.[1] It will give written notice to the expert that he is still required to send the report by the required date, give written notice to the expert substituting a later date as the required date or if, but only if, it considers that it would be in the interests of justice to replace the expert, revoke, by notice in writing to the expert, the requirement to prepare a report. The tribunal will not take any of these steps before it has informed the parties of the action it proposes to take and given each party the opportunity to make representations.[2] Where a tribunal has revoked the requirement made upon an expert to prepare a report under this power it will require another expert to prepare a report by proceeding as if it had just determined to require an expert to prepare a report, and the Rules apply accordingly.[3] Where in giving the reasons for any delay the expert has stated that an action by a party has contributed to the delay, the tribunal considers whether the party has unreasonably delayed the preparation of the expert's report. If it considers that to be the case it will either make a costs order under and in accordance with rule 12,[4] or strike out the whole or part of the originating application, or, as the case may be, of the notice of appearance. Where appropriate, the tribunal will direct that a respondent shall be debarred from defending altogether.[5] The tribunal will not exercise these powers without giving the party an opportunity to make representations.[6]

1 This also applies where the expert does not send his report to the tribunal by the required date: Equal Value Rules, rule 8A(10B).
2 Equal Value Rules, rule 8A(10A).
3 Equal Value Rules, rule 8A(10C).
4 The tribunal may, in making an order under rule 12 under this power order that the party pay to the Secretary of State the whole, or any part, of any fees and allowances paid or payable to the expert in respect of the time so far spent by him in carrying out work pursuant to the requirement to prepare a report: Equal Value Rules: rule 8A(10E).
5 Equal Value Rules, rule 8A(10D).
6 Equal Value Rules, rule 8A(10D).

18.110 Where a tribunal has received the report of the expert on the question asked of him, it sends a copy of the report to each party and fixes a date for the hearing of the case to be resumed. The date so fixed will be the earliest reasonably practicable date after the expiration of 14 days from the date on which the report is sent to the parties.[1] Upon the resumption of the hearing of the case the report is admitted as evidence in the case unless the tribunal has exercised its power not to admit the report.[2] Where the tribunal, on the application of one or more of the parties or otherwise, forms the view that the expert has not complied with a stipulation in the requirement, or that the conclusion contained in the report is one which, taking due account of the information supplied and representations made to the expert, could not reasonably have been reached, or that for some other material reason (other than disagreement with the conclusion that the applicant's work is or is not of equal value or with the reasoning leading to that conclusion) the report is unsatisfactory, the tribunal, may if it thinks fit, determine not to admit the report. In such a case the tribunal proceeds as if it had just determined to require an expert to prepare a report.[3] In forming its view on these matters the tribunal should take account of any representations of the parties thereon and may in that connection[4] permit any party to give evidence upon, to call witnesses and to question any witness upon any matter relevant thereto.[5] Where a tribunal has determined not to admit a report under this provision, that report will be treated for all purposes connected with the proceedings (other than the award of costs or allowances under rule 12 of the Equal Value Rules) as if it had not been received by the tribunal and no further account will be taken of it, and the requirement on the expert to prepare a report lapses.[6]

1 Equal Value Rules, rule 8A(11). The tribunal can hear oral evidence from the expert on the report: *Aldridge v British Telecommunications plc* [1989] ICR 790, EAT.
2 Equal Value Rules, rule 8A(12). The independent expert's report has unusual authority and importance, but there is no provision or principle that the tribunal can only reject it if the evidence is such as to show that it is so plainly wrong that it cannot be accepted: *Tennants Textile Colours Ltd v Todd* [1989] IRLR 3, NICA.
3 Equal Value Rules, rule 8A(13).

4 Subject to the Equal Value Rules, rule 9(2A) and (2B).
5 Equal Value Rules, rule 8A(14).
6 Equal Value Rules, rule 8A(18).

18.111 The tribunal may, at any time after it has received the report of an expert, require that expert (or, if that is impracticable, another expert) to explain any matter contained in the report or, having regard to such matters as may be set out in the requirement, to give further consideration to the question.[1] Such a requirement should stipulate that the expert will make his reply in writing to the tribunal, giving his explanation or, as the case may be, setting down any conclusion which may result from his further consideration and his reasons for that conclusion.[2] When the tribunal has received the reply from the expert it sends a copy of the reply to each of the parties and allows the parties to make representations thereon, and the reply should be treated as information furnished to the tribunal and be given such weight as the tribunal thinks fit.[3]

1 Equal Value Rules, rule 8A(15).
2 Equal Value Rules, rule 8A(16). See the Equal Value Rules, rule 8A(16A) for appropriate amendments to the provisions of rule 8A in these circumstances.
3 Equal Value Rules, rule 8A(17).

The hearing

18.112 The hearing of an equal value claim is conducted in similar fashion to other equal pay claims before tribunals. If an expert has been asked to report there are amendments as are appropriate to accommodate the involvement of the expert. The tribunal may, and will upon the application of a party, require the attendance of the expert who has prepared a report in connection with an equal value claim in any hearing relating to that claim. Where an expert attends in compliance with such requirement any party may cross-examine the expert on his report and on any other matter pertaining to the question on which the expert was required to report.[1] At any time after the tribunal has received the report of the expert, any party may, on giving reasonable notice of his intention to do so to the tribunal and to any other party to the claim, call one witness to give expert evidence on the question on which the tribunal has required the expert to prepare a report. Where such evidence is given, any other party may cross-examine the person giving that evidence upon it.[2] Except as provided in rule 8A(14) of the Equal Value Rules or as mentioned below, no party may give evidence upon, or question any witness upon, any matter of fact upon which a conclusion in the report of the expert is based.[3] Subject to these rules, a tribunal may permit a party to give evidence, to call witnesses and to question any witness upon any such matters of fact if, either the matter of fact is relevant to and is raised in connection with the issue contained in s 1(3) of the Equal Pay Act 1970 (defence of genuine material factor) upon which the determination of the tribunal is being sought, or the expert's report contains no conclusion on the question of whether the applicant's work and the work of the comparator identified in the tribunal's requirement of the expert are of equal value and the tribunal is satisfied that the absence of that conclusion is wholly or mainly due to the refusal or deliberate omission of a person required by the tribunal to furnish information or to produce documents to comply with that requirement.[4] The tribunal may, on the application of a party, if in the circumstances of the case, having regard to the general considerations as to conduct of hearings, it considers that it is appropriate so to proceed, hear evidence upon and permit the parties to address it upon the issue contained s 1(3) of the Equal Pay Act 1970 before determining whether to require an expert to prepare a report.[5]

1 Equal Value Rules, rule 9(2A). Tribunals bear in mind the desirability of limiting evidence and costs, see *Reed Packaging Ltd v Boozer* [1988] ICR 391 at p 399, EAT.
2 Equal Value Rules, rule 9(2B).
3 Equal Value Rules, rule 9(2C). The rule does not prevent a party from making submissions to contradict the conclusions of the independent expert or inhibit the tribunal from asking questions: *Tennants Textile Colours Ltd v Todd* [1989] IRLR 3, NICA. The tribunal is entitled to look at the totality of the evidence before reaching its conclusion, including evidence from the expert concerning issues of fact arising out of the report or the case itself: *Aldridge v British Telecommunications plc* [1989] ICR 790, EAT.
4 Equal Value Rules, rule 9(2D).
5 Equal Value Rules, rule 9(2E).

The decision

18.113 The usual requirements as to decisions apply in respect of equal value claims.[1] A copy of the expert's report (if any) received by the tribunal in the course of the proceedings is appended to the decision and reasons.[2] In effect, for the purposes of the Equal Value Rules, references to the decision and reasons of the tribunal are to that document with the expert's report appended.

1 Equal Value Rules, rule 10.
2 Equal Value Rules, rule 10(4A).

Costs

18.114 In addition to awards of costs mentioned at **18.109**, tribunals are able to award costs in connection with equal value claims as in other equal pay cases.[1] The costs in respect of which a tribunal may make an order include costs incurred by the party in whose favour the order is to be made in or in connection with any investigations carried out by an expert in preparing his report.[2]

1 Equal Value Rules, rule 12.
2 Equal Value Rules, rule 12(2A).

Miscellaneous powers

18.115 The powers of the tribunal and its officers and other matters relating to the proceedings before the tribunal in connection with equal value claims are generally similar to those in connection with other equal pay cases.[1] A tribunal may, before determining an application for an interlocutory order, or for joinder,[2] require the party making the application or, in an appropriate case, the expert, to give notice of it to every other party (or, in the case of an application by the expert, to the parties and any other person on whom the tribunal is asked, in the application, to impose a requirement). The notice should give particulars of the application and indicate the address to which and the time within which any objection to the application should be made, being an address and time specified for the purposes of the application by the tribunal.[3] The tribunal will, before proceeding to hear the parties on an equal value claim, invite them to apply for an adjournment for the purpose of seeking to reach a settlement of the claim and will, if both or all the parties agree to such a course, grant an adjournment for that purpose.[4] If, after the tribunal has adjourned the hearing for the expert to prepare his report but before the tribunal has received the report of the expert, the applicant gives notice of the withdrawal of his originating application, the tribunal will notify the expert that the requirement to prepare a report has ceased. The notice will be without prejudice to the operation of rules as to the award of costs.[5] The recorded delivery postal service is used for service of witness orders in connection with equal value claims in the same way as in other claim for equal pay.[6]

1 Equal Value Rules, rule 13.
2 Under rule 17.
3 Equal Value Rules, rule 13(5).
4 Equal Value Rules, rule 13(6A). This is often dealt with at a preliminary hearing; see *Reed Packaging Ltd v Boozer* [1988] ICR 391 at p 399, EAT. It is common for other interlocutory matters to be dealt with at such hearings.
5 Equal Value Rules, rule 13(6B).
6 Equal Value Rules, rule 20(5).

Scotland

18.116 The procedure of industrial tribunals in Scotland is governed by differing rules of procedure.[1] Subject only to the use of appropriate Scots terminology, the Scottish Rules are very similar to the Rules.[2] There is one Scottish Central Office of the Industrial Tribunals and three Area Offices.[3] There are no Regional Offices of Industrial Tribunals in Scotland. Despite the similarity between the Scottish Rules and the Rules, there are fairly substantial differences in practice between tribunals in England and in Scotland. Opening addresses are rarely allowed in Scotland and the practice in England and Wales of allowing all witnesses to be present throughout the hearing is not usually followed in Scotland. There, witnesses are usually absent from the tribunal hearing until they are called on to give evidence. Before a Scots tribunal the first closing address is usually made on behalf of the party who first called evidence. Unlike his counterpart in England and Wales a chairman in Scotland will almost never be asked by the Employment Appeal Tribunal to produce his note. Decisions are reserved in most cases in Scotland and are not given ex tempore. For this reason it is usual for factors relating to both merits and remedy to be dealt with together at one hearing rather than in two stages as is often the position in England and Wales.

1 Industrial Tribunals (Constitution and Rules of Procedure)(Scotland) Regulations 1993, SI 1993/2688, as amended by SI 1994/538 and SI 1996/1758. In this chapter referred to as 'the Scottish Rules'.
2 'Discovery' of documents is 'recovery' of documents, 'joinder' is 'sist' , 'costs' are 'expenses' and references which in the Rules are made to the county court are made to the sheriff court.
3 It is very important to note that originating applications can only be presented at the Scottish Central Office. They *cannot* be presented at Area Offices: *Craig v Associated Dairies Ltd* (1980) unreported.

Chapter 19

Appeals from industrial tribunals

Introduction

Appeals from industrial tribunals lie to the Employment Appeal Tribunal and not to the ordinary courts, see **19.09–19.10**.

Appeals can only be made on a point of law and cannot made with regard to findings of fact unless those findings were perverse, see **19.11–19.14**.

Notices of appeal have to be delivered to the appropriate office of the Employment Appeal Tribunal within 42 days from the date on which the extended reasons, or order, of the industrial tribunal were sent to the appellant. The fact that the appellant is awaiting assistance from one of the statutory Commissions, or for legal aid is not normally an acceptable reason for lodging an appeal out of time, see **19.21–19.23**.

There is a procedure for preliminary hearings, if there is doubt whether a point of law is raised on the appeal. This is also used to ensure that full hearings are efficiently conducted, see **19.28**. There are also arrangement for fast-tracking certain appeals, see **19.48**.

There are specific requirements as to documents for use at the hearing, for lodging skeleton arguments and otherwise as to the conduct of appeals, see **19.36–19.39** and **19.45–19.47**.

The power of the Employment Appeal Tribunal to award costs is more limited than that of the ordinary courts, see **19.59**.

Appeals from the Employment Appeal Tribunal lie to the Court of Appeal or the Court of Session as the case may be, see **19.61**.

Employment Appeal Tribunal

Constitution

19.01   The Employment Appeal Tribunal was created by the Employment Protection Act 1975.[1] It consists of a number of judges, nominated from time to time by the Lord Chancellor (other than himself) from judges of the High Court and Court of Appeal. It has at least one judge from the Court of Session, nominated by the Lord President of that court. One of the judges is appointed President of the Employment Appeal Tribunal by the Lord Chancellor.[2] The first President was Phillips J. The present incumbent is Morison J. In addition to the judges, Her Majesty the Queen appoints such number of other members of the Appeal Tribunal as she may appoint from time to time on the joint recommendation of the Lord Chancellor and the Secretary of State.[3] These members are persons who appear to the Lord Chancellor and the Secretary of State to have special knowledge, or experience, of industrial relations, either as representatives of employers, or of workers.[4] The Central Office of the Tribunal is at Audit House, 58, Victoria

Embankment, London EC4Y 0DS and the Scottish divisional office at 11, Melville Crescent, Edinburgh.

1 Section 87(1). The Employment Appeal Tribunal has some similarities to the defunct National Industrial Relations Court.
2 Industrial Tribunals Act 1996, s 22(3). Prior to the appointment, the Lord Chancellor consults with the Lord President of the Court of Session.
3 Industrial Tribunals Act 1996, s 22(1)(c).
4 Industrial Tribunals Act 1996, s 22(2).

19.02 The members of the Employment Appeal Tribunal in addition to the judges are persons appointed on the joint recommendation of the Lord Chancellor and the Secretary of State, and they hold and vacate office in accordance with the terms of their appointment.[1] They may resign at any time,[2] and if the Lord Chancellor, after consultation with the Secretary of State, is satisfied that a member has been absent from sittings of the Appeal Tribunal for a period longer than six consecutive months without the permission of the President of the Appeal Tribunal, or has become bankrupt, or made an arrangement with his creditors, or is incapacitated by physical or mental illness, or is otherwise unable, or unfit, to discharge the functions of a member, the Lord Chancellor may declare his office as a member of the Employment Appeal Tribunal to be vacant and notify the declaration in such manner as he thinks fit, and thereupon the office becomes vacant.[3]

1 Industrial Tribunals Act 1996, s 25(1).
2 Industrial Tribunals Act 1996, s 25(2). Members vacate office on their 70th birthday.
3 Industrial Tribunals Act 1996, s 25(4).

19.03 The Lord Chancellor can nominate another judge to act as President of the Employment Appeal Tribunal in the temporary absence of the President,[1] and judges may be appointed to act in the place of judges nominated to the Employment Appeal Tribunal who are themselves temporarily absent.[2] Temporary lay members may be appointed jointly by the Lord Chancellor and the Secretary of State.[3] The Lord Chancellor may also appoint temporary additional judges when it appears to him to be expedient to do so.[4]

1 Industrial Tribunals Act 1996, s 23(1).
2 Industrial Tribunals Act 1996, s 23(2). The appointment made when the judge who is absent was nominated by the Lord President of the Court of Session is made by him pursuant to s 23(2)(b).
3 Industrial Tribunals Act 1996, s 23(3).
4 Industrial Tribunals Act 1996, s 24.

19.04 The Employment Appeal Tribunal came into being on 30 March 1976.[1] It is a superior court of record and has an official seal which is judicially noticed.[2] Although the present offices of the Appeal Tribunal are situate as mentioned above, the Appeal Tribunal may sit at any time, and in any place, in Great Britain.[3] The President of the Employment Appeal Tribunal may direct that it sits in one, or more, divisions concurrently.[4] If the parties to proceedings consent, a case may be heard by a judge and one appointed member or by a judge and three appointed members, but in default of such consent, proceedings before the Appeal Tribunal should be heard by a judge and either two, or four, appointed members, so that in either case there are equal numbers of persons whose experience is as representatives of employers and of workers.[5] The Appeal Tribunal usually consists of a judge and two members. Appeals from proceedings heard by a chairman of industrial tribunals sitting alone pursuant to s 4(1)(a) of the Industrial Tribunals Act 1996, are heard by a judge alone, unless a judge directs otherwise.[6] Where a minister of the Crown so directs in relations to any proceedings on grounds of national security, the proceedings are heard by the President of the Employment Appeal Tribunal sitting alone.[7]

1 Employment Protection Act 1975 (Commencement No 3) Order 1976, SI 1976/321.
2 Industrial Tribunals Act 1996, s 20(3).
3 Industrial Tribunals Act 1996, s 20(2), and has done so.
4 Industrial Tribunals Act 1996, s 28(1).
5 Industrial Tribunals Act 1996, s 28(2).
6 Industrial Tribunals Act 1996, s 28(4).
7 Industrial Tribunals Act 1996, s 28(5).

19.05   The Secretary of State appoints officers and staff of the Appeal Tribunal, subject to the approval of the minister for the Civil Service as to numbers and terms and conditions of service.[1] There are provisions enabling the payment of remuneration and travelling and other allowances to the appointed members[2] and for payment of pensions, allowances and gratuities due to or in respect of, them, and, in certain circumstances, for the payment of compensation when a person ceases to be a member.[3]

1 Industrial Tribunals Act 1996, s 26.
2 Industrial Tribunals Act 1996, s 27(1), including those appointed temporarily.
3 Industrial Tribunals Act 1996, s 27(3) and (4).

The rules

19.06   The Lord Chancellor is empowered to make rules with respect to proceedings for the Employment Appeal Tribunal.[1] The Employment Appeal Tribunal Rules 1993[2] have been made by him pursuant to these powers. Subject to the rules for the time being in force the Employment Appeal Tribunal has power to regulate its own procedure.[3] Practice directions have been made by the President of the Employment Appeal Tribunal in the exercise of this power.[4]

1 Industrial Tribunals Act 1996, s 30(1). The rules are made after consultation with the Lord President of the Court of Session.
2 Employment Appeal Tribunal Rules 1993, SI 1993/2854.
3 Industrial Tribunals Act 1996, s 30(3).
4 That at present in force is set out at [1996] IRLR 430. See also *Blue Circle Staff Association v Certification Officer* [1977] 2 All ER 145; [1977] ICR 224, EAT.

19.07   On disposing of an appeal the Employment Appeal Tribunal may exercise any power of the industrial tribunal from which the appeal was brought, or remit the case to the industrial tribunal.[1] Any decision, or award, of the Appeal Tribunal on an appeal has the same effect and may be enforced in the same manner as a decision, or award, of the industrial tribunal.[2] The Appeal Tribunal has, in relation to the attendance and examination of witnesses, the production and inspection of documents, and all other matters incidental to its jurisdiction, the like powers, rights, privileges and authority, in England and Wales, as the High Court, and in Scotland, as the Court of Session.[3] No person may be punished for contempt of the Appeal Tribunal except by, or with consent of, a judge.[4]

19.07 *Appeals from industrial tribunals*

1 Industrial Tribunals Act 1996, s 35(1). Cases have been remitted where the Appeal Tribunal is satisfied not necessarily that something has gone wrong but it looked likely that something might have been amiss, requiring the matter to be properly investigated: *Askew v Victoria Sporting Club Ltd* [1976] ICR 302, EAT. However cases are only remitted if it is practical to do so: *Times Newspapers Ltd v Bartlett* (1976) 11 ITR 106, EAT. See also *Westminster City Council v Cabaj* [1996] IRLR 399, CA.
2 Industrial Tribunals Act 1996, s 35(2).
3 Industrial Tribunals Act 1996, s 29(2).
4 Industrial Tribunals Act 1996, s 36(4).

19.08 Legal aid is available for proceedings in the Employment Appeal Tribunal subject to the Civil Legal Aid (General) Regulations 1989.[1]

1 Civil Legal Aid (General) Regulations 1989, SI 1989/339, reg 149.

Grounds of appeal

19.09 Appeals lie to the Employment Appeal Tribunal on questions of law arising from any decision of, or arising in any proceedings before, an industrial tribunal under, or by virtue of:
(1) the Equal Pay Act 1970,
(2) the Sex Discrimination Act 1975,
(3) the Race Relations Act 1976,
(4) the Trade Union and Labour Relations (Consolidation) Act 1992,
(5) the Disability Discrimination Act 1995, or
(6) the Employment Rights Act 1996.[1]
The Employment Appeal Tribunal has other roles, in particular in connection with appeals from the Certification Officer, and some areas of original jurisdiction which are outside the scope of this book.

1 Industrial Tribunals Act 1996, s 21(1).

19.10 No appeal lies from any decision of an industrial tribunal under these statutes except to the Employment Appeal Tribunal.[1] The restriction of the grounds of appeal to those raising matters of law is of immense importance. The determination of facts by the industrial tribunal cannot be challenged on appeal (unless the decision is perverse).[2] Thus it is essential from the point of view of the parties that the facts are properly presented to the industrial tribunal at the hearing.

1 Industrial Tribunals Act 1996, s 21(2).
2 See Chapter 18.

Points of law

19.11 Whether or not there are points of law meriting an appeal depends upon the circumstances of each case.[1] Deductions as to the legal effects of factual situations are matters of law.[2] If the facts found by the tribunal do not support its decision, an appeal may be successfully prosecuted. A party may also appeal if he can show that the evidence was such that no reasonable tribunal could reach the tribunal's conclusion.[3] Questions as to the construction of statutes are matters of law,[4] as are points touching on the construction of contracts,[5] and whether, or not, a term may be implied in a contract.[6] An error in reasoning by a tribunal has also been the subject of a successful appeal,[7] as has the failure by an individual tribunal chairman to consider the primary ground of an application for review when deciding whether or not to grant a rehearing of an application for a remedy for unfair dismissal.⁸ Once the Employment Appeal Tribunal finds that the industrial tribunal has misdirected itself in law then the decision of the industrial tribunal should only stand if it is plainly and unarguably right.⁹

1 For the classic definition of a point of law for the purposes of bringing an appeal, see the speech of Lord Radcliffe in *Edwards v Bairstow* [1956] AC 14; [1955] 3 All ER 48, HL. Reference may also be made to *Moberley v Commonwealth Hall (University of London)* [1977] ICR 791, EAT; 'Some Notes on the Employment Appeal Tribunal' by Phillips J in (1978) 7 ILJ 137; and *British Telecommunications plc v Sheridan* [1990] IRLR 27, CA.
2 For instance, whether a contract created an employment relationship: *Davies v Presbyterian Church of Wales* [1986] ICR 280, HL.
3 *O'Hara v Fram Gerrard Ltd* [1973] IRLR 94, NIRC; *Hilti (Great Britain) Ltd v Windridge* [1974] ICR 352, NIRC; *Palmer v Vauxhall Motors Ltd* [1977] ICR 24, EAT. Or if the tribunal assessed compensation at a figure unwarranted by the evidence, or failed to take into account some element of compensation which they were legally bound to take into account: *Nohar v Granite Stone (Galloway) Ltd* [1974] ICR 273, NIRC. The Appeal Tribunal will not interfere with an award of compensation unless the error is something which could be described as more than trifling: *Fougere v Phoenix Motor Co Ltd* [1977] 1 All ER 237; [1976] ICR 495, EAT. In appeals based on quantum the notice of appeal should state precisely what is complained of and the order which it is suggested ought to have been made, with supporting figures: *Askew v Victoria Sporting Club Ltd* [1976] ICR 302, EAT.
4 See for instance *Lord Advocate v de Rosa* [1974] 2 All ER 849; [1974] ICR 480, HL. For a helpful explanation of judicial 'guidelines' see *Wells v Derwent Plastics Ltd* [1978] ICR 424, EAT. Guidelines are not 'tram lines' relieving industrial tribunals of the task of examining the facts of individual cases: *Ministry of Defence v Hunt* [1996] IRLR 139, EAT.
5 An example being *Cole v Midland Display Ltd* [1973] IRLR 62, NIRC.
6 *O'Brien v Associated Fire Alarms Ltd* [1969] 1 All ER 93; [1968] 1 WLR 1916, CA.
7 *Mercia Rubber Mouldings Ltd v Lingwood* [1974] ICR 256, NIRC.
8 *Berkeley Garage (Southampton) Ltd v Edmunds* [1975] ICR 228, QBD. On appeals the Employment Appeal Tribunal may exercise the discretions granted to the industrial tribunal: *Masters of Beckenham Ltd v Green* [1977] ICR 535, EAT; *Morris v Griffiths* [1977] ICR 153, EAT.
9 *Dobie v Burns International Security Services (UK) Ltd* [1984] IRLR 329, CA.

19.12 When considering appeals from industrial tribunals Phillips J said:¹
'The authorities on what amounts to a point of law are endless, and they express the matter in all sorts of different ways but it all in the end comes down to the same thing. An appellant who claims that there is an error of law must establish one of three things: he must establish either that the tribunal misdirected itself in law, or misunderstood the law, or misapplied the law; or, secondly, that the tribunal misunderstood the facts, or misapplied the facts; or, thirdly – and this again is put in all sorts of different ways – that although they apparently directed themselves properly in law, and did not misstate, or misunderstand, or misapply the facts, the decision was "perverse" to use a word which to modern ears, or (which is another way of saying the same thing) that there was no evidence to justify the conclusion which the tribunal reached. There are other variants. In *Cooper v British Steel Corpn*² I said that the court would usually interfere in a case where, looking at all the primary facts, the decision on what was a point of fact appeared to the appellate court to be plainly wrong. That perhaps is another way of putting the same thing, and I do not go back on what I said there – making it clear that by "plainly wrong" I mean something which is beyond a mere matter of opinion or approach: where the court, looking at all the facts, is satisfied that the decision is just wrong, it can readily deduce that, although they have not expressed some wrong approach, in fact the tribunal must have followed one. It is really another way – a lighter way,

perhaps – of saying that a decision below is "perverse". So the argument comes back to where it started.'

1 In *Watling v William Bird & Son Contractors Ltd* (1976) 11 ITR 70 at p 71, QBD.
2 [1975] ICR 454, QBD.

19.13   Appeals from industrial tribunals have also taken place where there have been irregularities in the conduct of the hearing.[1] For instance in *Lamont v Fry's Metals Ltd*[2] the chairman of the industrial tribunal announced the decision of the tribunal orally and a week later the parties were invited to make further representations as to an aspect of the case. In another case,[3] where an applicant was given no opportunity to cross-examine the respondent's witnesses, the case was remitted to a tribunal for rehearing. There was a similar outcome when it appeared that the chairman of the industrial tribunal had tried to combine the taking of evidence in two distinct cases when the tribunal did not have the jurisdiction to do so.[4] If there are irregularities, for instance when the chairman wrongly instructs a party's solicitor as to the order in which to present evidence, it is likely that the Employment Appeal Tribunal will look to see if there is a real possibility of prejudice to the injured party. If not, the decision of the industrial tribunal will not be overruled.[5] When a respondent was prevented by transport difficulties from attending the hearing, which proceeded in his absence, the Court of Session ordered that the case be reheard.[6]

1 It is usually alleged in such appeals that the rules of natural justice have not been complied with.
2 [1985] IRLR 470, CA.
3 *McBride v British Railways Board* (1972) 7 ITR 84, NIRC. See also *Estorffe v Smith* [1973] ICR 542, NIRC and *Wilcox v HGS* [1976] IRLR 222, CA.
4 *Strowger v David Rosenfield Ltd* (1972) 7 ITR 373, NIRC.
5 *Barnes v BPC (Business Forms) Ltd* [1976] 1 All ER 237; [1975] ICR 390, DC. The Appeal Tribunal should not substitute its own decision if that is not the only possible conclusion of a correct application of the law by the industrial tribunal: *Westminster City Council v Cabaj* [1996] IRLR 399, CA.
6 *Murrays (Turf Accountants) v Laurie* (1972) 7 ITR 22, Ct of Sess; *Priddle v Fisher & Sons* [1968] 3 All ER 506; [1956] 1 WLR 1478, DC. See also *Berkeley Garage (Southampton) Ltd v Edmunds* [1975] ICR 228, DC (employer did not attend the hearing with witness because he was misled by an official of the Department of Employment).

19.14   The task of the Employment Appeal Tribunal is to correct errors of law. It may be that its members would have decided a case differently from the industrial tribunal, but this does not mean that the Appeal Tribunal will overrule the decision of the industrial tribunal unless the industrial tribunal's members have misdirected themselves. The industrial tribunal is the 'industrial jury' which has had the advantage of hearing the evidence and seeing the witnesses in person. The Court of Appeal has pointed out that the Appeal Tribunal should take care to avoid concluding that an experienced industrial tribunal by not expressly mentioning some point or breach has overlooked it.[1] The Employment Appeal Tribunal can interfere if the decision of the industrial tribunal is perverse. However, the tests are stringent. The Appeal Tribunal must consider the industrial tribunal's decision 'not a permissible option'[2] or that it has reached a conclusion which offends reason or is one to which 'no reasonable industrial tribunal could come' or 'so very clearly wrong that it just cannot stand'. The decision of the industrial tribunal should not be disturbed unless the Appeal Tribunal can say 'My goodness, that was certainly wrong'.[3]

1 *Retarded Children's Aid Society Ltd v Day* [1978] 1 WLR 763; [1978] ICR 437, CA. It is not for the Employment Appeal Tribunal to decide on the weight to be attached to particular facts and the inferences to be drawn from them: *Eclipse Blinds Ltd v Wright* [1992] IRLR 133, Ct of Sess; *British Telecommunications plc v Sheridan* [1990] IRLR 27, CA; and *McLaren v National Coal Board* [1988] IRLR 215, CA.
2 *Piggott Bros v Jackson* [1991] IRLR 309, CA; and *Stewart v Cleveland Guest (Engineering) Ltd* [1994] IRLR 440, EAT.
3 *Neale v Hereford and Worcester County Council* [1986] IRLR 168, CA. See also *Council of Civil Service Unions v Minister for the Civil Service* [1985] IRLR 28, HL and *East Berkshire Health Authority v Matadeen* [1992] IRLR 336, EAT. In *Stewart v Cleveland Guest (Engineering) Ltd* [1994] IRLR 440, EAT, gave examples of cases where the Appeal Tribunal may interfere where the industrial decision is 'irrational', 'offends reason', 'is certainly wrong', 'must be wrong', 'is plainly wrong', 'is outrageous', 'makes absolutely no sense', etc.

New evidence

19.15   New evidence will be admitted on appeal only in rare and exceptional cases.[1] The test which the Employment Appeal Tribunal follows is that laid down in *Ladd v Marshall*[2] as applicable to appeals to the Court of Appeal in civil cases. These are that the evidence could not have been obtained with reasonable diligence for use at the trial; the evidence would probably have had an important influence on the outcome of the trial; and the evidence must be apparently credible. Where there is an application for a review, or an appeal to the Employment Appeal Tribunal, in either case seeking to introduce fresh evidence, it is essential that there be lodged, either with the application for review or with the notice of appeal, a statement in the form of a proof of evidence which it is sought to introduce.[3] The Appeal Tribunal will allow points which were not raised at the industrial tribunal hearing to be canvassed only in very limited circumstances.[4]

1 *Wileman v Minilec Engineering Ltd* [1988] IRLR 144, EAT. It is only in most unusual circumstances that new evidence will be admitted in view of the right of industrial tribunals to review their decisions, see **18.95–18.103.**
2 [1954] 1 WLR 1489, CA.
3 *Vauxhall Motors Ltd v Henry* (1978) 13 ITR 332, EAT.
4 *GKN (Cwmbran) Ltd v Lloyd* [1972] ICR 214, NIRC; *Bishop v John Brignell and Co (Builders) Ltd* (1974) 9 ITR 307, CA; *Kumchyk v Derby City Council* [1978] ICR 1116, EAT, having reviewed most of the authorities, the Employment Appeal Tribunal held that the consideration of the new point of law was not totally excluded but that in almost every conceivable case it would be unjust to do so. It might be just to consider a case where there has been some deception on the part of the respondent to the appeal, which could not be condoned by the appellate tribunal. It certainly is not enough to enable the Appeal Tribunal to consider a new point because of lack of skill or experience on behalf of the applicant, that a wrong tactical decision was made, or that the omission could have been made good by the industrial tribunal. This approach differs in some respects from that adopted by the Court of Appeal in appeals from the High Court and county court; see *Wilson v Liverpool Corpn* [1971] 1 WLR 302 at p 307, CA and *Hellyer Bros Ltd v McLeod* [1987] IRLR 232 at p 248, CA. For a more recent discussion of the position *Barber v Thames Television plc* [1991] IRLR 236, EAT, may be referred to.

Agreed decisions

19.16   Where both parties to an application to an industrial tribunal agree that the decision of the tribunal was in error, and agree a proposed settlement, the parties may not themselves reverse that decision but should refer the matter to the Employment Appeal Tribunal sitting in open court. It is best if the parties draft a formal order and request the Appeal Tribunal to accept it, ratify it and make it part of the order of the Appeal Tribunal.[1]

1 For a helpful exposition of the position see *J Sainsbury plc v Moger* [1994] ICR 800, EAT. See **19.56.**

19.17 *Appeals from industrial tribunals*

Reviews by industrial tribunals

19.17 In many cases when it is sought to challenge the decision of an industrial tribunal the right of review given to industrial tribunals should be made use of. However, a review is not an alternative, or preliminary, to an appeal.[1] The time limit for appealing is not postponed by the application for a review.

1 *Dean v Polytechnic of North London* [1973] ICR 490, NIRC. For the powers of industrial tribunals to review their decisions, see **18.95–18.103**.

Complaints as to conduct of an industrial tribunal hearing

19.18 The Employment Appeal Tribunal will not normally consider complaints of bias, or relating to the conduct of an industrial tribunal at the hearing, unless full and sufficient particulars are set out in the grounds of appeal. In any such case the Registrar may enquire of the party making the complaint whether it is the intention to proceed with the complaint, in which case the Registrar will give appropriate directions for hearing.[1] There is a special procedure to be adopted in these cases which is set out in the Employment Appeal Tribunal Practice Directions.[2] Complaints of this kind cannot be raised unless this procedure is followed.[3]

1 See **19.41**.
2 Employment Appeal Tribunal *Practice Direction* [1996] IRLR 430, r 9.
3 Employment Appeal Tribunal *Practice Direction* [1996] IRLR 430, r 9(5).

19.19 It is possible for the supervisory jurisdiction of the High Court to be exercised with regard to industrial tribunals by use of the prerogative orders of certiorari, mandamus and prohibition.[1] Their use in relation to industrial tribunals is very rare, and in view of the exclusive jurisdiction conferred on the Employment Appeal Tribunal,[2] and the comparative ease and cheapness of the system of review and appeals, it is unlikely that there will be any increase in their frequency. It may also be possible to obtain a judicial declaration with regard to proceedings before an industrial tribunal.[3]

1 Such appeals may be heard by a single judge. See the application for certiorari in *R v Industrial Tribunal, ex p George Green and Thompson Ltd* (1967) 2 ITR 360. This is the only case of certiorari of which the authors are aware. Applications for orders of prohibition and mandamus were made in *R v Industrial Tribunal, ex p Cotswold Collotype Co Ltd* [1979] ICR 190, QBD.
2 By the Industrial Tribunals Act 1996, s 21(2) and the Trade Union and Labour Relations (Consolidation) Act 1992, s 291(3).
3 See Whitesides and Hawker *Industrial Tribunals* (London, 1975) p 73.

Vexatious litigants

19.20 The Trade Union Reform and Employment Rights Act 1993 gave the Employment Appeal Tribunal new powers in connection with vexatious litigants. These are effective when, on an application made by the Attorney-General, or the Lord Advocate,[1] the Employment Appeal Tribunal is satisfied that any person has habitually and persistently and without any reasonable ground instituted vexatious proceedings, whether in an industrial tribunal or before the Employment Appeal Tribunal, and whether against the same person or different persons, or made vexatious applications in any proceedings whether in an industrial tribunal or before the Appeal Tribunal. In these circumstances the Employment Appeal Tribunal may after hearing the person, or giving him an opportunity to be heard, make a restriction of proceedings order.[2] A 'restriction of proceedings order' is an order that no proceedings can, without leave of the Appeal Tribunal, be instituted in any industrial tribunal or before the Appeal Tribunal by the person against whom the order is made. Any proceedings instituted by him in any industrial tribunal cannot be continued by him without leave of the Appeal Tribunal and no application (other than for leave under s 33 of the Industrial Tribunals Act 1996) can be made by him in any proceedings in any industrial tribunal, or in the Appeal Tribunal, without leave of the Appeal Tribunal.[3] A copy of the restriction of proceedings order is published in the London Gazette and the Edinburgh Gazette.[4] The Employment Appeal Tribunal will not give leave to proceed to the person subject to an order unless it is satisfied that the proceedings, or application in respect of which leave is sought, are not an abuse of the process of the tribunal in question and there are reasonable grounds for the proceedings or application.[5] No appeal lies from the decision of the Employment Appeal Tribunal refusing leave for the institution or continuance of, or for the making of an application in, proceedings by a person who is the subject of a restricted proceedings order.[6]

1 Industrial Tribunals Act 1996, s 33(1).
2 Industrial Tribunals Act 1996, s 33(1).
3 Industrial Tribunals Act 1996, s 33(2). The order may provide that it is to cease to have effect at the end of a specified period, but otherwise remains in force indefinitely: Industrial Tribunals Act 1996, s 33(3).
4 Industrial Tribunals Act 1996, s 33(5).
5 Industrial Tribunals Act 1996, s 33(4).
6 Industrial Tribunals Act 1996, s 37(3).

Procedure

Notice of appeal

19.21   Appeals to the Employment Appeal Tribunal are instituted by serving a notice of appeal on the Tribunal, within 42 days of the date on which the extended written reasons for the decision, or order, appealed from was sent to the appellant. The notice of appeal should be in, or substantially in, accordance with Form 1 (see Appendix 2) set out in the Schedule to the Employment Appeal Tribunal Rules 1993.[1] The notice should be accompanied by a copy of the extended reasons, or order, of the industrial tribunal which is appealed against.[2] Where a request for extended reasons has been refused by the industrial tribunal, an appellant may appeal against the refusal and may also apply to the Appeal Tribunal to exercise its discretion to hear the appeal on summary reasons only.[3] The notice of appeal must clearly identify the point of law which forms the ground of appeal from the decision of the industrial tribunal. It may also state the order which the appellant will ask the Appeal Tribunal to make at the hearing.[4] The processing of the appeal will be accelerated if the appellant serves on the Appeal Tribunal with the notice of appeal a copy of the originating application and notice of appearance in the tribunal proceedings.[5]

1 Employment Appeal Tribunal Rules 1993, SI 1993/2854, r 3(1). The present Employment Appeal Tribunal Rules came into operation on 16 December 1993: Employment Appeal Tribunal Rules 1993, SI 1993/2854, r 1. For the position where the law or its interpretation have changed

after the decision of the industrial tribunal, see *Setiya v East Yorkshire Health Authority* [1995] IRLR 348, EAT; and *Foster v South Glamorgan Health Authority* [1988] IRLR 277, EAT.
2 See footnote 1 above.
3 Employment Appeal Tribunal *Practice Direction* [1996] IRLR 430, para 2(2). See *Wolesley Centres Ltd v Simmons* [1994] ICR 503, EAT.
4 Employment Appeal Tribunal *Practice Direction* [1996] IRLR 430, para 2(3).
5 Employment Appeal Tribunal *Practice Direction* [1996] IRLR 430, para 2(7).

19.22   The notice of appeal should be served within the time limit. The time for the appeal runs even though the question of remedy and the assessment of compensation has been adjourned, or an application has been made for review.[1] It is not usually a good excuse for delay in appealing that legal aid had been applied for, and not yet determined, or that support is being sought from a body such as a trade union or the Equal Opportunities Commission or the Commission for Racial Equality.[2] If the notice of appeal is not delivered within the time limit it must be accompanied by an application for an extension of time explaining clearly and concisely the reasons for the delay.[3] The application cannot be considered until a notice of appeal in the prescribed form has been served.[4] Unless otherwise ordered, the application for extension of time will be considered and determined as if it were an interlocutory application.[5] The Registrar will normally determine the application in the first instance after inviting and considering written representations from both sides.[6] An interlocutory appeal from the Registrar's decision lies to a judge. Such appeals must be notified within five days of the Registrar's decision.[7] It is provided by the *Practice Direction* that in case of doubt or difficulty, a notice of appeal should be presented in time and an application made to the Registrar for directions.[8]

1 Employment Appeal Tribunal *Practice Direction* [1996] IRLR 430, para 3(1). The time starts to run after the decision is sent to the parties even if the other matters (for instance remedies) are still to be determined: *Firestone Tyre and Rubber Co Ltd v Challoner* [1977] IRLR 223, EAT.
2 Employment Appeal Tribunal *Practice Direction* [1996] IRLR 430, para 3(6).
3 Employment Appeal Tribunal *Practice Direction* [1996] IRLR 430, para 3(2). If reliance is to be placed on particular factors when applying for an extension of time in which to appeal it is desirable that it is supported by affidavit evidence by the person who can depose as to the facts: *Firestone Tyre and Rubber Co Ltd v Challoner* [1977] IRLR 223, EAT.
4 Employment Appeal Tribunal *Practice Direction* [1996] IRLR 430, para 3(3).
5 Employment Appeal Tribunal *Practice Direction* [1996] IRLR 430, para 3(4).
6 See footnote 5 above.
7 See footnote 5 above.
8 Employment Appeal Tribunal *Practice Direction* [1996] IRLR 430, para 3(7).

Extending time for appeal

19.23   In determining whether to extend time for appealing particular attention will be paid to whether any good excuse for the delay has been shown. The guidance contained in the decision of the Employment Appeal Tribunal in the case of *United Arab Emirates v Abdelghafar*[1] is of particular importance.[2] The approach used is similar to that adopted by the civil courts. Several factors are taken into account by the courts when deciding whether to exercise their discretion to extend time limits. The grant or refusal of an extension of time is a matter of judicial discretion. It is not exercised subjectively but in a principled manner in accordance with reason and justice. The public interest in the expeditious despatch of ligation (that time limits are requirements to be met) is balanced against the interest of the appellant to have his claim adjudicated on the merits and that this should not be denied because there has been a procedural fault (unless the default causes prejudice to the other party which an award of costs cannot compensate). The approach indicated by these principles is modified according to the stage which the proceedings had reached. In the case of an appeal, since the party has had a trial, he should act promptly. The interests of the parties and the public make the courts more strict about time limits on appeals. There is no reasonable or legitimate expectation of receiving an extension of time in which to appeal. An extension of time is an indulgence requested by a party. In the case of appeals to the Employment Appeal Tribunal the timetable set by the Rules should be adhered to. The limit is only relaxed in rare and exceptional cases, where the Appeal Tribunal is satisfied that there is a reason which justifies the departure from the Rules. The Appeal Tribunal will only exercise its discretion if there is a full and honest explanation for the non-compliance which is a good excuse for the default. If there is such an explanation other factors may be considered. Matters such as possible procedural abuse, the length of the delay and the merits of the case may be looked at. 'Thus the questions which must be addressed by the Appeal Tribunal, the parties and their representatives on an application for an extension are: (a) What is the explanation for the default? (b) Does it provide a good excuse for the default? (c) Are there exceptional circumstances which justify the Tribunal taking the exceptional step of granting an extension of time?'[3] If it appears to the Registrar that a notice of appeal gives insufficient particulars of, or lacks clarity in identifying, a point of law the Registrar may postpone his decision on an application under rule 3(3) pending amplification or clarification of the notice of appeal as regards the question of law or grounds of appeal by the intended appellant.[4]

1 [1995] ICR 65, at pp 69–72, EAT, upon which this paragraph is based. In that case it was held that since the State Immunity Act 1978, s 1(2) imposed a positive duty on the industrial tribunal to satisfy itself that effect had been given to the immunity conferred by the Act, it was the duty of the Employment Appeal Tribunal to correct the position where it had not done so, notwithstanding no acceptable explanation of the delay in the application for appeal had been put forward. Examples were given of excuses which had been rejected by the Appeal Tribunal, include ignorance and oversight of the time limit, the existence of applications for review of the industrial tribunal decision, prior notification of intention to appeal and delay in obtaining legal aid or advice or support from the Equal Opportunities Commission or the Commission for Racial Equality. The relevant authorities are reviewed by the then President of the Appeal Tribunal in this decision. For the position where the law or its interpretation has changed see **19.21**, n 1.
2 Employment Appeal Tribunal *Practice Direction* [1996] IRLR 430, para 3(5).
3 *United Arab Emirates v Abdelghafar* [1995] ICR 65 at pp 69–72, EAT.
4 Employment Appeal Tribunal *Practice Direction* [1996] IRLR 430, para 2(4).

Inadequate notice of appeal

19.24   In a case where it appears to the Registrar that the grounds of appeal stated in the notice of appeal do not give the Employment Appeal Tribunal jurisdiction to entertain the appeal the Registrar will notify the appellant accordingly informing him of the reasons for the opinion. In such cases, subject to rules 3(4) and (6), no further action will be taken on the appeal.[1] Where such notification has been given the appellant may serve a fresh notice of appeal within the time remaining, or within 28 days from the date on which the Registrar's notification was sent to him, whichever is the longer period.[2]

1 Employment Appeal Tribunal Rules 1993, SI 1993/2854, r 3(3).
2 Employment Appeal Tribunal Rules 1993, r 3(4). The fresh notice is considered as though an original notice of appeal: r 3(5).

19.25 It is not permissible for the parties to reserve a right to amend, alter, or add to any pleading in the Employment Appeal Tribunal. Such right is not inherent and may only be exercised if permitted by order for which an interlocutory application should be made as soon as the need for the amendment is known[1].The Registrar may consider the fresh notice of appeal with regard to jurisdiction as though it were an original notice of appeal. Where an appellant expresses dissatisfaction in writing with the reasons given by the Registrar for his opinion that the grounds of appeal stated in the notice of appeal do not give the Appeal Tribunal jurisdiction to entertain the appeal, the Registrar will place the papers before the President or a judge for his direction.[2]

1 Employment Appeal Tribunal *Practice Direction* [1996] IRLR 430, para 2(6).
2 Employment Appeal Tribunal Rules 1993, SI 1993/2854, r 3(6).

Failure to give notice of appearance

19.26 If the appellant in a case has not entered a notice of appearance before the industrial tribunal and has not applied to the industrial tribunal for an extension of time for doing so, or has applied for such an extension and been refused it, the notice of appeal will be immediately set down to be heard as a preliminary hearing.[1] The appellant will not be permitted to pursue the appeal unless the Employment Appeal Tribunal is satisfied at the preliminary hearing that:
(1)   there is a good excuse for failing to enter a notice of appearance and (if that be the case) for failing to apply for such an extension of time; and
(2)   there is a reasonably arguable defence to the claim in the originating application.[2]

1 Employment Appeal Tribunal *Practice Direction* [1996] IRLR 430, para 16(1). See *Charlton v Charlton Thermosystems (Romsey) Ltd* [1995] IRLR 79, EAT.
2 Employment Appeal Tribunal *Practice Direction* [1996] IRLR 430, para 16(2).

19.27 In order to satisfy the Employment Appeal Tribunal on these matters, the appellant must swear and lodge with the Appeal Tribunal an affidavit explaining in detail the circumstances in which there has been a failure to serve a notice of appearance in time or apply for such an extension of time, the reason for that failure to do so, and the facts and matters relied upon for contesting the claim on the merits. There should be exhibited to the affidavit all relevant documents and a completed draft notice of appearance.[1] The respondent to the appeal may swear and lodge with the Appeal Tribunal an affidavit in reply to the appellant's affidavit.[2]

1 Employment Appeal Tribunal *Practice Direction* [1996] IRLR 430, para 16(3).
2 Employment Appeal Tribunal *Practice Direction* [1996] IRLR 430, para 16(4).

Preliminary hearing

19.28 The present *Practice Direction* provides a procedure for preliminary hearings. It does not apply to appeals heard in Scotland. At the discretion of the Employment Appeal Tribunal appeals may be listed as ex parte preliminary hearings to determine whether the grounds in the notice of appeal raise a reasonably arguable point of law so as to give the Appeal Tribunal jurisdiction to entertain and determine it at a full hearing.[1] Both parties will be notified of the decision to list the appeal as a preliminary hearing, but only the appellant and/or a representative should attend to make submissions to the Appeal Tribunal on the issue whether the notice of appeal raises a reasonably arguable point of law.[2] The respondent is not required to attend the hearing and is not usually permitted to take part in it.[3] If the appellant does not attend, the appeal may nevertheless be dealt with on written submissions and dismissed.[4] The preliminary hearing will normally last no more than one hour.[5] If satisfied that a reasonably arguable point of law is established, the Appeal Tribunal will give appropriate directions (for example, a time estimate, leave to amend the notice of appeal, or the production of chairman's notes, the exchange and lodging of skeleton arguments) to enable the appeal to proceed to a full hearing without unnecessary delay, on all or only some of the grounds of appeal.[6] If not satisfied that a reasonably arguable point of law is raised by the appeal, the Appeal Tribunal will give a judgment explaining why the appeal is dismissed at that stage.[7] Some preliminary hearings are listed to be heard in the list of the President of the Appeal Tribunal and will not be assigned for hearing by a particular tribunal until the day of the hearing. The appellant and/or his representative will be notified on their arrival at the Appeal Tribunal of the arrangements for the hearing of the appeal.[8] It is open to any respondent to an appeal to make a written application to the Appeal Tribunal on the service of the respondent's answer for the appeal to be listed as a preliminary hearing to determine whether it shall proceed further.[9] The preliminary hearing procedure may be applied to cross-appeals as well as to appeals.[10]

1 Employment Appeal Tribunal *Practice Direction* [1996] IRLR 430, para 14(1).
2 Employment Appeal Tribunal *Practice Direction* [1996] IRLR 430, para 14(2).
3 Employment Appeal Tribunal *Practice Direction* [1996] IRLR 430, para 14(2).
4 Employment Appeal Tribunal *Practice Direction* [1996] IRLR 430, para 14(2).
5 Employment Appeal Tribunal *Practice Direction* [1996] IRLR 430, para 14(3).
6 Employment Appeal Tribunal *Practice Direction* [1996] IRLR 430, para 14(4).
7 Employment Appeal Tribunal *Practice Direction* [1996] IRLR 430, para 14(5).
8 Employment Appeal Tribunal *Practice Direction* [1996] IRLR 430, para 14(6).
9 Employment Appeal Tribunal *Practice Direction* [1996] IRLR 430, para 14(7).
10 Employment Appeal Tribunal *Practice Direction* [1996] IRLR 430, para 14(8).

Procedural steps

19.29 On receipt of the notice of appeal, the Registrar seals the original notice, and serves sealed copies on the appellant and the other parties to the proceedings before the industrial tribunal, on the Secretary of Industrial Tribunals and on the Secretary of State for Trade and Industry in the case of an appeal relating to the redundancy payments provisions.[1]

1 Employment Appeal Tribunal Rules 1993, SI 1993/2854, r 4 and also r 5.

The answer

19.30 As soon as practicable, the Registrar notifies every respondent of the date which the Employment Appeal Tribunal has appointed by which any answer must be delivered.[1] A respondent who wishes to resist an appeal, should within this time limit deliver to the Appeal Tribunal an answer in writing, in, or substantially in, accordance with Form 3 in the Schedule to the Rules.[2] If a respondent has not delivered an answer as directed by the Registrar, he may be precluded from taking part in the appeal unless leave is granted to serve an answer out of time.[3] The answer should set out the grounds on which the respondent relies. If he wishes to rely on any ground which is the same as the ground relied on by the industrial tribunal for making the decision, or order, appealed from it is sufficient to state this in the answer.[4] A respondent may cross-appeal by including in the answer a statement of the grounds of his cross-appeal. In that event an appellant who wishes to resist the cross-appeal, should, within the time appointed by the Appeal Tribunal, deliver to it a reply in writing setting out the grounds on which he relies.[5] The Registrar serves a copy of every answer and reply to a cross-appeal on every party, other than the party by whom it was delivered.[6] Should the respondent not wish to resist an appeal the parties may deliver to the Appeal Tribunal an agreed draft of an order allowing the appeal and the Appeal Tribunal may, if it thinks it right to do so, make an order allowing the appeal in the terms agreed.[7]

1 Employment Appeal Tribunal Rules 1993, SI 1993/2854, r 6(1).
2 Employment Appeal Tribunal Rules 1993, r 6(2). For form, see Appendix 2.
3 Employment Appeal Tribunal *Practice Direction* [1996] IRLR 430, para 2(8).
4 Employment Appeal Tribunal Rules 1993, r 6(2).
5 Employment Appeal Tribunal Rules 1993, r 6(3).
6 Employment Appeal Tribunal Rules 1993, r 6(4).
7 Employment Appeal Tribunal Rules 1993, r 6(5).

19.31   As soon as practicable the Registrar gives notice of the arrangements made by the Employment Appeal Tribunal for hearing the appeal. The notice is given to every party to the proceedings, the Secretary of Industrial Tribunals and the Secretary of State for Trade and Industry, in the case of an appeal relating to the redundancy payments provisions, if he is not a respondent.[1] The notice will state the date appointed by the Appeal Tribunal by which any interlocutory application must be made.[2] On the application of any person, or of its own motion, the Appeal Tribunal may direct that any person not already a party to the proceedings, be added as a party, or that any party in the proceedings shall cease to be a party, and in either case may give such consequential directions as it considers necessary.[3]

1 Employment Appeal Tribunal Rules 1993, SI 1993/2854, r 7(1).
2 Employment Appeal Tribunal Rules 1993, r 7(2).
3 Employment Appeal Tribunal Rules 1993, r 18.

Interlocutory applications

19.32   Interlocutory application may be made to the Employment Appeal Tribunal by giving notice in writing specifying the direction and order sought.[1] The Registrar then serves a copy on every other party to the proceedings who appears to be concerned in the matter to which the notice relates, and notifies the applicant and every such party of the arrangements made by the Appeal Tribunal for disposing of the application.[2] Every interlocutory application is considered in the first place by the Registrar who will have regard to the just and economical disposal of the application, and to the expense which may be incurred by the parties in attending an oral hearing and where applicable r 23(5).[3] On receipt of an interlocutory application the Registrar sends a copy to the other side and will indicate that, if it is not intended to oppose the application it may be unnecessary for the parties to be heard and that the appropriate order may be made without an oral hearing.[4] Where the application is opposed the Registrar will usually determine the application on the basis of written submissions.[5]

1 Employment Appeal Tribunal Rules 1993, SI 1993/2854, r 19(1).
2 Employment Appeal Tribunal Rules 1993, r 19(2).
3 Employment Appeal Tribunal Rules 1993, r 20(1).
4 Employment Appeal Tribunal *Practice Direction* [1996] IRLR 430, para 4(1).
5 Employment Appeal Tribunal *Practice Direction* [1996] IRLR 430, para 4(2).

19.33 Every interlocutory application, other than for a restricted report-ing order, is disposed of by the Registrar, except that any matter which he thinks should properly be decided by the President, or a judge, is referred to the President or a judge. The President or judge may dispose of the matter himself, or refer it to a full Employment Appeal Tribunal or refer it back to the Registrar with such directions as he thinks fit.[1] Every applica-tion for a restricted reporting order is disposed of by the President or a judge or, if he so directs is referred to a full Appeal Tribunal to dispose of it.[2] Save where the President or any judge directs otherwise, every inter-locutory application to strike out an appeal or pleading, or to debar a party from taking any further part in the proceedings, will be heard on the day appointed for the hearing of the appeal immediately preceding the hearing thereof.[3] When an application is disposed of by the Registrar, a party who is aggrieved by his decision may appeal to a judge, and in that case the judge may determine the appeal himself, or refer the matter in whole, or in part, to the Appeal Tribunal.[4] Such notice of appeal may be given to the Appeal Tribunal, either orally or in writing, within five days of the decision appealed from, and the Registrar notifies every other party who appears to him to be concerned with the appeal, and informs those parties and the appellant of the arrangements made by the Appeal Tribunal for the disposing of it.[5] When hearing interlocutory applications the Appeal Tribunal may sit either in private or in public.[6] In a case where a minister of the Crown has given directions under s 28(5) of the Industrial Tribunals Act 1996 the hearing of the interlocutory application is heard by the President sitting alone.[7]

1 Employment Appeal Tribunal Rules 1993, SI 1993/2854, r 20(2).
2 Employment Appeal Tribunal Rules 1993, r 20(3).
3 Employment Appeal Tribunal *Practice Direction* [1996] IRLR 430, para 4(3).
4 Employment Appeal Tribunal Rules 1993, r 21(1).
5 Employment Appeal Tribunal Rules 1993, r 21 (2).
6 Employment Appeal Tribunal Rules 1993, r 22(1).
7 Employment Appeal Tribunal Rules 1993, r 22(2).

Directions

19.34 The Employment Appeal Tribunal may, either on its own motion, or application, at any stage in the proceedings appoint a date for giving of direc-tions as to the future conduct of proceedings, where it appears to it that their future conduct would thereby be facilitated.[1] In some cases the Registrar may, where necessary, appoint a day when the parties should attend on an appoint-ment for directions after the service of the respondents answer, or of a reply to a cross-appeal.[2] The Registrar normally gives written directions including fixing a date for hearing the appeal.[3] The Registrar gives to each party notice of the date appointed and any party applying for directions should, if practic-able, before that date give to the Appeal Tribunal particulars of the directions which he seeks.[4] The Registrar will then take such steps as may be practicable to inform the other parties of any directions which are sought.[5] On the date appointed, the Appeal Tribunal considers every application for directions, and any written representations relating to the applications submitted to the Appeal Tribunal, and gives such directions as it thinks fit for the purposes of securing the just, expeditious and economical disposal of the proceedings, including, where appropriate, directions as to conciliation to ensure that the parties are enabled to avail themselves of opportunities for conciliation.[6] Amongst other directions, the Appeal Tribunal has the right to direct as it thinks fit, as to the amendment of any notice, answer or any other document, the admission of any facts or documents, the admission in evidence of any documents, the mode in which evidence is to be given at the hearing and the consolidation of proceedings with any other proceedings pending before the Employment Appeal Tribunal.[7] In addition the Appeal Tribunal can, of course, issue directions as to the place and date of hearing,[8] and has power to deal with applications for further, or variation of, directions.[9] The Appeal Tribunal may of its own motion, at any stage, give parties directions as to any steps to be taken in relation to the proceedings.[10]

1 Employment Appeal Tribunal Rules 1993, SI 1993/2854, r 24(1).
2 Employment Appeal Tribunal *Practice Direction* [1996] IRLR 430, para 5.
3 Employment Appeal Tribunal *Practice Direction* [1996] IRLR 430, para 5.
4 Employment Appeal Tribunal Rules 1993, r 24(2).
5 Employment Appeal Tribunal Rules 1993, r 24(3).
6 Employment Appeal Tribunal Rules 1993, r 24(4). For conciliation, see **18.17–18.18**.
7 Employment Appeal Tribunal Rules 1993, r 24(5).
8 Employment Appeal Tribunal Rules 1993, r 24(5).
9 Employment Appeal Tribunal Rules 1993, r 24(6).
10 Employment Appeal Tribunal Rules 1993, r 25.

Failure to act in time

19.35 If a respondent fails to deliver an answer within the time appointed, or if a party fails to comply with an order, or direction, of the Appeal Tribunal, it may order that he be debarred from taking any further part in the proceedings or make such other order as it thinks just.[1]

1 Employment Appeal Tribunal Rules, SI 1993/2854, r 25. This is also the position if in the case of an application under the Trade Union and Labour Relations (Consolidation) Act 1992, ss 67, 176 or 136A there is a failure to deliver a notice appearance in time.

Exhibits and documents for use at the hearing

19.36 The Employment Appeal Tribunal will prepare copies of all documents for use by its members at the hearing, in addition to those which the Registrar is required to serve on the parties under the Employment Appeal Tribunal Rules.[1] The parties and their advisers should ensure that only those documents are included which are relevant to the point of law raised in the appeal and are likely to be referred to at the hearing. The relevant contract of employment should usually be included.[2] It is the responsibility of the parties or their advisers to ensure that all exhibits and documents used before the industrial tribunal which are considered to be necessary for use at the hearing of the appeal are sent to the Appeal Tribunal as soon as possible after the service of the notice of appeal, and at least six weeks before the date fixed for the hearing of the appeal. This enables the Appeal Tribunal staff to prepare in advance of the hearing sufficient copies, to number pages and to compile an index for the use of the members of the Appeal Tribunal at the hearing.[3] The parties should ensure that all documents submitted for consideration at the hearing are capable of being legibly photocopied.[4] At least four weeks before a full hearing a copy of the index is sent by the Appeal Tribunal to the parties or their advisers so that they may prepare their bundles of documents in the same order.[5]

1 Employment Appeal Tribunal *Practice Direction* [1996] IRLR 430, para 6(1).
2 Employment Appeal Tribunal *Practice Direction* [1996] IRLR 430, para 6(3).
3 Employment Appeal Tribunal *Practice Direction* [1996] IRLR 430, para 6(4).
4 Employment Appeal Tribunal *Practice Direction* [1996] IRLR 430, para 6(2).
5 Employment Appeal Tribunal *Practice Direction* [1996] IRLR 430, para 6(5).

Admissibility of documents

19.37 Where an application is made by a party to an appeal to put in at the hearing of the appeal any agreed document which was not before the industrial tribunal, the application should be submitted in writing as soon as practicable after the service of the respondent's answer along with copies of the documents sought to be admitted at the hearing. Such documents may include a note of evidence given to the industrial tribunal only if that note is agreed by both parties.[1] The Registrar will forthwith communicate the nature of the application and of the documents sought to be admitted to the other party and, where appropriate, to the chairman of the industrial tribunal for comments by him and, if appropriate, by the lay members.[2] A copy of the comments will be forwarded to the party making the application by the Registrar, who will either dispose of it in accordance with the Employment Appeal Tribunal Rules or refer it for a ruling at the hearing. A copy of the comments received from the chairman and lay members of the tribunal will be sent to both parties.[3]

1 Employment Appeal Tribunal *Practice Direction* [1996] IRLR 430, para 10(1).
2 Employment Appeal Tribunal *Practice Direction* [1996] IRLR 430, para 10(2).
3 Employment Appeal Tribunal *Practice Direction* [1996] IRLR 430, para 10(3).

Chairman's notes of evidence

19.38 In Scotland it is not the practice to provide the Appeal Tribunal with the chairman's notes of evidence. In England and Wales the position is different. The general rule is that the chairman's notes of evidence will not be provided to the parties.[1] An appellant who considers that a point of law raised in the notice of appeal cannot be argued without access to the chairman's notes of evidence should submit with the notice of appeal an application for production of the chairman's notes. If he does not do so he should make an application in writing as soon as possible after service of the notice of appeal.[2] Any other party seeking production of chairman's notes of evidence should make a written application for them to the Appeal Tribunal (not to the industrial tribunal) as soon as possible after the service of the notice of appeal and, in the case of a respondent, the application should accompany the respondent's answer.[3] In either case the application must explain why it is considered necessary to refer to the chairman's notes in order to argue the point of law raised in the notice of appeal or respondent's answer. In particular the application must identify:
(1)   the issues in the notice of appeal or respondent's answer to which the notes of evidence are relevant; and

(2) the names of the witnesses whose evidence is considered relevant; and
(3) the parts of their evidence alleged to be relevant.[4]

1 *Webb v Anglian Water Authority* [1981] IRLR 494, EAT.
2 Employment Appeal Tribunal *Practice Direction* [1996] IRLR 430, para 7(1).
3 Employment Appeal Tribunal *Practice Direction* [1996] IRLR 430, para 7(2).
4 Employment Appeal Tribunal *Practice Direction* [1996] IRLR 430, para 7(3). See *Piggott Bros and Co Ltd v Jackson* [1991] IRLR 309, CA, as to the position where perversity is alleged. The notes will only be ordered to be produced if necessary. So that if the grounds of appeal depend on a proposition of law which can be advanced on the assumption that the facts set out in the decision are correct, production of the notes is not necessary and will not normally be ordered: *Hawkins v Ball and Barclays Bank plc* [1996] IRLR 258, EAT.

19.39 The application for production of the chairman's notes will be considered in the first instance by the Registrar who may determine the application on written representations.[1] A party dissatisfied with the Registrar's decision on the application may request that the matter be referred to the President, or to a judge of the Employment Appeal Tribunal, who may direct an oral hearing of the application.[2] The Appeal Tribunal will only order production of the chairman's notes, and the supply of copies to the parties, if satisfied that all or parts of such notes are necessary for the purpose of arguing the point of law on the appeal.[3] Notes of evidence are not ordered to be produced and supplied to the parties to enable them to check, or double check, the reasoning or findings in the decision against evidence given to or submissions made at the hearing, or to enable the parties to embark on a 'fishing expedition' to establish grounds of appeal or additional grounds of appeal.[4]

1 Employment Appeal Tribunal *Practice Direction* [1996] IRLR 430, para 7(4).
2 Employment Appeal Tribunal *Practice Direction* [1996] IRLR 430, para 7(5).
3 Employment Appeal Tribunal *Practice Direction* [1996] IRLR 430, para 7(6).
4 Employment Appeal Tribunal *Practice Direction* [1996] IRLR 430, para 7(7).

19.40 Where there is a conflict between a chairman's notes of evidence and findings of facts as they appear in the reasons, the Employment Appeal Tribunal will be guided by the findings of fact in the reasons, unless there are pending circumstances which lead it to the conclusion that the reasons may inaccurately state the substance of the evidence.[1]

1 *Ogidi-Olu v Board of Governors of Guys Hospital* [1973] ICR 645, NIRC.

Complaints about the conduct of the hearing by the industrial tribunal

19.41 A special procedure is applicable if the appeal contains a complaint about the conduct of the hearing by the industrial tribunal. The Appeal Tribunal will not permit complaints of this kind to be raised or developed at the hearing of the appeal unless this procedure has been followed.[1] A party who intends to complain about the conduct of the industrial tribunal (for example, bias or improper conduct by the chairman or lay members, or procedural irregularities at the hearing) must include in the notice of appeal full and sufficient particulars of the complaint.[2] In any such case the Registrar may enquire of the party making the complaint whether it is intended to proceed with it. If so, the Registrar will give appropriate directions for the hearing.[3] The directions will normally include the swearing and filing of affidavits by the complainant, or his or her advisers, or other witnesses, or by the respondent, or his or her advisers, or any others, who can give relevant evidence as to the facts which form the basis of the complaint and the provision of further particulars of the matters relied on.[4] When the directions have been complied with the Registrar will notify the chairman of the industrial tribunal and provide copies of the notice of appeal, the affidavits and other relevant documents to the chairman so that he has and, if appropriate, the lay members of the industrial tribunal have, an opportunity to comment on them. Those comments will be supplied by the Appeal Tribunal to the parties.[5] A copy of any affidavit or of directions for further particulars will be supplied to the other side.[6]

1 Employment Appeal Tribunal *Practice Direction* [1996] IRLR 430, para 9(6).
2 Employment Appeal Tribunal *Practice Direction* [1996] IRLR 430, para 9(1).
3 Employment Appeal Tribunal *Practice Direction* [1996] IRLR 430, para 9(2).
4 Employment Appeal Tribunal *Practice Direction* [1996] IRLR 430, para 9(3).
5 Employment Appeal Tribunal *Practice Direction* [1996] IRLR 430, para 9(4).
6 Employment Appeal Tribunal *Practice Direction* [1996] IRLR 430, para 9(5).

Witness orders

19.42   The Employment Appeal Tribunal has power, on the application of any party, to order any person to attend before it as a witness, or to produce any document.[1] A person to whom such an order is directed is not treated as having failed to obey the order, unless at the time at which it was served on him, there was tendered a sufficient sum of money to cover his costs of attending before the Appeal Tribunal.[2] The Appeal Tribunal may, either on its own motion, or on application, require any evidence to be given on oath.[3]

1 Employment Appeal Tribunal Rules 1993, SI 1993/2854, r 27(1).
2 Employment Appeal Tribunal Rules 1993, r 27(2).
3 Employment Appeal Tribunal Rules 1993, r 28.

Time limits

19.43   Time limits prescribed by the Employment Appeal Tribunal Rules, or by order of the Employment Appeal Tribunal, may be extended (whether they have already expired or not), or abridged, and the date appointed for any purposes may be altered, by order of the Appeal Tribunal.[1] When the last day for doing any act falls on a day when the appropriate office of the Appeal Tribunal is closed, and by reason thereof the act cannot be done on that day, it may be done on the next day on which that office is open.[2] An application for the extension of the time prescribed for the doing of an act, including the institution of an appeal[3] is heard and determined as an interlocutory application.[4]

1 Employment Appeal Tribunal Rules, SI 1993/2854, r 37(1). It is possible that the Employment Appeal Tribunal has no power to extend time limits applicable before the industrial tribunal, for instance that relating to review. It may be that such matters are within the industrial tribunal's discretion only. See *Archbold Freightage Ltd v Wilson* (1974) 9 ITR 133 at p 135, NIRC.
2 Employment Appeal Tribunal Rules 1993, r 37(2).
3 Under the Employment Appeal Tribunal Rules 1993, r 3.
4 Employment Appeal Tribunal Rules 1993, r 37(3).

Notices

19.44   Failure to comply with requirements of the Employment Appeal Tribunal Rules does not invalidate proceedings unless the Employment Appeal Tribunal directs otherwise.[1] The Appeal Tribunal may even dispense with the taking of any step required, or authorised, by the Employment Appeal Tribunal Rules, or may direct that any such step be taken in some manner other than prescribed by the Employment Appeal Tribunal Rules, if it considers that to do so would lead to the more expeditious, or economical, disposal of any proceedings, or would otherwise be desirable in the interests of justice.[2] The Employment Appeal Tribunal Rules lay down specific provisions as to the service of notices and documents.[3] They may be sent to any person by post to his address for service, or where no address for service has been given, to his registered office, principal place of business, head, or main office, or last known address, as the case may be. Notices, or other documents, required, or authorised, to be served on, or delivered to, the Employment Appeal Tribunal may be sent by post, or delivered to, the Registrar. In the case of a notice instituting proceedings this should be sent by post or delivered to the Registrar at the Central Office, or any other office of the Appeal Tribunal, or in other cases at the office of the Appeal Tribunal in which the proceedings are being dealt with.[4] Notices, or documents, to be served on, or delivered to, an unincorporated body may be sent to its secretary, manager or similar officer.[5] Documents served by post are assumed in the absence of evidence to the contrary, to have been delivered in the normal course of post.[6] The Appeal Tribunal can inform itself in such manner as it thinks fit of the posting of any document by its officers,[7] and it has power to direct that service of any document be dispensed with, or effected otherwise than in a manner prescribed by the Employment Appeal Tribunal Rules.[8]

1 Employment Appeal Tribunal Rules 1993, SI 1993/2854, r 39(1).
2 Employment Appeal Tribunal Rules 1993, r 39(2). This power extends to authorising the institution of an appeal notwithstanding that the period for the appeal has not commenced: r 39(3).
3 Employment Appeal Tribunal Rules 1993, r 35.
4 Employment Appeal Tribunal Rules 1993, r 35(1).
5 Employment Appeal Tribunal Rules 1993, r 35(2).
6 Employment Appeal Tribunal Rules 1993, r 35(3).
7 Employment Appeal Tribunal Rules 1993, r 35(4).
8 Employment Appeal Tribunal Rules 1993, r 35(5).

Preparation for the hearing

Skeleton arguments

19.45 The 1996 *Practice Direction* makes specific provisions for the provision of skeleton arguments to the Employment Appeal Tribunal.[1] The provisions do not apply to appeals heard in Scotland, unless otherwise directed by the Employment Appeal Tribunal Office in Edinburgh. In England and Wales, skeleton arguments should be provided by all parties in the case of all appeals, unless the Appeal Tribunal otherwise directs in individual cases. The skeleton argument is an important document since in the view of the Appeal Tribunal well-structured skeleton argument helps the members and the parties to focus on the point of law raised by the appeal and thereby makes the oral hearing more effective.[2] It is the practice of the Appeal Tribunal for all the members to read the papers (including the skeleton arguments) in advance. Where a party is represented before the Appeal Tribunal it is the duty of the representative to obtain the instructions necessary to enable him or her to comply with the procedure as to skeleton arguments within the time limits. Failure to follow this procedure may lead to an adjournment of an appeal or even to dismissal for non-compliance with the *Practice Direction*.[3]

1 Employment Appeal Tribunal *Practice Direction* [1996] IRLR 430, para 8.
2 Employment Appeal Tribunal *Practice Direction* [1996] IRLR 430, para 8(1).
3 Employment Appeal Tribunal *Practice Direction* [1996] IRLR 430, para 8(9) and (10).

19.46 A skeleton argument should be concise and identify and summarise the points of law, the steps or stages in the legal argument and the statutory provisions and authorities to be relied upon, identifying them by name, page and paragraph and stating the legal proposition sought to be derived from them. The well-prepared skeleton argument will do this, but it should be remembered that the purpose of a skeleton argument is not to argue the case on paper in detail.[1] In addition to setting out argument the skeleton should state the form of order which the party will ask the Employment Appeal Tribunal to make on the appeal: for example, in the case of the appellant, whether the Appeal Tribunal will be asked to remit the whole or part of the case to the same industrial tribunal, or to a different industrial tribunal, or whether the Appeal Tribunal will be asked to substitute a different decision for that of the industrial tribunal.[2] The appellant's skeleton argument should be accompanied by a written chronology of events relevant to the appeal which, if possible, should be agreed by the parties. That will normally be taken as an uncontroversial document, unless corrected by the respondent or the Appeal Tribunal.[3] In a case where notes of evidence of the chairman of the industrial tribunal have been produced the skeleton argument should identify the parts of the notes to which that party wishes to refer. The skeleton argument should cross-refer to the particular passages in the notes relied on.[4] Where practicable the skeleton argument should be prepared using the pagination in the index to the appeal bundle.[4]

1 Employment Appeal Tribunal *Practice Direction* [1996] IRLR 430, para 8(2).
2 Employment Appeal Tribunal *Practice Direction* [1996] IRLR 430, para 8(3).
3 Employment Appeal Tribunal *Practice Direction* [1996] IRLR 430, para 8(4).
4 Employment Appeal Tribunal *Practice Direction* [1996] IRLR 430, para 8(7).

19.47 The skeleton argument should be prepared in good time. It may be served by the appellant with the notice of appeal or by the respondent with the respondent's answer or cross-appeal.[1] Skeleton arguments should be exchanged by the parties and copies should be served on the Appeal Tribunal not less than two weeks before the date fixed for the hearing of the full appeal. In the case of preliminary hearings, the skeleton argument should be served by the appellant on the Appeal Tribunal at least seven days before the hearing or, if the preliminary hearing is fixed at less than seven days' notice, as soon as possible after the hearing date has been notified.[2] The fact that settlement negotiations are in progress in relation to the appeal does not excuse delay in lodging and exchanging skeleton arguments.[3]

1 Employment Appeal Tribunal *Practice Direction* [1996] IRLR 430, para 8(5).
2 Employment Appeal Tribunal *Practice Direction* [1996] IRLR 430, para 8(6).
3 Employment Appeal Tribunal *Practice Direction* [1996] IRLR 430, para 8(8).

Fast-track appeals

19.48 Although full appeals are normally heard in the order in which they are received, the Employment Appeal Tribunal has introduced an helpful system to enable certain appeals to be fast-tracked. In these cases it is deemed expedient to hear the appeal as soon as it can be fitted into the list. Appeals are placed in this category at the discretion of the President, or the Registrar. They normally fall into the following categories:

(1) appeals involving new legislation or changes to industrial tribunal procedures;

(2) appeals involving reinstatement, re-engagement or interim relief;

(3) appeals on the outcome of which other applications to the industrial tribunal depend;

(4) appeals which are likely to go forward to the Court of Appeal or to the European Court of Justice;

(5) appeals (including appeals on time limits) against decisions of an industrial tribunal as to a party's entitlement to bring or contest proceedings;

(6) appeals concerning trade union rights under s 67(2) of the Trade Union and Labour Relations (Consolidation) Act 1992;

(7) appeals against interlocutory orders and directions of an industrial tribunal (for example, adjournments, particulars, amendments, discovery and witness orders);

(8) appeals where the parties have made a reasoned case on the merits for an expedited hearing.[1]

1 Employment Appeal Tribunal *Practice Direction* [1996] IRLR 430, para 12(1).

Listing

Estimates of length of hearing

19.49 In particular because of the membership of the Employment Appeal Tribunal by part-time lay members, estimating the length of hearings is of special importance to the Appeal Tribunal. To avoid inconvenience to the parties and to the Appeal Tribunal, and to avoid additional delay and costs suffered as a result of adjournment of part-heard appeals, both parties are required to ensure that the estimates of length of hearing are accurate when first given and that any change in the estimate is notified immediately to the listing office, even if it is made as late as the day of the hearing. If the tribunal concludes that the hearing is likely to exceed the estimate, it may seek to avoid such adjournment by placing each side under appropriate time limits in order to complete the presentation of the submissions within the estimated time.[1]

1 Employment Appeal Tribunal *Practice Direction* [1996] IRLR 430, para 12(2).

Listing practice in England and Wales

19.50 When all the appeal documents have been received and an index compiled, the parties will be contacted by the Employment Appeal Tribunal to agree a hearing date. Once the agreed date is fixed the appeal will be set down in the list. In addition to this fixed date procedure a list (called an 'undated warned list') is drawn up at the beginning of each calendar month. Parties or their representatives are notified that their case has been included in this list and preferred dates will be sought. When 'fixed date' cases are settled or withdrawn, cases from the 'undated warned list' will be substituted and parties notified as soon as possible of the hearing date. If a case in that list has been 'warned' but not reached, the parties may apply for a fixed date for hearing.[1] A party finding that the date which has been agreed causes serious difficulties may apply to the listing office to change the date before the 15th of the month in which the case first appears on the list. No change will be made to the listing, unless the listing officer agrees, but reasonable efforts will be made to accommodate parties in serious difficulties. Changes after the 15th of the month in which the list appears can only be made on application to the President or Registrar of the Employment Appeal Tribunal. Arrangements for the making of such an application should be through the listing office.[2] Other cases may be put in the list by the listing officer with the consent of the parties at shorter notice: for example, where other cases have been settled or withdrawn or where it appears that they will take less time than originally estimated. Parties who wish their cases to be taken as soon as possible and at short notice should notify the listing officer.[3] Each week an up-to-date list for the following week is prepared, including any changes which have been made, in particular specifying cases which by then have been given fixed dates.[4]

1 Employment Appeal Tribunal *Practice Direction* [1996] IRLR 430, para 12(3)(a).
2 Employment Appeal Tribunal *Practice Direction* [1996] IRLR 430, para 12(3)(b).
3 Employment Appeal Tribunal *Practice Direction* [1996] IRLR 430, para 12(3)(c).
4 Employment Appeal Tribunal *Practice Direction* [1996] IRLR 430, para 12(3)(d).

Listing practice in Scotland

19.51 When the respondent's answer has been received and a copy served on the appellant, both parties will be notified in writing that the appeal must be ready for hearing in approximately six weeks. The proposed date of hearing will be notified to the parties three or four weeks ahead. Any party who wishes to apply for a different date must do so within seven days of the receipt of such notification. Thereafter a formal notice of the date fixed for the hearing will be issued not less than 14 days in advance. This will be a peremptory direction. It will not be discharged, except by the judge on cause shown.[1]

1 Employment Appeal Tribunal *Practice Direction* [1996] IRLR 430, para 12(4).

The hearing

19.52 The oral hearings at which any proceedings before the Employment Appeal Tribunal are finally disposed of, take place before such members of the Appeal Tribunal as the President may nominate subject to the rule mentioned above. The hearing will normally take place in public,[1] but the Appeal Tribunal may sit in private for the purpose of:
(1) hearing evidence which in the opinion of the Appeal Tribunal relates to matters of such a nature that it would be against the interests of national security to allow the evidence to be given in public; or
(2) to hear evidence from any person which in its opinion is likely to consist of:
    (a) information he could not disclose without contravening a prohibition imposed by, or under, any enactment; or
    (b) any information which has been communicated to him in confidence, or which he otherwise obtained in consequence of the confidence reposed in him by another person; or

(c)   information the disclosure of which would cause substantial injury to an undertaking of his or any undertaking in which he works for reasons other than its effect on any negotiations with respect to matters mentioned in s 244(1) of the Trade Union and Labour Relations (Consolidation) Act 1992.[2]

The Appeal Tribunal will sit in private in circumstances in which an industrial tribunal is required to sit in private (see **18.65**).

1 Employment Appeal Tribunal Rules 1993, SI 1993/2854, r 29(1).
2 Employment Appeal Tribunal Rules 1993, r 29(2).

Representation and authority

19.53   Parties may appear before the Employment Appeal Tribunal in person, or be represented by counsel, or by a solicitor, or a representative of a trade union, or employers' association, or by any other person whom they desire to represent them.[1] The Appeal Tribunal is bound by decisions of the Court of Appeal and the House of Lords on matters of law of England and of the Court of Session Inner House and House of Lords on matters of law in Scotland which are binding on it. Decisions of the National Industrial Relations Court, the High Court in England and the Court of Session Outer House in Scotland are of great persuasive authority and the Appeal Tribunal does not lightly differ from the principles which are found therein.[2]

1 Industrial Tribunals Act 1996, s 29(1).
2 *Portec (UK) Ltd v Mogensen* [1976] ICR 396 at p 400, EAT. In England and Wales it will only depart from a decision of the Court of Session on a point of employment law on a matter which purely relates to English law and will only depart from a decision of the Court of Appeal on a point of employment law on a matter which purely relates to Scots law: *Brown v Rentokil Ltd* [1992] IRLR 302, EAT.

Citation of authorities

19.54   Lists of authorities, limited to those necessary for arguing the point of law on the appeal, should be sent to the librarian of the Employment Appeal Tribunal using the form provided or by fax not less than 24 hours before the appeal is due to be heard.[1] It is undesirable for parties to cite the same case from different sets of reports. The parties should, if practicable, agree upon which report will be used at the hearing.[2] If an unreported case is to be cited by a party, it is the responsibility of the party citing such a case to provide photocopies for the use of each member of the Tribunal and to the other party to the hearing. The same applies to cases not reported in the principal series of law reports, to foreign cases and to extracts from textbooks and periodicals.[3] Parties are advised not to cite an unnecessary number of authorities either in skeleton arguments or in oral argument at the hearing. It is rarely necessary to cite more than one case for a legal proposition. It is a waste of the parties' time and of the Appeal Tribunal's time for parties or representatives to cite cases unnecessarily. It is of assistance to the Appeal Tribunal if parties attach photocopies of the most important authorities to the skeleton arguments submitted by them and highlight the passages relied on by them.[4] Only in exceptional circumstances will it be necessary to cite any authority at a preliminary hearing.[5] In the case of reports of decisions of the European Court of Justice, the official report should be used where possible, although it is appreciated by the Appeal Tribunal that there is a long time-lag in the reporting of cases in the official series.[6] It is often unnecessary for a party citing a case in oral argument to read it in full to the Appeal Tribunal. Whenever a case is cited in a skeleton argument or in an oral argument the legal proposition for which it is cited should be stated. References need only be made to the relevant passages in the report. If the formulation of the legal proposition based on the authority cited is not in dispute, further examination of the authority will often be unnecessary.[7]

1 Employment Appeal Tribunal *Practice Direction* [1996] IRLR 430, para 15(1).
2 Employment Appeal Tribunal *Practice Direction* [1996] IRLR 430, para 15(2).
3 Employment Appeal Tribunal *Practice Direction* [1996] IRLR 430, para 15(3).
4 Employment Appeal Tribunal *Practice Direction* [1996] IRLR 430, para 15(4).
5 Employment Appeal Tribunal *Practice Direction* [1996] IRLR 430, para 15(5).
6 Employment Appeal Tribunal *Practice Direction* [1996] IRLR 430, para 15(6).
7 Employment Appeal Tribunal *Practice Direction* [1996] IRLR 430, para 15(7).

The decision

19.55 If the members of the Appeal Tribunal are not unanimous the decision is taken by the majority.[1] Orders of the Appeal Tribunal are drawn up by the Registrar and a copy bearing the Appeal Tribunal's seal is served by the Registrar on every party to the proceedings to which it relates, and so far as appeals from industrial tribunals and restricted proceedings orders are concerned, on the Secretary of Industrial Tribunals.[2] On the application of any party made within 14 days after the making of an order finally disposing of proceedings, the Appeal Tribunal will give its reasons in writing for the order, unless it was made after the delivery of a reasoned judgment.[3] The Employment Appeal Tribunal can dismiss or uphold the appeal. Where the Appeal Tribunal finds that the industrial tribunal erred in law in finding that an employee was unfairly dismissed it will remit the case to the industrial tribunal unless no industrial tribunal, properly directing itself, could have come to the conclusion that the employee was not unfairly dismissed.[4]

1 A former President of the Employment Appeal Tribunal has said that where the expert members of the Appeal Tribunal are not in agreement upon a matter which is particularly within their competence to decide, the correct approach is to come down in favour of affirming the decision appealed from, especially where the expert members of the industrial tribunal were in agreement: *Marley Tile Co Ltd v Shaw* [1978] IRLR 238, EAT. This decision was overruled on other grounds [1980] IRLR 25, CA. Where the knowledge and experience of the industrial members of the Appeal Tribunal has played a decisive part in its decision the precise considerations should be spelled out: *British Coal Corpn v Cheesbrough* [1988] IRLR 351, CA.
2 Employment Appeal Tribunal Rules 1993, SI 1993/2854, r 31(1).
3 Employment Appeal Tribunal Rules 1993, r 31(2).
4 *Morgan v Electrolux Ltd* [1991] IRLR 89, CA. The Appeal Tribunal should remit the case unless there was only one possible outcome if the law was applied properly: *Westminster City Council v Cabaj* [1996] IRLR 399, CA.

Disposal of appeals by consent

19.56 An appellant who wishes to abandon or withdraw an appeal should notify the respondent and the Employment Appeal Tribunal immediately. If a settlement is reached the parties should inform the Appeal Tribunal as soon as possible.[1] The appellant should submit to the Appeal Tribunal a letter signed by the appellant, or on the appellant's behalf, and signed also by, or on behalf of, the respondent, asking the Appeal Tribunal for leave to withdraw the appeal and to make a consent order in the form of an attached draft signed by both parties dismissing the appeal, together with any other agreed order.[2] If the respondent does not agree to the proposed order (where, for example, the respondent wishes to apply for an order for costs against the appellant) the Appeal Tribunal should be informed. In such cases it will be necessary to fix an oral hearing to determine the outstanding matters in dispute between the parties.[3] If the parties reach an agreement that the appeal should be allowed by consent and that an order made by the industrial tribunal should be reversed or varied or the matter remitted to the industrial tribunal on the ground that the decision contains an error of law, it is usually necessary for the matter to be heard by the Appeal Tribunal to determine whether there is a good reason for making the order which both parties agree should be made. In order to save costs, it may be appropriate for the appellant or a representative only to attend to argue the case for allowing the appeal and making the order that the parties wish the Appeal Tribunal to make.[4] If the application for leave to withdraw an appeal is made close to the hearing date the Appeal Tribunal may require the attendance of the appellant and/or a representative to explain the reasons for delay in making a decision not to pursue the appeal.[5]

1 Employment Appeal Tribunal *Practice Direction* [1996] IRLR 430, para 13(1).
2 Employment Appeal Tribunal *Practice Direction* [1996] IRLR 430, para 13(2).
3 Employment Appeal Tribunal *Practice Direction* [1996] IRLR 430, para 13(3).
4 Employment Appeal Tribunal *Practice Direction* [1996] IRLR 430, para 13(4). See *J Sainsbury plc v Moger* [1994] ICR 800, EAT. In general the Appeal Tribunal will not make an order by consent if there is no overall settlement of the issue between the parties.
5 Employment Appeal Tribunal *Practice Direction* [1996] IRLR 430, para 13(5).

Handing down judgments

19.57 When the Employment Appeal Tribunal reserves judgment, the parties will be notified of the date when it is ready to be handed down.[1] Copies of the judgment may be made available to the parties or their representatives on the morning of the day on which it is handed down.[2] Copies may be made available on the previous day, subject to terms as to confidentiality, if so directed by the President or a judge of the Appeal Tribunal after request by the representatives of both parties to the clerk to the President or the judge of the Appeal Tribunal. Copies will be made available to recognised law reporters.[3] The judgment will be pronounced without being read aloud.[4] Applications for leave to appeal to the Court of Appeal and other applications (for example, costs) may be made either when the judgment is handed down or by written application soon after.[5]

1 Employment Appeal Tribunal *Practice Direction* [1996] IRLR 430, para 17(1).
2 Employment Appeal Tribunal *Practice Direction* [1996] IRLR 430, para 17(2).
3 Employment Appeal Tribunal *Practice Direction* [1996] IRLR 430, para 17(2).
4 Employment Appeal Tribunal *Practice Direction* [1996] IRLR 430, para 17(3).
5 Employment Appeal Tribunal *Practice Direction* [1996] IRLR 430, para 17(4).

Reviews

19.58 The Employment Appeal Tribunal may, either on its own motion, or on application, review any order made by it and may on such review revoke, or vary, the order. This can take place on the grounds that the order was wrongly made as a result of an error on the part of the Appeal Tribunal or its staff, a party did not receive proper notice of the proceedings leading to the order, or the interests of justice require such review.[1] The application for review should be made within 14 days of the date of the order.[2] There is a 'slip rule' providing for a clerical mistake in any order arising from an accidental slip or omission to be corrected at any time by or on the authority of a judge or member.[3] As a superior court of record the Employment Appeal Tribunal has an inherent power to reconsider any judgment or order before it is perfected.[4] This not superseded by the right of review contained in the Employment Appeal Rules.[5]

1 Employment Appeal Tribunal Rules 1993, SI 1993/2854, r 33(1). It is good practice for the Appeal Tribunal to give brief written reasons for refusing an application for review: *Persson v Matra Marconi Space UK Ltd* (1996) Times, 10 December, CA.
2 Employment Appeal Tribunal Rules 1993, r 33(2).
3 Employment Appeal Tribunal Rules 1993, r 33(3).
4 *Bass Leisure Ltd v Thomas* [1994] IRLR 104, EAT.
5 *Bass Leisure Ltd v Thomas* [1994] IRLR 104, EAT.

Costs

19.59 Where it appears to the Employment Appeal Tribunal that any proceedings were unnecessary, improper or vexatious, or that there has been unreasonable delay, or other unreasonable conduct in bringing, or conducting, the proceedings, the Appeal Tribunal may order the party at fault pay to any other party the whole, or such part as it thinks fit, of the costs or expenses incurred by that other party in connection with the proceedings.[1] When making such an order the Appeal Tribunal may assess the sum to be paid, or direct that it be assessed by a taxing officer from whose decision an appeal lies to a judge.[2] The judge may determine the appeal himself, or refer it to the Employment Appeal Tribunal, which may sit either in private or in public to deal with the appeal.[3]

1 Employment Appeal Tribunal Rules 1993, SI 1993/2854, r 34(1). An error of law is not sufficient: see *White v Manchester University* [1976] ICR 419, EAT. In this case the then President of the Appeal Tribunal, Phillips J, drew attention to the particularly restrictive nature of the costs rule. In a case where the application was made on a wholly mistaken basis, a careful review had been carried out by the industrial tribunal and the Registrar had written to the applicant explaining the difficulty and had drawn attention to the possible peril in relation to costs, but the applicant still persevered with her appeal, she was ordered to pay £25 towards the respondent's costs: *Wilson v Underhill House School Ltd* [1977] IRLR 475, EAT. An example of unreasonable delay occurred in *TVR Engineering Ltd v Johnson* [1978] IRLR 555, EAT. The employers entered a notice of appeal on 10 February 1978 and made a request for the notes of evidence taken at the industrial tribunal hearing. These were sent to the employer's solicitors on 19 April 1978. The hearing was fixed to take place on 21 July and on 12 July notice was sent to the Employment Appeal Tribunal and to the respondent employee's solicitors stating that the appellants withdrew the appeal. The respondent's solicitors asked for the whole of the costs incurred as a result of the appeal. The Appeal Tribunal of which the then President, Slynn J, was chairman, held that it was justifiable for the notice of appeal to be entered, but a period of two months was sufficient for solicitors and counsel to consider the notes of evidence and advise the appellants as to whether they should proceed with the appeal. Thus if the appellants and their advisers had behaved with reasonable despatch the decision could readily have been arrived at by the middle of June. Accordingly the appellants were ordered to pay the respondent's costs incurred subsequent to 15 June 1978. In *Croydon v Greenham (Plant Hire) Ltd* [1978] ICR 415, EAT, an employee who appealed and made written submissions asking that the Appeal Tribunal should hear his appeal in his absence was ordered to pay £50 towards the costs of the appeal of the respondents. In a case where, had the company taken counsel's opinion before launching the appeal they would have been advised that the appeal would be a non-starter because no point of law could be raised which had the remotest chance of success, their conduct was found to be unreasonable and costs were awarded against them in favour of the respondent employee: *Redland Roof Tiles Ltd v Eveleigh* [1979] IRLR 11, EAT. In

delivering the decision of the Appeal Tribunal Bristow J said (at p 12) 'Counsel's opinion is of course in some situations a luxury, but hardly a luxury in this situation for this company'. For recent examples where costs were awarded see *South Durham Health Authority v UNISON* [1995] IRLR 407, EAT; and *Reddington v Straker & Sons Ltd* [1994] ICR 172, EAT.
2 Employment Appeal Tribunal Rules 1993, r 34(2). For an example see *McConnell v Bolik* [1979] IRLR 422, EAT.
3 Employment Appeal Tribunal Rules 1993, r 34(3), applying rr 21 and 22.

Conciliation

19.60 The Tribunal does have power at any stage in the proceedings where it appears to it that there is reasonable prospect of agreement being reached between the parties, to take such steps as it thinks fit to enable them to avail themselves of any opportunities for conciliation whether by adjournment of proceedings, or otherwise.[1]

1 Employment Appeal Tribunal Rules 1993, SI 1993/2854, r 36. For conciliation, see **18.17–18.18.** For an example of a direction in accordance with the rule, see *Pambakian v Brentford Nylons Ltd* [1978] ICR 665, EAT.

Appeals from the Employment Appeal Tribunal

19.61 Subject to the above provisions, and without prejudice to the rules laid down in the Administration of Justice Act 1960, s 13 (appeals in cases of contempt of court), an appeal lies on any question of law from a decision or order of the Employment Appeal Tribunal with leave of the Tribunal, or of the Court of Appeal, or as the case may be, the Court of Session, in the case of proceedings in England and Wales to the Court of Appeal, or in the case of proceedings in Scotland, to the Court of Session.[1] Subject to any order made by the Court of Appeal, or Court of Session, and to any directions given by the Appeal Tribunal, an appeal from the Tribunal does not suspend the enforcement of any order by it.[2] Legal aid is available on such an appeal according to the usual rules. The normal requirements apply to appeals from the Court of Appeal or Court of Session.

1 Industrial Tribunals Act 1996, s 37. The fact that a case is the first before the Employment Appeal Tribunal under a new statutory provision is not of itself a reason for granting leave: *Medhurst v NALGO* [1992] IRLR 229, CA.
2 Employment Appeal Tribunal Rules 1993, SI 1993/2854, r 31(3).

Inspecting the register and documents and taking copies

19.62 As mentioned above, the Employment Appeal Tribunal maintains a register. The public have certain rights to inspect the register and to take copies of certain documents including judgments of the Appeal Tribunal.[1]

1 Details can be found in the Employment Appeal Tribunal *Practice Direction* [1996] IRLR 430, para 11.

Appendix 1

Checklists

Checklist 1

On engagement

1.   Use of employment application form.[1]
2.   Is the applicant eligible for the employment?[2]
3.   No discrimination on grounds of:
     (a) sex or marital status;[3]
     (b) race or colour;[4]
     (c) disability.[5]
4.   Is a work permit necessary?
5.   Convictions for criminal offences by applicant.
6.   Fixed term contract? Exclusion of statutory rights.
7.   A probationary period?[6] If so, ensure that it is explained and expressed as such in letter of appointment.
8.   Explain the provisions of the contract which affect the applicant. A useful way of dealing with this could be to refer to the statement of written particulars of terms of employment to be issued in accordance with the statutory obligation.[7]
9.   As a matter of practice, in the letter of appointment refer to the statement of written particulars of terms of employment.[8]
10.   If the statement of written particulars of terms of employment refers to other documents, explain to the prospective employee where these are available.[9]
11.   If the applicant is to be a replacement for an employee suspended on medical grounds, or for an employee absent wholly, or partly, because of pregnancy or confinement, and it is intended in due course to dismiss the replacement to allow the other employee to resume work, the statutory procedure must be gone through.[10]

---

1   The practice of using a written form of application for employment has much to commend it. See specimen job application form below.
2   Specific requirements of statutes and regulations (for instance those made under the Health and Safety at Work etc Act 1974). Does the applicant have the qualifications necessary for the employment?
3   See 7.07.
4   See 7.53.
5   See 7.120.
6   This may be advantageous in resisting a claim for unfair dismissal. However, any benefit from such an arrangement will usually only arise if the employee is aware that the appointment is probationary when it is accepted by him.
7   If the statement is used in this way, the terms of employment will be clear to the employee on engagement.
8   See Chapter 9 for provisions as to the statement. There is no requirement for the statement to be supplied at this stage but to do so avoids misunderstandings.

9 It is essential that any document referred to is available to the employee when the statement under the Employment Rights Act 1996 has to be given to the employee, and an explanation on engagement may prevent future difficulties.
10 See 7.100.

Job application form

XYZ & Co Limited

EMPLOYMENT APPLICATION

Please complete by inserting replies to all the following questions. If you have any difficulties please ask for help.

Surname   ....   Forenames   ....
Title: Mr/Miss/Mrs/Ms/other   ....
Address   ....
   ....
   ....
Telephone number   ....

Contact name, telephone and address for contact in cases of emergency. Please give details of relationship to you – for instance, husband, wife, partner, friend ....
....

[*If you wish, this information need not be given at the present time, but must be given as soon as possible if appointed*]

Sex   ....

Date of birth   ....

Marital status: single/married/divorced   ....

Number of children   ....

Job applied for   ....

How did you learn of the vacancy   ....

Have you been convicted of, or warned of any possible proceedings in respect of, any offence? [*Note: do not give details of a 'spent conviction' under the Rehabilitation of Offenders Act*] If so set out details   ....
....

Driving licence. Please complete details of current driving licence:

No   ....   Type   ....
Date of expiry   ....
When did you pass the test for this licence?   ....
(a)   Have you been convicted of any motoring offence?   ....
(b)   Have you been warned of, or know of, any circumstances which may give rise to possible proceedings in respect of any motoring offence?   ....
If the answer to (a) or (b) is yes please give details   ....
....

Give details of education since and excluding secondary school:

Institution	Subjects studied	Dates	Full-time/ part-time

Give details of qualifications relevant to the post applied for:

Qualification	Awarding body	Subjects included	Class of award (if applicable)	Date of award

Give details of prior experience relevant to the post applied for (in reverse chronological order, ie most recent experience first):

Company	Job	Dates of employment	Reason for leaving

Do you know of anyone who works here? If so, who? ....

Are you a member of a professional body/bodies? If so, please provide full details ....

Medical and health particulars

These details are required in the interest of yourself and your fellow workers. They will be dealt with in confidence.

Please list any diseases, disorders, allergies, medical, physical or psychological from which you suffer ....
....

Provide details of any medicine, drugs, treatment or therapy which you receive regularly ....
....

I confirm that all the above information is correct and that I wish to be considered for appointment for the job to which it relates.

Signed .... Date ....

Checklist 2

Preparation of written statement of terms of employment[1]

1. Name and address of employer.
2. Name and address of employee.
3. Date on which terms are to be stated.[2]
4. Date of commencement of period of continuous employment.
5. Title of employment.

6.   Job description.
7.   Place of employment.
8.   Remuneration. [*Be certain to include all matters such as details of overtime payments, bonuses etc.*]
9.   Hours. [*Include some provision for overtime or other extra hours if required from time to time.*]
10.   Holidays. [*Rules as to holidays and payment in respect of holiday pay on leaving.*]
11.   Incapacity due to sickness or injury and absences from work. [*Rules as to payment, reporting, medical examination etc.*]
12.   Pensions. [*Whether employer does or does not operate a pension scheme applicable to the employment. Is a contracting-out certificate in force in respect of the employment?*]
13.   Provisions as to notice by employee and employer.
14.   Disciplinary rules.
15.   Redress of grievances.
16.   Additional particulars, for instance relating to probationary period.
17.   Amendment. [*Consider whether to include any provision as to amendment.*]

1   This checklist should be readily adapted to fit most situations encountered in practice. If there are no particulars to be included under any head this should be stated. For the requirements for the written particulars, see Chapter 9.
2   This date must be a date not more than seven days before the statement is given.

Checklist 3

Constructive dismissal[1]

1.   Was there a contractual term:
    (a) express?
    (b) implied?
2.   If so, what were its provisions?
3.   Was it broken? Were the employer's actions authorised by the contract?
4.   If so, was the breach repudiatory? Did it go to the basis of the relationship between the parties?
5.   Was the breach 'accepted' by the employee? Did the employee terminate the employment? Was the termination caused by the repudiatory breach of contract by the employee and not some other factor?
6.   Was the 'acceptance' before the employee had affirmed the contract?

1   See 15.47.

Checklist 4

Time limits

	Time limits	Extending time	Qualification period	Reference in text
Particulars of employment	3 months	Not reasonably practicable	1 month	Chapter 9
Unlawful deductions	3 months	Not reasonably practicable	None	Chapter 6
Arrears of pay	3 months	Not reasonably practicable	None	Chapter 6
Holiday pay	3 months	Not reasonably practicable	None	Chapter 6, 4.52–4.54
Medical suspension	3 months	Not reasonably practicable	1 month	4.24–4.28
Written reasons for dismissal	3 months	Not reasonably practicable	2 years	13.54–13.57
Guarantee payment	3 months	Not reasonably practicable	1 month	4.35–4.45
Itemised pay statement	3 months	Not reasonably practicable	None	4.12–4.16
Equal pay	6 months from end of employment		None	Chapter 5
Sex discrimination	3 months	Just and equitable	None	Chapter 7
Time off work for ante-natal care	3 months	Not reasonably practicable	None	Chapter 7
Right to return to work after maternity leave	3 months	Not reasonably practicable	None	Chapter 7
Unfair dismissal because of pregnancy	3 months	Not reasonably practicable	None	Chapter 7
Race discrimination	3 months	Just and equitable	None	Chapter 7
Disability discrimination	3 months	Just and equitable	None	Chapter 7
Breach of contract	3 months	Not reasonably practicable	None	13.60
Money in lieu of notice	3 months	Not reasonably practicable	None	13.60
Counterclaim	6 weeks	Not reasonably practicable	None	13.60
Time off for trade union activities	3 months	Not reasonably practicable	None	14.34–14.37
Time off for public duties	3 months	Not reasonably practicable	None	4.55–4.59
Time off for pension trustee	3 months	Not reasonably practicable	None	4.61
Time off for safety representative	3 months	Not reasonably practicable	None	4.66
Time off to look for work when redundant	3 months	Not reasonably practicable	2 years	16.95
Dismissal for union or non-union membership	3 months	Not reasonably practicable	None	14.28–14.34
Refusal to employ for union and non-union membership	3 months	Not reasonably practicable	None	14.01–14.09
Action short of dismissal	3 months	Not reasonably practicable	None	14.11–14.27
Interim relief	7 days	Not reasonably practicable	None	14.32–14.33 and 15.167
Unfair dismissal	3 months	Not reasonably practicable	2 years	Chapter 15
Unfair dismissal as a result of medical suspension	3 months	Not reasonably practicable	1 month	15.14

Redundancy	6 months	6 months if reasonable	2 years	Chapter 16 16.112–16.118
Redundancy consultation	3 months	Not reasonably practicable	None	12.31–12.35
TUPE consultation	3 months	Not reasonably practicable	None	
Rights in insolvency	3 months	Not reasonably practicable	None	17.02–17.06

1 The time limits shown relate to claims to industrial tribunals.

2 The information given is that generally applicable to claims under the stated head. Reference should also be made to the appropriate paragraph in the text. The information given may be subject to certain further limits or to exceptions.

3 Time commences on the date which is appropriate to the claim. Generally 'extensions' to dates, for example, to the effective date of termination, do **not** extend to the time for making claims to industrial tribunals.

4 The two year time limit is subject to challenge.

Checklist 5

Handling redundancies[1]

1.   Number of employees at any one establishment to be dismissed (exclude those previously taken into account)?
2.   Are there employees' representatives? If not, should employees be invited to elect employees' representatives?
3.   Is there an independent trade union[s] recognised in respect of employees?
4.   Ascertain period during which dismissals are to take effect?
5.   Are there special circumstances for departing from the statutory procedure?
6.   Consider methods of selection.
     (a) Is there a customary arrangement or an agreed procedure relating to redundancy? If so, is it to be followed? If not, what steps are to be taken to change it?
     (b) Ensure that no dismissal will be on grounds relating to union membership or activities.
     (c) Consider dismissal of those over retiring age and volunteers.
     (d) Establish justifiable, clear and objective criteria for selection of those to be made redundant.
     (e) Ensure that there are procedures established to apply the criteria objectively to effect selection.
     (f) Make arrangements to ascertain whether those to be redundant can be offered alternative employment, be redeployed, trained or found employment with any associated employer.
     (g) Consider whether criteria could lead to claims of unlawful discrimination on grounds of sex, race or disability.
7.   Begin consultation with appropriate representatives in good time. Remember the statutory provisions as to minimum periods and disclosure in writing.
8.   Give proper warning of redundancy.
9.   Notify Secretary of State under provisions as to handling redundancies. Bear in mind minimum notice.
10.   Consider and reply to representations made by appropriate representatives.
11.   Consider holding 'at risk' interviews with those likely to be selected.
12.   Continue the consultation process for as long as it is productive.
13.   Effect selection of those to be made redundant, taking care to ensure that selection takes place objectively in accordance with the established criteria. At all times ensure the employer acts fairly.
14.   Offer alternative employment if available for redundant employees (even if it may mean what may be thought to be unacceptable reduction in status).
15.   Having ensured that the redundancies comply with agreed procedures and employer has acted fairly, issue dismissal notices.
16.   Comply with requirements for redundant employees to be given time off for training and to seek other employment.
17.   At time dismissal takes effect pay redundancy payments, giving statement of calculation and obtain receipts.
18.   Ensure redundant employees paid other entitlements: payment in lieu of notice, accrued holiday pay, bonus payments, etc.

19.   Advise redundant employees as to their options and entitlements under pension and life assurance schemes.

20.   Outplacement advice for redundant employees?

1 See **16.110**. Ensure that at all stages contemporaneous records are kept of all action taken by employer so that it can be referred to at any tribunal hearing.

Checklist 6

Claims for redundancy payments: applicant's representative

(in cases of claims other than in circumstances of lay-off and short-time)

1.   Is the potential claim pursuant to the statutory provisions of the Employment Rights Act 1996, another statutory scheme or another 'exempt' scheme?[1] If not within the Employment Rights Act 1996, obtain details of the scheme.

2.   Ascertain the date from which time in which to make application to the tribunal runs and latest date by which application must be lodged at the Office (or a Regional Office) of the Industrial Tribunals.[2]

3.   Is the applicant entitled to claim a redundancy payment? Ie:
   (a) was the applicant an employee?[3]
   (b) was the employment within the scope of the redundancy payment provisions?[4]
   (c) does the applicant have sufficient continuity of employment? Has the applicant received a redundancy payment in respect of earlier service?[5] and
   (d) does the applicant's age preclude a claim for redundancy payment?[6]
   (e) is the contract of employment illegal?[7]
   (f) was the right to claim a redundancy payment excluded by agreement where the dismissal is the expiry of a fixed term contract?[8]

4.   Do the circumstances of the termination of the employment constitute a dismissal?[9] [*Bear in mind that dismissal includes constructive dismissal and certain other events.*] Check that the contract of employment was not discharged by either consensual agreement or those events which do not amount to dismissal.

5.   Was the dismissal for redundancy alone? Should the application include claims for unfair dismissal, and/or for sex and/or race and/or disability discrimination and/or under the Employment Rights Act 1996 and/or for breach of contract.[10] Remember that the time limits for such claims are not the same as for redundancy.[11]

6.   Does the employer have a defence based on the offer of suitable alternative employment?[12]

7.   Does the employer have a defence based on the employee's conduct?[13]

8.   Check the identity of the employer. Ensure that name and address of employer is correct. Is the address of a corporate employer its registered office?

9.   Is there an issue as to who was the applicant's employer? Should any other respondent be joined?

10.   Is the employer solvent? Should application be made under the insolvency provisions?[14]

11.   Consider continuity of employment;[15] in particular whether there has been continuity of employment where there has been a change in the identity of the employer and whether or not a redundancy payment has been made which breaks the continuity.[16]

12.   Consider whether any payment made purports to be a redundancy payment and, if so, whether it complies with the statutory requirements and is correctly calculated.[17]

13.   Are there circumstances in which a payment made or pension to be paid may be set off against the redundancy payment?[18]

14.   Draw, complete and lodge originating application to industrial tribunal in good time.[19]

15.   Consider checklist as to interlocutory matters before industrial tribunals.

16.   Consider checklists for advocates before industrial tribunals.

17.   Was the applicant in an occupational pension and/or life assurance scheme? What was the nature of the scheme? Consider any options there are for the applicant under that scheme and whether he should receive specialist professional advice with regard to it. [*It is to be noted that the time allowed for exercise of some options, particularly those enabling former employees to continue life assurance at standard rates, is often very short.*]

18.   Consider all matters in the checklists for interlocutory matters and preparation for tribunal hearing.

1   See Chapter 16.
2   In Scotland the application should be presented at the Glasgow office only. See time limit checklist, Checklist 4.
3   See 3.15.
4   See 16.05.
5   See 16.02.
6   See 16.09.
7   See 16.01.
8   See 16.10.
9   See 16.26.
10   See time limit checklist, Checklist 4.
11   See Checklist 4.
12   See 16.60.
13   See 16.76.
14   See Chapter 17.
15   See 16.02.
16   See Chapter 12.
17   See 16.94.
18   See 16.78.
19   See 18.30.

Claims for redundancy payments: respondent's representative

(in cases of claims other than in circumstances of lay-off and short-time)

1.   Does the originating application have other claims such as unfair dismissal implicit within it?[1]

2.   Is the claim pursuant to the statutory provisions of the Employment Rights Act 1996, another statutory scheme or another 'exempt' scheme?[2] If not within the Employment Rights Act 1996, obtain details of the scheme.

3.   Is the application within time?[3]

4.   Is the applicant entitled to claim a redundancy payment? Ie:
  (a) was the applicant an employee?[4]
  (b) was the employment within the scope of the redundancy payment provisions?[5]

(c) does the applicant have sufficient continuity of employment?[6] Has the applicant received a redundancy payment in respect of earlier service?[7] and

(d) does the applicant's age preclude a claim for redundancy payment?[8]

(e) was the right to claim a redundancy payment excluded by agreement where the dismissal is the expiry of a fixed term contract?[9]

5. Was there a dismissal or did the employment come to an end by resignation, agreement, frustration or other reason not amounting to dismissal for the redundancy payment provisions?[10] [*Bear in mind that constructive dismissal will found a redundancy claim.*[11]]

6. If there was a dismissal, what was the reason for the dismissal? [*Consider whether contesting the claim for redundancy may invite a potentially more expensive claim for unfair dismissal.*]

7. Is the employee disentitled from receiving a redundancy payment (in whole or in part) as a result of his conduct?[12]

8. Is the employee precluded from a redundancy payment by virtue of having turned down suitable alternative employment?[13]

9. Consider the provisions as to 'relevant date'.[14]

10. Calculate the length of the applicant's continuous service. Has the employee received a redundancy payment in respect of any of this service?[15]

11. Ascertain the age of the employee at the 'relevant date'.

12. Is the amount of the redundancy payment to be reduced because of pension or other payments?[16]

13. Is the employee's redundancy payment to be reduced in whole or in part by virtue of misconduct?[17] [*If so, bear in mind that the employer has to establish the fact of misconduct and not merely the reasonable belief in such misconduct. If this matter is pursued the steps set out in the checklist for unfair dismissal may be relevant.*]

14. Complete notice of appearance to industrial tribunal and lodge within prescribed 21-day time limit. If not, seek extension of time.

15. Consider all matters in the checklists for interlocutory matters and preparation for tribunal hearing.

16. Calculate possible redundancy payment.

1 See Chapter 1, p 8.
2 See 16.11.
3 See Checklist 4.
4 See 16.01 and 3.06.
5 See 16.08.
6 See 16.01.
7 See 16.02.
8 See 16.09.
9 See 16.10.
10 See 16.26.
11 See 16.32.
12 See 16.76.
13 See 16.60.
14 See 16.02.
15 See 16.02.
16 See 16.78.
17 See 16.76.

Checklist 7

Claims for unfair dismissal

Applicant's representative

1. Is the potential claim pursuant to the statutory provisions of the Employment Rights Act 1996, or a dismissals procedure agreement?[1] If not within the Employment Rights Act 1996, obtain details of the agreement.
2. Ascertain the date from which time in which to make application to tribunal runs and latest date by which application must be lodged at the Office (or Regional Office) of the Industrial Tribunals.[2] If interim relief is a possibility, act immediately.[3]
3. Are there written reasons for dismissal? If not, consider requesting written reasons.[4]
4. Is the applicant entitled to claim a remedy for unfair dismissal? Ie:
    (a) was the applicant an employee?[5]
    (b) was the employment within the scope of the unfair dismissal provisions?[6]
    (c) does the applicant have sufficient continuity of employment? Has there been a break in the applicant's service?[7] and
    (d) does the applicant's age preclude a claim for unfair dismissal?[8]
    (e) was the contract of employment illegal?[9]
    (f) was the right excluded by agreement where the claim arises from the expiry of a fixed term contract?[10]
5. Do the circumstances of the termination of the employment constitute a dismissal?[11] [*Bear in mind that dismissal includes constructive dismissal and certain other events.*] Check that the contract of employment was not discharged by either consensual agreement or events which do not amount to dismissal.
6. Should the application include claims for a redundant payment, and/or for sex and/or race and/or disability discrimination and/or under other claims under the Employment Rights Act 1996 and/or for breach of contract?[12] Remember that the time limits for such claims are not the same as for unfair dismissal. Should [Have] other proceedings be [been] instituted? If so, should a stay be sought.[13]
7. Check the identity of the employer. Ensure that name and address of employer is correct. Is the address of a corporate employer its registered office?
8. Is there an issue as to who was the applicant's employer? Should any other respondents be joined?
9. Is the employer solvent? Should application be made under the insolvency provisions?[14]
10. Was the reason for the dismissal automatically unfair?[15]
11. Consider continuity of employment;[16] in particular whether there has been continuity of employment where there has been a change in the identity of the employer and whether or not there has been a break in the continuity of employment.[17] Does the requirement of two years' service apply? Is it satisfied?[18]
12. Is interim relief available? If so, the time limit is very short and there may be documentary requirements.[19]

13.   Draw, complete and lodge originating application to industrial tribunal in good time.[20] If the applicant wishes to be reinstated, make this clear on originating application.[21]

14.   Consider the provisions as to 'effective date of termination'.[22]

15.   Calculate the length of the applicant's continuous service.[23]

16.   Ascertain the age of the employee at the 'effective date of termination'.[24]

17.   Is the amount of compensation to be reduced because of ex gratia or other payments?

18.   Consider checklist as to interlocutory matters before industrial tribunals.

19.   Consider checklists for advocates before industrial tribunals.

20.   Is settlement possible? Can the matter be settled with the assistance of ACAS or by a compromise agreement?

21.   Was the applicant in an occupational pension and/or life assurance scheme and what was the nature of the scheme? Consider any options there are for the applicant under that scheme and whether he should receive specialist professional advice with regard to it. [*It is to be noted that the time allowed for exercise of some options, particularly those enabling former employees to continue life assurance at standard rates, is often very short.*]

1   See 15.20.
2   In Scotland the application must be presented at the Office in Glasgow. See time limit checklist, Checklist 4.
3   See 14.32 and 15.74.
4   See 13.54.
5   See 15.01 and 3.06.
6   See 15.02.
7   See 15.12.
8   See 15.07
9   See 15.05.
10   See 15.17.
11   See 15.29. For a list of time limits, see Checklist 4.
12   See Chapters 7 and 13.
13   See Chapter 18.
14   See Chapter 17.
15   See 15.71.
16   See 15.12.
17   See Chapters 11 and 12.
18   See Chapter 15.
19   See 15.168.
20   See Checklist 4.
21   See 15.49.
22   See 15.12.
23   See 15.07.
24   See 15.216.

Respondent's representative

1.   Does the originating application have other claims such as a claim for a redundancy payment, claims under the discrimination legislation, other rights under the Employment Rights Act 1996, or for breach of contract implicit within it?[1]

2.   If there is claim for breach of contract, consider making a counterclaim. Remember time limit for this.[2]

3.   Is the claim pursuant to the statutory provisions of the Employment Rights Act 1996 or a dismissals procedure agreement? If not within the Employment Rights Act 1996, obtain details of the agreement.

4. Is the application within time?[3]
5. Is the applicant entitled to claim a remedy for unfair dismissal? Ie:
   (a) was the applicant an employee?[4]
   (b) was the employment within the scope of the unfair dismissal provisions?[5]
   (c) does the applicant have sufficient continuity of employment?[6] Has his period of service been broken?[7] and
   (d) does the applicant's age preclude a claim for a remedy for unfair dismissal?[8]
   (e) was the contract of employment illegal?[9]
   (f) was the right excluded by agreement where the claim arises from the expiry of a fixed term contract?

6. Was there a dismissal, or did the employment come to an end by resignation, agreement, or another reason not amounting to dismissal for the redundancy payment provisions?[10] [*Bear in mind that constructive dismissal will found a claim.*[11]]

7. If there was a dismissal, what was the reason for the dismissal? Was it a reason resulting in automatic unfairness or one of the five statutory reasons?[12]

8. Was the dismissal procedurally fair?

9. Consider the provisions as to 'effective date of termination'.[13]

10. Calculate the length of the applicant's continuous service.[14]

11. Ascertain the age of the employee at the 'effective date of termination'.[15]

12. Has the applicant received a redundancy payment?

13. Should the amount of any compensation be reduced because of ex gratia or other payments?[16]

14. Complete notice of appearance to industrial tribunal and lodge within prescribed 21-day time limit. If not, seek extension of time.

15. Should other respondents be joined?

16. Should [Have] other proceedings be [been] taken against the applicant? If so, should a stay of the tribunal proceedings be sought?

17. Consider all matters in the checklists for interlocutory matters and preparation for tribunal hearing.

18. Calculate possible cost of claim.

1   See Chapter 1, p 8.
2   See Chapter 13 and Checklist 4.
3   See 15.155.
4   See 15.01 and 3.06.
5   See 15.02.
6   See 15.12.
7   See 15.12.
8   See 15.01.
9   See 15.05.
10 See 15.17.
11 See 15.29.
12 See 15.71.
13 See 15.59.
14 See 15.12.
15 See 15.07.
16 See 15.216.

Checklist 8

Other claims to tribunals

Applicant's representative

1. Is the potential claim pursuant to the statutory provisions of the Employment Rights Act 1996, the Transfer of Undertakings (Protection of Employment) Regulations 1981, the Trade Union and Labour Relations (Consolidation) Act 1992, or for breach of contract?[1] Obtain agreements and sources for all claims. If unfair dismissal or redundancy refer to checklists for those claims.
2. Ascertain the date from which time in which to make application to tribunal runs and latest date by which application must be lodged at the Office (or Regional Office) of the Industrial Tribunals. If interim relief is a possibility, act immediately.
3. Are there written reasons for a dismissal? If not, consider requesting written reasons.
4. Is the applicant entitled to claim the remedy/ies sought? Ie:
    (a) was the applicant an employee/worker as applicable?
    (b) was the employment within the scope of the statutory provisions?
    (c) does the applicant have sufficient continuity of employment for claim[s]? Has there been a break in the applicant's service? and
    (d) does the applicant's age preclude claim[s]?
    (e) was the contract of employment illegal?
    (f) was the right excluded by agreement where the claim arises from the expiry of a fixed term contract?
5. If dismissal is a necessary ingredient to the claim, do the circumstances of the termination of the employment constitute a dismissal? [*Bear in mind that dismissal includes constructive dismissal and certain other events.*] Check that the contract of employment was not discharged by either consensual agreement or events which do not amount to dismissal.
6. What claims under the Employment Rights Act 1996 should be included in the application? Should claims be included for unfair dismissal, a redundant payment, and/or for sex and/or race and/or disability discrimination and/or under other claims and/or for breach of contract? Note the difference between claims for unlawful deductions from wages and breach of contract and the possibility of proceeding in the courts for breach of contract. Remember that the time limits for all claims are not the same. Should [Have] other proceedings be [been] instituted? If so, should a stay be sought?
7. Check the identity of the employer. Ensure that name and address of employer is correct. Is the address of a corporate employer its registered office?
8. Is there an issue as to who was the applicant's employer? Should any other respondents be joined?
9. Is the employer solvent? Should application be made under the insolvency provisions?
10. Do continuous service requirements apply? Are they satisfied? If so, consider continuity of employment; in particular whether there has been continuity of employment where there has been a change in the identity of the employer and whether or not there has been a break in the continuity of employment.

11.   Is interim relief available? If so the time limit is very short and there may be documentary requirements.

12.   Draw, complete and lodge originating application to industrial tribunal in good time. If the applicant wishes to be reinstated, make this clear on originating application.

13.   Draw and consider issuing writ or county court summons.

14.   Consider the provisions as to 'effective date of termination' and/or 'relevant date' if applicable.

15.   Calculate the length of the applicant's continuous service.

16.   Ascertain the age of the employee at the 'effective date of termination'/ 'relevant date' if applicable.

17.   Is the amount of compensation to be reduced because of ex gratia or other payments.

18.   Consider checklist as to interlocutory matters before industrial tribunals.

19.   Consider checklists for advocates before industrial tribunals.

20.   Is settlement possible? Can the matter be settled with the assistance of ACAS or by a compromise agreement?

21.   Was the applicant in an occupational pension and/or life assurance scheme and what was the nature of the scheme? Consider any options there are for the applicant under that scheme and whether he should receive specialist professional advice with regard to it. [*It is to be noted that the time allowed for exercise of some options, particularly those enabling former employees to continue life assurance at standard rates, is often very short.*]

1   See other checklists for references in the text.

Respondent's representative

1.   Identify claims made in the originating application. If in doubt, seek further particulars.[1] If unfair dismissal or redundancy, refer to checklists for those claims.

2.   If there is claim for breach of contract, consider making a counterclaim. Remember time limit for this.

3.   Is the claim based on some agreement or other source. If so, obtain copy/details?

4.   Is the application within time?

5.   Is the applicant entitled to claim the remedy[ies] sought? Ie:

    (a) was the applicant an employee/worker as applicable?

    (b) was the employment within the scope of the statutory provisions?

    (c) does the applicant have sufficient continuity of employment for claim[s]? Has there been a break in the applicant's service? and

    (d) does the applicant's age preclude claim[s]?

    (e) was the contract of employment illegal?

    (f) was the right excluded by agreement where the claim arises from the expiry of a fixed-term contract?

6.   If dismissal is essential to the claim, was there a dismissal, or did the employment come to an end by resignation, agreement, or another reason not amounting to dismissal?

7.   Consider the provisions as to 'effective date of termination'/'relevant date'.

8.   If appropriate, calculate the length of the applicant's continuous service.

9. If appropriate, ascertain the age of the employee at the 'effective date of termination'/'relevant date'.

10. Should the amount of any compensation be reduced because of ex gratia or other payments?

11. Complete notice of appearance to industrial tribunal and lodge within prescribed 21-day time limit. If not, seek extension of time. Remember possible counterclaim and time limit.

12. Should other respondents be joined?

13. Should other proceedings be taken against the applicant? If so, when? Should a stay of the tribunal proceedings be sought?

14. Consider all matters in the checklists for interlocutory matters and preparation for tribunal hearing.

15. Calculate possible cost of claims.

1   See other checklists for references in the text.

Checklist 9

Claims of direct sex and race discrimination

1. What are the relevant facts?

2. Has the applicant been less favourably treated than others?

3. If so, are the circumstances consistent with the treatment being on grounds of race or sex?

4. If so, what is the respondent's explanation for the less favourable treatment? Is it credible? Is it an innocent and reasonable explanation?

5. If not, is it appropriate to draw the inference that the less favourable treatment was due to his or her race or sex?

6. Ignoring the respondent's intention and motive, would the applicant have received the same treatment from the respondent **but for** his or her race or sex?

7. When all these matters have been considered it is often useful to ask whether, in the round, the facts show that the applicant was the subject of unlawful discrimination.

8. If the discrimination is proved:

   (a) is the discrimination unlawful under s 6 of the Sex Discrimination Act 1975 or s 4 of the Race Relations Act 1976?

   (b) is the discrimination unlawful in view of the defences of genuine occupational qualification?

   (c) are the facts such that they are within the ambit of the legislation?

   (d) is the applicant within the definition of employment which is protected?

9. If so, was the unlawful act of discrimination done by the discriminator in the course of his or her employment?

10. If the answer is yes, the employer (assuming he is the respondent) is still liable unless he shows that he took all such steps as were reasonably practicable to prevent the employee from carrying out the act or acts of discrimination.

11. Is the application within the time limits or, if not, is it just and equitable for the tribunal to allow the application to proceed?

12. Are the facts such that the employee should also make other claims (for instance claiming unfair dismissal and/or a redundancy payment)?

Checklist 10

Claims of indirect sex and race discrimination

1. What are the relevant facts?
2. Is the employer imposing a requirement or condition which an employee, or prospective employee, must comply with as opposed to indicating a preference or series of preferences which are regarded as desirable but not an essential prerequisite for appointment?
3. If so, is that requirement or condition one which a considerably smaller proportion of persons of a particular gender or race can comply? In considering this the appropriate pools of persons being compared have to be determined. It is a matter of what occurs in practice whether or not persons can comply with the requirement or condition.
4. If so, is the imposition of the requirement or condition justifiable balancing the needs of the employer (considered objectively) and the discriminatory effects of the requirement or condition?
5. If not, consider paragraphs 8 onwards on checklist 9.

Checklist 11

Claims of disability discrimination

1. Is the applicant a person who is within the definition of employment?
2. If so, does the applicant come within the following categories:
    (a) a person who is deemed to be disabled?
    (b) a person currently suffering from a disability?
    (c) a person who in the past has suffered a disability?
    (d) a person who is suffering from a progressive condition?
    (e) a person who has been victimised for asserting a 'statutory' disability right?
3. If so, has the applicant been treated less favourably than others without his disability?
4. If so, are the circumstances consistent with the treatment being on grounds of his disability?
5. If so, what is the respondent's explanation for the less favourable treatment? Is it credible? Is it an innocent and reasonable explanation?
6. If not, is it appropriate to draw the inference that the less favourable treatment was due to his disability?
7. Ignoring the respondent's intention and motive: would the applicant have received the same treatment from the respondent **but for** his disability?
8. Has the employer complied with the duty to make reasonable adjustments?
9. Can the employer justify the treatment of the disabled employee on objective grounds unrelated to the disability?
10. Is the employer able to rely on the small employer exemption?
11. Did the act of discrimination take place in the course of the discriminator's employment?

12.   If so, can the employer rely on the defence that he took such steps as were reasonably practicable to prevent the employee committing the discriminatory act?

13.   Is the application in time?

14.   If not, is it just and equitable for the tribunal to allow the application to proceed?

15.   When all these matters have been considered it is often helpful to ask whether, in the round, the facts show that the applicant was the subject of unlawful discrimination.

Checklist 12

Addresses of Industrial Tribunal Offices

1.   The Office of Industrial Tribunals (England and Wales)
> 19–29 Woburn Place
> LONDON
> WC1 0LU

2.   The Office of Industrial Tribunals (Scotland)
> St Andrew House
> 141 West Nile Street
> GLASGOW
> G12 RU

3.   In England and Wales originating applications are usually presented at Regional Offices of Tribunals in the appropriate area corresponding to the postal codes of the place of work or of the employer's place of business.

4.   Addresses for Regional Offices of Tribunals in England and Wales

London South – Montague Court
101 London Road
WEST CROYDON
CR0 2RF
Tel: 0181 667 9131
Fax: 0181 649 9470

Bedford
8–10 Howard Street
BEDFORD
MK40 3HS
Tel: 01234 351306
Fax: 01234 352315

Birmingham – Phoenix House
1–3 Newhall Street
BIRMINGHAM
B3 3NH
Tel: 0121 236 6051
Fax: 0121 236 6029

Bristol – The Crescent Centre
Temple Back
BRISTOL
BS1 6EZ
Tel: 0117 929 8261
Fax: 0117 925 3452

Cardiff – Caradog House
1–6 St Andrew's Place
CARDIFF
CF1 3BE
Tel: 01222 372693
Fax: 01222 225906

Leeds – 3rd Floor
11 Albion Street
LEEDS
LS1 5ES
Tel: 0113 245 9741
Fax: 0113 242 8843

Manchester – Alexandra House
14–22 The Parsonage
MANCHESTER
M3 2JA
Tel: 0161 833 0581
Fax: 0161 832 0249

Nottingham – 3rd Floor
Byron House
2A Maid Marion Way
NOTTINGHAM
NG1 6HS
Tel: 0115 947 5701
Fax: 0115 950 7612

London North
19–29 Woburn Place
LONDON
WC1 0LU
Tel: 0171 273 8575
Fax: 0171 278 5068

Newcastle – 110 Quayside
NEWCASTLE UPON TYNE
NE1 3DX
Tel: 0191 232 8865
Fax: 0191 222 1680

Southampton – Duke's Keep
3rd Floor
Marsh Lane
SOUTHAMPTON
SO1 1EX
Tel: 01703 639555
Fax: 01703 635506

Checklist 13

Preparation of proceedings

1. Application in time?
2. Are there other proceedings which require an application for a stay of tribunal proceedings?
3. Should other parties be joined?
4. If there is a claim for breach of contract should a counterclaim be made? Take into account the short time limit.
5. Take statements for all witnesses.
6. Interlocutory orders?
7. All evidence relating to claim obtained? Statements signed and arrangements for witnesses to attend hearing confirmed?
8. If expert witnesses, usual procedure followed?
9. Consider length of hearing. Notify tribunal as soon as possible if hearing likely to last longer than one day.
10. Should hearing be in private? If so, seek directions.
11. Evidence as to income and/or loss obtained?
12. Evidence as to mitigation?
13. Information with regard to pension loss?
14. Evidence as to practicability of reinstatement?
15. Statements exchanged?
16. Bundle agreed, indexed and paginated?
17. Chronology agreed?
18. Statement of agreed facts prepared?

Checklist 14

Interlocutory matters[1]

1. Are pleadings in order?
2. Ask for further particulars?
3. If not satisfactory response, apply for order for further particulars.
4. Request discovery and inspection.
5. If not satisfactory response, apply for order for discovery and inspection.
6. Ask interrogatories?
7. If not satisfactory response, ask for order for interrogatories.
8. Take statements from witnesses.
9. Ask witnesses to attend. If will not do so, apply for witness orders (with documents?).
10. Other directions required?

1 All actions to be taken well in advance of hearing.

Checklist 15

Advocate's checklist

1. All interlocutory orders and directions complied with?
2. Witnesses all available, and arrangements made for them, to attend hearing?
3. Six copies of witness statements required.
4. Six copies of agreed bundle required.
5. Six copies of chronology required.
6. Six copies of statement of agreed facts?
7. Notes for cross-examination?
8. List and five copies of authorities to be cited?
9. Calculation of basic award and copies?
10. Calculation and schedule of losses and copies?
11. Skeleton arguments and copies.
12. Consider application(s) for costs.
13. Extended/full reasons required?

Checklist 16

Appeals to Employment Appeal Tribunal

Checklist for appellant on appeal

1. Extended/full reasons.
2. Identify points of law for appeal.
3. Draw grounds of appeal.
4. Lodge notice of appeal in good time.
5. Include copy of extended/full reasons and to accelerate appeal copy of originating application and notice of appearance.
6. Should application be made for fast-tracking?

7.   Apply to county court for stay of execution if respondent against whom an award has been made?

8.   Agreed decision as to appeal?

9.   Is new evidence necessary? If so, obtain statements and follow procedure.

10.   If complaint as to conduct of hearing, obtain affidavits and proceed as mentioned in the text.

11.   [*In England and Wales*] ask Employment Appeal Tribunal to request notes of evidence.

12.   Include copy of extended/full reasons and to accelerate appeal copy of originating application and notice of appearance.

13.   Follow preliminary hearing procedure.

14.   Consider answer.

15.   Should hearing be in private? If so, apply for directions.

16.   Apply for directions (hearing)?

17.   Admissibility of documents for use at the hearing.

18.   Documents for use at hearing.

19.   Witness orders?

20.   Estimate length of hearing, discuss with other side and notify Registrar.

21.   [*In England and Wales*] prepare and lodge skeleton argument in good time.

22.   Form of order requested.

23.   List of authorities.

24.   Costs.

25.   Leave to appeal?

Appendix 2

Precedents

1 Specimen service agreement[1] (with variations as to remuneration)

A2.01

THIS AGREEMENT is made the [   ] day of [   ]

BETWEEN [   ] LIMITED whose Registered Office is situate at [   ] of [   ] (hereinafter called 'the Company') of the one part and [   ] of [   ] (hereinafter called 'the Employee') of the other part

WHEREBY IT IS AGREED as follows:

1.   This Agreement will govern the relationship between the Company and the Employee from the [   ] day of [   ] and any former agreements subsisting between the parties will cease to have effect on that day.

2.   The Company will, subject to the provisions set out below, employ the Employee and he will serve the Company as [Director] or in such other capacity as the Board of Directors of the Company shall in its absolute discretion decide until the [   ] day of [   ][2] [and thereafter until the employment hereunder is terminated by either party giving to the other not less than six months' notice in writing so as to expire on or at any time after the said [   ] day of [   ]. [Provided that if the Employee ceases to be a director of the Company his employment under this Agreement will continue unaffected and he will perform executive duties on the Company's behalf.][3]

3.   The Employee will carry out such duties and comply with such instructions as the Board of Directors of the Company shall from time to time determine [at such place or places within Great Britain or abroad as the Board of Directors shall decide][4] and during his employment hereunder the Employee will devote the whole of his time and attention to the Company's affairs and use his best endeavours to promote its interests.

4.   The Company may at any time appoint any person or persons to act jointly with the Employee in discharging his duties hereunder.[5]

5.   The Employee will be entitled by way of remuneration to a salary at the rate of [   ] per annum. The salary will accrue from day to day and be payable by monthly instalments on the last day of the month.[6]

6. The Employee is eligible to join the [   ] Pension Scheme, subject to the rules of that Scheme.[7]

7. The Company will repay to the Employee all expenses incurred by him with its authority in connection with his employment.

8. The Company will during his employment so long as the Employee is legally entitled to drive supply to him a motor car for his use and will bear the cost and running expenses of the motor car. [[The Employee will pay to the Company the sum of [   ] per annum for his private use of the motor car] [and will supply the fuel for such use at his own expense].]

9. The Employee will be entitled to [   ] working days' holiday in each holiday year in addition to the statutory Bank Holidays. Holidays other than Bank Holidays will be taken within the period of 12 months starting on the first day of April in each year (the 'holiday year') at such times as are agreed by the Employee with the Board of Directors of the Company. Holidays may not be carried forward from one holiday year to the next and no payment will be made at any time in respect of holidays which have not been taken during a holiday year.[8]

10. During his employment by the Company the Employee will not be engaged, concerned or interested in any business or undertaking whatsoever other than in connection with his employment hereunder and the holding of shares or securities quoted on a public stock exchange.[9]

11. The Employee will not during his employment by the Company or for one year afterwards endeavour to solicit orders or custom from any person, firm or company who within the period of one year before the termination of his employment had been a customer of the Company [or any associated employer] or endeavour to influence in any way the relationship between any supplier or employee and the Company [or any associated employer].[9]

12. The Employee will not during his employment by the Company or afterwards communicate or divulge to any person, except to those officials of the Company whose province is to know the same, any confidential information relating to the business affairs, processes, or trade secrets of the Company or of any associated employer.[9]

13.—(1) If the Employee is absent from his duties as a result of sickness or injury for a period of [   ] days or more he will produce to the Company a medical certificate in respect of such absence.

(2) If the Employee is absent from his duties as a result of sickness or injury he will be entitled to payment of his salary at the full rate less any Social Security or other benefits payable to him for a period (whether consecutive or in aggregate) of no more than [   ] weeks in any period of 12 months and shall thereafter be entitled to no further payment from the Company during his absence. The Employee will make application for all Social Security benefits to which he may be entitled and will on request provide details to the Company.[10]

14. The Company will be entitled to determine the Employee's employment hereunder if:

(1) the Employee breaks any term of this Agreement;

(2) the Employee neglects, omits, or refuses to discharge his duties hereunder or to comply with any instruction given to him by the Board of Directors of the Company;

(3) the Employee is guilty of gross misconduct or is convicted of any criminal offence involving dishonesty;

(4) the Employee is declared bankrupt or a Receiving Order is made against him or he makes or attempts to make any composition with his creditors;

(5) the Employee as a result of mental or physical illness becomes incapable of performing his duties;

(6) for a period of [   ] weeks (whether consecutive or in aggregate) in any period of two years the Employee has been absent from his duties as a result of sickness or injury.

15. The Employee will have no claim against the Company in respect of the determination of his employment under this Agreement by reason of the liquidation of the Company for the purposes of amalgamation or reconstruction if he is offered employment on terms not less favourable than those contained in this Agreement with any person, firm, or company which acquires the whole or part of the undertaking of the Company as a result of such amalgamation or reconstruction.[11]

16. The term 'associated employer' in this Agreement means any company of which the Company has control (directly or indirectly) or which has control (directly or indirectly) over the Company or any company of which a third person having control over the Company has control whether directly or indirectly.

17. Notices given under this Agreement should be in writing and if to be given to the Company delivered or despatched by registered or recorded delivery post to its registered office and if to be given to the Employee handed to him or sent to his last known residential address in Great Britain by registered or recorded delivery post. A notice despatched by post is deemed to be given three days after despatch.

IN WITNESS, etc[12]

1   The form is a specimen only and will require adaptation to meet particular circumstances. If it is desired to include a clause excluding the right to a redundancy payment and/or compensation for unfair dismissal, see **A2.07**. That form may be adapted for inclusion in the service agreement.

2   It is intended to exclude the statutory rights on the expiration of the employment and discussion of 'fixed term' contracts at **A2.07** should be considered.

3   The purpose of the proviso being to prevent it being contended by the employee that removal from the board of directors amounts to a repudiation of the contract. The clause may be adapted by the inclusion of a further provision that the employee will not resign his directorship or refuse to seek re-election as a director of the company.

4   This provision is important to employers with several national or international bases.

5   The clause which is self-explanatory will enable the employer to appoint an employee to act jointly with the employee without repudiating the contract.

6   For other clauses as to remuneration, see **A2.02–A2.06**.

7   For the position as to pensions, see Chapter 8.

8   For holidays, see **8.52–8.54**. The requirements of Pt I of the Employment Rights Act 1996 as to details of holidays to be given in the written statement supplied pursuant to that section are discussed at **9.16**.

9   For the duty of good faith and restrictive agreements, see Chapter 10. If the employer has particular areas of knowledge which he wishes to protect there should be totally separate covenants with regard to each providing the minimum protection required, see **10.13–10.22**.

10   For consideration of the position during sickness and injury, see **4.46–4.51**.

11   This clause is an attempt to prevent the employee having a claim for breach of contract in situations of amalgamation and reconstruction.

12   No arbitration clause included, particularly since industrial tribunals now have some jurisdiction to determine disputes as to breaches of contract, see **13.60**. The agreement may be entered into as a deed and is exempt from stamp duty.

A2.02

Clause providing for specified increases in salary[1]

5.   The Employee will be entitled to a salary at the rate of [   ] per annum until 31 December [   ], to a salary at the rate of [   ] per annum from that date until 31 December [   ] and to a salary of [   ] per annum for the remainder of the period of the Employee's employment hereunder. The salary to which the Employee is entitled hereunder will accrue from day to day and be payable in arrears on the last day of each month by equal monthly instalments.

1   Clauses of this type are usually only suitable for short-term contracts.

A2.03

Clause providing for bonus by reference to profits[1]

5.—(1) The Employee will be entitled to a salary of [   ] per annum payable in arrears on the last day of each month. The salary will accrue from day to day.

(2) In addition to the salary mentioned in subclause (1) the Employee will be entitled to a bonus calculated at the rate of [   ] per centum of the Company's net profits declared by the Board of Directors to be available for the purposes of bonus calculation. Such profits will be computed after making such charges and setting aside such reserves as the Board in its absolute discretion considers appropriate but before charging bonus payments payable to any other employee. A certificate of the Company's profit for such purposes given by the Secretary of the Company will be final and binding on the parties hereto. The bonus will be paid within six months of the ending of the Company's financial year. It will be deemed to accrue from day to day and if the Employee ceases to be employed by the Company for whatever reason during a financial year will be apportioned on a daily basis in respect of the period during which the Employee was employed by the Company.

1   The definition of profits used in this clause leaves the right to determine the profits for the purpose of bonus calculation with the board of directors of the company. If a more exact definition is used difficulties may be encountered in its application. This clause may be unsatisfactory in theory but if several employees have similar provisions in their contracts it works surprisingly well in practice. It may be prudent to provide a maximum or a graduated or banded rate of bonus, or to provide a limit to the bonus.

A2.04

Clause providing for commission by reference to turnover[1]

5.—(1) The Employee will be entitled to a salary of [   ] per annum payable in arrears on the last day of each month. The salary will accrue from day to day.

(2) In addition to the salary hereinbefore mentioned the Employee will be entitled to a commission of [   ] per centum of the turnover of the Company. A certificate of the Company's turnover will be given by the Company's auditors which will be final and binding on the parties hereto. The commission will be paid within six months of the ending of the Company's financial year. It will be deemed to accrue from day to day and if the Employee ceases to be employed by the Company for whatever reason during a financial year will be apportioned on a daily basis in respect of the period during which the Employee was employed by the Company.

1 This type of clause is frequently encountered. It may be varied by including turnover over a threshold only or by using varying rates of commission for 'bands' of turnover. It has inherent dangers because there is no reference to profitability. A limit to the sum payable should be considered.

A2.05

Clause providing for schedule of increases[1]

5.   The Employee will be entitled by way of remuneration to a salary at the rate of [   ] per annum from the date hereof. The rate of salary may be increased as agreed between the Company and the Employee and if so agreed the particulars will be set out in the Schedule endorsed hereon and initialled by the Employee and by a[nother] director on the Company's behalf. The most recent of these particulars will be treated as if they are incorporated in this Agreement. The salary payable hereunder will accrue from day to day and be payable in arrears on the last day of each month by equal monthly instalments.

Schedule of increased salary in accordance with Clause 5

Date from which new salary is to commence	Rate per annum of new salary	Initialled by Employee	Initialled on behalf of the Company

1 Theoretical difficulties can be raised regarding this clause. However, it appears to work well in practice.

A2.06

Variation of salary by reference to the index of retail prices[1]

5.—(1) Subject as mentioned below the Employee will be entitled by way of remuneration to a salary at the rate of [   ] per annum. The Employee's salary hereunder will accrue from day to day and will be payable in arrears on the last day of each month by equal monthly instalments.

(2) The salary payable hereunder will be reviewed on 2 January in each year ('the review date'). The salary of the Employee during the year commencing with the review date will be the sum which is produced by

multiplying the amount of salary hereinbefore provided for by the fraction in which [   ]^2 is the denominator and the numerator is the figure for the Index of Retail Prices last published by [the appropriate government department] (or its successor) before the review date and calculated using the same basis for its compilation as is used at the date hereof. If that basis changes or no figure for the Retail Prices Index on that basis is published during the period of three months immediately preceding the review date the numerator is the figure which the Index would have been on the review date if the basis had not been changed or the figure had been published. If it is impossible to calculate this figure the numerator will be such figure as is agreed between the parties or failing agreement as is determined by an Arbitrator appointed in accordance with Clause [   ] hereof as being a reasonable estimate of that figure.^{3}

1   Salary increases by reference to published indices were much used in days of high inflation.

2   The figure of the Index of Retail Prices published immediately before the entry into the service agreement is inserted here.

3   This clause requires the inclusion of an arbitration clause in the service agreement.

A2.07

Agreement to exclude the right to redundancy payment and remedies for unfair dismissal where the employee is employed for a fixed term of two years or more^1

TO: [*Employer*]

I [   ] being employed by you under a contract of employment for a fixed term of [   ] years commencing on the [   ] hereby agree to exclude any right to a redundancy payment pursuant to the Employment Rights Act 1996 and to exclude any claim in respect of rights under Pt X of that Act, and in each case in pursuance of any statutory modification or re-enactment thereof, on the expiry of the fixed term without its being renewed.

Date

Signature   [*of Employee*]

1   See the Employment Rights Act 1996, s 197(3) discussed at **15.18** and **16.10**. An agreement to exclude the right to a redundancy payment in respect of a term which is renewed is not construed as applying to the term as renewed but this is without prejudice to making a further such agreement (Employment Rights Act 1996, s 197(5)).

2 Statements of terms and conditions of employment

A2.08

General form of statement of terms of employment[1]

Employer:

Address:

Employee:

Address:

Particulars of the terms of your employment as at [   ].[2]

The following particulars constitute the written statement required to be given to you by statute in respect of your employment with the above-named employer which began on [   ] [and which forms part of a continuous period of employment which began on [   ] with [   ]. [No employment with a previous employer counts as part of your continuous employment with the employer.]

1.   *Title of Employment.*

2.   *Job Description.* A job description is set out in appendix [   ] to this statement.[3]

3.   *Place of Employment.* [   ] You may be required to work [   ].

4.   *Remuneration.* Your rate of pay will be [   ] per [   ] paid on the [   ] day of each [   ]. Overtime is paid for on the following basis

[*Other special provisions as to payment – shift allowances, details of commission payments, no obligation to pay overtime etc. If some payments are non-contractual this should be made clear*]

5.   *Hours.* You are required to work [   ] days per week from Monday to Friday inclusive between the hours of [   ] am and [   ] pm with a break of [   ] hour for lunch, [and in addition you should work such overtime as may be reasonably required by the Employer].[4]

6.   *Holidays.* Rules as to holidays and holiday pay are set out in appendix [   ] to this statement.[5]

7.   *Incapacity due to sickness or injury and absences from work.* Rules relating to absence from work due to sickness and injury (including provision relating to sick pay) are set out in [appendix   to this statement][5] [in the rules copies of which are in the Wages Office]. If for any reason you are absent from work when expected to be present you or someone on your behalf should notify the employer (or arrange for the employer to be notified) as soon as possible and in any event no later than two hours after you were expected to be present.

8. *Pensions.* Your Employer [does not] operate[s] a pension scheme applicable to your employment [a summary of the rules of the pension scheme is herewith] [details of the scheme are available for inspection in the [   ] Office] [in the rules copies of which are in the Wages Office]. A contracting-out certificate is [not] in force in respect of your employment.

9. *Notice.*

(1) You are obliged to give a minimum period of [one week's][6] notice to terminate your employment.

(2) Except in circumstances when your employer is entitled to dismiss you summarily you are entitled to receive a period of notice of:
- (a) [one week] for continuous employment with the employer for any period of up to two years; or
- (b) [one week] for each complete year of such employment between two and 12 years; or
- (c) [12 weeks] for such employment of 12 years or more.[7]

[If contract for a fixed term, see A2.09]

10. *Disciplinary Rules.* A copy of the disciplinary rules applicable to your employment is set out [in appendix   to this statement]. [in the rules copies of which are in the Wages Office].

11. *Redress of Grievances.* Details of a procedure available in cases where you have grievance in connection with your employment is set out in appendix [   ] to this statement. You are encouraged to use this procedure if you have any grievance to which it applies.

12. *[Additional particulars, for instance relating to probationary period]*[8]

Notes:

1   The Employer reserves the right to amend the provisions of your contract from time to time. If matters included in this statement are altered you will be notified of the alteration as required by statute.
2   Where this statement refers to the rules copies of which are in the Wages Office, the rules may be referred to by you at any time during your normal working hours. Changes in those rules from time to time made in accordance with them shall be applicable to you.
3   Please sign the copy of this statement where indicated and return to me as soon as possible.

Dated

Signed   *[Company Secretary]*[9]

Acknowledgement by employee. I acknowledge receipt of a statement of which the foregoing is a true copy [and agree that the preceding provisions including those contained in the documents referred to (as varied from time to time in accordance herewith) form the basis of my contract of employment].[10]

Date

Signature   [*Employee*]

1   This form should be readily adapted to fit most situations encountered in practice. If there are no particulars to be included under any head, this should be stated.
2   This date must be a date not more than seven days before the statement is given.
3   This is not a requirement of the Act. As a matter of practice it may be useful to include, or refer to, a job description.
4   The words in brackets should be included if the employee is obliged to work overtime.
5   See **9.18**.
6   The minimum period is shown. A longer period may be agreed.
7   The minimum periods of notice required by the Employment Rights Act 1996, s 86(1) are shown. It may be agreed that the employee is entitled to longer notice but not shorter if the provisions of the Act as to notice apply, see **13.28–13.43**.
8   Although there is no statutory requirement it may be convenient to include any special provisions in the statement.
9   A signature is not required by the Act but does help avoid disputes if the contents of the statement are relevant to any dispute.
10   There is no requirement in the 1996 Act for the employee to sign a copy of the statement. However, it can be useful from an employer's point of view to obtain such signature as evidence that a statement was given and received and that the employee accepts the statement as correctly setting out the terms of the employment.

A2.09

Variation of provisions as to notice where contract for a fixed term including a provision as to notice

9.   *Fixed Term and Notice.*

   (1)   Your contract is for a fixed term to expire on [   ].

   (2)   During the fixed term you cannot give notice to terminate your employment.

   (3)   During the fixed term the Employer can give notice to terminate your employment in the following circumstances [   ]. In which case the period of notice to which you are entitled is [   ] months.

A2.10

Statement of terms of employment where terms are contained in a collective agreement[1]

Employer:

Address:

Employee:

Address:

Particulars of the terms of your employment as at [   ].[2]

The following particulars constitute the written statement required to be given to you by statute in respect of your employment with the above-named employer which began on [   ] [and which forms part of a continuous period of employment which began on [   ] with [   ]]. [No employment with a previous employer counts as part of your continuous employment with the employer.]

1. *Title of Employment.*

2. *Job Description.* A job description is set out in appendix [   ] to this statement.[3]

3. *Place of Employment.* [   ] You may be required to work [   ].

4. *Collective agreement(s).* Some of the terms of and other provisions relating to your employment are contained in [an] agreement[s] ('the Collective Agreement') between [   ] and [   ]. These include the provisions as to [incapacity to work due to sickness or injury (including provision as to sick pay)], [pensions] and [notice]. These provisions are subject to alteration as provided in the relevant terms of [that] [those] agreement[s]. A copy of the Collective Agreement as amended from time to time is available for inspection in the Wages Office at all times during normal working hours.

5. *Remuneration.* Your rate of pay will be [   ] per [   ] paid on the [   ] day of each [   ]. Overtime is paid for on the following basis

[*Other special provisions as to payment – shift allowances, details of commission payments, no obligation to pay overtime etc. If some payments are non-contractual this should be made clear*]

6. *Hours.* You are required to work [   ] days per week from Monday to Friday inclusive between the hours of [   ] am and [   ] pm with a break of [   ] hour for lunch, [and in addition you should work such overtime as may be required by your employers].[4]

7. *Holidays.* Rules as to holidays and holiday pay are set out in appendix [   ] to this statement.

8. *Incapacity due to sickness or injury and absences from work.* Rules relating to absence from work due to sickness and injury (including provision relating to sick pay) are [contained in the Collective Agreement] [set out in appendix [   ] to this statement].[5] If for any reason you are absent from work when expected to be present you should notify the employer (or arrange for the employer to be notified) as soon possible and in any event no later than two hours after you were expected to be present.

9. *Pensions.* [The provisions relating to pensions applicable to you are contained in the Collective Agreement] [Your Employer [does not] operate[s] a pension scheme applicable to your employment [a summary of the rules of the pension scheme is herewith] [details of the scheme are available for inspection in the [   ] Office]]. A contracting-out certificate is [not] in force in respect of your employment.

10. *Notice*. [The provisions relating to the notice to terminate your employment to be given by the Employer and the Employee are contained in the Collective Agreement.]

[(1) You are obliged to give a minimum period of [one week's][6] notice to terminate your employment.

(2) Except in circumstances when your employer is entitled to dismiss you summarily you are entitled to receive a period of notice of:
- (a) [one week] for continuous employment with the employer for any period of up to two years; or
- (b) [one week] for each complete year of such employment between two and 12 years; or
- (c) [12 weeks] for such employment of 12 years or more.[7]]

[*If contract for a fixed term, see A2.09*]

11. *Disciplinary Rules*. A copy of the disciplinary rules applicable to your employment is set out in appendix [   ] to this statement.

12. *Redress of Grievances*. Details of a procedure available in cases where you have grievance in connection with your employment is set out in appendix [   ] to this statement. You are encouraged to use this procedure if you have any grievance to which it applies.

13. [*Additional particulars, for instance relating to probationary period*][8]

Notes:

1   The Employer reserves the right to amend the provisions of your contract from time to time. If matters included in this statement are altered you will be notified of the alteration as required by statute.
2   If any of the provisions referred to in this statement arise from the Collective Agreement any change in that Agreement which is relevant to your employment will be incorporated in the contract between the employee and employer whether or not it is specifically agreed to by the Employee.
3   Please sign the copy of this statement where indicated and return to me as soon as possible.[9]

Date

Signed   [*Company Secretary*]

Acknowledgement by employee.[10] I acknowledge receipt of a statement of which the foregoing is a true copy [and agree that the preceding provisions including those contained in the documents referred to (as varied from time to time in accordance herewith) form the basis of my contract of employment].[10]

Date

Signature   [*Employee*]

1   This form should be readily adapted to fit most situations encountered in practice. If there are no particulars to be included under any head, this should be stated.

2   This date must be a date not more than seven days before the statement is given.

3   This is not a requirement of the Act.

4   Words such as those in brackets should be included if the employee is obliged to work overtime.

5   The employee should have reasonable opportunities of reading documents referred to in the course of his employment or they should be made reasonably accessible to him in some other way: Employment Rights Act 1996, s 2(3) and (4) and see **13.28–13.43**.

6   The minimum period is shown. A longer period may be agreed.

7   The minimum periods of notice required by the Employment Rights Act 1996, s 86(1) are shown. It may be agreed that the employee is entitled to longer notice but not shorter if the provisions of the Act as to notice apply, see **13.28–13.43**.

8   Although there is no statutory requirement it may be convenient to include any special provisions in the statement.

9   A signature is not required by the Employment Rights Act 1996 but does help avoid disputes if the contents of the statement are relevant to any dispute.

10   There is no requirement in the 1996 Act for the employee to sign a copy of the statement. However, it can be useful from an employer's point of view to obtain such signature as evidence that a statement was given and received and that the employee accepts the statement as correctly setting out the terms of the employment.

A2.11

Statement of written particulars of terms of employment when a service agreement has been entered into between the employer and the employee[1]

Employer:

Address:

Employee:

Address:

Particulars of the terms of your employment as at [   ].[2]

The following particulars constitute the written statement required to be given to you by statute in respect of your employment with the above-named employer which began on [   ] [and which forms part of a continuous period of employment which began on [   ] with [   ]]. [No employment with a previous employer counts as part of your continuous employment with the employer.]

1.   *Title of Employment.*

2.   *Remuneration.* Your entitlement to remuneration is as set out in the Service Agreement (the Service Agreement) with the Employer dated [   ], a copy of which is attached.

3.   *Hours.* The periods of time for which you are obliged to work are as set out in the Service Agreement.

4.   *Holidays.* Rules as to holidays and holiday pay are set out in the Service Agreement.

5.   *Absences from work.* Rules relating to absence from work due to sick-

ness and injury (including provisions relating to sick pay) are [set out in the Service Agreement] [are set out in appendix [   ] to this statement].[3] [If for any reason you are absent from work when expected to be present you should notify the employer (or arrange for the employer to be notified) as soon possible and in any event no later than two hours after you were expected to be present.]

6. *Pensions*. Your Employer [does not] operate[s] a pension scheme applicable to your employment. [Provisions relating to this are set out in the Service Agreement] [a summary of the rules of the pension scheme is herewith] [details of the scheme are available for inspection in the [   ] Office].[3] A contracting-out certificate is [not] in force in respect of your employment.

7. *Notice*. [The circumstances in which your employment may be terminated are set out in the Service Agreement.] [Your employment is for a fixed term as set out in the Service Agreement subject to termination as therein provided.]

8. *Disciplinary Rules*. The disciplinary rules applicable to your employment are [as set out in the Service Agreement] [set out in appendix [   ] to this statement].

9. *Redress of Grievances*. Details of a procedure available in cases where you have grievance in connection with your employment [are set out in the Service Agreement] [are set out in appendix [   ] to this statement]. You are encouraged to use this procedure if you have any grievance to which it applies.

10.   Other provisions relating to your employment are contained in the Service Agreement.

Note that the provisions set out in the Service Agreement may be changed in accordance with the provisions of that Agreement.

Date

Signed   [*Company Secretary*]

Acknowledgement by employee. I acknowledge receipt of a statement of which the foregoing is a true copy.

Date

Signature   [*Employee*]

1   This form should be readily adapted to fit most situations encountered in practice. If there are no particulars to be included under any head, this should be stated.
2   This date must be a date not more than seven days before the statement is given.
3   The employee should have reasonable opportunities of reading documents referred to in the course of his employment or they should be made reasonably accessible to him in some other way: Employment Rights Act 1996, s 2(2) and see **13.28–13.43**.

A2.12

Notification of change in terms of employment[1]

Employer

To Employee

This statement is given[2] to you pursuant to the obligation on the Employer to notify you of changes in the particulars of your employment.

The following changes [have been made] to the terms of your employment, as previously notified to you [have taken place by mutual agreement] [arise from alterations in the provisions of   ]:

From the [   ].

1. [Your remuneration is paid monthly instead of weekly from the [   ] day of [   ]. Payment will be made on the [   ] day of each month.]

2. A pension scheme which is applicable to your employment has been introduced. [A summary of the rules of the pension scheme is herewith] [details of the scheme are available for inspection in the [   ] Office]. A contracting-out certificate is [not] in force in respect of your employment.

The documents referred to above as being available in the Office are open to inspection at any time during normal working hours, are referred to as amended from time to time and future changes will be recorded in them.

Note: Please keep this document with the statement of particulars of your employment (and changes, if any) previously given to you.

Signed [*Signature of employer or duly authorised agent*]

Acknowledgement by employee. I acknowledge receiving the document of which the above is a copy.

Date

[*Signed by employee*]

  1   The employee should be informed of the nature of the change at the earliest opportunity and no later than one month after the change. See the detailed provisions of the Employment Rights Act 1996, s 4 and 9.22–9.24. The form should be varied as appropriate in the circumstances.
  2   The safest course is to give the statement to the employee and obtain a receipt. See 9.28.

A2.13

Notification of change of name of employer when terms of employment remain the same[1]

Employer

To Employee

This statement is given[2] to you pursuant to the obligation on the Employer to notify you of changes in the particulars of your employment.

With effect from [   ] the name of your Employer was changed to [   ]. Your Employer remains the same [company] [firm] and your terms of employment and period of continuous employment are not affected by the change.

Note: Please keep this document with the statement of particulars of your employment (and changes, if any) previously given to you.

Signed [*Signature of employer or duly authorised agent*]

Acknowledgement by employee. I acknowledge receiving the document of which the above is a copy.

Date

[*Signed by employee*]

   1   The employee should be informed of the nature of the change at the earliest opportunity and no later than one month after the change. See the detailed provisions of the Employment Rights Act 1996, s 4 and **9.22–9.24**. The form may be varied as appropriate in the circumstances.
   2   The safest course is to give the statement to the employee and obtain a receipt. See **9.28**.

A2.14

Notification of change of employer when terms of employment remain the same[1]

New Employer

To Employee

This statement is given[2] to you pursuant to the obligation on the Employer to notify you of changes in the particulars of your employment.

You are hereby notified that with effect from [   ] [the business carried on by your employer was transferred to [*New Employer*]]. Your terms of employment are not affected by the change. Your period of continuous employment with [*Former Employer*] is preserved and counts with your [*New Employer*].

Appendix 2

Note: Please keep this document with the statement of particulars of your employment (and changes, if any) previously given to you.

Signed [*Signature of employer or duly authorised agent*]

Acknowledgement by employee. I acknowledge receiving the document of which the above is a copy.

Date

[*Signed by employee*]

1   The employee should be informed of the nature of the change at the earliest opportunity and no later than one month after the change. See the detailed provisions of the Employment Rights Act 1996, s 4 and **9.22–9.24.** The form should be varied as appropriate in the circumstances.
2   The safest course is to give the statement to the employee and obtain a receipt. See **9.28.**

3   Rules as to absence due to sickness and injury, holidays and disciplinary and grievance procedures

A2.15

Specimen rules as to absence due to sickness and injury

1.   An employee absent from work as a result of sickness or injury should notify (or cause to be notified) the Company of the reason for his absence as soon as possible and no later than two hours after he is due in to work.

2.   A Medical Certificate as to the reason for the absence must be sent to the Company if the employee is absent for any period of seven or more consecutive working days, or three working days in one working week.

3.   Employees will be entitled to Statutory Sick Pay in accordance with the appropriate rules. The Company's additional sickness payments will be made in accordance with the following rules.

4.—(1) No payment will be made in respect of periods of absence through sickness or injury to an employee with less than [   ] months' continuous service with the Company immediately preceding the first day of the absence.

(2) For those continuously employed for a period of [   ] months or more immediately preceding the first day of the absence payment will be made at the normal basic rate to include Statutory Sick Pay (less any benefits from the Department of Health and Social Security or other state benefits payable to the employee) for up to a maximum of [   ] weeks' absence in any 12-month period. The employee must notify the Company as to benefit payable by the Department of Health and Social Security and other benefits receivable by him.

5.   It is a term of an employee's employment that if requested to do so at any time by the Company he will consent to be examined by a registered medical practitioner specified by it (the specified medical practitioner) and will consent to his own medical attendant reporting to the specified medical practitioner and to the specified medical practitioner reporting to the Personnel Director of the Company as to any medical matter which in the reasonable opinion of the specified medical practitioner may affect the employee's ability to carry out his work for the Company.

A2.16

Specimen rules relating to holidays and holiday pay

1.   Employees shall be entitled to the following customary holidays with pay:

New Year	New Year's Day
Easter	Easter Monday and Tuesday
May	May Day
Spring	Spring Bank Holiday Monday

| Summer/Autumn | Late Summer Bank Holiday Monday |
| Christmas | Christmas Day and Boxing Day (or in appropriate years two other days appointed by the employer). |

2.   Annual holidays are to be taken in such periods and at such times as may be agreed with the employer.

3.   The holiday year begins on the first day of January in each year, and ends on the last day of December of that year. Holidays which have not been taken in respect of a holiday year cannot be carried forward and no payment will be made in lieu thereof to continuing employees.

4.   Subject to rule 5 and as below, employees employed on the 1 January in each holiday year and throughout that year are entitled to [   ] weeks annual holiday with pay.

5.   Employees who have been employed for a continuous period of five years or more, prior to the 1 January each year and who are employed throughout that year are entitled to [   ] weeks annual holiday with pay.

6.   The annual holidays of employees engaged, or re-engaged, during a holiday year for that holiday year will be agreed at the time of engagement, or re-engagement, as the case may be.

7.   Employees leaving the Company's employment during a holiday year who have not taken accrued holidays are entitled to payment in lieu of untaken holiday. For these purposes holidays of all employees are taken as accruing at the rate of [   ] days for each complete and continuous month of employment during the holiday year, subject to a maximum of [   ] days in the case of employees to whom rule 4 applies, and [   ] days for employees to whom rule 5 applies. In the calculation of any payment due, a day's pay will be one-fifth of the normal weekly basic payment. No other payment for holiday entitlements will be made.

A2.17

Specimen grievance procedure[1]

1.   An employee having a grievance relating to his employment should raise the matter orally in the first instance with his foreman or immediate superior to ascertain whether it is possible for the difficulty to be resolved informally.

2.   If the matter is not resolved informally the employee should raise the matter again with the foreman or immediate supervisor in writing. The document should set out briefly the nature of the complaint.

3.   If the foreman or supervisor is not able to deal with the grievance at the time he should within the next [   ] working days look into the matter and give the results of the investigation to the employee.

4. If the grievance is not satisfactorily resolved at that time the employee should hand in brief written details of the grievance to the Works Office for the attention of the Works Manager.

5. Within [   ] days the Works Manager will arrange a meeting between himself or someone nominated by him, the aggrieved employee and his Shop Steward or any other employee the employee raising the grievance wishes to attend with him, and the foreman or immediate superior. At that meeting the employee will have the right to explain the grievance which will be discussed.

6. After the meeting the Works Manager, or his deputy, will give his decision on the matter as soon as practicable.

7. Should the grievance not be resolved, then the Works Manager will arrange for a written report of the meeting to be prepared for an Appeals Committee which will consist of the Personnel Director of the Company or some other person nominated by him, and another senior manager who has not previously been involved in connection with the grievance.

8. The Appeals Committee will consider:
    (1) the outline of the grievance prepared by the employee;
    (2) the report of the meeting with the Works Manager, or his deputy, as to the meeting conducted by him;
    (3) further written comments made by or on behalf of the employee;
    (4) written comments made by or on behalf of the foreman or immediate superior; and
    (5) any other matters which the Committee considers material.

9. There will then be a meeting of the Appeals Committee which the employee and his representative will attend and at which they may make such further comments as they wish and the foreman (or immediate superior) and Works Manager may do likewise.

10. The decision of the Appeals Committee will be final and binding on all parties. If the two members of the Appeals Committee do not agree then the Personnel Director or his representative will have a casting vote. A short note of the reasons for the decision of the Appeals Committee will be given to the employee.

1 The procedure should be established with employee representatives or trade unions concerned. It is preferable for there to be a formal procedure in the cases of all employers.

A2.18

Specimen disciplinary procedure[1]

Application

1. This procedure applies to all the employees of [   ] Limited ('the Company').

Purpose

2. The purpose of the procedure is to enable those employees who are falling below the standards expected of them to have their shortcomings drawn to their attention to assist them in correcting any shortcomings.

Suspension with pay

3. The Company reserves the right to suspend an employee on pay whilst it investigates an employee's conduct or for any other purpose connected with the application of its disciplinary procedure. An employee suspended under this power is entitled to be paid his basic rate of pay during the period of the suspension.

Gross misconduct

4. (1) The Company reserves the right in its discretion to suspend for such period as it shall decide (whether with or without pay) or dismiss summarily employees guilty of gross misconduct, such as theft, dishonesty or dangerous conduct. The examples given of gross misconduct are not exhaustive. Gross misconduct involves any activity of the employee which is of a serious nature going to the basis of his relationship with his employer.

   (2) In cases of gross misconduct the Company may suspend or dismiss the employee having conducted a disciplinary hearing in accordance with these rules, without having given the employee any prior warning. If the right of suspension or dismissal is exercised the employee will be given a written statement of the reasons for that action.

Sanctions

5. (1) With the exception of cases of gross misconduct, following a first breach of discipline the employee will be given an oral warning, or in the case of more serious misconduct, a written warning, setting out the circumstances giving rise to the complaint. Details of the warning will be recorded in the Company's records relating to the employee, and he will be told that the warning constitutes the first formal stage of the formal disciplinary procedure.

   (2) If in a case where a warning has been given, the conduct of the employee complained of is repeated, or continues, or the employee falls below the standard reasonably expected of him in some other way, a warning in writing will be given where the first warning was oral. This warning will set out the circumstances in which it is given and will be recorded in the Company's records relating to the employee. The employee will be informed that the warning is given in accordance with the disciplinary procedure.

   (3) If, after a written warning has been given, the conduct complained of is repeated or continues, or the employee falls below the standard reasonably expected of him in some other way, a final warning in writing will be given. This will state that any further breach of the Company's disciplinary rules could lead to suspension or dismissal. The warning will be recorded in the Company's records relating to the employee.

   (4) If, notwithstanding the final written warning, the conduct complained of continues, or is repeated, or the employee falls below the

standard reasonably expected of him in some other way, the Company may suspend or dismiss the employee. In a case where the employee is suspended the suspension shall be with or without pay and for such period as the Company shall decide.

(5) Warnings given to an employee cease to have effect one year after they have been given if during the period no further disciplinary action has been taken against the employee although they will remain recorded on the employee's file.

The procedure in action

6. No disciplinary action will be taken against an employee without him having the opportunity to explain his version of what took place at a disciplinary hearing.

7. Prior to a disciplinary hearing the employee will be notified in writing of the allegations against him and that the employee has the right to be accompanied by a colleague at the hearing.

8. The Works Manager or the person he nominated to act in his place will conduct a disciplinary hearing. He may be accompanied by a member of the Personnel Department. The member of the Personnel Department will act in an advisory role only. The colleague who accompanies the employee to the disciplinary hearing may act as his representative at the hearing if the employee so wishes.

9. A member of the Company's management other than those conducting the hearing will present details of the allegations against the employee and of matters in support. The employee will have the opportunity of explaining his version of what occurred and to call witnesses. He or his representative will have the opportunity of summing up on the employee's behalf, as will the Company's representative.

Decision

10. The employee will be informed of the outcome of the hearing either when it concludes or as soon as reasonably practicable thereafter. The decision and reasons for it will be confirmed in writing.

Appeal

11. If the employee is dissatisfied with the outcome of the disciplinary hearing he should notify the Personnel Director in writing that he wishes to appeal. In his notice he should set out a summary of his grounds of the appeal. This should be done within seven days of the employee being notified of the outcome of the disciplinary hearing.

12. If the employee does appeal the person conducting the disciplinary hearing will arrange for a written report of the disciplinary hearing to be prepared for an Appeals Committee and a copy will be supplied to the employee.

13. The Appeals Committee will consist of a Director of the Company, or some other person nominated by the Board of Directors of the Company,

and another member of the Company's senior management not previously involved. The members of the Appeals Committee may be accompanied by a member of the Personnel Department other [than the person (if any) who advised at the disciplinary hearing].

14.   Prior to the appeal hearing the Appeals Committee will consider:

(1)   the letter in which the employee exercises his right of appeal;
(2)   any further written representations which the employee may care to make, or which are made on his behalf;
(3)   the report prepared by the person conducting the disciplinary hearing; and
(4)   any further written comments made by or on behalf of the employee, and the Company.

Copies of all these documents will be made available to the employee and the Company's representative no later than two days before the appeal hearing.

15.   An appeal hearing will be convened as soon as practicable. At the appeal hearing the Appeals Committee will consider all documents before it and such further information and comments as the employee and the Company raise at the appeal hearing.

Decision of the Appeals Committee

16.   The Appeals Committee may confirm the original disciplinary decision, quash that decision, or substitute another in its place.

17.   The employee will be informed of the outcome of the appeal hearing, either when it concludes or as soon as reasonably practicable thereafter.

18.   The decision of the Appeals Committee will be final and binding on all parties. If the two members do not agree then the Director, or person nominated by the Board of Directors, will have a casting vote. A short note of the reasons for the decision will be given to the employee.

Termination of employment

19.   If practicable, steps will be taken to ensure that in the case of an employee given notice of dismissal, the above procedure will be implemented and the decision of the Appeals Committee given before the notice takes effect. However, an employee who is dismissed shall cease to be an employee of the Company on the expiration of his notice, or with immediate effect in the case of employees who are instantly dismissed, notwithstanding that the appeal hearing has not taken place, or the outcome of his appeal is not known.

1   See 15.143 and 15.148–15.149.

4 Forms applicable in circumstances of redundancy

A2.19

Calculation of redundancy payment [and receipt]

[*Employer*]

To   [*Name and address of employee*]

We hereby give you written particulars of the calculation of the redundancy payment to be made to you.

1.   Your period of continuous employment with the Company began on [   ].

2.   Your date of birth is [   ].

3.   The relevant date applicable in respect of your redundancy is [   ] and your age at that date is [   ] years.

4.   Yours week's pay calculated in accordance with the Employment Rights Act 1996 is £[   ]. [This sum is calculated by [*here insert method of calculation in accordance with the Schedule if this is not straightforward*].] [This is subject to the statutory maximum of £[   ].]

5.   Your redundancy payment is calculated as follows:

[multiplier] × [week's pay] = £[   ]

[**6.**   In addition on the termination of your employment you will be paid [   ] weeks' pay in lieu of notice, [   ] days' holiday pay (less tax of £[   ]) totalling £[   ] and £[   ] being sums due to you of £[   ] for [*reason*].

Thus the total sum due to you will be:

Redundancy payment	[ ]	
Payment in lieu of notice	[ ]	
Accrued holiday pay	[ ]	
[*Reason*]	[ ]	
Total	[ ]]	

Acknowledgement.[1]   I hereby acknowledge receipt of [the sums set out above including] the redundancy payment calculated as set out above.

[Date]

Signature   [*Employee*]

---

1   On duplicate copy.

Appendix 2

A2.20

Notice by the employee to terminate the employment prior to the expiry of the employer's notice and by the employer of intention to contest liability to pay a redundancy payment

Employee's notice[1]

Following receipt of notice to terminate my employment by reason of redundancy, I hereby give notice to terminate my contract of employment on [   ].

Date

Signature

  1   This notice is given pursuant to the Employment Rights Act 1996, s 136(3). See **16.72**.

Employer's counter-notice[1]

To [   ]

Take notice that you are required to withdraw your notice dated [   ] terminating your contract of employment and to continue in our employment until the date on which our notice dated [   ] expires, namely [*date*]. If you fail to do so we shall contest our liability to pay you a redundancy payment in respect of the termination of your contract of employment, see the Employment Rights Act 1996, s 142.

Date

Signature

  1   The notice is given in accordance with the Employment Rights Act 1996, s 142. See **16.72**. For the provisions as to service, see the Employment Rights Act 1996, s 179 and **16.130**.

A2.21

Offer of new contract made by employer to redundant employee[1]

The following are the particulars of employment which I, [*name and address of employer*], am offering you, [*name and address of employee*], to begin on [*date*].

1.   Description of employment [   ].

2.   Place of employment [   ].

3.   Scale or rate of remuneration or method of calculating remuneration [   ].

4.   Intervals at which remuneration is paid [   ].

5.   Normal hours of work and any other terms and conditions relating to hours of work [   ].

6. Holidays and holiday pay [   ].

7. Terms and conditions relating to incapacity for work due to sickness or injury and particulars of any sick pay [   ].

8. There is no pension scheme applicable to you [or particulars of pension scheme].

9. Amount of notice[2] to terminate contract to be given by:

    (1) employee [   ]
    (2) employer [   ].

10. All other terms and conditions of employment will remain as set out in the Statement of Written Particulars of Terms of Employment given to you on [   ], a copy of which is attached.

Date

Signature

1 See the Employment Rights Act 1996, ss 141 and 146 and **16.60–16.63**. The offer must be made to the employee while still employed by the employer and must take effect either immediately on the ending of that employment or after an interval of not more than four weeks. It is no longer a requirement that the offer should be in writing but it is best practice if it is.
2 If the contract is for a fixed term the date of expiry should be given.

A2.22

Agreement to extend trial period[1]

THIS AGREEMENT is made the [   ]

BETWEEN [('the Employer')] and

[('the Employee')]

WHEREBY IT IS AGREED as follows:

1. That upon the determination of the Employee's present employment by reason of redundancy he will undergo a period of retraining for the post of [   ].

2. That for the purposes of the Employment Rights Act 1996, s 138, the trial period therein mentioned will commence on the [   ] and continue until the [   ].

3. Both during the training period and thereafter the Employee's terms and conditions of employment will be as set out on the attached Statement.[2]

Signed by the Employee

Signed on behalf of the Employer

1 Employment Rights Act 1996, s 138(3). See **16.65**.
2 Attach statement setting out the terms and conditions of employment. The document setting out written particulars of terms of employment could be used for this purpose.

A2.23

Notice by employee requiring employer to give a written statement indicating how the amount of a redundancy payment has been calculated[1]

To [*Name and address of employer*]

This notice is given to you under the Employment Rights Act 1996, s 165, and requires you to give to me not later than [*date*][1] a written statement indicating how the amount of the redundancy payment received by me on [*date*] has been calculated.

Date

Signature   [*Employee*]

1 Employment Rights Act 1996, s 165. The minimum period is not less than one week beginning with the day on which the notice is given. 'Not less than' means a clear or whole week; see *McQueen v Jackson* [1903] 2 KB 163 and *Re Hector Whaling Ltd* [1936] Ch 208; [1935] All ER 302. For provisions as to service, see the Employment Rights Act 1996, s 179 and **16.130**.

A2.24

'Notice of extension' to be given by employer[1]

Form A

(For use when the participation in the strike has concluded and the number of days lost is ascertainable)

To [*Name and address of employee*]

This notice is served on you in accordance with the Employment Rights Act 1996, s 143. You are requested to agree to extend your contract of employment beyond the time of expiry, ie [   ][2] by an additional period of [   ].[3] We make this request because you took part in a strike of our employees from [   ] to [   ] [which resulted in the contract not being completed on time]. Unless you comply with this request or we are satisfied that, in consequence of sickness, injury or otherwise, you are unable to comply with it or that (notwithstanding that you are able to comply with it) in the circumstances it is reasonable for you not to do so, we shall contest any liability to pay you a redundancy payment in respect of your dismissal.

Date

[*Signature on behalf of employer*]

For and on behalf of [*employer*]

1 Employment Rights Act 1996, s 143. See **16.73**.
2 Insert the date of expiry of the employer's notice of termination (see the Employment Rights Act 1996, s 143(3)).

3   Insert the number of working days lost by striking (see the Employment Rights Act 1996, s 143(2)).

Form B

(For use during the period of participation in the strike)

To   [*Name and address of employee*]

This notice is served on you in accordance with the Employment Rights Act 1996, s 143. You are requested to agree to extend your contract of employment beyond the time of expiry, ie [   ],[1] by an additional period comprising as many available days as the number of working days lost by striking which period is not yet ascertainable. We make this request because you began to take part in a strike of our employees on [   ]. Unless you comply with this request or we are satisfied that, in consequence of sickness, injury or otherwise, you are unable to comply with it or that (notwithstanding that you are able to comply with it) in the circumstances it is reasonable for you not to do so, we shall contest any liability to pay you a redundancy payment in respect of your dismissal.

Date

[*Signature on behalf of employer*]

For and on behalf of [*employer*]

1   Insert the date of expiry of the employer's notice of termination (see the Employment Rights Act 1996, s 144(2)).

A2.25

Notice by employee of intention to claim redundancy payment in respect of lay-off or short-time, combined with notice terminating contract[1]

I [*name and address of employee*] hereby give you as my employer notice under the Employment Rights Act 1996, s 148, that I intend to claim a redundancy payment in respect of lay-off [or in respect of short-time] having been laid off [or kept on short-time] for the period of [   ] consecutive weeks ended on [   ] [*or having been laid off (or kept on short-time) for a series of six or more weeks within the meaning of the Employment Rights Act 1996, s 148, the last of such weeks having ended on the*   ] and I further[1] give you one week's[2] notice to terminate my employment by you on the [*date*].

Date

Signature   [*Employee*]

To   [*Name and address of employer*]

This notice was served[3] [   ] by [   ] on the [   ].

1   The notice is given pursuant to the Employment Rights Act 1996, s 148(1)(a) which specifically provides for some informality by including the words '... notice in writing to his employer indicating (in whatever terms) his intention to claim a redundancy payment ...'. The

above wording is in no way essential, but whatever words are used the statutory provisions must be accurately complied with.

2   The minimum contractual period not being less than one week is the minimum, see the Employment Rights Act 1996, s 150.

3   Here insert date and means of service. See the Employment Rights Act 1996, s 179 and **16.130** as to methods of service and **16.58** as to relevance of date of service.

A2.26

Counter-notice by employer of intention to contest liability given in reply to employee's notice of intention to claim[1]

To   [*Name and address of employee*]

In reply to your notice of intention to claim served on [   ] please take notice pursuant to the Employment Rights Act 1996, s 149, that I intend to contest any liability to pay you a redundancy payment in pursuance of your said notice.

Date

[*Signature on behalf of employer*][2]

For and on behalf of [*employer*]

This notice was served[3] [   ] by [   ] on [   ].

1   This notice is given in accordance with the Employment Rights Act 1996, s 149. The notice must be given to the employee within seven days after service of notice of intention to claim.

2   When the employer is a limited company the contract must be signed by a person acting under its authority.

3   Here insert date and means of service. See **16.130**, as to methods of service.

A2.27

Notice of withdrawal of counter-notice given by employer[1]

To: [*Name and address of employee*]

I hereby give you notice under the Employment Rights Act 1996, s 149 that I withdraw my counter-notice served upon you on [*date of service of counter-notice*].

Date

[*Signature by or on behalf of employer*][2]

For and on behalf of [*employer*]

This notice was served[3] [   ] by [   ] on [   ].

1   The notice is given as is mentioned in the Employment Rights Act 1996, s 149. See **16.58**.

2   When the employer is a limited company the contract must be signed by a person acting under its authority.

3   Here insert date and means of service. See the Employment Rights Act 1996, s 179 and **16.130**.

A2.28

Agreement by employee under a fixed term contract to exclude the right to a redundancy payment on its expiry[1]

To   [*Name and address of employer*]

I, [*name and address of employee*], being employed by you under a contract of employment for a fixed term of [   ][2] commencing on [   ] hereby agree that I am not entitled to a redundancy payment under the Employment Rights Act 1996 or any modification or re-enactment thereof, in respect of the expiry of that term without its being renewed.

Date

Signature   [*Employee*]

1   See the Employment Rights Act 1996, s 197(3) and **16.10**. This may be contained either in the contract itself or in a separate agreement, Employment Rights Act 1996, s 197(4). See also the form at **A2.07**.
2   Two years or more. See **16.10**.

A2.29

Specimen letter inviting consultation[1]

To   The [   ] of [*Recognised Independent Trade Union*][2]

Dear Sir

I have to inform you that as a result of financial difficulties which have been occasioned to this Company by the loss of the contract with [   ], resulting in a substantial decline in sales, it has been decided to reorganise our production facilities. Unfortunately this will result in the complete closure of the [   ] Works during the present financial year. The proposed reorganisation will have the following effects:

1.   350 manual workers and 50 office workers will be made redundant out of a total of 400 manual workers and 65 office workers at [   ] Works.

2.   It is proposed to select the number to be made redundant on a ['last in, first out'] basis. The employees remaining will assist in closing down plant and offices and will then be offered work at our [   ] Works in [   ].

3.   It is anticipated that the dismissals will take place over a period of three months in accordance with the agreed procedure. We propose that approximately one-third of those redundant should be dismissed at the end of [   ]; another third at the end of the following month; and the remainder on the last day of [   ]. The selection for order of dismissals will also be made on a 'last in, first out' basis.

4.   It is proposed to pay those employees made redundant half a week's pay (not subject to the statutory maximum) for each year of service with the

Appendix 2

Company in addition to statutory redundancy payments. Payment will be made to each employee on the last day of his employment.

The Board of Directors very much regret having to take this action and I will be pleased to discuss the matter with you and your colleagues.

Yours faithfully

1   The obligation to consult arises from the Trade Union and Labour Relations (Consolidation) Act 1992, s 188, see **16.110–16.124**.
2   For 'appropriate representatives', see **16.113**. For service, see the Trade Union and Labour Relations (Consolidation) Act 1992, s 188(5).

A2.30

Specimen letter to representatives of trade union after negotiations with and consideration of representations made by the trade union[1]

Dear Sir

Thank you for your assistance in the consideration of proposed redundancies at our [   ] Works. We have noted and carefully considered the representations which you have made and the other points raised both in writing and at our several meetings.

As a result of our discussions it has proved possible to avoid the proposed dismissals in the [maintenance department by altering the relevant shift pattern] and to reduce [to 35] the number of employees to be dismissed [in the machine room by carrying on in-house some processes previously undertaken by sub-contractors].

The Company appreciates that it will be easier for the redundant employees if the dismissals are all postponed for one month so that none take effect during the holiday period, and I can confirm that this will be done. Accordingly, the first redundancies will not now take place until [   ].

Unfortunately, your suggestion that redundancies would not be necessary if our other plants all went on short-time, is not acceptable, nor is the Company able to implement the other suggestions which you made. The financial position of the Company is such that unless the action which we propose is taken and carried out very quickly, serious damage will be caused to the remainder of our business and other jobs will be endangered.

Yours faithfully

1   See **16.114**.

5 Letters for use on transfers of undertakings

A2.31

Letter to appropriate representatives[1]

Dear

I write to inform you that we are proposing to transfer [the part of] our business to [   ] Limited. The Transfer of Undertakings (Protection of Employment) Regulations 1981 (TUPE) apply [will apply] to the transfer.

It is anticipated that the transfer will take place [on] [during] [some time after].

The reasons for the transfer are:

The following employees will be affected by the transfer:

TUPE will protect the employment rights of the employees concerned [with the exception of pension rights] and employees' periods of continuous employment with this Company will be preserved.

[There are no economic or social implications of the proposed transfer.] [The economic implications of the transfer are likely to be .]

[The social implications of the transfer are likely to be .]

We have been told that [ ] Limited will [not] be taking [the following] measures in connection with the transfer in relation to employees affected:

You will be receiving full information as to the pension position from [ ] in the [ ] Department shortly and I understand that Mr [ ] of [ ] Limited is also writing to you.

Please contact me or Mr [ ] so that we may discuss the proposals and consult with you regarding them.

Thank you for your efforts in the past.

Yours

1 See **12.24–12.36**.

A2.32

Letter to employee – pending transfer

Dear

I write to inform you that [the   part of] our business is to be transferred to [   ] Limited. The Transfer of Undertakings (Protection of Employment) Regulations 1981 apply [will apply] to the transfer.

Your period of continuous employment with this company will count with your new employer and the terms of your employment[, with the exception of those as to your pension,] will be unaffected.

You will be receiving full information as to the pension position from [   ] in the [   ] Department shortly and I understand that Mr [   ] of [   ] Limited is also writing to you.

If you have any doubts or queries as to your position please contact me or Mr [   ].

Thank you for your efforts in the past.

Yours

A2.33

Letter to employee – transfer having taken place

Dear

I write to inform you that [the   part of] our business was transferred to [   ] Limited. The Transfer of Undertakings (Protection of Employment) Regulations 1981 apply to the transfer.

With effect from [   ] your employer is [   ] Limited. Your period of continuous employment with this company counts with your new employer and the terms of your employment, with the exception of those as to your pension, are unaffected.

You will be receiving full information as to the pension position from [   ] in the [   ] Department shortly and I understand that Mr [   ] of [   ] Limited is also writing to you.

If you have any doubts or queries as to your position please contact me or Mr [   ].

Thank you for your efforts in the past.

Yours

6   Letters relating to disciplinary meetings

A2.34

Letters informing employee of disciplinary meeting and of its result

Dear

On 5 May 1996 you were suspended following an incident when it is alleged you struck the foreman. As you will see from the disciplinary rules (paragraph [4]), physical violence to another employee constitutes gross misconduct.

The disciplinary procedure is outlined at paragraph [6] onwards. There will be a disciplinary meeting at 2.15 pm on 8 May 1997 in the production manager's office. You are entitled to bring a fellow employee to speak on your behalf and any witnesses you may wish to call.

Please acknowledge receipt of this letter by returning the enclosed copy letter.

Yours

Dear

On 8 May 1997 you attended at a disciplinary meeting and at its conclusion you were informed of the company's decision to dismiss you on the ground of misconduct.

I was satisfied on the information before me that you had sworn at the foreman when he had made a perfectly proper request to you and that, when he told you that he was going to report you, you struck him in the face, breaking his glasses and cutting his eye. You were shown the statements taken from the three witnesses.

You did not deny these facts but said that you were provoked because the foreman had been getting at you over several months. I did not accept this explanation, but even if it was true it would not constitute an acceptable explanation.

In my view the company was entitled to dismiss you for gross misconduct forthwith. [However, I am well aware that you have given many years of loyal service to the company and, having spoken to the managing director, although we do not consider we are under any legal liability to do so, we are paying you 12 weeks' pay in lieu of notice. You must appreciate that we make this payment purely as an act of kindness and not as a matter of legal liability.][1]

When you were told you were to be dismissed you commented that you had been expecting that decision and you could not really complain. However, I remind you that you have the right to appeal against the decision and if you wish to do so, you should inform me within seven days of the date of this letter.

Yours

1 Wording in square brackets may be used in a case where the employer is prepared to make some payment.

A2.35

Letter in case of appeal when there has been a procedural defect at the first disciplinary hearing

Dear

On 3 October 1996 you attended an appeal hearing and at its conclusion you were informed that the appeal was to be dismissed. I am now writing to confirm to you the reasons why your appeal was rejected.

On 25 of September 1996 you attended a disciplinary hearing and you were dismissed for misconduct in pirating the company's software program and giving it to one of your friends who ran a business. In your grounds of appeal you pointed out that you had not been shown any of the statements which the company had obtained and that you had not been allowed to call witnesses to the contrary.

On receipt of your appeal I convened a preliminary meeting on 1 October 1996 and I showed you and your trade union representative all the statements the company has obtained and arranged the appeal hearing for your witness to attend on 3 October 1996.

The appeal hearing took the form of a complete rehearing of the matter and not merely a review of the earlier decision to dismiss. On the basis of the information before us which included your explanation and the account of your witness we came to the view that you had improperly used the company's software and that this constituted misconduct of such gravity that the only appropriate decision was that you should be dismissed.

Yours

A2.36

Appeal in which the decision to dismiss was allowed

Dear

On 5 March 1996 your appeal against the decision to dismiss was heard and at its conclusion we allowed your appeal but issued you with a final warning.

We accepted that the paint you removed from the finishing shop was a small quantity and that the company had no further commercial use for it. Moreover we accepted a practice had grown up whereby employees had been taking paint in these circumstances and that foremen had been turning a blind eye to this. In these circumstances we felt that the dismissal of a long-serving employee was too severe a penalty.

Nevertheless we were satisfied that you knew that removal of company property was against the company rules. You are therefore warned that if in the next 12 months you break any of the company rules you will be liable to dismissal. You are referred to paragraph [   ] of the disciplinary rules.

Yours

A2.37

Letter to all employees

It has come to our attention that a practice has grown up of employees removing tins of paint when there is still a small quantity of paint contained therein. The employee concerned was dismissed, but on appeal he was allowed to keep his job because in all the circumstances we felt that dismissal was inappropriate.

However, we must emphasise that removal of the company's property is strictly against the rules and will lead to instant dismissal. The fact that we did not dismiss the employee on this particular occasion cannot be used as a precedent on any future occasions since we have now clarified the position.

The foremen have now been instructed that this practice must cease. When tins of paint have been exhausted and the amount of paint left is so small that it is of no use to the company the tins must be left in the pallet designated for that purpose.

7 Pleadings

A2.38

GENERAL NOTE

The function of pleadings is to identify the issues of fact and law which have to be determined. In tribunals there are no formal rules of pleadings. No legal aid is available and applicants are frequently unrepresented or represented by those who do not have professional qualifications. Even large companies are often represented by their personnel managers.

In many of the following precedents the originating application is quite specifically drafted in the form in which an applicant would submit it. The fact that the notice of appearance is in many cases much longer and more sophisticated reflects the position which pertains in practice.

Tribunals eschew technicality and in tribunal cases there is rarely the extensive correspondence and elaborate pre-trial procedures which exist in court proceedings. It is therefore vital that the other side and the tribunal know what the issues are. Deploying professional ingenuity to conceal the issues in the hope that a tribunal will feel it wrong to adjudicate on an issue which has not been raised in the pleadings is unwise. Tribunals adopt an interventionist approach.

The precedents and forms do not purport to be exhaustive. They are, it is hoped, genuinely representative of what is encountered in practice.

APPLICATIONS TO AN INDUSTRIAL TRIBUNAL AND NOTICES OF APPEARANCE

Although there is no requirement to use the officially supplied forms for originating applications it is helpful to do so to ensure that all required information is provided.

When completing the forms particular care should be taken in providing details of the claims made, the name(s) and address(es) of the respondents and particulars of the claim(s).

In the originating application, box 1 should include all heads of claim which the applicant wishes the industrial tribunal to consider. The particulars of the respondents (in box 5) should include the correct and full names and addresses of all persons against whom claims are being or may be made.

When completing the notice of appearance it is important to ensure that the grounds of resistance are accurate and consistent with the evidence which will be given to the tribunal in due course. Considerable embarrassment may be avoided by making certain that the facts stated are those which will be given in evidence in due course. Best practice is to take the witness statements before completing the form of notice of appearance.

Set out below are the forms of originating application and notice of appearance, together with examples of particulars of claims and grounds of resistance. The specimens are examples of what may be encountered in practice and it is hoped they will be of assistance in actual cases.

Application to an Industrial Tribunal in England and Wales

For proceedings in Scotland use IT1(Scot)

Guidance Notes

If you think you have a case for an Industrial Tribunal:

- Read booklet ITL1(E/W). It tells you about:

  what types of complaint they can consider;

  the Industrial Tribunal procedure;

  which booklet describes your complaint more fully.

- Read the Employment booklet which describes your complaint. It tells you about:

  who to contact if you need advice or representation;

  qualifying periods – how long do you have to work for an employer before you can apply for a Tribunal;

  time limits – you must send us your application form within the time allowed for your complaint.

You can get the booklets free from any Employment Service Jobcentre.

If we do not receive your application within the time-limit stipulated for your type of complaint, we may not be able to deal with it. If you are in doubt, please contact the Advisory Conciliation and Arbitration Service (ACAS) (Booklet ITL1(E/W) gives addresses and telephone numbers) or contact your local Employment Service Jobcentre.

If you need advice or help to complete your application, you can seek help from for example, your Trade Union or local Citizens Advice Bureau.

You can present the case yourself or have a representative to act for you. If you name a representative, all further communications will be sent to them and not to you. Please arrange for them to keep you informed of the progress of the case.

If your complaint concerns equal pay or sex discrimination you may wish to contact the Equal Opportunities Commission for advice about representation. If your complaint concerns race discrimination you may wish to contact the Commission for Racial Equality.

If you have a disability and need any special arrangements when visiting the Industrial Tribunal, please inform the staff at the office dealing with your case in advance. They do all they can to help you.

If you have a question about the Industrial Tribunal procedure and cannot find the answer in the booklets, please ring the Industrial Tribunal Enquiry line on 0345 959775. (All calls are charged at local rate).

Please answer all the questions on the application that apply to your complaint.

When you have completed the form detach and retain these notes and send the application form to the relevant Tribunal Office.

Applications can be faxed, delivered by hand or posted. If you fax your application do not post a copy as well. If you post the application take a copy for your records.

Guidance on where to send your application is overleaf.

Industrial Tribunal Offices in England and Wales

Ashford – Tufton House, Tufton Street, Ashford, Kent TN23 1RJ, Fax: 01233 624423

Bedford – 8-10 Howard Street, Bedford MK40 3HS, Fax: 01234 352315

Birmingham – Phoenix House, 1-3 Newhall Street, Birmingham B3 3NH, Fax: 0121 236 6029

Bury St Edmunds – 100 Southgate Street, Bury St Edmunds IP33 2AQ, Fax: 01284 706064

Bristol – The Crescent Centre, Temple Back, Bristol BS1 6EZ, Fax: 0117 925 3452

Cardiff – Caradog House, 1-6 St Andrews Place, Cardiff CF1 3BE, Fax: 01222 225906

Exeter – Renslade House, Bonhay Road, Exeter EX4 3BX, Fax: 01392 430063

Leeds – Albion Tower, 11 Albion Street, Leeds LS1 5ES, Fax: 01132 428843

Leicester – 5A New Walk, Leicester LE1 6TE, Fax: 01162 255 6099

Liverpool – Union Court, Cook Street, Liverpool L2 4UJ, Fax: 0151 231 1484

London South – Registration Section, Montagu Court, 101 London Road, West Croydon CR0 2RF, Fax: 0181 649 9470

London North – 19-29 Woburn Place, London WC1H 0LU, Fax: 0171 273 8686

Manchester – Applications Dept., PO Box 210, Manchester M60 3BW, Fax: 0161 907 2048

Newcastle – Quayside House, 110 Quayside, Newcastle Upon Tyne NE1 3DX, Fax: 0191 222 1680

Nottingham – 3rd Floor, Byron House, 2A Maid Marian Way, Nottingham NG1 6HS, Fax: 01159 507612

Reading – 5th Floor, 30-31 Friar Street, Reading RG1 1DY, Fax: 01734 568066

Sheffield – 14 East Parade, Sheffield S1 2ET, Fax: 0114 276 2551

Shrewsbury – Prospect House, Belle Vue Road, Shrewsbury SY3 7NR, Fax: 01743 244186

Southampton – 3rd Floor, Dukes Keep, Marsh Lane, Southampton SO1 1EX, Fax: 01703 635506

Stratford – 44 The Broadway, Stratford, London E15 1XH, Fax: 0181 221 0398

Appendix 2

Where to send your application

- You will need to know the postcode for the place where you worked. If you have never worked for the employer use the postcode for the place where the matter which you are complaining about occurred.

- Refer to the chart below and send it to the tribunal office listed against the code e.g. PE10, 11 or 12 should go to Nottingham Office. (The full address of each office is on the reverse of these notes).

- Sending your application to the wrong office may cause delay. If you are in doubt where to send it, call the Industrial Tribunal Enquiry line on **0345 959775.**

Post Code Area	Tribunal Office	Post Code Area	Tribunal Office	Post Code Area	Tribunal Office	Post Code Area	Tribunal Office
AL	Bedford	GU1-10	London South	PE1-6	Leicester	SW1-2	London South
B	Birmingham	GU11-14	Southampton	PE7	Bury St Eds	SW3	London North
BA1-16	Bristol	GU15-16	London South	PE8	Bedford	SW4	London North
BA20-22	Exeter	GU17	Reading	PE9	Leicester	SW5-7	London North
BB	Manchester	GU18-25	London South	PE10-12	Nottingham	SW8-9	London South
BD	Leeds	GU26-35	Southampton	PE13-19	Bury St Eds	SW10	London North
BH	Southampton	HA	London North	PE20-25	Nottingham	SW11-20	London South
BL	Manchester	HD	Leeds	PE30-38	Bury St Eds	SY1-22	Shrewsbury
BN	Southampton	HG	Leeds	PL	Exeter	SY23-25	Cardiff
BR	Ashford	HP1-5	London North	PO	Southampton	TA1-5	Exeter
BS	Bristol	HP6-22	Reading	PR1-7	Manchester	TA6-9	Bristol
CA	Newcastle	HP23	London North	PR8-9	Liverpool	TA10-24	Exeter
CB	Bury St Eds	HP27	Reading	RG1-13	Reading	TD****	Newcastle
CF	Cardiff	HR	Cardiff	RG14-15	Southampton	TF	Shrewsbury
CH1-3	Liverpool	HU	Leeds	RG16-20	Reading	TN1-4	Ashford
CH4-8	Shrewsbury	HX	Leeds	RG21-28	Southampton	TN5-7	London South
CM	Stratford	IG	Stratford	RG29-45	Reading	TN8-18	Ashford
CO	Bury St Eds	IP	Bury St Eds	RH1-14	London South	TN19-22	Southampton
CR	London South	KT	London South	RH15-17	Southampton	TN23-31	Ashford
CT	Ashford	L	Liverpool	RH18-20	London South	TN32-33	Southampton
CV	Birmingham	LA1-6	Manchester	RM	Stratford	TN34-38	Ashford
CW1-5	Shrewsbury	LA7-23	Newcastle	S1-62	Sheffield	TN39-40	Southampton
CW6-10	Liverpool	LD	Cardiff	S63-64	Leeds	TQ	Exeter
CW11-12	Shrewsbury	LE	Leicester	S65-66	Sheffield	TR	Exeter
DA	Ashford	LL	Shrewsbury	S70-75	Leeds	TS	Newcastle
DE1-7	Nottingham	LN	Nottingham	S80-81	Sheffield	TW	London South
DE11-15	Leicester	LS	Leeds	SA	Cardiff	UB	London North
DE21-75	Nottingham	LU	Bedford	SE	London South	W	London North
DH	Newcastle	M	Manchester	SG1-7	Bedford	WA1-2	Liverpool
DL	Newcastle	ME	Ashford	SG8-14	Bury St Eds	WA3	Manchester
DN1-20	Leeds	MK	Bedford	SG15-19	Bedford	WA4-13	Liverpool
DN21	Nottingham	N	London North	SK	Manchester	WA14-16	Manchester
DN22	Sheffield	NE	Newcastle	SL	Reading	WC	London North
DN31-40	Leeds	NG	Nottingham	SM	London South	WD	London North
DT1-5	Southampton	NN1-13	Bedford	SN1-6	Bristol	WF	Leeds
DT6-8	Exeter	NN14-18	Leicester	SN7	Reading	WN1-7	Manchester
DT9-11	Southampton	NN29	Bedford	SN8-16	Bristol	WN8	Liverpool
DY	Birmingham	NP	Cardiff	SO	Southampton	WR	Birmingham
E	Stratford	NR	Bury St Eds	SP	Southampton	WS	Birmingham
EC	Stratford	NW	London North	SR	Newcastle	WV	Birmingham
EN	Stratford	OL1-13	Manchester	SS	Stratford	YO1-18	Leeds
EX	Exeter	OL14	Leeds	ST1-13	Shrewsbury	YO21-22	Newcastle
FY	Manchester	OL15-16	Manchester	ST14	Leicester	YO25	Leeds
GL	Bristol	OX	Reading	ST15-21	Birmingham	****TD post code area – English locations only – Scotland has its own tribunals	

Applications to an Industrial Tribunal

INDUSTRIAL TRIBUNAL SERVICE

Received at ITO

FOR OFFICE USE

Case Number

Code

Initials   ROIT

- This form has to be photocopied. If possible please use BLACK INK and CAPITAL letters.
- Where there are tick boxes, please tick the one that applies.

1 Please give the type of complaint you want the tribunal to decide (for example: unfair dismissal, equal pay). A full list is given in Booklet ITL1. If you have more than one complaint list them all.

4 Please give the dates of your employment

From   To

5 Please give the name and address of the employer, other organisation or person against whom this complaint is being brought

Name of the employer, organisation or person

Address

Postcode

Telephone

Please give the place where you worked or applied to work if different from above

Address

Postcode

2 Please give your details

Mr ☐   Mrs ☐   Miss ☐   Ms ☐

First names

Surname

Date of birth

Address

Postcode

Telephone

Daytime Telephone

Please give an address to which we should send documents if different from above

Postcode

3 If a representative is acting for you please give details

Name

Address

Postcode

Telephone

Reference

6 Please say what job you did for the employer (or what job you applied for). If this does not apply, Please say what your connection was with the employer

IT1(E/W)

page 3

567

Appendix 2

7 Please give the number of normal basic hours worked each week

Hours per week

9 If your complaint is NOT about dismissal, please give the date when the matter you are complaining about took place

8 Please give your earning details

Basic wage/salary

£   :   per

Average take home pay

£   :   per

Other bonuses/benefits

£   :   per

10 Unfair dismissal applicants only

Please indicate what you are seeking at this stage, if you win your case.

☐ Reinstatement: to carry on working in your old job as before (An order for reinstatement normally includes an award of compensation for loss of earnings.)

☐ Re-engagement: to start another job or new contract with your old employer. (An order for re-engagement normally includes an award of compensation for loss of earnings.)

☐ Compensation only: to get an award of money

11 Please give details of your complaint

If there is not enough space for your answer, please continue on a separate sheet and attach it to this form.

12 Please sign and date this form, then send it to the address given on page 1.

Signed

Date

THE INDUSTRIAL TRIBUNALS
NOTICE OF APPEARANCE BY RESPONDENT

In the application of

Case Number

(please quote in all correspondence)

* This form has to be photocopied, if possible please use Black Ink and Capital letters
* If there is not enough space for your answer, please continue on a separate sheet and attach it to this form

1. Full name and address of the Respondent:

3. Do you intend to resist the application? (Tick appropriate box)

YES   NO

4. Was the applicant dismissed? (Tick appropriate box)

YES   NO

Please give
reason below

Reason for dismissal:

5. Are the dates of employment given by the applicant correct? (Tick appropriate box)

YES   NO

please give correct dates below

Post Code:

Began on

Telephone number:

Ended on

2. If you require documents and notices to be sent to a representative or any other address in the United Kingdom please give details:

6. Are the details given by the applicant about wages/salary, take home or other bonuses correct? (Tick appropriate box)

YES   NO

Please give correct details
below

Basic Wages/Salary	£	per
Average Take Home Pay	£	per
Other Bonuses/Benefits	£	per

PLEASE TURN OVER

for office use only
Date of receipt   Initials

Post Code:

Reference:

Telephone number:

Form IT3 E&W - 1/95

Appendix 2

7. Give particulars of the grounds on which you intend to resist the application.

8. Please sign and date the form.

Signed   Dated

DATA PROTECTION ACT 1984
We may put some of the information you give on this form on to a computer. This helps us to monitor progress and produce statistics. We may also give information to:
* the other party in the case
* other parts of the Employment Department Group and organisations such as ACAS (Advisory Conciliation and Arbitration Service), the Equal Opportunities Commission or the Commission for Racial Equality.

Please post or fax this form to : The Regional Secretary Industrial Tribunals, Phoenix House, 1-3 Newhall Street, Birmingham, B3 3NH.

* IF YOU FAX THE FORM, DO NOT POST A COPY AS WELL
* IF YOU POST THE FORM, TAKE A COPY FOR YOUR RECORDS

Form IT3 E&W - 1/95

UNLAWFUL DEDUCTIONS FROM WAGES

Originating application

My employer unlawfully deducted £100 from my pay in respect of a mistake which they claim I made. I did not make the mistake.

My employer unlawfully deducted £100 from my pay in respect of a mistake which they claim I made. They had no right to make the deduction.

My employer failed to pay me holiday pay on the termination of my employment. This amounted to an unlawful deduction as is provided in s 13 of the Employment Rights Act 1996.

Notice of appearance

The applicant was paid all sums due to him.

The deduction claimed by the applicant was made but was authorised by his contract of employment.

The deduction claimed by the applicant was made. The applicant had consented in writing to the deduction.

EQUAL PAY

Originating application

Like work

I work as an invoice clerk for the respondents. A male, Mr J White, works as a clerk for them at the same factory. His work is the same or broadly similar to that which I do and he is paid more than me. I claim equal pay with Mr White.

Work rated as equivalent

I work as a general administrator for the respondents. A male, Mr A Green, works as a sales representative for them based at the same office. His work has been rated as at the same level as mine in a job evaluation study and yet he is paid more than me. I claim equal pay with Mr Green.

Work of equal value

I work as a machine minder working at the respondents' [   ] factory. A female, Miss L Brown, works as a warehousewoman at the same factory. Her work is of the same value as that which I do in terms of the demands on us and yet she is paid more than me. I claim equal pay with Miss Brown.

Appendix 2

Notice of appearance

Like work

[   ] is employed by us at [our   works] as is Mr White.
However, her work is not like work with that of Mr White. Mr White's work
is not the same as, or broadly similar to, that of the applicant's. Mr White
deals with a far wider variety of work of a much higher value than does the
applicant. His work entails taking decisions as to authorisation of payment of
suppliers whereas the applicant's work does not. In addition Mr White stands
in for the Purchasing Manager when that person is absent.

Work rated as equivalent

1   The work undertaken by [   ] is not rated as equivalent as that of
Mr Green under our job evaluation scheme.

2   Work is being undertaken towards the implementation of a job evaluation
scheme for our employees, but no job evaluation study has been finalised.
What the applicant refers to is a preparatory document which has since been
the subject of considerable amendment, in particular affecting the valuation
of the posts of administrator and sales representative.

Work of equal value

The work undertaken by [   ] is not of equal value with that undertaken by Miss Brown. Her work is much more demanding than the applicant's work in terms of effort, skill and decision-making.

Genuine material factor defence

It is accepted that the applicant's work is of equal value to that of Mrs Blue.
However, a higher salary is paid to Mrs Blue because she qualifies for the
bonus paid to all employees who have ten years' service with the Company.
Mr Orange will qualify for this bonus in four years if he is still employed by
the Company.

DISMISSAL AND REDUNDANCY

Constructive dismissal and redundancy

Originating application

I was the night-shift worker at Smith and Company. I was paid £10 per week
extra. They shut the night shift down and offered me a job on the day shift. I
refused and left. I was unfairly dismissed. I want compensation.

Notice of appearance

It is accepted that the applicant worked as a night-shift employment operative. However, under the terms upon which the applicant was employed, the
respondents were entitled to deploy him on either night or day shift. It is
therefore submitted that the respondents were entitled to require him to work
on the day shift and the applicant was not constructively dismissed.

If, contrary to the respondents' contention, it is adjudged that the applicant has been constructively dismissed, the respondent will contend that such dismissal was not unfair. The reason for the requirement for the applicant to work on the day shift was because the night shift was ended due to a shortage of orders. The respondents will contend that the reason for the changes was a reason which was fair, namely redundancy.

If it is to be claimed that the applicant was entitled to a redundancy payment, the respondents will contend that the applicant is not eligible for a redundancy payment since he unreasonably refused an offer of suitable alternative employment, namely a job on the day shift.

Request to amend

I want to amend my claim to include a claim for a redundancy payment.[1] I was not unreasonable in refusing to take the job on the day shift. My wife works during the day and it is necessary for me to work on the night shift to look after the children. In addition I live some 15 miles away from the factory in a village from which I cannot get to the factory by public transport. I do not have a car. I was able to get a lift with a friend who works on the night shift at another factory and I could not have got a lift for the day shift.

1 As the applicant claimed unfair dismissal as of right he was within time to make the application for a redundancy payment, see the Employment Rights Act 1996, s 164(1)(d).

Unfair dismissal for dishonesty when it is alleged that another employee was not dismissed in similar circumstances

Originating application

I was employed by Brown and Co for ten years. We are allowed to buy car components at a reduced rate. I did not know if the car alarm fitted my car so I decided to take it home to try it out. I intended to pay for the alarm. I was prosecuted for theft but was acquitted. Three weeks before I was dismissed an employee was stopped with property by a security guard and he was not dismissed. I want reinstatement, re-engagement and compensation.

Notice of appearance

It is accepted that the applicant was dismissed. It is, however, contended that the dismissal was fair because the respondents believed on reasonable grounds that he was guilty of dishonesty and/or misconduct and that decision was reached after the respondents had made such enquiries as were reasonable in the circumstances. The applicant was stopped by a security guard, interviewed by his manager and when asked for an explanation merely said: 'Please do not sack me; my wife is expecting a baby next month.'

In any event there is a company rule that under no circumstances shall company property be taken out of the premises. This is set out in the company handbook which each employee is given. It is accepted that there was an occasion when an employee was stopped with company property and was not dismissed. However, the facts were very different. The property concerned was a small screwdriver (value about £3). The employee gave the explanation that he wished to work on his car and needed this particular screwdriver to do the job. He claimed that he had left a note on his foreman's desk saying what he intended to do. The employee was taken back into the factory and the company accepted that such a note was left for the foreman. In view of this he was warned. A letter was sent to all employees pointing out that removal of company property was in any circumstances a serious offence which would result in instant dismissal. It was pointed out that the employee had not been dismissed because his explanation had been accepted, but that in future it was made clear that this was a wholly exceptional case.

The fact that the applicant was acquitted is not relevant. In any event the respondents will claim that the applicant should not receive any compensation since he contributed to the dismissal by removing company property and by failing to give any explanation which would suggest he was not acting dishonestly.

Claim for unfair dismissal alleging partiality; claim on behalf of respondents that no compensation should be awarded because of matters discovered after the dismissal

Originating application

I was caught fighting at work with Bill Smith. I was dismissed. My dismissal was unfair because the real reason why I was dismissed when Bill Smith was not is that he is the foreman's nephew.

Notice of appearance

The applicant was dismissed for fighting. The matter was thoroughly investigated and the evidence which the company accepted was that the applicant was the aggressor. The only explanation the applicant gave for his attack was that Smith had been asking for it.

The fact that Bill Smith was the nephew of the foreman was known to management, but was not a relevant consideration; he received a written warning. The company has a tradition of employing members of the same family and it will adduce at the hearing instances of cases in which members of the family of those in a managerial capacity have been dismissed.

In any event the applicant contributed to his dismissal for the reasons set out above.

If the tribunal finds that the applicant was unfairly dismissed, it is submitted that the applicant should not receive any compensation. Unbeknown to the members of the management who dismissed the applicant a security check was being carried out on employees' lockers. The applicant was found to have concealed in his locker items of company property worth £250. He was prosecuted, convicted and fined. It would not be just and equitable for the applicant to receive any compensation and in any event he would have been dismissed for dishonesty forthwith on discovery of his dishonesty.

Unfair dismissal and redundancy when there are changes in the job function

Originating application

I have worked for the company for 15 years. Initially I was employed as a wages clerk and it was my job to make up the wages. After the company introduced direct payment I was moved to other clerical duties involved with chasing up people who had not paid their bills within the 28 days allowed.

The company then introduced computerisation and I was sent on a course, but I did not find it easy to familiarise myself with the new techniques and I received warnings about my work. Eventually I was dismissed. I think my dismissal was unfair since I was never appointed as a computer operator. I want a redundancy payment.

Notice of appearance

The respondent company is a small company employing in total some 100 operatives of whom 85 are direct hourly paid workers; five are supervisory staff and ten are employed in the office.

At the time when the applicant was employed she was told that she was to be a wages clerk, but she was also told that she would be expected to help in general office work as well. Her particulars of employment described her work as clerical assistant. When the company moved to paying wages by a direct payment system the applicant was transferred to credit control and she raised no objection.

As part of the reorganisation of its procedures the company introduced computerisation. The applicant was one of three members of the staff who were involved and the company set about an elaborate training operation. There were inevitable difficulties in the changeover to computerisation but these were exacerbated by the negative attitude displayed by the applicant. She continued to make frequent mistakes and was not able and/or was unwilling to acquire the skills the company needed.

Matters came to a head when the applicant was found apparently going through the motions of operating the computer – she had not been able to access files and had not entered any information as required. She was interviewed and adopted an intransigent attitude. At first she denied any pretence with regard to operating the computer, but then admitted that she was fed up with asking others how to access files and enter information. The company decided that in view of the failure of the applicant to acquire the necessary skills despite a significant input by management and the computer consultants, it would be futile to spend more time in training the applicant. Moreover its faith in the honesty of the applicant was breached by her attempt to mislead management about what she was doing. This is a small company and there was no other position in the company to which she could be transferred.

In that the applicant is claiming that she was unfairly dismissed it is contended that an employee must be prepared to meet new challenges which modern technology requires and that the dismissal was for a fair reason, being one that related to her capability and/or conduct. In that the applicant is claiming redundancy it is denied that the reason for the dismissal constituted redundancy within the meaning of the Employment Rights Act 1996 as evidenced by the fact that thereafter the company recruited another employee to take her place.

Claim for a redundancy payment by an employee away due to long-term disability

Originating application

I was employed by the company as a labourer. Three years ago I was involved in an accident at work and hurt my back. The trade union is handling my case against my employers. I have had a number of operations, but I am still off sick. The company has now closed down its factory and moved employees to another factory on another site. A number of my old workmates have received redundancy payments. I want the company to pay me a redundancy payment.

Notice of appearance alleging frustration

It is admitted that the applicant was employed as a labourer and that he has been absent from work for some three years. He was involved in an accident at work. He has brought a claim against the company and the company has copies of medical reports obtained on behalf of the applicant which state that the applicant will by reason of his injuries never be able to do his pre-accident work again. The applicant was replaced after a period of three months.

Having studied the description of the applicant's injuries and the prognosis with regard to them in the medical reports, the company came to the conclusion that the applicant would never be able to work again. The company will therefore contend that the applicant's contract of employment has been frustrated and that he is not entitled to a redundancy payment.

The company did not dismiss the applicant on the grounds of ill-health because it seemed an unnecessary and humiliating option.

Unfair dismissal on the grounds of ill-health

Originating application

I have been employed by the company for 12 years and in the last 12 months have been away from work due to ill-health for a number of different reasons. I have produced a number of medical notes, but as many of the absences have only been for less than five days, I have certified myself as sick on those occasions.

After having been given warnings I was dismissed. Other employees have been away for longer periods and they have not been dismissed.

Notice of appearance

It is admitted that the applicant was dismissed, but the reason for the dismissal was a fair one in that it related either to conduct and/or capability.

Over the last five years the applicant has been persistently absent from work due to ill-health as shown in the schedule of absences. An analysis of the schedule shows that the applicant has been away in each of these years for at least 25 days and in the last 12 months prior to her dismissal she had 35 days' sick leave.

An analysis of the duration of the sick leave shows that in general terms no absence has lasted more than five days and that in every year between April and September there is a heavy incidence of sick leave on a Friday and the following Monday.

The applicant has been advised and warned as to the amount of sick leave taken, but the situation has not improved. It is true that on individual occasions employees may have had substantial periods off work for major surgery, but this is a contingency with which we can deal.

The company cannot deal with repeated and unforeseen absences for relatively trivial ailments. We are not in a position to say whether the illnesses and conditions are genuine or not.

Notwithstanding a final warning the applicant was absent on the Friday and the Monday on six out of eight of the last weekends prior to her dismissal. The applicant was interviewed and the company came to the view that it had no alternative but to dismiss the applicant because of her repeated absences due to what she claimed was her ill-health.

Unfair dismissal – breach of confidentiality and duty of trust

Originating application

I worked as a gardener and odd-job man at the company's factory. Recently they have cut my hours. I was offered and accepted the job of doing the lawns at a neighbouring firm. The managing director was driving past and he saw me working in the grounds of the other company. He later called me in and said that he was not having me working for a competitor and sacked me. I think that this was unfair. I want my job back.

Notice of appearance

It is admitted that the applicant was dismissed. The company accepts that it would not be fair to dismiss someone occupying the position which the applicant held merely because he was working for another firm in his free time. However, Snodgrass Ltd where he worked is our main competitor.

Many of the respondent company's customers are also customers or potential customers of Snodgrass Ltd. It has come to the attention of the managing director that the applicant has frequently chatted with this company's customers when they have been visiting Snodgrass Ltd and inevitably they have asked him if he has changed his job. He has told them that although he was still working for this company he thought it was only a matter of time before he was made redundant because this company was in a bad way. He has revealed to the customers that we have had difficulties with one of the components which we manufacture and that we have had a large number of warranty claims which has seriously affected the company. Although this is an exaggerated version of what has happened, we have had difficulties and revealing this information has had serious consequences. Two of our main customers have withdrawn orders for this component.

The applicant owed us a duty of confidentiality and trust and we believe he has abused that trust by revealing information which has had serious repercussions for us. The applicant was seen and these allegations were put to him. At first he denied it and then when the names of the customers concerned were given to him he said it was only said in jest. He was therefore dismissed for misconduct and it was fair to treat that as a sufficient reason for dismissal.

Unfair dismissal in which it is claimed that the dismissal was not for an isolated incident

Originating application

I was working at the factory on a hot Friday afternoon when the foreman suddenly told me that I had to work overtime. I refused at first, but he swore at me and told me I had to. I was planning to go away with my girl friend for the weekend so I was pretty upset at this. I was repairing this machine when the foreman came along and told me that I was taking too long and that they were losing production time because I was a right prat. I lost my temper and told him where to go. On the Monday I was called in by the manager and dismissed.

Notice of appearance

The applicant was dismissed for misconduct. The applicant was not dismissed for an isolated act of swearing at the foreman, but for a course of conduct which undermined the authority of the management.

The applicant has been on the rota to do overtime. When he was reminded of this on the Friday he used offensive language to the foreman. The foreman sought to be flexible and told the applicant he need only work an hour extra. When approached by the foreman who asked him how long he would be the applicant used offensive language which was clearly heard by others in the workshop.

The applicant has received several warnings for his behaviour and when he was dismissed was subject to a final written warning for gross insubordination to the same foreman. It is within the knowledge of the respondents that the applicant when he received the last written warning went back into the workshop, tore up the final written warning and said that the management were a group of spineless idiots who would not have the guts to dismiss him because his brother had been dismissed and had taken them to a tribunal.

When the applicant was seen he said merely that the foreman was out of order and refused to elaborate. The applicant was dismissed for misconduct and the company contends that it was fair to dismiss him because any other course would undermine management's authority amongst the workforce.

Unfair dismissal; claim by the respondent company that any procedural defect in the original decision to dismiss was cured by the subsequent appeal

Originating application

I have been employed as a lorry driver and as such make long-term deliveries all over England, Wales and Scotland. When I got back to the depot on 18 October 1996 I was called in to see the manager. He said that I have been seen on a motorway service station removing items from the load and giving them to another lorry driver and receiving payment.

I asked where it was alleged that this had happened and who it was who had informed the company. The manager merely said that this information was confidential and I was dismissed.

Notice of appearance

It is admitted that the applicant was dismissed for misconduct in that the company believed on reasonable grounds that he had been guilty of selling part of a consignment of video recorders.

The applicant appealed. The appeal took the form of a total re-hearing and not merely a review. The applicant was represented by his shop steward.

At the appeal hearing the applicant and his representative were given a copy of the statement of the informant who was a director of the company for whom the respondent company were transporting the load. That statement identified the registration of the applicant's lorry and gave the time and the details of where it was claimed the incident took place. It also contained the registration number of the lorry of the driver who had purchased the video recorder. There was a statement from the transport manager of that firm which confirmed that their lorry driver had admitted he had stopped at that motorway service station and that he had purchased a video machine but claimed that the applicant had said it was his own property and he had won it in a raffle.

In addition the applicant and his representative were shown the original of the delivery note which showed that there had been an alteration to the number of video recorders.

The applicant and his representative were asked if they wanted an adjournment to another day to call evidence on the applicant's behalf. After a short recess the applicant and his representative returned and said that they wanted the matter dealt with on that day.

When asked for his explanation the applicant said that he may have been at this service station, but nothing like what was described in the statements had happened.

In view of the weight of evidence, the manager conducting the appeal stated that he believed on reasonable grounds that the applicant had been selling a customer's property and therefore confirmed the dismissal. It should be emphasised that in confirming the dismissal he had totally re-heard all the evidence and took the decision without reference to the original decision to dismiss.

Case raising the status of employee

Originating application

I have been employed as a manager of the company's newspaper shop for three years and before that I had been the assistant branch manager at various of their shops.

When I took over as manager I was told that I was to be self-employed and pay my own tax and National Insurance. I was to received 15% of the turnover out of which I had to employ such staff as I needed and meet the business rates, the electricity and telephone bills.

The company met the rent of the premises, supplied all the stock and dictated what hours the shop should open. If I was away through illness or ill-health the company provided the relief manager. I was required to adhere to the company banking procedures and I was issued with a disciplinary code.

We have a quarterly stock check and for three quarters there were shown to be deficiencies which were above what I was told was the national norm. I was issued with a final warning that if the position did not improve my contract would be terminated.

On the last quarterly check there was still a deficiency. I was dismissed. They did not listen to my arguments as to why we had greater stock deficiencies than other shops, nor did they give any credit for the fact that over the last four quarters there has been a real improvement in the deficiencies. For practical purposes I was an employee and I claim I have been unfairly dismissed.

Notice of appearance

The tribunal does not have jurisdiction in this case since the applicant was not an employee. The applicant was initially employed as an assistant manager in which capacity he was involved in relief work at a number of stores.

He was then offered the position as permanent manager and it was explained to him that in such a position he would no longer be an employee but would be self-employed. The applicant was enthusiastic about this change and notwithstanding our advice that he should take home the contract and seek advice about its implications, he nevertheless insisted on signing the agreement.

The respondent company will refer to the terms of the contract at the hearing. Under the terms of the contract the applicant was allowed extensive discretion as to how to run the business and the amount he earned was directly related to the prosperity of the business.

His status as self-employed was accepted by both the tax and the National Insurance authorities.

Redundancy payment and unfair dismissal

Originating application

The applicant started work with the company on 1 April 1994. In the early part of 1996 there were persistent rumours of redundancies. On 28 March 1996 the applicant was summoned into the manager's office and informed that he had been fiddling his travelling expenses and that he was to be dismissed forthwith.

It is the applicant's case that the employers were not entitled to dismiss him without notice; that he was therefore entitled to have the statutory notice of one week added to his continuous service and that therefore he has two years' continuous service.

The applicant's case is that the summary dismissal was a pretext on the part of the company to avoid paying him a redundancy payment and that his selection for redundancy was in any event unfair since it was based on a personality clash between him and his manager rather than on any proper assessment of the needs of the company.

The applicant therefore claims a redundancy payment and/or unfair dismissal and money in lieu of notice.

Notice of appearance

The applicant does not have two years' continuous service. Thus he has not acquired the right not to be unfairly dismissed and is not entitled to a redundancy payment.

The respondents were entitled to dismiss the applicant summarily. He had claimed a mileage allowance for travelling to a depot. Our enquiries revealed that he had not visited that depot, but was seen at the time attending a football match.

In any event he does not have the right to a redundancy payment since although it is accepted he commenced employment on 1 April 1994, he did not attain the age of 18 until 1 June 1994 and would not qualify for such payment even if the period of statutory notice was included.

If contrary to our contention it is adjudged that the company was not entitled to dismiss the applicant summarily and the tribunal does have jurisdiction to hear the case of unfair dismissal, it is contended that the dismissal was for a fair reason, namely for misconduct.

In any event the respondents will contend as being relevant to any issue of compensation that the applicant would, on the balance of probabilities, have been dismissed on the grounds of redundancy by 5 April 1996 when substantial redundancies took place. It is absolutely certain the applicant would have been dismissed on the ground of redundancy by 30 May 1996 when the office was closed completely.

DISCRIMINATION ON THE GROUNDS OF SEX AND RACE

Sex discrimination – genuine occupational requirement

Originating application

I was made redundant from my last job as a fitter and therefore I decided to train as a chef. I completed the course and I saw an advert in the local paper for the position of a cook at an old people's home. I wrote a letter and they wrote back inviting me to an interview. They were obviously surprised that I was a man. My first name is Lesley, so there may have been some confusion from my letter. They said to me that they wanted a female. I have been discriminated against on ground of my sex. I want compensation.

Notice of appearance

It is accepted that the applicant applied for the job and that he was turned down on the basis that he was male. The reason for this was that there is a genuine occupational requirement that the position should be held by a woman.

The respondent operates a small old people's home with ten residents of whom eight are women. Because of the absolute necessity of maintaining the highest standards of hygiene we require the cook to take trays of food to those who are bedridden and, on occasions, to feed those patients who are incapable of feeding themselves. A cook would have access to residents' bedrooms for the reasons outlined above and inevitably some will be on a commode or, in the case of those who are senile, may well be in a state of undress. A cook has always to make sure that residents are clean before eating meals. Even in the dining room it is not unknown for residents to urinate and defecate.

Although the female residents will accept that doctors may be male when we canvassed with them the possibility of employing male care assistants there was a widespread protest and five of the residents either themselves or through their family threatened to leave the home.

We advertised for the post of a cook but in reality the job description (which we enclose) makes it clear that there is a need for the cook to carry out many of the functions of a care assistant for the reasons we have given. In view of our size we cannot justify employing a cook who did not have this degree of flexibility.

We accept that it would have been wiser to have spelt out this requirement in our advertisement in the local press and we apologise for any inadvertent offence we have caused. We are a small commercial organisation relying on fee-paying residents and we believe that if we were to employ a man in this capacity we would lose and not replace a significant proportion of our residents.

Sex discrimination – job application

Originating application

I applied for a job as a consultant physician. I am a woman and am now 38 years old. I have been a senior registrar and not only have had my fellowship for some years but have published several articles in the professional journals.

At the interview I was asked a number of questions about my family commitments. I was not appointed. At the de-briefing afterwards I was told that although the appointing body had been impressed by my academic qualifications and my clinical experience it was felt that I would not fit in at that particular hospital. They appointed a candidate with less experience and inferior academic qualifications. I believe that I have been discriminated against on the grounds of gender and that I was only shortlisted as a token gesture.

Notice of appearance

It is accepted that the applicant did have extensive experience and was highly qualified in academic terms. It is true that the applicant was asked questions about her family commitments but so too were the male candidates.

A consultant physician does not operate in a discrete area but has many functions which overlap with other disciplines. During the interview the view was formed that the applicant had a somewhat abrasive personality and that she would stimulate a certain amount of animosity with other working colleagues. This view of the applicant was foreshadowed in the references which she provided. It is denied that the applicant's gender was an issue in the decision as to whether she should be dismissed.

Unfair dismissal, discrimination in respect of sex and married status in cases in which confidentiality is of paramount importance

Originating application

I have been employed by my firm for ten years as the managing partner's secretary. About three years ago I started going out with the person who is now my husband who was an employee at the same firm. We married six months ago.

Appendix 2

Three months ago my husband left the firm and went to work for a competitor. After we came back from the honeymoon the managing partner called me in and said that he could not continue employing me as I saw sensitive material which would be of use to my husband's firm. He offered me a job working as the receptionist. This was a less interesting job and I was hurt by the suggestion that I would not be able to keep confidences. I refused the offer and I was dismissed. This was unfair.

I believe that this is sex discrimination. I do not believe that a man would have been treated this way and I am being discriminated against because of my marital status.

Notice of appearance

It is accepted that the applicant was dismissed but it is contended that this was for a substantial reason and it was fair to treat that as a sufficient reason for the dismissal.

The respondent is a firm of patent agents dealing with extremely confidential information which is potentially worth millions of pounds. The applicant's husband now works for the firm's main competitor.

Because of the extreme urgency of some of the firm's work the applicant is occasionally required to work overtime at short notice. To enable her to do some of her work at home she has a computer which will enable her to access information held in the firm's computer.

It was never suggested that the applicant would deliberately pass information to her husband. The fear is that quite inadvertently she will mention some aspect of her work which may well be of a routine nature and thus enable her husband to make an intelligent guess as to patents upon which the firm is working. The second concern was that even though this was not the case it would be an obvious inference for the firm's clients to make if they lost the right to a patent of an invention. This would lead to a loss of confidence in the firm and the threat of protracted litigation.

Patent agents pay extremely high insurance premiums – amounting to a significant proportion of their turnover. This is because if the firm is negligent, its clients can sue the firm not only for years of abortive research, but for the loss of profit which would have accrued had they obtained the patent.

The respondent firm and the firm which employs the applicant's husband share the same insurer and each firm informed the insurer of the position. The insurer indicated that it would not renew the respective policies if the position continued.

When the applicant's husband came to talk to the firm about moving, it raised no objection since he had been engaged on work which was coming to fruition. The respondent agreed to release him from his covenants but pointed out that it did not think it tenable that he and his wife could work for different firms in such a highly sensitive area. He said that they recognised this would be the position, but that the salary increase he would receive was considerably in excess of his wife's income and that she would be leaving very shortly as they hoped to have a family. The firm advised that the applicant had certain maternity rights to return to work.

The firm is a small firm employing fewer than 50 employees. Whilst the applicant was on her honeymoon the receptionist resigned. This was the one position in the firm for which the applicant was suitable which did not give access to sensitive and confidential material.

When the position was discussed with the applicant, the firm offered the post of receptionist at her current salary even though that job normally carried a lower salary.

The respondent did not discriminate against the applicant either on grounds of her gender or her marital status. Exactly the same course would have been taken in the case of a comparable male or single person who was living in the household of an employee of this competitor.

The firm accepts that it dismissed the applicant, but for the reasons set out above the dismissal was not unfair.

Pregnancy dismissal – defence of justification

Originating application

The applicant was employed as a domestic servant at a hotel from 11 May 1996. On 5 June 1996 she told the manager she was pregnant and later on that date she was called into the manager's office and was informed she would have to leave because of her pregnancy.

The applicant was unfairly dismissed on the grounds of pregnancy and subjected to unlawful sex discrimination in that she was dismissed whilst she was pregnant or for a reason related to pregnancy.

Notice of appearance

The respondents are a married couple who operate a small seaside hotel. The bulk of their business is carried out between 1 June and 30 September. During the season they employ three full-time and five part-time employees on a temporary basis. For the rest of the year they run the hotel themselves subject to engaging staff for particular functions.

The applicant is a student and she asked for a vacation job. Throughout it was made clear to her that the job would only be for the summer season and indeed she said that she had to return to her college on 1 October. It was also made clear that during the period of the school holidays the applicant would be required to work overtime since this was the period of peak pressure and the applicant readily agreed to this.

On 5 June the applicant refused to help in moving a bed and gave as the reason the fact that she was four months pregnant. The applicant admitted that she knew she was pregnant at the time she was interviewed for the job. In view of the proximity to the really busy part of the season the respondents decided that the applicant would have to be dismissed.

It is denied that the respondents have been guilty of sex discrimination. The applicant was employed for a specific time-limited job and she knew at the time when she applied for and accepted the position that by reason of her pregnancy she would be unable to meet the requirements of the job.

If the respondents are found to have unlawfully dismissed the applicant for the reasons set out above, it is contended that she is not entitled to compensation.

Return to work after pregnancy – small employer

Originating application

The applicant was employed as an accounts clerk by the respondent. When she took maternity leave on 5 January 1996 she had over three years' continuous service. When she sought to exercise her statutory right to work the respondent refused saying that unfortunately it was no longer feasible for her to return.

In the circumstances the applicant was unfairly dismissed in being denied her statutory right to work and was unfairly subject to unlawful sex discrimination.

Notice of appearance

The respondent is a solicitor who is a sole practitioner who employs fewer than five employees. Prior to the applicant's departure on maternity leave the respondent had already set in train extensive reorganisation of the office administration which included the introduction of a sophisticated computer system.

The introduction of the system took place over several months between April and August whilst the applicant was away on maternity leave. It included an expensive training programme for two of the employees. Had the applicant been present she would have been one of the employees who would have received such training.

When the applicant wished to return to work the new system was operative and it was not reasonably practical for her to return to work since she had not received the requisite training. It is not financially viable or practical to train her to operate this system as such training was included in the overall costs of the introduction of the new computer system. The applicant was not dismissed in accordance with s 96 of the Employment Rights Act 1996.

If it is to be argued that the applicant is entitled to a redundancy payment,[1] it will be contended that the acquisition of the computer skills which are now necessary was no more than the introduction of technological change to her previous job and that there was no redundancy as evidenced by the fact that the same number of employees are still employed.

It is denied that the applicant has been discriminated against on grounds of sex since the decision not to permit her to return was not gender based, but was due to the inability of the applicant to meet the changed demands of her old job.

If, contrary to the contentions set out above, it is adjudged that the applicant was dismissed, the dismissal was not unfair by the criteria of s 98 in that the dismissal related to a reason which was fair, namely some substantial other reason and/or capability and/or redundancy.

1   The applicant has not claimed a redundancy payment. However, it might be argued that the job function had changed sufficiently to say that there was no longer a need for work of a particular kind as an accounts clerk as opposed to a computer operator. Since as a result of her claim for unfair dismissal the applicant has the right to include a claim for a redundancy payment as of right, it is a matter of judgment as to whether to seek to preempt a claim not yet made. The reality is that a claim for redundancy is much less expensive than a claim for unfair dismissal and the fact that there has been a change in the demands of the job – whether defined as a business reorganisation and a substantial other reason or a redundancy – is a potentially fair reason for the purposes of s 98.

Race discrimination – job application

Originating application

I heard that there were jobs at Smith & Co and I went and asked if there were vacancies. I was told that there were no vacancies. I rang up and repeated the question and I was put through to the manager who said they did have occasional short-term jobs and promised to send an application form.

I filled in the application form and a week later I was telephoned to say that they had a labouring job for a few days and could I come straight in. When I got there they seemed surprised. I waited for 20 minutes in the reception area and then a manager came down and said there had been a mistake and actually there was no job available for that day. In the following six weeks I did not hear from them at all.

I am a West Indian but I was born here and speak with a Birmingham accent. My name does not suggest that I am West Indian. I believe I have been discriminated against on the grounds of race because whenever I was seen by Smith & Co I was told there were no jobs, but when I rang up I was encouraged to believe that there were short-term jobs. I want compensation.

Notice of appearance

The respondents are concerned with the transportation of heavy loads for export. This means that occasionally there is a need to engage labourers for short periods of time.

Appendix 2

The receptionist who initially saw the applicant was a temporary receptionist and when asked about vacancies she said that she did not know anything about it, which was correct.

When the applicant phoned again a different receptionist was on duty and she put the call through to one of the managers who explained that the company did sometimes have occasional short-term jobs available.

The applicant was called in to assist with getting a job loaded so that it could be transported from Immingham on the next day. After that phone call and before he arrived, a fax had been received putting back the departure by 48 hours because shipping had been delayed due to inclement weather. Therefore there was no need for the applicant as the company could deal with the matter with the existing labour. Unfortunately, the manager who called the applicant was engaged elsewhere at the time the applicant arrived and the full position was not explained to him.

In the seven weeks before the company received the documentation in respect of this case four phone calls were made to the applicant's home informing him of occasional jobs, but on each occasion there was no reply to the calls. The company is still prepared to keep the applicant on its books as an occasional labourer.

The respondents have a work force of 15 and a pool of occasional labourers of six. Four of the 15 employees are of West Indian or Asian backgrounds and two of the six occasional labourers are West Indians.

Indirect race discrimination

Originating application

I am of Indian origin and I have a degree in history from the University of Delhi. The respondent is a private educational establishment and I applied for a job to coach pupils on their 'A' level retakes.

I was interviewed but was not appointed and I was told that I was not considered eligible as I did not have a degree from a British university. I was unable to comply with this condition and the proportion of teachers of Indian origin who can comply with this condition or requirement is considerably smaller than the number of teachers of British origin.

I seek:
(1) a declaration that the respondent unlawfully discriminated against me on grounds of race by failing to appoint me to the post;
(2) a recommendation that the respondent takes action within such time as the tribunal considers practicable to amend the said requirement or condition so as not to constitute an act of racial discrimination; and
(3) compensation.

Notice of appearance

It is admitted that the applicant applied for, but was not appointed to, the post. He was one of three candidates all of whom were interviewed.

The applicant had a lower second class degree and no 'A' level teaching experience and his overall teaching experience was small. He had no teaching diploma. The candidate who was successful had an upper second class history degree, a teaching diploma and had, until taking early retirement, been head of the history department at a well-known public school. He had also been an 'A' level examiner.

When the applicant was told he was not to be appointed he claimed that we were prejudiced against Indian universities. We said we had a preference for degrees from universities the standard of whose degrees we knew and we said that this applied to British as well as Indian universities.

At no stage was he told that it was a condition of eligibility that he had to have a degree from a British university. However, we do consider it is justified to take into account that in history there is a close correspondence between the core 'A' level courses and the core British university course and that inevitably a graduate in history from an overseas university may well not have covered the ground of an 'A' level course.

The 'A' level course we take concerns 16th and 17th century English history and 19th century European history. The applicant had only covered 19th century British Imperial history and we believe on this ground alone he was not eligible for appointment.

Race discrimination – unfair dismissal

Originating application

I am an Indian and I was employed as a machine operator and had 15 years' service in the company. There was talk of redundancy, but I believed I was safe because selections for redundancy had always been on the basis of last in, first out.

I was amazed to be told that I was to be made redundant. In our pool there were five of us and I was the only one to be made redundant but I was the third longest serving employee.

I believe that I have been unlawfully discriminated against on ground of race and that I have been unfairly dismissed. I want my job back and compensation.

Notice of appearance

The redundancy exercise in which the applicant was made redundant was the fourth redundancy exercise in the last six years. It is accepted that on previous occasions the company had used the criteria of last in, first out. The result is that the company has an elderly workforce and has lost many skilled operatives who it would have wished to retain.

Because of a fall in orders the company needed to make redundancies but it did need to retain a workforce who were sufficiently flexible to meet all the requirements of the company. The company therefore devised a matrix based on skills, time lost and disciplinary proceedings and said that last in, first out was only to apply when employees had equal points on the matrix.

There is no recognised trade union so the company informed the workforce by letter and called a meeting to explain the position. Although there was some opposition, the majority of the workforce saw the need for altering the criteria and the company did alter certain aspects of the matrix in view of the points which were raised.

The applicant and the others were assessed according to the matrix and he scored the lowest marks. He was seen and the position explained to him. He merely said it was discrimination and refused to accept that an assessment had been carried out. Of the pool of five with whom he was considered the applicant was the only employee who had warnings for poor workmanship and absenteeism. The calculation of absenteeism was based on wage records.

The applicant was not unfairly dismissed nor was he discriminated against on grounds of race. We have 150 direct workers of whom 30 are of Asian or West Indian backgrounds. Of the 24 redundancies amongst direct employees there were only three redundancies amongst the ethnic minority. There are no grounds for inferring any general policy of racial discrimination in the introduction of the matrix.

BREACH OF CONTRACT

Breach of contract; payment of commission

Originating application

I am a representative and I was paid £12,000 basic salary. My contract stated that the employment was terminated on a month's notice. I had been employed with the company for 15 months when I was told that in view of the financial difficulties the company was having I was to be dismissed with a month's notice. They said I had to go straight away. Although my basic salary is only £12,000 I regularly earn at least another £1,000 commission a month. I asked if I could work the month's notice and they said I could not. I asked if I could receive the extra £1,000 that I would have received and they said I was not entitled to it.

Notice of appearance

By the terms of the applicant's contract he was eligible for a month's notice and there was a term in the contract that the company could pay a month's salary in lieu of notice. The respondents have acted in accordance with the term of the contract and they are under no obligation to pay the applicant any sum in respect of the commission he might have earned had he remained in employment.

TRADE UNION AND RELATED RIGHTS

Refusal of employment on grounds of refusal to join trade union

Originating application

I would like the tribunal to determine whether I have been refused employment because I would not join the ABC Union.[1]

On 21 October 1996 I attended an interview for a job as a factory hand with the respondent. I discussed my previous work experience with the foreman who told me that I could start the following Monday. As I was leaving he asked me to pick up an application form to join the ABC Union. I told him that I did not want to join the union.

The next day the foreman rang me at home and told me that he could not give me a job. I believe I have been refused employment because I will not join the ABC Union and I seek a declaration to that effect and an award of compensation.[2]

Notice of appearance of first respondent

It is admitted that the applicant was not offered employment because he would not join the ABC Union. The union threatened strike action if a non-member was employed. The respondent is a small company and has recently received a large order. This order would have been lost if a strike had been called and redundancies would have followed.

The respondent therefore requests that the ABC Union be joined as a party to these proceedings and should be ordered to pay all or some of any compensation awarded to the applicant.[3]

Notice of appearance of ABC Union (the second respondent)

It is denied that the second respondent threatened industrial action should the applicant be employed. The employee who threatened strike action is a member of the ABC Union but is not an official and had no authority from the union to make such a threat. Any strike would have been unofficial and would have had no support from the second respondent. The first respondent failed to renew its offer of employment to the applicant despite the second respondent's assurance that it would not call any industrial action.

1 See Trade Union and Labour Relations (Consolidation) Act 1992 (TULR(C)A), s 137.
2 See TULR(C)A, s 140.
3 See TULR(C)A, s 142.

Appendix 2

Refusal to offer employment on grounds of trade union membership

Originating application

My claim is that I have been refused employment by the respondent as a result of my membership of the ABC Union.[1]

On 30 September 1997 I read an advertisement in the *Anywhere Times* offering a position as general operative with the respondent. The advertisement stated:

'XYZ Limited is committed to full employee flexibility. We do not recognise any trade unions and will only employ those who share our commitment to modern flexible working practices.'

I believe that this advertisement indicated that employment would only be offered to those who are not members of a trade union.[2]

On 25 October 1997 I attended an interview with the respondent. During the interview I was asked if I was a trade union member and replied that I was. Two days later I was informed that I had not been given the job. I believe I have been refused employment because I am a member of the ABC Union.

Notice of appearance

The respondent denies that their advertisement indicated or might reasonably be taken to indicate that employment would be limited to those who are not members of a trade union. The respondent employs both members and non-members of trade unions.

The applicant was refused employment because he had no experience as a fork truck driver and was not prepared to undergo training to be part of our flexible workforce.

1 See TULR(C)A, s 137.
2 By TULR(C)A, s 137(3) where an advertisement is published which indicates or might reasonably be understood to indicate that employment will be limited to members or non-members of a trade union and a person who does not comply with the requirement is refused the job advertised it will be conclusively presumed that he was refused by reason of his trade union membership.

Action short of dismissal

Originating application

Would the tribunal please decide whether action short of dismissal has been taken against me by the respondent because I am a member of the ABC Union?[1]

On 19 August 1996 I was offered a new contract of employment by the respondent which would introduce flexible working and increase my wages by £10 per week. The contract also required that I would negotiate any future pay increases individually and not be represented by my trade union in collective bargaining. I was not prepared to give up my right to collective bargaining and so have not been given a pay rise this year.[2] I am also no longer eligible for shift bonus. I consider that action short of dismissal has been taken against me as a result of my membership of the ABC Union.

Notice of appearance

It is admitted that the applicant was offered a new contract of employment at a higher rate of salary which would have required him to give up his right to collective bargaining. The respondent's purpose was to increase flexibility in its pay structure not to deter the applicant from being a member of the ABC Union.[3]

The failure to offer the applicant a pay rise is an omission and so cannot amount to action short of dismissal.[4]

1　See TULR(C)A, s 146.

2　Note that such a claim would not now be maintainable due to the House of Lords' decision in *Associated Newspapers v Wilson; Associated British Ports v Palmer* [1995] ICR 407.

3　Where an employer's intention is to further a change in relationship with his employees and the employer also had a purpose that falls within TULR(C)A, s 146, s 148(3) provides a statutory presumption that the tribunal shall have regard only to the former purpose unless no reasonable employer could have taken the action complained of.

4　In *Associated Newspapers v Wilson; Associated British Ports v Palmer* [1995] ICR 407 the House of Lords held that a failure to grant a pay rise was an omission and so could not amount to action short of dismissal.

Dismissal for taking part in the activities of an independent trade union

Originating application

I would like it determined whether I have been dismissed for taking part in the activities of an independent trade union.[1]

I am a shop steward in the ABC Union. On 14 October 1996 I called a meeting of union members on my shift to discuss pay negotiations taking place with the respondent. On 18 October 1996 I received a letter stating that I had been guilty of misconduct at the shift meeting and asking me to a disciplinary hearing. At the end of the hearing I was dismissed. I believe I have been dismissed for taking part in trade union activities.

I also wish to apply for interim relief pending the determination of my unfair dismissal complaint and enclose a certificate signed by an authorised official of the ABC Union stating that I was a member of the ABC Union at the time of my dismissal and that there appear to be reasonable grounds for supposing that the reason for my dismissal was that I was taking part in the activities of an independent trade union.[2]

Notice of appearance

It is denied that the applicant was dismissed for taking part in the activities of an independent trade union at an appropriate time.

The applicant did not seek approval before calling the shift meeting and did not hold it at the customary time during the lunch break. Therefore the meeting was not at an appropriate time.[3]

The applicant called the meeting when he did in order to disrupt the delivery of a large quantity of perishable goods. As a result of the meeting the goods were not processed in time and £5,000 of damage was done. In the circumstances the respondent denies that the applicant was taking part in trade union activities.[4]

1 See TULR(C)A, s 152.
2 See TULR(C)A, s 161.
3 See TULR(C)A, s 152(1)(b).
4 Wholly unreasonable, extraneous or malicious acts done in support of trade union activities may provide grounds for a fair dismissal: *Lyon and Scherk v St James Press Ltd* [1976] ICR 413.

Paid time off for official of independent recognised trade union

Originating application

My application is to determine whether the respondent has refused to pay me for time off to carry out my trade union duties.[1]

I am employed by the respondent as a printer. I am an official of the ABC Union which is recognised by the respondent in respect of printers. On 12 September 1997 I took off a day to prepare for pay negotiations with the respondent. They have failed to pay me for this day.

Notice of appearance

It is admitted that the respondent failed to pay the applicant for the day he was absent on 12 September 1997. It is denied that the applicant used the day to prepare for negotiations with the union as he was seen by the respondent's managing director at the National races on the day in question. In any event, it would not have been reasonable for the applicant to take another day off work to prepare for negotiations as he had taken off three days in the previous month allegedly for that purpose.

1 See TULR(C)A, s 168.

Dismissal of health and safety representative during unofficial industrial action

Originating application

The tribunal is requested to determine whether I was dismissed during an unofficial 'go-slow' because I am a health and safety representative.

I am a trade union appointed health and safety representative and have held this post for five years. On 12 August 1997 I was taking part in an unofficial 'go-slow' and was dismissed by the respondent.

The respondent did not dismiss any other employees taking part in the 'go-slow' and I believe that I have been dismissed because I am a health and safety representative and that the 'go-slow' has been used as a cloak to disguise this fact.[1]

Notice of appearance

The industrial tribunal does not have jurisdiction to hear the applicant's complaint as he was taking part in unofficial strike action at the date of his dismissal. It is denied that the applicant was dismissed because he was a health and safety representative. All those who were taking part in the 'go-slow' who were employed on B shift were dismissed along with the applicant. No other staff were dismissed as the 'go-slow' then ended.

1   An employee who is dismissed while taking part in unofficial industrial action has no right to claim unfair dismissal unless the reason for the dismissal is forbidden by s 100 (health and safety), s 103 (employee representatives) or s 99 (pregnancy) of the Employment Rights Act 1996.

Other strikes and industrial action

Originating application

My claim is that I have been unfairly dismissed.

I was employed by the respondent as a kitchen operative for four years. On 26 June 1996 I and all other kitchen operatives employed in the hospitals of the XYZ Health Authority went out on official strike. During the strike I was dismissed.

Within three months of the date of my dismissal a large number of those who had been on strike were re-engaged but I was not. I believe that I have been unfairly dismissed.[1]

Notice of appearance

It is admitted that the applicant was dismissed while taking part in an official strike. The applicant was employed at the A District Hospital. No kitchen operatives employed at the A Hospital were re-engaged within three months of the strike action. It is admitted that the kitchen operatives employed at the B, C and D General Hospitals were re-engaged two months after the official strike. However, the respondent will contend that the A, B, C and D General Hospitals are separate establishments within the meaning of the Trade Union and Labour Relations (Consolidation) Act 1992, s 238(3)(b).

1   See TULR(C)A, s 238.

Health and safety

Originating application

Can the tribunal rule as to whether the respondent has caused me to suffer a detriment by reason of my health and safety activities?[1]

Appendix 2

I am employed as a food operative at the XYZ Company. For a number of months I have complained of fumes coming from a meat processing machine. I consider that these fumes constitute a grave risk to the health and safety of myself and my fellow workers.

On 6 August 1997 the fumes were particularly bad and I believed that they constituted a serious risk to my safety. Accordingly, I left my place of work and did not return until the next day. The respondent has refused to pay me for my day's absence and I claim that I have been subjected to a detriment contrary to s 44 of the Employment Rights Act 1996.

Notice of appearance

It is denied that any fumes are given off by the respondent's meat processing machinery. The machine gives off certain odours. The respondent has organised an inspection of the machine by a safety consultant who has concluded that the machine poses no risk to the health and safety of the applicant or other staff working in the area. The applicant was informed of this in writing on 8 July 1997. Accordingly it is denied that the applicant reasonably considered that there was a serious or imminent risk to her health and safety and the respondent contends that it was entitled to dock pay for a day on which the applicant did not attend work.

1 See s 44 of the Employment Rights Act 1996.

8 Applications in connection with tribunal proceedings

APPLICATIONS FOR JOINDER

Application by applicant

Dear

[*Case name and number*]

I refer to my application to the tribunal.

I have now discovered that although I carried out work for the respondent Smith Limited, my employer may have been Smiths Employee Services Limited whose registered office is [   ]. Please join Smith Employee Services Limited as an additional respondent in the proceedings.

Application by respondent

(*to be included in notice of appearance or in letter, as appropriate*)

The applicant ceased to be an employee of this company when we sold our [distribution operations] to [Greens Distribution Limited whose registered office is   ]. The applicant has carried on working for that company. Please join [Greens Distribution Limited] as an additional respondent in these proceedings.

APPLICATIONS FOR INTERLOCUTORY ORDERS OF INDUSTRIAL TRIBUNALS

Further and better particulars

1. Letter addressed to the applicant

Dear

[*Title and number of case*]

I have received a copy of your originating application to an industrial tribunal. To enable the respondents to consider your claim and prepare their notice of appearance I request that you provide me with the following information within [seven] days of the date of this letter:
[(1) The precise nature of your claim.
 (2) The statutory basis for your claim.
 (3) The facts on which you seek to rely for your claim. Etc.]

If this information is not provided in the time stated I will apply for an order of the tribunal to compel you to provide it.

Yours

Appendix 2

2. Letter addressed to regional secretary

Dear

[*Title and number of case*]

I am unclear as to the basis of the applicant's claim. I wrote to him on [*date*] requesting further particulars of his claim (a copy of my letter is attached) and [I have not received a reply] [the applicant's reply (a copy of which is also herewith) is unsatisfactory].

I request that an order be made requiring the applicant to provide me with the [following particulars] [particulars requested in my letter] within [seven] days of the order.

[Particulars required:
(1) The precise nature of the claim.
(2) The statutory basis for the claim.
(3) The facts on which the applicant seeks to rely for his claim. Etc.]

Yours

3. Letter addressed to respondents

Dear

[*Title and number of case*]

I have received a copy of your notice of appearance in response to my application to an industrial tribunal. So that I can consider your defence and prepare for the hearing I request that you provide me with the following information within [seven] days of the date of this letter:
[(1) The precise nature of the respondents' defence to my claim.
 (2) The statutory basis of the respondents' defence to my claim.
 (3) The facts on which you seek to rely for your statement that   etc.]

If this information is not provided in the time stated I will apply for an order of the tribunal that you do so.

Yours

4. Letter addressed to regional secretary

Dear

[*Title and number of case*]

I am unclear as to the basis of the respondents' defence to my claim. I wrote to them on [*date*] requesting further particulars of the notice of appearance (a copy of my letter is attached) and [I have not received a reply] [the applicant's reply (a copy of which is also herewith) is unsatisfactory].

I request that an order be made requiring the respondents to provide me with the [following particulars] [particulars requested in my letter] within [seven] days of the order.

[Particulars required:
(1) The precise nature of the respondents' defence to my claim.
(2) The statutory basis of the respondents' defence to my claim.
(3) The facts on which the respondents seek to rely for your statement that etc.]

Yours

Discovery

1. Letter to other party

Dear

[*Title and number of case*]

I write in connection with the industrial tribunal proceedings in which [I am] [we are] the [applicant] [respondents].

Please provide me within [seven] days of the date of this letter by way of discovery, details of all documents in your possession or under your control relating to [my terms and conditions of employment] [the company's disciplinary procedures] [the contract with X Limited] etc.

If this information is not provided in the time stated I will apply for an order of the tribunal that you do so.

Yours

2. Letter addressed to regional secretary

Dear

[*Title and number of case*]

I wrote to [   ] on [*date*] for details of all documents in their possession or under their control (a copy of my letter is attached) and [I have not received a reply] [the applicant's] [respondent's] reply (a copy of which is also herewith) is unsatisfactory].

I request that an order be made requiring [   ] to provide me with full discovery of the [following documents] [particulars requested in my letter] within [seven] days of the order.

[Details of documents required:]

Yours

Appendix 2

Inspection

1.   Letter to other party

Dear

I write in connection with the industrial tribunal proceedings in which [I am] [we are] the [applicant] [respondents].

Please provide me within [seven] days of the date of this letter with copies, or details of arrangements whereby I can within normal working hours inspect and take copies, of all documents in your possession or under your control relating to [my terms and conditions of employment] [the company's disciplinary procedures] [the contract with X Limited] [the documents set out on the attached list] etc.

If this information is not provided in the time stated I will apply for an order of the tribunal that you do so.

Yours

2.   Letter addressed to regional secretary

Dear

[*Title and number of case*]

I wrote to [   ] on [*date*] seeking copies or to make arrangements to inspect and take copies of documents in his possession or under his control (a copy of my letter is attached) and [I have not received a reply] [the applicant's reply (a copy of which is also herewith) is unsatisfactory].

I request that an order be made requiring [   ] to allow me to inspect and take copies at   of the [following documents] [particulars requested in my letter] within [seven] days of the order.

[Details of documents in respect of which inspection is required:]

Yours

Interrogatories

1.   To other party

Dear

[*Title and number of case*]

I write in connection with the industrial tribunal proceedings in which [I am] [we are] the [applicant] [respondents].

600

To enable me to prepare [my] [our] case for hearing please answer the following questions within the next [seven] days:

[(1) Identify the pool of employees from which I was selected for redundancy.]

[(2) Who was the person nominated to hear appeals pursuant to the disciplinary procedure?]

[(3) Who were the other employees you claim were not treated in a manner consistent with you?]

etc.

Yours

2. Letter addressed to regional secretary

Dear

[*Title and number of case*]

I wrote to [   ] on [*date*] seeking a reply to questions to enable me to prepare my case for hearing (a copy of my letter is attached) and [I have not received a reply] [the applicant's reply (a copy of which is also herewith) is unsatisfactory].

I request that an order be made requiring [   ] to answer the [following questions] [questions set out in my letter] within [seven] days of the order.

[Details of questions to which answers are required:]

Yours

Witness orders

1. To witness

Dear

You may be aware that [I] [the Company] is involved in proceedings in an industrial tribunal [making a claim against   Limited] [brought against it by Mr/s   ].

I believe that you are able to give important evidence relating to [   ]. Would you kindly contact me within the next [seven] days so that we can make arrangements to meet and I can take a statement from you? It may be necessary for you to attend the hearing in due course to give evidence to the tribunal. I will notify you of the arrangements for the hearing as soon as a date has been set for it.

Yours

2.   To regional secretary

Dear

[*Title and number of case*]

I write to seek an order requiring [*name*] of [*address*] to attend as a witness at the hearing of the above case which is to take place on [   ].

The attendance of [   ] is important for the proper presentation of my case because [   ]. [I enclose a copy of a statement taken from   ] [will say].

On [*date*] I asked [   ] to attend voluntarily but [he has refused] [he has not replied to my letter] [he says he will only attend if ordered to do so]. [   ] was notified of the date of hearing on [*date*].

Yours

SETTLEMENT AGREEMENTS

Settlement on ACAS Form COT 3

1.   Basic form

Settlement reached as a result of conciliation action

We the undersigned have agreed that the Respondents will pay to the Applicant and the Applicant agrees to accept [the sum of   ] in full and final settlement of these tribunal proceedings and of all other claims whatso-ever which the Applicant may have against the Respondents arising out of his contract of employment and its termination, with the exception of claims in relation to industrial accident, injury and/or disease or in relation to pensions schemes or entitlement.

The Respondents will pay the sum agreed to be paid within [   ] days of the date [hereof] [of the date of the tribunal decision giving effect to this agreement].

2.   Alternative form

Settlement reached as a result of conciliation action

1.   We the undersigned have agreed that in full and final settlement of these tribunal proceedings and of all other claims whatsoever which the Applicant may have against the Respondents arising out of his contract of employment and its termination the Respondents will:
   (a) pay to the Applicant [the sum of   ] within [   ] days of the [date hereof] [date of the decision of the tribunal giving effect to this agreement]; and
   (b) provide a reference for the applicant on request in the form set out in the Schedule attached.

2. This settlement is made without prejudice to the Applicant's rights (if any) in relation to industrial accident, injury and/or disease or in relation to pensions schemes or entitlement.

3. Obligations on applicant

Settlement reached as a result of conciliation action

1. We the undersigned have agreed that in full and final settlement of these tribunal proceedings and of all other claims whatsoever which the Applicant may have against the Respondents arising out of his contract of employment and its termination:
    (a) The Respondents will:
        (i) pay to the Applicant [the sum of   ] within [   ] days of the [date hereof] [date of the decision of the tribunal giving effect to this agreement]; and
        (ii) provide a reference for the applicant on request in the form set out in the Schedule attached.
    (b) The Applicant will:
        (i) no later than [return to the Respondents all the property of the Respondents in his possession, including in particular and   ]; and
        (ii) withdraw the application made to the industrial tribunal under Case Number [   ].

2. This settlement is made without prejudice to the Applicant's rights (if any) in relation to industrial accident, injury and/or disease or in relation to pensions schemes or entitlement.

4. Agreement not to disclose terms of settlement

Settlement reached as a result of conciliation action

1. We the undersigned have agreed that in full and final settlement of these tribunal proceedings and of all other claims whatsoever which the Applicant may have against the Respondents arising out of his contract of employment and its termination:
    (a) The Respondents will [   ].
    (b) The Applicant will [   ].

2. The parties agree that they will not disclose to any third party the terms of this agreement or the basis of the settlement between them.

3. This settlement is made without prejudice to the Applicant's rights (if any) in relation to industrial accident, injury and/or disease or in relation to pensions schemes or entitlement.

5. Alternative form

Settlement reached as a result of conciliation action

1. The Respondents and the Applicant have agreed that:
    (a) The Respondents will:
        [(i) pay to the Applicant the sum of [   ] within [   ] days of [today] [the decision of the tribunal made in consequence of this agreement]; and

       (ii) provide a reference for the applicant in the form set out in the Schedule attached on receipt of requests for a reference in respect of the applicant made at any time after the date hereof]; and

   (b) The Applicant will no later than [return to the Respondents all the property of the Respondents in his possession, including in particular and   ].

2.   This agreement is made without prejudice to the Applicant's rights (if any) in relation to industrial accident, injury and/or disease or in relation to pensions schemes or entitlement.

3.   The parties agree that the provisions of clause [   ] of the Service Agreement of [*date*] made between the parties hereto shall remain in full force and effect.

4.   This agreement is in full and final settlement of these tribunal proceedings and of all other claims whatsoever which the Applicant may have against the Respondents arising out of his contract of employment and its termination.

6. Alternative form

Settlement reached as a result of conciliation action

We the undersigned have agreed that the Respondents will pay to and the Applicant agrees to accept [the sum of   ] in full and final settlement of all claims of whatsoever nature which the Applicant may have against the Respondents arising out of his contract of employment and its termination whether under common law, statute (including without prejudice to the generality of the foregoing unfair dismissal, sex discrimination, race discrimination and   ), delegated legislation, European law or otherwise with the exception of claims in relation to industrial accident, injury and/or disease or in relation to pensions schemes or entitlement.

The Respondents will pay the sum agreed to be paid within [   ] days of the date [hereof] [of the date of the tribunal decision giving effect to this agreement].

COMPROMISE AGREEMENT[1]

Agreement to withdraw proceedings before an industrial tribunal

THIS AGREEMENT is made the [   ] day of [   ]

BETWEEN [   ] of [   ] (the Employee)

and

[   ] of [   ] (the Employer)

WHEREBY IT IS AGREED that:

1.   The Employer will pay to the Employee the sum of £[   ] within [   ] days of the date [hereof] [of the promulgation of a decision by the industrial tribunal dismissing the application the subject of this compromise agreement.]

2.   The Employee will [on payment of the sum payable hereunder] [immediately] withdraw his complaint against the Employer before the industrial tribunal (Case Number   ).

3.   The Employee accepts the payment made by the Employer in full and final settlement of this complaint and of all and any claims which he has or may have against the Employer arising out of his employment and its termination being claims in respect of which an industrial tribunal does not have jurisdiction.

4.   The Employee confirms that he has not commenced any proceedings against the Employer other than those referred to in clause 2.

[The Employer denies that it is under any liability whatsoever to the Employee [, which is acknowledged by the Employee.]

[The parties hereto will not disclose the terms of this agreement to any third person [other than to their legal advisers and members of the Employee's immediate family.]]

5.   The Employee acknowledges that, before signing this Agreement, he received independent legal advice from Mr/s,   a member of Messrs   of   , solicitors, a qualified lawyer, as to the terms and effect of this Agreement and in particular its effect on his ability to pursue his rights before an industrial tribunal.

6.   The statutory requirements as to compromise agreements have been satisfied in relation to this agreement.

Signed by

[*Employee*]

in the presence of

Signed by

on behalf of [*Employer*]

in the presence of

1   For the requirements as to compromise agreements, see **18.19** and Chapter 7.

REVIEW

Application for review[1]

To Regional Secretary

Dear

[*Case name and number*]

I apply for the review of the decision of the industrial tribunal promulgated on [   ].

Appendix 2

The grounds for this application are:

[A member of the tribunal staff made an error [in the written decision by transposing the award of compensation made in my favour at the hearing with that made to [Mr Smith] whose case was heard at the same time as mine].]

[[We] [I] did not receive notice of the proceedings and so was/were not able to be present to present [our] [my case].]

[[We] [I] did not receive notice of the hearing and so was/were absent when the decision was made. If [we] [I] had known of the hearing [we] would have attended and presented [our] [my] case.]

[Following the hearing evidence has come to light which was not known to [us] [me] and which [we] [I] could not reasonably known of, or have foreseen at the time of the hearing. The evidence is [from the applicant's new employer to the effect that the applicant's statement that his expected earnings in his new job are £150 a week was untrue. The applicant's anticipated earnings are £250 a week]. This is material to the issues decided by the tribunal because [the tribunal assumed that the applicant's statement was correct when calculating compensation].]

[In the interests of justice a review is required because [in calculating pension loss for the purpose of the compensation calculation the tribunal mistakenly assumed that the normal retirement age under that   pension scheme is 65 when it is 60.   The tribunal heard no evidence as to the point].]

Yours

1   See 18.95–18.103.

9 Appeals to the Employment Appeal Tribunal

Forms for appeals to the Employment Appeal Tribunal are provided in the Employment Appeal Tribunal Rules 1993, SI 1993/2854, Sch. Forms 1 and 3 are set out below. Specimens are included for paragraph 6 in Form 1 which it is hoped will be of assistance.

FORM 1

Notice of appeal from decision of industrial tribunal

1. The appellant is (*name and address of appellant*).

2. Any communication relating to this appeal may be sent to the appellant at (*appellant's name and address for service, including telephone number if any*).

3. The appellant appeals from
(*here give particulars of the decision of the industrial tribunal from which the appeal is brought including the date*).

4. The parties to the proceedings before the industrial tribunal, other than the appellant, were (*names and addresses of other parties to the proceedings resulting in decision appealed from*).

5. A copy of the industrial tribunal's decision or order and of the extended written reasons for that decision or order are attached to this notice.

6. The grounds upon which this appeal is brought are that the industrial tribunal erred in law in that (*here set out in paragraphs the various grounds of appeal*).

Date

Signed

FORM 3

Respondent's answer

1. The respondent is (*name and address of respondent*).

2. Any communication relating to this appeal may be sent to the respondent at (*respondent's name and address for service, including telephone number if any*).

3. The respondent intends to resist the appeal of (*here give the name of appellant*). The grounds on which the respondent will rely are [the grounds relied upon by the industrial tribunal/Certification Officer for making the decision or order appealed from] [and] [the following grounds]:
(*here set out any grounds which differ from those relied upon by the industrial tribunal or Certification Officer, as the case may be*).

4. The respondent cross-appeals from
(*here give particulars of the decision appealed from*).

5. The respondent's grounds of appeal are:
(*here state the grounds of appeal*).

Date

Signed

By applicant – specimen paragraph 6

The industrial tribunal erred in law in finding that the Applicant was not constructively dismissed in that:

(1) In paragraph [   ] of the Full Reasons the industrial tribunal stated:

'We have every sympathy with the Applicant. We consider that, as stated, his employer was guilty of a very serious breach going to the root of the contract. However, in our view he lost his right to treat himself as constructively dismissed since he delayed too long in leaving the job.'

That was a misdirection of law since the test is whether the Applicant affirmed the contract; delay is merely evidence of affirmation.

(2) At paragraph [   ] the tribunal set out the reasons for the delay in the Applicant resigning but made no finding as to the relevance of such reasons in considering whether the Applicant had affirmed the contract by not resigning.

By respondents – specimen paragraph 6

The industrial tribunal erred in law in finding that the Applicant was an employee in that:

(1) In paragraph [   ] of the decision the industrial tribunal stated 'We are satisfied that the control which the Respondents had over the Applicant as a manager running one of their shops was such that he was an employee.' That was a misdirection of law since the test of whether the Applicant was an employee did not depend solely on the question of control but on the much wider test of whether the Applicant was in business on his own account.

(2) Having misdirected themselves as to the proper test the tribunal failed to have regard to the evidence that:
   (a) the Applicant received 12% of the turnover from which to defray various expenses;
   (b) the Applicant had a wide discretion as to how many staff were to be engaged;
   (c) he had the right to 'hire and fire' such staff and he had the responsibility to pay them and make appropriate deductions for tax and National Insurance;
   (d) his right under the contract to use a proportion of the floor space to sell such items (not supplied by the appellant) as he wished;
   (e) he had a wide discretion as to how the business was to run in terms of opening hours, shop display, and manning levels.

By respondents – specimen paragraph 6

The industrial tribunal erred in law in finding that the Applicant was unfairly dismissed in that:

(1) The tribunal promulgated a decision with summary reasons. When Extended Reasons were sought the Chairman directed that the reasons previously given stand as the Extended Reasons.

(2) In paragraph [   ] the tribunal states:

'We have heard the Applicant give evidence and we accept he has given us an honest account. He may have acted unwisely but we do not think he acted dishonestly and we would not have dismissed him. We therefore find the dismissal unfair.'

That was a misdirection in law in that the proper test is whether the employer believed, on reasonable grounds, having made such enquiries as are appropriate, that the employee had acted dishonestly and that having regard to such belief whether the decision to dismiss was within the range of reasonable responses having regard to the statutory criteria of fairness.

The tribunal made no findings of fact as these issues and merely narrate the evidence given.

(3) The tribunal made no findings as to the contention that in any event the Applicant had contributed to his dismissal by removing company property from the premises notwithstanding that they state that the Applicant acted *unwisely.*

10   Pleadings in connection with county court proceedings

IN THE RIGHTWAY COUNTY COURT   Case No:

BETWEEN

HARD-UP PLC   *Plaintiffs*

and

JAY LIGHTHEART   *Defendant*

PARTICULARS OF CLAIM

1.   By an oral agreement made on or about ...th ...., the Defendant agreed to serve the Plaintiffs and the Plaintiffs agreed to employ the Defendant as a cake decorator at the Plaintiffs' premises at Juanita Street, Dundee.

2.   It was an express term of the agreement that the Defendant's employment could be terminated by reasonable notice given by either party to the agreement. Reasonable notice was three months' notice.

3.   On ...th .... in breach of the said agreement the Defendant wrongfully failed to attend his said place of employment and has not presented himself there for work since.

4.   In breach of the said agreement the Defendant did not and has not given the required or any notice of his intention to terminate his employment.

5.   By reason of the matters aforesaid, the Plaintiffs have suffered inconvenience and disruption of its manufacturing process, have incurred extra costs and have lost profit due to being unable to obtain the services of an alternative cake decorator.

PARTICULARS

6.   Further, pursuant to section 69 of the County Courts Act 1984, the Plaintiffs are entitled to and claim interest on the amount found to be due at such rates and for such periods as the Court thinks fit.

AND the Plaintiff claims:
  (a)   damages not in excess of £5,000;
  (b)   interest as pleaded above.

[Signature]

SERVED *etc*

IN THE RIGHTWAY COUNTY COURT   Case No:

BETWEEN

HARD-UP PLC   *Plaintiffs*

and

JAY LIGHTHEART   *Defendant*

DEFENCE
---

1.   Paragraphs 1 and 2 of the Particulars of Claim are admitted.

2.   Save that it is denied that the Defendant was absent wrongfully, paragraph 3 of the Particulars of Claim is admitted.

3.   It is denied that the Defendant terminated the said agreement as alleged or at all. On or about ...th .... the Plaintiffs told the Defendant that his salary was to be cut by 25%. The Defendant did not agree to such a cut in his salary. The Plaintiffs therefore told the Defendant not to bother attending for work. The Defendant accepted this instruction as immediate termination by the Plaintiffs of his contract of employment.

4.   It is denied that the Plaintiffs have suffered the alleged or any loss or damage.

5.   Except as expressly admitted above, each and every allegation of the Particulars of Claim is denied as if set out and traversed seriatim.

6.   Further or in the alternative, if which is denied the Defendant is liable to the Plaintiffs in the sum claimed or at all, then the Defendant will seek to set off so much of its counterclaim hereunder as may be necessary in extinction or diminution thereof.

COUNTERCLAIM

7.   The said agreement provided inter alia that if the Plaintiffs should determine his employment without giving the Defendant three months' notice they would pay to the Defendant the sum of £...... as agreed damages.

8.   The Defendant repeats paragraph 3 hereof and says that the Plaintiffs have thereby determined his employment without giving the Defendant the required or any notice.

9.   Further the Defendant is entitled to and claims pursuant to section 69 of the County Courts Act 1984 interest on the amount found to be due to him at such rates and for such periods as the Court thinks fit.

AND the Defendant counterclaims:

    (a) the sum of £   as agreed damages;

    (b) interest as pleaded above.

[Signature]

SERVED *etc*

IN THE END-OF-THE-EARTH COUNTY COURT   Case No:

BETWEEN

FELIX MALINGERER   *Plaintiff*

and

TIGHTFIST LIMITED   *Defendants*

PARTICULARS OF CLAIM

1. By an agreement in writing made on the ...th .... the Defendants agreed to employ the Plaintiff and the Plaintiff agreed to serve the Defendants as warehouse manager.

2. It was an express term of the agreement that the Defendants would pay to the Plaintiff an annual salary of £.... in equal monthly instalments.

3. It was an implied term of the agreement that temporary illness would not terminate the contract and that full salary should be paid during any absence through such temporary illness.

4. The Plaintiff commenced his duties for the Defendants on ...th ...., and continued to perform those duties until ...th .... when he fell ill.

5. By letter dated ...th .... the Plaintiff informed the Defendants of his illness and of the advice of his General Practitioner that he would be unable to perform his duties for several weeks.

6. The Plaintiff was unable to perform his duties due to illness for a period of ... weeks, from ...th .... until ...th ...., during which time he informed the Defendants of his progress on ... occasions by letters dated ....

7. The Defendants paid to the Plaintiff his due salary in accordance with the agreement from ...th .... until ...th .... Thereafter the Defendants made no payment to the Plaintiff.

8. On ... occasions, by letters dated ...th ...., the Plaintiff respectfully requested payment of the sums due to him. The Defendants gave no acknowledgement or reply to the Plaintiff's request, and made no salary payments to the Plaintiff after ...th ....

9. On ...th .... the Plaintiff presented himself at the Defendant company's work premises and informed ...., his supervisor, that he was now able and willing to resume his duties. The supervisor informed the Plaintiff that the agreement between the Plaintiff and the Defendants had been terminated by the Plaintiff's absence and escorted him off the premises.

10.   Since ...th .... the Plaintiff has repeatedly sought an interview with any representative of the Defendant company but the Defendants have refused any communication with the Plaintiff, and have paid no salary due to him.

11.   In the premises the Defendants have wrongfully dismissed the Plaintiff and has repudiated his contract, which repudiation the Plaintiff has accepted by letter dated ...th ....

12.   By reason of matters aforesaid the Plaintiff has suffered loss and damage and has been unable to obtain other suitable employment.

PARTICULARS OF SPECIAL DAMAGE

Salary from ...th .... until ...th .... pro rata at £......
per month after deducting the Plaintiff's tax liability: £......

13.   Further the Plaintiff is entitled to and claims interest pursuant to section 69 of the County Courts Act 1984 on the amounts found to be due at such rate and for such period as the Court sees fit.

AND the Plaintiff claims:
    (a)   damages in excess of £5,000;
    (b)   interest as pleaded above.

[Signature]

SERVED *etc*

IN THE END-OF-THE-EARTH COUNTY COURT   Case No:

BETWEEN

FELIX MALINGERER   *Plaintiff*

and

TIGHTFIST LIMITED   *Defendants*

_____

DEFENCE

1.   Paragraphs 1 and 2 of the Particulars of Claim are admitted.

2.   Paragraph 3 of the Particulars of Claim is admitted save that it is averred that it was further an implied term of the agreement that the Defendants should have the right to terminate it in the event of the Plaintiff becoming permanently incapacitated.

3.   Paragraphs 4 and 5 of the Particulars of Claim are admitted. By letter dated ...th .... the Defendants gave the Plaintiff permission to be absent on grounds of sickness.

4.   Save that it is denied that the Plaintiff was able to perform his duties after ...th ...., paragraphs 6 and 7 of the Particulars of Claim are admitted.

5.   Save that it is admitted that the Plaintiff frequently requested payment after ...th ...., paragraph 8 of the Particulars of Claim is denied. By letter dated ....th .... the Defendants informed the Plaintiff that they would regard the agreement as terminated if the Plaintiff failed to return to work within one month. By reason of his sickness the Plaintiff became permanently incapacitated and the contract was accordingly terminated by letter to the Plaintiff dated ...th ....

6.   The Defendants admit that the Plaintiff presented himself for work on or about ...th ...., but deny that he then was or at any time since has been able to perform his duties under the agreement, by reason of ill-health. Save as aforesaid, paragraph 9 of the Particulars of Claim is denied.

7.   Paragraphs 10, 11 and 12 of the Particulars of Claim are denied.

8.   The Defendants have at all material times been and still are willing to pay to the Plaintiff the sum of £......... in lieu of notice and that sum, which was tendered before action on ...th ...., is now brought into Court. The Defendants deny that they are liable to the Plaintiff for any other sum or that the Plaintiff has suffered damage.

[Signature]

SERVED *etc*

615

Appendix 3

Codes of practice

ACAS Code of Practice 1: Disciplinary Practice and Procedures in Employment (1977)

NOTES

Authority: Employment Protection Act 1975, s 6. (Now the Trade Union and Labour Relations (Consolidation) Act 1992, ss 199, 200. For the legal status of the Code see ibid, s 207.)

It was brought into force on 20 June 1977 by the Employment Protection Code of Practice (Disciplinary Practice and Procedures) Order 1977, SI 1977/867. A draft code which would have replaced this Code was prepared by ACAS in 1987 and submitted to the Secretary of State for Employment. but was not approved. The draft code was developed into a Handbook published by ACAS in 1988, 'Discipline at Work', which although it has no formal legal status is of considerable influence in tribunal proceedings to which it is relevant. Copies may be obtained from ACAS.

Notes to paras 3, 4 and 5 are as in the Code. See 15.47.

Introduction

1 This document gives practical guidance on how to draw up disciplinary rules and procedures and how to operate them effectively. Its aim is to help employers and trade unions as well as individual employees—both men and women—wherever they are employed regardless of the size of the organisation in which they work. In the smaller establishments it may not be practicable to adopt all the detailed provisions, but most of the features listed in paragraph 10 could be adopted and incorporated into a simple procedure.

Why have disciplinary rules and procedures?

2 Disciplinary rules and procedures are necessary for promoting fairness and order in the treatment of individuals and in the conduct of industrial relations. They also assist an organisation to operate effectively. Rules set standards of conduct at work; procedure helps to ensure that the standards are adhered to and also provides a fair method of dealing with alleged failures to observe them.

3 It is important that employees know what standards of conduct are expected of them and the Contracts of Employment Act 1972 (as amended by the Employment Protection Act 1975) (now Part I, Employment Rights Act 1996) requires employers to provide written information for their employees about certain aspects of their disciplinary rules and procedures.[1]

NOTES

1 Contracts of Employment Act 1972, s 4(2) (now Part I, Employment Rights Act 1996) requires employers to provide employees with a written statement of the main terms and conditions of their employment. Such statements must also specify any disciplinary rules applicable to them and indicate the person to whom they should apply if they are dissatisfied with any disciplinary decision. The statement should explain any further steps which exist in any procedure for dealing with disciplinary decisions or grievances. The employer may satisfy these requirements by referring the employees to a reasonably accessible document which provides the necessary information.

4 The importance of disciplinary rules and procedures has also been recognised by the law relating to dismissals, since the grounds for dismissal and the way in which the dismissal has been handled can be challenged before an industrial tribunal.[1] Where either of these is found by a tribunal to have been unfair the employer may be ordered to reinstate or re-engage the employees concerned and may be liable to pay compensation to them.

NOTES
1 The Trade Union and Labour Relations Act 1974, Sch 1, para 21(4), as amended by the Employment Protection Act 1975, Sch 16, Pt III (now s 111, Employment Rights Act 1996) specifies that a complaint of unfair dismissal has to be presented to an Industrial Tribunal before the end of the three-month period beginning with the effective date of termination.

Formulating policy

5 Management is responsible for maintaining discipline within the organisation and for ensuring that there are adequate disciplinary rules and procedures. The initiative for establishing these will normally lie with management. However, if they are to be fully effective the rules and procedures need to be accepted as reasonable both by those who are to be covered by them and by those who operate them. Management should therefore aim to secure the involvement of employees and all levels of management when formulating new or revising existing rules and procedures. In the light of particular circumstances in different companies and industries trade union officials[1] may or may not wish to participate in the formulation of the rules but they should participate fully with management in agreeing the procedural arrangements which will apply to their members and in seeing that these arrangements are used consistently and fairly.

NOTES
1 Throughout this Code, trade union official has the meaning assigned to it by s 30(1) of the Trade Union and Labour Relations Act 1974 (now s 119, Trade Union and Labour Relations (Consolidation) Act 1992) and means, broadly, officers of the union, its branches and sections, and anyone else, including fellow employees, appointed or elected under the union's rules to represent members.

Rules

6 It is unlikely that any set of disciplinary rules can cover all circumstances that may arise; moreover the rules required will vary according to particular circumstances such as the type of work, working conditions and size of establishment. When drawing up rules the aim should be to specify clearly and concisely those necessary for the efficient and safe performance of work and for the maintenance of satisfactory relations within the workforce and between employees and management. Rules should not be so general as to be meaningless.

7 Rules should be readily available and management should make every effort to ensure that employees know and understand them. This may be best achieved by giving every employee a copy of the rules and by explaining them orally. In the case of new employees this should form part of an induction programme.

8 Employees should be made aware of the likely consequences of breaking rules and in particular they should be given a clear indication of the type of conduct which may warrant summary dismissal.

Essential features of disciplinary procedures

9 Disciplinary procedures should not be viewed primarily as a means of imposing sanctions. They should also be designed to emphasise and encourage improvements in individual conduct.

10 Disciplinary procedures should:

(a) Be in writing.
(b) Specify to whom they apply.
(c) Provide for matters to be dealt with quickly.
(d) Indicate the disciplinary actions which may be taken.
(e) Specify the levels of management which have the authority to take the various forms of disciplinary action, ensuring that immediate superiors do not normally have the power to dismiss without reference to senior management.

(f) Provide for individuals to be informed of the complaints against them and to be given an opportunity to state their case before decisions are reached.

(g) Give individuals the right to be accompanied by a trade union representative or by a fellow employee of their choice.

(h) Ensure that, except for gross misconduct, no employees are dismissed for a first breach of discipline.

(i) Ensure that disciplinary action is not taken until the case has been carefully investigated.

(j) Ensure that individuals are given an explanation for any penalty imposed.

(k) Provide a right of appeal and specify the procedure to be followed.

The procedure in operation

11 When a disciplinary matter arises, the supervisor or manager should first establish the facts promptly before recollections fade, taking into account the statements of any available witnesses. In serious cases consideration should be given to a brief period of suspension while the case is investigated and this suspension should be with pay. Before a decision is made or penalty imposed the individual should be interviewed and given the opportunity to state his or her case and should be advised of any rights under the procedure, including the right to be accompanied.

12 Often supervisors will give informal oral warnings for the purpose of improving conduct when employees commit minor infringements of the established standards of conduct. However, where the facts of a case appear to call for disciplinary action, other than summary dismissal, the following procedure should normally be observed:

(a) In the case of minor offences the individual should be given a formal oral warning or if the issue is more serious, there should be a written warning setting out the nature of the offence and the likely consequences of further offences. In either case the individual should be advised that the warning constitutes the first formal stage of the procedure.

(b) Further misconduct might warrant a final written warning which should contain a statement that any recurrence would lead to suspension or dismissal or some other penalty, as the case may be.

(c) The final step might be disciplinary transfer, or disciplinary suspension without pay (but only if these are allowed for by an express or implied condition of the contract of employment), or dismissal, according to the nature of the misconduct. Special consideration should be given before imposing disciplinary suspension without pay and it should not normally be for a prolonged period.

13 Except in the event of an oral warning, details of any disciplinary action should be given in writing to the employee and if desired, to his or her representative. At the same time the employee should be told of any right of appeal, how to make it and to whom.

14 When determining the disciplinary action to be taken the supervisor or manager should bear in mind the need to satisfy the test of reasonableness in all the circumstances. So far as possible, account should be taken of the employee's record and any other relevant factors.

15 Special consideration should be given to the way in which disciplinary procedures are to operate in exceptional cases. For example:

(a) *Employees to whom the full procedure is not immediately available.* Special provisions may have to be made for the handling of disciplinary matters among

619

nightshift workers, workers in isolated locations or depots or others who may pose particular problems, for example because no one is present with the necessary authority to take disciplinary action or no trade union representative is immediately available.

(b) *Trade union officials.* Disciplinary action against a trade union official can lead to a serious dispute if it is seen as an attack on the union's functions. Although normal disciplinary standards should apply to their conduct as employees, no disciplinary action beyond an oral warning should be taken until the circumstances of the case have been discussed with a senior trade union representative or fulltime official.

(c) *Criminal offences outside employment.* These should not be treated as automatic reasons for dismissal regardless of whether the offence has any relevance to the duties of the individual as an employee. The main considerations should be whether the offence is one that makes the individual unsuitable for his or her type of work or unacceptable to other employees. Employees should not be dismissed solely because a charge against them is pending or because they are absent through having been remanded in custody.

Appeals

16   Grievance procedures are sometimes used for dealing with disciplinary appeals though it is normally more appropriate to keep the two kinds of procedure separate since the disciplinary issues are in general best resolved within the organisation and need to be dealt with more speedily than others. The external stages of a grievance procedure may, however, be the appropriate machinery for dealing with appeals against disciplinary action where a final decision within the organisation is contested or where the matter becomes a collective issue between management and a trade union.

17   Independent arbitration is sometimes an appropriate means of resolving disciplinary issues. Where the parties concerned agree, it may constitute the final stage of procedure.

Records

18   Records should be kept, detailing the nature of any breach of disciplinary rules, the action taken and the reasons for it, whether an appeal was lodged, its outcome and any subsequent developments. These records should be carefully safeguarded and kept confidential.

19   Except in agreed special circumstances breaches of disciplinary rules should be disregarded after a specific period of satisfactory conduct.

Further action

20   Rules and procedures should be reviewed periodically in the light of any developments in employment legislation or industrial relation practice and, if necessary, revised in order to ensure their continuing relevance and effectiveness. Any amendments and additional rules imposing new obligations should be introduced only after reasonable notice has been given to all employees and where appropriate, their representatives have been informed.

Commission for Racial Equality: Code of Practice for the Elimination of Racial Discrimination and the Promotion of Equality of Opportunity in Employment (1983)

NOTES

This Code of Practice was made by the Commission for Racial Equality under s 47 of the Race Relations Act 1976 and came into effect on 1 April 1984 (see the Race Relations Code of Practice Order 1983, SI 1983/1081). For the legal effect of the Code see s 47 of the 1976 Act. Notes are as in the Code, unless otherwise indicated. See Chapter 7.

1.1 This Code aims to give practical guidance which will help employers, trade unions, employment agencies and employees to understand not only the provisions of the Race Relations Act and their implications, but also how best they can implement policies to eliminate racial discrimination and to enhance equality of opportunity.

1.2 The Code does not impose any legal obligations itself, nor is it an authoritative statement of the law—that can only be provided by the courts and tribunals. If, however, its recommendations are not observed this may result in breaches of the law where the act or omission falls within any of the specific prohibitions of the Act. Moreover its provisions are admissible in evidence in any proceedings under the Race Relations Act before an Industrial Tribunal and if any provision appears to the Tribunal to be relevant to a question arising in the proceedings it must be taken into account in determining that question. If employers take the steps that are set out in the Code to prevent their employees from doing acts of unlawful discrimination they may avoid liability for such acts in any legal proceedings brought against them.

1.3 Employees of all racial groups have a right to equal opportunity. Employees ought to provide it. To do so is likely to involve some expenditure at least in staff time and effort. But if a coherent and effective programme of equal opportunity is developed it will help industry to make full use of the abilities of its entire workforce. It is therefore particularly important for all those concerned—employers, trade unions and employees alike—to co-operate with goodwill in adopting and giving effect to measures for securing such equality. We welcome the commitment already made by the CBI and TUC to the principle of equal opportunity. The TUC has recommended a model equal opportunity clause for inclusion in collective agreements and the CBI has published a statement favouring the application by companies of constructive equal opportunity policies.

1.4 A concerted policy to eliminate both race and sex discrimination often provides the best approach. Guidance on equal opportunity between men and women is the responsibility of the Equal Opportunities Commission.

2 The application of the Code

2.1 The Race Relations Act applies to all employers. The Code itself is not restricted to what is required by law, but contains recommendations as well. Some of its detailed provisions may need to be adapted to suit particular circumstances. Any adaptations that are made, however, should be fully consistent with the Code's general intentions.

2.2 Small firms

In many small firms employers have close contact with their staff and there will therefore be less need for formality in assessing whether equal opportunity is being achieved, for example, in such matters as arrangements for monitoring.

621

Moreover it may not be reasonable to expect small firms to have the resources and administrative systems to carry out the Code's detailed recommendations. In complying with the Race Relations Act, small firms should, however, ensure that their practices are consistent with the Code's general intentions.

3   Unlawful discrimination

3.1   The Race Relations Act 1976 makes it unlawful to discriminate against a person, directly or indirectly, in the field of employment (s 4).

Direct discrimination consists of treating a person, on racial grounds,[1] less favourably than others are or would be treated in the same or similar circumstances.

Segregating a person from others on racial grounds constitutes less favourable treatment (s 1(1)(a)).

NOTES
1 Racial grounds are the grounds of race, colour, nationality—including citizenship—or ethnic or national origins, and groups defined by reference to these grounds are referred to as racial groups.

3.2   Indirect discrimination consists of applying in any circumstances covered by the Act a requirement or condition which, although applied equally to persons of all racial groups, is such that a considerably smaller proportion of a particular racial group can comply with it and it cannot be shown to be justifiable on other than racial grounds. Possible examples are:

—a rule about clothing or uniforms which disproportionately disadvantages a racial group and cannot be justified;
—an employer who requires higher language standards than are needed for safe and effective performance of the job.

3.3   The definition of indirect discrimination is complex, and it will not be spelt out in full in every relevant Section of the Code. Reference will be only to the terms 'indirect discrimination' or 'discriminate indirectly'.

3.4   Discrimination by victimisation is also unlawful under the Act. For example, a person is victimised if he or she is given less favourable treatment than others in the same circumstances because it is suspected or known that he or she has brought proceedings under the Act, or given evidence or information relating to such proceedings, or alleged that discrimination has occurred.

Many of the Code's provisions show the close link between equal opportunity and good employment practice. For example, selection criteria which are relevant to job requirements and carefully observed selection procedures not only help to ensure that individuals are appointed according to their suitability for the job and without regard to racial group; they are also part of good employment practice. In the absence of consistent selection procedures and criteria, decisions are often too subjective and racial discrimination can easily occur.

5   Positive action

Opportunities for employees to develop their potential through encouragement, training and careful assessment are also part of good employment practice. Many employees from the racial minorities have potential which, perhaps because of previous discrimination and other causes of disadvantage, they have not been able to realise, and which is not reflected in their qualifications and experience. Where members of particular racial groups have been under-represented over the previous twelve months in particular work, employers and specified training bodies are allowed under the Act to encourage them to take advantage of opportunities for doing that work and to provide training to enable them to attain the skills needed for it. In the case of employers, such training can be provided for persons currently in their employment (as defined by the Act) and in certain circumstances for others too, for example if they have been designated as training bodies. This Code encourages employers to make use of these provisions, which are covered in detail in paragraphs 1.44 and 1.45 (ss 37, 38).

6 Guidance papers

The guidance papers referred to in the footnotes contain additional guidance on specific issues but do not form part of the statutory Code.

PART 1   THE RESPONSIBILITIES OF EMPLOYERS

1.1 Responsibility for providing equal opportunity for all job applicants and employees rests primarily with employers. To this end it is recommended that they should adopt, implement and monitor an equal opportunity policy to ensure that there is no unlawful discrimination and that equal opportunity is genuinely available.

1.2 This policy should be clearly communicated to all employees—eg through notice boards, circulars, contracts of employment or written notifications to individual employees.

1.3 An equal opportunity policy aims to ensure:

(a) that no job applicant or employee receives less favourable treatment than another on racial grounds;

(b) that no applicant or employee is placed at a disadvantage by requirements or conditions which have a disproportionately adverse effect on his or her racial group and which cannot be shown to be justifiable on other than racial grounds;

(c) that, where appropriate and where permissible under the Race Relations Act, employees of under-represented racial groups are given training and encouragement to achieve equal opportunity within the organisation.

1.4 In order to ensure that an equal opportunity policy is fully effective, the following action by employers is recommended:

(a) allocating overall responsibility for the policy to a member of senior management;

(b) discussing and, where appropriate, agreeing with trade union or employee representatives the policy's contents and implementation;

(c) ensuring that the policy is known to all employees and if possible, to all job applicants;

(d) providing training and guidance for supervisory staff and other relevant decision makers (such as personnel and line managers, foremen, gatekeepers and receptionists) to ensure that they understand their position in law and under company policy;

(e) examining and regularly reviewing existing procedures and criteria and changing them where they find that they are actually or potentially unlawfully discriminatory;

(f) making an initial analysis of the workforce and regularly monitoring the application of the policy with the aid of analyses of the ethnic origins of the workforce and of job applicants in accordance with the guidance in paragraphs 1.34–1.35.

Recruitment, promotion, transfer, training and dismissal

Sources of recruitment

Advertisements

1.5 *When advertising job vacancies it is unlawful for employers:*

—to publish an advertisement which indicates, or could reasonably be understood as indicating, an intention to discriminate against applicants from a particular racial group. (For exceptions see the Race Relations Act (s 29).)

1.6 It is therefore recommended that:

(a) employers should not confine advertisements unjustifiably to those areas or publications which would exclude or disproportionately reduce the numbers of applicants of a particular racial group;
(b) employers should avoid prescribing requirements such as length of residence or experience in the UK and where a particular qualification is required it should be made clear that a fully comparable qualification obtained overseas is as acceptable as a UK qualification.

1.7 In order to demonstrate their commitment to equality of opportunity it is recommended that where employers send literature to applicants, this should include a statement that they are equal opportunity employers.

Employment agencies

1.8 *When recruiting through employment agencies, job centres, careers offices and schools, it is unlawful for employers:*

(a) to give instructions to discriminate, for example by indicating that certain groups will or will not be preferred. (For exceptions see the Race Relations Act);
(b) to bring pressure on them to discriminate against members of a particular racial group. (For exceptions, as above.)

1.9 In order to avoid indirect discrimination it is recommended that employers should not confine recruitment unjustifiably to those agencies, job centres, careers offices and schools which, because of their particular source of applicants, provide only or mainly applicants of a particular racial group.

Other sources

1.10 *It is unlawful to use recruitment methods which exclude or disproportionately reduce the numbers of applicants of a particular racial group and which cannot be shown to be justifiable.* It is therefore recommended that employers should not recruit through the following methods:

(a) recruitment, solely or in the first instance, through the recommendations of existing employees where the workforce concerned is wholly or predominantly white or black and the labour market is multiracial;
(b) procedures by which applicants are mainly or wholly supplied through trade unions where this means that only members of a particular racial group, or a disproportionately high number of them, come forward.

Sources for promotion and training

1.11 *It is unlawful for employers to restrict access to opportunities for promotion or training in a way which is discriminatory* (ss 4, 28). It is therefore recommended that:

—job and training vacancies and the application procedure should be made known to all eligible employees, and not in such a way as to exclude or disproportionately reduce the numbers of applicants from a particular racial group.

Selection for recruitment, promotion, transfer, training and dismissal

1.12 *It is unlawful to discriminate,[1] not only in recruitment, promotion, transfer and training, but also in the arrangements made for recruitment and in the ways of affording access to opportunities for promotion, transfer or training.*

NOTES

1 It should be noted that discrimination in selection to achieve 'racial balance' is not allowed. The clause in the 1968 Race Relations Act which allowed such discrimination for the purpose of securing or preserving a reasonable balance of persons of different racial groups in the establishment is not included in the 1976 Race Relations Act.

Selection criteria and tests

1.13 In order to avoid direct or indirect discrimination it is recommended that selection criteria and tests are examined to ensure that they are related to job requirements and are not unlawfully discriminatory (ss 4, 28). (See Introduction, para 3.2.) For example:

(a) a standard of English higher than that needed for the safe and effective performance of the job or clearly demonstrable career pattern should not be required, or a higher level of educational qualification than is needed;

(b) in particular, employers should not disqualify applicants because they are unable to complete an application form unassisted unless personal completion of the form is a valid test of the standard of English required for safe and effective performance of the job;

(c) overseas degrees, diplomas and other qualifications which are comparable with UK qualifications should be accepted as equivalents, and not simply be assumed to be of an inferior quality;

(d) selection tests which contain irrelevant questions or exercises on matters which may be unfamiliar to racial minority applicants should not be used (for example, general knowledge questions on matters more likely to be familiar to indigenous applicants);

(e) selection tests should he checked to ensure that they are related to the job's requirements, ie an individual's test markings should measure ability to do or train for the job in question.

Treatment of applicants, shortlisting, interviewing and selection

1.14 In order to avoid direct or indirect discrimination it is recommended that:

(a) gate, reception and personnel staff should be instructed not to treat casual or formal applicants from particular racial groups less favourably than others. These instructions should be confirmed in writing;

(b) in addition, staff responsible for shortlisting, interviewing and selecting candidates should be:
   —clearly informed of selection criteria and of the need for their consistent application;
   —given guidance or training on the effects which generalised assumptions and prejudices about race can have on selection decisions;
   —made aware of the possible misunderstandings that can occur in interviews between persons of different cultural background;

(c) wherever possible, shortlisting and interviewing should not be done by one person alone but should at least be checked at a more senior level.

Genuine occupational qualification

1.15 *Selection on racial grounds is allowed in certain jobs where being of a particular racial group is a genuine occupational qualification for that job* (s 5(2)(d)). An example is where the holder of a particular job provides persons of a racial group with personal services promoting their welfare, and those services can most effectively be provided by a person of that group.

Transfers and training

1.16 In order to avoid direct or indirect discrimination (s 4(2)(b)) it is recommended that:

(a) staff responsible for selecting employees for transfer to other jobs should be instructed to apply selection criteria without unlawful discrimination;

(b) industry or company agreements and arrangements of custom and practice on job transfers should be examined and amended if they are found to contain requirements or conditions which appear to be indirectly discriminatory. For example, if employees of a particular racial group are concentrated in particular sections, the transfer arrangements should be examined to see if they are unjustifiably and unlawfully restrictive and amended if necessary;

(c) staff responsible for selecting employees for training, whether induction, promotion or skill training should be instructed not to discriminate on racial grounds;

(d) selection criteria for training opportunities should be examined to ensure that they are not indirectly discriminatory.

Dismissal (including redundancy) and other detriment

1.17 *It is unlawful to discriminate on racial grounds in dismissal, or other detriment to an employee* (s 4(2)(c)).

It is therefore recommended that:

(a) staff responsible for selecting employees for dismissal, including redundancy, should be instructed not to discriminate on racial grounds;

(b) selection criteria for redundancies should be examined to ensure that they are not indirectly discriminatory.

Performance appraisals

1.18 *It is unlawful to discriminate on racial grounds in appraisals of employee performance* (s 4(2)).

1.19 It is recommended that:

(a) staff responsible for performance appraisals should be instructed not to discriminate on racial grounds;

(b) assessment criteria should be examined to ensure that they are not unlawfully discriminatory.

Terms of employment, benefits, facilities and services

1.20 It is unlawful to discriminate on racial grounds in affording terms of employment and providing benefits, facilities and services for employees (s 4(2)). It is therefore recommended that:

(a) all staff concerned with these aspects of employment should be instructed accordingly;

(b) the criteria governing eligibility should be examined to ensure that they are not unlawfully discriminatory.

1.21 In addition, employees may request extended leave from time to time in order to visit relations in their countries of origin or who have emigrated to other countries. Many employers have policies which allow annual leave entitlement to be accumulated, or extra unpaid leave to be taken to meet these circumstances. Employers should take care to apply such policies consistently and without unlawful discrimination.

Grievance, disputes and disciplinary procedures

1.22 *It is unlawful to discriminate in the operation of grievance, disputes and disciplinary procedures,* (ss 2, 4(2)) for example by victimising an individual through disciplinary measures because he or she has complained about racial discrimination, or given evidence about such a complaint. Employers should not ignore or treat lightly grievances from members of particular racial groups on the assumption that they are over-sensitive about discrimination.

1.23 It is recommended that in applying disciplinary procedures consideration should be given to the possible effect on an employee's behaviour of the following:

—racial abuse or other racial provocation;
—communication and comprehension difficulties;
—differences in cultural background or behaviour.

Cultural and religious needs

1.24 Where employees have particular cultural and religious needs which conflict with existing work requirements, it is recommended that employers should consider whether it is reasonably practicable to vary or adapt these requirements to enable such needs to be met. For example, it is recommended that they should not refuse employment to a turbanned Sikh because he could not comply with unjustifiable uniform requirements.

Other examples of such needs are:

(a) observance of prayer times and religious holidays;[1]
(b) wearing of dress such as sarees and the trousers worn by Asian women.

NOTES
1 The CRE has issued a guidance paper entitled 'Religious Observance by Muslim Employees'.

1.25 *Although the Act does not specifically cover religious discrimination, work requirements would generally be unlawful if they have a disproportionately adverse effect on particular racial groups and cannot be shown to be justifiable*[1] (ss 4(2), 28).

NOTES
1 Genuinely necessary safety requirements may not constitute unlawful discrimination.

Communications and language training for employees

1.26 Although there is no legal requirement to provide language training, difficulties in communication can endanger equal opportunity in the workforce. In addition, good communications can improve efficiency, promotion prospects and safety and health and create a better understanding between employers, employees and unions. Where the workforce includes current employees whose English is limited it is recommended that steps are taken to ensure that communications are as effective as possible.

1.27 These should include, where reasonably practicable:

(a) provision of interpretation and translation facilities, for example, in the communi-
    cations of grievance and other procedures, and of terms of employment;
(b) training in English language and in communication skills;[1]
(c) training for managers and supervisors in the background and culture of racial
    minority groups;
(d) the use of alternative or additional methods of communication, where employees
    find it difficult to understand health and safety requirements, for example:
    —safety signs; translations of safety notices;
    —instructions through interpreters;
    —instruction combined with industrial language training.

NOTES
1 Industrial language training is provided by a network of Local Education Authority units throughout the country. Full details of the courses and the comprehensive services offered by these units are available from the National Centre for Industrial Language Training, The Havelock Centre, Havelock Road, Southall, Middlesex.

Instructions and pressure to discriminate

1.28 *It is unlawful to instruct or put pressure on others to discriminate on racial grounds* (ss 30, 31).

Appendix 3

(a) An example of an unlawful instruction is:
—an instruction from a personnel or line manager to junior staff to restrict the numbers of employees from a particular racial groups in any particular work;
(b) An example of pressure to discriminate is:
—an attempt by a shop steward or group of workers to induce an employer not to recruit members of particular racial groups, for example by threatening industrial action.

1.29 *It is also unlawful to discriminate in response to such instructions or pressure.*

1.30 The following recommendations are made to avoid unlawful instructions and pressure to discriminate:

(a) guidance should be given to all employees, and particularly those in positions of authority or influence on the relevant provisions of the law;
(b) decision-makers should be instructed not to give way to pressure to discriminate;
(c) giving instructions or bringing pressure to discriminate should be treated as a disciplinary offence.

Victimisation

1.31 *It is unlawful to victimise individuals who have made allegations or complaints of racial discrimination or provided information about such discrimination, for example by disciplining them or dismissing them (s 2). (See Introduction, para 3.4.)*

1.32 It is recommended that:
—guidance on this aspect of the law should be given to all employees and particularly to those in positions of influence or authority.

Monitoring equal opportunity

NOTES
See the CRE's guidance paper on 'Monitoring an Equal Opportunity Policy'.

1.33 It is recommended that employers should regularly monitor the effects of selection decisions and personnel practices and procedures in order to assess whether equal opportunity is being achieved.

1.34 The information needed for effective monitoring may be obtained in a number of ways. It will best be provided by records showing the ethnic origins of existing employees and job applicants. It is recognised that the need for detailed information and the methods of collecting it will vary according to the circumstances of individual establishments. For example, in small firms or in firms in areas with little or no racial minority settlement it will often be adequate to assess the distribution of employees from personal knowledge and visual identification.

1.35 It is open to employers to adopt the method of monitoring which is best suited to their needs and circumstances, but whichever method is adopted, they should be able to show that it is effective. In order to achieve the full commitment of all concerned the chosen method should be discussed and agreed, where appropriate, with trade union or employee representatives.

1.36 Employers should ensure that information on individuals' ethnic origins is collected for the purpose of monitoring equal opportunity alone and is protected from misuse.

1.37 The following is the comprehensive method recommended by the CRE.[1]
Analyses should be carried out of:

(a) the ethnic composition of the workforce of each plant, department, section, shift and job category, and changes in distribution over periods of time;
(b) selection decisions for recruitment, promotion, transfer and training, according to the racial group of candidates, and reasons for these decisions.

NOTES
1 This is outlined in detail in 'Monitoring an Equal Opportunity Policy'.

1.38   Except in cases where there are large numbers of applicants and the burden on resources would be excessive, reasons for selection and rejection should be recorded at each stage of the selection process, eg initial shortlisting and final decisions. Simple categories of reasons for rejection should be adequate for the early sifting stages.

1.39   Selection criteria and personnel procedures should be reviewed to ensure that they do not include requirements or conditions which constitute or may lead to unlawful indirect discrimination.

1.40   This information should be carefully and regularly analysed and, in order to identify areas which may need particular attention, a number of key questions should be asked.

1.41   Is there evidence that individuals from any particular racial group:

(a) do not apply for employment or promotion, or that fewer apply than might be expected?
(b) are not recruited or promoted at all, or are appointed in a significantly lower proportion than their rate of application?
(c) are under-represented in training or in jobs carrying higher pay, status or authority?
(d) are concentrated in certain shifts, sections or departments?

1.42   If the answer to any of these questions is yes, the reasons for this should be investigated. If direct or indirect discrimination is found action must be taken to end it immediately (ss 4, 28).

1.43   It is recommended that deliberate acts of unlawful discrimination by employees are treated as disciplinary offences.

Positive action

NOTES
The CRE has issued a guidance paper on Positive Action, entitled 'Equal Opportunity in Employment—Why Positive Action?'.

1.44   *Although they are not legally required, positive measures are allowed by the law to encourage employees and potential employees and provide training for employees who are members of particular racial groups which have been under- represented[1] in particular work* (s 38). (See Introduction, para 5.) Discrimination at the point of selection for work, however, is not permissible in these circumstances.

NOTES
1 A racial group is under-represented if, at any time during the previous twelve months, either there was no one of that group doing the work in question, or there were disproportionately few in comparison with the group's proportion in the workforce at that establishment, or in the population from which the employer normally recruits for work at that establishment.

1.45   Such measures are important for the development of equal opportunity. It is therefore recommended that, where there is under-representation of particular racial groups in particular work, the following measures should be taken wherever appropriate and reasonably practicable:

(a) job advertisements designed to reach members of these groups and to encourage their applications: for example, through the use of the ethnic minority press, as well as other newspapers;

(b) use of the employment agencies and careers offices in areas where these groups are concentrated;

(c) recruitment and training schemes for school leavers designed to reach members of these groups;

(d) encouragement to employees from these groups to apply for promotion or transfer opportunities;

(e) training for promotion or skill training for employees of these groups who lack particular expertise but show potential: supervisory training may include language training.

PART 2   THE RESPONSIBILITIES OF INDIVIDUAL EMPLOYEES

2.1   While the primary responsibility for providing equal opportunity rests with the employer, individual employees at all levels and of all racial groups have responsibilities too. Good race relations depend on them as much as on management, and so their attitudes and activities are very important.

2.2   *The following actions by individual employees would be unlawful:*

(a) discrimination in the course of their employment against fellow employees or job applicants on racial grounds (ss 4, 33), for example, in selection decisions for recruitment, promotion, transfer and training;

(b) inducing, or attempting to induce other employees, unions or management to practice unlawful discrimination (s 31). For example, they should not refuse to accept other employees from particular racial groups or refuse to work with a supervisor of a particular racial group;

(c) victimising individuals who have made allegations or complaints of racial discrimination or provided information about such discrimination (s 2). (See Introduction, para 3.4.)

2.3   To assist in preventing racial discrimination and promoting equal opportunity it is recommended that individual employees should:

(a) co-operate in measures introduced by management designed to ensure equal opportunity and non-discrimination;

(b) where such measures have not been introduced, press for their introduction (through their trade union where appropriate);

(c) draw the attention of management and, where appropriate, their trade unions to suspected discriminatory acts or practices;

(d) refrain from harassment or intimidation of other employees on racial grounds, for example, by attempting to discourage them from continuing employment. Such action may be unlawful if it is taken by employees against those subject to their authority.

2.4   In addition to the responsibilities set out above individual employees from the racial minorities should recognise that in many occupations advancement is dependent on an appropriate standard of English. Similarly an understanding of the industrial relations procedures which apply is often essential for good working relationships.

2.5   They should therefore:

(a) where appropriate, seek means to improve their standards of English;

(b) co-operate in industrial language training schemes introduced by employers and/or unions;

(c) co-operate in training or other schemes designed to inform them of industrial relations procedures, company agreements, work rules, etc;

(d) where appropriate, participate in discussions with employers and unions, to find solutions to conflicts between cultural or religious needs and production needs.

PART 3   THE RESPONSIBILITIES OF TRADE UNIONS

3.1   Trade unions, in common with a number of other organisations, have a dual role as employers and providers of services specifically covered by the Race Relations Act.

3.2   In their role as employer, unions have the responsibilities set out in Part 1 of the Code. They also have a responsibility to ensure that their representatives and members do not discriminate against any particular racial group in the admission or treatment of members, or as colleagues, supervisors, or subordinates.

3.3   In addition, trade union officials at national and local level and shopfloor representatives at plant level have an important part to play on behalf of their members in preventing unlawful discrimination and in promoting equal opportunity and good race relations. Trade unions should encourage and press for equal opportunity policies so that measures to prevent discrimination at the workforce can be introduced with the clear commitment of both management and unions.

Admission of members

3.4   *It is unlawful for trade unions to discriminate on racial grounds:*

(a) by refusing membership;
(b) by offering less favourable terms of membership (s 11(2)).

Treatment of members

3.5   *It is unlawful for trade unions to discriminate on racial grounds against existing members:*

(a) by varying their terms of membership. depriving them of membership or subjecting them to any other detriment (s 11(3));
(b) by treating them less favourably in the benefits, facilities or services provided.
These may include:
  training facilities;
  welfare and insurance schemes;
  entertainment and social events;
  processing of grievances;
  negotiations;
  assistance in disciplinary or dismissal procedures.

3.6   In addition, it is recommended that unions ensure that in cases where members of particular racial groups believe that they are suffering racial discrimination, whether by the employer or the union itself, serious attention is paid to the reasons for this belief and that any discrimination which may be occurring is stopped.

Disciplining union members who discriminate

3.7   It is recommended that deliberate acts of unlawful discrimination by union members are treated as disciplinary offences.

Positive action

3.8   *Although they are not legally required, positive measures are allowed by the law to encourage and provide training for members of particular racial groups which have been under-represented*[1] *in trade union membership or in trade union posts* (s 38(3), (4), (5)). (Discrimination at the point of selection, however, is not permissible in these circumstances.)

NOTES

1 A racial group is under-represented in trade union membership, if at any time during the previous twelve months no persons of that group were in membership, or disproportionately few in comparison with the proportion of persons of that group among those eligible for membership (s 38(5)). Under-representation in trade union posts applies under the same twelve month criteria where there were no persons of a particular racial group in those posts or disproportionately few in comparison with the proportion of that group in the organisation (s 38(4)).

3.9 It is recommended that, wherever appropriate and reasonably practicable, trade unions should:

(a) encourage individuals from these groups to join the union. Where appropriate, recruitment material should be translated into other languages;

(b) encourage individuals from these groups to apply for union posts and provide training to help fit them for such posts.

Training and information

3.10 Training and information play a major part in the avoidance of discrimination and the promotion of equal opportunity. It is recommended that trade unions should:

(a) provide training and information for officers, shop stewards and representatives on their responsibilities for equal opportunity. This training and information should cover:

the Race Relations Act and the nature and causes of discrimination;
the backgrounds of racial minority groups and communication needs;
the effects of prejudice;
equal opportunity policies;
avoiding discrimination when representing members.

(b) ensure that members and representatives, whatever their racial group, are informed of their role in the union, and of industrial relations and union procedures and structures. This may be done, for example:

through translation of material;
through encouragement to participate in industrial relations courses and industrial language training.

Pressure to discriminate

3.11 *It is unlawful for trade union members or representatives to induce or to attempt to induce those responsible for employment decisions to discriminate* (s 31):

(a) in the recruitment, promotion, transfer, training or dismissal of employees;

(b) in terms of employment, benefits, facilities or services.

3.12 For example, they should not:

(a) restrict the numbers of a particular racial group in a section, grade or department;

(b) resist changes designed to remove indirect discrimination, such as those in craft apprentice schemes, or in agreements concerning seniority rights or mobility between departments.

Victimisation

3.13 *It is unlawful to victimise individuals who have made allegations or complaints of racial discrimination or provided information about such discrimination* (s 2). (See Introduction, para 3.4.)

Avoidance of discrimination

3.14 *Where unions are involved in selection decisions for recruitment, promotion, training or transfer, for example through recommendation or veto, it is unlawful for them to discriminate on racial grounds* (ss 31, 33).

3.15 It is recommended that they should instruct their members accordingly and examine their procedures and joint agreements to ensure that they do not contain indirectly discriminatory requirements or conditions, such as: unjustifiable restriction on transfers between departments or irrelevant and unjustifiable selection criteria which have a disproportionately adverse effect on particular racial groups.

Union involvement in equal opportunity policies

3.16 It is recommended that:

(a) unions should co-operate in the introduction and implementation of full equal opportunity policies, as defined in paras 1.3 and 1.4;
(b) unions should negotiate the adoption of such policies where they have not been introduced or the extension of existing policies where these are too narrow;
(c) unions should co-operate with measures to monitor the progress of equal opportunity policies, or encourage management to introduce them where they do not already exist. Where appropriate (see paras 1.33–1.35) this may be done through analysis of the distribution of employees and job applicants according to ethnic origin;
(d) where monitoring shows that discrimination has occurred or is occurring, unions should co-operate in measures to eliminate it;
(e) although positive action[1] is not legally required, unions should encourage management to take such action where there is under-representation of particular racial groups in particular jobs, and where management itself introduces positive action representatives should support it;
(f) similarly, where there are communication difficulties, management should be asked to take whatever action is appropriate to overcome them.

NOTES
1 See 1.44—Positive Action recommendations.

PART 4   THE RESPONSIBILITIES OF EMPLOYMENT AGENCIES

4.1 Employment agencies, in their role as employers, have the responsibilities outlined in Part 1 of the Code. In addition, they have responsibilities as suppliers of job applicants to other employers.

4.2 *It is unlawful for employment agencies: (for exceptions see Race Relations Act)*

(a) *to discriminate on racial grounds in providing services to clients* (s 14(1));
(b) *to publish job advertisements indicating, or which might be understood to indicate that applications from any particular group will not be considered or will be treated more favourably or less favourably than others* (s 29);
(c) *to act on directly discriminatory instructions from employers to the effect that applicants from a particular racial group will be rejected or preferred or that their numbers should be restricted* (s 14(1));
(d) *to act on indirectly discriminatory instructions from employers ie that requirements or conditions should be applied that would have a disproportionately adverse effect on applicants of a particular racial group and which cannot be shown to be justifiable* (ss 14(1), 16(1)(b)).

4.3 It is recommended that agencies should also avoid indicating such conditions or requirements in job advertisements unless they can be shown to be justifiable. Examples in each case may be those relating to educational qualifications or residence.

4.4 It is recommended that staff should be given guidance on their duty not to discriminate and on the effect which generalised assumptions and prejudices can have on their treatment of members of particular racial group.

4.5   In particular staff should be instructed:

(a) not to ask employers for racial preferences;
(b) not to draw attention to racial origin when recommending applicants unless the employer is trying to attract applicants of a particular racial group under the exceptions in the Race Relations Act;
(c) to report a client's refusal to interview an applicant for reasons that are directly or indirectly discriminatory to a supervisor, who should inform the client that discrimination is unlawful. If the client maintains this refusal the agency should inform the applicant of his or her right to complain to an industrial tribunal and to apply to the CRE for assistance. An internal procedure for recording such cases should be operated;
(d) to inform their supervisor if they believe that an applicant, though interviewed, has been rejected on racial grounds. If the supervisor is satisfied that there are grounds for this belief, he or she should arrange for the applicant to be informed of the right to complain to an industrial tribunal and to apply to the CRE for assistance. An internal procedure for recording such cases should be operated;
(e) to treat job applicants without discrimination. For example, they should not send applicants from particular racial groups to only those employers who are believed to be willing to accept them, or restrict the range of job opportunities for such applicants because of assumptions about their abilities based on race or colour.

4.6   It is recommended that employment agencies should discontinue their services to employers who give unlawful discriminatory instructions and who refuse to withdraw them.

4.7   It is recommended that employment agencies should monitor the effectiveness of the measures they take for ensuring that no unlawful discrimination occurs. For example, where reasonably practicable they should make periodic checks to ensure that applicants from particular racial groups are being referred for suitable jobs for which they are qualified at a similar rate to that for other comparable applicants.

Equal Opportunities Commission: Code of Practice for the Elimination of Discrimination on the Grounds of Sex and Marriage and the Promotion of Equality of Opportunity in Employment (1985)

NOTES
This Code of Practice was issued by the Equal Opportunities Commission under s 56A of the Sex Discrimination Act 1975 and was brought into effect on 30 April 1985 by the Sex Discrimination Code of Practice Order 1985, SI 1985/387. The Legal Annex. which summarises the relevant provisions of the 1975 Act, is omitted. For the legal effect of the Code see s 56A of the 1975 Act. Notes are as in the Code. See Chapter 7.

INTRODUCTION

1   The EOC issues this Code of Practice for the following purposes:

(a) for the elimination of discrimination in employment;
(b) to give guidance as to what steps it is reasonably practicable for employers to take to ensure that their employees do not in the course of their employment act unlawfully contrary to the Sex Discrimination Act (SDA);
(c) for the promotion of equality of opportunity between men and women in employment.

The SDA prohibits discrimination against men, as well as against women. It also requires that married people should not be treated less favourably than single people of the same sex.

It should be noted that the provisions of the SDA—and therefore of this Code—apply to the UK-based subsidiaries of foreign companies.

2   The Code gives guidance to employers, trade unions and employment agencies on measures which can be taken to achieve equality. The chances of success of any organisation will clearly be improved if it seeks to develop the abilities of all employees, and the Code shows the close link which exists between equal opportunity and good employment practice. In some cases, an initial cost may be involved, but this should be more than compensated for by better relationships and better use of human resources.

Small businesses

3   The Code has to deal in general terms and it will be necessary for employers to adapt it in a way appropriate to the size and structure of their organisations. Small businesses, for example, will require much simpler procedures than organisations with complex structures and it may not always be reasonable for them to carry out all the Code's detailed recommendations. In adapting the Code's recommendations, small firms should, however, ensure that their practices comply with the Sex Discrimination Act.

Employers' responsibility

4   The primary responsibility at law rests with each employer to ensure that there is no unlawful discrimination. It is important, however, that measures to eliminate discrimination or promote equality of opportunity should be understood and supported by all employees. Employers are therefore recommended to involve their employees in equal opportunity policies.

Individual employees' responsibility

5   While the main responsibility for eliminating discrimination and providing equal opportunity is that of the employer, individual employees at all levels have responsibilities too. They must not discriminate or knowingly aid their employer to do so.

Trade union responsibility

6   The full commitment of trade unions is essential for the elimination of discrimination and for the successful operation of an equal opportunities policy. Much can be achieved by collective bargaining and throughout the Code it is assumed that all the normal procedures will be followed.

7   It is recommended that unions should co-operate in the introduction and implementation of equal opportunities policies where employers have decided to introduce them, and should urge that such policies be adopted where they have not yet been introduced.

8   Trade Unions have a responsibility to ensure that their representatives and members do not unlawfully discriminate on grounds of sex or marriage in the admission or treatment of members. The guidance in this Code also applies to trade unions in their role as employers.

Employment agencies

9   Employment agencies have a responsibility as suppliers of job applicants to avoid unlawful discrimination on the grounds of sex or marriage in providing services to clients. The guidance in this Code also applies to employment agencies in their role as employers.

Appendix 3

Definitions

10 For ease of reference, the main employment provisions of the Sex Discrimination Act, including definitions of direct and indirect sex and marriage discrimination, are provided in a Legal Annex to this Code.

PART 1 THE ROLE OF GOOD EMPLOYMENT PRACTICES IN ELIMINATING SEX AND MARRIAGE DISCRIMINATION

11 This section of the Code describes those good employment practices which will help to eliminate unlawful discrimination. It recommends the establishment and use of consistent criteria for selection, training, promotion, redundancy and dismissal which are made known to all employees. Without this consistency, decisions can be subjective and leave the way open for unlawful discrimination to occur.

Recruitment

12 It is unlawful: UNLESS THE JOB IS COVERED BY AN EXCEPTION:[1] TO DISCRIMINATE DIRECTLY OR INDIRECTLY ON THE GROUNDS OF SEX OR MARRIAGE:

—IN THE ARRANGEMENTS MADE FOR DECIDING WHO SHOULD BE OFFERED A JOB.
—IN ANY TERMS OF EMPLOYMENT.
—BY REFUSING OR OMITTING TO OFFER A PERSON EMPLOYMENT.
[*Section 6(1)(a); 6(1)(b); 6(1)(c)*]

NOTES
1 There are a number of exceptions to the requirements of the SDA, that employers must not discriminate against their employees or against potential employees.

13 It is therefore recommended that:

(a) each individual should be assessed according to his or her personal capability to carry out a given job. It should not be assumed that men only or women only will be able to perform certain kinds of work;
(b) any qualifications or requirements applied to a job which effectively inhibit applications from one sex or from married people should be retained only if they are justifiable in terms of the job to be done;
[*Section 6(1)(a) together with section 1(1)(b) or 3(1)(b)*]
(c) any age limits should be retained only if they are necessary for the job. An unjustifiable age limit could constitute unlawful indirect discrimination, for example, against women who have taken time out of employment for child-rearing;
(d) where trade unions uphold such qualifications or requirements as union policy, they should amend that policy in the light of any potentially unlawful effect.

Genuine occupational qualifications (GOQs)

14 It is unlawful: EXCEPT FOR CERTAIN JOBS WHEN A PERSON'S SEX IS A GENUINE OCCUPATIONAL QUALIFICATION (GOQ) FOR THAT JOB to select candidates on the ground of sex.
[*Section 7(2); 7(3) and 7(4)*]

15 There are very few instances in which a job will qualify for a GOQ on the ground of sex. However, exceptions may arise for example, where considerations of privacy and decency or authenticity are involved. The SDA expressly states that the need of the job for strength and stamina does not justify restricting it to men. When a GOQ exists for a job, it applies also to promotion, transfer or training for that job, but cannot be used to justify a dismissal.

16   In some instances, the GOQ will apply to some of the duties only. A GOQ will not be valid, however, where members of the appropriate sex are already employed in sufficient numbers to meet the employer's likely requirements without undue inconvenience. For example, in a job where sales assistants may be required to undertake changing room duties, it might not be lawful to claim a GOQ in respect of *all* the assistants on the grounds that any of them might be required to undertake changing room duties from time to time.

17   It is therefore recommended that:

—A job for which a GOQ was used in the past should be re-examined if the post falls vacant to see whether the GOQ still applies. Circumstances may well have changed, rendering the GOQ inapplicable.

Sources of recruitment

18   It is unlawful: UNLESS THE JOB IS COVERED BY AN EXCEPTION:

—TO DISCRIMINATE ON GROUNDS OF SEX OR MARRIAGE IN THE ARRANGEMENTS MADE FOR DETERMINING WHO SHOULD BE OFFERED EMPLOYMENT WHETHER RECRUITING BY ADVERTISEMENTS, THROUGH EMPLOYMENT AGENCIES, JOBCENTRES, OR CAREER OFFICES.
—TO IMPLY THAT APPLICATIONS FROM ONE SEX OR FROM MARRIED PEOPLE WILL NOT BE CONSIDERED.
[*Section 6(1)(a)*]
—TO INSTRUCT OR PUT PRESSURE ON OTHERS TO OMIT TO REFER FOR EMPLOYMENT PEOPLE OF ONE SEX OR MARRIED PEOPLE UNLESS THE JOB IS COVERED BY AN EXCEPTION.
[*Sections 39 and 40*]

It is also unlawful WHEN ADVERTISING JOB VACANCIES:

—TO PUBLISH OR CAUSE TO BE PUBLISHED AN ADVERTISEMENT WHICH INDICATES OR MIGHT REASONABLY BE UNDERSTOOD AS INDICATING AN INTENTION TO DISCRIMINATE UNLAWFULLY ON GROUNDS OF SEX OR MARRIAGE.

Advertising

19   It is therefore recommended that:
(a) job advertising should be carried out in such a way as to encourage applications from suitable candidates of both sexes. This can be achieved both by wording of the advertisements and, for example, by placing advertisements in publications likely to reach both sexes. All advertising material and accompanying literature relating to employment or training issues should be reviewed to ensure that it avoids presenting men and women in stereotyped roles. Such stereotyping tends to perpetuate sex segregation in jobs and can also lead people of the opposite sex to believe that they would be unsuccessful in applying for particular jobs;
(b) where vacancies are filled by promotion or transfer, they should be published to all eligible employees in such a way that they do not restrict applications from either sex;
(c) recruitment solely or primarily by word of mouth may unnecessarily restrict the choice of applicants available. The method should be avoided in a workforce predominantly of one sex, if in practice it prevents members of the opposite sex from applying;
(d) where applicants are supplied through trade unions and members of one sex only come forward, this should be discussed with the unions and an alternative approach adopted.

Appendix 3

Careers service schools

20   When notifying vacancies to the Careers Service, employers should specify that these are open to both boys and girls. This is especially important when a job has traditionally been done exclusively or mainly by one sex. If dealing with single sex schools, they should ensure, where possible, that both boys' and girls' schools are approached; it is also a good idea to remind mixed schools that jobs are open to boys and girls.

Selection methods

Tests

21   (a) If selection tests are used, they should be specifically related to job and/or career requirements and should measure an individual's actual or inherent ability to do or train for the work or career.
     (b) Tests should be reviewed regularly to ensure that they remain relevant and free from any unjustifiable bias, either in content or in scoring mechanism.

Application and interviewing

22   It is unlawful: UNLESS THE JOB IS COVERED BY AN EXCEPTION:

TO DISCRIMINATE ON GROUNDS OF SEX OR MARRIAGE BY REFUSING OR DELIBERATELY OMITTING TO OFFER EMPLOYMENT.
[*Section 6(1)(c)*]

23   It is therefore recommended that:

(a) employers should ensure that personnel staff, line managers and all other employees who may come into contact with job applicants, should be trained in the provisions of the SDA, including the fact that it is unlawful to instruct or put pressure on others to discriminate;
(b) applications from men and women should be processed in exactly the same way. For example, there should not be separate lists of male and female or married and single applicants. All those handling applications and conducting interviews should be trained in the avoidance of unlawful discrimination and records of interviews kept, where practicable, showing why applicants were or were not appointed;
(c) questions should relate to the requirements of the job. Where it is necessary to assess whether personal circumstances will affect performance of the job (for example, where it involves unsocial hours or extensive travel) this should be discussed objectively without detailed questions based on assumptions about marital status, children and domestic obligations. Questions about marriage plans or family intentions should not be asked, as they could be construed as showing bias against women. Information necessary for personnel records can be collected after a job offer has been made.

Promotion, transfer and training

24   It is unlawful: UNLESS THE JOB IS COVERED BY AN EXCEPTION, FOR EMPLOYERS TO DISCRIMINATE DIRECTLY OR INDIRECTLY ON THE GROUNDS OF SEX OR MARRIAGE IN THE WAY THEY AFFORD ACCESS TO OPPORTUNITIES FOR PROMOTION, TRANSFER OR TRAINING.
[*Section 6(2)(a)*]

25   It is therefore recommended that:
(a) where an appraisal system is in operation, the assessment criteria should be examined to ensure that they are not unlawfully discriminatory and the scheme monitored to assess how it is working in practice;

(b) when a group of workers predominantly of one sex is excluded from an appraisal scheme, access to promotion, transfer and training and to other benefits should be reviewed, to ensure that there is no unlawful indirect discrimination;

(c) promotion and career development patterns are reviewed to ensure that the traditional qualifications are justifiable requirements for the job to be done. In some circumstances, for example, promotion on the basis of length of service could amount to unlawful indirect discrimination, as it may unjustifiably affect more women than men;

(d) when general ability and personal qualities are the main requirements for promotion to a post, care should be taken to consider favourably candidates of both sexes with differing career patterns and general experience;

(e) rules which restrict or preclude transfer between certain jobs should be questioned and changed if they are found to be unlawfully discriminatory. Employees of one sex may be concentrated in sections from which transfers are traditionally restricted without real justification;

(f) policies and practices regarding selection for training, day release and personal development should be examined for unlawful direct and indirect discrimination. Where there is found to be an imbalance in training as between sexes, the cause should be identified to ensure that it is not discriminatory;

(g) age limits for access to training and promotion should be questioned.

Health and safety legislation

26   Equal treatment of men and women may be limited by statutory provisions which require men and women to be treated differently. For example, the Factories Act 1961 places restrictions on the hours of work of female manual employees, although the Health and Safety Executive can exempt employers from these restrictions, subject to certain conditions. The Mines and Quarries Act 1954 imposes limitations on women's work and there are restrictions where there is special concern for the unborn child (eg lead and ionising radiation). However the broad duties placed on employers by the Health and Safety at Work, etc, Act 1974 makes no distinctions between men and women. Section 2(1) requires employers to ensure, so far as is reasonably practicable, the health and safety and welfare at work of *all* employees. SPECIFIC HEALTH AND SAFETY REQUIREMENTS UNDER EARLIER LEGISLATION ARE UNAFFECTED BY THE ACT.
It is therefore recommended that:

—company policy should be reviewed and serious consideration given to any significant differences in treatment between men and women, and there should be well-founded reasons if such differences are maintained or introduced.

Terms of employment, benefits, facilities and services

27   It is unlawful: UNLESS THE JOB IS COVERED BY AN EXCEPTION: TO DISCRIMINATE ON THE GROUNDS OF SEX OR MARRIAGE, DIRECTLY OR INDIRECTLY, IN THE TERMS ON WHICH EMPLOYMENT IS OFFERED OR IN AFFORDING ACCESS TO ANY BENEFITS,[1] FACILITIES OR SERVICES.
[*Sections 6(1)(b); 6(2)(a); 29*]

NOTES
1 Certain provisions relating to death and retirement are exempt from the Act.

28   It is therefore recommended that:

(a) all terms of employment, benefits, facilities and services are reviewed to ensure that there is no unlawful discrimination on grounds of sex or marriage. For example, part-time work, domestic leave, company cars and benefits for dependants should be available to both male and female employees in the same or not materially different circumstances.

Appendix 3

29 In an establishment where part-timers are solely or mainly women, unlawful indirect discrimination may arise if, as a group, they are treated less favourably than other employees without justification.

It is therefore recommended that:

(b) where part-time workers do not enjoy pro-rata pay or benefits with full-time workers, the arrangements should be reviewed to ensure that they are justified without regard to sex.

Grievances, disciplinary procedures and victimisation

30 It is unlawful: TO VICTIMISE AN INDIVIDUAL FOR A COMPLAINT MADE IN GOOD FAITH ABOUT SEX OR MARRIAGE DISCRIMINATION OR FOR GIVING EVIDENCE ABOUT SUCH A COMPLAINT.
[Section 4(1); 4(2); and 4(3)]

31 It is therefore recommended that:

(a) particular care is taken to ensure that an employee who has in good faith taken action under the Sex Discrimination Act or the Equal Pay Act does not receive less favourable treatment than other employees, for example by being disciplined or dismissed;
(b) employees should be advised to use the internal procedures, where appropriate, but this is without prejudice to the individual's right to apply to an industrial tribunal within the statutory time limit, ie before the end of the period of three months beginning when the act complained of was done. (There is no time limit if the victimisation is continuing);
(c) particular care is taken to deal effectively with all complaints of discrimination, victimisation or harassment. It should not be assumed that they are made by those who are over-sensitive.

Dismissals, redundancies and other unfavourable treatment of employees

32 It is unlawful: TO DISCRIMINATE DIRECTLY OR INDIRECTLY ON GROUNDS OF SEX OR MARRIAGE IN DISMISSALS OR BY TREATING AN EMPLOYEE UNFAVOURABLY IN ANY OTHER WAY.
[Section 6(2)(b)]

It is therefore recommended that:

(a) care is taken that members of one sex are not disciplined or dismissed for performance or behaviour which would be overlooked or condoned in the other sex;
(b) redundancy procedures affecting a group of employees predominantly of one sex should be reviewed, so as to remove any effects which could be disproportionate and unjustifiable;
(c) conditions of access to voluntary redundancy benefit[1] should be made available on equal terms to male and female employees in the same or not materially different circumstances;
(d) where there is down-grading or short-time working (for example, owing to a change in the nature or volume of an employer's business) the arrangements should not unlawfully discriminate on the ground of sex;
(e) all reasonably practical steps should be taken to ensure that a standard of conduct or behaviour is observed which prevents members of either sex from being intimidated, harassed or otherwise subjected to unfavourable treatment on the ground of their sex.

NOTES
1 Certain provisions relating to death and retirement are exempt from the Act.

PART 2   THE ROLE OF GOOD EMPLOYMENT PRACTICES IN PROMOTING
EQUALITY OF OPPORTUNITY

33 This section of the Code describes those employment practices which help to promote equality of opportunity. It gives information about the formulation and implementation of equal opportunities policies. While such policies are not required by law, their value has been recognised by a number of employers who have voluntarily adopted them. Others may wish to follow this example.

Formulating an equal opportunities policy

34 An equal opportunities policy will ensure the effective use of human resources in the best interests of both the organisation and its employees. It is a commitment by an employer to the development and use of employment procedures and practices which do not discriminate on grounds of sex or marriage and which provide genuine equality of opportunity for all employees. The detail of the policy will vary according to size of the organisation.

Implementing the policy

35 An equal opportunities policy must be seen to have the active support of management at the highest level. To ensure that the policy is fully effective, the following procedure is recommended:

(a) the policy should be clearly stated and, where appropriate, included in a collective agreement;
(b) overall responsibility for implementing the policy should rest with senior management;
(c) the policy should be made known to all employees and, where reasonably practicable, to all job applicants.

36 Trade unions have a very important part to play in implementing genuine equality of opportunity and they will obviously be involved in the review of established procedures to ensure that these are consistent with the law.

Monitoring

37 It is recommended that the policy is monitored regularly to ensure that it is working in practice. Consideration could be given to setting up a joint Management/ Trade Union Review Committee.

38 In a small firm with a simple structure it may be quite adequate to assess the distribution and payment of employees from personal knowledge.

39 In a large and complex organisation a more formal analysis will be necessary, for example, by sex, grade and payment in each unit. This may need to be introduced by stages as resources permit. Any formal analysis should be regularly updated and available to Management and Trade Unions to enable any necessary action to be taken.

40 Sensible monitoring will show, for example, whether members of one sex:

(a) do not apply for employment or promotion, or that fewer apply than might be expected;
(b) are not recruited, promoted or selected for training and development or are appointed/selected in a significantly lower proportion than their rate of application;
(c) are concentrated in certain jobs, sections or departments.

Appendix 3

Positive action

Recruitment, training and promotion

41 Selection for recruitment or promotion must be on merit, irrespective of sex. However, the Sex Discrimination Act does allow certain steps to redress the effects of previous unequal opportunities. Where there have been few or no members of one sex in particular work in their employment for the previous 12 months, the Act allows employers to give special encouragement to, and provide specific training for, the minority sex. Such measures are usually described as Positive Action.
[*Section 48*]

42 Employers may wish to consider positive measures such as:

(a) training their own employees (male or female) for work which is traditionally the preserve of the other sex, for example, training women for skilled manual or technical work;

(b) positive encouragement to women to apply for management posts—special courses may be needed;

(c) advertisements which encourage application from the minority sex but make it clear that selection will be on merit without reference to sex;

(d) notifying job agencies, as part of a Positive Action Programme that they wish to encourage members of one sex to apply for vacancies, where few or no members of that sex are doing the work in question. In these circumstances, job agencies should tell both men and women about the posts and, in addition, let the under-represented sex know that applications from them are particularly welcome. Withholding information from one sex in an attempt to encourage applications from the opposite sex would be unlawful.

Other working arrangements

43 There are other forms of action which could assist both employer and employee by helping to provide continuity of employment to working parents, many of whom will have valuable experience or skills.

Employers may wish to consider with their employees whether:

(a) certain jobs can be carried out on a part-time or flexi-time basis;

(b) personal leave arrangements are adequate and available to both sexes. It should not be assumed that men may not need to undertake domestic responsibilities on occasion, especially at the time of childbirth;

(c) child-care facilities are available locally or whether it would be feasible to establish nursery facilities on the premises or combine with other employers to provide them;

(d) residential training could be facilitated for employees with young children. For example, where this type of training is necessary, by informing staff who are selected well in advance to enable them to make childcare and other personal arrangements; employers with their own residential training centres could also consider whether childcare facilities might be provided;

(e) the statutory maternity leave provisions could be enhanced, for example, by reducing the qualifying service period, extending the leave period, or giving access to part-time arrangements on return.

These arrangements, and others, are helpful to both sexes but are of particular benefit to women in helping them to remain in gainful employment during the years of child-rearing.

ACAS Code of Practice: Time off for Trade Union Duties and Activities (1991)

NOTES

Authority: Employment Protection Act 1975, s 6 (now the Trade Union and Labour Relations (Consolidation) Act 1992, ss 199, 200).

The original ACAS Code on this subject was issued in 1977 and came into force on 1 April 1978 (SI 1977/2076). It was revised, following amendments to the substantive law made by the Employment Act 1989, s 14, and in the light of comments received in a consultation exercise. The current Code came into force on 13 May 1991 (see SI 1991/968). For the legal status of the Code see the Trade Union and Labour Relations (Consolidation) Act 1992, s 207 (TULR(C) A 1992). The Annex, which reproduces the relevant statutory provisions, is omitted. See Chapter 14.

Introduction

1 Under s 6 of the Employment Protection Act 1975 the Advisory, Conciliation and Arbitration Service (ACAS) has a duty to provide practical guidance on the time off to be permitted by an employer:

(a) to a trade union official in accordance with section 27 of the Employment Protection (Consolidation) Act 1978 [now TULR(C) A 1992, s 168]; and

(b) to a trade union member in accordance with section 28 of the Employment Protection (Consolidation) Act 1978 [now TULR(C) A 1992, s 170].

This Code, which replaces the Code of Practice issued by the Service in 1978, is intended to provide such guidance.

The background

2 The Employment Protection Act 1975 gave trade union officials a statutory right to reasonable paid time off from employment to carry out trade union duties and to undertake trade union training. Union officials and members were also given a statutory right to reasonable unpaid time off when taking part in trade union activities. These rights were subsequently re-enacted as sections 27 and 28 of the Employment Protection (Consolidation) Act 1978 [now TULR(C) A 1992, ss 168–170].

3 Section 14 of the Employment Act 1989, which came into force on 26 February 1990, amends the statutory provisions. In particular, it introduces restrictions on the range of issues for which paid time off for trade union duties can be claimed to those covered by recognition agreements between employers and trade unions. Additionally union duties must relate to the official's own employer and not, for example, to any associated employer.

General purpose of the Code

4 The general purposes of the statutory provisions and this Code of Practice is to aid and improve the effectiveness of relationships between employers and trade unions. Employers and unions have joint responsibility to ensure that agreed arrangements seek to specify how reasonable time off for union duties and activities and for training can work to their mutual advantage.

Structure of the Code

5 Section 1 of this Code provides guidance on time off for trade union duties. Section 2 deals with time off for training of trade union officials. Section 3 considers time off for trade union activities. In each case the amount and frequency of time off, and the purposes for which and any conditions subject to which time off may be taken, are to be those that are reasonable in all the circumstances. Section 4 describes the responsibilities which employers and trade unions share in considering reasonable time off. Section 5 notes the advantages of reaching formal agreements with time off. Section 6 deals with industrial action and section 7 with methods of appeal.

Appendix 3

6 The annex of this Code reproduces the relevant statutory provisions on time off. To help differentiate between these and practical guidance, the summary of statutory provisions relating to time off which appears in the main text of the Code is in bold type. Practical guidance is in ordinary type. While every effort has been made to ensure that the summary of the statutory provisions included in this Code is accurate, only the courts can interpret the law authoritatively.

Status of the Code

7 The provisions of this Code are admissible in evidence and may be taken into account in determining any question arising during industrial proceedings relating to time off for trade union duties and activities. However, failure to observe any provision of the Code does not of itself render a person liable to any proceedings.

Section 1 Time off for trade union duties

ENTITLEMENT

8 Employees who are officials of an independent trade union recognised by their employer are to be permitted reasonable time off during working hours to carry out certain trade union duties.

9 An official is an employee who has been elected or appointed in accordance with the rules of the union to be a representative of all or some of the union's members in the particular company or workplace.

10 Officials are entitled to time off where the duties are concerned with:

- negotiations with the employer about matters which fall within section 29(1) of the Trade Union and Labour Relations Act 1974 (TULRA) [now TULR(C) A 1992, s 244] and for which the union is recognised for the purposes of collective bargaining by the employer; or
- any other functions on behalf of employees of the employer which are related to matters falling within s 29(1) TULRA and which the employer has agreed the union may perform.

Matters falling within s 29(1) TULRA are listed in the sub-headings of paragraph 12 below.

11 An independent trade union is recognised by an employer when it is recognised to any extent for the purposes of collective bargaining. Where a trade union is not so recognised by an employer, employees have no statutory right to time off to undertake any duties.

Examples of trade union duties

12 Subject to the recognition or other agreement, trade union officials should be allowed to take reasonable time off for duties concerned with negotiations or, where their employer has agreed, for duties concerned with other functions related to or connected with:

(a) terms and conditions of employment, or the physical conditions in which workers are required to work. Examples could include:
- pay
- hours of work
- holidays and holiday pay
- sick pay arrangements
- pensions

644

- vocational training
- equal opportunities
- notice periods
- the working environment
- utilisation of machinery and other equipment;

(b) engagement or non-engagement, or termination or suspension of employment or the duties of employment, of one or more workers. Examples could include:
- recruitment and selection policies
- human resource planning
- redundancy and dismissal arrangements;

(c) allocation of work or the duties of employment as between workers or groups of workers. Examples could include:
- job grading
- job evaluation
- job descriptions
- flexible working practices;

(d) matters of discipline. Examples could include:
- disciplinary procedures
- arrangements for representing trade union members at internal interviews
- arrangements for appearing on behalf of trade union members, or as witnesses, before agreed outside bodies or industrial tribunals;

(e) trade union membership or non-membership. Examples could include:
- representational arrangements
- any union involvement in the induction of new workers;

(f) facilities for officials of trade unions. Examples could include any agreed arrangements for the provisions of:
- accommodation
- equipment
- names of new workers to the union;

(g) machinery for negotiation or consultation and other procedures. Examples could include arrangements for:
- collective bargaining
- grievance procedures
- joint consultation
- communicating with members
- communicating with other union officials also concerned with collective bargaining with the employer.

13   The duties of an official of a recognised trade union must be connected with or related to negotiations or the performance of functions both in time and subject matter. Reasonable time off may be sought, for example to:

- prepare for negotiations
- inform members of progress
- explain outcomes to members
- prepare for meetings with the employer about matters for which the trade union has only representational rights.

PAYMENT FOR TIME OFF FOR TRADE UNION DUTIES

14   An employer who permits officials time off for trade union duties must pay them for the time off taken. The employer must pay either the amount that the officials would have earned had they worked during the time off taken or, where earnings vary with the work done, an amount calculated by reference to the average hourly earnings for the work they are employed to do. There is no statutory requirement to pay for time of where the duty is carried out at a time when the official would not otherwise have been at work.

Appendix 3

Section 2   Training of officials in aspects of industrial relations

ENTITLEMENT

15   Employees who are officials of an independent trade union recognised by their employer are to be permitted reasonable time off during working hours to undergo training relevant to the carrying out of their trade union duties.[1] These duties must be concerned with:

- negotiations with the employer about matters which fall within s 29(1) TULRA and for which the union is recognised to any extent for the purposes of collective bargaining by the employer; or
- any other functions on behalf of employees of the employer which are related to matters falling within s 29(1) TULRA [now TULR(C)A 1992, s 244] and which the employer has agreed the union may perform.

Matters falling within s 29(1) TULRA are set out in paragraph 12 above.

NOTES
1 Section 1 of this Code gives a more complete summary of the statutory entitlement of officials to time off to undertake trade union duties.

What is relevant industrial relations training?

16   Training should be in aspects of industrial relations relevant to the duties of an official. There is no one recommended syllabus for training as an official's duties will vary according to:

- collective bargaining arrangements at the place of work, particularly the scope of the recognition or other agreement
- the structure of the union
- the role of the official.

17   The training must also be approved by the Trades Union Congress or by the independent trade union of which the employee is an official.

18   Trade union officials are more likely to carry out their duties effectively if they possess skills and knowledge relevant to their duties. In particular, employers should be prepared to consider releasing trade union officials for initial training in basic representational skills as soon as possible after their election or appointment, bearing in mind that suitable courses may be infrequent. Reasonable time off could also be considered, for example:

- for further training particularly where the official has special responsibilities
- where there are proposals to change the structure and topics of negotiations about matters for which the union is recognised; or where significant changes in the organisation of work are being contemplated
- where legislative change may affect the conduct of industrial relations at the place of work and may require the reconsideration of existing agreements.

PAYMENT FOR TIME OFF FOR TRAINING

19   An employer who permits time off for officials to attend training relevant to their duties at the workplace must pay them for the time off taken. The employer must pay either the amount that the officials would have earned had they worked during the time off taken or, where earnings vary with the work done, an amount calculated by reference to the average hourly earnings for the work that they are employed to do. There is no statutory requirement to pay for time off where training is undertaken at a time when the official would not otherwise have been at work.

Section 3 Time off for trade union activities

ENTITLEMENT

20 To operate effectively and democratically, trade unions need the active partici-pation of members. It can be very much in employers' interests that such participa-tion is assured. An employee who is a member of an independent trade union recognised by the employer in respect of that description of employee is to be per-mitted reasonable time off during working hours to take part in any trade union activity.

What are examples of trade union activities?

21 The activities of a trade union member can be, for example:

- attending workplace meetings to discuss and vote on the outcome of negotiations with the employer
- meeting full-time officials to discuss issues relevant to the workplace
- voting in properly conducted ballots on industrial action
- voting in union elections.

22 Where the member is acting as a representative of a recognised union activities can be, for example, taking part in:

- branch, area or regional meetings of the union where the business of the union is under discussion
- meetings of official policy making bodies such as the executive committee or annual conference
- meetings with full-time officials to discuss issues relevant to the workplace.

23 There is no right to time off for trade union activities which themselves consist of industrial action.

PAYMENT FOR TIME OFF FOR TRADE UNION ACTIVITIES

24 There is no requirement that union members or representatives be paid for time off taken on trade union activities. Nevertheless employers may want to consider payment in certain circumstances, for example to ensure that workplace meetings are fully representative.

Section 4 The responsibilities of employers and trade unions

GENERAL CONSIDERATIONS

25 The amount and frequency of time off should be reasonable in all the circum-stances. Although the statutory provisions apply to all employers without exception as to size and type of business or service, trade unions should be aware of the wide variety of difficulties and operational requirements to be taken into account when seeking or agreeing arrangements for time off, for example:

- the size of the organisation and the number of workers
- the production process
- the need to maintain a service to the public
- the need for safety and security at all times.

26 Employers in turn should have in mind the difficulties for trade union officials and members in ensuring representation and communications with, for example:

- shift workers
- part-time workers
- those employed at dispersed locations
- workers with particular domestic commitments.

27   For time off arrangements to work satisfactorily trade unions should:

- ensure that officials are aware of their role, responsibilities and functions
- inform management, in writing, as soon as possible of appointments or resignations of officials
- ensure that officials receive any appropriate written credentials promptly.

28   Employers should consider making available to officials the facilities necessary for them to perform their duties efficiently and communicate effectively with their members, fellow lay officials and full-time officers. Where resources permit the facilities could include:

- accommodation for meetings
- access to a telephone and other office equipment
- the use of notice boards
- where the volume of the official's work justifies it, the use of dedicated office space.

REQUESTING TIME OFF

29   Trade union officials and members requesting time off to pursue their industrial relations duties or activities should provide management with as much notice as possible and give details of:

- the purpose of such time off
- the intended location
- the timing and duration of time off required.

30   In addition, officials who request paid time off to undergo relevant training should:

- give at least a few weeks' notice to management of nominations for training courses
- if asked to do so, provide a copy of the syllabus or prospectus indicating the contents of the training course.

31   When deciding whether request for paid time off should be granted, consideration would need to be given as to their reasonableness, for example to ensure adequate cover for safety or to safeguard the production process or the provision of service. Similarly managers and unions should seek to agree a mutually convenient time which minimises the effect on production or services. Where workplace meetings are requested consideration should be given to holding them, for example:

- towards the end of a shift or the working week
- before or after a meal break.

32   Employers need to consider each application for the time off on its merits; they might also need to consider the reasonableness of the request in relation to agreed time off already taken or in prospect.

Section 5   Agreements on time off

33   To take account of the wide variety of circumstances and problems which can arise, there can be positive advantages for employers and trade unions in establishing agreements on time off in ways which reflect their own situations. A formal agreement can help to:

- provide clear guidelines against which applications for time off can be determined
- avoid misunderstanding
- facilitate better planning
- ensure fair and reasonable treatment.

34   Agreements could specify:

● the amount of time off permitted
● the occasions on which time off can be taken
● in what circumstances time off will be paid
● to whom time off will be paid
● the procedure for requesting time off.

35   In addition, it would be sensible for agreements to make clear:

● arrangements for the appropriate payment to be made when time off relates in part to union duties and in part to union activities
● whether payment (to which there would be no statutory entitlement) might be made to shift and part-time employees undertaking trade union duties outside their normal working hours.

36   Agreements for time off and other facilities for union representation should be consistent with wider agreements which deal with such matters as constituencies, number of representatives and the election of officials.

37   In smaller organisations, it might be thought more appropriate for employers and unions to reach understandings about how requests for time off are to be made; and more broadly to agree flexible arrangements which can accommodate their particular circumstances.

38   The absence of a formal agreement on time off, however, does not in itself deny an individual any statutory entitlement. Nor does any agreement supersede statutory entitlement to time off.

Section 6   Industrial action

39   Employers and unions have a responsibility to use agreed procedures to settle problems and avoid industrial action. Time off may therefore be permitted for this purpose particularly where there is a dispute. **There is no right to time off for trade union activities which themselves consist of industrial action.** However, where an official is not taking part in industrial action but represents members involved, normal arrangements for time off with pay for the official should apply.

Section 7   Making a complaint

40   Every effort should be made to resolve any dispute or grievance in relation to time off work for union duties or activities. There is advantage in agreeing ways in which such disputes can be settled and any appropriate procedures to resolve disputes should be followed. Where the grievance remains unresolved, trade union officials or members have a right to complain to an industrial tribunal that their employer has failed to allow reasonable time off or, in the case of an official, has failed to pay for all or part of the time off taken. Such complaints may be resolved by conciliation by ACAS and if this is successful, no tribunal hearing will be necessary. ACAS assistance may also be sought without the need for a formal complaint to a tribunal.

NOTE
The Annex, which reproduces the relevant statutory provisions (now re-enacted in the Trade Union and Labour Relations (Consolidation) Act 1992) is omitted.

Code of Practice for the Elimination of Discrimination in the Field of Employment Against Disabled Persons or Persons who have had a Disability

NOTES

Commencement: 2 December 1996 (SI 1996/1386, art 3).

This Code was issued by the Secretary of State for Education and Employment on 25 July 1996 under the Disability Discrimination Act 1995, s 53(1)(a), following consultations pursuant to s 54(1) of that Act and the laying of a draft before both Houses of Parliament on 6 June 1996. The legal status of the Code is as stated in s 53(4)–(6).

The introductory provisions (paras 1 and 2 not reproduced) and Annexes do not form part of the Code and do not have effect as such. The text of the Code itself and notes thereto (appropriately amended) are reproduced below. See Chapter 7 and the guidance on p 687.

3   GENERAL GUIDANCE TO HELP AVOID DISCRIMINATION

Be flexible

3.1   There may be several ways to avoid discrimination in any one situation. Examples in this Code are *illustrative only*, to indicate what should or should not be done in those and other broadly similar types of situations. They cannot cover every possibility, so it is important to consider carefully how the guidance applies in any specific circumstances. **Many ways of avoiding discrimination will cost little or nothing.** The Code should not be read narrowly; for instance, its guidance on recruitment might help avoid discrimination when promoting employees.

Do not make assumptions

3.2   It will probably be helpful to talk to each disabled person about what the real effects of the disability might be or what might help. There is less chance of a dispute where the person is involved from the start. Such discussions should not, of course, be conducted in a way which would itself give the disabled person any reason to believe that he was being discriminated against.

Consider whether expert advice is needed

3.3   It is possible to avoid discrimination using personal, or in-house, knowledge and expertise, particularly if the views of the disabled person are sought. The Act does not oblige anyone to get expert advice but it could help in some circumstances to seek independent advice on the extent of a disabled person's capabilities. This might be particularly appropriate where a person is newly disabled or the effects of someone's disability become more marked. It may also help to get advice on what might be done to change premises or working arrangements, especially if discussions with the disabled person do not lead to a satisfactory solution. Annex 2 gives information about getting advice or help.

Plan ahead

3.4   Although the Act does not require an employer to make changes in anticipation of ever having a disabled applicant or employee, nevertheless when planning for change it could be cost-effective to consider the needs of a range of possible future disabled employees and applicants. There may be helpful improvements that could be built into plans. For example, a new telecommunications system might be made accessible to deaf people even if there are currently no deaf employees.

Promote equal opportunities

3.5   If an employer has an equal opportunities policy or is thinking of introducing one, it would probably help to avoid a breach of the Act if that policy covered disability issues. Employers who have, and follow, a good policy—including monitoring its effectiveness—are likely to have that counted in their favour by a tribunal if a complaint is made. But employers should remember that treating people equally will not always avoid a breach of the Act. An employer may be under a duty to make a reasonable adjustment. This could apply at any time in the recruitment process or in the course of a disabled person's employment.

4   THE MAIN EMPLOYMENT PROVISIONS OF THE ACT

Discrimination

What does the Act say about discrimination?

4.1   *The Act makes it unlawful* for an employer to discriminate against a disabled person in the field of employment (s 4). *The Act says* 'discrimination' occurs in two ways.

4.2   One way in which discrimination occurs is when—

- for a reason which relates to a disabled person's disability, the employer treats that disabled person less favourably than the employer treats or would treat others to whom the reason does not or would not apply; *and*
- the employer cannot show that this treatment is justified (s 5(1)).
      A woman with a disability which requires use of a wheelchair applies for a job. She can do the job but the employer thinks the wheelchair will get in the way in the office. He gives the job to a person who is no more suitable for the job but who does not use a wheelchair. The employer has therefore treated the woman *less favourably* than the other person because he did not give her the job. The treatment was *for a reason related to the disability*—the fact that she used a wheelchair. And the reason for treating her less favourably *did not apply to the other person* because that person did not use a wheelchair.
      If the employer could not justify his treatment of the disabled woman then he would have unlawfully discriminated against her.
      An employer decides to close down a factory and makes all the employees redundant, including a disabled person who works there. This is not discrimination as the disabled employee is not being dismissed for a reason which relates to the disability.

4.3   A disabled person may not be able to point to other people who were actually treated more favourably. However, it is still 'less favourable treatment' if the employer would give better treatment to someone else to whom the reason for the treatment of the disabled person did not apply. This comparison can also be made with other disabled people, not just non-disabled people. For example, an employer might be discriminating by treating a person with a mental illness less favourably than he treats or would treat a physically disabled person.

4.4   The other way *the Act says* that 'discrimination' occurs is when—

- an employer fails to comply with a duty of reasonable adjustment imposed on him by section 6 in relation to the disabled person; *and*
- he cannot show that this failure is justified (s 5(2)).

4.5   The relationship between the duty of reasonable adjustment and the need to justify less favourable treatment is described in paragraphs 4.7–4.9. The duty itself is described from paragraph 4.12 onwards and the need to justify a failure to comply with it is described in paragraph 4.34.

What will, and what will not, be justified treatment?

4.6   *The Act says* that less favourable treatment of a disabled person will be justified only if the reason for it is both material to the circumstances of the particular case *and* substantial (s 5(3)). This means that the reason has to relate to the individual circumstances in question and not just be trivial or minor.

Someone who is blind is not shortlisted for a job involving computers because the employer thinks blind people cannot use them. The employer makes no effort to look at the individual circumstances. A general assumption that blind people cannot use computers would not in itself be a material reason—it is not related to the particular circumstances.

A factory worker with a mental illness is sometimes away from work due to his disability. Because of that he is dismissed. However, the amount of time off is very little more than the employer accepts as sick leave for other employees and so is very unlikely to be a substantial reason.

A clerical worker with a learning disability cannot sort papers quite as quickly as some of his colleagues. There is very little difference in productivity but he is dismissed. That is very unlikely to be a substantial reason.

An employer seeking a clerical worker turns down an applicant with a severe facial disfigurement solely on the ground that other employees would be uncomfortable working alongside him. This will be unlawful because such a reaction by other employees will not in itself justify less favourable treatment of this sort—it is not substantial. The same would apply if it were thought that a customer would feel uncomfortable.

An employer moves someone with a mental illness to a different workplace solely because he mutters to himself while he works. If the employer accepts similar levels of noise from other people, the treatment of the disabled person would probably be unjustified—that level of noise is unlikely to be a substantial reason.

Someone who has psoriasis (a skin condition) is rejected for a job involving modelling cosmetics on a part of the body which in his case is severely disfigured by the condition. That would be lawful if his appearance would be incompatible with the purpose of the work. This is a substantial reason which is clearly related—material—to the individual circumstance.

4.7 *The Act says* that less favourable treatment cannot be justified where the employer is under a duty to make a reasonable adjustment but fails (without justification) to do so, *unless* the treatment would have been justified even after that adjustment (s 5(5)).

An employee who uses a wheelchair is not promoted, solely because the work station for the higher post is inaccessible to wheelchairs—though it could readily be made so by rearrangement of the furniture. If the furniture had been rearranged, the reason for refusing promotion would not have applied. The refusal of promotion would therefore not be justified.

An applicant for a typing job is not the best person on the face of it, but only because her typing speed is too slow due to arthritis in her hands. If a reasonable adjustment—perhaps an adapted keyboard—would overcome this, her typing speed would not in itself be a substantial reason for not employing her. Therefore the employer would be unlawfully discriminating if on account of her typing speed he did not employ her and provide the adjustment.

An employer refuses a training course for an employee with an illness which is very likely to be terminal within a year because, even with a reasonable adjustment to help in the job after the course, the benefits of the course could not be adequately realised. This is very likely to be a substantial reason. It is clearly material to the circumstances. The refusal of training would therefore very likely be justified.

Someone who is blind applies for a job which requires a significant amount of driving. If it is not reasonable for the employer to adjust the job so that the driving duties are given to someone else, the employer's need for a driver might well be a substantial reason for not employing the blind person. It is clearly material to the particular circumstances. The non-appointment could therefore be justified.

How does an employer avoid unlawful discrimination?

4.8   An employer should not treat a disabled employee or disabled job applicant less favourably, for a reason relating to the disability, than others to whom that reason does not apply, unless that reason is material to the particular circumstances and substantial. If the reason is material and substantial, the employer may have to make a reasonable adjustment to remove it or make it less than substantial (s 5(3) and (5)).

4.9   Less favourable treatment is therefore justified if the disabled person cannot do the job concerned, and no adjustment which would enable the person to do the job (or another vacant job) is practicable (s 5(3) and (5)). (See paragraph 4.20 for examples of adjustments which employers may have to make.)

4.10   *The Act says* that some charities (and Government-funded supported employment) are allowed to treat some groups of disabled people more favourably than others. But they can do this only if the group being treated more favourably is one with whom the charitable purposes of the charity are connected and the more favourable treatment is in pursuance of those purposes (or, in the case of supported employment, those treated more favourably are severely disabled people whom the programme aims to help) (s 10).

What does the Act say about helping others to discriminate?

4.11   *The Act says* that a person who knowingly helps another to do something made unlawful by the Act will also be treated as having done the same kind of unlawful act (s 57(1)).

   A recruitment consultant engaged by an engineering company refuses to consider a disabled applicant for a vacancy, because the employer has told the consultant that he does not want the post filled by someone who is 'handicapped'. Under the Act the consultant could be liable for aiding the company.

Reasonable adjustment

What does the Act say about the duty of 'reasonable adjustment'?

4.12   *The Act says* that the duty applies where any physical feature of premises occupied by the employer, or any arrangements made by or on behalf of the employer, cause a substantial disadvantage to a disabled person compared with non-disabled people. An employer has to take such steps as it is reasonable for him to have to take in all the circumstances to prevent that disadvantage—in other words the employer has to make a 'reasonable adjustment' (s 6(1)).

   A man who is disabled by dyslexia applies for a job which involves writing letters within fairly long deadlines. The employer gives all applicants a test of their letter-writing ability. The man can generally write letters very well but finds it difficult to do so in stressful situations. The *employer's arrangements* would mean he had to begin his test immediately on arrival and to do it in a short time. He would be *substantially disadvantaged compared to non-disabled people* who would not find such arrangements stressful or, if they did, would not be so affected by them. The employer therefore gives him a little time to settle in and longer to write the letter. These new arrangements do not inconvenience the employer very much and only briefly delay the decision on an appointment. These are *steps that it is reasonable for the employer to have to take in the circumstances to prevent the disadvantage*—a 'reasonable adjustment'.

4.13   If a disabled person cannot point to an existing non-disabled person compared with whom he is at a substantial disadvantage, then the comparison should be made with how the employer would have treated a non-disabled person.

4.14 How to comply with this duty in recruitment and during employment is explained in paragraphs 5.1–5.29 and 6.1–6.21. The following paragraphs explain how to satisfy this duty more generally.

What 'physical features' and 'arrangements' are covered by the duty?

4.15 *Regulations define* the term 'physical features' to include anything on the premises arising from a building's design or construction or from an approach to, exit from or access to such a building; fixtures, fittings, furnishings, furniture, equipment or materials; and any other physical element or quality of land in the premises. All of these are covered whether temporary or permanent.[1]

NOTES
1 Disability Discrimination (Employment) Regulations 1996, SI 1996/1456.

4.16 *The Act says* that the duty applies to 'arrangements' for determining to whom employment should be offered and any term, condition or arrangement on which employment, promotion, transfer, training or any other benefit is offered or afforded (s 6(2)). The duty applies in recruitment and during employment; for example, selection and interview procedures and the arrangements for using premises for such procedures as well as job offers, contractual arrangements, and working conditions.

The design of a particular workplace makes it difficult for someone with a hearing impairment to hear. That is a disadvantage caused by the *physical features*. There may be nothing that can reasonably be done in the circumstances to change these features. However, requiring someone to work in such a workplace is an *arrangement made by the employer* and it might be reasonable to overcome the disadvantage by a transfer to another workplace or by ensuring that the supervisor gives instructions in an office rather than in the working area.

What 'disadvantages' give rise to the duty?

4.17 *The Act says* that only substantial disadvantages give rise to the duty (s 6(1)). Substantial disadvantages are those which are not minor or trivial.

An employer is unlikely to be required to widen a particular doorway to enable passage by an employee using a wheelchair if there is an easy alternative route to the same destination.

4.18 An employer cannot be required to prevent a disadvantage caused by premises or by non-pay arrangements by increasing the disabled person's pay (see paragraph 5.29).

4.19 The duty of reasonable adjustment does not apply in relation to benefits under occupational pension schemes or certain benefits under other employment-related benefit schemes although there is a duty not to discriminate in relation to such benefits (see paragraphs 6.9–6.16).

What adjustments might an employer have to make?

4.20 *The Act gives* a number of examples of 'steps' which employers may have to take, if it is reasonable for them to have to do so in all the circumstances of the case (s 6(3)). Steps other than those listed here, or a combination of steps, will sometimes have to be taken. The steps in the Act are—

● *making adjustments to premises*
An employer might have to make structural or other physical changes such as: widening a doorway, providing a ramp or moving furniture for a wheelchair user; relocating light switches, door handles or shelves for someone who has difficulty in reaching; providing appropriate contrast in decor to help the safe mobility of a visually impaired person.

● *allocating some of the disabled person's duties to another person*

Minor or subsidiary duties might be reallocated to another employee if the disabled person has difficulty in doing them because of the disability. For example, if a job occasionally involves going onto the open roof of a building an employer might have to transfer this work away from an employee whose disability involves severe vertigo.

● *transferring the person to fill an existing vacancy*

If an employee becomes disabled, or has a disability which worsens so she cannot work in the same place or under the same arrangements and there is no reasonable adjustment which would enable the employee to continue doing the current job, then she might have to be considered for any suitable alternative posts which are available. (Such a case might also involve reasonable retraining.)

● *altering the person's working hours*

This could include allowing the disabled person to work flexible hours to enable additional breaks to overcome fatigue arising from the disability, or changing the disabled person's hours to fit with the availability of a carer.

● *assigning the person to a different place of work*

This could mean transferring a wheelchair user's work station from an inaccessible third floor office to an accessible one on the ground floor. It could mean moving the person to other premises of the same employer if the first building is inaccessible.

● *allowing the person to be absent during working hours for rehabilitation, assessment or treatment*

For example, if a person were to become disabled, the employer might have to allow the person more time off during work, than would be allowed to non-disabled employees, to receive physiotherapy or psychoanalysis or undertake employment rehabilitation. A similar adjustment might be appropriate if a disability worsens or if a disabled person needs occasional treatment anyway.

● *giving the person, or arranging for him to be given, training*

This could be training in the use of particular pieces of equipment unique to the disabled person, or training appropriate for all employees but which needs altering for the disabled person because of the disability. For example, all employees might need to be trained in the use of a particular machine but an employer might have to provide slightly different or longer training for an employee with restricted hand or arm movements, or training in additional software for a visually impaired person so that he can use a computer with speech output.

● *acquiring or modifying equipment*

An employer might have to provide special equipment (such as an adapted keyboard-phone for someone with a hearing impairment or modified equipment (such as longer handles on a machine). There is no requirement to provide or modify equipment for personal purposes unconnected with work, such as providing a wheelchair if a person needs one in any event but does not have one: the disadvantage in such a case does not flow from the employer's arrangements or premises.

● *modifying instructions or reference manuals*

The way instruction is normally given to employees might need to be revised when telling a disabled person how to do a task. The format of instructions or manuals may need to be modified (eg produced in braille or on audio tape) and instructions for people with learning disabilities may need to be conveyed orally with individual demonstration.

● *modifying procedures for testing or assessment*

This could involve ensuring that particular tests do not adversely affect people with particular types of disability. For example, a person with restricted manual dexterity might be disadvantaged by a written test, so an employer might have to give that person an oral test.

- *providing a reader or interpreter*

  This could involve a colleague reading mail to a person with a visual impairment at particular times during the working day or, in appropriate circumstances, the hiring of a reader or sign language interpreter.
- *providing supervision*

  This could involve the provision of a support worker, or help from a colleague, in appropriate circumstances, for someone whose disability leads to uncertainty or lack of confidence.

When is it 'reasonable' for an employer to have to make an adjustment?

4.21   Effective and practicable adjustments for disabled people often involve little or no cost or disruption and are therefore very likely to be reasonable for an employer to have to make. *The Act lists* a number of factors which may, in particular, have a bearing on whether it will be reasonable for the employer to have to make a particular adjustment (s 6(4)). These factors make a useful checklist, particularly when considering more substantial adjustments. The effectiveness and practicability of a particular adjustment might be considered first. If it is practicable and effective, the financial aspects might be looked at as a whole—cost of the adjustment and resources available to fund it. Other factors might also have a bearing. The factors in the Act are listed below.

The effectiveness of the step in preventing the disadvantage

4.22   It is unlikely to be reasonable for an employer to have to make an adjustment involving little benefit to the disabled employee.

A disabled person is significantly less productive than his colleagues and so is paid less. A particular adjustment would improve his output and thus his pay. It is more likely to be reasonable for the employer to have to make that adjustment if it would significantly improve his pay, than if the adjustment would make only a relatively small improvement.

The practicability of the step

4.23   It is more likely to be reasonable for an employer to have to take a step which is easy to take than one which is difficult.

It might be impracticable for an employer who needs to appoint an employee urgently to have to wait for an adjustment to be made to an entrance. How long it might be reasonable for the employer to have to wait would depend on the circumstances. However, it might be possible to make a temporary adjustment in the meantime, such as using another, less convenient entrance.

The financial and other costs of the adjustment and the extent of any disruption caused

4.24   If an adjustment costs little or nothing and is not disruptive, it would be reasonable unless some other factor (such as practicability or effectiveness) made it unreasonable. The costs to be taken into account include staff and other resource costs. The significance of the cost of a step may depend in part on what the employer might otherwise spend in the circumstances.

It would be reasonable for an employer to have to spend at least as much on an adjustment to enable the retention of a disabled person—including any retraining—as might be spent on recruiting and training a replacement.

4.25   The significance of the cost of a step may also depend in part on the value of the employee's experience and expertise to the employer.

Examples of the factors that might be considered as relating to the value of an employee would include—

- the amount of resources (such as training) invested in the individual by the employer;
- the employee's length of service;
- the employee's level of skill and knowledge;
- the employee's quality of relationships with clients;
- the level of the employee's pay.

4.26 It is more likely to be reasonable for an employer to have to make an adjustment with significant costs for an employee who is likely be in the job for some time than for a temporary employee.

4.27 An employer is more likely to have to make an adjustment which might cause only minor inconvenience to other employees or the employer than one which might unavoidably prevent other employees from doing their job, or cause other significant disruption.

The extent of the employer's financial or other resources

4.28 It is more likely to be reasonable for an employer with substantial financial resources to have to make an adjustment with a significant cost, than for an employer with fewer resources. The resources in practice available to the employer as a whole should be taken into account as well as other calls on those resources. The reasonableness of an adjustment will depend, however, not only on the resources in practice available for the adjustment but also on all other relevant factors (such as effectiveness and practicability).

4.29 Where the resources of the employer are spread across more than one 'business unit' or 'profit centre' the calls on them should also be taken into account in assessing reasonableness.

A large retailer probably could not show that the limited resources for which an individual shop manager is responsible meant it was not reasonable for the retailer to have to make an adjustment at that shop. Such an employer may, however, have a number—perhaps a large number—of other disabled employees in other shops. The employer's expenditure on other adjustments, or his potential expenditure on similar adjustments for other existing disabled employees, might then be taken into account in assessing the reasonableness of having to make a new adjustment for the disabled employee in question.

4.30 It is more likely to be reasonable for an employer with a substantial number of staff to have to make certain adjustments, than for a smaller employer.

It would generally be reasonable for an employer with many staff to have to make significant efforts to reallocate duties, identify a suitable alternative post or provide supervision from existing staff. It could also be reasonable for a small company covered by the Act to have to make any of these adjustments but not if it involved disproportionate effort.

The availability to the employer of financial or other assistance to help make an adjustment

4.31 The availability of outside help may well be a relevant factor.

An employer, in recruiting a disabled person, finds that the only feasible adjustment is too costly for him alone. However, if assistance is available, eg from a Government programme or voluntary body, it may well be reasonable for him to have to make the adjustment after all.

A disabled person is not required to contribute to the cost of a reasonable adjustment. However, if a disabled person has a particular piece of special or adapted equipment which he is prepared to use for work, this might make it reasonable for the employer to have to take some other step (as well as allowing use of the equipment).

An employer requires his employees to use company cars for all business travel. One employee's disability means she would have to use an adapted car or an alternative form of transport. If she has an adapted car of her own which she is willing to use on business, it might well be reasonable for the employer to have to allow this and pay her an allowance to cover the cost of doing so, even if it would not have been reasonable for him to have to provide an adapted company car, or to pay an allowance to cover alternative travel arrangements in the absence of an adapted car.

Other factors

4.32 Although the Act does not mention any further factors, others might be relevant depending on the circumstances. For example—

● *effect on other employees*
Employees' adverse reaction to an adjustment being made for the disabled employee which involves something they too would like (such as a special working arrangement) is unlikely to be significant.
● *adjustments made for other disabled employees*
An employer may choose to give a particular disabled employee, or group of disabled employees, an adjustment which goes beyond the duty—that is, which is more than it is reasonable for him to have to do. This would not mean he necessarily had to provide a similar adjustment for other employees with a similar disability.
● *the extent to which the disabled person is willing to cooperate*
An employee with a mobility impairment works in a team located on an upper floor, to which there is no access by lift. Getting there is very tiring for the employee, and the employer could easily make a more accessible location available for him (though the whole team could not be relocated). If that was the only adjustment which it would be reasonable for the employer to have to make but the employee refused to work there then the employer would not have to make any adjustment at all.

Could an employer have to make more than one adjustment?

4.33 Yes, if it is reasonable for the employer to have to make more than one.
A woman who is deafblind is given a new job with her employer in an unfamiliar part of the building. The employer (i) arranges facilities for her guide dog in the new area, (ii) arranges for her new instructions to be in Braille and (iii) suggests to visitors ways in which they can communicate with her.

Does an employer have to justify not making an adjustment?

4.34 *The Act says* that it is discrimination if an employer fails to take a step which it is reasonable for him to have to take, and he cannot justify that failure (s 5(2)). However, if it is unreasonable (under s 6) for an employer to have to make any, or a particular, adjustment, he would not then also have to justify (under s 5) not doing so. Failure to comply with the duty of reasonable adjustment can only be justified if the reason for the failure is material to the circumstances of the particular case and substantial (s 5(4)).
An employer might not make an adjustment which it was reasonable for him to have to make because of ignorance or wrong information about appropriate adjustments or about the availability of help with making an adjustment. He would then need to justify failing in his duty. It is unlikely that he could do so unless he had made a reasonable effort to obtain good information from a reputable source such as contacting the local Placing Assessment and Counselling Team or an appropriate disability organisation.
If either of two possible adjustments would remove a disadvantage, but the employer has cost or operational reasons for preferring one rather than the other,

it is unlikely to be reasonable for him to have to make the one that is not preferred. If, however, the employee refuses to cooperate with the proposed adjustment the employer is likely to be justified in not providing it.

A disabled employee refuses to follow specific occupational medical advice provided on behalf of an employer about methods of working or managing his condition at work. If he has no good reason for this and his condition deteriorates as a result, the refusal may justify the employer's subsequent failure to make an adjustment for the worsened condition.

Building regulations, listed buildings, leases

How do building regulations affect reasonable adjustments?

4.35   A building or extension to a building may have been constructed in accordance with Part M of the building regulations (or the Scottish parallel, Part T of the Technical Standards) which is concerned with access and facilities for disabled people. *Regulations provide* in these circumstances that the employer does not have to alter any physical characteristic of the building or extension which still complies with the building regulations in force at the time the building works were carried out.[1]

Where the building regulations in force at the time of a building's construction required that a door should be a particular width, the employer would not have to alter the width of the door later. However, he might have to alter other aspects of the door (eg the type of handle).

NOTES
1   Disability Discrimination (Employment) Regulations 1996, SI 1996/1456, reg 8.

4.36   Employers can only rely upon this defence if the feature still satisfies the requirement of the building regulations that applied when the building or extension was constructed.

What about the need to obtain statutory consent for some building changes?

4.37   Employers might have to obtain statutory consent before making adjustments involving changes to premises. Such consents include planning permission, listed building consent, scheduled monument consent and fire regulations approval. The Act does not override the need to obtain such consents (s 59). Therefore an employer does not have to make an adjustment if it requires a statutory consent which has not been given.

4.38   The time it would take to obtain consent may make a particular adjustment impracticable and therefore one which it is not reasonable for the employer to have to take. However, the employer would then also need to consider whether it was reasonable to have to make a temporary adjustment—one that does not require consent—in the meantime.

4.39   Employers should explore ways of making reasonable adjustments which either do not require statutory consent or are likely to receive it. They may well find it useful to consult their local planning authority (in England and Wales) or planning authority (in Scotland).

An employer needs statutory consent to widen an internal doorway in a listed building for a woman disabled in an accident who returned to work in a wheelchair. The employer considers using a different office but this is not practicable. In the circumstances the widening would be a reasonable adjustment. The employer knows from the local planning authority that consent is likely to be given in a few weeks. In the meantime the employer arranges for the woman to share an accessible office which is inconvenient for both employees, but does not prevent them doing their jobs and is tolerable for that limited period.

What happens where a lease says that certain changes to premises cannot be made?

4.40 Special provisions apply where a lease would otherwise prevent a reasonable adjustment involving an alteration to premises. *The Act modifies* the effect of the lease so far as necessary to enable the employer to make the alteration if the landlord consents, and to provide that the landlord must not withhold consent unreasonably but may attach reasonable conditions to the consent (**s 16**).

How will arrangements for getting the landlord's consent work?

4.41 *The Act says* that the employer must write to the landlord (called the 'lessor' in the Act) asking for consent to make the alteration. If an employer fails to apply to the landlord for consent, anything in the lease which would prevent that alteration must be ignored in deciding whether it was reasonable for the employer to have to make that alteration (**Sch 4, para 1**). If the landlord consents, the employer can then carry out the alteration. If the landlord refuses consent the employer must notify the disabled person, but then has no further obligation. Where the landlord fails to reply within 21 days or a reasonable period after that he is deemed to have withheld his consent. In those circumstances the withholding of the consent will be unreasonable (see paragraph 4.44).[1]

NOTES
1 Disability Discrimination (Employment) Regulations 1996, SI 1996/1456.

4.42 If the landlord attaches a condition to the consent and it is reasonable for the employer to have to carry out the alteration on that basis, the employer must then carry out the alteration. If it would not be reasonable for the employer to have to carry out the alteration on that basis, the employer must notify the disabled person, but then has no further obligation.[1]

NOTES
1 Disability Discrimination (Employment) Regulations 1996, SI 1996/1456.

When is it unreasonable for a landlord to withhold consent?

4.43 This will depend on the circumstances but a trivial or arbitrary reason would almost certainly be unreasonable. Many reasonable adjustments to premises will not harm a landlord's interests and so it would generally be unreasonable to withhold consent for them.

> A particular adjustment helps make a public building more accessible generally and is therefore likely to benefit the landlord. It would very probably be unreasonable for consent to be withheld in these circumstances.

4.44 *Regulations provide* that withholding consent will be unreasonable where—

● a landlord has failed to act within the time limits referred to in paragraph 4.41 above (ie 21 days of receipt of the employer's application or a reasonable period after that); or
● the lease says that consent will be given to alterations of that type or says that such consent will be given if it is sought in a particular way and it has been sought in that way.[1]

NOTES
1 Disability Discrimination (Employment) Regulations 1996, SI 1996/1456.

When is it reasonable for a landlord to withhold consent?

4.45 This will depend on the particular circumstances.

> A particular adjustment is likely to result in a substantial permanent reduction in the value of the landlord's interest in the premises. The landlord would almost certainly be acting reasonably in withholding consent.

A particular adjustment would cause significant disruption or inconvenience to other tenants (for example, where the premises consist of multiple adjoining units). The landlord would be likely to be acting reasonably in withholding consent.

What conditions would it be reasonable for a landlord to make when giving consent?

4.46 This will depend on the particular circumstances. However, *Regulations provide* that it would be reasonable for the landlord to require the employer to meet any of the following conditions—

- obtain planning permission and other statutory consents;
- submit any plans to the landlord for approval (provided that the landlord then confirms that approval will not be withheld unreasonably);
- allow the landlord a reasonable opportunity to inspect the work when completed;
- reimburse the landlord's reasonable costs incurred in connection with the giving of his consent;
- reinstate the altered part of the premises to its former state when the lease expires but only if it would have been reasonable for the landlord to have refused consent in the first place.[1]

NOTES
1 Disability Discrimination (Employment) Regulations 1996, SI 1996/1456.

What happens if the landlord has a 'superior' landlord?

4.47 The employer's landlord may also hold a lease which prevents him from consenting to the alteration without the consent of the 'superior' landlord. The statutory provisions have been modified by regulations to cover this. The employer's landlord will then be acting reasonably by notifying the employer that consent will be given if the superior landlord agrees. The employer's landlord must then apply to the superior landlord to ask for agreement. The provisions in paragraphs 4.41–4.46, including the requirements not to withhold consent unreasonably and not to attach unreasonable conditions, then apply to the superior landlord.[1]

NOTES
1 The Disability Discrimination (Sub-leases and Sub-tenancies) Regulations 1996.

What if some agreement other than a lease prevents the premises being altered?

4.48 An employer or landlord may be bound by the terms of an agreement or other legally binding obligation (for example, a mortgage or charge or restrictive covenant or, in Scotland, a feu disposition) under which the employer or landlord cannot alter the premises without someone else's consent. In these circumstances *Regulations provide* that it is always reasonable for the employer or landlord to take steps to obtain the necessary consent so that a reasonable adjustment can be made. Unless or until that consent is obtained the employer or landlord is not required to make the alteration in question. The step of seeking consent which it is always reasonable to have to take does not extend to having to apply to a court or tribunal.[1] Whether it is reasonable for the employer or landlord to have to apply to a court or tribunal would depend on the circumstances of the case.

NOTES
1 Disability Discrimination (Employment) Regulations 1996, SI 1996/1456.

Agreements which breach the Act's provisions

Can a disabled person waive rights, or an employer's duties, under the Act ?

4.49 *The Act says* that any term in a contract of employment or other agreement is 'void' (ie not valid) to the extent that it would require a person to do anything that would breach any of the Act's employment provisions, or exclude or limit the operation of those provisions (**s 9**).

4.50 An employer should not include in an agreement any provision intended to avoid obligations under the Act, or to prevent someone from fulfilling obligations. An agreement should not, therefore, be used to try to justify less favourable treatment or deem an adjustment unreasonable. Moreover, even parts of agreements which have such an effect (even though unintended) are made void if they would restrict the working of the employment provisions in the Act. However, special arrangements cover leases and other agreements which might prevent a change to premises which could be an adjustment under the Act but where the possible restrictions to the Act's working were unintentional. These are described in paragraphs 4.40–4.48.

4.51 The Act also says that a contract term is void if it would prevent anyone from making a claim under the employment provisions in an industrial tribunal (**s 9**). Further information is given in Annex 3 about such agreements.

What about permits issued in accordance with the Agricultural Wages Acts?

4.52 Under the Agricultural Wages Act 1948 and the Agricultural Wages (Scotland) Act 1949 minimum wages, and terms and conditions, can be set for agricultural workers. Permits can be issued to individuals who are 'incapacitated' for the purposes of those Acts and they can then be paid such lower minimum rates or be subject to such revised terms and conditions of employment that the permit specifies. *Regulations provide* that the treatment of a disabled person in accordance with such a permit would be taken to be justified.[1] This would not prevent the employer from having to comply with the duty not to discriminate, including the duty of reasonable adjustment, for matters other than those covered by the permit.

NOTES
1 Disability Discrimination (Employment) Regulations 1996, SI 1996/1456.

Victimisation

What does the Act say about victimisation?

4.53 Victimisation is a special form of discrimination covered by the Act. *The Act makes* it unlawful for one person to treat another (the victim) less favourably than he would treat other people in the same circumstances because the 'victim' has—

● brought, or given evidence or information in connection with, proceedings under the Act (whether or not proceedings are later withdrawn);
● done anything else under the Act; or
● alleged someone has contravened the Act (whether or not the allegation is later dropped);

or because the person believes or suspects that the victim has done or intends to do any of these things (**s 55**).

It is unlawful for an employer to victimise either disabled or non-disabled people.
    A disabled employee complains of discrimination. It would be unlawful for the employer to subject non-disabled colleagues to any detriment (eg suspension) for telling the truth about the alleged discrimination at an industrial tribunal hearing or in any internal grievance procedures.

4.54 It is not victimisation to treat a person less favourably because that person has made an allegation which was false and not made in good faith (**s 55(b)**).
(Harassment is covered in paragraphs 6.22–6.23.)

Setting up management systems to help avoid discrimination

What management systems might be set up to help avoid discrimination?

4.55 *The Act says* that employers are responsible for the actions done by their employees in the course of their employment. In legal proceedings against an employer based on actions of an employee, it is a defence that the employer took such steps as were reasonably practicable to prevent such actions. It is not a defence for the employer simply to show the action took place without his knowledge or approval. Employers who act through agents will also be liable for the actions of their agents done with the employer's express or implied authority (s 58).

> An employer makes it clear to a recruitment agency that the company will not take kindly to recruits with learning disabilities being put forward by the agency. The agency complies by not putting such candidates forward. Both the employer and the agency will be liable if such treatment cannot be justified in an individual case.

4.56 Employers should communicate to their employees and agents any policy they may have on disability matters, and any other policies which have elements relevant to disabled employees (such as health, absenteeism or equal opportunities). All staff should be made aware that it is unlawful to discriminate against disabled people, and be familiar with the policies and practices adopted by their employer to ensure compliance with the law. Employers should provide guidance on non-discriminatory practices for all employees, so they will be aware what they should do and how to deal with disabled colleagues and disabled applicants for vacancies in the organisation, and should ensure so far as possible that these policies and practices are implemented. Employers should also make it clear to their agents what is required of them with regard to their duties under the Act, and the extent of their authority.

4.57 *The Act says* that an employer is not under an obligation to make an adjustment if he does not know, and could not reasonably be expected to know, that a person has a disability which is likely to place the person at a substantial disadvantage (s 6(6)). An employer must therefore do all he could reasonably be expected to do to find out whether this is the case.

> An employee has a disability which sometimes causes him to cry at work although the cause of this behaviour is not known to the employer. The employer's general approach on such matters is to tell staff to leave their personal problems at home and to make no allowance for such problems in the work arrangements. The employer disciplines the employee without giving him any opportunity to explain that the problem in fact arises from a disability. The employer would be unlikely to succeed in a claim that he could not reasonably be expected to have known of the disability or that it led to the behaviour for which the employee was disciplined.
>
> An employer has an annual appraisal system which specifically provides an opportunity to notify the employer in confidence if any employees are disabled and are put at a substantial disadvantage by the work arrangements or premises. This practice enables the employer to show that he could not reasonably be expected to know that an employee was put at such a disadvantage as a result of disability, if this was not obvious and was not brought to the employer's attention through the appraisal system.

4.58 In some cases a reasonable adjustment will not work without the co-operation of other employees. Employees may therefore have an important role in helping to ensure that a reasonable adjustment is carried out in practice.

> It is a reasonable adjustment for an employer to communicate in a particular way to an employee with autism (a disability which can make it difficult for someone to understand normal social interaction among people). As part of the reasonable adjustment it is the responsibility of that employer to seek the co-operation of other employees in communicating in that way.

4.59 It may be necessary to tell one or more of a disabled person's colleagues (in confidence) about a disability which is not obvious and/or whether any special assistance is required. This may be limited to the person's supervisor, or it may be necessary to involve other colleagues, depending on the nature of the disability and the reason they need to know about it.

In order for a person with epilepsy to work safely in a particular factory, it may be necessary to advise fellow workers about the effects of the condition, and the methods for assisting with them.

An office worker with cancer says that he does not want colleagues to know of his condition. As an adjustment he needs extra time away from work to receive treatment and to rest. Neither his colleagues nor the line manager needs to be told the precise reasons for the extra leave but the latter will need to know that the adjustment is required in order to carry it out effectively.

4.60 The extent to which an employer is entitled to let other staff know about an employee's disability will depend at least in part on the terms of employment. An employer could be held to be discriminating in revealing such information about a disabled employee if the employer would not reveal similar information about another person for an equally legitimate management purpose; or if the employer revealed such information without consulting the individual, whereas the employer's usual practice would be to talk to an employee before revealing personal information about him.

4.61 The Act does not prevent a disabled person keeping a disability confidential from an employer. But this is likely to mean that unless the employer could reasonably be expected to know about the person's disability anyway, the employer will not be under a duty to make a reasonable adjustment. If a disabled person expects an employer to make a reasonable adjustment, he will need to provide the employer—or, as the case may be, someone acting on the employer's behalf—with sufficient information to carry out that adjustment.

An employee has symptomatic HIV. He prefers not to tell his employer of the condition. However, as the condition progresses, he finds it increasingly difficult to work the required number of hours in a week. Until he tells his employer of his condition—or the employer becomes or could reasonably be expected to be aware of it—he cannot require the employer to change his working hours to overcome the difficulty. However, once the employer is informed he may then have to make a reasonable adjustment.

4.62 If an employer's agent or employee (for example, an occupational health officer, a personnel officer or line manager) knows in that capacity of an employee's disability, then the employer cannot claim that he does not know of that person's disability, and that he is therefore excluded from the obligation to make a reasonable adjustment. This will be the case even if the disabled person specifically asked for such information to be kept confidential. Employers will therefore need to ensure that where information about disabled people may come through different channels, there is a means—suitably confidential—for bringing the information together, so the employer's duties under the Act are fulfilled.

In a large company an occupational health officer is engaged by the employer to provide him with information about his employees' health. The officer becomes aware of an employee's disability, which the employee's line manager does not know about. The employer's working arrangements put the employee at a substantial disadvantage because of the effects of her disability and she claims that a reasonable adjustment should have been made. It will not be a defence for the employer to claim that he did not know of her disability. This is because the information gained by the officer on the employer's behalf is imputed to the employer. Even if the person did not want the line manager to know that she had a disability, the occupational health officer's knowledge means that the employer's duty under the Act applies. It might even be necessary for the line manager to implement reasonable adjustments without knowing precisely why he has to do so.

4.63 Information will not be imputed to the employer if it is gained by a person providing services to employees independently of the employer. This is the case even if the employer has arranged for those services to be provided.

An employer contracts with an agency to provide an independent counselling service to employees. The contract says that the counsellors are not acting on the employer's behalf while in the counselling role. Any information about a person's disability obtained by a counsellor during such counselling would not be imputed to the employer and so could not itself place a duty of reasonable adjustment on the employer.

What if someone says they have a disability and the employer is not convinced?

4.64 If a candidate asks for an adjustment to be made because of an impairment whose effects are not obvious, nothing in the Act or Regulations would prohibit the employer from asking for evidence that the impairment is one which gives rise to a disability as defined in the Act.

An applicant says she has a mental illness whose effects require her to take time off work on a frequent, but irregular, basis. If not satisfied that this is true, the employer would be entitled to ask for evidence that the woman has a mental illness which was likely to have the effects claimed and that it is clinically well recognised (as required by the Act).

Effects of other legislation

What about the effects of other legislation?

4.65 An employer is not required to make an adjustment—or do anything under the Act—that would result in a breach of statutory obligations (s 59).

If a particular adjustment would breach health and safety or fire legislation then an employer would not have to make it. However, the employer would still have to consider whether he was required to make any other adjustment which would not breach any legislation. For instance, if someone in a wheelchair could not use emergency evacuation arrangements such as a fire escape on a particular floor, it might be reasonable for the employer to have to relocate that person's job to an office where that problem did not arise.

An employer shortlisting applicants to fill a junior office post is considering whether to include a blind applicant who the employer believes might present a safety risk moving around the crowded office. A reasonable adjustment might be to provide mobility training to familiarise the applicant with the work area, so removing any risk there might otherwise be.

What about legislation which places restrictions on what employers can do to recruit disabled people?

4.66 The Disability Discrimination Act does not prevent posts being advertised as open only to disabled candidates. However, the requirement, for example, under Section 7 of the Local Government and Housing Act 1989 that every appointment to local authorities must be made on merit means that a post cannot be so advertised. Applications from disabled people can nevertheless be encouraged. However, this requirement to appoint 'on merit' does not exclude the duty under the 1995 Act to make adjustments so a disabled person's 'merit' must be assessed taking into account any such adjustments which would have to be made.

5   RECRUITMENT

Discrimination against applicants

How does the Act affect recruitment?

5.1   *The Act says* that it is unlawful for an employer to discriminate against a disabled person—

- in the arrangements made for determining who should be offered employment;
- in the terms on which the disabled person is offered employment; or
- by refusing to offer, or deliberately not offering, the disabled person employment s 4(1).

5.2   The word 'arrangements' has a wide meaning. Employers should avoid discrimination in, for example, specifying the job, advertising the job, and the processes of selection, including the location and timing of interviews, assessment techniques, interviewing, and selection criteria.

Specifying the job

Does the Act affect how an employer should draw up a job specification?

5.3   Yes. The inclusion of unnecessary or marginal requirements in a job specification can lead to discrimination.

An employer stipulates that employees must be 'energetic', when in fact the job in question is largely sedentary in nature. This requirement could unjustifiably exclude some people whose disabilities result in them getting tired more easily than others.

An employer specifies that a driving licence is required for a job which involves limited travelling. An applicant for the job has no driving licence because of the particular effects in his case of cerebral palsy. He is otherwise the best candidate for that job, he could easily and cheaply do the travelling involved other than by driving and it would be a reasonable adjustment for the employer to let him do so. It would be discriminatory to insist on the specification and reject his application solely because he had no driving licence.

5.4   Blanket exclusions (ie exclusions which do not take account of individual circumstances) may lead to discrimination.

An employer excludes people with epilepsy from all driving jobs. One of the jobs, in practice, only requires a standard licence and normal insurance cover. If, as a result, someone with epilepsy, who has such a licence and can obtain such cover, is turned down for the job then the employer will probably have discriminated unlawfully in excluding her from consideration.

An employer stipulates that candidates for a job must not have a history of mental illness, believing that such candidates will have poor attendance. The employer rejects an applicant solely because he has had a mental illness without checking the individual's probable attendance. Even if good attendance is genuinely essential for the job, this is not likely to be justified and is therefore very likely to be unlawful discrimination.

Can an employer stipulate essential health requirements?

5.5   Yes, but the employer may need to justify doing so, and to show that it would not be reasonable for him to have to waive them, in any individual case.

Can employers simply prefer a certain type of person?

5.6   Stating that a certain personal, medical or health-related characteristic is desirable may also lead to discrimination if the characteristic is not necessary for the performance of the job. Like a requirement, a preference may be decisive against an otherwise well-qualified disabled candidate and may have to be justified in an individual case.

An employer prefers all employees to have a certain level of educational qualification. A woman with a learning disability, which has prevented her from obtaining the preferred qualification, is turned down for a job because she does not have that qualification. If the qualification is not necessary in order to do the job and she is otherwise the best candidate, then the employer will have discriminated unlawfully against her.

Publicising the vacancy

What does the Act say about how an employer can advertise vacancies?

5.7 Where a job is advertised, and a disabled person who applies is refused or deliberately not offered it and complains to an industrial tribunal about disability discrimination, the Act requires the tribunal to assume (unless the employer can prove otherwise) that the reason the person did not get the job was related to his disability if the advertisement could reasonably be taken to indicate—

● that the success of a person's application for the job might depend to any extent on the absence of a disability such as the applicant's; or
● that the employer is unwilling to make an adjustment for a disabled person (s 11).

An employer puts in an advertisement for an office worker, 'Sorry, but gaining access to our building can be difficult for some people'. A man, who as a result of an accident some years previously can only walk with the aid of crutches but can do office work, applies for the job and is turned down. He complains to an industrial tribunal. Because of the wording of the advertisement, the tribunal would have to assume that he did not get the job for a reason relating to his disability unless the employer could prove otherwise.

What is an 'advertisement' for the purposes of the Act?

5.8 *According to the Act* 'advertisement' includes every form of advertisement or notice, whether to the public or not (s 11(3)). This would include advertisements internal to a company or office.

Does an employer have to provide information about jobs in alternative formats?

5.9 In particular cases, this may be a reasonable adjustment.

A person whom the employer knows to be disabled asks to be given information about a job in a medium that is accessible to her (in large print, in braille, or on tape or on computer disc). It is often likely to be a reasonable adjustment for the employer to comply, particularly if the employer's information systems, and the time available before the new employee is needed, mean it can easily be done.

Can an employer say that he would welcome applications from disabled people?

5.10 Yes. *The Act does not prevent* this and it would be a positive and public statement of the employer's policy.

Can an employer include a question on an application form asking whether someone is disabled?

5.11 Yes. *The Act does not prevent* employers including such a question on application forms. Employers can also ask whether the individual might need an adjustment and what it might be.

Appendix 3

Selection

Does the duty of reasonable adjustment apply to applicants?

5.12 *The Act says* that the duty to make a reasonable adjustment does not apply where the employer does not know, and could not reasonably be expected to know, that the disabled person in question is or may be an applicant for the post, or, that a particular applicant has a disability which is likely to place him at a disadvantage (s6(a)).

Does an employer have to take special care when considering applications?

5.13 Yes. Employers and their staff or agents must not discriminate against disabled people in the way in which they deal with applications. They may also have to make reasonable adjustments.

> Because of his disability, a candidate asks to submit an application in a particular medium, different from that specified for candidates in general (eg typewritten, by telephone, or on tape). It would normally be a reasonable adjustment for the employer to allow this.

Whom can an employer shortlist for interview?

5.14 If an employer knows that an applicant has a disability and is likely to be at a substantial disadvantage because of the employer's arrangements or premises, the employer should consider whether there is any reasonable adjustment which would bring the disabled person within the field of applicants to be considered even though he would not otherwise be within that field because of that disadvantage. If the employer could only make this judgement with more information it would be discriminatory for him not to put the disabled person on the shortlist for interview if that is how he would normally seek additional information about candidates.

What should an employer do when arranging interviews?

5.15 Employers should think ahead for interviews. Giving applicants the opportunity to indicate any relevant effects of a disability and to suggest adjustments to help overcome any disadvantage the disability may cause, could help the employer avoid discrimination in the interview and in considering the applicant, by clarifying whether any reasonable adjustments may be required.

5.16 Nevertheless, if a person, whom the employer previously did not know, and could not have known, to be disabled, arrives for interview and is placed at a substantial disadvantage because of the arrangements, the employer may still be under a duty to make a reasonable adjustment from the time that he first learns of the disability and the disadvantage. However, what the employer has to do in such circumstances might be less extensive than if advance notice had been given.

What changes might an employer have to make to arrangements for interviews?

5.17 There are many possible reasonable adjustments, depending on the circumstances.

> A person has difficulty attending at a particular time because of a disability. It will very likely be reasonable for the employer to have to rearrange the time.
>
> A hearing impaired candidate has substantial difficulties with the interview arrangements. The interviewer may simply need to ensure he faces the applicant and speaks clearly or is prepared to repeat questions. The interviewer should make sure that his face is well lit when talking to someone with a hearing or visual impairment. It will almost always be reasonable for an employer to have to provide such help with communication support if the interviewee would otherwise be at a substantial disadvantage.

An employer who pays expenses to candidates who come for interview could well have to pay additional expenses to meet any special requirements of a disabled person arising from any substantial disadvantage to which she would otherwise be put by the interview arrangements. This might include paying travelling expenses for a support worker or reasonable cost of travel by taxi, rather than by bus or train, if this is necessary because of the disability.

A job applicant does not tell an employer (who has no knowledge of her disability) in advance that she uses a wheelchair. On arriving for the interview she discovers that the room is not accessible. The employer did not know of the disability and so could not have been expected to make changes in advance. However, it would still be a reasonable adjustment for the employer to hold the interview in an alternative accessible room, if a suitable one was easily available at the time with no, or only an acceptable level of, disruption or additional cost.

Should an employer consider making changes to the way the interview is carried out?

5.18 Yes, although whether any change is needed—and, if so, what change—will depend on the circumstances.

It would almost always be reasonable to allow an applicant with a learning disability to bring a supportive person such as a friend or relative to assist when answering questions that are not part of tests.

It would normally be reasonable to allow a longer time for an interview to someone with a hearing impairment using a sign language interpreter to communicate.

Does an employer have to make changes to anticipate *any* disabled person applying for a job?

5.19 No. An employer is not required to make changes in anticipation of applications from disabled people in general. It is only if the employer knows or could be reasonably expected to know that a particular disabled person is, or may be, applying and is likely to be substantially disadvantaged by the employer's premises or arrangements, that the employer may have to make changes.

Should an employer ask about a disability?

5.20 The Act does not prohibit an employer from seeking information about a disability but an employer must not use it to discriminate against a disabled person. An employer should ask only about a disability if it is, or may be, relevant to the person's ability to do the job—after a reasonable adjustment, if necessary. Asking about the effects of a disability might be important in deciding what adjustments ought to be made. The employer should avoid discriminatory questions.

An applicant whose disability has left him using a wheelchair but healthy, is asked by an employer whether any extra leave might be required because of the condition. This is unlikely to be discriminatory because a need for extra time off work may be a substantial factor relevant to the person's ability to do the job. Therefore such a question would normally be justified. Similarly, a reasonable question about whether any changes may need to be made to the workplace to accommodate the use of the wheelchair would probably not be discriminatory.

Does the Act prevent employers carrying out aptitude or other tests in the recruitment process?

5.21 No, but routine testing of all candidates may still discriminate against particular individuals or substantially disadvantage them. If so, the employer would need to revise the tests—or the way the results of such tests are assessed—to take account of specific disabled candidates, except where the nature and form of the test were necessary to assess a matter relevant to the job. It may, for instance, be a reasonable adjustment to accept a lower 'pass rate' for a person whose disability inhibits performance in such a test. The extent to which this is required would depend on how closely the test is related to the job in question and what adjustments the employer might have to make if the applicant were given the job.

An employer sets a numeracy test for prospective employees. A person with a learning disability takes the test and does not achieve the level the employer normally stipulates. If the job in fact entails very little numerical work and the candidate is otherwise well suited for the job it is likely to be a reasonable adjustment for the employer to waive the requirement.

An employer sets candidates a short oral test. An applicant is disabled by a bad stammer, but only under stress. It may be a reasonable adjustment to allow her more time to complete the test, or to give the test in written form instead, though not if oral communication is relevant to the job and assessing this was the purpose of the test.

Can an employer specify qualifications?

5.22 An employer is entitled to specify that applicants for a job must have certain qualifications. However, if a disabled person is rejected for the job because he lacks a qualification, the employer will have to justify that rejection if the reason why the person is rejected (ie the lack of a qualification) is connected with his disability. Justification will involve showing that the qualification is relevant and significant in terms of the particular job and the particular applicant, and that there is no reasonable adjustment which would change this. In some circumstances it might be feasible to reassign those duties to which the qualification relates, or to waive the requirement for the qualification if this particular applicant has alternative evidence of the necessary level of competence.

An employer seeking someone to work in an administrative post specifies that candidates must have the relevant NVQ Level 4 qualification. If Level 4 fairly reflects the complex and varied nature and substantial personal responsibility of the work, and these aspects of the job cannot reasonably be altered, the employer will be able to justify rejecting a disabled applicant who has only been able to reach Level 3 because of his disability and who cannot show the relevant level of competence by other means.

An employer specifies that two GCSEs are required for a certain post. This is to show that a candidate has the general level of ability required. No particular subjects are specified. An applicant whose dyslexia prevented her from passing written examinations cannot meet this requirement, but the employer would be unable to justify rejecting her on this account alone if she could show she nevertheless had the skill and intelligence called for in the post.

Can an employer insist on a disabled person having a medical examination?

5.23 Yes. However, if an employer insists on a medical check for a disabled person and not others, without justification, he will probably be discriminating unlawfully. The fact that a person has a disability is unlikely in itself to justify singling out that person to have a health check, although such action might be justified in relation to some jobs.

An employer requires all candidates for employment to have a medical examination. That employer would normally be entitled to include a disabled person.

An applicant for a job has a disabling heart condition. The employer routinely issues a health questionnaire to job applicants, and requires all applicants who state they have a disability to undergo a medical examination. Under the Act, the employer would not be justified in requiring a medical examination whenever an applicant states he has a disability—for example, this would not normally be justified if the disability is clearly relevant neither to the job nor to the environment in which the job is done. However, the employer would probably be justified in asking the applicant with the disabling heart condition to have a medical examination restricted to assessing its implications for the particular job in its context. If, for example, the job required lifting and carrying but these abilities were limited by the condition, the employer would also have to consider whether it would be reasonable for him to have to make a change such as providing a mechanical means of lifting and/or carrying, or arranging for the few items above the person's limit to be dealt with by another person, whilst ensuring that any health and safety provisions were not breached.

How can an employer take account of medical evidence?

5.24   In most cases, having a disability does not adversely affect a person's general health. Medical evidence about a disability can justify an adverse employment decision (such as dismissing or not promoting). It will not generally do so if there is no effect on the person's ability to do the work (or any effect is less than substantial), however great the effects of the disability are in other ways. The condition or effects must be relevant to the employer's decision.

An applicant for a post on a short-term contract has a progressive condition which has some effects, but is likely to have substantial adverse effects only in the long term. The likelihood of these long-term effects would not itself be a justifiable reason for the employer to reject him.

An employer requires all candidates for a certain job to be able to work for at least two years to complete a particular work project. Medical evidence shows that a particular candidate is unlikely to be able to continue working for that long. It would be lawful to reject that candidate if the two-year requirement was justified in terms of the work, and it would not be reasonable for the employer to have to waive it in the particular circumstances.

Advice from an occupational health expert simply that an employee was 'unfit for work' would not mean that the employer's duty to make a reasonable adjustment was waived.

What will help an employer decide to select a particular disabled person?

5.25   The employer must take into account any adjustments that it is reasonable for him to have to make. Suggestions made by the candidate at any stage may assist in identifying these.

What if a disabled person just isn't the right person for the job?

5.26   An employer must not discriminate against a disabled candidate, but there is no requirement (aside from reasonable adjustment) to treat a disabled person more favourably than he treats or would treat others. An employer will have to assess an applicant's merits as they would be if any reasonable adjustments required under the Act had been made. If, after allowing for those adjustments, a disabled person would not be the best person for the job the employer would not have to recruit that person.

Terms and conditions of service

Are there restrictions on the terms and conditions an employer can offer a disabled person?

5.27   Terms and conditions of service should not discriminate against a disabled person. The employer should consider whether any reasonable adjustments need to be made to the terms and conditions which would otherwise apply.

An employer's terms and conditions state the hours an employee has to be in work. It might be a reasonable adjustment to change these hours for someone whose disability means that she has difficulty using public transport during rush hours.

Does that mean that an employer can never offer a disabled person a less favourable contract?

5.28   No. Such a contract may be justified if there is a material and substantial reason and there is no reasonable adjustment which can be made to remove that reason.

> A person's disability means she has significantly lower output than other employees doing similar work, even after an adjustment. Her work is of neither lower nor higher quality than theirs. The employer would be justified in paying her less in proportion to the lower output if it affected the value of her work to the business.

Can employers still operate performance-related pay?

5.29   *Regulations provide* that this is justified so long as the scheme applies equally to all employees, or all of a particular class of employees. There would be no requirement to make a reasonable adjustment to an arrangement of this kind to ensure (for example) that a person's pay was topped up if a deteriorating condition happened to lead to lower performance.[1] However, there would still be a duty to make a reasonable adjustment to any aspect of the premises or work arrangements if that would prevent the disability reducing the employee's performance.

NOTES
1   Disability Discrimination (Employment) Regulations 1996, SI 1996/1456, reg 3.

6   EMPLOYMENT

Discrimination against employees

Does the Act cover all areas of employment?

6.1   Yes. *The Act* says that it is unlawful for an employer to discriminate against a disabled person whom he employs—

● in the terms of employment which he affords him;
● in the opportunities which he affords him for promotion, a transfer, training or receiving any other benefit;
● by refusing to afford him, or deliberately not affording him, any such opportunity; or
● by dismissing him, or subjecting him to any other detriment (s 4(2)).

6.2   Therefore, an employer should not discriminate in relation to, for example: terms and conditions of service, arrangements made for induction, arrangements made for employees who become disabled (or who have a disability which worsens), opportunities for promotion, transfer, training or receiving any other benefit, or refusal of such opportunities, pensions, dismissal or any detriment.

Induction

What is the effect on induction procedures?

6.3   Employers must not discriminate in their induction procedures. The employer may have to make adjustments to ensure a disabled person is introduced into a new working environment in a clearly structured and supported way with, if necessary, an individually tailored induction programme (s 4(2) and s 6(1)).

> An employer runs a one day induction course for new recruits. A recruit with a learning disability is put at a substantial disadvantage by the way the course is normally run. The employer might have to make an alternative arrangement: for example running a separate, longer course for the person, or permitting someone to sit in on the normal course to provide support, assistance or encouragement.

Promotion and transfer

What are an employer's duties as far as promotion and transfer are concerned?

6.4 Employers must not discriminate in assessing a disabled person's suitability for promotion or transfer, in the practical arrangements necessary to enable the promotion or transfer to take place, in the operation of the appraisal, selection and promotion or transfer process, or in the new job itself—and may have to make a reasonable adjustment (s 4(2)(b) and (c) and s 6(1)).

A garage owner does not consider for promotion to assistant manager a clerk who has lost the use of her right arm, because he wrongly and unreasonably believes that her disability might prevent her performing competently in a managerial post. The reason used by the employer to deny the clerk promotion has meant that she was discriminated against.

An employer considering a number of people for a job on promotion is aware that one of the candidates for interview has a hearing impairment, but does not find out whether the person needs any special arrangements for the interview, for example a sign language interpreter. If the candidate requires such an adjustment, and it would be reasonable for the employer to have to make it, the employer would fail in his duty if he did not make that adjustment.

A civil engineer whose disability involves kidney dialysis treatment, is based in London and regularly visits hospital for the treatment. She wishes to transfer to a vacant post in her company's Scottish office. She meets all the requirements for the post, but her transfer is turned down on the ground that her need for treatment would mean that, away from the facilities in London, she would be absent from work for longer. The employer had made no attempt to discuss this with her or get medical advice. If the employer had done so, it would have been clear that similar treatment would be equally available in the new locality. In these circumstances, the employer probably could not show that relying on this reason was justified.

Someone disabled by a back injury is seeking promotion to supervisor. A minor duty involves assisting with the unloading of the weekly delivery van, which the person's back injury would prevent. In assessing her suitability for promotion, the employer should consider whether reallocating this duty to another person would be a reasonable adjustment.

What should an employer do to check that promotion and transfer arrangements do not discriminate?

6.5 The employer should review the arrangements to check that qualifications required are justified for the job to be done. He should also check that other arrangements, for example systems which determine other criteria for a particular job, do not exclude disabled people who may have been unable to meet those criteria because of their disability but would be capable of performing well in the job.

Training and other benefits provided by the employer

Does the Act apply to the provision of training?

6.6 Yes. Employers must not discriminate in selection for training and must make any necessary reasonable adjustments (s 4(2)(b) and (c) and s 6(1)).

An employer wrongly assumes that a disabled person will be unwilling or unable to undertake demanding training or attend a residential training course, instead of taking an informed decision. He may well not be able to justify a decision based on that assumption.

An employer may need to alter the time or the location of the training for someone with a mobility problem, make training manuals, slides or other visual media accessible to a visually impaired employee, perhaps by providing braille versions or having them read out, or ensure that an induction loop is available for someone with a hearing impairment.

673

An employer refuses to allow a disabled employee to be coached for a theory examination relating to practical work which the disability prevented the employee from doing. The employer would almost always be justified in refusing to allow the coaching because it was designed to equip employees for an area of work for which, because of the disability, the person could not be suited even by a reasonable adjustment.

What about other benefits provided by employers?

6.7 An employer must not discriminate in providing disabled people with opportunities for receiving benefits (which include 'facilities' and 'services') which are available to other employees (s 4(2)(b) and (c)). The employer must make any necessary reasonable adjustment to the way the benefits are provided (s 6(1)) although this does not apply to benefits under occupational pension schemes or certain other employment related benefit schemes (paragraph 6.16).

Benefits might include canteens, meal vouchers, social clubs and other recreational activities, dedicated car parking spaces, discounts on products, bonuses, share options, hairdressing, clothes allowances, financial services, healthcare, medical assistance/insurance, transport to work, company car, education assistance, workplace nurseries, and rights to special leave.

If physical features of a company's social club would inhibit a disabled person's access it might be a reasonable adjustment for the employer to make suitable modifications.

An employer provides dedicated car parking spaces near to the workplace. It is likely to be reasonable for the employer to have to allocate one of these spaces to a disabled employee who has significant difficulty getting from the public car parks further away that he would otherwise have to use.

6.8 If an employer provides benefits to the public, or to a section of the public which includes the disabled employee, provision of those benefits will normally fall outside the duty not to discriminate in employment. Instead, the duty in the Act not to discriminate in providing goods, facilities and services will apply. However, the employment duty will apply if the benefit to employees is materially different (eg at a discount), is governed by the contract of employment, or relates to training (s 4(2) and (3)).

A disabled employee of a supermarket chain who believes he has been discriminated against when buying goods as a customer at any branch of the supermarket would have no claim under the employment provisions. However, if that employee were using a discount card provided only to employees, then the employment provisions would apply if any less favourable treatment related to his use of the card.

Occupational pension schemes and insurance

What does the Act say about occupational pension schemes?

6.9 *The Act inserts* into every scheme a 'non-discrimination' rule. The trustees or managers of the scheme are prohibited by that rule from doing—or omitting to do—anything to members or non-members of schemes that would be unlawful discrimination if done by an employer (s 17). References to employers in paragraphs 6.11–6.15 should therefore be read as if they also apply to trustees or managers when appropriate.

When is less favourable treatment justified?

6.10 Less favourable treatment for a reason relating to a disability can be justified only if the reason is material and substantial.

Trustees of a pension scheme would not be justified in excluding a woman simply because she had a visual impairment. That fact, in itself, would be no reason why she should not receive the same pension benefits as any other employee.

6.11 There are circumstances when a disabled person's health or health prognosis is such that the cost of providing benefits under a pension scheme is substantially greater than it would be for a person without the disability. In these circumstances *Regulations provide* that an employer is regarded as justified in treating a disabled person less favourably in applying the eligibility conditions for receiving the benefit. Employers should satisfy themselves, if necessary with actuarial advice and/or medical evidence, of the likelihood of there being a substantially greater cost. [1]

NOTES
1 Disability Discrimination (Employment) Regulations 1996, SI 1996/1456.

When could the justification be used?

6.12 The justification would be available whenever the disabled person is considered for admission to the scheme. However, the justification cannot be applied to a disabled member, unless a term was imposed at the time of admission which allowed this.

Which benefits does this justification apply to?

6.13 The justification can apply to the following types of benefits provided by an occupational pension scheme: termination of service, retirement, old age or death, accident, injury, sickness or invalidity.[1]

NOTES
1 Disability Discrimination (Employment) Regulations 1996, SI 1996/1456.

Would a minor degree of extra cost amount to a justification for less favourable treatment?

6.14 No. Only the likelihood of a substantial additional cost should be taken to be a justification. Substantial means something more than minor or trivial.[1]

An employer receives medical advice that an individual with multiple sclerosis is likely to retire early on health grounds. The employer obtains actuarial advice that the cost of providing that early retirement benefit would be substantially greater than an employee without MS and so the individual is refused access to the scheme. This is justified.

NOTES
1 Disability Discrimination (Employment) Regulations 1996, SI 1996/1456.

What happens to an employee's rate of contributions if the employer is justified in refusing the employee access to some benefits but not others?

6.15 *Regulations provide* that if the employer sets a uniform rate of contribution the employer would be justified in applying it to a disabled person. A disabled person could therefore be required to pay the same rate of contributions as other employees, even if not eligible for some of the benefits.[1]

NOTES
1 Disability Discrimination (Employment) Regulations 1996, SI 1996/1456.

Does the duty to make a reasonable adjustment apply?

6.16 No. The duty of reasonable adjustment does not apply to the provision of benefits under an occupational pension scheme or any other benefit payable in money or money's worth under a scheme or arrangement for the benefit of employees in respect of—

● termination of service;
● retirement, old age or death; or

● accident, injury, sickness or invalidity (s 6(11)). (Although there is power to add other matters to this list by regulations, none have been added at the date of this Code.)

Therefore, neither the employer nor the scheme's trustees or managers need to make any adjustment for a disabled person who, without that adjustment, will be justifiably denied access either to such a scheme or to a benefit under the scheme. Nor will they have to make an adjustment for someone receiving less benefit because they justifiably receive a lower rate of pay.

Does the Act cover the provision of insurance schemes for individual employees?

6.17 The Act also applies to provision of group insurance, such as permanent health insurance or life insurance, by an insurance company for employees under an arrangement with their employer. A disabled person in, or who applies or is considering applying to join, a group of employees covered by such an arrangement is protected from discrimination in the provision of the insurance services in the same way as if he were a member of the public seeking the services of that insurance company under the part of the Act relating to the provision of goods, facilities and services. However, the right of redress in this case would be exercised through an industrial tribunal (and not the courts) (s 18).

Does the Act cover the provision of insurance to an employer?

6.18 The employer may have to make reasonable adjustments to remove any disadvantage caused to a disabled person which arose from the arrangements made by the employer to provide himself with insurance cover. Such adjustments could include measures which would reduce any risk otherwise posed by the disabled person, so that the insurer would then provide cover, or seeking alternative cover. If cover could not be obtained at all at realistic cost it is most unlikely that the employer would have to bear the risk himself.

>   It comes to an employer's attention that someone who works for his antiques business has epilepsy. The employer is obliged to notify his insurance company who refuse to cover the employer against damage caused by the disabled person. To avoid dismissing the employee, it might be reasonable for the employer to have to bar the person from contact with valuable items, if this would mean the insurance company then provided cover.

Retention of disabled employees

6.19 An employer must not discriminate against an employee who becomes disabled, or has a disability which worsens (s 4(2)). The issue of retention might also arise when an employee has a stable impairment but the nature of his employment changes.

6.20 If as a result of the disability an employer's arrangements or a physical feature of the employer's premises place the employee at a substantial disadvantage in doing his existing job, the employer must first consider any reasonable adjustment that would resolve the difficulty. The employer may also need to consult the disabled person at appropriate stages about what his needs are and what effect the disability might have on future employment, for example, where the employee has a progressive condition. The nature of the reasonable adjustments which an employer may have to consider will depend on the circumstances of the case.

>   It may be possible to modify a job to accommodate an employee's changed needs. This might be by rearranging working methods or giving another employee certain minor tasks the newly disabled person can no longer do, providing practical aids or adaptations to premises or equipment, or allowing the disabled person to work at different times or places from those with equivalent jobs (for instance, it may be that a change to part-time work might be appropriate for someone who needed to spend some time each week having medical treatment).

A newly disabled employee is likely to need time to readjust. For example, an employer might allow: a trial period to assess whether the employee is able to cope with the current job, or a new one; the employee initially to work from home; a gradual build-up to full time hours; or additional training for a person with learning disabilities who moves to another workplace.

It may be a reasonable adjustment for an employer to move a newly disabled person to a different post within the organisation if a suitable vacancy exists or is expected shortly.

Additional job coaching may be necessary to enable a disabled person to take on a new job.

In many cases where no reasonable adjustment would overcome a particular disability so as to enable the disabled person to continue with similar terms or conditions, it might be reasonable for the employer to have to offer a disabled employee a lower-paying job, applying the rate of pay that would apply to such a position under his usual pay practices.

If new technology (for instance a telephone or information technology system) puts a disabled person at a substantial disadvantage compared with non-disabled people, then the employer would be under a duty to make a reasonable adjustment. For example, some telephone systems may interfere with hearing aids for people with hearing impairments and the quality of the inductive coupler may need to be improved.

Termination of employment

6.21 Dismissal—including compulsory early retirement—of a disabled person for a reason relating to the disability would need to be justified and the reason for it would have to be one which could not be removed by any reasonable adjustment.

It would be justifiable to terminate the employment of an employee whose disability makes it impossible for him any longer to perform the main functions of his job, if an adjustment such as a move to a vacant post elsewhere in the business is not practicable or otherwise not reasonable for the employer to have to make.

It would be justifiable to terminate the employment of an employee with a worsening progressive condition if the increasing degree of adjustment necessary to accommodate the effects of the condition (shorter hours of work or falling productivity, say) became unreasonable for the employer to have to make.

An employer who needs to reduce the workforce would have to ensure that any scheme which was introduced for choosing candidates for redundancy did not discriminate against disabled people. Therefore, if a criterion for redundancy would apply to a disabled person for a reason relating to the disability, that criterion would have to be 'material' and 'substantial' and the employer would have to consider whether a reasonable adjustment would prevent the criterion applying to the disabled person after all.

Harassment

What does the Act say about harassment?

6.22 The Act does not refer to harassment as a separate issue. However, harassing a disabled person on account of a disability will almost always amount to a 'detriment' under the Act. (Victimisation is covered in paragraphs 4.53–4.54.)

Are employers liable for harassment by their employees?

6.23 An employer is responsible for acts of harassment by employees in the course of their employment unless the employer took such steps as were reasonably practicable to prevent it. As a minimum first step harassment because of disability should be made a disciplinary matter and staff should be made aware that it will be taken seriously.

Appendix 3

7 PARTICULAR PROVISIONS

Discrimination against contract workers

7.1 The Act deals specifically with work which is carried out by individuals ('contract workers') for a person (a 'principal') who hires them under contract from their employer (generally an employment business)—referred to below as the 'sending' employer.

What does the Act say about contract workers?

7.2 *The Act says* that it is unlawful for a principal to discriminate against a disabled person—

- in the terms on which the person is allowed to do the contract work;
- by not allowing the person to do, or continue to do, the contract work;
- in the way he affords the person access to, or by failing to afford him access to, benefits in relation to contract work; or
- by subjecting the person to any other detriment in relation to contract work (s 12(1)).

7.3 *The Act and Regulations apply* as if the principal were, or would be, the actual employer of the contract worker. Therefore, the same definition of 'discrimination'— including the need to justify less favourable treatment—applies as for employers (s 12(3)).

   The employer of a labourer, who some years ago was disabled by clinical depression but has since recovered, proposes to supply him to a contractor to work on a building site. Although his past disability is covered by the Act, the site manager refuses to accept him because of his medical history. Unless the contractor can show that the manager's action is justified, the contractor would be acting unlawfully.

What will be the effect of the duty to make adjustments for principals?

7.4 The duty to make a reasonable adjustment applies to a principal as to an employer (s 12(3)).

7.5 In deciding whether any, and if so, what, adjustment would be reasonable for a principal to have to make, the period for which the contract worker will work for the principal is important. It might well be unreasonable for a principal to have to make certain adjustments if the worker will be with the principal for only a short time.

   An employment business enters into a contract with a firm of accountants to provide an assistant for two weeks to cover an unexpected absence. The employment business wishes to put forward a person who, because of his disability, finds it difficult to travel during the rush hour and would like his working hours to be modified accordingly. It might not be reasonable for the firm to have to agree given the short time in which to negotiate and implement the new hours.

Will the principal and the 'sending' employer both have duties to make reasonable adjustments?

7.6 Both the 'sending' employer and the principal may separately be under a duty of reasonable adjustment in the case of a contract worker who is disabled. If the 'sending' employer's own premises or arrangements place the contract worker at a substantial disadvantage, then the 'sending' employer may have a duty to make a reasonable adjustment (s 6(1)). The 'sending' employer may also have a duty to make a reasonable adjustment where a similar substantial disadvantage is likely to affect a contract worker as a result of the arrangements or premises of all or most of the principals to whom he might be supplied. The employer would not have to take separate steps in relation to each principal, but would have to make any reasonable adjustment within his power which would overcome the disadvantage wherever it might arise. The principal would not have to make any adjustment which the employer should make.[1] However, subject to that the principal would be responsible only for any additional reasonable adjustment which is necessary solely because of the principal's own arrangements or premises (s 6(1) applied by s 12(3)). It would also usually be reasonable for a principal and a 'sending' employer to have to cooperate with any steps taken by the other to assist a disabled contract worker.

A travel agency hires a clerical worker from an employment business to fulfil a three month contract to file travel invoices during the busy summer holiday period. The contract worker is a wheelchair user, and is quite capable of doing the job if a few minor, temporary changes are made to the arrangement of furniture in the office. It would be reasonable for the travel agency to make this adjustment.

A bank hires a blind word processor operator as a contract worker from an employment business. The employment business provides her with a specially adapted portable computer because she would otherwise be at a similar substantial disadvantage in doing the work wherever she does it. (In such circumstances the bank would not have to provide a specially adapted computer if the employment business did not.) The bank would have to cooperate by letting the contract worker use her computer whilst working for the bank if it is compatible with the bank's systems. If not, it could be a reasonable adjustment for the bank to make the computer compatible and for the employment business to allow that change to be made.

NOTES
1 Disability Discrimination (Employment) Regulations 1996, SI 1996/1456.

What about contract workers in small firms?

7.7 The Act applies to any employment business which has 20 or more employees (including people currently employed by it but hired out to principals). It also applies to any principal who has 20 or more workers (counting both the principal's own employees and any contract workers currently working for the principal). It does not apply to employment businesses or principals with fewer than 20 employees. Note the extended definition of 'employment' in the Act (see paragraph 2.8).

An employment business has 15 employees (including people currently hired out to others) and enters a contract to provide a worker in a shop. The shop employs 29 people. Neither the duty not to discriminate nor the duty to make a reasonable adjustment applies to the employment business, but both duties apply to the owner of the shop. However, the length of time the worker was contracted to work at the shop would be an important factor in assessing whether the shop-owner had to make any significant adjustment.

A deaf individual is employed by an employment business that has 100 employees (including people currently hired out to others). He is hired regularly to do contract work and, as a reasonable adjustment, the business provides a portable induction loop for assignments. If he works for a principal with, say, 17 workers, (counting both employees and contract workers) that principal would not be required to cooperate with use of the induction loop. However, if the principal has 20 or more such workers the principal would be obliged to cooperate.

What about the Supported Placement Scheme (SPS)?

7.8 These arrangements also apply to the Employment Service's Supported Placement Scheme (SPS) for severely disabled people. The 'contractor' under the scheme (usually a local authority or voluntary body) is the equivalent of the 'sending' employer, and the 'host employer' is the equivalent of the principal. A local authority can even be both the contractor and the host employer at the same time (as can a voluntary body) in which case the duty not to discriminate and the duty of reasonable adjustment would apply to it as to an employer.

Provisions applying to trade organisations

What does the Act say about trade organisations?

7.9 A trade organisation is defined as an organisation of workers or of employers, or any other organisation whose members carry on a particular profession or trade for the purposes of which the organisation exists (s 13(4)). Therefore trade unions, employers' associations, and similar bodies like the Law Society and chartered professional institutions, for example, must comply with the legislation.

7.10 *The Act says* that it is unlawful for a trade organisation to discriminate against a disabled person—

● in the terms on which it is prepared to admit the person to membership; or
● by refusing to accept, or deliberately not accepting, an application for membership.

It is also unlawful for a trade organisation to discriminate against a disabled member of the organisation—

● in the way it affords the person access to any benefits or by refusing or deliberately omitting to afford access to them;
● by depriving the person of membership, or varying the terms of membership; or
● by subjecting the person to any other detriment (s 13).

Trade organisations should therefore check that they do not discriminate as regards, for example, training facilities, welfare or insurance schemes, invitations to attend events, processing of grievances, assistance to members in their employers' disciplinary or dismissal procedures.

7.11 *The Act defines* discrimination by a trade organisation in similar terms to the definition relating to discrimination by an employer. Therefore, the need to justify less favourable treatment for a reason relating to disability applies as in the case of an employer (s 14(3)).

A trade organisation is arranging a trip to some of its members' workplaces but it decides to exclude a member in a wheelchair because too many of the sites are inaccessible to make participation worthwhile. This could well be justified. (Note, however, paragraph 7.12.)

Do trade organisations have a duty to make adjustments?

7.12 *The Act includes* a requirement on trade organisations to make reasonable adjustments (s 15). However, this duty will not be brought into force until after the other employment provisions, at a date which will be subject to consultation.

What about the actions of employees or representatives of trade organisations?

7.13 Individual employees or agents of trade organisations who have dealings with members or applicants are treated in the same way as individual employees or agents of employers who deal with job applicants or employees: the trade organisation is responsible for their actions (s 58).

8 RESOLVING DISAGREEMENTS WITHIN THE EMPLOYING ORGANISATION

What does the Act say about resolving disagreements?

8.1 The Act does not require employers to resolve disputes within their organisations. However, it is in an employer's interests to resolve problems as they arise where possible. This should be in a non-discriminatory way to comply with the Act's general provisions.

8.2 One method might be the use of a grievance procedure. Grievance procedures provide an open and fair way for employees to make known their concerns and enable grievances to be resolved quickly before they become major difficulties. Use of the procedures can highlight areas where the employer's duty of reasonable adjustment may not have been observed, and can prevent misunderstandings in this area leading to tribunal complaints.

Do existing grievance and disciplinary procedures need changing?

8.3 Where grievance or disciplinary procedures are in place, the employer might wish to review, and where necessary adapt, them to ensure that they are flexible enough to be used by disabled employees. Where a formal grievance (or disciplinary) procedure operates, it must be open, or applied, to disabled employees on the same basis as to others. Employers will have to ensure that grievance (or disciplinary) procedures do not, in themselves, discriminate against disabled employees and may have to make reasonable adjustments to enable some disabled employees to use grievance procedures effectively or to ensure disciplinary procedures have the same impact on disabled employees as on others.

> An employee with a learning disability has to attend an interview under the employer's disciplinary procedures. The employee would like his guardian or a friend to be present. The employer agrees to this but refuses to rearrange the interview to a time which is more convenient to the guardian or friend. The employer may be in breach of the duty to make a reasonable adjustment. (See Annex 3 for information about industrial tribunals.)

ANNEX 1   WHAT IS MEANT BY DISABILITY

1   This Annex is included to aid understanding about who is covered by the Act and should provide sufficient information on the definition of disability to cover the large majority of cases. The definition of disability in the Act is designed to cover only people who would generally be considered to be disabled. A Government publication *Guidance on matters to be taken into account in determining questions relating to the definition of disability*,[1] is also available.

NOTES
1 See p 687.

When is a person disabled?

2   A person has a disability if he has a physical or mental impairment which has a substantial and long-term adverse effect on his ability to carry out normal day-to-day activities.

What about people who have recovered from a disability?

3   People who have had a disability within the definition are protected from discrimination even if they have since recovered.

What does 'impairment' cover?

4   It covers physical or mental impairments; this includes sensory impairments, such as those affecting sight or hearing.

Are all mental impairments covered?

5   The term 'mental impairment' is intended to cover a wide range of impairments relating to mental functioning, including what are often known as learning disabilities. However, the Act states that it does not include any impairment resulting from or consisting of a mental illness, unless that illness is a clinically well-recognised illness.

A clinically well-recognised illness is one that is recognised by a respected body of medical opinion.

What is a 'substantial' adverse effect?

6   A substantial adverse effect is something which is more than a minor or trivial effect. The requirement that an effect must be substantial reflects the general understanding of disability as a limitation going beyond the normal differences in ability which might exist among people.

What is a 'long-term' effect?

7   A long-term effect of an impairment is one—

● which has lasted at least 12 months; or
● where the total period for which it lasts is likely to be at least 12 months; or
● which is likely to last for the rest of the life of the person affected.

8   Effects which are not long-term would therefore include loss of mobility due to a broken limb which is likely to heal within 12 months and the effects of temporary infections, from which a person would be likely to recover within 12 months.

What if the effects come and go over a period of time?

9   If an impairment has had a substantial adverse effect on normal day-to-day activities but that effect ceases, the substantial effect is treated as continuing if it is likely to recur; that is if it is more probable than not that the effect will *recur*. To take the example of a person with rheumatoid arthritis whose impairment has a substantial adverse effect, which then ceases to be substantial (ie the person has a period of remission). The effects are to be treated as if they are continuing, and are likely to continue beyond 12 months, *if*—

● the impairment remains; and
● at least one recurrence of the substantial effect is likely to take place 12 months or more after the initial occurrence.

This would then be a long-term effect.

What are 'normal day-to-day activities'?

10   They are activities which are carried out by most people on a fairly regular and frequent basis. The term is not intended to include activities which are normal only for a particular person or group of people, such as playing a musical instrument, or a sport, to a professional standard or performing a skilled or specialised task at work. However, someone who is affected in such a specialised way but is *also* affected in normal day-to-day activities, would be covered by this part of the definition. The test of whether an impairment affects normal day-to-day activities is whether it affects one of the broad categories of capacity listed in Schedule 1 to the Act. They are—

● mobility;
● manual dexterity;
● physical co-ordination;
● continence;
● ability to lift, carry or otherwise move everyday objects;
● speech, hearing or eyesight;
● memory or ability to concentrate, learn or understand; or
● perception of the risk of physical danger.

What about treatment?

11   Someone with an impairment may be receiving medical or other treatment which alleviates or removes the effects (though not the impairment). In such cases, the treatment

is ignored and the impairment is taken to have the effect it would have had without such treatment. This does not apply if substantial adverse effects are not likely to recur even if the treatment stops (ie the impairment has been cured).

Does this include people who wear spectacles?

12   No. The sole exception to the rule about ignoring the effects of treatment is the wearing of spectacles or contact lenses. In this case, the effect while the person is wearing spectacles or contact lenses should be considered.

Are people who have disfigurements covered?

13   People with severe disfigurements are covered by the Act. They do not need to demonstrate that the impairment has a substantial adverse effect on their ability to carry out normal day-to-day activities.

What about people who know their condition is going to get worse over time?

14   Progressive conditions are conditions which are likely to change and develop over time. Examples given in the Act are cancer, multiple sclerosis, muscular dystrophy and HIV infection. Where a person has a progressive condition he will be covered by the Act from the moment the condition leads to an impairment which has *some* effect on ability to carry out normal day-to-day activities, even though not a *substantial* effect, if that impairment is likely eventually to have a substantial adverse effect on such ability.

What about people who are registered disabled?

15   Those registered as disabled under the Disabled Persons (Employment) Act 1944 both on 12 January 1995 and 2 December 1996 will be treated as being disabled under the Disability Discrimination Act 1995 for three years from the latter date. At all times from 2 December 1996 onwards they will be covered by the Act as people who have had a disability. This does not preclude them from being covered as having a current disability any time after the three year period has finished. Whether they are or not will depend on whether they—like anyone else—meet the definition of disability in the Act.

Are people with genetic conditions covered?

16   If a genetic condition has no effect on ability to carry out normal day-to-day activities, the person is not covered. Diagnosis does not in itself bring someone within the definition. If the condition is progressive, then the rule about progressive conditions applies.

Are any conditions specifically excluded from the coverage of the Act?

17   Yes. Certain conditions are to be regarded as not amounting to impairments for the purposes of the Act. These are—

● addiction to or dependency on alcohol, nicotine, or any other substance (other than as a result of the substance being medically prescribed);
● seasonal allergic rhinitis (eg hayfever), except where it aggravates the effect of another condition;
● tendency to set fires;
● tendency to steal;
● tendency to physical or sexual abuse of other persons;
● exhibitionism;
● voyeurism.

Also, disfigurements which consist of a tattoo (which has not been removed), non-medical body piercing, or something attached through such piercing, are to be treated as not having a substantial adverse effect on the person's ability to carry out normal day-to-day activities.[1]

Appendix 3

NOTES
1 Disability Discrimination (Meaning of Disability) Regulations 1996, SI 1996/1455.

ANNEX 2   HOW TO GET FURTHER INFORMATION, HELP AND ADVICE

1   A range of leaflets about various aspects of the Act is available. To obtain copies, call 0345 622 633 (local rate), or textphone 0345 622 644. Copies of the leaflets are also available in braille and audio cassette.

2   Statutory Guidance on the definition of disability is produced separately. This can be obtained from HMSO bookshops . . . This Guidance should prove helpful where it is not clear whether or not a person has or has had a disability.

3   There is a wide range of practical help and advice available to assist employers in the recruitment and employment of people, including disabled people, for example from Jobcentres, Careers Service offices, Training and Enterprise Councils (in England and Wales) and Local Enterprise Companies (in Scotland). Addresses and telephone numbers are available in local telephone directories.

4   Where necessary, specialist help and advice for disabled people and for employers who might, or do, employ disabled people is available from the Employment Service through its local Placing, Assessment and Counselling Teams (PACTs). PACTs can help with issues related to employing disabled people, but cannot advise on an employer's specific legal obligations.

5   PACTs may be able to provide help with special aids, equipment and other measures to overcome the effects of disability in the working environment.

6   The addresses and telephone numbers of PACTs are listed in local telephone directories under 'Employment Service', or can be obtained from the nearest Jobcentre.

7   Many specialist organisations for disabled people also offer a range of employment help and advice. The Employment Service publish a booklet called *Sources of Information and Advice (Ref: PGP6)* which lists many of the specialist organisations offering help to employers on employment and disability issues. The booklet can be obtained from PACTs.

8   The Advisory, Conciliation and Arbitration Service (ACAS) can help employers and individuals with factual information on the legislation and assistance related to its effects on industrial relations practices and procedures. The address and telephone numbers of ACAS offices are listed in local telephone directories under 'ACAS'.

9   Employers working in historic buildings, or other heritage properties, may also wish to obtain a copy of *Easy Access to Historic Properties* from English Heritage at 23 Savile Row, London, W1X 1AB. Tel: 0171 973 3434.

10   Disability can take a very large number of forms and the action an employer may be required to take will depend to a very large extent on the particular circumstances of the case. Any advice and information employers receive should be considered in that light. In some circumstances employers may wish to consider whether they should seek legal advice.

ANNEX 3   COMPLAINTS UNDER THE EMPLOYMENT PROVISIONS

What does the Act say about making complaints?

1   *The Act says* that a person who believes that an employer has unlawfully discriminated or failed to make a reasonable adjustment, or that a person has aided an employer to do such an act, may present a complaint to an industrial tribunal (s 8(1)).

684

What does the Act say about conciliation?

2   When a formal complaint has been made to an industrial tribunal *the Act places a duty* on the Advisory, Conciliation and Arbitration Service's (ACAS) conciliation officers to try to promote settlement of the dispute without a tribunal hearing (**Sch 3, para 1**). ACAS can also assist in this way without a formal application to a tribunal being made.

What does the Act say about obtaining a remedy for unlawful discrimination?

3   *The Act says* that a disabled person who believes someone has unlawfully discriminated against him or failed to make a reasonable adjustment, in breach of the employment provisions of the Act or Regulations, may present a complaint to an industrial tribunal (**s 8(1)**).

4   If the tribunal upholds the complaint it may—

● declare the rights of the disabled person (the complainant), and the other person (the respondent) in relation to the complaint;
● order the other person to pay the complainant compensation; and
● recommend that, within a specified time, the other person take reasonable action to prevent or reduce the adverse effect in question (**s 8(2)**).

5   *The Act allows* compensation for injury to feelings to be awarded whether or not other compensation is awarded (**s 8(4)**).

6   *The Act says* that if a respondent fails, without reasonable justification, to comply with an industrial tribunal's recommendation, the tribunal may—

● increase the amount of compensation to be paid; or
● order the respondent to pay compensation if it did not make such an order earlier (**s 8(5)**).

Who can be taken to an Industrial Tribunal?

7   The tribunal complaints procedure applies to anyone who, it is claimed, has discriminated in the employment field—employers (and their employees and agents for whose acts they are responsible), trade organisations, people who hire contract workers and people who aid any of these to discriminate.

Complaints involving landlords

8   If a reasonable adjustment requiring the consent of the employer's landlord (or a superior landlord) is not made, for whatever reason, the disabled person may bring a complaint against the employer in an industrial tribunal. Either the disabled person or the employer may ask the tribunal to make the landlord a party to the proceedings. If the industrial tribunal finds that the landlord acted unreasonably in withholding consent, or gave consent but attached an unreasonable condition, it can make any appropriate declaration, order that the alteration may be made, or award compensation against the landlord (**s 27 and Sch 4, para 2**).

Complaining about pension schemes

9   A disabled person who considers that the trustees or managers of a pension scheme have discriminated against him, may complain through the pensions dispute resolution mechanism. Information about the scheme should give details about this. If necessary, a complaint may be made to the Pensions Ombudsman.

10   From April 1997, all occupational pension schemes will be required to set up and operate procedures for resolving disputes between individual pension scheme members and the trustees or managers.

11 The Occupational Pensions Advisory Service (OPAS) can provide an advice and conciliation service for members of the public who have problems with their occupational pension. OPAS can be contacted at 11 Belgrave Road, London, SW1U 1RB. Tel: 0171 233 8080.

12 A disabled person who considers that an employer has discriminated against him in providing access to a pension scheme can complain to an industrial tribunal following the same process for other complaints against employers.

What is the 'Questionnaire Procedure'?

13 *The Act provides* for a procedure (the questionnaire procedure) to assist a person who believes that discrimination has occurred, to decide whether or not to start proceedings and, if the person does, to formulate and present a case in the most effective manner (s 56). Questionnaire forms are obtainable from Jobcentres.

Can compromise agreements be an alternative to making tribunal complaints?

14 *The Act says* that, in general, the terms of an agreement (such as a contract of employment) cannot prevent a disabled person from complaining to an industrial tribunal, or force a complaint to be stopped (s 9). However, *the Act also says* that in some circumstances a disabled person can make an agreement not to make a complaint or to stop one (s 9).

15 These circumstances are if—

● an ACAS conciliation officer has acted under the Act on the matter; *or* the following conditions apply—
● the disabled person must have received independent legal advice from a qualified lawyer about the terms and effects of the agreement, particularly its effect on his ability to complain to a tribunal;
● the adviser must have an insurance policy covering any loss arising from the advice; and
● the agreement must be in writing, relate to the complaint, identify the adviser and say that these conditions are satisfied.

16 It may be in the interests of some disabled people to make such 'compromise' agreements instead of pursuing complaints to industrial tribunal hearings, but care should be taken to ensure that the above conditions are met.

How is a complaint made to an Industrial Tribunal?

17 Complaints to an industrial tribunal can be made on an application form (IT1). Forms are obtainable from Jobcentres. Completed applications should be returned to the Industrial Tribunals Central Office. The address is on the form.

18 Applications to an industrial tribunal must be made within three months of the time when the incident being complained of occurred. The time limit will not normally be extended to allow for the time it might take to try to settle the dispute within the organisation eg by way of internal grievance procedures (see paragraphs 8.1–8.3). A tribunal may, however, consider a complaint which is out of time, if it considers, in all the circumstances of the case, that it is just and equitable to do so (**Sch 3, para 3**).

What does the Act say about reporting restrictions?

19 *The Act empowers* a tribunal to make 'restricted reporting orders' if it considers that evidence of a personal nature is likely to be heard by the tribunal. Such orders prohibit the publication, for example in a newspaper, of any matter likely to lead members of the public to identify the complainant or any other person mentioned in the order, until the tribunal's decision is promulgated.

Guidance on Matters to be taken into Account in Determining Questions Relating to the Definition of Disability

NOTES
Commencement: 31 July 1996 (SI 1996/1996, art 2).

This guidance was issued by the Secretary of State for Education and Employment on 25 July 1996 under the Disability Discrimination Act 1995, s 3, following consultation and the laying of a draft before both Houses of Parliament on 6 June 1996. The statutory effect of the guidance is as stated in s 3. The guidance is reproduced in full below.

PART I INTRODUCTION

Using the guidance

1 Although this guidance is primarily designed for courts and tribunals, it is likely to be of value to a range of people and organisations. **In the vast majority of cases there is unlikely to be any doubt whether or not a person has or has had a disability, but this guidance should prove helpful in cases where it is not clear.**

2 The definition of disability has a number of elements. The guidance covers each of these elements in turn. Each section contains an explanation of the relevant provisions of the Act which supplement the basic definition; guidance and examples are provided where relevant. Those using this guidance for the first time may wish to read it all, as each part of the guidance builds upon the part(s) preceding it.

3 Part II of this guidance relates to matters to be taken into account when considering whether an effect is substantial and/or long term. Most of the examples are to be found here, and particularly in **Section C**. Because the purpose of this guidance is to help in the cases where there is doubt, examples of cases where there will not be any doubt are not included.

4 Throughout the guidance descriptions of the provisions in the legislation are immediately preceded by bold italic text. They are immediately followed by a reference to the relevant provision of the Act or Regulations. References to sections of the Act are marked 's'; references to schedules are marked 'Sch'; and references to paragraphs in schedules are marked 'para'. References in footnotes to 'Definition Regulations' mean the Disability Discrimination (Meaning of Disability) Regulations 1996.[1]

NOTES
1 SI 1996/1455.

Main elements of the definition of disability

5 *The Act defines* 'disabled person' as a person with '**a physical or mental impairment which has a substantial and long-term adverse effect on his ability to carry out normal day-to-day activities**' (s 1).

6 This means that—

- the person must have an *impairment*, that is either physical or mental (see paragraphs 10–15 below);
- the impairment must have adverse effects which are *substantial* (see **Section A**);
- the substantial effects must be *long-term* (see **Section B**); and
- the long-term substantial effects must be *adverse* effects on *normal day-to-day activities* (see **Section C**).

This definition is subject to the provisions in Schedule 1 (**Sch 1**).

Inclusion of people who have had a disability in the past

7   *The Act says* that Part I of the Act (definition), Part II (employment) and Part III (goods, facilities, services and premises) also apply in relation to a person who has had a disability as defined in paragraphs 5 and 6 above. For this purpose, those Parts of the Act are subject to the provisions in Schedule 2 to the Act (**s 2, Sch 2**).

Exclusions from the definition

8   Certain conditions are not to be regarded as impairments for the purposes of the Act. These are—

● addiction to or dependency on alcohol, nicotine, or any other substance (other than in consequence of the substance being medically prescribed);
● the condition known as seasonal allergic rhinitis (eg hayfever), except where it aggravates the effect of another condition;
● tendency to set fires;
● tendency to steal;
● tendency to physical or sexual abuse of other persons;
● exhibitionism;
● voyeurism.

Also, disfigurements which consist of a tattoo (which has not been removed), non-medical body piercing, or something attached though such piercing, are to be treated as not having a substantial adverse effect on the person's ability to carry out normal day-to-day activities.[1]

NOTES
1   SI 1996/1455.

Registered disabled people

9   The introduction of the employment provisions in the Act coincides with the abolition of the Quota scheme which operated under the Disabled Persons (Employment) Act 1944. *The Disability Discrimination Act says* that anyone who was registered as a disabled person under the Disabled Persons (Employment) Act 1944 and whose name appeared on the register both on 12 January 1995 and on 2 December 1996 (the date the employment provisions come into force) is to be treated as having a disability for the purposes of the Disability Discrimination Act during the period of three years starting on 2 December 1996. This applies regardless of whether the person otherwise meets the definition of 'disabled person' during that period. Those who are treated by this provision as being disabled for the three-year period are also to be treated after this period has ended as having had a disability in the past (**Sch 1, para 7**).

Impairment

10   The definition requires that the effects which a person may experience arise from a physical or mental impairment. In many cases there will be no dispute whether a person has an impairment. Any disagreement is more likely to be about whether the effects of the impairment are sufficient to fall within the definition. Even so, it may sometimes be necessary to decide whether a person has an impairment so as to be able to deal with the issues about its effects.

11   It is not necessary to consider how an impairment was caused, even if the cause is a consequence of a condition which is excluded. For example, liver disease as a result of alcohol dependency would count as an impairment.

12 *Physical or mental impairment* includes sensory impairments, such as those affecting sight or hearing.

13 *Mental impairment* includes a wide range of impairments relating to mental functioning, including what are often known as learning disabilities (formerly known as 'mental handicap'). However, *the Act states* that it does not include any impairment resulting from or consisting of a mental illness unless that illness is a clinically well-recognised illness (**Sch 1, para 1**).

14 A *clinically well-recognised illness* is a mental illness which is recognised by a respected body of medical opinion. It is very likely that this would include those specifically mentioned in publications such as the World Health Organisation's International Classification of Diseases.

15 *The Act states* that mental impairment does not have the special meaning used in the Mental Health Act 1983 or the Mental Health (Scotland) Act 1984, although this does not preclude a mental impairment within the meaning of that legislation from coming within the definition in the Disability Discrimination Act (**s 68**).

PART II GUIDANCE ON MATTERS TO BE TAKEN INTO ACCOUNT IN DETERMINING QUESTIONS RELATING TO THE DEFINITION OF DISABILITY

A Substantial

Meaning of 'substantial' adverse effect

A1 The requirement that an adverse effect be substantial reflects the general understanding of 'disability' as a limitation going beyond the normal differences in ability which may exist among people. A 'substantial' effect is more than would be produced by the sort of physical or mental conditions experienced by many people which have only minor effects. A 'substantial' effect is one which is more than 'minor' or 'trivial'.

The time taken to carry out an activity

A2 The time taken by a person with an impairment to carry out a normal day-to-day activity should be considered when assessing whether the effect of that impairment is substantial. It should be compared with the time that might be expected if the person did not have the impairment.

The way in which an activity is carried out

A3 Another factor to be considered when assessing whether the effect of an impairment is substantial is the way in which a person with that impairment carries out a normal day-to-day activity. The comparison should be with the way the person might be expected to carry out the activity if he or she did not have the impairment.

Cumulative effects of an impairment

A4 *The Act provides* that an impairment is to be taken to affect the ability of a person to carry out normal day-to-day activities only if it affects that person in one (or more) of the respects listed in paragraph C4 (**Sch 1, para 4**). An impairment might not have a substantial adverse effect on a person in any one of these respects, but its effects in more than one of these respects taken together could result in a substantial adverse effect on the person's ability to carry out normal day-to-day activities.

A5 For example, although the great majority of people with cerebral palsy will experience a number of substantial effects, someone with mild cerebral palsy may experience minor effects in a number of the respects listed in paragraph C4 which together could create substantial adverse effects on a range of normal day-to-day activities: fatigue may hinder walking, visual perception may be poor, co-ordination and balance may cause some difficulties. Similarly, a person whose impairment causes breathing difficulties may experience minor effects in a number of respects but which overall have a substantial adverse effect on their ability to carry out normal day-to-day activities. For some people, mental illness may have a clear effect in one of the respects in C4. However, for others, depending on the extent of the condition, there may be effects in a number of different respects which, taken together, substantially adversely affect their ability to carry out normal day-to-day activities.

A6 A person may have more than one impairment, any one of which alone would not have a substantial effect. In such a case, account should be taken of whether the impairments together have a substantial effect overall on the person's ability to carry out normal day-to-day activities. For example a minor impairment which affects physical co-ordination and an irreversible but minor injury to a leg which affects mobility, taken together, might have a substantial effect on the person's ability to carry out certain normal day-to-day activities.

Effects of behaviour

A7 Account should be taken of how far a person can reasonably be expected to modify behaviour to prevent or reduce the effects of an impairment on normal day-to-day activities. If a person can behave in such a way that the impairment ceases to have a substantial adverse effect on his or her ability to carry out normal day-to-day activities the person would no longer meet the definition of disability.

A8 In some cases people have such 'coping' strategies which cease to work in certain circumstances (for example, where someone who stutters or has dyslexia is placed under stress). If it is possible that a person's ability to manage the effects of an impairment will break down so that effects will sometimes still occur, this possibility must be taken into account when assessing the effects of the impairment.

A9 If a disabled person is advised by a medical practitioner to behave in a certain way in order to reduce the impact of the disability, that might count as treatment to be disregarded (see paragraph A11 below).

Effects of environment

A10 Whether adverse effects are substantial may depend on environmental conditions which may vary; for example, the temperature, humidity, the time of day or night, how tired the person is or how much stress he or she is under may have an impact on the effects. When assessing whether adverse effects are substantial, the extent to which such environmental factors are likely to have an impact should also therefore be considered.

Effects of treatment

A11 *The Act provides* that where an impairment is being *treated or corrected* the impairment is to be treated as having the effect it would have without the measures in question (Sch 1, para 6(1)). *The Act states* that the treatment or correction measures to be disregarded for these purposes include medical treatment and the use of a prosthesis or other aid (Sch 1, para 6(2)).

A12 This applies even if the measures result in the effects being completely under control or not at all apparent.

A13 For example, if a person with a hearing impairment wears a hearing aid the question whether his or her impairment has a substantial adverse effect is to be decided by reference to what the hearing level would be without the hearing aid. And in the case of someone with diabetes, whether or not the effect is substantial should be decided by reference to what the condition would be if he or she was not taking medication.

A14 However, *the Act states* that this provision does not apply to sight impairments to the extent that they are capable of correction by spectacles or contact lenses. In other words the only effects on ability to carry out normal day-to-day activities to be considered are those which remain when spectacles or contact lenses are used (or would remain if they were used). This does not include the use of devices to correct sight which are not spectacles or contact lenses (**Sch 1, para 6(3)**).

Progressive conditions

A15 A progressive condition is one which is likely to change and develop over time. *The Act gives* the following examples of progressive conditions: cancer, multiple sclerosis, muscular dystrophy, HIV infection. *The Act provides* for a person with such a condition to be regarded as having an impairment which has a substantial adverse effect on his or her ability to carry out normal day-to-day activities before it actually does so. Where a person has a progressive condition, he or she will be treated as having an impairment which has a *substantial* adverse effect from the moment any impairment resulting from that condition first has *some* effect on ability to carry out normal day-to-day activities. The effect need not be continuous and need not be substantial. For this rule to operate medical diagnosis of the condition is not by itself enough (**Sch 1, para 8**).

Severe disfigurements

A16 *The Act provides* that where an impairment consists of a severe disfigurement, it is to be treated as having a substantial adverse effect on the person's ability to carry out normal day-to-day activities. There is no need to demonstrate such an effect (**Sch 1, para 3**). *Regulations provide* that a disfigurement which consists of a tattoo (which has not been removed) is not to be considered as a severe disfigurement. Also excluded is a piercing of the body for decorative purposes including anything attached through the piercing.[1]

NOTES
1 SI 1996/1455.

A17 Examples of disfigurements include scars, birthmarks, limb or postural deformation or diseases of the skin. Assessing severity will be mainly a matter of the degree of the disfigurement. However, it may be necessary to take account of where the feature in question is (eg on the back as opposed to the face).

B Long term

Meaning of long-term effects

B1 *The Act states* that, for the purpose of deciding whether a person is disabled, a long-term effect of an impairment is one—

● which has lasted at least twelve months; or
● where the total period for which it lasts, from the time of the first onset, is likely to be at least twelve months; or
● which is likely to last for the rest of the life of the person affected (**Sch 1, para 2**).

For the purpose of deciding whether a person has had a disability in the past, a long-term effect of an impairment is one which lasted at least 12 months (**Sch 2, para 5**).

B2　It is not necessary for the effect to be the same throughout the relevant period. It may change, as where activities which are initially very difficult become possible to a much greater extent. The main adverse effect might even disappear—or it might disappear temporarily—while one or other effects on ability to carry out normal day-to-day activities continue or develop. Provided the impairment continues to have, or is likely to have, such an effect throughout the period, there is a long-term effect.

Recurring effects

B3　*The Act states* that if an impairment has had a substantial adverse effect on a person's ability to carry out normal day-to-day activities but that effect ceases, the substantial effect is treated as continuing if it is likely to recur; that is, it is more likely than not that the effect will recur. (In deciding whether a person has had a disability in the past, the question is whether a substantial adverse effect has in fact recurred.) Conditions which recur only sporadically or for short periods (eg epilepsy) can still qualify (**Sch 1, para 2(2), Sch 2, para 5**). *Regulations specifically exclude* seasonal allergic rhinitis (eg hayfever) from this category, except where it aggravates the effects of an existing condition.[1]

NOTES
1　SI 1996/1455.

B4　For example, a person with rheumatoid arthritis may experience effects from the first occurrence for a few weeks and then have a period of remission. But, if the effects are likely to recur, they are to be treated as if they were continuing. If the effects are likely to recur beyond twelve months after the first occurrence, they are to be treated as long-term.

B5　Likelihood of recurrence should be considered taking all the circumstances of the case into account. This should include what the person could reasonably be expected to do to prevent the recurrence; for example, the person might reasonably be expected to take action which prevents the impairment from having such effects (eg avoiding substances to which he or she is allergic). This may be unreasonably difficult with some substances. In addition, it is possible that the way in which a person can control or cope with the effects of a condition may not always be successful because, for example, a routine is not followed or the person is in an unfamiliar environment. If there is an increased likelihood that the control will break down, it will be more likely that there will be a recurrence. That possibility should be taken into account when assessing the likelihood of a recurrence.

Effects of treatment

B6　If medical or other treatment is likely to cure an impairment, so that recurrence of its effects would then be unlikely even if there were no further treatment, this should be taken into consideration when looking at the likelihood of recurrence of those effects. However, as **Section A** describes, if the treatment simply delays or prevents a recurrence, and a recurrence would be likely if the treatment stopped, then the treatment is to be ignored and the effect is to be regarded as likely to recur.

Meaning of 'likely'

B7　It is *likely* that an event will happen if it is more probable than not that it will happen.

B8　In assessing the likelihood of an effect lasting for any period, account should be taken of the total period for which the effect exists. This includes any time before the point when the discriminatory behaviour occurred as well as time afterwards. Account should also be taken of both the typical length of such an effect on an individual, and any relevant factors specific to this individual (for example, general state of health, age).

Assessing whether a past disability was long-term

B9 *The Act provides* that a person who has had a disability within the definition is protected from discrimination even if he or she has since recovered or the effects have become less than substantial. In deciding whether a past condition was a disability, its effects count as long-term if they lasted twelve months or more after the first occurrence, or if a recurrence happened or continued until more than twelve months after the first occurrence (**s 2, Sch 2, para 5**).

C   Normal day-to-day activities

Meaning of 'normal day-to-day activities'

C1   *The Act states* that an impairment must have a long-term substantial adverse effect on normal day-to-day activities (**s 1**).

C2   The term 'normal day-to-day activities' is not intended to include activities which are normal only for a particular person or group of people. Therefore in deciding whether an activity is a 'normal day-to-day activity' account should be taken of how far it is normal for most people and carried out by most people on a daily or frequent and fairly regular basis.

C3   The term 'normal day-to-day activities' does not, for example, include work of any particular form, because no particular form of work is 'normal' for most people. In any individual case, the activities carried out might be highly specialised. The same is true of playing a particular game, taking part in a particular hobby, playing a musical instrument, playing sport, or performing a highly skilled task. Impairments which affect only such an activity and have no effect on 'normal day-to-day activities' are not covered. The examples included in this section give an indication of what are to be taken as normal day-to-day activities.

C4   *The Act states* that an impairment is only to be treated as affecting the person's ability to carry out *normal day-to-day activities* if it affects one of the following—

● mobility;
● manual dexterity;
● physical co-ordination;
● continence;
● ability to lift, carry or otherwise move everyday objects;
● speech, hearing or eyesight;
● memory or ability to concentrate, learn or understand; or
● perception of the risk of physical danger (**Sch 1, para 4**).

C5   In many cases an impairment will adversely affect the person's ability to carry out a range of normal day-to-day activities and it will be obvious that the overall adverse effect is substantial or the effect on at least one normal day-to-day activity is substantial. In such a case it is unnecessary to consider precisely how the person is affected in each of the respects listed in paragraph C4. For example, a person with a clinically well-recognised mental illness may experience an adverse effect on concentration which prevents the person from remembering why he or she is going somewhere; the person would not also have to demonstrate that there was an effect on, say, speech. A person with an impairment which has an adverse effect on sight might be unable to go shopping unassisted; he or she would not also have to demonstrate that there was an effect on, say, mobility.

C6   Many impairments will, by their nature, adversely affect a person directly in one of the respects listed in C4. An impairment may also indirectly affect a person in one or more of these respects, and this should be taken into account when assessing whether the impairment falls within the definition. For example—

● medical advice: where a person has been professionally advised to change, limit or refrain from a normal day-to-day activity on account of an impairment or only do it in a certain way or under certain conditions;
● pain or fatigue: where an impairment causes pain or fatigue in performing normal day-to-day activities, so the person may have the capacity to do something but suffer pain in doing so; or the impairment might make the activity more than usually fatiguing so that the person might not be able to repeat the task over a sustained period of time.

C7   Where a person has a mental illness such as depression account should be taken of whether, although that person has the physical ability to perform a task, he or she is, in practice, unable to sustain an activity over a reasonable period.

C8   Effects of impairments may not be apparent in babies and young children because they are too young to have developed the ability to act in the respects listed in C4. *Regulations provide* that where an impairment to a child under six years old does not have an effect in any of the respects in C4, it is to be treated as having a substantial and long-term adverse effect on the ability of that child to carry out normal day-to-day activities where it would normally have a substantial and long-term adverse effect on the ability of a person aged six years or over to carry out normal day-to-day activities.[1]

NOTES
1   SI 1996/1455.

C9   In deciding whether an effect on the ability to carry out a normal day-to-day activity is a substantial adverse effect, account should be taken of factors such as those mentioned under each heading below. The headings are exhaustive—the person must be affected in one of these respects. The lists of examples are not exhaustive; they are only meant to be illustrative. The assumption is made in each example that there is an adverse effect on the person's ability to carry out normal day-to-day activities. A person only counts as disabled if the substantial effect is adverse.

C10   The examples below of what it would, and what it would not, be reasonable to regard as substantial adverse effects are indicators and not tests. They do not mean that if a person can do an activity listed then he or she does not experience any substantial adverse effects; the person may be inhibited in other activities, and this instead may indicate a substantial effect.

C11   In reading examples of effects which it would not be reasonable to regard as substantial, the effect described should be thought of as if it were the only effect of the impairment. That is, if the effect listed in the example were the only effect it would not be reasonable to regard it as substantial in itself.

C12   Examples of effects which are obviously within the definition are not included below. So for example, inability to dress oneself, inability to stand up, severe dyslexia or a severe speech impairment would clearly be covered by the definition and are not included among the examples below. The purpose of these lists is to provide help in cases where there may be doubt as to whether the effects on normal day-to-day activities are substantial.

C13   The examples below describe the effect which would occur when the various factors described in Parts A and B above have been allowed for. This includes, for example the effects of a person making such modifications of behaviour as might reasonably be expected, or of disregarding the impact of medical or other treatment.

Mobility

C14   This covers moving or changing position in a wide sense. Account should be taken of the extent to which, because of either a physical or a mental condition, a person is inhibited in getting around unaided or using a normal means of transport, in leaving home with or without assistance, in walking a short distance, climbing stairs, travelling in a car or completing a journey on public transport, sitting, standing, bending, or reaching, or getting around in an unfamiliar place.

Examples

It **would be reasonable** to regard as having a substantial adverse effect—

- inability to travel a short journey as a passenger in a vehicle;
- inability to walk other than at a slow pace or with unsteady or jerky movements;
- difficulty in going up or down steps, stairs or gradients;
- inability to use one or more forms of public transport;
- inability to go out of doors unaccompanied.

It **would not be reasonable** to regard as having a substantial adverse effect—

- difficulty walking unaided a distance of about 1.5 kilometres or a mile without discomfort or having to stop—the distance in question would obviously vary according to the age of the person concerned and the type of terrain;
- inability to travel in a car for a journey lasting more than two hours without discomfort.

Manual dexterity

C15   This covers the ability to use hands and fingers with precision. Account should be taken of the extent to which a person can manipulate the fingers on each hand or co-ordinate the use of both hands together to do a task. This includes the ability to do things like pick up or manipulate small objects, operate a range of equipment manually, or communicate through writing or typing on standard machinery. Loss of function in the dominant hand would be expected to have a greater effect than equivalent loss in the non-dominant hand.

Examples

It **would be reasonable** to regard as having a substantial adverse effect—

- loss of function in one or both hands such that the person cannot use the hand or hands;
- inability to handle a knife and fork at the same time;
- ability to press the buttons on keyboards or keypads but only much more slowly than is normal for most people.

It **would not be reasonable** to regard as having a substantial adverse effect—

- inability to undertake activities requiring delicate hand movements, such as threading a small needle;
- inability to reach typing speeds standardised for secretarial work;
- inability to pick up a single small item, such as a pin.

Physical co-ordination

C16 This covers balanced and effective interaction of body movement, including hand and eye co-ordination. In the case of a child, it is necessary to take account of the level of achievement which would be normal for a person of the particular age. In any case, account should be taken of the ability to carry out 'composite' activities such as walking and using hands at the same time.

Examples

It **would be reasonable** to regard as having a substantial adverse effect—

- ability to pour liquid into another vessel only with unusual slowness or concentration;
- inability to place food into one's own mouth with fork/spoon without unusual concentration or assistance.

It **would not be reasonable** to regard as having a substantial adverse effect—

- mere clumsiness;
- inability to catch a tennis ball.

Continence

C17 This covers the ability to control urination and/or defecation. Account should be taken of the frequency and extent of the loss of control and the age of the individual.

Examples

It **would be reasonable** to regard as having a substantial adverse effect—

- even infrequent loss of control of the bowels;
- loss of control of the bladder while asleep at least once a month;
- frequent minor faecal incontinence or frequent minor leakage from the bladder.

It **would not be reasonable** to regard as having a substantial adverse effect—

- infrequent loss of control of the bladder while asleep;
- infrequent minor leakage from the bladder.

Ability to lift, carry or otherwise move everyday objects

C18 Account should be taken of a person's ability to repeat such functions or, for example, to bear weights over a reasonable period of time. Everyday objects might include such items as books, a kettle of water, bags of shopping, a briefcase, an overnight bag, a chair or other piece of light furniture.

Examples

It **would be reasonable** to regard as having a substantial adverse effect—

- inability to pick up objects of moderate weight with one hand
- inability to carry a moderately loaded tray steadily.

It **would not be reasonable** to regard as having a substantial adverse effect—

- inability to carry heavy luggage without assistance;
- inability to move heavy objects without a mechanical aid.

Speech, hearing or eyesight

C19 This covers the ability to speak, hear or see and includes face-to-face, telephone and written communication.

SPEECH

Account should be taken of how far a person is able to speak clearly at a normal pace and rhythm and to understand someone else speaking normally in the person's native language. It is necessary to consider any effects on speech patterns or which impede the acquisition or processing of one's native language, for example by someone who has had a stroke.

Examples

It **would be reasonable** to regard as having a substantial adverse effect—

- inability to give clear basic instructions orally to colleagues or providers of a service;
- inability to ask specific questions to clarify instructions;
- taking significantly longer than average to say things.

It **would not be reasonable** to regard as having a substantial adverse effect—

- inability to articulate fluently due to a minor stutter, lisp or speech impediment;
- inability to speak in front of an audience;
- having a strong regional or foreign accent;
- inability to converse in a language which is not the speaker's native language.

HEARING

If a person uses a hearing aid or similar device, what needs to be considered is the effect that would be experienced if the person were not using the hearing aid or device. Account should be taken of effects where the level of background noise is within such a range and of such a type that most people would be able to hear adequately.

Examples

It **would be reasonable** to regard as having a substantial adverse effect—

- inability to hold a conversation with someone talking in a normal voice in a moderately noisy environment;
- inability to hear and understand another person speaking clearly over the voice telephone.

It **would not be reasonable** to regard as having a substantial adverse effect—

- inability to hold a conversation in a very noisy place, such as a factory floor;
- inability to sing in tune.

EYESIGHT

If a person's sight is corrected by spectacles or contact lenses, or could be corrected by them, what needs to be considered is the effect remaining while they are wearing such spectacles or lenses, in light of a level and type normally acceptable to most people for normal day-to-day activities.

Examples

It **would be reasonable** to regard as having a substantial adverse effect—

- inability to see to pass the eyesight test for a standard driving test;
- inability to recognise by sight a known person across a moderately-sized room;
- total inability to distinguish colours;
- inability to read ordinary newsprint;
- inability to walk safely without bumping into things.

It **would not be reasonable** to regard as having a substantial adverse effect—

- inability to read very small or indistinct print without the aid of a magnifying glass;

- inability to distinguish a known person across a substantial distance (eg playing field);
- inability to distinguish between red and green.

Memory or ability to concentrate, learn or understand

C20 Account should be taken of the person's ability to remember, organise his or her thoughts, plan a course of action and carry it out, take in new knowledge, or understand spoken or written instructions. This includes considering whether the person learns to do things significantly more slowly than is normal. Account should be taken of whether the person has persistent and significant difficulty in reading text in standard English or straightforward numbers.

Examples

It **would be reasonable** to regard as having a substantial adverse effect—

- intermittent loss of consciousness and associated confused behaviour;
- persistent inability to remember the names of familiar people such as family or friends;
- inability to adapt after a reasonable period to minor change in work routine;
- inability to write a cheque without assistance;
- considerable difficulty in following a short sequence such as a simple recipe or a brief list of domestic tasks.

It **would not be reasonable** to regard as having a substantial adverse effect—

- occasionally forgetting the name of a familiar person, such as a colleague;
- inability to concentrate on a task requiring application over several hours;
- inability to fill in a long, detailed, technical document without assistance;
- inability to read at faster than normal speed;
- minor problems with writing or spelling.

Perception of the risk of physical danger

C21 This includes both the underestimation and overestimation of physical danger, including danger to well-being. Account should be taken, for example, of whether the person is inclined to neglect basic functions such as eating, drinking, sleeping, keeping warm or personal hygiene; reckless behaviour which puts the person or others at risk; or excessive avoidance behaviour without a good cause.

Examples

It **would be reasonable** to regard as having a substantial adverse effect—

- inability to operate safely properly-maintained equipment;
- persistent inability to cross a road safely;
- inability to nourish oneself (assuming nourishment is available);
- inability to tell by touch that an object is very hot or cold.

It **would not be reasonable** to regard as having a substantial adverse effect—

- fear of significant heights;
- underestimating the risk associated with dangerous hobbies, such as mountain climbing;
- underestimating risks—other than obvious ones—in unfamiliar workplaces.

Appendix 4

Aids to calculation of redundancy payments and compensation for unfair dismissal

1 Redundancy payment calculator

COMPLETE YEARS OF CONTINUOUS EMPLOYMENT

Age	2	3	4	5	6	7	8	9	10	11	12	13	14	15	16	17	18	19	20
20	1	1	1	1	–														
21	1	1½	1½	1½	1½	–													
22	1	1½	2	2	2	2	–												
23	1½	2	2½	3	3	3	3	–											
24	2	2½	3	3½	4	4	4	4	–										
25	2	3	3½	4	4½	5	5	5	5	–									
26	2	3	4	4½	5	5½	6	6	6	6	–								
27	2	3	4	5	5½	6	6½	7	7	7	7	–							
28	2	3	4	5	6	6½	7	7½	8	8	8	8	–						
29	2	3	4	5	6	7	7½	8	8½	9	9	9	9	–					
30	2	3	4	5	6	7	8	8½	9	9½	10	10	10	10	–				
31	2	3	4	5	6	7	8	9	9½	10	10½	11	11	11	11	–			
32	2	3	4	5	6	7	8	9	10	10½	11	11½	12	12	12	12	–		
33	2	3	4	5	6	7	8	9	10	11	11½	12	12½	13	13	13	13	–	
34	2	3	4	5	6	7	8	9	10	11	12	12½	13	13½	14	14	14	14	–
35	2	3	4	5	6	7	8	9	10	11	12	13	13½	14	14½	15	15	15	15½
36	2	3	4	5	6	7	8	9	10	11	12	13	14	14½	15	15½	16	16	16
37	2	3	4	5	6	7	8	9	10	11	12	13	14	15	15½	16	16½	17	17
38	2	3	4	5	6	7	8	9	10	11	12	13	14	15	16	16½	17	17½	18
39	2	3	4	5	6	7	8	9	10	11	12	13	14	15	16	17	17½	18	18½
40	2	3	4	5	6	7	8	9	10	11	12	13	14	15	16	17	18	18½	19
41	2	3	4	5	6	7	8	9	10	11	12	13	14	15	16	17	18	19	19½
42	2½	3½	4½	5½	6½	7½	8½	9½	10½	11½	12½	13½	14½	15½	16½	17½	18½	19½	20½
43	3	4	5	6	7	8	9	10	11	12	13	14	15	16	17	18	19	20	21
44	3	4½	5½	6½	7½	8½	9½	10½	11½	12½	13½	14½	15½	16½	17½	18½	19½	20½	21½
45	3	4½	6	7	8	9	10	11	12	13	14	15	16	17	18	19	20	21	22
46	3	4½	6	7½	8½	9½	10½	11½	12½	13½	14½	15½	16½	17½	18½	19½	20½	21½	22½
47	3	4½	6	7½	9	10	11	12	13	14	15	16	17	18	19	20	21	22	23
48	3	4½	6	7½	9	10½	11½	12½	13½	14½	15½	16½	17½	18½	19½	20½	21½	22½	23½
49	3	4½	6	7½	9	10½	12	13	14	15	16	17	18	19	20	21	22	23	24
50	3	4½	6	7½	9	10½	12	13½	14½	15½	16½	17½	18½	19½	20½	21½	22½	23½	24½
51	3	4½	6	7½	9	10½	12	13½	15	16	17	18	19	20	21	22	23	24	25
52	3	4½	6	7½	9	10½	12	13½	15	16½	17½	18½	19½	20½	21½	22½	23½	24½	25½
53	3	4½	6	7½	9	10½	12	13½	15	16½	18	19	20	21	22	23	24	25	26
54	3	4½	6	7½	9	10½	12	13½	15	16½	18	19½	20½	21½	22½	23½	24½	25½	26½
55	3	4½	6	7½	9	10½	12	13½	15	16½	18	19½	21	22	23	24	25	26	27
56	3	4½	6	7½	9	10½	12	13½	15	16½	18	19½	21	22½	23½	24½	25½	26½	27½
57	3	4½	6	7½	9	10½	12	13½	15	16½	18	19½	21	22½	24	25	26	27	28
58	3	4½	6	7½	9	10½	12	13½	15	16½	18	19½	21	22½	24	25½	26½	27½	28½
59	3	4½	6	7½	9	10½	12	13½	15	16½	18	19½	21	22½	24	25½	27	28	29
60	3	4½	6	7½	9	10½	12	13½	15	16½	18	19½	21	22½	24	25½	27	28½	29½
61	3	4½	6	7½	9	10½	12	13½	15	16½	18	19½	21	22½	24	25½	27	28½	30
62	3	4½	6	7½	9	10½	12	13½	15	16½	18	19½	21	22½	24	25½	27	28½	30
63	3	4½	6	7½	9	10½	12	13½	15	16½	18	19½	21	22½	24	25½	27	28½	30
64	3	4½	6	7½	9	10½	12	13½	15	16½	18	19½	21	22½	24	25½	27	28½	30

(Left margin vertical label: AGE IN COMPLETE YEARS AT RELEVANT DATE)

The numbers to the left of the left hand column show the age in years of the ex-employee at the relevant date (if appropriate as 'extended'), see **16.02**. The numbers above the horizontal line are the ex-employee's period of continuous employment with the employer (see Chapter 11) in complete years calculated to that relevant date.

The right to a redundancy payment may be lost in certain circumstances, see **16.60–16.79** and the amount payable reduced in others, see **16.98**.

2 Unfair dismissal – calculation of the basic award

COMPLETE YEARS OF CONTINUOUS EMPLOYMENT

AGE IN COMPLETE YEARS AT EFFECTIVE DATE OF TERMINATION

Age	1	2	3	4	5	6	7	8	9	10	11	12	13	14	15	16	17	18	19	20
17	½																			
18	½	1																		
19	½	1	1½																	
20	½	1	1½	2																
21	½	1	1½	2	2½															
22	½	1	1½	2	2½	3														
23	1	1½	2	2½	3	3½	4													
24	1	2	2½	3	3½	4	4½	5												
25	1	2	3	3½	4	4½	5	5½	6											
26	1	2	3	4	4½	5	5½	6	6½	7										
27	1	2	3	4	5	5½	6	6½	7	7½	8									
28	1	2	3	4	5	6	6½	7	7½	8	8½	9								
29	1	2	3	4	5	6	7	7½	8	8½	9	9½	10							
30	1	2	3	4	5	6	7	8	8½	9	9½	10	10½	11						
31	1	2	3	4	5	6	7	8	9	9½	10	10½	11	11½	12					
32	1	2	3	4	5	6	7	8	9	10	10½	11	11½	12	12½	13				
33	1	2	3	4	5	6	7	8	9	10	11	11½	12	12½	13	13½	14			
34	1	2	3	4	5	6	7	8	9	10	11	12	12½	13	13½	14	14½	15		
35	1	2	3	4	5	6	7	8	9	10	11	12	13	13½	14	14½	15	15½	16	
36	1	2	3	4	5	6	7	8	9	10	11	12	13	14	14½	15	15½	16	16½	17
37	1	2	3	4	5	6	7	8	9	10	11	12	13	14	15	15½	16	16½	17	17½
38	1	2	3	4	5	6	7	8	9	10	11	12	13	14	15	16	16½	17	17½	18
39	1	2	3	4	5	6	7	8	9	10	11	12	13	14	15	16	17	17½	18	18½
40	1	2	3	4	5	6	7	8	9	10	11	12	13	14	15	16	17	18	18½	19
41	1	2	3	4	5	6	7	8	9	10	11	12	13	14	15	16	17	18	19	19½
42	1½	2½	3½	4½	5½	6½	7½	8½	9½	10½	11½	12½	13½	14½	15½	16½	17½	18½	19½	20½
43	1½	3	4	5	6	7	8	9	10	11	12	13	14	15	16	17	18	19	20	21
44	1½	3	4½	5½	6½	7½	8½	9½	10½	11½	12½	13½	14½	15½	16½	17½	18½	19½	20½	21½
45	1½	3	4½	6	7	8	9	10	11	12	13	14	15	16	17	18	19	20	21	22
46	1½	3	4½	6	7½	8½	9½	10½	11½	12½	13½	14½	15½	16½	17½	18½	19½	20½	21½	22½
47	1½	3	4½	6	7½	9	10	11	12	13	14	15	16	17	18	19	20	21	22	23
48	1½	3	4½	6	7½	9	10½	11½	12½	13½	14½	15½	16½	17½	18½	19½	20½	21½	22½	23½
49	1½	3	4½	6	7½	9	10½	12	13	14	15	16	17	18	19	20	21	22	23	24
50	1½	3	4½	6	7½	9	10½	12	13½	14½	15½	16½	17½	18½	19½	20½	21½	22½	23½	24½
51	1½	3	4½	6	7½	9	10½	12	13½	15	16	17	18	19	20	21	22	23	24	25
52	1½	3	4½	6	7½	9	10½	12	13½	15	16½	17½	18½	19½	20½	21½	22½	23½	24½	25½
53	1½	3	4½	6	7½	9	10½	12	13½	15	16½	18	19	20	21	22	23	24	25	26
54	1½	3	4½	6	7½	9	10½	12	13½	15	16½	18	19½	20½	21½	22½	23½	24½	25½	26½
55	1½	3	4½	6	7½	9	10½	12	13½	15	16½	18	19½	21	22	23	24	25	26	27
56	1½	3	4½	6	7½	9	10½	12	13½	15	16½	18	19½	21	22½	23½	24½	25½	26½	27½
57	1½	3	4½	6	7½	9	10½	12	13½	15	16½	18	19½	21	22½	24	25	26	27	28
58	1½	3	4½	6	7½	9	10½	12	13½	15	16½	18	19½	21	22½	24	25½	26½	27½	28½
59	1½	3	4½	6	7½	9	10½	12	13½	15	16½	18	19½	21	22½	24	25½	27	28	29
60	1½	3	4½	6	7½	9	10½	12	13½	15	16½	18	19½	21	22½	24	25½	27	28½	29½
61	1½	3	4½	6	7½	9	10½	12	13½	15	16½	18	19½	21	22½	24	25½	27	28½	30
62	1½	3	4½	6	7½	9	10½	12	13½	15	16½	18	19½	21	22½	24	25½	27	28½	30
63	1½	3	4½	6	7½	9	10½	12	13½	15	16½	18	19½	21	22½	24	25½	27	28½	30
64	1½	3	4½	6	7½	9	10½	12	13½	15	16½	18	19½	21	22½	24	25½	27	28½	30

The numbers to the left of the left hand column show the age in years of the ex-employee at the effective date of termination (if appropriate as 'extended'), see **15.59–15.69**. The numbers above the horizontal line are the ex-employee's period of continuous employment with the employer (see Chapter 11) in complete years calculated to that effective date of termination.

There are certain circumstances in which the basic award is of a different figure, see **15.191** and **15.192**. The basic award may be reduced or extinguished, see **15.193**.

3 Unfair dismissal – calculation of pension loss

'Industrial Tribunals: Compensation for Loss of Pension Rights' (HMSO)
Appendix 1: Loss of pension rights from date of dismissal to the hearing

Unless there are arguments to the contrary we consider that the following formula should apply:
(1) Ascertain the employer's contribution as a percentage of the applicant's pay. It may be necessary to adjust this figure if exceptional circumstances pertain; if for example the pension fund is over-funded and the employer is having a pension contribution holiday. If the pension is a non-contributory one which is not funded, for example, a civil service pension, then it may be necessary to impute a notional employer's contribution.
(2) If the figure for the employer's contribution is not readily forthcoming then assume that the employer's contribution is 10% (15% in the case of non-contributory schemes).
(3) Treat the employer's contribution as a weekly loss, in the same manner as a weekly loss of earnings.

Loss of future pension rights

Use the same rate of contributions as for 1 and the same multiplier as for assessment of future loss of earnings.

Loss of enhancement of accrued pension rights

Assume no loss of enhancement of accrued pension benefit unless the contrary is proved in:
(1) Schemes in which pension benefits are referable to contributions made and not final salary (ie company money purchase schemes, personalised plans etc).
(2) Public sector schemes – funded and non-funded.
(3) Private sector final salary schemes where the applicant has less than five years until retirement.

Loss of enhancement of accrued benefit in final salary schemes (where condition 5 c(i) and c(ii) do not apply):
(1) Ascertain the deferred pension he will receive (ignoring any anticipated increases or additional benefits).
(2) Ascertain the applicant's present age and his anticipated age of retirement.
(3) Apply the appropriate multiplier as set out it in the table.
(4) Reduce the resulting figure by a reasonable percentage for the likelihood of withdrawal (ie that he would have left before retirement for reasons other than death or disability).

Appendix 4

Appendix 2, table 1: Flow chart for calculation of loss of pension rights from date of dismissal to the hearing

1. Ascertain the employee's gross weekly pensionable pay	£
2. Ascertain the employer's normal contribution as a % of the payroll	
3. If the figure for the employer's contribution is not readily forthcoming then assume that the employer's contribution is 10% (15% for non-contributory schemes)	
Weekly continuing pension loss	£
4. Multiply by number of weeks between effective date of termination and date of hearing	×
AWARD	

NB   This is not part of the prescribed element.

Aids to calculation of redundancy payments and compensation

Appendix 2, table 2: Flow chart for calculation of loss of future pension rights

1. Ascertain the employee's gross weekly
    pensionable pay

2. Ascertain the employer's normal
    contribution as a % of the payroll

3. If the figure for the employer's
    contribution is not readily
    forthcoming then assume that the
    employer's contribution is 10%
    (15% for non-contributory schemes)

Weekly continuing pension loss

4. Multiply by number of weeks allowed
    for future loss of earnings whether
    total or partial

AWARD

£

£

×

Appendix 2, table 3: Flow chart for calculation of loss of enhancement of accrued pension rights

1. Is it a final salary or a money purchase scheme?

    Final Salary   Money Purchase

2. Is it a private sector or public sector scheme?

    Private Sector   Public Sector
                            (fully index linked)

3. Has the applicant less than five years until retirement?

    No   Yes

4. (i) Ascertain the deferred pension
    he will receive (ignoring any
    anticipated increase in benefit)

    £

    (ii) Apply the appropriate multiplier
    as set out in the table

    ×

    sub-total

    (iii) Reduce the resulting figure by a
    reasonable percentage for the
    likelihood of withdrawal (ie that he
    would have left before the retirement
    for reasons other than death or
    disability)

    less %

    AWARD   £   NO AWARD

Appendix 4: Table of multipliers to be applied to the deferred annual pension to assess compensation for loss of enhancement of accrued pension rights

Age last birthday at dismissal	Normal retirement age 60	Normal retirement age 65
Under 35	1.9	1.5
35–44	1.8	1.5
45–49	1.7	1.4
50	1.6	1.4
51	1.5	1.4
52	1.4	1.3
53	1.3	1.3
54	1.1	1.3
55	1.0	1.2
56	0.8	1.2
57	0.6	1.1
58	0.3	1.0
59	0.1	0.9
60	NIL	0.8
61		0.6
62		0.4
63		0.3
64		0.2

4   Unfair dismissal – compensation calculator

The following table may be a useful tool for practitioners in calculating compensation for unfair dismissal. It is not applicable in all circumstances but should be of assistance in the majority of cases.

	£	£	£
BASIC AWARD			
Multiplier (from table 2) = X			
Week's pay (subject to maximum) Y			
X × Y	....		
Less			
Redundancy payment	....	....	
Conduct %		....	
NET BASIC AWARD =			....
COMPENSATORY AWARD			
Loss of statutory rights	[200]		
Loss of wages to date of decision			
(after taking into account failure to mitigate)	....		
Future loss			
Net average weekly income from former			
employment = P			
Period of future loss in weeks = Q			
Loss to date of new employment			
(including 'notional' employment)			
P × Q =	....		
Continuing loss thereafter			
Period C			
Loss D			
C × D =	....		
Pension loss (Appendix 4, table 3)	....		
Expenses	....		
Other losses	....	....	
Less			
Payments from respondent			
(including excess over statutory			
redundancy payment)		....	
Total		....	
Less			
Contributory fault by applicant % =		....	
NET COMPENSATORY AWARD			....
ADDITIONAL AWARD			....
SPECIAL AWARD			....
GRAND TOTAL			....

As to basic awards, see **15.190–15.193** and Appendix 4, table 2.
As to compensatory awards, see **15.194–15.218**.
For pension loss, see Appendix 4, table 3.
In some circumstances an additional or special award may be payable, see **15.187–15.188** and **15.219**.

Index